The GALE
ENCYCLOPEDIA
of SCIENCE

The GALE ENCYCLOPEDIA
of SCIENCE

VOLUME 1
Aardvark – Calendars

Bridget Travers,
Editor

Gale Research

An ITP Information/Reference Group Company

I(T)P
Changing the Way the World Learns

NEW YORK • LONDON • BONN • BOSTON • DETROIT
MADRID • MELBOURNE • MEXICO CITY • PARIS
SINGAPORE • TOKYO • TORONTO • WASHINGTON
ALBANY NY • BELMONT CA • CINCINNATI OH

The GALE ENCYCLOPEDIA *of* SCIENCE

Bridget Travers, *Editor*

Sheila M. Dow, *Coordinating Editor (Advisors)*
James Edwards, *Coordinating Editor (Databases)*
Paul Lewon, *Coordinating Editor (Illustrations)*
Jacqueline Longe, *Coordinating Editor (Contributors)*
Donna Olendorf, *Coordinating Editor (Submissions, Indexing)*

Christine B. Jeryan, Kyung-Sun Lim, Kimberley A. McGrath, Robyn V. Young, *Contributing Editors*

Kristine M. Binkley, Zoran Minderovic, *Associate Editors*

Nicole Beatty, Pamela Proffitt, Carley Wellman, *Assistant Editors*

Linda R. Andres, Shelly Andrews, Dawn R. Barry, Ned Burels, Melissa Doig, David Oblender, *Contributors*

Marlene S. Hurst, *Permissions Manager*
Margaret A. Chamberlain, *Permissions Specialist*
Susan Brohman, *Permissions Associate*

Victoria B. Cariappa, *Research Manager*
Maureen Richards, *Research Specialist*

Mary Beth Trimper, *Production Director*
Evi Seoud, Assistant *Production Manager*
Shanna Heilveil, *Production Assistant*

Cynthia Baldwin, *Product Design Manager*
Mary Krzewinski, *Art Director*
Barbara Yarrow, *Graphic Services Manager*
Randy Bassett, *Image Database Supervisor*
Robert Duncan, *Digital Imaging Specialist*
Pamela A. Hayes, *Photography Coordinator*

Benita L. Spight, Manager, *Data Entry Services*
Gwendolyn S. Tucker, *Data Entry Supervisor*
Beverly Jendrowski, *Senior Data Entry Associate*
Francis L. Monroe, *Data Entry Associate*

Jeffrey Muhr, Roger M. Valade, III, *Editorial Technical Services Associates*

Indexing provided by the Electronic Scriptorium

This book is printed on recycled paper that meets Environmental Protection Agency standards.

The paper used in this publication meets the minimum requirements of American National Standard for Information Sciences—Permanence Paper for Printed Library Materials, ANSI Z39.48-1984.

Gale encyclopedia of science / Bridget E. Travers, editor.
      p.   cm.
   Includes bibliographical references and index.
   Summary: Contains 2,000 entries ranging from short definitions to major overviews of concepts in all areas of science.
      ISBN 0–08103–9892–3 (alk. paper)
      1. Science--Encyclopedias, Juvenile.   [1. Science-
-Encyclopedias.]   I. Travers, Bridget.
   Q121.G35 1995
503--dc20   95-25402
                                                      CIP
                                                      AC

CONTENTS

ORGANIZATION OF THE ENCYCLOPEDIA

The Gale Encyclopedia of Science has been designed with ease of use and ready reference in mind.

- Entries are **alphabetically arranged** in a single sequence, rather than by scientific field.
- Length of entries varies from **short definitions** of one or two paragraphs to longer, more **detailed entries** on complex subjects.
- Longer entries are arranged so that an **overview** of the subject appears first, followed by a detailed discussion conveniently arranged under subheadings.
- A list of **key terms** are provided where appropriate to define unfamiliar terms or concepts.

- Longer entries conclude with a **further reading** section, which points readers to other helpful sources.
- The **contributor's name** appears at the end of longer entries. His or her affiliation can be found in the "Contributors" section at the front of each volume.
- **"See-also" references** appear at the end of entries to point readers to related entries.
- **Cross-references** placed throughout the encyclopedia direct readers to where information on subjects without their own entries can be found.
- A comprehensive **general index** guides readers to all topics and persons mentioned in the book.

ADVISORY BOARD

A number of experts in the library and scientific communities provided invaluable assistance in the formulation of this encyclopedia. Our advisory board performed a myriad of duties, from defining the scope of coverage to reviewing individual entries for accuracy and accessibility. We would therefore like to express our appreciation to them:

Academic Advisors

Bryan Bunch
Adjunct Instructor
Department of Mathematics
Pace University

David Campbell
Head
Department of Physics
University of Illinois at Urbana
    Champaign

Neil Cumberlidge
Professor
Department of Biology
Northern Michigan University

Bill Freedman
Professor
Department of Biology and
    School for Resource and Environmental Studies
Dalhousie University

Clayton Harris
Assistant Professor
Department of Geography and
    Geology
Middle Tennessee State University

William S. Pretzer
Curator
Henry Ford Museum and Greenfield Village
Dearborn, Michigan

Theodore Snow
Fellow and Director
Center for Astrophysics and
    Space Research
University of Colorado at Boulder

Robert Wolke
Professor emeritus
Department of Chemistry
University of Pittsburgh

Richard Addison Wood
Meteorlogical Consultant
Tucson, Arizona

Librarian Advisors

Donna Miller
Director
Craig-Moffet County Library
Craig, Colorado

Judy Williams
Media Center
Greenwich High School
Greenwich, Connecticut

Carol Wishmeyer
Science and Technology Department
Detroit Public Library
Detroit, Michigan

CONTRIBUTORS

Nasrine Adibe
Professor Emeritus
Department of Education
Long Island University
Westbury, New York

Mary D. Albanese
Department of English
University of Alaska
Juneau, Alaska

James L. Anderson
Soil Science Department
University of Minnesota
St. Paul, Minnesota

Susan Andrew
Teaching Assistant
University of Maryland
Washington, D.C.

John Appel
Director
Fundación Museo de Ciencia y
Tecnología
Popayán, Colombia

David Ball
Assistant Professor
Department of Chemistry
Cleveland State University
Cleveland, Ohio

Dana M. Barry
Editor and Technical Writer

Center for Advanced Materials
Processing
Clarkston University
Potsdam, New York

Puja Batra
Department of Zoology
Michigan State University
East Lansing, Michigan

Donald Beaty
Professor Emeritus
College of San Mateo
San Mateo, California

Eugene C. Beckham
Department of Mathematics and
Science
Northwood Institute
Midland, Michigan

Martin Beech
Research Associate
Department of Astronomy
University of Western Ontario
London, Ontario

Massimo D. Bezoari
Associate Professor
Department of Chemistry
Huntingdon College
Montgomery, Alabama

John M. Bishop III
Translator
New York, New York

T. Parker Bishop
Professor
Middle Grades and Secondary
Education
Georgia Southern University
Statesboro, Georgia

Carolyn Black
Professor
Incarnate Word College
San Antonio, Texas

Larry Blaser
Science Writer
Lebanon, Tennessee

Jean F. Blashfield
Science Writer
Walworth, Wisconsin

Richard L. Branham Jr.
Director
Centro Rigional de
Investigaciones Científicas y
Tecnológicas
Mendoza, Argentina

Patricia Braus
Editor
American Demographics
Rochester, New York

David L. Brock
Biology Instructor
St. Louis, Missouri

Leona B. Bronstein
Chemistry Teacher (retired)
East Lansing High School
Okemos, Michigan

Brandon R. Brown
Graduate Research Assistant
Oregon State University
Corvallis, Oregon

Lenonard C. Bruno
Senior Science Specialist
Library of Congress
Chevy Chase, Maryland

Scott Christian Cahall
Researcher
World Precision Instruments, Inc.
Bradenton, Florida

G. Lynn Carlson
Senior Lecturer
School of Science and
    Technology
University of Wisconsin—
    Parkside
Kenosha, Wisconsin

James J. Carroll
Center for Quantum Mechanics
The University of Texas at Dallas
Dallas, Texas

Steven B. Carroll
Assistant Professor
Division of Biology
Northeast Missouri State
    University
Kirksville, Missouri

Rosalyn Carson-DeWitt
Physician and Medical Writer
Durham, North Carolina

Yvonne Carts-Powell
Editor
Laser Focus World
Belmont, Massachustts

Chris Cavette
Technical Writer
Fremont, California

Kenneth B. Chiacchia
Medical Editor

University of Pittsburgh Medical
    Center
Pittsburgh, Pennsylvania

M. L. Cohen
Science Writer
Chicago, Illinois

Robert Cohen
Reporter
KPFA Radio News
Berkeley, California

Sally Cole-Misch
Assistant Director
International Joint Commission
Detroit, Michigan

George W. Collins II
Professor Emeritus
Case Western Reserve
Chesterland, Ohio

Jeffrey R. Corney
Science Writer
Thermopolis, Wyoming

Tom Crawford
Assistant Director
Division of Publication and
    Development
University of Pittsburgh Medical
    Center
Pittsburgh, Pennsylvania

Pamela Crowe
Medical and Science Writer
Oxon, England

Clinton Crowley
On-site Geologist
Selman and Associates
Fort Worth, Texas

Edward Cruetz
Physicist
Rancho Santa Fe, California

Frederick Culp
Chairman
Department of Physics
Tenneesse Technical
Cookeville, Tennessee

Neil Cumberlidge
Professor

Department of Biology
Northern Michigan University
Marquette, Michigan

Mary Ann Cunningham
Environmental Writer
St. Paul, Minnesota

Les C. Cwynar
Associate Professor
Department of Biology
University of New Brunswick
Fredericton, New Brunswick

Paul Cypher
Provisional Interpreter
Lake Erie Metropark
Trenton, Michigan

Stanley J. Czyzak
Professor Emeritus
Ohio State University
Columbus, Ohio

Rosi Dagit
Conservation Biologist
Topanga-Las Virgenes Resource
    Conservation District
Topanga, California

David Dalby
President
Bruce Tool Company, Inc.
Taylors, South Carolina

Lou D'Amore
Chemistry Teacher
Father Redmund High School
Toronto, Ontario

Douglas Darnowski
Postdoctoral Fellow
Department of Plant Biology
Cornell University
Ithaca, New York

Sreela Datta
Associate Writer
Aztec Publications
Northville, Michigan

Sarah K. Dean
Science Writer
Philadelphia, Pennsylvania

Sarah de Forest
Research Assistant
Theoretical Physical Chemistry
  Lab
University of Pittsburgh
Pittsburgh, Pennsylvania

Louise Dickerson
Medical and Science Writer
Greenbelt, Maryland

Marie Doorey
Editorial Assistant
Illinois Masonic Medical Center
Chicago, Illinois

Herndon G. Dowling
Professor Emeritus
Department of Biology
New York University
New York, New York

Marion Dresner
Natural Resources Educator
Berkeley, California

John Henry Dreyfuss
Science Writer
Brooklyn, New York

Roy Dubisch
Professor Emeritus
Department of Mathematics
New York University
New York, New York

Russel Dubisch
Department of Physics
Sienna College
Loudonville, New York

Carolyn Duckworth
Science Writer
Missoula, Montana

Peter A. Ensminger
Research Associate
Cornell University
Syracuse, New York

Bernice Essenfeld
Biology Writer
Warren, New Jersey

Mary Eubanks

Instructor of Biology
The North Carolina School of
  Science and Mathematics
Durham, North Carolina

Kathryn M. C. Evans
Science Writer
Madison, Wisconsin

William G. Fastie
Department of Astronomy and
  Physics
Bloomberg Center
Baltimore, Maryland

Barbara Finkelstein
Science Writer
Riverdale, New York

Mary Finley
Supervisor of Science Curriculum
  (retired)
Pittsburgh Secondary Schools
Clairton, Pennsylvania

Gaston Fischer
Institut de Géologie
Université de Neuchâtel
Peseux, Switzerland

Sara G. B. Fishman
Professor
Quinsigamond Community
  College
Worcester, Massachusetts

David Fontes
Senior Instructor
Lloyd Center for Environmental
  Studies
Westport, Maryland

Barry Wayne Fox
Extension Specialist,
  Marine/Aquatic Education
Virginia State University
Petersburg, Virginia

Ed Fox
Charlotte Latin School
Charlotte, North Carolina

Kenneth L. Frazier
Science Teacher (retired)
North Olmstead High School

North Olmstead, Ohio

Bill Freedman
Professor
Department of Biology and
  School For Resource and
  Environmental Studies
Dalhousie University
Halifax, Nova Scotia

T. A. Freeman
Consulting Archaeologist
Quail Valley, California

Elaine Friebele
Science Writer
Cheverly, Maryland

Randall Frost
Documentation Engineering
Pleasanton, California

Robert Gardner
Science Education Consultant
North Eastham, Massachusetts

Gretchen M. Gillis
Senior Geologist
Maxus Exploration
Dallas, Texas

Kathryn Glynn
Audiologist
Portland, Oregon

Natalie Goldstein
Educational Environmental
  Writing
Phoenicia, New York

David Gorish
TARDEC
U.S. Army
Warren, Michigan

Louis Gotlib
South Granville High School
Durham, North Carolina

Hans G. Graetzer
Professor
Department of Physics
South Dakota State University
Brookings, South Dakota

Jim Guinn
Assistant Professor
Department of Physics
Berea College
Berea, Kentucky

Steve Gutterman
Psychology Research Assistant
University of Michigan
Ann Arbor, Michigan

Johanna Haaxma-Jurek
Educator
Nataki Tabibah Schoolhouse of
  Detroit
Detroit, Michigan

Monica H. Halka
Research Associate
Department of Physics and
  Astronomy
University of Tennessee
Knoxville, Tennessee

Jeffrey C. Hall
Astronomer
Lowell Observatory
Flagstaff, Arizona

C. S. Hammen
Professor Emeritus
Department of Zoology
University of Rhode Island

Beth Hanson
Editor
The Amicus Journal
Brooklyn, New York

Clay Harris
Associate Professor
Department of Geography and
  Geology
Middle Tennessee State
  University
Murfreesboro, Tennessee

Catherine Hinga Haustein
Associate Professor
Department of Chemistry
Central College
Pella, Iowa

Dean Allen Haycock
Science Writer
Salem, New York

Paul A. Heckert
Professor
Department of Chemistry and
  Physics
Western Carolina University
Cullowhee, North Carolina

Darrel B. Hoff
Department of Physics
Luther College
Calmar, Iowa

Dennis Holley
Science Educator
Shelton, Nebraska

Leonard Darr Holmes
Department of Physical Science
Pembroke State University
Pembroke, North Carolina

Rita Hoots
Instructor of Biology, Anatomy,
  Chemistry
Yuba College
Woodland, California

Selma Hughes
Department of Psychology and
  Special Education
East Texas State University
Mesquite, Texas

Mara W. Cohen Ioannides
Science Writer
Springfield, Missouri

Zafer Iqbal
Allied Signal Inc.
Morristown, New Jersey

Sophie Jakowska
Pathobiologist, Environmental
  Educator
Santo Domingo, Dominican
  Republic

Richard A. Jeryan
Senior Technical Specialist
Ford Motor Company
Dearborn, Michigan

Stephen R. Johnson
Biology Writer
Richmond, Virginia

Kathleen A. Jones
School of Medicine
Southern Illinois University
Carbondale, Illinois

Harold M. Kaplan
Professor
School of Medicine
Southern Illinois University
Carbondale, Illinois

Anthony Kelly
Science Writer
Pittsburgh, Pennsylvania

Amy Kenyon-Campbell
Ecology, Evolution and
  Organismal Biology Program
University of Michigan
Ann Arbor, Michigan

Eileen M. Korenic
Institute of Optics
University of Rochester
Rochester, New York

Jennifer Kramer
Science Writer
Kearny, New Jersey

Pang-Jen Kung
Los Alamos National Laboratory
Los Alamos, New Mexico

Marc Kusinitz
Assistant Director Media
  Relations
John Hopkins Medical Instituition
Towsen, Maryland

Arthur M. Last
Head
Department of Chemistry
University College of the Fraser
  Valley
Abbotsford, British Columbia

Nathan Lavenda
Zoologist
Skokie, Illinios

Jennifer LeBlanc
Environmental Consultant
London, Ontario

Benedict A. Leerburger
Science Writer
Scarsdale, New York

Betsy A. Leonard
Education Facilitator
Reuben H. Fleet Space Theater
  and Science Center
San Diego, California

Scott Lewis
Science Writer
Chicago, Illinois

Frank Lewotsky
Aerospace Engineer (retired)
Nipomo, California

Karen Lewotsky
Cartographer
Portland, Oregon

Kristin Lewotsky
Editor
Laser Focus World
Nashua, New Hamphire

Stephen K. Lewotsky
Architect
Grants Pass, Oregon

Sarah Lee Lippincott
Professor Emeritus
Swarthmore College
Swarthmore, Pennsylvania

David Lunney
Research Scientist
Centre de Spectrométrie
  Nucléaire et de Spectrométrie de
  Masse
Orsay, France

Steven MacKenzie
Ecologist
Spring Lake, Michigan

J. R. Maddocks
Consulting Scientist
DeSoto, Texas

Gail B. C. Marsella
Technical Writer
Allentown, Pennsylvania

Karen Marshall
Research Associate
Council of State Governments
  and Centers for Environment
  and Safety
Lexington, Kentucky

Liz Marshall
Science Writer
Columbus, Ohio

James Marti
Research Scientist
Department of Mechanical
  Engineering
University of Minnesota
Minneapolis, Minnesota

Elaine L. Martin
Science Writer
Pensacola, Florida

Lilyan Mastrolla
Professor Emeritus
San Juan Unified School
Sacramento, California

Iain A. McIntyre
Manager
Electro-optic Department
Energy Compression Research
  Corporation
Vista, California

G. H. Miller
Director
Studies on Smoking
Edinboro, Pennsylvania

J. Gordon Miller
Botanist
Corvallis, Oregon

Christine Miner Minderovic
Nuclear Medicine Technologist
Franklin Medical Consulters
Ann Arbor, Michigan

David Mintzer
Professor Emeritus
Department of Mechanical

Engineering
Northwestern University
Evanston, Illinois

Christine Molinari
Science Editor
University of Chicago Press
Chicago, Illinois

Frank Mooney
Professor Emeritus
Fingerlake Community College
Canandaigua, New York

Partick Moore
Department of English
University of Arkansas at Little
  Rock
Little Rock, Arkansas

Robbin Moran
Department of Systematic Botany
Institute of Biological Sciences
University of Aarhus
Risskou, Denmark

J. Paul Moulton
Department of Mathematics
Episcopal Academy
Glenside, Pennsylvania

Otto H. Muller
Geology Department
Alfred University
Alfred, New York

Angie Mullig
Publication and Development
University of Pittsburgh Medical
  Center
Trafford, Pennsylvania

David R. Murray
Senior Associate
Sydney University
Sydney, New South Wales
Australia

Sutharchana Murugan
Scientist Three Boehringer
  Mannheim Corp.
Indianapolis, Indiana

Muthena Naseri
Moorpark College

Moorpark, California

David Newton
Science Writer and Educator
Ashland, Oregon

F. C. Nicholson
Science Writer
Lynn, Massachusetts

James O'Connell
Department of Physical Sciences
Frederick Community College
Gaithersburg, Maryland

Dónal P. O'Mathúna
Associate Professor
Mount Carmel College of
  Nursing
Columbus, Ohio

Marjorie Pannell
Managing Editor, Scientific
  Publications
Field Museum of Natural History
Chicago, Illinois

Gordon A. Parker
Lecturer
Department of Natural Sciences
University of Michigan—
  Dearborn
Dearborn, Michigan

David Petechuk
Science Writer
Ben Avon, Pennsylvania

John R. Phillips
Department of Chemistry
Purdue University, Calumet
Hammond, Indiana

Kay Marie Porterfield
Science Writer
Englewood, Colorado

Paul Poskozim
Chair
Department of Chemistry, Earth
  Science and Physics
Northeastern Illinois University
Chicago, Illinois

Andrew Poss
Senior Research Chemist
Allied Signal Inc.
Buffalo, New York

Satyam Priyadarshy
Department of Chemistry
University of Pittsburgh
Pittsburgh, Pennsylvania

Patricia V. Racenis
Science Writer
Livonia, Michigan

Cynthia Twohy Ragni
Atmospheric Scientist
National Center for Atmospheric
  Research
Westminster, Colorado

Jordan P. Richman
Science Writer
Phoenix, Arizona

Kitty Richman
Science Writer
Phoenix, Arizona

Vita Richman
Science Writer
Phoenix, Arizona

Michael G. Roepel
Researcher
Department of Chemistry
University of Pittsburgh
Pittsburgh, Pennsylvania

Perry Romanowski
Science Writer
Chicago, Illinois

Nancy Ross-Flanigan
Science Writer
Belleville, Michigan

Gordon Rutter
Royal Botanic Gardens
Edinburgh, Great Britain

Elena V. Ryzhov
Polytechnic Institute
Troy, New York

David Sahnow
Associate Research Scientist

John Hopkins University
Baltimore, Maryland

Peter Salmansohn
Educational Consultant
New York State Parks
Cold Spring, New York

Peter K. Schoch
Instructor
Department of Physics and
  Computer Science
Sussex County Community
  College
Augusta, New Jersey

Patricia G. Schroeder
Instructor
Science, Healthcare, and Math
  Division
Johnson County Community
  College
Overland Park, Kansas

Randy Schueller
Science Writer
Chicago, Illinois

Kathleen Scogna
Science Writer
Baltimore, Maryland

William Shapbell Jr.
Launch and Flight Systems
  Manager
Kennedy Space Center, Florida

Anwar Yuna Shiekh
International Centre for
  Theoretical Physics
Trieste, Italy

Raul A. Simon
Chile Departmento de Física
Universidad de Tarapacá
Arica, Chile

Michael G. Slaughter
Science Specialist
Ingham ISD
East Lansing, Michigan

Billy W. Sloope
Professor Emeritus
Department of Physics

Virginia Commonwealth
University
Richmond, Virginia

Douglas Smith
Science Writer
Milton, Massachusetts

Lesley L. Smith
Department of Physics and
Astronomy
University of Kansas
Lawrence, Kansas

Kathryn D. Snavely
U.S. General Accounting Office
Policy Analyst, Air Quality Issues
Raleigh, North Carolina

Charles H. Southwick
Professor
Environmental, Population, and
Organismic Biology
University of Colorado at
Boulder
Boulder, Colorado

John Spizzirri
Science Writer
Chicago, Illinois

Frieda A. Stahl
Professor Emeritus
Department of Physics
California State University, Los
Angeles
Los Angeles, California

Robert L. Stearns
Department of Physics
Vassar College
Poughkeepsie, New York

Ilana Steinhorn
Science Writer
Boalsburg, Pennsylvania

David Stone
Conservation Advisory Services
Gai Soleil
Chemin Des Clyettes
Le Muids, Switzerland

Eric R. Swanson
Associate Professor

Department of Earth and Physical
Sciences
University of Texas
San Antonio, Texas

Cheryl Taylor
Science Educator
Kailua, Hawaii

Nicholas C. Thomas
Department of Physical Sciences
Auburn University at
Montgomery
Montgomery, Alabama

W. A. Thomasson
Science and Medical Writer
Oak Park, Illinois

Marie L. Thompson
Science Writer
Ben Avon, Pennsylvania

Melvin Tracy
Science Educator
Appleton, Wisconsin

Karen Trentelman
Research Associate
Archaeometric Laboratory
University of Toronto
Toronto, Ontario

Robert K. Tyson
Senior Scientist
W. J. Schafer Assoc.
Jupiter, Florida

James Van Allen
Professor Emeritus
Department of Physics and
Astronomy
University of Iowa
Iowa City, Iowa

Julia M. Van Denack
Biology Instructor
Silver Lake College
Manitowoc, Wisconsin

Kurt Vandervoort
Department of Chemistry and
Physics
West Carolina University
Cullowhee, North Carolina

Chester Vander Zee
Naturalist, Science Educator
Volga, South Dakota

Jeanette Vass
Department of Chemistry
Cuyahoga Community College
Timberlake, Ohio

R. A. Virkar
Chair
Department of Biological
Sciences
Kean College
Iselin, New Jersey

Kurt C. Wagner
Instructor
South Carolina Governor's
School for Science and
Technology
Hartsville, South Carolina

Cynthia Washam
Science Writer
Jensen Beach, Florida

Joseph D. Wassersug
Physician
Boca Raton, Florida

Tom Watson
Environmental Writer
Seattle, Washington

Jeffrey Weld
Instructor, Science Department
Chair
Pella High School
Pella, Iowa

Frederick R. West
Astronomer
Hanover, Pennsylvania

Glenn Whiteside
Science Writer
Wichita, Kansas

John C. Whitmer
Professor
Department of Chemistry
Western Washington University
Bellingham, Washington

CONTRIBUTORS

Donald H. Williams
Department of Chemistry
Hope College
Holland, Michigan

Robert L. Wolke
Professor Emeritus
Department of Chemistry
University of Pittsburgh
Pittsburgh, Pennsylvania

Jim Zurasky
Optical Physicist
Nichols Research Corporation
Huntsville, Alabama

ACKNOWLEDGEMENTS

Photographs appearing in the *Gale Encyclopedia of Science* were received from the following sources:

© Account Phototake/Phototake: **Genetic disorders**; © James Allem, Stock Market: **Gazelles**; © A. W. Ambler, National Audubon Society Collection/Photo Researchers, Inc.: **Goats, Newts, Sedimentary rock**; © Toni Angermayer, National Audubon Society Collection/Photo Researchers, Inc.: **Hamsters**; © Mark Antman/Phototake: **Textiles**; AP/Wide World Photos: **Elements, formation of**; © Archiv, National Audubon Society Collection/Photo Researchers, Inc.: **Astrolabe**; © Bachman, National Audubon Society Collection/Photo Researchers, Inc.: **Wombats**; © Bill Bachman, National Audubon Society Collection/Photo Researchers, Inc.: **Grasslands**; Baiyer River Sanctuary, New Guinea © Tom McHugh, National Audubon Society Collection/Photo Researchers, Inc.; © M. Baret/RAPHU, National Audubon Society Collection/Photo Researchers, Inc.: **Biotechnology**; Jen and Des Bartlett, National Audubon Society Collection/Photo Researchers, Inc.: **Sea lions**; © Jen and Des Bartlett, National Aububon Society Collection/Photo Researchers, Inc.: **Cicadas, Langurs and leaf monkeys, Aardvark, Bandicoots, Grebes, Lorises, Monitor lizards, Opossums, Pipefish, Sea horses, Secretary bird, Spiny anteaters**; © Bat Conservation Int'l: **Bats**; © John Bavosi, National Audubon Society Collection/ Photo Researchers, Inc.: **Hernia**; Tom Bean: **Archaeology**; © Tom Bean, Stock Market: **Volcano**; © James Bell, National Audubon Society Collection/Photo Researchers, Inc.: **Buds and budding**; © Pierre Berger, National Audubon Society Collection/Photo Researchers, Inc.: **Beech family**; © J. Bernholc et al, North Carolina State University/Science Photo Library, National Audubon Society Collection/Photo Researchers, Inc.: **Buckminsterfullerene**; © The Bettmann Archive: **Chemical warfare, Photography**; © Art Bileten, National Audubon Society Collection/Photo Researchers, Inc.: **North America**; © Biophoto Associates, National Audubon Society Collection/Photo Researchers, Inc.: **Acne, Chromosome, Tropical diseases, Spina bifida**; © Wesley Bocxe, National Audubon Society Collection/Photo Researchers, Inc.: **Oil spills**; © Mark Boulton, National Audubon Society Collection/Photo Researchers, Inc.: **Bustards, Erosion**; © Malcolm Boulton, National Audubon Society Collection/Photo Researchers, Inc.: **Porcupines, Baboons**; © Mark N. Boulton, National Audubon Society Collection/Photo Researchers, Inc.: **Yak**; © Dr. Tony Brain/Science Photo Library, National Audubon Society Collection/Photo Researchers, Inc.: **Aerobic**; © Thomas H. Brakefield, Stock Market: **Cats**; © Tom Brakefield, Stock Market: **Wolverine**; © 1980 Ken Brate, National Audubon Society Collection/Photo Researchers, Inc.: **Citrus trees**; Andrea Brizzi, Stock Market: **Sewage treatment**; © S. Brookens, Stock Market: **Mynah birds**; © John R. Brownlie, National Audubon Society Collection/Photo Researchers, Inc.: **Lyrebirds**; © Dr. Jeremy Brugess/Science Photo Library, National Audubon Society Collection/ Photo Researchers, Inc.: **Leaf, Chloroplast, Aphids, Battery**; © John Buitenkant 1993, National Audubon Society Collection/Photo Researchers, Inc.: **Buttercup**; © 1994, Michele Burgess/Bikderberg, Stock Market: **Elephant**; © Michele Burgess, Stock Market: **Flightless birds**; © Jane Burton, National Audubon Society Collection/Photo Researchers, Inc.: **Pangolins**; © Diana Calder/Bikderberg, Stock Market: **Barometer**; © Scott Camazinr, National Audubon Society Collection/Photo Researchers, Inc.: **AIDS**; © Tardos Camesi/Bikderberg, Stock

Market: **Transformer**; © John Cancalosi: **Numbat**; © Robert Caputo, National Audubon Society Collection/Photo Researchers, Inc.: **Hyena**; © Alan D. Carey, National Audubon Society Collection/Photo Researchers, Inc.: **Captive breeding and reintroduction, Coffee plant**; © Carolina Biological Supply Company/Phototake: **Chemoreception, Microscopy, Plant, Cashew family, Yeast**; © Tom Carrill/Phototake: **Pollution control**; © Tom Carroll/Phototake: **Air pollution, Bridges, Freeway**; © CBC/CBC/Phototake: **Petrels and shearwaters**; © Jean-Loup Charmet, National Audubon Society Collection/Photo Researchers, Inc.: **Anesthesia, Rabies**; © Ann Chawatsky/Phototake: **Burn**; © Ron Church, National Audubon Society Collection/Photo Researchers, Inc.: **Barracuda**; © Geoffrey Clifford,Stock Market: **Fractal**; © CNRI/ Science Photo Library, Nationa Audubon Society Collection/Photo Researchers, Inc.: **Influenza**; © CNRI/Phototake: **Leprosy**; © CNRI/Science Photo Library, National Audubon Society Collection/ Photo Researchers, Inc.: **Enterobacteria**; © Pedro Coll, Stock Market: **Cave, Machine tools**; © Holt Confer/Phototake: **Cranes**; © Judd Cooney/Phototake: **Weasels**; © Tony Craddock, National Audubon Society Collection/Photo Researchers, Inc.: **Microwave communication**; © Allan D. Cruickshank, National Audubon Society Collection/Photo Researchers, Inc.: **Cuckoos, Gila monster**; © Russell D. Curtis, National Audubon Society Collection/ Photo Researchers, Inc.: **Sleep disorders**; © Tim Davis, National Audubon Society Collection/Photo Researchers, Inc.: **Colobus monkeys, Finches**; © John Deeks, National Audubon Society Collection/Photo Researchers, Inc.: **Clouds**; © E.R. Degginger, National Audubon Society Collection/Photo Researchers, Inc.: **Tundra**; © Nigel Dennis, National Audubon Society Collection/Photo Researchers, Inc.: **Flamingos**; © Jack Dermid, National Audubon Society Collection/Photo Researchers, Inc.: **Dune**; © Jack Dermid 1979, National Audubon Society Collection/Photo Researchers, Inc.: **Bromeliad family**; © Jack Dermid, National Audubon Society Collection/Photo Researchers, Inc.: **Puffer fish**; © 1992 Alan L. Detrick, National Audubon Society Collection/Photo Researchers, Inc.: **Amaranth family**; © Mike Devlin, National Audubon Society Collection/Photo Researchers, Inc.: **Prosthetics**; © Richard Dibon-Smith, National Audubon Society Collection/Photo Researchers, Inc.: **Sheep**; © Gregory G. Dimijian 1990, National Audubon Society Collection/Photo Researchers, Inc.: **Coca**; © Thomas Dimock, Stock Market: **Crabs**; © Martin Dohrn, National Audubon Society Collection/Photo Researchers, Inc.: **Interference, Skeletal system**; © Martin Dohrn/Science Photo Library, National Audubon Society Collection/Photo Researchers, Inc.: **Wave motion**; © Dopamine-CNRI, National Audubon Society Collection/Photo Researchers, Inc.: **Ulcers**; © A. B. Dowsett/Science Photo Library, National Audubon Society Collection/ Photo Researchers, Inc.: **Virus**; © John Dudak/Phototake: **Arrowroot, Composite family**; © Richard Duncan,National Audubon Society Collection/Photo Researchers, Inc.: **Geometry**; © Hermann Eisenbeiss, National Audubon Society Collection/Photo Researchers, Inc.: **Surface tension**; © Thomas Ernsting, Stock Market: **Metric system**; © Thomas Ernsting/Bikderberg, Stock Market: **Virtual reality**; © 1992 Robert Essel/Bikderberg, Stock Market: **Electricity**; © Robert Essel, Stock Market: **Moose**; © Kenneth Eward/BioGrafx, National Audubon Society Collection/Photo Researchers, Inc.: **Atom**; © Dr. Brian Eyden, National Audubon Society Collection/Photo Researchers, Inc.: **Cancer**; © Douglas Faulkner, National Audubon Society Collection/Photo Researchers, Inc.: **Manatee, Coral reef**; © Fawcett, National Audubon Society Collection/ Photo Researchers, Inc.: **Cell**; © Fawcett/Phillips, National Audubon Society Collection/Photo Researchers, Inc.: **Flagella**; © Kenneth W. Fink, National Audubon Society Collection/Photo Researchers, Inc.: **Turacos**; © Cecil Fox/Science Source, National Audubon Society Collection/Photo Researchers, Inc.: **Alzheimer's disease**; © Carl Frank, National Audubon Society Collection/Photo Researchers, Inc.: **Rivers**; © Stephen Frink, Stock Market: **Squirrel fish**; © Petit Fromat/Nestle, National Audubon Society Collection/Photo Researchers, Inc.: **Embryo and embryonic development**; © G.R. Gainer, Stock Market: **Spiral**; Gale Research Inc.: **Jet engine**; © Gordon Garrado/Science Photo Library, National Audubon Society Collection/Photo Researchers, Inc.: **Thunderstorm**; © Frederica Georgia, National Audubon Society Collection/Photo Researchers, Inc.: **Hydrothermal vents**; © Ormond Gigli, Stock Market: **Frigate birds**; © 1989 Ned Gillette, Stock Market: **Mass wasting**; © A. Glauberman, National Audubon Society Collection/Photo Researchers, Inc.: **Cigarette smoke**; © F. Gohier 1982, National Audubon Society Collection/Photo Researchers, Inc.: **Amaryllis family**; © Francois Gohier, National Audubon Society Collection/Photo Researchers, Inc.: **Stromatolites**; © Spencer Grant, National Audubon Society Collection/Photo Researchers, Inc.: **Robotics**; © Stephen Green-Armytage, Stock Market:

Boas; © Al Greene and Associates, National Audubon Society Collection/Photo Researchers, Inc.: **Coast and beach**; © Barry Griffiths, National Audubon Society Collection/Photo Researchers, Inc.; © Tommaso Guicciardini/Science Photo Library, National Audubon Society Collection/Photo Researchers, Inc.: **Gravity**; © Dan Guravich 1987, National Audubon Society Collection/Photo Researchers, Inc.: **Atmospheric optical phenomena**; © Dan Guravich, National Audubon Society Collection/Photo Researchers, Inc.: **Alluvial systems**; © A. Gurmankin 1987/Phototake: **Begonia**; © Clem Haagner, National Audubon Society Collection/Photo Researchers, Inc.: **Giraffes and okapi**; © Hugh M. Halliday, National Audubon Society Collection/Photo Researchers, Inc.: **Shrikes**; © David Halpern, National Audubon Society Collection/Photo Researchers, Inc.: **Oil drilling**; © Chris Hamilton, Stock Market: **Waterwheel**; © Craig Hammell/Bikderberg, Stock Market: **Caliper**; © Hammond Incorporated, Maplewood, New Jersey.: **Bar code**; © 1993 Brownie Harris, Stock Market : **Antenna**; © Brownie Harris, Stock Market: **Turbine**; © Adam Hart-Davis/Science Photo Library, National Audubon Society Collection/Photo Researchers, Inc.: **Electrostatic devices**; © Adam Hart-Davis, National Audubon Society Collection/Photo Researchers, Inc.: **Thermometer, Integrated circuit**; © Anne Heimann, Stock Market: **Horseshoe crabs**; © Robert C. Hermes,National Audubon Society Collection/Photo Researchers, Inc.: **Mayflies**; © John Heseltine, National Audubon Society Collection/Photo Researchers, Inc.: **Geodesic dome**; © Andrew Holbrooke, Stock Market: **Landfill, Prosthetics**; © Holt Studios International, National Audubon Society Collection/Photo Researchers, Inc.: **Cashew family**; © Eric Hosking, F.R.P.S., National Audubon Society Collection/Photo Researchers, Inc.: **Auks**; © Eric Hosking, National Audubon Society Collection/Photo Researchers, Inc.: **Kingfishers, Loons, Mice, Stilts and avocets**; © John Howard, National Audubon Society Collection/Photo Researchers, Inc.: **Electromagnetic Field**; Robert J. Huffman/Field Mark Publications.: **Anoles, Anteaters, Armadillos, Bison, Blackbirds, Butterflies, Cactus, Capybaras, Carnivorous plants, Carnivorous plants, Composting, Cormorants, Cranes, Crayfish, Crows and jays, Deer, Ducks, Eagles, Falcons, Fossil and fossilization, Frogs, Fungi, Geese, Goats, Gulls, Hawks, Herons (2 photos), Horsetails, Ibises, Iguanas, Juniper, Koalas, Mockingbirds and thrashers, Moths (2 photos), Nuclear fission, Nuthatches, Oaks, Owls (2 photos), Parrots, Peafowl, Peccaries, Pelican, Pheasants, Pigeons and doves, Prairie dog, Praying mantis, Quail, Recycling, Rhinoceros, Sandpipers, Seals, Sparrows and buntings, Squirrels, Starfish, Swallows and martins, Swans, Terns, Thistle, Thrushes, Turkeys, Turtles, Tyrant flycatchers, Warblers, Waste management, Wetlands, Wrens, Zebras**; IBM Almaden: **Compact disc**; © Institut Pastuer/Phototake: **Immune system**; © Bruce Iverson/Science Photo Library, National Audubon Society Collection/Photo Researchers, Inc.: **Electric motor**; © Jacana, National Audubon Society Collection/Photo Reasearchers, Inc.: **Tuna**; © Y. Lanceau Jacana, National Audubon Society Collection/Photo Researchers, Inc.: **Carp**; JLM Visuals: **Acid rain, Africa, Agricultural machines, Agronomy, Alternative energy sources, Animal breeding, Antarctica, Arachnids, Astroblemes, Australia, Barrier Islands, Bitterns, Blue revolution, Brick, Bridges, Buoyancy, Principle of, Camels, Carnivore, Chameleons, Coal, Cotton, Crop rotation, Cycads, Deposit, Desert, Dinosaur, Disturbance, ecological, Dogwood tree, Dust devil, Earthquake, Endangered species, Europe, Fault, Ferns, Ferrets, Flax, Flooding, Fold, Fossil and fossilization, Freshwater, Gerbils, Ginger, Ginkgo, Glaciers, Goatsuckers, Gourd family, Grasses, Grasshoppers, Groundwater, Heath family, Hornbills, Horse chestnut, Ice ages, Igneous rocks, Introduced species, Iris family, Irrigation, Karst topography, Lagomorphs, Lake, Land use, Legumes, Lice, Lichens, Liverwort, Lobsters, Mangrove tree, Marmots, Mass wasting, Milkweeds, Mint family, Mistletoe, Mulberry family, Muskoxen, Mutation, Myrtle family, Nightshade, Octopus, Olive family, Orchid family, Oviparous, Paleobotany, Palms, Pandas, Penguins, Peninsula, Petroleum, Pigs, Pike, Plate tectonics, Pollination, Poppies, Prairie chicken, Pythons, Radio astronomy, Rushes, Savanna, Saxifrage family, Scavenger, Scorpionfish, Sculpins, Sea anemones, Sea level, Sedges, Sediment and sedimentation, Segmented worms, Sequoia, Shrimp, Silk cotton family, Skinks, Snails, Species, Spiderwort family, Storks, Swamp cypress family, Symbiosis, Tea plant, Terracing, Territoriality, Thermal expansion, Tides (2 photos), Trains and railroads, Turbulence, Vireos, Volcano, Vultures, Walnut family, Waterlilies, Wheat, Woodpeckers**; © Mark A. Johnson, Stock Market: **Jellyfish**; © Verna Johnston 1972, National Audubon Society Collection/Photo Researchers, Inc.: **Amaryllis family**; © Verna R. Johnston, National Audubon Society Collection/Photo

Researchers, Inc.: **Gophers**; © Darrell Jones, Stock Market: **Marlins**; © Chris Jones Photo, Stock Market: **Mining**; © Chris Jones, Stock Market: **Mass Production**; © Joyce Photographics, National Audubon Society Collection /Photo Researchers, Inc.: **Soil, Eutrophication**; © Robert Jureit, Stock Market: **Desert**; © John Kaprielian, National Audubon Society Collection/Photo Researchers, Inc.: **Buckwheat**; © Ed Kashi/Phototake: **CAD/CAM/CIM**; © Ted Keane, National Audubon Society Collection/Photo Researchers, Inc.: **Arum family**; © Michael A. Keller 1989, Stock Market: **Nutrition**; © Tom Kelly/Phototake : **Submarine**; © Karl W. Kenyon, National Audubon Society Collection/Photo Researchers, Inc.: **Otters**; © Paolo Koch, National Audubon Society Collection/Photo Researchers, Inc.: **Ore**; © Carl Koford, National Audubon Society Collection/Photo Researchers, Inc.: **Condors**; © Stephen J. Krasemann, National Audubon Society Collection/Photo Researchers, Inc.: **Prescribed burn**; © Charles Krebs, Stock Market: **Dating techniques, Walruses**; © J. Kubec A. NR.m, Stock Market: **Glass**; © Dr. Dennis Kunkel/Phototake: **Membrane, Natural fibers**; © Dennis Kunkel/Phototake : **Blood**; Dennis Kunkel (2) /Phototake: **Mites**; © Maurice & Sally Landre, National Audubon Society Collection/Photo Researchers, Inc.: **Bromeliad family**; © Lawrence Livermore National Laboratory/Science Photo Library, National Audubon Society Collection/Photo Researchers, Inc.: **States of matter**; © Lawrence Berkeley Laboratory/Science Photo Library, National Audubon Society Collection/Photo Researchers, Inc.: **Cyclotron, Particle detectors**; © Francis Leroy, Biocosmos/Science Photo Library, National Audubon Society Collection/Photo Researchers, Inc.: **Hydrothermal vents**; © Tom & Pat Lesson, National Audubon Society Collection/Photo Researchers, Inc.: **Old-growth forests**; © Yoav Levy/Phototake: **Acupuncture, Motion, Machines, simple, Phases of matter, Superconductor, Viscosity, Water pollution**; © Dr. Andrejs Liepins, National Audubon Society Collection/Photo Researchers, Inc.: **Hodgkin's disease**; © Norman Lightfoot, National Audubon Society Collection/Photo Researchers, Inc.: **Albinism**; © Suen-O Linoblad,National Audubon Society Collection/Photo Researchers, Inc.: **Eland**; © R. Ian Lloyd, Stock Market: **Island**; © Paul Logsdon/Phototake: **Contour plowing**; Courtesy of Jacqueline Longe.: **Ultrasonics**; © Dr. Kari Lounatimaa/ Science Photo Library, National Audubon Society Collection/Photo Researchers, Inc.: **Asexual reproduction**; © Alexander Lowry, National Audubon Society Collection/Photo Researchers, Inc.: **Hazardous wastes**; © Renee Lynn, National Audubon Society Collection/Photo Researchers, Inc.: **Capuchins**; © John Madere, Stock Market: **Mass transportation**; © Dr. P. Marazzi, National Audubon Society Collection/Photo Researchers, Inc.: **Edema**; © Andrew J. Martinez, National Audubon Society Collection/Photo Researchers, Inc.: **Flatfish**; © Bob Masini/Phototake: **Radial keratotomy**; © Karl H. Maslowski, National Audubon Society Collection/Photo Researchers, Inc.: **Caribou, Weaver finches**; © Don Mason, Stock Market: **Bats**; © Cynthia Matthews, Stock Market: **Birth**; © C. G. Maxwell, National Audubon Society Collection/Photo Researchers, Inc.: **Cattails**; © Henry Mayer, National Audubon Society Collection/Photo Researchers, Inc.: **Beech family**; © Fred McConnaughey, National Audubon Society Collection/Photo Researchers, Inc.: **Boxfish, Cuttlefish, Mackerel**; © Tom McHugh/Science Source, National Audubon Society Collection/Photo Researchers, Inc.: **Fossil and fossilization**; © Tom McHugh, National Audubon Society Collection/Photo Researchers, Inc.: **Bowerbirds, Canines, Elapid snakes, Elephant shrew, Gibbons and siamangs, Gorillas, Mole-rats, Skates, Sturgeons, Vipers, Salamanders**; © Will and Deni McIntyre, National Audubon Society Collection/Photo Researchers, Inc.: **Canal, Dyslexia, Amniocentesis, Lock**; © Eamonn McNulty, National Audubon Society Collection/Photo Researchers, Inc.: **Pacemaker**; © Dilip Mehia/Contact Giza, Stock Market: **Pyramid**; © Anthony Mercieca Photo, National Audubon Society Collection/Photo Researchers, Inc.: **Bluebirds**; © Astrid & Hanns-Frieder Michler/Science Photo Library, National Audubon Society Collection/Photo Researchers, Inc.: **Precipitation**; © 1983 Lawrence Midgale, National Audubon Society Collection/Photo Researchers, Inc.: **Composite family**; Courtesy of J. Gordon Miller.: **Horses**; © Mobil Solar Energy Corporation/Phototake: **Photovoltaic cell**; © Viviane Moos, Stock Market: **Perpendicular, Smog**; © Moredun Animal Health LTD, National Audubon Society Collection/Photo Researchers, Inc.: **Thrombosis**; © Hank Morgan, National Audubon Society Collection/Photo Researchers, Inc.: **In vitro fertilization**; © Hank Morgan, National Audubon Society Collection/Photo Researchers, Inc.: **Radiation detectors**; © Roy Morsch, Stock Market: **Bioluminescence, Seeds, Toucans**; © Roy Morsch/Bikderberg, Stock Market: **Dams**; © John Moss, National Audubon Society Collection/Photo Researchers, Inc.: **Aqueduct**; © Prof. P. Motta/Dept. of Anatomy/University La Sapienza,

Rome/Science Photo Library, National Audubon Society Collection/Photo Researchers, Inc.: **Connective tissue, Skeletal system, Osteoporosis**; © Prof. P. Motta/G. Macchiarelli/University La Sapienza, Rome/Science Photo Library, National Audubon Society Collection/ Photo Researchers, Inc.: **Heart**; © Mug Shots, Stock Market: **Electrocardiogram**; © Joe Munroe, National Audubon Society Collection/Photo Researchers, Inc.: **Amaranth family, Starlings**; © Dr. Gopal Murti, National Audubon Society Collection/Photo Researchers, Inc.: **Sickle cell anemia**; © S. Nagendra, National Audubon Society Collection/Photo Researchers, Inc.: **Spider monkeys**; © NASA/Science Photo Library, National Audubon Society Collection/Photo Researchers, Inc.: **Radar**; © NASA, National Audubon Society Collection/Photo Researchers, Inc.: **Satellite**; NASA: **Aircraft (2 photos), Airship, Balloon, Black Hole, Comets, Constellation, Dark Matter, Earth, Jupiter (3 photos), Mars (3 photos), Mercury (2 photos), Meteors and meteorites, Moon (3 photos), Neptune (2 photos), Planetary nebulae, Pluto, Rockets and missiles, Saturn (2 photos), Saturn, Solar flare, Solar system, Space Shuttle, Spacecraft, manned, Sun (2 photos), Sunspots, Telephone, Tropical cyclone, Uranus (2 photos), Venus (2 photos)**; © National Aububon Society Collection/Photo Researchers, Inc.: **Monoculture, Aye-ayes, Bass, Chinchilla, Crocodiles, Fossa, Lemur, Plastics, Pneumonia**; © Tom Nebbia, Stock Market: **Drought**; © Nelson-Bohart & Associates/Phototake: **Metamorphosis**; © Ray Nelson/Phototake: **Amplifier**; © Joseph Nettis, National Audubon Society Collection/Photo Researchers, Inc.: **Computerized axial tomography**; © Mark Newman/Phototake: **Glaciers**; © Newman Laboratory of Nuclear Studies, Cornell University, National Audubon Society Collection/Photo Researchers, Inc.: **Subatomic particles**; © NIH, National Audubon Society Collection/Photo Researchers, Inc.: **Artificial heart and heart valve**; © Novosti Press Agency, National Audubon Society Collection/Photo Researchers, Inc.: **Nuclear fusion, Spacecraft, manned**; © Richard Nowitz/Phototake: **Engraving and etching**; © Gregory Ochocki, National Audubon Society Collection/Photo Researchers, Inc.: **Ocean sunfish**; © John Olson , Stock Market : **Brewing, Metal production**; © Omikron, National Audubon Society Collection/Photo Researchers, Inc.: **Lampreys and hagfishes, Squid**; © Omikron, National Audubon Society Collection/Photo Researchers, Inc.: **Tarsiers**; © Stan Osolinski 1993, Stock Market: **Predator**; © Stan Osolinski 1992, Stock Market: **Evolution**; © 1992 Gabe Palmer/Bikderberg, Stock Market: **Sextant**; © David Parker, ESA/National Audubon Society Collection/Photo Researchers, Inc.: **Rockets and missiles**; © David Parker/Science Photo Library, National Audubon Society Collection/Photo Researchers, Inc.: **Oscilloscope**; © David Parker, National Audubon Society Collection/Photo Researchers, Inc.: **Computer, digital**; © Claudia Parks, Stock Market: **Coast and beach**; © David Parler, National Audubon Society Collection/Photo Researchers Inc.: **Particle detector**; © Pekka Parviatnen, National Audubon Society Collection/Photo Researchers, Inc.: **Auroras**; © Alfred Pasieka/Science Photo Library, National Audubon Society Collection/Photo Researchers, Inc.: **Magnetism**; © Bryan F. Peterson, Stock Market: **Natural Gas**; © David M. Phillips/The Population Council/Science Source, National Audubon Society Collection/Photo Researchers, Inc.: **Fertilization**; © Mark D. Phillips, National Audubon Society Collection/Photo Researchers, Inc.: **Monkeys**; © Phototake: **Oryx**; Phototake (CN) /Phototake: **Abscess**; © Photri, Stock Market: **Explosives**; © 1973 Photri/Bikderberg, Stock Market: **Tornado**; © Roy Pinney, National Audubon Society Collection/Photo Researchers, Inc.: **Arum family**; © Philippe Plailly, National Audubon Society Collection/Photo Researchers, Inc.: **Hologram and holography, Microscopy, Gene therapy**; © Philippe Plailly/Eurelious/Science Photo Library, National Audubon Society Collection/Photo Researchers, Inc.: **Microscopy**; © Philippe Plailly/Eurelios, National Audubon Society Collection/Photo Researchers, Inc.: **Electrostatic devices**; © Rod Planck, National Audubon Society Collection/Photo Researchers, Inc.: **Mosquitoes**; © Planet Earth: **Coelacanth, Crocodiles, Orang-utan, Tapirs**; © 1986 David Pollack/Bikderberg, Stock Market: **Concrete**; © J. Polleross, Stock Market: **Emission**; © Marco Polo/Phototake: **Slash-and-burn agriculture**; © Cecilia Posada/Phototake: **Assembly line**; © Masud Quraishy, National Audubon Society Collection/Photo Researchers, Inc.: **Cats**; © E. Hanumantha Rao, National Audubon Society Collection/Photo Researchers, Inc.: **Bee-eaters**; © Rapho, National Audubon Society Collection/Photo Researchers, Inc.: **Dik-diks**; © G. Carleton Ray, National Audubon Society Collection/Photo Researchers, Inc.: **Sharks**; © Hans Reinhard/Okapia 1990, National Audubon Society Collection/Photo Researchers, Inc.: **Carrot family**; © H. Reinhard/Okapia, National Audubon Society Collection/Photo Researchers, Inc.: **Buzzards**; © Roger Ressmeyer/Starlight/for the W. M. Keck Observatory, courtesy of California Associate for Research and Astronomy.: **Telescope**; © Chris Rogers/Bikderberg, Stock Market: **Laser**; © Otto Rogge, Stock Market: **Precious metals**; © Frank Rossotto, Stock Market: **Temperature regulation**; © Martin M. Rotker/Phototake: **Adrenals, Aneurism**; Neasaphus Rowalewkii: **Fossil and fossilization**; © Royal Greenwhich Observatory, National Audubon Society Collection/Photo Researchers, Inc.: **Atomic clocks**; © Royal Observatory, Edinburgh/AATB/Science Photo Library, National Audubon Society Collection/Photo Researchers, Inc.: **Star cluster**; © Royal Observatory, Edinburgh/National Audubon Society Collection/Photo Researchers, Inc.: **Telescope**; © Ronald Royer/Science Photo Library, National Audubon Society Collection/Photo Researchers, Inc.: **Star**; © Leonard Lee Rue III, National Audubon Society Collection/Photo Researchers, Inc.: **Groundhog, Kangaroos and wallabies, Mongooses, Muskrat, Coatis, Rats, Rusts and smuts, Seals**; © Leonard Lee Rue, National Audubon Society Collection/Photo Researchers, Inc.: **Camels**; © Leonard Lee Rue, National Audubon Society Collection/Photo Researchers, Inc.: **Shrews**; © Len Rue Jr., National Audubon Society Collection/Photo Researchers, Inc.: **Badgers**; © S.I.U.,National Audubon Society Collection/Photo Researchers, Inc.: **Lithotripsy**; © 1994 Ron Sanford, Stock Market: **Behavior**; © Nancy Sanford, Stock Market: **Mink**; © Ron Sanford, Stock Market: **Beavers, Raccoons**; © Science Photo Library, National Audubon Society Collection/Photo Researchers, Inc.: **Arthritis, Gangrene, Artificial fibers**; Science Photo Library: **Binary star, Galaxy, Halley's comet, Milky Way, Paleontology, Star formation**; Science Source: **Eclipses, Quasar**; © Secchi-Lecague/Roussel-UCLAF/CNRI/Science Photo Library, National Audubon Society Collection/Photo Researchers, Inc.: **Neuron**; © Nancy Sefton, National Audubon Society Collection/Photo Researchers, Inc.: **Sponges**; © Dr. Gary Settles/Science Source, National Audubon Society Collection/Photo Researchers, Inc.: **Aerodynamics**; James Lee Sikkema: **Elm , Gesnerias, Grapes, Holly family, Lilac, Lily family, Lily family, Maples, Mustard family, Nightshade, Pines, Rose family, Spruce, Spurge family, Swamp cypress family, Willow family**; © Lee D. Simon, National Audubon Society Collection/Photo Researchers, Inc.: **Bacteriophage**; © James R. Simon, National Audubon Society Collection/Photo Researchers, Inc.: **Sloths**; © Ben Simon, Stock Market: **Elephant;** © SIU, National Audubon Society Collection/Photo Researchers, Inc.: **Frostbite**; © SIU, National Audubon Society Collection/ Photo Researchers, Inc.: **Birth**; © Prof. D. Skobeltzn, National Audubon Society Collection/Photo Researchers, Inc.: **Cosmic rays**; © Howard Sochurek, Stock Market: **Gene**; © Dr. M.F. Soper, National Audubon Society Collection/Photo Researchers, Inc.: **Plovers**; Courtesy of Charles H. Southwick: **Macaques, Rhesus monkeys**; © James T. Spencer, National Audubon Society Collection/Photo Researchers, Inc.: **True eels**; © Hugh Spencer, National Audubon Society Collection/Photo Researchers, Inc.: **Spore**; © Spielman/CNRI/Phototake: **Lyme disease**; © St Bartholomew's Hospital, National Audubon Society Collection/Photo Researchers, Inc.: **Bubonic Plague**; © Alvin E. Staffan, National Audubon Society Collection/Photo Researchers, Inc.: **Walkingsticks**; © S. Stammers, National Audubon Society Collection/Photo Researchers, Inc.: **Interferons**; © Peter Steiner, Stock Market: **LED**; © Tom Stewart, Stock Market: **Icebergs**; © David Stoeklein, Stock Market: **Partridges**; © Streinhart Aquarium, National Audubon Society Collection/Photo Researchers, Inc.: **Geckos**; © Mary M. Thacher, National Audubon Society Collection/Photo Researchers, Inc.: **Genets**; © Mary M. Thatcher, National Audubon Society Collection/Photo Researchers, Inc.: **Carrot family**; © Asa C. Thoresen, National Audubon Society Collection/Photo Researchers, Inc.: **Slash-and-burn agriculture**; Geoff Tompkincon, National Audubon Society Collection/Photo Researchers, Inc.: **Surgery**; © Geoff Tompkinson, National Audubon Society Collection/Photo Researchers, Inc.: **Cryogenics**; © Tom Tracy, National Audubon Society Collection/Photo Researchers, Inc.: **Refrigeration**; © Alexander Tsiaras, National Audubon Society Collection/Photo Researchers, Inc.: **Cauterization, Transplant, surgical**; © George Turner, National Audubon Society Collection/Photo Researchers, Inc.: **Cattle family;** © U.S. Fish & Wildlife Service: **Canines, Kangaroo rats, Toads, Turtles**; © Akira Uchiyama, National Audubon Society Collection/Photo Researchers, Inc.: **Saiga antelope**; © Howard Earl Uible, National Audubon Society Collection/Photo Researchers, Inc.: **Marmosets and tamarins**; © Howard E. Uible, National Audubon Society Collection/Photo Researchers, Inc.: **Tenrecs**; © R. Van Nosstrand, National Audubon Society Collection/Photo Researchers, Inc.: **Gibbons and siamang**; © G. Van Heijst and J. Flor, National Audubon Society Collection/Photo Researchers, Inc.: **Chaos**; © Irene Vandermolen, National Audubon Society Collection/Photo Researchers, Inc.: **Banana**; © K. G. Vock/Okapia, National Audubon Society Collection/Photo

Researchers, Inc.: **Birch family**; © Ken Wagner/Phototake: **Herbicides, Agrochemicals**; © Susan Woog Wagner, National Audubon Society Collection/Photo Researchers, Inc.: **Down's syndrome**; © M. I. Walker/Science Photo Library, National Audubon Society Collection/Photo Researchers, Inc.: **Copepods**; © Kennan Ward, Stock Market: **Chimpanzees, Salmon**; Bill Wassman: **Dinosaur**; © C. James Webb/Phototake: **Smallpox**; C. James Webb/Phototake: **Elephantiasis**; © Ulrike Welsch, National Audubon Society Collection/Photo Researchers, Inc.: **Deforestation**; © Jerome Wexler 1981, National Audubon Society Collection/Photo Researchers, Inc.: **Carnivorous plants**; © Herbert Wexler, National Audubon Society Collection/Photo Researchers, Inc.: **Livestock;** © Jeanne White, National Audubon Society Collection/Photo Researchers, Inc.: **Hippopotamuses, Dragonflies**; © George Whiteley, National Audubon Society Collection/Photo Researchers, Inc.: **Horticulture**; © Mark Wilson, National Audubon Society Collection/Photo Researchers, Inc.: **Falcons**; © Charles D. Winters, National Audubon Society Collection/Photo Researchers, Inc.: **Centrifuge**; © Anthony Wolff/Phototake: **Boobies and Gannets**; Illustrations reprinted by permission of Robert L. Wolke.: **Air pollution (2 illustrations), Aluminum, Amino acid, Atom, Barbiturates, Calorimetry, Carbon (3 illustrations), Chemical bond (3 illustrations), Chemical compound (2 illustrations), Crystal, Deoxyribonucleic Acid (DNA), Earth's interior, Electrolysis, Electrolyte, Electromagnetic spectrum, Ester, Fatty acids, Gases, properties of (4 illustrations), Hydrocarbon (3 illustrations), Metric system, Metabolism, Molecule, Nuclear fission (2 illustrations), Plastics, Radiation, Soap, Solution, States of matter (2 illustrations), Water, X rays**; © David Woods, Stock Market: **Cockatoos**; © Norbert Wu, Stock Market: **Courtship, Rays**; © Zefa Germany, Stock Market: **Codfishes, Forests, Hummingbirds, Mole, Rain forest**; © 1994 Zefa Germany, Stock Market: **Bears, Mimicry, Pollination**.

Line art illustrations provided by Hans and Cassady of Westerville, Ohio.

A

A young aardvark in Kenya.

Aardvark

Aardvarks are nocturnal, secretive, termite– and ant–eating mammals, and are one of Africa's strangest animals. Despite superficial appearances, aardvarks are not classified as true anteaters; they have no close relatives and are the only living species of the order Tubulidentata and family Orycteropodidae. Aardvarks are large piglike animals weighing from 88–143 lb (40–65 kg) and measuring nearly 6 ft (20 m) from nose to tip of tail. They have an arched body with a tapering piglike snout at one end and a long tapering tail at the other. Their legs are powerful and equipped with long, strong claws for digging. The first white settlers in South Africa named these peculiar animals aardvarks, which means earth pigs in Afrikaans.

Aardvarks are found throughout Africa south of the Sahara Desert. They spend the daylight hours in burrows and forage for food at night. Grunting, shuffling, and occasionally pressing their nose to the ground, aardvarks zigzag about in search of insect prey. Fleshy tentacles around the nostrils may be chemical receptors that help locate prey. Their favorite food is termites. Using their powerful limbs and claws, aardvarks tear apart concrete–hard termite mounds and lick up the inhabitants with their sticky foot–long tongue. Aardvarks also eat ants, locusts, and the fruit of wild gourds. Adapted for eating termites and ants, the teeth of aardvarks are found only in the cheeks, and have almost no enamel or roots.

Female aardvarks bear one offspring per year. A young aardvark weighs approximately 4 lb (2 kg) when born, and is moved to a new burrow by its mother about every eight days. After two weeks the young aardvark accompanies its mother as she forages, and after about six months it can dig its own burrow.

Hyenas, lions, cheetahs, wild dogs, and humans prey on aardvarks. Many Africans regard aardvark meat as a delicacy, and some parts of the animal are valued by many tribes for their supposed magical powers. If caught in the open, aardvarks leap and bound away with surprising speed; if cornered, they roll over and lash out with their clawed feet. An aardvark's best defense is digging, which it does with astonishing speed even in sun–baked, rock–hard soil. In fact, aardvarks can penetrate soft earth faster than several men digging frantically with shovels.

Aardwolf see **Hyena**

Abacus

The abacus is an ancient calculating machine. This simple apparatus is about 5,000 years old and is thought to have originated in Babylon. As the concepts of zero and Arabic number notation became widespread, basic math functions became simpler, and the use of the abacus diminished. Most of the world employs adding machines, calculators, and computers

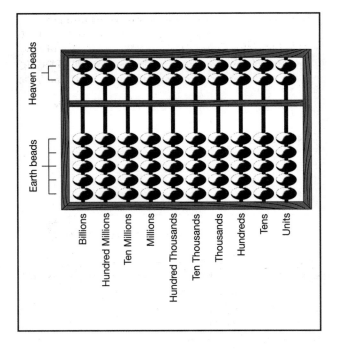

ABOVE: A Chinese abacus called a *suan pan* (reckoning board). NEXT PAGE: An example of addition on a *suan pan*. The heaven beads have five times the value of the earth beads below them.

for mathematical calculations, but today Japan, China, the Middle East, and Russia still use the abacus, and school children in these countries are often taught to use the abacus. In China, the abacus is called a suan pan, meaning counting tray. In Japan the abacus is called a soroban. The Japanese have yearly examinations and competitions in computations on the soroban.

Before the invention of counting machines, people used their fingers and toes, made marks in mud or sand, put notches in bones and wood, or used stones to count, calculate, and keep track of quantities. The first abaci were shallow trays filled with a layer of fine sand or dust. Number symbols were marked and erased easily with a finger. Some scientists think that the term *abacus* comes from the Semitic word for dust, *abq*.

A modern abacus is made of wood or plastic. It is rectangular, often about the size of a shoe–box lid. Within the rectangle, there are at least nine vertical rods strung with movable beads. The abacus is based on the decimal system. Each rod represents columns of written numbers. For example, starting from the right and moving left, the first rod represents ones, the second rod represents tens, the third rod represents hundreds, and so forth. A horizontal crossbar is perpendicular to the rods, separating the abacus into two unequal parts. The moveable beads are located either above or

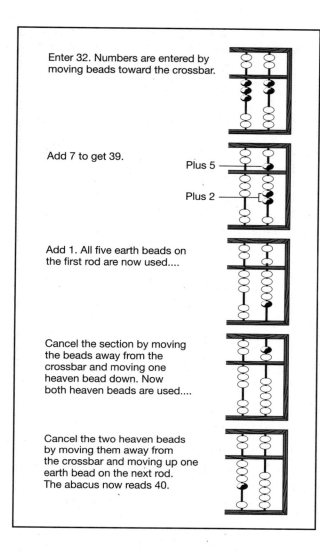

Enter 32. Numbers are entered by moving beads toward the crossbar.

Add 7 to get 39.

Plus 5

Plus 2

Add 1. All five earth beads on the first rod are now used....

Cancel the section by moving the beads away from the crossbar and moving one heaven bead down. Now both heaven beads are used....

Cancel the two heaven beads by moving them away from the crossbar and moving up one earth bead on the next rod. The abacus now reads 40.

one earth (one unit) bead. The number 24 would use four earth beads on the first rod and two earth beads on the second rod. The number 26 then, would use one heaven and one earth bead on the first rod, and two earth beads on the second rod. Addition, subtraction, multiplication, and division can be performed on an abacus. Advanced abacus users can do lengthy multiplication and division problems, and even find the square root or cube root of any number.

See also Arithmetic; Mathematics.

Abalones see **Snails**

Abrasives

Abrasive materials are hard crystals that are either found in nature or manufactured. The most commonly used of such materials are aluminum oxide, silicon carbide, cubic boron nitride, and diamond (see Table 1). Other materials such as garnet, zirconia, glass, and even walnut shells are used for special applications.

Abrasives are primarily used in metalworking because their grains can penetrate even the hardest metals and alloys. However, their great hardness also makes them suitable for working with such other hard materials as stones, glass, and certain types of plastics. Abrasives are also used with relatively soft materials, including wood and rubber, because their use permits high stock removal, long–lasting cutting ability, good form control, and fine finishing.

Applications for abrasives generally fall in the following categories: 1) cleaning of surfaces and the coarse removal of excess material, such as rough off–hand grinding in foundries; 2) shaping, as in form grinding and tool sharpening; 3) sizing, primarily in precision grinding; and 4) separating, as in cut–off or slicing operations.

For the past 100 years or so, manufactured abrasives such as silicon carbide and aluminum oxide have largely replaced natural abrasives—even natural diamonds have nearly been supplanted by synthetic diamonds. The success of manufactured abrasives arises from their superior, controllable properties as well as their dependable uniformity.

Both silicon carbide and aluminum oxide abrasives are very hard and brittle, and as a result they tend to form sharp edges. These edges help the abrasive to

below the crossbar. Beads above the crossbar are called heaven beads, and beads below are called earth beads. Each heaven bead has a value of five units and each earth bead has a value of one unit. A Chinese suan pan has two heaven and five earth beads, and the Japanese soroban has one heaven and four earth beads. These two abaci are slightly different from one another, but they are manipulated and used in the same manner. The Russian version of the abacus has many horizontal rods with moveable, undivided beads, nine to a column.

To operate, the soroban or suan pan is placed flat, and all the beads are pushed to the outer edges, away from the crossbar. Usually the heaven beads are moved with the forefinger and the earth beads are moved with the thumb. For the number one, one earth bead would be pushed up to the crossbar. Number two would require two earth beads. For number five, only one heaven bead would to be pushed to the crossbar. The number six would require one heaven (five units) plus

TABLE 1. COMMON INDUSTRIAL ABRASIVES	
Abrasive	**Used for**
aluminum oxide	grinding plain and alloyed steel in a soft or hardened condition
silicon carbide	cast iron, nonferrous metals, and nonmetallic materials
diamond	grinding cemented carbides, and for grinding glass, ceramics, and hardened tool steel
cubic boron nitride	grinding hardened steels and wear-resistant superalloys

penetrate the work material and reduce the amount of heat generated during the abrasion. This type of abrasive is used in precision and finish grinding. Tough abrasives, which resist fracture and last longer, are used for rough grinding.

Industry uses abrasives in three basic forms: 1) bonded to form solid tools such as grinding wheels, cylinders, rings, cups, segments, or sticks; 2) coated on backings made of paper or cloth in the form of sheets (such as sandpaper), strips or belts; 3) loose, held in some liquid or solid carrier as for polishing or tumbling, or propelled by force of air or water pressure against a work surface (such as sandblasting for buildings).

How do abrasives work?

Abrasion most frequently results from scratching a surface. As a general rule, a substance is only seriously scratched by a material that is harder than itself. This is the basis for the Mohs scale of hardness (see Table 2) in which materials are ranked according to their ability to scratch materials of lesser hardness. Abrasives are therefore usually considered to be refractory materials with hardness values ranging from six to 10 on the Mohs scale that can be used to reduce, smooth, clean, or polish the surfaces of other, less hard substances such as metal, glass, plastic, stone, or wood.

During abrasion, abrasive particles first penetrate the abraded material and then cause a tearing off of particles from the abraded surface. The ease with which the abrasive particles dig into the surface depends on the hardness of the abraded surface; the ease with which the deformed surface is torn off depends on the strength and, in some cases, on the toughness of the material. Between hardness, strength, and toughness, hardness is usually the most important factor determining a material's resistance to abrasion.

When two surfaces move across each other, peaks of microscopic irregularities must either shift position, increase in hardness, or break. If local stresses are sufficiently great, failure of a tiny volume of abraded material will result, and a small particle will be detached. This type of abrasion occurs regardless of whether contact of the two surfaces is due to sliding, rolling, or impact.

Some forms of abrasion involve little or no impact, but in others the energy of impact is a deciding factor in determining the effectiveness of the abrasive. Brittle materials, for example, tend to shatter when impacted, and their abrasion may resemble erosion more than fracture.

See also Crystal.

Further Reading:

Green, Robert E., ed. *Machinery's Handbook,* New York: Industrial Press, 1992.

Randall Frost

Abscess

An abscess is a circumscribed collection of pus usually caused by microorganisms. Abscesses can occur anywhere in the body—in hard or soft tissue, organs or confined spaces. Due to their fluid content, abscesses can assume various shapes. Their internal pressure can cause compression and displacement of surrounding tissue, resulting in pain. An abscess is part of the body's natural defense mechanism; it localizes infection to prevent the spread of bacteria.

TABLE 2. MOHS HARDNESSES OF SELECTED MATERIALS	
Abrasive	*Mohs Hardness*
wax (0 deg C)	0.2
graphite	0.5 to 1
talc	1
copper	2.5 to 3
gypsum	2
aluminum	2 to 2.9
gold	2.5 to 3
silver	2.5 to 4
calcite	3
brass	3 to 4
fluorite	4
glass	4.5 to 6.5
asbestos	5
apatite	5
steel	5 to 8.5
cerium oxide	6
orthoclase	6
vitreous silica	7
beryl	7.8
quartz	8
topaz	9
aluminum oxide	9
silicon carbide (beta type)	9.2
boron carbide	9.3
boron	9.5
diamond	10

Any trauma such as injury, bacterial or amoebic infection, or surgery can result in an abscess. Microorganisms causing an abscess may enter tissue following penetration (e.g., a cut or puncture) with an unsterile object or be spread from an adjacent infection. These microorganisms also are disseminated by the lymph and circulatory systems.

Abscesses are more likely to occur if the urinary, biliary, respiratory, or immune systems have impaired function. A foreign object such as a splinter or stitch can predispose an area to an abscess. The body's inflammatory response mechanism reacts to trauma. The area involved has increased blood flow; leukocytes (mostly neutrophils) and exudates (fluid, typically serum and cellular debris) escape from blood vessels at the early stage of inflammation and collect in any available space. Neutrophils release enzymes which are thought to help establish the abscess cavity. The exudate attracts water, causing swelling in the affected area. Usually the body removes various exudates with its circulatory and lymphatic systems. When the body's immune response is altered by disease, extreme fatigue, or other predisposing factors as mentioned above, resolution of the inflamed area is slow to occur. If the affected area does not heal properly, an abscess can form.

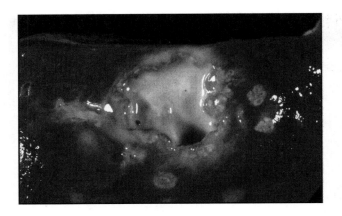

An amoebic abscess caused by *Entameoba histolytica*.

Symptoms of an abscess vary according to location. Fever and pain can be present while dysfunction of an organ system sometimes is the symptom. An abscess can rupture and drain to the outside of the body or into surrounding tissue where the fluid and debris can be reabsorbed into the blood stream. Occasionally surgical drainage or antibiotics are needed to resolve an abscess.

See also Immune system; Inflammation.

Absolute zero see **Temperature**

Absolute temperature see **Temperature**

Absolute dating see **Dating techniques**

Absorption spectrum see **Atomic spectroscopy**

Abyssal plain

Abyssal plains are the vast, flat, sediment–covered areas of the deep ocean floor. They are the flattest, most featureless areas on the Earth, and have a slope of less than one foot of elevation difference for each thousand feet of distance. The lack of features is due to a thick blanket of sediment that covers most of the surface.

These flat abyssal plains occur at depths of over 6,500 ft (1,980 m) below sea level. They are underlain by the oceanic crust, which is predominantly basalt — a dark, fine–grained volcanic rock. Typically, the basalt is covered by layers of sediments, much of which is

deposited by deep ocean turbidity currents (caused by the greater density of sediment–laden water), or biological materials, such as minute shells of marine plants and animals, that have "rained" down from the ocean's upper levels, or a mixture of both.

Other components of abyssal plain sediment include wind–blown dust, volcanic ash, chemical precipitates, and occasional meteorite fragments. Abyssal plains are often littered with nodules of manganese containing varying amounts of iron, nickel, cobalt, and copper. These pea– to potato–sized nodules form by direct precipitation of minerals from the seawater onto a bone or rock fragment. Currently, deposits of manganese nodules are not being mined from the sea bed, but it is possible that they could be collected and used in the future.

Of the 15 billion tons of river–carried clay, sand, and gravel that is washed into the oceans each year, only a fraction of this amount reaches the abyssal plains. The amount of biological sediments that reaches the bottom is similarly small. Thus, the rate of sediment accumulation on the abyssal plains is very slow, and in many areas, less than an inch of sediment accumulates per thousand years. Because of the slow rate of accumulation and the monotony of the topography, abyssal plains were once believed to be a stable, unchanging environment. However, deep ocean currents have been discovered that scour the ocean floor in places. Some currents have damaged trans–oceanic communication cables laid on these plains.

Although they are more common and widespread in the Atlantic and Indian ocean basins than in the Pacific, abyssal plains are found in all major ocean basins. Approximately 40% of our planet's ocean floor is covered by abyssal plains. The remainder of the ocean floor topography consists of hills, cone–shaped or flat–topped mountains, deep trenches, and mountain chains such as the mid–oceanic ridge systems.

The abyssal plains do not support a great abundance of aquatic life, though some species do survive in this relatively barren environment. Deep sea dredges have collected specimens of unusual–looking fish, worms, and clam–like creatures from these depths.

See also Ocean.

Acceleration

The term acceleration, used in physics, is a vector quantity. This means that acceleration contains both a number which is called its magnitude and a specific direction. An object is said to be accelerating if its rate of change of velocity is increasing or decreasing over a period of time and/or if its direction of motion is changing. The units for acceleration include a distance unit and two time units. Examples are m/s^2 and mi/hr/s. Sir Isaac Newton in his Second Law of Motion defined acceleration as the ratio of an unbalanced force acting on an object to the mass of the object.

History

The study of motion by Galileo Galilei (1564–1642) in the late 16th and early 17th centuries and by Sir Isaac Newton (1642–1727) in the mid–17th century was one of the major cornerstones of modern Western experimental science. Over a period of 20 years, Galileo observed the motions of objects rolling down various inclines and attempted to time these events. He discovered that the distance an object traveled was proportional to the square of the time that it was in motion. From these experiments came the first correct concept of accelerated motion. Newton wanted to know why acceleration occurred. In order to produce a model that would help explain how the known universe of the seventeenth century worked, Newton had to give to science and physics the concept of a force which was mostly unknown at that time. With his Second Law of Motion, he clearly demonstrated that acceleration is caused by an unbalanced force (commonly called a push or a pull) acting on an object. What we call gravity, Newton showed was nothing more than a special type of acceleration. The interaction of the acceleration of gravity on the mass of our body produces the force which is called weight. A general definition of mass is that it refers to the quantity of matter in a body.

Linear acceleration

An object that is moving in a straight line is accelerating if its velocity (sometimes incorrectly referred to as speed) is increasing or decreasing during a given period of time. Acceleration (a) can be either positive or negative depending on whether the velocity is increasing (+a) or decreasing (–a). An automobile's motion can help explain linear acceleration. The speedometer measures the velocity. If the auto starts from rest and accelerates to 60 mph in 10 seconds, what is the acceleration? The auto's velocity changed 60 mph in 10 seconds. Therefore, its acceleration is 60 mph/10 s = + six mi/hr/s. That means its acceleration changed six miles per hour every second it was moving. Notice there are one distance unit and two time units in the answer. If the auto had started at 60 mph and then

stopped in 10 seconds after the brakes were applied, the acceleration would be = –6 mi/hr/s. If this automobile changes direction while moving at this constant acceleration, it will have a different acceleration because the new vector will be different from the original vector. The mathematics of vectors are quite complex.

Circular acceleration

In circular motion, the velocity may remain constant but the direction of motion will change. If our automobile is going down the road at a constant 60 mph and it goes around a curve in the road, the auto undergoes acceleration because its direction is constantly changing while it is in the curve. Roller coasters and other amusement park rides produce rapid changes in acceleration (sometimes called centripetal acceleration) which will cause such effects as "g" forces, "weightlessness" and other real or imaginary forces to act on the body, causing dramatic experiences to occur. The astronauts experience as much as 7 "gs" during lift–off of the space shuttle but once in orbit it appears that they have lost all their weight. The concept of "weightlessness" in space is a highly misunderstood phenomena. It is not caused by the fact that the shuttle is so far from the Earth; it is produced because the space shuttle is in free fall under the influence of gravity. The shuttle is traveling 17,400 mph around the Earth and it is continually falling toward the Earth, but the Earth falls away from the shuttle at exactly the same rate.

Force and acceleration

Before the time of Sir Isaac Newton, the concept of force was unknown. Newton's Second Law was a simple equation and an insight that significantly affected physics in the seventeenth century as well as today. In the Second Law, given any object of mass (m), the acceleration (a) given to that object is directly proportional to the net force (F) acting on the object and inversely proportional to the mass of the object. Symbolically, this means a = F/m or in its more familiar form F = ma. In order for acceleration to occur, a net force must act on an object.

See also Accelerators; Gravity and gravitation; Laws of motion; Vector; Velocity.

Further Reading:

Cohen, I. Bernard. *Introduction to Newton's Principia.* Cambridge, MA: Harvard University Press, 1971.
Galilei, Galileo (trans. by H. Crew and A. DiSalvo). *Dialogues Concerning Two New Sciences.* Glendale, CA: Prometheus Books, 1991.

Hewitt, Paul. *Conceptual Physics.* New York: Harper-Collins Publishers, Inc., 1992.

Olenick, Richard, et al. *The Mechanical Universe: Introduction to Mechanics and Heat.* New York: Cambridge University Press, 1985.

Serway, Raymond and J. Faughn. *College Physics.* 3rd ed. Knoxville, TN: SPC Publishers, Inc., 1992.

Methods of Motion: An Introduction to Mechanics. Washington, D.C.: National Science Teachers Association, 1992.

Kenneth L. Frazier

Accelerators

The term accelerators most commonly refers to particle accelerators, devices for increasing the velocity of subatomic particles such as protons, electrons, and positrons. Particle accelerators were originally invented for the purpose of studying the basic structure of matter, although they later found a number of practical applications. Particle accelerators can be subdivided into two large sub–groups: linear and circular accelerators. Machines of the first type accelerate particles as they travel in a short line, sometimes over very great distances. Circular accelerators move particles along a circular or spiral path in machines that vary in size from less than a few feet to many miles in diameter.

The simplest particle accelerator was invented by Alabama–born physicist Robert Jemison Van de Graaff (1901–1967) in about 1929. The machine that now bears his name illustrates the fundamental principles on which all particle accelerators are based.

In the Van de Graaff accelerator, a silk conveyor belt collects positive charges from a high–voltage source at one end of the belt and transfers those charges to the outside of a hollow dome at the other end of the belt located at the top of the machine. The original Van de Graaff accelerator operated at a potential difference of 80,000 volts, although later improvements raised that value to 5,000,000 volts.

The Van de Graaff accelerator can be converted to a particle accelerator by attaching a source of positively charged ions, such as protons or He^+ ions, to the hollow dome. These ions feel an increasingly strong force of repulsion as positive charges accumulate on the dome. At some point, the ions are released from their source, and they travel away from the dome with high energy and at high velocities. If this beam of rapidly–moving particles is directed at a target, the ions of which it consists may collide with atoms in the target and break them apart. An analysis of ion–atom collisions such as these can provide a great deal of information about the structure of the target atoms, about the ion "bullets" and about the nature of matter in general.

Linear accelerators

In a Van de Graaff generator, the velocity of an electrically charged particle is increased by exposing that particle to an electric field. The velocity of a proton, for example, may go from zero to 100,000 miles per second (160,000 km per second) as the particle feels a strong force of repulsion from the positive charge on the generator dome. Linear accelerators (linacs) operate on the same general principle except that a particle is exposed to a series of electrical fields, each of which increases the velocity of the particle.

A typical linac consists of a few hundred or a few thousand cylindrical metal tubes arranged one in front of another. The tubes are electrically charged so that each carries a charge opposite that of the tube on either side of it. Tubes 1, 3, 5, 7, 9, etc., might, for example, be charged positively, and tubes 2, 4, 6, 7, 10, etc., charged negatively.

Imagine that a negatively charged electron is introduced into a linac just in front of the first tube. In the circumstances described above, the electron is attracted by and accelerated toward the first tube. The electron passes toward and then into that tube. Once inside the tube, the electron no longer feels any force of attraction or repulsion and merely drifts through the tube until it reaches the opposite end. It is because of this behavior that the cylindrical tubes in a linac are generally referred to as drift tubes.

At the moment that the electron leaves the first drift tube, the charge on all drift tubes is reversed. Plates 1, 3, 5, 7, 9, etc. are now negatively charged, and plates 2, 4, 6, 8, 10, etc. are positively charged. The electron exiting the first tube now finds itself repelled by the tube it has just left and attracted to the second tube. These forces of attraction and repulsion provide a kind of "kick" that accelerates the electron in a forward direction. It passes through the space between tubes 1 and 2 and into tube 2. Once again, the electron drifts through this tube until it exits at the opposite end.

The electrical charge on all drift tubes reverses, and the electron is repelled by the second tube and attracted to the third tube. The added energy it receives is manifested in a greater velocity. As a result, the electron is moving faster in the third tube than in the second and can cover a greater distance in the same amount of time. To make sure that the electron exits a tube at just the right moment, the tubes must be of different lengths. Each one is slightly longer than the one before it.

The largest linac in the world is the Stanford Linear Accelerator, located at the Stanford Linear Accelerator Center (SLAC) in Stanford, California. An underground tunnel 2 mi (3 km) in length passes beneath U.S. highway 101 and holds 82,650 drift tubes along with the magnetic, electrical, and auxiliary equipment needed for the machine's operation. Electrons accelerated in the SLAC linac leave the end of the machine traveling at nearly the speed of light with a maximum energy of about 32 GeV (gigaelectron volts).

The term electron volt (ev) is the standard unit of energy measurement in accelerators. It is defined as the energy lost or gained by an electron as it passes through a potential difference of one volt. Most accelerators operate in the megaelectron volt (million electron volt; MeV), gigaelectron volt (billion electron volt; GeV), or teraelectron volt (trillion electron volt; TeV) range.

Circular accelerators

The development of linear accelerators is limited by some obvious physical constraints. For example, the SLAC linac is so long that engineers had to take into consideration the Earth's curvature when they laid out the drift tube sequence. One way of avoiding the problems associated with the construction of a linac is to accelerate particles in a circle. Machines that operate on this principle are known, in general, as circular accelerators.

The earliest circular accelerator, the cyclotron, was invented by University of California professor of physics Ernest Orlando Lawrence in the early 1930s. Lawrence's cyclotron added to the design of the linac one new fundamental principle from physics: a charged particle that passes through a magnetic field travels in a curved path. The shape of the curved path depends on the velocity of the particle and the strength of the magnetic field.

The cyclotron consists of two hollow metal containers that look as if a tuna fish can had been cut in half vertically. Each half resembles a uppercase letter D, so the two parts of the cyclotron are known as dees. At any one time, one dee in the cyclotron is charged positively and the other negatively. But the dees are connected to a source of alternating current so that the signs on both dees change back and forth many times per second.

The second major component of a cyclotron is a large magnet that is situated above and below the dees. The presence of the magnet means that any charged particles moving within the dees will travel not in straight paths, but in curves.

Imagine that an electron is introduced into the narrow space between the two dees. The electron is accelerated into one of the dees, the one carrying a positive charge. As it moves, however, the electron travels toward the dee in a curved path.

After a fraction of a second, the current in the dees changes signs. The electron is then repelled by the dee toward which it first moved, reverses direction, and heads toward the opposite dee with an increased velocity. Again, the electron's return path is curved because of the magnetic field surrounding the dees.

Just as a particle in a linac passes through one drift tube after another, always gaining energy, so does a particle in a cyclotron. As the particle gains energy, it picks up speed and spirals outward from the center of the machine. Eventually, the particle reaches the outer circumference of the machine, passes out through a window, and strikes a target.

Lawrence's original cyclotron was a modest piece of equipment— only 4.5 in (11 cm) in diameter—capable of accelerating protons to an energy of 80,000 electron volts (80 kiloelectron volts). It was assembled from coffee cans, sealing wax, and leftover laboratory equipment. The largest accelerators of this design ever built were the 86 in (218 cm) and 87 in (225 cm) cyclotrons at the Oak Ridge National Laboratory and the Nobel Institute in Stockholm, Sweden, respectively.

Cyclotron modifications

At first, improvements in cyclotron design were directed at the construction of larger machines that could accelerate particles to greater velocities. Soon, however, a new problem arose. Physical laws state that nothing can travel faster than the speed of light. Thus, adding more and more energy to a particle will not make that particle's speed increase indefinitely. Instead, as the particle's velocity approaches the speed of light, additional energy supplied to it appears in the form of increased mass. A particle whose mass is constantly increasing, however, begins to travel in a path different from that of a particle with constant mass. The practical significance of this fact is that, as the velocity of particles in a cyclotron begins to approach the speed of light, those particles start to fall "out of synch" with the current change that drives them back and forth between dees.

Two different modifications—or a combination of the two—can be made in the basic cyclotron design to deal with this problem. One approach is to gradually change the rate at which the electrical field alternates between the dees. The goal here is to have the sign change occur at exactly the moment that particles have reached a certain point within the dees. As the particles speed up and gain weight, the rate at which electrical current alternates between the two dees slows down to "catch up" with the particles.

In the 1950s, a number of machines containing this design element were built in various countries. Those machines were known as frequency modulated (FM) cyclotrons, synchrocyclotrons, or, in the Soviet Union, phasotrons. The maximum particle energy attained with machines of this design ranged from about 100 MeV to about 1 GeV.

A second solution for the mass increase problem is to alter the magnetic field of the machine in such a way as to maintain precise control over the particles' paths.

This principle has been incorporated into the machines that are now the most powerful cyclotrons in the world, the synchrotrons.

A synchrotron consists essentially of a hollow circular tube (the ring) through which particles are accelerated. The particles are actually accelerated to velocities close to the speed of light in smaller machines before they are injected into the main ring. Once they are within the main ring, particles receive additional jolts of energy from accelerating chambers placed at various locations around the ring. At other locations around the ring, very strong magnets control the path followed by the particles. As particles pick up energy and tend to spiral outward, the magnetic fields are increased, pushing particles back into a circular path. The most powerful synchrotrons now in operation can produce particles with energies of at least 400 GeV.

In the 1970s, nuclear physicists proposed the design and construction of the most powerful synchrotron of all, the superconducting super collider (SSC). The SSC was expected to have an accelerating ring 82.9 kilometers (51.5 miles) in circumference with the ability to produce particles having an energy of 20 TeV. Estimated cost of the SSC was originally set at about $4 billion. Shortly after construction of the machine at Waxahachie, Texas began, however, the United States Congress decided to discontinue funding for the project.

Applications

By far the most common use of particle accelerators is basic research on the composition of matter. The quantities of energy released in such machines are unmatched anywhere on Earth. At these energy levels, new forms of matter are produced that do not exist under ordinary conditions. These forms of matter provide clues about the ultimate structure of matter.

Accelerators have also found some important applications in medical and industrial settings. As particles travel through an accelerator, they give off a form of radiation known as synchrotron radiation. This form of radiation is somewhat similar to x rays and has been used for similar purposes.

See also Subatomic particles.

Further Reading:

Glashow, Sheldon L., and Leon M. Lederman, "The SSC: A Machine for the Nineties," *Physics Today*, March 1985, pp. 28–37.

Livingston, M. Stanley, and John P. Blewett. *Particle Accelerators*. New York: McGraw–Hill, 1962.

Newton, David E. *Particle Accelerators: From the Cyclotron to the Superconducting Super Collider*. New York: Franklin Watts, 1989.

Winick, Herman, "Synchrotron Radiation," *Scientific American*, November 1987, pp. 88–99.

David E. Newton

Accretion disk

An accretion disk is an astronomical term that refers to the rapidly spiraling matter that is in the process of falling into an astronomical object. In principle, any star could have an accretion disk, but in practice, accretion disks are often associated with highly collapsed stars such as black holes or neutron stars.

The matter that serves as the base of the accretion disk can be obtained when a star passes through a region where the interstellar matter is thicker than normal. Normally, however, a star gets an accretion disk from a companion star. When two stars orbit each other there is an invisible figure eight around the two stars, called the *Roche lobes*. The Roche lobes represent all the points in space where the gravitational potential from each star is equal. Therefore any matter on the Roche lobes could just as easily fall into either star. If one star in a binary system becomes larger than the Roche lobes, matter will fall from it onto the other star, forming an accretion disk.

The matter falling into a collapsing star hole tends to form a disk because a spherical mass of gas that is spinning will tend to flatten out. The faster it is spinning, the flatter it gets. So, if the falling material is orbiting the central mass, the spinning flattens the matter into an accretion disk.

Black holes are objects that have collapsed to the point that nothing, not even light, can escape the incredible force of their gravity. Because no light can escape, however, there is no way to directly observe it. However, if the black hole has an accretion disk, we can observe the black hole indirectly by observing the accretion disk, which will emit x rays. Without accretion disks there would be little hope of astronomers ever observing black holes.

Accretion disks can also occur with a white dwarf in a binary system. A white dwarf is a collapsed star that is the final stage in the evolution of stars similar to the Sun. White dwarfs contain as much mass as the Sun, compressed to about the size of Earth. Normally the nuclear reactions in a white dwarf have run out of fuel, but the hydrogen from the accretion disk falling onto a white dwarf fuels additional nuclear reactions. White dwarfs have some unusual properties that do not allow them to expand slowly to release the heat pressure generated by these nuclear reactions. This heat pressure therefore builds up until the surface of the white dwarf explodes. This type of explosion is called a nova (not to be confused with a supernova), and typically releases as much energy in less than a year as the Sun does in 100,000 years.

See also Black hole; Interstellar matter; Neutron star; White dwarf.

Accuracy

Accuracy is how close an experimental reading or calculation is to the true value. Lack of accuracy may be due to error or due to approximation. The less total error in an experiment or calculation, the more accurate the results. Error analysis can provide information about the accuracy of a result.

Accuracy in measurements

Errors in experiments stem from incorrect design, inexact equipment, and approximations in measurement. Imperfections in equipment are a fact of life, and sometimes design imperfections are unavoidable as well. Approximation is also unavoidable and depends on the fineness and correctness of the measuring equipment. For example, if the finest marks on a ruler are in centimeters, then the final measurement is not likely to have an accuracy of more than half a centimeter. But if the ruler includes millimeter markings, then the measurements can be an order of magnitude more accurate.

Accuracy differs from precision. Precision deals with how repeatable measurements are—if multiple measurements return numbers that are close to each other, then the experimental results are precise. The results may be far from accurate, but they will be precise.

In calculations

Approximations are also unavoidable in calculations. Neither people nor computers can provide a totally accurate number for 1/3 or pi or any of several other numbers, and often the desired accuracy does not require it. The person calculating does, however make sure that the approximations are sufficiently small that they do not endanger the useful accuracy of the result. Accuracy becomes an issue in computations because rounding errors accumulate, series expansions are attenuated, and other methods that are not analytical tend to include errors.

Rounding

If you buy several items, all of which are subject to a sales tax, then you can calculate the total tax by summing the tax on each item. However, for the total tax to be accurate to the penny, you must do all the calculations to an accuracy of tenths of a penny (in other words, to three significant digits), then round the sum to the nearest penny (two significant digits). If you calculated only to the penny, then each measurement might be off by as much as half a penny ($0.005) and the total possible error would be this amount multiplied by the number of items bought. If you bought three items, then the error could be as large as 1.5 cents; if you bought 10 items then your total tax could be off by as much as five cents.

As another example, if you want to know the value of pi to an accuracy of two decimal places, then you could express it as 3.14. This could also be expressed as 3.14 +/- 0.005 since any number from 3.135 to 3.145 could be expressed the same way—to two significant decimal points. Any calculations using a number accurate to two decimal places are only accurate to one decimal place. In a similar example, the accuracy of a table can either refer to the number of significant digits of the numbers in a table or the number of significant digits in computations made from the table.

Acetic acid

Acetic acid is an organic acid with the chemical formula CH_3COOH. It is found most commonly in vinegar.

In the form of vinegar, acetic acid is one of the earliest chemical compounds known to and used by humans. It is mentioned in the Bible as a condiment and was used even earlier in the manufacture of white lead and the extraction of mercury metal from its ores. The first reasonably precise chemical description of the acid was provided by the German natural philosopher Johann Rudolf Glauber in about 1648.

Acetic acid is a colorless liquid with a sharp, distinctive odor and the characteristic taste associated with vinegar. In its pure form it is referred to as *glacial acetic acid* because of its tendency to crystallize as it is cooled. Glacial acetic acid has a melting point of 62°F (16.7°C) and a boiling point of 244°F (118.0°C). The acid mixes readily with water, ethyl alcohol, and many other liquids. Its water solutions display typical acid behaviors such as neutralization of oxides and bases and reactions with carbonates. Glacial acetic acid is an extremely caustic substance with a tendency to burn the skin. This tendency is utilized by the medical profession for wart removal.

Originally acetic acid was manufactured from pyroligneous acid which, in turn, was obtained from the destructive distillation of wood. Today the compound is produced commercially by the oxidation of butane, ethylene, or methanol (wood alcohol). Acetic acid forms naturally during the aerobic fermentation of sugar or alcoholic solutions such as beer, cider, fruit juice, and wine. This process is catalyzed by the bacterium *Acetobacter*, a process from which the species gets its name.

Although acetic acid is best known to the average person in the form of vinegar, its primary commercial use is in the production of cellulose acetate, vinyl acetate, and terephthalic acid. The first of these compounds is widely used as a rubber substitute and in photographic and cinematic film, while the latter two compounds are starting points for the production of polymers such as adhesives, latex paints, and plastic film and sheeting.

A promising new use for acetic acid is in the manufacture of calcium–magnesium acetate (CMA), a highly effective and biodegradable deicer. CMA has had limited use in the past because it is 50 times more expensive than salt. In 1992, however, Shang–Tian Yang, an engineer at Ohio State University, announced a new method for making acetic acid from wastes produced during cheese making. Yang's process may soon make CMA competitive with salt as a commercial deicer.

Most commonly vinegar is prepared commercially by the fermentation of apple cider, malt, or barley. The fermentation product is a brownish or yellow liquid consisting of 4–8% acetic acid. It is then distilled to produce a clear colorless liquid known as *white vinegar*.

See also Fermentation.

Acetaminophen see **Analgesia**

Acetone

Acetone is a colorless, flammable, and volatile liquid with a characteristic odor that can be detected at very low concentrations. It is used in consumer goods such as nail polish remover, model airplane glue, lacquers, and paints. Industrially, it is used mainly as a solvent and an ingredient to make other chemicals.

Acetone is the common name for the simplest of the ketones. The formula of acetone is $CH_3 \cdot CO \cdot CH_3$.

The International Union of Pure and Applied Chemistry's (IUPAC) systematic name for acetone is 2–propanone; it is also called dimethyl ketone. The molecular weight is 58.08. Its boiling point is 133°F (56.2°C) and the melting point is −139.63°F (−95.35°C). The specific gravity is .7899.

Acetone is the simplest and most important of the ketones. It is a polar organic solvent and therefore dissolves a wide variety of substances. It has low chemical reactivity. These traits, and its relatively low cost, make it the solvent of choice for many processes. About 25% of the acetone produced is used directly as a solvent.

About 20% is used in the manufacture of methyl methacrylate to make plastics such as acrylic plastic, which can be used in place of glass. Another 20% is used to manufacture methyl isobutyl ketone, which serves as a solvent in surface coatings. Acetone is important in the manufacture of artificial fibers, explosives, and polycarbonate resins.

Because of its importance as a solvent and as a starting material for so many chemical processes, acetone is produced in the United States in great quantities. Acetone was 42nd in industrial volume in 1993 when 2.463 billion lbs (1 billion kg) were produced. Today, acetone is available at low cost and high purity

to laboratories, so it is rarely synthesized outside of industry.

Acetone is normally present in low concentrations in human blood and urine. Diabetic patients produce it in larger amounts. Sometimes "acetone breath" is detected on the breath of diabetics by others and wrongly attributed to the drinking of liquor. If acetone is splashed in the eyes, irritation or damage to the cornea will result. Excessive breathing of fumes causes headache, weariness, and irritation of the nose and throat. Drying results from contact with the skin.

Acetylcholine see **Neurotransmitters**
Acetyline see **Hydrocarbon**

Acetylsalicylic acid

Acetylsalicylic acid, commonly known as aspirin, is the most popular therapeutic drug in the world. It is an analgesic (pain–killing), antipyretic (fever–reducing), and anti–inflammatory sold without a prescription as tablets, capsules, powders, or suppositories. The drug reduces pain and fever, is believed to decrease the risk of heart attacks and strokes, and may deter colon cancer and help prevent premature birth. Often called the wonder drug, aspirin can have serious side effects, and its use results in more accidental poisoning deaths in children under five years of age than any other drug.

History

In the mid–to–late 1700s, English clergyman Edward Stone chewed on a piece of willow bark and discovered its analgesic property after hearing an "old wives' tale" that declared a brew from the bark was "good for pain and whatever else ails you." The bark's active ingredient was isolated in 1827 and named salicin for the Greek word *salix*, meaning willow. Salicylic acid, first produced from salicin in 1838 and synthetically from phenol in 1860, was effective in treating rheumatic fever and gout but caused severe nausea and intestinal discomfort. In 1898, a chemist named Hoffmann, working at Bayer Laboratories in Germany and whose father suffered from severe rheumatoid arthritis, synthesized acetylsalicylic acid in a successful attempt to eliminate the side effects of salicylic acid, which, until then, was the only drug that eased his father's pain. Soon the process for making large quantities of acetylsalicylic acid was patented, and aspirin—named for its ingredients acetyl and spiralic (salicylic) acid—became available by prescription. Its popularity was immediate and worldwide. Huge demand in the United States brought manufacture of aspirin to that country in 1915 when it also became available without a prescription.

Mechanism of action

Analgesic/anti–inflammatory action

Aspirin's recommended therapeutic adult dosage ranges from 600–1000 milligrams and works best against "tolerable" pain; extreme pain is virtually unaffected, as is pain in internal organs. Aspirin inhibits (blocks) production of hormones (chemical substances formed by the body) called prostaglandins which may be released by an injured cell, triggering release of two other hormones which sensitize nerves to pain. The blocking action prevents this response and is believed to work in a similar way to prevent tissue inflammation. Remarkably, aspirin only acts on cells producing prostaglandins—for instance, injured cells. Its effect lasts approximately four hours.

Antipyretic action

This action is believed to occur at the anterior (frontal) hypothalamus, a portion of the brain which regulates such functions as heart rate and body temperature. The body naturally reduces its heat through perspiration and the dilation (expansion) of blood vessels. Prostaglandins released in the hypothalamus inhibit the body's natural heat–reducing mechanism. As aspirin blocks these prostaglandins, the hypothalamus is free to regulate body temperature. Aspirin lowers abnormally high body temperatures while normal body temperature remains unaffected.

Blood–thinning action

One prostaglandin, thromboxane A_2, aids platelet aggregation (accumulation of blood cells). Because aspirin inhibits thromboxane production, thus "thinning the blood," it is frequently prescribed in low doses over long periods for at–risk patients to help prevent heart attacks and strokes.

Adverse affects

Poisoning

Aspirin's availability and presence in many prescription and non–prescription medications makes the

---

KEY TERMS

Analgesic—Compound which relieves pain without loss of consciousness.

Antipyretic—Anything that reduces fever.

Hypothalamus—A small area near the base of the brain where release of hormones influence such involuntary bodily functions as temperature, sexual behavior, sweating, heart rate, and moods.

Placenta—An organ which develops in the uterus during pregnancy to which the fetus is connected by the umbilical cord and through which the fetus receives nourishment and eliminates waste.

Platelets—Irregularly shaped disks found in the blood of mammals which aid in clotting the blood.

Prostaglandins—Groups of hormones and active substances produced by body tissue which regulate important bodily functions, such as blood pressure.

Suppository—Medication placed in a body cavity, usually the vagina or rectum, which melts and is absorbed by the body.

---

risk of accidental overdose relatively high. Children and the elderly are particularly susceptible, as their toxicity thresholds are much lower than adults. About 10% of all accidental or suicidal episodes reported by hospitals are related to aspirin.

Bleeding

As aspirin slows down platelet accumulation, its use increases risk of bleeding, a particular concern during surgery and childbirth. Aspirin's irritant effect on the stomach lining may cause internal bleeding, sometimes resulting in anemia.

Reye's syndrome

Reye's syndrome is an extremely rare disease, primarily striking children between the ages of three and 15 years after they have been treated with aspirin for a viral infection. Reye's syndrome manifests as severe vomiting, seizures, disorientation, and sometimes coma, which can result in permanent brain damage or death. The cause of Reye's is unknown, but the onset strongly correlates to the treatment of viral infections with aspirin, and incidents of Reye's in children on aspirin therapy for chronic arthritis is significant. In 1985, these observations were widely publicized and warning labels placed on all aspirin medications, resulting in a decline in the number of children with viruses being treated with aspirin and a corresponding decline in cases of Reye's syndrome.

Other adverse affects

Aspirin can adversely affect breathing in people with sinusitis or asthma, and long–term use may cause kidney cancer or liver disease. There is some evidence it delays the onset of labor in full term pregnancies and, as it crosses the placenta, may be harmful to the fetus.

See also Analgesia; Anti–inflammatory agents; Anticoagulants; Reye's syndrome.

Further Reading:

Feinman, Susan E., ed. *Beneficial and Toxic Effects of Aspirin*, Florida: CRC Press, Inc., 1994.

Ray, Oakley and Charles Ksir, *Drugs, Society & Human Behavior*, St. Louis/Toronto/Boston: Times Mirror/ Mosby College Publishing, 1990.

"Aspirin's Next Conquest: Does it Prevent Colon Cancer?" *Journal of the National Cancer Institute*, (February 2, 1994): 166–68.

Marie L. Thompson

Trees killed by acid rain in the Great Smoky Mountains.

Acid, organic see **Carboxylic acid**

Acid rain

"Acid rain" is a popularly used phrase that refers to the deposition of acidifying substances from the atmosphere and the environmental effects that this causes. Acid rain became a prominent issue around 1970, and since then research has demonstrated that depositions of atmospheric chemicals are causing widespread acidification of lakes and streams, and possibly soils. The resulting biological effects include the extirpation of many populations of fish. Scientific understanding of the causes and consequences of acid rain, in conjunction with lobbying of government by environmental organizations, has resulted in large reductions in the atmospheric emissions of pollutants in North America and parts of Europe. If these reduc-

tions prove to be large enough, acid rain will be less an environmental problem in those regions.

Atmospheric depositions

Strictly speaking, "acid rain" should only refer to rainfall, or so–called wet precipitation. However, the proper meaning of acid rain is "the deposition of acidifying substances from the atmosphere." This is because acidification is not just caused by acidic rain, but also by chemicals in snow and fog, and by inputs of gases and particulates when precipitation is not occurring.

Of the many chemicals that are deposited from the atmosphere, the most important in terms of causing acidity in soil and in surface waters (such as lakes and streams) are: (1) dilute solutions of sulfuric and nitric acids (H_2SO_4 and HNO_3, respectively), deposited as acidic rain or snow, (2) the gases sulfur dioxide (SO_2) and oxides of nitrogen (NO and NO_2, together called

NO_x), and (3) very small particulates, such as ammonium sulfate ($[NH_4]_2SO_4$ and ammonium nitrate [NH_4NO_3]).

The depositions of these gases and particulates primarily occur when it is not raining or snowing. This type of atmospheric input is known as "dry deposition."

Large regions of Europe and North America are exposed to these acidifying depositions. However, only certain types of ecosystems are vulnerable to becoming acidified by these atmospheric inputs. These usually have a thin cover of soil, containing little calcium, and sitting upon a bedrock of hard minerals such as granite or quartz. There is convincing evidence that atmospheric depositions have caused an acidification of freshwater ecosystems. Many lakes, streams, and rivers have become acidic, resulting in declining or locally extirpated populations of some plants and animals. However, there is not yet conclusive evidence that terrestrial ecosystems have been degraded by acidic deposition (except for cases of severe pollution by toxic SO_2).

Chemistry of precipitation

The acidity of an aqueous solution is measured as its concentration of hydrogen ions (H^+). The pH scale expresses this concentration in logarithmic units to the base 10, ranging from very acidic solutions of pH 0, through the neutral value of pH 7, to very alkaline (or basic) solutions of pH 14. It is important to recognize that a one–unit difference in pH (for example, from pH 3 to pH 4) implies a 10–fold difference in the concentration of hydrogen ions. The pHs of some common solutions include: lemon juice, pH 2; table vinegar, pH 3; milk, pH 6.6; milk of magnesia, pH 10.5.

As just noted, an acidic solution, strictly speaking, has a pH less than 7.0. However, in environmental science the operational definition of acidic precipitation is a pH less than 5.65. This is the pH associated with the weak solution of carbonic acid (H_2CO_3) that forms when water droplets in clouds are in chemical equilibrium with carbon dioxide (CO_2), an atmospheric gas with a concentration of about 355 ppm (parts per million; a unit of concentration).

Water in precipitation contains a mixture of positively charged ions (or cations) and negatively charged ions (or anions). The most abundant cations are usually hydrogen (H^+), ammonium (NH_4^+), calcium (Ca^{2+}), magnesium (Mg^{2+}), and sodium (Na^+), while the major anions are sulfate (SO_4^{2-}), chloride (Cl^-), and nitrate (NO_3^-). The principle of conservation of electrochemi-cal neutrality of aqueous solutions states that the total number of cation charges must equal that of anions, so the net electrical charge is zero. Following from this principle, the quantity of H^+ in an aqueous solution is related to the difference in concentration of the sum of all anions, and the sum of all cations other than H^+. That is: $H^+ = SO_4^{-2} + NO_3^- + Cl^- - Na^+ - NH_4^+ - Ca^{2+} - Mg^{2+}$.

Data for the chemistry of precipitation in a region experiencing severe acid rain are available from Hubbard Brook, New Hampshire, where one of the world's best, long–term studies of this phenomenon has been undertaken. The average pH of precipitation at Hubbard Brook is 4.2, and H^+ accounts for 71% of the total amount of cations, and SO_4^{-2} and NO_3^- for 87% of the anions. Therefore, most of the acidity of precipitation at Hubbard Brook occurs as dilute sulfuric and nitric acids. The SO_4^{-2} is believed to originate from SO_2 emitted from power plants and industries, and oxidized by photochemical reactions in the atmosphere to SO_4^{-2}. The NO_3^- originates with emissions of NO_x (i.e., NO and NO_2) gases from these sources and automobiles. Not surprisingly, air masses that pass over the large emissions sources of Boston and New York produce storms with the largest concentrations of H^+, SO_4^{-2}, and NO_3^- at Hubbard Brook.

Regions differ greatly in their precipitation chemistry. This can be demonstrated using data for precipitation chemistry monitored during an extensive study in eastern Canada. The village of Dorset in southern Ontario is close to large sources of emission of SO_2 and NO_x. On average, the precipitation at Dorset is very acidic at pH 4.1, and the large concentrations of SO_4^{-2} and NO_3^- suggest that the acidity is caused by dilute sulfuric and nitric acids. In comparison, the Experimental Lakes Area (ELA) is in a remote landscape in northwestern Ontario, infrequently affected by polluted air masses. The ELA site has a less acidic precipitation (average pH 4.7) and smaller concentrations of SO_4^{-2} and NO_3^- than at Dorset. Another site near the Atlantic Ocean in Nova Scotia receives air masses that pass over large sources of emissions in New England and southeastern Canada. However, by the time Nova Scotia is reached much of the acidic SO_4^{-2} and NO_3^- have been removed by prior rain–out, and the precipitation is only moderately acidic (pH 4.6). Also, because Nova Scotia is influenced by the ocean, its precipitation chemistry is characterized by large concentrations of Na^+ and Cl^-. Finally, Lethbridge in southern Alberta is in a prairie landscape, and its precipitation is not acidic (average pH 6.0) because of the influence of calcium–rich, acid–neutralizing dusts that are blown into the atmosphere from agricultural fields.

In some places, fog moisture can be especially acidic. For example, fogwaters at coastal locations in New England can be as acidic as pH 3.0–3.5. At high–elevation locations where fog is frequent there can be large depositions of cloudwater and acidity. At a site in New Hampshire where fog occurs 40% of the time, cloudwater deposition to a conifer forest is equivalent to 47% of the water input by rain and snow, and because of its large concentrations of some chemicals, fog deposition accounted for 62% of the total inputs of H^+, and 81% of those of SO_4^{-2} and NO_3^-.

Spatial patterns of acidic precipitation

Large regions are affected by acidic precipitation in North America, Europe, and elsewhere. A relatively small region of eastern North America is known to have experienced acidic precipitation before 1955, but this has since expanded so that most of the eastern United States and southeastern Canada is now affected.

Interestingly, the acidity of precipitation is not usually greater close to large point–sources of emission of important gaseous precursors of acidity, such as smelters or power plants that emit SO_2 and NO_x. This observation emphasizes the fact that acid rain is a regional phenomenon, and not a local one. For example, the acidity of precipitation is not appreciably influenced by distance from the world's largest point-source of SO_2 emissions, a smelter in Sudbury, Ontario. Furthermore, when that smelter was temporarily shut down by a labor dispute, the precipitation averaged pH 4.49, not significantly different from the pH 4.52 when there were large emissions of SO_2.

Deposition of acidifying substances

Dry deposition occurs in the intervals of time between precipitation events. Dry deposition includes inputs of tiny particulates from the atmosphere, as well as the uptake of gaseous SO_2 and NO_x by plants, soil, and water. Unlike wet deposition, rates of dry deposition can be much larger close to point–sources of emission, compared with further away.

Once they are dry deposited, certain chemicals can generate important quantities of acidity when they are chemically transformed in the receiving ecosystem. For example, SO_2 gas can dissolve into the water of lakes or streams, or it can be absorbed by the foliage of plants. This dry–deposited SO_2 is then oxidized to SO_4^{-2}, which is electrochemically balanced by H^+, so that acidity results. Dry–deposited NO_x gas can similarly be oxidized to NO_3^- and also balanced by H^+.

In relatively polluted environments close to emissions sources, the total input of acidifying substances (i.e., wet + dry depositions) is dominated by the dry deposition of acidic substances and their acid–forming precursors. The dry deposition is mostly associated with gaseous SO_2 and NO_x, because wet deposition is little influenced by distance from sources of emission.

For example, within a 25 mi (40 km) radius of the large smelter at Sudbury, about 55% of the total input of sulfur from the atmosphere is due to dry deposition, especially of SO_2. However, less than 1% of the SO_2 emission from the smelter is deposited in that area, because the tall smokestack is so effective at dispersing the emissions.

Because they have such a large surface area of foliage and bark, forests are especially effective at absorbing atmospheric gases and particles. Consequently, dry inputs accounted for about 33% of the total sulfur deposition to a hardwood forest in New Hampshire, 56–63% of the inputs of S and N to a hardwood forest in Tennessee, and 55% of their inputs to a conifer forest in Sweden.

Chemical changes in the forest canopy

In any forest, leaves and bark are usually the first surfaces encountered by precipitation. Most rainwater penetrates the foliar canopy and then reaches the forest floor as so–called throughfall, while a smaller amount runs down treetrunks as stemflow. Throughfall and stemflow have a different chemistry than the original precipitation. Because potassium is easily leached out of leaves, its concentration is especially changed. In a study of several types of forest in Nova Scotia, the concentration of potassium (K^+) was about 10 times larger in throughfall and stemflow than in rain, while calcium (Ca^{+2}) and magnesium (Mg^{+2}) were three to four times more concentrated. There was less of a change in the concentration of H^+; the rainwater pH was 4.4, but in throughfall and stemflow of hardwood stands pH averaged 4.7, and it was 4.4–4.5 in conifer stands. The decreases in acidity were associated with ion-exchange reactions occurring on foliage and bark surfaces, in which H^+ is removed from solution in exchange for Ca^{+2}, Mg^{+2}, and K^+. Overall, the "consumption" of hydrogen ions accounted for 42%–66% of the input of H^+ by precipitation to these forests. Similarly, H^+ consumption by the tree canopy was 91% in a hardwood forest at Hubbard Brook, New Hampshire, 21%–80% among seven stands in New Brunswick, and 14%–43% in stands in upstate New York.

In areas polluted by SO_2 there can be large increases in the sulfate concentration of throughfall and stemflow, compared with ambient precipitation. This is caused by the washoff of SO_2 and SO_4 that had previously been dry–deposited to the canopy. At Hubbard Brook this SO_4 enhancement is about four times larger than ambient precipitation, while in central Germany it is about two to three times greater. These are both regions with relatively large concentrations of particulate SO_4 and gaseous SO_2 in the atmosphere.

Chemical changes in soil

Once precipitation reaches the forest floor, it percolates into the soil. Important chemical changes take place as: (1) microbes and plants selectively absorb, release, and metabolize chemicals; (2) ions are exchanged at the surfaces of particles of clay and organic matter; (3) minerals are made soluble by so–called acid–weathering reactions; and (4) secondary minerals such as certain clays and metal oxides are formed through chemical precipitations of soluble ions of aluminum, iron, and other metals. These various chemical changes can contribute to soil acidification, the leaching of important chemicals such as calcium and magnesium, and the mobilization of toxic ions of aluminum, especially Al^{3+}. These are all natural, closely linked processes, occurring wherever there is well established vegetation, and where water inputs by precipitation are greater than evapotranspiration (i.e., evaporation from vegetation and non–living surfaces). A potential influence of acid rain is to increase the rates of some of these processes, such as leaching of toxic H^+ and Al^{3+} to lakes and other surface waters.

Some of these effects have been examined by experiments in which simulated "rainwater" of various pHs was added to soil contained in plastic tubes. These experiments have shown that very acidic solutions can cause: (1) an acidification of soil; (2) increased leaching of the so–called "basic cations" Ca, Mg, and K, resulting in nutrient loss, decreased base saturation of cation exchange capacity, and increased vulnerability of soil to acidification; (3) increased solubilization of toxic ions of metals such as aluminum, iron, manganese, lead, and zinc; and (4) saturation of the ability of soil to absorb sulfate, after which sulfate leaches at about the rate of input. The leaching of sulfate has a secondary influence on soil acidification if it is accompanied by the loss of base cations, and it can cause acidifying and toxic effects in surface waters if accompanied by Al^{3+} and H^+.

Soil acidification can occur naturally. This fact can be illustrated by studies of ecological succession on newly exposed parent materials of soil. At Glacier Bay, Alaska, the melting of glaciers exposes a mineral sub-

strate with a pH of about 8.0, with up to seven to 10% carbonate minerals. As this material is colonized and modified by vegetation and climate, its acidity increases, to about pH 4.8 after 70 years when a conifer forest has established. Accompanying this acidification is a reduction of carbonates to less than 1%, caused by leaching and uptake by plants.

Several studies have attempted to determine whether naturally occurring soil acidification has been intensified as a result of acid rain and associated atmospheric depositions. So far, there is no conclusive evidence that this has occurred on a wide scale. It appears that soil acidification is a potential, longer–term risk associated with acid rain.

Chemistry of surface waters

Compared with precipitation, lakes, ponds, streams, and rivers are relatively concentrated in ions, especially in calcium, magnesium, potassium, sodium, sulfate, and chloride. These chemicals have been mobilized from the terrestrial part of the surface waters. In addition, some surface waters are brown because of large concentrations of dissolved organic compounds, usually leached out of nearby bogs. Brown–water lakes are often naturally acidic, with a pH of about 4 to 5.

Seasonal variations in the chemistry of surface waters are important. Where a snowpack accumulates, meltwater in the springtime can be quite acidic. This happens because soils are frozen and/or saturated during snowmelt, so there is little possibility to neutralize the acidity of meltwater. So–called "acid shock" events in streams have been linked to the first meltwaters of the snowpack, which are generally more acidic than later fractions.

A widespread acidification of weakly–buffered waters has affected the northeastern United States, eastern Canada, Scandinavia, and elsewhere. In 1941, for example, the average pH of 21 lakes in central Norway was 7.5, but only 5.4–6.3 in the 1970s. Before 1950 the average pH of 14 Swedish waterbodies was 6.6, but 5.5 in 1971. In New York's Adirondack Mountains, 4% of 320 lakes had pH less than 5 in the 1930s, compared with 51% of 217 lakes in that area in 1975 (90% were also devoid of fish). The Environmental Protection Agency recently sampled a large number of lakes and streams in the United States. Out of 10,400 lakes, 11% were acidic, mostly in the eastern United States. Atmospheric depositions were attributed as the cause of acidification of 75% of the lakes, while 3% had been affected by acidic drainage from coal mines, and 22% by organic acids from bogs. Of the 4,670 streams considered acidic, 47% had been acidified by atmospheric deposition, 26% by acid–mine drainage, and 27% by bogs.

Surface waters that are vulnerable to acidification generally have a small acid–neutralizing capacity. Usually, H^+ is absorbed until a buffering threshold is exceeded, and there is then a rapid decrease in pH until another buffering system comes into play. Within the pH range of 6 to 8, bicarbonate alkalinity is the natural buffering system that can be depleted by acidic deposition. The amount of bicarbonate in water is determined by geochemical factors, especially the presence of mineral carbonates such as calcite ($CaCO_3$) or dolomite ($Ca,MgCO_3$) in the soil, bedrock, or aquatic sediment of the watershed. Small pockets of these minerals are sufficient to supply enough acid–neutralizing capacity to prevent acidification, even in regions where acid rain is severe. In contrast, where bedrock, soil, and sediment are composed of hard minerals such as granite and quartz, the acid–neutralizing capacity is small and acidification occurs readily. Vulnerable watersheds have little alkalinity and are subject to large depositions of acidifying substances, and these are especially common in glaciated regions of eastern North America and Scandinavia, and at high altitude in more southern mountains (such as the Appalachians), where crustal granite has been exposed by erosion.

High–altitude, headwater lakes and streams are often at risk because they usually have a small watershed. Because there is little opportunity for rainwater to interact with the thin soil and bedrock typical of headwater systems, little of the acidity of precipitation is neutralized before it reaches surface water.

In overview, the acidification of freshwaters can be conceptualized as a titration of a dilute bicarbonate solution with sulfuric and nitric acids derived from atmospheric depositions. In waters with little alkalinity, and where the watershed provides large fluxes of sulfate accompanied by hydrogen and aluminum ions, the waterbody is vulnerable to acidification.

Effects of acidification on terrestrial plants

Few studies have demonstrated injuries to terrestrial plants caused by an exposure to ambient acid rain. Although many experiments have demonstrated injuries to plants after treatment with artificial "acid rain" solutions, the toxic thresholds are usually at substantially more acidic pHs than normally occur in nature.

For example, some Norwegian experiments involved the treating of young forests with simulated acid rains. Lodgepole pine watered for three years grew 15–20% more quickly at pHs 4 and 3, compared with a "control" treatment of pH 5.6–6.1. The height growth of spruce was not affected over the pH range 5.6 to 2.5, while Scotch pine was stimulated by up to 15% at pHs of 2.5 to 3.0, compared with pH 5.6–6.1. Birch trees were also stimulated by the acid treatments. However, feather mosses that dominated the ground vegetation were negatively affected by acid treatments.

Because laboratory experiments are well controlled, they are useful for the determination of dose–response effects of acidic rainwaters on plants. In general, growth reductions are not observed unless treatment pHs are more acidic than about 3.0, and some species are stimulated by more acidic pHs than this. In one experiment, the growth of white pine seedlings was greater after treatment at pHs of 2.3 to 4.0 than at pH 5.6. In another experiment, seedlings of 11 tree species were treated over the pH range 2.6 to 5.6. Injuries to foliage occurred at pH 2.6, but only after a week of treatment with this very acidic pH.

Overall, it appears that trees and other vascular plants are rather tolerant of acidic rains, and they may not be at risk of suffering direct, short–term injuries from ambient acidic precipitation. It remains possible, however, that even in the absence of obvious injuries, stresses associated with acid rain could decrease plant growth. Because acid rain is regional in character, these yield decreases could occur over large areas, and this would have important economic implications. This potential problem is most prevalent in forests and other natural vegetation. This is because agricultural lands are regularly treated with liming agents to reduce soil acidity, and because acid production by cropping and fertilization is much larger than that caused by atmospheric depositions.

Studies in western Europe and eastern North America have examined the possible effects of acid rain on forest productivity. Recent decreases in productivity have been shown for various tree species and in various areas. However, progressive decreases in productivity are natural as the canopy closes and competition intensifies in developing forests. So far, research has not separated clear effects of regional acid rain from those caused by ecological succession, insect defoliation, or climate change.

Effects of acidification on freshwater organisms

The community of microscopic algae (or phytoplankton) of lakes is quite diverse in species. Non–acidic, oligotrophic (i.e., unproductive) lakes in a temperate climate are usually dominated by golden-brown algae and diatoms, while acidic lakes are typically dominated by dinoflagellates, cryptomonads, and green algae.

An important experiment was performed in a remote lake in Ontario, in which sulfuric acid was added to slowly acidify the entire lake, ultimately to about pH 5.0 from the original pH of 6.5. During this whole–lake acidification, the phytoplankton community changed from an initial domination by golden–brown algae to dominance by green algae. There was no change in the total number of species, but there was a small increase in algal biomass after acidification, because of an increased clarity of the water.

In some acidified lakes the abundance of larger plants (called macrophytes) has decreased, sometimes accompanied by increased abundance of a moss known as *Sphagnum*. In itself, proliferation of *Sphagnum* can cause acidification, because these plants efficiently remove cations from the water in exchange for H^+, and their mats interfere with acid neutralizing processes in the sediment.

Zooplankton are small crustaceans living in the water column of lakes. These animals can be affected by acidification through: (1) the toxicity of H^+ and associated metals ions, especially Al^{3+}; (2) changes in their phytoplankton food; and (3) changes in predation, especially if plankton–eating fish become extirpated by acidification. Surveys have demonstrated that some zooplankton species are sensitive to acidity, while others are more tolerant. In general, higher–pH lakes are richer in zooplankton species. For example, a survey of lakes in Ontario found nine to 16 species with three to four dominants at pH greater than pH 5, but only one to seven species with one to two dominants at more acidic pHs.

In the whole–lake experiment mentioned previously, the abundance of zooplankton increased by 66%–93% after acidification, a change attributed to an increase in algal biomass. Although there was little change in dominant species, the less common species were extirpated.

Fish are the best–known victims of acidification. Loss of populations of trout, salmon, and other species have occurred in many acidified freshwaters. A survey of 700 Norwegian lakes, for example, found that brown trout were absent from 40% of the waterbodies and sparse in another 40%, even though almost all of the lakes had supported healthy fish populations prior to the 1950s. Surveys during the 1930s in the Adirondack Mountains of New York found brook trout in 82% of the lakes. However, in the 1970s fish did not occur in 43% of 215 lakes in the same area, including 26 def-inite extirpations of brook trout in re–surveyed lakes. This dramatic change paralleled the known acidification of these lakes. Other studies documented the loss of fish populations from lakes in the Killarney region of Ontario, where there are known extirpations of lake trout in 17 lakes, while smallmouth bass have disappeared from 12 lakes, largemouth bass and walleye from four, and yellow perch and rock bass from two.

Many studies have been made of the physiological effects of acidification on fish. Younger life–history stages are generally more sensitive than adults, and most losses of fish populations can be attributed to reproductive failure, rather than mortality of adults (although adults have sometimes been killed by acid–shock episodes in the springtime).

There are large increases in concentration of certain toxic metals in acidic waters, most notably ions of aluminum. In many acidic waters aluminum ions can be sufficient to kill fish, irrespective of any direct effects of H^+. In general, survival and growth of larvae and older stages of fish are reduced if dissolved aluminum concentrations are larger than 0.1 ppm, an exposure regularly exceeded in acidic waters. The most toxic ions of aluminum are Al^{3+} and $AlOH^{2+}$.

Although direct effects of acidification on aquatic birds have not been demonstrated, changes in their habitat could indirectly affect their populations. Losses of fish populations would be detrimental to fish–eating waterbirds such as loons, mergansers, and osprey. In contrast, an increased abundance of aquatic insects and zooplankton, resulting from decreased predation by fish, could be beneficial to diving ducks such as common goldeneye and hooded merganser, and to dabbling ducks such as the mallard and black duck.

Reclamation of acidified waterbodies

Fishery biologists especially are interested in liming acidic lakes to create habitat for sportfish. Usually, acidic waters are treated by adding limestone ($CaCO_3$) or lime [$Ca(OH)_2$], a process analogous to a whole–lake titration to raise pH. In some parts of Scandinavia liming is used extensively to mitigate the biological damages of acidification. By 1988 about 5,000 waterbodies had been limed in Sweden, mostly with limestone, along with another several hundred lakes in southern Norway. In the early 1980s there was a program to lime about 800 acidic lakes in the Adirondack region of New York.

Although liming rapidly decreases the acidity of a lake, the water later re–acidifies at a rate determined by size of the drainage basin, the rate of flushing of the

KEY TERMS

Acidic rain (acidic precipitation)—(1) Rain, snow, or fog water having a pH less than 5.65. (2) The deposition of acidifying substances from the atmosphere during a precipitation event.

Acidification—An increase over time in the content of acidity in a system, accompanied by a decrease in the acid–neutralizing capacity of that system.

Acidifying substance—Any substance that causes acidification. The substance may have an acidic character and therefore act directly, or it may initially be non–acidic but generate acidity as a result of its chemical transformation, as happens when ammonium is nitrified to nitrate, and when sulfides are oxidized to sulfate.

Acidity—The ability of a solution to neutralize an input of hydroxide ion (OH^-). Acidity is usually measured as the concentration of hydrogen ion (H^+), in logarithmic pH units (see also pH). Strictly speaking, an acidic solution has a pH less than 7.0.

Acid–mine drainage—Surface water or ground water that has been acidified by the oxidation of pyrite and other reduced–sulfur minerals that occur in coal mines and coal–mine wastes.

Acidophilous—Refers to organisms that only occur in acidic habitats, and are tolerant of the chemical stresses of acidity.

Acid shock—A short–term event of great acidity. This phenomenon regularly occurs in fresh–water systems that receive intense pulses of acidic water when an accumulated snowpack melts rapidly in the spring.

Conservation of electrochemical neutrality—Refers to an aqueous solution, in which the number of cation equivalents equals the number of anion equivalents, so that the solution does not have a net electrical charge.

Equivalent—Abbreviation for mole–equivalent, and calculated as the molecular or atomic weight multiplied times the number of charges of the ion. Equivalent units are necessary for a charge–balance calculation, related to the conservation of electrochemical neutrality (above).

Leaching—The movement of dissolved chemicals with water that is percolating downward through soil.

pH—The negative logarithm to the base 10 of the aqueous concentration of hydrogen ions in units of moles per liter. An acidic solution has pH less than 7, while an alkaline solution has pH greater than 7. Note that a one–unit difference in pH implies a 10–fold difference in the concentration of hydrogen ions.

lake, and continued atmospheric inputs. Therefore, small headwater lakes have to be re–limed more frequently. In addition, liming initially stresses the acid–adapted biota of the lake, causing changes in species dominance until a new, steady–state ecosystem is achieved. It is important to recognize that liming is a temporary management strategy, and not a long–term solution to acidification.

Avoiding acid rain

Neutralization of acidic ecosystems treats the symptoms, but not the sources of acidification. Clearly, large reductions in emissions of the acid–forming gases SO_2 and NO_x are the ultimate solution to this widespread environmental problem. However, there is controversy over the amount that the emissions must be reduced in order to alleviate acidic deposition, and about how to pursue the reduction of emissions. For

example, should large point sources such as power plants and smelters be targeted, with less attention paid to smaller sources such as automobiles and residential furnaces? Not surprisingly, industries and regions that are copious emitters of these gases lobby against emission controls, for which they argue the scientific justification is not yet adequate.

In spite of many uncertainties about the causes and magnitudes of the damages associated with acid rain and related atmospheric depositions, it is intuitively clear that what goes up (that is, the acid–precursor gases) must come down (as acidifying depositions). This common–sense notion is supported by a great deal of scientific evidence, and because of public awareness and concerns about acid rain in many countries, politicians have began to act effectively. Emissions of sulfur dioxide and oxides of nitrogen are being reduced, especially in western Europe and North America. For example, in 1992 the governments of the United States and Canada signed an air–quality agreement aimed at reducing acidifying depositions in both countries. This agreement calls for large expenditures by governments and industries to achieve substantial reductions in the emissions of air pollutants during the 1990s.

However, so far the actions to reduce emissions of the precursor gases of acidifying deposition have only been vigorous in western Europe and North America. Actions are also needed in other, less wealthy regions where the political focus is on industrial growth, and not on control of air pollution and other environmental degradations that are so often used to subsidize that growth. In the coming years, much more attention will have to be paid to acid rain and other pollution problems in eastern Europe and the former USSR, China, India, southeast Asia, Mexico, and other so–called "developing" nations. Emissions of important air pollutants are rampant in these places, and are increasing rapidly.

See also Air pollution; Forests; pH; Sulfur dioxide.

Further Reading:

Freedman, B. *Environmental Ecology*, 2nd ed. San Diego: Academic Press, 1994.
Anonymous. *National Acid Precipitation Assessment Program*. Integrated Assessment Report. Washington, D.C.: Superintendent of Documents, U.S. Government Printing Office, 1989.
Schindler, D.W. "Effects of Acid Rain on Freshwater Ecosystems." *Science*, 239: 149–57, 1988.

Bill Freedman

Acids and bases

Acids and bases are chemical compounds that have certain specific properties in aqueous solutions. In most chemical circumstances, acids are chemicals that produce positively–charged hydrogen ions, H^+, in water, while bases are chemicals that produce negatively–charged hydroxide ions, OH^-, in water. Bases are sometimes called *alkalis*. Acids and bases react with each other in a reaction called *neutralization*. In a neutralization reaction, the hydrogen ion and the hydroxide ion react to form a molecule of water:

$$H^+ + OH^- \rightarrow H_2O$$

Chemically, acids and bases may be considered opposites of each other. The concept of acids and bases

is so important in chemistry that there are several useful definitions of "acid" and "base" that pertain to different chemical environments, although the definition above is the most common one.

Acids and bases have some general properties. Many acids have a sour taste (those that are an accepted part of the diet, that is!). Citric acid, found in oranges and lemons, is one example where the sour taste is related to the fact that the chemical is an acid. Molecules that are bases usually have a bitter taste, like caffeine. Bases make solutions that are slippery. Many acids will react with metals to dissolve the metal and at the same time generate hydrogen gas, H_2. Perhaps the most obvious behavior of acids and bases is their abilities to change colors of certain other chemicals. Historically, an extract of lichens (*V. lecanora* and *V. rocella*) called *litmus* has been used since it turns blue in the presence of bases and red in the presence of acids. Litmus paper is still commonly used to indicate whether a compound is an acid or a base. Extracts made from red onions, red cabbage, and many other fruits and vegetables change colors in the presence of acids and bases. Such materials are called *indicators*.

Classic definition of acids and bases

Although acids and bases have been known since prehistoric times (vinegar, for example, is an acid), the first attempt to define what makes a compound an acid or a base was made by the Swedish chemist Svante Arrhenius (1859–1927), who proposed the definition that an acid was any compound that produced hydrogen ions, H^+, when dissolved in water, and a base was any compound that produced hydroxide ions, OH^-, when dissolved in water. Although this was and still is a very useful definition, it has two major limitations. First, it was limited to water, or aqueous, solutions. Second, it practically limited acids and bases to ionic compounds that contained the H^+ ion or the OH^- ion (compounds like hydrochloric acid, HCl, or sodium hydroxide, NaOH). Limited though it might be, it was an important step in the understanding of chemistry in solutions, and for his work on solution chemistry Arrhenius was awarded the 1903 Nobel Prize in Chemistry.

Many common acids and bases are consistent with the Arrhenius definition. The following table shows a few common acids and bases and their uses. In all cases it is assumed that the acid or base is dissolved in water.

Many acids release only a single hydrogen ion per molecule into solution. Such acids are called *monoprotic*. Examples include hydrochloric acid, HCl, and nitric acid, HNO_3. *Diprotic* acids can release two

Acid	Name	Use	Base	Name	Use
HCl	hydrochloric acid	cleaning, drugs, plastics	NaOH	sodium hydroxide	drain cleaner, soap
H_2SO_4	sulfuric acid	chemical synthesis, batteries	KOH	potassium hydroxide	soaps
$HC_2H_3O_2$	acetic acid	vinegar	$Mg(OH)_2$	magnesium hydroxide	antacids

hydrogen ions per molecule. H_2SO_4 is an example. *Triprotic* acids, like H_3PO_4, can release three hydrogen ions into solution. Acetic acid has the formula $HC_2H_3O_2$ and is a monoprotic acid because it is composed of one H^+ ion and one acetate ion, $C_2H_3O_2^-$. The three hydrogen atoms in the acetate ion do not act as acids.

Strong and weak acids and bases

An important consideration when dealing with acids and bases is their *strength*; that is, how chemically reactive they act as acids and bases. The strength of an acid or base is determined by the degree of ionization of the acid or base in solution—that is, the percentage of dissolved acid or base molecules that release hydrogen or hydroxide ions. If all of the dissolved acid or base separates into ions, it is called a *strong acid* or *strong base*. Otherwise, it is a *weak acid* or *weak base*. There are only a few strong acids: hydrochloric acid (HCl), hydrobromic acid (HBr), hydriodic acid (HI), perchloric acid ($HClO_4$), nitric acid (HNO_3), and sulfuric acid (H_2SO_4). Similarly, there are only a few strong bases: lithium hydroxide (LiOH), sodium hydroxide (NaOH), potassium hydroxide (KOH), calcium hydroxide (Ca[OH]$_2$), strontium hydroxide (Sr[OH]$_2$), and barium hydroxide (Ba[OH]$_2$). These strong acids and bases are 100% ionized in aqueous solution. All other Arrhenius acids and bases are weak acids and bases. For example, acetic acid ($HC_2H_3O_2$) and oxalic acid ($H_2C_2O_4$) are weak acids, while iron hydroxide, $Fe(OH)_3$, and ammonium hydroxide, NH_4OH (which is actually just ammonia, NH_3, dissolved in water), are examples of weak bases. The percentage of the acid and base molecules that are ionized in solution varies and depends on the concentration of the acid. For example, a 2% solution of acetic acid in water, which is about the concentration found in vinegar, is only 0.7% ionized. This means that fully 99.3% of the acetic acid molecules are unionized

and exist in solution as the complete acetic acid molecule.

Brønsted–Lowry definition of acids and bases

Although the Arrhenius definitions of acids and bases are simplest and most useful, they are not the most widely applicable. Some compounds, like ammonia, NH_3, act like bases in aqueous solution even though they are not hydroxide–containing compounds. Also, the Arrhenius definition assumes that the acid–base reactions are occurring in aqueous solution. In many other cases, water is indeed the solvent. In many cases, however, water is not the solvent. What was necessary was to formulate a definition of acid and base that were independent of the solvent and the presence of H^+ and OH^- ions.

Such a definition was proposed in 1923 by English chemist Thomas Lowry (1874–1936) and Danish chemists J. N. Brønsted (1879–1947) and N. Bjerrum (1879–1958) and is called the Brønsted–Lowry definition of acids and bases. (Bjerrum seems to have been forgotten.) The central chemical species of this definition is H^+, which consists merely of a proton. By the Brønsted–Lowry definition, an acid is any chemical species that donates a proton to another chemical species. Conversely, a base is any chemical species that accepts a proton from another chemical species. Simply put, a Brønsted–Lowry acid is a proton donor and a Brønsted–Lowry base is a proton acceptor.

The Brønsted–Lowry definition includes all Arrhenius acids and bases, since the hydrogen ion is a proton donor (in fact, it is a proton) and a hydroxide ion accepts a proton to form water:

$$H^+ \;+\; OH^- \;\rightarrow\; H_2O$$

proton donor   proton acceptor

But the Brønsted–Lowry definition also includes chemical species that are not Arrhenius–type acids or bases. The classic example is ammonia, NH_3. Ammonia dissolves in water to make a slightly basic solution even though ammonia does not contain OH^- ions. What is happening is that an ammonia molecule is accepting a proton from a water molecule to make an ammonium ion (NH_4^+) and a hydroxide ion:

$$NH_3 \ + \ H_2O \rightarrow NH_4^+ \ + \ OH^-$$

B-L base ⠀⠀ B-L acid

In essence, the water molecule is donating a proton to the ammonia molecule. The water molecule is therefore acting as the Brønsted–Lowry acid and the ammonia molecule is acting as the Brønsted–Lowry base.

In order to better understand the Brønsted–Lowry definition, it needs to be understood what is meant by a proton. The descriptions proton donor and proton acceptor are easy to remember. But are there actually bare protons floating around in solution? Not really. In aqueous solution, the protons are attached to the oxygen atoms of water molecules, giving them a positive charge. This species is called the *hydronium ion* and has the chemical formula H_3O^+. It is more accurate to use the hydronium ion instead of the bare hydrogen ion when writing equations for chemical reactions between acids and bases in aqueous solution. For example, the reaction between the hydronium ion and the hydroxide ion, the typical Arrhenius acid–base reaction, would produce two molecules of water.

Chemical reactions can go forward or backward; when the rates of the reverse reactions are equal, it is at *chemical equilibrium*. It can be shown that each side of the equilibrium has a Brønsted–Lowry acid and base. For example:

$$NH_3 \ + \ H_2O \longleftrightarrow NH_4^+ \ + \ OH^-$$

B-L base ⠀ B-L acid ⠀ B-L acid ⠀ B-L base

On each side of the reaction there is an acid and a base. The NH_4^+ ion is an acid because in the reverse reaction it donates a proton (H^+) to the OH^- ion to form NH_3 and H_2O. With respect to the reaction above, the H_2O and OH^- species make up an acid–base pair, called a conjugate acid–base pair, while the NH_3 and NH_4^+ species make up another conjugate acid–base pair. All Brønsted–Lowry acid–base reactions can be separated into reactions between two conjugate acid–base pairs. The conjugate acid always has one more H^+ than the conjugate base.

Lewis definition of acids and bases

The Brønsted–Lowry acid–base definition, while broader than the Arrhenius definition, is still limited to hydrogen–containing compounds, and is dependent on a hydrogen ion (that is, a proton) transferring from one molecule to another. Ultimately, a definition of acid and base that is completely independent of the presence of a hydrogen atom is necessary.

Such a definition was provided in 1923 by American chemist Gilbert N. Lewis (1875–1946). Instead of focusing on protons, Lewis's definition focuses on electron pairs. Since all compounds contain electron pairs, the Lewis definition is applicable to a wide range of chemical reactions.

A Lewis acid is defined as the reactant in a chemical reaction that accepts an electron pair from another reactant. A Lewis base is defined as the reactant in a chemical reaction that donates an electron pair to another reactant. Like the Brønsted–Lowry definition of acids and bases, the Lewis definition is reaction–dependent. A compound is not an acid or base in its own right; rather, how that compound reacts with another compound is what determines whether it is an acid or a base.

To show that the Lewis definition is not in conflict with previous definitions of acid and base, consider the fundamental acid–base reaction of H^+ with OH^- to give H_2O. The oxygen atom in the hydroxide ion has three unbonded electron pairs around it, and during the course of the reaction one of those electron pairs is "donated" to the hydrogen ion, making a chemical bond. Thus, OH^- is the electron pair donor and the Lewis base, whereas H^+ is the electron pair acceptor and, therefore, the Lewis acid. These assignments are consistent with both the Arrhenius definition and the Brønsted–Lowry definitions of acid and base.

However, the Lewis acid/base definition is much broader than the previous two definitions. Consider the reaction of BF_3 and NH_3 in the gas phase, in which NH_3 is donating an electron pair to the BF_3 molecule:

$$
\begin{array}{ccccc}
\ddot{F} & \ddot{H} & & \ddot{F} \ H \\
\ddot{F}\!:\!B & \ddot{:}N\!:\!H & \rightarrow & \ddot{F}\!:\!\ddot{B}\!:\!\ddot{N}\!:\!H \\
\ddot{F} & \ddot{H} & & \ddot{F} \ H
\end{array}
$$

Lewis acid ⠀⠀ Lewis base

Compounds like F_3BNH_3 are stable and can be purchased as solutions in organic solvents or even as pure compounds. In the above chemical reaction, BF_3 is accepting an electron pair and therefore is the Lewis acid; NH_3 is donating the electron pair and so is the Lewis base. However, in this case neither the Arrhenius definition nor the Brønsted–Lowry definition are applicable. Therefore, while the Lewis acid/base definition includes acids and bases from the other two definitions, it expands the definitions to include compounds that are not otherwise considered "classic" acids and bases.

Organic acids

Organic chemistry is the study of compounds of the element carbon. Organic chemistry uses the ideas of acids and bases in two ways. The more general way is that the concept of Lewis acids and bases is used to classify organic chemical reactions as acid/base reactions because the donation of electron pairs is quite common.

The second way that organic chemistry uses the concepts of acids and bases is in the definition of certain groupings of atoms within an organic molecule called *functional groups* as acidic or basic. An organic base is, in the true Lewis base style, any molecule with electron pairs that can be donated. The most common organic base involves a nitrogen atom, N, bonded to carbon–containing groups. One important class of such compounds is known as amines. In these compounds, the nitrogen atom has an unbonded electron pair that it can donate as it reacts as a Lewis base. Several of these compounds are gases and have a somewhat putrid, fish–like odor. These compounds are relatively simple molecules; there are larger organic molecules, including many of natural origin, that contain a nitrogen atom and so have certain base–like properties. These compounds are called *alkaloids*. Examples include quinine, caffeine, strychnine, nicotine, morphine, and cocaine.

Organic chemistry uses the acid concept not only in the definition of the Lewis acid but also by defining a particular collection of atoms as an acid functional group. Any organic molecule containing a carboxyl group, –COOH, is called a *carboxylic acid*. (Non–organic acids are sometimes called *mineral acids*). Examples include formic acid, which has the formula HCOOH and is produced by some ants and causes their bites to sting. Another example is acetic acid, CH_3COOH, which is the acid in vinegar.

Uses of acids and bases

Many specific uses of acids and bases have been discussed above. Generally, strong acids and bases are used for cleaning and, most importantly, for synthesizing other compounds. Their utility is illustrated by the fact that three of the top 10 chemicals produced in the US in 1994 are acids or bases: sulfuric acid (#1, 89 billion lbs/40 billion kg produced), sodium hydroxide (#8, 26 billion lbs/12 billion kg produced), and phosphoric acid (#9, 25 billion lbs/11 billion kg produced). Weak acids and bases have specific uses in society which are so variable that the specific compound entry should be consulted.

KEY TERMS

....

Functional group—In organic chemistry, certain specific groupings of atoms in a molecule.

Ionic compound—Any compound composed of positively– and negatively–charged ions.

See also Acetic acid; Alkaloid; Amine; Carboxylic acids; Citric acid; Neutralization; Nitric acid; pH; Sodium hydroxide; Sulfuric acid.

Further Reading:

Ihde, A. *The Development of Modern Chemistry*. New York: Dover, Inc., 1984.
Snyder, C.H. *The Extraordinary Chemistry of Ordinary Things*. New York: John Wiley and Sons, 1992.

David W. Ball

Acne

Acne, also called *acne vulgaris*, is a chronic inflammation of the sebaceous glands embedded in the skin. These glands secrete sebum, an oily lubricant. The condition, normally acquired in adolescence, usually resolves itself by the time the individual is 20–30 years old.

Contrary to popular myth, acne is not caused or aggravated by eating greasy foods or chocolate. Acne is associated with heavy sebum secretion caused by hormones. Androgens (male hormones) stimulate sebum secretion and estrogen (a female hormone) reduces sebum production.

While the tendency to develop acne is passed from parent to child, certain behaviors can aggravate acne outbreak. Acne can be caused by mechanical irritation, including pulling or stretching the skin, as often happens in athletic activities. Because steroid drugs contain androgens, taking steroids can also aggravate acne. Adolescent women who use oil–based cosmetics and moisturizers can have an aggravated case of acne.

The inflammation of acne results from the plugging of the sebaceous ducts, which lead from the sebaceous gland to the surface of the skin. Once plugged, the duct becomes inflamed and pustular. In some individuals the acne pustules are few, infrequent, and iso-

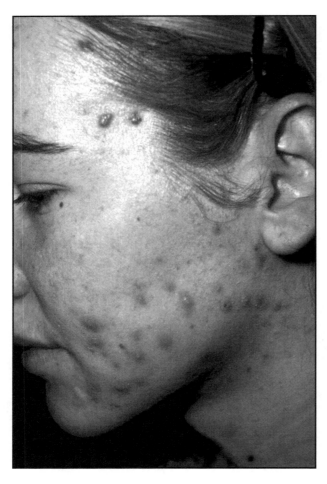

Acne vulgaris affecting a woman's face. Acne is the general name given to a skin disorder in which the sebaceous glands become inflamed.

lated. In others the condition is pronounced, with widespread pustule development.

Manipulating acne pustules can cause deep and permanent scarring. Washing the affected area with a germicidal soap and an abrasive sponge will help dislodge the material plugging the duct. Because estrogen inhibits the development of acne, taking birth–control pills may help alleviate acne in young women. A topical antibiotic may also prove helpful. For deeper acne, injected antibiotics may be necessary.

Acorn worm

Acorn worms are fragile tube worms that live in sand or mud burrows in the intertidal areas of the world's oceans. Acorn worms are members of the phylum Hemichordata, which includes two classes—the Enteropneusta (acorn worms) and the Pterobranchia (pterobranchs). Acorn worms, also known as tongue worms, belong to one of four genera, *Balanoglossus, Glossobalanus, Ptychodera,* and *Saccoglossus.* They are mostly burrowing animals that vary in size from 1–39 in (1–100 cm) in length (*Balanoglossus gigas*). The body of acorn worms consists of proboscis, collar, and trunk. The proboscis is a digging organ and together with the collar (and a lot of imagination) it resembles an acorn, hence its name.

The embryos of the hemichordates show affinities with both the phylum Echinodermata (starfish and sand dollars) and with the phylum Chordata (which includes the vertebrates). The relationships between these phyla are tenuous and are not demonstrable in all forms. The larvae of the Chordata subphylum Cephalochordata, which includes *Amphioxus*, resemble the larvae of the Hemichordata, indicating that the Hemichordata may have given rise to the Chordata, and therefore the vertebrates.

The phylum Chordata is characterized by a dorsal, hollow nerve cord, a notochord, pharyngeal "gill" slits or pouches, and a coelom, the fluid–filled main body cavity. Acorn worms resemble chordates in that these worms have pharyngeal gill slits, a nerve cord, and a coelom. A small structure in the anterior trunk was once thought to be a notochord. but it has been shown to be an extension of the gut.

Acoustics

Acoustics is the science that deals with the production, transmission, and reception of sound. Sound may be produced when a material body vibrates; it is transmitted only when there is some material body, called the medium, that can carry the vibrations away from the producing body; it is received when a third material body, attached to some indicating device, is set into vibratory motion by that intervening medium. However, the only vibrations that are considered sound (or sonic vibrations) are those in which the medium vibrates in the same direction as the sound travels, and for which the vibrations are very small. When the rate of vibration (see below) is below the range of human hearing, the sound is termed infrasonic; when it is above that range, it is called ultrasonic. (The term supersonic refers to bodies moving at speeds greater than the speed of sound, and is not normally involved in the study of acoustics.)

Production of sound

There are many examples of vibrating bodies producing sounds. Some are as simple as a string in a violin or piano, or a column of air in an organ pipe or in a clarinet; some are as complex as the vocal chords of a human. Sound may also be caused by a large disturbance which causes parts of a body to vibrate, such as sounds caused by a falling tree.

Vibrations of a string

To understand some of the fundamentals of sound production and propagation it is instructive to first consider the small vibrations of a stretched string held at both ends under tension. While these vibrations are not an example of sound, they do illustrate many of the properties of importance in acoustics as well as in the production of sound. The string may vibrate in a variety of different ways, depending upon whether it is struck or rubbed to set it in motion, and where on the string the action took place. However, its motion can be analyzed into a combination of a large number of simple motions. The simplest, called the fundamental (or the first harmonic), appears in Figure 1, which shows the outermost extensions of the string carrying out this vibration.

The second harmonic is shown in Figure 2; the third harmonic in Figure 3; and so forth (the whole set of harmonics beyond the first are called the overtones). The rate at which these vibrations take place (number of times per second the motion is repeated) is called the frequency, denoted by f (the reciprocal of the frequency, which is the time for one cycle to be competed, is called the period). A single complete vibration is normally termed a cycle, so that the frequency is usually given in cycles per second, or the equivalent modern unit, the hertz (abbreviated Hz). It is characteristic of the stretched string that the second harmonic has a frequency twice that of the fundamental; the third harmonic has a frequency three times that of the fundamental; and so forth. This is true for only a few very simple systems, with most sound–producing systems having a far more complex relationship among the harmonics.

Those points on the string which do not move are called the nodes; the maximum extension of the string (from the horizontal in the Figures) is called the amplitude, and is denoted by A in Figures 1–3. The distance one must go along the string at any instant of time to

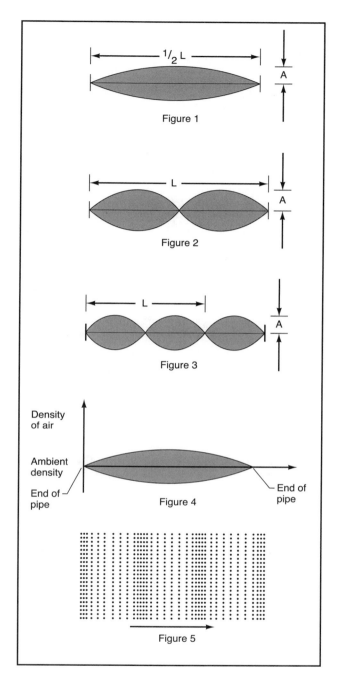

Figure 1

Figure 2

Figure 3

Density of air

Ambient density

End of pipe

End of pipe

Figure 4

Figure 5

reach a section having the identical motion is called the wavelength, and is denoted by L in Figures 1–3. It can be seen that the string only contains one–half wavelength of the fundamental, that is, the wavelength of the fundamental is twice the string length. The wavelength of the second harmonic is the length of the string. The string contains one–and–one–half (3/2) wavelengths of the third harmonic, so that its wavelength is two–thirds (2/3) of the length of the string. Similar relationships hold for all the other harmonics.

If the fundamental frequency of the string is called f_0, and the length of the string is l, it can be seen from the above that the product of the frequency and the wavelength of each harmonic is equal to $2f_0 l$. The dimension of this product is a velocity (e.g., feet per second or centimeters per second); detailed analysis of the motion of the stretched string shows that this is the velocity with which a small disturbance on the string would travel down the string.

Vibrations of an air column

When air is blown across the entrance to an organ pipe, it causes the air in the pipe to vibrate, so that there are alternate small increases and decreases of the density of the air (condensations and rarefactions). These alternate in space, with the distance between successive condensations (or rarefactions) being the wavelength; they alternate in time, with the frequency of the vibration. One major difference here is that the string vibrates transversely (perpendicular to the length of the string), while the air vibrates longitudinally (in the direction of the column of air). If the pipe is open at both ends, then the density of the air at the ends must be the same as that of the air outside the pipe, while the density inside the pipe can vary above or below that value. Again, as for the vibrations of the string, the density of the air in the pipe can be analyzed into a fundamental and overtones. If the density of the air vibrating in the fundamental mode (of the open pipe) is plotted across the pipe length, the graph is as in Figure 4.

The "zero value" at the ends denotes the fact that the density at the ends of the pipe must be the same as outside the pipe (the ambient density), while inside the pipe the density varies above and below that value with the frequency of the fundamental, with a maximum (and minimum) at the center. The density plot for the fundamental looks just like that for the fundamental of the vibrating stretched string (Figure 1). In the same manner, plots of the density for the various overtones would look like those of the string overtones. The frequency of the fundamental can be calculated from the fact that the velocity, which is analogous to that found for vibrations of the string, is the velocity with which sound travels in the air, usually denoted by c. Since the wavelength of the fundamental is twice the pipe length, its frequency is $c/2l$, where l is the length of the organ pipe. (While the discussion here is in terms of the density variations in the air, these are accompanied by small variations in the air pressure, and small motions of the air itself. At places of increased density the pressure is increased; where the pressure is changing rapidly, the air motion is greatest.)

When a musician blows into the mouthpiece of a clarinet, the air rushing past the reed causes it to vibrate which then causes the column of air in the clarinet to vibrate in a manner similar to, but more complicated than, the motion of the organ pipe. These vibrations (as for all vibrations) can also be analyzed into harmonics. By opening and closing the keyholes in the clarinet, different harmonics of the clarinet are made to grow louder or softer causing different tones to be heard.

Sound production in general

Thus, the production of sound depends upon the vibration of a material body, with the vibration being transmitted to the medium that carries the sound away from the sound producer. The vibrating violin string, for example, causes the body of the violin to vibrate; the "back–and–forth" motion of the parts of the body of the violin causes the air in contact with it to vibrate. That is, small variations in the density of the air are produced by the motion of the violin body, and these are carried forth into the air surrounding the violin. As the sound is carried away, the small variations in air density are propagated in the direction of travel of the sound.

Sounds from humans, of course, are produced by forcing air across the vocal cords, which causes them to vibrate. The various overtones are enhanced or diminished by the size and shape of the various cavities in the head (the sinuses, for example), as well as the placement of the tongue and the shape of the mouth. These factors cause specific wavelengths, of all that are produced by the vocal cords, to be amplified differently so that different people have their own characteristic voice sounds. These sounds can be then controlled by changing the placement of the tongue and the shape of the mouth, producing speech. The frequencies usually involved in speech are from about 100 to 10,000 Hz. However, humans can hear sounds in the frequency range from about 20 to 18,000 Hz. These outer limits vary from person to person, with age, and with the loudness of the sound. The density variations (and corresponding pressure variations) produced in ordinary speech are extremely small, with ordinary speech producing less than one–millionth the power of a 100 watt light bulb!

In the sonic range of frequencies (those produced by humans), sounds are often produced by loudspeakers, devices using electronic and mechanical components to produce sounds. The sounds to be transmitted are first changed to electrical signals by a microphone (see Reception of sounds, below), for example, or from an audio tape or compact disc; the frequencies carried by the electrical signals are those to be produced as the sound signals. In the simplest case, the wires carrying the electrical signals are used to form an electromagnet which attracts and releases a metal diaphragm. This, in turn, causes the variations in the density in the air adjacent to the diaphragm. These variations in density will have the same frequencies as were in the original electrical signals.

Ultrasonic vibrations are of great importance in industry and medicine, as well as in investigations in pure science. They are usually produced by applying an alternating electric voltage across certain types of crystals (quartz is a typical one) that expand and contract slightly as the voltage varies; the frequency of the voltage then determines the frequency of the sounds produced.

Transmission of sound

In order for sound to travel between the source and the receiver there must be some material between them that can vibrate in the direction of travel (called the propagation direction). (The fact that sound can only be transmitted by a material medium means that an explosion outside a spaceship would not be heard by its occupants!) The motion of the sound–producing body causes density variations in the medium (see Figure 5, which schematically shows the density variations associated with a sound wave), which move along in the direction of propagation. The transmission of sounds in the form of these density variations is termed a wave since these variations are carried forward without significant change, although eventually friction in the air itself causes the wave to dissipate. (This is analogous to a water wave in which the particles of water vibrate up and down, while the "wave" propagates forward.) Since the motion of the medium at any point is a small vibration back and forth in the direction in which the wave is proceeding, sound is termed a longitudinal wave. (The water wave, like the violin string, is an example of a transverse wave.) The most usual medium of sound transmission is air, but any substance that can be compressed can act as a medium for sound propagation. A fundamental characteristic of a wave is that it carries energy and momentum away from a source without transporting matter from the source.

Since the speed of sound in air is about 331 meters per second (about 1,088 feet per second), human speech involves wavelengths from about 3.3 meters to 3.3 centimeters (from about 11 feet to 1.3 inches). Thus, the wavelengths of speech are of the size of ordinary objects, unlike light, whose wavelengths are extremely small compared to items that are part of everyday life. Because of this, sound does not ordinar-

ily cast "acoustic shadows" but, because its wavelengths are so large, can be transmitted around ordinary objects. For example, if a light is shining on a person, and a book is placed directly between them, the person will no longer be able to see the light (a shadow is cast by the book on the eyes of the observer). However, if one person is speaking to another, then placing a book between them will hardly affect the sounds heard at all; the sound waves are able to go around the book to the observer's ears. On the other hand, placing a high wall between a highway and houses can greatly decrease the sounds of the traffic noises if the dimensions of the wall (height and length) are large compared with the wavelength of the traffic sounds. Thus, sound waves (as for all waves) tend to "go around" (e.g., ignore the presence of) obstacles which are small compared with the wavelength of the wave; and are reflected by obstacles which are large compared with the wavelength. For obstacles of approximately the same size as the wavelength, waves exhibit a very complex behavior known as diffraction, in which there are enhanced and diminished values of the wave amplitude, but which is too complicated to be described here in detail.

The speed of sound in a gas is proportional to the square root of the pressure divided by the density. Thus, helium, which has a much lower density than air, transmits sound at a greater speed than air. If a person breathes some helium, the characteristic wavelengths are still determined by the shape of the mouth, but the greater sound speed causes the speech to be emitted at a higher frequency—thus the "Donald Duck" sounds from someone who speaks after taking a breath of helium from a balloon.

In general, the speed of sound in liquids is greater than in gases, and greater still in solids. In sea water, for example, the speed is about 1,447 meters per second (about 4,750 feet per second); as for a gas, the speed increases as the pressure increases, and as the density decreases. Typical speeds of sound in solids are 5,000 meters per second, but vary considerably from one solid to another.

Reception of sound

By far the most important sound receiver in use is the human ear. While the details of the workings of the ear are too complicated to be described here, the process consists of the sound wave (the density variations carried through the air) striking the eardrum, causing it to vibrate with the same set of frequencies as had been carried in the wave. This vibration is transmitted through a set of bones in the ear to a liquid–filled chamber; small hairs in the liquid are set

KEY TERMS

Amplitude—The maximum displacement of the material that is vibrating.

Condensations—When air is the vibrating medium there are alternate small increases and decreases of the density of the air; the increases are called condensations.

Cycle—A single complete vibration.

Cycles per second—The number of complete vibrations per second.

Frequency—The rate at which vibrations take place (number of times per second the motion is repeated), denoted here by f and given in cycles per second or in hertz.

Fundamental—The lowest frequency of vibration of a sound–producing body (also called the first harmonic).

Harmonics (first, second, etc.)—The various frequencies of vibration of a sound–producing body, numbered from the one of lowest frequency to higher frequencies.

Hertz—A hertz (abbreviated as Hz) is one cycle per second.

Infrasonic vibrations—When the rate of vibration is below the range of human hearing, e.g., below about 10 cycles per second.

Longitudinal wave—The case where the motion of the vibrating body is in the wave propagation direction.

Loudspeaker—A device to produce sounds from an electric current, by electrical and mechanical means, in the range of frequencies around the sonic range (that is produced by humans).

Medium—A material body that carries the acoustic vibrations away from the body producing them.

Microphone—A device to change sounds, by electrical and mechanical means, into an electric current having the same frequencies as the sound, in the range of frequencies around the sonic range (that is produced by humans).

Nodes—Places where the amplitude of vibration is zero.

Overtones—The set of harmonics, beyond the first, of a sound–producing body.

Period—The length of time for one cycle to be completed; the reciprocal of the frequency.

Propagation direction—The direction in which the wave is traveling.

Rarefactions—When air is the vibrating medium there are alternate small increases and decreases of the density of the air; the decreases are called rarefactions.

Sonar—A device utilizing sound to determine the range and direction to an underwater object.

Supersonic—Refers to bodies moving at speeds greater than the speed of sound (not normally involved in the study of acoustics).

Transverse wave—The case where the motion of the vibrating body is perpendicular to the wave propagation direction.

Ultrasonic vibrations—When the rate of vibration is above the range of human hearing, e.g., above about 20,000 cycles per second.

Wave—A motion, in which energy and momentum is carried away from some source, which repeats itself in space and time with little or no change.

Wavelength—The distance, at any instant of time, between parts of a vibrating body having the identical motion, denoted here by L.

---

into motion and excite nerves which then transmit these frequencies to the brain.

In the sonic range of frequencies, the microphone, a device using electrical and mechanical components, is the common method of receiving sounds. One simple form is to have a diaphragm as one plate of an electrical condenser. When the diaphragm vibrates under the action of a sound wave, the current in the circuit varies due to the varying capacitance of the condenser. This varying current can then be used to activate a meter or oscilloscope or, after suitable processing, make an audio tape or some such permanent record.

Applications

The applications of acoustical devices are far too numerous to describe; one only has to look around our homes to see some of them: telephones, radios and television sets, compact disc players and tape recorders;

even clocks that "speak" the time! Probably one of the most important from the human point of view is the hearing aid, a miniature microphone–amplifier–loud-speaker that is designed to enhance whatever range of frequencies a person finds difficulty hearing.

However, one of the first large–scale "industrial" uses of sound propagation was by the military in World War I, in the detection of enemy submarines by means of sonar (for *sound navigation and ranging*). This was further developed during the period between then and World War II, and since then. The ship hunting submarine has a sound source and receiver projecting from the ship's hull that can be used for either listening or in an echo–ranging mode; the source and receiver are directional, so that they can send and receive an acoustic signal from only a small range of directions at one time. In the listening mode of operation, the operator tries to determine what are the sources of any noise that might be heard: the regular beat of an engine heard underwater can tell that an enemy might be in the vicinity. In the echo–ranging mode, a series of short bursts of sound is sent out, and the time for the echo to return is noted; that time interval multiplied by the speed of sound in water indicates (twice) the distance to the reflecting object. Since the sound source is directional, the direction in which the object lies is also known. This is now such a well developed method of finding underwater objects that commercial versions are available for fishermen to hunt for schools of fish.

Ultrasonic sources, utilizing pulses of frequencies in the many millions of cycles per second (and higher!), are now used for inspecting metals for flaws. The small wavelengths make the pulses liable to reflection from any imperfections in a piece of metal. Castings may have internal cracks which will weaken the structure; welds may be imperfect, possibly leading to failure of a metal–to–metal joint; metal fatigue may produce cracks in areas impossible to inspect by eye. The use of ultrasonic inspection techniques is increasingly important for failure prevention in bridges, aircraft, and pipelines, to name just a few.

The use of ultrasonics in medicine is also of growing importance. The detection of kidney stones or gallstones is routine, as is the imaging of fetuses to detect suspected birth defects, cardiac imaging, blood flow measurements, and so forth.

Thus, the field of acoustics covers a vast array of different areas of use, and they are constantly expanding. Acoustics in the communications industry, in various phases of the construction industries, in oil field exploration, in medicine, in the military, and in the entertainment industry, all attest to the growth of this field and to its continuing importance in the future.

Further Reading:

Albers, Vernon. *The World of Sound.* Cranbury, New Jersey: A. S. Barnes and Co., Inc., 1970.

Child, Graham. *Sound.* Garden City, New York: Doubleday Science Series, Doubleday and Company, Inc., 1970.

Johnston, Ian. *Measured Tones.* London: Institute of Physics Publishing, 1989.

Scott, David M. *The Physics of Vibrations and Waves.* Columbus, Ohio: Merrill Publishing Company, 1986.

David Mintzer

Acquired immunodeficiency syndrome see **AIDS**

Acrylic see **Artificial fibers**

Actinides

Actinides or actinoids is a generic term that refers to a series of 15 chemical elements. Denoted by the generic symbol An, these elements are all radioactive heavy metals, positioned in the seventh period and elaborated upon at the bottom of the periodic table.

Occurrence

Only actinium (atomic symbol, Ac), thorium (Th), protactinium (Pa), and uranium (U) are extracted from deposits in nature. In Canada, the United States, South Africa, and Namibia, thorium and protactinium are available in large quantities. All other actinides are synthetic or man made.

To understand the physical and chemical properties of actinides, a basic foundation of atomic structure, radioactivity, and the periodic table is required. The atomic structure can be pictured like a solar system. In the middle of the atom is the nucleus, composed of neutrons (no charge) and protons (positively charged). Around the nucleus, electrons (negatively charged) are rotating on their own axis, as well as circulating in definite energy levels. Each energy level (or shell) is designated by a principal quantum number (n) as K, L, M, N, O, etc. or 1, 2, 3, 4, 5, etc. respectively. Each shell has sub–shells, or orbitals. The first energy level consists of one orbital (s); the second level consists of two orbitals (s and p); the third level consists of three orbitals (s, p, and d), and from the fourth level on up there are four orbitals (s, p, d, and f). The orbitals closer to the nucleus are lower in energy level than the orbitals further away from the nucleus.

The electrons are distributed according to Pauli's exclusion principle. In any atom, the number of protons is equal to the number of electrons, thus bringing the neutrality in charge. These stable and abundant atoms exist in nature only. In the unstable and less abundant atoms, the number of neutrons is more than the number of electrons (one element with the same atomic number but with a different atomic mass). These unstable atoms are known as isotopes, some of which are radioactive.

Radioactive isotopes become nonradioactive by the decaying process. The decaying process may involve an emission of: (1) electrons or negative beta particles; (2) helium nuclei or alpha particles; (3) gamma rays or very high frequency electromagnetic waves; (4) positrons or positively charged electrons or positive beta particles.

The decaying process may also be due to K–capture (an orbital electron of a radioactive atom that may be captured by the nucleus and taken into it). Each of the above mentioned decay processes results in a isotope of a different element (an element with a different atomic number). The emission of alpha particles also results in elements with different atomic weights.

The most important decay process in actinides is K–capture, followed by the splitting, or fission, of the nucleus. This fission results in enormous amounts of energy and two or more extra neutrons. These newly formed neutrons can further start K–capture, with the subsequent reactions going on like a chain reaction. Atomic reactors and atomic bombs depend on the chain reactions.

A scheme of the classification of all known (both discovered and man-made) elements is represented in the modern periodic table. The periodical table is divided into vertical columns and horizontal rows representative of the periods with increasing atomic numbers. Each box contains one element and is represented by its symbol, a single or double letter, with the atomic number as a superscript, and the atomic weight as a subscript. Note that in the sixth and seventh periods, there are breaks between atomic numbers 57 and 72 (Lanthanides) and 89 and 104 (Actinides). Fourteen elements are present between the atomic numbers 89 and 104, and are elaborated upon at the bottom of the periodic table. These 14 elements, plus actinium, are known as Actinides.

General preparation

All actinide metals are prepared on a scale by the reduction of AnF_3 or AnF_4 with vapors of lithium (Li), magnesium (Mg), calcium (Ca), or barium (Ba) at 2,102–2,552°F (1,100–1,400°C); sometimes chlorides or oxides are used. The Van Arkel–de Boer process is a special preparation method used for thorium and protactinium.

Physical and chemical properties

A common feature of actinides is the possession of multiple oxidation states. The term oxidation state refers to the number of electron(s) that are involved or that can possibly become involved in the formation of chemical bond(s) in that compound, when one element combines with another element during a chemical reaction. The oxidation state is designated by a plus sign (when an electron is donated or electro–positive) or by a minus sign (when the electron is accepted or electronegative). An element can have more than one oxidation state. An electron configuration can provide the information about the oxidation state of that element. The most predominant oxidation state among Actinides is +3, which is similar to lanthanides. The crystal structure (geometry), solubility property, and the formation of chemical compounds are based on the oxidation state of the given element.

Actinides ions in an aqueous solution are colorful, containing colors such as red purple (U^{3+}), purple (Np^{3+}), pink (Am^{3+}), green (U^{4+}), yellow green (Np^{4+}), and pink red (Am^{4+}). Actinides ions U, Np, Pu, and Am undergo hydrolysis, disproportionation, or formation of polymeric ions in aqueous solutions with a low pH.

All actinides are characterized by partially filled 5f, 6d, and 7s orbitals. Actinides form complexes easily with certain ligands as well as with halide, sulfate, and other ions. Organometallic compounds (compounds with a sign bond between the meta and carbon atom of organic moiety) of uranium and thorium have been prepared and are useful in organic synthesis. Several alloys of protactinium with uranium have been prepared.

Uses of actinides

Even though hazards are associated with radioactivity of actinides, many beneficial applications exist as well. Radioactive nuclides are used in cancer therapy, analytical chemistry, and in basic research in the study of chemical structures and mechanisms. The explosive power of uranium and plutonium are well exploited in making atom bombs. In fact, the uranium enriched atom bomb that exploded over Japan was the first uranium bomb released. Nuclear reactions of uranium–235 and plutonium–239 are currently utilized in atomic energy powerplants to generate electric power. Thorium is economically useful for the reason that fissionable uranium–233 can be produced from thorium–232. Plutonium–238 is used in implants in the human body to power the heart pacemaker, which is does not need to be replaced for at least 10 years. Curium–244 and plutonium–238 emit heat at 2.9 watts and 0.57 watts per gram, respectively. Therefore, curium and plutonium are used as power sources on the Moon to provide electrical energy for transmitting messages to Earth.

See also Elements, families of; Periodic table.

Sutharchanadevi Murugen

Actinium see **Actinides**

Activated complex

The term activated complex refers to the molecular compound or compounds which exist in the highest energy state, or *activated stage*, during a chemical reaction. An activated complex acts as an intermediary between the reactants and the products of the reaction.

A chemical reaction is the reorganization of atoms of chemically compatible and chemically reactive molecular compounds, called *reactants*. A chemical reaction goes through three stages, the initial stage consisting of the reactants, the transition stage of the activated complex, and the final stage, in which the products are formed.

For example, consider the chemical reaction

$$A + B \rightleftarrows A—B \rightarrow C + D$$

where A and B are reactants, A—B is the activated complex, and C and D are the products. For a chemical reaction to occur, the reactant molecules should collide. Collisions between molecules are facilitated by an increase in the concentration of reactant, an increase in temperature, or the presence of a catalyst. Not every collision is successful, that is, produces a chemical reaction. For a successful collision to occur, reactants require a minimum amount of energy, called the *activation energy*. Once the reactant reaches the energy level, it enters the transition stage and forms the activated complex.

The energy of the activated complex is higher than that of reactants or the products, and the state is temporary. If there is not sufficient energy to sustain the chemical reaction, the activated complex can reform into the reactants in a backward reaction. With proper energy, though, the activated complex forms the products in a forward reaction.

See also Compound, chemical; Reaction; Element, chemical.

Active galactic nuclei

Active galactic nuclei (AGNs) are perhaps the most violently energetic objects in the universe. Active galaxies emit a tremendous amount of energy, most of which is generated in the relatively small nucleus. The nucleus of the Milky Way galaxy has many of the characteristics of active galactic nuclei, but to a much lesser extent. A galactic nucleus is not considered an active galactic nucleus unless it has at least 100 times the energy output of the nucleus of the Milky Way (at least 10^{37} Watts).

Much of the energy from active galactic nuclei is emitted as radio waves rather than as optical light. These radio waves are emitted by electrons moving in a helical path in a strong magnetic field at speeds near the speed of light and are called *synchrotron radiation*. Active galactic nuclei also often have jets of material streaming out from the nucleus. They tend to vary in brightness on rapid cycles of days to months in length. The rapid variations indicate that the energy–producing nucleus is small, ranging in size from a few light days to a few light months. There are several varieties of active galactic nuclei, including radio galaxies, Seyfert galaxies, BL Lacertae objects, and quasars.

Compact radio galaxies appear as giant elliptical galaxies. Radio telescopes, however, reveal a very energetic compact nucleus at the center, which is the source of most of the energy emitted by the galaxy. Perhaps the best known compact radio galaxy is M87. Recent observations from the provide strong evidence that this core contains a supermassive black hole.

Seyfert galaxies look like spiral galaxies with a hyperactive nucleus. The normal looking spiral arms surround an abnormally bright nucleus. BL Lacertae objects look like stars, but in reality are most likely to be very active nuclei of galaxies. BL Lacertae objects have unusual behavior, including extremely rapid and erratic variations in observed properties, and their exact nature is not known for certain. Quasars also look like stars, but they are perhaps the most distant and energetic type of active galactic nuclei.

The fundamental problem with active galactic nuclei is understanding how they can produce such large amounts of energy in such small volumes. The rapid variations in brightness tell us that active galactic nuclei are generally less than a few light months in size compared to a normal galaxy which might be 100,000 light years across. Most astronomers currently think that the energy source is a supermassive black hole.

See also BL Lacertae object; Black hole; Galaxy; Quasar; Radio waves.

Acupressure

Acupressure is an ancient method of improving a person's health by applying pressure to specific sites on the body. Acupressure is similar to acupuncture, but does not break the skin. Instead, the acupressure practitioner relies on pressure invoked by fingertip or knuckle to accomplish his purpose.

Also called Shiatzu, acupressure originated in ancient China approximately 500 years B.C. and spread throughout the Orient. It is the oldest form of physical therapy for which instructions are written. A basic level of acupressure can be practiced by anyone for the relief of pain or tension, and the practice is in active use by those who practice alternative forms of medicine.

Like acupuncture, acupressure recognizes certain pressure points located along meridians that extend the length of the body. Certain meridians and their connectors are associated with given organs or muscles, and pressure points on the meridian will affect the pain level in the organ. The pressure points are often located far from the organ they affect. This is a reflection of the belief that energy flows through the body along the meridians and that pain develops in an area when the energy flow through the corresponding meridian is stopped or reduced. Acupressure opens the energy and eases pain or discomfort.

Anyone who would practice acupressure must first learn the location of the meridians and their connectors. More than a thousand pressure points have been mapped along the meridians, but the amateur practitioner need not know them all. Generally the individual with a recurrent or chronic pain can learn the point that best eases his pain and learn how much pressure to apply to accomplish his purpose.

Reports from various Oriental and American institutions indicate that acupressure can be an effective way to ease pain and relax stressed muscles without the aid of medications. It has even been employed to provide anesthesia for certain types of surgery.

See also Acupuncture; Alternative medicine.

Larry Blaser

Acupuncture

Acupuncture is an ancient method of therapy that originated in China more than 2,000 years ago. It consists of inserting needles through the skin at very specific sites to achieve a cure of a disease or to relieve pain. Although it is not part of standard American medical treatment, it has achieved some acceptance for specific applications such as alleviating pain. Many physicians remain skeptical about its use as an anesthetic for surgery or cure for grave diseases, however.

In the Far East, acupuncture remains in wide use. It is considered one part of a total regimen that includes herbal medicine, closely guided dietetics, and psychological counseling. Ancient Chinese myths form the basic set of rules that guide the practitioner in the placement of the needles. The acupuncturist sees the human body as a collection of acupuncture points that are connected by a series of meridians or channels. Twelve pairs of meridians are found on the body, with one of each pair lying on each side of the body. An additional two meridians run along the midline of the front and back. So–called extrameridians are scattered about and connect the 14 meridians on each side. Other points outside the meridians on the hands, ears, and face have specific reflex effects. Altogether there are more than 1,000 acupuncture points lying along the courses of the meridians and in the extrameridian areas. Supposedly the concept of meridians developed as the ancient Chinese discovered that pain in a given area responded not only to pressure or puncture in its immediate area but also to pressure on distant points. Pain in one arm, for example, often responds to acupuncture in the opposite arm in the area corresponding to the painful arm. It is the Chinese theory that vital energy (Chi) flows along the meridians or channels and that an excess or deficiency of energy along a given channel is the cause of the pain or disfunction of an organ. As the concept of acupuncture took shape, the ancient Chinese learned that points on

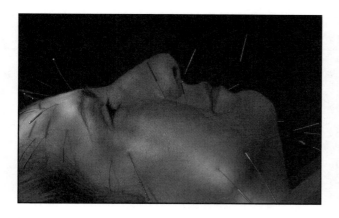

A woman undergoing acupuncture.

the body, when stimulated, helped to ease pain or heal internal diseases. They also discovered other points that were distant from the affected area that could be stimulated to achieve pain relief in the affected area. As the number of points grew, they were connected by the imaginary meridians and were labeled by their function. The large intestine meridian, for example, originates at the root of the fingernail of the first finger. The channel courses along the thumb side of the arm, over the shoulder, up the neck to the face where it ends at the nostril. The stomach meridian begins below the eye, courses across the face, then up to the forehead, and then reverses direction to run down the throat, along the chest and abdomen, down the front of the thigh and lower leg, across the ankle and foot to end at the lateral side of the root of the second toenail. The Conception Vessel is the name given to one of the midline meridians. Its route is from the genital area straight up the middle of the abdomen to end at the center of the lower lip. The posterior midline meridian, the Governor Vessel, starts at the tailbone, courses up the spine, over the midline of the head and ends on the front of the upper gum.

The needles used in acupuncture may be specially made for the procedure or they may be the needles used in giving injections, such as the ones commonly used in physician's offices. Short needles are used for areas that are less fleshy and longer needles may be used in areas of deep flesh and muscle. The acupuncturist simply inserts the needle to a prescribed depth then rotates it. When the needle enters the skin, the patient will feel a transient pain. When the needle tip reaches the depth of the meridian, the patient will have a sensation of radiating warmth or fullness. The insertion points nearest the painful area should be treated first, then the distant points treated. Once the needles are in place they are rotated to stimulate the channel.

Needles may be left in place for 15 minutes to half an hour, then withdrawn. For acute conditions, the treatment may be given twice a day. For a longlasting condition (chronic pain), the treatment can be given every second or third day for up to 20 treatments, after which no acupuncture should be given for several weeks.

Because the acupuncture points are very specifically located and because people are different sizes, a special system of measuring the body has been developed to locate the points. To accommodate various body sizes and limb lengths, the Chinese developed the "human inch" or cun. This term has since been modernized to the Acupuncture Unit of Measurement (AUM). The AUM is a system that simply divides a given distance on the human body into equal parts no matter how long that distance is. For example, the AUM of the chest is the division of the distance between the nipples into eight AUM. The distance from the lower end of the breastbone (sternum) to the umbilicus also is eight AUM. Thus, a broadchested man may have a distance of 12 inches between the nipples on his chest and the smaller man may have only 10 inches. Nevertheless, whatever the distance is it is divided into eight units because it is eight AUM across the thorax. The upper arm from crease of the elbow to armpit is nine AUM, the lower arm from crease of the elbow to crease of the wrist is 12 AUM, and so on until all the areas of the body have been given standard AUM dimensions.

Because the needles must be manipulated for stimulation once they have been inserted, means other than rotation are used for conditions that require a large number of needles. In some cases, a small electric current can be passed through the needles to the meridian

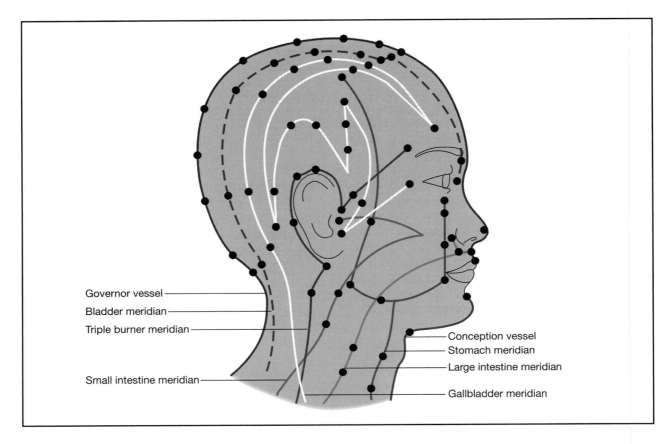

Acupuncture sites and meridians on the face and neck.

to provide the stimulation. Another technique known as moxibustion uses heat to stimulate the meridian. In this case, the needle is inserted and a small bit of the dried leaves of the plant, *Artemisia vulgaris*, is placed in the cup of the needle and lighted. The heat from the smoldering plant is passed through the needle to the area of pain. A few points on the body are not suited to needle insertion. These points may have a small, smoldering cone of Artemisia vulgaris placed directly on the skin and the heat is allowed to penetrate. Why acupuncture seems to be effective in some patients remains a matter of investigation. The meridians or channels seem to be pathways of nerve fibers that are stimulated by the needles. Changes in the area being treated can be demonstrated clinically, showing that the pain threshold has been raised so that pain is no longer felt. Whatever the mechanism, the patient who undergoes acupuncture must have a degree of faith in its effectiveness and must be relaxed during the procedure. At times, changes in muscle tension may bend the needles and make them difficult to remove, but this is less a problem among patients who are not tense at the prospect of having several needles inserted into their bodies.

See also Acupressure; Alternative medicine.

Further Reading:

"Acupuncture." (fact sheet), National Institutes of Health Office of Alternative Medicine, 1993.

"Acupuncture Illustrated." *Consumer Reports* 59 (January 1994): 54–57.

Botello, J.G. "Acupuncture: Getting the Point." *Lears* 6 (November 1993): 43–44.

ADA (adenosine deaminase) deficiency

ADA deficiency is an inherited condition that occurs in fewer than one in 100,000 live births worldwide. Individuals with ADA deficiency inherit defective ADA genes and are unable to produce the enzyme adenosine deaminase in their cells. This enzyme is needed to break down metabolic byproducts that become toxic to T cell lymphocytes. Most of the body's cells have other means of removing the metabolic byproducts that ADA helps break down and remain unaffected by ADA deficiency. However, T cell lymphocytes, white blood cells that help fight infection, are not able to remove the byproducts in the absence of ADA.

Without ADA, the toxins derived from the metabolic byproducts kill the T cells shortly after they are produced in the bone marrow. Instead of having a normal life span of a few months, T cells of individuals with ADA deficiency live only a few days. Consequently, their numbers are greatly reduced, and the body's entire immune system is weakened.

The body's immune system includes T cell lymphocytes and B cell lymphocytes; these lymphocytes play different roles in fighting infections. B cells produce antibodies that lock on to disease–causing viruses and bacteria, thereby marking the pathogens for destruction. Unlike B cells, T cells cannot produce antibodies, but they do control B cell activity. T cell helpers enable antibody production, whereas T cell suppressors turn off antibody production. Another T cell subtype kills cancer cells and virus–infected cells.

Because T cells control B cell activity, the reduction of T cells results in an absence of both T cell and B cell function called severe combined immunodeficiency (SCID). Individuals with SCID are unable to mount an effective immune response to any infection. Prior to present–day treatments, most ADA–deficient SCID victims died from infections before reaching the age of two.

Treatments for ADA deficiency

The treatment of choice for ADA deficiency is bone marrow transplantation from a matched sibling donor. Successful bone marrow transplants cure ADA deficiency. Unfortunately, only 20–30% of patients with ADA deficiency have a matched sibling donor. Another treatment involves injecting the patient with PEG–ADA, polyethylene glycol–coated bovine ADA. Supplying the missing enzyme in this way helps some patients fight infections, while others are helped very little.

The newest treatment for ADA deficiency is gene therapy. Gene therapy provides victims with their own T cells into which a normal copy of the human ADA gene has been inserted. ADA deficiency is the first disease to be treated with human gene therapy.

The first person to receive gene therapy for ADA deficiency was four–year–old Ashanthi DeSilva. The treatment was developed by three physicians—W. French Anderson, Michael Blaese, and Kenneth Culver. DeSilva received her first treatment, an infusion of

---

KEY TERMS

B cell lymphocytes—Immune–system white blood cells that produce antibodies.

PEG–ADA—A drug, polyethylene–coated bovine ADA, used for treating ADA–deficiency. The polyethylene coating prevents rapid elimination of the ADA from the blood.

Retrovirus—A type of virus that inserts its genetic material into the chromosomes of the cells it infects.

Stem cells—Bone marrow cells that produce the blood cells, such as T cells and B cells; they can also replicate themselves.

T cell lymphocytes—Immune–system white blood cells that enable antibody production, suppress antibody production, or kill other cells.

---

her own T cells implanted with normal ADA genes, on 14 September 1990 at the National Institutes of Health in Bethesda, Maryland.

How did DeSilva's T cells acquire the normal ADA genes? A. Dusty Miller of the Fred Hutchinson Research Center in Seattle, Washington, made the vectors for carrying the normal ADA genes into the T cells. These vectors were made from a retrovirus, a type of virus that inserts its genetic material into the cell it infects. By replacing harmful retroviral genes with normal ADA genes, Miller created the retrovirus vectors to deliver the normal ADA genes into DeSilva's T cells. The retrovirus vectors—carrying normal ADA genes—were mixed with T cells that had been extracted from DeSilva's blood and grown in culture dishes. The retrovirus vectors entered the T cells and implanted the normal ADA genes into the T cell chromosomes. The T cells were then infused back into DeSilva's blood where the normal ADA genes in them produced ADA.

When doctors saw that DeSilva benefited and suffered no harmful effects from gene therapy, they repeated the same treatment on nine–year–old Cynthia Cutshall on 30 January 1991. Both girls developed functioning immune systems. However, since T cells have a limited life span, DeSilva and Cutshall needed to receive periodic infusions of their genetically–corrected T cells, and they both continued with PEG–ADA injections.

Subsequent research is focusing on developing a permanent cure for ADA deficiency using gene therapy. In May and June of 1993, Cutshall and three newborns with ADA deficiency received their own stem cells that had been implanted with normal ADA genes. Stem cells are the bone marrow cells that produce the blood cells. Unlike T cells which only live for a few months, stem cells live throughout the patient's life, and thus the patient should have a lifetime supply of ADA without requiring further treatment. The results of these initial trials have not yet been published.

See also Immune system.

Further Reading:

Bishop, Jerry E., and Michael Waldholz. *Genome*. New York: Simon and Schuster, 1990.

Blaese, Michael R. "Development of Gene Therapy for Immunodeficiency: Adenosine Deaminase Deficiency." *Pediatric Research* 33 (1993): S49–S55.

Culver, Kenneth W. "Splice of Life." *The Sciences* 33 (1993): 18–24.

Culver, Kenneth W., W. French Anderson, and R. Michael Blaese. "Lymphocyte Gene Therapy." *Human Gene Therapy* 2 (1991): 107–109.

Drlica, Karl. *Understanding DNA and Gene Cloning*. 2nd ed. New York: John Wiley & Sons, Inc., 1992.

Elmer–Dewitt, Philip. "The Genetic Revolution." *Time* (17 January 1994): 46–53.

Jaroff, Leon. "Brave New Babies." *Time* (31 May 1993): 56–57.

Svitil, Kathy. "Help for Kids With SCIDs." *Discover* 15 (January 1994): 91.

Thompson, Larry. "The First Kids With New Genes." *Time* (7 June 1993): 50–51.

Pamela Crowe

Adaptation

The term adaptation encompasses three biological concepts. In physiology, adaptation refers to the process of adjustment by individual organisms in response to short–term changes in their environment. In evolutionary biology, adaptation refers to the process of natural selection which results in adaptations in living things. To an evolutionary biologist, adaptations are the features of organisms that enable them to survive and reproduce in a particular environment. The grasping hands of primates, the sensitive antennae of insects, and the flowers and fruits of plants are all adaptations that promote survival and/or reproduction. Adaptation is the gradual accumulation of beneficial traits over time, that is, the "fine–tuning" of organisms to the demands of their environment.

Historical background

That living things are adapted to survive in particular habitats was obvious to scientists long before Charles Darwin published his influential book *On the Origin of Species* (1859), in which he discussed the adaptations of organisms as the product of natural selection. Many features of living things—the bee's sting, the vertebrate eye, the human brain—appeared to some to have been designed by a master engineer as if to serve their specific purpose. Different species that live in similar environments often exhibit similar characteristics. Fish, whales, and penguins all use fins or flippers to propel themselves through water, although the evolutionary lineages of these three groups diverged long ago. The common plan of such features demanded an explanation.

One effort to explain such traits was a school of thought called natural theology. Proponents of natural theology, including the English naturalist John Ray (1627–1705) and the Reverend William Paley (1743–1805), argued that the elegant and often complex features of organisms were best explained as the products of a direct design by a divine intelligence. Another effort to explain adapted traits was the notion of the inheritance of acquired characters, also known as Lamarckism—although its famous proponent, Jean–Baptiste Lamarck (1744–1829), was not the first to suggest it. This theory argued that the short–term traits that organisms acquire during their life in response to the demands of the environment were passed directly on to their offspring. This is not widely accepted by biologists today.

Biologists now recognize natural selection to be the mechanism that produces evolutionary adaptation. Natural selection is undirected and unconscious, and is blind with respect to any eventual outcome. Exactly how specific adaptations arise, however, is far from solved. It is easy to imagine how natural selection might produce relatively simple adaptations such as camouflage: a rabbit that lives in regions covered by snow in winter is better adapted to its environment if it produces a white coat during the winter months. The difficulty arises in explaining the evolution of extremely complex and multifaceted adaptations, such as the vertebrate eye. Of course, the functioning, perfectly–formed eye is a superb adaptation for visual processing; but its evolution could hardly have come about overnight. The question may be asked, what good is half an eye?

Darwin suggested the answer lies in gradual change over many generations, in which the intermediate stages leading to a fully–formed eye each have some adaptive value. Perhaps a simple spot of light–sensitive cells concentrates and becomes larger in one region of the proto–eye; if the area folds inward to form a small chamber with a pin–hole opening, it is a structure that functions like a simple camera. In fact, this kind of structure is found in the marine mollusc, *Nautilus*. If the proto–eye is protected by the addition of a transparent membrane, it is a precursor to the cornea; if part of the fluid that fills the chamber differentiates, it is a lens. All the parts making up a fully functioning eye could evolve independently, in small steps, each one building on, and interacting with earlier changes. In this scenario, "half an eye" could be quite advantageous—indeed, could mean the difference between life and death—relative to no eye at all.

Examples of adaptation

Physiological adaptation

The condition of low oxygen in the blood (hypoxia) is commonly encountered by people traveling to high altitudes, where the decreasing barometric pressure means that less oxygen is available for respiration. People who visit or live at high altitudes undergo physiological changes (adaptations) to adjust to the low–oxygen environment. Short–term visitors increase ventilation rate and cardiac output, and produce more red blood cells to carry oxygen to body tissues. Over a longer period, as acclimatization happens, the heart output and ventilation rate return to normal levels, while the red blood cell count continues to climb. This adaptation occurs because tissue cells become more metabolically efficient, and are thus capable of more work with relatively less fuel. The most famous of all high–altitude people are the Sherpas of Nepal, whose climbing feats are legendary. The ability to adapt or acclimatize in this way is itself an evolved adaptation.

Evolutionary adaptation

Kettlewell's study of the peppered moth, *Biston betularia,* is one of the most widely cited cases of natural selection producing adaptation. Before the industrial revolution in Britain, this moth was predominantly light–colored, which afforded perfect camouflage from predatory birds on the light–colored lichen–covered tree trunks on which it rested. When pollution from factories caused the lichens on the trees to die, the moths' resting place became the darker color of the bark beneath. Kettlewell observed that, as this transformation occurred, a dark, or melanic, form of the moth became increasingly common, eventually coming to make up more than 90% of the population of moths in the affected areas. In the unpolluted areas, however, the original, light form of the moth remained common. Kettlewell attributed the moth's color change to selection by predatory birds, which locate the moths visually, and so remove individual moths that do not conform to the background coloration of trees in their environment. He tested his idea that the moths' color protected them from predation by placing each of the two forms on trees in different areas, photographing birds in the act of capturing moths, and measuring the rates at which the two moth forms were taken. Kettlewell concluded that the moths' color was, indeed, the result of adaptation to conditions in its habitat.

Some of the most interesting cases of adaptation occur when two species evolve together, so that each benefits from the association. The mutualistic association between the ant *Formica fusca* and the larval stage of the lycaenid butterfly *Glaucopsyche lygdamus* is an example. The butterfly caterpillar produces a sweet "honeydew" solution which the ants harvest as food. In return, the ants defend the caterpillar against parasitic wasps and flies. The mutual adaptation of two species in this manner is known as coadaptation. Different species of lycaenid butterflies and ants have evolved such mutualistic associations numerous times, suggesting that the two groups have been evolving together for a long period.

Not all species interactions are beneficial for both members, however. Some organisms have evolved specialized adaptations to reduce the negative impact of a cooperating species. *Heliconius* butterflies disperse the pollen from the flowers of *Passiflora* vines (so benefitting the plant), but female butterflies also lay single eggs on young *Passiflora* shoots, and the developing larva may consume the entire shoot (a definite cost to the plant). The female butterfly typically does not lay an egg on a shoot that already has an egg, since the larvae are cannibalistic, and the one that is laid and hatches first will likely eat any others. Several *Passiflora* species produce new shoots featuring a small structure that closely resembles a *Heliconius* egg. A female butterfly that sees this egg mimic will avoid laying there, and the shoot will be spared. The plant's adaptation to avoid herbivory by the butterfly larvae is almost certainly made possible by their long association in another context, namely pollination.

Current approaches to adaptation

Evolutionary biologists who study adaptation use a comparative method to explain similar characteristics of organisms by analyzing the genealogical links between species and synthesizing ideas about evolutionary change using statistical analysis.

Some researchers favor a restricted meaning of the term adaptation: for a feature to be considered an adaptation, it must be derived from a more primitive state in response to natural selection. In the case of snowshoe hares that turn white in winter, it would be necessary to show that individuals possessing this trait evolved from a population that lacked this feature, perhaps remaining brown year–round. In restricting the definition of adaptation, researchers draw a distinction between current utility and the historical origin of adaptive traits. The observation that a white coat helps camouflage a snowshoe hare in the snow is not especially informative about the origin of white fur in these creatures. This distinction has led researchers Stephen J. Gould and Elisabeth Vrba to suggest the term exaptation, to denote traits of organisms that provide beneficial effects, but which were actually selected for a different function—whereby the white fur had evolved for its improved heating properties, for instance, and only incidentally proved advantageous as camouflage. In some cases, therefore, the features we recognize as adaptive represent new uses of traits that originally arose for other reason. In practical terms, the emergence of solutions to ecological problems will depend on what selection has to work with.

See also Evolution; Natural selection.

Further Reading:

Ciba Foundation. Symposium 102: *Origins and Development of Adaptation*. London: Pitman, 1984.

Dawkins, Richard. *The Blind Watchmaker*. New York: Norton, 1985.

Gould, Stephen J., and Elisabeth Vrba. "Exaptation—a missing term in the science of form." *Paleobiology* 8, No. 1 (1982):4–15.

Harvey, Paul H., and Mark D. Pagel. *The Comparative Method in Evolutionary Biology*. New York: Oxford University Press, 1991.

Williams, George C. *Adaptation and Natural Selection*. Princeton, NJ: Princeton University Press, 1966.

Susan Andrew

ADD (attention deficit disorder) see **Hyperactivity**

Adder see **Snakes; Viper**

Addiction

Addiction is a compulsion to engage in unhealthy or detrimental behavior. It is estimated that up to 25% of the American population has some form of addictive behavior.

Addiction is usually a desire for drugs such as heroin, cocaine, or alcohol. There are other forms of addiction, however, and seemingly harmless behaviors can become the focus of the addict's life. Gambling, eating, running, working, smoking, or sexual activity can all become addictive behaviors.

Addiction and addictive substances have long been a part of human culture. The use of alcoholic beverages, such as beer, was recorded by the ancient Egyptians. The Romans and other early civilizations fermented, drank, and traded in wine. The infamous "opium dens" of the Far East offered crude opium. The discovery of America was accompanied by the discovery of tobacco, grown by the indigenous population.

Addiction today, especially addiction to illegal drugs, takes a heavy toll on modern society. Illegal drugs are easy enough to obtain, but they have a high price. In order to get money to feed their addiction, some addicts resort to theft or prostitution.

Addictions

Addiction is not limited to substances that are ingested or injected. A hobby or a job can be the object of an addiction.

Chemical addictions

Chemical addiction is the general description for an addiction to a substance that must be injected or ingested. Alcohol, opiates, and cocaine are the most common of these chemicals. Though each of them is addictive, they have different effects on the body.

Addiction to alcohol, for example, may be the result of heavy drinking coupled with a malfunctioning type of cell in the liver of the alcoholic. Many adults can drink large quantities of alcoholic beverages and suffer only a "hangover"—headache and nausea. The malfunctioning liver in the alcoholic, however, does not detoxify the byproducts of alcohol ingestion rapidly. The resultant accumulation of a chemical called *acetaldehyde* causes several symptoms, including pain, which can be relieved by the intake of more alcohol. The consumption of ever–increasing amounts of alcohol with greater frequency can lead to organ failure and death if the alcoholic is left untreated.

Opium, produced by a species of poppy, is an ancient addictive substance that is still produced for its cash value. Although raw opium is not the form that most addicts encounter, purified, powdered opium has been used in many forms for hundreds of years. Tincture of opium, or laudanum, was introduced about 1500. Paregoric, a familiar household remedy today, dates from the early 1700s.

Heroin, a derivative of opium, has become a common addictive drug. Heroin is a powder that is dissolved in water and injected into the user's vein, giving an immediate sensation of warmth and relaxation. Physical or mental pain is relieved, and the user enters a deeply relaxed state for a few hours. The powder also can be inhaled for a milder effect. Heroin is extremely addictive and with only a few doses the user is "hooked."

Morphine, a refinement of opium, was discovered in the early 1800s. It was first used as an effective analgesic, or painkiller, and it is still used for that purpose. Its fast action makes it a drug of choice to ease the pain of wounded soldiers during wartime. Morphine has one–fifth the addictive power of heroin.

Cocaine in its various forms is another class of addictive compounds. In fact, it is the most addictive of these drugs; some people need only a single exposure to the drug to become addicted. Cocaine is processed from the coca plant and is used in the form of a white powder. It can be inhaled, ingested, injected, or mixed with marijuana and smoked. It is also further processed into a solid crystalline substance marketed as "crack." Unlike the opiates, which bring on a warm feeling and immobility, cocaine makes its users energetic.

Any of these chemical substances can become the object of intense addiction. Addicts of the opiates and cocaine must have increasingly frequent doses to maintain their desired physiological effects. Soon the addict has difficulty focusing on anything else, making it nearly impossible to hold a job or maintain a normal life. These drugs are of economic importance not only because of the amount of money that is spent on obtaining them, but also because of the crimes committed to obtain the cash to buy the drugs and the drug enforcement resources that are dedicated to policing those crimes.

Some experts consider drinking large amounts of coffee or cola beverages as evidence of an addiction to caffeine. In fact, these substances do provide a short–term mood lift to the user. The first cup of coffee in the morning, the midmorning coffee break, the cola at lunch, and the dinner coffee are habitual. Withdrawal from caffeine can cause certain mood changes and a longing for caffeine for many months afterward.

Tobacco use is also addictive. Cigarette smoking, for example, is one of the most difficult habits to stop. Withdrawal symptoms are more pronounced in the smoker than in the coffee drinker. Reforming smokers are subject to swift mood swings and intense cravings for a cigarette. A long–time smoker may never overcome the desire for cigarettes.

Withdrawal symptoms are caused by psychological, physical, and chemical reactions in the body. As the amount of addictive chemical in the blood begins to fall, the urge to acquire the next dose is strong. The hard drugs such as heroin and cocaine produce intense withdrawal symptoms that, if not eased by another dose of the addictive substance or an appropriate medication, can leave the user in painful helplessness. Strong muscle contractions, nausea, vomiting, sweating, and pain increase in strength until it becomes extremely difficult for the user to stay away from the drug.

The non–chemical addictions

Addictions can involve substances or actions not including addictive chemicals. Some of these addictions are difficult to define and may seem harmless enough, but they can destroy the lives of those who cannot escape them.

Gambling is one such form of addiction, affecting 6–10% of the American population, according to some experts. Gamblers begin as most others do, by placing small bets on horses or engaging in low–stakes card games or craps. Their successes are a form of ego enhancement, however, so they strive to repeat them. Their bets become larger, more frequent, and more irrational. Gamblers have been known to lose their jobs, their homes, and their families as a result of their activities. Their pattern is to place ever–larger bets to make up for their losses. Gamblers are difficult to treat because they refuse to recognize that they have an abnormal condition. After all, nearly everyone gambles—on the lottery, the horses, home poker games, or football or baseball games. Once a compulsive gambler is convinced that his or her problem is serious, an addiction program may be successful in treating the condition.

Food addiction can be a difficult condition to diagnose. Food addicts find comfort in eating. The physical sensations that accompany eating can become addictive, even though an addict may not taste the food. Food addicts may indulge in binge eating in which they consume prodigious quantities of food in one sitting, or they may consume smaller quantities of food over a longer period of time, but eat constantly during that time.

A food addict can become grossly overweight, with extremely low self-esteem, which becomes more pronounced as he or she gains weight. The addict then seeks comfort by eating more food, setting up a cycle that probably will lead to a premature death if not interrupted.

The opposite of addiction to eating is addiction to not eating. This addiction often starts as an attempt to lose weight and ends in malnutrition. To do this, young people, usually females, will reject food almost entirely (a condition called anorexia) or will purge any food that they take in as soon after eating as possible (a condition called bulimia). Some experts say that nearly a hundred people a year die of malnutrition that results from anorexia or bulimia. Others say the number is much larger because the deaths are not recorded as anorexia or bulimia, but as heart failure or kidney failure, either of which can result from malnutrition.

Anorexia and bulimia are difficult to treat. In the minds of victims, they are bloated and obese even though they may be on the brink of starvation, and so they often resist treatment. Hospitalization may be required even before the official diagnosis is made. Treatment includes a long, slow process of psychiatric counseling.

The sex addict also is difficult to diagnose because "normal" sex behavior is not well–defined. Generally, any sex act between two consenting adults is condoned if neither suffers harm. Frequency of sexual activity is not used as a deciding factor in diagnosis. More likely the sex addict is diagnosed by his or her attitude toward sex partners.

The sex addict has difficulty in forming lasting relationships. The primary goal of a relationship is to have sex, not to form a bond with anyone. He or she seeks a succession of mates or more than one at a time to obtain physical satisfaction. When the sex addict is not with a partner, he or she may masturbate to feed the addiction.

Other compulsions or addictions include exercise, especially running. Running releases certain hormones called endorphins in the brain, giving a feeling of euphoria or happiness. This is the "high" that runners often describe. They achieve it when they have run sufficiently to release endorphins and have felt their effects. So good is this feeling that the compulsive runner may practice his hobby in spite of bad weather, injury, or social obligation. Because running is considered a healthful hobby, it is difficult to convince an addict that he is overdoing it and must temper his activity.

The addict

Because addictive behavior has such serious effects on the health and social well–being of the addict and those around him or her, why would anyone start? One characteristic that marks addicts, whether to chemicals or nonchemical practices, is a low sense of self esteem. The addict may arise from any social or economic situation, and there is no way to discern among a group of people who will become an addict and who will not.

It has been a basic tenet that the individual who uses drugs heavily will become addicted. However, soldiers who served in Vietnam reported heavy use of marijuana and heroin while they were in the combat zone, yet the vast majority gave up the habit upon returning home. There are reports, however, of people becoming addicted to a drug with exposure to only once or a few times.

See also Alcoholism; Amphetamines; Barbiturates; Cocaine; Marijuana; Morphine; Narcotic; Nicotine.

Further Reading:

Bender, D. and Leone, B. *Drug Abuse: Opposing Viewpoints.* San Diego: Greenhaven Press, Inc. 1994.

Meintz, S.L. and Larson, C. "Can you spot this kind of addiction?" *RN* 57 (July, 1994): 42–45.

O'Brien, W.B. and Henican, E. *You Can't Do It Alone: The Daytop Way to Make Your Child Drug Free.* New York: Simon & Schuster, 1993.

Silverstein, A., V. Silverstein, and R. Silverstein, *The Addictions Handbook.* Hillside, NJ: Enslow Publishers, 1991.

Larry Blaser

Some experts believe people are born with the predisposition to become addicted. Children of addicts have a greater probability of becoming addicts than do children whose parents are not drug users. Thus the probability of addiction may be at least partially hereditary. On the other hand, a psychological problem may lead the individual into addiction. The need for instant gratification, a feeling of being socially ostracized, and an inability to cope with the "downs" of life all have been cited as possible springboards to addiction.

Treatment of addiction

Addiction of any form is difficult to treat. Many programs instituted to break the grip of addictive substances have had limited success. The "cure" depends upon the resolve of the addict, and he or she often struggles with the addiction even after treatment.

Trying to stop chemical intake without benefit of medical help is a difficult task for the addict because of intense physical withdrawal symptoms. Pain, nausea, vomiting, sweating, and hallucinations must be endured for several days. Most addicts are not able to cope with these symptoms, and they will relieve them by indulging in their addiction.

The standard therapy for the chemical addict is the so–called 12–step program, which provides physical and emotional support during withdrawal and recovery. The addict is also educated about drug and alcohol addiction. "Kicking" a habit, though, is difficult, and backsliding is frequent. Many former addicts have enough determination to avoid drugs for the remainder of their lives, but an equal number will take up the habit again.

Addison's disease

Addison's disease, also called adrenocortical deficiency or primary adrenal hypofunction, is a rare condition caused by destruction of the cortex of the adrenal gland, one of several glands the endocrine system. Because Addison's disease is treatable, those who develop the illness can expect to have a normal life span.

The adrenal glands

The adrenal glands, also called suprarenal glands, sit like flat, triangular caps atop each kidney. They are divided into two distinct areas—the medulla at the center and cortex surrounding the outside. The cortex, which makes up about 80% of the adrenal gland, secretes three types of hormones—sex hormones, mineralocorticoids (principally aldosterone) and glucocorticoids (primarily cortisol or hydrocortisone). Scientists believe these hormones perform hundreds of regulatory functions in the body, including helping to regulate metabolism, blood pressure, the effects of insulin in the breakdown of sugars, and the inflammatory response of the immune system. Addison's disease results from an injury or disease that slowly destroys the adrenal cortex, therefore shutting down the production of these hormones.

The production of cortisol by the adrenal cortex is precisely metered by a control loop that begins in an area in the brain called the *hypothalamus*, a collection of specialized cells that control many of the functions of the body. When necessary, the hypothalamus secretes a releasing factor that tells the pituitary gland to secrete another hormone to stimulate the adrenal gland to release more cortisol. The increased cortisol levels signal the pituitary to stop producing the adrenal stimulant. This is a finely tuned loop, and if it is interrupted or shut down, as in Addison's disease, profound changes occur in the body.

History of Addison's disease

The disease is named for its discoverer, Dr. Thomas Addison, a British surgeon who described adrenal insufficiency in 1849, though endocrine functions had yet to be explained. Addison described the condition from autopsies he performed. At the time, there was no cure for adrenal insufficiency, so victims died after contracting it. Addison also noted that 70–90% of patients with adrenal insufficiency had tuberculosis as well.

Addison's disease is no longer a fatal illness if it is properly diagnosed. Today, doctors note that up to 70% of cases are the result of the adrenal cortex being destroyed by the body's own immune system, so Addison's is called an *autoimmune disease*. Those who have sustained an injury to the adrenal gland and people who have diabetes are at increased risk of Addison's disease. Tuberculosis is also linked to the disease, but since this disease can now be cured, Addison's disease is rarely caused by tuberculosis today.

Addison's disease

The effects of adrenal insufficiency do not manifest themselves until more than 90% of the adrenal cortex has been lost. Then weakness and dizziness occur, and the skin darkens, especially on or near the elbows, knees, knuckles, lips, scars, and skin folds. These symptoms begin gradually and worsen over time.

The patient becomes irritable and depressed and often craves salty foods. Some people do not experience these progressive symptoms, but become aware of the disease during what is called an *addisonian crisis*. In this case, the symptoms appear suddenly and require immediate medical attention. Severe pain develops in the lower back, abdomen, or legs; vomiting and diarrhea leave the patient dehydrated. A person may become unconscious and may even die.

A doctor's examination reveals low blood pressure that becomes even lower when the patient rises from a sitting or lying position to a standing position. A blood test shows low blood sugar (hypoglycemia), low blood sodium (hyponatremia), and low levels of cortisol. Other tests are carried out to determine whether the condition is the result of adrenal insufficiency or if the low levels of cortisol are the result of problems with the hypothalamus or pituitary.

Treatment

Once diagnosed, Addison's disease is treated by replacing the natural cortisol with an oral medication. The medicine is adjusted by a doctor to bring cortisol levels in the blood up to normal and maintain them. A patient also is advised to eat salty foods, not skip any meals, and carry a packet containing a syringe with cortisone to be injected in case of an emergency.

With the loss of the ability to secrete cortisol under stress, a patient must take extra medication when he undergoes dental treatments or surgery. Even though Addison's disease is not curable, a patient with this condition can expect to live a full life span.

See also: Adrenals; Autoimmune disease; Diabetes mellitus; Endocrine system; Hormones; Immune system; Insulin; Metabolism; Tuberculosis.

Further Reading:

Kessler, Christine A. "Adrenal Gland (Adrenal disorders and other problems)," in *Endocrine Problems: Nurse Review*. Springhouse, PA: Springhouse Corp.

Larson, David E., ed. *Mayo Clinic Family Health Book*. New York: William Morrow, 1990.

National Institute of Diabetes and Digestive and Kidney Diseases. "Addison's Disease" (fact sheet). National Institutes of Health Publication No. 90–3054.

Larry Blaser

Addition

Addition, indicated by a + sign, is a method of combining numbers. The result of adding two numbers is called their sum.

Adding natural numbers

Consider the natural, or counting, numbers 1,2,3, 4,... Each natural number can be defined in terms of sets. The number 1 is the name of the collection containing every conceivable set with one element, such as the set containing 0 or the set containing the Washington Monument. The number 2 is the name of the collection containing every conceivable set with two elements, and so on. The sum of two natural numbers is determined by counting the number of elements in the union of two sets chosen to represent them. For example, let the set {A,B,C} represent 3 and the set {W,X,Y,Z} represent 4. Then 3 + 4 is determined by counting the elements in {A,B,C,W,X,Y,Z}, which is the union of {A,B,C} and {W,X,Y,Z}. The result is seven, and we write 3 + 4 = 7. In this way, the operation of addition is carried out by counting.

The addition algorithm

Addition of natural numbers is independent of the numerals used to represent the numbers being added. However, some forms of notation make addition of large numbers easier than other forms. In particular, the Hindu–Arabic positional notation (in general use today) facilitates addition of large numbers, while the use of Roman numerals, for instance, is quite cumbersome. In the Hindu–Arabic positional notation, numerals are arranged in columns, each column corresponding to numbers that are 10 times larger than those in the column to the immediate right. For example, 724 consists of 4 ones, 2 tens, and 7 hundreds. The addition algorithm amounts to counting by ones in the right hand column, counting by tens in the next column left, counting by hundreds in the next column left and so on. When the sum of two numbers in any column exceeds nine, the amount over 10 is retained and the rest transferred or "carried" to the next column left. Suppose it is desired to add 724 and 897. Adding each column gives 11 ones, 11 tens, and 15 hundreds. But 11 ones is equal to 1 ten and 1 one so we have 1 one, 12 tens and 15 hundreds. Checking the tens column we find 12 tens equals 2 tens and 1 hundred, so we actually have 1 one, 2 tens and 16 hundreds. Finally, 16 hundreds is 6 hundreds and 1 thousand, so the end result is 1 thousand, 6 hundreds, 2 tens, and 1 one, or 1,621.

Adding common fractions

Historically, the number system expanded as it became apparent that certain problems of interest had no solution in the then-current system. Fractions were included to deal with the problem of dividing a whole thing into a number of parts. Common fractions are numbers expressed as a ratio, such as 2/3, 7/9, and 3/2. When both parts of the fraction are integers, the result is a rational number. Each rational number may be thought of as representing a number of pieces; the numerator (top number) tells how many pieces the fraction represents; the denominator (bottom number) tells us how many pieces the whole was divided into. Suppose a cake is divided into two pieces, after which one half is further divided into six pieces and the other half into three pieces, making a total of nine pieces. If you take one piece from each half, what part of the whole cake do you get? This amounts to a simple counting problem if both halves are cut into the same number of pieces, because then there are a total of six or 12 equal pieces, of which you take two. You get either 2/6 or 2/12 of the cake. The essence of adding rational numbers, then, is to turn the problem into one of counting equal size pieces. This is done by rewriting one or both of the fractions to be added so that each has the same denominator (called a common denominator). In this way, each fraction represents a number of equal size pieces. A general formula for the sum of two fractions is $a/b + c/d = (ad + bc)/bd$.

Adding decimal fractions

Together, the rational and irrational numbers constitute the set of real numbers. Addition of real numbers is facilitated by extending the positional notation used for integers to decimal fractions. Place a period (called a decimal point) to the right of the ones column, and let each column to its right contain numbers that are successively smaller by a factor of ten. Thus, columns to the right of the decimal point represent numbers less than one, in particular, "tenths," "hundredths," "thousandths," and so on. Addition of real numbers, then, continues to be defined in terms of counting and carrying, in the manner described above.

Adding signed numbers

Real numbers can be positive, negative, or zero. Addition of two negative numbers always results in a negative number and is carried out in the same fashion that positive numbers are added, after which a negative sign is placed in front of the result, such as $-4 + (-21) = -25$. Adding a positive and a negative number is the equivalent of subtraction, and, while it also proceeds by counting, the sum does not correspond to counting the members in the union of two sets, but to counting the members not in the intersection of two sets.

Addition in algebra

In algebra, which is a generalization of arithmetic, addition is also carried out by counting. For example, to sum the expressions $5x$ and $6x$ we notice that $5x$ means we have five xs and $6x$ means we have six xs, making a total of 11 xs. Thus $5x + 6x = (5 + 6)x = 11x$, which is usually established on the basis of the distributive law, an important property that the real numbers obey. In general, only like variables or powers can be added algebraically. In adding two polynomial expressions, only similar terms are combined; thus, $(3x^2 + 2x$

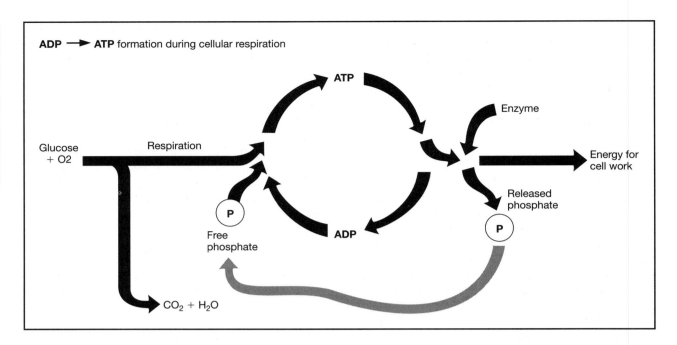

ADP → ATP formation during cellular respiration

ADP is formed during cellular respiration with energy released by the breakdown of glucose molecules.

$+7y + z) + (x^3 + 3x + 4z + 2yz) = (x^3 + 3x^2 + 5x + 7y + 5z + 2yz)$.

See also Algebra; Fraction, common; Natural numbers; Rational number; Real numbers; Subtraction.

Further Reading:
Boyer, Carl B. *A History of Mathematics.* 2nd ed. Revised by Uta C. Merzbach. New York: John Wiley and Sons, 1991.
McKeague, Charles P. *Elementary Algebra.* 5th ed. Fort Worth: Saunders College Publishing, 1995.
Pascoe, L. C. *Teach Yourself Mathematics.* Lincolnwood, IL: NTC Publishing Group, 1992.
Paulos, John Allen. *Beyond Numeracy, Ruminations of a Numbers Man.* New York: Alfred A. Knopf, 1991.

J. R. Maddocks

Adenosine diphosphate

Adenosine diphosphate (ADP) is a key intermediate in the body's energy metabolism—it serves as the "base" to which energy–producing reactions attach an additional phosphate group, forming adenosine triphosphate (ATP). ATP then diffuses throughout the cell to drive energy–requiring reactions.

Structurally, ADP consists of the purine base adenine (a complex, double–ring molecule containing five nitrogen atoms) attached to the five–carbon sugar ribose; this combination is known as adenosine. Attaching two connected phosphate groups to the ribose produces ADP. Schematically, the structure may be depicted as Ad–Ph–Ph, where Ad is adenosine and Ph is a phosphate group.

See also Adenosine triphosphate; Metabolism.

Adenosine triphosphate

Adenosine triphosphate (ATP) is often described as the body's "energy currency"—energy–producing metabolic reactions store their energy in the form of ATP, which can then drive energy–requiring syntheses and other reactions anywhere in the cell.

Structurally ATP consists of the purine base adenine (a complex, double–ring molecule containing five nitrogen atoms) attached to the five–carbon sugar ribose; this combination is known as adenosine. Attaching a string of three connected phosphate groups to the ribose produces ATP. Schematically, one may depict the structure of ATP as Ad–Ph–Ph–Ph, where Ad is adenosine and Ph is a phosphate group. If only two phosphate groups are attached, the resulting compound is adenosine diphosphate (ADP).

The final step in almost all the body's energy–producing mechanisms is attachment of the third phosphate group to ADP. This new phosphate–phosphate bond, known as a high–energy bond, effectively stores the energy that has been produced. The ATP then diffuses throughout the cell, eventually reaching sites where energy is needed for such processes as protein synthesis or muscle cell contraction. At these sites, enzyme mechanisms couple the energy–requiring processes to the breakdown of ATP's high–energy bond. This regenerates ADP and free phosphate, both of which diffuse back to the cell's energy–producing sites and serve as raw materials for production of more ATP.

The ATP–ADP couple is thus analogous to a rechargeable storage battery, with energy production sites representing the battery charger. ATP is the fully charged battery that can supply energy to a flashlight or transistor radio. ADP is the used battery that is returned for charging.

ADP is not a fully drained battery, however. It still possesses one high–energy phosphate–phosphate bond. When energy is short and ATP is scarce, the second phosphate can be transferred from one ADP to another. This creates a new ATP molecule, along with one of adenosine monophosphate (AMP). Since the "fully drained" AMP will probably be broken down and disposed of, however, this mechanism represents an emergency response that is inhibited when ATP is plentiful.

ATP is also a building block in DNA synthesis, with the adenosine and one phosphate being incorporated into the growing helix. (The "A" in ATP is the same as in the A–C–G–T "alphabet" of DNA.) This process differs from most other ATP–using reactions, since it releases *two* phosphate groups—initially still joined, but soon separated. With very little pyrophosphate (Ph–Ph) available in the cell, the chance that it will break the DNA chain and again form —though all enzyme reactions are theoretically reversible—is effectively infinitesimal. Since breaking the DNA chain would probably kill the cell, what at first might appear to be energy wastage turns out to be quite worthwhile. The cell also converts ATP to AMP and pyrophosphate in a few other cases where the reaction must always go only in a single direction.

See also Adenosine diphosphate; Enzyme; Metabolism.

Adhesive

Adhesives bond two or more materials at their surface, and may be classified as structural or non–structural. Structural adhesives can support heavy loads, while non–structural adhesives cannot. Most adhesives exist in liquid, paste, or granular form, although film and fabric–backed tape varieties are also commercially available.

Adhesives have been used since ancient times. The first adhesives were probably made from boiled–down animal products such as hides or bones. Organic, i.e., carbon–based, adhesives have also been derived from plant products for use with paper products. While many of these organic glues have proven effective in the adhesion of furniture and other indoor products, they have not been effective in outdoor use where they are exposed to harsher environmental conditions.

Although inorganic adhesives, which are based on materials not containing carbon, such as the sodium silicates (water glasses) for bonding paper board, are sold commercially, most adhesives in common use are made of synthetic, organic materials. By far, the most widely used adhesives today are synthetic, polymer–based adhesives.

Synthetic adhesives may be made of amorphous thermoplastics above their glass transition temperatures; thermosetting monomers as in the case of epoxy glues and cyanoacrylates; low molecular weight reactive species as in the case of urethane adhesives; or block copolymers, suspensions, or latexes.

Types of adhesive bonding

Adhesive bonding may originate in a variety of ways. It may be the result of mechanical interlocking of the adhesive with the bonded surface, covalent bonding between bonded surfaces, or secondary electronic interactions between the bonded materials.

In mechanical adhesion, the adhesive flows around the substrate surface roughness so that interlocking of the two materials takes place. The adhesive may penetrate the substrate surface. Surface interpenetration often involves polymer diffusion; this type of bonding depends on the ability of the polymer adhesive to diffuse into the bonded surface.

Secondary electronic bonding may result from hydrogen bonds between the adhesive and substrate, from the interactions of overlapping polymer chains, or from such nonspecific forces as Van der Waals interactions.

In the case of covalent bonding, actual primary chemical bonds are formed between the bonded materials. For example, graft or block copolymers may bond different phases of a multicomponent polymeric material together.

Bonding applications

Adhesives are characterized by their shelf life, which is defined as the time that an adhesive can be stored after manufacture and still remain usable, and by their working life, defined as the time between mixing or making the adhesive and when the adhesive is no longer usable. The best choice of adhesive depends on the materials to be bonded.

Bonding metals

Epoxy resin adhesives perform well in the structural bonding of metal parts to each other. Non–structural adhesives such as polysulfides, neoprene, or rubber–based adhesives are also available for bonding metal foils. Ethylene cellulose cements are used for filling recesses in metal surfaces.

When bonding metals to non–metals, the choices of adhesives are more extensive. In the case of structural bonding, for example, polyester–based adhesives may be used to bond plastic laminates to metal surfaces; low–density epoxy adhesives may be used to adhere light plastics such as polyurethane foam to various metals; and liquid adhesives made of neoprene and synthetic resins may be used to bond metals to wood. General purpose rubber, cellulose, and vinyl adhesives may be used to non–structurally bond metals to other materials such as glass and leather.

Bonding plastics

Thermoplastic materials including nylon, polyethylene, acetal, polycarbonate, polyvinyl chloride, cellulose nitrate, and cellulose acetate are easily dissolved by solvents and softened by heat. These limitations restrict the use of adhesives with such materials, and solvent or heat welding may prove better bonding alternatives for adhering these materials.

Solvent cements can frequently be used to bond thermoplastics together. These cements combine a solvent with a base material that is the same as the thermoplastic to be adhered. In view of environmental considerations, however, many adhesives manufacturers are now reformulating their solvent–based adhesives. General purpose adhesives such as cellulosics, vinyls, rubber cements, and epoxies have also been used successfully with thermoplastics.

Thermosetting plastics, including phenolics, epoxies, and alkyds, are easily bonded with epoxy–based adhesives, neoprene, nitrile rubber, and polyester–based cements. These adhesives have been used to bond both thermosets and thermoplastics to other materials, including ceramics, fabric, wood, and metal.

KEY TERMS

. . . .

Composite—A mixture or mechanical combination (on a macroscopic level) of materials that are solid in their finished state, that are mutually insoluble, and that have different chemistries.

Inorganic—Not containing compounds of carbon.

Monomer—A substance composed of molecules that are capable of reacting together to form a polymer.

Organic—Containing carbon atoms, when used in the conventional chemical sense.

Polymer—A substance, usually organic, composed of very large molecular chains that consist of recurring structural units.

Synthetic—Referring to a substance that either reproduces a natural product or that produces a unique material not found in nature, and that is produced by means of chemical reactions.

Thermoplastic—A high molecular weight polymer that softens when heated and that returns to its original condition when cooled to ordinary temperatures.

Thermoset—A high molecular weight polymer that solidifies irreversibly when heated; also called a thermosetting plastic.

Bonding wood

Animal glues, available in liquid and powder form, are frequently used in wood bonding. But animal glues are very sensitive to variations in temperature and moisture. Casein–type adhesives offer moderate resistance to moisture and high temperature, as do urea resin adhesives, which can be used to bond wood to wood, or wood to plastic.

Vinyl–acetate emulsions are excellent for bonding wood to materials that are especially porous, such as metal and some plastic laminates, but these adhesives also tend to be sensitive to temperature and moisture. Rubber, acrylic, and epoxy general–purpose adhesives also perform well with wood and other materials.

Fabric and paper bonding

General purpose adhesives including rubber cements and epoxies are capable of bonding fabrics together, as well as fabrics to other materials. When coated fabrics must be joined, the base adhesive material must be the same as the fabric coating. Rubber cements, gum mucilages, wheat pastes, and wood rosin adhesives can be used to join paper or fabric assemblies.

Further Reading:

Green, Robert E. *Machinery's Handbook,* 24th ed. New York: Industrial Press, 1992.
Sperling, L. H. *Introduction to Physical Polymer Science.* New York: John Wiley & Sons, 1992.
Wu, S. *Polymer Interfaces and Adhesion.* New York: Marcel Dekker, 1982.

Randall Frost

Adolescence see **Puberty**

ADP see **Adenosine diphosphate**

Adrenals

The adrenal glands are a pair of endocrine glands that sit atop the kidneys and that release their hormones directly into the bloodstream. The adrenals are flattened, somewhat triangular bodies that, like other endocrine glands, receive a rich blood supply. The phrenic (from the diaphragm) and renal (from the kidney) arteries send many small branches to the adrenals, while a single large adrenal vein drains blood from the gland.

Each adrenal gland is actually two organs in one. The inner portion of the adrenal gland, the adrenal medulla, releases substances called catecholamines, specifically epinephrine, adrenaline, norepinephrine, noradrenaline, and dopamine. The outer portion of the adrenal gland, the adrenal cortex, releases steroids, which are hormones derived from cholesterol.

There are three somewhat distinct zones in the adrenal cortex: the outer part, the zona glomerulosa (15% of cortical mass) made up of whorls of cells; the middle part, the zona fasciculata (50% of cortical mass) made up of columns of cells and that are continuous with the whorls; and an innermost area called the zona reticularis (7% of cortical mass), which is separated from the zona fasciculata by venous sinuses.

The cells of the zona glomerulosa secrete steroid hormones known as mineralocorticoids, which affect the fluid balance in the body, principally aldosterone, while the zona fasiculata and zona reticularis secrete glucocarticoids, notably cortisol and the androgen testosterone, which are involved in carbohydrate, protein, and fat metabolism.

The secretion of the adrenal cortical hormones is controlled by a region of the brain called the hypothalamus, which releases a corticotropin–releasing hormone. This hormone targets the anterior part of the pituitary gland, situated directly below the hypothalamus. The corticotropin–releasing hormone stimulates the release from the anterior pituitary of adreno-corticotropin (ACTH), which, in turn, enters the blood and targets the adrenal cortex. There, it binds to receptors on the surface of the gland's cells and stimulates them to produce the steroid hormones.

Steroids contain as their basic structure three 6–carbon (hexane) rings and a single 5–carbon (pentane) ring. The adrenal steroids have either 19 or 21 carbon atoms. These important hormones are collectively called corticoids. The 21–carbon steroids include glucocorticoids and mineralocorticoids, while the 19–carbon steroids are the androgens. Over 30 steroid hormones are made by the cortex, but only a few are secreted in physiologically significant amounts. These hormones can be classified into three main classes, glucocorticoids, mineralocorticoids, and corticosterone.

Cortisol (hydrocortisone) is the most important glucocorticoid. Its effect is the opposite to that of insulin. It causes the production of the sugar glucose from amino acids and glycogen stored in the liver, called gluconeogenesis, so increasing blood glucose. Cortisol also decreases the use of glucose in the body (except for the brain, spinal cord and heart), and it stimulates the use of fatty acids for energy.

Glucocorticoids also have anti–inflammatory and antiallergenic action, so they are often used in the treatment of rheumatoid arthritis. The excessive release of glucocorticoids causes Cushing's disease, which is characterized by fatigue and loss of muscle mass due to the excessive conversion of amino acids into glucose. In addition, there is the redistribution of body fat to the face, causing the condition known as "moon face."

The mineralocorticoids are essential for maintaining the balance of sodium in the blood and body tissues and the volume of the extracellular fluid in the body. Aldosterone, the principal mineralocorticoid produced by the zona glomerulosa, enhances the uptake and retention of sodium in cells, as well as the cells' release of potassium. This steroid also causes the tubules of the kidneys to retain sodium, thus maintaining levels of this ion in the blood, while increasing the excretion of potassium into the urine. Simultaneously, aldosterone increases reabsorption of bicarbonate by the kidney, thereby decreasing the acidity of body fluids.

A deficiency of adrenal cortical hormone secretion causes Addison's disease, characterized by fatigue, weakness, skin pigmentation, a craving for salt, extreme sensitivity to stress, and increased vulnerability to infection.

The adrenal androgens are weaker than testosterone, the male hormone produced by the testes. However, some of these androgens, including androstenedione, dehydroepiandrosterone (DHEA), and dehydroepiandrosterone sulfate can be converted by other tissues to stronger androgens, such as testosterone. The cortical output of androgens increases dramatically after puberty, giving the adrenal gland a major role in the developmental changes in both sexes. The cortex also secretes insignificant amounts of estrogen.

The steroid hormones are bound to steroid–binding proteins in the bloodstream, from which they are released at the surface of target cells. From there they move into the nucleus of the cell, where they may either stimulate or inhibit gene activity.

The release of the cortical hormones is controlled by adrenocorticotropic (ACTH) from the anterior pituitary gland. The level of ACTH has a diurnal periodicity, that is, it undergoes a regular, periodic change during the 24–hour time period. ACTH concentration in the blood rises in the early morning, peaking just before awaking, and reaching its lowest level shortly before sleep.

Several factors control the release of ACTH from the pituitary, including corticotropin–releasing hormone from the hypothalamus, free cortisol concentration in the plasma, stress (e.g., surgery, hypoglycemia, exercise, emotional trauma), and the sleep–wake cycle.

Mineralocorticoid release is also influenced by factors circulating in the blood. The most important of these factors is angiotensin II, the end–product of a series of steps starting in the kidney. When the body's blood pressure declines, this change is sensed by a special structure in the kidney called the juxtaglomerular apparatus. In response to this decreased pressure in kidney arterioles the juxtaglomerular apparatus releases an enzyme called renin into the kidney's blood vessels. There, the renin is converted to angiotensin I, which undergoes a further enzymatic change in the bloodstream outside the kidney to angiotensin II. Angiotensin II stimulates the adrenal cortex to release aldosterone, which causes the kidney to retain sodium. The increased concentration of sodium in the blood–filtering tubules of the kidney causes an osmotic movement of water into the blood, thereby increasing the blood pressure.

The adrenal medulla, which makes up 28% of the mass of the adrenal glands, is composed of irregular strands and masses of cells that are separated by venous sinuses. These cells contain many dense vesicles, which contain granules of catecholamines.

The cells of the medulla are modified ganglion (nerve) cells that are in contact with preganglionic fibers of the sympathetic nervous system. There are two types of medullary secretory cells, called chromaffin cells: the epinephrine (adrenalin)–secreting cells, which have large, less dense granules, and the norepinephrine (noradrenalin)–secreting cells, which contain smaller, very dense granules that do not fill their vesicles. Most chromaffin cells are the epinephrine–secreting type. These substances are released following stimulation by the acetylcholine–releasing sympathetic nerves that form synapses on the cells. Dopamine, a neurotransmitter, is secreted by a third type of adrenal medullar cell, different from those that secrete the other amines.

The extensive nerve connections of the medulla essentially mean that this part of the adrenal gland is a sympathetic ganglion, that is, a collection of sympathetic nerve cell bodies located outside the central nervous system. Unlike normal nerve cells, the cells of the medulla lack axons and instead, have become secretory cells.

The catecholamines released by the medulla include epinephrine, norepinephrine and dopamine. While not essential to life, they help to prepare the body to respond to short–lived but intense emergencies.

Most of the catecholamine output in the adrenal vein is epinephrine. Epinephrine stimulates the nervous system and also stimulates glycogenolysis (the breakdown of glycogen to glucose) in the liver and in skeletal muscle. The free glucose is used for energy production or to maintain the level of glucose in the blood. In addition, it stimulates lipolysis (the breakdown of fats to release energy–rich free fatty acids) and stimulates metabolism in general. Epinephrine also increases the force and rate of heart muscle contraction, which results in an increase in cardiac output.

The only significant disease associated with the adrenal medulla is pheochromocytoma. This tumor is highly vascular and secretes its hormones in large amounts. The symptoms of this disease include hypertension, sweating, headaches, excessive metabolism, inflammation of the heart, and palpitations.

See also Cholesterol; Dopamine; Endocrine system; Hormones; Metabolism; Proteins.

Further Reading:
Tortora, Gerard J., and Sandra R. Grabowski. *Principles of Anatomy and Physiology.* 7th ed. New York: Harper-Collins, 1993.

Marc Kusinitz

Adrenocortical insufficiency see **Addison's disease**

Aerobic

Aerobic means that an organism needs oxygen to live. Some microorganisms can live without oxygen and they are called *anaerobic*. Bacteria are not dependent on oxygen to burn food for energy, but most other living organisms do need oxygen. Fats, proteins, and sugars in the diet of organisms are chemically broken down in the process of digestion to release energy to drive life activities. If oxygen is present, maximum energy is released from the food, and the process is referred to as aerobic respiration. The analogy of a bonfire with the energy metabolism of living organisms is appropriate up to the point that both processes require fuel and oxygen to produce energy and yield simpler compounds as a result of the oxidation process. There are, however, a number of important differences between the energy produced by the fire and the energy that comes from organism metabolism. The fire burns all at once and gives off large quantities of heat and light. Aerobic oxidation in an organism, on the other hand, proceeds in a series of small and controlled steps. Much of the energy released in each step is recaptured in the high-energy bonds of a chemical called adenosine triphosphate, a compound found in all cells and serving as an energy storage site. Part of the energy released is given off as heat.

Energy metabolism begins with an anaerobic sequence known as glycolysis. Since the reactions of glycolysis do not require the presence of oxygen, it is termed the anaerobic pathway. This pathway does not produce too much energy for the body, but it establishes a base for further aerobic steps that do have a much higher yield of energy. It is believed that cancer cells do not have the necessary enzymes to utilize the aerobic pathway. Since these cells rely on glycolysis for their energy metabolism, they place a heavy burden on the rest of the body.

The aerobic pathway is also known as the Krebs citric acid cycle and the cytochrome chain. In these two steps the by–products of the initial anaerobic glycolysis

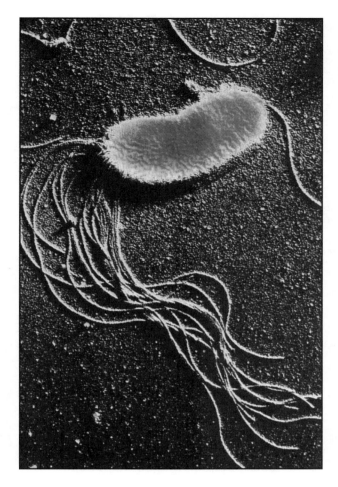

A scanning electron micrograph (SEM) of the aerobic soil bacterium *Pseudomonas fluorescens*. The bacterium uses its long, whip-like flagellae to propel itself through the water layer that surrounds soil particles.

step are oxidized to produce carbon dioxide, water, and many energy–rich ATP molecules. All together, all these steps are referred to as cell respiration. Forty percent of the glucose "burned" in cell respiration provides the organism with energy to drive its activities, while 60% of the oxidized glucose is dissipated as heat. This ratio of heat and energy is about the same as a power plant that produces electricity from coal.

See also Adenosine diphosphate; Adenosine triphosphate; Anaerobic; Krebs cycle; Metabolism; Oxygen; Respiration.

Aerodynamics

Aerodynamics is the science of air flow over airplanes, cars, buildings, and other objects. Aerodynamic

Wind tunnel testing of an aircraft model.

principles are used to find the best ways in which airplanes can get lift, reduce drag, and remain stable by controlling the shape and size of the wing, the angle at which it is positioned with respect to the airstream, and the flight speed. The flight characteristics change at higher altitudes as the surrounding air becomes colder and thinner. The behavior of the air flow also changes dramatically at flight speeds close to, and beyond, the speed of sound. The explosion in computational capability has made it possible to understand and exploit the concepts of aerodynamics and to design improved wings for airplanes. Increasingly sophisticated wind tunnels are also available to test new models.

Basic air flow principles

Air properties that influence flow

Air flow is governed by the principles of fluid dynamics which deal with the motion of liquids and gases in and around solid surfaces. The viscosity, density, compressibility, and temperature of the air determine how the air will flow around a building or a plane. The viscosity of a fluid is its resistance to flow. Even though air is 55 times less viscous than water, viscosity is important near a solid surface since air, like all other fluids, tends to stick to the surface and slow down the flow. A fluid is compressible if its density can be increased by squeezing it into a smaller volume. At flow speeds less than 220 mph (354 kph), 1/3 the speed of sound, we can assume that air is incompressible for all practical purposes. At speeds closer to that of sound (660 mph [1,622 kph]), however, the variation in the density of the air must be taken into account. The effects of temperature change also become important at these speeds. A regular commercial airplane, after landing, will feel cool to the touch. The Concorde jet, which flies at twice the speed of sound, will feel hotter than boiling water.

Laminar and turbulent flow

Flow patterns of the air may be laminar or turbulent. In laminar or streamlined flow, air, at any point in the flow, moves with the same speed in the same direction at all times so that the flow appears to be smooth and regular. The smoke then changes to turbulent flow, which is cloudy and irregular, with the air continually changing speed and direction.

Laminar flow, without viscosity, is governed by Bernoulli's principle: the sum of the static and dynamic pressures in a fluid remains the same. A fluid at rest in a pipe exerts static pressure on the walls. If the fluid now starts moving, some of the static pressure is converted to dynamic pressure, which is proportional to the square of the speed of the fluid. The faster a fluid moves, the greater its dynamic pressure and the smaller the static pressure it exerts on the sides.

Bernoulli's principle works very well far from the surface. Near the surface, however, the effects of viscosity must be considered since the air tends to stick to the surface, slowing down the flow nearby. Thus, a boundary layer of slow–moving air is formed on the surface of an airplane or automobile. This boundary layer is laminar at the beginning of the flow, but it gets thicker as the air moves along the surface and becomes turbulent after a point.

Numbers used to characterize flow

Air flow is determined by many factors, all of which work together in complicated ways to influence flow. Very often, the effects of factors such as viscosity, speed, and turbulence cannot be separated. Engineers have found smart ways to get around the difficulty of treating such complex situations. They have defined some characteristic numbers, each of which tells us something useful about the nature of the flow by taking several different factors into account.

One such number is the Reynolds number, which is greater for faster flows and denser fluids and smaller for more viscous fluids. The Reynolds number is also higher for flow around larger objects. Flows at lower Reynolds numbers tend to be slow, viscous, and laminar. As the Reynolds number increases, there is a transition from laminar to turbulent flow. The Reynolds number is a useful similarity parameter. This means that flows in completely different situations will behave in the same way as long as the Reynolds number and the shape of the solid surface are the same. If the Reynolds number is kept the same, water moving around a small stationary airplane model will create exactly the same flow patterns as a full–scale airplane of the same shape, flying through the air. This principle makes it possible to test airplane and automobile designs using small–scale models in wind tunnels.

At speeds greater than 220 mph (354 kph), the compressibility of air cannot be ignored. At these speeds, two different flows may not be equivalent even if they have the same Reynolds number. Another similarity parameter, the Mach number, is needed to make them similar. The Mach number of an airplane is its flight speed divided by the speed of sound at the same altitude and temperature. This means that a plane flying at the speed of sound has a Mach number of one.

The drag coefficient and the lift coefficient are two numbers that are used to compare the forces in different flow situations. Aerodynamic drag is the force that opposes the motion of a car or an airplane. Lift is the upward force that keeps an airplane afloat against gravity. The drag or lift coefficient is defined as the drag or lift force divided by the dynamic pressure, and also by the area over which the force acts. Two objects with similar drag or lift coefficients experience comparable forces, even when the actual values of the drag or lift force, dynamic pressure, area, and shape are different in the two cases.

Skin friction and pressure drag

There are several sources of drag. The air that sticks to the surface of a car creates a drag force due to skin friction. Pressure drag is created when the shape of the surface changes abruptly, as at the point where the roof of an automobile ends. The drop from the roof increases the space through which the air stream flows. This slows down the flow and, by Bernoulli's principle, increases the static pressure. The air stream is unable to flow against this sudden increase in pressure and the boundary layer gets detached from the surface creating an area of low–pressure turbulent wake or flow. Since the pressure in the wake is much lower than the pressure in front of the car, a net backward drag or force is exerted on the car. Pressure drag is the major source of drag on blunt bodies. Car manufacturers experiment with vehicle shapes to minimize the drag. For smooth or "streamlined" shapes, the boundary layer remains attached longer, producing only a small wake. For such bodies, skin friction is the major source of drag, especially if they have large surface areas. Skin friction comprises almost 60% of the drag on a modern airliner.

Airfoil

An airfoil is the two–dimensional cross–section of the wing of an airplane as one looks at it from the side. It is designed to maximize lift and minimize drag. The upper surface of a typical airfoil has a curvature greater than that of the lower surface. This extra curvature is known as camber. The straight line, joining the front tip or the leading edge of the airfoil to the rear tip or the trailing edge, is known as the chord line. The angle of attack is the angle that the chord line forms with the direction of the air stream.

Lift

The stagnation point is the point at which the stream of air moving toward the wing divides into two streams, one flowing above and the other flowing below the wing. Air flows faster above a wing with greater camber since the same amount of air has to flow through a narrower space. According to Bernoulli's principle, the faster flowing air exerts less pressure on the top surface, so that the pressure on the lower surface is higher, and there is a net upward force on the wing, creating lift. The camber is varied, using flaps and slats on the wing in order to achieve different degrees of lift during take–off, cruise, and landing.

Since the air flows at different speeds above and below the wing, a large jump in speed will tend to arise when the two flows meet at the trailing edge, leading to a rearward stagnation point on top of the wing. Wilhelm Kutta (1867–1944) realized that a circulation of air around the wing would ensure smooth flow at the trailing edge. According to the Kutta condition, the strength of the circulation, or the speed of the air around the wing, is exactly as much as is needed to keep the flow smooth at the trailing edge.

Increasing the angle of attack moves the stagnation point down from the leading edge along the lower surface so that the effective area of the upper surface is increased. This results in a higher lift force on the wing. If the angle is increased too much, however, the boundary layer is detached from the surface, causing a sudden loss of lift. This is known as a stall and the angle at which this occurs for an airfoil of a particular shape, is known as the stall angle.

Induced drag

The airfoil is a two–dimensional section of the wing. The length of the wing in the third dimension, out to the side, is known as the span of the wing. At the wing tip at the end of the span, the high–pressure flow below the wing meets the low–pressure flow above the wing, causing air to move up and around in wing–tip vortices. These vortices are shed as the plane moves forward, creating a downward force or downwash behind it. The downwash makes the airstream tilt downward and the resulting lift force tilt backward so that a net backward force or drag is created on the wing. This is known as induced drag or drag due to lift. About 1/3 of the drag on a modern airliner is induced drag.

Stability and control

In addition to lift and drag, the stability and control of an aircraft in all three dimensions is important since an aircraft, unlike a car, is completely surrounded by air. Various control devices on the tail and wing are used to achieve this. Ailerons, for instance, control rolling motion by increasing lift on one wing and decreasing lift on the other.

Supersonic flight

Flight at speeds greater than that of sound are supersonic. Near a Mach number of one, some portions of the flow are at speeds below that of sound, while other portions move faster than sound. The range of speeds from Mach number 0.8 to 1.2 is known as transonic. Flight at Mach numbers greater than five is hypersonic.

The compressibility of air becomes an important aerodynamic factor at these high speeds. The reason for this is that sound waves are transmitted through the successive compression and expansion of air. The compression due to a sound wave from a supersonic aircraft does not have a chance to get away before the next compression begins. This pile up of compression creates a shock wave, which is an abrupt change in pressure, density, and temperature. The shock wave causes a steep increase in the drag and loss of stability of the aircraft. Drag due to the shock wave is known as wave drag. The familiar "sonic boom" is heard when the shock wave touches the surface of the earth.

Temperature effects also become important at transonic speeds. At hypersonic speeds above a Mach number of five, the heat causes nitrogen and oxygen molecules in the air to break up into atoms and form new compounds by chemical reactions. This changes the behavior of the air and the simple laws relating pressure, density, and temperature become invalid.

The need to overcome the effects of shock waves has been a formidable problem. Swept–back wings have helped to reduce the effects of shock. The supersonic Concorde that cruises at Mach 2 and several military airplanes have delta or triangular wings. The

---

KEY TERMS

Air foil—The cross–section of an airplane wing parallel to the length of the plane.

Angle of attack—The angle that the length of the airfoil forms with the oncoming airstream.

Camber—The additional curvature of the upper surface of the airfoil relative to the lower surface.

Induced drag or drag due to lift—The drag on the airplane due to vortices on the wingtips created by the same mechanism that produces lift.

Similarity parameter—A number used to characterize a flow and compare flows in different situations.

Stall—A sudden loss of lift on the airplane wing when the angle of attack increases beyond a certain value known as the stall angle.

Supersonic speed—A speed greater than that of sound.

Wave drag—Drag on the airplane due to shock waves that are produced at speeds greater than sound.

---

supercritical airfoil designed by Richard Whitcomb of the NASA Langley Laboratory has made air flow around the wing much smoother and has greatly improved both the lift and drag at transonic speeds. It has only a slight curvature at the top and a thin trailing edge. The proposed hypersonic aerospace plane is expected to fly partly in air and partly in space and to travel from Washington to Tokyo within two hours. The challenge for aerodynamicists is to control the flight of the aircraft so that it does not burn up like a meteor as it enters the atmosphere at several times the speed of sound.

See also Aircraft; Airship; Balloon; Bernoulli's principle; Fluid dynamics; Mach number; Viscosity.

Further Reading:

Anderson, John D. Jr. *Introduction to Flight*. New York: McGraw–Hill, 1989.

Hucho, Wolf–Heinrich. "Aerodynamics of Road Vehicles." *Annual Review of Fluid Mechanics* (1993): 485.

Smith, H. C. *The Illustrated Guide to Aerodynamics*. Blue Ridge Summit, PA: Tab Books, 1992.

Wegener, Peter P. *What Makes Airplanes Fly?* New York: Springer–Verlag, 1991.

Sreela Datta

Aerosols

Aerosols are collections of tiny particles of solid and/or liquid suspended in a gas. The size of particles in an aerosol ranges from about 0.001 to about 100 microns. The defining characteristic of an aerosol is that it is very stable and tends not to settle out over long periods of time due to the molecular bombardment. The most familiar form of an aerosol is the pressurized spray can. Aerosols are produced by a number of natural processes and are now manufactured in large quantities for a variety of commercial uses. They are also involved in a number of environmental problems, including air pollution and destruction of ozone in the atmosphere.

Classification

Aerosols are commonly classified into various subgroups based on the nature and size of the particles of which they are composed and, to some extent, the manner in which the aerosol is formed. Although relatively strict scientific definitions are available for each subgroup, these distinctions may become blurred in actual practical applications. The most important of these subgroups are the following:

Fumes

Fumes consist of solid particles ranging in size from 0.001 to one micron. Some typical fumes are those produced by the dispersion of carbon black, rosin, petroleum solids, and tobacco solids in air. Probably the most familiar form of a fume is smoke. Smoke is formed from the incomplete combustion of fuels such as coal, oil, or natural gas. The particles of which it consists are smaller than 10 microns in size.

Dusts

Dusts also contain solid particles suspended in a gas, usually air, but the particles are larger in size than those in a fume. They range from about one to about 100 microns (and even larger) in size. Dust is formed by the release of materials such as soil and sand, fertilizers, coal dust, cement dust, pollen, and fly ash into the atmosphere. Because of their larger particle size, dusts tend to be more unstable and settle out more rapidly than is the case with fumes, which do not settle out at all.

Mists

Mists are dispersions in a gas of liquid particles less than about 10 microns in size. The most common type of mist is that formed by tiny water droplets suspended in the air, as on a cool summer morning. If the concentration of liquid particles becomes high enough to affect visibility, it is then called a fog. A particular form of fog that has become significant in the last half century is smog. Smog forms when natural moisture in the air interacts with human–produced components, such as smoke and other combustion products, to form chemically active materials.

Sprays

Sprays form when relatively large (10+ microns) droplets of a liquid are suspended in a gas. Sprays can be formed naturally, as along an ocean beach, but are also produced as the result of some human invention such as aerosol can dispensers of paints, deodorants, and other household products.

Sources

About three–quarters of all aerosols found in the Earth's atmosphere come from natural sources. The most important of these natural components are sea salt, soil and rock debris, products of volcanic emissions, smoke from forest fires, and solid and liquid particles formed by chemical reactions in the atmosphere. As an example of the last category, gaseous organic compounds released by plants are converted by solar energy in the atmosphere to liquid and solid compounds that may then become components of an aerosol. A number of nitrogen and sulfur compounds released into the atmosphere as the result of living and non–living changes undergo similar transformations.

Volcanic eruptions are major, if highly irregular, sources of atmospheric aerosols. The eruptions of Mount Hudson in Chile in August, 1991, and Mount Pinatubo in the Philippines in June, 1991, produced huge volumes of aerosols that had measurable effects on the Earth's atmosphere.

The remaining atmospheric aerosols result from human actions. Some, such as the aerosols released from spray–can products, go directly to form aerosols in the atmosphere. Others undergo chemical changes similar to those associated with natural products. For example, oxides of nitrogen and sulfur produced during the combustion of fossil fuels may be converted to liquid or solid nitrates and sulfates, which are then incorporated into atmospheric aerosols.

Physical properties

The physical and chemical properties of an aerosol depend to a large extent on the size of the particles that make it up. When those particles are very large, they tend to have the same properties as a macroscopic (large size) sample of the same material. The smaller the particles are, however, the more likely they are to take on new characteristics different from those of the same material in bulk.

Aerosols tend to coagulate, or to collide and combine with each other to form larger bodies. A cloud, for example, consists of tiny droplets of water and tiny ice crystals. These particles move about randomly within the cloud, colliding with each other from time to time. As a result of a collision, two water particles may adhere (stick) to each other and form a larger, heavier particle. This process results in the formation of droplets of water or crystals of ice heavy enough to fall to the Earth as rain, snow, or some other form of precipitation.

Synthetic production

The synthetic production of aerosols for various commercial purposes has become such a large industry that the term aerosol itself has taken on a new meaning. Average citizens who know little or nothing about the scientific aspects of aerosols recognize the term as referring to devices for dispensing a wide variety of products.

Aerosol technology is relatively simple in concept. A spray can is filled with a product to be delivered (such as paint), a propellant, and, sometimes, a carrier to help disperse the product. Pressing a button on the can releases a mixture of these components in the form of an aerosol.

The simplicity of this concept masks, however, some difficult technological problems involved in the manufacture of certain "spray" (aerosol) products. An aerosol pesticide, for example, must be formulated in such a way that a precise amount of poison is released, enough to kill pests, but not so much as to produce an environmental hazard. Similarly, a therapeutic spray such as a throat spray must deliver a carefully measured quantity of medication. In cases such as these, efforts must be taken to determine the optimal particle size and concentration in the aerosol by monitoring the CFC propellants, which destroy the ozone layer.

The production of commercial aerosols fell slightly in the late 1980s because of concerns about the ozone and other environmental effects. By 1992, however, their manufacture had rebounded. In that year 990 million container units (bottles and cans) of personal aerosol products and 695 million container units of household products were manufactured.

Combustion aerosols

Aerosol technology has made possible vastly improved combustion systems, such as those used in fossil–fueled power generator plants and in rocket engines. The fundamental principle involved is that any solid or liquid fuel burns only at its surface. The combustion of a lump of coal proceeds relatively slowly because inner parts of the coal can not begin to burn until the outer layers are burned off first.

The rate of combustion can be increased by dividing a lump of coal or a barrel of fuel oil into very small particles, the smaller the better. Power–generating plants today often run on coal that has been pulverized to a dust, or oil that has been converted to a mist. The dust or mist is then thoroughly mixed with an oxidizing agent, such as air or pure oxygen, and fed into the combustion chamber. The rate of combustion of such aerosols is many times greater than would be the case for coal or oil in bulk.

Environmental factors

A number of environmental problems are associated with aerosols, the vast majority of them associated with aerosols produced by human activities. For example, smoke released during the incomplete combustion of fossil fuels results in the formation of at least two major types of aerosols that may be harmful to plant and animal life. One type consists of finely divided carbon released from unburned fuel. This soot can damage plants by coating their leaves and reducing their ability to carry out photosynthesis. It can also clog the alveoli, air sacs in human lungs, and interfere with a person's respiration.

A second type of harmful aerosol is formed when stack gases, such as sulfur dioxide and nitrogen oxides, react with oxygen and water vapor in the air to form sulfuric and nitric acids, respectively. Mists containing these acids may be carried hundreds of miles from their original source before conglomeration occurs and the acids fall to Earth as "acid rain." Considerable disagreement exists about the precise nature and extent of the damage caused by acid rain. But there seems to be little doubt that in some locations it has caused severe harm to plant and aquatic life.

Ozone depletion

A particularly serious environmental effect of aerosol technology has been damage to the Earth's ozone layer. This damage appears to be caused by a group of compounds known as chlorofluorocarbons (CFCs) which, for more than a half century, were by far the most popular of all propellants used in aerosol cans.

Scientists originally felt little concern about the use of CFCs in aerosol products because they are highly stable compounds at conditions encountered on the Earth's surface. They have since learned, however, that CFCs behave very differently when they diffuse into the upper atmosphere and are exposed to the intense solar radiation present there.

In those circumstances, CFCs decompose and release chlorine atoms that, in turn, react with ozone in the stratosphere. The result of this sequence of events is that the concentration of ozone in portions of the atmosphere has been decreasing over at least the past decade, and probably for much longer. This change is not a purely academic concern since the Earth's ozone layer absorbs ultraviolet radiation from the Sun and protects animals on the Earth's surface from the harmful effects of that radiation.

Technological solutions

Methods for reducing the harmful environmental effects of aerosols such as those described above have received the serious attention of scientists for many years. As a result, a number of techniques have been invented for reducing the aerosol components of things like stack gases. One device, the electrostatic precipitator, is based on the principle that the particles of which an aerosol consists (such as unburned carbon in stack gases) carry small electrical charges. By lining a smokestack with charged metal grids, the charged aerosol particles can be attracted to the grids and precipitated out of the emitted smoke.

Efforts aimed at solving the CFC/ozone problem have not yet been as successful as those used in other forms of air pollution. Chemists have developed and tested a number of substitutes for CFCs as aerosol propellants. One group of special interest has been the hydrochlorofluorocarbons (HCFCs), CFC–like compounds that also contain hydrogen atoms. Most CFC–substitutes tried so far, however, are too expensive, not efficient enough as a propellant, or equally harmful to the environment.

Aerosol sniffing

Another risk associated with commercial aerosols is their use as recreational drugs. Inhalation of some consumer aerosol preparations may produce a wide variety of effects, including euphoria, excitement, delusions, and hallucinations. Repeated sniffing of aerosols can result in addiction that can cause intoxica-

> ## KEY TERMS
> . . . .
>
> **Acid rain**—A form of precipitation that is significantly more acidic than neutral water, often produced as the result of industrial processes.
>
> **Chlorofluorocarbons (CFCs)**—A group of organic compounds once used widely as propellants in commercial sprays, but outlawed in the United States in 1978 because of their harmful environmental effects.
>
> **Dust**—An aerosol consisting of solid particles in the range of 1 to 100 microns suspended in a gas.
>
> **Electrostatic precipitator**—A device for removing pollutants from a smokestack.
>
> **Fume**—A type of aerosol consisting of solid particles in the range 0.001 to 1 micron suspended in a gas.
>
> **Mist**—A type of aerosol consisting of droplets of liquid less than 10 microns in size suspended in a gas.
>
> **Ozone layer**—A region of the upper atmosphere in which the concentration of ozone is significantly higher than in other parts of the atmosphere.
>
> **Smog**—An aerosol form of air pollution produced when moisture in the air combines and reacts with the products of fossil fuel combustion.
>
> **Smoke**—A form of smoke formed by the incomplete combustion of fossil fuels such as coal, oil, and natural gas.
>
> **Spray**—A type of aerosol consisting of droplets of liquid greater than 10 microns in size suspended in a gas.
>
> **Stack gases**—Gases released through a smokestack as the result of some power–generating or manufacturing process.

tion, damaged vision, slurred speech, and diminished mental capacity.

See also Acid rain; Air pollution; Chlorofluorocarbons; Emission; Ozone layer depletion; Precipitation; Smog.

Further Reading:

Browell, Edward V., *et al.* "Ozone and Aerosol Changes during the 1991–1992 Airborne Arctic Stratospheric Expedition." *Science* (1993): 1155–158.

Charlson, R. J., *et al.* "Climate Forcing by Anthropogenic Aerosols." *Science* (1992): 423–30.

Charlson, Robert J., and Tom M. L. Wigley. "Sulfate Aerosol and Climatic Change." *Scientific American* (1994): 48–55.

Friedlander, S. K. *Smoke, Dust and Haze: Fundamentals of Aerosol Behavior.* New York: John Wiley & Sons, 1977.

Haggin, Joseph. "Pressure to Market CFC Substitutes Challenges Chemical Industry." *Chemical & Engineering News* 69 (1991): 27–8.

Hidy, G. M. "Aerosols" in Robert A. Meyers, ed. *Encyclopedia of Physical Science and Technology.* San Diego: Academic Press, 1987.

Hobbs, Peter V., and M. Patrick McCormick, eds. *Aerosols and Climate.* Hampton, VA: A. Deepak, 1988.

Miller, Norman S., and Mark S. Gold. "Organic Solvent and Aerosol Abuse." *American Family Physician* 44 (1991): 183–89.

Osborne, Elizabeth G. "Administering Aerosol Therapy." *Nursing* 23 (1993): 24C–24E.

Reist, Parker C. *Introduction to Aerosol Science.* New York: Macmillan, 1989.

"War Spurs Aerosol Research." *Geotimes* 37 (1992): 10–11.

David E. Newton

Africa

Africa is the world's second largest continent. From the perspective of geologists and paleontologists (scientists studying ancient life forms), Africa also takes center stage in the physical history and development of life on earth. Africa possesses the world's richest and most concentrated deposits of minerals such as gold, diamonds, uranium, chromium, cobalt, and platinum. It is also the cradle of human evolution and the birthplace of many other animal and plant species, as well as having the earliest evidence of reptiles, dinosaurs, and mammals.

Origin of Africa

Present–day Africa, occupying one–fifth of the Earth's land surface, is the central remnant of the ancient southern supercontinent called Gondwanaland, a landmass once made up of South America, Australia, Antarctica, India, and Africa. This massive supercontinent broke apart between 195 million and 135 million years ago, cleaved by the same geological forces that continue to transform the earth's crust today.

Plate tectonics are responsible for the rise of mountain ranges, the gradual drift of continents, earthquakes, and volcanic eruptions. The fracturing of Gondwanaland took place during the Jurassic Period, the middle segment of the Mesozoic Era when dinosaurs flourished on earth. It was during the Jurassic that flowers made their first appearance, and dinosaurs like the carnivorous Allasaurus and plant eating Stegasaurus lived.

Geologically, Africa is 3.8 billion years old, which means that in its present form or joined with other continents as it was in the past, Africa has existed for four–fifths of the earth's 4.6 billion years. Africa's age and geological continuity are unique among continents. Structurally, Africa is composed of five *cratons* (structurally stable, undeformed regions of the earth's crust). These cratons, in South, Central, and West Africa are mostly igneous granite, gneiss, and basalt, and formed separately between 3.6 and 2 billion years ago, during the Precambrian Era.

The Precambrian, an era which comprises more than 85% of the planet's history, was when life first evolved and the earth's atmosphere and continents developed. Geochemical analysis of undisturbed African rocks dating back two billion years has enabled paleoclimatologists to determine that Earth's atmosphere contained much higher levels of oxygen than today.

Continental drift

Africa, like other continents, "floats" on a plastic layer of the earth's upper mantle called the asthenosphere. The overlying rigid crust or lithosphere, as it is known, can be as thick as 150 mi (240 km) or under 10 mi (16 km), depending on location. The continent of Africa sits on the African plate, a section of the earth's crust bounded by mid–oceanic ridges in the Atlantic and Indian Oceans. The entire plate is creeping slowly toward the northwest at a rate of about 0.75 in (2 cm) per year.

The African plate is also spreading or moving outward in all directions, and therefore Africa is growing in size. Geologists say that sometime in the next 50 million years, East Africa will split off from the rest of the continent along the East African rift which stretches 4,000 miles (6,400 km) from the Red Sea in the north to Mozambique in the south.

General features

Considering its vast size, Africa has few extensive mountain ranges and fewer high peaks than any other

Mount Kilimanjaro in Tanzania is the highest point in Africa at 19,340 ft (5,895 m).

continent. The major ranges are the Atlas Mountains along the northwest coast and the Cape ranges in South Africa. Lowland plains are also less common than on other continents.

Geologists characterize Africa's topography as an assemblage of swells and basins. Swells are rock strata warped upward by heat and pressure while basins are masses of lower lying crustal surfaces between swells. The swells are highest in East and central West Africa where they are capped by volcanic flows originating from the seismically active East African Rift system. The continent can be visualized as an uneven tilted plateau, one that slants down toward the north and east from higher elevations in the east and south.

During much of the Cretaceous period, from 130 million to 65 million years ago, when dinosaurs like tyrannosaurus, brontosaurus, and triceratops walked the earth, Africa's coastal areas and most of the Sahara Desert were submerged underwater. Global warming during the Cretaceous period melted polar ice and caused ocean levels to rise. Oceanic organic sediments from this period were transformed into the petroleum and natural gas deposits now exploited by Libya and

Algeria, Nigeria and Gabon. Today, oil and natural gas drilling is conducted both on land and offshore on the continental shelf.

The continent's considerable geological age has allowed more than enough time for widespread and repeated erosion, yielding soils leached of organic nutrients but rich in iron and aluminum oxides. Such soils are high in mineral deposits such as bauxite (aluminum ore), manganese, iron, and gold, but they are very poor for agriculture. Nutrient–poor soil, along with deforestation and desertification (expansion of deserts) is just one of the daunting challenges facing African agriculture in modern times.

East African rift system

The most distinctive and dramatic geological feature in Africa is undoubtedly the East African Rift system. The rift opened up in the Tertiary period, approximately 65 million years ago, shortly after the dinosaurs became extinct. The same tectonic forces that formed the rift valley and which threaten to eventually split East Africa from the rest of the continent have caused the northeast drifting of the Arabian plate, the opening of the Red Sea to the Indian Ocean, and the volcanic uplifting of Africa's highest peaks including its highest, Kilimanjaro in Tanzania. Mount Kibo, the higher of Kilimanjaro's two peaks, soars 19,320 feet (5,796 m) and is permanently snowcapped despite its location near the equator.

Both Kilimanjaro and Africa's second highest peak, Mount Kenya (17,058 ft/5,117 m) sitting astride the equator, are actually composite volcanos, part of the vast volcanic field associated with the East African Rift Valley. The rift valley is also punctuated by a string of lakes, the deepest being Lake Tanganyika with a maximum depth of 4,708 ft (1,412 m). Only Lake Baikal in Eastern Russia is deeper at 5,712 ft (1714 m).

Seismically the rift valley is very much alive. Lava flows and volcanic eruptions occur about once a decade in the Virunga Mountains north of Lake Kivu along the western stretch of the rift valley. One volcano in the Virunga area in eastern Zaire which borders Rwanda and Uganda actually dammed a portion of the valley formerly drained by a tributary of the Nile River, forming Lake Kivu as a result.

On its northern reach, the 4,000 mi (6,400 km) long rift valley separates Africa from Asia. The rift's eastern arm can be traced from the Gulf of Aqaba separating Arabia from the Sinai peninsula, down along the Red Sea which divides Africa from Arabia. The East African rift's grabens (basins of crust bounded by fault lines) stretch through the extensive highlands of central Ethiopia which range up to 15,000 ft (4,500 m) and then along the Awash River. Proceeding south, the rift valley is dotted by a series of small lakes from Lake Azai to Lake Abaya and then into Kenya by way of Lake Turkana.

Slicing through Kenya, the rift's grabens are studded by another series of small lakes from Lake Baringo to Lake Magadi. The valley's trough or basin is disguised by layers of volcanic ash and other sediments as it threads through Tanzania via Lake Natron. However, the rift can be clearly discerned again in the elongated shape of Lake Malawi and the Shire River Valley, where it finally terminates along the lower Zambezi River and the Indian Ocean near Beira in Mozambique.

The rift valley also has a western arm which begins north of Lake Albert (Lake Mobutu) along the Zaire–Uganda border continuing to Lake Edward. It then curves south along Zaire's eastern borders forming that country's boundaries with Burundi as it passes through Lake Kivu and Tanzania by way of Lake Tanganyika. Lake Tanganyika is not only the second deep-

est lake in the world but also at 420 mi (672 km) the second longest, second in length and depth only to Lake Baikal in Eastern Russia.

The rift's western arm then extends toward Lake Nysasa (Lake Malawi). Shallow but vast Lake Victoria sits in a trough between the rift's two arms. Although the surface altitude of the rift valley lakes like Nyasa and Tanganyika are hundreds of feet above sea level, their floors are hundreds of feet below due to their great depths. In that sense they resemble the deep fjords found in Norway.

The eastern arm of the rift valley is much more active than the western branch, volcanically and seismically. There are more volcanic eruptions in the crust of the eastern arm with intrusions of magma (subterranean molten rock) in the middle and lower crustal depths. Geologists consider the geological forces driving the eastern arm to be those associated with the origin of the entire rift valley and deem the eastern arm to be the older of the two.

Human evolution

It was in the great African Rift Valley that hominids, or human ancestors, arose. Hominid fossils of the genus *Australopithicus* dating from 3 million to 4 million years ago have been unearthed in Ethiopia and Tanzania. And the remains of a more direct ancestor of man, *Homo erectus,* who was using fire 500,000 years ago, have been found in Olduvai Gorge in Tanzania as well as in Morocco, Algeria, and Chad.

Paleontologists, who study fossil remains, employ radioisotope dating techniques to determine the age of hominid and fossil remains of other species. This technique measures the decay of short–lived radioactive isotopes like carbon and argon to determine a fossil's age. This is based on the radioscope's atomic half–life, or the time required for half of a sample of a radioisotope to undergo radioactive decay. Dating is typically done on volcanic ash layers and charred wood associated with hominid fossils rather than the fossils themselves, which usually do not contain significant amounts of radioactive isotopes.

Volcanic activity

Present–day volcanic activity in Africa is centered in and around the East African Rift valley. Volcanos are found in Tanzania at Oldoinyo Lengai and in the Virunga range on the Zaire–Uganda border at Nyamlagira and Nyiragongo. But there is also volcanism in West Africa. Mount Cameroon, which stands 13,350 ft (4,005 m), along with smaller volcanos in its vicinity,

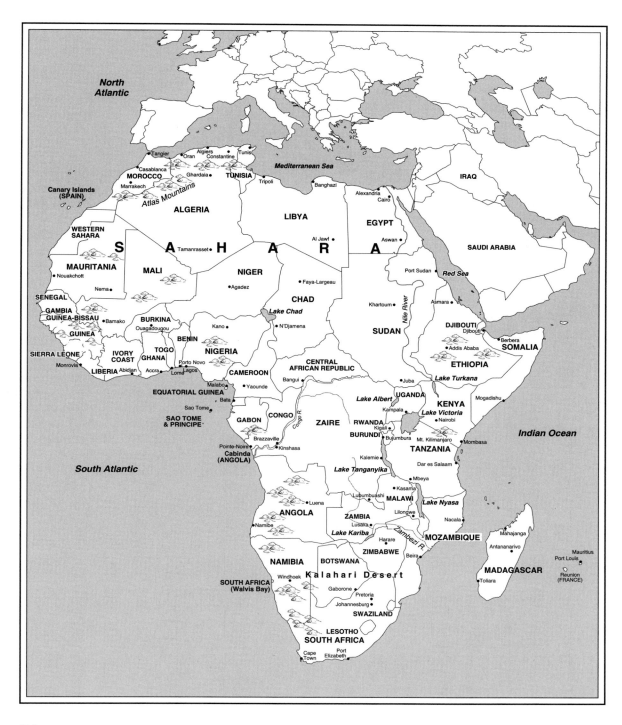

Africa.

on the bend of Africa's West Coast in the Gulf of Guinea are the exception. They are the only active volcanos on the African mainland not in the rift valley.

However, extinct volcanos and evidence of their activity are widespread on the continent. The Ahaggar Mountains in central Sahara contain more than 300 volcanic necks which rise above their surroundings in vertical columns of a thousand feet or more. Also in the central Sahara, several hundred miles to the east in the Tibesti Mountains, there exist huge volcanic craters or calderas. The Trou au Natron is 5 mi (8 km) wide and over 3,000 ft (900 m) deep. In the rift valley, the Ngorongoro Crater in Tanzania, surrounded by teeming wildlife and spectacular scenery is a popular tourist attraction. Volcanism formed the diamonds found in South Africa and Zaire. The Kimberly diamond mine in South Africa is actually an ancient volcanic neck.

Folded mountains

The only folded mountains in Africa are found at the northern and southern reaches of the continent. Folded mountains result from the deformation and uplift of the earth's crust, followed by deep erosion. Over millions of years this process built ranges like the Atlas Mountains, which stretch from Morocco to Algeria and Tunisia.

Geologically, the Atlas Mountains are the southern tangent of the European Alps, geographically separated by the Strait of Gibraltar in the west and the Strait of Sicily in the east. The Atlas are strung across northwest Africa in three parallel arrays, the coastal, central, and Saharan ranges. By trapping moisture, the Atlas Mountains carve out an oasis along a strip of northwest Africa compared with the dry and inhospitable Sahara Desert just to the south.

The Atlas Mountains are relatively complex folded mountains featuring horizontal thrust faults and ancient crystalline cores. The Cape ranges on the other hand are older, simpler structures, analogous in age and erosion to the Appalachian mountains of the eastern United States. The Cape ranges rise in a series of steps from the ocean to the interior, flattening out in plateaus and rising again to the next ripple of mountains.

Islands

For a continent of its size Africa has very few islands lying off its coast. The major Mediterranean islands of Corsica, Sardinia, Sicily, Crete, and Cyprus owe their origins to the events that formed Europe's Alps, and are a part of the Eurasian plate, not Africa. Islands lying off Africa's Atlantic Coast like the Canaries, Azores, and even the Cape Verde Islands near North Africa are considered Atlantic structures. Two islands in the middle of the South Atlantic, Ascension and St. Helena, also belong to the Atlantic. Islands belonging to Equatorial Guinea as well as the island country of Sao Tome and Principe at the sharp bend of Africa off of Cameroon and Gabon are related to volcanic peaks of the Cameroon Mountains, the principal one being Mount Cameroon.

Madagascar, the world's fourth largest island after Greenland, New Guinea, and Borneo, is a geological part of ancient Gondwanaland. The island's eastern two–thirds are composed of crystalline igneous rocks, while the western third is largely sedimentary. Although volcanism is now quiescent on the island, vast lava flows indicate widespread past volcanic activity. Madagascar's unique plant and animal species testify to the island's long separation from the mainland.

Ocean inundations in North Africa

Marine fossils, notably tribolites dating from the Cambrian Period (505–570 million years ago; the first period of the Paleozoic Era) have been found in southern Morocco and Mauritania. Rocks from the succeeding period, the Ordovician (500 million to 425 million years ago) consist of sandstones with a variety of fossilized marine organisms; these rocks occur throughout northern and western Africa, including the Sahara.

The Ordovician was characterized by the development of brachiopods (shellfish similar to clams), corals, starfish, and some organisms that have no modern counterparts, called sea scorpions, conodonts, and graptolites. At the same time the African crust was extensively deformed. The continental table of the central and western Sahara was lifted up almost a mile (1.6 km). The uplifting alternated with crustal subsidings, forming valleys that were periodically flooded.

Glaciation

During the Ordovician Period, Africa, then part of Gondwanaland, was situated in the southern hemisphere on or near the South Pole. It was toward the end of this period that huge glaciers formed across the present–day Sahara and the valleys were filled by sandstone and glacial deposits. Although Africa today sits astride the tropics, it was once the theater of the Earth's most spectacular glacial activity. In the next period, the Silurian (425 million to 395 million years ago) further marine sediments were deposited.

Tectonics in North Africa

The Silurian was followed by the Devonian, Mississippian, and Pennsylvanian periods (408–286 million years ago), the time interval when insects, reptiles, amphibians, and forests first appeared. A continental collision between Africa (Gondwanaland) and the North American plate formed a super–supercontinent (Panagaea) and raised the ancient Mauritanide mountain chain which once stretched from Morocco to Senegal. During the late Pennsylvanian period, layer upon layer of fossilized plants were deposited, forming seams of coal in Morocco and Algeria.

When Pangaea and later Gondwanaland split apart in the Cretaceous Period (144–66 million years ago), a shallow sea covered much of the northern Sahara and Egypt as far south as the Sudan. Arabia, subjected to many of the same geological and climatic influences as northern Africa, was thrust northward by tectonic movements at the end of the Oligocene and beginning of the Miocene epochs (around 30 million years ago). During the Oligocene and Miocene (5–35 million years ago; segments of the modern Cenozoic Era) bears, monkeys, deer, pigs, dolphins, and early apes first appeared.

Arabia at this time nearly broke away from Africa. The Mediterranean swept into the resulting rift, forming a gulf that was plugged by an isthmus at present–day Aden on the Arabian peninsula and Djibouti near Ethiopia. This gulf had the exact opposite configuration of today's Red Sea, which is filled by waters of the Indian Ocean.

As the Miocene Epoch drew to a close about five million years ago, the isthmus of Suez was formed and the gulf (today's Red Sea) became a saline (salty) lake. During the Pliocene (5 million to 1.6 million years ago) the Djibouti-Aden isthmus subsided, permitting the Indian Ocean to flow into the rift that is now the Red Sea.

Origin of Sahara desert

In the Pleistocene Epoch (1.6 million to 11,000 years ago), the Sahara was subjected to humid and then to dry and arid phases, spreading the Sahara desert into adjacent forests and green areas. About 5,000 to 6,000 years ago in the post glacial period of our modern epoch, the Holocene, a further succession of dry and humid stages further promoted desertification in the Sahara as well as the Kalahari in southern Africa.

Earth scientists say the expansion of the Sahara is still very much in evidence today, causing the desertification of farm and grazing land and presenting the omnipresent specter of famine in the Sahel (Saharan) region.

Minerals and resources

Africa has the world's richest concentration of minerals and gems. In South Africa, the Bushveld Complex, one of the largest masses of igneous rock on Earth, contains major deposits of strategic metals such as platinum, chromium, and vanadium—metals that are indispensable in tool making and high tech industrial processes. The Bushveld complex is about 2 billion years old.

Another spectacular intrusion of magmatic rocks composed of olivine, augite, and hypersthene occurred in the Archean Eon over 2.5 billion years ago in Zimbabwe. Called the Great Dyke, it contains substantial deposits of chromium, asbestos, and nickel. Almost all of the world's chromium reserves are found in Africa. Chromium is used to harden alloys, to produce stainless steels, as an industrial catalyst, and to provide corrosion resistance.

Unique eruptions that occurred during the Cretaceous in southern and central Africa formed kimberlite pipes—vertical, near–cylindrical rock bodies caused by deep melting in the upper mantle. Kimberlite pipes are the main source of gem and industrial diamonds in Africa. Africa contains 40% of the world's diamond reserves, which occur in South Africa, Botswana, Namibia, Angola, and Zaire.

In South Africa uranium is to be found side-by-side with gold, thus decreasing costs of production. Uranium deposits are also found in Niger, Gabon, Zaire, and Namibia. South Africa alone contains half the world's gold reserves. Mineral deposits of gold also occur in Zimbabwe, Zaire, and Ghana. Alluvial gold (eroded from soils and rock strata by rivers) can be found in Burundi, Cote d'Ivoire and Gabon.

As for other minerals, half of the world's cobalt is in Zaire and a continuation into Zimbabwe of Zairian cobalt–bearing geological formations gives the former country sizable reserves of cobalt as well. One quarter of the world's aluminum ore is found in a coastal belt of West Africa stretching 1,200 mi (1,920 km) from Guinea to Togo, with the largest reserves in Guinea.

Major coal deposits exist in southern Africa, North Africa, Zaire, and Nigeria. And North Africa is awash in petroleum reserves, particularly in Libya, Algeria, Egypt, and Tunisia. Nigeria is the biggest petroleum producer in West Africa, but Cameroon, Gabon, and the Congo also contain oil reserves. There are also

KEY TERMS
. . . .

Composite volcano—A large, steep–sided volcano composed of alternating layers of volcanic ash and lava flows.

Craton—Structurally stable, undeformed regions of the earth's crust usually dating to the Archean Era (2.5 billion or more years ago).

Gondwanaland—The ancient supercontinent comprised of present–day Africa, South America, Australia, Antarctica, and India.

Graben—A depressed area of the Earth's crust that is bounded by faults; a down-dropped block of the Earth's crust.

Lava domes—Small dome–shaped masses of volcanic rock formed in the vent of a volcano.

Paleoclimatologist—A geologist who studies climates of the earth's geologic past.

Swells—Rock strata warped upward by heat and pressure.

Volcanic neck—A massive column of volcanic rock, formed in the vent of a volcano, that has been exposed by erosion of the flanks of the volcano.

Such environmental degradation has been exacerbated by overgrazing, agricultural abuse, and manmade climatic change, including possible global warming caused by the buildup of manmade carbon dioxide, chlorofluorocarbons (CFCs) and other greenhouse gases.

Deforestation, desertification, and soil erosion pose threats to Africa's manmade lakes and thereby Africa's hydroelectric capacity. Africa's multiplying and undernourished populations exert ever greater demands on irrigated agriculture but the continent's water resources are increasingly taxed beyond their limits. To stabilize Africa's ecology and safeguard its resources and mineral wealth many earth scientists say greater use must be made of sustainable agricultural, and pastoral practices. Progress in environmental and resource management, as well as population control is also vital.

Further Reading:
Petters, Sunday W. *Regional Geology of Africa.* 1989.

Robert Cohen

African antelopes see **Dik-Diks; Duikers**
African violet see **Gesnerias**

petroleum reserves in southern Africa, chiefly in Angola.

Most of Africa's iron reserves are in western Africa, with the most significant deposits in and around Liberia, Guinea, Gabon, Nigeria, and Mauritania. In West Africa as well as in South Africa where iron deposits are also found, the ore is bound up in Precambrian rock strata.

Modern–day climatic and environmental factors

Africa, like other continents, has been subjected to gyrating swings in climate during the Quarternary Period of the last 2 million years. These climatic changes have had dramatic affects on landforms and vegetation. Some of these cyclical changes may have been driven by cosmic or astronomical phenomena including asteroid and comet collisions.

But the impact of humankind upon the African environment has been radical and undeniable. Beginning 2,000 years ago and accelerating to our present day, African woodland belts have been deforested.

Agent Orange

Agent Orange is one of several herbicide preparations used by the U.S. Defense Department to destroy forests and enemy crops in Vietnam in the 1960s. Agent Orange contains a 50:50 mixture of two herbicides: 2,4–D (2,4–dichlorophenoxyacetic acid) and 2,4,5–T (2,4,5–trichlorophenoxyacetic acid). A contaminant of 2,4,5–T is TCDD (2,3,7,8–tetrachlorodibenzo–*p*–dioxin), which is highly toxic to animals.

History

During the Vietnam conflict, North Vietnamese guerrillas found cover in the lush jungles of South Vietnam. To deprive their opponents of cover and food crops, the U.S. military sprayed Agent Orange and other herbicides on about 6,600 sq mi (1,709,000 ha), an area equivalent to one tenth of the land mass of South Vietnam. This military strategy is regarded as having saved the lives of many U.S. combat soldiers. The bulk of the herbicides were applied by "Operation

64

Ranch Hand," a tactical program for spraying herbicides from airplanes by the Air Force.

Developed and tested during World War II, 2,4–D and 2,4,5–T were commonly used agricultural herbicides in the United States. In 1950, more than 10 million lbs (4.5 million kg) of these herbicides were applied annually for weed control in the United States. By 1960, their use had increased to 35 million lbs (16 million kg).

Between 1962 and 1971, over 10.5 million gal (40.5 million l) of Agent Orange were sprayed in Vietnam. Peak use occurred between 1967 and 1969. Agent Orange was sprayed in Vietnam at a rate that was approximately ten times that normally used in U.S. forestry. U.S. forces sprayed approximately 90% of Agent Orange on tropical forests in Vietnam; the remainder fell on crops and mangrove swamps. The herbicide was sprayed on the boundaries of military bases and river banks from sprayers on boats and trucks and backpack sprayers carried by men.

Concerns arise over health effects

In 1969, a scientific study found that 2,4,5–T, one of the chemicals in Agent Orange, causes birth defects when given to mice in high doses. A later study revealed that 2,3,7,8 TCDD (tetrachlorodibenzo-*p*-dioxin), a contaminant of 2,4,5–T, actually caused the birth defects. In 1970, the American Association for the Advancement of Science (AAAS) established a commission to study the effects of herbicides on the ecology and population of South Vietnam. The commission reported that herbicides had not only destroyed vegetation and food, but 2,4,5–T and its associated dioxin contaminant might possibly have caused birth defects in South Vietnamese people.

A second study sponsored by the South Vietnamese Ministry of Health found no difference in the number of stillbirths and birth defects in the years during and after the herbicide spraying. The National Academy of Sciences also found no evidence for a higher rate of birth defects resulting from herbicide spraying in South Vietnam. However, a North Vietnamese study published in 1971 reported a high frequency of retarded and malformed children born to more than 900 South Vietnamese who had been exposed to herbicide spraying and later hospitalized in Hanoi.

On April 15, 1970, federal agencies responsible for regulating health and agriculture suspended all use of 2,4,5–T in the U.S, except for killing weeds and brush on non–crop land. On May 9, 1970, Operation

Ranch Hand flew its last mission in Vietnam. U.S. forces ceased herbicide spraying in Vietnam in 1971.

Agent Orange components: toxicity to animals

Like aspirin and caffeine, 2,4–D and 2,4,5–T are moderately toxic: they can alter the body's normal chemical activities, but substantial quantities must be absorbed into the body to produce visible harmful effects. A substantial dose—0.0045 oz per lb of body weight (300 milligrams per kg body weight)—of these herbicides produces death in laboratory animals. An acute reaction occurs only at high doses because animals rapidly excrete these chemicals in the urine. Long–term exposure to 2,4–D and 2,4,5–T does not cause accumulated tissue damage.

The toxicity of TCDD, a contaminant of 2,4,5–T, is the subject of continuing controversy and study. The TCDD content of 2,4,5–T samples used in the 1969 animal studies was 30 parts per million, or 0.003%. In later studies, scientists found that when the level of the dioxin contaminant in 2,4,5–T samples was much lower, no birth defects occurred in test animals.

Since the early 1970s, TCDD has been known as the most toxic of all chlorodibenzodioxins. However, while some animals are very sensitive to TCDD, others are moderately tolerant to it. As little as 0.25 micrograms (a millionth of a gram) per lb body weight (0.6 microgram per kg) can kill 50% of the guinea pigs exposed to TCDD. But it takes a dose of TCDD that is 10,000 times larger to cause the same number of deaths in hamsters.

Toxicity to humans

Workers involved in accidents or spills at factories where 2,4,5–T is manufactured have developed a condition called *chloracne*, a rash of skin lesions on the face, neck, and back. This condition is an easily observed toxic effect resulting from exposure to TCDD.

TCDD is formed during the synthesis of trichlorophenol, an ingredient needed to produce 2,4,5–T. After the TCDD contaminant was identified, researchers developed a method to produce trichlorophenol with a reduced level of TCDD in the final product. This change substantially decreased the number of chloracne cases among factory workers in the herbicide industry.

Since the liver is the body's specialized organ for handling poisons, it is not surprising that chemical plant workers exposed to TCDD in occupational accidents or activities suffered from enlarged livers and impaired liver functions. They also reported having neurological problems.

Investigation of health effects

In 1977, veterans of the Vietnam war began to report serious health symptoms, which they believed to result from exposure to Agent Orange. In response to veterans' concerns, the White House established an Interagency Work Group to study possible long–term health effects of phenoxy herbicides and contaminants in 1979.

The Veterans Administration (VA) sponsored studies of Vietnam veterans and their families to evaluate any relationship between health problems and the spraying of Agent Orange. The agency also endorsed studies of exposure of workers in the herbicide industry to TCDD.

Evidence of exposure: TCDD levels in the body

Inadequate records of herbicide spraying and troop movements have made it difficult to determine to what degree individuals were exposed to herbicides and TCDD in Vietnam. The blood and tissue levels of TCDD in Vietnam veterans suggest that, with the exception of Operation Ranch Hand personnel, troops in Vietnam received substantially lower exposures than did workers in chemical factories. Interpreting the measurements is difficult because TCDD comes from widespread sources in the United States: cigarette smoke, incinerator emissions, automobile emissions, charcoal grilled steaks, and paper products. The average level of TCDD in fatty tissue of Americans is four to seven parts per trillion (ppt).

Studies of workers at herbicide factories and Vietnam veterans have determined the following facts about exposure to TCDD: TCDD concentrations in the blood serum of chemical plant workers were strongly correlated with the length of time that the workers had been exposed to TCDD; median blood levels of TCDD in over 800 Ranch Hand veterans who were heavily exposed to Agent Orange were significantly higher (12.8 ppt) than in a comparable group of veterans (4.2 ppt); the average TCDD concentrations in fatty tissues and blood sera of Vietnam veterans who, based on records of herbicide spraying and troop positions, might have been exposed to Agent Orange on the ground, did not differ significantly from that of other veterans and civilians; the number of deaths or birth defects among people who suffered from chloracne after accidental exposure to TCDD at manufacturing plants did not differ significantly from those of other industrial workers.

Agent Orange and cancer

As Vietnam veterans continued to express concern about the possible health effects of Agent Orange, the U.S. Congress passed Public Law 102–4, the "Agent Orange Act of 1991." This law ordered a comprehensive review and evaluation of information regarding the health effects of exposure to Agent Orange and its components by the National Academy of Sciences (NAS).

The NAS found that, except for individuals directly involved in the spraying of Agent Orange, information on the degree of herbicide exposure among Vietnam veterans was insufficient to make any conclusions about health effects. Therefore, the NAS evaluated studies of people who were actually exposed to herbicides—often at high levels and for long periods of time. After an extensive review of all available information, the NAS classified possible health effects in four categories, according to their likelihood of being caused by TCDD exposure:

I. Sufficient evidence of an association: Soft tissue sarcoma, Non–Hodgkin's lymphoma, Hodgkin's disease, chloracne, and porphyria cutanea tarda (a skin condition in genetically susceptible individuals). The CDC (Centers for Disease Control) found that service in Vietnam was associated with an increased risk of non–Hodgkin's lymphoma, but the evidence suggests that 2,4–D, rather than TCDD, is responsible.

II. Limited/suggestive evidence of an association: Respiratory cancers (lung, larynx, trachea), prostate cancer, multiple myeloma (cancer of bone marrow cells). Respiratory cancers were found to be related to TCDD only when workers were exposed to high levels of TCDD for prolonged periods of time. No conclusions could be made from studies of Vietnam veterans.

III. Insufficient evidence to determine whether an association exists: Liver, nasal, bone, female reproductive, kidney, testicular cancers, leukemia, spontaneous abortion, birth defects, stillbirths, low birthweight, childhood cancer in offspring, infertility, cognitive, neurological disorders, motor/coordination dysfunction, nervous system, metabolic and digestive, immune system, circulatory, and respiratory disorders.

IV. Limited/suggestive evidence of no association: Skin cancer, gastrointestinal tumors, bladder cancer, brain tumors.

Evidence gathered to date from animal studies and occupational exposures in the herbicide industry is still inadequate to resolve many of the veterans' concerns over possible health effects of Agent Orange. Consequently, the NAS recommends continuing the health study of Air Force Ranch Hand personnel and including in that study Army Chemical Corps veterans who also applied Agent Orange. In addition, the NAS concludes that if scientists can adequately estimate herbicide exposures by reconstructing the timing of Agent Orange applications and troop movements in Vietnam, they might be able to link the level of exposure to health effects—or lack of them—in veterans.

Ecological effects

The damage to the flora of Indochina caused by the spraying of Agent Orange is still visible today. Although Agent Orange applications affected foliage over the diverse areas of Vietnam, the most severe damage occurred in the mangrove forests of coastal areas. About 306,280 acres (124,000 ha/1,240 sq km) of coastal mangrove, comprising about 40% of the mangrove swamps in South Vietnam, was sprayed at least once. The spraying killed extensive thickets of the dominant mangrove species, *Rhizophora apiculata*, which is very sensitive to Agent Orange herbicides, leaving barren, badly eroded coastlines. A 1970 National Academy of Sciences report described the harvesting of dead mangroves for fuel, an occupation that would sustain fewer people than it did before the war, as the supply of mangrove wood was not being renewed. The report warned of a future economic loss when the forest would be stripped, unless a vigorous replanting program was undertaken. The destruction of mature seed–bearing trees has made regeneration of mangroves slow and sporadic, and "weed" species have become dominant. The Academy of Sciences estimates that full recovery of the mangrove forest to its former state will take at least 100 years.

After the mangrove trees were destroyed, the number of coastal birds declined dramatically. The web of channels winding beneath the mangrove trees provide important breeding and nursery grounds for a rich variety of fish and crustaceans. The wartime spraying of mangrove swamps is thought to be the cause of a post–war decline in South Vietnam's offshore fishery.

Aerial spraying of Agent Orange over 14 million acres (5.8 million ha) of dense inland forests killed about 10% of the tall trees comprising the forest canopy. Defoliation of the trees was extensive, but some defoliated trees continued to live. Smaller shrubs, protected from the herbicides by the high canopy, or those which replaced dying trees—now comprise the majority of vegetation in affected areas. The total loss of commercially useful timber caused by the military application of herbicides in South Vietnam is estimated to be 26–61 million cu yards (20–47 million cu m). In areas that were sprayed repeatedly (approximately 34% of the sprayed land), all woody plants, except for a few resistant, commercially unimportant species (*Irvingia malayana* and *Parinari annamense*), were replaced by tussock grasses and bamboo. In the dry season, the stands of grass easily catch fire, and, if burned repeatedly, the lands are less likely to return to forests. The beginnings of natural recovery can be seen, but if the lands are left to natural processes, it will be many years before the forests will approach their former productivity.

As the rich, diverse tropical forests disappeared, so did animal habitat. A uniform grassland has poor habitat diversity compared to the complex, multilayered tropical forest. As a result, the number of bird and mammal species living in the areas that were sprayed declined dramatically. Most of the forest animals are adapted to living in one specific type of habitat and are unable to adjust to survival in the grassland. Wild boar, wild goat, water buffalo, tiger, and various species of deer became less common once the cover and food resources of the forest were removed. Domestic animals such as water buffalo, zebus, pigs, chickens, and ducks were also reported to become ill after the spraying of Agent Orange.

Because Agent Orange herbicides might remain in the soil, there is concern that these residues might inhibit the growth of crops and other plants. Soil bacteria break down the herbicides into smaller molecules, but complete decomposition of 2,4,5–T requires that two types of bacteria be present in the soil. Studies performed 15 years after the spraying in South Viet Nam found degradation products of Agent Orange in the soil. These byproducts, which can be toxic, can be passed through the food web.

How much Agent Orange actually reached the soil is subject to question. A large proportion of the herbicides falling onto the forest are trapped by the canopy; few drops reach the soil directly. In open areas, however, virtually the entire application reached the soil.

The contaminant TCDD is quite persistent in soil, with a half–life of three to five years. (In that period of time, one half of the dioxin originally applied would still be present in the soil.) In studies conducted in the United States, samples from inland soils and sediments in mangrove areas treated with TCDD had substantial levels of the chemical after 10 years.

An indirect effect of the Agent Orange spraying is the poor fertility of soils in many areas, due to erosion following the destruction of soil–binding vegetation.

See also Herbicides.

KEY TERMS

Chloracne—A rash of skin lesions on the face, neck, and back caused by exposure to TCDD.

Exposure dose—Quantity of a chemical which an organism receives from the environment a through inhalation, ingestion, or contact with the skin.

Non–Hodgkin's lymphoma—Tumors derived from cells in lymph nodes, bone marrow, spleen, liver, or other sites in the body.

Soft tissue sarcoma—A rare but diverse group of tumors that arise in the muscles, connective tissue, inner layer of skin, bone, and other tissues.

Toxicity—The degree to which a chemical, in sufficient quantities, can poison humans and other organisms.

Further Reading:

Gough, Michael. *Dioxin, Agent Orange: The Facts* New York: Plenum Press, 1986.

Hanson, David. "Dioxin Toxicity: New Studies Prompt Debate, Regulatory Action." *Chemical and Engineering News* (August 12, 1991).

National Academy of Sciences Institute of Medicine. *Veterans and Agent Orange: Health Effects of Herbicides Used in Vietnam.* Washington, D.C.: National Academy Press, 1993.

Young, A.L. and G.M. Reggiani, eds. *Agent Orange and Its Associated Dioxin: Assessment of a Controversy.* Amsterdam: Elsevier, 1988.

Elaine Friebele

Aging and death

Aging is the natural effect of time and the environment on living organisms, and death is its end result. No living thing can avoid the physiological progression from birth to maturity to aging and death. Although a number of physical losses are often associated with aging, there are some things that are also gained by aging. Whereas with age most people lose height, weight, body water, and agility, age also imparts wisdom and experience.

Gerontology is the study of all aspects of aging. No single theory on how and why people age is able to account for all facets of aging. Although great strides have been made to postpone death as the result of certain illnesses, less headway has been made in delaying aging.

Life–span is species–specific. Members of the same species have similar life expectancies. In most species, death occurs not long after the reproductive phase of life ends. This is obviously not the case for humans. However, there are some changes that occur in women with the onset of menopause when estrogen levels drop. Post–menopausal women produce less facial skin oil (which serves to delay wrinkling) and are at greater risk of developing osteoporosis (brittle bones). Men continue to produce comparable levels of facial oils and are thus less prone to early wrinkling. Osteoporosis occurs as calcium leaves bones and is used elsewhere; hence, sufficient calcium intake in older women is important, because bones which are brittle break more easily.

Theories on aging

Most theories of aging take one of two approaches. Some theories attribute aging to a process of a general systems failure which eventually cripples a person to the point of death. Considerably more theories, however, center around the notion that aging is controlled by a programmed, biological clock. The species–specific aspect of life–span supports a biological clock. If cats and humans live in the same environment, why do they live different lengths of time? Is it their body structure (the result of their genes), their genes themselves, or how their various cells and organs interact that give them different life–spans?

The strongest arguments favor one of, or a combination of, the following: hormonal control, limited cell division, gene theory, gene mutation theory, protein cross–linkage theory, and free radicals. In support of hormonal control, there is the observation that the thymus gland (under the sternum) begins to shrink at adolescence, and aging is more rapid in people without a thymus. Another hormonal approach focuses on the hypothalamus (at the base of the brain) which controls the production of growth hormones in the pituitary gland. It is thought that the hypothalamus either slows down normal hormonal function or that it becomes more error–prone with time, leading eventually to physiological aging.

More recent theories on aging come from cell biology and molecular biology. Cells in culture in the laboratory keep dividing only up to a point, and then they die. Cells taken from embryos or infants divide more than those taken from adults. Hence, it is thought that this is the underlying mechanism of aging—that once cells can no longer divide to replenish themselves, a person will begin to die. However, most scientists now think that most cells (other than brain and muscle cells) never get to their final division.

Gene theory and gene mutation theory, both offer explanations for aging at the level of DNA. Gene theory suggests that genes are somehow altered over time such that they naturally cause aging. Gene mutation theory is based on the observation that mutations accumulate over time, and that it is mutations that cause aging and disease. This view is supported by the fact that samples of cells from older people do generally have more genetic mutations than cells taken from younger people. In addition, some diseases associated with age do result from genetic mutations. Cancer is often the result of multiple mutations. And some mutations reveal underlying genetic weaknesses which cause disease in some people. Gene mutation theory also notes that for mutations to accumulate, normal DNA–repair mechanisms must have weakened. All cells have inherent repair mechanisms which routinely fix DNA errors. For these errors to build up, the repair system must have gone awry, and DNA–repair failure is thought to be a factor in cancer.

Protein cross–linkage and free radicals are also thought to contribute to aging. Faulty bonds (cross–linkages) can form in proteins with important structural and functional roles. Collagen makes up 25–30% of the body's protein and provides support to organs and elasticity to blood vessels. Cross–linkage in collagen molecules alters the shape and function of the organs it supports and decreases vessel elasticity. Free radicals are normal chemical byproducts resulting from the body's use of oxygen. However, free radicals bind unsaturated fats into cell membranes, alter the permeability of membranes, bind chromosomes, and generally alter cellular function, causing damage. Antioxidants, such as vitamins C and E, block free radicals and so are suggested to prolong life.

Diseases associated with aging

Some consequences of aging are age–related changes in vision, hearing, muscular strength, bone strength, immunity, and nerve function. Glaucoma and cataracts are ocular problems associated with aging that can be treated to restore failing vision in older people. Hearing loss is often noticeable by age 50, and the range of sounds heard decreases. Muscle mass and nervous system efficiency decrease, causing slower reflex times and less physical strength, and the immune syste-

m weakens, making older people more susceptible to infections.

More serious diseases of aging include Alzheimer's and Huntington's diseases. Alzheimer's patients exhibit loss and diminished function of a vast number of brain cells responsible for higher functions; learning, memory, and judgment are all affected. Huntington's disease is a severely degenerative malady which is inherited as a dominant gene. Although its symptoms do not appear until after age 30, it is fatal, attacking major brain regions. There is no treatment for either of these age–related diseases.

Death

Death is marked by the end of blood circulation, the end of oxygen transport to organs and tissues, the end of brain function, and overall organ failure. The diagnosis of death can occur legally when breathing and the heart beat have stopped and when the pupils are unresponsive to light. The two major causes of death in the U.S. are heart disease and cancer.

Other causes of death include stroke, accidents, infectious diseases, murder, suicide, and euthanasia. While most of these phenomena are understood, the concept of stroke may be unclear. A stroke occurs when blood supply to part of the brain is impaired or stopped, severely diminishing some neurological function. Some cases of dementia result from several small strokes that may not have been detected. Some causes of death, such as Alzheimer's disease and AIDS (Acquired Immunodeficiency Syndrome), get a good deal of attention in the press, but they are not as prevalent as cardiac disease and cancer.

Further Reading:
Kanungo, M. *Genes and Aging*. New York: Cambridge University Press. 1994.
Nuland, S. *How We Die: Reflections on Life's Final Chapter*. New York: Alfred A. Knopf. 1993.
Spence, A. *Biology of Human Aging*. Englewood Cliffs, N.J.: Prentice Hall. 1989.

Louise Dickerson

> **KEY TERMS**
>
> **Gerontology**—The scientific study of aging with regard to its social, physical, and psychological aspects.
>
> **Life–span**—The duration of life.

Agouti

The twelve species of agoutis are the best–known members of the family Dasyproctidae (genus Dasyprocta) of the order Rodentia. Agoutis are found from southern Mexico through Central America to southern Brazil, including the Lesser Antilles. They are long–legged, slender–bodied, rabbit–like mammals with short ears and a short tail. The body length of agoutis measures 16–24 in (41.5–62 cm), and adults weigh 3–9 lbs (1.3–4 kg). The fur is quite coarse and glossy, and is longest and thickest on the back. The fur ranges from pale orange through shades of brown to black on the backside, with a whitish, yellowish, or buff–colored underside. The back may be striped.

The forelimbs each have four digits, while the hind limbs have three hoof–like claws. The cheek teeth have high crowns and short roots, a condition known as hypsodont.

Agoutis live in cool damp lowland forests, grassy stream banks, thick bush, high dry hillsides, savannas, and in cultivated areas. These animals are active during the day, feeding on fruit, vegetables, and various succulent plants, as well as corn, plantain, and cassava root. Agoutis eat sitting erect, holding the food with their forelimbs.

Female agoutis have eight mammary glands, and usually two, but up to four, young are born. Mating may occur twice a year, and there is a three–month gestation period. The young are born in a burrow which is dug out among limestone boulders, along river banks, or under the roots of trees. The nest is lined with leaves, roots, and hair. The life span of agoutis in captivity is 13–20 years.

Other members of the family Dasyproctidae, include pacas, Itapeizcuinte, Ihei, or Iconejos pintados of the genus Cuniculus, which are bigger than agoutis and have spotted stripes, and the members of the genus Myoprocta, known as Iacushi or Iacuchi, agouti, Icutia de rabo, Icutiaia or Icotiara, which are much smaller than agoutis and have a longer tail. Agoutis (genus Dasyprocta), are also known in their geographical range as Iagutis, Inequis, Icutias, Icotias, Ikonkoni, Icotuzas, and Ipicure.

Members of the genus Plagiodontia inhabit the Dominican Republic (IP. aedium) and Haiti (IP. hylaeum), and the latter is sometimes incorrectly referred to as agouti or Izagouti. The genus Plagiodontia are rodents of the family I Capromydae and correctly called I Hispaniolan hutias or jutias.

See also Rodents.

Agricultural machines

Agriculture is an endeavor practiced in all countries. From the earliest times, humankind has engaged in some form of planting, herding, or gathering. From about 11,000–8,000 B.C. in the Middle East, where many consider civilization to have begun, early farmers used crude flint–edged wooden sickles to harvest wild grains growing on the river banks. The harvested grain was often stored in caves for use during the fall and winter. Unfortunately, there was often not enough to gather and store to feed the growing population.

Soon local tribes learned how to plant and cultivate the seeds of wild grasses and raise them as food. About 9,000 B.C. these same Middle Eastern tribes learned to domesticate sheep and raise them for both their skins and food. Communities grew along the rich, fertile banks between the Tigris and Euphrates rivers in Mesopotamia (now Iraq). Here in the "cradle of civilization" the first true machine, the wheel, was invented and used on animal–drawn carts in the expanding fields. For the first time canals were built linking the principal rivers with local tributaries. Pulleys were used to draw water from the canals creating the first irrigation system.

Early farmers quickly learned that a supply of water was essential to farming. Thus, the primary fields of grain were planted alongside the great rivers of the Middle East. However, getting water from the rivers to the fields became a problem. The invention of the shaduf, or chain–of–pots, helped solve this problem. This human–powered primitive device consisted of buckets attached to a circular rope–strung over a horizontal wooden wheel with wooden teeth projecting at the rim. The buckets were lowered into the water by this revolving "chain," and water was lifted from the river and carried to the fields.

The first farming tool was a pointed stick called a digging stick. The food gatherers used it to dig roots; later farmers used it to dig holes for seeds. The spade was invented by the farmer who simply added a cross bar to his digging stick so that he could use his foot to drive it deeper into the earth. A stick with a sharp branch at one end was the first hoe. Later a stone or shell was added to the stick to give it a more effective cutting edge. Sharp stones cut along one edge converted a stick into a sickle.

After animals were domesticated for food, they were soon trained to become beasts of burden. Sometime around 2,300 B.C. along the Indus River of northern India, water buffalo and zebu cattle were used to

A combine harvesting wheat in Oklahoma.

pull crude wooden plows through the earth, thus developing the practices of plowing and cultivating.

The discovery of metal in the end of the Neolithic period enabled farmers to have sharper, stronger blades for hoes, plows, points, and sickles. The Romans improved the design of their agricultural implements, leading to vastly improved plows and sickles using metal parts. They raised olive and fig trees as well as cereal grains; they also kept vineyards, many of which are still bearing.

The Roman plow consisted of two wooden planks in the shape of a "V." At the tip of the "V" was attached a metal tip. At the back of the "V" an upright wooden post allowed a farmer to guide the implement. A pair of oxen were required to pull the crude plow known as an aratrum. This rather basic tool could not plow a furrow or cut a slice of soil and turn it over as our modern plows do. Since this two–ox aratrum merely scratched the soil, it was necessary to go back over the first–plowed earth again and cross–plow it at right angles to the initial pass.

The basic plow was one of the farmer's most important implements, yet it remained unchanged for centuries. Until the 1800s the plow was still a heavy, pointed piece of wood which was pulled by several oxen and dug an irregular furrow. It didn't turn the soil. In 1793, Thomas Jefferson developed a curved iron moldboard, made according to a mathematical plan, that would lift and turn the soil yet offer little resistance to the motion of the plow. Yet his idea was never tested. However, four years later, a New Jersey farmer, Charles Newbold, patented a plow with a cast iron curved moldboard similar to the idea Jefferson proposed. Ironically, farmers were slow to accept the device, many claiming that cast iron would poison the soil and encourage the growth of weeds. In 1819, Jethro Wood followed Newbold's design with a cast–iron plow with detachable parts that could be replaced when worn. Soon more and more farmers recognized the advantages of the new design and slowly began to accept the concept of a metal, curved blade or moldboard.

However, as men began to plow the plains, cast iron plows proved to have a major disadvantage: soft or damp soil easily clung to the blade and made a full furrow difficult to achieve. When James Oliver, a Scottish–American iron founder developed an iron plow with a face hardened by chilling in the mold when it was cast. His device solved some of the previous problems. By the time of his death in 1908, his invention had made him the richest man in Iowa. Yet even the Oliver plow had problems with the heavy, sticky soil of the prairies. Soil still stuck to the moldboard instead of turning over.

The steel plow was the answer to this problem. In 1833, John Lane, a blacksmith from Lockport, Illinois, began covering moldboards with strips of saw steel. For the first time a plow was successful in turning the prairie soil. Then, in 1837, a blacksmith from Grand Detour, Illinois, named John Deere began making a one–piece share and moldboard of saw steel, and within 25 years the steel plow had replaced the cast iron plow on the prairies. Demand for Deere's plow was so great he had to import steel from Germany. Today, the company that bears his name is one of the world's leading manufacturers of farming implements.

The Romans are also credited with the invention of a crude machine used to cut or "reap" wheat. It was called Pliny's Reaper, not because Pliny was the inventor but because the great Roman historian mentioned it in his writings around 60 A.D. Pliny's Reaper consisted of a wooden comb affixed to the front of a wooden cart. The cart was pushed through the fields by an ox. A farm hand guided the grain into the comb's teeth and manually sliced off the heads of the wheat, allowing the grain to fall into a trailing cart and leaving the straw standing. This was a disadvantage where the straw was valuable as fodder.

Another agricultural development also occurred about this time. For thousands of years the only tool used to separate or "thresh" the grain from the straw was a stick that was used to literally beat the grain from the straw. In warm climates animals were used to walk on the wheat, or "tread out the corn." However, in the colder climates of central and northern Europe, where the weather was uncertain, threshing was done by hand in barns.

Then, during Roman times, a farmer decided to lash two strong pieces of wood together with a leather thong. By using one stick as a handle and whipping the grain with the other stick, he could swing his device in a circular motion rather than the up–and–down motion used previously. Thus, a great deal more grain could be threshed. The invention was called a *flagullum* after the Latin word meaning a whip. It was later simply called a flail. After the fall of Rome, no further advances in reaping machines were made for 15 centuries.

During the Middle Ages, agricultural hardware also made slow progress, yet some gains were recorded. Around 1,300 A.D. a new type of harness was developed which radically changed farming. This simple device allowed a horse, rather than an ox, to be hitched to a plow. Since a horse can plow three or four times faster than on ox, horses gradually replaced oxen as the chief source of power.

During the early 1700s, several major changes in agricultural machines were made. In this period known today as the "Agricultural Revolution," inventors in Great Britain and the United States introduced machines that decreased the amount of labor needed and increased productivity.

For centuries farmers had planted seeds by sowing or scattering them on the soil and trusting chance to provide for germination and a decent crop. Sowing seeds was both labor intensive and extremely wasteful, as many seeds never grew into plants. Next, farmers tried digging a small trench and burying their seeds. This method improved the yield, but was even more labor intensive. Then, in 1701, an English farmer named Jethro Tull invented a horse–drawn device that drilled a pre–set hole in the soil and deposited a single seed. It was the first successful farm machine with inner moving parts and the ancestor of today's modern farm machinery.

Harvesting of grain is perhaps the most difficult job for farmers, and for hundreds of years all the work was performed by human hands. Horses and oxen had been used to pull plows, but harrows and carts were of no avail at harvest time, when only hours of back-breaking toil could cut and bind the grain before it rotted on the ground, a window of about 10 days. At best, bringing in all the grain was uncertain; in cases of bad weather or too few laborers, it could result in famine.

The principal implement of the harvest in the earliest recorded days of history was the sickle, a curved knife with which a strong man could cut a half acre in the course of a day. Harvesting with a sickle, however, is grueling labor. Each bunch of grain must be grasped in one hand and cut by the sweep of the blade. In 1830, the sickle was still in general use under certain crop conditions.

The scythe was an ancient tool used for cutting standing grain. With it, a man could cut two acres a day. During the 18th century the scythe was improved by the addition of wooden fingers. With this implement, called a cradle, grain could be cut and at the same time gathered and thrown into swaths, making it simpler for others following to bind it into sheaves.

It was during the late 18th and early 19th centuries that American ingenuity altered centuries of farming practices. In 1793 for example, a young Connecticut resident, Eli Whitney, graduated from Yale University and went to live on a cotton plantation in Georgia. There he observed the slaves picking cotton. Each slave slowly separated and stripped the cotton fiber from its seed. However, the cotton clung so tenaciously to the green seeds that a slave working all day could only clean a single pound of cotton. Whitney recognized the problem and designed a machine to separate the cotton fibers from their seeds.

His device, called a cotton engine (the word "engine" was soon slurred to "gin"), consisted of a cylinder from which hundreds of wires (later changed to saw–toothed disks) projected. The pieces of wires worked in slots wide enough for the cotton but not wide enough for the seeds. As the hooks pulled the cotton through the slots, a revolving brush removed the cotton from the cylinder.

The cotton gin alone altered the entire economy of the South and the nation. The year following Whitney's invention the cotton crop increased from five to eight million pounds. Six years later, in 1800, 35 million pounds were produced. By the time Whitney died in 1825, more than 225 million pounds of cotton were produced each year. The invention of the cotton gin led to the expansion of the plantation system with its use of slave labor and led to the South's dependence upon a single staple crop. It also encouraged the economic development of the entire nation by providing large sums for use in foreign exchange.

The invention of the reaper was probably the most influential in the history of agriculture. It greatly reduced the threat of famine in America and released thousands of men from the farm. Before the early 1800s, 95% of the world's population was needed to work on the farm. In 1830, 91% of the 220 million Americans were living in cities and small towns, with only 4% living on farms.

Many inventors worked on animal–powered machines for harvesting grain. In 1828 alone there were four patents issued in England for reaping machines. None were successful. However, in 1826, a Scottish man named Patrick Bell developed a machine that consisted of two metal strips, one fixed and the other oscillating back and forth against it. As the machine moved forward the metal strips sliced the grain. Although Bell's machine was an effective grain harvester, he was discouraged from requesting a patent by angry farm workers who feared for their jobs.

About the same time as Bell was working on his machine, a Virginian of Scotch–Irish parentage, Cyrus H. McCormick, was also trying to produce a machine that would successfully harvest grain. In 1831 McCormick demonstrated his first reaper before a skeptical gathering near his father's farm near Steel's Tavern, Virginia. The trial failed because the field was too hilly, but when another farmer offered his acreage on a flatter field, the test was a success. Although McCormick's first device was still in a crude state, it cut as much grain as six laborers working with scythes or as much as 24 could cut with sickles.

His harvester combined a number of elements, none of which were new, but had never been combined before. He used a reciprocating blade similar to Bell's design. A reel pushed the grain against a blade. The harvested grain fell onto a wooden platform located beneath the blade and was swept into swaths by a laborer standing astride it.

Despite the fact that the machine worked, no one was interested in buying one for $50.00. The following year McCormick demonstrated an improved model at Lexington, California, and still found no buyers. By 1840 his total sales amounted to one. He increased the price to $100.00 and in 1842 sold seven. By 1845 he had sold close to 100 reapers and word of their successful achievements began to spread. McCormick moved to Chicago and formed his own company to manufacture reapers. By the time he retired as a wealthy man, his son had taken over the business, which was later merged to become the International Harvester Company, now Navistar.

Other horse–drawn machines followed the improved plows and grain reapers. In 1834, threshing machines were first brought from Scotland, where they had been used since 1788. A successful American thresher was patented in 1837. The following year the combine was introduced on the American farm, and for the first time a machine combined both the harvesting and threshing of grain. These early machines were large and bulky and required horse or mule teams to pull them. It was not until the 1920s, with the successful introduction of gasoline–engine tractors, that combines were accepted on farms. By 1935 a one–man combine was in use, and by the agricultural boom of the Second World War, self–propelled combines were common.

Other American patents were granted in the 1840s and 1850s for an improved grain drill (thus making obsolete the sowing of seeds by hand), a mowing machine, a disk harrow, a corn planter, and a straddle row cultivator. The Marsh harvester, patented in 1858, used a traveling apron to lift the cut grain into a receiving box where men riding on the machine bound it in bundles. Early in the 1870s, an automatic wire binder was perfected, but it was superseded by a twine binder late in the decade.

Although animal power was still required, the new agricultural implements greatly saved both time and labor. During the period between 1830 and 1840, for example, the time required to harvest an acre of wheat was reduced from 37 hours to about 11 hours.

With the introduction of steam power in the early part of the 19th century, the days of animal powered machines were numbered. Shortly before the Civil War the first steam engines were used on farms. Initially, these heavy, rather crude devices were used in the field to provide belt power for threshing machines or other farming jobs that could be accomplished at a stationary location. During the 1850s, self propelled steam tractors were developed. However, they required a team of men to operate them. A constant supply of water and fuel (usually wood or coal) was required; someone was also needed to handle the controls and monitor the boiler.

Huge steam tractors were sometimes used to pull a plow, but their use was extremely limited. Because of its cost, size, and the general unwieldiness of the machine, it could only be employed profitably on the immense acreages of the west. The first internal combustion tractors built near the beginning of the 20th century were patterned after the steam models. And, like their steam predecessors, the first gasoline tractors embodied many of the same faults: they were still too heavy; they were unreliable and broke down about as often as they ran; and, nearly all of them had an alarming tendency to dig themselves into mud holes in wet soil.

During those early years, designers were convinced that there could be neither power nor traction without great weight. The efforts of all progressive farm tractor manufacturers have since been directed toward lessening a tractor's weight per horsepower. The early steam giants weighted more than 1,000 lbs (450 kg) per horsepower. Today's farm tractor weighs about 95 lbs (43 kg) per horsepower.

Gas powered tractors were tested on farms in the early 1900s; however, the first all–purpose gas tractor was not introduced until 1922. It had a high rear wheel drive for maximum clearance under the rear axle, narrow front wheels designed to run between rows, and a power connection to attach other implements on either the front or rear end. This power take–off was standard on all farm tractors by 1934. The use of the power

take–off allowed all harvesting machinery to employ a wider cut and high speed gearing. It meant that rotary power from the engine could be transmitted through a flexible shaft to drive such field implements as mowing machines, balers, combines, etc.

In 1933, pneumatic tires were introduced and, for the first time, allowed tractors to be used on paved highways, a valuable aid in moving equipment from one field to another on farms crossed by paved roads.

The continued development of farm machinery has kept pace with the rapid expansion of technology. The modern farm, for example, can use a single multipurpose machine for precision tillage, planting, shaping the beds, and fertilizing the soil, all in a single pass. For the farmer who needs to grade his field to an exact slope for proper surface irrigation, he can use special laser–leveling equipment. A laser bean is transmitted at the pre–set angle of slope and its signal is received on a mobile scraper. The scraper blade is constantly changing pitch to assure the angle of slope is leveled accurately. With laser leveling, farmers have achieved a 20–30% savings in irrigation water compared with traditional methods.

The use of aircraft in farming has also revolutionized many farming techniques. Fertilizers and pesticides are now widely broadcast over large fields by low–flying crop dusting planes. In some parts of the world, rice is sown over flooded fields by air, which saves a tremendous amount of manual labor traditionally used to plant rice.

Harvesting techniques have also been modernized since the days when McCormick's reaper was pulled across the fields. Today, almost all small grains are harvested by self–propelled combines that cut the crop, strip it if necessary, and deliver the grain to a waiting bin. Although some corn is harvested and chopped for silage, most is grown for grain. Special harvester heads strip and shell the ears, delivering clean kernels ready for bundling or storage in waiting silos. To ease the burden of handling large hay bales, machines can now harvest a hay crop, compress the hay into compact 1.6 inch square cubes, and unload the compressed feed nuggets into a waiting cart attached to the rear of the harvester.

Harvesting fruits and vegetables has always been the most labor intensive farming operation. Traditionally, harvesters simply cross a field and slice off the head of cabbage, lettuce, or celery with a sharp disk or series of knives. Most of these harvesters are non–selective, and there can be considerable waste from harvesting under– or over–ripe produce. Selection for color or grade is dependent on workers at the site or at grading stations.

Today, special electronic equipment attached to a harvester can determine the correct size, color and density of certain types of produce. Tomatoes, for example, now pass through special harvesters where an optical sensor inspects each tomato as it passes at high speed. The sensor judges whether the tomato is mature or not mature, red or green, and rejects the green fruit. Today more than 95% of California's vast tomato crop is harvested mechanically. The tomatoes have been genetically altered to toughen their skin, allowing mechanical harvesting.

Asparagus harvesters can determine the pre–set length before cutting, while a lettuce harvester electronically determines which heads meet the proper size and density standards. Yet despite the tremendous advances in agricultural technology, many fruits and vegetables are still best harvested by hand. These include most citrus fruits, melons, grapes, broccoli, etc.

In dairy farming, modern equipment such as automated milking machines, coolers, clarifiers, separators, and homogenizers has allowed the farmer to increase his herds as well as the productivity of his cattle. Yet the dairy farmer still puts in more man–hours of labor per dollar return than does the field–crop farmer. According to a study by the U.S. Department of Agriculture, the average number of labor–hours of labor used to produce an acre of corn in a Midwestern state was reduced from 19.5 in 1910 to 10.3 in 1938 and to less than seven in 1995. In contrast, no change was reported in the man–hours required in the production of beef cattle and egg-laying hens, while a 5% increase was noted in the labor associated with dairy farming.

Benedict A. Leerburger

Agrochemicals

An agrochemical is any substance that humans use to help in the management of an agricultural ecosystem. Agrochemicals include: (1) fertilizers, (2) liming and acidifying agents, (3) soil conditioners, (4) pesticides, and (5) chemicals used in animal husbandry, such as antibiotics and hormones.

The use of agrochemicals is an increasingly prominent aspect of modern industrial agriculture. The use of agrochemicals has been critically important in increasing the yields of agricultural crops. However, some uses of agrochemicals cause substantial environmental and ecological damages, which detract significantly from the benefits of the use of these materials.

Fertilizers

Fertilizers are substances that are added to agricultural lands to alleviate nutrient deficiencies, allowing large increases in the rates of crop growth. Globally, about 152 million tons (138 million metric tons) of fertilizer are used in agriculture each year. In the United States, the average rate of fertilizer application is about 218 lbs per 2.5 acres (99 kilograms per hectare), and about 21 million tons (19 million metric tons) are used in total each year.

The most commonly used fertilizers are inorganic compounds of nitrogen. Under conditions where agricultural plants have access to sufficient water, their productivity is most often constrained by the supply of available forms of nitrogen, especially nitrate (NO_3^-), and sometimes ammonium (NH_4^+). Farmers commonly increase the availability of these inorganic forms of nitrogen by applying suitable fertilizers, such as urea or ammonium nitrate. The rate of fertilization in intensive agricultural systems is commonly several hundred pounds of nitrogen per acre per year, but it can be as large as 1,103 lbs per 2.25 acres per year (500 kg per hectare per year).

Phosphorus and potassium are other commonly applied nutrients in agriculture. Most phosphorus fertilizers are manufactured from rock phosphate, and are known as superphosphate and triple–superphosphate. Some phosphorus fertilizers are also made from bone meal and seabird guano. Potassium fertilizers are mostly manufactured from mined potash.

Often, these three macronutrients are applied in a combined formulation that includes nitrogen, in what is known as an N–P–K fertilizer. For example, a 10–10–10 fertilizer would contain materials equivalent to 10% of each of nitrogen, phosphorus, and potassium, while a 4–8–16 would contain these nutrients in concentrations of 4%, 8%, and 16%, respectively. The desired ratios of these three nutrients are governed by the qualities of the soil that is being fertilized, and by the needs of the specific crop that is being cultivated.

Sometimes other nutrients must also be supplied to agricultural crops. Sulfur, calcium, or magnesium, for example, are limiting to crop productivity in some places. Rarely, micronutrients such as copper, molybdenum, or zinc must be applied to achieve proper crop growth.

Agrochemical spraying in a Michigan orchard.

Liming and acidifying agents

Agricultural soils are commonly too acidic or too alkaline for the optimal growth of many crop species. When this is the case, chemicals may be added to the soil to cause its pH to change to a more appropriate range.

Acidic soils are an especially common problem in agriculture. Acidic soils can be caused by various factors, including the removal of acid–neutralizing bases contained in the biomass of harvested crops, the use of certain types of fertilizers, acid rain, the oxidation of sulfide minerals, and the presence of certain types of organic matter in soil. Because soil acidification is such a common occurrence, acid–neutralizing (or liming) materials are among the most important agrochemicals, in terms of the total quantities that are added to soil each year.

Acidic soils are commonly neutralized by adding calcium–containing minerals, usually as calcite ($CaCO_3$) in the form of powdered limestone or crushed oyster or mussel shells. Alternatively, soil acidity may be neutralized using faster–acting lime ($Ca[OH]_2$). The rate of application of acid–neutralizing substances in agriculture can vary greatly, from several hundred pounds per acre per year to more than 1,000 pounds per acre per year. The rates used depend on the acidity of the soil, the rate at which new acidity is generated, and the needs of specific crops.

Much less commonly, soils are alkaline in reaction, and they may have to be acidified somewhat to bring them into a pH range suitable for the growth of most crops. This problem can be especially common in soils developed from parent materials having large amounts of limestone ($CaCO_3$) or dolomite ($Ca,MgCO_3$). Soils can be acidified by adding sulfur compounds, which generate acidity as they are oxidized, or by adding certain types of acidic organic matter, such as peat mined from bogs.

Soil conditioners

Soil conditioners are organic–rich materials that are sometimes added to soils to improve aeration and water–holding capacity, both of which are very important aspects of soil quality. Various materials can be utilized as soil conditioners, including peat, crop residues, livestock manure, sewage sludge, and even shredded newspapers. However, compost is probably the most desirable of the soil conditioners. Compost contains large quantities of well–humified organic compounds, and also supplies the soil with nutrients in the form of slow–release organic compounds.

Pesticides

Pesticides are agrochemicals that are used to reduce the abundance of pests, that is, organisms that are considered to interfere with some human purpose. Many kinds of pesticides are used in agriculture, but they can be categorized into simple groups on the basis of the sorts of pests that are the targets of the use of these chemicals. Herbicides are used to kill weeds, that is, non–desired plants that interfere with the growth of crops and thereby reduce their yield. Fungicides are used to protect agricultural plants from fungal pathogens, which can sometimes cause complete failure of crops. Insecticides are used to kill insects that defoliate crops, or that feed on stored grains or other agricultural products. Acaricides are used to kill mites, which are important pests of crops such as apples, and ticks, which can carry debilitating diseases of livestock. Nematicides are used to kill nematodes, which are important parasites of the roots of some crop species. Rodenticides are used to kill rats, mice, gophers, and other rodents that are pests in fields or that eat stored crops. Preservatives are agrochemicals that are added to processed foods to help prevent spoilage.

Pesticides are chemically diverse substances. About 300 different insecticides are now in use, along with about 290 herbicides, 165 fungicides, and other pesticides. However, each specific pesticidal chemical (also known as the "active ingredient") may be marketed in a variety of formulations, which contain additional substances that act to increase the efficacy of the actual pesticide. These so–called "inert" ingredients of the formulations can include solvents, detergents, emulsifiers, and chemicals that allow the active ingredient to better adhere to foliage. In total, at least 3,000 different pesticidal formulations exist.

Pesticides can also be classified according to the similarities of their chemical structures. Inorganic pesticides, for example, are simple compounds of toxic elements such as arsenic, copper, lead, and mercury. Inorganic pesticides were formerly used in large quantities, especially as fungicides. However, they have largely been replaced by various types of organic pesticides.

A few of the commonly used organic pesticides are based on substances that are synthesized naturally by plants as biochemical defenses, and can be extracted and used against pests. Pyrethrum, for example, is an insecticide obtained from a species of chrysanthemum, while rotenone is a rodenticide extracted from a tropical shrub.

Most organic pesticides, however, have been synthesized by chemists. The synthetic organic pesticides include well–known groups such as the chlorinated hydrocarbons (including the insecticide DDT, and the herbicides 2,4–D and 2,4,5–T), organophosphates (such as parathion and malathion), carbamates (for example, carbaryl and carbofuran), and triazine herbicides (such as atrazine and simazine).

A final class of pesticidal organochemicals is based on the actions of bacteria, fungi, or viruses that are pathogenic to specific pests, and can be applied as a pesticidal formulation. The most commonly used biological insecticide is manufactured using spores of the bacterium *Bacillus thuringiensis*, also known as B.t. These spores can be mass–produced in laboratory–like factories, and then used to prepare an insecticidal solution. Insecticides based on B.t. are mostly used against leaf–eating moths and biting flies, such as blackflies and mosquitoes. Most other insects are little affected by B.t.–based insecticides, so the unintended nontarget effects of their usage are relatively small.

Very large quantities of pesticides are used in modern agriculture. Globally, about 4.4–6.6 billion lbs (2–3 billion kg) of pesticides are used each year, having a total value of about $20 billion. The United States alone accounts for about one–third of all pesticide usage, even though that country only supports about 4% of the world's population.

Agrochemicals used for animal husbandry

Contagious diseases of livestock can be a very important problem in modern agriculture. This is especially true of conditions in which animals are being reared at a large density, for example, in feed–lots. Various agrochemicals may be used to control infectious diseases and parasites under such conditions. Antibi-

otics are especially important in this respect. These chemicals may be administered by injection whenever bacterial diseases are diagnosed. However, antibiotics are sometimes administered routinely with the feed, as a prophylactic treatment to prevent the occurrence of infections. Because of the extremely crowded conditions that exist when livestock are reared in "factory farms," antibiotics must be administered routinely to animals grown under those circumstances.

Sometimes, hormones and other animal–growth regulators are used to increase the productivity of livestock. For example, bovine growth hormone (BGH) is routinely administered in some agricultural systems to increase the growth rates of cows and their milk production.

Environmental effects of the use of agrochemicals

Many important benefits are achieved by the use of agrochemicals. These are largely associated with increased yields of plant and animal crops, and less spoilage during storage. These benefits are substantial, and in combination with genetically improved varieties of crop species, agrochemicals have made very important contributions to the successes of the "green revolution." This has helped to increase the food supply for the rapidly increasing population of humans on Earth.

However, the use of certain agrochemicals has also been associated with some important environmental and ecological damages. Excessive use of fertilizers, for example, can lead to the contamination of groundwater with nitrate, rendering it unfit for consumption by humans or livestock. Water containing large concentrations of nitrate can poison animals by immobilizing some of the haemoglobin in blood, reducing the ability to transport oxygen. In addition, the run–off of agricultural fertilizers into streams, lakes, and other surface waters can cause increased production of those aquatic ecosystems, a problem known as eutrophication. The ecological effects of eutrophication can include an extensive mortality of fish and other aquatic animals, along with excessive growths of nuisance algae, and off–tastes of drinking water.

The use of pesticides can also result in many environmental problems. As was previously noted, pesticides are used in agriculture to reduce the abundance of species of pests (that is, the "targets") to below a level of acceptable damages, which is economically determined. Unfortunately, during many uses of pesticides in agriculture the exposures of other organisms, including humans, are not well controlled. This is especially true when entire fields are sprayed, for example, using application equipment drawn by a tractor, or mounted on an airplane or helicopter. During these sorts of broadcast applications, many nontarget organisms are exposed to the pesticide. This occurs on the treated site, and on nearby off–sites as well, as a result of "drift" of the sprayed agrochemical. These nontarget exposures cause many unnecessary poisonings and deaths of organisms that are not agricultural pests.

In addition, there is a widespread, even global contamination of the environment with some types of persistent pesticides, especially with organochlorines such as DDT, dieldrin, and aldrin. This contamination involves widespread occurrences of pesticide residues in virtually all wildlife, well waters, foods, and even in humans. Residues of some of the chemicals used in animal husbandry are also believed by some people to be a problem, for example, when traces of antibiotics and bovine growth hormones occur in consumer products such as meat or milk.

Some of the worst examples of environmental damages caused by pesticides have been associated with the use of relatively persistent chemicals, such as DDT. Most modern usage of pesticides usually involves chemicals that are less persistent than DDT and related chlorinated hydrocarbons. However, severe damages are still caused by the use of some newer pesticides. In North America, for example, millions of wild birds are probably killed each year as a nontarget effect of the routine use of carbofuran, an agricultural insecticide. This is a substantial ecological price to pay for the benefits associated with the use of this agrochemical.

The use of some pesticides is also quite risky for humans. About 1 million pesticide poisonings occur globally every year, resulting in 20,000 fatalities. About one–half of the human poisonings occur in poorer, less–developed countries, even though these places account for only 20% of the world's use of pesticides. This disproportionate risk is due to greater rates of illiteracy in poorer countries, and to lax enforcement of regulations concerning the use of pesticides.

There have been a few examples of pesticides causing extensive toxicity to humans. The most famous case occurred at Bhopal, India in 1984, in the vicinity of a factory that was manufacturing an agricultural insecticide. In that case, there was an accidental release of about 40 tonnes of deadly methyl isocyanate vapor to the atmosphere. This agrochemical–related emission caused the deaths of about 3,000 people, and more than 20,000 others were seriously injured.

These and other environmental effects of the use of some agrochemicals are unfortunate consequences of the application of these chemical tools to deal with

---

KEY TERMS

. . . .

Agrochemical—Any substance used in the management of an agricultural ecosystem, including fertilizers, pH–adjusting agents, soil conditioners, pesticides, and crop–growth regulators.

Fertilizer—An agrochemical that is added to soil to reduce or eliminate nutrient–caused constraints to crop productivity.

Nontarget effects—Effects on organisms other than the intended pest target of a pesticide treatment.

Pest—An organism that is considered to be undesirable, from the perspective of humans.

pH—The negative logarithm to the base 10 of the aqueous concentration of hydrogen ion in units of moles per liter. An acidic solution has a pH less than 7, while an alkaline solution has a pH greater than 7. Note that a one–unit difference in pH implies a 10–fold difference in the concentration of hydrogen ion.

Soil conditioners—This refers to substances added to soil to improve its aeration and water–holding capacity, with great benefits in terms of crop growth. Various organic compounds can be used as soil conditioners, but compost is the best.

---

agricultural problems. Researchers are constantly searching for nonchemical ways of dealing with many of these agricultural needs. Much attention is being paid, for example, to developing nonchemical, or "organic," methods of enhancing soil fertility and dealing with pests. Unfortunately, economically effective alternatives to most uses of agrochemicals have not yet been discovered. Consequently, our modern agricultural industries will continue to rely heavily on the use of agrochemicals to manage their problems of fertility, soil quality, and pests.

See also Fertilizers; Fungicide; Herbicides; Pesticides.

Further Reading:

Briggs, D. J. and F. M. Courtney. *Agriculture and Environment*. New York: Longman, 1989.

Briggs, S. A. *Basic Guide to Pesticides: Their Characteristics and Hazards*. Washington, D.C.: Taylor & Francis, 1992.

Freedman, B. *Environmental Ecology*. 2nd ed. San Diego: Academic Press, 1994.

Pimentel, D., et. al. "Environmental End Economic Costs of Pesticide Use." *Bioscience,* 41 (1992): 402–409.

Soule, J. D. and J. K. Piper. *Farming in Nature's Image: An Ecological Approach to Agriculture.* Island Press, 1992.

Wild, A. *Soils and the Environment.* Cambridge, U.K.: Cambridge University Press, 1993.

Bill Freedman

Agronomy

Agronomy can be defined as those branches of agricultural science that deal with the production of both plant and animal crops, and the management of soil. The subject matter of agronomy is quite diverse, but falls into three major categories: (1) crop breeding and the genetic improvement of varieties; (2) methods of cultivation of crops (both plants and animals); and (3) sustainability of the agricultural enterprise, especially with respect to fertility of the soil.

Crop improvement

Most varieties of agricultural crops look and grow very differently than their wild progenitors. In fact, almost all of the domesticated species of plants and animals that humans depend upon as sources of food, materials, or energy have been selectively bred for various desirable traits. This evolutionary process has resulted in the development of substantial genetic differences between domesticated varieties and their wild ancestors—differences that have arisen because of deliberate selection of desirable traits by humans.

Selective breeding of agricultural species has been very important in improving their productivity under cultivation. Enormous increases in the useful yields of cultivated plants have been attained through genetically–based improvements of growth rates. These include responses to the addition of fertilizer, along with modifications of the growth form, anatomy, and chemistry of crops. Similarly, domesticated animals have been selectively bred for growth rates, compliant behavior, chemical quality of their produce, and other desirable traits.

Selective breeding of some agricultural species has been so intensive and thorough that they can no longer survive without the assistance of humans, that is, in the absence of cultivation. For example, the seeds of maize can no longer disperse from their cob because of the tightly enclosing leaves that have evolved as a result of selective breeding. Similarly, our dairy cows are no longer capable of surviving on their own—they require humans to milk them, or they die from the complications of mastitis.

Selective breeding of existing and potential agricultural species still has a great deal to contribute to future developments in agronomy. Existing crops require continual genetic refinements to make them more suitable to the changing environmental conditions of agricultural ecosystems, to improve their resistance to diseases and pests, and to improve their nutritional qualities. At the same time, continuing surveys of the diversity of wild species will discover many plants and animals that are of potential benefit to humans. Selective breeding will be a critical part of the process by which those new biodiversity resources are domesticated.

Managing the soil

The quality of agricultural soils can be easily degraded by various cultural influences, but especially: (1) nutrient removals; (2) losses of organic matter; (3) acidification; and (4) erosion that is caused when soils are plowed and crops are harvested. Soil degradation is one of the most important problems associated with agricultural activities, because of the obvious implications for the longer–term sustainability of productivity and harvests. Understanding the causes of soil degradation and devising ways of preventing or mitigating this problem are among the most important objectives of agronomy.

Nutrient losses from agricultural soils are caused by a number of influences:

1. Whenever crop biomass is removed from the land during harvesting, nutrients such as nitrogen, phosphorus, potassium, calcium, and others are also extracted. These removals occur in the form of nutrients contained in the biomass. Depending on the crop, nutrient removals during annual harvesting are not necessarily large, but over a longer period of time the cumulative losses become significant, and the soil becomes impoverished.

2. Severe disturbance of the integrity of the soil surface, for example, by plowing, makes the soil quite susceptible to erosion by water and wind. Associated with the physical losses of soil are losses of the nutrients that are contained.

3. Nutrient losses are also encouraged when there are decreases in the concentrations of organic matter in the soil, a phenomenon that is also associated with

An irrigated area along a river near Yazd, Iran. Note the unirrigated desert in the background.

tillage of the land. Organic matter is important because it helps to bind nutrients in relatively immobile and insoluble forms, thereby helping to ensure their continuous supply, and preventing the leaching of nutrients from the site.

When nutrient losses from soil have been severe, it may be possible to compensate for the losses of fertility by adding nutrients. Fertilization is an important activity in modern agriculture. However, fertilization is expensive, and it causes important environmental impacts. Therefore, many agronomists are engaged in research designed to reduce the dependence of modern agriculture on intensive fertilization, and on increasing the efficiency of nutrient uptake by crops.

Losses of soil organic matter are another important problem that agronomists must address. Soil organic matter is important because of its great influence on the tilth, or physical structure of soil, which is closely associated with the concentration of humified organic matter. Tilth is very influential on the water– and nutrient–holding capacities of the soil, and is highly beneficial to the growth of crops. The emerging field of organic agriculture is largely involved with managing

and optimizing the concentration of organic matter in soils. Commonly used techniques in organic agriculture include the use of green manures and composts to maintain the concentration of organic matter in soil, as well as the use of carefully designed crop rotations and mixed–cropping systems.

Soil acidification is another important agricultural problem. Acidification is caused by the removal of calcium and magnesium during cropping, through erosion, leaching, and actions of certain nitrogen–containing fertilizers, such as ammonium nitrate and urea.

Acidification may also be partially caused by atmospheric pollution, especially in regions where the air is contaminated by sulfur dioxide, and where acidic precipitation is important. Acidification is routinely countered in agriculture by mixing limestone or lime into the soil.

Erosion is another common agricultural problem that is largely caused by disturbance of the soil surface through plowing. Erosion represents a mass wasting of the soil resource, with great implications for fertility and other important aspects of land capability. Erosion also causes secondary impacts in the aquatic ecosystems that typically receive the large wastage of eroded materials. Erosion is particularly severe on lands with significant slopes and coarse soils, especially if these occur in a region with abundant precipitation. Erosion can be substantially prevented by plowing along contour lines rather than down–slope, and by maximizing the amount of time during which the land has a well–established plant cover. The latter can be accomplished through the use of no–tillage agricultural systems, and wherever possible, by cultivating perennial crops on sites that are vulnerable to erosion.

Managing pests and diseases

Pests and their control are another significant problem agronomists must deal with. Pests can be defined as any organisms that interfere with some human purpose. In agriculture, the most important pests are weeds, insects and other defoliators, and disease–causing pathogens. The use of such pesticides as herbicides, insecticides, fungicides, and antibiotics is a very important aspect of modern agriculture. Unfortunately, many pesticides cause important environmental damages, and many agronomists are attempting to develop systems that would decrease the reliance on pesticides in agriculture, while not compromising yields.

Animal husbandry

Devising better systems in which to raise animals as crops is another important aspect of agronomy. Considerations in animal husbandry include optimization of the productivity of the animals, achieved through selective breeding, and careful management of diet, disease, and housing. Agronomists concerned with animal husbandry are also interested in improving the nutritional quality of the food products, disposal of waste materials, and humane treatment of the livestock.

Agricultural systems

Ultimately, the goal of agronomy is to develop agricultural systems that are sustainable over the long term. An agricultural system involves particular combinations of crop species, along with methods of tillage, seeding, pest management, and harvesting. Furthermore, agricultural systems may involve the growth of successive crops in a carefully designed rotation, or perhaps the growth of several crops at the same time, for example, by row cropping or intercropping.

The ultimate judgement of the success of agronomy will be the sustainability of the agricultural systems that agronomists develop, and then persuading agriculturalists to use them.

KEY TERMS

Agricultural system—A combination of the choice of crop species, and the methods of tillage, seeding, pest management, and harvesting. The crop may be grown in successive monocultures, or the system may involve rotations of different crops, or polyculture systems such as row cropping and intercropping.

Agronomy—The application of agricultural science to the production of plant and animal crops, and the management of soil fertility.

Organic matter—Any biomass of plants or animals, whether living or dead. Dead organic matter is the most important form in soils, particularly when occurring as humic substances.

Nutrient—Any chemical required for life. The most important nutrients that plants obtain from soil are compounds of nitrogen, phosphorus, potassium, calcium, magnesium, and sulfur.

Tilth—The physical structure of soil, closely associated with the concentration of humified organic matter. Tilth is important in water– and nutrient–holding capacity of the soil, and is highly beneficial to the growth of crops.

See also Acid rain; Agrochemicals; Animal breeding; Contour plowing; Crop rotation; Crops; Erosion; Fertilizers; Genetic engineering; Integrated pest management; Organic farming; Pests; Pesticides; Soil conservation.

Further Reading:

Briggs, D.J. and F.M. Courtney. *Agriculture and Environment*. New York: Longman, 1989.

Carroll, R.C., J.H. Vandermeer, and P.M. Rossett. *Agroecology*. New York: McGraw–Hill, 1990.

Freedman, B. *Environmental Ecology,* 2nd ed. San Diego: Academic Press, 1984.

Hartmann, H.T., A.M. Kofranek, V.E. Rubatzky, and W.J. Flocker. *Plant Science: Growth, Development, and Utilization of Cultivated Plants*. Englewood Cliffs, NJ: Prentice–Hall, 1988.

Miller, R.W. and R.L. Donahue. *Soils. An Introduction to Soils and Plant Growth*. New York: Prentice–Hall, 1989.

Soule, J.D. and J.K. Piper. *Farming in Nature's Image: An Ecological Approach to Agriculture*. Island Press, 1992.

Wild, A. *Soils and the Environment*. Cambridge, U.K.: Cambridge University Press, 1993.

Bill Freedman

AIDS

Acquired Immune Deficiency Syndrome (AIDS) is a viral disease that is almost invariably fatal. AIDS destroys the immune system of its victims, leaving them vulnerable to a variety of illnesses. No cure has been found and no vaccine is available to prevent the disease. AIDS patients may live as long as 10 years, but most die within a year to 18 months after diagnosis.

History and spread of AIDS

AIDS first appeared in the United States in 1980 and is believed to have originated in Africa. The presence of AIDS was initially made known when two patients were diagnosed with *Pneumocystis carinii* and Kaposi's sarcoma. Kaposi's sarcoma is a form of cancer that appears as large purple blotches on the skin. Until the advent of AIDS, it was known only to occur in people of Mediterranean origin aged 60 years and older. The appearance of Kaposi's sarcoma in younger persons of different origins prompted an investigation by the U.S. Centers for Disease Control and Prevention (CDC).

Physicians outside the CDC, such as immunologist Michael Gottlieb of the University of California, Los Angeles, were also involved in the investigation. Gottlieb was called in as a consultant for three patients experiencing thrush (infection in the mouth or throat by a fungus called Candida, which forms large, white plaques over the oral mucosa) and *Pneumocystis carinii*, a lung parasite. One of Gottlieb's most telling findings was that nearly all of the patients were devoid of a white blood cell called a T–helper lymphocyte. This kind of white blood cell is crucial to the function of the immune system, so their destruction indicated that he was observing a disease that destroyed the patient's immune system and allowed the invasion of other disease–causing agents. The disease was named Acquired Immune Deficiency Syndrome; *acquired* because the person was not born with it but acquired it later; *immunodeficiency*, of course, because the disease completely disrupted the immune system; and *syndrome* because the cases all presented with similar histories and clinical signs.

Invariably the patients' immune systems were severely compromised. This led investigators to believe that perhaps a virus was the cause. However, no virus had been found and the available drugs that were useful against viral diseases were totally ineffective in treating individuals with AIDS.

The first reported cases of AIDS came predominantly from the homosexual communities of major urban centers, which seemed to indicate that the disease could be sexually transmitted. Throughout the early 1980s, other high–risk groups were identified. These included hemophiliacs and intravenous (IV) drug users.

Hemophilia is an inherited disease in which a factor is missing that causes blood to clot. A hemophiliac can experience a serious bleeding episode from only a minor cut. The disease has no cure, but can be controlled by injections of one of the blood factors called Factor VIII. To prepare a vial of Factor VIII the blood of up to 20,000 donors is mixed and the blood is broken down into its components—plasma, red blood cells, white blood cells, and clotting factors. It was evident that the preparation of Factor VIII allowed the causal agent of AIDS to go through the preparatory cycle unharmed and able to transmit AIDS to the recipient of the clotting agent. It was evident, too, that the causal agent of AIDS could invade the blood supply, so anyone who received a blood transfusion was at risk of contracting AIDS.

Drugs such as cocaine and heroin can be taken intravenously—into a vein—using a syringe and needle. Blood is drawn into the syringe to mix with the drug before it is injected. Frequently the syringe and needle are shared with other users who inject themselves without cleaning the apparatus. The small amount of blood remaining in the bore of the needle is sufficient to transmit infectious agents from one person to another, such as the agent responsible for AIDS. Intravenous drug users eventually would comprise the largest percentage of AIDS patients.

AIDS spread to people outside of the high–risk groups through sexual contact and the transmission of infected blood. Babies born to women with AIDS were also found to be susceptible to the disease. As more cases were reported, it became evident that the disease could be transmitted by people who carried the infectious agent but did not have symptoms of AIDS. It was also discovered, however, that AIDS cannot be transmitted through casual contact, such as kissing or touching.

In 1985, a test was devised to detect the presence of the virus. Called the enzyme-linked immunosorbic assay (ELISA), the test immediately found use to screen blood donations. Another test called the Western blot test also was developed, though it was much more intricate and time–consuming than ELISA. The Western blot test is used to double–check any blood specimen that the ELISA test indicates is positive for the virus.

Individuals and donated blood are checked for presence of the AIDS virus to prevent spread of the disease. Having the means to detect the presence of the

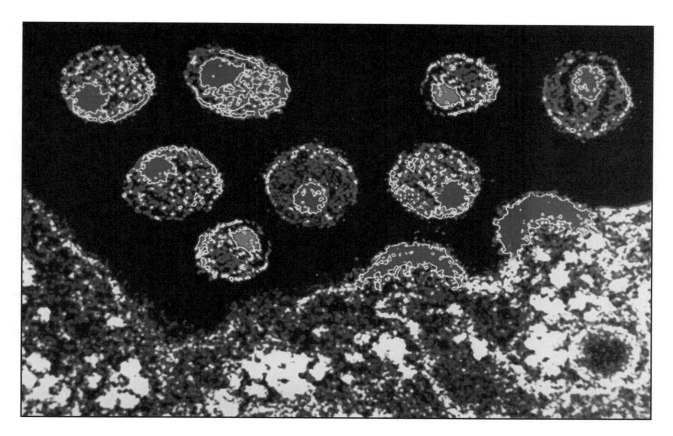

Mature HIV-1 viruses (above) and the lymphocyte from which they emerged (below). Two immature viruses can be seen budding on the surface of the lymphocte (right of center).

virus, however, has not stopped its spread, and the epidemic has continued unchecked. By 1991, the CDC reported that 161,073 people had AIDS in the United States and 100,777 had died of the disease. An estimated one million Americans were infected with the virus. The statistics are even more devastating in Third World nations. Only 2% of AIDS cases are in the United States, and the rest are scattered around the world, primarily in developing countries.

The virus that causes AIDS

The search to identify the infectious agent for AIDS began immediately after the first few cases were reported. An agent that could be transmitted sexually or by blood exchange suggested a bacterium, a virus, or a fungal agent. Bacteria and fungi can be seen through the ordinary light microscope, but none could be detected in the blood or other body fluids of AIDS patients. Viruses are much smaller than bacteria and cannot be seen using a light microscope. Still, using more sophisticated means of detection, scientists had not seen a virus in the blood of infected patients. The

very nature of the AIDS virus, in fact, made it next to impossible to observe the virus itself.

It was not until 1983 that the virus was identified. By then, the World Health Organization estimated that some 14 million people worldwide carried the virus and more than 3 million had developed AIDS.

In 1983, scientists at the Pasteur Institute in Paris recovered a virus from the lymph node of a patient who had lymphadenopathy. Lymphadenopathy is a condition of swollen lymph nodes indicating that the body is fighting an infection. It is for these swollen nodes that the physician feels along the neck and under the arms of an ill person, to find evidence that an infection may be present. Early in the history of AIDS, physicians considered that lymphadenopathy involving the nodes in the neck, throat, and armpit was an early part of the AIDS progression. At first the virus recovered from the lymph node was thought to be one that already had been described—the human T–cell leukemia virus or HTLV. The description of the virus published by French investigator Luc Montagneir appeared at the same time that American scientist Robert Gallo published the description of a virus he had isolated from an AIDS patient.

Both scientists described a retrovirus of the lenti virus variety. As a class, lenti viruses are associated with diseases that have a long incubation period and they also suppress the immune system. However, the HTLV was ruled out as a possibility. The HTLV, for one thing, was difficult to culture in the laboratory so it would be unlikely to survive the process of preparing blood factors from whole blood. Also, the HTLV did not destroy lymphocytes, so the devastation of the helper T–cell in AIDS victims could not have been the result of HTLV infection.

The French dubbed their virus lymphadenopathy-associated virus (LAV) and the Americans, still looking at the HTLV, named theirs a variant of the HTLV: HTLV-III. Their choice was based on reactions of HTLV–III with some proteins from HTLV–I and HTLV-II, so a relationship was assumed. This cross–reaction was later proved incorrect.

Further research demonstrated the French and American viruses to be lenti viruses whose proteins were different from the HTLV. To simplify reference to the AIDS virus the International Committee on Taxonomy of Viruses in 1986 recommended that the AIDS–causing virus be named the human immunodeficiency virus (HIV). Since that time, the HIV has been isolated from many AIDS patients as well as from patients who do not have symptoms of AIDS. The latter are called HIV positive, indicating they have the virus but not the disease. Further research showed that the HIV can be subdivided into HIV-1 and HIV-2. Individuals who have the HIV–2 seem to take longer to develop AIDS and the disease runs its course at a slower rate.

Like all viruses, the HIV cannot reproduce itself unless it invades a host cell. It is called a retrovirus because it carries its genetic material in the form of RNA instead of DNA. Once inside a cell, an enzyme called reverse transcriptase converts the RNA to DNA and the viral material is then inserted into the host cell DNA so that it will replicate the virus.

In form, the HIV is spherical and has a diameter of approximately 1/10,000th of a millimeter. A millimeter is about 1/25th of an inch, so approximately 250,000 of the viruses could be placed side by side in an inch–long space. The outer coat or envelope of the virus is made up of a double layer of lipids, or fat–like molecules. The virus constructs this coat for itself as it breaks out of a human cell. It simply wraps itself in the same material that forms the envelope of the host cell. A number of mushroom–shaped structures protrude from the surface of the virus. The mushroom cap, made of four glycoprotein molecules called gp120, is the attachment mechanism for the virus to grasp a host cell before invading it. The mushroom–shaped cap is supported by a stem consisting of four gp41 molecules, the stem buried in the viral envelope.

Inside the virus a cone–shaped core made of another protein, p24, encloses the viral RNA. Each strand of RNA contains the virus's genetic material arranged in nine genes. Scientists have identified each of the nine genes, but have not fully explained their functions. Three of the genes, gag, pol, and env, direct the formation of structural proteins. The remaining six genes, three regulatory—tat, rev, and nef—and three auxiliary genes—vif, vpr, and vpu—provide for construction of the proteins that control cell invasion, production of new viruses, and the ability to cause disease. Also included in the core are other proteins to support the virus and the enzymes reverse transcriptase, to convert the viral RNA into DNA, and integrase, which splices the viral DNA into the DNA of the host cell. The HIV prefers host cells that have on their surfaces a cluster of cells that form a receptor site called cluster designation 4 (CD4). The white blood cell called the T–helper cell is one such designated host, but other cells within the immune system also qualify.

Macrophages are cells that devour invading foreign materials and use parts of the invading cell to stimulate the T cells. Macrophages engulf the HIV and thus become reservoirs of infection, so the virus has no means to locate a favorable host cell. It has no means of locomotion, so once in the bloodstream the virus simply is pushed around the circulatory system until it bumps into a CD4–containing cell. Then, the HIV surface protein gp120 binds to the CD4 molecule on the potential host and the surface membranes of the virus and the cell fuse. The core of the virus with its RNA and enzymes is released into the host and infection begins. The enzyme reverse transcriptase converts the viral RNA to DNA which then migrates to the host cell's nucleus, the area in the cell in which the DNA of the host cell resides. With the aid of its other enzyme, integrase, the viral DNA is inserted into the host DNA. After that, each time the host cell divides, the viral DNA is reproduced as well.

Copies of the viral DNA are made in the form of messenger RNA, which passes from the nucleus into the body of the host cell so that the cell's protein–manufacturing structures can reproduce the viral proteins and enzymes. Thus new viruses are made. The new, immature viral particles gather inside the host cell's membrane and then bud out from the cell and pinch off, taking with them an envelope formed of the host cell's double–layer lipid membrane. Further processing by an enzyme called protease transposes the particles into infectious viruses that are now capable of beginning the cycle over again. During the early stages of infection the blood contains many viruses that have been reproduced quickly after the initial infection. They spread throughout the body seeking host cell's. The CD4 T cells in the blood will decrease by up to 40% in number during the first two weeks or so.

AIDS and its symptoms

Early in the infection, within two to four weeks, the person invaded by the HIV will experience a flu–like illness: high fever, headaches, sore throat, muscle and joint pains, nausea and vomiting, open ulcers in the mouth, swollen lymph nodes, and perhaps a rash. As the immune system begins to fight the HIV invasion, some cells in the immune system produce antibodies to neutralize the viruses that are free floating in the blood stream. Killer T cells destroy many other cells infected with the HIV and the CD4 T cell count rebounds to nearly normal levels. Now the patient enters a phase of the disease in which no symptoms are present, which may extend for a period of up to 10 years. During that time the patient may feel healthy, but the HIV is not at rest. It is replicating itself and invading other cells, many of them in the lymphoid system. Lymph tissue such as that in the lymph nodes, tonsils, and spleen is the center of disease–fighting activity. Some of the white blood cells in the immune system migrate to these tissues, where they are replicated and released in greater numbers back into the blood stream.

Over the years, the virus will disrupt the structure of the lymph nodes so that they no longer function as infection fighters. The networks within lymph tissue that trap foreign cells for destruction are themselves destroyed and special precursor cells within the bone marrow and thymus gland that were slated for special immune duties also are destroyed, further suppressing the immune system. Some white blood cells infected with the HIV circulate through the brain and lungs, seeding the HIV as they go. People with AIDS exhibit abnormalities within the central nervous system. Killer T cells and macrophages continue to destroy the HIV and HIV–infected cells, but the number of these guardian cells is decreasing. Killer T cells may kill uninfected cells that have particles of the HIV on their surfaces. Also, by a means not yet known, the HIV can signal CD4 T cells to "turn off" or deactivate so they will not respond to stimulation by other cells in the immune system. Thus, by one means or another, the HIV shuts down the body's immune response.

With an unresponsive immune system, the HIV carrier becomes vulnerable to any number of opportunistic infections. These are infections that normally would be quickly disposed of by the immune reaction, but that now can gain a foothold with the immune system not functioning. Kaposi's sarcoma is seen frequently, though it is not an infection but a cancer. *Pneumocystis carinii* is an infectious agent that affects the lungs. HIV infection of the brain leads to a form of dementia that worsens over time.

The search for a cure for AIDS has been unsuccessful. A few drugs now are approved for use, but none has been demonstrated to increase the patient's life span. They do lessen the severity of the disease, however, and may serve to lengthen the time before conversion from HIV positive to full–blown AIDS. Ziduvudine (AZT) was the first drug used to treat AIDS patients. AZT interrupts the life cycle of the virus by preventing reverse transcriptase from converting HIV RNA to DNA. Many patients are unable to withstand the effects of AZT for a long period of time. The drug itself may further deplete the white blood cell count, which means it must be discontinued. Also, the effectiveness of AZT fades over time, possibly because the virus mutates to a form that can resist the drug. Because the step in the virus life cycle in which reverse transcriptase is used is inside the host cell, it is difficult for AZT to reach its target without destroying the white blood cell. A second drug, DdI, may be substituted for AZT or used in conjunction with it. DdI does not deplete the white cell count, but may cause painful inflammation of the pancreas and nerve damage. Opportunistic infections are treated with appropriate drugs, but that does not affect the HIV infection. These opportunistic infections are frequently the immediate cause of death in AIDS patients.

The search for an effective vaccine to prevent AIDS has also been unsuccessful. Many vaccines are prepared from the infectious organism itself. The outer coating of a vaccine is sufficient to trigger the development of antibodies in the human body, which will initiate a resistance to the live virus if it attempts to invade. The HIV, however, is able to change its outer coating to confound any vaccine that might be compounded from it. Like the common cold virus, the HIV can assume many guises, at least for benefit of the immune system, and the search for a vaccine is stymied. AIDS is a disease that is spread by exchange of blood or by sexual contact. In the time that it has been known to exist it has never been demonstrated to spread by casual contact. It is not dangerous to have an HIV–infected student in school with other students, and AIDS patients do not need to be isolated from other people.

See also Immune system; Retrovirus; Virus.

Further Reading:

"AIDS, the Unanswered Questions." *Science* (special issue) 260 (May 28, 1993).

Greene, Warner C. "AIDS and the Immune System." *Scientific American* 269 (September, 1993): 99–105.

Grimes, D.E. and Grimes, R.M. *AIDS and HIV Infection.* St. Louis: Mosby, 1994.

"HIV infection and AIDS." Background statement from the National Institute of Allergy and Infectious Diseases. 1992.

"Women and HIV Infection." 1994. National Institute of Allergy and Infectious Diseases.

Larry Blaser

Aildebeeste see **Antelopes and gazelles**

Aircraft

An aircraft is a machine used for traveling through the atmosphere supported either by its own buoyancy or by some sort of engine that propels the ship through the air. Aircraft of the former type are known as lighter–than–air ships, while those of the latter type tend to be heavier–than–air machines. Included in the general term aircraft are such specific machines as dirigibles, gliders, airplanes, and helicopters.

Early theories of air travel

Humans have dreamed of flying like birds for centuries. A Chinese myth dating to at least 1500 B.C. tells of men flying through the air in a carriage driven by something very much like a modern propeller. The Greek legend of Daedalus and Icarus is closer to the image that early humans had of flight, however. According to that legend, Daedalus constructed a set of wings that he attached to his son, Icarus, as a means of escaping from the island of Crete. Icarus flew so high, however, that the wax holding the wings to his body melted, and he fell to his death.

For more than 20 centuries, humans repeated Daedalus's experiment, with ever more sophisticated attempts to duplicate the flight of birds. All such attempts failed, however, as inventors failed to recognize that the power generated by a single human could never be sufficient to lift a person off the Earth's surface.

Lighter–than–air aircraft

The first real success experienced by humans in designing aircraft made use of the concept of buoyancy. Buoyancy refers to the fact that an object tends to rise if it is placed in a medium whose density is greater than its own. A cork floats in water, for example, because the cork is less dense than the water. Buoyant aircraft became possible when scientists discovered that certain gases—especially hydrogen and helium—are less dense than air. Air that has been heated is also less dense than cooler air. Thus, a container filled with one of these gases will rise in air of its own accord.

Balloons were the first aircraft to make use of this principle. The fathers of ballooning are sometimes said to be the Montgolfier brothers, Joseph and Jacques. In 1782, the brothers constructed a large balloon which they filled with hot air produced by an ordinary bonfire under the balloon. The balloon rose more than a mile into the air. A year later, the Montgolfiers sent up a second balloon, this one carrying a tub that held a duck, a rooster, and a sheep. Then, only two months later, they constructed yet another balloon, this one large enough to carry a human into the atmosphere.

Balloon transportation suffers from one major drawback: The balloon goes wherever the winds carry it, and passengers have almost no control over the direction or speed of their travel. The additions needed to convert a balloon into a useable aircraft are a motor

The first supersonic transport to fly, the Soviet Union's Tupolev-144. It flew on December 31, 1968, two months before the Concorde's inaugural flight, yet the Anglo-French Concordes are the only aircraft of this type still in use.

to propel the balloon in any given direction and a rudder with which to steer the balloon. The modified form of a balloon with these features is known as a dirigible.

The father of the modern dirigible is generally said to be Count Ferdinand von Zeppelin. Zeppelin's dirigible consisted of a rigid aluminum framework supporting a fabric covering and filled with hydrogen gas. On July 2, 1900, Zeppelin's dirigible took its initial flight; his first working ship was 420 ft (125 m) long and 40 ft (12 m) in diameter. It was capable of lifting 27,000 lb (12,000 kg) and traveling at air speeds comparable to those of airplanes then available. At their peak, Zeppelin–styled dirigibles were able to carry a maximum of 72 passengers in an elaborate gondola that also held a dining room, bar, lounge, and walkways.

The end of commercial dirigible travel came in the 1930s as the result of two events. One was the continuing improvement in heavier–than–air travel which made the much slower dirigible obsolete. The other event was the dramatic explosion and destruction of the dirigible *Hindenburg* as it attempted to moor at Lakehurst, New Jersey, on May 6, 1937. The ever–present danger that the highly flammable hydrogen gas used to inflate dirigibles would ignite and burn up had finally come to realization at Lakehurst. Although later dirigibles were designed to fly with non–flammable helium, they never really regained the popularity of the pre–Lakehurst period. Today, dirigibles are widely used for advertising purposes. The "Goodyear blimp" and its cousins have now become familiar sights at outdoor sporting events all over the United States.

Heavier–than–air aircraft

The father of heavier–than–air machines is said to be Sir George Cayley (1773–1857). Cayley carried out a careful study of the way birds fly and, in 1810, wrote a pioneering book on flight, *On Aerial Navigation.* Cayley's research laid the foundations of the modern science of aerodynamics, the study of the forces experienced by an object flying through the air. In 1853, he constructed his first working aircraft, a glider which his coachman rode above the valleys on the Cayley estate in Yorkshire, England.

Gliders

Cayley's glider is now regarded as the earliest version of the modern airplane. The glider—also known as a sailplane—differs from a modern airplane only in that it has no power source of its own. Instead, it uses updrafts and winds for propulsion and maneuvering. Cayley was well aware of the need for a powerful engine for moving a heavier–than–air machine, but only steam engines were then available, and they were much too heavy for use in an aircraft. So Cayley designed an airship (his glider) that could make use of natural air movements.

The modern sailplane retains the characteristics that Cayley found to be crucial in the design of his own glider. In particular, both aircrafts have very large wings, are made of the lightest possible material, and have extremely smooth surfaces. The protrusion of a single rivet can produce enough friction to interfere with the successful maneuvering of a sailplane or glider. Properly designed sailplanes can remain in the air for hours and can travel at speeds of up to 150 mph (240 kmp) using only natural updrafts.

Four fundamental aerodynamic forces

The age of modern aviation can be said to have begun on December 17, 1903 at Kitty Hawk, North Carolina. On that date, Wilbur and Orville Wright, two bicycle makers from Dayton, Ohio, flew the world's first powered aircraft, a biplane (double–winged aircraft) with a wing span of 40 ft 4 in (12 m 1.5 cm) and weighing 605 lb (275 kg). The plane remained in the air a total of only 12 seconds and covered only 120 ft (37 m). But both brothers knew, as Wilbur then said, that "the age of flight had come at last."

The problems that the Wright brothers had to solve in the early 1900s were essentially the same as those confronting aeronautical engineers today. In order to make a heavier–than–air machine fly, four factors have to be taken into consideration: weight, lift, drag, and thrust.

The B-2 Stealth Bomber.

Weight is, of course, caused by the pull of the Earth's gravitational field on the airplane itself, its passengers, and its cargo. The plane will never leave the ground unless some method is found for counteracting the gravitational effect of weight. The way in which weight is counterbalanced is by means of lift, a force equal to and opposite in direction to the pull of gravity. Lift is provided by means of the flow of air over the airplane's wings.

Imagine that a strong wind blows over the wings of an airplane parked on a landing strip. Airplane wings are always designed so that the flow of air across the top surface and across the bottom surface of the wing is not identical. For example, the upper surface of the wing might have a slightly curved shape, like half of a tear drop. The lower surface of the same wing might then have a perfectly flat shape.

When air passes over a wing of this design, it moves more quickly over the top surface than it does the bottom surface. The effect produced was first observed by Swiss mathematician Daniel Bernoulli in the 1730s and is now known by his name, the Bernoulli effect. Bernoulli discovered that the faster a fluid moves over a surface, the less pressure it exerts on that surface.

In the case of an airplane wing, air moving over the top of the wing travels faster and exerts less pressure than air moving over the bottom of the wing. Since the pressure under the wing is greater than the pressure on top of the wing, air tends to push upward on the wing, raising the airplane off the ground.

A number of factors determine the amount of lift a wing can provide an airplane. One factor is the size of the wing. The larger the wing, the greater the total force exerted on the bottom of the wing compared to the reduced pressure on top of the wing. A second factor is speed. The faster air moves over a wing, the less pressure it exerts and the greater the lifting force provided the airplane. A third factor is the relative orientation of the wing to the air flow coming toward it. This factor is known as the angle of attack. In general, the greater the angle of attack, the greater the lifting force provided by the wing.

A pilot has control over all three of these factors in an airplane. Speed is controlled by increasing or decreasing the rate at which the engine turns, thereby changing the speed at which the propeller turns. Wing size is also under the pilot's control because of flaps that are attached to the following edge of a wing. These flaps can be extended during takeoff and landing to increase the total wing area and then retracted during level flights to reduce drag. Wing flaps and flap–like sections on the tail—the elevators—change the angle at which the wing or tail meets oncoming air and, thus, the airplane's angle of attack.

Thrust and drag

An airplane does not fly, of course, simply by setting it out on the runway and waiting for a strong wind to blow over its wings. Instead, the airplane is caused to move forward, forcing it to rush through still air at a high rate of speed. The forward thrust for the aircraft comes from one of two sources: a rotating propeller blade powered by some kind of engine or a rocket engine. The propeller used to drive the Wrights' first flight at Kitty Hawk was a home built engine that weighed 180 lb (82 kg) and produced 180 horsepower.

The forward thrust provided by a propeller can be explained in exactly the same way that the lift of a wing can be explained. Think of a propeller as a short, narrow mini–wing pivoted at the center and connected to an engine that provides rotational motion. The mini–wing is shaped like a larger wing, with a convex forward surface and a flat back surface. As the mini–wing is caused to rotate around its pivot point, the wing sweeps through the air, which passes over the forward surface of the mini–wing faster than it does over the back surface. As a result, the pressure on the forward surface of the mini–wing is less than it is on the back, and the mini–wing is driven forward, carrying the airplane along with it.

The pitch and angle of attack of the mini–wing—the propeller—can be changed just as can the angle of attack of the airplane's main wings. During level flight, the pitch of the propeller is turned at a sharp angle to the oncoming airflow, allowing the aircraft to maintain air speed with minimal fuel consumption. During take-

off and landing, the pitch of a propeller is reduced, exposing a maximum surface area to airflow and attaining a maximum thrust. At landing, the propeller direction can actually be reversed, causing the direction of force on the propellers to shift by 180°. As a result, the propeller becomes a brake on the airplane's forward motion.

The term drag refers to a variety of factors, each of which tends to slow down the forward movement of an aircraft. The most obvious type of drag is friction drag, a retarding force that results simply from the movement of a body such as an airplane through a fluid. The amount and effect of friction drag are very much a function of the shape and design of the aircraft.

Perhaps the most complex type of drag is that caused by the very air movements that lift an aircraft off the ground. The discussion of the Bernoulli effect above assumed that air flows smoothly over a surface. Such is never the case, however. Instead, as air travels over an airplane wing, it tends to break apart and form eddies and currents. The interaction of these eddies and currents with the overall air flow and with the airplane wing itself results in a retarding force: induced drag. One of the great challenges facing aeronautical engineers is to design aircraft in which all forms of drag are reduced to a minimum.

Aircraft stability

Once it is in flight, an airplane is subject to three major types of movements: pitch, yaw, and roll. These three terms describe the possible motion of an airplane in each of three dimensions. Pitch, for example, refers to the tendency of an airplane to rotate in a forward or backward direction, tail–over–nose, or vice versa. Yaw is used to describe a horizontal motion, in which the airplane tends to rotate with the left wing forward and the right wing backward, or vice versa. Roll is the phenomenon in which an airplane twists vertically around the body, with the right wing sliding upward and the left wing downward, or vice versa.

Each of the above actions can, of course, result in an airplane's crashing, so methods must be available for preventing each. The horizontal tail at the back of an airplane body helps to prevent pitching. If the plane's nose should begin to dip or rise, the angle of attack on the tail changes, and the plane adjusts automatically. The pilot also has control over the vertical orientation of the plane's nose.

Roll is prevented by making a relatively modest adjustment in the orientation of the aircraft's wings. Instead of their being entirely horizontal to the ground, they are tipped upward at their outer edges in a very wide V shape. The shape is called a dihedral. When the airplane begins to roll over one direction or the other, the movement of air changes under each wing and the plane rights itself automatically.

Yawing is prevented partly by means of the vertical tail at the back of the airplane. As a plane's nose is pushed in one direction or the other, airflow over the tail changes, and the plane corrects its course automatically. A pilot also has control over vertical tail flaps and can adjust for yawing by shifting the plane's ailerons, flaps on the following edge of the wings and the rear horizontal tail.

Jet engines

Until the 1940s, the only system available for powering aircraft was the piston–driven propeller engine. In order to increase the speed and lifting power of an airplane, the only option that aeronautical engineers had was to try to increase the efficiency of the engine or to add more engines to the airplane. During World War II, the largest power plants consisted of as many as 28 cylinders, capable of developing 3,500 horsepower.

At the very end of World War II, German scientists produced an entirely new type of power system, the jet engine. As "new" as the jet airplane was in 1944, the scientific principles on which it is based had been around for more than 2,000 years. You can think of a jet engine as a very large tin can, somewhat fatter in the middle and more narrow at both ends. Both ends of the tin can have been removed so that air can pass in the front of the can (the engine) and out the back.

The center of the engine contains the elements necessary for its operation. Compressed air is mixed with a flow of fuel and ignited. As combustion gases are formed, they push out of the rear of the engine. As the gases leave the engine, they also turn a turbine which compresses the air used in the middle of the engine.

The principle on which the jet engine operates was first enunciated by Sir Isaac Newton in the seventeenth century. According to Newton's Second Law, for every action, there is an equal and opposite reaction. In the jet engine, the action is the surge of burned gases flowing out of the back of the engine. The reaction to that stream of hot gases is a forward push that moves the engine—and the wing and airplane to which it is attached—in a forward direction.

Because the exiting gases turn a turbine as well as powering the engine, a jet of this kind is also known as a turbojet. The first airplanes of this kind—the German Messerschmitt 262 and the British Gloster Meteor—were available for flight in the spring of 1944, only months before the end of the war. The first turbojet planes were capable of speeds of about 540 mph (865 kmp), about 20 mph (33 kmp) faster than any piston–driven aircraft then in flight.

Wind tunnels

No matter what kind of power system is being used in an aircraft, aeronautical engineers are constantly searching for new designs that will improve the aerodynamic properties of aircraft. Perhaps the single most valuable tool in that search is the wind tunnel. A wind tunnel is a closed space in which the model of a new airplane design is placed. A powerful fan at one end of the tunnel is then turned on, producing a very strong wind across the surface on the airplane model. In this respect, the wind tunnel matches the airplane–on–the–landing–strip example used above. The flow of air from the fan, across the model, and out the back of the tunnel can be followed by placing small amounts of smoke into the wind produced by the fan. Engineers can visually observe the path of smoke as it flows over the plane, and they can take photographs to obtain permanent records of these effects.

The wind tunnel was first suggested by the great Russian physicist Konstantin Tsiolkovsky. In 1897, Tsiolkovsky constructed the first wind tunnel in the town of Kaluga and investigated the effects of various aircraft bodies and wing designs on the flow of air over an aircraft. Today, wind tunnels of various sizes are in use, allowing the test of small models of airframes and wings as well as of full–size aircraft.

Specialty airplanes

Many people may think of the modern aircraft business as being dominated by military jet fighters and bombers, commercial jetliners and prop planes, and other similar large aircraft. But flying has become a popular hobby among many people in the world today, and, as a result, a number of special kinds of aircraft have been developed for use by ordinary people. One example is the bicycle drive light plane.

One of the most successful examples of this aircraft design is known as *Daedalus '88*. *Daedalus '88* was designed to be so light and so aerodynamically sound that it could be flown by means of a single person turning the pedals of a bicycle. The bicycle pedals in *Daedalus '88* are attached to a shaft that turns the aircraft's propeller, providing the thrust needed to get the plane off the ground. The wings are more than 100 ft (31 m) wide and the boom connecting the propeller to the tail of the plane is 29 ft (9 m) long.

Most of *Daedalus '88*'s success is due to the use of the lightest possible materials in its construction: polyester for wing coverings, styrofoam and balsa wood for wing ribs, and aluminum and graphite epoxy resins for wing spars. The final aircraft weighs no more than 70 lb (32 kg). In the late 1980s, *Daedalus '88* was flown for a record–breaking 70 mi (110 km) at a speed of 18 mph (29 kph) by Greek bicyclist Kanellos Kanellopoulos.

Helicopters

A helicopter is an aircraft that has the capability of maneuvering in both horizontal and vertical directions. It accomplishes these maneuvers by means of a single elaborate and rather remarkable propeller–like device mounted to its top. Although the device looks like an ordinary propeller, it is much more complicated. In fact, the device is more properly thought of as a pair of wings (rotor blades) that spin around a common center. By varying the pitch, position, and angle of attack of the rotor blades, the helicopter pilot can direct the their thrust upward, downward, forward, backward, or at an angle. For example, if the pilot wants the aircraft to go upward, he or she increases the pitch in each blade of the rotor, increasing the upward lift that is generated. If the pilot wants to move the aircraft in a forward direction, the whole rotor shift can be tipped forward to change the lifting action to a forward thrust.

Helicopters present some difficult design problems for aeronautical engineers. One of the most serious problems is that the spinning of the rotor causes—as Newton's Second Law would predict—a reaction in the helicopter body itself. As the rotors spin in one direction, the aircraft has a tendency to spin at an equal speed in the opposite direction. A number of inventions have been developed to deal with this problem. Some helicopters have two sets of rotors, one turning in one direction, and the other in the opposite direction. A more common approach is to add a second propeller on the rear tail of the helicopter, mounted either horizontally or vertically. Either design helps to stabilize the helicopter and to prevent it from spinning out of control.

Navigation

Guiding the motion of aircraft through the skies is a serious problem for two reasons. First, commercial and military aircraft now fly in all kinds of weather, often under conditions that prevent their seeing other

KEY TERMS

Dirigible—A balloon that is capable of being steered.

Drag—A force of resistance caused by the movement of an aircraft through the air, such as the friction that develops between air and the aircraft body.

Glider—A motorless aircraft that remains in the air by riding on rising currents of air.

Helicopter—An aircraft with the capability of flying upward, downward, forward, backward, or in other directions.

Jet engine—An engine that obtains its power from burning a fuel within the engine, creating a backward thrust of gases that simultaneously pushes the engine forward.

Lift—The upper force on the wings of an aircraft created by differences in air pressure on top of and underneath the wings.

Pitch—The tendency of an aircraft to rotate in a forward or backward direction, tail–over–nose, or vice versa.

Roll—The tendency of an aircraft to twist vertically around its body, the right wing sliding upward and the left wing downward, or vice versa.

Thrust—The forward force on an aircraft provided by the aircraft's power system.

Wind tunnel—A closed space in which the movement of air flow over various types of aircraft bodies can be studied.

Yaw—The tendency of an aircraft to rotate in a horizontal motion, with the left wing forward and the right wing backward, or vice versa.

aircraft, the ground, or the airports at which they are supposed to land. Second, there is so much traffic in the air at any one time in many parts of the world that precautions must be taken to prevent collisions.

The crucial invention that made the control of air flight possible was the development of radar in the 1930s by the Scottish physicist Sir Robert Watson–Watt. Radar is a system by which radio beams are sent out from some central location (such as an airport tower) in all directions. When those beams encounter an object in the sky—such as an aircraft—they bounce off that object and are reflected to the sending station. A controller at the sending station is able to "see" the location of all aircraft in the vicinity and, knowing this, can then direct their movements to make landings and takeoffs possible and to prevent in–air collisions of the aircraft.

Today, every movement of every aircraft is constantly monitored using radar and radio signals. The moment a commercial airliner is ready to leave its gate for a flight, for example, the pilot notifies the control tower. One controller in the tower directs the airplane's movement on the ground, telling it when to back away from the gate and what runway to use for departure. Once the airplane is airborne, the pilot switches to a new radio channel and receives instructions from departure control. Departure control guides the aircraft's movements through the busiest section of the air near the airport, a distance about 30 mi (50 km) in radius. Finally, departure control "hands over" control of the airplane to a third system, one that guides the aircraft through various sections of the sky between its takeoff and landing points. As the plane approaches its final destination, the series of "hand offs" described above is reversed.

See also Aerodynamics; Airship; Balloon; Buoyancy; Jet engine; Radar.

Further Reading:

Garrison, Paul. *Lift, Thrust & Drag—A Primer of Modern Flying.* Blue Ridge, PA: TAB Books, Inc., 1981.
Stever, H. Guyford, James J. Haggerty, and the Editors of *Life. Flight.* New York: Time Incorporated, 1965.

David E. Newton

Air see **Atmosphere, composition and structure of**

Air currents see **Atmospheric circulation; Atmosphere, compostion and structure of**

Air masses and fronts

An air mass is an extensive body of air that has a relatively homogeneous temperature and moisture content over a significant altitude. Air masses typically cover areas of a few hundreds or thousands or millions of square kilometers. A front is the boundary at which two air masses of different temperature and moisture

content meet. The role of air masses and fronts in the development of weather systems was first appreciated by the Norwegian father and son team of Vilhelm and Jacob Bjerknes in the 1920s. Today, these two phenomena are still studied intensively as predictors of future weather patterns.

Source regions

Air masses form when a body of air comes to rest over an area large enough for it to take on the temperature and humidity of the land or water below it. Certain locations on the Earth's surface possess the topographical characteristics that favor the development of air masses. The two most important of these characteristics are topographic regularity and atmospheric stability. Deserts, plains, and oceans typically cover very wide areas with relatively few topographical irregularities. In such regions, large masses of air can accumulate without being broken apart by mountains, land/water interfaces, and other features that would break up the air mass.

The absence of consistent wind movements also favors the development of an air mass. In regions where cyclonic or anticyclonic storms are common, air masses obviously cannot develop easily.

Classification

The system by which air masses are classified reflects the fact that certain locations on the planet possess the topographic and atmospheric conditions that favor air mass development. That system uses two letters to designate an air mass. One letter, written in upper case, indicates the approximate latitude (and, therefore, temperature) of the region: A for arctic; P for polar; E for equatorial; T for tropical. The distinctions between arctic and polar on the one hand and equatorial and tropical on the other are relatively modest. The first two terms (arctic and polar) refer to cold air masses, and the second two (equatorial and tropical) to warm air masses.

A second letter, written in lower case, indicates whether the air mass forms over land or sea and, hence, the relative amount of moisture in the mass. The two designations are c for continental (land) air mass and m for maritime (water) air mass.

The two letters are then combined to designate both temperature and humidity of an air mass. One source region of arctic air masses, for example, is the northern–most latitudes of Alaska, upper Canada, and Greenland. Thus, air masses developing in this source region are designated as cA (cold, land) air masses.

Similarly, air masses developing over the Gulf of Mexico, a source region for maritime tropical air masses, are designated as mT (warm, water) air masses.

Properties of air masses

The movement of air masses across the Earth's surface is an important component of the weather that develops in an area. For example, weather patterns in North America are largely dominated by the movement of about a half dozen air masses that travel across the continent on a regular basis.

Two of these air masses are the cP and cA systems that originate in Alaska and central Canada and sweep down over the northern United States during the winter months. These air masses bring with them very cold temperatures, strong winds, and heavy precipitation, such as the snowstorms commonly experienced in the Great Lakes states and New England. The name "Siberian Express" is sometimes used to describe some of the most severe storms originating from these cP and cA air masses.

From the south, mT air masses based in the Gulf of Mexico, the Caribbean, and western Atlantic Ocean move northward across the southern states, bringing hot, humid weather that is often accompanied by thunderstorms in the summer.

Weather along the western coast of North America is strongly influenced by mP air masses that flow across the region from the north Pacific Ocean. These masses actually originate as cP air over Siberia, but are modified to mP masses as they move over the broad expanse of the Pacific, where they can pick up moisture. When an mP mass strikes the west coast of North America, it releases its moisture in the form of showers and, in northern regions, snow.

Fronts

The term front was suggested by the Bjerknes because the collisions of two air masses reminded them of a battlefront during a military operation. That collision often results in war–like weather phenomena between the two air masses.

Fronts develop when two air masses with different temperatures and, usually, different moisture content come into contact with each other. When that happens, the two bodies of air act almost as if they are made of two different materials, such as oil and water. Imagine what happens, for example, when oil is dribbled into a glass of water. The oil seems to push the water out of its way and, in return, the water pushes back on the oil. A similar shoving match takes place between warm and cold air masses along a front. The exact nature of that shoving match depends on the relative temperature and moisture content of the two air masses and the relative movement of the two masses.

Cold fronts

One possible situation is that in which a mass of cold air moving across the Earth's surface comes into contact with a warm air mass. When that happens, the cold air mass may force its way under the warm air mass like a snow shovel wedging its way under a pile of snow. The cold air moves under the warm air because the former is more dense. The boundary formed between these two air masses is a cold front.

Cold fronts are usually accompanied by a falling barometer and the development of large cumulonimbus clouds that bring rain showers and thunderstorms. During the warmer seasons, the clouds form as moisture–rich air inside the warm air mass, which is cooled and water condenses out as precipitation.

Cold fronts are represented on weather maps by means of solid lines that contain solid triangles at regular distances along them. The direction in which the triangles point shows the direction in which the cold front is moving.

Warm fronts

A situation opposite to the preceding is one in which a warm air mass approaches and then slides up and over a cold air mass. The boundary formed in this case is a warm front. As the warm air mass comes into contact with the cold air mass, it is cooled and some of the moisture held within it condenses to form clouds. In most cases, the first clouds to appear are high cirrus clouds, followed sometime later by stratus and nimbostratus clouds.

Warm fronts are designated on weather maps by means of solid lines to which are attached solid half circles. The direction in which the half circles point shows the direction in which the warm front is moving.

Occluded front

A more complex type of front is one in which a cold front overtakes a slower–moving warm front. When that happens, the cold air mass behind the cold front eventually catches up and comes into contact with the cold air mass underneath the warm front. The boundary between these two cold air masses is an occluded front.

A distinction can be made depending on whether the approaching cold air mass is colder or warmer than

Moran, Joseph M., and Michael D. Morgan. *Essentials of Atmosphere and Weather*. New York: Macmillan Publishing Company, 1994.

David E. Newton

KEY TERMS

Anticyclonic—Referring to an area of high pressure around which winds blow in a clockwise direction in the northern hemisphere.

Continental—Referring to very large land masses.

Cyclonic—Referring to an area of low pressure around which winds blow in a counter–clockwise direction in the northern hemisphere.

Humidity—The amount of moisture in the air.

Maritime—Referring to the oceans.

Topographical—Referring to the surface features of an area.

Air pollution

Air pollution occurs when the atmosphere contains large concentrations of gases, vapors, or particulates that are potentially toxic to people, animals, or vegetation, or that are damaging to buildings, art, or other materials.

the second air mass beneath the warm front. The former is called a cold–type occluded front, while the latter is a warm–type occluded front.

Once again, the development of an occluded front is accompanied by the formation of clouds and, in most cases, by steady and moderate precipitation. An occluded front is represented on a weather map by means of a solid line that contains, alternatively, both triangles and half circles on the same side of the line.

Stationary fronts

In some instances, the collision of two air masses results in a stand–off. Neither mass is strong enough to displace the other, and essentially no movement occurs. The boundary between the air masses in this case is known as a stationary air mass and is designated on a weather map by a solid line with triangles and half circles on opposite sides of the line. Stationary fronts are often accompanied by fair, clear weather, although some light precipitation may occur.

See also Atmosphere, composition and structure of; Precipitation; Storm; Weather forecasting; Weather mapping.

Further Reading:

Ahrens, C. Donald. *Meteorology Today*, Second Edition. St. Paul, MN: West Publishing Company, 1985.

Eagleman, Joe R. *Meteorology: The Atmosphere in Action*, Second Edition. Belmont, CA: Wadsworth Publishing Company, 1985.

"Genesis of Fronts and Airmasses," *Weatherwise*, December 1985, 324–328.

Lutgens, Frederick K., and Edward J. Tarbuck. *The Atmosphere: An Introduction to Meteorology*, Fourth Edition. Englewood Cliffs, NJ: Prentice Hall, 1989.

The most important gaseous air pollutants are ammonia (NH_3), carbon dioxide (CO_2), carbon monoxide (CO), fluoride (F, occurring in various chemical forms, such as hydrogen fluoride, HF), methane (CH_4), nitric oxide and nitrogen dioxide (NO and NO_2, together known as oxides of nitrogen, or NO_x), ozone (O_3), peroxyacetyl nitrate (PAN), and sulfur dioxide (SO_2).

Vapors of hydrocarbons and elemental mercury can also be air pollutants, as are tiny particulates with very small, less than one–micrometer diameters (μm, or 10^{-6} meters) that physically behave like gases in the atmosphere and can remain suspended for a long time. These tiny particulates include non–reactive minerals such as silicates, dusts containing toxic elements such as arsenic, copper, lead, nickel, and vanadium, and aerosols of organic compounds that are emitted as smoke during combustions, including relatively large and toxic molecules such as polycyclic aromatic hydrocarbons.

Some so–called "trace toxics" also occur in the atmosphere in very small concentrations. The trace toxics include persistent organochlorines, such as the pesticide DDT, polychlorinated biphenyls (PBCs), and the dioxin, TCDD. Other less persistent pesticides may also be air pollutants close to places where they are used.

These various air pollutants can influence environmental quality in many ways. When present in sufficiently large amounts, gases such as ozone and sulfur dioxide can cause toxicity to plants and animals. As is described later in the specific sections dealing with these gases, the toxicity to plants can result in severe ecological damages, sometimes causing extensive forest diebacks and even deforestation. In other cases,

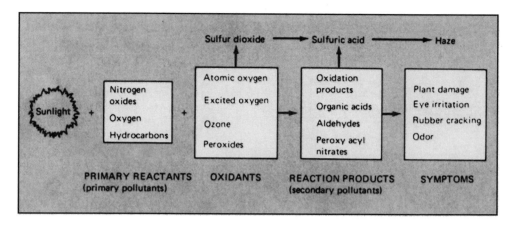

The chemistry of photochemical smog.

such as the trace toxics, the amounts of the potentially toxic chemicals in air or atmospheric deposition are usually minute and too small to cause measurable biological damages. In such cases the occurrence of the chemicals in the atmosphere is considered to represent a trace contamination, rather than damage–causing pollution. The effects of emissions of carbon dioxide do not occur through direct biological damages, but through a possible intensification of Earth's greenhouse effect, which could result in enormous ecological damages occurring in response to changes in climate.

Sources of air pollutants

Air pollutants can be emitted to the atmosphere by natural sources, as well as through the activities of humans (the latter are also known as *anthropogenic emissions*). Natural sources of emissions of air pollutants include volcanoes, forest fires, and outgassings from soils and wetlands. On the global scale, the natural emissions of some gases exceed those associated with human activities, as are the cases of hydrogen sulfide, carbon dioxide, and methane. More locally or regionally, however, anthropogenic emissions may be more important for all of these chemicals.

For some gaseous pollutants, global human emissions rival the scale of, or are larger than natural sources, as are the cases for sulfur dioxide and oxides of nitrogen. Moreover, the human emissions are increasing rapidly in quantity. This is happening as a result of the growth of the human population, and also because the increasingly widespread industrial and economic development of nations is resulting in greater numbers of vehicles, fossil–fueled generating stations, metal smelters, and other sources of industrial emissions. Prior to this century, none of these sources

of emissions of air pollutants were important, and most did not even exist.

Sulfur dioxide, soot, and reducing smog

Sulfur dioxide is emitted from many anthropogenic sources, including metal smelters, coal– and oil–fired power plants, and homes that are heated using fuel oil. As a result, urban environments and their surrounding regions are commonly polluted with this gas.

Severe conditions of air pollution can occur when atmospheric conditions are relatively stable, and at the same time there are large emissions of sulfur dioxide and commonly associated pollutants, such as soot from coal burning. This can happen when there is an *atmospheric inversion*, in which a layer of relatively cool air is trapped beneath a layer of warmer air. The usual condition in the atmosphere is for air temperature to decrease with increasing altitude. However, under certain conditions a layer of cooler air can become trapped beneath a higher layer of warmer air. Usually, this circumstance is associated with cloudless skies at night, which promotes rapid cooling of the surface, and sometimes with the drainage of dense, cooler air from nearby uplands into a valley or lowland. Very stable atmospheric conditions occur beneath inversion layers. If an inversion event occurs in an urban or industrial area with large emissions of air pollutants, large concentrations of toxic chemicals can accumulate, and damages can be caused to humans, vegetation, and structures. These air pollution events last until the air–temperature inversion is alleviated by warming of the surface atmosphere during the day, or until strong winds break up the inversion, allowing the relatively polluted air mass to be diluted with cleaner, ambient air.

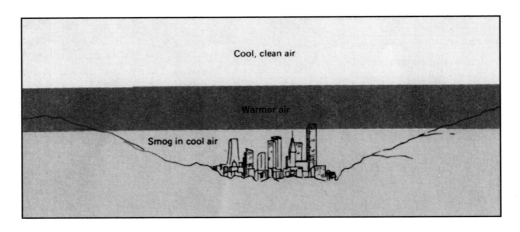

A diagram of a temperature inversion.

The word "smog" is derived from "smoke" and "fog." So–called "reducing smog" is characterized by large concentrations of sulfur dioxide and particulates of sulfate and soot, and these events occur most intensely during atmospheric temperature inversions. Reducing smogs became rather common occurrences during the mid–19th century after the beginning of the industrial revolution, when the burning of coal in industry and for space heating began to cause severe air pollution by sulfur dioxide and soot in the larger cities of Europe and North America. It had long been suspected that reducing smog and similar types of urban air pollution were unhealthy for humans, and damaging to vegetation and buildings. These fears were confirmed when a number of incidents of increased rates of human illness and deaths occurred that were clearly attributable to reducing smogs, with people with chronic respiratory or heart diseases being especially at risk.

The most famous reducing smogs were a series of episodes that afflicted London, most notably the "killer smog" of the early winter of 1952. This event developed under conditions of persistent atmospheric stability and cold during which much of southern England was covered by a natural, white fog. However, as the concentrations of sulfur dioxide and sooty particulates accumulated in London, the atmospheric conditions transformed into a noxious "black fog" with virtually zero visibility. This happened because of the continued emissions of air pollutants by heavy industry and for the generation of electricity and from homes as people tried to keep warm by burning coal in domestic fireplaces and furnaces. This killer smog is estimated to have resulted in a period of 18 days during which human mortality rates were greater than normal, resulting in 3,900 so–called "excess deaths" (that is, calcu-

lated on the basis of the increased rate of mortality), mostly of very young or elderly people, especially those with pre–existing respiratory or coronary diseases. Of course, much larger numbers of people were made ill during the killer smog of 1952.

A smaller but even more intense killer smog occurred in 1948 in Donora, a town of about 14,000 people located in a valley near Pittsburgh. In this case there was also a fog and stagnant air occurring beneath a persistent atmospheric inversion over a four–day period in late autumn. Donora was an industrial town with large factories that manufactured steel, zinc, and sulfuric acid. The continued large emissions of sulfur dioxide and particulates from these heavy industries caused severe air pollution during the smog event. There was a statistically enormous increase in the death rate of humans during and soon after this smog, with 20 deaths occurring in a relatively small population, while 43% of the population was made clinically ill, 10% with severe symptoms.

Reducing smogs used to be rather common in the larger, industrialized cities of western Europe and North America. More recently, however, governments have established policies and legislation to achieve cleaner air in cities, especially through changes in the amounts and methods by which coal can be burned. As a result, air quality has improved in most cities, and the severe effects of reducing smogs are less important in those countries that have effective laws to regulate air pollution of this sort. However, rapidly industrializing regions of eastern Europe, the former Soviet Union, China, and elsewhere still have substantial problems with reducing smogs. The social and economic priorities in those regions are to achieve rapid growth in the size of the industrial economy, and much less emphasis is placed on managing environmental quality. Because

Smog over Los Angeles, California.

the emissions of pollutants are not well controlled, reducing smogs are still an important problem in those places, and in fact they are becoming more common and more intense.

Point sources of air pollution

Sulfur dioxide has also caused some severe damages to ecosystems in the vicinity of industrial point sources of emission, especially around large metal smelters that are roasting sulfide–rich ores, and to a lesser degree around coal– and oil–fired generating stations. One of the world's most notorious cases of damages of this sort has occurred in the vicinity of the town of Sudbury, Ontario, where there have been large emissions of sulfur dioxide by the metal processing industry for about a century.

The metal ores mined at Sudbury are sulfide minerals. The first step in the processing of these minerals is oxidation of the sulfide with atmospheric oxygen at a

high temperature, resulting in the production of enormous quantities of sulfur dioxide as a waste gas. Over the years the sulfur dioxide wastes have been dealt with in various ways, but mostly by emitting them to the atmosphere for disposal.

Roast beds were the first method used to process metal ores at Sudbury. The roast beds were immense heaps of sulfide ore piled upon locally harvested firewood. The wood was ignited, and this started a combustion of the ore, which would burn and smolder for several months. After the roast bed cooled, the metal concentrates were gathered, shipped to a refinery, and processed into pure metals for use in manufacturing. Atmospheric emissions from the roast beds occurred at ground level, and the plumes were intensely toxic fumigations of sulfur dioxide, acidic mists, and metals, especially nickel and copper. Although all of these chemicals are toxic to plants and animals, the sulfur dioxide caused the greatest damages. As many as 30 roast beds operated in the Sudbury area, and these devastated the local ecosystems through the directly toxic effects of sulfur dioxide, acidity, and metals. After the vegetation cover was killed by the toxic fumigations, the soil freely eroded from slopes, exposing the naked bedrock of granite and gneiss, which became blackened by reaction with the acidic gases and mists.

Recognizing the obvious damages to ecosystems, and the likely effects on people, the government forbade the use of roast beds after 1928, and three smelters with tall stacks (they were at least 492 ft ([150 m] in height) were constructed to roast the sulfide ores. At the time, these were among the tallest smokestacks in the world. The smokestacks vented pollutants relatively high into the atmosphere, which significantly improved local air quality because ground–level fumigations occurred much less frequently. However, depending on the location, surface fumigations still occurred. Consequently, the sulfur dioxide continued to damage vegetation and cause lakes and soils to acidify, and toxic metals were spread over a large area.

After about four decades of operation of the large point sources at Sudbury, well defined patterns of ecological damages developed in their vicinity. The most devastated conditions occurred closest to the smelters, where there was very little or no cover of vegetation, because few plants could survive the toxic conditions. The environment in those places was characterized by frequent fumigations by toxic concentrations of sulfur dioxide, and soils and surface waters were very acidic and had large concentrations of nickel, copper, aluminum, and other metals. The toxic metals were either deposited as a result of emissions from the smelters, or they were solubilized from soil minerals because of the extreme acidification.

Because the smelters are point sources, environmental pollution and ecological damages became less intensive farther away, decreasing at a roughly exponential rate with increasing distance. Beyond about 9–12 mi (15–20 km) from the smelters it was difficult to detect obvious ecological damages to terrestrial ecosystems, although contamination by nickel and copper could be demonstrated at these and farther distances, and many lakes were acidified by the deposition of sulfur dioxide to at least 25–31 mi (40–50 km) away.

A major improvement of regional air quality occurred in 1972, when a very tall, 1,247–foot (380 m) "superstack" was built at the largest of the Sudbury smelters. This smokestack allowed an even more effective dispersion of smelter emissions, so that local fumigations became much less frequent. At the same time one of the smelters was closed, the industry began to reduce the actual emissions of sulfur dioxide by recovering some of the sulfur from the waste gases (this process is called *flue–gas desulfurization*), and by selectively processing ores having smaller concentrations of sulfur. All of these changes resulted in very substantial improvements of the local air quality. The improved environmental conditions have allowed plant species to invade sites close to the smelters as they became less toxic and acidic. Consequently, the vegetation cover has increased close to the smelters, an ecological recovery that has been actively enhanced by managed revegetation along roadways and other places where soil had not completely eroded away. In addition, lakes close to the sources of emissions have become less acidic, and there has been somewhat of a recovery of their plant and animal systems.

However, it is important to understand that while the superstack and other actions at Sudbury have substantially improved local air quality, there are still problems associated with the continued large emissions of pollutants. The Sudbury smelters are still major sources of sulfur dioxide, a precursor of atmospheric sulfate, itself important in the phenomenon of acid rain. It is even possible that the height of the superstack will be reduced in order to decrease the amount of sulfur dioxide emitted from Sudbury that is transported over long distances where it contributes to acid rain.

Smelters located at Anaconda, Montana, Ducktown, Tennessee, Superior, Arizona, Trail, British Columbia, and Wawa, Ontario are some other North American examples of industrial point sources of air pollution that have caused significant ecological damages.

Ozone and oxidizing smog

In any consistently sunny places where large numbers of people live and work in an industrialized society, oxidizing smogs (also known as photochemical, and sometimes as Los Angeles–type smogs) have mostly replaced reducing smogs in importance. Oxidizing smogs form as a result of chemical reactions occurring in the atmosphere, and this condition is therefore caused indirectly by the emitted, or primary, pollutants. Oxidizing smogs commonly form where there are large emissions of nitric oxide and hydrocarbons, occurring in an environment where the weather is often sunny and atmospheric conditions are frequently stable during the early part of the day. These conditions favor a complex of photochemical reactions involving the emitted pollutants, which result in the formation of non–emitted, or secondary, pollutants, including the strongly oxidizing gases, ozone and peroxyacetyl nitrate. These secondary gases are the most important chemicals in oxidizing smogs that are harmful to people and cause damages to agricultural and natural vegetation.

The atmospheric concentrations of the various chemical components of photochemical smog vary during the day in a rather predictable manner. This has been well studied in the vicinity of Los Angeles where ozone concentrations are largest in the early–to–mid afternoon and then decrease as these gases are replaced and diluted by the cleaner air of winds that originate over the Pacific Ocean. However, those oceanic winds also blow the polluted photochemical smog inland where agricultural regions of the coastal lowlands are affected as are natural pine forests on the windward slopes of the fringing mountains. The concentrations of ozone and other components of oxidizing smog are also strongly influenced by the daily patterns of traffic volume, since vehicles are the major sources of emission of the primary pollutants. Because sunlight is not available, the photochemical reactions do not occur at night. This general, daily cycle of pollutant concentrations is typical of places that experience oxidizing smog.

Humans are sensitive to ozone, which irritates and damages the membranes of the respiratory system and eyes and commonly induces asthma. People vary greatly in their sensitivity to ozone, but highly sensitive individuals suffer considerable discomfort from exposure to oxidizing smogs of an intensity that commonly occurs in large, sunny cities in industrialized countries. The physiological stresses of oxidizing smogs may decrease the longevity of these hypersensitive people, but in contrast to the worse events of reducing smog, oxidizing smogs do not appear to cause episodes of high mortality of humans. The damages to people are important, but they occur over a longer term and in a more chronic fashion.

Ozone is by far the most important gaseous air pollutant in North America in terms of causing damages to agricultural and wild plants. Most plants suffer acute injury (or obvious tissue damages) from exposures to 200–300 ppb (parts per billion, or 10^{-9}) ozone for several hours, while longer–term exposures to about 100 ppb are sufficient to reduce yields, even in the absence of obvious injuries (this is called "hidden injury"). However, very sensitive species can be damaged by much smaller concentrations, for example, as little as 50–60 ppb in the cases of tobacco (*Nicotiana tobacco*) and spinach (*Spinacea oleracea*). Because concentrations larger than these toxic thresholds are very common in places that experience photochemical air smogs, ozone is an economically important pollutant. The air quality standard for ozone in the United States sets a maximum concentration of 120 ppb for an average, one–hour concentration, but this concentration is exceeded many days each year in much of the southwestern U.S. and in other sunny regions as well. Studies have suggested that each year, the economic value of crop losses associated with ozone damage exceeds $5 billion.

Natural vegetation is also damaged by ozone in some regions. The best known damages are caused to forests of ponderosa pine (*Pinus ponderosa*) in southern California. The forest damages to pine forests was first noticed in the 1950s in the San Bernardino Mountains, although the damages were not diagnosed as caused by ozone until 1963. Severe damages to ponderosa pine have occurred over at least 100,000 hectares, and lesser damages over about 1/2 million hectares. Trees that have been stressed by needle losses due to ozone are relatively vulnerable to secondary damages caused by bark beetles and fungal root pathogens, which are often the ultimate cause of death of weakened trees.

Chlorofluorocarbons and stratospheric ozone

Chlorofluorocarbons (CFCs) are very useful chemicals that have been synthesized and used in refrigeration as propellants and for cleaning microelectronics. After many of these uses, CFCs are routinely or accidentally vented into the atmosphere. However, these chemicals are very stable in the lower atmosphere, and as a result they enter the global atmospheric circulation and slowly penetrate to the upper atmosphere or stratosphere, where they degrade as a result of the intense photochemical conditions that exist there. The breakdown of chlorofluorocarbons results in the formation of simple compounds of chlorine, which then consume stratospheric ozone. Ozone is a relatively abundant gas in the stratosphere, where it is formed by natural photochemical reactions.

The concentration of ozone in the stratosphere is typically about 0.2–0.3 ppm, more than 10 times larger than typically occurs in unpolluted environments at ground level. Beginning in the early 1980s, scientists began to notice distinct but temporary decreases in the concentration of stratospheric ozone (called ozone "holes"), occurring during the late winter and early springtime over Antarctica. Between the late 1970s and the late 1980s the average decrease in springtime stratospheric ozone was 30–40%. Ozone holes have also been documented over the Arctic, although these are less intense than over Antarctica. The ozone depletions are believed to be caused by atoms or simple compounds of chlorine, which mostly originate indirectly through emissions of CFCs.

Although the ozone holes only occur over Antarctica and the Arctic, concentrations of stratospheric ozone at lower latitudes can be also affected when the ozone–depleted, high–latitude air disperses widely through the stratosphere in the late spring. It has been estimated that the seasonal concentrations of stratospheric ozone over 50° S latitude may have decreased by 3–8% during the 1980s.

Stratospheric ozone is biologically important because it absorbs incoming solar ultraviolet radiation, especially in the wavelength range of 200–290 nm, and to a lesser degree over 290–320 nm. Because of this role, ozone serves as an ultraviolet shield, protecting life on Earth's surface from some of the damaging effects of this energetic radiation. It is well known that ultraviolet radiation can damage genetic material and can increase the risks of developing skin cancers, including deadly melanoma, as well as other maladies such as cataracts and other corneal damages such as snowblindness and suppression of the immune system. Plants are also affected, partly because their photosynthetic pigments are degraded by ultraviolet radiation.

Clearly, stratospheric ozone provides a beneficial function, in contrast to ozone at ground level, which as described earlier is generally viewed as harmful to organisms. The effect of CFCs on stratospheric ozone concentrations appears to be an important environmental problem.

Carbon dioxide and the greenhouse effect

It is well known that the concentration of carbon dioxide in Earth's atmosphere has been rapidly increasing from about 280 ppm in the mid–1800s to more than 350 ppm today. This environmental change has mostly been caused by two types of human activities: (1) the burning of large quantities of fossil fuels, such as coal, petroleum, and natural gas. These materials have all developed over geological time from partially decomposed plant biomass, and their combustion leads to large emissions of fossil carbon into the atmosphere; (2) the conversion of forests, which contain larger quantities of biomass and store more carbon than any other type of ecosystem, into agricultural ecosystems which store much less carbon. The difference in stored carbon that results from this ecological conversion is balanced by a large emission of carbon dioxide into the atmosphere.

Overall, during the past several centuries, the burning of fossil fuels and deforestation have had a similarly sized influence on the concentration of carbon dioxide in the atmosphere, although in recent decades fossil fuels have been somewhat more important.

The increasing concentrations of atmospheric carbon dioxide are important because this gas is highly influential in the process known as the greenhouse effect by which Earth maintains its surface temperature. In the absence of this greenhouse effect, Earth's surface temperature would average about 17.6°F (–8°C) which is much colder than life could tolerate, largely because water is frozen at this temperature. By slowing the rate at which Earth cools itself, the greenhouse effect helps maintain the planet's surface temperature at an average of about 77°F (25°C), and therefore within the range of tolerance of organisms and ecosystems. Carbon dioxide is influential in the greenhouse effect, because it is an effective absorber of long–wavelength infrared energy of the sort that Earth radiates in order to cool itself of the energy that it gains by absorbing incoming, shorter–wavelength solar radiation.

In view of the well–known influence of carbon dioxide on Earth's greenhouse effect, scientists have hypothesized that the increasing concentrations of this gas could lead to an intensification of the greenhouse process, possibly leading to global warming. If this prediction was to prove correct there could be catastrophic ecological implications, because the present distributions of Earth's ecosystems and species are

KEY TERMS

Anthropogenic—Associated with the activities of humans.

Flue–gas desulfurization—Various chemical processes used on sulfur dioxide from waste gases before they are dispersed into the environment.

Hidden injury—Refers to plant damage, such as decreased productivity, that occurs as a result of an exposure to toxic pollution that is not sufficient to cause acute injuries, such as discolored or dead foliage.

Inversion—Refers to a condition in which there is an atmospheric zone in which temperature increases with altitude, instead of the usual decrease with increasing altitude.

Stratosphere—Earth's upper atmosphere, in which temperature does not decrease with increasing altitude. The height of the stratosphere varies seasonally, but is typically higher than about 12–19 mi (20–30 km). The lower atmosphere, or troposphere, occurs beneath the stratosphere.

largely determined by the patterns of climate, especially those of rainfall and temperature. Therefore, substantial changes in climate would require enormous adjustments by both natural and agricultural ecosystems, and the corresponding damages would probably be enormous. Other potential effects of an intensification of Earth's greenhouse effect include a rise in sea level due both to the melting of glaciers and the expansion of warmed sea water. There would also be large changes in oceanic circulation.

It has also been suggested that increased concentrations of atmospheric carbon dioxide could be favorable to certain plants that are growing in fertile soils and whose productivity might be limited by the rate at which they can assimilate this nutrient gas from the atmosphere. This effect would be especially important for some plants in agriculture, but it is unlikely to be important in natural ecosystems. Although carbon–dioxide fertilization would be somewhat beneficial, this would not compensate for the much more negative effects of potential climatic responses to an intensification of the greenhouse effect.

See also Acid rain; Atmosphere, composition and structure of; Carbon cycle; Carbon dioxide; Carbon monoxide; Chlorofluorocarbons; Contamination; DDT;

Dioxin; Emission; Greenhouse effect; Ozone; Ozone layer depletion; Point source; Pollution; Pollution control; Sulfur dioxide.

Further Reading:

Freedman, B. *Environmental Ecology*, 2nd ed. San Diego: Academic Press, 1994.

Hemond, H. F., and E. J. Fechner. *Chemical Fate and Transport in the Environment*. San Diego: Academic Press, 1994.

Bill Freedman

The Santos Dumont airship in flight over Paris in 1903.

Airship

A technologically advanced cousin of the balloon, airships are streamlined vessels buoyed by gases and controlled by means of propellers, rudders, and pressurized air systems. More commonly referred to as blimps and dirigibles, the airship is comprised of non–rigid, semi–rigid, and rigid types that rely on lighter–than–air gases such as helium and hydrogen for lift. Since the turn of the twentieth century, they have been engaged commercially in the transport of passengers and cargo and have proven a successful means of advertising.

Airships derive their lift from forward motion, just as an airplane does, and all three types have long used the internal–combustion engine, like the type used in automobiles, to propel their massive bodies through the air. These have included the earliest motorcycle engines, the diesel engines of the mammoth American ships *Akron* and *Macon*, and the beefed–up Porsche engines used to power a new generation of airships. Traditional pressure airships house the engine, propeller, and gear box on an outrigger that extends from the side of the car, while the modern British Skyship's 500 and 600 use inboard engines that turn long prop shafts which allow the propellers to be vectored outboard. The introduction of pivoted, or vectored, engines gave airships the ability to change the direction of thrust and afforded it such amenities as near–vertical lift–off, thus reducing the need for long runways. Capable of airborne refueling, airships can remain aloft for weeks at a time, reaching an average airspeed of 60 miles (96.5 km) per hour.

History and type

Non–rigid airships

Mastery of the skies proved a dominant preoccupation with French inventors in the latter half of the eighteenth century. In 1783, Jacques and Joseph Montgolfier designed the first balloon used for manned flight, while concurrently, Jean–Baptiste–Marie Meusnier had thought to streamline the balloon and maneuver it by some mechanized means. While several airships of similar design met with limited success from 1852, Meusnier's idea did not officially get off the ground until 1898. That year, the Brazilian aeronaut Alberto Santos–Dumont became the first pilot to accurately navigate a hydrogen–filled envelope and basket by means of a propeller mounted to a motorcycle engine.

Because of their non–rigid structure, the first blimps, like the balloon, were prone to collapsing as the gas contracted during descent. To counter this, Santos–Dumont introduced the ballonet, an internal airbag that helps maintain the envelope's structure and regulates pitch as well as lift, or buoyancy. Modern blimps continue to use ballonets positioned at the front and rear of the envelope, permitting the engineer to pump air into one or the other to change the pitch angle. For example, by increasing the amount of air in the aft ballonet, the airship becomes tail heavy, thus raising the nose skyward. Steering is further achieved by controlling rudders affixed to one of several types of tail fin

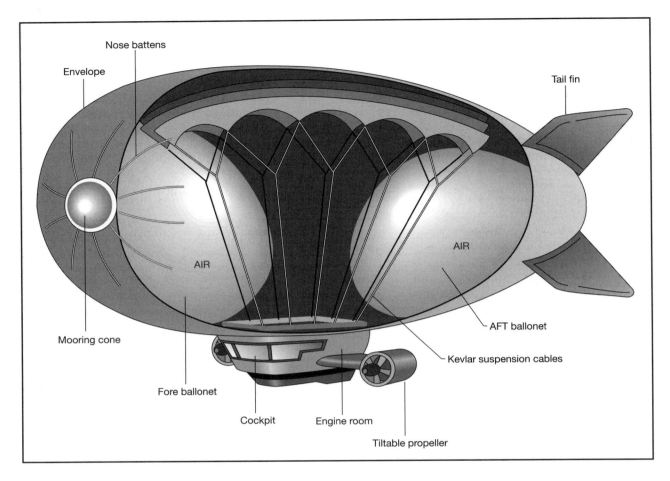

Nose battens

Envelope

Tail fin

AIR

AIR

AFT ballonet

Mooring cone

Kevlar suspension cables

Fore ballonet

Cockpit

Engine room

Tiltable propeller

The internal structure of an airship.

configurations, allowing for basic left, right, up, and down directions. The long standard cross–shaped fin is slowly being replaced by an X–shaped configuration. While the X is more complicated, requiring a combination of rudders to complete a maneuver, it provides better ground clearance.

The car or gondola serves as the control center, passenger quarters and cargo hold of the airship. The envelope and car are connected by a series of suspended cables attached to the envelope by different types of load–sharing surfaces. Many modern airships use a curtain structure glued or bonded along the length of the envelope which evenly distributes the weight of the car and engines.

Rigid airships

The German inventor, Count Ferdinand von Zeppelin took the guesswork out of airship aerodynamics by building a rigid structure of lightweight, aluminum girders and rings that would hold the vessel's streamlined shape under varying atmospheric conditions.

Unlike Dumont's single–unit envelope, von Zeppelin incorporated a number of drum–shaped gasbags within compartments of the structure to maintain stabilization should one of the bags become punctured or deflate. The dirigible was then encapsulated by a fabric skin pulled tightly across its framework. Buoyancy was controlled by releasing water ballast to ascend or by slowly releasing the hydrogen gas through a venting system as the ship descended.

Von Zeppelin was among the first airship designers to realize, in practice, the functionality of greater size in lighter–than–air vessels. As he increased the surface area of the envelope, the volume increased by a greater proportion. Thus, a larger volume afforded better lift to raise the aluminum hull and maximized the dirigible's cargo carrying capacity. Airships like the *Graf Zeppelin*, the *Hindenburg*, and their American counterparts, the *Macon* and the *Akron*, reached lengths of up to 800 ft (244 m) with volume capacities nearing seven million cubic feet. Hydrogen was, in part, responsible for such engineering feats because it is the lightest gas known to man and it is inexpensive. Its major drawback, one that would virtually close the chapter on non–rigid airship aviation, was its flammability. While passenger quarters, cargo, and fuel could be secured to or stored within the dirigible's metal structure, its engines were housed independently and suspended to reduce the possibility of friction–caused ignition of the gas.

Little did English writer Horace Walpole know how closely he had prophesied the future of airships when, upon the launch of the *Montgolfier* balloon, he wrote, "I hope these new mechanic meteors will prove only playthings for the learned or the idle, and not be converted into engines of destruction . . . ." While zeppelins, as they had become known, were initially put into commercial service, successfully completing nearly 1,600 flights in a four–year period, they were engaged in the service of Germany during World War I as giant bombers, raiding London itself in May of 1915. After the war, the rigid dirigible was employed as both a trans–Atlantic luxury liner and airborne aircraft carrier, but eventually fell out of favor after the *Hindenburg* disaster in Lakehurst, New Jersey, on May 6, 1936.

Semi–rigid airships

An intermediate version of the rigid and non–rigid types, the envelope of the semi–rigid airship was fitted with a keel similar to that of a boat. The keel acted as a sort of metal spine which helped maintain the envelope's shape and supported the gondola and engines. Interest in the semi–rigid airship was short–lived, though it met with some success. In 1926, the Italian pilot Umberto Nobile navigated the airship *Norge* across the North Pole, accompanied by the Norwegian explorer Roald Amundsen.

The modern age of airships

Helium succeeded hydrogen as the gas of choice for the following generation of airships and continues as such in the latter half of the 20th century. Though its lifting capacity is less than that of hydrogen, helium is considered a safe resource because it is inflammable. During the 1920s, the United States discovered an abundant source of the gas in its own backyard and reinstated the blimp as a surveillance mechanism during World War II, maintaining a fleet of some of the largest non–rigid airships ever built. "It was the American monopoly of helium that made possible this Indian Summer of the small airship—long after every other country had abandoned the whole concept," wrote Patrick Abbott in his book *Airship*.

By the 1950s, the Goodyear Tire and Rubber Co. had become involved in the production of airships as part of the Navy's intended early warning defense system, and remained one of the largest manufacturers of blimps until the late 1980s. The Goodyear blimp is probably most noted as a high–flying billboard and camera mobile that has offered millions of television viewers a bird's–eye view of sporting events for several decades.

The early 1990s marked a resurgence in airships with the design of such models as the 222–foot (67.6 m) long *Sentinel 1000*. Built by Westinghouse Airships, Inc., its envelope is made of a lightweight, heavy–duty Dacron/Mylar/Tedlar composite that may eventually replace the traditional rubberized fabrics used by the *Sentinel*'s predecessors. According to *Aviation Week and Space Technology*, the craft "has a 345,000–cu.–ft. envelope and is powered by two modified Porsche automotive engines fitted with propellers that can be tilted through a range of plus 120 to minus 90 degrees."

Its potential for transporting heavy payloads, its quietness, and relative stability, have brought the airship back to design rooms around the world. Based partly on its fuel efficiency and the fact that its shape and skin make it virtually invisible to other radar, the United States has plans to reintroduce the blimp as a radar platform for its Air Defense Initiative. French scientists have used the airship to navigate and study rainforests by treetop, while environmentalists have considered its usefulness as a means of monitoring coastal pollution. The future may see airships powered by helicopter rotor systems and solar power, as well as the return of the rigid airship.

See also Aerodynamics; Aircraft; Balloon.

Further Reading:
Abbott, Patrick. *Airship*. New York: Charles Scribner's Sons, 1973.
Bell, Adrian. "On the Roof of the Rainforest." *New Scientist* 129 (1991): 48–51.
Garvey, William. "Rebirth of the Blimp." *Popular Mechanics* 168 (1991): 30–33+.
Hamer, Mick. "Airships Face a Military Future." *New Scientist* 115 (1987): 38–40.
Hollister, Anne. "Blimps." *Life Magazine* 4 (1988): 65–69.
Hughes, David. "New Westinghouse Airship Designed for Early Warning Surveillance." *Aviation Week and Space Technology* 135 (1991): 24–25.
Meyer, Henry Cord. *Airshipmen, Businessmen and Politics 1890–1940*. Washington D.C.: Smithsonian Institution Press, 1991.

John Spizzirri

Albatrosses

Found primarily in the southern oceans, albatrosses are large, long–lived seabirds in the family Diomedeidae, which contains some 13 species. All are superb fliers, and may be found far from land, soaring with their wings set in a characteristic bowed position. Together with petrels, shearwaters, and fulmars, albatrosses are grouped in the order Procellariformes, which includes hook–billed sea birds commonly known as "tubenoses." The extremely large nostrils on top of the bill lead to a pair of internal tubes, then to a highly developed olfactory center in the brain. Thus, unlike many other bird species, albatrosses possess a keen sense of smell; some people think that albatrosses can locate other individuals, food, and breeding and nesting areas by smell alone.

Flight and navigation

Albatrosses in flight are soaring birds, "floating" on the air for extended periods without flapping their wings. They have the greatest wingspan of any bird; the wings of the wandering albatross may reach 12 feet in length. Their slender wings have a very high aspect ratio, that is, a high ratio of wing length to wing width. A high aspect ratio minimizes drag (air resistance) dur-

ing flight because the area at the tip of the wing is relatively small compared to the overall wing length. In addition, since albatrosses are large, relatively heavy birds, the amount of load on the wing is also rather high. It is thought that albatrosses may be close to the structural limits of wing design. In spite of this, albatrosses can soar even in windless conditions if waves on the water below create a slight updraft of air.

While albatrosses are remarkably graceful on the wing, they are rather ungainly on land and on the surface of the water, to which they must descend to feed on fish and squid. To become airborne again, albatrosses must run across the surface of the water into the wind until they can hoist themselves aloft. Perhaps this ungraceful appearance is the reason the Laysan albatross of Midway Island was dubbed the "Gooney Bird." Many unfortunate birds were struck by airplanes there during World War II.

The navigational powers of albatrosses are impressive. They often spend many days at sea searching for food, out of sight of land and obvious geographical landmarks. Some 82% of Laysan albatrosses transported experimentally to unfamiliar sites up to 4,740 mi (7,630 km) from their home site were able to find their way back. In contrast, only 67% of Leach's storm–petrels were able to successfully navigate back to their home area over much shorter distances—up to 540 mi (870 km).

Salt regulation

Because albatrosses, and indeed all tubenoses, remain out at sea for days or even weeks while foraging, these birds must be physiologically capable of drinking seawater without harm. The potentially serious problem of salt/fluid balance is resolved by means of internal salt glands located at the base of the bill which support the salt and water regulation of the kidneys. Salt glands help regulate the birds' blood salt content, which rises following ingestion of seawater, by producing a concentrated, salty fluid which drips out of the tube on top of the bill. Consequently, all tubenoses have the habit of sneezing and shaking their heads frequently to clear this fluid.

Courtship rituals

Albatross courtship is unique among seabirds, both in its complexity and its duration. Both males and females engage in a coordinated "dancing" display, in which partners face one another and perform stereotyped and often synchronized behaviors such as bill "clappering" (where the bill is opened and closed

KEY TERMS

Aspect ratio of a wing—The ratio of a wing's length to its width; a higher value indicates less air resistance in flight.

Courtship rituals—Stereotyped displays performed by male and female prior to forming a partnership for rearing offspring.

Soaring—Sustained flight with wings extended without flapping, characteristic of albatrosses, hawks, vultures, and other birds.

Tubenoses—A group of marine birds including albatrosses, shearwaters, petrels, and fulmars, characterized by paired nasal tubes and salt glands.

repeatedly so that it is almost a blur); "sky calling" (in which the bird lifts its bill to the sky, uttering a call like the "moo" of a cow); and fanning the wings while prancing in place. These displays are performed in repeating cycles for up to an hour each, numerous times per day. It is thought that this behavior allows potential mates to evaluate each others' suitability as long–term partners.

Once formed, pair bonds in albatrosses appear to be permanent. After the initial courtship phase is over, the elaborate courtship rituals are much reduced or abandoned altogether in subsequent years. Researchers believe that these displays function more in pair formation than in the maintenance of the pair bond.

Care of the young

Albatrosses produce a single helpless chick, which in most species requires a full year to leave the nest, longer than any other seabird. This is almost certainly because of the great effort required to collect food for the chick, who may be left alone while the parent forages at sea for periods of 30–40 days, or even up to 80 days in the case of the wandering albatross.

To compensate for their lengthy absences, adults feed their chicks a rich meal of oil, procured from their fishy diet. As a result, albatrosses have been called the "oil tankers" of the bird world: a stream of oil, produced in the adult stomach, is delivered into the hungry chick's bill. In this way the young birds are able to develop a layer of fat to sustain them during long parental foraging trips.

Further Reading:

Ehrlich, Paul R., David S. Dobkin, and Darryl Wheye. *The Birder's Handbook: A Field Guide to the Natural History of North American Birds.* New York: Simon & Schuster, 1988.

Gill, Frank B. *Ornithology.* New York: Freeman, 1990.

Susan Andrew

Albedo

Albedo means *reflecting power* and comes from the Latin word, *albus,* for white or whiteness. The scientific meaning of albedo is the ability of a surface to reflect a certain proportion of visible light. A perfect mirror has an albedo of 100%; the polished surface of white metals like aluminum or silver comes close to that figure. Some metals like brass or copper, however, are colored, and they do not reflect all visible light equally well. This shows that albedo is dependent on the wavelength of the light being reflected.

In astronomy and meteorology, albedo describes the proportion of sunlight reflected back into outer space, for example, by a planet or a satellite. Without this reflection all the planets and their satellites would be invisible to us since, unlike the Sun, they are not self–luminous. The light from the Sun is white or yellowish because it is emitted from a star whose temperature is very high, close to 9,900°F (5,800°k).

The albedo of the Earth is around 30–35%. It is higher over snow–covered surfaces, or where there is a cloud cover, and lower over clear oceans. After 30–35% of the sunlight is reflected back to space, the remaining 65–70% is first absorbed by the Earth and its atmosphere and is re–emitted at the much longer wavelengths corresponding to the average temperature of our planet, 60°F (20.6°C). This re–emitted radiation is in the infrared part of the spectrum, and while we feel it as heat, it is not visible. Astronauts in outer space would not be able to see the Earth if it had no albedo. Earth is known as the *blue planet* because the albedo reflects the particular wavelength that lies in the blue area of the spectrum. Mars, on the other hand, appears reddish to us, probably because its surface formations contain a large proportion of iron oxide, which reflects red light.

The albedo plays a crucial role in determining the Earth's climate, as the average temperature at its sur-

A man with albinism stands with his normally pigmented father.

face is closely tied to the 65–70% of absorbed sunlight or solar energy. The light which is directly reflected back does not contribute to the warming of our planet. If, therefore, the albedo were to increase, the temperature at the Earth's surface would drop. If the albedo were to decrease, temperature would rise.

See also Weather.

Albinism

Albinism is a recessive inherited defect in melanin metabolism in which pigment is absent from hair, skin, and eyes (oculocutaneous albinism) or just from the eyes (ocular albinism). Melanin is a dark biological pigment that is formed as an end product of the metabolism of the amino acid tyrosine. When human skin is exposed to sunlight it gradually darkens or tans due to an increase in melanin. Tanning helps protect the underlying skin layers from the sun's harmful ultraviolet rays.

The most common examples of albinism are the white rats, rabbits, and mice found at pet stores. The characteristic white coats and pink eyes of these albino animals contrast dramatically with the brown or gray fur and dark eyes of genetically normal rats, rabbits, and mice. Domestic white chickens, geese, and horses are partial albinos. They retain pigment in their eyes, legs, and feet.

In the past, albinos were often regarded with fear or awe. Sometimes they were killed at birth, although albino births were common enough in some groups not to cause any excitement. For example, among the San Blas Indians of Panama, one in approximately 130 births is an albino. In the mid–nineteenth century, albinos were exhibited in carnival sideshows. Whole families were displayed at times and were described as a unique race of night people. They were said to live underground and to come out only at night when the light was dim and would not hurt their eyes.

In humans, albinism is rare. One person in 17,000 has some type of albinism. Researchers have currently identified 10 different types of oculocutaneous albinism and five types of ocular albinism based on clinical appearance. Humans who have oculocutaneous albinism are unable to produce melanin; they have white, yellow, or yellow–brown hair, very light eyes (usually blue or grayish rather than pink), and very fair skin. The irises of their eyes may appear violet or pinkish because they have very little pigment and allow light to reflect back from the reddish retina in the back of the eye. People with albinism may also suffer from a variety optical disorders such as near– or far–sightedness, nystagmus (rapid irregular movement of the eyes back and forth), or strabismus (muscle imbalance of the eyes causing crossed eyes or lazy eye). They are very sensitive to bright light and sunburn easily. They must take great care to remain covered, wear a hat, and apply sunscreen anytime they are outdoors, since their skin is highly susceptible to precancerous and cancerous growths. People with albinism often wear sunglasses or tinted lenses even indoors to reduce light intensity to a more bearable level.

In ocular albinism only the eyes lack melanin pigment, while the skin and hair show normal or near–normal color. People with this condition have a variety of eye disorders because the lack of pigment impairs normal eye development. They are extremely sensitive to bright light and especially to sunlight (photophobia). Treatment of ocular albinism includes the use of visual aids and sometimes surgery for strabismus.

Albinism occurs when melanocytes (melanin–producing cells) fail to produce melanin. This absence of melanin production happens primarily in two ways. In tyrosinase–negative albinism (the most common form), the enzyme tyrosinase is missing from the melanocytes. Tyrosinase is a catalyst in the conversion of tyrosine to melanin. When the enzyme is missing no melanin is produced. In tyrosinase–positive albinism, a defect in the body's tyrosine transport system impairs melanin production. One in every 34,000 persons in the United States has tyrosinase–negative albinism. It is equally common among blacks and whites, while more blacks than whites are affected by tyrosinase–positive albinism. Native Americans have a high incidence to both forms of albinism.

Albinism cannot be cured, but people with this condition can expect to live a normal lifespan. Protection of the skin and eyes from sunlight is of primary importance for individuals with albinism. The gene carrying the defect that produces albinism is recessive, so both parents must carry this recessive gene in order to produce a child with the condition. When both parents carry the gene (and neither has albinism), there is a one in four chance with each pregnancy that their child will have albinism. The inheritance pattern of ocular albinism is somewhat different. This condition

KEY TERMS

Catalyst—Any agent that accelerates a chemical reaction without entering the reaction or being changed by it.

Melanin—A dark biological pigment found in the hair, skin, and eyes. Melanin absorbs harmful ultraviolet rays and is an important screen against the sun.

Melanocyte—A melanin–producing cell.

Tyrosinase—An enzyme that catalyzes the conversion of tyrosine to melanin.

Tyrosine—An amino acid that is a precursor of thyroid hormones and melanin.

is X–linked, meaning that the recessive gene for ocular albinism is located on the X chromosome. X–linked ocular albinism appears almost exclusively in males who inherit the condition from their mothers. Recently a blood test has been developed to identify carriers of the gene that causes tyrosinase–negative albinism, and a similar test can identify this condition in the fetus by amniocentesis.

Vitiglio is another pigmentation disorder that resembles partial albinism. In this condition the skin exhibits stark white patches resulting from the destruction or absence of melanocytes. About 1% of the U. S. population has this disorder and it primarily affects people between the ages of 10 and 30. Unlike albinism, the specific cause of vitiglio is not known, although there seems to be a hereditary component, since about 30% of those who have vitiglio have family members with the condition. A link also exists between vitiglio and several other disorders with which it is often associated, including thyroid dysfunction, Addison's disease, and diabetes. Chemicals such as phenols may also cause vitiglio.

Further Reading:

Haefemeyer, J. W. and J. L. Knuth. "Albinism." *Journal of Ophthalmic Nursing and Technology* 10 (1991): 55–62.

Haefemeyer, J. W., R. A. King, and Bonnie LeRoy. *Facts about Albinism*. Minneapolis: International Albinism Center, 1992.

"Ocular Albinism." Philadelphia: National Organization for Albinism and Hypopigmentation.

Professional Guide to Diseases. 4th ed. Springhouse, PA: Springhouse Corp., 1992.

"What Is Albinism." Philadelphia: National Organization for Albinism and Hypopigmentation.

Larry Blaser

Alchemy

Alchemy was a system of thinking about nature that preceded and contributed to the development of the modern science of chemistry. It was popular in ancient China, Persia, and western Europe throughout antiquity and the Middle Ages. A combination of philosophy, metallurgical arts, and magic, alchemy was based on a world view postulating an integral correspondence between the microcosm and the macrocosm—the smallest and largest parts of the universe. Its objectives were to find ways of accelerating the rates at which metals were thought to "grow" within the earth in their development toward perfection (gold) and of accomplishing a similar perfection in humans by achieving eternal life.

Origin

While it is not known when alchemy originated, historians agree that alchemistic ideas and practices flourished in the ancient world within several cultural traditions, as evidenced by manuscripts dating from the early centuries of the Christian era. The term "alchemy" has remained mysterious; scholars have identified "al" as an Arabic article, and proposed various etymologies for the word "chem," but a clear explanation of the term is still lacking.

Alchemy in China

Alchemical practices, namely, attempts to attain immortality, are believed to have arisen in China in the fourth century B.C. in conjunction with spread of Taoism, a mystical spiritualist doctrine which emerged in reaction to the practical spirit of Confucianism, the dominant philosophy of the period. The main emphasis in Chinese alchemy, it seems, was not on transmutation—the changing of one metal into another—but on the search for human immortality. In their search for an elixir of immortality, court alchemists experimented with mercury, sulfur, and arsenic, often creating venomous potions; several emperors died after drinking them. Such spectacular failures eventually led to the disappearance of alchemy in China.

Arabic alchemy

Alchemy flourished in the Islamic Arab caliphate of Baghdad in the eighth and ninth centuries, when court scientists, encouraged by their rulers, began studying and translating Syriac manuscripts of Greek philosophical and scientific works. The greatest representative of Arabic alchemy was ar–Razi (c. 850–925), who worked in Baghdad. In their quest for gold, Arabic alchemists diligently studied and classified chemical elements and chemicals. Ar–Razi speculated about the possibility of using "strong waters," which were in reality corrosive salt solutions, as the critical ingredient for the creation of gold. Experimentation with salt solutions led to the discovery of mineral acids, but scholars are not sure if Arabic alchemy should be credited with this discovery.

Alchemy in the Western world

The history of Western alchemy probably begins in the Egyptian city of Alexandria, a great center of Greek learning during the Hellenistic period, a time of Greek cultural expansion and dominance following Alexander the Great's military conquests. Among the most prominent Alexandrian alchemists was Zosimos of Panopolis, Egypt, who may have lived in the third or fourth century A.D. In accordance with older traditions, Zosimos believed that a magical ingredient was needed for the creation of gold. Greek alchemists called this ingredient *xerion*, which is Greek for powder. Through Arabic, this word came into Latin and modern European languages as *elixir*, and later became known as the elusive "philosophers' stone."

After the fall of the Western Roman Empire in the fifth century, Greek science and philosophy, as well as alchemy, sank into oblivion. In was not until the 11th century that scholars rediscovered Greek learning, translating Syriac and Arabic manuscripts of Greek scientific and philosophical works into Latin, the universal language of educated Europeans. The pioneers of medieval science, such as Roger Bacon (c. 1219–c. 1292), viewed alchemy as a worthwhile intellectual pursuit, and alchemy continued to exert a powerful influence on intellectual life throughout the Middle Ages. However, as in ancient China, alchemists' failure to produce gold eventually provoked scepticism and led to the decline of alchemy. In the 16th century, however, alchemists, frustrated by their fruitless quest for gold, turned to more practical matters, such as the use of alchemy to create medicines. The greatest representative of this practical alchemy, which provided the basis for the development of chemistry as a science, was the Swiss physician and alchemist Philippus Aureolus Paracelsus (1493–1541), who successfully used chemicals in medicine. Although a believer in magic, astrology, and alchemy, Paracelsus was also an empirical scientist who significantly contributed to the development of medicine.

Although eclipsed by the development of empirical science, alchemy continued as a spiritual counterpart to modern science, which is viewed by some

KEY TERMS

Elixir—In alchemy, a substance supposed to have the power to change base metals into gold or to bring about human immortality.

Macrocosm—The whole extent of the universe.

Microcosm—A small part of the whole universe, as, for example, an individual human life.

Philosopher's Stone—A material thought by alchemists to have the power to bring about the transmutation of metals.

Transmutation—The conversion of one substance into another, as in the conversion of lead or iron into gold.

thinkers as too narrow in scope. While alchemy is often defined as "unscientific," great scientists, including Isaac Newton (1643–1727), took it seriously enough to conduct alchemical experiments. In addition, alchemy is credited with laying the foundation of chemistry. Not only did alchemists systematize and classify the knowledge of elements and chemicals, they also made a number of important discoveries, including sal ammoniac, saltpeter, alcohol, and mineral acids. They also developed a number of laboratory techniques, including distillation and crystallization.

See also Chemistry.

Further Reading:

Burckhardt, Titus. *Alchemy: Science of the Cosmos, Science of the Soul*. Translated by William Stoddart. Baltimore: Penguin Books, 1971.

Bynum, W. F., E. J. Browne, and Roy Porter. *Dictionary of the History of Science*. Princeton, NJ: Princeton University Press, 1981.

Holmyard, E. J. *Alchemy*. Edinburgh: T. & A. Constable, 1957.

Lapp, Ralph E., and the Editors of *Life. Matter*. New York: Time, 1963.

Partington, J. R. *A Short History of Chemistry*. 3rd edition. London: Macmillan, 1957.

Reed, John. *Prelude to Chemistry: An Outline of Alchemy, Its Literature and Relationships*. New York: Macmillan, 1937.

Taylor, F. Sherwood. *The Alchemists: Founders of Modern Chemistry*. New York: H. Schuman, 1949.

David E. Newton and Zoran Minderovic

Alcids see **Auks**

Alcohol

Alcohol is commonly thought of as either rubbing alcohol, the active ingredient in an alcoholic drink, or the additive that makes gasoline into gasohol. Chemists generalize its meaning to include almost any carbon–hydrogen compound with at least one hydroxyl group (symbolized as –OH) in its molecular structure. Categorized by the number and placement of the –OH groups, and the size and shape of the attached carbon molecule, alcohols are fundamental to organic chemical synthesis. The chemical industry produces and uses many different kinds of alcohols.

History

Techniques for producing the first alcoholic beverages, beer and wine, were developed millennia ago by various Middle Eastern and Far Eastern cultures. The word alcohol is of Arabic derivation. Ancient Egyptian papyrus scrolls exist with directions for making beer from dates and other plant foods. The alcohol in these drinks was ethanol (ethyl alcohol). Pure alcohol could not be made at that time; it was always mixed with the water, flavorings, and plant residue from the original fermentation. Almost all the ethanol produced was used for drinking, consumed as is perhaps after filtering or allowing the sediment to settle.

Fermentation, the oldest kind of alcohol production and possibly the oldest chemical technology in the world, is the action of yeast on sugars in solution. When fruits, vegetables, honey, molasses, or grains such as barley are mashed up in water and undergo fermentation, the yeast's metabolism of the sugars produces ethanol as a byproduct. Wood and starches can also be fermented, although their complex molecules must be broken down somewhat first. They always give small amounts of other larger alcohols (collectively called fusel oil) in addition to ethanol. Fermentation has been developed to an advanced technology and after distillation provides much of the fuel ethanol for addition to gasoline.

The process of distillation was discovered sometime after the first century A.D. Purer ethanol distilled from crude fermentation mixtures was then available for consumption, medicinal, and chemical uses. Eventually people learned to make methanol (wood alcohol) by destructively distilling wood but ethanol and methanol were the only alcohols available before the modern era.

The discovery and understanding of the alcohols as a group of chemical compounds has only happened in the last century. In 1926 the first industrial process for generating methanol was developed and since then many different alcohols have been made by direct chemical synthesis (the making of chemical compounds from simpler ones). The industrial processes that generate and consume alcohols change to keep up with modern technology and discoveries but the alcohols continue to occupy a central place in the science of chemical synthesis.

Names, properties, and uses

The formal name of an alcohol tells the number of hydroxyl (–OH) groups and the number of carbon atoms in the molecule, the names of any other atoms, and the attachment of the atoms in the molecule, although many older names are still used. Most simple alcohols end with the –ol suffix, added to the name of the molecule that had the same number of carbon atoms, but with a hydrogen atom in place of the hydroxyl group. Methanol, for example, has one carbon atom (like methane) and one hydroxyl group. Ethanol has two carbon atoms (like ethane) and one hydroxyl group. Two isomers of propanol exist (1–propanol and 2–propanol) because the hydroxyl group can be attached either at the end or in the middle of the three–carbon–atom chain. Rubbing alcohol contains mostly 2–propanol (also called isopropanol or isopropyl alcohol).

As the number of carbon atoms increases, the alcohol's solubility in water decreases. But as the number of hydroxyl groups grows, the solubility of the alcohol in water increases, as does its boiling point. Alcohols with two hydroxyl groups on adjacent carbon atoms are called glycols or diols. Ethylene glycol's properties of high water solubility, high boiling point, and low freezing point make it a good antifreeze for cars. These characteristics are due to the hydrogen bonding making the glycol associate firmly with water. Alcohols with more than three hydroxyl groups are called polyols. The sweetener sorbitol, often found in packaged baked goods and sugar–free gum, is a polyol with six carbon atoms and six hydroxyl groups in its molecules.

Most alcohols burn in air; ethanol has been frequently used as fuel. Methanol can sometimes be used as a fuel, though it evaporates too quickly for regular use in cars. Isopropyl alcohol is widely used in industry as a solvent for paints and chemical processes. In addition to its presence in alcoholic beverages, ethanol also is used as a solvent for food extracts such as vanilla, perfumes, and some types of paints and lacquers. Some alcohols can be ingested, although methanol is extremely toxic, and even ethanol is poiso-

The molecular structures of some alcohols:

METHANOL

ETHANOL

PROPYL ALCOHOL (PROPANOL)

ISOPROPYL ALCOHOL (ISOPROPANOL)

ETHYLENE GLYCOL

GLYCEROL

nous in large quantities. Glycerol, an alcohol with three carbon atoms and three hydroxyl groups in its molecules, has very low toxicity. It also possesses good moisturizing properties, so about 50% of the amount produced goes into foods and cosmetics.

Almost any organic chemical can be made by starting with the smaller alcohols, so both methanol and ethanol are in the top 50 industrial chemicals in the United States. Methanol occupies a particularly important place in industrial organic synthesis: it is used in the synthesis of organic chemicals such as formaldehyde (used to make various polymers), methyl–tert–butyl ether (the octane enhancer that replaced lead in unleaded gasoline), acetic acid, and synthetic gasoline, though this use has not yet become common.

Production

Alcohols are produced industrially from petroleum, coal, or other natural products. The "cracking" of crude petroleum yields many lower–molecule–weight

KEY TERMS

Alcohol—Any of the large number of molecules containing a hydroxyl (–OH) group bonded to a carbon atom to which only other carbon atoms or hydrogen atoms are bonded.

Azeotrope—A mixture of certain substances that distill together at the same boiling temperature, instead of separately.

Destructive distillation—An antiquated process for obtaining small amounts of alcohols, particularly methanol, from wood. The wood is heated to a high temperature in the absence of air, and gradually decomposes into a large number of chemicals.

Distillation—Collecting and condensing the vapor from a boiling solution. Each distinct, volatile chemical compound boils off individually at a specific temperature, so distillation is a way of purifying the volatile compounds in a mixture.

Ester—A molecule with a carbon both bonded to an ether linkage (carbon–oxygen–carbon), and double bonded to an oxygen.

Fermentation—The action of yeast metabolism on sugar solutions, resulting in the production of ethanol.

Glycol—An alcohol with two hydroxyl groups bonded to adjacent carbons in the molecule. Also called a diol.

Grignard synthesis—A classic laboratory method of preparing alcohols. An alkyl halide is first reacted with magnesium, and then the addition of an aldehyde or ketone results in the formation of the alcohol.

Hydroxyl group—The –OH group attached to a carbon atom in a molecule. If the carbon atom itself is attached to only other carbon atoms or hydrogen atoms, the molecule is an alcohol.

Intermediate—In a chemical synthesis, any compound that is generated only to be used in the next step of the process.

Polyol—An alcohol with many hydroxyl groups bonded to the carbon atom backbone of the molecule.

Primary alcohol—An alcohol with the hydroxyl group at one end of the chain of carbon atoms.

Secondary alcohol—An alcohol with the hydroxyl group in the middle of a straight chain of carbon atoms.

Synthesis gas—A mixture of carbon monoxide and hydrogen gases, obtainable both from coal and natural gas, and used widely for the synthesis of alcohols and other organic compounds in the chemical industry.

Tertiary alcohol—An alcohol with the hydroxyl group in the middle of a branched chain of carbon atoms.

---

chemical compounds, including some starting materials for alcohols such as ethylene and propylene. Ethylene reacts with hot steam over a catalyst to yield ethanol directly. A process known as hydration produces isopropyl alcohol when water is chemically added to propylene.

When "gasified," coal yields a mixture of hydrogen gas and carbon monoxide called synthesis gas, an important starting material for a variety of low– or high–molecular–weight alcohols. Methanol is now made almost entirely from synthesis gas. Before direct chemical synthesis was available, methanol was produced by the destructive distillation of wood (hence its older name, wood alcohol). Wood heated to a high temperature without air does not burn in the regular sense but decomposes into a very large number of different

chemicals, of which methanol and some other alcohols are a small fraction.

Distilling the ethanol from fermentation products gives a mixture of 95% ethanol and 5% water, resulting in an azeotrope. This is when two chemicals distill together instead of separating at their different boiling temperatures. Most industrial ethanol is 95% alcohol unless there is specific need for very dry ethanol.

Reactions

The plastics industry is a major consumer of all types of alcohols, because they are intermediates in a large variety of polymer syntheses. The hydroxyl group is the part of an alcohol that makes the molecule relatively reactive and thus very useful in synthesis. Dozens of reactions are possible. Important esters made from ethanol include the insecticide malathion, the fragrance compound ethyl cinnamate, and the polymer building blocks ethyl acrylate and ethyl methacrylate. Examples of esters made from methanol include methyl salicylate (oil of wintergreen), the perfume ingredients methyl paraben and methyl benzoate, and the polymer starting material methyl acrylate. High–molecule–weight alcohols converted into esters are widely used as plasticizers in the polymer industry, and very high–molecule–weight alcohols with 12 to 18 carbon atoms are used to make biodegradable surfactants (detergents).

Alcohols can also be oxidized. If the alcohol's hydroxyl group is at the end of a carbon atom chain, an oxidation reaction produces either a carboxylic acid or an aldehyde. If the hydroxyl group is attached in the middle of a straight carbon atom chain, an oxidation reaction produces a ketone. An alcohol whose hydroxyl group is attached to a carbon atom that also has three other carbon branches attached to it cannot be oxidized.

The formation of double bonds in hydrocarbons can be accomplished by the dehydration of alcohols. Acid added to the alcohol removes not only the hydroxyl group, but also a hydrogen atom from an adjacent carbon atom. The reaction is called a dehydration, because H–O–H (water) is removed from the molecule and a double bond forms between the two carbon atoms.

See also Distillation; Ethanol; Fermentation.

Further Reading:

Kent, J. A., ed. *Riegel's Handbook of Industrial Chemistry*. 9th ed. New York: Van Nostrand–Reinhold, 1992.

Morrison, R. T., and R. N. Boyd. *Organic Chemistry*. 6th ed. Englewood Cliffs, NJ: Prentice–Hall, 1992.

Partington, J. R. *Origins and Development of Applied Chemistry*. New York: Arno Press, 1975.

Szmant, H. H. *Organic Building Blocks of the Chemical Industry*. New York: Wiley, 1989.

Gail B. C. Marsella

Alcoholism

Alcoholism is a serious, chronic, potentially fatal condition manifested by a person's powerful addiction to alcoholic beverages. While experts have linked alcoholism to physiological (possibly hereditary), psychological, socioeconomic, ethnic, cultural, and other fac-

tors, there is no clear explanation of its genesis. Alcoholism occurs in all economic strata of society, in all age groups, from teenagers to the elderly, and in all races. Thus the popular stereotype of the alcoholic as a down–and–out person is misleading: alcoholics can be sufficiently functional to maintain a successful professional career. Particularly dangerous is the stereotype of alcoholism as an adult disease. Children and teenagers can become alcoholics—no age group is immune. While the abuse of alcoholic beverages has been known from time immemorial, the term alcoholism was coined in the 19th century by the Swedish physician Magnus Huss.

The psychology of alcoholism

It is commonly held that an alcoholic drinks in order to attain a euphoric state of mind. However, some researchers believe that it is not euphoria that the alcoholic seeks, but, more specifically, an escape from psychological pain. According to this view, to an alcoholic, sobriety is painful, and alcohol eases the pain. Most researchers, however, have not been able to explain alcoholism as simply a reaction to psychological distress. Instead, it is widely believed that physiological factors influence the alcoholic's drinking pattern.

The physiology of alcoholism

Some adults can drink alcohol–containing beverages in moderate amounts without experiencing significant side effects. There is evidence that having a glass or two of wine each day may be beneficial for the heart and digestive process.

Alcohol is a potent source of energy and calories. The ready availability of calories in alcohol gives an individual—alcoholic or nonalcoholic—a jolt of energy. These are, however, called empty calories, because alcohol contains no nourishment—vitamins, minerals, or other substances that the body needs. Some of the symptoms of alcoholism are the result of this phenomenon. The alcoholic can obtain the calories he needs from alcohol, but alcohol does not contain the nourishment his body needs to maintain such functions as the repair or replacement of cells.

Normally when alcohol enters the body it is rapidly absorbed from the stomach and distributed to all parts of the body in the blood. The alcohol is detoxified or broken down by first being changed into acetaldehyde when it flows through the liver. Acetaldehyde is a chemical that can cause painful reactions in the body. A second reaction in the liver alters acetaldehyde to form acetate, which is then changed into sugar. The liver of the alcoholic, however, is abnormally slow at the second–stage reaction.

Scientists have suggested that this conversion of acetaldehyde into acetate in the livers of alcoholics occurs at about half the speed that it does in the livers of nonalcoholics. Acetaldehyde thus accumulates in the bodies of alcoholics and causes many of the symptoms they exhibit, such as staggering gait, shaking hands, blinding headaches, and hallucinations.

Acetaldehyde is a very reactive and dominant chemical. In body cells it can block the normal chemical processes that should occur, including those in the brain. It can react with any other chemical in the immediate vicinity and produce byproducts of unpredictable reaction. Often the result of high levels of acetaldehyde is pain. The alcoholic may enter a cycle of drinking which leads to pain that is eased only by further drinking. The symptoms exhibited by some alcoholics when they begin to enter sobriety are collectively called delirium tremens or DTs. These symptoms can include hallucinations, illusions, trembling, and sweating.

The stages of alcoholism

The alcoholic, if he does not receive effective treatment, will progress through three stages of increasing deterioration. Alcoholism is difficult to diagnose in the early or adaptive stage. The alcoholic may drink heavily and remain functional. He does not experience any withdrawal symptoms other than the standard hangover following excessive drinking. The cells of the body adapt to large quantities of alcohol and still function. The alcohol provides a ready source of energy for cell functions and the cells become adept at using it. Even at this stage, however, alcohol intake will exact a penalty. The alcohol begins to attack cell structures, eroding cell membranes, altering cellular chemical balances, and otherwise upsetting a finely tuned system.

In this early stage of the condition the alcoholic can show a tremendous tolerance for alcoholic beverages. He might consume quantities that render normal adults hopelessly inebriated, yet not lose his ability to function. Only when his blood alcohol level begins to lessen does the alcoholic show symptoms of impairment. Thus, even though he does not exhibit signs of delirium tremens, the alcoholic in the early stage will know that he feels better when he drinks, functions more efficiently, and thinks more clearly. He will increase the frequency and amount of his drinking and will cross over into the middle stage of alcoholism.

No definite signpost marks the border between the early stage and middle stage of alcoholism, and the change may take years. Eventually, however, the alcoholic drinks to effect a cure, not to attain euphoria or efficiency in functioning. Deterioration of the cells of the body's organs and systems by steady infusion of alcohol begins to exert itself. The alcoholic experiences withdrawal symptoms that bring on physical and psychological pain that persists until it is eased by taking in more alcohol. These withdrawal symptoms soon worsen and require increased amounts of alcohol to erase them. The alcoholic will experience severe headaches, trembling, chills, and nausea when his blood alcohol level begins to ebb.

Full–blown DTs will eventually follow as the alcoholic continues to drink and his cellular metabolism becomes more and more dependent upon alcohol. He may have hallucinations, may become frightened and shrink into a corner, or may become dangerous as he lashes out to protect himself from an imaginary attack. He may manipulate his hands as if playing a game of cards or throwing dice or whittling. These symptoms are not benign, but signify a deep–seated stress on the body, especially the nervous system, and require immediate medical attention. The trauma of DTs may bring about a heart attack, stroke, or respiratory failure. Up to 25% of alcoholics experiencing DTs may die if not treated. At this stage, the alcoholic's body will no longer tolerate a state of low blood alcohol. His withdrawal symptoms become unimaginably painful, and he can no longer limit his consumption to socially acceptable times; he must have a drink when he arises in the morning, and will probably drink on the job to alleviate his withdrawal symptoms.

But as the alcoholic's drinking increases, so does the cellular demand for alcohol, to the extent that he can no longer forestall his painful symptoms without being constantly in a state of drunkenness. This is the final, deteriorative stage of alcoholism. At this stage the alcoholic's tolerance to alcohol lessens because of widespread organ damage, especially in the liver and nervous system. A minority, probably about 10%, die as a result of late–stage organ damage such as cirrhosis. The liver simply cannot perform its functions, and the blood has a steadily increasing level of toxins. Perhaps a third of those in the late stages of alcoholism die from accidents such as falling down stairs or drowning, or by committing suicide. The physiological damage is widespread: the heart, pancreas, digestive system, and respiratory system all have characteristic changes in the late–stage alcoholic. The liver, however, suffers the most extensive damage.

Larson, J.M. *Alcoholism: The Biochemical Connection.* New York: Villard Books, 1992.

Sandmaier, M. *The Invisible Alcoholics: Women and Alcohol.* 2nd ed. Bradenton, Fla.: Human Services Institute, 1992.

Thompson, L. *Correcting the Code: Inventing the Genetic Cure for the Human Body.* New York: Simon and Schuster, 1994.

Larry Blaser and Zoran Minderovic

KEY TERMS

Detoxification—The process of removing a poison or toxin from the body. The liver is the primary organ of detoxification in the body.

Metabolism—The physical and chemical processes that produce and maintain a living organism, including the breakdown of substances to provide energy for the organism.

Physiology—Study of the function of the organs or the body.

Treatment

There is no cure for alcoholism. Treatment consists of bringing the alcoholic to realization of his condition and the need to avoid alcohol. It is often unsuccessful, and many alcoholics relapse into their drinking habits even after a period of abstinence..

Long–term therapeutic programs of about four weeks usually are considered necessary to arm the alcoholic to function without drinking. He is first sedated to sleep through the initial, painful withdrawal symptoms. After that he is subjected to an educational program to reveal to him the reasons for his condition and its inevitably fatal outcome. He is introduced to a supportive network such as Alcoholics Anonymous, the oldest such program in existence, to provide guidance for the remainder of his life. Ideally, family members participate in the treatment process to some degree, since they too can benefit from an educated understanding of alcoholism and from a support network. During his institutional stay the alcoholic receives appropriate therapy for organ damage and a concentrated nutritional regimen to restore his metabolism to normalcy rather than to an alcohol dependency.

Upon completion of therapy, the alcoholic is released into the world to resume a normal life without the physiological need for alcohol. Statistically, he has about a 50–50 chance of success. While many alcoholics return to drinking in the face of everyday stress, many others do recover, frequently finding greater peace of mind in their recovery than they possessed even before their drinking became excessive.

See also Addiction; Alcohol; Cirrhosis; Fetal alcohol syndrome; Korsakoff's syndrome.

Further Reading:

Blum, K. and J.E. Payne, *Alcohol and the Addictive Brain.* New York: The Free Press, 1991.

Aldehydes

Aldehydes are a class of highly reactive organic chemical compounds that contain a carbonyl group (in which a carbon atom is double–bound to an oxygen atom) and at least one hydrogen atom bound to the alpha carbon (the central carbon atom in the carbonyl group). The aldehydes are similar to the ketones, which also contain a carbonyl group. In the aldehydes, however, the carbonyl group is attached to the end of a chain of carbon atoms, which is not the case with the ketones. The word aldehyde is a combination of parts of the words al(cohol) and dehyd(rogenated), because the first aldehyde was prepared by removing two hydrogen atoms (dehydrogenation) from ethanol. Molecules that contain an aldehyde group can be converted to alcohols by the addition of two hydrogen atoms to the central carbon oxygen double bond (reduction). Organic acids are the result of the introduction of one oxygen atom to the carbonyl group (oxidation). Aldehydes are very easy to detect by smell. Some are very fragrant, and others have a smell resembling that of rotten fruit.

Principal aldehydes

Formaldehyde is the simplest aldehyde. The central carbon atom in the carbonyl group is bound to two hydrogen atoms. Its chemical formula is $H_2C=O$. Formaldehyde, discovered in Russia by A. M. Butlerov in 1859, is a gas in its pure state. It is either mixed with water and sold as Formalin solutions or as a solid polymer called paraformaldehyde. The rather small formaldehyde molecule is very reactive and has found applications in the manufacture of many organic chemicals such as dyes and medical drugs. Formaldehyde is also a good insecticide, and it is used to kill germs in warehouses and ships. It is probably most familiar to the general public in its application as a preservative. In biology laboratories, animals and organs are suspended in formaldehyde solutions, which are also used as embalming fluid to preserve dead bodies from decay.

Acetaldehyde is the name of the shortest carbon chain aldehyde. It has a central carbon atom that has a double bond to an oxygen atom (the carbonyl group), a single bond to a hydrogen atom, and a single bond to another carbon atom connected to three hydrogen atoms (methyl group). Its chemical formula is written as CH_3CHO. Acetaldehyde is one of the oldest known aldehydes and was first made in 1774 by Carl Wilhelm Scheele. Its structure was not completely understood until 60 years later, when Justus von Liebig determined the constitution of acetaldehyde, described its preparation from ethanol, and gave the name of aldehydes to the chemical group.

The next larger aldehyde molecules have longer carbon atom chains with each carbon atom connected to two hydrogen atoms. This group of aldehydes is called aliphatic and has the general formula $CH_3(CH_2)_nCHO$, where n=1–6. When n=1, the aldehyde formula is CH_3CH_2CHO and is named propionaldehyde; when n=2, $CH_3(CH_2)_2CHO$ or butyraldehyde. The aliphatic aldehydes have irritating smells. For example, the smell of butyraldehyde, in low concentrations, resembles that of rotten butter. These medium–length aldehyde molecules are used as intermediates in the manufacture of other chemicals such as acetone and ethyl acetate used in finger nail polish remover. They are also important in the production of plastics.

Fatty aldehydes contain long chains of carbon atoms connected to an aldehyde group. They have between eight and 13 carbon atoms in their molecular formula. The fatty aldehydes have a very pleasant odor, with a fruity or a floral aroma, and can be detected in very low concentrations. Because of these characteristics, the fatty aldehydes are used in the formulation of many perfumes. The aldehyde that contains eight carbon atoms in its molecular formula is called octyl aldehyde and smells like oranges. The next longer aldehyde molecule is nonyl aldehyde, with nine carbon atoms in its structure, and has the odor of roses. A very powerful smelling compound is the 10–carbon aldehyde (decyl aldehyde), which has a scent of orange peel and is present in small concentration in most perfumes. Citral, a more complicated 10–carbon aldehyde, has the odor of lemons. Lauryl aldehyde, the 12–carbon aldehyde, smells like lilacs or violets. Fatty aldehydes are also added to soaps and detergents to give them their "fresh lemon scent."

The aromatic aldehydes have a benzene or phenyl ring connected to the aldehyde group. The aromatic aldehyde molecules have very complex structures but are probably the easiest to identify. Anisaldehyde smells like licorice. The odor of cinnamon found in various products is due to an aromatic aldehyde of complex structure named cinnamaldehyde. The aldehyde vanillin is a constituent in many vanilla–scented perfumes.

KEY TERMS

Aldehyde—A class of organic chemical compounds that contain a –CHO group.

Carbonyl group—A combination of a central carbon atom and an oxygen atom that have a double bond.

Dehydrogenation—The process of removing hydrogen atoms from a compound.

Methyl group—A terminal carbon atom connected to three hydrogen atoms.

Oxidation—The conversion of one chemical (compound) to another by the addition of oxygen atoms.

Reduction—The conversion of one chemical (compound) to another by deoxidation, which is accomplished by the addition of hydrogen atoms.

Further Reading:

Arctander, S. *Perfume and Flavor Materials of Natural Origin.* Elizabeth, NJ: S. Arctander, 1960.

Kirk–Othmer Encyclopedia of Chemical Technology, vol. 16. New York: John Wiley and Sons, 1991.

McMurry, J. *Organic Chemistry.* Pacific Grove, CA: Brooks/Cole Publishing Company, 1992.

Walker, J.F. *Formaldehyde.* New York: Reinhold Publishing Corp., 1974.

Andrew Poss

Alder trees see **Birch family**

Alewife see **Herrings**

Alfalfa see **Legumes**

Algae

Algae (singular: alga) are photosynthetic, eukaryotic organisms that do not develop multicellular sex organs. Algae can be unicellular, or they may be large,

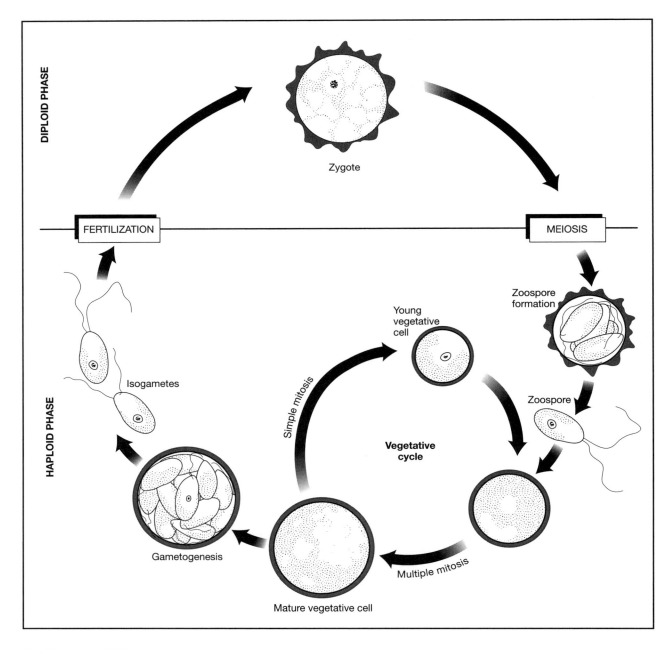

DIPLOID PHASE

Zygote

FERTILIZATION

MEIOSIS

Zoospore formation

Young vegetative cell

Isogametes

HAPLOID PHASE

Simple mitosis

Vegetative cycle

Zoospore

Gametogenesis

Multiple mitosis

Mature vegetative cell

The life cycle of *Chlorococcum,* a green alga.

multicellular organisms. Algae can occur in salt or fresh waters, or on the surfaces of moist soil or rocks. The multicellular algae develop specialized tissues, but they lack the true stems, leaves, or roots of the more complex, higher plants.

The algae are not a uniform group of organisms. They actually consist of seven divisions of distantly related organisms. These are considered together more as a matter of human convenience, than as a reflection of their ordered, biological, or evolutionary relation-

ships. Therefore, the term "algae" is a common one, rather than a word that connotes a specific, scientific meaning.

Algae and their characteristics

As considered here, all of the algae are eukaryotic organisms, meaning their cells have nuclear material of deoxyribonucleic acid (DNA) organized within a discrete, membrane–bounded organelle, known as the nucleus. In view of this definition, the so–called blue–green algae are not discussed in this article, because those organisms are prokaryotic (that is, without an organized nucleus) and are more appropriately referred to as blue–green bacteria, or as Cyanobacteria. The Cyanobacteria are also different from the true algae in that they do not contain the photosynthetic pigment known as chlorophyll a, they do not have cell walls made of cellulose, and they do not store energy as starch or related polysaccharides.

Virtually all species of algae are photosynthetic. They have a relatively simple anatomy, which can range in complexity from single–celled organisms to colonial filaments, plates, or spheres, to the large, multicellular structures of the brown algae, known as thalli. Algal cell walls are generally made of cellulose, but can contain pectin, a class of hemi–cellulose polysaccharides that give the algae a slimy feel. The larger, multicellular algae have relatively complex tissues, which can be organized into organ–like structures that serve particular functions.

Types of algae

The actual term "algae" is not very useful in formal biology, because a number of disparate groups of unrelated organisms are aggregated under this broad term. The seven divisions of organisms that are considered within the algae are the Euglenophyta, Chrysophyta, Pyrrophyta, Chlorophyta, Rhodophyta, Paeophyta, and Xanthophyta. These divisions are separated on the basis of various features including their morphology and the biochemistry of their pigments, cell walls, and energy–storage compounds. The colors of these various algae types differ according to their particular mixtures of photosynthetic pigments, which typically include a combination of one or more chlorophylls and various accessory pigments. The latter can include carotenoids, xanthophylls, and phycobilins (these mask the green of the primary chlorophylls in various ways). The major differences among the seven divisions of algae are briefly summarized below.

Euglenophyta (eulenoids)

The Euglenophyta or Euglenoids are 800 species of unicellular, protozoan–like algae, most of which occur in fresh waters. The euglenoids lack a true cell wall, and are bounded by a proteinaceous cell covering known as a pellicle. Euglenophytes have one to three flagellae for locomotion, and they store carbohydrate reserves as paramylon. The primary photosynthetic pigments of euglenophytes are chlorophylls a and b, while their accessory pigments are carotenoids and xanthophylls.

Most euglenoids have chloroplasts, and are photosynthetic. Some species, however, are heterotrophic, and feed on organic material suspended in the water. Even the photosynthetic species, however, are capable of surviving for some time if kept in the dark, as long as they are "fed" with suitable organic materials.

Chrysophyta (golden–brown algae)

The Chrysophyta are the golden–brown algae and diatoms, which respectively account for 1,100 and 40,000-100,000 species of unicellular algae. These algae occur in both marine and fresh waters, although most species are marine. The cell walls of golden–brown algae and diatoms are made of cellulose and pectic materials, a type of hemi–cellulose. In the diatoms especially, the cell wall is heavily impregnated with silica and is therefore quite rigid and resistant to decay. These algae store energy as a carbohydrate called leucosin, and also in oil droplets. The golden–brown algae achieve locomotion using one to two flagellae. The photosynthetic pigments of these algae are chlorophylls a and c, and the accessory pigments are carotenoids and xanthophylls, including a specialized pigment known as fucoxanthin.

Communities of diatoms (class Bacillariophyceae) can be extremely diverse, with more than 500 species commonly recorded from the phytoplankton, periphyton, and surface muds of individual ponds and lakes. Diatoms have double shells, or frustules, that are largely constructed of silica (SiO_2), the two halves of which (called valves) fit together like a pillbox. Diatom species are distinguished on the basis of the shape of their frustules, and the exquisite markings on the surface of these structures.

The golden–brown algae (class Chrysophyceae) are much less diverse than the diatoms. Some species of golden–brown algae lack cell walls, while others have pectin–rich walls. Golden–brown algae are especially important in open waters of the oceans, where they may dominate the productivity and biomass of the especially tiny size fractions of the phytoplankton. These are known as the nannoplankton, consisting of cells smaller than about 0.05 mm in diameter.

Pyrrophyta (fire algae)

The Pyrrophyta are the fire algae, including the dinoflagellates, which together account for 1,100 species of unicellular algae. Most of these species occur in marine ecosystems, but some are in fresh waters. The dinoflagellates have cell walls constructed of cellulose, and have two flagellae. These algae store energy as starch. The photosynthetic pigments of the

Pyrrophyta are chlorophylls *a* and *c*, and the accessory pigments are carotenoids and xanthophyll, including fucoxanthin.

Some species of dinoflagellates can temporarily achieve a great abundance, as events that are commonly known as "red tides" because of the resulting color of the water. Red tides can be toxic to marine animals, because of the presence of poisonous chemicals that are synthesized by the dinoflagellates. Some species of dinoflagellates develop a bioluminescence, which can be clearly seen at night, and may cause the surface of the ocean to look as if it were aflame.

Chlorophyta (green algae)

The Chlorophyta or green algae consist of about 7,000 species, most of which occur in fresh water, although some others are marine. Most green algae are microscopic, but a few species, such as those in the genus *Cladophora*, are multicellular and macroscopic. The cell walls of green algae are mostly constructed of cellulose, with some incorporation of hemicellulose, and calcium carbonate in some species. The food reserves of green algae are starch, and their cells can have two or more organelles known as flagella, which are used in a whip–like fashion for locomotion. The photosynthetic pigments of green algae are chlorophylls *a* and *b*, and their accessory pigments are carotenoids and xanthophylls.

Some common examples of green algae include the unicellular genera *Chlamydomonas* and *Chlorella*, which have species dispersed in a wide range of habitats. More complex green algae include *Gonium*, which forms small, spherical colonies of four to 32 cells, and *Volvox*, which forms much larger, hollow–spherical colonies consisting of tens of thousands of cells. Some other colonial species are much larger, for example, *Cladophora*, a filamentous species that can be several meters long, and *Codium magnum*, which can be as long as 26 ft (8 m).

The stoneworts (class Charophyceae) are a very distinctive group of green algae, which are sometimes treated as a separate division (the Charophyta). These algae can occur in fresh or brackish waters, and they have cell walls that contain large concentrations of calcium carbonate. Charophytes have relatively complex growth forms, with whorls of "branches" developing at their tissue nodes. Charophytes are also the only algae that develop multicellular sex organs, although these are not comparable to those of the higher plants.

Rhodophyta (red algae)

The Rhodophyta or red algae are 4,000 species of mostly marine algae, which are most diverse in tropical waters. Species of red algae range from microscopic to macroscopic in size. The larger species typically grow attached to a hard substrate, or they occur as epiphytes on other algae. The cell walls of red algae are constructed of cellulose and polysaccharides, such as agar and carrageenin. These algae lack flagellae, and they store energy as a specialized polysaccharide known as floridean starch. The photosynthetic pigments of red algae are chlorophylls *a* and *d*, and their accessory pigments are carotenoids, xanthophyll, and phycobilins.

Some examples of red algae include filamentous species such as *Pleonosporum* spp., so–called coralline algae such as *Porolithon* spp., which become heavily encrusted with calcium carbonate and contribute greatly to the building of tropical reefs, and thalloid species, such as the economically important Irish moss (*Chondrus crispus*).

Paeophyta (brown algae)

The Paeophyta or brown algae number about 1,500 species, almost all of which occur in marine environments. These seaweeds are especially abundant in cool waters. Species of brown algae are macroscopic in size, including the giant kelps that can routinely achieve lengths of tens of meters. Brown algae have cell walls constructed of cellulose and polysaccharides known as alginic acids. Some brown algae have relatively complex, differentiated tissues, including a hold-fast that secures the organism to its substrate, air bladders to aid with buoyancy, a supporting stalk or stipe, wide blades that provide the major surface for nutrient exchange and photosynthesis, and spore–producing, reproductive tissues. The specialized, reproductive cells of brown algae are shed into the water and are motile, using two flagella to achieve locomotion. The food reserves of these algae are carbohydrate polymers known as laminarin. Their photosynthetic pigments are chlorophylls *a* and *c*, while the accessory pigments are carotenoids and xanthophylls, including fucoxanthin, a brown–colored pigment that gives these algae their characteristic dark color.

Some examples of brown algae include the sargassum weed (*Sargassum* spp.), which dominates the extensive, floating ecosystem in the mid–Atlantic gyre known as the Sargasso Sea. Most brown seaweeds, however, occur on hard–bottom, coastal substrates, especially in cooler waters. Examples of these include the rockweeds (*Fucus* spp. and *Ascophyllum* spp.), the kelps (*Laminaria* spp.), and the giant kelps (*Macrocystis* spp. and *Nereocystis* spp.). The giant kelps are by far the largest of the algae, achieving a length as great as 328 ft (100 m).

Xanthophyta (yellow–green algae)

The Xanthophyta or yellow–green algae are 450 species that primarily occur in fresh waters. They are unicellular or small–colonial algae, with cell walls made of cellulose and pectic compounds, and sometimes containing silica. The yellow–green algae store carbohydrate as leucosin, and they can have two or more flagellae for locomotion. The primary photosynthetic pigment of yellow–green algae is chlorophyll *a*, and the accessory pigments are carotenoids and xanthophyll.

Ecological relationships

Many types of algae are microscopic, occurring in single cells or small colonies. The usual habitat of many of the microscopic algae is open waters, in which case they are known as phytoplankton. Many species, however, live on the surfaces of rocks and larger plants within shallow–water habitats, and these are known as periphyton. Other microscopic algae live on the moist surfaces of soil and rocks in terrestrial environments.

Microscopic algae are at the base of their ecological food web — these are the photosynthetic, primary producers that are fed upon by herbivores. In the open waters of ponds, lakes, and especially the vast oceans, the algal phytoplankton is the only means by which diffuse solar radiation can be fixed into biological compounds. In these open–water (or pelagic) habitats the phytoplankton are consumed by small, grazing animals known as zooplankton, most of which are crustaceans. The zooplankton are in turn fed upon by larger zooplankton or by small fish (these predators are known as planktivores), which may then be eaten by larger fish (or piscivores). At the top of the open–water food web may be fish–eating birds, seals, whales, very large fish such as sharks or bluefin tuna, or humans. Therefore, the possibility of all of the animals occurring higher in the food web, including the largest of the top predators, are ultimately dependent on the productivity of the microscopic phytoplankton of the pelagic marine ecosystem.

Other algae are macroscopic, meaning they can be readily observed without the aid of magnification. Some of these algae are enormous, with some species of kelps commonly reaching lengths greater than tens of meters long. Because they are primary producers, these macroscopic algae are also at the base of their ecological food web. In most cases, however, relatively few herbivores can directly consume the biomass of macroscopic algae, and the major trophic interaction of these plants is through the decomposer, or detritivore part of the food web. In addition, because of their large size macroscopic algae are critically important components of the physical structure of their ecosystems, providing habitat for a wide range of other organisms. The largest kelps develop a type of ecosystem that is appropriately referred to as a marine "forest" because of the scale and complexity of its habitat structure.

Some species of green algae occur as mutualistic symbionts with fungi, in an association of two organisms known as lichens. Lichens are common in many types of habitats (see entry on lichen). Other green algae occur in a mutualism with certain animals. In general, the host animal benefits from access to the photosynthetic products of the green alga, while the alga benefits from protection and access to inorganic nutrients. For example, species of unicellular *Chlorella* live inside of vacuoles within host cells of various species of freshwater protozoans, sponges, and hydra. Another species of green alga, *Platymonas convolutae*, occurs in cells of a marine flatworm, *Convoluta roscoffensis*. Various other green algae occur inside of marine mollusks known as nudibranchs. Similarly, various species of dinoflagellates occur as symbionts with marine corals.

Each species within an algal community has its particular ecological requirements and tolerances. Consequently, algal species tend to segregate along gradients in time and space, according to varying patterns of environmental resources, and of biological interactions, such as competition and predation. For example, during the growing season there is a time–series of varying abundances of phytoplankton species in open-water habitats. At certain times, particular species or closely related groups of species are abundant, but then these decline and other species of phytoplankton become dominant. This temporal dynamic is not totally predictable; it may vary significantly from year to year. The reasons for these patterns in the abundances and productivity of algal species are not understood, but they are likely associated with differences in their requirements for nutrients and other environmental factors, and perhaps with differing competitive abilities under resource–constrained conditions.

In a similar way, species of seaweeds tend to sort themselves out along stress–related environmental gradients associated with varying distances above and below the high–tide mark on rocky marine shores. The most important environmental stress for intertidal organisms is desiccation (drying), caused by exposure to the atmosphere at low tide, with the intensity of drying being related to the amount of time that is spent out of the water, and therefore to the distance above the high–tide line. For sub–tidal seaweeds the most important stress is the physical forces associated with waves, especially during storms. The various species of brown and red algae are arranged in rather predictable zonations along transects perpendicular to rocky shores. The largest kelps only occur in the sub–tidal habitats, because they are intolerant of desiccation. Within this near–shore habitat the species of algae are arranged in zones on the basis of their tolerance to the mechanical forces of wave action, as well as their competitive abilities in the least stressful, deeper–water habitats somewhat farther out to sea, where the tallest species grow and develop a kelp forest. In the intertidal habitat, the various species of wracks and rockweeds dominate particular zones at various distances from the low–tide mark, with the most desiccation–tolerant species occurring closest to the high–tide mark. Competition, however, also plays an important role in the distributions of the intertidal seaweeds.

Factors limiting the productivity of algae

Some species of algae can occur in extreme environments. For example, species of green algae have been observed in hot–water springs at Yellowstone National Park, in highly acidic volcanic lakes, in the extremely saline Great Salt Lake and Dead Sea, and on the surfaces of glaciers and snow. Some algae even survive suspended in the atmosphere as spores or in droplets of moisture.

These are, however, extremely stressful environmental conditions. Most algae occur in less stressful habitats, where their productivity tends to be limited by the availability of nutrients (assuming that sufficient light is available to support the photosynthetic process). In general, the productivity of freshwater algae is primarily limited by the availability of the nutrient phosphate (PO_4^{-3}), while that of marine algae is limited by nitrate (NO_3^-) or ammonium (NH_4^+). Some algal species, however, may have unusual nutrient requirements, and their productivity may be limited by certain micronutrients, such as silica, in the case of diatoms.

The structure of algal communities may also be greatly influenced by ecological interactions, such as competition and herbivory. For example, when herbivorous sea urchins are abundant, they can sometimes overgraze species of kelps in subtidal ecosystems of the west coast of North America, degrading the kelp forests. However, where sea otters (*Enhydra lutris*) are

abundant this does not happen because the otters are effective predators of the urchins.

Another example of a biological influence on the structure of an algal community concerns the zebra mussel (*Dreissena polymorpha*). This is a bivalve mollusk that has been accidentally introduced by ocean–going ships to the Great Lakes of North America, where it has become an important pest because it clogs water pipes with its prolific growths, and can displace native species by competitively appropriating hard–substrate habitats. More to the present point, however, the zebra mussel is such an effective filter–feeder on phytoplankton, that its large populations in parts of the Great Lakes are apparently responsible for some of the clarification of the water that has occurred in recent years. Grazing by the zebra mussel has actually resulted in decreased standing crops of phytoplankton, even in well–fertilized waters.

Economic products obtained from algae

The most important economic products obtained from algae are associated with brown and red seaweeds, which can be utilized as food for people, and as resources for the manufacturing of industrial products. These seaweeds are mostly harvested from the wild, although increasing attention is being paid to the cultivation of large algae.

Some species of algae can be directly eaten by humans, and in eastern Asia they can be especially popular, with various species used as foods. An especially common food is the red alga known as nori in Japan and as laver in western Europe (*Porphyra* spp.), which has long been eaten by coastal peoples of China and Japan. This alga is often used as a wrapper for other foods, such as rice or plums, or it may be cooked into a clear soup. Nori has been cultivated for centuries in eastern Asia. Another alga known as dulse or sea kale (*Rhodymenia palmata*) is consumed dried or cooked into various stews or soups. Other commonly eaten seaweeds include the sea lettuce (*Ulva lactuca*), and murlins or edible kelp (*Alaria esculenta*).

Potentially, seaweeds are quite nutritious foods, because about 50% of their weight occurs as carbohydrates, with smaller concentrations of proteins and fats, and diverse micronutrients, including iodine. In practice, however, seaweeds are not very nutritious foods for humans, because we do not have the enzymes necessary to metabolize the most abundant of the complex, algal carbohydrates.

In some places, coastal livestock such as sheep and cattle, and wild ungulates such as deer, will graze algal biomass from the intertidal zone at low tide. These animals can take better advantage of the algal carbohydrates than can humans, largely because of the digestive abilities of the symbiotic microorganisms in their rumens and guts. Sometimes, algal biomass is harvested by humans and added to the fodder of livestock as a source of micronutrients.

The major economic importance of brown seaweeds, however, is as a natural resource for the manufacturing of a class of industrial chemicals known as alginates. These chemicals are extracted from algal biomass, and are used as thickening agents and as stabilizers for emulsions in the industrial preparation of foods and pharmaceuticals, and for other purposes.

Agar is another seaweed product, prepared from the mucilaginous components of the cell walls of certain red algae. Agar is used in the manufacturing of pharmaceuticals and cosmetics, as a culture medium for laboratory microorganisms, and for other purposes, including the preparation of jellied desserts and soups. Carrageenin is another, agar–like compound obtained from red algae that is widely used to stabilize emulsions in paints, pharmaceuticals, ice cream, and other products. Irish moss (*Chondrus crispus*) is a purplish alga that is a major source of carrageenin.

Researchers are investigating methods for the economic cultivation of red and brown seaweeds for the production of alginates, agar, and carrageenin. In California, use has been made of rafts anchored to float about 12 meters below the surface, in shallow, less than 100–meter–deep water, to grow the highly productive, giant kelp *Macrocystis* as an industrial feedstock. Seaweeds are also cultivated on floating devices in coastal China, and research is investigating whether growth rates in dense plantings can be economically increased by enriching the seawater with nitrogen–containing fertilizers.

In some places, large quantities of the biomass of brown and red algae wash ashore, especially after severe storms that detach these algae from their substrates. This material, known as wrack, is an excellent substrate for composting into an organic–rich material that can greatly improve soil qualities in terms of aeration and water– and nutrient–holding capacity.

Over extremely long periods of time, the frustules of diatoms can accumulate in large quantities. This material is known as diatomaceous earth, and its small reserves are mined for use as a fine polishing substrate, as a fine filtering material, and for other industrial purposes.

Algae as environmental problems

Red tides are events of great abundance (or "blooms") of red, brown, or yellow–colored dinoflagellates of various species. These algae synthesize biochemicals, such as saxitoxin and domoic acid, which are extremely poisonous and can kill a wide range of marine animals, as well as humans who eat shellfish containing the toxins. The toxic syndromes of humans associated with dinoflagellate toxins are known as paralytic, diarrhetic, and amnesic shellfish poisoning.

Scientists cannot yet predict the environmental conditions that cause red tides to develop, although it seems that they are related to the availability and ratio of nutrients to temperature. Red tides are natural phenomena, but some scientists believe that human interference may have increased the frequency of these phenomena in some regions.

The dinoflagellates involved with toxic dinoflagellate blooms are commonly of the genera *Alexandrium*, *Dinophysis*, *Nitzchia*, or *Ptychodiscus*. The algal toxins can be accumulated by filter–feeding shellfish such as clams and oysters. If these are eaten while they contain red–tide toxins, they can poison humans or animals in the local ecosystem. Even creatures the size of large whales can die from eating fish containing large concentrations of dinoflagellate toxins.

In addition, freshwater algae can cause problems when they are overly abundant. Algal blooms can cause foul tastes in the water stored in reservoirs, which may be required by nearby towns or cities as drinking water. This can be a significant problem in naturally productive, shallow–water lakes of the prairies in North America.

Eutrophication is another major problem that is associated with algal blooms in lakes that are receiving large inputs of nutrients through sewage disposal or the runoff of agricultural fertilizers. Eutrophication can result in severe degradation of the aquatic ecosystem when large quantities of algal biomass sink to deeper waters and consume most of the oxygen during their decomposition. The anoxic (deficiency in oxygen) conditions that develop are lethal to the animals that live in the sediment and deep waters, including most species of fish. Because the primary limiting nutrient in fresh waters is usually phosphate, inputs of this nutrient can be specifically controlled by sewage treatment, and by the banning of detergents containing phosphorus. This has been done in many areas in North America, and eutrophication is now less an environmental problem than it used to be.

KEY TERMS

. . . .

Accessory pigments—Pigments such as the carotenoids, xanthophylls, and phycobilins, which can absorb solar radiation, and pass some of the absorbed energy to chlorophyll pigments for use in photosynthesis.

Bloom—An event of great abundance of phytoplankton, to the degree that the water is distinctly colored by the algal pigments.

Epiphyte—A plant that is using another plant as a platform upon which to grow.

Eukaryotic—This refers to organisms that have their nuclear material bounded by a membrane, and occurring within a cellular organelle called a nucleus.

Gyre—A zone of spirally circulating oceanic water, that tends to retain floating materials, as in the Sargasso Sea of the Atlantic Ocean.

Macroscopic—A size range that can be seen without magnification.

Microscopic—A size range that cannot be seen without magnification.

Mutualism—A symbiotic relationship between two species that is mutually beneficial.

Periphyton—Unicellular algae that occur on the surfaces of the rocks and larger plants of aquatic ecosystems.

Phytoplankton—Microscopic algae that occur suspended in the water column.

Primary photosynthetic pigment—This refers to the green–colored, chlorophyll pigments of algae and higher plants. These absorb red and blue light, to make the energy available to drive photosynthesis.

Thallus (plural: thalli)—A type of plant biomass that is not clearly differentiated into discrete tissues or organs.

Zooplankton—Tiny animals that occur in the water column. Most zooplankton graze on phytoplankton.

See also Biological community; Eukaryotae; Eutrophication; Food chain/web; Red tide; Symbiosis.

Further Reading:

Dawson, E.Y. *Marine Botany*. New York: Holt, Reinhart & Winston, 1968.

Freedman, B. *Environmental Ecology, 2nd ed*. San Diego: Academic Press, 1994.

Pritchard, H.N. and P.T. Bradt. *Biology of Non–vascular Plants. St. Louis Times Mirror* / Mosby: 1984.

Raven, P.H., R.F. Evert, and H. Curtis. *Biology of Plants*. New York: Worth Publishers Inc., 1976.

Bill Freedman

Algebra

Algebra is often referred to as a generalization of arithmetic. As such, it is a collection of rules: rules for translating words into the symbolic notation of mathematics, rules for formulating mathematical statements using symbolic notation, and rules for rewriting mathematical statements in a manner that leaves their truth unchanged.

The power of elementary algebra, which grew out of a desire to solve problems in arithmetic, stems from its use of variables to represent numbers. This allows the generalization of rules to whole sets of numbers. For example, the solution to a problem may be the variable x or a rule such as ab=ba can be stated for all numbers represented by the variables a and b.

Elementary algebra is concerned with expressing problems in terms of mathematical symbols and establishing general rules for the combination and manipulation of those symbols. There is another type of algebra, however, called abstract algebra, which is a further generalization of elementary algebra, and often bears little resemblance to arithmetic. Abstract algebra begins with a few basic assumptions about sets whose elements can be combined under one or more binary operations, and derives theorems that apply to all sets, satisfying the initial assumptions.

Elementary algebra

Algebra was popularized in the early ninth century by Al–Khowarizmi, an Arab mathematician, and the author of the first algebra book, Al-jabr wa'l Muqabalah, from which the English word algebra is derived. An influential book in its day, it remained the standard text in algebra for a long time. The title translates roughly to "restoring and balancing," referring to the primary algebraic method of performing an operation on one side of an equation and restoring the balance, or equality, by doing the same thing to the other side. In his book, Al–Khowarizmi did not use variables as we recognize them today, but concentrated on procedures and specific rules, presenting methods for solving numerous types of problems in arithmetic. Variables based on letters of the alphabet were first used in the late 16th century by the French mathematician François Viète. The idea is simply that a letter, usually from the English or Greek alphabet, stands for an element of a specific set. For example, x, y, and z are often used to represent a real number, z to represent a complex number, and n to stand for an integer. Variables are often used in mathematical statements to represent unknown quantities.

The rules of elementary algebra deal with the four familiar operations of addition $(+)$, multiplication $(\times)$, subtraction $(-)$, and division $(\div)$ of real numbers. Each operation is a rule for combining the real numbers, two at a time, in a way that gives a third real number. A combination of variables and numbers that are multiplied together, such as $64x^2$, $7yt$, $s/2$, $32xyz$, is called a monomial. The sum or difference of two monomials is referred to as a binomial, examples include, $64x^2+7yt$, $13t+6x$, and $12y-3ab/4$. The combination of three monomials is a trinomial $(6xy+3z-2)$, and the combination of more than three is a . All are referred to as algebraic expressions.

One primary objective in algebra is to determine what conditions make a statement true. Statements are usually made in the form of comparisons. One expression is greater than $(>)$, less than $(<)$, or equal to $(=)$ another expression, such as $6x+3 > 5$, $7x^2-4 < 2$, or $5x^2+6x = 3y+4$. The application of algebraic methods then proceeds in the following way. A problem to be solved is stated in mathematical terms using symbolic notation. This results in an equation (or inequality). The equation contains a variable; the value of the variable that makes the equation true represents the solution to the equation, and hence the solution to the problem. Finding that solution requires manipulation of the equation in a way that leaves it essentially unchanged, that is, the two sides must remain equal at all times. The object is to select operations that will isolate the variable on one side of the equation, so that the other side will represent the solution. Thus, the most fundamental rule of algebra is the principle of Al–Khowarizmi: whenever an operation is performed on one side of an equation, an equivalent operation must be performed on the other side bringing it back into balance. In this way, both sides of an equation remain equal.

Applications

Applications of algebra are found everywhere. The principles of algebra are applied in all branches of mathematics, for instance, calculus, geometry, topology. They are applied every day by men and women working in all types of business. As a typical example of applying algebraic methods, consider the following problem. A painter is given the job of whitewashing three billboards along the highway. The owner of the billboards has told the painter that each is a rectangle, and all three are the same size, but he does not remember their exact dimensions. He does have two old drawings, one indicating the height of each billboard is two feet less than half its width, and the other indicating each has a perimeter of 68 feet. The painter is interested in determining how many gallons of paint he will need to complete the job, if a gallon of paint covers 400 square feet. To solve this problem three basic steps must be completed. First, carefully list the available information, identifying any unknown quantities. Second, translate the information into symbolic notation by assigning variables to unknown quantities and writing equations. Third, solve the equation, or equations, for the unknown quantities.

Step one, list available information: (a) three billboards of equal size and shape, (b) shape is rectangular, (c) height is 2 feet less than 1/2 the width, (d) perimeter equals 2 times sum of height plus width equals 68 feet, (e) total area, equals height times width times 3, is unknown, (f) height and width are unknown, (g) paint covers 400 sq.ft. per gallon, (h) total area divided by 400 equals required gallons of paint.

Step two, translate. Assign variables and write equations.

Let: A = area; h = height; w = width; g = number of gallons of paint needed.

Then:(1) $h = 1/2w - 2$ (from [c] in step 1) (2) $2(h+w) = 68$ (from [d] in step 1) (3) $A = 3hw$ (from [e] in step 1) (4) $g = A/400$ (from [h] in step 1)

Step three, solve the equations. The right hand side of equation (1) can be substituted into equation (2) for h giving $2(1/2w-2+w) = 68$. By the commutative property, the quantity in parentheses is equal to $(1/2w+w-2)$, which is equal to $(3/2w-2)$. Thus, the equation $2(3/2w-2)=68$ is exactly equivalent to the original. Applying the distributive property to the left hand side of this new equation results in another equivalent expression, $3w-4 = 68$. To isolate w on one side of the equation, add 4 to both sides giving $3w-4+4 = 68+4$ or $3w = 72$. Finally, divide the expressions on each side of this last expression by 3 to isolate w. The result is w = 24 ft. Next, put the value 24 into equation (1) wherever w appears, $h = (1/2(24)-2)$, and do the arithmetic to find $h = (12-2) = 10$ft. Then, put the values of h and w into equation (3) to find the area, $A = 3\times10\times24 = 720$ sq. ft. Finally, substitute the value of A into equation (4) to find $g = 720/400 = 1.8$ gallons of paint.

Graphing algebraic equations

The methods of algebra are extended to geometry, and vice versa, by graphing. The value of graphing is two–fold. It can be used to describe geometric figures using the language of algebra, and it can be used to depict geometrically the algebraic relationship between two variables. For example, suppose that Fred is twice the age of his sister Irma. Since Irma's age is unknown, Fred's age is also unknown. The relationship between their ages can be expressed algebraically, though, by letting y represent Fred's age and x represent Irma's age. The result is y = 2x. Then, a graph, or picture, of the relationship can be drawn by indicating the points (x,y) in the Cartesian coordinate system for which the relationship y = 2x is always true. This is a straight line, and every point on it represents a possible combination of ages for Fred and Irma (of course negative ages have no meaning so x and y can only take on positive values). If a second relationship between their ages is given, for instance, Fred is three years older than Irma, then a second equation can be written, y = x+3, and a second graph can be drawn consisting of the ordered pairs (x,y) such that the relationship y = x+3 is always true. This second graph is also a straight line, and the point at which it intersects the line y = 2x is the point corresponding to the actual ages of Irma and Fred. For this example, the point is (3,6), meaning that Irma is three years old and Fred is six years old.

Linear algebra

Linear algebra involves the extension of techniques from elementary algebra to the solution of systems of linear equations. A linear equation is one in which no two variables are multiplied together, so that terms like xy, yz, x^2, y^2, and so on, do not appear. A system of equations is a set of two or more equations containing the same variables. Systems of equations arise in situations where two or more unknown quantities are present. In order for a unique solution to exist there must be as many independent conditions given as there unknowns, so that the number of equations that can be formulated equals the number of variables. Thus, we speak of two equations in two unknowns, three equations in three unknowns, and so forth. Consider the example of finding two numbers such that the first is six times larger than the second, and the second is 10 less that the first. This problem has two unknowns, and contains two independent conditions. In order to determine the two numbers, let x represent the first number and y represent the second number. Using the information provided, two equations can be formulated, x = 6y, from the first condition, and x–10 = y, from the second condition. To solve for y, replace x in the second equa-

tion with 6y from the first equation, giving 6y–10=y. Then, subtract y from both sides to obtain 5y–10=0, add 10 to both sides giving 5y=10, and divide both sides by 5 to find y=2. Finally, substitute y=2 into the first equation to obtain x=12. The first number, 12, is six times larger than the second, 2, and the second is 10 less than the first, as required. This simple example demonstrates the method of substitution. More general methods of solution involve the use of matrix algebra.

Matrix algebra

A matrix is a rectangular array of numbers, and matrix algebra involves the formulation of rules for manipulating matrices. The elements of a matrix are contained in square brackets and named by row and then column. For example the matrix has two rows and two columns, with the element (–6) located in row one column two. In general, a matrix can have i rows and j columns, so that an element of a matrix is denoted in double subscript notation by a_{ij}. The four elements in A are $a_{11} = 1$, $a_{12} = -6$, $a_{21} = 3$, $a_{22} = 2$. A matrix having m rows and n columns is called an "m by n" or (m x n) matrix. When the number of rows equals the number of columns the matrix is said to be square. In matrix algebra, the operations of addition and multiplication are extended to matrices and the fundamental principles for combining three or more matrices are developed. For example, two matrices are added by adding their corresponding elements. Thus, two matrices must each have the same number of rows and columns in order to be compatible for addition. When two matrices are compatible for addition, both the associative and commutative principles of elementary algebra continue to hold. One of the many applications of matrix algebra is the solution of systems of linear equations. The coefficients of a set of simultaneous equations are written in the form of a matrix, and a formula (known as Cramer's rule) is applied which provides the solution to n equations in n unknowns. The method is very powerful, especially when there are hundreds of unknowns, and a computer is available.

Abstract algebra

Abstract algebra represents a further generalization of elementary algebra. By defining such constructs as groups, based on a set of initial assumptions, called axioms, provides theorems that apply to all sets satisfying the abstract algebra axioms. A group is a set of elements together with a binary operation that satisfies three axioms. Because the binary operation in question may be any of a number of conceivable operations, including the familiar operations of addition, subtraction, multiplication, and division of real numbers, an asterisk or open circle is often used to indicate the operation. The three axioms that a set and its operation must satisfy in order to qualify as a group, are: (1) members of the set obey the associative principle [a × (b × c) = (a × b) × c]; (2) the set has an identity element, I, associated with the operation ×, such that a × I = a; (3) the set contains the inverse of each of its elements, that is, for each a in the set there is an inverse, a', such that a∗a' = I. A well known group is the set of integers, together with the operation of addition. If it happens that the commutative principle also holds, then the group is called a commutative group. The group formed by the integers together with the operation of addition is a commutative group, but the set of integers together with the operation of subtraction is not a group, because subtraction of integers is not associative. The set of integers together with the operation of multiplication is a commutative group, but division is not strictly an operation on the integers because it does not always result in another integer, so the integers together with division do not form a group. The set of rational numbers, however, together with the operation of division is a group. The power of abstract algebra derives from its generality. The properties of groups, for instance, apply to any set and operation that satisfy the axioms of a group. It does not matter whether that set contains real numbers, complex numbers, vectors, matrices, functions, or probabilities, to name a few possibilities.

See also Associative property; Arithmetic; Calculus; Commutative property; Complex numbers; Geometry; Identity element; Integers; Linear algebra; Matrix; Solution of equation; Topology; Variable.

Further Reading:

Algebra Blaster 3. CD–ROM for Windows. Davidson and Associates Inc., Torrance CA, 1994.

Davison, David M., Marsha Landau, Leah McCracken, and Linda Thompson. *Prentice Hall Pre–Algebra.* Needham, MA: Prentice Hall, 1992.

Immergut, Brita and Jean Burr Smith. *Arithmetic and Algebra Again.* New York: McGraw Hill, 1994.

McKeague, Charles P. *Intermediate Algebra, 5th ed.* Fort Worth: Saunders College Publishing, 1995.

J.R. Maddocks

Algorithm

An algorithm is a set of instructions which indicate a method for accomplishing a task. If followed cor-

---

rectly, an algorithm guarantees successful completion even without the use of any intelligence. The term algorithm is derived from the name Al–Khowarizmi, a ninth century Arabian mathematician who is credited for discovering algebra. With the advent of computers, which are particularly adept at utilizing algorithms, the creation of new and faster algorithms has become an important consideration in the study of theoretical computer science.

Algorithms can be written to solve any conceivable problem. For example, an algorithm can be developed for tying a shoe, making cookies, or determining the area of a circle. In an algorithm for tieing a shoe each step, from obtaining a shoe with a lace to releasing the string after it is tied, is spelled out. The individual steps are written in such a way that no judgement is ever required to successfully carry them out. The length of time required to complete an algorithm is directly dependent on the number of steps involved. The more steps, the longer it takes to complete. Consequently, algorithms are classified as fast or slow depending on the speed at which they allow a task to be completed. Typically, fast algorithms are usable while slow algorithms are unusable.

See also Computer, analog; Computer, digital.

Aliphatic hydrocarbon see **Hydrocarbon**

Alkali see **Acids and bases**

Alkali metals

The first column on the periodic table of the chemical elements is collectively called the alkali metal group: lithium, sodium, potassium, rubidium, cesium, and francium. Because their outer electron structure is similar, they all have somewhat similar chemical and physical properties. All are shiny, soft enough to cut with a knife, and most are white (cesium is yellow white). All react with water to give hydrogen gas and the metal hydroxide; the heavier alkali metals react with such vigorous evolution of heat that the hydrogen often bursts into flame. They also react with the oxygen in the air to give either an oxide, peroxide, or superoxide, depending on the metal. Alkali metals almost always form ions with a positive (+1) charge, and are so reactive as elements that virtually all occur in nature only in compound form. Sodium is the most abundant, followed by potassium, rubidium, lithium, and cesium. Francium is intensely radioactive and extremely rare; only the tiniest traces occur in the Earth's crust.

Most of the alkali metals glow with a characteristic color when placed in a flame; lithium is bright red, sodium gives off an intense yellow, potassium is violet, rubidium is a dark red, and cesium gives off blue light. These flame tests are useful for identifying the metals. Additionally, a striking use of sodium's characteristic emitted yellow light is in highly specialized lightbulbs, such as the very bright sodium vapor lights that appear along highways. In these bulbs, sodium atoms are excited with electricity, not a flame. Lightbulbs made with sodium use less electricity than conventional bulbs and are brighter, because the sodium gives off a larger percentage of its energy as light rather than heat.

Lithium

Lithium was discovered in 1817 by the J.A. Arfvedson, but it was not isolated as the free metal until 1821, by W.T. Brande. It occurs naturally in small quantities (about 20 parts per million in the earth's crust), normally bound up with aluminum and silica in minerals. It is the smallest alkali metal, with an atomic number of 3 and an atomic weight of 6.94 amu. It has a melting point of 357°F (180.5°C), and a boiling point of 2,419°F (1,326°C).

Lithium carbonate is well known for its ability to calm the mood swings of manic–depressive psychosis, a serious mental disorder. Industrially, however, it is used in lubricants, in batteries, in glass (to make it harder), and in alloys of lead, aluminum, and magnesium to make them less dense and stronger.

Sodium

Sodium is the second element in the alkali metal group, with an atomic number of 11 and an atomic weight of 22.99 amu. Its melting point (208°F/97.8°C) and boiling point (1,621°F/883°C) are both lower than those of lithium, a trend that continues in the alkali metal group; as the atomic mass and size increase, the melting and boiling points decrease. Humphrey Davy first isolated sodium metal by passing electricity through molten sodium hydroxide in 1807. It occurs naturally, in compound form, in relatively large amounts—about 20,000 parts per million in the earth's crust, plus a large concentration in seawater. Sodium chloride (or common salt) is one of the most common compounds on earth, followed closely by sodium carbonate (also called soda ash or washing soda.) Both of these are obtained now largely by mining.

Sodium compounds of various kinds are vital to industry. Sodium nitrite is a principle ingredient in gunpowder. The pulp and paper industry uses large amounts of sodium hydroxide, sodium carbonate, and sodium sulfate; the latter helps dissolve the lignin from wood pulp in the Kraft process so it can be made into cardboard and brown paper. In addition to paper pulping, sodium carbonate is also used by power companies to absorb sulfur dioxide, a serious pollutant, from smokestack gases. Sodium carbonate is also important to the glass and detergent industries. Sodium hydroxide is one of the top 10 industrially produced chemicals, heavily used in manufacturing. Sodium chloride is used in foods, in water softeners, and as a de–icer for roads and sidewalks. Sodium bicarbonate (baking soda) is produced for the food industry as well.

Many useful chemicals and processes, particularly those of the "chlor–alkali" industry, can trace their production back to sodium chloride. Passing electricity through a concentrated salt water solution (the electrolysis of brine) produces sodium hydroxide and chlorine gas. Electrolysis of molten sodium chloride, on the other hand, yields elemental sodium and chlorine gas. Sodium sulfate is prepared in large quantities by reacting sulfuric acid with sodium chloride.

Biochemically, sodium is a vital nutrient, although excesses of it can aggravate high blood pressure. Sodium compounds regulate nerve transmission, alter membrane permeability, and perform myriad other tasks for living organisms.

Potassium

Potassium, the third element in the alkali metal group, has an atomic number of 19 and an atomic mass of 39.10 amu. Its melting point and boiling point are 147°F (63.7°C) and 1,393°F (756°C) respectively. Davy discovered and isolated potassium in 1807, by passing electricity through molten potassium hydroxide to obtain the free metal. Potassium is nearly as abundant as sodium in the earth's crust (21,000 parts per million). Much less potassium than sodium is present in seawater, however, partly because the plant life of the world absorbs potassium in large quantities. The chief minerals of potassium are sylvite, sylvinite, and carnallite.

Almost all the potassium used industrially goes into fertilizer, although small amounts of potassium hydroxide, potassium chlorate, and potassium bromide are important, respectively, in the detergent, explosive, and photography industries. Like sodium, potassium is a vital nutrient for organisms in a variety of ways.

Rubidium and cesium

Rubidium, the fourth element in the alkali metal group, has an atomic number of 37 and an atomic weight of 85.47 amu. Its melting point is 102°F (38.98°C), and its boiling point is 1,270°F (688°C). Cesium, the second to last element in the group, has an atomic number of 55, an atomic weight of 132.90 amu, a melting point of 257.4°F (28.59°C), and a boiling point of 1,274°F (690°C). Both were discovered in 1860–61 by R.W. Bunsen and G.R. Kirchoff. They were the first two elements to be discovered with a spectroscope.

Both rubidium and cesium are rare in the Earth's crust (rubidium at 90 parts per million and cesium only 3 parts per million.) The main mineral in which cesium can be found is pollucite. Rubidium can be found in pollucite, lepidolite, and carnallite. Rubidium is used almost exclusively for research, but cesium has some highly specialized industrial uses, including special glasses and radiation detection equipment.

Francium

Marguerite Perey discovered francium in 1939, and named it after her homeland, France. Almost no francium occurs naturally on the earth, except very small amounts in uranium ores. Additionally, it is very radioactive, so the very tiny amounts produced by bombarding radium with neutrons are used almost exclusively for pure research. Presumably it has chemistry resembling the other alkali metals, although much of that must remain speculative.

See also Elements, families of; Lithium; Periodic table; Sodium.

Further Reading:
Emsley, J., *The Elements*, 2nd ed. Clarendon Press, 1991.

Greenwood, N.N. and A. Earnshaw, *Chemistry of the Elements*. New York: Pergamon Press, 1986.

Gail B.C. Marsella

Alkaline earth metals

The second column on the periodic table of the chemical elements is collectively called the alkaline earth metal group: beryllium, magnesium, calcium, strontium, barium, and radium. Because the outer electron structure in all of these elements is similar, they all have somewhat similar chemical and physical properties. All are shiny, fairly soft—although harder than the alkali metals—and most are white or silvery colored. The steady increase in melting and boiling points with increasing molecular mass noticed in the alkali metal group is less pronounced in the alkaline earths; beryllium has the highest rather than the lowest melting point, for example, and the other metals do not follow a consistent pattern.

All the alkaline earth metals react with water to give hydrogen gas and the metal hydroxide, although somewhat less vigorously than the alkali metals. Magnesium metal can be set on fire, and burns with an extremely intense white light as it combines with oxygen in the air to form magnesium oxide. Strontium, barium, and calcium react readily with oxygen in the air to form their oxides.

Alkaline earth metals almost always form ions with a positive (+2) charge, and are sufficiently reactive as elements that they usually occur in nature only in compound form, frequently as carbonates or sulfates. Calcium is by far the most abundant, followed by magnesium, and then in much lesser amounts barium, strontium, and beryllium. Radium is radioactive and fairly rare; what exists in the Earth's crust occurs almost exclusively in uranium deposits.

Several of the alkaline earth metals glow with a characteristic color when placed in a flame; calcium gives off an orange light, strontium a very bright red, and barium an apple green. These flame tests are useful for identifying the metals. Strontium compounds are often added to fireworks displays to obtain the most vivid reds.

Beryllium

Beryllium, the smallest alkaline earth metal, is atomic number 4 on the periodic table, has an atomic weight of 9.01 amu, and melting and boiling points of 2,349°F (1,287°C) and about 4,712°F (2,500°C), respectively. It was discovered by N. L. Vauquelin in 1797 after a mineralogist named R.J. Hauy noticed that emeralds and beryl possessed many similar properties and might be identical substances, but it was not until 30 years later that the free metal was isolated (independently) by F. Wohler and A. Bussy. It occurs naturally in the precious stones emerald and aquamarine, which are both forms of the mineral beryl, a beryllium aluminosilicate compound.

Beryllium has no biochemical function and is extremely toxic to human beings, but small amounts (about 2%) impart superior characteristics, such as high strength, wear resistance, and temperature stability, to alloys. Copper–beryllium alloys make good hand tools in industries that use flammable solvents, because the tools do not cause sparks when struck against other objects. Nickel–beryllium alloys are used for specialized electrical connections and various high temperature applications. Beryllium is used instead of glass in x ray tubes because it lets through more of the x ray radiation than glass would.

Magnesium

Magnesium is atomic number 12, has an atomic weight of 24.31 amu, and has melting and boiling points of 1,200°F (649°C) and 2,021°F (1,105°C), respectively. It was isolated (as were many other alkali and alkaline earth metals) by British chemist Humphry Davy in 1808, although its existence had been known since 1755. Magnesium, like calcium, is one of the most common elements, existing at about 23,000 parts per million in the Earth's crust. Its most common mineral forms in nature are dolomite and magnesite (both carbonates), and carnallite (a chloride); relatively large amounts (about 1,200 parts per million) are also present in seawater. Asbestos is a magnesium silicate mineral, as are soapstone (or talc) and mica.

Magnesium performs a critical role in living things because it is a component of chlorophyll, the green pigment that captures sunlight energy for storage in plant sugars during photosynthesis. Chlorophyll is a large molecule called a porphyrin; the magnesium occupies the center of the porphyrin molecule. (In the animal kingdom, a similar porphyrin called heme allows hemoglobin to transport oxygen around in the bloodstream; in heme's case, however, iron rather than magnesium occupies the central place in the porphyrin.)

Elemental magnesium is a strong, light metal, particularly when alloyed with other metals like aluminum or zinc, and has many uses in construction; airplane parts are often made of magnesium alloys. Some of magnesium's rare earth alloys are so temperature resistant that they are used to make car engine parts. In organic chemistry, magnesium combines with alkyl halides to give Grignard reagents, vitally important in organic chemical synthesis because of their versatility. Almost any type of organic compound can be prepared by the proper selection, preparation, and reaction of a Grignard reagent.

Calcium

Calcium is atomic number 20, has an atomic weight of 40.08, and has melting and boiling points of 1,536°F (839°C) and 2,721°F (1,494°C), respectively. Davy isolated it in 1808 by electrolytic methods. It is the third most common metal on earth, exceeded only by iron and aluminum, and the fifth most common element (41,000 parts per million in the Earth's crust, and about 400 parts per million in seawater.) The principle sources of calcium are limestone and dolomite (both carbonates), and gypsum (the sulfate.) Other natural materials made of calcium carbonate include coral, chalk, and marble.

Calcium is an essential nutrient for living things, and its compounds find use in myriad industries. Both limestone and gypsum have been used in building materials since ancient times; in general, gypsum was used in drier climates. Marble is also a good building material. Limestone and dolomite are the principle sources of slaked lime (calcium hydroxide) and quick lime (calcium oxide) for the steel, glass, paper, dairy, and metallurgical industries. Lime can act as a flux to remove impurities from steel, as a neutralizing agent for acidic industrial waste, as a reagent for reclaiming sodium hydroxide from paper pulping waste, and as a "scrubbing" compound to remove pollutants from smokestack effluent. The paper industry uses calcium carbonate as an additive to give smoothness and opacity to the finished paper, and the food, cosmetic, and pharmaceutical industries use it in antacids, toothpaste, chewing gum, and vitamins.

Strontium

Strontium is atomic number 38, has an atomic weight of 87.62, and has melting and boiling points of 1,614°F (768°C) and 2,518°F (1,381°C), respectively. A. Crawford identified it as an element in 1790, and in 1808, Davy produced it as the free metal. It occurs in the Earth's crust at about 370 parts per million, mostly as the minerals celestite (the sulfate) and strontianite (the carbonate), and occurs in the ocean at about eight parts per million. In addition to its use in fireworks, strontium is also a glass additive.

Barium

Barium is atomic number 56, has an atomic weight of 137.3, and has melting and boiling points of 1,341°F (727°C) and about 3,362°F (1,850°C), respectively. It was isolated in 1808 by Davy, using a variation of his usual electrolytic process. Barite (the sulfate) is the main ore from which barium can be obtained, although witherite (the carbonate) was at one time also mined. It is not particularly plentiful, occurring in about 500 parts per million in the Earth's crust, and on the average about 10 parts per billion in seawater. By far, most of the barium sulfate mined is used to make a sort of lubricating mud used in well–drilling operations, although small amounts of barium are alloyed with nickel for specialized uses, and some barium sulfate is used in medicine. Barium itself is toxic and has no biochemical function in living things.

Radium

Radium is atomic number 88, has an atomic weight of 226.0 amu, and has melting and boiling points of about 1,292°F (700°C) and about 3,092°F (1,700°C), respectively. It was discovered by Marie and Pierre Curie in 1898; they extracted a small quantity as radium chloride by processing tons of the uranium ore called pitchblende. Radium exists in the Earth's crust in only about .6 parts per trillion, and almost none can be found in seawater. All of the isotopes of radium are radioactive, and consequently hazardous to living things. It was formerly used in medicine to treat various kinds of cancer and other conditions, but its use has declined as safer radioisotopes have been discovered. Radium was also used to paint the luminous numbers on watch dials, but that use has been stopped for safety reasons.

See also Calcium; Chlorophyll; Elements, families of; Periodic table.

Further Reading:

Emsley, J., *The Elements*, 2nd ed. Clarendon Press, 1991.
Greenwood, N.N. and A. Earnshaw, *Chemistry of the Elements*. New York: Pergamon Press, 1986.

Gail B.C. Marsella

Alkaloid

Alkaloids are chemical compounds found in plants that can react with acids to form salts. All alkaloids contain the element nitrogen, usually in complex, multi–ring structures.

Role in the plant

Between 10% and 15% of all plants contain some type of alkaloid. It is unclear why alkaloids are so common, and it is a matter of controversy among scientists. Some believe that plants rid themselves of excess nitrogen through the production of alkaloids just as humans and other mammals convert excess nitrogen into urea to be passed in the urine. Some modify this theory by suggesting that plants use alkaloids to temporarily store nitrogen for later use, instead of discarding altogether this difficult–to–obtain element.

Perhaps the most likely theory is that the presence of alkaloids discourages insects and animals from eating plants. The poisonous nature of most alkaloids supports this theory, although various alkaloids that are employed in small quantities for specific purposes can be useful to man.

Role in animals

Many alkaloids act by blocking or intensifying the actions of neurotransmitters, chemicals released by nerve cells in response to an electrical impulse called a neural signal. Neurotransmitters diffuse into neighboring cells where they produce an appropriate response, such as an electrical impulse, in another nerve cell or contraction in a muscle cell.

Each nerve cell produces only one type of neurotransmitter; acetylcholine and norepinephrine are the most common. Cells may respond to more than one type of neurotransmitter, however, and the response to each type may be different.

Medical use

A number of alkaloids are used as drugs. Among the oldest and best known of these is quinine, derived from the bark of the tropical cinchona tree. Indians of South America have long used cinchona bark to reduce fever, much as willow bark was used in Europe as a source of aspirin. In the 1600s Europeans discovered that the bark could actually cure malaria—one of the most debilitating and fatal diseases of tropical and subtropical regions.

Quinine was purified as early as 1823, and soon it replaced crude cinchona bark as the standard treatment for malaria. Not until the 1930s was quinine replaced by synthetic analogues that offered fewer side effects and a more reliable supply. Quinine is still used as the principal flavoring agent in tonic water—a beverage named for its ability to prevent malarial symptoms.

Cinchona bark also produces quinidine. It is used primarily to control abnormalities of heart rhythm such as fibrillation, a series of rapidly quivering beats that do not pump any blood, and heart block, a condition in which electrical currents fail to coordinate the contractions of the upper and lower chambers of the heart.

Vincaleukoblastine and vincristine, two alkaloids derived from the periwinkle plant (*Catharanthus roseus*), are used effectively for the treatment of white–blood–cell cancers. Vincaleukoblastine is especially useful against lymphoma (cancer of the lymph glands), while vincristine is used against the most common form of childhood leukemia.

Atropine is an alkaloid produced by several plants, including deadly nightshade (*Atropa belladonna*), Jimson weed (*Datura stramonium*), and henbane (*Hyoscyamus niger*). It has a variety of medical uses, as it is able to relax smooth muscle by blocking action of the neurotransmitter acetylcholine. Atropine is most commonly used to dilate the pupil during eye examinations. Atropine also relieves nasal congestion and as serves as an antidote to nerve gas and insecticide poisoning.

Pilocarpine, derived from several Brazilian shrubs of the genus *Pilocarpus*, is another alkaloid used in ophthalmology, the medical specialty that treats the eye. This drug stimulates the drainage of excess fluid from the eyeball, relieving the high pressure in the eye caused by glaucoma. If untreated, glaucoma can lead to blindness.

Introduction of reserpine in the 1950s revolutionized high blood pressure treatment and brought new hope to those suffering from this previously untreatable and life–threatening condition. Derived from tropical trees and shrubs of the genus Aauwolfia, reserpine works by depleting the body's stores of the neurotransmitter norepinephrine. Among its other functions, norepinephrine contracts the arteries and thereby contributes to high blood pressure.

Unfortunately, reserpine also causes drowsiness and sometimes severe depression. Medications without these side effects have been developed in recent decades, and reserpine is rarely used.

Alkaloids for pain and pleasure

Many medically useful alkaloids act by way of the peripheral nervous system; others work directly on the brain. Prominent among the latter are the pain relievers morphine and codeine, derived from the opium poppy (*Papaver somniferum*). Morphine is the stronger of the two, but codeine is often prescribed for moderate pain. Codeine is also an effective cough suppressant; for years it was a standard component of cough syrups. Now, however, it has been replaced for the most part by drugs that do not have the psychological side effects of codeine.

Both morphine and codeine are addictive drugs that produce a state of relaxed, dreamy euphoria—an exaggerated state of "feeling good," referred to by drug addicts as a "high." The equivalent street drug is heroin, derived from morphine by a simple chemical modification. Heroin addicts typically believe that their drug is stronger and produces a more pronounced "high" than morphine; however, since heroin is rapidly converted to morphine once it enters the body, most medical scientists consider the two drugs completely equivalent.

The effects of cocaine are almost the opposite of those of morphine; cocaine's legal classification as a narcotic—a drug that produces stupor—is misleading from a medical standpoint. This product of the coca plant, native to the Andes Mountains in South America, produces a state of euphoric hyperarousal. The user feels excited, elated, and intensely aware of his or her surroundings, with an impression of enhanced physical strength and mental ability. These feelings are accompanied by the physical signs of arousal: elevated heart rate and blood pressure. The increased heart rate caused by a high dose may lead to fibrillation and death.

A cocaine "high," unlike the "highs" from most abused drugs, lasts less than half an hour—often much less. Once an individual becomes addicted, he or she needs large amounts of the expensive drug. Users' enhanced aggressiveness and physical self–confidence further increase cocaine's social dangers. Cocaine usage over time can result in paranoid schizophrenia, a type of insanity characterized by unfounded suspicion and fantasies of persecution; when this psychological condition is combined with continued cocaine use, the addict may perform violent acts against the supposed plotters.

Cocaine is also a local anesthetic, and was used medically for that purpose in the early part of the century. Procaine and xylocaine, synthetic local anesthetics introduced during mid–century, have replaced cocaine as a medical drug.

Another pleasurable yet addictive drug is nicotine, usually obtained by either smoking or chewing leaves of the tobacco plant, *Nicotiana tabacum*. Ground–up leaves, known as snuff, may be placed in the nose or cheek, allowing the nicotine to diffuse through the linings of the cavities into the bloodstream.

With the possible exception of alcohol, nicotine is the world's most widely used addictive drug. Its attractiveness undoubtedly results from the drug's paradoxical combination of calming and stimulating properties—it can produce either relaxation or arousal, depending on the user's state. Its physical effects, however, are primarily stimulatory. By increasing the heart rate and blood pressure while constricting the arteries—including those in the heart—nicotine significantly increases the risk of a heart attack.

Some alkaloid stimulants are not addictive, however. These include caffeine and the related compounds theophylline and theobromine. Caffeine is found in coffee, made from beans of *Coffea arabica*; in tea, from leaves of *Camellia sinensis*; in cocoa and chocolate, from seeds of *Theobroma cacao*; and in cola drinks, which contain flavorings derived from nuts of *Cola* plants. In northern Argentina and southern Brazil, leaves of *Ilex paraguariensis* (a type of holly) are used to make maté, a drink more popular there than either coffee or tea.

In addition to caffeine, tea also contains small amounts of theophylline, while theobromine is the major stimulant in cocoa. Large amounts of coffee, tea, cocoa, or cola drinks (more than 6–12 cups of coffee a day, for example), can produce nervousness, shakiness (muscle tremors), and insomnia, and may increase the risk of heart attack. Adverse effects from smaller amounts of these beverages have been claimed but never clearly demonstrated.

Black pepper falls into an entirely different category of the pain/pleasure grouping. This spice derives its burning flavor primarily from the alkaloids piperine, piperidine, and chavicine.

Addiction

Addiction was originally defined by the appearance of physical symptoms—such as sweating, sniffling, and trembling—when a drug was withdrawn from an addicted person or animal. It was also thought that addiction was accompanied by adaptation, in which more and more of the drug is required to produce the same effect.

So long as the focus was on opium–derived drugs such as morphine and heroin, this definition was appropriate. Beginning in the 1960s, however, scientists realized that it did not define the properties that render cocaine and other drugs so dangerous. Cocaine does not produce adaptation, and its withdrawal does not result in physical symptoms that can be seen in laboratory animals. Cocaine withdrawal does, however, produce an intense depression that disappears when the drug is again available. Similarly, nicotine withdrawal produces psychological symptoms such as restlessness, anxiety, irritability, difficulty in concentrating, and a craving for the drug. Today these psychological withdrawal symptoms are recognized as valid indicators of addiction.

Poisonous alkaloids

Nearly all of the alkaloids mentioned so far are poisonous in large amounts. Some alkaloids, however, are almost solely known as poisons. One of these is strychnine, derived from the small Hawaiian tree *Strychnos nux–vomica*. Symptoms of strychnine poisoning begin with feelings of restlessness and anxiety, proceeding to muscle twitching and exaggerated reflexes. In severe poisoning, a loud sound can cause severe muscle spasms throughout the entire body. These spasms may make breathing impossible and result in death.

In the early part of the twentieth century, strychnine was widely used as a rat poison. In recent decades, however, slower–acting poisons have been used for rodent control; since rats can remember which foods have made them sick, one that receives a non–fatal dose of a fast–acting poison such as strychnine will never again take that type of poisonous bait.

A number of other plants also derive their lethal properties from alkaloids of one type or another. Among these are poison hemlock (*Conium maculatum*) and plants of the genus *Aconitum*, commonly called monkshood—known by devotees of werewolf stories as wolfsbane. Other examples include shrubs of the genus *Calycanthus*, known as Carolina allspice, spicebush, and sweet betty, among other names; vines of the genus *Solandra*, such as the chalice vine, cup–of–gold, silver cup, and trumpet plant; trees or shrubs of the genus *Taxus*, such as yews; plants of the lily–like genus *Veratrum*, including false hellebore; and the golden chain or bean tree (*Laburnum anagyroides*).

Although vines and non–woody plants of the genus *Solanum* pose a real danger only to children, they represent an extremely varied group. Poisonous members of this genus range from the common potato to the nightshade (not the same as the deadly nightshade that produces atropine). The group also includes the Jerusalem cherry, the false Jerusalem cherry, the love apple, the Carolina horse nettle, the bittersweet, the nipplefruit, the star–potato vine, and the apple of Sodom.

Poisoning by ordinary potatoes usually results from eating uncooked sprouts or sun–greened skin. These parts should be cut away and discarded. For other plants in the group, it is the immature fruit that is most likely to be poisonous. In contrast to the nervous–system effects of most alkaloids, the alkaloids found in the genus *Solanum* produce mainly fever and diarrhea.

See also Addiction; Antipsychotic drugs; Caffeine; Cocaine; Codeine; Morphine; Neurotransmitter; Nicotine; Nux vomica tree; Poisons and toxins; Quinine.

Further Reading:

Lampe, Kenneth F., and Mary Ann McCann. *AMA Handbook of Poisonous & Injurious Plants*. Chicago: Chicago Review Press, 1985.

Pelletier, S. W. *Alkaloids: Chemical and Biological Perspectives*. New York: John Wiley & Sons, 1983.

W. A. Thomasson

Alkanes see **Alkyl group; Hydrocarbon**
Alkenes see **Alkyl group; Hydrocarbon**

Alkyl group

An alkyl group is a paraffinic hydrocarbon group that may be derived from an alkane by dropping one hydrogen from the structure. Such groups are often represented in chemical formulas by the letter R and have the generic name C_nH_{2n+1}.

Alkanes

Aliphatic compounds, of which the alkanes are one example, have an open chain of carbon atoms as a skeleton. This open chain may be straight or branched. Alkanes, also known as paraffins, are composed of carbon and hydrogen only; they have the generic formula C_nH_{2n+2}, and are the simplest and least reactive of the aliphatic compounds. Alkanes with straight chains are known as normal alkanes. (Branched chain alkanes are treated as alkyl derivatives of the straight chain com-

pounds.) The first four members of the normal alkane series are methane, ethane, propane, and butane (see below). The names of the remaining normal alkanes are composed of a prefix that indicates the number of carbon atoms in the compound, followed by the termination –ane. Thus, n–hexane is the name given to the normal alkane having a chain of six carbon atoms.

The n–alkanes exist on a continuum that extends from simple gases to molecules of very high molecular weights. Table 1 shows how the physical properties and uses of the n–alkane change with the number of repeating CH_2 units in the chain.

Alkyl radicals

Alkanes from which one atom of hydrogen has been removed become monovalent radicals. These radicals, which are molecular fragments having an unpaired electron, are known as alkyl groups. The names of the alkyl groups are formed by substituting the suffix –yl for –ane in the names of the alkanes from which they are derived.

As indicated in Table 2, the methyl group (CH_3–) is formed from methane, CH_4. The ethyl group, C_2H_5–, is formed from ethane, C_2H_6. Two different alkyl groups can be formed from propane, CH_3–CH_2–CH_3. Removal of a hydrogen atom from one of the carbon atoms at the end of the chain forms C_3H_7–. This CH_3–CH_2–CH_2– group is called a normal propyl group (n–propyl group). Removing a hydrogen from the second carbon produces an isopropyl group (i–propyl group).

The next member of the alkanes has the formula C_4H_{10}. There are four isomers of this molecular formula. Removal of a hydrogen from one of the end carbons in n–butane, CH_3–$(CH_2)_2$–CH_3, produces the n–butyl group (CH_3–CH_2–CH_2–CH_2–). Removing a hydrogen atom from carbon 2 or 3 produces the secondary butyl group (sec–butyl group; CH_3–CH–CH_2–CH_3). Removal of a hydrogen from carbon atoms

TABLE 1. PROPERTIES OF THE ALKANE SERIES

Number of CH2 units in chain	Appearance at room temperature	Uses
1 to 4	simple gas	cooking gas
5 to 11	simple liquid	gasoline
9 to 16	medium viscosity liquid	kerosene
16 to 25	high viscosity liquid	oil and grease
25 to 50	simple solid	paraffin wax candles
1,000 to 3,000	tough plastic solid	polyethylene bottles and containers

TABLE 2. ALKYL GROUPS DERIVED FROM ALKANES

Alkane	Alkyl Group
methane (CH_4)	methyl (CH_3-)
ethane (CH_3- CH_3)	ethyl (CH_3 -CH_2-)
propane (CH_3-CH_2 -CH_3)	n-propyl (CH_3-CH_2 -CH_2-) i-propyl(CH_3-ICH-CH_3)

TABLE 3. ALKENES DERIVED FROM ALKYL GROUPS

Alkyl Group	Alkene
methyl (CH_3-)	methylene (-CH_2 -)
ethyl (CH_3 -CH_2-)	ethylene (CH_2 = CH_2)
n-propyl (CH_3-CH_2 -CH_2-) i-propyl(CH_3-ICH_2-CH_3)	propylene (CH_3 -CH = CH_2)
n-butyl (CH_3 -CH_2 -CH_2 -CH_2-)	butylene (CH_2 = CH -CH_2 -CH_3) or (CH_3 - CH = CH -CH_3)

1, 3, or 4 forms the isobutyl group (i–butyl group; CH_3–CH(CH_2–)–CH_3). Finally, removing a hydrogen from carbon 2 gives the tertiary butyl group (t–butyl group; CH_3–C(CH_3)–CH_3).

Frequently the terms primary, secondary, and tertiary are used to describe carbon atoms in a molecule. A primary carbon atom is one that is attached to only one other carbon atom; a secondary carbon atom is attached to two other carbon atoms; and a tertiary carbon atom is attached to three other carbon atoms in the molecule. Thus the ethyl group defined above is a primary group, since the carbon atom that has lost the hydrogen is attached to only one other carbon atom in the molecule. The n–propyl group is also a primary group for the same reason. But the i–propyl group is a secondary group, because the central carbon atom from which the hydrogen has been removed is attached to

two other carbon atoms. The n–butyl and i–butyl groups are both primary groups; the secondary butyl group is a secondary group; and the tertiary butyl group is tertiary, because the central atom is attached to the three other carbon atoms in the molecule. The methyl group, however, cannot be defined using this classification scheme.

In general, the letter R is used to designate any alkyl group (R = CH_3, C_2H_5, etc.). With this convention, the alkanes are represented by the general formula R–H, and the alkyl halides by R–X, where X is a halogen.

Alkenes

The series of compounds derived from the alkanes by removing one hydrogen atom from each of two adjacent carbon atoms, thereby introducing a double bond into the molecule, bears the name olefin. The systematic names are formed by substituting the suffix –ENE for –ANE in the name of the alkane from which they are derived. Thus the series as a whole is called the alkenes (see Table 3).

See also Butyl group; Ethyl group; Hydrocarbon; Methyl group; Propyl group.

Further Reading:

Baumgarten, Reuben L. *Organic Chemistry.* New York: John Wiley and Sons, 1978.
Sperling, L.H. *Introduction to Physical Polymer Science.* New York: John Wiley and Sons, 1992.

Randall Frost

Allergy

An allergy is an excessive or hypersensitive response of the immune system to harmless substances in the environment. Instead of fighting off a disease–causing foreign substance, the immune system launches a complex series of actions against an irritating substance, referred to as an allergen. The immune response may be accompanied by a number of stressful symptoms, ranging from mild to severe to life–threatening. In rare cases, an allergic reaction leads to anaphylactic shock—a condition characterized by a sudden drop in blood pressure, difficulty in breathing, skin irritation, collapse, and possible death.

The immune system may produce several chemical agents that cause allergic reactions. One of the main immune system substances responsible for the symptoms of allergy are the histamines that are produced after an exposure to an allergen. Along with other treatments and medicines, the use of antihistamines helps to relieve some of the symptoms of allergy by blocking out histamine receptor sites. The study of allergy medicine includes the identification of the different types of allergy, immunology, and the diagnosis and treatment of allergy.

Types of allergy

The most common cause of allergy is pollens that are responsible for seasonal or allergic rhinitis. The popular name for rhinitis, hay fever, a term used since the 1830s, is inaccurate because the condition is not caused and its symptoms do not include fever.

Throughout the world during every season, pollens from grasses, trees, and weeds produce allergic reactions like sneezing, runny nose, swollen nasal tissues, headaches, blocked sinuses, and watery, irritated eyes. Of the 46 million allergy sufferers in the United States, about 25 million have rhinitis.

Dust and the house dust mite constitute another major cause of allergies. While the mite itself is too large to be inhaled, its feces are about the size of pollen grains and can lead to allergic rhinitis. Other types of allergy can be traced to the fur of animals and pets, food, drugs, insect bites, and skin contact with chemical substances or odors. In the United States there are about 12 million people who are allergic to a variety of chemicals. In some cases an allergic reaction to an insect sting or a drug reaction can cause sudden death. Serious asthma attacks are associated with seasonal rhinitis and other allergies. About nine million people in the United States suffer from asthma.

Role of immune system

Some people are allergic to a wide range of allergens, while others are allergic to only a few or none. The reasons for these differences can be found in the makeup of an individual's immune system. The immune system is the body's defense against substances that it recognizes as dangerous to the body. Lymphocytes, a type of white blood cell, fights viruses and bacteria and other antigens by producing antibodies. When an allergen first enters the body, the lymphocytes produce an antibody called immunoglobulin E (IgE). The IgE antibodies attach to mast cells, large cells that are found in connective tissue and contain histamines along with a number of other chemical substances.

Studies show that allergy sufferers produce an excessive amount of IgE, indicating a hereditary factor for their allergic responses. How individuals adjust over time to allergens in their environments also determines their degree of susceptibility to allergic disorders.

The second time any given allergen enters the body, it becomes attached to the newly–formed Y–shaped IgE antibodies. These antibodies, in turn, stimulate the mast cells to discharge its histamines and other anti–allergen substances. There are two types of histamine: H_1 and H_2. H_1 histamines travel to receptor sites located in the nasal passages, respiratory system, and skin, dilating smaller blood vessels and constricting airways. The H_2 histamines, which constrict the larger blood vessels, travel to the receptor sites found in the salivary and tear glands and in the stomach's

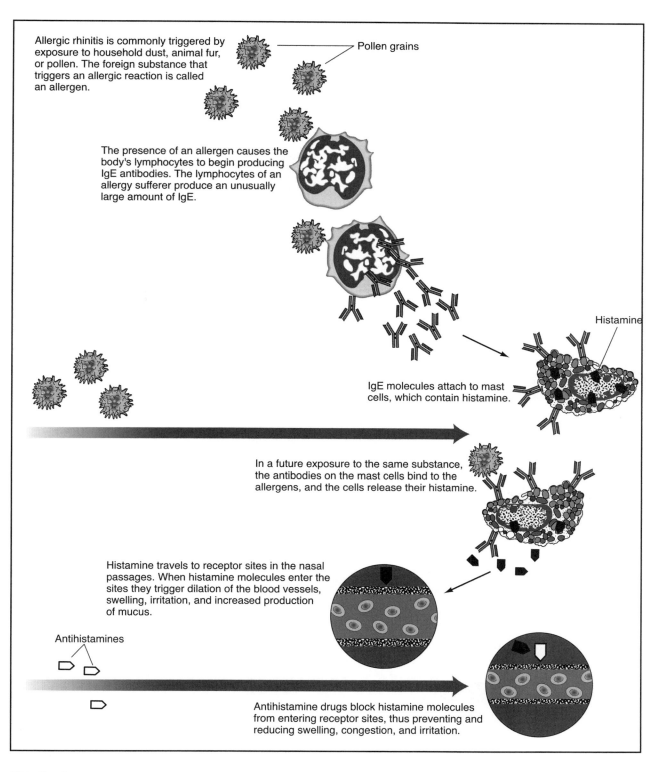

Allergic rhinitis is commonly triggered by exposure to household dust, animal fur, or pollen. The foreign substance that triggers an allergic reaction is called an allergen.

Pollen grains

The presence of an allergen causes the body's lymphocytes to begin producing IgE antibodies. The lymphocytes of an allergy sufferer produce an unusually large amount of IgE.

Histamine

IgE molecules attach to mast cells, which contain histamine.

In a future exposure to the same substance, the antibodies on the mast cells bind to the allergens, and the cells release their histamine.

Histamine travels to receptor sites in the nasal passages. When histamine molecules enter the sites they trigger dilation of the blood vessels, swelling, irritation, and increased production of mucus.

Antihistamines

Antihistamine drugs block histamine molecules from entering receptor sites, thus preventing and reducing swelling, congestion, and irritation.

The allergic response.

KEY TERMS

. . . .

Allergen—An otherwise harmless substance that causes a fixed allergic response.

Anaphylactic shock—A violent, sometimes fatal, response to an allergen after initial contact.

Corticosteroids—Drugs that stimulate the adrenal gland and are highly effective in treating asthma and allergies but also have many side effects.

Decongestants—Drugs used for a short term to reduce mucous membrane congestion.

Histamines—One of the main products of the immune system to trigger allergic reactions.

IgE—The chief immunoglobulin responsible for producing the compounds that cause allergic reactions.

Lymphocyte—A white blood cell that stimulates antibody formation.

Mast cell—A tissue white blood cell located at the site of small blood vessels.

Receptor sites—Places on the mast cell where Y-shaped antibodies stimulate histamine production.

Rhinitis—Nasal congestion, inflammation, and sneezing caused by seasonal pollens or other allergens.

Weal—The reddened, itchy swelling caused by a skin patch test.

times attempted by exposing the patient to slight amounts of the allergen at regular intervals.

Antihistamines, which are now prescribed and sold over the counter as a rhinitis remedy, were discovered in the 1940s. There are a number of different ones, and they either inhibit the production of histamine or block them at receptor sites. After the administration of antihistamines, IgE receptor sites on the mast cells are blocked, thereby preventing the release of the histamines that cause the allergic reactions. The allergens are still there, but the body's "protective" actions are suspended for the period of time that the antihistamines are active. Antihistamines also constrict the smaller blood vessels and capillaries, thereby removing excess fluids. Recent research has identified specific receptor sites on the mast cells for the IgE. This knowledge makes it possible to develop medicines that will be more effective in reducing the symptoms of various allergies.

Corticosteroids are sometimes prescribed to allergy sufferers as anti–inflammatories. Decongestants can also bring relief, but these can be used for a short time only, since their continued use can set up a rebound effect and intensify the allergic reaction.

See also Antibody and antigen; Immune system.

Further Reading:

Bierman W. and D. Pearlman, eds. *Allergic Diseases from Infancy to Adulthood.* Reprint. Philadelphia: W. B. Saunders, 1987.

Davies, Robert and Susan Ollier. *Allergy: The Facts.* Oxford: Oxford University Press, 1989.

Joneja, Janice Vickerstaff and Leonard Bielory. *Understanding Allergy, Sensitivity, & Immunity.* New Brunswick, NJ: Rutgers University Press, 1990.

Steinman, Marion. *A Parent's Guide to Allergies and Asthma.* New York: Dell Publishing, 1992.

Jordan P. Richman

Alligators see **Crocodiles**

mucosal lining. H$_2$ histamines play a role in stimulating the release of stomach acid, thus creating a seasonal stomach ulcer condition.

Diagnosis and treatment

The patient's medical history provides the primary basis for diagnosis. Skin patch tests are sometimes used to determine exactly which potential allergens the patient is allergic to. A group of substances are placed in patches under the skin; any actual allergen will raise a weal at the site of the patch. The weal is a circular area of swelling that itches and is reddened. The tests at times produce false positives, so that they cannot be relied on exclusively.

The simplest form of treatment is the avoidance of the allergic substance, but that is not always possible. In such cases, desensitization to the allergen is some-

Allotrope

Allotropes are two or more forms of the same element in the same physical state (solid, liquid, or gas) that differ from each other in their physical, and sometimes chemical, properties. The most notable examples of allotropes are found in groups 4A, 5A, and 6A of the periodic table. Gaseous oxygen, for example, exists in three allotropic forms: monatomic oxygen (O), a diatomic molecule (O_2), and in a triatomic molecule known as ozone (O_3).

A striking example of differing physical properties among allotropes is the case of carbon. Solid carbon exists in two allotropic forms: diamond and graphite. Diamond is the hardest naturally occurring substance and has the highest melting point (more than 6,335°F [3,500°C]) of any element. In contrast, graphite is a very soft material, the substance from which the "lead" in lead pencils is made.

The allotropes of phosphorus illustrate the variations in chemical properties that may occur among such forms. White phosphorus, for example, is a waxy white solid that bursts into flame spontaneously when exposed to air. It is also highly toxic. On the other hand, a second allotrope of phosphorus known as red phosphorus is far more stable, does not react with air, and is essentially nontoxic.

Allotropes differ from each other structurally depending on the number of atoms in a molecule of the element. There are allotropes of sulfur, for example, that contain 2, 6, 7, 8, 10, 12, 18, and 20 atoms per molecule (formulas S_2 to S_{20}). Several of these, however, are not very stable.

The term allotrope was first suggested by Swedish chemist J. J. Berzelius (1779–1848). He took the name from the Greek term *allotropos*, meaning other way. Berzelius was unable to explain the structure of allotropes, however. The first step in that direction was accomplished by British father and son crystallographers W. H. and L.W. Bragg in 1914. The Braggs used x ray diffraction to show that diamond and graphite differ from each other in their atomic structure.

Alloy

A mixture of two or more metals is called an alloy. Alloys are distinguished from composite metals in that alloys are thoroughly mixed, creating, in effect, a synthetic metal. In metal composites, the introduced metal retains its identity within the matrix in the form of fibers, beads, or other shapes.

Alloys can be created by mixing the metals while in a molten state or by bonding metal powders. Various alloys have different desired properties such as strength, visual attractiveness, or malleability. The number of possible alloy combinations is almost endless since any metal can be alloyed in pairs or in multiples.

An entire period of human prehistory is named for the earliest known alloy—bronze. During the Bronze Age (c. 3500–1000 B.C.) humans first fashioned tools and weapons from something other than basic materials found in nature. Humans combined copper and tin to form a strong metal that was still easily malleable. Modern bronze contains a 25:75 ratio of tin to copper. The use of bronze in early times was greatest in nations where tin deposits were most plentiful, like Asia Minor, and among countries that traded with tin–mining nations.

Brass is an alloy of copper and zinc. It is valued for its light weight and rigid strength. It has a ratio of about one–third zinc to two–thirds copper. The exact ratio of metals determines the qualities of the alloy. For example, brass, having less than 63% copper, must be heated to be worked. Brass is noted for its beauty when polished. Brass was perhaps first produced in Palestine from 1400 to 1200 B.C. It was later used by the Romans for coins. Many references to brass in the Bible and other ancient documents are really mistranslations of mentions of bronze.

Pewter is an alloy of copper, tin, and antimony. It is a very soft mixture that can be worked when cold and beat repeatedly without becoming brittle. It was used in Roman times, but its greatest period of popularity began in England in the 14th century and continued into the 18th. Colonial American metalworks produced some notable pewter work. As a cheaper version of silver, it was used in plates, cups, pitchers, and candelabras.

The various types of steel and iron are all alloys classifiable by their content of other materials. For instance, wrought iron has a very small carbon content, while cast iron has at least 2% carbon.

Steels contain varying amounts of carbon and metals such as tungsten, molybdenum, vanadium, and cobalt, giving them the strength, durability, and anti–corrosion capabilities required by their different uses. Stainless steel, which has 18% chromium and 8% nickel alloyed to it, is valued for its anti–corrosive qualities.

Duraluminum contains one–third steel and two–thirds aluminum. It was developed during World War I for the superstructures of the Zeppelin airships built in Germany.

Many alloys add function to physical beauty. For example, sterling silver is made with 8% copper to add strength so that it can be made into chalices and silver-ware.

All American coins are made from copper alloy, sometimes sandwiched between layers of silver.

Alloys greatly enhance the versatility of metals. Without them there would be total dependency on pure metals, which would affect their cost and availability. Alloys are a very important part of humankind's past and future.

See also Metal; Metallurgy; Steel.

Allspice see **Myrtle family**

Alluvial systems

An alluvial system is a landform produced when a stream or river, that is, some channelized flow (geologists call them all streams no matter what their scale) slows down and deposits sediment that was transported either as bedload or in suspension. The basic principle underlying alluvial deposits is that the more rapidly water is moving, the larger the particles it can hold in suspension and the farther it can transport those particles.

For example, suppose that a river is flowing across a mountainous region, eroding rock, sand, gravel, silt, and other materials from the stream bed. As long as the stream is flowing rapidly, a considerable quantity of materials such as these can be transported, either along the bottom or as particles suspended in the water column. But then imagine that the stream rushes out of the mountainous region and onto a valley floor. As the river slows down, suspended materials begin to be deposited. The larger bedload materials (for example, rocks and stones) accumulate first, and the lighter suspended materials (sand, silt, and clay) later. Any collection of materials deposited by a process such as this is known as *alluvium*. The conditions under which an alluvial system forms are found in both arid and humid climates, and in areas of both low slope (river deltas or swamps) and high slope (mountain streams).

Commmon components

Although the system above was in a mountainous setting, any river or stream is part of an alluvial system. Many stream systems consist of several features with which you may already be familiar. These include the channel, head, mouth, meanders, point bars and cut

banks, floodplains, levees, oxbow lakes, and stream terraces, to name a few.

The channel is the sloping trough–like depression down which water flows from the stream's origin, or head, to its destination, or mouth. All channels naturally curve, or meander. At the outside of a bend in a channel meander, the flow is concentrated and so erosion causes undercutting, and a cutbank forms. On the inside of the meander, flow decreases, so deposition occurs; a sand bar, or point bar, forms.

When a stream floods, several processes naturally follow. As the water flows out of its channel, it immediately begins to slow down, since it spreads out over a large area, increasing the resistance to flow. Coarser sediments are therefore deposited very close to the channel. This forms a very gently sloping lump of alluvium that parallels the channel, known as a natural levee. As the natural levee builds up over thousands of years, it helps prevent flooding. That is why humans build man–made levees—to emulate natural levees. Finer sediments flow with the stream water out onto the flat area behind the levee, known as the floodplain.

During the same flood, if the water is especially high, or the channel is highly meandering, the flood may cut a new channel, connecting two closely positioned meanders, a neck, in what is called a neck cut–off. Once the neck is cut, the channel is much straighter, and the meander is abandoned to become a part of the floodplain. This abandoned meander then forms a lake known as an oxbow. If you look down from the airplane the next time you fly over a large river, you can probably see some old abandoned meanders in the river's floodplain.

Another common feature of alluvial systems is the stream terrace. A stream terrace is simply an old floodplain that is now abandoned. Abandonment occurred when the erosive power of the stream increased and it began to rapidly downcut to a lower elevation. The stream did not have time to erode its old floodplain by meandering over it, so it was preserved. The abandoned floodplain, or stream terrace, can be seen well above the new stream channel elevation. Multiple terraces can sometimes be seen, looking like steps in a giant staircase.

Coastal alluvial plains

When an alluvial system operates over a long period of time, perhaps millions of years, it works to flatten the surrounding landscape, and significantly decrease its average elevation. Areas that were originally mountainous can be worn down to rolling hills, and eventually produce extensive plains composed of

This delta formed downstream of a break in a natural levee. Note the marsh growth that developed along the banks of the distributaries.

alluvial sediment. The sediment is eroded from high-lands that may be tens, hundreds, or perhaps thousands of miles from the coast, and the alluvium serves to bury existing coastal features beneath a blanket of sediment. During periods of lower sea level in the geologic past, coastal plains extended far out on the margins of the continents. Today, these alluvial sediments are hundreds of feet below sea level.

Alluvial fans

As a stream emerges from a mountain valley, its waters are dispersed over a relatively wide region of valley floor. Such is the case, for example, along the base of the Panamint Mountains that flank California's Death Valley. A stream flowing down a mountain side tends to deposit heavier materials near the foot of the mountain, somewhat lighter materials at a greater distance from the mountain, and still lighter materials at a still greater distance from the mountain.

Often, the flow of water ends within the deposited material itself. This material tends to be very porous, so water is more likely to soak into the ground than to flow across its surface. Thus, there is no preferred

direction of deposition from side to side at the mouth of the stream, and as the alluvium accumulates it forms a cone–shaped pattern on the valley floor known as an alluvial fan.

The idealized model described above would suggest that an alluvial fan should have a gradually changing composition, with heavier materials such as rocks and small stones at the base of the mountain and lighter materials such as sand and silt at the base ("toe") of the fan. In actual fact, alluvial fans seldom have this idealized structure. One reason for the more varied structure found in a fan is that stream flows change over time. During flows of low volume, lighter materials are deposited close to the mountain base on top of heavier materials deposited during earlier flows of high volume. During flows of high volume, heavier materials are once more deposited near the base of the mountain, now on top of lighter materials. A vertical cross–section of an alluvial fan is likely to be more heterogeneous, therefore, than would be suggested by an idealized depositional model.

Alluvial fans tend to have small slopes that may be no more than a foot every half a mile (a few tenths of a meter per kilometer). The exact slope of the fan depends on a number of factors. For example, streams that drain an extensive area, that have a large volume of water, or that carry suspended particles of smaller size are more likely to form fans with modest slopes than are streams with the opposite characteristics.

Under some circumstances, a river or stream may continue to flow across the top of an alluvial fan as well as soak into it. For example, the volume of water carried during floods may cause water to cut across an alluvial fan and empty onto the valley floor itself. Also, over time, sediments may become compacted within the fan, and it may become less and less porous. Then, the stream or river that feeds the fan may begin to cut a channel through the fan itself and to lay down a new fan at the base of the older fan. As the fans in a valley become more extensive, their lateral edges may begin to overlap each other. This feature is known as a bajada or piedmont alluvial plain.

In some regions, piedmont alluvial plains have become quite extensive. The city of Los Angeles, for example, is largely constructed on such a plain. Other extensive alluvial systems can be found in the Central Valley of California and along the base of the Andes Mountains in Paraguay, western Argentina, and eastern Bolivia.

Alluvial fans have certain characteristics that make them attractive for farming. In the first place, they generally have a somewhat reliable source of water (except in a desert): the stream or river by which they were formed. Also, they tend to be relatively smooth and level, making it easy for planting, cultivating, and harvesting.

Deltas

Deltas are common alluvial features, and can be found at the mouths of most streams that flow into a lake or ocean. When rivers and streams flow into standing water, their velocity decreases rapidly. They then deposit their sediment load, forming a fan–shaped, sloping deposit very similar to an alluvial fan, but located in the water rather than on dry land. This is known as a delta. Deltas show a predictable pattern of decreasing sediment size as you proceed farther and farther from shore.

The Mississippi River Delta is the United States' best known delta. Other well known deltas are the Nile Delta of northern Africa and the Amazon Delta of South America. When Aristotle observed the Nile Delta, he recognized it was shaped like the Greek letter, delta, hence the name. Most deltas clog their chan-

nels with sediment and so must eventually abandon them. If the river then flows to the sea along a significantly different path, the delta will be abandoned and a new delta lobe will form. This process, known as delta switching, helps build the coastline outward, forming new land for agriculture, as well as other uses.

See also Rivers.

Further Reading:
Bull, W. B. "Alluvial fans," *Journal of Geological Education*, vol. 26, no. 3: 101–06.

David E. Newton

Almond see **Rose family**

Aloe see **Lily family**

Alpacas see **Camels**

Alpha particles see **Radioactivity; Subatomic particles**

Alternating current see **Electric current**

Alternative energy sources

Coal, oil, and natural gas provide over 85% of the total primary energy used around the world. Although figures differ in various countries, nuclear reactors and

Wind generators in Whitewater, California.

hydroelectric power together produce less than 10% of the total world energy. Wind power, active and passive solar systems, and geothermal energy are examples of alternative energy sources. Collectively, these make up the final small fraction of total energy production.

The exact contribution alternative energy sources make to the total primary energy used around the world is not known. Conservative estimates place their share at 3–4%, but some energy experts dispute these figures. Amory Lovins has argued that the statistics collected are based primarily on large electric utilities and the regions they serve. They fail to account for areas remote from major power grids, which are more likely to use solar energy, wind energy, or other sources. When these areas are taken into consideration, Lovins claims, alternative energy sources contribute as much as 11% to the total primary energy used in the United States. Animal manure, furthermore, is widely used as an energy source in India, parts of China, and many African nations, and when this is taken into account the percentage of the worldwide contribution alternative sources make to energy production could rise as high as 10–15%.

Wind power

Now an alternative energy source, wind power is one of the earliest forms of energy used by humankind. Wind is caused by the uneven heating of the earth's surface, and its energy is equal to about 2% of the solar energy that reaches the earth. In quantitative terms, the amount of kinetic energy within Earth's atmosphere is equal to about 10,000 trillion kilowatt hours.

The kinetic energy of wind is proportional to the wind velocity, and the ideal location for a windmill generator is an area with constant and relatively fast winds and no obstacles such as buildings or trees. An efficient windmill can produce 175 watts per square meter of propeller blade area at a height of 75 ft (25 m). The estimated cost of generating one kilowatt hour by wind power is about eight cents, as compared to five cents for hydropower and 15 cents for nuclear power. The largest two utilities in California purchase wind–generated electricity, and though this state leads the country in the utilization of wind power, Denmark leads the world. The Scandinavian nation has refused to use nuclear power, and by the turn of the century it expects to obtain 10% of its energy needs from windmills.

Solar power

Solar energy can be utilized either directly as heat or indirectly by converting it to electrical power using photovoltaic cells. Greenhouses and solariums are the most common examples of the direct use of solar energy, with glass windows concentrating the visible light from the sun but restricting the heat from escaping. Flatplate collectors are another direct method, and mounted on rooftops they can provide one third of the energy required for space heating. Windows and collectors alone are considered passive systems; an active solar system uses a fan, pump, or other machinery to transport the heat generated from the sun.

Photovoltaic cells are made of semiconductor materials such as silicon. These cells are capable of absorbing part of the solar flux to produce a direct electric current with about 14% efficiency. The current cost of producing photovoltaic current is about four dollars a watt. However, a thin–film technology is being perfected for the production of these cells, and the cost per watt will eventually be reduced because less materials will be required. Photovoltaics are now being used economically in lighthouses, boats, rural villages, and other remote areas. Large solar systems have been most effective using trackers that follow the sun or mirror reflectors that concentrate its rays.

Geothermal energy

Geothermal energy is the natural heat generated in the interior of the earth, and like solar energy it can also be used directly as heat or indirectly to generate electricity. Steam is classified as either dry (no water droplets), or wet (mixed with water). When it is generated in certain areas containing corrosive sulfur compounds, it is known as sour steam, and when generated in areas that are free of sulfur it is known as sweet steam. Geothermal energy can be used to generate electricity by the flashed steam method, in which high temperature geothermal brine is used as a heat exchanger to convert injected water into steam. The produced steam is used to turn a turbine. When geothermal wells are not hot enough to create steam, a fluid which evaporates at a much lower temperature than water, such as isobutane or ammonia, can be placed in a closed system where the geothermal heat provides the energy to evaporate the fluid and run the turbine.

There are 20 countries worldwide that utilize this energy source, and they include the United States,

Mexico, Italy, Iceland, Japan, and the former Soviet Union. Unlike solar energy and wind power, geothermal energy is not free of environmental impact. It contributes to air pollution, it can emit dissolved salts, and, in some cases, toxic heavy metals such as mercury and arsenic.

Though there are several ways of utilizing energy from the ocean, the most promising are the harnessing of tidal power and ocean thermal energy conversion. The power of ocean tides is based on the difference between high and low water. In order for tidal power to be effective the differences in height need to be very great, more than 15 ft (3 m), and there are only a few places in the world where such differences exist. These include the Bay of Fundy and a few sites in China. Ocean thermal energy conversion utilizes temperature changes rather than tides. Ocean temperature is stratified, especially near the tropics, and the process takes advantage of this fact by using a fluid with a low boiling point, such as ammonia. The vapor from the fluid drives a turbine, and cold water from lower depths is pumped up to condense the vapor back into liquid. The electrical power generated by this method can be shipped to shore or used to operate a floating plant such as a cannery.

Other sources of alternative energy

Other sources of alternative energy are currently being explored, some of which are still experimental. These include harnessing the energy in biomass through the production of wood from trees or the production of ethanol from crops such as sugar cane or corn. Methane gas can be generated from the anaerobic breakdown of organic waste in sanitary landfills and from wastewater treatment plants. With the cost of garbage disposal rapidly increasing, the burning of garbage is becoming a viable option as an energy source. Adequate air pollution controls are necessary, but trash can be burned to heat buildings, and municipal garbage is currently being used to generate electricity in Hamburg, Germany. In an experimental method known as magnetohydrodynamics, hot gas is ionized (potassium and sulfur) and passed through a strong magnetic field where it produces an electrical current. This process contains no moving parts and has an efficiency of 20–30%.

Of all the alternative sources, energy conservation is perhaps the most important, and improving energy efficiency is the best way to meet energy demands without adding to air and water pollution. Experts have estimated that it is possible to double the efficiency of electric motors, triple the intensity of light bulbs, quadruple the efficiency of refrigerators and air conditioners, and quintuple the gasoline mileage of automobiles. Several automobile manufacturers in Europe and Japan have already produced prototype vehicles with very high gasoline mileage. Volvo has developed the LCP 2000, a passenger sedan that holds four to five people, meets all United States safety standards, accelerates from 0 to 50 mph in eleven seconds, and has a high fuel efficiency rating.

See also Pollution; Waste Management.

Further Reading:

Alternative Energy Handbook. Englewood Cliffs, NJ: Prentice Hall, 1993.

Brower, M. *Cool Energy: Renewable Solutions to Environmental Problems.* Cambridge: MIT Press, 1992.

Goldemberg, J. *Energy for a Sustainable World.* New York: Wiley, 1988.

Schaeffer, J. *Alternative Energy Sourcebook: A Comprehensive Guide to Energy Sensible Technologies.* Ukiah, CA: Real Goods Trading Corp., 1992.

Shea, C. P. *Renewable Energy: Today's Contribution, Tomorrow's Promise.* Washington, D.C.: Worldwatch Institute, 1988.

Muthena Naseri and Douglas Smith

Alternative medicine

No precise definition of alternative medicine exists. In general it is a practice that fits three criteria: it is not taught in the standard medical school curriculum; there is not sufficient scientific evidence that the treatment is safe and effective against a specific disease; and insurance companies do not reimburse the patient for its cost.

Such a definition could include nearly all unproven but ineffective practices that offer little in benefit but draw billions of health care dollars from desperate patients. The use of laetrile (a derivative of apricot pits) to treat cancer and chelation therapy to remove cholesterol deposits from severely affected arteries are cases in point. Both are highly touted by their practitioners, both have been tested under rigid scientific research standards, and both have been found ineffective and useless. The primary harm of such treatments lies in the fact that patients who utilize them often do not seek more effective, mainstream medical care.

The first known example of alternative medicine in the United States was the introduction and patenting in 1797 of a "mechanical tractor" to pull bad electricity, the source of all illnesses, from the body. A chief justice of the Supreme Court, several members of Congress, and the retired president, George Washington, all used this device. Although some alternative medical practices are clearly ineffective and sometimes dangerous, others have achieved a degree of acceptability in the eyes of organized medicine. Among these are biofeedback, acupuncture, chiropractic medicine, and relaxation techniques.

Lifestyle changes

Lifestyle changes can be as simple as getting more exercise or as complex as completely redesigning the diet. Exercise in moderation is a preventive measure against heart disease, stroke, and other serious conditions. It is only when such exercise programs become excessive or all consuming that they may be harmful. Some people use very high daily doses of vitamins in an attempt to forestall the aging process or to assist the body in ridding itself of cancer or the HIV virus. Megadoses of vitamins have not been proven effective for these purposes. Vitamins play a specific role in the metabolism and excess vitamins simply are stored in the fat or are eliminated from the body through the kidneys.

Changes to achieve a more balanced intake of nutrients or to reduce the amount of fat in the diet are beneficial, but dietary programs that add herbal supplements to the diet may be ineffective or even harmful. Chinese and Far Eastern cultures use herbal therapy to achieve weight loss, delay aging, or increase strength. Dietary supplements of Chinese herbs have become increasingly popular among Westerners, although most Americans do not know specifically what herbs they are consuming. Laboratory tests have raised questions about the effectiveness of many of these herbs; some may have high lead content and therefore are potentially toxic.

Relaxation

Many practices are included under the general term of relaxation. Relaxation techniques are generally accepted as beneficial to individuals who are otherwise unable to sleep, in pain, under ongoing job–related stress, or recovering from surgery. Various relaxation techniques frequently are used in hospitals to help patients deal with pain or to help them sleep.

In the simplest form of relaxation therapy, the individual is taught to lie quietly and to consciously relax each part of the body. Beginning with the feet and progressing through the ankles, calves, thighs, abdomen, and so forth up to the neck and forehead, each part of the body is told to relax and the individual focuses his thoughts on the body part that is being told to relax. It is possible to feel the muscles of the leg or the arm relaxing under this focused attention.

The ancient practice of yoga is also considered a relaxation technique. The practice of assuming a specified position (the lotus position, for example), clearing the mind of the sources of stress, and concentrating on one's inner being for a short time can be beneficial. Following a yoga session, the individual often is less stressed and can order his thoughts in a more organized manner. Transcendental Meditation is a variation of yoga that consists of assuming specific body positions and chanting a mantra, a word or two that is repeated and that serves to concentrate the mind. This practice also clears the mind of stressful thoughts and anxiety, and enables the practitioner to reorder his priorities in a more relaxed manner.

Yet another variation on relaxation came into widespread use in the late 1960s. Biofeedback became a popular practice that initiated an industry devoted to manufacturing the devices needed to practice it effectively. Biofeedback is a process by which an individual consciously controls certain physiologic processes. These can be processes that normally are subject to thought control, such as muscle tension, or those that are not, such as heart rate. To effect such control, the person is connected to a gauge or signal device that changes tone with changes in the organ being controlled. This visual or auditory signal provides evidence of the effectiveness of the person's effort. The heart rate can be monitored by the scale of a tone or a blip on a small screen. The tone lowers in pitch or the blip appears with decreasing frequency as the heart rate slows. The goal is for the individual to learn to influence the signal in front of him and, having acquired this proficiency, to be able to accomplish the same physiologic changes without the visual or auditory signal. Biofeedback has been used successfully to reduce stress, eliminate headaches, control asthma attacks, and relieve pain.

Hypnotism, despite its use for entertainment purposes, also has a place in medical practice. Hypnotism was first introduced to the medical community in the late eighteenth century by a German physician, Franz Anton Mesmer (1734–1815), and was first called mesmerism. Mesmerism fell out of favor in France when a scientific committee failed to verify Mesmer's claims for the practice. The name was later changed to hypnotism (from the Greek word *hypnos* for sleep) by James Braid (1795–1860), an English ophthalmologist. Although technically hypnotism is not sleep, the name stuck.

Sigmund Freud (1856–1939), the father of modern psychiatry, adopted hypnotism into his practice in the 19th century. Early in his use of the practice he praised its benefits, writing two scientific papers on hypnotism and employing it to treat his patients. By the early 1890s, however, Freud abandoned hypnotism in favor of his own methods of analysis. It was not until the 1950s that the British and American medical societies approved the use of hypnosis as an adjunct to pain treatment.

In clinical use hypnotism is called hypnotherapy, and it is used to treat both physical and psychological disorders. The patient is placed in a trancelike state so that the physician may delve into the deepest levels of the mind to relieve such conditions as migraine headaches, muscle aches, chronic headaches, and postoperative pain. This trancelike condition can be induced by the practitioner or by the patient. It is achieved by first relaxing the body and then by concentrating the patient's attention on a single object or idea, shifting his thoughts away from the immediate environment. In the lightest form of hypnosis, the superficial level, the patient may accept suggestions but will not always take steps to carry them out. Therapists try to reach the deeper state of hypnosis, the somnambulistic stage, in which the patient is readily susceptible to suggestion and carries out instructions while hypnotized as well as after he has come out of the trance (post–hypnotic suggestion).

While in the trance the patient can be induced to ignore pain, to fully relax, or to carry out other beneficial suggestions by the therapist. Also the therapist may suggest that the patient can hypnotize himself when he needs relief from pain or needs to blunt his appetite. The patient is given a simple ritual to follow including specific words to say to place himself in a hypnotic trance. He will then convince himself that his pain has been relieved or that he has eaten a sufficient amount. Upon recovering his normal level of consciousness he will find that his pain is less or that he has no need of additional food.

Unlike portrayals of hypnotists in films, a therapist cannot hypnotize anyone who does not want to be hypnotized. It is essential that the patient and therapist have a close rapport, that the patient fully believes the practice will be of benefit to him, and that the surroundings are devoid of distracting stimuli. Even when in a trance, the patient will not carry out any act that he would find morally unacceptable in his waking state.

The hypnotist cannot place someone in a trance, for example, and direct him to steal a car or rob a bank. The subject will awaken with the shock of the suggestion.

Chiropractic medicine

Chiropractic medicine is founded on the theory that many human diseases and disorders stem from deviations or subluxations of the spine, which impinge on the spinal nerves, causing pain or disfunction of the affected organs. Treatment consists of determining which of the vertebrae have shifted and then realigning them properly. This may be accomplished in a single treatment or may require a series of treatments over time.

Chiropractic, derived from the Greek words for "practice by the hands," was developed by a Canadian–born Iowa grocer, Daniel David Palmer (1845–1913), in 1895. Palmer believed that the source of illness was the misalignment, or subluxation, of the spinal column in such a way that the vertebrae impinged upon the spinal nerves that passed from the spinal cord, between the vertebrae, to the various organs and muscles of the body. This constriction of the spinal nerve prevented the neural impulses from flowing properly, thus making it impossible for the brain to regulate body functions and leaving tissues susceptible to diseases. Correcting the subluxation would, therefore, restore the neural impulses and strengthen the body.

In 1898, Palmer established the Palmer College of Chiropractic in Davenport, Iowa. In 1910 he published a textbook on chiropractic which outlined his theories. Since then the number of chiropractic schools has increased to 16 with a total enrollment of approximately 10,000. To practice as a Doctor of Chiropractic (D.C.) an individual must complete the four years of chiropractic school and pass a licensing test. Some states specify that entry into a chiropractic college requires only a high school diploma and others require two years of college prior to entry.

Chiropractors themselves differ in the definition of their specialty—this has led to the formation of two separate professional organizations. The International Chiropractors Association advocates chiropractic therapy limited to spinal manipulation only, while members of the American Chiropractors Association endorse a wider range of therapeutics including physical therapy, diathermy (heating of body tissues with electromagnetic radiation, electric current, and ultrasonic waves), and dietary counseling in addition to the basic spinal manipulation.

Chiropractors do not prescribe medication or perform surgery. Only with great reluctance did the American Medical Association recognize chiropractic as a legitimate specialty. The practice is still approached with skepticism by many in the mainstream medical community because no chiropractic school is recognized by any accrediting body and because the practice itself is based on unsound, unscientific principles. Still, many physicians refer patients with back pain to chiropractors who are more skilled at manipulating misaligned vertebrae.

Acupuncture

Acupuncture is a form of therapy developed by the ancient Chinese and subsequently refined by Chinese practitioners. It consists of inserting needles through the skin in very specific places to alleviate pain, cure disease, or provide anesthesia for surgery. Acupuncture as a palliative is accepted among the medical community. Its use as a cure for serious disease or for anesthesia is not endorsed by many physicians.

For the practitioner of acupuncture, the human body is a collection of thousands of acupuncture points that lie along specific lines or meridians. Twelve pairs of meridians are plotted on the body, one of each pair on each side. An additional meridian, the Conception Vessel, courses along the midline of the front of the body and another, the Governor Vessel, along the spine. The meridians are connected by extrameridians. Additional acupuncture points lie outside the meridians on areas such as the ear lobes, fingers, toes, and so forth.

Each meridian is a course for the flow of energy through the body and that flow may be connected to an organ removed from the actual location of the meridian. Needles are inserted at points along the meridian that are specific for a given organ. For example, although the liver lies in the right side of the abdomen, the acupuncture points for liver disease may include areas on the opposite side of the body as well as one of the earlobes.

Acupuncture therapy consists of first locating the source of pain, then deciding upon the appropriate meridian and acupuncture points. Needles used in acupuncture may be short, for use in less–fleshy areas, or long for use in areas with copious flesh or muscle. The needle simply is inserted into the proper acupuncture point and rotated. The needles are left in place for a given time and rotated periodically while they are in place. Some patients find dramatic relief from pain with acupuncture and a number of physicians have incorporated the procedure into their practices.

In the Orient, acupuncture is a recognized form of therapy, and it is combined with herbal medicine, diet restrictions, and exercise. Not only is it used for pain relief, but it is also used frequently as anesthesia during surgery and for the treatment of serious diseases such as cancer. No scientific proof has been offered that it is effective against serious diseases, though its anesthetic and analgesic properties have been demonstrated.

Homeopathy

Homeopathy is a term derived from the Greek words meaning "similar suffering." It is a system in which diluted plant, mineral, or animal substances are given to stimulate the body's natural healing powers. Homeopathy was developed in the late eighteenth century by Samuel Hahnemann (1755–1843), a German physician. Hahnemann conducted experiments to improve standard therapy, which then consisted of bloodletting and administering purgatives made with mercury, which were highly toxic. In one of his experiments he ingested an extract of cinchona, the bark from a Peruvian tree used by the natives to treat malaria. Hahnemann consumed large doses of the bark and developed the symptoms of malaria. From this he concluded that if large doses resulted in symptoms of the disease, small doses should stimulate the body's own disease–fighting mechanism.

Homeopathy is based upon three principles formulated by Hahnemann. The first is the law of similars, stating that like cures like. The second is the law of infinitesimal dose, stating that the potency of a remedy is a reflection of how much it is diluted. Third is the holistic medical model, stating that any illness is specific to the individual who has it.

The law of similars is seen in more traditional medical practice in the use of immunizations. Inoculations of attenuated or dead viruses or bacteria are given to stimulate the production of antibodies to resist a full–scale invasion of the same virus or bacterium. Thus, immunizing a child against poliomyelitis consists of administering a solution containing the dead polio virus; this results in the formation of antibodies that are available to repel the living polio virus if the child is exposed to it.

Homeopathy is much more accepted in Europe, Latin America, and India than it is in the United States. It is touted as a low–cost, nontoxic, effective means of delivering medication that can cure even chronic diseases, including those that conventional medications fail to cure. In France pharmacies are required to stock homeopathic remedies in addition to regular pharmaceutical drugs. Hospital and outpatient clinics specializing in homeopathy are part of the British health care system and the practice of homeopathy is a recognized postgraduate medical specialty.

In the United States homeopathy has only begun to be accepted by the mainstream medical community. Approximately 3,000 physicians or other health care providers endorse the practice. Though it excites little enthusiasm among practicing physicians in America, homeopathy is an ongoing specialty, and the production of homeopathic remedies is regulated by the Food and Drug Administration to assure their purity, and proper labeling and dispensing.

Naturopathy

The practitioner of naturopathic medicine considers the person as a whole, treats symptoms such as fever as a natural manifestation of the body's defense mechanism that should not be interrupted, and works to heal disease by altering the patient's diet, lifestyle, or work habits. The basis of naturopathy can be traced back through Native American practices, to India, China, and ancient Greece.

Two of the most important influences on naturopathy in the United States were the brothers John Harvey Kellogg (1952–1943) and Will Keith Kellogg (1860–1951) of Battle Creek, Michigan, and C. W. Post (1854–1914), one of their employees. John Harvey Kellogg was a physician who established a sanitarium that used natural therapies such as hydrotherapy and vegetarianism to cure diseases. His brother, Will, built a factory that produced cereal and granola. C. W. Post established another cereal manufacturing company. Both manufacturing facilities remain major cereal producers today.

In naturopathy, the body's power to heal is acknowledged to be a powerful process that the practitioner should enhance using natural remedies. Fever, inflammation, and other symptoms are not the underlying cause of disease, but are reflections of the body's attempt to rid itself of the underlying cause. The disease itself originates from spiritual, physical, or emotional roots, and the cause must be identified in order that effective therapy may be applied. The patient is viewed holistically and not as a collection of symptoms; the cure is gauged to be safe and not harmful to the patient. The practitioner is a teacher who is trained to recognize the underlying problems and to teach the patient to adopt a healthier lifestyle, diet, or attitude to forestall disease. The naturopathic practitioner is a specialist in preventive medicine who believes that prevention can best be achieved by teaching patients to live in ways that maintain good health.

In addition to advising the patient on lifestyle changes to prevent disease, the naturopathic practitioner may also call upon acupuncture, homeopathy, physical therapy, and other means to strengthen the patient's ability to fight disease. Herbal preparations as well as vitamin and mineral supplements may be used to strengthen weakened immune systems. Stressful situations must be eased so that the digestive system can function properly, and any spiritual disharmony is identified and corrected.

Naturopaths are trained in herbal medicine, clinical dietetics, hydrotherapy, acupuncture, and other noninvasive means to treat disease. They provide therapy for chronic as well as acute conditions, and may work beside physicians to help patients recover from major surgery. The naturopath does only minor surgery and depends upon natural remedies for the bulk of patient therapy. Naturopathy is not widely accepted by physicians, although some practitioners are also Doctors of Medicine.

See also Acupressure; Acupuncture; Biofeedback.

Further Reading:

Alternative Medicine: The Definitive Guide. Puyallup, WA: Future Medicine Publishing, 1993.

Beardsley, T. "Fads and Feds." *Scientific American* 269 (September 1993): 39.

Botello, J. G. "Acupuncture: Getting the Point." *Lears* 6 (November 1993): 43–44.

Callahan, J. "Hypnosis Can Bring Pain Relief." *New Choices for Retirement Living* 33 (July/August 1993): 44–47.

Fugh–Berman, A. "The Case for 'Natural' Medicine." *The Nation* 257 (6–13 September 1993): 240–244.

Gill, M. S. "New Ways to Heal." *Redbook* 181 (July 1993): 63–64.

McLellan, D. "Medicine Man." *Washingtonian* 28 (May 1993): 46–47+.

McLeod, Don. "Medical Quacks: Trading on Fear." *AARP Bulletin* 35 (October 1994): 20.

Phalon, R. "New Support for Old Therapies." *Forbes* 152 (20 December 1993): 254–255.

Larry Blaser

Altruism

Altruism refers to animal behavior that benefits other animals of the same species. Living in the company of other animals presents numerous drawbacks, including increased competition for food, nest sites, and mates, and increased visibility to predators, to name just a few. We might expect animals to strive to outdo the competition whenever possible, to take the best food and other resources for themselves, and to put other individuals between themselves and the lurking predator. Yet many animals are observed to act in ways that help one another: a ground squirrel, spotting a hunting hawk, stands tall and gives a shrill alarm call, potentially drawing the hawk's attention to itself; a lioness allows cubs that are not her own to suckle alongside her cubs; a honeybee comes to the defense of its hive by stinging an encroacher, an act which proves fatal to the bee. Such self–sacrificing acts of altruism require an explanation, because they seem to contradict what we would expect in a world shaped by natural selection. If competition is the name of the game, why should animals sometimes place the interests of another creature before their own, even to the point of suicide?

Biologists recognize altruism when an animal, like an alarm–calling ground squirrel, sustains some cost to its present or future reproduction by aiding another animal, whose reproductive success is thereby given a boost. The alarm–calling squirrel presumably risks attack by calling attention to itself; in addition, if the squirrel is watching out for predators, it will not be able to forage or perform other activities well. Squirrels nearby can profit, however, as they scatter for cover from the predator. Evolutionary biologists have puzzled over how altruistic behavior of all kinds could evolve, since evolution requires maximizing reproductive success, not sacrificing it. An explanation was provided by William D. Hamilton in 1964, who showed that if a helper directs aid to a genetic relative, it may be more than compensated, in reproductive terms, by the increased reproduction of that relative—with whom it typically shares many genes. The key to genetic representation in future generations—and evolutionary success—can thus be brought about either by having offspring, or by helping relatives to do so, in a phenomenon known as kin selection.

The altruistic behavior of honeybees, lionesses, and ground squirrels is almost certainly facilitated by the social context in which these animals live: they are surrounded by genetic relatives, whose welfare is of direct interest to a potential helper. More difficult to explain is altruism that occurs between individuals who are not related. Unrelated male olive baboons in Africa team up to steal a sexually receptive female from a higher–ranking rival male: as one interloper harasses the dominant male, the other solicits and mates with the female. The next time, the two allies may switch roles, so that each benefits by the association. Helping relationships based on such reciprocity have been identified as reciprocal altruism by sociobiologist Robert L. Trivers. Reciprocal altruism does not require that the actor and the recipient be genetic relatives, but the actor has the expectation that the aid will be returned in kind at a later time. Individuals who defect or cheat in these relationships are likely to be abandoned or even punished by the defrauded partner.

Many acts of altruism performed by human beings—especially those that are made anonymously—are especially challenging to explain. Newspapers and other media are full of accounts of numerous acts of heroism: people donate blood and other organs, dive in a raging river to save a floundering stranger, or leave the waitress a tip in a restaurant even though the tipper will never return. Sociobiologists argue that while the benefits of such actions are delayed in time, they may be cumulative and profound. In a supremely social species like humans, reputation may be everything; individuals who establish themselves as reliable partners in social exchange are likely to be highly desirable as associates in reciprocity. With this in mind, it may not be surprising to discover that many "anonymous" acts of altruism are not anonymous at all: for example, although blood donors never learn who receives their blood, and never reap a reward directly from the recipient, they often wear a sticker proclaiming, "Be nice to me—I gave blood today!" The reward may come from other individuals who become favorably inclined toward the donor, and the donor further buttresses his or her reputation as a desirable partner in reciprocal altruism.

See also Evolution; Natural selection.

Susan Andrew

Alum see **Potassium aluminum sulfate**

Aluminum

Aluminum is the metallic chemical element of atomic number 13. Its symbol is Al, its atomic weight is 26.98, its specific gravity is 2.70, its melting point is 660°C, and its boiling point is 2,467°C.

Aluminum is a metal in group three of the periodic table. Its atoms consist of a single stable isotope, ^{27}Al. Known as *aluminium* in other English–speaking countries, it was named after *alum*, one of its salts that has been known for thousands of years and was used by the Egyptians, Greeks, and Romans as a *mordant*—a chemical that helps dyes stick to cloth.

General properties

Aluminum is a light–weight, silvery metal, familiar to every household in the form of pots and pans, beverage cans, and aluminum foil. It is attractive, non–toxic, corrosion–resistant, non–magnetic, and easy to form, cast, or machine into a variety of shapes. It is one of the most useful metals we have; four million tons of it are produced every year in the United States alone—a production rate that among metals is second only to that of iron.

Pure aluminum is relatively soft and not the strongest of metals, but when melted together with other elements such as copper, manganese, silicon, magnesium, and zinc, it forms alloys with a wide range of useful properties. Aluminum alloys are used in airplanes, highway signs, bridges, storage tanks, and buildings. The world's tallest buildings, the World Trade Center towers in New York, are covered with aluminum. Aluminum is being used more and more in automobiles because it is only one–third as heavy as steel and therefore decreases fuel consumption.

Where aluminum comes from

Aluminum is the third most abundant element in the earth's crust, after only oxygen and silicon, and it is the most abundant of all metals. It constitutes 8.1% of the crust by weight and 6.3% of all the atoms in the crust. Because it is a very active metal, aluminum is never found in the metallic form, but only in a wide variety of earthy and rocky minerals, including feldspar, mica, granite, and clay. Kaolin is an especially fine, white aluminum–containing clay that is used in making porcelain.

Aluminum oxide, Al_2O_3, often called alumina, does not melt until over 3,632° F (2,000° C), and is used to line furnaces. Other forms of alumina are corundum and emery, which are very hard and are used as abrasives. Among the many other mineral forms that aluminum is found in are several semiprecious gemstones, including garnet ($Fe_3Al_2Si_3O_{12}$), beryl ($Be_3Al_2Si_6O_{18}$), and ruby and sapphire, which are Al_2O_3 containing impurities of chromium and iron, respectively. Artificially made rubies and sapphires are used in lasers.

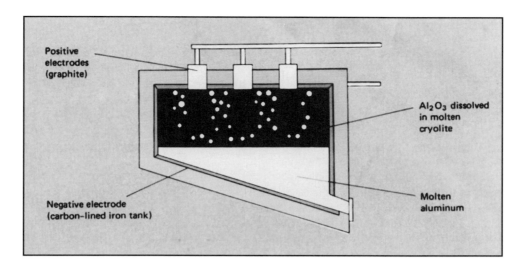

A typical Hall-process electrolysis cell used to make molten aluminum. Molten aluminum is denser than the molten cryolite mixture, and so it collects at the bottom of the cell.

How the metal is obtained

As a highly reactive metal, aluminum is very difficult to separate from the other elements that are combined with it in its minerals and compounds. In spite of its great abundance on Earth, the metal itself remained unknown for centuries. In 1825, some impure aluminum metal was finally isolated by H. C. Oersted by treating aluminum chloride, $AlCl_3$, with potassium amalgam—potassium dissolved in mercury. Then in 1827, H. Wöhler obtained pure aluminum by the reaction of metallic potassium with $AlCl_3$. He is generally given credit for the discovery of this element.

But it was still very expensive to produce aluminum metal in any quantity, and for a long time it remained a rare and valuable metal. In 1852, aluminum was selling for about $545 a pound. The big breakthrough came in 1886, when Charles M. Hall, a 23–year–old student at Oberlin College in Ohio, and Paul L–T. Héroult, another college student in France, independently invented what is now known as the Hall or Hall–Héroult process. It consists of dissolving alumina in melted *cryolite*, Na_3AlF_6, a common aluminum–containing mineral, and then passing an electric current through the hot liquid. Molten aluminum metal collects at the cathode (negative electrode). (See Electrolysis.) Not long after the development of this process, the price of aluminum metal plummeted to around 30 cents a pound.

In the production of aluminum today by the Hall–Héroult process, the aluminum oxide is dissolved in a molten mixture of sodium, calcium, and aluminum fluorides, which melts at a lower temperature than cryolite. The aluminum oxide is in the form of bauxite, a white, brown, or red earthy clay; it was first found near Les Baux, France, in 1821 by P. Berthier, and is now the main source of all aluminum. It is mined in various parts of Africa and in France, Surinam, Jamaica, and the U.S.—mainly in Alabama, Arkansas, and Georgia. The world's supply of bauxite appears to be immense enough to last for hundreds of years at the rate it is being mined today.

How we use it

In spite of the fact that aluminum is very active chemically, it does not corrode in moist air the way iron does. Instead, it quickly forms a thin, hard coating of aluminum oxide. Unlike iron oxide or rust, which flakes off, the aluminum oxide sticks tightly to the metal and protects it from further oxidation. The oxide coating is so thin that it is transparent, so the aluminum retains its silvery metallic appearance. Sea water, however, will corrode aluminum unless it has been given an unusually thick coating of oxide by the anodizing process.

When aluminum is heated to high temperatures in a vacuum, it evaporates and condenses onto any nearby cool surface such as glass or plastic. When evaporated onto glass, it makes a very good mirror, and aluminum has largely replaced silver for that purpose because it does not tarnish and turn black, as silver does when exposed to impure air. Many food–packaging materials and shiny plastic novelties are made of paper or plastic with an evaporated coating of bright aluminum. The "silver" helium balloons that we see at birthday parties are made of a tough plastic called Mylar, covered with a thin, evaporated coating of aluminum metal.

Aluminum conducts electricity about 60% as well as copper, which is still very good among metals. Because it is also light in weight and highly ductile (can be drawn out into thin wires), it is used instead of copper in almost all of the high–voltage electric transmission lines in the U.S.

Aluminum is used to make kitchen pots and pans because of its high heat conductivity. It is handy as an air– and water–tight food wrapping because it is very malleable; it can be pressed between steel rollers to make foil (a thin sheet) less than a thousandth of an inch thick. Claims are occasionally made that aluminum is toxic and that aluminum cookware is therefore dangerous, but no clear evidence for this belief has ever been found. Many widely used antacids in the drug store contain thousands of times more aluminum (in the form of aluminum hydroxide) than a person could ever get from eating food cooked in an aluminum pot. Aluminum is the only light element that has no known physiological function in the human body.

Chemistry and compounds

Aluminum is an unusual metal in that it reacts not only with acids, but with bases as well. Like many active metals, aluminum dissolves in strong acids to evolve hydrogen gas and form salts. In fact, cooking even weakly acidic foods such as tomatoes in an aluminum pot can dissolve enough aluminum to give the dish a "metallic" taste. But aluminum also dissolves in strong bases such as sodium hydroxide, commonly known as lye. Most oven cleaners, which are designed to work on steel and porcelain, contain sodium or potassium hydroxide; the user must take care not to get it on any aluminum parts of the range because it will cause adverse effects. Some commercial drain cleaners contain lye mixed with shavings of aluminum metal; the aluminum dissolves in the sodium hydroxide solution to produce bubbles of hydrogen gas, which add a mechanical clog–breaking action to the grease–dissolving action of the lye.

Hydrated aluminum chloride, $AlCl_3 \cdot H_2O$, also called aluminum chlorohydrate, is used in antiperspirants because, like alum (potassium aluminum sulfate), it has an astringent effect—a tissue–shrinking effect—that closes up the sweat–gland ducts and stops perspiration.

Over one million tons of aluminum sulfate, $Al_2(SO_4)_3$, are produced in the U.S. each year by dis-

solving aluminum oxide in sulfuric acid, H_2SO_4. It is used in water purification because when it reacts with lime (or any base), it forms a sticky precipitate of aluminum hydroxide that sweeps out tiny particles of impurities. Sodium aluminum sulfate, $NaAl(SO_4)_2 \cdot 12H_2O$, a kind of alum, is used in "double–acting" baking powders. It acts as an acid, reacting at oven temperatures with the sodium bicarbonate in the powder to form bubbles of carbon dioxide gas.

See also Metal production; Metallurgy; Periodic table.

Further Reading:

Kirk–Othmer Encyclopedia of Chemical Technology, "Aluminum." John Wiley, 1991.
Lide, David R., ed., Handbook of Chemistry and Physics, 73rd Edition, CRC Press, 1992–93.
Umland, Jean B., General Chemistry, West Publishing, 1993.
Wolke, Robert L., Chemistry Explained, Prentice Hall, 1980.

Robert L. Wolke

Aluminum hydroxide

A common compound of aluminum, hydrogen, and oxygen which can be considered either a base with the formula $Al(OH)_3$, or an acid with the formula H_3AlO_3. In addition, the compound is frequently treated as a hydrate—a water–bonded compound—of aluminum oxide and designated variously as hydrated alumina, or aluminum hydrate or trihydrate, hydrated aluminum, or hydrated aluminum oxide, with the formula $Al_2O_3(H_2O)_x$.

Properties

Aluminum hydroxide is found in nature as the mineral bayerite or gibbsite (also called hydrargillite). A mixed aluminum oxide–hydroxide mineral is known as diaspore or boehmite.

In a purified form, aluminum hydroxide is either a white bulky powder or granules with a density of about 2.42 g/mL. It is insoluble in water, but soluble in strong acids and bases. In water, aluminum hydroxide behaves as an amphoteric substance. That is, it acts as an acid in the presence of a strong base and as a base in the presence of a strong acid. This behavior can be represented by the following somewhat oversimplified equation.

$$3\,H^+ + AlO_3^{3-} \leftrightarrows Al(OH)_3 \leftrightarrows Al^{3+} + 3OH^-$$

In the presence of a strong acid such as hydrochloric acid, the above equilibrium shifts to the right, and aluminum chloride is formed.

$$Al(OH)_3 + 3\ HCl \rightarrow 3H_2O + AlCl_3$$

In the presence of a strong base such as sodium hydroxide, the equilibrium is driven to the left and a salt of the aluminate ion (AlO_2^-) is formed.

$$NaOH + H_3AlO_3 \rightarrow NaAlO_2 + 2H_2O$$

Sodium aluminate, $NaAlO_2$, has a number of practical applications, such as in water softening, the sizing of paper, the manufacture of soap and milk glass, and in the printing of textiles and fabrics.

Uses

Aluminum hydroxide and its closely related compounds have a number of practical uses. In one process of water purification, for example, aluminum sulfate, $Al_2(SO_4)_3$, or alum (usually potassium aluminum sulfate, $KAl(SO_4)_2$, is mixed with lime (calcium hydroxide, $Ca(OH)_2$) in a container of water to be purified. The reaction between these compounds results in the formation of a gelatinous precipitate aluminum hydroxide. As the precipitate settles out of solution, it adsorbs on its surface particles of dirt and bacteria that were suspended in the impure water, which can then be removed by filtering off the aluminum hydroxide precipitate.

The ability of aluminum hydroxide to adsorb substances on its surface explains a number of its other applications. It is used in a number of chemical operations, for example, as a filtering medium and in ion–exchange and chromatography devices.

Aluminum hydroxide is popular as an antacid. It behaves as a base, reacting with and neutralizing excess stomach acid (hydrochloric acid) to bring relief from "heartburn." A few of the more common commercial antacids containing aluminum hydroxide are Amphojel, Di–Gel, Gelusil, and Maalox. Ingredients can change without notice, however, so the labels should always be checked.

Aluminum hydroxide is also used as a mordant in dyeing. In most cases, the compound is precipitated out of a water solution onto the fibers to be dyed. The material is then immersed into the dye bath. The color of the final product depends on the combination of dye and mordant used in the process. A similar process is used in the manufacture of certain paint pigments. A given dye and aluminum hydroxide are precipitated together in a reaction vessel and the insoluble compound thus formed is then filtered off.

KEY TERMS

Adsorption—The process by which atoms, ions, or molecules of one substance adhere to the surface of a second substance.

Amphoterism—The property of being able to act as either an acid or a base.

Equilibrium—A state in which the products of a reaction are being produced at the same rate as the rate at which they are being used up to produce the original reactants.

Mordant—A material that is capable of binding a dye to a fabric.

Pigment—Any substance that imparts color to another substance.

Additional uses of aluminum hydroxide include the manufacture of aluminosilicate glass, a high melting point glass used in cooking utensils, the waterproofing of fabrics, and the production of fire clay, paper, pottery, and printing inks.

A close chemical relative of aluminum hydroxide, aluminum hydroxychloride $Al_2(OH)_5Cl$, is an ingredient in many commercial anti–perspirants. The compound acts as an astringent, a substance that closes pores and stops the flow of perspiration.

Further Reading:

Brown, Theodore L., and H. Eugene LeMay, Jr. *Chemistry: The Central Science*, 3rd edition. Englewood Cliffs, NJ: Prentice–Hall, 1985.

Budavari, Susan, ed. *The Merck Index*, 11th edition. Rahway, NJ: Merck and Company, 1989.

Hawley, Gessner G., ed. *The Condensed Chemical Dictionary*, 9th edition. New York: Van Nostrand Reinhold, 1977.

David E. Newton

Alveoli see **Respiratory system**

Alzheimer's disease

Alzheimer's disease is a progressive brain disease that produces devastating mental deterioration. Its symptoms, which include increasingly poor memory, personality changes, and loss of concentration and judgment, are caused by the death of brain cells and decreased connections between the cells that survive. The disease affects approximately four million persons in the United States. Although most victims are over age 65, Alzheimer's disease is not a normal result of aging. Medication can relieve some symptoms but there is no effective treatment or cure. Its cause is unknown.

History

People have long assumed that physical and mental decline were normal and unavoidable features of old age. Such deterioration was called senility. As recently as the early 1970s, much of the public and many physicians and nurses were not familiar with Alzheimer's disease. It was not until the 1980s that scientists and physicians realized that Alzheimer's disease was the most common cause of senility in middle–aged and older people. Since then, the public has become more aware of the disease, especially since Alzheimer's disease has stricken popular celebrities like artist Norman Rockwell, actress Rita Hayworth, and former President Ronald Reagan.

The term Alzheimer's disease is less than a century old. A German neurologist, Dr. Alois Alzheimer (1864–1915), was the first person to describe the disease. In 1906, he studied a 51–year–old woman whose personality and mental abilities were obviously deteriorating: she forgot things, became paranoid, and acted strangely. She died approximately four and one–half years after Alzheimer first treated her. Following an autopsy, Alzheimer examined sections of her brain under a microscope. He noted deposits of an unusual substance in her cerebral cortex—the outer, wrinkled layer of the brain, where many of the higher brain functions such as memory, speech, and thought originate. The substance Alzheimer saw under the microscope is now known to be a protein called amyloid ß–protein.

Many scientists today believe this protein plays an important role in causing Alzheimer's disease. Others believe it is not the primary cause of the disease, but rather a response to it. Eighty years or so after Alzheimer described the first case of the disease, researchers have found that a small percentage of Alzheimer's disease cases are apparently caused by genetic mutations. Most cases, however, are the result of unknown causes.

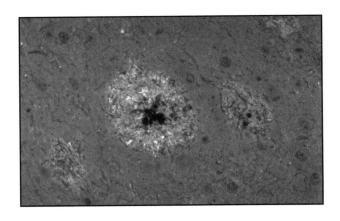

Diseased tissue from the brain of an Alzheimer's patient showing senile plaques within the brain's gray matter.

Alzheimer's disease is a progressive disorder

The first symptom of Alzheimer's disease is usually memory loss of recent events. A slight decline in recent, as opposed to long term, memory is typical in healthy elderly adults. The memory loss seen in Alzheimer's disease, however, is much more severe. As years pass, memory loss becomes greater, and personality and behavioral changes occur. Although victims may remain physically healthy for years, their mental faculties progressively decline. Later symptoms include disorientation, confusion, speech impairment, restlessness, irritability, and inability to care for oneself. Finally, the brain loses the ability to control basic physical functions such as swallowing.

Alzheimer's disease slowly destroys its victim's brains and robs them of the thoughts and memories that make them unique human beings. It creates tremendous problems and stress for those who care for patients. Persons with Alzheimer's disease typically live between five and 10 years after diagnosis, although improvements in health care in recent years have enabled some victims to survive for 15 or even more years. Life–prolonging therapy and treatment, however, does nothing to stop the progression of the disease—they only delay the inevitable. In the absence of other diseases such as heart disease or cancer, Alzheimer's patients usually die from pneumonia or from complications resulting from other infections.

Diagnosing Alzheimer's disease

It is not a simple procedure to diagnose Alzheimer's disease. Physicians must use a process of elimination, because there is no simple, standard diagnostic procedure, such as a blood test, for determining who has the disease. Also, Alzheimer's disease symptoms can be mimicked by other medical conditions, such as brain tumors, dietary deficiencies, and side–effects of medication. About one–third of persons with early symptoms who visit physicians on their own or are taken by family members do not have Alzheimer's disease. The only possible physical procedure for definitively diagnosing Alzheimer's disease is to open the skull and to remove a sample of brain tissue, a biopsy, for microscopic examination. This is rarely done, because brain surgery is too drastic a procedure to use simply to obtain a sample of tissue. Ninety years after Alois Alzheimer first saw the amyloid ß–protein under his microscope, direct microscopic examination of the brain is still the only certain method of diagnosis. Nevertheless, by combining the results of medical histories, physical examinations, laboratory tests, and neurological exams to rule out other causes of dementia, physicians can accurately diagnose 90% or more of cases.

Prescription drugs are useful for treating symptoms like insomnia, anxiety, and depression, but there is no cure or drug that will stop the progressive degeneration produced by the disease. A drug called Tacrine has provided temporary improvement for only a few patients.

Alzheimer's disease is a growing problem

Estimates by the Alzheimer's Association indicate that Alzheimer's disease is the fourth leading cause of death in the United States, after heart disease, cancer, and stroke. It causes the deaths of more than 100,000 adults in the United States each year.

There were an estimated 2.5 million Alzheimer's disease cases in the United States in the mid–1970s. Today the number of cases has increased to four million, according to estimates by the National Institute on Aging. The Alzheimer's Association claims the cost of caring for these patients is $80–90 billion per year.

The apparent increase in the number of Alzheimer's disease cases—from 0.4 per 100,000 in 1979 to 4.2 per 100,000 in 1987—could be the result of more accurate reporting of cases, an increase in the actual number of cases, or a combination of both, according to the Centers for Disease Control. Canada, Australia, and parts of Europe report similar increases. As more and more citizens live into their 80s and 90s, the number of Alzheimer's disease cases could reach 12–14 million or more before the middle of the next century.

Alzheimer's disease is in most cases a disease of old persons. Ten per cent of everyone 65 years of age

or older and 40–50% of everyone 85 or older has or will get the disease. Except for a small number of cases of inherited Alzheimer's disease, the disease is rarely seen in persons in their 30s or 40s.

Alzheimer's disease causes drastic changes in the brain

The brains of Alzheimer's disease victims appear shrunken compared to nondiseased brains. The atrophy is particularly apparent in large parts of the neocortex, the outer layer of gray matter responsible for higher brain functions such as thought and memory. The hippocampus (a part of the brain near the temple) and the area around it are also heavily affected in Alzheimer's disease patients. This area plays an important role in forming memories. Much of the shrinkage of the brain is due to loss of brain cells and decreased numbers of connections, or synapses, between them.

In the surviving brain cells of an Alzheimer's patient, two hallmark features of the disease can be seen under the microscope: neurofibrillary tangles and amyloid plaques. Neurofibrillary tangles are abnormal collections of bunched and twisted fibrils in neurons. The fibrils are derived from components of a network of tubules and filaments that provide cells with structure and organization. The protein in neurofibrillary tangles is called tau. Such tangles are not specific to Alzheimer's disease but are also found in a dozen or so other brain diseases. The severity of mental impairment, however, correlates best with loss of connections between brain cells (synaptic loss), followed by neurofibrillary tangles; plaques appear to correlate only slightly or not at all.

Amyloid plaques consist of a core of amyloid ß–protein and other proteins surrounded by neurites. Neurites are the long projections of nerve cell bodies called axons and dendrites. Axons send signals to other cells and dendrites receive them. In addition to amyloid ß–protein, plaques contain other proteins, such as those normally found in blood serum.

Scavenger cells called microglia can be found in the center of plaques, and astrocytes, a type of cell that usually helps protect neurons, are found around the outside of the spherical plaques. The microglia may be part of an inflammatory response of the body to the plaques. Some researchers believe this response may actually end up killing brain cells rather than destroying plaques.

Amyloid plaques can be found in the brains of healthy persons in small numbers, but they are greatly increased in the brains of Alzheimer's disease patients.

The disease, in fact, is defined by the presence of a large number of plaques in a section of brain tissue. The concentrations of many types of neurotransmitters (chemical messengers used by brain cells to communicate with one another) are also lower in the brains of Alzheimer's disease victims.

Risk factors for Alzheimer's disease

Scientists are studying many factors that may contribute to Alzheimer's disease. These include toxins, metabolic abnormalities, and infectious agents alone and in combination with each other. Among the known risk factors for Alzheimer's disease are head trauma, age, Down's syndrome, and in a small percentage of cases—approximately 10%—gene mutations.

Several studies have indicated that head injury suffered late in life and serious enough to produce unconsciousness is a significant risk factor for the disease. Both former President Ronald Reagan and artist Norman Rockwell suffered head injuries prior to developing Alzheimer's disease. It is not known if these injuries contributed to the onset of their dementia, but their cases are consistent with studies linking head trauma and Alzheimer's disease.

Down's syndrome is a genetic disorder that causes retardation. It results when a person is born with three copies of chromosome 21 instead of two. Virtually everyone with Down's syndrome develops plaques and tangles typical of Alzheimer's disease if they live long enough. It is intriguing that the gene for amyloid ß–protein is found on chromosome 21.

Familial Alzheimer's disease, an inherited form of the disease, accounts for approximately 10% of cases. Approximately 100 families in the world are known to have rare genetic mutations that are linked with early onset of disease symptoms. Some of these families have an aggressive form of the disease in which symptoms appear before age 40. The early onset genes are on chromosome 21, chromosome 14, and an unidentified chromosome. The mutation on chromosome 14 accounts for more than 80% of familial or inherited Alzheimer's disease cases.

In the majority of Alzheimer's disease cases, symptoms appear after age 65 and are not linked to a specific mutation. Some scientists suspect that the genes that are mutated in persons with familial Alzheimer's may play some role in the disease in victims without the mutations. While genes alone may cause 10% of all cases, the remaining 90% may be caused by various combinations of genetic and as yet undefined environmental factors. It is possible that most cases result from a genetic predisposition combined in varying ways with other factors.

Recently scientists have discovered that the gene for apolipoprotein E (ApoE), a protein that moves cholesterol in the bloodstream and can bind to amyloid ß–protein and other proteins, can affect a person's risk of developing the disease. There are three forms of the ApoE gene: ApoE2, ApoE3, and ApoE4. These three forms of the gene are not mutations but are normally occurring variations found in many populations. Unlike the genes inherited by the families with familial Alzheimer's disease, it is not a mutation in the ApoE gene that increases the risk factor; rather, it is the variety or type of ApoE gene someone inherits that affects his or her chances of developing Alzheimer's disease.

No one knows how this gene contributes to Alzheimer's disease, but it is known that inheritance of ApoE4 increases the risk and lowers the age of onset of the disease. Inheritance of ApoE2 decreases the risk and increases the age of onset. The ApoE gene seems to be a "susceptibility gene."

Current research

Researchers are attacking the problem of Alzheimer's disease by studying the basic biology of the disease and by trying to develop drugs they hope will affect those changes. Because no one knows what causes Alzheimer's disease, or how brain lesions like plaques form, or why connections between brain cells are destroyed, it is difficult to know what kind of drugs will help. Until the exact biological causes of Alzheimer's disease are identified, drug trials may be used more for research than therapy.

Many scientists are convinced that the key to understanding the disease and the best hope for an effective treatment lies in understanding ß–amyloid protein. This is the same substance Alois Alzheimer saw in plaques in the brain of his demented patient in 1906. Scientists still want to know how it is made and what its purpose is. These researchers hope one day to decrease the production of ß–amyloid protein or of the larger protein, amyloid precursor protein, from which it is derived.

After years of effort, several research groups have succeeded in producing animal models of Alzheimer's disease. By introducing genes for mutated human ß–amyloid protein into mice, they have created animals which experience brain degeneration and plaques. Tests with these animals may one day help determine

KEY TERMS

. . . .

ß–amyloid protein—A protein that accumulates in the brains of Alzheimer's disease victims.

Dementia—Deterioration and loss of most higher mental functions, including the abilities to reason, remember, and concentrate.

Neurofibrillary tangles—Abnormal, dense bundles of a protein called tau found in neurons in several brain diseases, including Alzheimer's disease.

Plaques–In Alzheimer's disease, abnormal, spherical structures found in large numbers. The centers of the plaques contain ß–amyloid protein.

Senility—Serious mental and physical deterioration once thought to be normal in old age.

the role of ß–amyloid protein in Alzheimer's disease and could help researchers find drugs for treatment.

Other scientists believe ß–amyloid protein is not the key to understanding and treating the disease. They believe accumulation of large amounts of ß–amyloid protein is a response to an as–yet undiscovered cause.

The pharmaceutical industry is developing drugs for a variety of therapeutic approaches to treating Alzheimer's disease. These include drugs that will inhibit the inflammatory response the brain appears to mount against plaques. In this approach, it is assumed that the inflammatory response contributes to cell death. By inhibiting it, the researchers hope to decrease the loss of brain cells in Alzheimer's disease. Other drug companies are continuing to develop drugs they hope will increase the amounts of neurotransmitters like acetylcholine in the brains of Alzheimer's disease patients. Acetylcholine is an important chemical messenger in the brain that is severely lowered in Alzheimer's disease. By preventing the breakdown of remaining acetylcholine, researchers hope to alleviate some of the symptoms of the disease.

See also Aging and death; Brain; Chromosomal abnormalities; Dementia; Down's syndrome; Mutation.

Further Reading:

Beardsley, Tim. "Putting Alzheimer's to the Tests: Several New Techniques May Detect the Disease." *Scientific American* 272, No. 2 (February 1995): 12.

Selkoe, Dennis J. "Amyloid Protein and Alzheimer's Disease." *Scientific American* (November 1991): 68–78.

Swerdlow, Joel L. "Quiet Miracle of the Brain." *National Geographic* 187, No. 6 (June 1995): 2–41.

Dean Allen Haycock

AM (amplitude modulation) see **Radio waves**

Amaranth family

The amaranth family, also called the pigweed family, is a large family of dicotyledonous flowering plants known to botanists as the amaranthaceae. It is a relatively large family having about 65 genera and about 900 species. The species in this family are mostly annual or perennial herbs, although a few species are shrubs or small trees. Botanists divide the Amaranthaceae into two subfamilies, the Amaranthoideae and the Gomphrenoideae, based on certain morphological characteristics of their flowers. All species have simple leaves, rather than compound leaves.

The flowers of most species in the Amaranthaceae are bisexual, meaning that they have both male and female reproductive organs. In all species, the flowers are very small and have radial symmetry. The flowers of most species arise in a dense inflorescence, or flower cluster, with each flower of the inflorescence subtended by one or more small red bracts (modified leaves). The small red bracts remain present as the flower matures into a fruit. The flowers of most species make nectar and are insect–pollinated. An exception is *Amaranthus*, a genus with about 50 species, whose flowers are wind pollinated and do not make nectar.

Many species in the Amaranthaceae have red inflorescences, fruits, and vegetative parts, due to the presence of betalain pigments. Betalains are a class of nitrogen–containing plant pigments which only occur in 10 evolutionarily related plant families, known as the Centrospermae. Interestingly, none of the species with betalain pigments also have flavonoid pigments. Flavonoids and betalains can be very similar in color, even though they have very different chemical structures.

Most of the 900 species of the Amaranthaceae grow in tropical and subtropical regions of Africa, Central America, and South America. The number of Amaranthaceae species declines as one approaches the northern and southern temperate zones. There are only about 100 species of this family in America and

A tumbleweed on a highway west of Valentine, Nebraska.

Canada. Many species of the Amaranthaceae can be considered weeds, since they invade disturbed areas, such as agricultural fields and roadsides.

Several species in the Amaranthaceae are used by mankind. Some species are important horticultural plants, such as *Amaranthus caudatus*, known as "Love–lies–bleeding." The seeds of several species in the Amaranthus genus were eaten by native cultures of North and South America, and were in cultivation over 5,000 years ago in the Tehuacan region of modern–day Mexico. Many health food stores currently sell amaranth grain, a flour–like substance which results from grinding amaranth seeds. Amaranth grain can be used with wheat to make bread, or can be cooked with water to make a side dish.

Amaryllis family (Amaryllidaceae)

Species in the amaryllis family are flowering plants, and are mostly long–lived, perennial herbs arising from a bulb or, less commonly, from rhizomes (underground stems). These plants have linear or strap

Love-lies-bleeding, a member of the Amaranth family.

shaped leaves, either crowded around the base of a leafless flowering stem, or arranged in two tight rows along a short stem, as in the common houseplant *Clivia*. The leaves are usually hairless and contain mucilage cells, or cells filled with calcium oxalate crystals known as raphides for defense against herbivores. Silica–filled (glass) cells, which are typical of many other monocotyledonous plant families, are absent from the amaryllis family.

The flowers of amaryllids are bisexual, with six perianth parts (or tepals) that sometimes have appendages that form a corona, as in the central, protruding part of a daffodil flower (*Narcissus* spp.). The flowers are white, yellow, purple, or red, but never blue. The flowers are pollinated by bees or moths, but many are also adapted to bird and some to bat pollination. The fruits are usually many–seeded capsules, or sometimes berries.

156

A Joshua tree (*Yucca brevifolia*) in bloom in the Mojave Desert, California.

Between 900 and 1,300 species of amaryllids have been recognized. Most are tropical or subtropical, with centers of distribution in South Africa, the western Mediterranean (especially Spain and Morocco), and to a lesser extent, Andean South America. Many species are drought–resistant xerophytes that produce leaves in the spring or when the rainy season begins, open their stomates only at night, have stomates located in the bottom of pits, and have thick waxy leaves—all to conserve water.

Many amaryllids are prized as ornamentals for home or garden because of their large, showy flowers, which are held high above the contrasting dark green leaves. The Cape belladona (*Amaryllis belladona*) is a native of dry regions of southwestern Cape Province, South Africa, and is widely cultivated for its large, pink, bell–shaped flowers, which are moth–pollinated. The genus Hippeastrum, which is native to the West Indies, Mexico, and as far south as Argentina, has also been called *Amaryllis* by some taxonomists. Whatever its correct identity, many species of this genus have spectacular, large flowers that have evolved for pollination by birds, and are commonly grown as ornamentals.

On the left a flowering century plant (*Agave shawii*), and on the right a cirio (*Idria columnaris*), Baja California, Mexico. Some plant taxonomists include agaves in the Amaryllis family, while others place it in its own family, the Agavaceae.

Many members of the tribe Narcisseae are also widely cultivated, both indoors and outdoors. Most of the horticultural varieties originate from Spain, Portugal, or Morocco, and are small to medium–sized herbs, with linear leaves around a leafless stem that typically bears one to several flowers. The spring–flowering species have been most intensively bred as garden ornamentals, especially the common daffodil (*Narcissus pseudonarcissus*). Snowdrops (*Galanthus nivalis*), an early blooming ornamental, and St. John's Lily (*Crinum asiaticum*), are also amaryllids. Clivia is a common houseplant, especially in Europe, that is prized for its deep–green, shiny leaves and its large salmon–colored flowers, and for the fact that it requires little light, water, or attention.

Agaves are often included in the amaryllis family. However, this taxonomic treatment is controversial, and agaves are sometimes put into their own family, the Agavaceae. About 300 species live in dry habitats from the southern United States to northern South America. These are conspicuous perennials, with a dense rosette of large, persistent sword–like leaves that bear spines at the tip, and often along the margins as well.

The scientific name *Agave* comes from the Greek *agaue,* which means noble, referring to the height of their flowering stalks. Their common name, century plant, refers to the long period of time that these plants remain in a non–sexual, vegetative state before flowering. This period generally lasts for five to 50 years, and not 100 years as the name implies. When they are ready to flower, *Agave* plants rapidly develop a thick flowering stem that may reach 20 ft (6 m) in height. Greenhouse keepers have sometimes come to work in the morning to find a flowering stem of an agave poking through the broken glass of their greenhouse. After this one episode of sexual activity, some species of agave plants die.

A few species of agaves are commercially important. *Agave americana,* commonly called American aloe or century plant, contains aloe, which is a commonly used ingredient in shampoos, moisturizers, and salves. Also important is the production of Mexico's national alcoholic beverage, pulque, which is mostly made from *Agave americana,* although a few other species of agave are also used. When the flowering stem is formed, a large amount of sap is produced. The bud at the end of the developing flowering stem is removed, and a cavity scooped out in which the sugary sap collects. As much as 238 gallons (900 liters) can be recovered from one plant over three to four months. The sap is fermented, resulting in a milky liquid with an alcohol concentration of four to eight percent. This beverage is pulque. A more potent liquor known as mescal is produced by distillation of pulque.

Many species of agave are valuable for the long fibers in their leaves. Aztecs used the fibers of henequen (*A. fourcroydes*) to make a twine, and the practice continues today. The stronger sisal hemp is derived from leaves of *A. sisalana,* native to the Americas but now grown in many parts of the tropics. Sisal is commonly used to manufacture baler twine for agriculture and a parcelling twine. The hard fibers of *Furcraea macrophylla* of Columbia have been used to make the large bags used for shipping coffee beans from that and other countries.

Further Reading:

Bateman, G., ed.. *Flowering Plants of the World.* Oxford: Oxford University Press, 1978.

Dahlgren, R.M.T., H.T. Clifford, and P.F. Yeo. *The Families of the Monocotyledons: Structure, Evolution, and Taxonomy.* Berlin: Springer–Verlag, 1985.

Les C. Cwynar

Amber see **Fossil and fossilization**

Ambush bugs see **True bugs**

American redstart see **Warblers**

Americum see **Element, transuranium**

Ames test

The Ames test, named for its developer, Dr. Bruce Ames, is a method to test chemicals for their cancer–causing properties. It is used by cosmetic companies, pharmaceutical manufacturers, and other industries that must prove that their products will not cause cancer in humans.

Dr. Ames, a cancer researcher at the University of California, began development of his method in the late 1950s. He believed an efficient, less–expensive means could be found to screen substances than the cumbersome methods in use. He hit upon the use of bacteria, which could be grown (cultured) cheaply, and grew rapidly so that testing could be completed quickly, yet could indicate the carcinogenic (cancer–causing) potential of many chemicals.

The bacterium used is a strain of *Salmonella typhimurium* that lacks an enzyme needed to form colonies. The bacterium is grown on agar culture (agar is a gelatin–like substance with nutrients). The substance to be tested is blotted on a bit of paper and placed on the agar. If the substance is a carcinogen it will cause mutations in the bacterium as the cells divide. The mutant cells will have the enzyme to form colonies. The test can be completed in a day.

Bacterial mutations are the result of DNA damage. Because DNA in bacteria is similar to that in the higher animals, it is assumed the substance also will damage DNA in those animals and cause cell mutations and possibly cancer.

The Ames test is a screening test; it is not the final test that any substance must undergo before being commercially produced. It is designed to detect a cancer–causing agent quickly and inexpensively.

Prior to development of this test the procedure to determine whether a substance was a carcinogen required feeding the test substance to or injecting it into laboratory animals such as rats or mice and then examining them for evidence of tumor formation. Testing took years to complete, hundreds of animals, and millions of dollars.

Any substance that causes bacterial mutation in the Ames test is not given further consideration for development. A substance that does not produce bacterial mutation still must undergo animal testing, but at least the manufacturer has a good idea that it is not a cancer–causing agent.

See also Cancer.

Amicable numbers

Two numbers are said to be amicable (i.e., friendly) if each one of them is equal to the sum of the *proper* divisors of the others, i.e., whole numbers less than the given numbers that divide the given number with no remainder. For example, 220 has proper divisors 1, 2, 4, 5, 10, 11, 20, 22, 44, 55, and 110. The sum of these divisors is 284. The proper divisors of 284 are 1, 2, 4, 71, and 142. Their sum is 220; so 220 and 284 are amicable. This is the smallest pair of amicable numbers.

The discovery of amicable numbers is attributed to the neo–Pythagorean philosopher Iamblichus (c. 250–330), who credited Pythagoras with the original knowledge of their nature. The Pythagoreans believed that amicable numbers, like all special numbers, had a profound cosmic significance. A biblical reference (a gift of 220 goats from Jacob to Esau, Genesis 23: 14) is thought by some to indicate an earlier knowledge of amicable numbers.

No pairs of amicable numbers other than 220 and 284 were discovered by European mathematicians until 1636, when the French mathematician Pierre de Fermat (1601–1665) found the pair 18,496 and 17,296. A century later, the Swiss mathematician Leonhard Euler (1707–1783) made an extensive search and found about 60 additional pairs. Surprisingly, however, he overlooked the smallest pair, 1184 and 1210, which was subsequently discovered in 1866 by a 16–year–old boy, Nicolo Paganini.

During the medieval period, Arabian mathematicians preserved and developed the mathematical knowledge of the ancient Greeks. For example, The polymath Thabit ibn Qurra (836–901) formulated an ingenious rule for generating amicable number pairs: Let $a = 3 \times 2^n - 1$, $b = 3 \times 2^{n-1} - 1$ and $c = 9 \times 2^{2n-1} - 1$; then, if a, b, and c are primes, $2^n \times ab$ and $2^n \times c$ are amicable. This rule produces 220 and 284 when n is 2. When n is 3, c is not a prime, and the resulting numbers are not amicable. For n = 4 it produces Fermat's pair, 17,296 and 18,416, skipping over Paganini's pair and others.

Amicable numbers serve no practical purpose, but professionals and amateurs alike have for centuries enjoyed seeking them and exploring their properties.

Amides

An amide is a nitrogen–containing compound that can be considered a derivative of ammonia, NH_3. Organic amides contain the group (–C=O). The simplest organic amide is methamide,

$$\begin{array}{c} HC=O \\ | \\ NH_2 \end{array}$$

Inorganic amides consist of a metal or some other cation combined with the amide ion (–NH_2), as in sodium amide ($NaNH_2$). In comparison with their better known organic cousins, the inorganic amides are less important. One member of the inorganic family, sodium amide, does find some application as a dehydrating agent and in the production of the dye indigo, the rocket fuel hydrazine, sodium cyanide, and other compounds.

Classification and properties

Like the amines, the amides can be classified as primary, secondary, or tertiary, depending on the number of hydrogen atoms substituted in the ammonia molecule. An amide containing the –NH_2 group is a primary amide, one containing the –NH group is asecondary amine, and one containing the –N– group is a tertiary amine.

Although amides and amines both contain an amino group (–NH$_2$, NH or N), the former are much weaker bases and much stronger acids than the latter. Amides undergo many of the same reactions as do other derivatives of organic acids. For example, they undergo hydrolysis to produce the parent carboxylic acid and ammonia. They can also be dehydrated with a strong agent such as diphosphorus pentoxide, P$_2$O$_5$. The product of this reaction, a nitrile, a compound containing the –C≡N group, is widely used in the synthesis of other organic compounds.

Some familiar amides

The synthesis of a protein results in a protein in the formation of an amide bond between adjacent amino acids. Proteins can be considered the most common examples of amides in the natural world. A naturally occurring amide is nicotinamide, one of the B vitamins. A third familiar natural amide is urea, also known as carbamide. Urea is the compound by which otherwise toxic wastes are excreted from mammalian bodies.

Important synthetic amides

Perhaps the best known of all synthetic amides is the fiber known as nylon. In 1931, the American chemist Wallace Hume Carothers discovered a process for making one of the first synthetic fibers. He found that the addition of adipic acid to hexamethylene diamine resulted in the formation of a strong, fiber–like product to which he gave the name Nylon 66. The 66 part of the name reflects the fact that adipic acid and hexamethylene diamine each contain six carbon atoms in their molecules.

The reaction between these two substances results in the formation of a long polymer, somewhat similar to the structure of natural protein. As in protein, the sub–units of nylon are joined by amide bonds. For this reason, both protein and nylon can be thought of as polyamides, compounds in which a large number of amide units are joined to each other in a long chain.

Other types of nylon were also developed at later dates. One form, known as Nylon 6, is produced by the polymerization of a single kind of molecule, 6–amino-hexanoic acid. The bonding between sub–units in Nylon–6—amide bonds—is the same as it is in Nylon 66. In all types of nylon, the fiber obtains its strength from hydrogen bonding that occurs between oxygen and hydrogen atoms on adjacent chains of the material.

Another type of polymer is formed when two of the simplest organic compounds, urea and formalde-

KEY TERMS

Amide ion—An anion with the formula –NH$_2$.

Hydrogen bond—A weak chemical bond that results from the electrical attraction between oppositely charged particles, usually a hydrogen ion and an oxygen–containing ion.

Nylon—A group of synthetic fibers that have in common the fact that they are large polymers held together by amide bonding.

Polymer—A large molecule made up of many small sub–units repeated over and over again.

Protein—Any large naturally occurring polymer made of many amino acids bonded to each other by means of amide bonds.

Synthetic detergent—A soap–like material that is manufactured from raw materials.

hyde, react with each other. In this reaction, amide bonds form between alternate urea and formaldehyde molecules, resulting in a very long polyamide chain. Urea formaldehyde polymers are in great demand by industry, where they are used as molding compounds, in the treatment of paper and textiles, and as a binder in particle board, to mention but a few uses.

An amide with which many people are familiar is acetaminophen, an analgesic (pain–killer). It is the active ingredient in products such as Amadil, Cetadol, Datril, Naprinol, Panadol, and Tylenol. Another amide analgesic is phenacetin, found in products such as APC (aspirin, phenacetin, and caffeine) tablets and Empirin.

Other commercially important amides include the insect repellant N,N–dimethyl–m–toluamide (Off, Deet), the local anesthetics lidocaine (Xylocaine) and dibucaine (Nupercaine), the tranquilizer meprobromate (Miltown, Equaine), and the insecticides Sevin and Mipcin.

See also Artificial fibers; Polymer.

Further Reading:
Embree, Harland D. *Brief Course: Organic Chemistry*. Glenview, IL: Scott, Foresman, 1983, pp. 362–67.
Joesten, Melvin D., David O. Johnston, John T. Netterville, and James L. Wood. *World of Chemistry*. Philadelphia: Saunders, 1991, pp. 429, 734.
Widom, Joanne M., and Stuart J. Edelstein. *Chemistry: An Introduction to General, Organic, and Biological Chemistry*. San Francisco: W. H. Freeman, 1981, pp. 525–30.

David E. Newton

Amine

An amine is an organic compound that may be considered a derivative of ammonia (NH_3) in which one or more hydrogen atoms have been replaced by organic groups. Amines are generally classified into subgroups, depending on the number of hydrogen atoms that have been replaced. If R stands for an organic substituent, then a primary amine can be designated as RNH_2, a secondary amine as R_2NH, and a tertiary amine as R_3N.

Occurrence

Amines occur widely in nature where they play important roles in a variety of biological processes. Most prominently, amino groups ($\equiv N$, $=NH$, or $-NH_2$) are found in amino acids, in alkaloids, and in vitamins. A number of amines have pronounced physiological activity in the body. Some naturally occurring amines are thiamine chloride (vitamin B^1), histamine, quinine, caffeine, codeine, morphine, and nicotine. Adrenalin and serotonin are two of the most familiar amines that function as neurotransmitters (nerve message carrying chemicals) in our nervous systems.

Properties

Amines constitute such a large number of compounds that relatively few generalizations can be made about their physical properties. One of the most interesting of those properties, however, is the strong and unpleasant odor associated with some of the simpler amines. They are produced along with ammonia during the decay of organic matter and tend to have a strong, offensive, ammonia–like odor. Two of the compounds with the most pronounced odors are putrescine [$(CH_2)(NH_2)_2$] and cadaverine [$(CH_2)_5(NH_2)_2$], which are largely responsible for the odor of dead fish and decaying meat.

Basicity of amines

The most prominent chemical property of the amines is their basicity. The nitrogen atom that occurs in every amine contains an unshared pair of electrons. According to the Brønsted–Lowry theory of acids and bases, that makes the nitrogen atom a base. In water solution, for example, an amine attracts a hydrogen ion (proton) from the water molecule, forming a positively charged ion and a hydroxide ion. An example of that reaction is given by the following equation.

$$CH_3NH_2 + H_2O \leftrightarrows CH_3NH_3^+ + OH^-$$

The basicity of an amine depends on the type of organic group(s) that is substituted in the ammonia molecule. In general, amines containing aliphatic (open chain) groups tend to be more basic than those containing aromatic (ring) groups. Also, the greater the number of substituted groups in an amine, the more basic it is. That is, tertiary amines are more basic than secondary amines which, in turn, are more basic than primary amines. In general, aliphatic amines are more basic than ammonia itself, while aromatic amines are less basic than ammonia.

Reactions of amines

Amines undergo many of the reactions that one would expect of any base. For example, they react with strong acids to form amine salts. The equation below illustrates the reaction between methylamine and hydrochloric acid, resulting in the formation of methylammonium chloride.

$$CH_3NH_2 + HCl \leftrightarrows CH_3NH_3^+ + Cl^-$$

Reactions with nitrous acid

One amine–acid reaction of particular commercial interest is the reaction of an amine with nitrous acid (HNO_2). When nitrous acid is added to most amines, the products formed are either unstable or are of relatively little commercial interest. One exception to that rule is the reaction between nitrous acid and primary aromatic amines—amines in which a single aromatic group has been substituted for one of the hydrogen atoms in ammonia. The product of this reaction is known as a diazonium salt. A diazonium salt has the general formula Ar–$N\equiv N$:X, where Ar is the aromatic group and X is usually a halogen. Diazonium salts are generally stable at temperatures below 41°F (5°C) although they quickly (and sometimes explosively) decompose above that temperature.

Coupling reactions

Diazonium salts are of interest to chemists because they can be converted into a great variety of other compounds. They are sometimes the only (or the best) way in which some of these compounds can be made. Of greater commercial interest is the reaction between diazonium salts and other aromatic compounds. The products of such reactions are known as azo compounds and the reactions themselves are called diazo coupling reactions.

The property of an azo compound that makes it commercially attractive is the presence of the $-N\equiv N-$ chromophore group. A chromophore group is an arrangement of atoms in a molecule that gives color to the compound. Azo dyes are intensely colored compounds produced by coupling reactions, often between the families known as naphthylamines and naphthols. Some examples of azo dyes are butter yellow, direct blue 2B, direct green B, bismarck brown 2R, para–red, and chrysoidine Y. The first of these compounds was previously used as a coloring agent in foods, but was later banned because of its suspected carcinogenic (cancer causing) properties.

Sulfa drugs

One of the great steps forward in modern medicine was the discovery of the antibiotic effects of a group of amines known as the sulfa drugs (not to be confused with the element sulfur). In 1935, a German doctor named Gerhard Domagk found that a newly invented dye called Prontosil was able to destroy the deadly streptococcus bacterium. A year later, the French scientist Ernest Fourneau demonstrated that Prontosil breaks down in the human body to form an aromatic amine, sulfanilamide, and it is the amine that is toxic to streptococci. These discoveries made possible the development of some of the earliest anti–bacterial drugs available to medical science.

Over the next decade, chemists synthesized a variety of compounds related to sulfanilamide that also have antibacterial action. These included sulfadiazine, sulfapyridine, sulfathiazole, and sulfacetamide. These drugs proved successful in treating a number of diseases including pneumonia, urinary tract infections, and gastrointestinal disorders.

Scientists now know how sulfa drugs work as antibacterial agents. Their structures are very similar to that of p–aminobenzoic acid (PABA), a compound essential to bacterial growth. When fed to bacteria, sulfa drug molecules take the place of PABA molecules in bacterial cells, prevent the formation of chemicals essential to bacterial metabolism, and cause the death of the bacteria.

History

Amines were discovered accidentally by the French chemist Charles Adolphe Wurtz in 1849. He produced methylamine (CH_3NH_2) ethylamine ($C_2H_5NH_2$) by treating nitrogen–containing compounds with alkali solution. The existence of such compounds had been predicted a decade earlier by Justus von Liebig, but Wurtz was the first to point out that amines could be thought of as derivatives of ammonia. His work on the amines was especially important in the development of his Theory of

KEY TERMS

Aliphatic—Organic compounds in which carbon atoms are arranged in open chains.

Alkaloids—Naturally occurring compounds whose molecules consist of cyclic structures containing nitrogen, nearly all with pronounced physiological and/or psychological effects on humans.

Amino acids—Organic compounds that contain both an amine and an acid group, the fundamental constituents of proteins.

Aromatic—Organic compounds in which carbon atoms are arranged in benzene–like rings.

Azo compound—A product of the reaction between a diazonium salt and an aromatic compound.

Basicity—The tendency of a substance to act chemically as a base.

Chromophore group—Any group of atoms that gives color to a substance.

Coupling reaction—A chemical reaction in which diazonium salts react with aromatic compounds to form azo compounds.

Diazonium salt—A compound that consists of an aromatic group, two nitrogen atoms bonded to each other in a triple bond, and an anion such as a halogen ion.

Sulfa drugs—A group of drugs that share a common structural feature and are effective in fighting various types of disease–causing bacteria.

Types, an early attempt to organize the young science of organic chemistry.

See also Alkaloid; Amino acid; Ammonia; Antibiotics; Neurotransmitter; Vitamin.

Further Reading:

Brown, William H., and Elizabeth P. Rogers. *General, Organic and Biochemistry*. Boston: Willard Grant, 1980. Chapter 17.
Hart, Harold. *Organic Chemistry: A Short Course*, 2nd edition. Boston: Houghton Mifflin, 1991. Chapter 11.
Solomons, T. W. Graham. *Organic Chemistry*, 2nd edition. New York: John Wiley, 1980.

David E. Newton

Amino acid

Amino acids are organic compounds made of carbon, hydrogen, oxygen, nitrogen and, in a few cases, sulfur. The basic structure of an amino acid molecule consists of a carbon atom that is bonded to an amino group (–NH$_2$), a carboxyl group (–COOH), a hydrogen atom and a fourth group that differs from one amino acid to another and which is often referred to as the –R group or the side chain. The –R group can vary widely and is responsible for the differences in the chemical properties. The name, amino acid, comes from the amino group and the acid group which are the most reactive parts of the molecule. The amino acids that are important in the biological world are referred to as α–amino acids because the amino group is bonded to the α–carbon atom, that is, the one adjacent to the carboxyl group.

A chemical reaction that is characteristic of amino acids involves the formation of a bond, called a peptide linkage, between the carboxyl group of one amino acid and the amino group of a second amino acid. Very long chains of amino acids can bond together in this way to form proteins. The importance of the amino acids in nature arises from their ability to form proteins, which are the basic building blocks of all living things.

The specific properties of each kind of protein are largely dependent on the kind and sequence of the amino acids in it. Other chemical behavior of these protein molecules is due to interactions between the amino and the carboxyl groups or between the various R– groups along the long chains of amino acids in the molecule. These chemical interactions confer a three–dimensional configuration on the protein which is essential to its proper functioning.

Chemical structure

Although most of the known amino acids were identified and isolated (sometimes in impure form) during the nineteenth century, the chemical structures of many of them were not known until much later. Understanding their importance in the formation of proteins, the basis of the structure and function of all cells is of even more recent origin, dating to the first part of the 20th century. Only about 20 amino acids are common in humans, with two others present in a few animal species. There are over 100 other lesser known ones that are found mostly in plants.

Each of the common amino acids has, in addition to its chemical name, a more familiar name and a three–letter abbreviation that is frequently used to identify it. They are often grouped by similarities in the chemical properties of the side chains. The side chain of glycine (gly) consists of a single hydrogen atom; alanine (ala), valine (val), leucine (leu), and isoleucine (ile) all have hydrocarbon (containing only hydrogen and carbon) side chains; proline (pro) has a hydrocarbon that is part of a ring structure; serine (ser) and threonine (thr) have an alcohol (–OH) side chain; cysteine (cys) and methionine (met) both have sulfur atoms as part of the –R group; phenlyalanine (phe), tyrosine (tyr), and tryptophan (trp) all contain an aromatic ring (related to the benzene ring) as part of the side chain; aspartic acid (asp) and glutamic acid (glu) have a second carboxylic acid group while asparagine (asn) and glutamine (gln) have a carboxylic acid derivative (a –CONH$_2$) group; and lysine (lys), arginine (arg), and histidine (his) have an –R group that contains a second amino group.

Although amino acid molecules contain an amino group and a carboxyl group, certain chemical properties are not consistent with this structure. Unlike the behavior of molecules with amino or carboxylic acid functional groups alone, amino acids exist mostly as crystalline solids that decompose rather than melt at temperatures over 392°F (200°C). They are quite soluble in water but insoluble in non–polar solvents like benzene or ether. Their acidic and basic properties are exceptionally weak for molecules that contain an acid carboxyl group and a basic amino group.

This problem was resolved when it was realized that amino acids are better represented as dipolar ions, sometimes called zwitterions (from the German, meaning hybrid ions). Although the molecule as a whole does not have a net charge, there is a transfer of an H$^+$ ion from the carboxyl group to the amino group ; consequently, the amino group is present as an –NH$_3^+$ and the carboxyl group is present as a –COO$^-$ (Fig. 1). This reaction is an acid–base interaction between two groups in the same molecule and occurs because the –COOH group is a rather strong acid and the –NH$_2$ group is a rather strong base. As a result of this structure, amino acids can behave as acids in the presence of strong bases or they can behave as bases in the presence of strong acids.

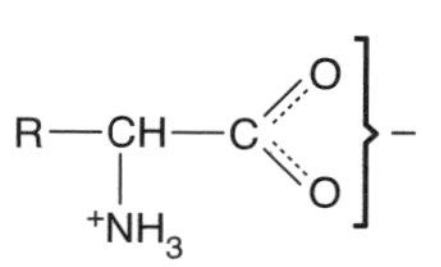

Figure 1.

Name	The XYZ group is	Shorthand	Name	The XYZ group is	Shorthand
Glycine	$-H$	Gly	Glutamine	$-CH_2CH_2C(=O)-NH_2$	Gln
Alanine	$-CH_3$	Ala	Lysine	$-CH_2CH_2CH_2CH_2NH_2$	Lys
Valine	$-CH(CH_3)CH_3$	Val	Arginine	$-CH_2CH_2CH_2N(H)-C(NH)-NH_2$	Arg
Leucine	$-CH_2CH(CH_3)CH_3$	Leu	Histidine	imidazole group	His
Isoleucine	$-CH(CH_3)CH_2CH_3$	Ile	Phenylalanine	$-CH_2-C_6H_5$	Phe
Serine	$-CH_2OH$	Ser	Tyrosine	$-CH_2-C_6H_4OH$	Tyr
Threonine	$-CH(CH_3)OH$	Thr	Tryptophan	indole group	Trp
Cysteine	$-CH_2SH$	Cys	Proline	pyrrolidine ring	Pro
Methionine	$-CH_2CH_2SCH_3$	Met			
Aspartic acid	$-CH_2C(=O)-OH$	Asp			
Asparagine	$-CH_2C(=O)-NH_2$	Asn			
Glutamic acid	$-CH_2CH_2C(=O)-OH$	Glu			

The 20 most common amino acids: $NH_2-CH(XYZ)-C(=O)-OH$

One other property of amino acids that is important to their chemical behavior is that all of the amino acids except glycine can exist as mirror images of each other; that is, right– or left–handed versions of the molecule. Like the positions of the thumb and fingers of a glove, the right hand being the mirror image of the left hand, the positions of the functional groups on the α carbon can be mirror images of each other. Interestingly, nearly all of the amino acids occurring in nature are the left–handed versions of the molecules. Right–handed versions are not found in the proteins of higher organisms but are present in some lower forms of life such as in the cell walls of bacteria. They are also found in some antibiotics such as streptomycin, actinomycin, bacitracin, and tetracycline. These antibiotics can kill bacterial cells by interfering with the formation of protein necessary for maintaining life and for reproducing.

Bonding

Amino acids are extremely important in nature as the monomers, or individual units, that join together in chains to form copolymers (polymers made of more than one kind of monomer). The chains may contain as few as two or as many as 3,000 amino acid units. Groups of only two amino acids are called dipeptides; three amino acids bonded together are called tripeptides; if there are more than 10 in a chain, they are called polypeptides; and if there are 50 or more, they are known as proteins.

In 1902 the German organic chemist, Emil Fischer, first proposed that the amino acids in polypeptides are linked together between the carboxyl group of one amino acid and the amino group of the other. This bond forms when the –OH from the carboxyl end of one molecule and the hydrogen from the amino end of another molecule split off and form a small molecule byproduct, H_2O or water. This type of reaction is called a condensation reaction. The new bond between the carbon atom and the nitrogen atom is called a peptide bond, also known as an amide linkage. Because every amino acid molecule has a carboxyl end and an amino end, each one can join to any other amino acid by the formation of a peptide bond.

All the millions of different proteins in living things are formed by the bonding of only 20 amino acids to form long polymer chains. Like the 26 letters of the alphabet that join together to form different words, depending on which letters are used and what the sequence is, the 20 amino acids can join together in different combinations and sequences to form proteins. But whereas words usually have only about 10 or fewer letters per word, proteins are usually made from at least 50 amino acids to more than 3,000. Because each amino acid can be used many times along the chain and because there are no restrictions on the length of the chain, the number of possible combinations for the formation of protein is truly enormous.

The amino acids in polypeptides can be represented in three ways: by writing out the complete chemical formulas; by writing the amino acid sequence using the standard, three–letter abbreviation for each acid as in gly–ser–ala (which represents glycine, serine and alanine); or by naming the polypeptide as in gly-cylserylalanine. The name is derived by dropping the –ine or –ic ending of each amino acid along the chain and replacing it with a –yl ending. The last acid of the chain is given its full name. It is common practice to write polypeptides with the free, unbonded amino group on the left and the free carboxylic acid group on the right.

Because order is important in the functioning of a protein, gly–ser–ala, gly–ala–ser, and ala–ser–gly, for example, are different peptides. In fact, there are 27 different tripeptides that are possible from these three amino acids. (Each may be used more than once.) There are about two quadrillion different proteins that can exist if each of the 20 amino acids present in humans is used only once. However, just as not all sequences of letters make sense, not all sequences of amino acids make functioning proteins and other sequences can cause undesirable effects. While small mistakes in the amino acid sequence can sometimes be tolerated in nature without serious problems, at other times malfunctioning proteins can be caused by a single incorrect amino acid in the polymer chain. Sickle cell anemia is a fatal disease caused by a single amino acid, glutamic acid being replaced by a different one, valine, at the sixth position from the end of the protein chain in the hemoglobin molecule. This small difference causes lower solubility of the sickle cell hemoglobin molecules. They precipitate out as small rods which give the cells the characteristic sickle shape and result in the often fatal disease.

The specific sequence of the amino acids along the protein chain is referred to as the primary structure of the protein. However, these chains are not rigid, but rather they are long and flexible like string. The strands of protein can twist to form helixes or fold into sheets. They can bend and fold back on themselves to form globs and several protein molecules sometimes combine into a larger molecule. All of these configurations are caused by interactions both within a single protein strand as well as between two or three separate strands of protein.

Just as proteins are formed when amino acids bond together to form long chains, they can be broken down again into their individual amino acids by a reaction called hydrolysis. This reaction is just the reverse of the formation of the peptide bond. In the process of digestion, proteins are once again broken down into their individual amino acid components. Special digestive enzymes are necessary to cause the peptide linkage to break and a molecule of water is added when the reaction occurs. The resulting amino acids are released into the small intestine where they can easily pass into the bloodstream and be carried to every cell of the organism. There, once again, each individual cell can use these amino acids to assemble the new and different proteins required for its specific functions. Life goes on by the continual breakdown of protein into the individual amino acid units followed by the buildup of new protein from these amino acids.

Of the 20 amino acids required by humans for making protein, 12 of them can be made within the body from other nutrients. But the other eight, called the essential amino acids, cannot be made by the body and must be obtained from the diet. These are isoleucine, leucine, lysine, methionine, phenlyalanine, threonine, tryptophan, and valine. In addition, arginine and histidine are believed to be essential to growing children but may not be essential to mature adults. An adequate protein is one that contains all of the essential amino acids in sufficient quantities for growth and repair of body tissue. Most proteins from animal sources (gelatin being the only exception), contain all the essential amino acids and are considered adequate proteins. Many plant proteins do not contain all of the essential amino acids. Corn, for example, does not contain the essential amino acids lysine and tryptophan. Rice is lacking in lysine and threonine, wheat is lacking in lysine, and soy beans are lacking in methionine. People who are vegetarians and do not consume animal protein in their diets sometimes suffer from malnutrition because of the lack of one or more amino acids in their diets even though they may consume enough food and plenty of calories.

See also Carboxyl group; Hydrolysis; Nutrition; Proteins.

Further Reading:

Ball, Philip. *Designing the Molecular World: Chemistry at the Frontier.* Princeton, NJ: Princeton University Press, 1994.

Bishop, Katherine. "Baby Boomers Fight Aging by Dropping Acid (Amino)," *New York Times*, (10 June 1992): B1(N).

KEY TERMS

α–amino acid—An amino acid in which the –NH$_2$ (amino) group is bonded to the α–carbon atom.

α–carbon atom—The carbon atom adjacent to the carboxyl group.

Amino group—An –NH$_2$ group.

Carboxyl group—A –COOH group; also written –CO$_2$H.

Essential amino acid—Amino acids that cannot be synthesized by the body and must be obtained from the diet.

Monomers—Small, individual subunits which join together to form polymers.

Peptide—Substances made up of chains of amino acids, usually less than 50.

Peptide bond—The bond formed when the carboxyl group of one amino acid joins with the amino group of a second amino acid and splits off a water molecule.

Newhouse, Elizabeth L., et al, eds. *Inventors and Discoverers: Changing Our World.* Washington, D. C.: National Geographic Society, 1988.

Leona B. Bronstein

Amino acid racemization see **Dating techinques**

Ammonia

Ammonia, composed of three parts hydrogen and one part nitrogen, is a sharp–smelling, flammable, and toxic gas which is very soluble in water, where it acts as a base in its chemical reactions.

Ammonia in the past

Ammonia was present in the primordial atmosphere of the earth, and may have been the source of nitrogen for the earliest forms of life, although much controversy exists over the details. In ancient Egypt, ammonium compounds were used in rites honoring the god Ammon, from which came the name we still use for the gas and its compounds. Early chemists learned to generate ammonia from animal parts such as deerhorn, and obtained ammonial preparations (spirits of hartshorn, etc.), but Joseph Priestley (1733–1804) first collected and experimented with the pure substance. C. L. Berthellot (1748–1822) proved that ammonia is composed of nitrogen and hydrogen.

In the nineteenth century, ammonia was sometimes manufactured by the action of steam on calcium cyanamide, called the cyanamide process, which in turn was made by reacting calcium carbide with nitrogen at high temperatures. In the early twentieth century, German chemists Fritz Haber and Carl Bosch learned how to make ammonia in large quantities by high–pressure catalytic reactions of nitrogen (from air) with hydrogen. Both men were awarded Nobel prizes—Haber in 1918 and Bosch in 1931. The Haber–Bosch process is the basis for modern ammonia production, although many improvements have been made in the details of the technology.

Physical and chemical properties of ammonia

Ammonia (boiling point –29.2°F/–34°C) can be made in the laboratory by heating ammonium chloride with lime, and the gas collected by downward displacement of air, or displacement of mercury. Water solutions of ammonia, called ammonium hydroxides, having as much as 28% ammonia by weight, can be obtained by this method. Ammonium hydroxide exhibits the characteristics of a weak base, turning litmus paper blue, and neutralizing acids with the formation of ammonium salts. Transition metal ions are either precipitated as hydroxides (iron [II], iron [III]) or converted to ammonia complexes (copper [II], nickel [II], zinc [II], silver [I]). The copper (II) ammonia complex, in solution, is deep blue in color, and serves as a qualitative test for copper. It also has the ability to dissolve cellulose, and has been used in the for making regenerated cellulose fibers, or rayon.

Ammonia molecules possess a pyramidal shape, with the nitrogen atom at the vertex. These molecules continually undergo a type of motion called inversion, in which the nitrogen atom passes through the plane of the three hydrogen atoms like an umbrella turning inside out in the wind. When ammonia acts as a base, the nitrogen atom bonds either to a proton (to form ammonium ion) or to a metal cation. Ammonium salts such as ammonium chloride, called sal ammoniac, are water soluble and volatile when heated. It is often found that considerable heat is absorbed when ammo-

nium salts dissolve in water, leading to dramatic reduction in temperature. Ammonium salts containing anions of weak acids (carbonate, sulfide) easily liberate ammonia owing to the tendency of a proton to break off the nitrogen atom and be bound by the weak acid anion.

In liquid or frozen ammonia, the molecules attract one another through sharing a hydrogen atom between one molecule and the next, called hydrogen bonding. In this attraction, called association, compounds apparently containing free electrons can be obtained by treating sodium/ammonia solutions with complexing agents.

Ammonia is a flammable gas, and reacts with oxygen to form nitrogen and water, or nitrogen (II) oxide and water. Oxidation of ammonia in solution leads to hydrazine, a corrosive and volatile ingredient in fuels. Ammonium salts of oxidizing anions—nitrate, dichromate, perchlorate—are unstable and can explode or deflagrate when heated. Ammonium nitrate is used as a high explosive; ammonium perchlorate as a component of rocket fuels. Ammonium dichromate is used in a popular artificial volcano demonstration, in which a conical pile of the salt is ignited and burns vigorously, throwing off quantities of green chromium (III) oxide—the lava.

When ammonium hydroxide is treated with iodine crystals, an explosive brown solid, nitrogen triiodide, is formed. When dry, this substance is so sensitive that the lightest touch will cause it to explode with a crackling sound and a puff of purple iodine vapor.

Sources and production of ammonia

Ammonia is manufactured by the reaction of hydrogen with nitrogen in the presence of an iron catalyst, which is known as the Haber–Bosch process. The reaction is exothermic and is accompanied by a concentration in volume. (The ammonia occupies less volume than the gases from which it is made.) High pressure conditions (150–250 bar) are used, and temperatures range from 752–932°F (400–500°C). The mixed gases circulate through the catalyst, ammonia is formed and removed, and the unconverted reactants are recirculated. Large ammonia plants can produce over 1,000 tons per day. Each ton of ammonia requires 3,100 cu yd (2,400 cu m) of hydrogen and 1,050 cu yd (800 cu m) of nitrogen, as well as 60 gigajoules of energy. Much of the energy is consumed in the compressors needed to attain the high pressure used in the synthesis, and in heating the reactants. Further energy is needed to produce the hydrogen from hydrocarbon feedstocks, and to separate nitrogen from air. The synthesis reaction itself produces some heat, and great attention is given to heat efficiency, and use of waste heat. The gases that enter the catalytic converter must be highly purified and free of sulfur compounds, which adversely affect the catalyst. The catalyst is prepared in place by hydrogen treatment of magnetite, an iron oxide containing potassium hydroxide and other oxides in small amounts as promoters. A large ammonia plant might have as much as 100 tons of catalyst.

Since the hydrogen is usually derived from a natural gas called methane, the price of ammonia is very sensitive to the availability or price of fuels. United States production of ammonia reached 17 million tons in 1991, and demand was even larger than U.S. production, leading to about two million tons of imports. World ammonia production is about 100 million tons per year, which amounts to about 40 lbs (18 kg) for each person on earth.

Ammonia is formed from nitrogen in air by the action of nitrogen–fixing bacteria that exist in the soil on the roots of certain plants like alfalfa. Nitrogen fixation can also be accomplished by blue–green algae in the sea. These bacteria and algae possess an enzyme called nitrogenase that permits them to convert nitrogen to ammonia at 77°F (25°C) and 1 bar of pressure, much milder conditions than those of the Haber–Bosch process. Nitrogenase is known to be a complex protein containing metal atoms, such as iron and molybdenum, and sulfide ions, but its structure and mode of action are imperfectly understood, even after decades of research. Recent research indicates that the nitrogen molecule may bind to iron atoms in the enzyme as a reaction step.

Ammonia can be formed in the human body, and may build up abnormally during serious illnesses such as Reyes syndrome. Much nitrogen is normally excreted by humans (and other mammals) as urea, a water soluble solid, but fish can excrete ammonia directly.

Urea eventually reacts with water to form ammonia, which therefore is usually present to some extent in waste water. Low concentrations of ammonia in water can be detected and measured using a solution called Nessler's reagent, which develops a strong color in the presence of ammonia. A recent toxic substance inventory done by the United States government estimated that in 1989 200,000 tons of ammonia were released into the environment. This figure does not include fertilizer applications of ammonia.

Although the earth's atmosphere is free of ammonia, liquid and solid ammonia exist on other planets, such as Jupiter, where it may have originally formed from metal nitrides reacting with water. Ammonia has also been detected in interstellar space by radioastronomy.

Uses of ammonia

The largest use of ammonia is in fertilizers, which are applied to the soil and help provide increased yields of crops such as corn, wheat, and soybeans. Liquid ammonia, ammonia/water solutions, and chemicals made from ammonia, such as ammonium salts and urea, are all used as sources of soluble nitrogen. Urea, which is made from ammonia and carbon dioxide, can also be used as a feed supplement for cattle, aiding in the rapid building of protein by the animals.

All other important nitrogen chemicals are now made from ammonia. Nitric acid results from oxidation of ammonia in the presence of a platinum catalyst, called the Ostwald process, followed by treatment of the resulting nitrogen oxides with water. Nitric acid and nitrates are needed for the manufacture of explosives like TNT, nitroglycerin, gunpowder, and also for the propellants in cartridges for rifles and machine guns.

Two types of polymers needed for artificial fibers require the use of ammonia, polyamides (nylon) and acrylics (orlon). The original polyamide named nylon, brought out by DuPont Chemical Co., was made from two components, adipic acid and hexamethylenediamine. The nitrogen in the second named component is derived from ammonia. Acrylics are made from a three–carbon nitrogen compound, acrylonitrile. Acrylonitrile comes from the reaction of propene, ammonia, and oxygen in the presence of a catalyst.

Because of its basic properties, ammonia is able to react with acidic gases such as nitrogen oxides and sulfur oxides to form ammonium salts. Thus ammonia is useful in scrubbers that remove acidic gases before they can be released into the environment.

Future prospects

Ammonia will continue to be important for agriculture and for the whole nitrogen chemicals industry. As countries in Asia and Latin America develop high standards of living and stronger economies, they will begin to need their own ammonia plants. For this reason, capacity and production will continue to grow. New uses may develop, particularly for ammonia as a relatively inexpensive base with unique properties, for

KEY TERMS

. . . .

Ammonia complexes—Species, usually positively charged ions, formed by linking several ammonia molecules through their nitrogen atoms to a transition metal ion.

Gigajoule—A billion joules. An amount of energy equal to 277 kilowatt hours, or about the electrical energy used by a family in a month.

Polyamide—A polymer such as nylon, containing recurrent amide groups linking segments of the polymer chain.

liquid ammonia as a solvent, and as a storage medium for hydrogen, as the nations evolve toward alternative fuels.

See also Amides; Fertilizers; Nitrogen; Urea.

Further Reading:

Buechner, W., R. Schleibs, G. Winter, and K.H. Buechel, *Industrial Inorganic Chemistry*. New York: VCH, 1989.

Cantrell, R.A. *Minerals Yearbook 1991*. U.S. Dept of the Interior, 1991.

Greenwood, N.N. and A. Earnshaw, *The Chemistry of the Elements*. Oxford: Pergamon, 1984.

John R. Phillips

Ammonification

Strictly speaking, ammonification refers to any chemical reaction that generates ammonia (NH_3) as an end product (or its ionic form, ammonium, NH_4^+). Ammonification can occur through various inorganic reactions or as a result of the metabolic functions of microorganisms, plants, and animals. In the ecological context, however, ammonification refers to the processes by which organically bound forms of nitrogen occurring in dead biomass (such as amino acids and proteins) are oxidized into ammonia and ammonium. The ecological process of ammonification is carried out in soil and water by a great diversity of microbes and is one of the many types of chemical transformations that occur during the decomposition of dead organic matter.

Ammonification is a key component in the nitrogen cycle of ecosystems. The nitrogen cycle consists of a complex of integrated processes by which nitrogen circulates among its major compartments in the atmosphere, water, soil, and organisms. During various phases of the nitrogen cycle, this element is transformed among various of its organic and inorganic compounds.

As with all components of the nitrogen cycle, the proper functioning of ammonification is critical to the health of ecosystems. In the absence of ammonification, organic forms of nitrogen would accumulate in large quantities. Because growing plants need access to inorganic forms of nitrogen, particularly ammonium and nitrate (NO_3^-), the oxidation of organic nitrogen of dead biomass through ammonification is necessary for maintenance of the productivity of species and ecosystems.

Ammonification

Nitrogen is one of the most abundant elements in the tissues of all organisms and is a component of many biochemicals, particularly amino acids, proteins, and nucleic acids. Consequently, nitrogen is one of the critically important nutrients and is required in relatively large quantities by all organisms. Animals receive their supply of nitrogen through the foods they eat, but plants must assimilate inorganic forms of this nutrient from their environment.

However, the rate at which the environment can supply inorganic nitrogen is limited and usually small in relation to the metabolic demands of plants. Therefore, the availability of inorganic forms of nitrogen is frequently a limiting factor for the productivity of plants. This is a particularly common occurrence for plants growing in terrestrial and marine environments, and to a lesser degree, in fresh waters (where phosphate supply is usually the primary limiting nutrient, followed by nitrate).

The dead biomass of plants, animals, and microorganisms contains large concentrations of organically bound nitrogen in various forms, such as proteins and amino acids. The process of decomposition is responsible for recycling the inorganic constituents of the dead biomass and preventing it from accumulating in large unusable quantities. Decomposition is, of course, mostly carried out through the metabolic functions of a diverse array of bacteria, fungi, actinomycetes, other microorganisms, and some animals. Ammonification is a particular aspect of the more complex process of organic decay, specifically referring to the microbial conversion of organic–nitrogen into ammonia (NH_3) or ammonium (NH_4^+).

Ammonification occurs under oxidizing conditions in virtually all ecosystems and is carried out by virtually all microorganisms that are involved in the decay of dead organic matter. In situations where oxygen is not present, a condition referred to as anaerobic, different microbial decay reactions occur, and these produce nitrogen compounds known as amines.

The microbes derive some metabolically useful energy from the oxidation of organic–nitrogen to ammonium. In addition, much of the ammonium is assimilated and used as a nutrient for the metabolic purposes of the microbes. However, if the microbes produce ammonium in quantities that exceed their own requirements, as is usually the case, the surplus is excreted into the ambient environment (such as the soil), and is available for use as a nutrient by plants, or as a substrate for another microbial process, known as nitrification (see below). Animals, in contrast, mostly excrete urea or uric acid in their nitrogen–containing liquid wastes (such as urine), along with diverse organic–nitrogen compounds in their feces. The urea, uric acid, and organic nitrogen of feces are all substrates for microbial ammonification.

One of the most elementary of the ammonification reactions is the oxidation of the simple organic compound, urea [$CO(NH_2)_2$], to ammonia through the action of a microbial enzyme known as urease. (Note that two units of ammonia are produced for every unit of urea that is oxidized.) Urea is a commonly utilized agricultural fertilizer, used to supply ammonia or ammonium for direct uptake by plants, or as a substrate for the microbial production of nitrate through nitrification (see below).

Ammonium is a suitable source of nitrogen uptake for many species of plants, particularly those that live in acidic soils and waters. However, most plants that occur in non–acidic soils cannot utilize ammonium very efficiently, and they require the anion nitrate (NO_3^+) as their source of nitrogen uptake. The nitrate is generally derived by the bacterial oxidation of ammonium to nitrite, and then to nitrate, in an important ecological process known as nitrification. Because the species of bacteria that carry out nitrification are extremely intolerant of acidity, this process does not occur at significant rates in acidic soils or waters. This is the reason why plants growing in acidic habitats can only rely on ammonium as their source of nitrogen nutrition.

Because ammonium is a positively charged cation, it is held relatively strongly by ion–exchange reactions

occurring at the surfaces of clay minerals and organic matter in soils. Consequently, ammonium is not leached very effectively by water as it percolates downward through the soil. This is in contrast to nitrate, which is highly soluble in soil water and is leached readily. As a result, nitrate pollution can be an important problem in agricultural areas that have been heavily fertilized with nitrogen–containing fertilizers.

Humans and ammonification

Humans have a major influence on the nitrogen cycle, especially through the use of fertilizers in agriculture. Under nutrient–limited conditions, farmers commonly attempt to increase the availability of soil nitrogen, particularly as nitrate, and to a lesser degree, as ammonium. Rates of fertilization in intensive agricultural systems can exceed 446.2 lbs/ac (500 kg/ha) of nitrogen per year. The nitrogen in the fertilizer may be added as ammonium nitrate (NO_4NH_4) or as urea. The latter compound must be ammonified before inorganic forms of nitrogen are present, that is, the ammonium and nitrate that can be taken up by plants. In some agricultural systems, compost or other organic materials may be added to soils as a conditioner and fertilizer. In such cases, the organic nitrogen is converted to available ammonium through microbial ammonification, and nitrate may subsequently be generated through nitrification.

In situations where the rates of fertilization are excessive, the ability of the ecosystem to assimilate the nitrogen input becomes satiated. Although the ammonium produced by ammonification does not leach readily, the nitrate does, and this can lead to the pollution of groundwater and surface waters, such as streams and rivers. Pollution of groundwater with nitrate poses risks for human health, while surface waters may experience an increased productivity through eutrophication.

See also: Ammonia; Nitrogen; Nitrogen cycle; Organic agriculture; Urea.

Further Reading:

Atlas, R.M. and R. Bartha. *Microbial Ecology.* Menlo Park, CA: Benjamin/Cummings, 1987.

Freedman, B. *Environmental Ecology, 2nd ed.* San Diego: Academic Press, 1994.

Russell, E.W. *Soil Conditions and Plant Growth, 10th ed.* London: Wm. Clowes & Sons, 1977.

Bill Freedman

Amnesia

Amnesia is a dissociative psychological disorder manifested by total or partial loss of memory and usually caused by a trauma. Unlike ordinary forgetfulness (the inability to remember a friend's telephone number), amnesia is a serious threat to a person's professional and social life. Amnesia, which depending on its cause can be either organic and psychogenic, has several types.

How amnesia is manifested

Global or generalized amnesia indicates the total loss of a person's identity: the individual has forgotten who she or he is. What makes this type of amnesia baffling is the fact that only personal memory is affected. The amnesiac does not remember who he or she is but displays no loss of general knowledge. A person suffering from retrograde amnesia cannot remember events that happened immediately before the trauma. In anterograde amnesia, all events following the trauma are forgotten. Finally, amnesia can also be selective, or categorical, manifested by a person's inability to remember events related to a specific incident.

Causes of amnesia

The causes of amnesia can be physiological and/or psychological. Amnesia caused by physical trauma is called organic amnesia, while the term psychogenic amnesia is used in reference to amnesia caused by psychological trauma.

Organic amnesia

Examples of organic amnesia include cases of memory loss following head injuries, brain lesions,

---

KEY TERMS

. . . .

Dissociative disorder—Referring to psychological conditions, such as psychogenic amnesia and multiple personality disorder, in which an area of personal memory is dissociated from a person's consciousness.

Etiology—The sum of disease–causing factors.

---

stroke, substance abuse, carbon monoxide poisoning, malnutrition, electro–convulsive therapy, surgery, and infections. Persons suffering from any kind of organic amnesia display a number of typical characteristics. Their memory loss is also anterograde: events after the trauma are forgotten. In addition, they can remember the distant past well, but their grasp of the immediate past is tenuous. If treatment is unsuccessful, the amnesiac's condition can worsen, leading to progressive memory loss. In such cases, memory loss is irreversible. If therapy is successful, the patient may partially regain memories blocked by retrograde amnesia, while anterograde amnesia usually remains.

Psychogenic amnesia

The causes of psychogenic amnesia are psychological, and they include career–related stress, economic hardship, and emotional distress. Experts have maintained that psychogenic amnesia has no physiological causes, although recent research has established that emotional trauma may alter the brain physiology, thus setting the stage for the interplay of psychological and physiological factors in the etiology of amnesia. In other words, psychogenic amnesia may have secondary causes which could be defined as organic. The most enigmatic psychogenic amnesia is identity loss; the person affected by this type of amnesia loses all personal memories, while retaining his or her general (impersonal) knowledge. For example, the amnesiac may not know his or her name, but can still be able to speak an acquired second language. Furthermore, in psychogenic amnesia, there is no anterograde memory loss. Finally, although psychogenic amnesia is reversible and can end within hours or days, it is a serious condition that can be difficult to treat.

See also Memory.

Further Reading:

American Psychiatric Association. *Diagnostical and Statistical Manual of Mental Disorders.* 4th ed. Washington, D.C.: APA, 1994.

Feldman, R. *Understanding Psychology*. New York: McGraw–Hill, 1993.

Rosenhan, David L., and Martin E. P. Seligman. *Abnormal Psychology*. 2nd ed. New York: W. W. Norton, 1989.

Zoran Minderovic

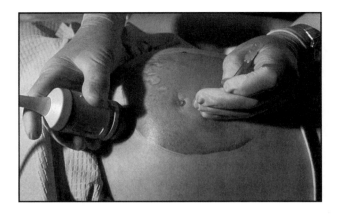

The physician uses an ultrasound monitor (left) to position the needle for insertion into the amnion when performing amniocentesis.

Amniocentesis

Amniocentesis is a procedure used to detect the presence of Down's syndrome and various central nervous system abnormalities (such as spina bifida or anencephaly) in a fetus. It is also used to determine the maturity level of a potentially premature baby. Amniocentesis is normally performed in the 14th–16th weeks of pregnancy in women considered to be at risk of Down's syndrome or other problems.

Window on the womb

Prior to the development of amniocentesis in the 1950s, there was no way to detect whether a baby might be born with serious health problems. Amniocentesis has changed the nature of pregnancy by offering greater information about the fetus and creating more decisions for the parents. If problems exist with the fetus, the pregnant woman must decide if she will continue the pregnancy.

Amniocentesis takes advantage of a wealth of 20th century technological and medical advances in genetics, fetal development, and diagnostic testing knowledge. The procedure is performed by inserting a hollow needle through the abdominal and uterine walls into the amniotic sac. The fluid in the amniotic sac is rich with cells from the fetus. Approximately half an ounce of fluid is removed.

The fluid is placed in a centrifuge which divides the cells from the liquid. The amniotic liquid and the cells are analyzed. The amniotic fluid is examined to determine the level of alpha fetoprotein a chemical normally present in the blood. High levels of alpha fetoprotein suggest a possible spinal–cord defect such as spina bifida, while low levels of the chemical suggest the possibility of Down's syndrome.

The cells are called amniocytes and may be examined for genetic abnormalities or for inborn metabolic errors. Some problems only can only be detected after the cells are cultured (the process of growing cells in a laboratory in special material which encourages cell growth). Other problems may be spotted in uncultured cells.

Amniocentesis is not without risk to the fetus. About 0.5% of all amniocentesis procedures cause spontaneous abortions. Other possible complications include injury to the fetus and infection of the fetus or the mother. Another disadvantage of the procedure is that it can not be performed until the 14th week of pregnancy, when the pregnancy is already well established. Test results can not be reported for two weeks.

Completion of amniocentesis depends on the accuracy of ultrasound, a technology which uses sound waves to detect the shape of body tissue, including fetuses. Ultrasound devices track echoes produced when sound waves bounce off objects in the body. This record is transformed to a photographic image. The image is used to determine where the fetus is within the pregnant woman's womb so the fetus can be avoided when inserting the amniocentesis needle into the body.

The most common genetic abnormality detected using amniocentesis is Down's syndrome. Down's syndrome occurs when children are born with 47 chromosomes in each cell instead of the normal 46. Children with this syndrome are mentally retarded and are more likely to have congenital heart disorders and other health problems. Women are at greater risk of giving birth to a Down's Syndrome child as they grow older. Women 35 and over are generally advised to have amniocentesis when they are pregnant in the United States because the risk of having a Down's syndrome child is higher than the risk of losing a baby due to amniocentesis at this age.

Spina bifida, a serious disorder in which the spine develops abnormally, is another health problem which can be detected by amniocentesis. Spina bifida usually causes some paralysis and may cause other physical disabilities.

Inborn metabolic abnormalities detected also include Tay–Sachs disease, a genetic disorder which causes blindness and paralysis. It is fatal in infancy.

Couples at risk of other health problems also are advised to have amniocentesis. This includes men or women with a previous child with a chromosome abnormality, neural tube defect, or metabolic disorder. A family history of certain genetic problems also leads some pregnant women to have amniocentesis.

Because amniocentesis can not be performed until the middle of pregnancy many women choose another method of prenatal diagnosis such as chorionic villus sampling, which can be performed as early as the first 8–10 weeks of pregnancy. Chorionic villus sampling takes cells from the placenta. This method has a higher risk of spontaneous abortion; about 3.2% chorionic villus sampling procedures cause spontaneous abortion. Many women are willing to take a greater risk to the fetus to gain information in a more timely fashion.

The long–term outlook on children born following amniocentesis suggests that the procedure does not cause health problems. A Canadian study compared the health of 1,298 children who had experienced amniocentesis before birth with 3,738 children who had not experienced the procedure. The study, which examined children ages 7–18, found no higher incidence of any health problems in the children who had experienced amniocentesis.

Future testing

While enthusiasm for chorionic villus sampling increased in the 1980s the technology remains riskier to the fetus than amniocentesis. As a result, amniocentesis remains the primary tool for prenatal diagnosis.

One dispute among experts concerns whether pregnant women younger than 35 should have amniocentesis. This stems from the fact that only 25% of the women who give birth to Down's syndrome babies are 35 or older. This means most births of Down's syndrome infants occur in women younger than 35. Some experts have suggested that women 30 and over should have amniocentesis.

Another dispute concerns whether amniocentesis should be used as a tool to select the sex of a fetus. Opinion on the issue has changed among genetics counselors who advise potential parents about genetic

---

KEY TERMS

Amniotic fluid—The fluid in which the fetus lives in the womb.

Anencephaly—A serious birth abnormality in which parts of the brain are missing.

Chorionic villus sampling—A prenatal test in which cells of the placenta are removed using a catheter.

Chromosomes—Structure in the nucleus of animal and human cells holding a strand of DNA which contains genetic information.

Ultrasound—A diagnostic test which records images derived from sound waves bouncing off tissues.

---

testing and interpreting the results. In 1975 only 1% of a group polled reported that they would perform amniocentesis for the purpose of sex selection. By 1988 a total of 62% said they would perform the procedure for this purpose.

As knowledge of genetics increases, the scope of information provided through amniocentesis should also increase. This will increase the number of choices facing pregnant women and their families. Critics say amniocentesis and other prenatal tests have changed pregnancy from a seamless nine months of preparation to a time of uncertainty and important decision–making. While this may be true, amniocentesis has also provided tools for the healthy birth of many infants, including many born to parents whose genetic heritage would have made the birth of healthy offspring unlikely.

See also Birth; Birth defects; Embryo and embryonic development.

Further Reading:

Baird, P.S., I.M.L. Yee, and A.D. Sadovnick. "Population-Based Study of Long–Term Outcomes After Amniocentesis." *The Lancet*. 344 (22 October 1994): 1134–36.

Boss, Judith A. "First Trimester Prenatal Diagnosis: Earlier Is Not Necessarily Better." *Journal of Medical Ethics*. 20 (1994): 146–51.

Merkatz, Irwin R., and Joyce E. Thompson. "Prenatal Diagnosis," in *New Perspectives on Prenatal Care*. New York: Elsevier, 1990.

Nicolaides, Kypros, Maria de Lourdes Brizot, Fatima Patel, and Rosalinde Snijders. "Comparison of Chorionic Villus Sampling and Amniocentesis for Fetal Karyotyping

At 10–13 Weeks' Gestation." *The Lancet.* 344 (13 August 1994): 435–39.

Rothman, Barbara Katz. *The Tentative Pregnancy.* New York: Viking Press, 1986.

Wilson, J. Robert, and Elsie Reid Carrington. "Amniocentesis," in *Obstetrics and Gynecology.* St. Louis: Mosby Year Book. 1991.

Patricia Braus

Amoeba

Amoeba are single–celled protozoans of the order Amoebida. They consist of a mass of cellular fluid surrounded by a membrane, and containing one or more nuclei (depending upon the species), as well as other cell organelles, such as food vacuoles.

The word amoeba is derived from the Greek word ameibein (to change), which describes the amoeba's most easily distinguishable feature, the continuous changing of shape by repeated formation of *pseudopods* (Greek: false feet).

Pseudopodal movement is based on a continual change in the state of protoplasm flowing into the foot–like appendage. An interior fluid (endoplasm), under pressure from an exterior gel (ectoplasm), flows forward in the cell. When the endoplasm reaches the tip of a developing pseudopod, the fluid is forced backward against the ectoplasm, and is turned into a gel. After returning to the body of the cell, the newly formed ectoplasm gel is converted back to fluid endoplasm, and again flows forward under the pressure of the exterior gel.

Pseudopods serve two important functions—locomotion and food capture, activities that are often interrelated. Amoeba use their pseudopods to ingest food by a method called phagocytosis (Greek: phagein, to eat).

The streaming of protoplasm inside the pseudopods moves the amoeba forward. When the organism contacts a food particle, the pseudopods surround the particle. After the food is corralled by the amoeba, an opening in the membrane allows the food particle to pass into the cell. Inside the cell, the food is enclosed within food vacuoles, digested by enzymes, and assimilated by the amoeba. The amoeba expels particles that are not acceptable as food.

The organisms generally implied by the term "amoeba" belong to the phylum Protozoa, class Mastigophora, which includes organisms with flagellae (whip–like organs of locomotion) such as *Chlamydomonas angulosa*, as well as those with pseudopods. The class Sarcodina, which has as its principle distinguishing feature the almost universal presence of pseudopods, includes *Amoeba proteus*, the best–known Protozoan.

The Rhizopoda (in some classifications a subclass of Sarcodina) contains all common "naked amoeba," which are either tubular or somewhat flattened. They move by means of protoplasmic flow, by producing pseudopodia, or by advancing as a single mass. Rhizopoda also includes sarcodinids known as giant amoebae and testaceous forms (those with tests, or shells). Some apparently "naked" amoebae have coatings of various kinds, such as scales, mucoid layers called *glycocalyces*, or complex filaments much smaller than scales.

In addition to the naked forms, many species of amoeba have tests, and are referred to as shelled amoebae. Most of these shelled amoebae are classified in the order Arcellinida. They have a test with a single opening, and are predominantly freshwater organisms. Shelled amoebae feed on a variety of organisms, such as bacteria, algae, and other protozoans.

Most members of the order of Amoebida are free–living in fresh or salt water or soil, and ingest bacteria. Larger members also feed on algae and other protozoans. Several amoeba of this group are pathogenic to humans.

The family Amoebidae includes mostly fresh–water species, whose pseudopodal movement is either monopodial (the entire protoplasmic mass moves forward) or polypodial (where several pseudopods advance simultaneously). One member, *Amoeba proteus* is commonly used for teaching and cell biology research. *Chaos carolinense,* one of the larger species, has multiple nuclei and can reach a length of 0.12 in (3 mm).

The Hartmannellidae family includes small and medium–sized amoebae that move forward monopodially, advancing by means of a steady flow. They feed on bacteria, although some species of the genus *Saccamoeba* also feed on unicellular algae.

The family Entamoebidae includes most of the obligately endozoic (parasitic inside a host) Amoebida organisms, including *Entamoeba histolytica*. Amebiasis (infection with *E. histolytica*) is a serious intestinal disease also called amoebic dysentery. It is characterized by diarrhea, fever, and dehydration. Although amebiasis is usually limited to the intestine, it can spread to other areas of the body, especially the liver.

Entamoeba histolytica exists as either a trophozoite or cyst. The trophozoite is motile, possesses a single nucleus, and lives in the intestine. It is passed from the body in diarrhea, but cannot survive outside the host. The cyst form, consisting of condensed protoplasm surrounded by a protective wall, is produced in the intestine, can survive outside the host, and even withstands the acid of the stomach when it is ingested with food or contaminated water. Once inside the intestine, *E. histolytica* multiplies by means of binary fission.

Another family, Acanthamoebidae (in the Amoebida suborder Acanthopodina), includes the genus *Acanthamoeba* genera, which are often isolated from fresh water and soil. *Acanthamoeba* cause primary amebic meningoencephalitis (PAM, inflammation of the brain and its protective membranes), especially in individuals who are ill and whose immune systems are weakened. *Acanthamoeba* infections have been traced to fresh water, hot tubs, soil, and homemade contact lens solutions. In the latter case, contamination of contact lens solution with the organism has caused keratitis, an inflammation of the cornea accompanied by pain and blurred vision. Severe cases can require a corneal transplant or even removal of the eye.

A member of the order Schizopyrenida, *Naegleria fowleri* is an especially dangerous human parasite, causing rapidly fatal PAM in people swimming in heated water, or warm, freshwater ponds and lakes, mainly in the southern United States. Both *Naegleria* and *Acanthamoeba* enter through the nasal mucosa and spread to the brain along nerves.

See also Cell; Protozoa.

Ampere see **Units and standards**

Amphetamines

Amphetamines are a group of nervous system stimulants, which includes amphetamine, dextroamphetamine, and methamphetamine. They are used to induce a state of alert wakefulness and euphoria, and since they inhibit appetite they also serve as diet pills. After World War II, they were widely prescribed by physicians as diet pills, but they are generally no longer recommended for weight loss programs since there are too many hazards in the prolonged use of amphetamines. Prolonged exposure may result in organ impairment, affecting particularly the kidneys. Amphetamines are addictive and may lead to compulsive behavior, hallucinations, paranoia, and suicidal actions. Their medical use has currently been narrowed to treating only two disorders. One is a condition known as attention–deficit hyperactivity disorder (ADHD) in children. When used to treat overactive children, amphetamines are carefully administered under controlled situations as part of a larger program. The other condition for which amphetamines are prescribed is a sleep disorder known as narcolepsy, the sudden uncontrollable urge to sleep during the hours of wakefulness.

In street language, amphetamines are known as pep pills, as speed (when injected), and as ice (when smoked in a crystalline form). The popularity of amphetamines as a street drug appears to have been facilitated originally by pilfering from the drug companies manufacturing the pills. They are now also illegally manufactured in secret laboratories.

History

Amphetamines were first synthesized in 1887 by the drug company Smith, Kline and French. They were not marketed until 1932, however, as Benzedrine inhalers for relief from nasal congestion due to hay fever, colds, or asthma. In 1935, after noting its stimulant effects, the drug company encouraged prescription of the drug for the chronic sleep disorder narcolepsy. Clinical enthusiasm for the drug led to its misapplication for the treatment of various conditions, including addiction to opiates. The harmful effects of the drug were first noted by the British press, and in 1939 amphetamines were placed on a list of toxic substances for the United Kingdom.

The early abuse of Benzedrine inhalers involved the removal of the strip containing the amphetamines from the casing of the inhaler. The strips were then either chewed or placed in coffee to produce an intense stimulant reaction. Since the inhalers were inexpensive and easily obtainable at local drug stores, they were purchased by young people searching for ways of getting "high."

But amphetamines became particularly popular in World War II. Soldiers on both sides were given large amounts of amphetamines as a way of fighting fatigue and boosting morale. The British issued 72 million tablets to the armed forces. Records also show that kamikaze pilots and German panzer troops were given large doses of the drug to motivate their fighting spirit. Hitler's own medical records show that he received eight injections a day of methamphetamine, a drug known to create paranoia and unpredictable behavior when administered in large dosages.

The demand for amphetamines was high in the 1950s and early 1960s. They were used by people who had to stay awake for long periods of time. Truck drivers who had to make long hauls used them to drive through the night. Those who had long tours of duty in the armed forces relied on them to stay awake. High school and college students cramming for tests took them to study through the nights before their examinations. Athletes looked to amphetamines for more energy, while English and American popular musicians structured their lives and music around them. The Food and Drug Administration (FDA) estimated that there were well over 200 million amphetamine pills in circulation by 1962 in the United States alone.

During that period of time about half of the quantity of amphetamines produced were used outside of the medically prescribed purposes mandated by the legal system. Of the 19 companies producing amphetamines then, nine were not required to show their registry of buyers to the FDA. It is believed that these nine companies supplied much of the illegal traffic in amphetamines for that period.

By 1975 a large number of street preparations were being passed off as amphetamine tablets. Tests indicated that only about 10% of the street drugs represented as amphetamines contained any amphetamine substance at all. The false amphetamines were in fact mixtures of caffeine and other drugs that resembled amphetamine, such as phenethylamine, an over–the–counter drug used to relieve coughs and asthma or to inhibit appetite. Other false amphetamine tablets contained such over–the–counter drugs as ephedrine and pseudoephedrine. These bootleg preparations came under such names as Black Beauty, Hustler, and Penthouse, and they were promoted in magazines that catered to counterculture sentiment.

The use of amphetamines and drugs like amphetamine showed a sharp decrease in the 1980s. The decrease was probably due to the increasing use of cocaine, which was introduced in the mid–1970s and continues to be a major street drug at the present time. Another reason was the introduction of newer types of appetite suppressants and stimulants on the pharmacological market and then to the street trade. Still, a survey done in 1987 showed that a large number of high school seniors (12%) had used drugs of the amphetamine type during the previous year.

Ice

Illegal users of methamphetamine originally took the drug in pill form or prepared it for injection. More recently, however, a crystalline form of the drug that is smoked like crack cocaine has appeared on the market. The practice of smoking methamphetamine began in Hawaii and then spread to California. Various names are given to smokable methamphetamine, such as Ice, LA Ice, and Crank. Ice is much cheaper than crack because it is made from easily available chemicals and does not require complicated equipment for its production. An illegal drug manufacturer can produce ice at a much lower cost than cocaine and therefore realize a much greater profit margin. Like cocaine, amphetamine reaches the brain faster when it is smoked. Users have begun to prefer ice over crack because the high lasts much longer, persisting for well over 14 hours. The side effects of an ice high can be quite severe, however. Such side effects as paranoia, hallucinations, impulsive behavior, and other psychotic effects may last for several days after a prolonged high from ice.

Action

Amphetamines, according to recent research, act on the neurotransmitters of the brain to produce their mood–altering effects. The two main neurotransmitters affected are dopamine and norepinephrine, produced by cells in the brain. Amphetamines appear to stimulate the production of these two neurotransmitters and then prevent their uptake by other cells. They further increase the amount of surplus neurotransmitters by inhibiting the action of enzymes that help to absorb them into the nervous system. It is believed that the excess amount of neurotransmitters caused by the amphetamines are also responsible for the behavioral changes that follow a high.

Drugs that pose a high risk of addiction like amphetamines, opiates, and cocaine all seem to arouse the centers of the brain that control the urge to seek out pleasurable sensations. Addictive drugs overcome those centers and displace the urge to find pleasure in food, sex, or sleep, or other types of activity that motivate people not addicted to drugs. The drug addict's primary concern is to relive the pleasure of the drug high, even at the risk of "crashing" (coming down from the high in a painful way) and in the face of the social disapproval the habit inevitably entails. Laboratory experiments have shown that animals self–administering amphetamines will reject food and water in favor of the drug. They eventually perish in order to keep up their supply of the drug.

Withdrawal symptoms for chronic users include depression, anxiety, and the need for prolonged periods of sleep.

Physical and psychological effects

Amphetamines inhibit appetite and stimulate respiration as a result. On an oral dose of 10–15 milligrams daily an individual feels more alert and more confident in performing both physical and mental work and is able to show an increase in levels of activity. It has not been determined how the drug affects the quality of work done under its influence. The drug also results in a rise in blood pressure and an increased, though sometimes irregular, heart rate.

Psychological dependency arises from the desire to continue and heighten the euphoric effects of the drug. During an amphetamine euphoria, the individual feels an enlargement of physical, mental, and sexual powers along with the absence of the urge to eat or sleep. Those who inject the drug feel a "rush" of the euphoric effect moments after the injection. They will feel energized and focused in an unusual way.

Depending on the user's medical history, the dosage, and the manner in which the drug was delivered to the body, a number of toxic effects can accompany amphetamine abuse. Large intravenous dosages can lead to delirium, seizures, restlessness, the acting out of paranoic fantasies, and hallucinations. In hot weather there is a danger of heat stroke, since amphetamines raise the body temperature. The increased blood pressure can lead to stroke. Heart conditions such as arrhythmia (irregular heartbeat) can develop and become fatal, especially for those with heart disease. Since the dosage levels of street drugs are not reliable, it is possible to overdose unknowingly when using the drug intravenously. The results can be coma and death. Chronic users will show much weight loss and chronic skin lesions. Those who are "shooting up" (injecting) street versions of amphetamine face the further dangers from contaminated substances, adulterations in the chemicals used, and a lack of sterilized needles. These conditions carry the same risks associated with heroin use, such as hepatitis and infections to vital organs, along with irreversible damage to blood vessels. Contaminated needles may also transmit the HIV virus that causes AIDS.

Treatment

It takes several days to help a person recover from an acute amphetamine reaction. It is important to control body temperature and to reassure a person undergoing the psychological effects of the drug. In order to control violent behavior, tranquilizers are administered to quiet the patient. Treatment of the depression which is an after–effect of heavy usage is also required.

KEY TERMS

. . . .

AIDS—Acquired Immune Deficiency Syndrome; a fatal viral disease contracted by a virus transmitted through the blood.

Attention–deficit hyperactivity disorder (ADHD)—A childhood condition marked by extreme restlessness and the inability to concentrate, which is sometimes treated with amphetamines.

Crashing—Coming down from a prolonged drug high such as that produced by amphetamines.

Euphoria—Feelings of elation and well–being produced by drugs like amphetamines.

HIV—Human immunodeficiency virus, which leads to AIDS.

Ice—Crystalline methamphetamine that is smoked to produce a high.

Neurotransmitters—Chemicals produced in the brain, which are responsible for different emotional states.

Paranoia—Delusions of persecution; one of the main psychotic conditions produced by an excess use of amphetamines.

Speed—An injectable form of methamphetamine.

Tranquilizers—Drugs used to pacify anxiety attacks.

Patients will seek to deal with the fatigue that comes after the body has eliminated the drug by resuming its use. A long–term program for maintaining abstinence from the drug has to be adhered to. Just as in the case of recovery from alcoholism and other forms of drug abuse, recovering addicts benefit from support groups.

See also Addiction.

Further Reading:

Chan, Paul, et al. "Fatal and Nonfatal Methamphetamine Intoxication in the Intensive Care Unit." *Journal of Toxicology: Clinical Toxicology*, 32 (June 1994): 147–56.

Shapiro, Harry. *Waiting for the Man*. New York: William Morrow, 1988.

Stimmel, Barry. *The Facts About Drug Use*. New York: Haworth Medical Press, 1991.

Jordan Richman

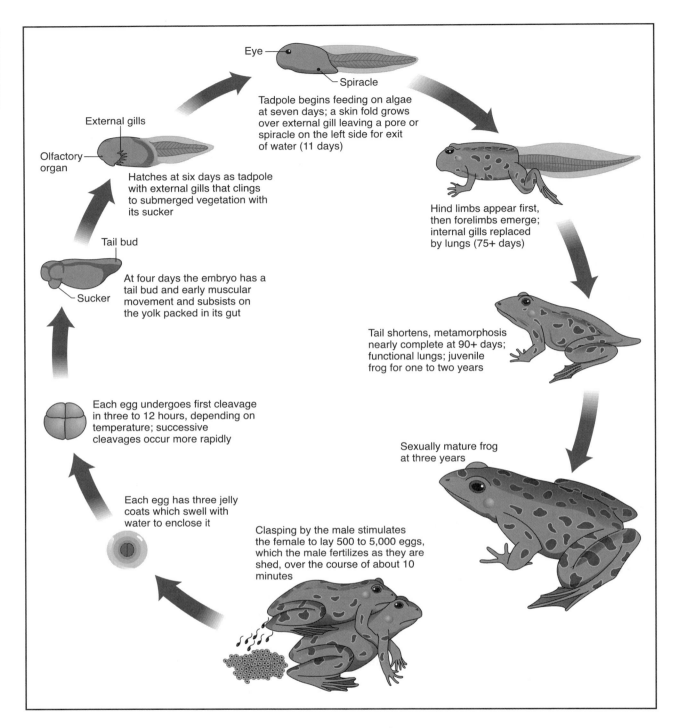

Eye

Spiracle

Tadpole begins feeding on algae at seven days; a skin fold grows over external gill leaving a pore or spiracle on the left side for exit of water (11 days)

External gills

Olfactory organ

Hatches at six days as tadpole with external gills that clings to submerged vegetation with its sucker

Hind limbs appear first, then forelimbs emerge; internal gills replaced by lungs (75+ days)

Tail bud

Sucker

At four days the embryo has a tail bud and early muscular movement and subsists on the yolk packed in its gut

Tail shortens, metamorphosis nearly complete at 90+ days; functional lungs; juvenile frog for one to two years

Each egg undergoes first cleavage in three to 12 hours, depending on temperature; successive cleavages occur more rapidly

Sexually mature frog at three years

Each egg has three jelly coats which swell with water to enclose it

Clasping by the male stimulates the female to lay 500 to 5,000 eggs, which the male fertilizes as they are shed, over the course of about 10 minutes

The life cycle of a frog.

Amphibians

The vertebrate class Amphibia today includes about 3,500 species in three orders: frogs and toads (order Anura), salamanders and newts (order Caudata), and caecilians (order Gymnophiona). There is, however, a much larger number of extinct species, because this ancient group of animals were the first vertebrates to begin to exploit terrestrial environments. Fossil amphibians are known from at least the Devonian era, about 400 million years ago. However, this group was most diverse during the late to Carboniferous and Triassic eras, about 360 to 230 million years ago.

None of the surviving groups of amphibians can be traced back farther than about 200 million years. All of the living amphibians are predators as adults, mostly eating a wide variety of invertebrates, although the largest frogs and toads can also eat small mammals, birds, fish, and other amphibians. In contrast with adults, larval frogs and toads (tadpoles) are mostly herbivorous, feeding on algae, rotting or soft tissues of higher plants, and infusions of microorganisms.

Amphibians are poikilothermic animals—their body temperature is not regulated, so it conforms to the environmental temperature. Amphibians have a moist, glandular, scaleless skin, which is poorly waterproofed in most species; this skin allows gaseous exchange and actively pumps salts. Most amphibians have tails, but the tail in adult frogs and toads is vestigial, and is fused with the pelvis and sacral vertebrae into a specialized structure called a urostyle. Some species of caecilians have lost their limbs and limb–girdles, and are worm-like in appearance.

All amphibians have a complex life cycle, which begins with eggs that hatch into larvae, which eventually metamorphose into adult animals. Usually, the eggs are laid into water and are externally fertilized. The larvae or tadpoles have gills or gill slits and are aquatic. Adult amphibians may be either terrestrial or aquatic, and breathe either through their skin (when in water) or by their simple saclike lungs (when on land). However, these are all generalized characteristics of the amphibian lifestyle; some species have more specialized life histories, and can display attributes that differ substantially from those described above. Rare idiosyncrasies of amphibian life history can include ovoviviparity, in which fully formed, self–nourishing, developing eggs are retained inside the female's body until they hatch as tadpoles, and even viviparity, in which larvae develop within the female but are nourished by the parent as well as by their incompletely formed egg until they are released as miniature frogs.

Frogs and toads lack tails, and have greatly enlarged hind legs that are well adapted for jumping and swimming. Most of the living species of amphibians are anurans, comprising about 3,000 species. Most anurans are aquatic, but some are well adapted to drier habitats. Some common anurans of North America include the bullfrog (*Rana catesbeiana*, family Ranidae), spring peeper (*Hyla crucifer*, family Hylidae), American toad (*Scaphiopus holbrooki*, family Pelobatidae). The latter species lives in arid regions, estivating during dry periods but emerging after rains

to feed, and taking advantage of heavy but unpredictable periods of rain to engage in frenzies of breeding. The largest frogs reach 11.8 in (30 cm) in length and weigh several pounds.

There are about 250 species of newts and salamanders, ranging in size from approximately 6 in (15 cm) to more than 5 ft (1.5 m). These amphibians have a tail and similarly sized legs well adapted to walking, but are usually found in or near water. Most species lay their eggs in water, but adults usually spend most of their time in moist habitats on land. An exception is the red–spotted newt (*Notophthalmus viridescens*, family Salamandridae) of eastern North America, which in its juvenile stage (the red eft) wanders in moist terrestrial habitats for several years before returning to water to develop into its aquatic adult stage. Some species, such as the lungless red–backed salamander (*Plethodon cinereus*, family Plethodontidae) of North America, are fully terrestrial. This species lays its eggs in moist places on the forest floor, where the animals develop through embryonic and larval stages and hatch directly as tiny versions of the adult stage.

Caecilians are legless, almost tailless, wormlike, burrowing amphibians found in moist, tropical habitats. They feed on soil invertebrates. There are at least 160 species of caecilians, reaching 5 ft (1.5 m) in length, but most are rarely seen despite their size.

See also Caecilieth; Chordates; Frogs; Newts; Salamanders; Toads.

Amphipods see **Zooplankton**

Amplifier

An amplifier is a device, usually electronic, which magnifies information to a more powerful signal at the amplifier's output. Amplifiers are usually based on electronic principles but may utilize hydraulics or magnetics.

Amplifiers are used when the electrical power of a signal must be increased. Audio amplifiers can increase the microwatts developed by a microphone to more than a million watts of power required to fill a stadium during a concert. Satellites use amplifiers to strengthen television and telephone signals so they can be received easily when beamed back to Earth.

Long–distance telephone circuits were made possible when amplifiers magnified power that had been

The power amplifier for the Antares fusion laser.

dissipated by the resistance of cross–country phone wires. Amplifiers were also needed to restore lost volume. Undersea telephone cables require amplifiers beneath the sea. Cable–television systems require as many as 100 sophisticated broad–band width amplifiers to serve subscribers.

Amplifiers and energy

Just as a faucet is not the source of the water it dispenses, an amplifier does not create the energy it controls. An amplifier draws on the power of the weak input signal and supplements it with energy provided by a power source, increasing the power of the signal.

A replacement battery installed in a portable cassette–tape player supplies it with all the energy that will eventually create sounds during the life of that battery. The battery contains no information about the music or speech the player will eventually produce. Amplifiers in the tape player make it possible for the program on a compact disc, cassette tape, or a radio signal to dispense the battery's energy at a controlled rate as needed to produce the desired sounds.

Efficiency

No amplifier can be 100% efficient. All amplifiers waste some of the energy supplied to them. For instance, an amplifier's efficiency may be improved, but the result may be increased distortion in the final output.

Cascading amplifiers

To process an extremely weak signal, an amplifier must be able magnify data power by a factor of millions. To achieve this, amplifier stages are frequently connected in series to multiply their gain. Each stage in a chain provides the signal for the following stage, an arrangement called a cascade. The total amplification of a cascade is equal to the product of the individual–stage gains. If each of three amplifiers in cascade has a voltage gain of 100, the overall voltage gain will equal one million. A 10–micro volt signal processed by this cascade increases to a 10–volt signal.

Discrete and integrated amplifiers

Electronic amplifiers using separate transistors, resistors, and capacitors wired into place one by one are called discrete amplifiers. Discrete amplifiers have been all but superseded by integrated circuits (ICs) for small–signal applications. Vast numbers of transistors and many supporting components are contained on an IC's single silicon crystal chip. Circuit boards now use just a few encapsulated chips in place of the hundreds of individual components once required. An engineer or technician normally does not need to be aware of an IC's internal circuitry, further simplifying their use.

See also Electronics.

Further Reading:

Cannon, Don L., *Understanding Solid–State Electronics, 5th ed.*, SAMS division of Prentice Hall Publishing Company, 1991.

Donald Beaty

Amplitude modulation see **Radio waves**

Amputation

The term amputation refers to the complete or partial severance of a limb or other body part. Surgical amputations may be performed because of an injury, congenital (birth) defect, malignant disease, infection, or vascular disease. Approximately 80% of all surgical amputations are performed on the lower limbs, such as the leg or foot. Artificial limbs (prosthetics) are often used to restore complete or partial functioning, such as walking, after amputation.

History

Although surgical amputations date back at least to the time of Hippocrates (c. 460–375 B.C.), amputating limbs to save lives did not become widespread until the 16th century. Many of the advances in amputation surgery were made by military surgeons during the course of wars. In 1529, French military surgeon Ambroise Pare rediscovered the use of ligation, in which a thread–like or wire material is used to tie off, or constrict, blood vessels. This surgical technique, which stops the flow of blood from a severed vein, greatly reduces the patient's chances of bleeding to death and helped to make amputation a viable surgical approach.

The introduction of the tourniquet in 1674 further advanced surgical amputation. Essentially, a tourniquet is a circling device that is wrapped around the limb above the area to be amputated and then twisted to apply pressure to stop the flow of blood.

In 1867, Lord Lister's introduction of antiseptic techniques to surgery further advanced amputation. Antiseptics, such as iodine and chloride, reduced the chances of infection by inhibiting the growth of infectious agents such as bacteria. Other advances at this time included the use of chloroform and ether as anesthetics to reduce pain and keep the patient unconscious during surgery.

Reasons for amputation

The reasons for surgical amputations can be classified under four major categories: trauma, disease, tumors, and congenital defects. Amputations resulting from trauma to the limb are usually the result of physical injury, for example, from an accident; thermal injury due to a limb being exposed to extreme hot or cold temperatures; or infections, such as gangrene. Certain diseases, such as diabetes mellitus and vascular disease, may also lead to complete or partial amputation of a limb. Vascular disease is a leading cause of amputation in people over 51 years of age. The development of either malignant or nonmalignant tumors may also lead to amputation. Finally, congenital deficiencies, such as absence of part of an arm or leg or some other deformity, may be severe enough to require amputation, particularly if the defect interferes with the individual's ability to function.

Levels and goals of amputation

In determining how much of a limb to amputate, the surgeon must take several factors into consideration. When dealing with amputation due to disease, the surgeon's first and most important goal is to remove enough of the appendage or limb to insure the elimination of the disease. For example, when amputating to stop the spread of a malignant tumor, the surgeon's objective is to remove any portion of the limb or tissue that may be infected by the malignancy.

Other considerations in determining the level of amputation include leaving enough of a stump so that an artificial limb (prosthesis) may be attached in a functional manner. As a result, whenever possible, the surgeon will try to save functioning joints like knees and elbows.

Further goals of amputation surgery include leaving a scar that will heal well and is painless, retaining as much functioning muscle as possible, successfully managing nerve ends, achieving hemostasis (stopping the flow of blood) in veins and arteries through ligation, and proper management of remaining bone.

Prosthetics and limb reattachment

The use of artificial limbs or prosthetics most likely dates back to prehistoric man's use of tree limbs and forked sticks for support or replacement of an appendage. In 1858, a copper and wood leg dating back to 300 B.C. was discovered in Italy. In the 15th century, a knight who had lost a hand in battle could acquire an iron replacement. Recent medical–surgical and engineering advances have led to the development of state–of–the–art prosthetics, some of which can function nearly as well as the original limb. For example, some individuals who lose a leg may even be able to run again with the aid of a modern prosthetic device.

Recent advances have also led to more and more accidentally amputated limbs being successfully reattached. Depending on a number of factors, including the condition of the limb and how long it has been severed, full functional ability may be regained. In a notorious case that occurred in 1993, a man's severed penis was reattached with full functional ability.

Phantom limb

A baffling medical phenomenon associated with amputation is the amputee's perception of a phantom limb. In these cases, which are quite common among amputees, the amputees will perceive their amputated limb as though it still exists as part of their body. This phantom limb may be so real to an amputee that he or she may actually try to stand on a phantom foot or perform some task such as lifting a cup with a phantom hand. Although amputees may feel a number of sensations in a phantom limb, including numbness, coldness, and heat, the most troubling sensation is pain. Approximately 70% of all amputees complain of feeling pain in their phantom limbs. Such pain ranges from mild and sporadic to severe and constant.

Although it probably is related to the central nervous system, the exact cause of the phantom limb phenomenon is unknown. Theories on the origin of the phantom limb phenomenon include impulses from remaining nerve endings and spontaneous firing of spinal cord neurons (nerve cells). More recent studies indicate that the phenomenon may have its origin in the brain's neuronal circuitry.

Treatments for phantom limb pain include excision (cutting out) of neuromas (nodules that form at the end of cut nerves), reamputation at a higher point on the limb, or operation on the spinal cord. Although success has been achieved with these approaches in some cases, the patient usually perceives pain in the phantom limb again after a certain interval of time.

See also Prosthetics.

Further Reading:

Atlas of Limb Prosthetics: Surgical, Prosthetic, and Rehabilitation Principles. 2nd ed. New York: Mosby Year Book, 1992.

McPhee, A.T. "Scientist Solves Mystery: Why a Missing Arm Itches." *Current Science* 78 (1993): 8–9.

Melzack, Ronald. "Phantom Limbs." *Scientific American* (April, 1994) : 120–126.

Mulvey, Martha A. "Traumatic Amputation." *RN* 54 (1991): 26–30.

David Petechuk

Amyotonia see **Neuromuscular diseases**

Anabolism

Anabolism, or, biosynthesis, is the process by which living organisms synthesize complex molecules of life from simpler ones. Anabolism, together with catabolism, are the two series of chemical processes in cells that are, together, called metabolism. Anabolic reactions are divergent processes. That is, relatively few types of raw materials are used to synthesize a wide variety of end products. This results in an increase in cellular size or complexity—or both.

Anabolic processes produce peptides, proteins, polysaccharides, lipids, and nucleic acids. These molecules comprise all the materials of living cells, such as membranes and chromosomes, as well as the specialized products of specific types of cells, such as enzymes, antibodies, hormones, and neurotransmitters.

Catabolism, the opposite of anabolism, produces smaller molecules used by the cell to synthesize larger molecules, as will be described below. Thus, in contrast to the divergent reactions of anabolism, catabolism is a convergent process, in which many different types of molecules are broken down into relatively few types of end products.

The energy required for anabolism is supplied by the energy–rich molecule adenosine triphosphate, or *ATP*. This energy exists in the form of the high–energy chemical bond between the second and third molecule of phosphate on ATP. ATP's energy is released when this bond is broken, turning ATP into adenosine diphosphate, or ADP. During anabolic reactions, the high–energy phosphate bond of ATP is transferred to a substrate (a molecule worked on by an enzyme) in order to energize it in preparation for the molecule's subsequent use as a raw material for the synthesis of a larger molecule. In addition to ATP, some anabolic processes also require high–energy hydrogen atoms that are supplied by the molecule NADPH.

Although anabolism and catabolism occur simultaneously in the cell, the rates of their chemical reactions are controlled independently of each other. For example, there are two enzymatic pathways for glucose metabolism. The anabolic pathway synthesizes glucose, while catabolism breaks down glucose. The two pathways share 9 of the 11 enzymatic steps of glucose metabolism, which can occur in either sequence (i.e., in the direction of anabolism or catabolism). However, two steps of glucose anabolism use an entirely different set of enzyme–catalyzed reactions.

There are two important reasons that the cell must separate complementary anabolic and catabolic pathways. First, catabolism is a so–called "downhill" process during which energy is released, while anabolism requires the input of energy, and is therefore an energetically "uphill" process. At certain points in the anabolic pathway, the cell must put more energy into a reaction than is released during catabolism. Such anabolic steps require a different series of reaction than are used at this point during catabolism.

Second, the different pathways permit the cell to control the anabolic and catabolic pathways of specific molecules independently of each other. This is important because there are times when the cell must slow or halt a particular catabolic or anabolic pathway in order to reduce breakdown or synthesis of a particular molecule. If both anabolism and catabolism used the same pathway, the cell would not be able control the rate of either process independent of the other: slowing the rate of catabolism would slow the rate of anabolism.

Opposite anabolic and catabolic pathways can occur in different parts of the same cell. For example, in the liver the breakdown of fatty acids to the molecule acetyl–CoA takes place inside mitochondria. Mitochondria are the tiny, membrane–bound organelles that function as the cell's major site of ATP production. The buildup of fatty acids from acetyl–CoA occurs in the cytosol of the cell, that is, in the aqueous area of the cell that contains various solutes.

Although anabolic and catabolic pathways are controlled independently, both metabolic routes share an important common sequence of reactions that is known collectively as the citric acid cycle, or Krebs cycle. The Krebs cycle is part of a larger series of enzymatic reactions collectively called oxidative phosphorylation. This pathway is an important means of breaking down glucose to produce energy, which is stored in the form of ATP. But the molecules produced by the Krebs cycle can also be used as precursor molecules, or raw materials, for anabolic reactions that make proteins, fats, and carbohydrates.

Despite the independence of anabolism and catabolism, the various steps of these processes are in some ways so intimately linked that they form what might be considered an "enzymatic ecological system." In this system, a change in one part of a metabolic series of reactions can have a ripple effect throughout the linked anabolic and catabolic pathways.

This ripple effect is the cell's way of counterbalancing an increase or decrease in anabolism of a molecule with an opposite increase or decrease in catabolism. This lets the cell adjust the rate of anabolic and catabolic reactions to meet its immediate needs, and prevent imbalance of either anabolic or catabolic products.

For example, when the cell needs to produce specific proteins, it produces only enough of each of the various amino acids needed to synthesize those proteins. Moreover, certain amino acids are used by the cell to make glucose, which appears in the blood, or glycogen, a carbohydrate stored in the liver. So the products of amino acid catabolism do not accumulate, but rather feed the anabolic pathways of carbohydrate synthesis. Thus, while many organisms store energy–rich nutrients such as carbohydrates and fat, most do not store other biomolecules, such as proteins, or nucleic acids, the building blocks of deoxyribonucleic acid (DNA).

The cell regulates the rate of anabolic reactions by means of allosteric enzymes. The activity of these enzymes increases or decreases in response to the presence or absence of the end product of the series of reactions. For example, if an anabolic series of reactions produces a particular amino acid, that amino acid inhibits the action of the allosteric enzyme, reducing the synthesis of that amino acid.

See also Adenosine diphosphate; Adenosine triphosphate; Catabolism; Krebs cycle; Metabolism.

Anconda see **Boas; Snakes**

Anaerobic

The term anaerobic refers to living processes (usually the release of energy from nutrients) that take place in the absence of molecular oxygen. The earliest organisms, the prokaryotic bacteria, lived in an oxygen deficient atmosphere and extracted energy from organic compounds without oxygen (that is, by anaerobic respiration). Most organisms alive today extract their energy from nutrients aerobically (in the presence of oxygen) although a few respire. Aerobic respiration releases a lot of energy from nutrients, whereas anaerobic respiration releases relatively little energy.

Anaerobic organisms

Microorganisms which cannot tolerate oxygen and which are killed in its presence are called obligate (or strict) anaerobes. Bacteria of the genus *Clostridium* which cause gas gangrene, tetanus, and botulism belong to this group as well as *Bacteroides gingivalis* which thrives in anaerobic crevices between the teeth. Strict anaerobes are killed by oxygen, which is why hydrogen peroxide (which releases oxygen) is frequently applied to wounds. Methane–producing bacteria (methanogens), can be isolated from the anaerobic habitats of swamp sludge sewage and from the guts of certain animals. Methanogens generate the marsh gases of swamps and sewage treatment plants by converting hydrogen and carbon dioxide gases to methane. Some organisms, such as yeast, have adapted to grow in either the presence or absence of oxygen and are termed facultative anaerobes.

Anaerobic respiration

All cells carry out the process of glycolysis, which is an example of anaerobic respiration. Glycolysis is the initial phase of cellular respiration which involves the splitting of the six–carbon glucose molecule into two three–carbon pyruvate fragments. This is the main energy–releasing pathway that occurs in the cytoplasm of all prokaryotes and eukaryotes, and no oxygen is required. During glycolysis, oxidation (the removal of electrons and hydrogen ions) is facilitated by the coenzyme NAD^+ (nicotinamide adenine dinucleotide), which is then reduced to NADH. Only two ATP molecules result from this initial anaerobic reaction. This is a small amount of energy when compared to the net aerobic energy yield of 36 ATP in the complete oxidation of one molecule of glucose.

Fermentation

Under anaerobic conditions, the pyruvate molecule can follow other anaerobic pathways to regenerate the NAD^+ necessary for glycolysis to continue. These include alcoholic fermentation and lactate fermentation. In the absence of oxygen the further reduction or addition of hydrogen ions and electrons to the pyruvate molecules that were produced during glycolysis is termed fermentation. This process recycles the reduced NADH to the free NAD^+ coenzyme which once again serves as the hydrogen acceptor enabling glycolysis to continue. Alcoholic fermentation, characteristic of some plants and many microorganisms, yields alcohol and carbon dioxide as its products. Yeast is used by the biotechnology industries to generate carbon dioxide gas necessary for bread–making and in the fermentation of hops and grapes to produce alcoholic beverages. Depending on the yeast variety used, the different alcohol levels realized act as a form of population control by serving as the toxic element which kills the producers. Birds have been noted to fly erratically after they have gorged themselves on the fermenting fruit of the *Pyracantha* shrub.

Reduction of pyruvate by NADH releasing NAD^+ necessary for the glycolytic pathway can also result in lactate fermentation, which takes place in some animal tissues and in some microorganisms. Lactic acid–producing bacterial cells are responsible for the souring of milk and production of yogurt. In working animal muscle cells, lactate fermentation follows the exhaustion of the ATP stores. Fast twitch muscle fibers store little energy and rely on quick spurts of anaerobic activity, but the lactic acid which accumulates within the cells eventually leads to muscle fatigue and cramp.

See also Aerobic; Bacteria; Cellular respiration; Fermentation; Yeast.

Analgesia

Analgesia is the loss of pain without the loss of consciousness.

Techniques for controlling and relieving pain include acupuncture, anesthesia, hypnosis, biofeedback, and the use of analgesic drugs. Acupuncture is the ancient Chinese practice of inserting fine needles along certain pathways of the body and is used to relieve pain, especially in surgery, and to cure disease. In Western medicine the discovery of ether was a landmark in the development of anesthesia. Other techniques for pain control include electrical stimulation of the skin, massage, and stress–management therapy.

Analgesia is of primary importance for the treatment of injury or illness. The main agents for accomplishing analgesia in medical practice are analgesic drugs. These fall into two main categories: addictive and nonaddictive. Nonaddictive analgesics are generally used for treating moderate to severe pain and can be purchased without a prescription as over-the-counter drugs. More powerful analgesics have the potential for addiction and other undesirable side effects. They are usually used in hospitals or prescribed for relief from severe pain.

Presently, efforts are underway to develop powerful nonaddictive pain–relieving drugs. In order to improve the effectiveness and minimize the harm of analgesic drugs, pharmacological research has focused on the mechanism of how analgesics accomplish the task of pain relief. *Mechanism* in this context means the way the drug works in the body to accomplish its results.

Nonaddictive analgesics

While sold under many different brand names, the three main nonaddictive analgesics are aspirin, acetaminophen, and ibuprofen.

Aspirin was first synthesized in 1853 from vinegar and salicylic acid (acetylsalicylic acid). It is a member of the salicin family, which is a bitter white chemical found in willow bark and leaves. The analgesic qualities of willow bark were known to the ancient Greeks and others throughout the ages. In 1898 a German company, Bayer, further developed and marketed acetylsalicylic acid from industrial dyes and one year later named it aspirin. It soon became enormously popular as a pain reliever and antifever medicine. Its use as an anti–inflammatory for the treatment of arthritis and rheumatism made it the "gold standard" for readily available pain relief.

One of the major drawbacks of aspirin, however, is its effect on the stomach. It acts as an irritant and can cause bleeding ulcers in persons who take it over a long period of time. Recent research shows that aspirin's effectiveness not only as an analgesic but also as an anticoagulant makes it useful in the treatment of heart attacks and stroke, as well as a preventive medicine for other diseases.

Acetaminophen, introduced in 1955, is an over–the–counter drug that has become a very popular alternative to aspirin, since it relieves moderate pain without irritating the stomach. For the treatment of arthritis and rheumatism, acetaminophen does not have aspirin's anti–inflammatory effect, but as a pain and fever reliever it is just as effective as aspirin.

Ibuprofen is a nonsteroidal anti–inflammatory drug (NSAID) first introduced as a prescription drug in 1974. The Food and Drug Administration allowed it to be marketed as an over–the–counter drug in 1984. As an analgesic for minor pain and fever, it has about the same performance as aspirin and acetaminophen. Unlike acetaminophen, however, it can be irritating to the stomach.

Mechanism of nonaddictive analgesics

Pain that is caused by trauma (injury) in the body sets off the creation of a chemical called prostaglandin. The initial pain is caused by the nerve impulse that relays the injury message to the brain. According to the prostaglandin theory, the pain that is felt afterward is due to the prostaglandin at the site of the injury sending pain messages to the spinal cord, which then transmits these messages to the brain.

In 1971, a Nobel prize–winning pharmacologist, Sir John R. Vane, theorized that by blocking the formation of certain prostaglandins, aspirin was able to relieve the inflammation and pain that accompanies the trauma of damaged cells. Even though analgesics like aspirin had been used for centuries, Vane's discovery was the first real breakthrough in understanding how they work, and interest in prostaglandin research grew rapidly.

How over–the–counter medicines like aspirin, acetaminophen, and ibuprofen are able to temporarily relieve mild to moderate pain and even some severe pain is not completely understood. The blocking of prostaglandin production throughout the body, not just at the site of the pain, is the major theory that is currently accepted among medical scientists, although there are other theories to explain how these drugs work. Recent research suggests that aspirin has the ability to shut off communication of pain–transmitting nerves in the spinal cord.

The effectiveness of over–the–counter pain medicine depends on the kind of pain being experienced. Some pain originates in the skin and mucous areas of the body, while other pain comes from the smooth muscles and organs within the body. This latter type of pain is often difficult to pinpoint; it may feel like a generalized dull ache or throb, or may be referred pain, meaning pain that is felt in a part of the body away from its actual source.

Addictive analgesics

The treatment of severe pain, like pain that accompanies heart attack, kidney stones, gallstones, or terminal cancer, requires the use of prescription medicines that are far more potent than nonprescription drugs. Morphine, a drug derived from opium, has a long history of effective relief of severe pain, but it also is addictive and has dangerous side effects. Morphine and other drugs like it are called opiates.

Unlike nonaddictive drugs, increasing dosages of opiates also increases their analgesic effects. Thus, when they are self–administered, as pain increases, there is a danger of an overdose. Morphine is both a depressant and a stimulant. As a stimulant, it may cause nausea and vomiting, constriction of the pupils of the eye, and stimulation of the vagus nerve which regulates heartbeat. This stimulation of the vagus nerve interferes with the treatment of pain in coronary thrombosis. Its main side effects—addictive potential, tolerance (dosages must be increased to get the same effect), constipation, and a marked depression of the respiratory system—restrict morphine's use as an analgesic.

Mechanism of addictive analgesics

The first line of defense against pain in the body is the endorphins. These chemicals are peptides (compounds of amino acids) found in the brain and parts of the central nervous system. Like opiates, they produce a sense of well being (euphoria) and relieve pain. Endorphins are released from a transmitting nerve cell and then bind to the receptor sites of a receiving cell. After an endorphin sends the message to block pain signals to the receptor site it is annihilated, thus allowing other endorphins to be produced.

Morphine molecules flow through the spaces (synapses) between these sending and receiving cells and position themselves on the receptor sites, locking out endorphins. The morphine molecule sends the same message as the endorphin to block the pain signal. With long–term use of morphine, the endorphins decline in number and so do the receptor sites, leading to the twin problems of addiction and drug tolerance.

Development of new analgesics

The first phase in the development of new analgesics came with the development of narcotic blockers used to help drug addicts who overdose on a narcotic. Since these drugs have the ability to block the effects of morphine, they are called antagonists. They do not, however, provide any pain relief.

A second generation of narcotic antagonists are called agonist–antagonist analgesics. An agonist drug does provide pain relief by occupying receptor sites that block pain signals to the brain. The new group of agonist–antagonist medications show improved performance over morphine for providing pain relief, with fewer side effects and less chance of addiction.

The present challenge for medical science is to find medicines that are as effective as the opiates and morphine for relieving pain but do not have their side effects. The recent research on the brain which has uncovered how endorphins and other related brain chemicals work holds out hope for improved analgesic drugs.

See also Acupuncture; Anesthesia; Morphine; Novocain; Pain.

Further Reading:

Gold, Mark S., and Michael Boyett. *Wonder Drugs: How They Work.* New York: Simon & Schuster, 1987.

Kehrer, James P., and Daniel M. Kehrer. *Pills and Potions.* New York: Arco, 1984.

The Merck Manual. Rahway, NJ: Merck, 1992.

McCaffery, Margo, and Alexandra Beebe. *Pain: Clinical Manual for Nursing Practice.* St. Louis: Mosby, 1989.

McKenry, Leda M., and Evelyn Salerno. *Mosby's Pharmacology in Nursing.* St. Louis: Mosby, 1989.

Jordan P. Richman

Analysis, mathematical see **Calculus**

Analytic geometry

Analytic geometry is a branch of mathematics which uses algebraic equations to describe the size and position of geometric figures on a coordinate system.

Developed during the seventeenth century, it is also known as Cartesian geometry or coordinate geometry. The use of a coordinate system to relate geometric points to real numbers is the central idea of analytic geometry. By defining each point with a unique set of real numbers, geometric figures such as lines, circles, and conics can be described with algebraic equations. Analytic geometry has found important applications in science and industry alike.

Historical development of analytic geometry

During the seventeenth century, finding the solution to problems involving curves became important to industry and science. In astronomy, the slow acceptance of the heliocentric theory of planetary motion required mathematical formulas which would predict elliptical orbits. Other areas such as optics, navigation and the military required formulas for things such as determining the curvature of a lens, the shortest route to a destination, and the trajectory of a cannon ball. Although the Greeks had developed hundreds of theorems related to curves, these did not provide quantitative values so they were not useful for practical applications. Consequently, many seventeenth–century mathematicians devoted their attention to the quantitative evaluation of curves. Two French mathematicians, Rene Descartes (1596–1650) and Pierre de Fermat (1601–1665) independently developed the foundations for analytic geometry. Descartes was first to publish his methods in an appendix titled *La geometrie* of his book *Discours de la methode* (1637).

Cartesian coordinate system

The link between algebra and geometry was made possible by the development of a coordinate system which allowed geometric ideas, such as point and line, to be described in algebraic terms like real numbers and equations. In the system developed by Descartes, called the rectangular cartesian coordinate system, points on a geometric plane are associated with an ordered pair of real numbers known as coordinates. Each coordinate describes the location of a single point relative to a fixed point, the origin, which is created by the intersection of a horizontal and a vertical line known as the x–axis and y–axis respectively. The relationship between a point and its coordinates is called one–to–one since each point corresponds to only one set of coordinates.

The x and y axes divide the plane into four quadrants. The sign of the coordinates is either positive or negative depending in which quadrant the point is located. Starting in the upper right quadrant and working clockwise, a point in the first quadrant would have a positive value for the abscissa and the ordinate. A point in the fourth quadrant (lower right hand corner) would have negative values for each coordinate.

The notation P (x,y) describes a point P which has coordinates x and y. The x value, called the abscissa, represents the horizontal distance of a point away from the origin. The y value, known as the ordinate, represents the vertical distance of a point away from the origin.

Distance between two points

Using the ideas of analytic geometry, it is possible to calculate the distance between the two points A and B, represented by the line segment AB which connects the points. If two points have the same ordinate but different abscissas, the distance between them $AB = x_2 - x_1$. Similarly, if both points have the same abscissa but different ordinates, the distance $AB = y_2 - y_1$. For points which have neither a common abscissa or ordinate, the Pythagorean Theorem is used to determine distance. By drawing horizontal and vertical lines through points A and B to form a right triangle, it can be shown using the distance formula that $AB = - (x_2 - x_1)^2 + (y_2 - y_1)^2$. The distance between the two points is equal to the length of the line segment AB.

In addition to length, it is often desirable to find the coordinates of the midpoint of a line segment. These coordinates can be determined by taking the average of the x and y coordinates of each point. For example, the coordinates for the midpoint M(x,y) between points P(2,5) and Q(4,3) are $x = (2 + 4)/2 = 3$ and $y = (5 + 3)/2 = 4$.

Algebraic equations of lines

One of the most important aspects of analytic geometry is the idea that an algebraic equation can relate to a geometric figure. Consider the equation $2x + 3y = 44$. The solution to this equation is an ordered pair (x,y) which represents a point. If the set of every point which makes the equation true (called the *locus*) were plotted, the resulting graph would be a straight line. For this reason, equations such as these are known as linear equations. The standard form of a linear equation is $Ax + By = C$, where A, B, and C are constants and A and B are not both 0. It is interesting to note that an equation such as $x = 4$ is a linear equation. The graph of this equation is made up of the set of all ordered pairs in which x = 4.

The steepness of a line relative to the x axis can be determined by using the concept of the slope. The slope of a line is defined by the equation

$$m = \frac{Y_2 - Y_1}{X_2 - X_1}$$

The value of the slope can be used to describe a line geometrically. If the slope is positive, the line is said to be rising. For a negative slope, the line is falling. A slope of zero is a horizontal line and an undefined slope is a vertical line. If two lines have the same slope, then these lines are parallel.

The slope gives us another common form for a linear equation. The slope–intercept form of a linear equation is written y = mx + b, where m is the slope of the line and b is the y intercept. The y intercept is defined as the value for y when x is zero and represents a point on the line which intersects the y axis. Similarly, the x intercept represents a point where the line crosses the x axis and is equal to the value of x when y is zero. Yet another form of a linear equation is the point–slope form, $y - y_1 = m(x - x_1)$. This form is useful because it allows us to determine the equation for a line if we know the slope and the coordinates of a point.

Calculating area using coordinates

One of the most frequent activities in geometry is determining the area of a polygon such as a triangle or square. By using coordinates to represent the vertices, the areas of any polygon can be determined. The area of triangle OPQ, where O lies at (0,0), P at (a,b), and Q at (c,d), is found by first calculating the area of the entire rectangle and subtracting the areas of the three right triangles. Thus the area of the triangle formed by points OPQ is = da – (dc/2) – (ab/2) – [(d–b)(a–c)]/2. Through the use of a determinant, it can be shown that the area of this triangle is

$$\text{Area of triangle} = \frac{1}{2} \begin{vmatrix} a & b \\ c & d \end{vmatrix}$$

This specific case was made easier by the fact that one of the points used for a vertex was the origin. The

$$\text{Area of triangle} = \frac{1}{2} \begin{vmatrix} x_1 & y_1 \\ x_2 & y_2 \end{vmatrix} + \frac{1}{2} \begin{vmatrix} x_2 & y_2 \\ x_3 & y_3 \end{vmatrix} + \frac{1}{2} \begin{vmatrix} x_3 & y_3 \\ x_1 & y_1 \end{vmatrix}$$

general equation for the area of a triangle defined by coordinates is represented by the previous equation.

In a similar manner, the area for any other polygon can be determined if the coordinates of its points are known.

Equations for geometric figures

In addition to lines and the figures that are made with them, algebraic equations exist for other types of geometric figures. One of the most common examples is the circle. A circle is defined as a figure created by the set of all points in a plane which are a constant distance from a central point. If the center of the circle is at the origin, the formula for the circle is $r^2 = x^2 + y^2$ where r is the distance of each point from the center and called the radius. For example, if a radius of 4 is chosen, a plot of all the x and y pairs which satisfy the equation $4^2 = x^2 + y^2$ would create a circle. Note, this equation, which is similar to the distance formula, is called the center–radius form of the equation. When the radius of the circle is at the point (a,b) the formula, known as the general form, becomes $r^2 = (x - a)^2 + (y - b)^2$.

The circle is one kind of a broader type of geometric figures known as conic sections. Conic sections are formed by the intersection of a geometric plane and a double–napped cone. After the circle the most common conics are parabolas, ellipses, and hyperbolas.

Curves known as parabolas are found all around us. For example, they are the shape formed by the sagging of telephone wires or the path a ball travels when it is thrown in the air. Mathematically, these figures are described as a curve created by the set of all points in a plane which are a constant distance from a fixed point, known as the focus, and a fixed line, called the directrix. This means that if we take any point on the parabola, the distance of the point from the focus is the same as the distance from the directrix. A line can be drawn through the focus which is perpendicular to the directrix. This line is called the axis of symmetry of the parabola. The midpoint between the focus and the directrix is the vertex.

The equation for a parabola is derived from the distance formula. Consider a parabola which has a vertex at point (h,k). The linear equation for the directrix can be represented by y = k – p, where p is the distance of the focus from the vertex. The standard form of the equation of the parabola is then $(x - h)^2 = 4p(y - k)$. In this case, the axis of symmetry is a vertical line. In the case of a horizontal axis of symmetry, the equation becomes $(y - k)^2 = 4p(x - h)$ where the equation for the directrix is x = h – p. This formula can be expanded to give the more common quadratic formula which is $y = Ax^2 + Bx + C$ such that $A \neq 0$.

Another widely used conic is an ellipse, which looks like a flattened circle. An ellipse is formed by the graph of the set of points the sum of whose distances from two fixed points (foci) is constant. To visualize this definition, imagine two tacks placed at the foci. A string, which is longer than the distance between them, is tied to each tack. The string is pulled taut with a pencil and an ellipse is formed by the path traced. Certain parts of the ellipse are given various names. The two points on an ellipse intersected by a line passing through both foci are called the vertices. The chord which connects both vertices is the major axis and the chord perpendicular to it is known as the minor axis. The point at which the chords meet is known as the center.

Again by using the distance formula, the equation for an ellipse can be derived. If the center of the ellipse is at point (h,k) and the major and minor axes have lengths of 2a and 2b respectively, the standard equation is

$$\frac{(x-h)^2}{a^2} + \frac{(y-k)^2}{b^2} = 1$$

Major axis is horizontal

$$\frac{(x-h)^2}{b^2} + \frac{(y-k)^2}{a^2} = 1$$

Major axis is vertical

If the center of the ellipse is at the origin, the equation simplifies to $(x^2/a^2) + (y^2/b^2) = 1$.

The "flatness" of an ellipse depends on a number called the eccentricity. This number is given by the ratio of the distance from the center to the focus divided by the distance from the center to the vertex. The greater the eccentricity value, the flatter the ellipse.

Another conic section is a hyperbola, which looks like two facing parabolas. Mathematically, it is similar in definition to an ellipse. It is formed by the graph of the set of points, the difference of whose distances from two fixed points (foci) is constant. Notice that in the case of a hyperbola, the difference between the two distances from fixed points is plotted and not the sum of this value as was done with the ellipse.

As with other conics, the hyperbola has various characteristics. It has vertices, the points at which a line passing through the foci intersects the graph, and a

KEY TERMS

Abscissa—The x–coordinate of a point representing its horizontal distance away from the origin.

Conic—A geometric figure created by a plane passing through a right circular cone.

Coordinate system—A system which relates geometric points to real numbers based on their location in space relative to a fixed point called the origin.

Directrix—A fixed line involved in defining the shape of a conic.

Ellipse—A conic section which appears as a "flat" circle.

Focus—A single point involved in defining the shape of a conic.

Hyperbola—A conic section created by a plane passing through the base of two cones.

Intercept—The point at which a curve meets the x or y axes.

Linear equations—A mathematical equation which represents a line.

Locus—The set of all points that make an equation true.

Ordinate—The y–coordinate of a point representing its vertical distance away from the origin.

Pythagorean theorem—An idea which suggests that the sum of the squares of the sides of a right triangle is equal to the square of the hypotenuse. It is used to find the distance between two points.

Slope—A value which measures the steepness of a line on a coordinate system.

center. The line segment which connects the two vertices is called the transverse axis. The simplified equation for a hyperbola with its center at the origin is $(x^2/a^2) - (y^2/b^2) = 1$. In this case, a is the distance between the center and a vertex, b is the difference of the distance between the focus and the center and the vertex and the center.

Three–dimensional coordinate systems and beyond

Geometric figures such as points, lines, and conics are two–dimensional because they are confined to a single plane. The term two–dimensional is used because each point in this plane is represented by two real numbers. Other geometric shapes like spheres and cubes do not exist in a single plane. These shapes, called surfaces, require a third dimension to describe their location in space. To create this needed dimension, a third axis (traditionally called the z–axis) is added to the coordinate system. Consequently, the location of each point is defined by three real numbers instead of two. For example, a point defined by the coordinates (2,3,4) would be located 2 units away from the x axis, 3 units from the y axis, and 4 units from the z axis.

The algebraic equations for three–dimensional figures are determined in a way similar to their two-dimensional counterparts. For example, the equation for a sphere is $x^2 + y^2 + z^2 = r^2$. As can be seen, this is slightly more complicated than the equation for its two–dimensional cousin, the circle, because of the additional variable z^2.

It is interesting to note that just as the creation of a third dimension was possible, more dimensions can be added to our coordinate system. Mathematically, these dimension can exist, and valid equations have been developed to describe figures in these dimensions. However, it should be noted that this does not mean that these figures physically exist and in fact, at present they only exist in the minds of people who study this type of multidimensional analytic geometry.

See also Circle; Conic sections; Geometry; Hyperbola; Parabola; Point.

Further Reading:

Paulos, John Allen. *Beyond Numeracy.* New York: Alfred A. Knopf Inc., 1991.

Perry Romanowski

Anaphylaxis

Anaphylaxis is a severe, sudden, often fatal bodily reaction to a foreign substance or antigen. C.R. Richet first coined the term to define the puzzling reactions that occurred in dogs following injection of an eel toxin. Instead of acquiring immunity from the toxin as expected, the dogs experienced acute reactions, including often fatal respiratory difficulties, shock, and internal hemorrhaging. In humans, anaphylaxis is a rare event usually triggered by an antiserum (to treat snake or insect bites), antibiotics (especially immunoglobu-

lin), or after wasp or bee stings. Certain foods can also trigger these severe reactions, including seafood, rice, potatoes, egg–whites, raw milk, and pinto beans.

In systemic or system–wide cases, symptoms occur just minutes (or in rare cases weeks) after introduction of the foreign substance and include flushed skin, itching of the scalp and tongue, breathing difficulties caused by bronchial spasms or swollen tissues, vomiting, diarrhea, a sudden drop in blood pressure, shock, and loss of consciousness. Less severe cases, usually caused by nonimmunologic mechanisms, may produce widespread hives or severe headache. These less severe cases are called anaphylactoid reactions.

While the exact biological process is poorly understood, anaphylaxis is thought to result from antigen–antibody interactions on the surface of mast cells, a connective tissue cell that is believed to contain a number of regulatory chemicals. This interaction damages cell membranes, causing a sudden release of chemicals, including histamine, heparin, serotonin, bradykinin, and other pharmacologic mediators. Once released, these mediators produce the frightening bodily reactions that characterize anaphylaxis.

Because of the severity of these reactions, treatment must begin as soon as possible. The most common emergency treatment involves injection of epinephrine (adrenaline), followed by administration of cortisone, antihistamines, and other drugs which can reduce the effects of the unleashed chemical mediators. For people with known reactions to antibiotics, foods, insect and snake bites, or other factors, avoidance of the symptom–inducing agent is the best form of prevention.

See also Antibody and antigen.

Anatomy

Anatomy, a subfield of biology, is the study of the structure of living things. There are three main areas of anatomy: cytology studies the structure of cell; histology examines the structure of tissues; and gross anatomy deals with organs and organ groupings called systems. Comparative anatomy, which strives to identify general structural patterns of families of plants and animals, provided the basis for the classification of species. Human anatomy is a crucial element of the medical curriculum.

Modern anatomy, as a branch of Western science, was founded by the Flemish scientist Andreas Vesalius (1514–1564), who in 1543 published *De humani cor-*

poris fabrica (*Structure of the Human Body*), one of the great works in the history of science. In addition to correcting numerous misconceptions about the human body, Vesalius's book was the first description of human anatomy that organized the organs into systems. Although initially rejected by many followers of classical anatomical doctrines, Vesalius's systematic conception of anatomy soon became the foundation of anatomical research and education throughout the world; anatomists still use his systematic approach.

Human anatomy

Human anatomy divides the body into the following distinct functional systems: cutaneous, muscular, skeletal, circulatory, nervous, digestive, urinary, endocrine, respiratory, and reproductive. This division helps the student understand the organs, their relationships, and the relations of individual organs to the body as a whole.

The cutaneous system consists of the integument—the covering of the body, including the skin, hair, and nails. The skin is the largest organ in the body, and its most important function is to act as a barrier between the body and the outside world. The skin's minute openings (pores) also provide an outlet for sweat, which regulates the body temperature. Melanin, a dark pigment found in the skin, provides protection from sunburn. The skin also contains oil–producing cells.

Beneath the skin is the muscular system. The muscles enable the body to move and provide power to the hands and fingers. There are two basic types of muscles. Voluntary (skeletal) muscles enable us to perform movements of our own decision, to walk, move our arms, or smile and frown. Involuntary (smooth) muscles are not consciously controlled, and operate on their own. For example, they play an important role in digestion. There is a third type of muscle, the heart muscle (myocardium), which is involuntary, but is striated, as in skeletal muscles. This life–sustaining muscle pumps blood throughout the body—constantly, without pause—from the embryonic stage to death.

The skeletal system, or the skeleton, is underneath the muscular system. This bony frame provides the support that the muscles need in order to function. Of the 206 bones in the human body, the largest is the femur, or thigh bone. The smallest are the tiny ear ossicles, three in each ear, and named the hammer, anvil, and stirrup. Often included in the skeletal system are the ligaments, which connect bone to bone; the joints, which allow the connected bones to move; and the tendons, which connect muscle to bone.

KEY TERMS

. . . .

Dissection—To cut apart or separate to reveal structures of the organism being studied.

The circulatory system comprises the heart, arteries, veins, capillaries, blood and blood–forming organs, and the lymphatic sub–system. The four chambers of the heart pump blood throughout the body and the lungs. From the heart, the blood circulates through arteries. The blood is distributed through smaller and smaller tubes until it passes into the microscopic capillaries which bathe every cell. The veins collect the "used" blood from the capillaries and return it to the heart.

The nervous system consists of the brain, the spinal cord, and the sensory organs that provide information to them. For example, our eyes, ears, nose, tongue, and skin receive stimuli and send signals to the brain. The brain then makes decisions about any needed action. The brain is an intricate system of complicated cells that allow us to think, read, hear, and enjoy a movie. It also regulates breathing, movement, body temperature, and many other functions.

The digestive system is essentially a long tube extending from the mouth to the anus. Food entering the mouth is conducted through the stomach, small intestine, and large intestine, where accessory organs contribute digestive juices to break down the food, extracting the molecules that can be used to nourish the body. The unusable parts of the ingested food are expelled through the anus as fecal matter. The salivary glands (in the mouth), the liver, and the pancreas are the primary digestive glands.

The urinary system consists of the kidneys, the bladder, and the connecting tubules. The kidneys filter water and waste products from the blood and pass them into the bladder. At intervals, the bladder is emptied through the urinary tract, ridding the body of unneeded substances.

The endocrine system consists of ductless (endocrine) glands which produce hormones that regulate various bodily functions. The pancreas secretes insulin to regulate sugar metabolism, for example. The pituitary gland in the brain is the principal gland that regulates the others.

The respiratory system includes the lungs, the diaphragm, and the tubes that connect them to the outside air. Respiration is the process whereby an organism absorbs oxygen from the air and returns carbon dioxide. The diaphragm is the muscle that enables the lungs to work.

Finally, the reproductive system enables sperm and egg to unite and the egg to remain in the uterus or womb to develop into a functional human.

See also Circulatory system; Digestive system; Endocrine system; Muscular system; Nervous system; Reproductive system; Respiratory system; Skeletal system.

Further Reading:

"Adam & Eve—Bit by Bit." *Science News* 145 (8 January 1994): 28.
Gray's Anatomy. Philadelphia: Lea & Febiger, 1992.

Larry Blaser

Anchovy

Anchovies are bony fish in the order Clupeiformes, which they share with herring, salmon, and trout. Anchovies are in the family Engraulidae and all of the more than 100 species are in the same genus (Engraulis). Anchovies are predominantly marine fish but are occasionally found in brackish waters and even in fresh water. Anchovies are found in the Mediterranean sea, Black sea, the European Atlantic coastal waters, and the Pacific coasts of Peru and Chile. The anchovy is about 4–8 in (10–20 cm) long, with smooth scales, and soft fins.

Anchovies live in schools made up of thousands of individuals often grouped according to size. The fish come to the surface waters during the spawning season (May–July). The eggs float on the surface of the water and hatch in three to four days. Anchovies eat while swimming with their mouths open and feed on plankton, small crustaceans, and fish larvae. When food is scarce, the anchovies take turns swimming at the front of the school (where they are likely to encounter the best food) so all have a chance to eat. When a school of anchovies senses danger, the school swims together to make a tight ball in which the fish on the inside are protected, while the fish on the outer part of the ball have a greater chance of being consumed. Anchovies are usually caught by fishermen at night–the lights on the boat serve as a lure.

In Peru, the anchovy known as anchovetta (*E. ringens*) is economically important as a source of fertil-izer. Other species of anchovy (*E. encrasicolus*) are canned in oil and salt and sold as a delicacy (these are the hairy–looking fish on pizza and the fish that make the dressing for Caesar salad). Other species of anchovy are used for fish bait or are added to pet food and livestock feed.

Anemia

Anemia means literally lack of blood. In fact it is a reduction in the number of red blood cells, plasma, or packed red blood cells to a level that is lower than necessary for normal functioning. This is the result of the inability to replace lost cells or plasma volume at the rate they are being lost. The underlying cause for anemia may be one of several conditions.

Causes of anemia

Anemia can result from a rapid loss of blood cells as with trauma, or from a reduced rate of replacement, or from an abnormally rapid destruction of blood cells within the body that outstrips the replacement ability of bone marrow.

Normally the red blood cell count for an adult male is 5.4 million per cubic mm of blood at sea level. The count for the adult female is 4.8 million per cubic mm. An adult male is considered anemic if his red cell count falls below 4.5 million per cubic mm, and the female if her count is less than 4 million per cubic mm. The normal rate of replacement for red blood cells is 40,000 to 50,000 new cells per cubic mm per day. Blood cells are generated within the bone marrow.

Trauma and surgery

Any time the integrity of the body is violated blood can be lost. An automobile accident, a wound, a fall, or a surgical procedure all can open the body to blood loss. A trauma or wound that opens a major blood vessel allows blood to be pumped from the closed circulatory system and depletes the blood volume. Certainly the body is not able to replace such a rapid loss of blood cells or plasma.

Surgical procedures have become more and more "bloodless." Refinements in techniques as well as in instrumentation have rendered modern surgical procedures blood–conserving transactions.

A great deal of surgery is carried out using flexible scopes and instruments that can be inserted into the body through very small incisions. The surgical procedure is carried out by the physician who can see the surgical field by means of a miniature camera on the tip of the instrument. Long incisions followed by clamping of bleeding arteries and veins have been replaced. The need for blood transfusions during surgery has been reduced markedly over the past decade. The patient who may need blood replacement is urged to have his own blood collected prior to surgery, so there will be no subsequent problems from the transfusion.

Low red blood cell production

A deficiency in red blood cell production is the most common cause of anemia, and a lack of iron is the most common reason for low cell production. Iron is the basic atom of hemoglobin, the substance that gives blood its red color and that is responsible for carrying oxygen and carbon dioxide through the body. The normal level of iron in the body is 0.1–0.2 oz (3 to 5 g), depending upon one's sex and size.

Iron deficiency occurs as the result of inadequate intake of iron, loss of iron in young women of childbearing age through menstruation and child bearing, impaired absorption of iron, which may occur following removal of part of the stomach and small intestine, or because of a chronic loss of low volumes of blood within the digestive system through polyps, cancer, or ulcerations brought on by excessive aspirin intake.

Old and nonfunctional red blood cells are culled from the blood stream by the spleen. The cells are destroyed and the iron molecule within the hemoglobin is transferred back to the bone marrow for reuse, a classic example of recycling. Red blood cells that escape the body, however, take iron with them. Of the usual iron intake of 10 to 20 mg daily in the diet, about one or two mg is absorbed to replace lost iron. Absorption is increased in women who are menstruating or are pregnant.

People with iron deficiency anemia will have abnormally small red blood cells and low hemoglobin levels even though the total red blood cell count may be normal. Supplementary iron intake may resolve the problem, but surgery may be necessary if the underlying cause is a polyp or other area bleeding internally.

Aplastic anemia

Aplastic anemia is a life–threatening form of anemia resulting from insufficient production of blood cells. The underlying cause of the disease is in the bone marrow itself. Aplastic anemia can be brought about by exposure to toxic chemicals or radiation or by exces-

---

KEY TERMS
. . . .

Bone marrow—The spongy center of many bones that manufactures the blood cells.

Hemolytic anemia—Hemolytic means destruction of the blood cell, an abnormal rate of which may lead to lowered levels of these cells.

Menstruation—The normal, nearly monthly bleeding cycle experienced by women of childbearing age. It is the result of lack of a fertilized egg that triggers the loss of the lining of the uterus (womb) and subsequent bleeding.

Spleen—An organ lying just under the diaphragm in the abdomen that removes old or damaged blood cells from circulation. The spleen is not a critical organ and can be removed if necessary.

---

sive intake of certain medications. Removal of the toxic agent or getting away from the source of radiation usually will allow the patient to recover without further events. However, a form of aplastic anemia known as idiopathic, which means a disease of unknown cause, may well result in death.

Aplastic anemia affects all cells in the blood including the white blood cells and blood platelets. Loss of white blood cells, the core of the immune system, leaves one susceptible to infection. Loss of blood platelets, which are functional in the clotting process, means bleeding into the skin, digestive system, urine, or nervous system may occur, as may repeated nosebleeds.

Treatment for this form of anemia is to remove the agent causing it, if known, and to provide supportive treatment until the bone marrow recovers. In extreme cases bone marrow transplantation from a compatible individual may be attempted and is sometimes successful.

Megaloblastic anemia

Megaloblastic refers to the large, immature blood cells seen with this kind of anemia. One form called pernicious anemia is the result of a digestive inadequacy in which vitamin B_{12} is not absorbed through the intestine. The condition also is caused by a parasitic infection, as with a tapeworm, certain digestive diseases, cancer, and anticancer chemotherapeutic agents, and most commonly by lack of folate. It is an anemia often seen in elderly people who suffer from malnutri-

---

tion, alcoholics, teenagers, (possibly also related to malnutrition) and pregnant women.

This form of anemia may be corrected easily by placing the individual on a balanced, adequate diet or by replacing lowered levels of folate or vitamins.

Sickle cell anemia

Although blood cell levels are not lowered in sickle cell anemia, the blood cells may be nonfunctional at times, resulting in oxygen starvation of some body tissues. See Sickle Cell Anemia for a more detailed discussion of this genetic condition.

Others

There are many other kinds of anemias, though they are rarely seen. Those discussed are the most common types. Others include a form called spherocytosis, which, as the name implies, results in a spherical form of red blood cell resulting from an abnormality in the cell membrane; a similar form called elliptocytosis; and others resulting from decreased or abnormal hemoglobin production.

See also Blood; Sickle cell anemia.

Further Reading:
Friedland, I. "The anemia epidemic." *Working Mother* 16 (July, 1993):18+.
National Heart, Lung, and Blood Institute, Bethesda, MD. Publications on anemia and sickle cell anemia.

Larry Blaser

Anesthesia

Anesthesia is the loss of feeling or sensation. It may be accomplished without the loss of consciousness, or with partial or total loss of consciousness.

Anesthesiology is a branch of medical science which relates to anesthesia and anesthetics. The anesthetist is a specialized physician in charge of supervising and administering anesthesia in the course of a surgical operation. Depending on the type of operation and procedures used, there are two types of anesthesia: general anesthesia, which causes a loss of consciousness, and local anesthesia, where the anesthetic "freezes" the nerves in the area covered by the operation. In local anesthesia, the patient may be conscious during the course of the operation or given a sedative, a drug that induces sleep.

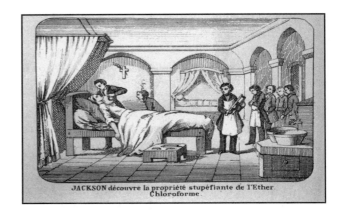

JACKSON découvre la propriété stupéfiante de l'Ether Chloroforme.

A 19th century physician administering ether prior to surgery (probably an amputation). Ether was one of the earliest anesthetics to be used, but was difficult to administer, as it made the patient choke. For a time it was replaced by chloroform, but made a comeback when chloroform proved even more dangerous.

History of anesthesia

While the search for pain control during surgery dates back to the ancient world, it was not until 1846 that it went on record that a patient was successfully rendered unconscious during a surgical procedure. Performed in a Boston hospital, the operation used a gas called ether to anesthetize the patient while a neck tumor was removed. In Western medicine, the development of anesthesia has made possible complex operations like open heart surgery and organ transplants. Medical tests that would otherwise be impossible to perform are routinely carried out with the use of anesthesia.

Before the landmark discovery of ether as an anesthetic, patients who needed surgery for either illness or injury had to face the surgeon's knife with only the help of alcohol, opium, or other narcotic. Often a group of men held the patient down during the operation in case the narcotic or alcohol wore off before it was over. Under these conditions many patients died just from the pain of the operation.

Nitrous oxide

In 1776 Joseph Priestly, the British chemist, discovered the gas nitrous oxide. Another British chemist, Humphry Davy, proposed nitrous oxide as a means for pain–free surgery, but his views were dismissed by other physicians of the day. In the next century, Horace Wells, a Connecticut dentist, began to experiment with nitrous oxide, and in 1845 attempted to demonstrate its anesthetic qualities to a public audience. However, the patient woke before the operation was over and began to scream in pain. Because of this spectacle, it took another 20 years before nitrous oxide again gained attention. By 1870, nitrous oxide was a commonplace dental anesthetic.

Ether

Ether, a gas, was discovered in 1540 and given its name in 1730. The gas was first successfully used by an American physician, Crawford W. Long, in an operation in 1842. The operation, however, was unrecorded, so official credit went instead to William Morton for his 1846 demonstration of an operation with the use of ether.

Chloroform

The credit for discovering the third major anesthetic of this period in medical history goes to James Young Simpson, a Scottish gynecologist and obstetrician. Simpson used ether in his practice but searched for an anesthetic that would make bearing children less painful for women. He tested several gases until he came upon chloroform in 1847 and began to use it on women in labor. Chloroform use, though, had higher risks than those associated with ether, and it called for greater skill from the physician. Neither ether nor chloroform are used in surgery today.

Emergence of anesthesiology

Anesthesiology as a medical specialty was slow to develop. By the end of the 19th century, ether, which was considered safer than chloroform, was administered by *etherizers* who had little medical experience, including students, new physicians, non–medical specialists, nurses, and caretakers. Eventually, nurses began to be used for this job, becoming the first anesthetists by the end of the 19th century.

While the practice of surgery began to make considerable progress by the turn of the century, anesthesiology lagged behind. In the 20th century, though, the need for specialists in anesthesia was sparked by two world wars and advanced surgical techniques. To meet these demands, the American Society of Anesthetists was formed in 1931 and specialists were then certified by the American Board of Anesthesiology in 1937. By 1986, the Board certified 13,145 specialists—physicians and nurses, called nurse anesthetists—in the field of anesthesiology.

Types of anesthesia

Modern anesthesiology can be divided into two types, pharmacological and non–pharmacological.

Pharmacological anesthesia uses a wide variety of anesthetic agents to obtain varying degrees of sedation and pain control. The anesthesia is administered orally, by injection, or with a gas mask for inhalation. Examples of non–pharmacological anesthesia are the use of breathing techniques during conscious childbirth (Lamaze method of natural childbirth) and the ancient art of Chinese acupuncture. Non–pharmacological anesthesia requires special skills on the part of its practitioners, and its effects are not as reliable as pharmacological techniques.

Pharmacological anesthesia is described as either general or local.

General anesthesia

There are three phases to general anesthesia. The anesthetist must first induce the state of unconsciousness (induction), keep the patient unconscious while the procedure is performed (maintenance), then allow the patient to emerge back into consciousness (emergence).

A drug commonly used to induce unconsciousness is thiopentone sodium. It is a barbiturate that produces unconsciousness within 30 seconds after being injected intravenously. Thiopentone does not reduce pain; it actually lowers the threshold of pain. It is used in the induction stage to bring about a quick state of unconsciousness before using other drugs to maintain the anesthetic condition during surgery.

Other agents used for the induction and maintenance of anesthesia are gases or volatile liquids such as nitrous oxide, halothane, enflurane, methoxyflurane and cyclopropane.

Nitrous oxide is still commonly used in dentistry, minor surgery, and major surgery when it is accompanied by other anesthetics. Though the gas has been used for many years, it is still uncertain how nitrous oxide accomplishes its anesthetic effect. Mixtures of oxygen and nitrous oxide appear to enhance its effect. Unlike other agents used today, it appears to have no toxic side effects on the body.

Halothane is a colorless liquid with a very low boiling point. Its use, though, may be connected to liver toxicity. Enflurane and methoxyflurane are also liquids that are useful as analgesics (pain relievers) and muscle relaxants, but they also may have undesirable side effects. Cyclopropane, which is an expensive and explosive gas used for rapid induction and quick recovery, has over the years been replaced with the use of halothane.

The anesthesiologist interviews the patient before the operation and examines his or her medical records to determine which of the many anesthetic agents available will be used. Cyclopropane or atropine may be given before the operation to relieve pain and anxiety. When a muscle relaxant is given for the surgical procedure, the anesthesiologist monitors the respiratory equipment to ensure patient is breathing properly.

Administration of the anesthetic is usually accomplished by the insertion of a cannula (small tube) into a vein. Sometimes a gas anesthetic may be introduced through a mask. If a muscle relaxant is used, the patient may not be able to breathe on his own, and a breathing tube is passed into the windpipe (trachea). The tube then serves either to deliver the anesthetic gases or to ventilate (oxygenate) the lungs.

During the course of the surgery, the anesthesiologist maintains the level of anesthetic needed to keep up the patient's level of anesthesia to the necessary state of unawareness while monitoring vital functions, such as heart beat, breathing, and blood/gas exchange.

Complications of general anesthesia

There are a number of possible complications that can occur under general anesthesia. They include loss of blood pressure, irregular heart beat, heart attack, vomiting and then inhaling the vomit into the lungs, coma, and death. Although mishaps do occur, the chance of a serious complication is extremely low. Avoidance of complications depends on a recognition of the condition of the patient before the operation, the choice of the appropriate anesthetic procedure, and the nature of the surgery itself.

Local anesthesia

Local anesthetics block pain in regions of the body without affecting other functions of the body or overall consciousness. They are used for medical examinations, diagnoses, minor surgical and dental procedures, and for relieving symptoms of minor distress, such as itching, toothaches, and hemorrhoids. They can be taken as creams, ointments, sprays, gels, or liquid; or they can be given by injection and in eye drops.

Some local anesthetics are benzocaine, bupivacaine, cocaine, lidocaine, procaine, and tetracaine. Some act rapidly and have a short duration of effect, while others may have a slow action and a short duration. They act by blocking nerve impulses from the immediate area to the higher pain centers. Regional anesthetics allow for pain control along a wider area of the body by blocking the action of a large nerve (nerve block). Sprays can be used on the throat and related

areas for a bronchoscopy, and gels can be used for the urethra to numb the area for a catherization or cystoscopy.

Spinal anesthesia is used for surgery of the abdomen, lower back and legs. Spinal or epidural anesthesia is also used for surgery on the prostate gland and hip. A fine needle is inserted between two vertebrae in the lumbar (lower part) of the spine and the anesthetic flows into the fluid which surrounds the spinal cord. The nerves absorb the anesthetic as they emerge from the spinal fluid. The area anesthetized is controlled by the location of the injection and the amount of absorption of the anesthetic by the spinal fluid.

Complications of local anesthesia

It is possible to have adverse reactions to local anesthetics, such as dizziness, hypotension (low blood pressure), convulsions, and even death. These effects are rare but can occur if the dose is too high or if the drug has been absorbed too rapidly. A small percentage of patients (1–5%) may develop headaches with spinal anesthesia.

Theory of the mechanism of anesthesia

Although scientists are not sure exactly how anesthesia works, there are many theories that have been proposed. In addition, different anesthetics may have different mechanisms of action. One theory proposes a relationship between the solubility of the anesthetic agent into the fat cells of the body (lipid solubility) as determining the degree of its potency as an anesthetic agent. Since nerve cell membranes are highly lipid, the brain, with its high nerve cell content, soaks up the anesthetic. Not all lipid soluble substances, however, are anesthetics. Lipid solubility, therefore, is only a partial explanation of the anesthetic's mechanism.

Another feature of anesthetic absorption is the way it is passed from the lungs to other cells in the body. At first there is a quick transmission from the lungs to the rest of the body, but as an equilibrium is reached, the anesthetic then begins to quickly pass out from the lungs. However, fat cells retain the anesthetic longer than other cells.

Studies have shown that some inhaled anesthetics are metabolized by the liver (hepatic metabolism). Here is where the skill of the anesthetist enters to control the amounts administered in order to avoid the problem of toxicity.

The future of anesthesia

Since World War II, many changes have taken place in anesthesiology. Important discoveries have

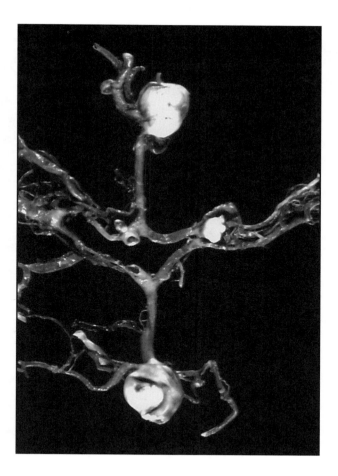

Three aneurisms can be seen in this section of cerebral artery removed from a human brain.

been made with such volatile liquids as halothane and synthetic opiates. The technology of delivery systems has been greatly improved. But with all these changes, the basic goal of anesthesia has been the same—the control of a motionless surgical field in the patient. In the next 50 years it is possible that the goals of anesthesia will be widened. The role of anesthesia will broaden as newer surgical techniques develop in the area of organ transplants. Anesthesia may also be used in the future to treat acute infectious illness, mental disorders, and different types of heart conditions. There may be a wide range of new therapeutic applications for anesthesia.

In the next 50 years, anesthesiologists will probably compete strongly for research funds. Better trained anesthesiologists will need to do research to gain further knowledge on the effects and mechanisms of anesthesia. Since understanding and controlling pain is the central problem of anesthesiology, it will be necessary to gain more knowledge about the mechanism of pain and pain control. New anesthetics, delivery, and monitoring systems will need to be developed to keep up with the pace of medical development as it moves closer to noninvasive surgical techniques.

See also Analgesia; Chloroform; Ether; Novocain; Pain.

Further Reading:

Barash, Paul G., Bruce F. Cullen, and Robert K. Stoelting. *Clinical Anesthesia*. Philadelphia: Lippincott, 1992.
Mckenry, Leda M. and Evelyn Salerno. *Mosby's Pharmacology in Nursing*. Philadelphia: Mosby, 1989.

Jordan P. Richman

Aneurism

An aneurism is a weak spot in the wall of an artery or a vein that dilates or balloons out, forming a blood–filled sack or pouch. Aneurisms can occur almost anywhere in the body and are found in all age groups, although they occur primarily in the elderly. The foremost cause of aneurisms is atherosclerosis, or fatty deposits in the arteries. If an aneurism bursts, a massive amount of blood is released, which results in an almost instantaneous drop in blood pressure and can cause death. Surgery can be a successful treatment for unruptured aneurisms.

Atherosclerotic aneurisms are the most common aneurisms. They are found primarily in the abdominal aorta (a larger elastic artery), typically occur after the age of 50, and are more common in men than women. Syphilitic (luetic) aneurisms occur primarily in the thoracic aorta and are due to syphilis, a sexually transmitted disease. Dissecting aneurisms occur when blood penetrates the arterial or venous wall, causing dissections between the wall's various layers. Aneurisms occurring from injury to the artery are known as false aneurisms.

Aneurisms are also classified by their size and shape. A berry aneurism is spherical, or circular, and usually 0.4 to 0.6 in (1 to 1.5 cm) in diameter. A saccular aneurism is a larger berry aneurism and may reach a size of 6 to 8 in (15 to 20 cm). Fusiform aneurisms are shaped like spindles, and cylindroid (or tubular) aneurisms are cylinder dilations that occur over a considerable length of the artery.

Although recent studies show that genetics can be a factor in the development of aneurisms, environmental factors, such as a bad diet resulting in high blood pressure, are a major cause of aneurisms. Cigarette smoking is considered to be the highest risk factor for developing an aneurism. As a result, treatment of hypertension through proper diet and prescription drugs and by refraining from smoking are approaches to preventing the likelihood of an aneurism forming.

A key to the successful treatment of aneurisms is to discover them before they burst. Diagnostic procedures for aneurisms include the use of ultrasound, computed tomography, and magnetic resonance angiography. Surgical "clipping" or "grafting" is the treatment of choice for most aneurisms. This process involves cutting out the aneurism and then reconnecting the artery or vein with a metallic clip or synthetic tube graft.

Angina see **Heart diseases**

Angiography

Angiography is a medical diagnostic test in which a fluid that is visible on x rays is used to make photographs of the arteries of the heart or other organs.

First used in the early 1950s, angiography now is a standard procedure to locate areas in which an artery is closed or constricted and interfering with the circulation of blood. Angiography applied to the heart is called coronary angiography. A constriction of one of the arteries feeding the heart can be serious enough that a person will experience chest pains when he or she exercises because the heart muscle has an insufficient supply of blood.

The heart is a special muscular organ that must continue beating at all times. When you are awake or asleep, resting or exercising, the heart must supply the body with blood. In times of extra need, as when you run or bicycle rapidly, the heart must work harder to supply oxygen–laden blood to the muscles. To accomplish its work the heart is given the first arteries that branch off the main artery leaving the heart, the aorta. In this way the heart has a source of blood at high pressure and with the most oxygen.

The arteries that supply the heart muscle are called the coronary arteries, and they course around the outside of the heart to carry blood to all parts of the hard–working muscle. As a person ages, however, these coronary arteries may begin to close down from cholesterol deposits, or they may have spasms in the muscle of the arteries, or a blood clot that has been circulating in the blood stream may lodge in one of the arteries. Any of these situations can result in pain or even death because the heart muscle is receiving too little oxygen. Pain in the chest that is caused by an oxygen–starved heart is called angina.

Angina is a serious condition requiring medical attention. It may indicate a blockage that is easily controlled by medications, or it may be that the blockage is life threatening and may require bypass to restore circulation. To treat angina, the physician must know the exact location of the blockage, whether only one artery is blocked or several are affected, and how severe the blockage is—whether it is only partially obscuring the artery or entirely plugging the blood passage.

To locate a blockage and discern its severity the doctor usually must resort to an angiogram. This is called an invasive study because it requires a catheter to be inserted into one of the patient's arteries.

To perform an angiogram the cardiologist inserts a long, thin tube—the catheter—into an artery in the thigh, usually. The patient is fully awake during an angiogram, which is performed under local anesthesia. In this way the patient can turn over or from side to side if the doctor needs a different view. The arteries do not have pain or touch senses, so the patient cannot feel the catheter as it progresses through his arteries.

The catheter is radio–opaque, that is, it can be seen on an x ray so the doctor can follow the progress of the catheter. He feeds the catheter into the artery and from there into the main artery of the body, the aorta. The tip of the catheter is slightly bent so that it can be steered from one artery into another by turning the catheter. The doctor follows the progress of the catheter on a

KEY TERMS

Diagnostic—A means to find the source of a condition or disease to enable to physician to apply the appropriate therapy.

Fluoroscope—An instrument consisting of an x ray machine and a television–like screen. The x rays are passed through the patient and focused on the screen so the physician can observe the structure that is being studied or the progress of a contrast medium.

Heart attack—Distress of the heart muscle in a locale fed by an artery that has become blocked. Without blood for only a short while, the heart muscle can cause chest pain called angina pectoris.

Spasm—A sudden flexing of the arterial wall that constricts the artery and slows blood flow. In a coronary artery, a spasm can cause a heart attack.

fluoroscope. The fluoroscope is a screen on which x rays are projected after they pass through the patient. The radio–opaque catheter shows up on the screen as a long, moving shadow.

The physician guides the tip of the catheter from the aorta into the main coronary artery and injects a contrast medium. This is a liquid that also is visible on x rays. As the contrast medium floods through the coronary arteries a videotape is made of the progress of the fluid into and through the arterial tree. The contrast medium is visible only for a few seconds on the fluoroscope and then is pumped out of the arteries, but the videotape can be reviewed at a slower pace. Any constriction or stoppage in the artery will be evident by looking at the pattern of the medium. It will show the artery coursing over the heart until the contrast medium reaches a constriction, where it is pinched into a small stream, or a stoppage, which the medium is not able to pass at all. The physician can move the tip of the catheter to position it at another artery as needed.

Once the troublesome area or areas have been located the doctor can decide what form of treatment is most appropriate.

A coronary angiogram is a form of test generally called an arteriogram, which means literally a picture of an artery. Arteries are long tubes with muscular walls that carry blood away from the heart. The arterial muscle enables the size of the artery to be enlarged or reduced in accordance with the demand for blood. Immediately after a meal, for example, the arteries to the digestive organs are enlarged to carry away the digested nutrients. The arteries in the arms and legs will be constricted to carry less blood. On the other hand, when a person runs or plays actively the arteries to the arms and legs and other muscles used in the activity are dilated to carry a full load of oxygen–rich blood to the muscles; the arteries to the digestive system are constricted.

Arteriograms are used to see the arteries in organs other than the heart. This diagnostic study can be carried out with the arteries in the brain, to find the location of a ruptured artery that has caused a stroke, for example; or in the kidneys and in the legs. In all cases the test consists of injecting a radio–opaque contrast medium into a suitable blood vessel and then capturing the image of the arteries made visible by the medium.

See also Circulatory system; X rays.

Further Reading:

Mayo Clinic Family Health Book. New York: William Morrow & Company, Inc. 1990.

Larry Blaser

Angiosperm

Angiosperm is the name given to those plants which produce flowers during sexual reproduction. The term literally means "vessel seed" and refers to the fact that seeds are contained in a highly specialized organ called an ovary.

Flowering plants are the most recently evolved of the major groups of plants, arising only about 130 million years ago. Despite their geological youthfulness, angiosperms are the dominant plants of the world today: about 80% of all living plant species are flowering plants. Furthermore, they occupy a greater variety of habitats than any other group of plants. Why have angiosperms become so successful? The ancestors of flowering plants are the gymnosperms (e.g., pine and fir), which are the other major group of plants that produce seeds. The gymnosperms, however, produce their seeds on the surface of leaf–like structures, which makes the seeds vulnerable to mechanical damage when winds whip the branches back and forth, and to drying out. Most importantly, conifer seeds are vulnerable to insects and other animals, which view seeds as nutritious, energy packed treats. In angiosperms, the margins of the seed–bearing leaves have become inrolled and fused, so the seeds are no longer exposed but are more safely tucked inside the newly evolved "vessel," which is the ovary.

The other major advance of the angiosperms over the gymnosperms was the evolution of the flower, which is the structure responsible for sexual reproduction in these plants. The function of sexual reproduction is to bring together genetic material from two individuals of differing ancestry, so that the offspring will have a new genetic makeup. The gymnosperms dealt with their immobility by packaging their male component into tiny pollen grains, which can be released into the wind to be blown to the female component of another individual of the same species. Although this method of pollination succeeds, it is wasteful and inefficient because most of the pollen grains land somewhere other than on a female, such as in your nose, where they cause hay fever. Furthermore, pollen grains are rich in fixed energy and nutrients such as nitrogen, so they are costly to make (aboriginal North Americans used to make pancakes out of the pollen of cattail). By evolving bright colors, scents, and nectar, the flowers of angiosperms served to attract animals. By travelling from one flower to another, these animals would accidentally move pollen as well, enabling sexual reproduction to take place. Because flower–seeking animals such as bees, butterflies, and hummingbirds can learn to recognize different types of flowers, they can move pollen from flower to flower quite efficiently. Therefore, animal–pollinated species of flowering plants do not need to produce as much pollen as gymnosperms, and the resources they save can be put into other important functions, such as growth and greater seed production. Therefore, the flower and its ovary have provided angiosperms with tremendous advantages, and have enabled them to become rapidly dominant over their gymnosperm ancestors.

See also Flower; Pollination; Sexual reproduction.

Les C. Cwynar

Angle

An angle is a geometric figure created by two line segments that extend from a single point or two planes which extend from a single line. The size of an angle, measured in units of degrees or radians, is related to the amount of rotation required to superimpose one of its sides on the other. First used by ancient civilizations, angles continue to be an important tool to science and industry today.

The study of angles has been known since the time of the ancient Babylonians (4,000–300 B.C.). These people used angles for measurement in many areas such as construction, commerce, and astronomy. The ancient Greeks developed the idea of an angle further and were even able to use them to calculate the circumference of the Earth and the distance to the moon.

A geometric angle is formed by two lines (rays) that intersect at a common endpoint called the vertex. The two rays are known as the sides of the angle. An angle can be specified in various ways. If the vertex of an angle is at point P, then the angle could be denoted by $\angle$P. It can be further described by using a point from each ray. For example, the angle $\angle$OPQ would have the point O on one ray, a vertex at point P, and the point Q on the remaining ray. An angle can also be denoted by a single number or character which is placed on it. The most common character used is the Greek letter θ (theta).

Units of measurement of an angle

An angle is commonly given an arithmetic value which describes its size. To specify its this value, an angle is drawn in a standard position on a coordinate system, with its vertex at the center and one side, called the initial side, along the x axis. The value of the angle then represents the amount of rotation needed to get from the initial side to the other side, called the terminal side. The direction of rotation indicates the sign of the angle. Traditionally, a counterclockwise rotation gives a positive value and a clockwise rotation gives a negative value. The three terms which are typically used to express the value of an angle include revolutions, degrees, or radians.

The revolution is the most natural unit of measurement for an angle. It is defined as the amount of rotation required to go from the initial side of the angle all the way around back to the initial side. One way to visualize a revolution is to imagine spinning a wheel around one time. The distance traveled by any point on the wheel is equal to one revolution. An angle can then be given a value based on the fraction of the distance a point travels divided by the distance traveled in one rotation. For example, an angle represented by a quarter turn of the wheel is equal to .25 rotations.

A more common unit of measurement for an angle is the degree. This unit was used by the Babylonians as early as 1,000 B.C. At that time, they used a number system based on the number 60, so it was natural for mathematicians of the day to divide the angles of an equilateral triangle into 60 individual units. These units became known as degrees. Since six equilateral triangles can be evenly arranged in a circle, the number of degrees in one revolution became $6 \times 60 = 360$. The unit of degrees was subdivided into 60 smaller units called minutes and in turn, these minutes were subdivided into 60 smaller units called seconds. Consequently, the notation for an angle which has a value of 44 degrees, 15 minutes, and 25 seconds would be 44° 15' 25''.

An angle may be measured with a protractor, which is a flat instrument in the shape of a semi–circle. There are marks on its outer edges which subdivide it into 180 evenly spaced units, or degrees. Measurements are taken by placing the midpoint of the flat edge over the vertex of the angle and lining the 0° mark up with the initial side. The number of degrees can be read off at the point where the terminal side intersects the curve of the protractor.

Another unit of angle measurement, used extensively in trigonometry, is the radian. This unit relates a unique angle to each real number. Consider a circle with its center at the origin of a graph and its radius along the x–axis. One radian is defined as the angle created by a counterclockwise rotation of the radius around the circle such that the length of the arc traveled is equal to the length of the radius. Using the formula for the circumference of a circle, it can be shown that the total number of radians in a complete revolution of 360° is 2π. Given this relationship, it is possible to convert between a degree and a radian measurement.

Geometric characteristics of angles

An angle is typically classified into four categories including acute, right, obtuse, and straight. An acute angle is one which has a degree measurement greater than 0° but less than 90°. A right angle has a 90° angle measurement. An obtuse angle has a measurement greater than 90° but less than 180°, and a straight angle, which looks like a straight line, has a 180° angle measurement.

Two angles are known as congruent angles if they have the same measurement. If their sum is 90°, then they are said to be complementary angles. If their sum is 180°, they are supplementary angles. Angles can be bisected (divided in half) or trisected (divided in thirds) by rays protruding from the vertex.

When two lines intersect, they form four angles. The angles directly across from each other are known as vertical angles and are congruent. The neighboring

---

KEY TERMS

Congruent angles—Angles which have the same measurement.

Degree—A unit of measurement used to describe the amount of revolution of an angle denoted by the symbol °. There are 360° in a complete revolution.

Initial side—The ray of an angle which falls on the x–axis when an angle is in its standard position.

Radian—A unit of angle measurement used to relate the amount of revolution of an angle in terms of a the radius of a circle. There are 2π radians in a complete revolution.

Terminal side—The ray of an angle in its standard position which extends away from the x–axis.

Vertex—The point at which the two sides of an angle meet.

Vertical angles—Angles created by the intersection of two lines which are directly across from each other and share a common vertex.

---

angles are called adjacent because they share a common side. If the lines intersect such that each angle measures 90°, the lines are then considered perpendicular or orthogonal.

In addition to size, angles also have trigonometric values associated with them such as sine, cosine, and tangent. These values relate the size of an angle to a given length of its sides. These values are particularly important in areas such as navigation, astronomy, and architecture.

See also Congruence; Geometry; Trigonometry.

Perry Romanowski

Anglerfish

Anglerfish are marine fish that attract prey by dangling a fleshy, bait–like appendage (the esca) in front of their heads. The appendage, which resembles a fishing pole, is attached to the end of the dorsal fin's foremost spine (the illicium), which is separated from the rest of the fin.

Anglerfish belong to the order Lophiiformes, which includes three suborders, 15 families, and about 215 species. The order Lophiiformes is in the class Osteichthyes, the bony fishes, which, in turn, is in the subphylum Vertebrata, phylum Chordata.

Anglerfish are distributed throughout the world and include both free–swimming (pelagic) species and seabed–dwelling (benthic) species. Most species of anglerfish live on the ocean floor and have bizarre body forms. They have small gill openings located at or behind the base of the pectoral fins, which are limblike in structure; some species also have limblike pelvic fins. The swim bladder of anglerfish is physoclistic, that is, it has no connection to the digestive tract.

The common names of many anglerfish are particularly colorful: for example, the flattened goosefish, the warty angler, and the spherical frogfish. The flattened goosefish inhabits the muddy bottom of the continental slopes of the Atlantic, Indian, and western Pacific Oceans and remains motionless as it angles for prey with its esca. The balloon–shaped warty angler is found in South Australia and New South Wales, and the spherical frogfish, which propels itself in hopping motions with pectoral fins modified into special "jumping" limbs, is found in tropical and subtropical seas.

The diet of anglerfish consists mostly of other fish, although some species consume marine invertebrates. For example, batfish, anglerfish with free flaps of skin, also eat marine snails, clams, crustacea, and worms; deep–sea anglers of the family Melanocetidae consume copepods and arrow worms in addition to fish.

Deep–sea anglerfish, which belong to the suborder Ceratioidei, live at depths between 4,920 and 8,200 ft (1,500 and 2,500 m). The deep–sea anglerfish lack pelvic fins, are free–swimming (pelagic) and do not remain still on the bottom, as do other anglerfish. Deep–sea anglerfish are distributed widely from subarctic to subantarctic waters, but are absent from the Mediterranean Sea.

Anglerfish range in length from about 4 in to 2 ft (10 to 60) cm. The males of four families of the suborder Ceratioidei show a dramatic sexual dimorphism, in that males are much smaller than the females. The male *Ceratias holboelli*, for example, grows to a maximum length of only 2.5 in (6 cm) while the females can reach up to 4 ft (1.2 m) in length.

Soon after birth, parasitic male deep–sea anglers use their pincerlike mouths to affix themselves to a female. The tissue of their mouths fuses completely with the tissues of the female, so that their blood supplies mingle. The female is the hunter, attracting prey with a luminous esca, while the male receives nourishment via the shared blood supply. The male, assured of a life without the need to hunt for food, ceases growth, except for development of reproductive organs. In turn, the female is assured a lifetime supply of sperm from the male to fertilize her eggs.

Some anglerfish are used by humans as food; for example, the European goosefish, *Lophius piscatorius*, also called monkfish, is highly prized; and frogfish are sometimes sold for home aquariums and are occasionally eaten.

Animal

Animals are creatures in the kingdom Animalia, one of the five major divisions of organisms (the others are: Monera or bacteria, Fungi, Protists or protozoans, and Plantae or plants). Animals are multicellular, eukaryotic organisms, with cells that do not have walls made of cellulose. Animals are capable of voluntary, spontaneous movements, often in response to sensory perceptions. For their nutrition, animals require sources of biologically fixed energy, that is, the biomass of either plants or other animals. Zoology is the scientific study of animals.

The time of the origin of animals during Earth's evolutionary history is not known, because the first animals were soft–bodied, multicellular life forms that did not preserve well as fossils. By the time that multicellular animals became represented in the geological record about 640–670 million years ago, there were already numerous phyla of animals, so the actual origin of the kingdom must have occurred earlier.

Most zoologists recognize the existence of 30–35 phyla of animals, some of which are extinct and only known from their fossil record. The simplest animals with the most ancient lineages are asymmetric or radially symmetric, for example, Porifera (sponges) and Cnidaria (jellyfish and sea anemones). The simplest of the bilaterally symmetric animals include Platyhelminthes (flatworms) and Nematoda (Nematodes). Coelomates are a functional group of animals with an enclosed body cavity, the best known of which are Mollusca (snails, clams, octopus, and squid), Annelida (segmented worms and leeches), Arthropoda (insects, spiders, and crustacea), Echinodermata (sea urchins and starfish), and Chordata (fish, amphibians, reptiles, birds, and mammals).

About one million species of animals have been named. However, biologists estimate that a much larger number of animals species has yet to be discovered, and that the actual total could be as large as 30–50 million species. The undiscovered species mostly occur in Earth's richest ecosystems, especially old–growth tropical rain forests, and perhaps the deep oceans. Most of the undiscovered species of terrestrial animals are believed to be insects, especially beetles.

See also Arrow worms; Arthropods; Brachiopods; Chordates; Flatworms; Horsehair worms; Mesozoa; Mollusks; Moss animals; Phoronids; Ribbon worms; Spiny–headed worms; Sponges.

Bill Freedman

Dairy cattle on a farm in southern Wisconsin.

Animal breeding

Animal breeding is the selective mating of animals to increase the possibility of obtaining desired traits in the offspring. It has been performed with most domesticated animals, especially cats and dogs, but its main use has been to breed better agricultural stock. The more modern techniques involve a wide variety of laboratory methods, including the modification of embryos, sex selection, and genetic engineering. These procedures are beginning to supplant traditional breeding methods, which focus on selectively combining and isolating livestock strains. In general, the most effective strategy for isolating traits is by selective inbreeding; but different strains are sometimes crossed to take advantage of hybrid vigor and to forestall the negative results of inbreeding, which include reduced fertility, low immunity, and the development of genetic abnormalities.

The genetic basis of animal breeding

The major purpose of both traditional and modern animal breeding is to exercise control over the traits that are produced in the offspring. Once the optimal environment for raising an animal to maturity has been established (i.e., the proper nutrition and care has been determined) the only way to manipulate an animal's potential is to manipulate its genetic information. In general, the genetic information of animals is both diverse and uniform: diverse, in the sense that a population will contain many different forms of the same gene (for instance, the human population has 300 different forms of the protein hemoglobin); and uniform,

in the sense that there is a basic physical expression of the genetic information which makes, for instance, most goats look similar to each other.

In order to properly understand the basis of animal breeding, it is important to distinguish between genotype and phenotype. Genotype refers to the information contained in an animal's DNA, or genetic material. An animal's phenotype is the physical expression of its genotype. Although every creature is born with a fixed genotype, the phenotype is a variable which is influenced by many factors in the animal's environment and development. For example, two cows with identical genotypes could develop quite different phenotypes if raised in different environments and fed different foods.

The close association of environment with the expression of the genetic information makes animal breeding a challenging endeavor, because the physical traits which a breeder desires to selectively breed for cannot always be attributed entirely to the animal's genes. Moreover, most traits are due not just to one or two genes, but to the complex interplay of many different genes.

The DNA consists of a set of chromosomes; the number of chromosomes varies between species (humans, for example, have 46 chromosomes). Mammals (and indeed most creatures) have two copies of each chromosome in the DNA (this is called diploidy). This means that there are two copies of the same gene in an animal's DNA. Sometimes each of these will be partially expressed. For example, in a person having one copy of a gene which codes for normal hemoglobin and one coding for sickle–cell hemoglobin, about half of the hemoglobin will be normal and the other half will be sickle–cell. In other cases, only one of the genes can be expressed in the animal's phenotype. The gene which is expressed is called dominant, and the gene which is not expressed is called recessive. For instance, a human being could have two copies of the gene coding for eye color, and one of them could code for blue, one for brown. The gene coding for brown eyes would be dominant, and the individual's eyes would be brown. But the blue–eyes gene would still exist, and could be passed on to the person's children.

Most of the traits an animal breeder might wish to select will be recessive, for the obvious reason that if the gene were always expressed in the animals, there would be no need to breed for it. If a gene is completely recessive, the animal will need to have two copies of the same gene for it to be expressed (another way to express this is to say that the animal is homozygous for that particular gene). For this reason, animal breeding is usually most successful when animals are selectively inbred. If a bull has two copies of a gene for a desirable recessive trait, it will pass one copy of this gene to each of its offspring. The other copy of the gene will come from the cow, and assuming it will be normal, none of the offspring will show the desirable trait in their phenotype. However, each of the offspring will have a copy of the recessive gene. If they are then bred with each other, some of their offspring will have two copies of the recessive gene. If two animals with two copies of the recessive gene are bred with each other, all of their offspring will have the desired trait.

There are disadvantages to this method, although it is extremely effective. One of these is that for animal breeding to be performed productively, a number of animals must be involved in the process. Another problem is that undesirable traits can also mistakenly be selected for. For this reason, too much inbreeding will produce sickly or unproductive stock, and at times it is useful to breed two entirely different strains with each other. The resulting offspring are usually extremely healthy; this is referred to as "hybrid vigor." Usually hybrid vigor is only expressed for a generation or two, but crossbreeding is still a very effective means to combat some of the disadvantages of inbreeding.

Another practical disadvantage to selective inbreeding is that the DNA of the parents is altered during the production of eggs and sperm. In order to make eggs and sperm, which are called gametes, a special kind of cell division occurs called meiosis, in which cells divide so that each one has half the normal number of chromosomes (in humans, each sperm and egg contains 23 chromosomes). Before this division occurs, the two pairs of chromosomes wrap around each other, and a phenomenon known as crossing over takes place, in which sections of one chromosome will be exchanged with sections of the other chromosome, so that new combinations are generated. The problem with crossing over is that some unexpected results can occur. For instance, the offspring of a bull homozygous for two recessive but desirable traits and a cow with "normal" genes will all have one copy of each recessive gene. But when these offspring produce gametes, one recessive gene may migrate to a different chromosome, so that the two traits no longer appear in one gamete. Since most genes work in complicity with others to produce a certain trait, this can make the process of animal breeding very slow, and it requires many generations before the desired traits are obtained—if ever.

Economic considerations

There are many reasons why animal breeding is of paramount importance to those who use animals for their livelihood. Cats have been bred largely for aesthetic beauty; many people are willing to pay a great deal of money for a Siamese or Persian cat, even though the affection felt for a pet has little to do with physical appearance. But the most extensive animal breeding has occurred in those areas where animals have been used to serve specific practical purposes. For instance, most dog breeds are the result of a deliberate attempt to isolate traits which would produce better hunting and herding dogs (although some, like toy poodles, were bred for traits that would make them desirable pets). Horses have also been extensively bred for certain useful qualities; some for size and strength, some for speed. But farm animals, particularly food animals, have been the subject of the most intensive breeding efforts.

The physical qualities of economic importance in farm animals vary for each species, but a generalized goal is to eliminate the effects of environment and nutrition. An ideal strain of milk cow, for instance, would produce a large amount of high–quality milk despite the type of food it is fed and the environment in which it is reared. Thus animals are generally all bred for feed efficiency, growth rate, and resistance to disease. However, a pig might be bred for lean content in its meat, while a hen would be bred for its laying potential. Many cows have been bred to be hornless, so that they cannot inadvertently or deliberately gore each other.

Although maximum food production is always a major goal, modern animal breeders are also concerned about nutritional value and the ability of animals to survive in extreme environments. Many parts of the world are sparsely vegetated or have harsh climatic conditions, and a high efficiency producer which could endure these environments would be extremely useful to the people who live there. In addition, many people of industrialized countries are concerned not about food availability but about the quality of this food; so breeders seek to eliminate the qualities which make meat or milk or eggs or other animal products unhealthy, while enhancing those qualities which make them nutritious.

Modern methods in biotechnology

Although earlier animal breeders had to confine themselves to choosing which of their animals should mate, modern technological advances have altered the face of animal breeding, making it both more selective and more effective. Techniques like genetic engineering, embryo manipulation, artificial insemination, and cloning are becoming more and more refined. Some, like artificial insemination and the manipulation of embryos to produce twins, are now used habitually. Others, like genetic engineering and cloning, are the subject of intense research and will probably have a great impact on future animal breeding programs.

Artificial insemination

Artificial insemination is the artificial introduction of semen from a male with desirable traits into females of the species to produce pregnancy, and is useful because a far larger number of offspring can be produced than would be possible if the animals were traditionally bred. Because of this, the value of the male as breeding stock can be determined much more rapidly, and the use of many different females will permit a more accurate evaluation of the hereditability of the desirable traits. In addition, if the traits which are produced in the offspring do prove to be advantageous, it is easier to disperse them within an animal population in this fashion, as there is a larger breeding stock available. One reason why artificial insemination has been an extremely important tool is that it allowed new strains of superior stock to be introduced into a supply of animals in an economically feasible fashion.

The process of artificial insemination requires several steps. The semen must be obtained and effectively diluted, so that the largest number of females can be inseminated consistent with a high probability of pregnancy. The semen must be properly stored so that it remains viable. The females must be tested before the sample is introduced to ensure that they are fertile, and following the procedure, they must be tested for pregnancy to determine its success. All these factors make artificial insemination more expensive and more difficult than traditional breeding methods, but the processes have been improved and refined so that the economic advantages far outweigh the procedural dis-

advantages, and artificial insemination is the most widely applied breeding technique.

Embryo manipulation

In order to understand the techniques of embryo manipulation, it is important to understand the early stages of reproduction. When the egg and sperm unite to form a zygote, each of the parents supply the zygote with half of the chromosomes necessary for a full set. The zygote, which is a single cell, then begins to reproduce itself by the cellular division process called mitosis, in which each chromosome is duplicated before separation so that each new cell has a full set of chromosomes. This is called the Morula Stage, and the new cells are called blastomeres. When enough cells have been produced (the number varies from species to species), cell differentiation begins to take place. The first differentiation appears to be when the blastocyst is formed, which is an almost hollow sphere with a cluster of cells inside; and the differentiation appears to be between the cells inside, which become the fetus, and the cells outside, which become the fetal membranes and placenta. However, the process is not entirely understood at the present time and there is some variation between species; so it is difficult to pinpoint the onset of differentiation, which some scientists believe occurs during blastomere division.

During the first stages of cell division, it is possible to separate the blastomeres with the result that each one develops into a separate embryo. Blastomeres with this capability are called totipotent. The purpose of this ability of a single blastomere to produce an entire embryo is probably to safeguard the process of embryo development against the destruction of any of the blastomeres. In theory, it should be possible to produce an entire embryo from each blastomere (and blastomeres are generally totipotent from the four to eight cell stage), but in practice it is usually only possible to produce two embryos. That is why this procedure is generally referred to as embryo splitting rather than cloning, although both terms refer to the same thing (cloning is the production of genetically identical embryos, which is a direct result of embryo splitting).

Interestingly enough, although the embryos which are produced from separated blastomeres usually have fewer cells than a normal embryo, the resulting offspring fall within the normal range of size for the species.

It is also possible to divide an embryo at other parts of development. For instance, the time at which embryo division is most successful is after the blastocyst has formed. Great care must be taken when dividing a blastocyst, since differentiation has already occurred to some extent, and it is necessary to halve the blastocyst very precisely.

Another interesting embryonic manipulation is the creation of chimaeras. These are formed by uniting two different gametes, so that the embryo has two distinct cell lineages. Chimaeras do not combine the genetic information of both lineages in each cell. Instead, they are a patchwork of cells which contain one lineage or the other. For this reason, the offspring of chimaeras are from one distinct genotype or the other, but not from both. Thus chimaeras are not useful for creating new animal populations beyond the first generation. However, they are extremely useful in other contexts. For instance, while embryo division as described above is limited in the number of viable embryos which can be produced, chimaeras can be used to increase the number. After the blastomeres are separated, they can be combined with blastomeres of a different genetic lineage. It has been found that with the additional tissue, the survival rate of the new embryos is more favorable. For some reason only a small percentage of the resulting embryos are chimaeric; this is thought to be because only one cell lineage develops into the cells inside the blastocyst, while the other lineage forms extraembryonic tissue. It is believed that the more advanced cells are more likely to form the inner cells.

Another application of chimaeras could be for breeding endangered species. Because of the different biochemical environments in the uterus, and the different regulatory mechanisms for fetal development, only very closely related species are able to bear each other's embryos to term. For example, when a goat is implanted with a sheep embryo or the other way around, the embryo is unable to develop properly. This problem can perhaps be surmounted by creating chimaeras in which the placenta stems from the cell lineage of the host species. The immune system of an animal attacks tissue which it recognizes as "non–self," but it is possible that the mature chimaeras would be compatible with both the host species and the target species, so that it could bear either embryo to term. This has already proved to be true in studies with mice.

A further technique which is being developed to manipulate embryos involves the creation of uniparental embryos and same–sex matings. In the former case, the cell from a single gamete is made to go through mitosis, so that the resulting cell is completely homozygous. In the latter case, the DNA from two females (parthogenesis) or two males (androgenesis) is combined to form cells that have only female– or male–derived DNA. These zygotes cannot be developed into live animals, as genetic information from male and female derived DNA is necessary for embryonic development. However, these cells can be used to generate chimaeras. In the case of parthogenetic cells, these chimaeras produce viable gametes. The androgenetic cells do not become incorporated in the embryo; they are used to form extra–embryonic tissue, and so no gametes are recovered.

Aside from these more ambitious embryo manipulation endeavors, multiple ovulation and embryo transfer (MOET) could soon become a useful tool. MOET is the production of multiple embryos from a female with desirable traits, which are then implanted in the wombs of other females of the same species. This circumvents the disadvantages of breeding from a female line (which are that a female can only produce a limited number of offspring due to the time investment and physical rigors of pregnancy). At the present time, MOET is still too expensive for commercial application, but is being applied experimentally.

Genetic engineering

Genetic engineering is being implemented to create animals which have had a new gene inserted directly into their DNA. These animals are called transgenic. The procedure involves microinjection of the desired gene into the nucleus of fertilized eggs. It has been found that in many cases, but with varying rates of success, the new gene is reproduced in all developing cells, and that the gene can be transcribed (which means that the information contained in the gene can be read and utilized by the cell). This is a startling breakthrough in animal breeding endeavors, because it means that a specific trait can be incorporated into a population in a single generation, rather than the several generations this takes when conventional breeding techniques are used.

However, there are some serious limitations to the procedure. The first of these has to do with the manner in which many genes work together to produce most traits. In fact, there are very few traits a breeder would like to include in an animal population which involve only one or two genes. Although it might some day be possible to incorporate any number of genes into an embryo's DNA, the complex interplay of genes is not understood very well, and the process of identifying all of the genes related to a desired trait is costly and time–consuming.

Another problem in the production of transgenic animals is that they pass their modified DNA on to their offspring with varying success rates and unpredictable results. In some cases, the new gene is present in the offspring but it is not utilized. The new gene may

KEY TERMS

Androgenesis—Reproduction from two male parents.

Artificial insemination—The artificial introduction of semen from a male with desirable traits into females of the species to produce pregnancy.

Blastocyst—An embryo at that stage of development in which the cells have differentiated to form embryonic and extraembryonic tissue. The blastocyst resembles a sphere with the extraembryonic tissue making up the surface of the sphere and the future embryonic tissue appearing as a cluster of cells inside the sphere.

Blastomere—The embryonic cell during the first cellular divisions, before differentiation has occurred.

Chimaera—An animal (or embryo) which is formed from two distinct cellular lineages which do not mingle in the cells of the animal, so that some cells contain genetic information from one lineage and some from the other.

Cloning—The production of multiple genetically identical embryos or zygotes.

Crossing over—A phenomenon which occurs during meiosis, in which genetic information from one chromosome can migrate to another chromosome.

Diploid—Having two sets of chromosomes.

Extraembryonic tissue—That part of the developmental tissue which does not form the embryo.

Fetus—The unborn or unhatched animal during the latter stages of development.

Genome—Half a diploid set of chromosomes; the genetic information from one parent.

Hybrid vigor—The quality of increased health and fertility (superior to either parent) usually produced when two different genetic strains are crossed.

Parthogenesis—Reproduction from two female parents.

Placenta—The organ to which a fetus is attached by the umbilical cord in the womb, which provides nutrients for the fetus.

Totipotent—Embryonic cells which are able to produce an entire fetus.

Transgenic—Cells or species which have undergone genetic engineering.

Uniparental—Having only one genetic parent.

also be altered or rearranged in some way, probably during the process of gamete production.

These factors have made it difficult to successfully produce a transgenic strain of animals. However, with further research into the mechanism by which the gene is incorporated into the genome, and by successfully mapping the target animal genome and identifying the genes responsible for various traits, genetic engineering will no doubt become a major tool for improving animal strains.

Sex selection

It would be extremely useful if a breeder were able to predetermine the sex of each embryo produced, because in many cases one sex is preferred. For instance, in a herd of dairy cows or a flock of laying hens, females are the only commercially useful sex. When the owner of a dairy herd has inseminated a cow at some expense, this issue becomes more crucial. In some cases, an animal is being bred specifically for use as breeding stock; in this case, it is far more useful to produce a male which can be bred with multiple females than a female which can only produce a limited number of offspring.

Whether or not an animal is male or female is determined by its sex chromosomes, which are called X and Y chromosomes. An animal with two X chromosomes will develop into a female, while an animal with one X and one Y chromosome will become a male. In mammals, the sex of the offspring is almost always determined by the male parent, because the female can only donate an X chromosome, and it is the presence or absence of the Y chromosome which causes maleness (this is not true in, for instance, birds; in that case it is the female which has two different sex chromosomes). The problem in sex selection is to separate the Y–carrying sperm from the X–carrying sperm. Thus far attempts to do so have been largely unsuccessful or too expensive for commercial application, but the economic advantages make this an area of intense research, and it is quite probable that an efficient and cost–effective method will soon be developed.

See also Biotechnology; Captive breeding and reintroduction; Embryonic transfer; Genetic engineering; Genetics; Livestock.

Further Reading:

Babiuk, Lorne A., and John J. Phillips, ed. *Animal Biotechnology*. New York: Pergamon Press, 1989.

Dawkins, Richard. *The Selfish Gene*. New York: Oxford University Press, 1989.

Hill, William G. and Trudy F.C. Mackay, ed. *Evolution and Animal Breeding*. Wallingford, UK: C.A.B. International, 1989.

Sarah A. de Forest

Anion

An anion is a negatively charged atom or group of atoms. Anions are attracted to the anode, or positive electrode, in an electrolytic cell. Some common anions are the hydroxide ion (OH^-), the chloride ion (Cl^-), the nitrate ion (NO_3^-), and the bicarbonate ion (HCO_3^-). The single minus signs indicate that these ions carry one electron's worth of negative charge. The carbonate ion (CO_3^{2-}), for example, carries two units of negative charge.

The names of anions consisting of single atoms (monatomic ions) end in the suffix –ide. Fluoride (F^-), sulfide (S^{2-}), and oxide (O^{2-}), are examples of such ions. A few polyatomic ions (ions with more than one atom) also have an –ide ending. The cyanide ion (CN^-) is an example.

The names of most polyatomic anions end in either –ate or –ite. For example, the most common polyatomic anions of sulfur are the sulfate (SO_4^{2-}) and sulfite (SO_3^-) ions. In pairs such as this one, the –ate suffix is used for the ion which contains sulfur in the higher oxidation number, and the –ite suffix for the ion with the lower oxidation number. The oxidation number of sulfur is six in the sulfate ion and four in the sulfite ion.

See also Atom.

Anise see **Carrot family**

Anode

The word anode is used in two different sets of circumstances: with respect to vacuum tubes and with respect to electrochemical cells.

Vacuum tubes

A vacuum tube is a tube (usually made of glass) with most of the air pumped out, and usually containing two electrodes—two pieces of metal with a potential difference (a voltage difference) applied between them. Electrons, being negatively charged, are repelled out of the negative electrode and fly through the vacuum toward the positive electrode, to which they are simultaneously being attracted. The positive electrode is called the anode; the negative electrode is called the cathode.

Common examples of vacuum tubes in which electrons flow from a cathode to an anode are cathode ray tubes, such as television tubes and computer monitors, and x ray tubes. In an x ray tube, the kind of metal that the anode is made of determines the kind of x rays (i.e., the x ray energy) that the tube emits.

Electrochemical cells

There are two kinds of electrochemical cells: those in which chemical reactions produce electricity—called galvanic cells or voltaic cells—and those in which electricity produces chemical reactions—called electrolytic cells. An example of a galvanic cell is a flashlight battery, and an example of an electrolytic cell is a cell used for electroplating silver or gold. In either case, there are two electrodes called the anode and the cathode.

Unfortunately, there has been much confusion about which electrode is to be called the anode in each type of cell. Chemists and physicists correctly consider electricity to be a flow of negative electrons, but for historical reasons, engineers have considered electricity to be a flow of positive charge in the opposite direction. Furthermore, even chemists have been confused because negative charge flows away from one of the electrodes inside the cell, but in the external circuit negative charge flows toward that same electrode. This has led to a variety of conflicting definitions of anodes in various textbooks and reference works.

The confusion can be cleared up by defining the anode and cathode in terms of the actual chemical reactions—the oxidation and reduction reactions—that are taking place inside the cell, whether the cell is generating electricity as a galvanic cell or consuming it as an electrolytic cell. The anode is now defined as the electrode at which an oxidation reaction is taking place in the cell. The cathode, then, is the electrode at which the corresponding reduction reaction is taking place.

Anodes in practical use

A sacrificial anode is a piece of metal that is made to act as an anode and therefore be oxidized, in order to protect another piece of metal from being oxidized. For example, to keep iron or steel from oxidizing (rusting) when in contact with air and moisture, such as when it is being used as a fence post, the post can be connected to a piece of zinc that is buried in the ground next to it. The iron and zinc in the moist soil constitute the two electrodes of a galvanic cell. But because zinc oxidizes more easily than iron does, the zinc acts as the anode and is preferentially oxidized. It is said to be "sacrificed" because it gradually gets eaten away by oxidation instead of the iron. For this reason, a cable made of zinc was buried alongside the Alaskan pipeline, the huge steel pipe that transports petroleum from the Alaskan oil fields to the lower states.

Galvanized iron is iron that has been coated with zinc so that it can be used outdoors or in the ground without rusting. The zinc oxidizes in preference to the iron. Galvanized iron is widely used in making garbage cans, pails, and chain–link fencing.

Anodizing is a process in which a piece of metal is made the anode in an electrolytic cell in order to oxidize it deliberately. When aluminum is anodized in this way, a coating of aluminum oxide is built up on its surface. This coating, unlike the metal itself, can take dyes. Many kinds of aluminum utensils and novelties in bright blue, green, red, and gold colors are made of anodized aluminum.

See also Cell, electrochemical; Oxidation–reduction reaction; Vacuum tube; X rays.

Robert L. Wolke

Anoles

Anoles are small lizards in the genus *Anolis* (family Iguanidae), found only in the Americas, mostly in the tropical countries. Because anoles can change the color of their skin according to their mood, temperature, humidity, and light intensity, these animals are sometimes called chameleons. However, none of the more than 300 species of anoles is closely related to the true chameleons (family Chamaeleonidae) of Eurasia and Africa.

Aggressive encounters and defense responses to predators prompt the extension of the throat fan, or

A brown anole (*Anolis sagrei*) on Estero Island, Florida. Anoles are the largest group of reptiles in the Western Hemisphere.

dewlap, of male anoles. This stereotyped visual display is often accompanied by a vigorous demonstration of head–bobbing, the frequency and amplitude of which are important among anoles in species recognition.

Because anoles spend a great deal of time engaged in displays and other activities associated with holding their breeding territory, the males are at a relatively greater risk of predation than the more inconspicuous females. However, the greater risks of predation are balanced by the better reproductive success that a male anole may achieve during the period of his life that he is able to hold a high–quality territory.

The green anole (*Anolis carolinensis*) is the only species native to North America, occurring in the southeastern United States, and also in Cuba and nearby islands. The green anole does not hibernate, and is active on warm, sunny days throughout the winter, remaining inactive in a sheltered place on colder days. The usual color of these animals is brown, but male animals quickly become green when they are engaged in aggressive encounters with other males, or when they are courting a female.

Four additional species of anoles have been introduced to Florida from their natural ranges in the West Indies or Central America. These are the brown anole (*Anolis sagrei*), the large–headed anole (*A. cybotes*), the bark anole (*A. distichus*), and the knight anole (*A. equestris*). Although these species are not part of the native fauna of Florida, they are now entrenched components of that state's ecosystems as are many other introduced species of plants and animals.

See also Chameleons.

Anorexia nervosa see **Eating disorders**

Antarctica

Of the seven continents on our planet Earth—North America, South America, Europe, Africa, Asia, Australia, and Antarctica—the last lies at the southernmost tip of the world. It is the coldest, driest, and windiest continent. Ice covers 98% of the land, and its 5,100,000 square miles (13,209,000 square kilometers) cover nearly one–tenth of the Earth's land surface, or the same size as Europe and the United States combined. Despite its barren appearance, Antarctica and its surrounding waters and islands teem with life all their own, and the continent plays a significant role in the climate and health of the entire planet.

Humans have never settled on Antarctica because of its brutal climate, but since its discovery in the early 1800s explorers and scientists have traveled across dangerous seas to study the continent's winds, temperatures, rocks, wildlife, and ice. Scientists treasure the unequaled chance at undisturbed research; as travel to the continent improves, tourists enjoy the opportunity to visit the last "frontier" on earth; environmentalists focus on Antarctica as the only place unspoiled by human hands; and, in an increasingly resource–hungry world, others look at the continent as a key source of oil and mineral resources. While some countries have tried to claim parts of the continent as their own, Antarctica is an independent continent protected by international treaty from ownership by any one country.

Antartica—an overview

Antarctica does not have a town, a tree, or even a blade of grass on the entire continent. That does not mean that Antarctica is not vital to life on earth. Seventy percent of the world's fresh water is frozen atop the continent. These icecaps reflect warmth from the Sun back into the atmosphere, preventing the planet from overheating. Huge icebergs break away from the stationary ice and flow north to mix with warm water from the equator, producing currents, clouds, and complex weather patterns. Creatures as small as microscopic phytoplankton and as large as whales live on and around the continent, including more than 40 species of birds. Thus, the continent provides habitat for a vital link in the world's food chain.

Archaeologists and geologists believe that millions of years ago Antarctica was part of a larger continent called Gondwanaland, according to similar fossils, rocks, and other geological features found on all of the other southern continents. About 200 million years ago, Gondwanaland broke apart and created the separate continents of Antarctica, Africa, Australia, South America, and India. Antarctica drifted away from the other continents as a result of shifting in the plates of the earth's crust, a process that continues today. The continent is currently centered roughly on the geographic South Pole, the point where all south latitudinal lines meet. It is the most isolated continent on earth, 600 miles or 1,000 kilometers from the southernmost tip of South America and more than 1,550 miles or 2,494 kilometers away from Australia.

Geology

Antarctica is considered an island—because it is surrounded by water—and a continent. The land itself is divided into two parts, east and west, and divided by the Transantarctic Mountains. The larger side, to the east, is located mainly in the eastern longitudes. West Antarctica is actually a group of islands held together by permanent ice.

Almost all of Antarctica is under ice, in some areas by as much as 2 mi (3 km). The ice has an average thickness of about 6,600 ft (2,000 m), which is higher than most mountains in warmer countries. This grand accumulation of ice makes Antarctica the highest continent on Earth, with an average elevation of 7,500 ft (2,286 m).

While the ice is extremely high in elevation, the actual land mass of the continent is, in most places, well below sea level due to the weight of the ice. If all of this ice were to melt, global sea levels would rise by about 200 ft (65 m), flooding the world's major coastal ports and vast areas of low–lying land. Even if one–tenth of Antarctica's ice were to slide into the sea, sea levels would rise by 20 ft (6 m), severely damaging the world's coastlines.

Under all that ice, the Antarctic continent is made up of mountains. The Transantarctic Mountains are the longest range on the continent, stretching 3,000 mi (4,828 km) from the Ross to Weddell Seas. Vinson Massif, at 16,859 ft (5,140 m), is the highest mountain peak. The few areas where mountains peak through the ice are called nunataks.

Among Antarctica's many mountain ranges lie three large, moon–like valleys—the Wright, Taylor, and Victoria—which are the largest continuous areas of ice–free land on the continent. Known as the "dry valleys," geologists estimate that it has not rained or snowed there for at least one million years. Any falling snow evaporates before it reaches the ground, because the air is so dry from the ceaseless winds and brutally cold temperatures. The dryness also means that nothing decomposes, including seal carcasses found to be more

A glacier system in Antarctica.

than 1,000 years old. Each valley is 25 mi (40 km) long and 3 mi (5 km) wide, and provides a rare glimpse of the rocks that form the continent and the Transantarctic Mountains.

Around several parts of the continent, ice forms vast floating shelves. The largest, known as the Ross Ice Shelf, is about the same size as Texas or Spain. The shelves are fed by glaciers on the continent, and thus the resulting shelves and icebergs are made up of frozen fresh water. The largest glacier on Earth, the Lambert Glacier on the eastern half of the continent, is 25 mi (40 km) wide and more than 248 mi (400 km) long.

Gigantic icebergs are a unique feature of Antarctic waters. They are created when huge chunks of ice separate from an ice shelf, a cliff or glacier, a process known as calving. Icebergs can be amazingly huge; an iceberg measured in 1956 was 208 mi (335 km) long by 60 mi (97 km) wide, larger than some small countries, and was estimated to contain enough fresh water to supply the water needs of London, England for 700 years. Only 10–15% of an iceberg normally appears above the water's surface, which can create great dangers to ships traveling in Antarctic waters. As these ice-

bergs break away from the continent, new ice is added to the continent by snowfall.

Icebergs generally flow northward and, if they do not become trapped in a bay or inlet, will reach the Antarctic Convergence, the point in the ocean where cold Antarctic waters meet with warmer waters. At this point, ocean currents usually sweep the icebergs from west to east until they melt. An average iceberg will last several years before melting.

Three oceans surround Antarctica—the Atlantic, Pacific, and Indian Oceans. Some oceanographers refer to the parts of these oceans around Antartica as the Southern Ocean. While the saltwater that makes up these oceans does not usually freeze, the air is so cold adjacent to the continent that even the salt and currents cannot keep the water from freezing. In the winter months, in fact, the ice covering the ocean waters may extend over an area almost as large as the continent. This ice forms a solid ring close to the continent, and loose chunks at the northern stretches. In October (early spring) as temperatures and strong winds rise, the ice over the oceans is broken up, creating huge icebergs.

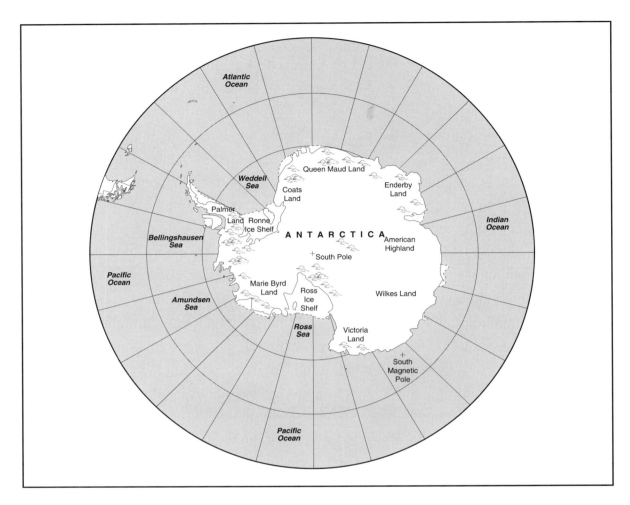

Antarctica.

Subantarctic islands are widely scattered across the ocean around Antarctica. Some, such as Tristan da Cunha and the Falkland Islands, have populations that live there year–round. Others, including the Marion Islands, the Crozets and Kerguelen, St. Paul, Amsterdam, Macquarie and Campbell Islands, have small scientific bases. Others are populated only by penguins, seals, and birds.

Strong winds blow constantly against the western shores of most of the northernmost islands, creating some of the stormiest seas in the world. Always wet in the summer, they are blanketed in snow in the winter and grasses in the summer. Further south in the colder subantarctic, the islands are covered with snow for much of the year and may have patches of mosses, lichen, and grasses in the summer. Seals and enormous populations of sea birds, including penguins and petrels, come to the islands' beaches and cliffs to breed in the summer.

The Falkland Islands, part of the British Commonwealth, are the largest group of subantarctic islands, lying 300 mi (480 km) east of South America. Two main islands, East and West, have about 400 smaller islets surrounding them. The islands cover 6,200 sq mi (16,000 sq km). Much of the ground is covered with wet, springy turf, overlying thick beds of peat. Primary industries are farming and ranching of cattle and sheep.

Climate

Antarctica is the coldest and windiest place on earth. The wind can gust up to 200 miles per hour, or twice as hard as the average hurricane. Surprisingly, little snow actually falls in Antarctica; because the air is so cold, what snow does fall turns immediately to ice.

Because of the way the Earth tilts on its axis as it rotates around the Sun, both polar regions experience long winter nights and long summer days. At the South

Pole itself, the sun shines around the clock during the six months of summer, and virtually disappears during the cold winter months. The tilt also affects the angle at which the Sun's radiation hits the Earth. While it is directly overhead over the Equator, it strikes the polar regions at more indirect angles. As a result, the Sun's radiation generates much less heat, even though the polar regions receive as much annual daylight as the rest of the world.

Even without the wind chill, the continent's temperatures can be almost incomprehensible to anyone who has not visited there. In winter, temperatures may fall to –100°F (–73°C). The world's record for lowest temperature was recorded on Antarctica in 1960, when it fell to –126.9°F (–89.8°C).

The coastal regions are generally warmer than the interior of the continent. The Antarctic Peninsula may get as warm as 50°F (10°C), although average coastal temperatures are generally around 32°F (0°C). During the dark winter months temperatures drop drastically, however, and the warmest temperatures range from –4 to –22°F (–20 to –30°C). In the colder interior, winter temperatures range from –40 to –94°F (–40 to –70°C).

The strong winds that constantly travel over the continent as cold air races over the high ice caps and then flows down to the coastal regions, are called katabatic winds. Winds associated with Antarctica blizzards commonly gust to more than 120 mi (193 km) per hour, and are among the strongest winds on Earth. Even at its calmest, the continent's winds can average 50–90 mi (80–145 km) per hour. Cyclones occur continually from west to east around the continent. Warm, moist ocean air strikes the cold, dry polar air, and gradually swirls its way toward the coast, usually losing its force well before it reaches land. These cyclones play a vital role in the exchange of heat and moisture between the tropics and the cold polar air.

While the Antarctic sky can be clear, a white–out blizzard may be occurring on the ground because the strong winds whip up the fallen snow. The wind redesigns the snow into irregularly shaped ridges, called sastrugi, which are difficult to traverse. Blizzards are common on the continent, and have hindered several exploration teams from completing their missions.

Surprisingly, Antarctica, with all its ice and snow, is the driest continent on Earth based on annual precipitation amounts. The constantly cold temperatures have allowed each year's annual snowfall to build up over the centuries, without melting. Along the polar ice cap, annual snowfall is only 1–2 in (2.5–5 cm). More precipitation falls along the coast and in the coastal moun-

tains, where it may snow 10–20 in (25–51 cm) per year.

Plants and animals

While the Arctic region teems with life, the Antarctic continent is nearly barren due to the persistently cold and dry climate. Plants that grow in the region reflect this climate and geology, including the pearlwort (*Colobanthus quitensis*) and grass (*deschampsia antarctica*), the only two flowering plants on the continent. Both grow in a small area on or near the warmest part of the continent, at the Antarctic Peninsula. Larger plants include mosses and lichen, a combination of algae and fungi found along the coast and on the peninsula. Green, nonflowering liverworts live on the western side of the peninsula. Brightly colored snow algae often form on top of the snow and ice, coloring it bright patches of red, yellow, or green.

A few hardy organisms live on rocks in the dry valleys, primarily lichens that hide inside the porous orange sandstone. These lichens, called *cryptoendoliths* or "hidden in rock," use up more than 99.9% of their photosynthetic productivity to simply stay alive. In contrast, a typical plant uses 90% for survival. Ironically, the lichens found in these valleys are one of the longest–living organisms on earth.

Few creatures can survive Antarctica's brutal climate. Except for a few mites and midges, native animals do not exist on Antarctica. Life in the sea and along the coast of Antarctica and its islands, however, is often abundant. A wide variety of animals make the surrounding waters their home, from zooplankton to large birds and mammals. A few fish have developed their own form of antifreeze over the centuries to prevent ice crystals from forming in their bodies, while others have evolved into cold–blooded species to survive the cold.

The base of Antarctica's marine food chain is phytoplankton, which feed on the rich nutrients found in coastal waters. The zooplankton feed on the phytoplankton, which are in turn consumed by the native fish, birds, and mammals. Antarctic krill, tiny shrimp-like creatures about 1.5 in (4 cm) long, are the most abundant zooplankton and are essential to almost every other life form in the region. They swim in large pools and look like red patches on the ocean. At night their crusts shimmer like billions of fireflies beneath the sea. Because of their abundance, krill have also been explored as a potential food source for humans.

Among the whales that make the southern oceans their home for at least part of the year include the blue, fin, sei, minke, humpback, and southern right whales.

Known as baleen whales, this whale group has a bristly substance called baleen located in plates in their mouths that filter food such as krill from the water. The blue whale in fact is the largest animal ever recorded to have lived on earth. The blue whale eats three tons—or six thousand pounds—of krill each day, and has been measured to weigh up to 180 tons (163,000 kg) and span 124 ft (38 m) in length. Once discovered in the 1800s, the blue whale was heavily hunted for its blubber, which was melted into oil for fuel. While scientists believe more than 200,000 existed before whaling, there are as few as 1,000 blue whales today. All baleen and toothed whales are now protected from hunting by international agreements.

Two toothed whales also swim in Antarctic waters, the sperm and the orca or killer whale. The sperm whale is the larger of the two, measuring as long as 60 feet (18 meters) and weighing as much as 70 tons (63,500 kg). It can dive up to 3,300 ft (1,006 m).

More than half the seals in the world live in the Antarctic—their blubber and dense fur insulate them from the cold. Five species of true or earless seals live in the region, the Weddell, Ross, leopard, crabeater, and elephant. The Weddell seal is the only one that lives in the Antarctic year–round, on or under the ice attached to the continent in the winter. Using their saw-like teeth to cut holes in the ice for oxygen, they can dive up to 2,000 ft (610 m) to catch fish and squid. The seals use a complex system to control their bodies' oxygen levels, which allows them to dive to such depths and stay underwater for as long as an hour.

The Ross seal, named for English explorer James Ross, is quick underwater and catches fish easily with its sharp teeth. It lives on the thickest patches of ice and is the smallest and least plentiful of the species. Leopard seals are long and sleek, and are fierce predators, living on the northern edges of pack ice, in the sea or near penguin rookeries, where they eat small penguins and their eggs as well as other seals. Crabeater seals are the most populated on earth, with an estimated 40 million or more in the Antarctic region alone. Elephant seals are the largest of their species, live on the subantarctic islands, and eat squid and fish. Unlike most seals, the males are much larger than the females. All five seal species are now protected under international law from hunting, which almost wiped out the Ross and elephant seals in the 1800s. One other type of seal, the southern fur seal, is also plentiful on Antarctica. It has a visible ear and longer flippers than the true seals, which makes it much more agile on land as well as in the water.

Several seabirds make the Antarctic their home, including 24 species of petrels, small seabirds that dart over the water and nest in rocks along the shore. Examples include the albatross, a gliding bird with narrow, long wings that may live up to 40 years, the southern giant fulmar, dove prion, and snow petrel. Shore birds that feed in the shallow waters near the shoreline include the blue–eyed cormorant, the Dominican gull, and the brown skua, which eats the eggs and young of other birds. The Arctic tern is the world's best at long–distance flying, since it raises its young in the Arctic but spends the rest of the year in the Antarctic, a distance of over 10,000 mi (16,090 km). Land birds include the wattled sheathbill, South Georgia pintail, and South Georgia pipit.

Of all the animals, penguins are the primary inhabitants of Antarctica. Believed to have evolved 40 to 50 million years ago, they have oily feathers that provide a waterproof coat and a thick layer of fat for insulation. Penguins' bones are not hollow, as are most birds' for flying, but solid. This prevents them from flying, but adds weight and makes it easier for them to dive into the water for food. And because they do not have predators that can live in the brutally cold climate, they do not need to fly. Thus their wings have evolved over the centuries to resemble flippers or paddles.

Seven of the 18 known species of penguins live on the Antarctic: the Adelie and emperor, both considered true Antarctic penguins because they live on the continent; the chinstrap, gentoo, macaroni, rockhopper, and king. The Adelie is the most plentiful species of penguin and can be found over the widest area of the continent. They spend their winters on the pack ice away from the continent, then return to land in October to nest in large rookeries or colonies, along the rocky coasts.

The emperor penguin is the largest of its species, and although it is the only Antarctic bird never to set foot on land, it breeds on sea ice attached to the mainland. The most popular type of penguin for zoos, emperor penguins are four feet tall and can weigh up to 80 pounds. It is the hardiest of all the animals that inhabit the Antarctic, staying throughout the year while other birds head north to escape the brutal winter. They breed on the ice surface during the winter months because of their immense size, which requires a longer incubation period. This schedule also ensures that the chicks will hatch in July or early spring in the Antarctic, providing the most days for the chicks to put on weight before the next winter's cold arrives.

The female lays one egg on the ice, then walks up to 50 mi (80 km) to open sea for food. When she returns, filled with food for the chick, the male—which has been incubating the egg atop the ice during the coldest winter months—makes the same trek out to sea to restore its body weight, which may drop by 50% during this period. The parents take turns traveling for food once the chick has hatched.

Because the emperor penguin is one of the few species that lives on Antarctica year–round, researchers believe it could serve as an indicator to measure the health of the Antarctic ecosystem. The penguins travel long distances and hunt at various levels of the ocean, covering wide portions of the continent. At the same time, they are easily tracked because the emperor penguins return to their chicks and mates in predictable ways. Such an indicator of the continent's health becomes more important as more humans travel to and explore Antarctica, and as other global conditions begin to affect the southernmost part of the world.

Exploration of the continent

Greek philosopher Aristotle hypothesized more than 2,000 years ago that the Earth was round, and that the southern hemisphere must have a landmass large enough to balance the lands in the northern hemisphere. He called the proposed land mass "Antarktikos," meaning the opposite of the Arctic.

The Greek geographer and astronomer Ptolemy called Antarctica the "Terra Australis Incognita" or "unknown southern land" in the second century A.D. He claimed the land was fertile and populated, but separated from the rest of the world by a region of torrid heat and fire around the equator. This concept was believed for several centuries, and the continent remained a mystery until James Cook crossed the Antarctic Circle and circumnavigated the continent in 1773. While he stated that the land was uninhabitable because of the ice fields surrounding the continent, he noted that the Antarctic Ocean was rich in whales and seals. For the next 50 years hunters exploited this region for the fur and oil trade.

As hunting ships began traveling further and further south in the early 1800s to find fur seals, it was inevitable that the continent would be found. Three countries claim first discovery rights to Antarctic land: Russia, due to explorer Fabian von Bellinghausen, on January 27, 1820; the British Commonwealth as a result of English explorer Edward Bransfield, on January 30, 1820; and American sealer Nathaniel Palmer, on November 18, 1820. In actuality, American sealer John Davis was the first person to actually step onto the continent, on February 7, 1821.

James Weddell was the next sealer to travel to the continent, on January 13, 1823. He found several previously unknown seal species, one of which later became known as the Weddell seal, then took his two ships—the *Jane* and the *Beaufoy*—farther south than any explorer had previously traveled. He reached 74 degrees south latitude on February 20, 1823, and the vast sea he had entered became known as the Weddell Sea.

In 1895, the first landing on the continent was accomplished by the Norwegian whaling ship *Antarctic*. The British were the first to spend a winter on Antarctica, in 1899. By 1911 a race had begun to see who would reach first reach the South Pole, an imaginary geographical center point at the bottom of the earth. Again, a Norwegian named Roald Amundsen was the first to reach it, on December 14, 1911. Robert Scott of England and his four men arrived a month later. While the first team made it home safely, the Scott team ran out of food and froze to death on their way home.

Airplanes first landed on Antarctica when Australian Hubert Wilkins flew 1,300 mi (2,092 km) over the Antarctic Peninsula in the 1920s, viewing terrain never before seen by another human. American Richard Byrd, the first person to fly over the North Pole in 1926, took his first Antarctic flight in 1929 and discovered a new mountain range he named Rockefeller. Thereafter, the continent was mapped and explored primarily from the air. Byrd continued his explorations to Antarctica over the next three decades, and revolutionized the use of modern vehicles and communications equipment for polar exploration.

Scientific exploration

While various countries were busy claiming rights to Antarctica, scientists were cooperating effectively on research as early as 1875. Twelve nations participated in the first International Polar Year in 1882 and 1883. While most of the research was done in the Arctic, one German station was located in the Antarctic region. A second International Polar Year occurred in 1932–33, followed by the International Geophysical Year (IGY) from July 1, 1957 to December 31, 1958. This time, all twelve nations conducted research in Antarctica and set up base camps in various locations, some of which are still used today. Topics of research included the pull of gravity, glaciology, cosmic rays, the southern lights, and changes in the atmosphere.

Several organizations and agreements have been signed since these cooperative research projects to ensure that political conflicts do not arise concerning research and use of Antarctica. The Scientific Committee on Antarctic Research (SCAR) was created in 1958 to provide a scientific advisory body between the different countries. The Antarctic Treaty was signed on December 1, 1959, by the 12 nations involved in the IGY projects, and made official on June 23, 1961, after each country ratified it within their own governments. As of April 1994, 42 countries had committed themselves to the spirit of cooperation outlined in the treaty, making it one of the most successful international agreements ever created.

The treaty commits all countries to relinquish any territorial claims indefinitely, ban military activity and weapons testing in the region, freely exchange and implement scientific plans, investigations, and results, and ban nuclear testing and the disposal of radioactive wastes. Any disputes that cannot be settled by negotiation or arbitration are sent to the International Court of Justice for settlement. The treaty thus sets aside 10% of the Earth as a nuclear–free, demilitarized zone.

The countries added the Agreed Measures for the Conservation of Antarctic Fauna and Flora to the treaty in 1964, and in 1991, the Protocol on Environmental Protection. The Protocol grew out of increasing concerns that poor habits by researchers and increasing numbers of tourists were exacerbating pollution problems on the continent. For example, the largest research station on the continent—U.S.–owned McMurdo Station built in 1955—had for decades dumped all garbage and wastes into nearby Winter Quarters Bay. Studies of the bay found that pollution had driven away most of the native organisms, replaced by others who can tolerate low water quality conditions.

The 1991 Protocol requires countries to protect the continent's ecosystem, particularly in how wastes are produced and disposed of while on the continent. The protocol also bans all exploration and mining of natural resources for the next 50 years, and requires the countries to complete environmental impact assessments for all activities and enact laws to ensure that citizens follow the protocol's provisions. The provision that protects Antarctica from mining is an increasingly important one, as scientists begin to discover that the land under all that ice contains rich amounts of coal, iron, copper, gold, and oil. While the cost to mine these resources is exorbitant today, new technologies and depletion of other resource reserves may prompt some countries to look to Antarctica for their supplies.

Other agreements that protect Antarctica from human abuse are the Convention for the Conservation of Antarctic Seals (CCAS), the Convention on the Conservation of Antarctic Marine Living Resources (CCAMLR), and several specific recommendations enacted by treaty countries. Together, these agreements make up the Antarctic Treaty System (ATS). As a result of these various treaties enacted to protect Antarctica and the species that call the continent their home, people may travel to learn from Antarctica, but not to conquer. Wars have never been fought on Antarctica, and the species that live on and around the continent have survived massive hunting intrusions to survive and even revive their populations.

Current events

A wide variety of research is continuing on Antarctica, primarily during the relatively warmer summer months from October to February when temperatures may reach a balmy 30–50°F (–1 to 10°C). The cold temperatures and high altitude of Antartica put astronomers' telescopes above the lower atmosphere, which lessens blurring. During the summer months they can study the Sun around the clock, since it shines 24 hours a day. Antarctica is also the best place to study interactions between solar wind and the Earth's magnetic field, temperature circulation in the oceans, unique animal life, ozone depletion, ice zone ecosystems, and glacial history. Buried deep in Antarctica ice lie clues to ancient climates, which may provide answers to whether the earth is due for global warming or the next ice age.

Scientists consider Antarctica to be a planetary bellwether, an early indicator of negative changes in the entire planet's health. For example, they have discovered that a hole is developing in the ozone layer over the continent, a protective layer of gas in the upper atmosphere that screens out the ultraviolet light that is harmful to all life on Earth. The ozone hole was first observed in 1980 during the spring and summer months, from September through November. Each year greater destruction of the layer can be seen during these months, and the first four years of the 1990s have produced the greatest rates of depletion thus far. The hole was measured to be about the size of the continental United States in 1994, and it lasts for longer intervals each year. Scientists have identified various chemicals created and used by humans, such as chlorofluorocarbons (CFCs) as the cause of this destruction, and bans on uses of these chemicals have begun in some countries.

Researchers have also determined that a major climate change may have occurred in Antarctica in the past 10–12 years, based on recorded changes in ozone levels and an increase in cloudiness over the South Pole. This, coupled with a recorded weakening of the

KEY TERMS

. . . .

Antarctic Circle—The line of latitude at 66 degrees 32′ South, where there are 24 hours of daylight in midsummer and 24 hours of darkness in midwinter.

Antarctic convergence—A 25–mile or 40–kilometer region where cold Antarctic surface water meets warmer, subantarctic water and sinks below it.

Antarctic Ocean—The seas surrounding the continent, where the Atlantic, Pacific, and Indian converge.

Blubber—Whale or seal fat used to create fuel.

Calving—When huge chunks of ice or icebergs break off from ice shelves and sheets.

Dry valleys—An area on the continent where no rain is known to have fallen for more than two million years, and the extremely dry katabatic winds cause any snow blown into the valleys to evaporate before hitting the ground. The Taylor, Victoria, and Wright valleys are the largest continuous areas of ice–free land on the continent.

Glacier—A river of ice that moves down a valley to the sea, where it breaks into icebergs.

Iceberg—A large piece of floating ice that has broken off a glacier or ice shelf.

Katabatic winds—Fierce winds that flow down along the steep slopes of the interior mountains of Antarctica, and along ice caps and glaciers on the subantarctic islands.

Krill—Tiny sea animals or zooplankton that are the main food for most larger species in the Antarctic region.

Nunataks—Mountain peaks that thrust through the ice and snow cover.

Pack ice—Ice from seawater, which forms a belt approximately 300–1,800 miles (483–2,897 kilometers) wide around the continent in winter.

Southern lights—Also known as the Aurora Australis, they are streamers of different colors in the sky, especially at night.

South Magnetic Pole—The point to which a compass is attracted and which is some distance from the geographic South Pole. It varies from year to year as the Earth's magnetic field changes.

South Pole—The geographically southernmost place on Earth.

Subantarctica—The region just north of Antarctica and the Antarctic Circle, but south of Australia, South America, and Africa.

ozone shield over North America in 1991, has led scientists to conclude that the ozone layer is weakening around the entire planet.

Others are studying the ice compact on Antarctica to determine if, in fact, the earth's climate is warming due to the burning of fossil fuels. The global warming hypothesis is based on the atmospheric process known as the greenhouse effect, in which the pollution prevents the heat energy of the earth from escaping into the outer atmosphere. Global warming could cause some of the ice cap to melt, flooding many cities and lowland areas. Because the polar regions are the engines that drive the world's weather system, this research is essential to identify the effect of human activity on these regions.

Most recently, a growing body of evidence is showing that the continent's ice has fluctuated dramatically in the past few million years, vanishing completely from the continent once and from its western third at least several times. These collapses in the ice structure might be triggered by climatic change, such as global warming, or by far less predictable factors, such as volcanic eruptions under the ice. While the east Antarctic ice sheet has remained relatively stable because it lies on a single tectonic plate, the western ice sheet is a jumble of small plates whose erratic behavior has been charted on satellite data. The west Antarctic is also dominated by two seas, the Ross and Weddell, whose landward regions are covered by thick, floating shelves of ice. Some researchers speculate that if warmer, rising oceans were to melt this ice, the entire western sheet might disintegrate quickly, pushing global sea levels up by 15–20 ft (5–6 m).

See also Gaia hypothesis; Greenhouse effect; Ozone layer depletion; Plate tectonics.

Further Reading:

Billings, Henry. *Antarctica—Enchantment of the World.* Chicago: Childrens Press, 1994.
Grotta, Daniel and Sally. "Antarctica: Whose Continent is it Anyway?" *Popular Science*, Volume 240, Number 1, 1992: 62–7, 90–1.

Horgan, John. "Antarctic Meltdown." *Scientific American,* Volume 266, Number 3: 19–28.

Monastersky, Richard. "Antarctic Ozone Level Reaches New Low." *Science News,* Volume 144, Number 16:247.

Monastersky, Richard. "Science on Ice." *Science News,* Volume 143, Number 15, 1993: 232–35.

Palca, Joseph. "Poles Apart, Science Thrives on Thin Ice." *Science,* Volume 255, Number 5042, 1992: 276–78.

Sally Cole–Misch

Antbirds and gnat–eaters

The antbirds and gnat–eaters are 231 species of birds that comprise the relatively large family, Formicariidae. These birds only occur in Central and South America, mostly in lowland tropical forests.

The antbirds and gnat–eaters are variable in their body form and size. Their body length ranges from 4–14 in (10–36 cm), and they have short, rounded wings, and a rounded tail that can be very short or quite long. Most species have a rather large head with a short neck, and the bill is stout and hooked at the tip. Species that live and feed in the forest canopy have a relatively long tail and wings, while those of ground–feeding species are shorter.

The colors of the plumage of most species are rather subdued hues of browns and greys, although there are often bold patterns of white, blue, or black. Males and females of most species have differing plumage. These birds generally occur in solitary pairs, which are permanent residents in a defended territory.

Species of antbirds forage widely in the forest floor or canopy for their food of insects, spiders, and other invertebrates. Species of antbirds are prominent members of the local, mixed–species foraging flocks that often occur in their tropical–forest habitat. These flocks can contain as many as 50 species, and are thought to be adaptive because they allow better detection of birds of prey.

Despite of their name, antbirds rarely eat ants. Antbirds received their common name from the habit of some species of following a column of army–ants as it moves through their tropical–forest habitat. These predatory assemblages of social insects disturb many insects as they move along the forest floor. Antbirds and other species of birds often follow these columns to capture insects and other prey that have been dis-

turbed by the army ants. About 27 species of antbirds have the habit of actively following army ants, while other species do this on a more casual, less focused basis.

Antbirds lay two to three eggs in a cup–shaped nest located in a low tree or on the ground. Both parents share in the incubation of the eggs and the nurturing of the young. Pairs of antbirds are monogamous for life, the partners remaining faithful to one another until death.

Species of antbirds are prominent elements of the avian community of the lowland tropical forests that are their usual habitat. In some cases in Amazonia, as many as 30–40 species of antbirds can occur in the same area, dividing the habitat up into subtly defined niches.

The white–faced ant–catcher (*Pithys albifrons*) is an ant–following species of tropical forests of Amazonian Brazil and Venezuela. The ocellated ant–thrush (*Phaenostictus mcclennani*) ranges from Nicaragua to Ecuador. The rufous–capped ant–thrush (*Formicarius colma*) forages on the floor of Amazonian forests of Brazil, Venezuela, Ecuador, and Peru.

Anteaters

Anteaters belong to the family Myrmecophagidae, which includes four species in three genera. They are found in Trinidad, and from southern Mexico to northern Argentina. The spiny anteater (echidna) of Australia is an egg–laying mammal and is not related to the placental anteaters of the New World. The banded anteater (or numbat) of Australia is a marsupial mammal, and not a close relative of the placental anteaters. The anteater's closest relatives are sloths, armadillos, and pangolins. All belong to the order Edentata, meaning without teeth, although only the anteaters are strictly toothless.

Anteaters feed by shooting their whiplike tongues in and out of insect nests up to 160 times per minute. Ants, along with sticks and gravel, stick to the sticky tongue like flies to flypaper. Horny papillae toward the rear of the two–foot–long tongue help this toothless mammal to grind its food, which is ground up further by the muscular stomach. It is thought that grit that the anteater swallows may actually help its stomach to grind up the food. In a typical day, a giant anteater, the largest of four species, will consume up to 30,000 ants.

A giant anteater (*Myrmecophaga tridactyla*).

Anteaters' bodies have a narrow head and torso and a long, slender snout that is kept close to the ground to sniff for insects. Anteaters have poor eyesight and hearing but a keen sense of smell. Their legs end in long, sharp claws that are used primarily to open ant and termite nests but double as defensive weapons. To protect their claws, anteaters walk on their knuckles with their claws turned inward.

A diet of ants and termites provides little energy, so anteaters have adapted by evolving an unusually low resting metabolic rate and low core body temperature, moving slowly, and spending much of the day sleeping. Female anteaters bear only one offspring per year and devote much of their energy to caring for the young.

The largest of the four New World species is the giant anteater (*Myrmecophaga tridactyla*), which is widely distributed throughout Central and South America east of the Andes to northern Argentina. The giant anteater is about the size of a large dog. It is covered with short, mostly gray hair, except on its tail, which has long, bushy fur. True to its name, the giant anteater subsists almost entirely on large, ground–dwelling ants. It moves between ant nests, taking just a little from each nest, thereby avoiding excessive ant bites and depletion of its food supplies.

Giant anteaters are solitary creatures, pairing up shortly before mating and parting just afterward. Females suckle their young for about six months and carry them on their back for up to a year, when the young anteaters are nearly fully grown. The giant anteater is an endangered species due to habitat destruction and hunting.

The lesser, or collared, anteater consists of two species, *Tamandua mexicana* and *T. tetradactyla*. *Tamandua mexicana* is found from southern Mexico to northwestern Venezuela and Peru, while *T. Tetradactyla* lives in Trinidad and South America, east of the Andes, from Venezuela to northern Argentina and southern Brazil. Lesser anteaters are distinguished from giant anteaters by their large ears, prehensile tail, and affinity for climbing trees. They are about half the size of giant anteaters and are covered with bristly hair that varies in color from blond to brown. The term collared anteater refers to the band of black fur encircling the abdomen, found in *T. mexicana* and *T. tetradactyla* from the southeastern part of their range. The tree–climbing lesser anteaters feed mostly on termites. Like the giant anteater, the female tamandua carries her offspring on her back.

The most elusive of the four species of anteater is the silky anteater (*Cyclopes didactylus*) This squirrel–sized animal spends most of the day sleeping in trees, and comes out to forage for ants at night. Silky anteaters are distributed from southern Mexico to most of the Amazon basin, and west of the Andes to northern Peru. These anteaters rest on branches of the silk cotton trees, where its silky, gold and gray fur blends with the tree's soft, silver fibers. This camouflage protects the silky anteater from owls, eagles, and other predators. In this species, both parents feed the young, and both carry their offspring on their backs.

See also Monotremes; Numbat; Spiny anteaters.

Further Reading:

Macdonald, David, ed. *The Encyclopedia of Mammals.* New York: Facts on File, 1984.

Nowak, Ronald M. *Walker's Mammals of the World.* Baltimore: The Johns Hopkins University Press, 1991.

"Quick–snacking anteater avoids attack." *Science* (8 August 1991): 88.

Cynthia Washam

Antelopes and gazelles

Antelopes and gazelles belong to the family Bovidae, which includes even–toed hoofed animals with hollow horns and a four–chambered stomach. Sheep, cattle, and goats are also bovids. The family Bovidae in Africa includes nine tribes of antelopes, one of which includes the 12 species of gazelles (Antilopini). Other tribes are the duikers (Cephalophini), dwarf antelopes (Neotragini), reedbuck, kob, and waterbuck (Reduncini), hartebeeste, topi, and wildebeeste (Alcelaphini), impala (Aepycerotini), bushbuck, kudu, and eland (Tragelaphini), rhebok (Peleini), and horse antelopes (Hippotragini). Most antelopes and gazelles are found in Africa where 72 of the 84 species live. The word gazelle comes from an Arabic word that means affectionate. Antelopes and gazelles can be found throughout the grasslands of Africa, in mountains, forests, and deserts. Antelopes range in size from small 15 lb (7 kg) antelopes to a 1,200 lb (545 kg) animal, the eland, of East and West Africa.

Antelopes and gazelles are noted for the beauty of their horns. Some are spiral in shape, others are ringed, lyre–shaped, or S–shaped. Gazelles have black–ringed horns 10–15 in (25 to 38 cm) long. Depending on the size of the species, the horns can be as short as 1 in (2.5 cm) or as long as 5 ft (1.5 m). The Grant's gazelle has horns that are as long as the shoulder height of the animal. In most species the females as well as the males have horns.

The prevailing color of antelopes and gazelles is brown or black and white, but different species show a range of coloration and markings. All antelopes and gazelles have scent glands that they use to mark territory and to signal, age, sex, & social status. Glands can be preorbital (below the eyes) or between the hooves (interdigital), subauricular (below the ears), or on the back, shins, and genital areas of the animals.

Smaller species of antelopes with well–developed hind quarters and coloration indicate a reliance on concealment and bounding escape runs. The larger species tend to inhabit open spaces, since they are able to escape predators by their ability to reach high speeds, some reaching 35 mph (56 kph).

Some species, such as the Dorcas gazelle and the oryx of the dry savanna regions, have developed effective ways to decrease the need for water. Some species are solitary in habit while others such as the impala live in herds, which are either single sex (all females) which mate only with the dominant male, or are herds of both males and females. They can be polygamous—one male to a number of females—or monogamous.

Some groups are adolescent males. Common to all species is the birth of one offspring. Pregnancy ranges from four to nine months depending on the size of the species.

See also Dwarf antelopes; Eland; Hartebeestes; Oryx; Waterbuck.

Antenna

An antenna is a device used to transmit and receive electromagnetic waves such as radio waves and microwaves. Antennas provide the transition between a guided wave (flowing in a wire) and a free–space wave (flowing in air or vacuum). An antenna can take high frequency pulses from an electrical signal generator, focus them, and launch them into space, like the antenna at a radio station. Conversely, it can pick up waves from space, focus them, and send them to a receiver, like the antenna on your car radio. You can think of an antenna as a soap bubble pipe: pulses (soap film) travel down the transmission line (pipe stem), reach the bowl (antenna), and are electrically shaped and pushed out into free space. In fact, the horn antennas used for microwave communication look very much like the diagram, and are designed to let the radiation spread out gradually rather than undergo an abrupt transition from the waveguide into free space. This is known as impedance matching, and contributes to the propagation of the radiation in the same way as cupping your hands around your mouth when shouting makes your voice travel further.

Basically there are two types of antennas: those that rotate and those that are stationary. Rotating antennas usually operate as search and detection systems. They are typically found on ships, airports, or weather stations. Often, an antenna will include a reflecting element to focus the radio waves, commonly parabolic or shaped something like an orange slice.

The stationary antenna type is generally found at radio or microwave transmitting sites. This antenna configuration can be a long wire between pylons, a single pylon with a long rod at the top, or include a number of unevenly spaced rods like an outdoor television antenna. The satellite dish, an antenna with a parabolic reflector, is another common type of stationary configuration.

See also Microwave communication; Radio; Radio waves; Radar.

Anther see **Flower**

Antenna for a Doppler weather radar site. Doppler radar can be used to detect wind shear and microburst weather conditions.

Anthropocentrism

Anthropocentrism is a world view that considers humans to be the most important factor and value in the universe. In contrast, the biocentric world view considers humans to be no more than a particular species of animal, without greater intrinsic value than any of the other species of organisms that occur on Earth. The ecocentric world view incorporates the biocentric one, while additionally proposing that humans are a natural component of Earth's ecosystem, and that humans have an absolute and undeniable requirement of the products and services of ecosystems in order to sustain themselves and their societies.

There are a number of important implications of the anthropocentric view, which strongly influence the ways in which humans interpret their relationships with other species and with nature and ecosystems. Some of these are discussed below:

1. The anthropocentric view suggests that humans have greater intrinsic value than other species. A result of this attitude is that any species that are of potential use to humans can be a "resource" to be exploited. This use often occurs in an unsustainable fashion that results in degradation, sometimes to the point of extinction of the biological resource, as has occurred with the dodo, great auk, and other animals.

2. The view that humans have greater intrinsic value than other species also influences ethical judgements about interactions with other organisms. These ethics are often used to legitimize treating other species in ways that would be considered morally unacceptable if humans were similarly treated. For example, animals are often treated very cruelly during the normal course of events in medical research and agriculture. This prejudiced treatment of other species has been labelled "speciesism" by ethicists.

3. Another implication of the anthropocentric view is the belief that humans rank at the acme of the natural evolutionary progression of species and of life. This belief is in contrast to the modern biological interpretation of evolution, which suggests that no species are "higher" than any others, although some clearly have a more ancient evolutionary lineage, or may occur as relatively simple life forms.

The individual, cultural, and technological skills of humans are among the attributes that make their species, *Homo sapiens*, special and different. The qualities of humans have empowered their species to a degree that no other species has achieved during the history of life on Earth, through the development of social systems and technologies that make possible an intense exploitation and management of the environment. This power has allowed humans to become the most successful species on Earth. This success is indicated by the population of humans that is now being maintained, the explosive growth of those numbers, and the increasing amounts of Earth's biological and environmental resources that are being appropriated to sustain the human species.

However, the true measure of evolutionary success, in contrast to temporary empowerment and intensity of resource exploitation, is related to the length of time that a species remains powerful— the sustainability of its enterprise. There are clear signals that the intense exploitation of the environment by humans is causing widespread ecological degradation and a diminished carrying capacity to sustain people, numerous other species, and many types of natural ecosystems. If this environmental deterioration proves to truly be important, and there are many indications that it will, then the recent centuries of unparalleled success of the human species will turn out to be a short–term phenomenon, and will not represent evolutionary success. This will be a clear demonstration of the fact that humans have always, and will always, require access to a continued flow of ecological goods and services to sustain themselves and their societies.

Antibiotics

Antibiotics are drugs used to fight infections and infectious diseases caused by bacteria. They are made from the natural substances of one microorganism to hinder the life activities of another. Fungi molds, such as the one from which the penicillins are derived, and special kinds of soil bacteria are the chief sources for these drugs.

In the current production of antibiotics these natural sources are combined with various synthetic chemicals manufactured in laboratories to form semisynthetic antibiotics. Semisynthetic antibiotics provide coverage against the newer antibiotic resistant strains of disease–causing bacteria. These strains have arisen in the past several decades as a result of the introduction and mass use of antibiotics since the early 1940s. Semisynthetics also widen the scope of coverage of an antibiotic to fight a larger number of different types of disease–causing bacteria.

The first use of the term antibiotic is credited to Selman Waksman, an American microbiologist who discovered the second major antibiotic after penicillin, streptomycin. Antibacterial drugs, which were made from chemicals in the dye industry rather than living microbes, preceded the introduction of antibiotics. The sulfa drugs introduced in the mid–1930s were called antibacterials. Though they are sometimes loosely referred to as antibiotics, antibacterials are bacteriostatic rather than bactericidal. Bacteriostatic drugs prevent bacteria from reproducing; bactericidal ones kill bacteria by either destroying their cell walls or by some other lethal action. The present day use of semisynthetic antibiotics has, however, narrowed the distinction between the two terms.

Most bacteria are actually beneficial to the planet and other animal life, including humans. About 3%, however, are pathogenic, or disease–causing. Another 10% may or may not be disease–causing depending on such varying conditions as where and when they appear. The other 87% are either harmless or play an important part in life processes.

Unlike antibiotics, antibacterials can be used to treat parasitical and fungal infections along with bacterial ones. Neither antibiotics nor antibacterials, however, are effective against viral infections, which are treated with an antiviral agent. Though antibiotics may adversely affect the life process of higher organisms, they are usually designed to attack and kill only a bacterial microorganism that causes disease, a pathogen.

Transmission of pathogens

Pathogens can be transmitted from one person to another by coughing and sneezing (droplet infection), physical contact with an infected person, food that is infected with pathogens, contaminated water, insect bites, and sexual contact. Toxins from pathogenic bacteria destroy vital body cells and stimulate the immune system. The immune system may destroy the bacteria, but the white blood cells can also damage and inflame the body's own cells.

The respiratory system and urogenital system are particularly vulnerable to pathogenic attack. Influenza and colds are from viruses that are much smaller than bacteria and more difficult to treat. Pneumonia may be caused by bacteria, viruses, fungi, or protozoa, while tuberculosis is caused by a specific type of bacteria. The two major sexually transmitted disease (STDs), syphilis and gonorrhea, are caused by pathogenic bacteria; herpes type 2 and AIDS are viral infections.

By the end of World War II syphilis and gonorrhea were thought to be well under control with the new antibiotics. But in the past few decades there has been a conspicuous increase of all STDs. Some of the contributing causes for this increase may be contraceptive pills that have replaced the use of condoms, changes in attitudes toward sex, and world tourism. The antibiotic cure for STDs and the other infectious diseases did not begin to take place until the early 1940s. Along with many other diseases, STDs are now becoming more difficult to treat with antibiotics because of the development of antibiotic resistant strains of pathogenic bacteria.

Classification of antibiotics

Antibiotics are classified by the way they act against bacteria (mechanism of action) and the effect they have on them. The effect can either be bactericidal or bacteriostatic, like the earlier antibacterials. Unlike human cells which are without cell walls (eukaryotic cells), bacteria do have cell walls over their cell membranes (prokaryotic cells). The antibiotics that fall into the penicillin and cephalothin groups restrict the growth of the bacteria's cell wall. That action kills the bacteria at the point it is about to divide because the increased mass of its contents can no longer be kept intact by its cell wall. Its contents then spill into the surrounding fluid. Human cells are unharmed by this action since they do not have cell walls.

Other antibiotics will block nutrients from passing through the cell membrane. If the bacteria can still live but not reproduce as a result of that action, the drug is then bacteriostatic and may either be an antibacterial or antifungal agent. Tetracyclines, aminoglycosides (streptomycin) and the macrolides, which includes erythromycin, disrupt the synthesis of protein within the bacterial cell. Other antibiotics will interfere with the genetic activity of the bacteria by disrupting its ability to replicate its genes. Only bactericidal drugs will be effective against life–threatening pathogens.

Antibiotics may also be described by their action against Gram–positive and Gram–negative bacteria. Bacteria are identified either by their shapes or the way they stain in reaction to certain chemical preparations. In 1880, Hans Christian Gram of Denmark was the first to note the differences in the way bacteria react to staining preparations. He called those that retained a deep purple stain even after washing "stain positive," and those that lost the stain and responded to another stain "stain negative." Today, bacteria are classified as either Gram–positive or Gram–negative as the two major types of bacteria. The staining test indicates the differences in the structure of the cell wall of the two types of bacteria.

Gram–positive and Gram–negative bacteria are each responsible for certain types of disease. Penicillin G, for example, is used for treating certain gram–positive infections but is ineffective against gram–negative ones. Other antibiotics are only effective against Gram–negative bacteria. Chloromycetin, discovered in 1947, was the first antibiotic to be effective against both Gram–positive and Gram–negative bacteria.

History of antibiotics

There is evidence that the ancient Romans were using some form of penicillin in their medicinal ointments 2,000 years ago. Medical records that date back to 1500 B.C. from Mesopotamia, Egypt, and China show that dung and soybean curd were used to extract moldy and fermented material for treating wounds and swellings. Before Fleming's discovery of penicillin, William Roberts in 1874 observed the antagonism

between fungi molds and bacteria. Louis Pasteur and Jules Francois Joubert also observed the failure of *Anthrax bacilli* to grow when covered with molds that were carried by the air. They realized the possibility of using their observations for the development of a pathogen killer, but instead most of their research and others' for the next 50 years centered on the development of vaccines, serums for immunity, and chemical germicides. It would not be until 1943 that penicillin would begin to gain widespread use as an effective antibiotic.

Until 1943, medical science had no effective medicine to kill pathogenic bacteria. Paul Ehrlich, the German bacteriologist at the turn of the century, theorized that "magic bullets" could be found to kill disease–causing organisms without harming the rest of the body. In 1910, he developed an arsenic compound that could kill the bacteria, *Treponema pallida*, responsible for syphilis. Though the arsenic did not kill the patient, it was not the single injection or "magic bullet" that Ehrlich had hoped for, since it took many injections over a long course of treatment to cure the disease. Nevertheless, his theory of a "magic bullet" anticipated the later discovery of antibiotics.

In 1928, Alexander Fleming, the British bacteriologist, while experimenting with a virulent strain of *Staphylococcus aureus* bacteria, noticed that some of the strains were killed from summer spores that entered from the outside into the laboratory. The spores were first misidentified as a red brush fungus, *Penicillium rubrum*, but much later identified as a near relative, *Penicillium notatum*. The penicillin fungi are a family of mold–producing fungus, the type used to ripen Camembert and Roquefort cheeses. Fleming called the chemical substance extracted from the mold responsible for killing the bacteria penicillin. Since these early extracts were impure and in such small quantity, it would take more than a decade before his discovery could be applied to the effective manufacturing and use of the first antibiotics.

Sulfa drugs

In 1935 before the bactericidal antibiotic penicillins were developed for use, however, the sulfa drugs were developed from chemicals used in the dye industry. The sulfonamides were the first effective antibacterials, that is, drugs that do not kill bacteria but keep them from multiplying. Their bacteriostatic action keeps the bacteria count fixed and thus gives the body time to mobilize a defense against infection.

Most of the sulfonamides since then have been replaced by other antibacterials. Some that can concentrate in the urinary tract are still being used for urinary infections. Many disease–causing bacteria have developed resistant strains against sulfonamides. Some bacteria that cause urinary infections have become resistant to sulfonamides, as well as those responsible for pneumonia, septicaemia (blood poisoning), and gonorrhea. Sulfonamides are still being used, along with newer antibacterials, for such conditions as leprosy, colitis, eye infections (used in eye drops), and as a prevention of infection from burns (used as a cream).

The early sulfonamides work against bacteria by preventing them from reproducing rather than by killing them. This group of antibacterials interfere with the bacteria's metabolic system to produce folic acid from para–aminobenzoic acid. Without the folic acid, the bacterial cell cannot divide. Newer antibacterials are now bactericidal. They interfere with other chemical processes brought about by folic acid chemistry. Trimethoprim interferes with the enzyme that changes folic acid to folinic acid. Without folinic acid, bacteria cannot build up their cell nuclei.

Antibacterials can have adverse effects, such as nausea, vomiting, rashes, depression, and other serious conditions. The sulfonamides have largely been replaced by the antibiotics, though they are still used for some of the special conditions which have been previously indicated. Some of the newer antibacterials, like trimethoprim, are also bactericidal.

Development of penicillin as an antibiotic

Early attempts to use extracts from Fleming's molds to treat bacterial infections were unsuccessful because the quantity and quality were not potent enough. In 1939 a group of Oxford University researchers attempted to improve penicillin as an antibiotic drug. In 1941 they used an improved version of the penicillin extract to treat a British policeman suffering from osteomyelitis, a bone disease caused by *Staphylococcus aureus*. Though the patient showed much improvement from the treatment, he died when the supply of penicillin was expended.

World War II acted as a further spur to the development of penicillin. Attempts to mass produce penicillin were carried over to the United States from England because of the war. A vial of the mold was brought to the United States and facilities were secured for mass production from beer mold liquor. In 1943 the first amounts of penicillin from this production began to be used to treat wounded soldiers. Penicillin was still so scarce that it had to be recycled from the patients' urine.

The search for other antibiotics

Several problems arose along with the successful use of the sulfonamides and penicillins. The penicillins are not effective against all forms of bacteria and they often cause serious allergic reactions. They usually have to be taken by injection at a hospital to be effective and penicillin resistant strains of bacteria have developed in hospital environments as a result of their widespread use. Several new families of antibiotics are now in use to answer some of the special needs for the current fight against microbes.

In 1939, René Dubos made the next major breakthrough in antibiotic medicine with his discovery of an antibiotic from a bacteria in the soil which he named *Bacillus brevis*. His experiments in this area started in the 1920s, and they were inspired by Pasteur's theories that the soil must hold some kind of pathogen–killing microbes, otherwise cattle that had the anthrax disease when they were buried would transmit the same disease to cattle who were safely grazing in the places where the dead cattle were buried.

Dubos found that his antibiotic, which he called tyrothricin, was effective against pneumonia in mice that he had infected with pneumococci. Unfortunately, however, the mice died because the tyrothricin also destroyed their red blood cells. Rather than giving up his work with his discovery, he was encouraged by physicians who were searching for new antibiotics to find external applications for tyrothricin. Ointments containing gramicidin and tyrocidine, derivatives from tyrothricin, proved effective medicines that Dubos and his fellow researchers developed. These drugs could even be used in mouthwashes for oral infections because the stomach acid kills the microbes before they enter the bloodstream.

Others soon followed in Dubos's path of finding antibiotics from the soil. In 1944 Selman Waksman, who had worked with Dubos in the discovery of tyrothricin, along with other researchers, developed the drug streptomycin from soil samples found in a poultry breeder's farm. The drug was successfully tested in an outbreak of the plague. It was also proven to be the first effective drug against tuberculosis. Some of the side effects of the streptomycin included fever, skin rashes, and lowered blood pressure. More serious ones were problems with vision that could lead to blindness, along with hearing loss and dizziness. By 1953 some of the side effects of streptomycin were either eliminated or reduced by a series of chemical refinements.

The aminoglycosides

A new class of antibiotic drugs called aminoglycosides grew out of the discovery of streptomycin. Such drugs as neomycin, kanamycin, and gentamicin have replaced the use of streptomycin since they are safer and more effective. The aminoglycosides are used against bacteria that resist penicillin's cell wall–breaking action. But since these drugs still retain the same side–effect problems of streptomycin—hearing loss, nerve cell damage and damage to the kidneys—they are only used in cases of serious infections for a short time. There is a continuous search for new drugs in this class because bacteria are quick to develop resistance to them.

Other antibiotic classes

After the discoveries of Fleming, Dubos, and Waksman, drug companies realized that a great number of potential antibiotics would have to be developed on a more systematic basis than the hit and miss procedures that had been followed in the early days of antibiotic discovery. Benjamin Duggar, a botanist working for Lederle Laboratories, had hundreds of soil samples collected from around the world tested in the company's laboratories. Aureomycin™ (chlortetracycline), an antibiotic that could kill penicillin–resistant bacteria as well as a wide range of other ones, came out of that concerted effort.

It was soon discovered that Aureomycin™ belonged to a third class of antibiotics after the penicillins and aminoglycosides—the tetracyclines. Another group, the cephalosporins, came from a bacteria group living in a drainage pipe on the Italian coast. The antibiotics in this group resemble the effects of penicillin. Another antibiotic, erythromycin, used for allergies and against penicillin–resistant bacteria came from soil samples located in the Philippines. These findings represent some of the worldwide search that took place for antibiotic molds and bacteria between 1945 and 1960. The search yielded an annual output of hundreds of tons of prescription antibiotics used in that period.

From the period of the 1960s to the present there has been an outpouring of designer type antibiotics—synthetic penicillin and streptomycin molecules combined with bacteria and mold ones to deal with the problems of resistant strains and side effects. In 1957 penicillin was synthesized in the laboratory for the first time, but the process was too costly to market the drug. Semi–synthetic antibiotics, which are part synthetic and part microbial, have led to more effective penicillin and streptomycin preparations. The unearthing of new soil molds such as the carbapenems and, in the 1980s, the monobactems, are producing antibiotics to deal with the problems of hospital–based infections.

Antibiotics used in treatment and prevention

Before treatment can begin with an antibiotic, a proper diagnosis has to be made. Specimens of body fluids and tissues are examined in order to detect the presence of a pathogen. Certain types of antibodies present in a blood sample may point to the infecting agent. Even after the laboratory tests have identified the illness, the physician must ask such questions as should an antibiotic be used; if yes, what kind, and do the benefits compensate for cost factors and adverse effects. In cases of severe illness the testing processes and administration of an antibiotic must be speeded up to avoid further complications or death. Adjustments of medication can then be made in follow–up treatment. The avoidance of using an antibiotic in less severe cases has the advantages of avoiding allergic or toxic responses for the patient, keeping in check the proliferation of resistant strains, and containing the costs of treatment.

The use of antibiotics for prevention, unlike vaccination, has limited effectiveness. An antibiotic may be prescribed as a preventive measure against the threat of a specific microbial infection or where one has recently entered the body. The attempt to give blanket coverage against any pathogen without specific targets, however, may do more harm than good. The unnecessary use of antibiotics makes the individual more susceptible to antibiotic–resistant strains of bacteria.

It has been estimated that 90% of antibiotic prescriptions are not called for and argued that the use of antibiotics in animal feed has increased the appearance of salmonella and other dangerous infections related to meat and poultry production. The justification for mixing antibiotics in animal feed is to prevent infections from taking place in the animals and to allow for extra growth. Animals will grow larger when their metabolic energy is not directed to fighting off low–grade infections, but using even minute traces of antibiotics in the feed encourages the development of more virulent strains of antibiotic–resistant bacteria. These strains then become harder to fight in both the animal and human population. Allowing the use of antibiotics not used by humans in animal feed is one way some countries deal with this problem.

The major problem of antibiotic resistance

The optimism that ushered in the antibiotic age in the second half of the 20th century is presently undergoing a period of serious revision. With the advent of such new diseases as AIDS, Lyme and Legionnaire's disease, the flesh–eating streptococcus A, hantavirus, and other newly appearing viral diseases in different parts of the world, there is a recognition of medicine's limitations in the war against infectious diseases. Along with these new diseases is a resurgence of the older ones in more resistant forms, such as the STDs, tuberculosis, cholera, diphtheria, typhoid, and pertussis (whooping cough) in the United States, Russia, and in other countries as well. Today there are third world countries experiencing outbreaks of bubonic plague, new strains of cholera, and AIDS.

Before the discovery and use of penicillin and other antibiotics, infectious diseases were fought off by the immune system. In that battle the patient either survived or perished. Antibiotics circumvented the immune system and went directly after the bacteria to kill them without killing the cells of the body. As soon as penicillin was used, the bacteria it killed began to mutate, that is change its genetic makeup to form new strains that could resist the attack against its cell wall. Some mutant bacteria even developed enzymes that could kill the antibiotic. Over the decades, from the first use of antibiotics most known diseases have built up an immunity against one or more antibiotics.

Bacterial mechanisms for conferring immunity against antibiotics

The ability of bacteria to resist antibiotics can be explained partly by the Darwinian theory of evolution. Darwin was the first to point out how the ability of organisms to spontaneously change their genetic identity to form mutant variations aided in their ability to survive sudden changes in the environment. Most of the mutations will not be to the organism's advantage, but some may help to overcome a sudden change in the environment. In most species this process takes long periods of time, but microbes reproduce about every 20 minutes. With their fast rate of mutation, it does not take very long until a survival adaptation takes place.

If an antibiotic destroys a colony of bacteria but there is one that survives as a result of a mutant change, that one, when it reproduces, will then form a new colony of antibiotic–resistant bacteria. Since antibiotics also attack and kill harmless bacteria, these harmless bacteria also begin to mutate to resistant strains. Harmful bacteria may be able to pick up the resistant gene from the harmless bacteria by a process known as conjugation. The two come together and transfer genetic material between themselves through a tube.

Toxic bacteria may become infected by viruses. These bacteria then pass their toxic genes to the infecting viruses. Later the viruses pass the toxic gene on to less harmful bacteria. That action results in a new population of pathogenic bacteria. The viral–bacterial exchange of genes is called transduction. Another mechanism of transmitting new pathogens through the human population comes as a consequence of clearing remote jungles or forests where animals in the area may infect people for the first time. The belief is that AIDS may have been transmitted that way through jungle monkeys. Lyme disease, which is a bacterial infection, was carried by deer and mice in the forests. As people began to enter these environments as hikers and home builders, they made contact with the ticks which carry the Lyme disease bacteria.

Measures to control the spread of antibiotic resistant disease

Medical scientists have been organizing to inform society of the dangers of the misuse of antibiotics. In 1981 an international organization called the Alliance for Prudent Use of Antibiotics was formed. Some of the practices that lead to antibiotic misuse are:

1) Patients stop taking antibiotics before the infection is cured. The weak pathogens are killed but the resistant ones stay on.

2) Antibiotics are sometimes used for viral infections even though they do not work against the viruses. This misuse leads to killing the harmless bacteria and opening the way for the more toxic ones.

3) Antibiotics are sold over the counter in many countries. People then begin to self–medicate themselves inappropriately.

4) Antibiotics in animal feed leads to bacterial immunity against antibiotics.

There is a growing consensus among doctors that vaccines are a better way to fight bacterial infections than antibiotics. Vaccines are safer than antibiotics and they prepare the immune system against an invading pathogen in such a way as to make it difficult for the invader to set up a defense against each individual's immune system. Vaccines against a wide range of diseases have proven effective over the years and new ones have been developed for pneumonia and tuberculosis. One is soon expected for streptococcus A as well.

The future use of antibiotics, the "wonder drugs" of earlier decades, has been challenged by the resistant mechanisms of the microbe world. If antibiotics will continue to play a vital role in the treatment of infectious disease in the future, then there will be a need for

KEY TERMS

Allergic response—Skin rashes from penicillin and other antibiotics.

Antibacterial—Bacteriostatic chemical antibiotics like the sulfa drugs.

Antibiotic resistance—The mutation of pathogens to fight off antibiotics.

Bactericidal—Antibiotics that kill bacteria by destroying their cell walls and other lethal mechanisms.

Fungi mold—Lower types of non–chlorophyll from which the first antibiotic, penicillin, is derived.

Gram–positive/negative—A staining process which divides bacteria into two major groups by the structure of their cell walls.

Pathogen—A disease–causing microbe.

Semisynthetic antibiotics—Combinations of synthetic antibiotics with natural ones.

Soil bacteria—Bacteria found in the soil which destroy other bacteria.

Sulfonamides—The second family of antibacterial drugs after the sulfa drugs.

continuous medical research for newer types of drugs, for educational programs for the best use of antibiotics, and for control measures to protect their continued use.

See also Infection.

Further Reading:

Clayman, Charles B., ed., *Guide to Prescription and Over–the–Counter Drugs*. New York: Random House, 1988.

Gold, Mark S. and Michael Boyette. *Wonder Drugs: How They Work*. New York: Simon & Schuster, 1987.

Lemonick, Michael D. "The Killers," *Time*, September 12, 1994, 60–69.

Levy, Stuart B. *The Antibiotic Paradox*. New York: Plenum Press, 1992.

Jordan P. Richman

Antibody and antigen

Antibodies, or Y–shaped immunoglobulins, are proteins found in the blood where they help to fight against foreign substances called antigens. Antigens, which are usually proteins or polysaccharides, stimulate the immune system to produce antibodies. The antibodies inactivate the antigen and help to remove it from the body. While antigens can be the source of infections from pathogenic bacteria and viruses, organic molecules detrimental to the body from internal or environmental sources also act as antigens.

Once the immune system has created an antibody for an antigen whose attack it has survived, it continues to produce antibodies for subsequent attacks from that antigen. This long–term memory of the immune system provides the basis for the practice of vaccination against disease. The immune system, with its production of antibodies, has the ability to recognize, remember, and destroy well over a million different antigens.

There are several types of simple proteins known as globulins in the blood: alpha, beta, and gamma. Antibodies are gamma globulins produced by B lymphocytes when antigens enter the body. The gamma globulins are referred to as immunoglobulins. In medical literature they appear in the abbreviated form as Ig. Each antigen stimulates the production of a specific antibody (Ig).

Antibodies are all in a Y–shape with differences in the upper branch of the Y. These structural differences of amino acids in each of the antibodies enables the individual antibody to recognize an antigen. An antigen has on its surface a combining site that the antibody recognizes from the combining sites on the arms of its Y–shaped structure. In response to the antigen that has called it forth, the antibody wraps its two combining sites like a "lock" around the "key" of the antigen combining sites to destroy it.

An antibody's mode of action varies with different types of antigens. With its two–armed Y–shaped structure, the antibody can attack two antigens at the same time with each arm. If the antigen is a toxin produced by pathogenic bacteria that cause an infection like diphtheria or tetanus, the binding process of the antibody will nullify the antigen's toxin. When an antibody surrounds a virus, such as one that causes influenza, it prevents it from entering other body cells. Another mode of action by the antibodies is to call forth the assistance of a group of immune agents which operate in what is known as the plasma complement system. First the antibodies will coat infectious bacteria and then white blood cells will complete the job by engulfing the bacteria, destroying them, and then removing them from the body.

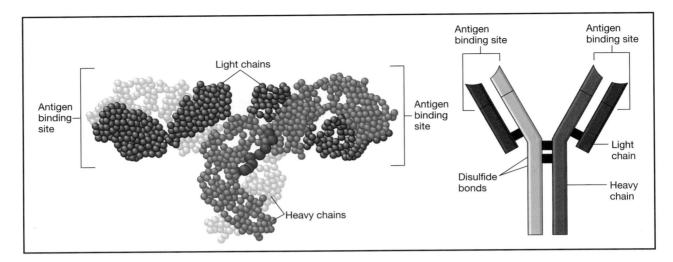

An IgG molecule (left) is shown schematically (right).

Functions of antibody types

There are five different antibody types, each one having a different Y–shaped configuration and function. They are the Ig G, A, M, D, and E antibodies.

IgG

IgG is the most common type of antibody. It is the chief Ig against microbes. It acts by coating the microbe to hasten its removal by other immune system cells. It gives lifetime or long–standing immunity against infectious diseases. It is highly mobile, passing out of the blood stream and between cells, going from organs to the skin where it neutralizes surface bacteria and other invading microorganisms. This mobility allows the antibody to pass through the placenta of the mother to her fetus, thus conferring a temporary defense to the unborn child.

After birth, IgG is passed along to the child through the mother's milk, assuming that she nurses the baby. But some of the Ig will still be retained in the baby from the placental transmission until it has time to develop its own antibodies. Placental transfer of antibodies does not occur in horses, pigs, cows, and sheep. They pass their antibodies to their offspring only through their milk.

IgA

This antibody is found in body fluids such as tears, saliva, and other bodily secretions. It is an antibody that provides a first line of defense against invading pathogens and allergens, and is the body's major defense against viruses. It is found in large quantities in the bloodstream and protects other wet surfaces of the body. While they have basic similarities, each IgA is further differentiated to deal with the specific types of invaders that present at different openings of the body.

IgM

Since this is the largest of the antibodies, it is effective against larger microorganisms. Because of its large size (it combines 5 Y–shaped units), it remains in the bloodstream where it provides an early and diffuse protection against invading antigens, while the more specific and effective IgG antibodies are being produced by the plasma cells.

The ratio of IgM and IgG cells can indicate the various stages of a disease. In an early stage of a disease there are more IgM antibodies. The presence of a greater number of IgG antibodies would indicate a later stage of the disease. IgM antibodies usually form clusters that are in the shape of a star.

IgD

This antibody appears to act in conjunction with B and T–cells to help them in location of antigens. Research continues on establishing more precise functions of this antibody.

IgE

The antibody responsible for allergic reactions, IgE acts by attaching to cells in the skin called mast cells and basophil cells (mast cells that circulate in the body). In the presence of environmental antigens like

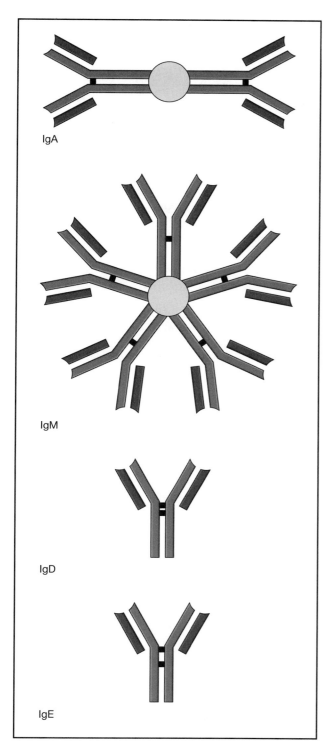

Diagrams of the other classes of antibody molecules.

pollens, foods, chemicals, and drugs, IgE releases histamines from the mast cells. The histamines cause the nasal inflammation (swollen tissues, running nose, sneezing) and the other discomforts of hay fever or other types of allergic responses, such as hives, asthma, and in rare cases, anaphylactic shock (a life–threatening condition brought on by an allergy to a drug or insect bite). An explanation for the role of IgE in allergy is that it was an antibody that was useful to early man to prepare the immune system to fight parasites. This function is presently overextended in reacting to environmental antigens.

The presence of antibodies can be detected whenever antigens such as bacteria or red blood cells are found to agglutinate (clump together), or where they precipitate out of solution, or where there has been a stimulation of the plasma complement system. Antibodies are also used in laboratory tests for blood typing when transfusions are needed and in a number of different types of clinical tests, such as the Wassermann test for syphilis and tests for typhoid fever and infectious mononucleosis.

Types of antigens

By definition, anything that makes the immune system respond to produce antibodies is an antigen. Antigens are such living foreign bodies as viruses, bacteria, and fungi that cause disease and infection. Or they can be dust, chemicals, pollen grains, or food proteins that cause allergic reactions.

Antigens which cause allergic reactions are called allergens. A large percentage of any population, in varying degrees, is allergic to animals, fabrics, drugs, foods, and products for the home and industry. Not all antigens are foreign bodies. They may be produced in the body itself. For example, cancer cells are antigens that the body produces. In an attempt to differentiate its "self" from foreign substances, the immune system will reject an organ transplant that is trying to maintain the body or a blood transfusion that is not of the same blood type as itself.

There are some substances such as nylon, plastic, or Teflon that rarely display antigenic properties. For that reason nonantigenic substances are used for artificial blood vessels, component parts in heart pacemakers, and needles for hypodermic syringes. These substances seldom trigger an immune system response, but there are other substances that are highly antigenic and will almost certainly cause an immune system reaction. Practically everyone reacts to certain chemicals, for example, the resin from the poison ivy plant, the venoms from insect and reptile bites, solvents, formalin, and asbestos. Viral and bacterial infections also generally trigger an antibody response from the immune system. For most people penicillin is not antigenic, but for some there can be an immunological response that ranges from severe skin rashes to death.

Another type of antigen is found in the tissue cells of organ transplants. If, for example, a kidney is transplanted, the surface cells of the kidney contain antigens which the new host body will begin to reject. These are called human leukocyte antigens (HLA), and there are four major types of HLA subdivided into further groups. In order to avoid organ rejection, tissue samples are taken to see how well the new organ tissues match for HLA compatibility with the recipient's body. Drugs will also be used to suppress and control the production of helper/suppressor T–cells and the amount of antibodies.

Red blood cells with the ABO antigens pose a problem when the need for blood transfusions arises. Before a transfusion, the blood is tested for type so that a compatible type is used. Type A blood has one kind of antigen and type B another. A person with type AB blood has both the A and B antigen. Type O blood has no antigens. A person with type A blood would require either type A or O for a successful transfusion. Type B and AB would be rejected. Type B blood would be compatible with a B donor or an O donor. Since O has no antigens, it is considered to be the universal donor. Type AB is the universal recipient because its antibodies can accept A, B, AB, or O.

One way of getting around the problem of blood types in transfusion came about as a result of World War II. The great need for blood transfusions led to the development of blood plasma, blood in which the red and white cells are removed. Without the red blood cells, blood could be quickly administered to a wounded soldier without the delay of checking for the blood antigen type.

Another antigenic blood condition can affect the life of newborn babies. Rhesus disease (also called erythroblastosis fetalis) is a blood disease caused by the incompatibility of Rh factors between a fetus and a mother's red blood cells. When an Rh negative mother gives birth to an Rh positive baby, any transfer of the baby's blood to the mother will result in the production of antibodies against Rh positive red blood cells. At her next pregnancy the mother will then pass those antibodies against Rh positive blood to the fetus. If this fetus is Rh positive, it will suffer from Rh disease. Tests for Rh blood factors are routinely administered during pregnancy.

Vaccination

Western medicine's interest in the practice of vaccination began in the eighteenth century. This practice probably originated with the ancient Chinese and was adopted by Turkish doctors. A British aristocrat, Lady Mary Wortley Montagu (1689–1762), discovered a crude form of vaccination taking place in a lower–class section of the city of Constantinople while she was traveling through Turkey. She described her experience in a letter to a friend. Children who were injected with pus from a smallpox victim did not die from the disease but built up an immunity to it. Rejected in England by most doctors who thought the practice was barbarous, smallpox vaccination was adopted by a few English physicians of the period. They demonstrated an almost 100% rate of effectiveness in smallpox prevention.

By the end of the eighteenth century, Edward Jenner (1749–1823) improved the effectiveness of vaccination by injecting a subject with cowpox, then later injecting the same subject with smallpox. The experiment showed that immunity against a disease could be achieved by using a vaccine that did not contain the specific pathogen for the disease. In the nineteenth century, Louis Pasteur (1822–1895) proposed the germ theory of disease. He went on to develop a rabies vaccine that was made from the spinal cords of rabid rabbits. Through a series of injections starting from the weakest strain of the disease, Pasteur was able after 13 injections to prevent the death of a child who had been bitten by a rabid dog.

There is now greater understanding of the principles of vaccines and the immunizations they bring because of our knowledge of the role played by antibodies and antigens within the immune system. Vaccination provides active immunity because our immune systems have had the time to recognize the invading germ and then to begin production of specific antibodies for the germ. The immune system can continue producing new antibodies whenever the body is attacked again by the same organism or resistance can be bolstered by booster shots of the vaccine.

Monoclonal antibodies

For research purposes there were repeated efforts to obtain a laboratory specimen of one single antibody in sufficient quantities to further study the mechanisms and applications of antibody production. Success came in 1975 when two British biologists, César Milstein (1927–) and Georges Kohler (1946–) were able to clone immunoglobulin (Ig) cells of a particular type that came from multiple myeloma cells. Multiple myeloma is a rare form of cancer in which white blood cells keep turning out a specific type of Ig antibody at the expense of others, thus making the individual more susceptible to outside infection. By combining the myeloma cell with any selected antibody–producing cell, large numbers of specific monoclonal antibodies can be produced. Researchers have used other animals, such as mice, to produce hybrid antibodies which increase the range of known antibodies.

Monoclonal antibodies are used as drug delivery vehicles in the treatment of specific diseases, and they also act as catalytic agents for protein reactions in various sites of the body. They are also used for diagnosis of different types of diseases and for complex analysis of a wide range of biological substances. There is hope that they will be as effective as enzymes in chemical and technological processes and that they will play a role in genetic engineering research.

See also Allergy; Anaphylaxis; Blood; Germ theory; Immune system; Rh factor; Smallpox; Transplant, surgical; Vaccine.

Further Reading:

Barrett, James T. *Textbook of Immunology.* St. Louis: Mosby, 1988.

Friedlander, Mark P., and Terry M. Phillips. *Winning the War Within.* Emmaus, PA: Rodale Press, 1986.

Joneja, Janice V., and Leonard Bielory. *Understanding Allergy, Sensitivity, and Immunity.* New Brunswick, NJ: Rutgers University Press, 1990.

Sell, Stewart. *Basic Immunology.* New York: Elsevier, 1987.

Weiner, Michael A. *Maximum Immunity.* Boston: Houghton Mifflin, 1986.

Jordan P. Richman

Anticoagulants

Anticoagulants are complex organic or synthetic compounds, often carbohydrates, that help prevent the clotting or coagulation of blood. The most widely used of these is heparin, which blocks the formation of thromboplastin, an important clotting factor in the blood. Most anticoagulants are used for treating existing thromboses (clots that form in blood vessels) to prevent further clotting. Oral anticoagulants, such as warfarin and dicumarol, are effective treatments for venous thromboembolisms (a blockage in a vein caused by a clot), but heparin is usually prescribed for treating the more dangerous arterial thrombosis.

Anticoagulants are often mistakenly referred to as blood thinners. Their real role is not to thin the blood but to inhibit the biochemical series of events that lead to the unnatural coagulation of blood inside unsevered blood vessels, a major cause of stroke and heart attack.

The coagulation process

In 1887, Russian scientist Ivan Pavlov first postulated the existence of natural anticlotting factors in animals and humans. His extensive studies of blood circulation led him to the realization that when blood reaches the lungs, it loses some of its ability to coagulate, a process aided, he believed, by the addition of some anticlotting substance. In 1892, A. Schmidt, the father of the enzymatic theory of blood coagulation, published the first data proving the existence of coagulation–inhibiting agents in liver, spleen, and lymph node cells. He later isolated this agent from liver tissue and demonstrated its anticoagulant properties. In 1905, P. Morawitz hypothesized that thrombosis might be effectively controlled by reducing the coagulation properties of the blood using antithrombins found in plasma.

Most modern theories of coagulation are scientifically complex and involve numerous substances known as clotting factors. The major mechanism of clot formation involves the conversion of fibrinogen, a highly soluble plasma protein, into fibrin, a stringy protein. There are a number of steps in this conversion process. First, when blood vessels are severed, prothrombin activator is produced. This agent's interaction with calcium ions causes prothrombin, an alpha globulin produced by the liver, to undergo conversion to thrombin. Next, thrombin, acting as an enzyme, triggers chemical reactions in fibrinogen, binding the molecules together end to end in long threads. Once these fibrin structures are formed, they adhere to the damaged area of the blood vessel, creating a mesh that traps blood cells and platelets. The resulting sticky mass, a clot, acts as a plug to seal the vessel and prevent further blood loss.

Thrombosis and embolism

Normally, clots form only in response to tissue injury. The natural flow of blood keeps thrombin from congregating in any one area. Clots can usually form only when the blood flows slowly or when wounds are opened. A clot that forms in a vessel abnormally is known as a thrombus; if the clot breaks free and is swept up along through the blood stream to another location, it is known as an embolus. These abnormal formations are thought to be caused by condition changes in the linings of blood vessels. Atherosclerosis and other diseases that damage arterial linings may lead directly to the formation of blood clots. Anticoagulants are used to treat these conditions.

Heparin

The first effective anticoagulant agent was discovered in 1916 by a medical student named McLean, who isolated a specific coagulation inhibitor from the liver of a dog. This substance, known as heparin because it is found in high concentrations in the liver, could not be widely produced until 1933, when Canadians Scott and Charles began extracting the substance from the lungs of cattle. In 1937, Crafford and Murray began using heparin to treat and prevent surgical thrombosis and embolism.

Heparin is a complex organic acid found in all mammalian tissues that contain mast cells (allergic reaction mediators). It plays a direct role in all phases of blood coagulation. In animals and humans, it is produced by mast cells or heparinocytes, which are found in the connective tissues of the capillaries, inside blood vessels, and in the spleen, kidneys, and lymph nodes. There are several types of heparin in widescale clinical use, all of which differ in physiologic activity. Various salts of heparin have been created, including sodium, barium, benzidine, and others. The most widely used form in medical practice is heparin sulfate.

How it works

Heparin works by inhibiting or inactivating the three major clotting factors—thrombin, thromboplastin, and prothrombin. It slows the process of thromboplastin synthesis, decelerates the conversion of prothrombin to thrombin, and inhibits the effects of thrombin on fibrinogen, blocking its conversion to fibrin. The agent also causes an increase in the number of negatively charged ions in the vascular wall, which helps prevent the formation of intravascular clots.

Heparin is administered either by periodic injections or by an infusion pump. The initial dose is usually 5,000 units, followed by 1,000 units per hour, depending on the patient's weight, age, and other factors. The therapy usually lasts for seven to 10 days. Heparin is also used in the treatment of deep vein thrombosis, a serious surgical complication which is also associated with traumatic injury. This condition can lead to immediate death from pulmonary embolism or produce long-term, adverse effects. Patients with pelvic or lower extremity fractures, spinal cord injuries, a previous thromboembolism, varicose veins, and those over age 40 are most at risk. Low-dose heparin is a proven therapy and is associated with only a minimal risk of irregular bleeding.

Oral anticoagulants

The development of oral anticoagulants can be linked directly to a widespread cattle epidemic in the U.S. and Canada during the mid-1920s. A scientist named Roderick traced the cause of this outbreak to the cattle feed, a fodder containing spoiled sweet clover, which caused the cattle to bleed to death internally. Mixing alfalfa, a food rich in vitamin K, into the fodder seemed to prevent the disease. In 1941, Campbell and Clay showed that the decaying sweet clover contained a substance which produced an anti-vitamin-K effect. They isolated this substance from the sweet clover, calling it dicumarol. During the 1940s, the agent was synthesized and widely used in the United States to treat postoperative thrombosis. In 1948, a more powerful synthetic compound was derived for use, initially as a rodenticide. This substance, known as warfarin, is now one of the most widely prescribed oral

KEY TERMS

Dicumarol—The first mass–produced oral anti-coagulant was derived from sweet clover.

Fibrinogen—A soluble plasma protein that, in the presence of thrombin, is converted into a more insoluble protein, fibrin, during the coagulation process.

Heparin—The most widely used and effective anticoagulant, it is found naturally in mammalian tissues.

Thrombin—This plasma substance works as an enzyme to cause a reaction in fibrinogen, chemically changing it into fibrin.

Thrombus—A blood clot that forms abnormally in a vessel.

anticoagulants. There are numerous other agents in clinical use. Acenocoumarol, ethyl biscoumacetate, and phenprocoumon, which are seldom used in the United States, are widely prescribed elsewhere in the world.

Most oral anticoagulants work by suppressing the action of vitamin K in the coagulation process. These agents are extremely similar in chemical structure to vitamin K and effectively displace it from the enzymatic process which is necessary for the synthesis of prothrombin and other clotting factors. Indeed, one of the ways to treat irregular bleeding, the most common side effect of oral anticoagulants, is vitamin K therapy.

In addition to bleeding, another side effect of oral anticoagulant use is negative interaction with numerous other drugs and substances. Even unaided, oral anticoagulants can have serious effects. For example, use of warfarin during pregnancy can cause birth defects, fetal hemorrhages, and miscarriage. Dicumarol, the original oral anticoagulant, is seldom used today because it causes painful intestinal problems and is clinically inferior to warfarin.

Over the past two decades, the search for new, less toxic anticoagulants has led to the development and use of a number of synthetic agents, including fibrinlysin, thrombolytin, and urokinase. The enzyme streptokinase, developed in the early 1980s, is routinely injected into the coronary artery to stop a heart attack. Another new agent, tissue plasminogen activator, a blood protein, is being generated is large quantities using recombinant–DNA techniques. The search is

on for a natural anticlotting factor that can be produced in mass quantities.

See also Acetylsalicylic acid; Blood; Embolism; Thrombosis.

Further Reading:

Gilman, Alfred and Alfred Gosh. *The Pharmacological Basis of Therapeutics*. New York: Pergamon Press, 1990.
Rubenstein, Edward and Daniel Federman, eds. *Scientific American Medicine*. New York: Scientific American, 1994.

Anticonvulsants

Anticonvulsants are drugs designed to prevent the seizures or convulsions typical of epilepsy or other convulsant disorders.

Petit mal seizures may be so subtle that an observer will not notice that an individual is having one. Grand mal seizures are more dramatic and unmistakable. The patient may cry out, lose consciousness, and drop to the ground with muscle spasms in the extremities, trunk, and neck. The patient may remain unconscious after the seizure.

Anticonvulsant drugs are available only by prescription because they are so potent and toxic if taken in excess. Their consumption must be carefully monitored by blood tests. Once an individual has been diagnosed with epilepsy he must continue taking the anticonvulsant drugs for life.

The barbiturates, such as phenobarbital, mephobarbital, and metharbital, are sometimes used as anticonvulsants. Of the family of barbiturate drugs, these are the only three that are satisfactory for use over a long period of time. They act directly on the central nervous system and can produce effects such as drowsiness, hypnosis, deep coma, or death, depending upon the dose taken. Because they are habit forming drugs, the barbiturates probably are the least desirable to use as anticonvulsant drugs.

Phenytoin is a close relative to the barbiturates, but differs in chemical structure. Phenytoin acts on the motor cortex of the brain to prevent the spread of the signal that initiates a seizure. Sudden withdrawal of the drug after a patient has taken it for a long period of time can have serious consequences. The patient can be plunged into a constant epileptic state (*staus epilepticus*). Lowering the dosage or taking the patient off phenytoin must be done gradually.

A third class of anticonvulsant drugs, the succinimides, suppress the brain wave pattern leading to seizures and stabilizes the cortex against them. These are useful drugs in the treatment of petit mal epilepsy, and like phenytoin, must be withdrawn slowly.

Valproic acid compounds also are antiepileptic drugs, though their mechanism of action is unknown. One of their major side effects is liver toxicity, though that appears most often in young patients and in those who are taking more than one anticonvulsant drug.

See also Epilepsy.

Antidepressants

Antidepressants are a group of medicines used in the treatment of clinical depression. Depression is a term used to describe a normal state of mind as well as a serious mental disorder. Normal depression is a mood state everyone experiences that involves short–lived states of sadness, pessimism, a sense of inadequacy, and other negative feelings. Clinical depression involves the same negative feelings as normal depression but in a more intense and long–lasting form. In addition, a number of physical symptoms are present, including problems sleeping, a loss of or great increase in appetite, and frequent fatigue. It appears that various degrees and types of depression exist. Those with severe depression may experience such psychotic symptoms as hallucinations or delusions, and some depressed individuals may try to injure themselves or attempt suicide. Four main types of antidepressants have been used to combat these symptoms: the sympathomimetic stimulants, tricyclics, monoamine oxidase inhibitors (MAOIs), and the newer heterocyclic or second–generation antidepressants.

The positive effects of drugs on depression were discovered accidentally in the 1950s when it was observed that MAOIs being used to treat tuberculosis elevated the mood of some of the individuals who were depressed. This discovery, eventually lead to the hypothesis that depression is related to the neurochemical catecholamine. This is because MAOIs inhibit the activity of the enzyme monoamine oxidase, which in turn increases the concentrations of catecholamines between nerve cells.

A very brief explanation of how neurochemicals and the nervous system work is in order. First, nerves do not actually connect physically. Instead they are separated by a space called the synaptic cleft. Because they do not connect, messages are sent between them through the synaptic cleft using neurotransmitters. Neurotransmitters are defined as chemical substances released into the synaptic cleft following nerve impulses. After release, the neurotransmitter binds with the receptor of the nerve that is across the synaptic cleft (the postsynaptic nerve) for a short time until it is released back into the cleft. Much of it will be reabsorbed into the original nerve cell from which it was released. MAO and a second enzyme act to metabolize a small portion of the neurotransmitter. So far, nine chemical substances that act as neurotransmitters have been identified, two of which show strong links to depression. These are norepinephrine and serotonin. Antidepressants act on one or more particular aspects of the transmission between nerve cells.

Sympathomimetic stimulants

These stimulants, which include drugs such as Amphetamine and Dextroamphetamine, encourage release of the stored neurotransmitter and block its reabsorption from the synaptic cleft. These drugs produce only short–lived effects and tend to be addictive. For these reasons their use as antidepressants has become uncommon.

Tricyclic antidepressants

Characterized by a three–ring chemical structure, tricyclic antidepressants were discovered in the 1950s and include drugs such as Imipramine and Desipramine. In the 1950s, doctors tested Imipramine on schizophrenic patients and found that, while it did not help the patients with their delusions or hallucinations, it did elevate the mood and energy of those who were depressed.

Generally, tricyclics prevent the reuptake of norepinephrine and/or serotonin from the synapse. Different specific tricyclics have different effects on norepinephrine and/or serotonin. While the exact antidepressant action of tricyclics is not fully understood, it appears that they cause certain types of receptor cells to sink back into the cell membrane and thus become temporarily inaccessible to neurotransmitter(s).

Most patients take from three to four weeks to notice changes in their symptoms after beginning to take tricyclics. They will usually show improved patterns of sleep after a few days, a general re–awakening of interest in life, an elevation in mood, and recognition of improved behavior from other people—even though the depressed person may not recognize this improvement in themselves.

Some side effects of tricyclic antidepressants are caused by their blocking the acetylcholine receptors just at the point where these receptors make contact with certain internal organs. This blockade occurs at the sites of the salivary glands, the iris of the eyes, and the intestinal tract, and thus may lead to dry mouth, blurred vision, and constipation. They are called anticholinergic effects, and they are more of an annoyance than a cause for undue concern. Drowsiness may also be a side effect of tricyclic use, and while this may help some individuals get better rest, others may be frustrated by not being able to do all the things they would normally be able to do. If they have to drive or operate machinery they may have to be switched to a tricyclic with a lower sedative effect. Some of these side effects can be minimized quite easily; for instance, candy or gum can help with the condition of dry mouth by stimulating the salivary glands, and constipation can be diminished by laxatives, high fiber diets, eating fruits and vegetables, and keeping fluid intake high.

Monoamine oxidase inhibitors (MAOIs)

MAOIs include drugs such as Isocarboxazid, Phenelzine, and Tranylcypromine. The first MAOI to be discovered was an antibiotic called iproniazid which was being used to treat patients with tuberculosis. It was found that while this antibiotic was not successful in treating tuberculosis, it did help to put the tubercular patients in such a cheerful state of mind that they began to neglect taking care of their illness. MAOIs inhibit the metabolic activity of the enzyme monoamine oxidase, which leads to an increased concentration of norepinephrine and other neurotransmitters in the synaptic cleft. It is believed that monoamine oxidase breaks down natural stimulants like norepinephrine. One theory of how MAOIs work maintains that the increased storage of these important neurotransmitters at critical sites in the nervous system relieves depressive effects caused by their absence.

One of the major drawbacks of MAOIs is the care that users have to exert in their diet as they are prohibited from eating a number of foods that can interact negatively with the MAOI. MAOIs may also have adverse side effects when used with other drugs. Additional side effects may include lowered blood pressure, reduced sex drive, insomnia, and anxiety. Indeed, because of their potential side effects and dietary restrictions, MAOIs are not used very frequently today. Nonetheless, MAOIs may be called for instead of tricyclic antidepressants for treating patients with cardiovascular disease. Also, they may be indicated for certain types of depression with symptoms such as anxiety, overeating, fear, and hypochondria.

Heterocyclic or second generation

These are non–tricyclic, non–MAOIs that were introduced in the 1980s. Specific drugs include Amoxapine, Maprotiline, Trazodone, Buproprion, and Fluoxetine. We will only cover only Fluoxetine (which has the trade name of Prozac) here as it is now widely prescribed to treat moderate to severe chronic depression.

Fluoxetine (Prozac)

Fluoxetine is a newer antidepressant that has received much attention because it seems to have fewer side effects than the tricyclics and MAOIs, and it has proven effective in treating those with moderate to severe chronic depression. This is as opposed to more severe, rapid onset depressions that usually respond to tricyclics. Unlike many of the tricyclics and MAOIs, fluoxetine's action is very specific, serving to inhibit the reuptake of serotonin alone. It may have fewer side effects than tricyclics and MAOIs because its action in the nervous system is more specific than theirs.

Generally, fluoxetine is very well tolerated by most people. Nonetheless, some of the possible side effects are nervousness, insomnia, headache, decreased sexual function, diarrhea, and nausea.

Fluoxetine is currently being used to treat a wide range of psychological problems other than depression and depression–related disorders. In 1993, total sales of fluoxetine equaled that of all other antidepressants combined, and an estimated 10 million people are currently using fluoxetine and its related medications world–wide.

Based on research, many physicians believe that fluoxetine, though it has fewer side effects and is easier to administer, is not really any more effective in treating depression than tricyclics or MAOIs. Indeed, some studies have found tricyclics to be more effective in treating some cases of depression than fluoxetine. Overall though, fluoxetine's major advantage over tricyclics is fewer side effects and its effectiveness in treating less severe types of depression.

See also Depression.

Further Reading:

Barnhart, E., ed. *Physician's Desk Reference*. Montvale, NJ: Medical Economics Data, 1992.
Begley, Sharon, Geoffrey Cowley, and Jerry Adler. "Beyond Prozac," *Newsweek*, February 7, 1994, pp. 36–43.

Papolos, Demitri and Janice Papolos. *Overcoming Depression.* New York: Harper & Row, 1987.

Sargent, Marilyn. *Depression* (pamphlet). Washington, D.C.: National Institute of Mental Health, 1990.

Simon, Gilbert I. and Harold Silverman. *The Pill Book*, 4th ed. New York: Bantam, 1990.

Wolman, B.B. and G Stricker. Editors. 1990. *Depressive Disorders: Facts, Theories, and Treatment Methods.* New York: John Wiley & Sons.

Jordan P. Richman and Marie Doorey

Antihelmintics

Antihelmintics are drugs used to kill parasitic worms (from the Greek word *helmins*, worm). These preparations are also called vermicides.

Worm infestations are among the most common parasitic diseases of man. Often the life cycle of the worm begins when a child playing in dirt ingests the eggs of the worm. The egg hatches in the child's digestive tract and the worms begin their unending quest to reproduce, to make more eggs to infect more humans.

Parasitic worms may be either round (called nematodes), or a segmented, flat configuration (called cestodes). Worms are most problematic in areas where sanitation is poor.

The most common parasitic worm infestation in nontropical climates is by the pinworm (*Enterobias vermicularis*), which is highly infectious and may affect an entire family before the infection is diagnosed. At any time, up to 20% of the childhood population has pinworms and may jump to 90% among children who are institutionalized, as in an orphanage.

Other roundworm infections are by the hookworm and whipworm, either of which can gain entrance to the body by penetrating the skin of a bare foot. Trichinosis derives from eating raw or undercooked pork containing the worm larva.

Flat, segmented worms, also called tapeworms, can originate in raw beef, pork, or fish. These worms attach their heads to the walls of the intestine and shed square segments that are packages of eggs.

Most roundworm infestations can be cleared by taking pyrantel pamoate, a drug recently approved for sale over the counter. It was developed in 1972 as a prescription drug. Because it is given in the form of a pill or syrup in a single dose, based on body weight, without serious side effects, pyrantel was approved for nonprescription sale. This medication relaxes the muscles the worm holds on to on the intestinal wall so the worm is passed out with the normal fecal movement.

Other, more potent drugs are available by prescription to treat worm infections. They include piperazine, tetrachloroethylene, and thiabendazole for roundworms and niclosamide for tapeworms.

See also Parasites.

Larry Blaser

Antihistamines

Antihistamines are substances that block the action of a naturally occurring chemical called histamine. Antihistamines are available by prescription and over–the–counter. They are given frequently to ease the symptoms of a head cold or allergy. However, scientific findings have demonstrated that antihistamines are not effective in treating symptoms of the common cold.

Histamine

Histamine is a chemical that under normal circumstances is bound in granules within certain types of connective tissue cells called mast cells, which are widely distributed throughout the body. In this form, histamine is inactive and without influence over any bodily function. When histamine is released by trauma or an encounter with certain allergy–initiating substances, its effect is rapid and dramatic.

Histamine is an important mediator in the early stages of inflammation. In its active form, histamine causes blood vessels to become more permeable, allowing fluid and white blood cells to leak out into the surrounding tissue. It also produces the sensation of itching. These effects of histamine produce the symptoms of an individual with a springtime allergy—watery eyes, sniffles, and an itchy nose.

Antihistamines

Antihistamines were developed in France, and introduced into medicine in 1942. A few years later they were introduced in the United States, where they have proved useful in easing symptoms of severe allergic reactions. Antihistamines block the effect of histamines by occupying the receptor site on the very cells that histamine seeks out. By occupying histamine receptors, the drug prevents histamine from causing blood vessels to become leaky, and reduces the sensation of itching. Other properties of antihistamines decrease fluid production. Thus, the individual who has an allergy can take an antihistamine and be relieved of the itchy nose and watery eyes that are symptoms of the allergy. The antihistamine does not cure the allergy; the patient continues to be sensitive to various allergens (allergens are those substances which trigger the allergic response, such as dust, pollen, cat hair, and tobacco smoke). However, when taking an antihistamine an individual can encounter an allergen, yet remain free of symptoms.

The human body has two types of histamine receptor. H1 receptors are active in the allergic response

---

KEY TERMS

....

Receptor—An area of specialized protein on the surface of a cell to which another chemical can attach and exert some influence on the cell.

---

described above. H2 receptors increase gastric acid secretion and are important in ulcer formation. Several drugs used in ulcer treatment block H2 receptors, thus limiting gastric acid secretion. These drugs include cimetidine (Tagamet) and ranitidine (Zantac); formerly available only by prescription, they are now available in lower strength over–the–counter.

The antihistamine drugs also have significant side effects, the most outstanding of which is drowsiness. Anyone taking an antihistamine should not drive, fly an airplane, operate any form of machinery, go scuba diving, work in a high place or on a ladder, or carry out any other form of occupation that may require full alertness. Also, anyone taking an antihistamine should not consume an alcoholic beverage or any tranquilizing medication. The antihistamine will enhance the soporific (sleep–inducing) effects of either of the other chemicals. The potency of the antihistamines' ability to induce sleep is further demonstrated by the fact that all sleep medications available without prescription are antihistamines. A new type of antihistamine (e.g., terfendine or Seldane) does not cross the blood–brain barrier and therefore does not cause sleepiness.

Strong antihistamines are available by prescription and others, of milder strength, are a prominent over–the–counter medication. Americans spend approximately $1 billion on over–the–counter anithistamines every year, many of which are incorrectly used to treat the common cold.

See also Allergy; Histamine.

Further Reading:

Griffith, H. W. *Complete Guide to Prescription and Non–Prescription Drugs.* Los Angeles, CA: The Body Press. 1991.

Zimmerman, D. R. *Zimmerman's Complete Guide to Nonprescription Drugs.* Detroit, MI: Visible Ink Press. 1993.

Larry Blaser

Anti–inflammatory agents

Anti–inflammatory agents counter the inflammatory process often associated with arthritis, gout, and other rheumatic conditions, as well as other ailments such as headaches. Inflammation causes a localized elevated temperature and, sometimes, pain. Some effective anti–inflammatories are available over–the–counter (without prescription), but for stubborn or long–term inflammatory conditions more powerful preparations are available by prescription.

Aspirin, ibuprofen, and naproxen are three nonsteroidal anti–inflammatory drugs (NSAIDs). They are classified as NSAIDs because they do not contain steroid compounds such as cortisone or their structure is not steroidal.

Aspirin

The oldest and most familiar anti–inflammatory drug is aspirin. It is inexpensive, effective, and well known in medical circles. Its side effects are readily understood and can be treated. Aspirin is commonly the first drug of choice for minor inflammations and pains.

Ancient Greeks chewed willow bark to relieve pain as did other civilizations through history. The active ingredient of willow bark was not synthesized until 1893. This ingredient is called acetylsalicylic acid (ASA). In 1900 the Bayer company marketed ASA powder and in 1918 the Sterling Company purchased the brand name and developed the first aspirin tablet.

Aspirin was a protected trade name until 1921 when a judge ruled that the word aspirin was so common that it could no longer be deemed a protected trademark. This decision allowed other drug companies to enter this lucrative market with their own products. Now aspirin is marketed as tablets, capsules, and powders with prices ranging from rock bottom to high cost. Whatever the form and whatever the cost, aspirin is acetylsalicylic acid and generally is produced in five–grain (325 mg) doses. This amount is considered to be the lowest an adult can take effectively.

How aspirin relieves inflammation is yet to be determined. The most accepted explanation is that aspirin inhibits prostaglandin production. Prostaglandins are a family of hydroxy fatty acids that can lower blood pressure, regulate acid secretion in the stomach, regulate body temperature, and control inflammatory processes, among other actions. There are six prostaglandins (designated A, B, C, etc.) and

each has a different action. They are likely targets for aspirin to counter inflammation.

Unfortunately aspirin also has toxic effects. As the technical name states it is an acid and it irritates the lining of the gastric tract possibly promoting bleeding or ulcers. People who have ulcers should take aspirin with caution and stop if bleeding or pain occurs. In high doses aspirin can be fatal.

Ibuprofen

A much newer product for relief of inflammation is the synthetic compound ibuprofen. Formerly available by prescription only, it was made available over–the–counter in 1984 in lower doses than used as a prescription drug. It is stronger than aspirin so its usage is recommended in lower doses. A 200 mg ibuprofen tablet is considered to be as effective as two aspirin (650 mg).

Although it does not have aspirin's history ibuprofen is considered safer because it has fewer side effects. (This may be the result of less experience.) It will not cause gastric problems or bleeding. It is especially useful for long–term treatment of arthritis inflammation. because ibuprofen and will not cause gastric problems or bleeding.

Naproxen

Naproxen is an NSAID for treatment of arthritis released onto the over–the–counter market in 1994. It has an advantage of fewer required dosages—twice daily as opposed to every four to six hours with aspirin or ibuprofen. Naproxen has side effects such as nausea, ringing in the ears, and skin rash. Its mechanism of action is believed to be similar to aspirin's, that is, it inhibits prostaglandin production.

See also Acetylsalicylic acid; Inflammation.

Further Reading:
The Complete Drug Reference: United States Pharmacopeia. Yonkers, NY: Consumer Report Books, 1992.
Zimmerman, David R. *Zimmerman's Complete Guide to Nonprescription Drugs.* Detroit: Gale Research, 1993.

Larry Blaser

Antimatter see **Antiparticle**

Antimetabolites

Antimetabolites are substances that interfere with the normal metabolism of an organism, thereby causing its death. They are widely used in the medical sciences because they have the ability to kill or inactivate microorganisms that cause disease. Terms such as antibacterials, antifungals, and antivirals are used to describe antimetabolites that act on bacteria, fungi, and viruses, respectively. In most cases, an antimetabolite works by inhibiting the action of an enzyme that is crucial to the process of metabolism. When the enzyme is immobilized, the series of reactions by which metabolism occurs is interrupted and the microorganism dies.

One of the classic examples of antimetabolite action is that of the sulfa drugs, discovered in the 1930s. Some examples of the sulfa drugs are sulfathiazole, sulfadiazine, and sulfacetamide. All sulfa drugs affect the metabolism of microorganisms in the same way. Under normal circumstances, a bacterium makes use of a compound known as para–aminobenzoic acid (PABA) to produce a second compound, folic acid. Folic acid is then used in the manufacture of nucleic acids in the bacterium.

Sulfa drugs have chemical structures that are very similar to that of PABA. When a sulfa compound is ingested by a bacterium, the microorganism attempts to make folic acid using the sulfa drug rather than PABA. The folic acid–like compound that is produced, however, can not be used to make nucleic acids. The bacterium's normal metabolism is interrupted, and it dies.

Antimetabolites generally work in one of three ways to interrupt the metabolism of an organism. First, as in the example above, they may prevent the formation of nucleic acids, essential for the production of DNA in the organism. Second, they may interfere with the synthesis of proteins in the cell of a microorganism. Third, they may interfere with the synthesis of a cell wall, causing the cell to break apart and die.

Today, a wide variety of antimetabolite drugs are available to physicians. In addition to the sulfa drugs described above, other examples of such drugs include members of the penicillin family, the tetracyclines, chloramphenicol, streptomycin, and the anti–cancer drug known as 5–fluorouracil.

Antimony see **Element, chemical**

Antioxidants

Antioxidants are vitamins that many scientists believe prevent and help to treat cancer and heart disease. They act by neutralizing circulating free radicals that are destructive to cells. The vitamins A, (beta–carotene), C, D, and E make up the antioxidant family.

Vitamins have vital functions in the body, but only minuscule amounts of vitamins are required to achieve their metabolic activities. Vitamin–deficiency conditions are well known and easily treated. The philosophical jump from vitamin deficiency to megavitamin therapy may be as harmful as beneficial. Since vitamins are present naturally in foods, most people who eat a balanced and adequate diet will consume sufficient quantities of vitamins. This does not mean that vitamin supplements or vitamin–mineral combinations are harmful if taken in recommended daily amounts. The problem lies in consuming these supplements in amounts far above the recommended doses.

The vitamins

Vitamin A is a fat–soluble vitamin necessary for bone development, bone growth, and the prevention of night blindness. Vitamin A has not been proven effective in prevention of respiratory infections, vision problems, or skin conditions, but there are vitamin A analogs that are very effective in treating some skin diseases. It is present in yellow fruits and vegetables such as peaches, carrots, and cantaloupe, and in dairy products, liver, and eggs.

Overuse of vitamin A can have serious consequences. A rash on the shoulders and back, blurred vision, and loss of appetite may occur. Because vitamin A is stored in the liver excessive amounts may cause serious liver damage (although huge doses of vitamin A would be required to cause such damage).

Vitamin C (also called ascorbic acid) is a water–soluble vitamin and is not stored in great quantities in the body. A well–nourished adult can store up to 1,500 mg of vitamin C, which is enough for four to five months. The primary condition associated with vitamin C deficiency is called scurvy, a condition characterized by aching muscles, spontaneous bleeding from the gums and other tissues, and swollen joints.

Dietary sources of vitamin C include citrus fruits, berries, and red peppers. No evidence has been found that vitamin C can prevent or cure the common cold, prevent hardening of the arteries, forestall aging, or is effective in treating mental illness. Some studies have shown that it may prevent cancer though evidence is controversial. Studies are underway to answer that question.

Vitamin D (the sunshine vitamin) is essential to prevent rickets, a deficiency disease affecting bone development in children. Normally it is synthesized from a substance in human skin when exposed to the Sun. Some foods such as milk and bread are fortified with small amounts of the vitamin to insure adequate intake. Natural dietary sources include fish, butter, and liver.

Vitamin D is a fat–soluble vitamin and excess amounts are not excreted from the body. The vitamin accumulates and can have serious health consequences such as kidney stones and heart problems. Claims that vitamin D can prevent osteoporosis (bone thinning) or reduce blood cholesterol levels have not been substantiated. However, there are vitamin D analogs that are effective. Because of serious side effects if consumed in large doses, the use of vitamin D as a supplement is not recommended.

Vitamin E, also a fat–soluble vitamin, can be consumed in large amounts without causing any serious side effects. The benefits of this vitamin remain vague. It may be needed for the routine functioning of nerves and muscles. There is some evidence that it can prevent heart disease if taken in high doses.

Vitamins as antioxidants

Free radicals are short–lived but very reactive molecules that carry an unpaired electron. Because they are produced through normal metabolic processes and their creation also is stimulated by external sources such as tobacco smoke and smog most of the body's cells are continually exposed to free radicals. Free radicals damage the DNA in cells, and some scientists believe that the resulting cell damage, if not repaired, can cause cancer, cataracts, or heart disease.

Theoretically vitamins A (beta–carotene), C, D, and E neutralize free radicals and prevent their cellular toxicity. The scientific evidence for this remains inconclusive, however, and research continues. Studies that conclude that antioxidant vitamins neutralize free radicals have been subject to criticism because the vitamins were taken as supplements to the diet. Critics point out that the benefits demonstrated by the research could have derived from the diet as well as the supplements.

See also Vitamin.

Further Reading:

Cowley, Geoffrey. "Are Supplements Still Worth Taking?" *Newsweek* 123 (25 April 1994): 47.

Adler, Tina. "Power Foods: Looking at How Nutrients May Fight Cancer." *Science News* 147 (22 April 1995): 248–49.

Larry Blaser

Antiparticle

An antiparticle is a subatomic particle identical with more familiar subatomic particles such as electrons or protons, but with the opposite electrical charge or, in the case of uncharged particles, the opposite magnetic moment. For example, an antielectron (also known as a positron) is identical with the more familiar electron, except that the former carries a single unit of positive electrical charge rather than a single unit of negative electrical charge. Antiparticles are not considered to be unusual or abnormal but are as fundamental a part of the natural world as are non–antiparticles. The main difference between the two classes of particles is that the world with which humans normally deal is constituted of protons, neutrons, and electrons rather than antiprotons, antineutrons, and antielectrons. To avoid suggesting that non–antiparticles are more "normal" than antiparticles, the name koinoparticle has been suggested for "ordinary" particles such as the proton, electron, and neutron.

Dirac's Hypothesis

During the late 1920s, the British physicist Paul Dirac attempted to modify the currently accepted model of the atom by including in it the relativistic properties of electrons. As a result of his analysis, Dirac found that electrons should be expected to exist in two energy states, one positive and one negative. The concept of positive energy presents no problems, of course, but Dirac and other physicists were uncertain as to the meaning of a negative energy state. What did it mean to say that an electron had less than zero energy?

Eventually Dirac concluded that the negative energy state for an electron might imply the existence of a kind of electron that no one had yet imagined, one that is identical with the familiar negatively–charged electron in every respect except its charge. It was, Dirac suggested, an electron with a positive charge, or an antielectron.

Within five years, Dirac's hypothesis had been confirmed. In 1932, the American physicist Carl Anderson found in photographs of a cosmic ray shower the tracks of a particle that satisfied all the properties predicted by Dirac for the antielectron. Anderson suggested the name positron for the new particle.

Other antiparticles

The existence of the positron strongly suggested to scientists that other antiparticles might exist. If there were a positively–charged electron, they asked, why could there also not be a negatively–charged proton . . . the antiproton. The search for the antiproton took much longer than the search for the antielectron. In fact, it was not until 1955 that Emilio Segre and Owen Chamberlain were able to prove that antiprotons are produced when protons from a powerful cyclotron collide with each other.

The antineutron is a fundamentally different kind of antiparticle than the antielectron or antiproton. Since neutrons have no electrical charge, an antineutron could not differ in this respect from its mirror image. Instead, an antineutron is a particle whose direction of spin is opposite that of the neutron. Since a particle's spin is expressed in the magnetic field that it generates — its magnetic moment — the antineutron is defined as the antiparticle with a magnetic moment equal in magnitude, but opposite in sign, to that of the neutron.

Other antiparticles also exist. For example, the electron is a member of a group of fundamental particles known as the leptons. Other leptons include the mu neutrino (muon) and the tau neutrino (tauon), electron–like particles that exist only at very high energy levels not observed under circumstances of our ordinary everyday world. Both muons and tauons have their own antiparticles, the antimuon and the antitauon.

Antimatter

Given the existence of the antiproton, antineutron, and antielectron, one might imagine the existence of antiatoms, atoms that are identical to the atoms of everyday life but have mirror image electrical charges and mirror image magnetic moments. In fact, some scientists believe that a whole universe of antimatter made of antiatoms may actually exist in some dimensions of which we are not aware.

Locating the existence of such an antiuniverse would be very difficult, however. When an antiparticle comes into contact with its mirror image — an antielectron with an electron, for example — the two particles annihilate each other and their mass is converted to energy. Thus, any time matter comes into contact with antimatter, both are destroyed and converted into energy.

Antiparticles and cosmology

The Swedish physicist Hans Alfvén has studied in some detail the possible role of antiparticles in the creation of the universe. At first glance, one would assume that the number of koinoparticles and antiparticles produced during the Big Bang would be equal. As it happens, however, the way in which the two classes of particles decay is very slightly different, a difference that would have become more and more important as the nascent universe aged during the first second of creation. Eventually, the very small difference in decay properties between particles might have produced a larger and larger difference, with koinomatter finally winning a predominance in terms of numbers throughout the universe. Until and if scientists can learn more about the presence of antimatter in other parts of the universe, however, questions such as these will remain unanswered.

See also Subatomic particles.

Further Reading:

Alfvén, Hans. *Worlds–Antiworlds: Antimatter in Cosmology.* San Francisco: W. H. Freeman and Company, 1966.

McGraw–Hill Encyclopedia of Science & Technology, 6th edition, Vol. 1. New York: McGraw–Hill Book Company, 1987.

Tipler, Paul A. *College Physics*. New York: Worth Publishers, Inc., 1987.

David E. Newton

Antipsychotic drugs

An antipsychotic drug, sometimes called a neuroleptic, is a prescription medication that is used to treat psychosis. A psychosis is a major psychiatric disorder characterized by derangement or disorganization of personality and/or by the inability to tell what is real from what is not real, often with hallucinations, delusions, and thought disorders. People who are psychotic often have a difficult time communicating with or relating to others. Sometimes they become agitated and violent. Among the conditions considered to be psychoses are schizophrenia, major depression, and bi–polar affective disorder (manic depression). Psychosis can arise from emotional or organic causes. Organic causes include brain tumors, drug interactions, and substance abuse.

The vast majority of antipsychotics work by blocking the absorption of dopamine, a chemical which occurs naturally in the brain and is responsible for causing psychotic reactions, especially those that happen as a result of mental illness. Dopamine is one of the substances in the brain responsible for transmitting messages across the gaps, or synapses, of nerve cells. Too much dopamine in a person's brain speeds up nerve impulses to the point of causing hallucinations, delusions, and thought disorders. By blocking the dopamine receptors, antipsychotics reduce the severity of these symptoms. The brain has several types of dopamine receptors, and their unselective blockage by antipsychotic drugs causes the side effects.

When a patient takes an antipsychotic drug, he or she enters what is called a neuroleptic state. Impulsiveness and aggression decrease as do concern and arousal about events going on in the environment outside the person. The person taking the drug has fewer hallucinations and delusions as well. Once these symptoms are controlled by antipsychotic drugs, he or she can live a more normal life, and physicians can more easily treat the cause of the psychosis.

Antipsychotic medications were not used in the United States before 1956. The first drug used to treat psychosis was reserpine, which is made from a plant called rauwolfia. Reserpine was first made in India, where rauwolfia had been used to treat psychotic symptoms for centuries. Chlorpromazine, which was invented at about the same time and marketed under the name Thorazine, soon became the most favored drug. Once these and other antipsychotic medicines were introduced in the United States, they gained widespread acceptance for the treatment of schizophrenia. The use of these drugs allowed the release of many people who had been confined to mental institutions.

Despite their benefits, antipsychotic medicines have a number of strong side effects. Although it usually takes at least two weeks for the drug to work on symptoms of psychosis, these side effects often show up sooner. The most severe include muscle rigidity, muscle spasms, twitching, and constant movement. Tardive dyskinesia (TD)—a rhythmic, uncontrollable movement of the tongue, lips, jaw, or arms and legs—develops after a mental patient has taken an anti–psychotic drug for a longer period of time. Twenty six percent of chronically mentally ill people who are or have been hospitalized develop TD. Often these side effects do not disappear when a person stops taking his or her medication.

Perhaps the most serious side effect of antipsychotic medications is neuroleptic malignant syndrome or NMS, a condition that occurs when someone taking an antipsychotic drug is ill or takes a combination of

KEY TERMS

Bi–polar affective disorder (manic depression)— A mental illness characterized by severe mood swings from depression to mania (great enthusiasm, energy, and joy).

Delusions— The belief in ideas that are clearly false.

Hallucinations— Seeing, feeling, or hearing something that is not there.

Schizophrenia— A severe mental disorder characterized by isolation from others, thought disturbances, and emotional disturbances.

drugs. People with NMS cannot move or talk. They also have unstable blood pressure and heart rates. Often NMS is fatal. Even when the person recovers, he or she has an 80% chance of experiencing NMS again if given antipsychotic drugs.

Today a new generation of antipsychotics has been developed as a result of recent molecular biology discoveries about how the brain works. These new drugs have fewer side effects. Some do not completely block dopamine receptors; others are more selective, blocking only one type of dopamine receptor. A few of the newer drugs block serotonin or glutamate, two other neurotransmitters.

See also Psychosis.

Further Reading:

American Psychiatric Association. *Let's Talk about Psychiatric Drugs.* Washington, D.C.: American Psychiatric Association, 1993.

Buelow, George, and Suzanne Hebert. *Counselor's Resource on Psychiatric Medications, Issues of Treatment and Referral.* Pacific Grove, CA: Brooks/Cole, 1995.

Shives, Rebraca Louise. *Basic Concepts of Psychiatric–Mental Health Nursing.* 3rd ed. Philadelphia: J. B. Lippincott Company.

Kay Marie Porterfield

Antisepsis

Antisepsis is the prevention or inhibition of an infection by the elimination or attenuation of an infectious agent. This is usually accomplished by application of an antiseptic or germicidal preparation. An antiseptic differs from an antibiotic.

An infection is the result of invasion of the body by an infectious agent such as a bacterium or virus. An infection may be contracted by airborne agents, by contact with an already infected patient, by contact with animals or the fleas on them, or by contact with articles used by an infected individual. Some infections are localized, signaled by a swelling and redness in a small area, as when a finger is cut, or they may be general as with the "black plague." The search for antiseptic agents is as old as humanity. In a hieroglyphic prescription, an ancient Egyptian ordered a mixture of grease and honey for treatment of a wound (ca. 1500 B.C.). For thousands of years no effective agent existed because the underlying cause of infections was not known.

Preparations of extracts of plants, broths of animal or plant materials, poultices of moss, mud, or dung, and other such natural materials were used in an effort to heal infections. Often the cure was worse than the infection. Not until the 18th century did progress begin to be made toward conquering everyday infections.

During the Middle Ages the accepted theory was that diabolical agents of some sort overwhelmed the body's natural balance of the four natural fluids— blood, phlegm, choler (yellow bile), and black bile— causing infections and disease. With no effective way to treat an infection or to prevent a simple wound from becoming infected, any minor injury could become life threatening. Personal hygiene was practically unknown, especially among the lower classes or commoners. In settled areas the streets were open sewers into which human waste and garbage were tossed. A simple cut finger could rapidly progress to gangrene of the limb or general sepsis and death. Therapeutic measures involved the attempt to reimpose balance among the fluids, often by bleeding and purging.

The first inkling of any etiology other than demons or a demonic curse was the work of Heironymous Fracastorius (1483–1553), who put forth the theory that disease is caused by imperceptible particles. Athanasius Kircher (1601–1680) later observed "tiny worms" in the blood and pus of plague victims and theorized that these were the source of the infection. This was the first theory that dealt with microbial agents as infectious organisms, and it could be rendered only after the invention of the microscope.

As late as the beginning of the 19th century, physicians had no knowledge of the septic process or its prevention. Although surgery had developed steadily, the mortality rate among patients was very high. Whether the patient would die from an infected organ or from the surgery to remove it often was a moot point. Surgeons went from one patient to the next without washing their hands or changing aprons. Thus, the bacteria from one patient were readily passed to the next and sepsis was an accepted fact.

A start toward effective antisepsis was made by Ignaz Sammelweiss (1818–1865), a Hungarian obstetrician, who studied puerperal fever (childbed fever), which was fatal to many women during childbirth. He proposed that the infectious agent could be spread by the attending physician and that washing hands between patients could prevent the infection. At first he was ridiculed, but when his rate of fatal puerperal fever infections declined rapidly with his practice of washing his hands, other obstetricians soon adopted the practice. This was the first introduction of antisepsis into medical practice.

Later, Louis Pasteur, the French chemist and bacteriologist, showed that various microorganisms could bring about changes in organic matter and that some of these organisms were airborne. Robert Koch was the first to demonstrate that different infections in animals were caused by different bacteria. He devised "four postulates" to demonstrate that a given microbe will cause a specific infection. Koch's postulates are: (1) the infectious agent can be isolated from an infected animal, (2) the microbe can be cultured in a laboratory setting, (3) it can be introduced into a healthy animal and will cause the infection that afflicted the first animal, and (4) the same infectious agent can be isolated from that animal. These postulates formed the basis of research into bacterial diseases and are still followed.

From these early efforts strides began to be made toward understanding and countering septic conditions. Individual microorganisms were identified as the causal agent in given diseases and efforts made to find a way to kill the microorganism or stop its growth. The bacterial etiology of the plague, tuberculosis, yellow fever, cholera, and other of humanity's most dread maladies eventually were discovered and their vulnerabilities found.

Bacterial infections

Bacteria are one-celled organisms that abound in the human ecosystem. Soil, air, and water all contain billions of such microorganisms in any given cubic inch. Bacteria generally assume the shape of a rod (a bacillus), a sphere (coccus), or a spiral (spirochete). Any of these forms may be aerobic (requiring air to live) or anaerobic (does not require oxygen to live),

free living, parasitic, or pathogenic (disease–causing). They may exist as single entities, as long chains (streptococcus) or bunched together (staphylococcus), and they may be mobile or not.

These microorganisms exist virtually everywhere in our surroundings and on the skin and in the mouth and nose of humans and other animals. Of course, not all bacteria cause diseases or infection and some species are considered beneficial. Many microorganisms cannot live in the human system and some that do are not harmful. Bacterial reactions are responsible for making cheese, and another microorganism (yeast) is the active agent in fermentation, as of wine. For those that are harmful, however, a bacterial infection can be contracted by the infectious agent gaining access to the interior of the body through an open cut or scrape or by the bite of a mosquito or flea or other insect, or by the bite of another human.

Although infectious agents abound in areas of poor hygiene, they also are present in any other surrounding. A seemingly innocuous cut on a finger can be the opening for a microorganism that will flourish in the warm, blood–washed interior of the body. Bacteria reproduce by cell division and once in the body that process begins and proceeds rapidly. A minor wound should not be neglected, especially in children who will play in dirt or other areas where they may be exposed to infectious agents.

Once in the body the bacterium begins to divide rapidly. Most of the time such an invasion is sensed by the body's immune system which begins its defensive response. Evidence of the battle between the bacterium and the elements of the immune system sometimes can be seen in the raised, red area of skin from which pus often exudes.

The immune system consists of specialized white blood cells. Some of these cells engulf the bacterium and carry parts of it through the blood to other white blood cells that marshall the defenses. In the time of need, white blood cells are produced at an accelerated rate to combat the infection. This is the basis of the "blood count" or white cell count in the laboratory. If the white cell count is high the physician knows that an infection is active someplace in the body.

Killer blood cells engulf the bacteria and digest it. The rapid reproduction of the bacterium provides a challenging foe for the immune system. The dead cells and detritus of the destroyed bacterium form the white exudate called pus. If the infectious agent reproduces at a rate beyond the control of the immune system the physician may provide help in the form of an antibiotic or he may lance (cut open) a superficial infection to allow it to drain and to provide access for an antiseptic agent.

If the bacterial invasion is minor the immune system soon dispatches the invader and the system returns to normal. Often some of the white blood cells form antibodies against such invading bacteria so the immune system will be better armed to combat any future invasions by the same microorganism. The white blood cell count returns to its normal level, but still with the capability of mobilizing the immune defense on short notice.

It is this response that is the basis for inoculations against certain infections such as whooping cough and tetanus. The inoculation uses dead or attenuated organisms to stimulate antibody formation in the body to prevent future, full–scale development of these diseases. The first use of such a vaccination was by an English physician, Edward Jenner, who noticed that milkmaids who had contracted a disease called cowpox did not contract the more deadly plague. He extracted material from the pustules formed by cowpox and used it to inject into his own children. They then developed cowpox but were never infected by plague–causing bacteria. The cowpox infection had resulted in the formation of antibodies that could react against any invading plague germs.

A more serious infection requires the use of antibiotics, which are injected into the body and are formulated to destroy the invading bacterium.

Current antisepsis

Because they are an ever–present threat in the human environment, bacteria and other microbes require special consideration in everyday life as well as in unusual circumstances, such as during surgery. The bacterial cell will lie dormant over long periods of time in an environment not favorable to its reproduction, but will begin cell division immediately upon being introduced into a nurturing environment.

Modern antisepsis is both preventive and therapeutic. Preventive measures consist of, for example, the surgeon washing his hands thoroughly with an antiseptic soap and wearing a sterile gown and gloves during surgery, similar treatment of the patient's skin to kill as many bacteria as possible in the operative field to prevent the entrance of bacteria into the interior of the body, sterilization of the instruments used to perform surgery, and wearing of masks by the entire surgical team. Therapeutic antisepsis, of course, is the application of a bactericidal agent to an infected area to kill the infectious agent.

KEY TERMS

Attenuated—A bacterium that has been killed or weakened, often used as the basis of a vaccine against the disease caused by the bacterium.

Etiology—The cause or origin of a disease.

Organic—Carbon based material. The word organism is derived from it, meaning any life form.

Pathogenic—Disease causing.

Sepsis—(From the Greek, meaning decay) the presence in the blood or other tissue of a microorganism that causes an infection or disease.

Antiseptics in use by consumers consist of those powders, liquids, or ointments that are applied to the surface of the skin to prevent infection of a cut, splinter, or other superficial wound. They are for external use only and each is effective against only one type of bacterium (e.g., gram positive bacteria). The early antiseptics were based on mercury (mercurochrome, merthiolate), but have fallen into disuse. Although mercury poses a serious health hazard if absorbed into the body, the small amounts of mercury in the mercury–based antiseptics were not such threats. They were discontinued simply because they were ineffective. Although they readily stopped bacteria from reproducing and spreading, they did not kill the microorganism. Once the merthiolate was washed away, the bacteria revived and resumed their invasion of the tissues.

Newer antiseptics are based on the quaternary ammonium compounds (benzalkonium chloride, benzethonium chloride), which are longstanding and very strong antiseptics; alcohols such as ethyl or isopropyl alcohols; hydrogen peroxide; and phenol. Each is effective against a narrow range of bacterial infections, but none is effective against viruses. These antiseptics often are mixed to provide a wider range of antibacterial activity. They are applied externally on a cut or scrape to prevent infection and they are gargled to kill bacteria that may cause a sore throat.

Antiseptics are designed to be used on superficial wounds in the skin. Antibiotics, also available over the counter in creams and salves, are useful also in these conditions, but additionally can be used to treat deeper wounds or wounds in creases of the body that provide a greater opportunity for infection.

It is not possible to rid one's environment of microbes, no matter how much hand washing or rinsing with bactericidal agents one employs. Microbes are always present, so any cut or opening in the skin must be attended with the idea of preventing a bacterial invasion. Use of an antiseptic soap and antibacterial medication coupled with the application of a mechanical barrier such as an adhesive strip will minimize the chance of infection. Any injury that becomes swollen, reddened, and begins to exude pus should be treated by a physician.

See also Infection.

Further Reading:
Purdy, C. "It's the Little Things That Count." *Current Health* 20 (March, 1994): 20–22.
Zimmerman, David R. *Zimmerman's Complete Guide to Nonprescription Drugs.* Detroit: Visible Ink Press, 1993.

Larry Blaser

Antlions

Antlions or doodlebugs are insects best known by their larvae, which have a small, fat body with a huge sickle–shaped pair of mandibles. Antlions belong to the family Myrmeleonidae, of the order Neuroptera, which also includes the lacewings. Members of this order are named for the delicate venation on the wings of the adult, but most people are probably more familiar with the larval stage of antlions.

Some species of antlions simply chase down their prey of small insects, while others construct a pitfall trap, or sand trap, which they dig in the loose soil. This is done by pushing the sand away from the center of a circle while walking backwards. This trap, shaped like a funnel, can measure up to 2 in (5 cm) across with the antlion larva hidden at the bottom.

Ants and other insects stumble upon the antlion trap and lose their footing. The loose nature of the soil prevents them from regaining their balance as they slide down the side of the pit into the waiting jaws of the antlion. The prey is caught and injected with a paralyzing secretion. The body fluids are then sucked out and the empty exoskeleton is discarded. If the prey manages to regain its balance and footing, it is greeted with a shower of sand that is thrown by the antlion, causing it to lose its footing again, often with the same deadly result.

Adult antlions superficially resemble damselflies. However, compared to the damselfly, the antlion is a very feeble flyer, has a very complex wing venation, and has clubbed antennae almost a quarter inch (0.6 cm) long. Unfortunately, adult antlions are not easy to find, and little is known about their behavior. Adult antlions mate in the summer and the female lays her fertilized eggs in sandy soils which are required by the larvae. Depending on species, from one to three years are spent as a larva which eventually pupates, usually in the spring, in a sand–encrusted silk cocoon at the bottom of the sand trap. One month later an adult antlion emerges from the pupal cocoon.

Ant–pipits

The ant–pipits are 10–11 species of birds that make up the family Conopophagidae. These birds are exclusively South American, occurring in tropical rain forests of Amazonia. The usual habitat of ant–pipits is thick and lush with foliage, and the birds are rather shy. Consequently, these small birds are difficult to see and demanding to study. Therefore, little is known about their biology and ecology.

Ant–pipits are small, stocky, wren–like birds, with a short tail, short wings, and long legs. The body length of these almost tail–less birds is 4–5.5 in (10–14 cm). Ant–pipits feed on the forest floor, mostly by using their strong legs and feet to scratch about in plant litter to expose their food of insects and other arthropods. Ant–pipits are permanent residents in their forest habitats, meaning they are not known to undertake long–distance, migratory movements.

The true ant–pipits are eight to nine species in the genus *Conopophaga*. The black–bellied ant–pipit (*Conopophaga melanogaster*) is a rather attractive species of tropical forests in Amazonian Brazil. Male individuals have a chestnut back, wings, and tail, a black head and breast, and a white eye–stripe that extends back into a distinctive plume at the back of the head. Coloration of the female black–bellied ant–pipit consists of more subdued hues of brown and grey.

The black–cheeked ant–pipit (*C. melanops*) of Amazonian Brazil has a chestnut cap, an olive back and wings, and a large, black cheek–patch. The chestnut–crowned ant–pipit (*C. castaneiceps*) occurs in Amazonian Columbia, Ecuador, and Peru, while the slaty ant–pipit (*C. ardesiaca*) occurs in Bolivia and southern Peru.

There are two species of *Corythopis* ant–pipits, the ringed ant–pipit (*Corythopis torquata*) and the southern ant–pipit (*C. delalandi*).

Ants

Ants are insects in the family Formicidae in the order Hymenoptera, which also includes bees and wasps. The body of ants is divided into three sections: head, thorax, and abdomen. The head bears two long, flexible antennae (for touch and chemical detection), two eyes, and a pair of powerful mandibles (jaws) for feeding and defense. Ants have three pairs of long legs that end with a claw. They are attached to the thorax, which is connected by a narrow petiole, or waist, to the segmented abdomen. At the tip of the abdomen are the reproductive organs and the stinging organ (in some species). Ants live in highly successful social communities called colonies, and are found worldwide in cool scrublands, hot deserts, inner cities, and tropical rain forests. Their nests are constructed underground or in tree–top leaf nests woven with silken thread.

Ants weigh between 0.28–1.41 oz (1–5 mg), depending on the species. In 1994, 9,500 species of ants in 300 genera were recognized, and it is expected that many more species will be added to this total.

Mandibles are elongated, saw–toothed, blade–like pinchers which snap together sideways, allowing for the efficient capture of living prey and providing excellent defense against predators. Females of ground–dwelling species of ants secrete an antibiotic substance, which they smear throughout the nest, thus protecting the entire colony from the fungi and bacteria that thrive in damp, decaying vegetation.

Social structure, development, and behavior

Ants live in eusocial communal societies where, typically, members are clearly segregated into breeding and working castes. In the colony, several generations of adults reside together, and the young are fed, nurtured, and protected deep within the mound. A typical colony of the *Pheidole tepicana* is comprised of the queen, the males, and six castes of workers.

Mating, reproduction, and life span

Ants undergo complete metamorphosis—from egg, to larva, to pupa, to adult. Each ant colony begins with, and centers on, the queen, whose sole purpose is to reproduce. Although the queen may copulate with several males during her brief mating period, she never mates again. She stores sperm in an internal pouch, the spermatheca, near the tip of her abdomen, where sperm remain immobile until she opens a valve that allows them to enter her reproductive tract to fertilize the eggs.

The queen controls the sex of her offspring. Fertilized eggs produce females (either wingless workers seldom capable of reproduction, or reproductive virgin queens). Unfertilized eggs develop into winged males which do no work, and exist solely to fertilize a virgin queen. The queen produces myriads of workers by secreting a chemical which retards wing growth and ovary development in the female larvae. Virgin queens are produced only when there are sufficient workers to allow for the expansion of the colony.

Queens live long lives in comparison with their workers and are prolific breeders. A queen of *Lasius niger*, a common ant found in Europe, lived for 29 years in captivity, while the queen of the urban Pharaoh's ant, *Monomorium pharaonis*, lives for only three months. The queen of the leafcutter ant from South America produces 150 million workers during her 14–year life span.

The first phase of colony development is the founding stage, beginning with mating, when winged males and virgin queens leave the nest in massive swarms called nuptial flights, searching out a mate from another colony. In colonies with large populations, like that of the fire ant *Solenopsis,* hundreds of thousands of young queens take to the air in less than an hour, but only one or two individuals will survive long enough to reproduce. Most are taken by predators such as birds, frogs, beetles, centipedes, spiders, or by defensive workers of other ant colonies. A similar fate awaits the male ants, none of which survive after mating.

After mating, queen ants and male ants lose their wings. The queen scurries off in search of a site to start her new nest. If she survives, she digs a nest, lays eggs, and single–handedly raises her first brood which consists entirely of workers. In leafcutter ants, adults emerge 40–60 days after the eggs are laid. The young daughter ants feed, clean, and groom the queen ant. The workers enlarge the nest, excavate elaborate tunnel systems, and transport new eggs into special hatching chambers. Hatchling larvae are fed and cleaned, and pupated larvae in cocoons are protected until the young adults emerge to become workers themselves.

The colony now enters the ergonomic stage, a time entirely devoted to work and expansion. It may take a single season or five years before the colony is large enough to enter the reproductive stage, when the queen ant begins to produce virgin queens and males which leave the nest at mating time to begin the entire cycle anew.

In some species, a new queen founds a new colony alone; in others species, several queens do so together. Sometimes, groups of workers swarm from the nest with a young queen to help her establish her nest. In colonies with several already fertile queens, such as in the Costa Rican army ant *Eciton burchelli,* entire groups break away with their individual queens to establish individual colonies. In single queen colonies, such as those of the fire ant, the death of the queen means the death of the colony, as she leaves no successors. Colonies with multiple queens survive and thrive.

Labor management

Some species of ant develop a caste of big, strong, major workers (soldiers) responsible for milling (chewing and pulverizing hard seed food), storing liquid food, and defense. Workers gather and store food for the entire colony, lugging loads much larger than themselves back to the nest. The workers of *Myrmecocystus mimicus,* the honeypot ant of the southwestern United States, collect nectar from flowers, sweet moisture from fruit, and honeydew produced by sucking insects like aphids. The food is carried back to the nest, where it is regurgitated into the crop of storage worker ants, which become living storage barrels. When a hungry ant touches the head or mouth of a storage worker ant, the storage worker responds by regurgitating food for the hungry ant.

Worker ants remove all waste (such as body parts and feces) from the nest, or bury objects too large for removal. Different species use different methods of disposing of their dead. Many simply eat the dead. Others, such as the army ant (*Eciton*), carry the corpses out of the nest, while the fire ant (*Solenopsis invicta*) scatters the corpses about the nest's periphery. In some instances, sick and dying ants actually leave the nest to die.

Defense and offense

Ants employ diverse strategies to protect their colony, territory, or food. Ants are aggressive, often raiding other ant colonies, fighting to the death and snapping off limbs, heads, and body parts of enemies with their strong, sharp mandibles. Minor workers grab the enemy by the legs, pinning them down so majors can attack the body. In some species, soldier ants do the fighting, while the minor workers scurry to and from the battleground, dragging corpses of both enemy

and kin back to the nest to feed the family. When moving colony sites, workers transport the queen, males, aged or ill workers, pupae, larvae, and eggs.

Communication

Ants secrete substances called pheromones, which are chemical messages detected by other ants through sense organs or the antennae. This process, called chemoreception, is the primary communication vehicle that facilitates mate attraction, kin, and non–kin recognition. It is also used to discriminate between egg, larva, and pupa, as warning signals, recruitment to defensive action or a new food source, the laying of odor trails from which workers or scouts find their way home or lead an entire colony to a new location, and delineation of territorial boundaries.

Chemoreception is supported by tactile (touch and feel), acoustic (hearing and vibration detection), and visual communication. Ants send tactile signals by touching and stroking each others' bodies with their antennae and forelegs. Ants produce high–pitched chirps known as stridulations by rubbing together specialized body parts on the abdomen called files and scrapers. Stridulations are sometimes heard, but most often felt, the vibrations being detected by sensitive receptors on the legs. The young queen stridulates frantically during mating season to announce a full sperm sac, deterring other would–be mates and allowing her to escape to begin nesting. Drumming and body–rapping are used primarily by tree–dwelling ants and carpenter ants, and involve banging the head or antenna on a hard surface, sending vibrational warning signals to nest mates. Some large–eyed species, such as Gigantiops, can see form and movement but vision in most ants is virtually nonexistent and the least important of all their communication senses.

Ants and the ecosystem

Earth–dwelling species of ants turn and enrich more soil than do earthworms; predatory species of ants control insect pests and spider populations, as well as animal litter by devouring rotting carcasses. Other species of ants spread seeds, thereby propagating valuable vegetation. Ants can also be serious pests; for example, leafcutter ants, which grow fungi gardens for food, also strip massive amounts of leaves and flowers. They haul the vegetation to their nests and pulverize it into a paste, which they feed to fungi that grows like mold on bread. Ant colonies are enormous: one nest of the Brazilian ant *Atta sexdens* housed about 8 million ants. A colony this size can strip as much vegetation as

KEY TERMS

Chemoreception—Detection of chemical substances which act as messengers.

Crop—Part of an ant's digestive tract which expands to form a sac in which liquid food is stored.

Eusocial—Truly social, with complex societal structures.

Mandibles—A pair of biting jaws in insects.

Milling—Chewing and pulverizing hard seed into a powdery texture.

Pheromones—Hormonal and chemical secretions.

Replete—Ants which receive regurgitated liquid food from many worker ants, storing it in the crop for future regurgitation back to other hungry ants.

Spermatheca—Oval pouch or sperm sac.

a cow in just one day, causing serious agricultural destruction.

See also Aphids.

Further Reading:

Holldobler, Bert, and Edward O. Wilson. *Journey to the Ants.* Cambridge, MA: Harvard University Press, 1994.

Holldobler, Bert and Edward O Wilson. *The Ants.* Cambridge, MA: Harvard University Press, 1990.

Williams, David F., ed. *Exotic Ants: Biology, Impact, and Control of Introduced Species.* Boulder, CO: Westview Press, 1994.

Marie L. Thompson

Ant-thrush see **Antbirds and gnat-eaters**

Anxiety

Anxiety is an unpleasant emotional state characterized by an often vague apprehension, uneasiness, or dread. Anxiety is often accompanied by physical sensations similar to those of fear such as perspiration, tightness of the chest, difficulty breathing or breathlessness, dry mouth, and headache. Unlike fear, in which the individual is usually aware of its cause, the cause of anxiety is often not clear.

Everyone experiences anxiety; it is a natural and healthy human response which many theorists believe has evolved to warn us of impending dangers so that we might better cope with them. If the anxiety, however, seems to be excessive in strength or duration, or happens without sufficient objective reasons, it might be considered an unhealthy, possibly "abnormal," response. There are numerous theories as to the causes and functions of anxiety. This entry will cover the four most extensive and influential theories: the existential, psychoanalytic, behavioral and learning, and cognitive.

Existential theorists generally distinguish between normal and neurotic anxiety. They believe normal anxiety is an unavoidable and natural part of being alive. It is the emotional accompaniment of the fear of death and of the immediate awareness of the meaninglessness of the world we live in. Anxiety is also felt on experiencing freedom and realizing that we can create and define our lives through the choices we make. In this sense, anxiety is positive, showing us we are basically free to do whatever we choose. Neurotic anxiety is a blocking of normal anxiety which interferes with self–awareness. Rather than facing and dealing with the threat causing the normal anxiety, the individual cuts him or herself off from it.

Sigmund Freud, the Austrian physician who founded the highly influential theory and treatment method called psychoanalysis, distinguished three types of anxiety: reality, neurotic, and superego or moral. Reality anxiety is fear of real and possible dangers in the outside world. Neurotic anxiety is fear of being punished by society for losing control of one's instincts, for instance by eating large amounts of food very rapidly, or openly expressing sexual desire. Moral or superego anxiety is fear of negative self–evaluation from the conscience or superego. The anxiety may be felt as guilt, and those with strong superegos may feel guilt or anxiety when they do (or even think of doing) something they were raised to believe was wrong. In Freudian theory, anxiety functions to warn individuals of impending danger, and it signals the ego to take actions to avoid or cope with the potential danger.

Learning and behavioral theories focus on how fears and anxieties can be learned through direct experience with a noxious stimulus, for example, touching a hot pan, or by indirect observation such as seeing someone else touching a hot pan and expressing pain. Most people learn to avoid the stimuli or situations that lead to anxiety, which is reinforcing as one then experiences less anxiety. But taken too far, avoidance can be very limiting. For example, if someone avoided all tests or job interviews, they would never succeed in school or have many job options. Extreme avoidance can also lead to extreme behaviors such as those seen in some phobias, which are persistent, intense, irrational fears of a thing or situation with a strong urge to flee from the source of fear. For example, someone with a phobia of pigeons might have difficulty walking calmly down a city street when pigeons are nearby. In both instances, avoidance prevents the individual from learning the original feared stimulus may not be dangerous.

Cognitive theories focus on the role of cognition, or thinking, in anxiety. They look at how interpretations or evaluations of situations affect reactions to the situations. This is based on evidence that internal mental statements or thoughts can dictate whether anxiety or other emotions are felt.

Some theorists believe anxiety plays a central role in most, if not all, mental disorders. Research suggests, for example, that there is almost always an element of anxiety in depression. There are a number of mental disorders in which anxiety plays the central role, such as phobias and generalized anxiety disorder. There is evidence that some individuals may be biologically predisposed toward experiencing strong anxiety.

Further Reading:

Kaplan, H.I., and B.J. Sadock. *Comprehensive Textbook of Psychiatry*, 6th ed. Baltimore, MD: Williams and Wilkins, 1995.
Wolman, B.B., and G. Stricker, eds. *Anxiety and Related Disorders: A Handbook*. New York: John Wiley and Sons, 1994.

Aorta see **Heart**

Apes

Apes are a group of primates that includes gorillas, orang–utans, chimpanzees, and gibbons. These are the primate species that are the most closely related to humans. The hands, feet, and face of an ape are hairless, while the rest of its body is covered with coarse black, brown, or red hair. Apes share some characteristics which set them apart from other primates: they have an appendix, lack a tail, and their skeletal structures have certain features not found in the skeletons of other primates.

Gorillas

Gorillas inhabit the forests of Central Africa and are the largest and most powerful of all primates. Adult males stand 6 ft (1.8 m) upright (although this is an unnatural position for a gorilla) and weigh up to 450 lbs (200 kg), while females are much smaller. Gorillas live to about 44 years and mature males (those usually over 13 years), called silverbacks, are marked by a band of silver–gray hair on their backs.

Gorillas live in small family groups of several females and their young, led by a dominant silverback male. The females comprise a harem for the silverback, who holds the sole mating rights in the troop. Like humans, female gorillas produce one infant after a gestation period of nine months. The large size and great strength of the silverback are advantages in competing with other males for leadership of the group and in defending the group against outside threats.

Despite its ferocious image, however, the gorilla is not an aggressive animal. Even in a clash between two adult males, most of the conflict consists of aggressive posturing, roaring, and chest–beating, rather than physical contact.

During the day these ground–living apes move slowly through the forest, selecting species of leaves, fruit, and stems from the surrounding vegetation. Their home range is about 9–14 square miles (25–40 sq km). At night the family group sleeps in trees, resting on platform nests that they make from branches; silverbacks usually sleep at the foot of the tree.

Gorilla numbers are declining rapidly and only 50,000 remain in the wild. Other than humans, gorillas have no real predators, although leopards will occasionally take young apes. Hunting, poaching (a mountain gorilla is worth $150,000), and habitat loss are causing gorilla populations to decline. The shrinking forest refuge of these great apes is being progressively felled in order to accommodate the ever–expanding human population.

Orang–utans

The orang–utan has its population restricted to the rainforests of the Indonesian islands of Sumatra and Borneo. The orang–utan is the largest living arboreal mammal, and it spends most of the daylight hours moving slowly and deliberately through the forest canopy in search of food. Sixty percent of its diet consists of fruit, and the remainder is composed of young leaves and shoots, tree bark, mineral–rich soil, and insects. Orang–utans are long–lived, with many individuals reaching 50–60 years of age in the wild. These large, chestnut–colored, long–haired apes are facing possible extinction from two different causes: habitat destruction and the wild animal trade.

Even though Indonesia has more than 400,000 sq mi (1,000,000 sq km) of rainforest habitat remaining, the rate of loss threatens the continued existence of the wild orang–utan population, which is now estimated at about 25,000 individuals. Both the Indonesian government and the Convention on International Trade in Endangered Species of Wild Fauna and Flora (CITES) have banned international trade of orang–utans, yet their population continues to be threatened by the black market. In order to meet the demand for these apes as pets around the world, poachers kill the mother orang–utan to secure the young, and the mortality rate of these orphans is extremely high, with less than 20% of those smuggled ever arriving alive at their final destination. Some hope for the species rests in a global effort to manage a captive propagation program in zoos.

Chimpanzees

Common chimpanzees are widespread in the forested parts of West, Central, and East Africa. Pygmy chimpanzees, or bonobos, are restricted to the swampy lowland forests of the Zaire basin. Despite their names, common chimpanzees are no longer common, and pygmy chimpanzees are no smaller than the other species.

Chimpanzees are partly arboreal and partly ground–dwelling. They feed in fruit trees by day, nest in other trees at night, and can move rapidly through treetops. On the ground, chimpanzees usually walk on all fours (called knuckle walking), since their arms are longer than their legs. Their hands have fully opposable thumbs and, although lacking a precision grip, can manipulate objects dexterously. Chimpanzees make and use a variety of tools: they shape and strip "fishing sticks" from twigs to poke into termite mounds, and they chew the ends of shoots to fashion fly whisks. They also throw sticks and stones as offensive weapons and hunt and kill young monkeys.

Chimpanzees live in small nomadic groups of three to six animals (common chimpanzee) or six to 15 animals (pygmy chimpanzee) which make up a larger community of 30–80 individuals that occupy a territory. Adult male chimpanzees cooperate in defending their territory against predators. Chimpanzee society consists of fairly promiscuous mixed–sex groups. Female common chimpanzees are sexually receptive for only a brief period in mid–month (estrous), while female pygmy chimpanzees are sexually receptive for

most of the month. Ovulating females capable of fertilization have swollen pink hindquarters and copulate with most of the males in the group. Female chimpanzees give birth to a single infant after a gestation period of about eight months.

Jane Goodall has studied common chimpanzees for almost 30 years in the Gombe Stream National Park of Tanzania. She has found that chimpanzee personalities are as variable as those of humans, that chimpanzees form alliances, have friendships, have personal dislikes, and run feuds. Chimpanzees also have a cultural tradition—that is, they pass learned behavior and skills from generation to generation. Chimpanzees have been taught complex sign language (the chimpanzee larynx will not allow speech) through which abstract ideas have been conveyed. These studies show that chimpanzees can develop a large vocabulary and that they can manipulate this vocabulary to frame new thoughts.

Humans share 98.4% of their genes with chimpanzees, so only 1.6% of human DNA is responsible for all the differences between the two species. The DNA of gorillas differs 2.3% from chimpanzees, which means that the closest relatives of chimpanzees are humans, not gorillas. Further studies of chimpanzees would undoubtedly help us better understand the origins of human social behavior and human evolution. Despite this special status, both species of chimpanzees are threatened by the destruction of their forest habitat by hunting and by capture for research.

Gibbons

Gibbons (genus *Hylobates*, meaning dweller in the trees) are the smallest members of the ape family. Gibbons are found in southeast Asia, China, and India, and nine species are recognized. They spend most of their lives at the tops of trees in the jungle, eating leaves and fruit. They are extremely agile, swinging with their long arms on branches to move from tree to tree, and they are often seen walking upright on tree branches. Gibbons are known for their loud calls and songs, which they use to announce their territory and warn away others. They are devoted parents, raising usually one or two offspring at a time and showing extraordinary affection in caring for them. Conservationists and animal protectionists who have worked with gibbons describe them as extremely intelligent, sensitive, and affectionate.

Gibbons have long been hunted for food, for medical research, and for sale as pets and zoo specimens. A common method of collecting them is to shoot the mother and capture the nursing or clinging infant, if it is still alive. The mortality rate in collecting and transporting gibbons to areas where they can be sold is extremely high, and this coupled with the destruction of their jungle habitat has resulted in severe depletion of their numbers. Despite a ban on international trade in gibbons, illegal trade in gibbons, particularly babies, continues on a wide scale in markets throughout Asia.

See also Chimpanzees; Gibbons and siamangs; Gorillas; Orang–utan; Primates.

Further Reading:
Benirschke, K. *Primates: The Road to Self–Sustaining Populations.* New York: Springer–Verlag, 1986.
Goodall, Jane. *Through a Window: My Thirty Years With the Chimpanzees of Gombe.* Boston: Houghton Mifflin, 1990.
Schaller, G. B. *The Year of the Gorilla.* Chicago: University of Chicago Press, 1988.
Speart, J. "Orang Odyssey." *Wildlife Conservation* 95 (1992): 18–25.

Eugene C. Beckham, Neil Cumberlidge, and Lewis G. Regenstein

Apgar score

Apgar score is the assessment of a newborn baby's physical condition based on skin color, heart rate, response to stimulation, muscle tone, and respiratory effort. Each criteria is rated from zero to two with a total score of 10 signifying the best possible physical condition. The assessment determines the need for immediate emergency treatment, helps prevent unnecessary emergency intervention, and indicates possible brain damage. Because the score corresponds closely to an infant's life expectancy, it is used as a guideline to advise parents on their baby's chances of survival.

Dr. Virginia Apgar published her scoring system in 1953 during her tenure as professor of anesthesiology at Columbia–Presbyterian Medical Center, New York, where she was involved in the birth of more than 17,000 babies. She observed the need for a quick, accurate, scientific evaluation of the newborn, primarily to aid in diagnosing asphyxiation (suffocation) and to determine the need for resuscitation (aided breathing). The evaluations, made and recorded one, five, and 10 minutes after birth, quickly became the standard by which modern medicine throughout the world measured the health of the newborn infant.

Apgar's name became an acronym for Appearance, Pulse, Grimace, Activity, and Respiration.

Appearance scores two if the baby's skin is a healthy tone such as pink, one if extremities are bluish, and zero if the entire body is blue. Pulse (heart rate) scores two for higher than 100 per minute, one for below 100, and zero if absent. Grimace scores two for an energetic cry (with or without the traditional slap on the bottom or soles of the feet), one for a slight wail, and zero for no response. Actively moving babies score two for muscle tone, one for some effort at movement, and zero if limp. Respiration scores two for strong efforts to breathe; one for irregular breathing, and zero for no effort. With a total five–minute score of seven to 10, the infant's chances of surviving the first month are almost 100%, approximately 80% with a score of four, and 50% with a score of zero to one.

In 1989, an article in *The Lancet* concluded the Apgar Score was outmoded in light of advanced diagnostic and treatment techniques. Magee Women's Hospital in Pittsburgh, Pennsylvania, the largest obstetrical services hospital in the United States, still uses the Apgar Score as an indicator of the newborn's chances of survival. However, immediate resuscitation needs are determined under the Neonatal Resuscitation Program, developed in 1986 by the American Council of Pediatrics and the American Heart Association, and whose guidelines are used across the United States and by modern medical centers throughout the world.

See also Birth.

Aphasia

Aphasia is a disorder caused by damage to the areas of the brain that direct the ability to speak, interpret, and understand language. Usually, aphasia is caused by a head injury, a brain tumor, a stroke, or a serious infection.

In adults, one of the most common causes of aphasia is a cerebro–vascular accident—a stroke. A stroke occurs when the blood and oxygen supply to the brain is blocked, either by a clogged blood vessel (cerebral thrombosis) or a burst blood vessel (cerebral hemorrhage). When an injury or stroke interferes with the blood and oxygen supply, the brain cells cut off from oxygen die.

The areas of the brain involved in communication and language—all located on the left side of the brain—include the auditory cortex, which sorts what is heard into categories that make sense; Wernicke's area, where words and word patterns are stored; and Broca's area, which receives information from Wernicke's area

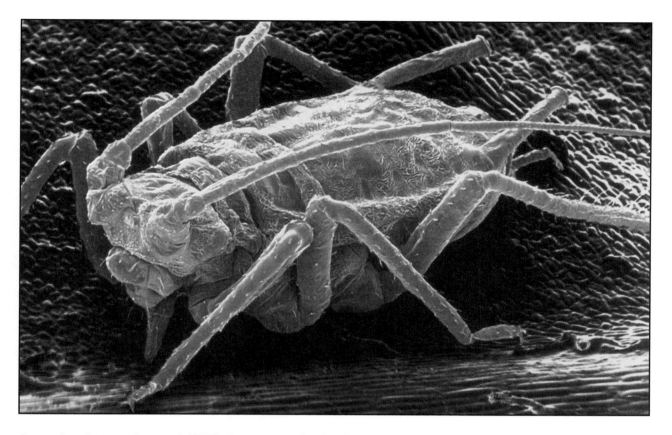

A scanning electron micrograph (SEM) of a green peach aphid (*Myzus persicae*) on the leaf of a Marvel of Peru (*Mirabilis jalapa*). This aphid winters on peach trees and migrates to other plants for the summer. It is an economic pest when it infests crops such as potatoes. The aphid is also a carrier of plant viruses, which are transmitted when it inserts its stylet into the veins of a leaf in search of sugar–carrying cells. The tubes on the aphid's back are siphons for sending pheromone signals.

and sends signals to the tongue, lips, and jaw that translate brain messages into actual speech.

Because these areas of the brain control different language skills, the communication problems that occur depend on what parts of the brain are damaged. For example, if the Broca area is injured, one may understand what is said and be able to think of an appropriate response. But because the link between thought and the physical act of speaking is damaged, one has trouble coordinating lips, tongue, and jaw to form understandable words. Damage to the Broca area may also make it difficult to communicate in writing; one knows what to write but the connection between thought and hand movement to form words on paper has been damaged.

There are several different systems for classifying aphasias. Some broad areas include

Wernicke's aphasia (difficulty understanding language because words spoken cannot be matched to words stored in the brain); conduction aphasia (a break in the fibers that connect the Wernicke and Broca areas of the brain; a person understands what is said, but can not repeat it); transcortical aphasia (repetition without understanding); and global aphasia (all language abilities are impaired because all portions of the brain related to language have been damaged). See also Stroke.

Aphids

Aphids are insects in the order Homoptera, which are also known as plant lice. Some 3,800 species of aphids have been identified worldwide with 1,300 species occurring in North American, which includes some 80 species that are pests of crops and ornamental plants. Aphids have a distinctive pear–shaped body, and most are soft and green in color. The wings are transparent and are held in a tent–like position over the abdomen, which has a short tail, called a cauda. The legs are long and thin, and the antennae are thin and have six segments. Two tube–like structures, called cornicles, project from the fifth or sixth abdominal segments of aphids. The cornicles excrete a defensive chemical when the aphid is threatened.

Reproductive habits

Aphids have a complicated life cycle and reproduction habits that make them extremely adaptable to their host plants and environments. When aphid eggs that have overwintered on their host plants hatch in the spring, they produce females without wings. These females and are capable of reproducing asexually, a process called parthenogenesis. Several asexual generations of aphids may be produced during a growing season.

When it becomes necessary to move to another plant, females with wings are produced and move to another host plant. As winter approaches, both males and females are produced and their fertilized eggs again overwinter until the next spring. Sometimes winged females that produce asexually also migrate to new hosts. The lack of wings among generations of aphids which have no need to migrate is seen as an adaptive advantage, since it helps keep them from being blown away in windy weather.

Ants and aphids

An intimate, symbiotic relationship exists between ants and aphids. They are often compared to cattle, with the ants acting as protectors and ranchers. What aphids have that ants want is something called honeydew, a sweet substance that is excreted by aphids through their anus and contains surplus sugar from the aphid's diet. Ants protect aphid eggs during the winter, and carry the newly hatched aphids to new host plants, where the aphids feed on the leaves and the ants get a supply of honeydew.

Because of their ability to reproduce rapidly and grow large colonies, their feeding on plants causes yellowing, stunting, mottling, browning, and curling of leaves, as well as inhibiting the ability of the host plant to produce crops. Infestations by aphids can cause plants to die, and the insects can carry other diseases, such as plant viruses, from one plant to another. Their saliva is also toxic to plant tissues. Among the biological controls of aphid infestations in agriculture and horticulture are lacewings, sometimes called "aphid

KEY TERMS

Exoskeleton—A hard, shell–like structure that serves both to protect the vital organs of animals without an internal skeleton and to support their muscle systems.

Honeydew—A sweet substance excreted by aphids that ants need.

Parthenogenesis—Asexual reproduction without the fertilization of eggs.

Spiracles—Openings that lead to a system of tubes which supply air to insects.

Symbiotic—Living together in a mutually beneficial relationship.

lions," lady beetles or lady bird beetles (ladybugs), and syrphid flies. Pesticides, including diazinon, disyston, malathion, nicotine sulfate, and others, are also used to control aphids. On a smaller scale, some gardeners control aphids by simply washing them off with a spray of soapy water.

See also Ants.

Further Reading:

Arnett, Ross H. *American Insects*. New York: Van Nostrand Reinhold, 1985.

Hubbell, Sue. *Broadsides from the Other Orders: A Book of Bugs*. New York: Random House, 1993.

Imes, Rick. *The Practical Entomologist*. New York: Simon & Schuster, 1992.

McGavin, George C. *Bugs of the World*. New York: Facts on File, 1993.

Vita Richman and Neil Cumberlidge

Approximation

In mathematics, making an approximation is the act or process of finding a number acceptably close to an exact value; that number is then called an approximation or approximate value. Approximating has always been an important process in the experimental sciences and engineering, in part because it is impossible to make perfectly accurate measurements. Approximation also arises because some numbers can never be expressed completely in decimal notation. In these cases approximations are used. For example, irrational numbers, such as π, are nonterminating, nonrepeating decimals. Every irrational number can be approximated by a rational number, simply by truncating it. Thus, π can be approximated by 3.14, or 3.1416, or 3.141593, and so on, until the desired accuracy is obtained.

Another application of the approximation process occurs in iterative procedures. Iteration is the process of solving equations by finding an approximate solution, then using that approximation to find successively better approximations, until a solution of adequate accuracy is found. Iterative methods, or formulas, exist for finding square roots, solving higher order polynomial equations, solving differential equations, and evaluating integrals.

The limiting process of making successively better approximations is also an important ingredient in defining some very important operations in mathematics. For instance, both the derivative and the definite integral come about as natural extensions of the approximation process. The derivative arises from the process of approximating the instantaneous rate of change of a curve by using short line segments. The shorter the segment the more accurate the approximation, until, in the limit that the length approaches zero, an exact value is reached. Similarly, the definite integral is the result of approximating the area under a curve using a series of rectangles. As the number of rectangles increases, the area of each rectangle decreases, and the sum of the areas becomes a better approximation of the total area under investigation. As in the case of the derivative, in the limit that the area of each rectangle approaches zero, the sum becomes an exact result.

Every function can be expressed as a series, the indicated sum of an infinite sequence. For instance, the sine function is equal to the sum: $\sin(x) = x - x^3/3! + x^5/5! - x^7/7!+....$ In this series the symbol (!) is read "factorial" and means to take the product of all positive integers up to and including the number preceding the symbol ($3! = 1 \times 2 \times 3$, and so on). Thus, the value of the sine function for any value of x can be approximated by keeping as many terms in the series as required to obtain the desired degree of accuracy. With the growing popularity of digital computers, the use of approximating procedures has become increasingly

important. In fact, series like this one for the sine function are often the basis upon which handheld scientific calculators operate.

An approximation is often indicated by showing the limits within which the actual value will fall, such as 25 ± 3, which means the actual value is in the interval from 22 to 28. Scientific notation is used to show the degree of approximation also. For example, 1.5×10^6 means that the approximation 1,500,000 has been measured to the nearest hundred thousand; the actual value is between 1,450,000 and 1,550,000. But 1.500×10^6 means 1,500,000 measured to the nearest thousand. The true value is between 1,499,500 and 1,500,500.

See also Derivative; Equation; Integral; Irrational number; Rational number.

Apraxia

Apraxia is a disorder of brain function in which a person is unable to perform learned motor acts even though the physical ability exists and the desire to perform them is there. Brain damage to the parietal lobes, particularly in the dominant hemisphere, results in apraxia. Unlike paralysis, movements remain intact but the patient can no longer combine them sequentially to perform desired functions like dressing. Damage to the parietal lobes can arise from a variety of causes including metabolic diseases, stroke, and head injuries.

The German neurologist Hugo Liepmann (1863–1925) introduced the term apraxia in 1900 after observation of an impaired patient. Based on anatomic data, he suggested that planned or commanded actions are controlled not in the frontal lobe of the brain but in the parietal lobe of the brain's dominant hemisphere. Liepmann then postulated that damage to this portion of the brain prevents the activation of "motor programmes," learned sequences of activities that produce desired results on command. He also divided apraxia into three types: ideational, ideomotor, and kinetic.

Ideational apraxia, sometimes called object blindness, renders patients incapable of making appropriate use of familiar objects upon command, even though they can name the object and describe how to use it. Ideomotor apraxia is the inability to follow verbal commands or imitate an action, such as waving goodbye. The harder the patient tries, the more difficult execution becomes. Ironically, the patient often performs the gesture spontaneously or as an emotional response, like waving good-

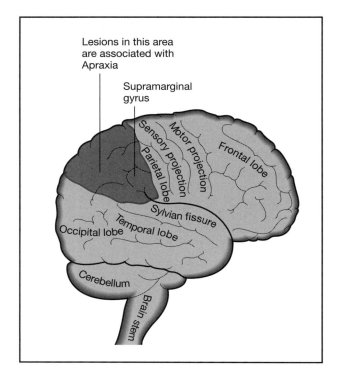

Lesions in this area are associated with Apraxia

Supramarginal gyrus

Sensory projection

Motor projection

Parietal lobe

Frontal lobe

Sylvian fissure

Occipital lobe

Temporal lobe

Cerebellum

Brain stem

The area of the brain associated with apraxia.

bye when a loved–one leaves. Kinetic apraxia refers to clumsiness in performing a skilled act that is not due to paralysis, muscle weakness, or sensory loss.

Other types of apraxia have been described since Liepmann's time. Apraxia of speech is the inability to program muscles used in speech, resulting in incorrect verbal output. It is frequently seen in conjunction with aphasia, the inability to select words and communicate via speech, writing, or signals. In dressing apraxia, patients can put clothes on but cannot program the appropriate movement sequences. Therefore, a coat goes on back–to–front, or socks over shoes. Facial apraxia leaves patients unable to move portions of their face upon command. They often, however, use other parts of their body to achieve a similar end. For example, when asked to blow out a match, the patient may step on it. Constructional apraxia refers to the inability to apply well–known and practiced skills to a new situation, like drawing a picture of a simple object from memory.

Although intense research has increased scientific understanding of this complex disorder, many mysteries remain.

Further Reading:

Brown, Jason W., *Aphasia, Apraxia and Agnosia, Clinical and Theoretical Aspects*. Springfield: Charles C. Thomas, 1972.

Brown, Jason W., ed. *Agnosia and Apraxia: Selected Papers of Liepmann, Lange, and Pixel*. Hillsdale: Lawrence Erlbaum Associates, 1988.

Hammond, Geoffrey R., ed. *Cerebral Control of Speech and Limb Movements*. Amsterdam: North–Holland, 1990.

Roy, E. A., ed. *Neuropsychological Studies of Apraxia and Related Disorders*. Amsterdam: North–Holland, 1985.

Williams, Moyra. *Brain Damage, Behavior, and the Mind*. New York: John Wiley & Sons, 1979.

Marie L. Thompson

Apricot see **Rose family**

Aquaculture see **Blue revolution**

Aqueduct

Aqueducts are structures used to carry water from a supply source to distant areas in need of water. The word aqueduct comes from two Latin words, aqua (water) and ducere (to lead). The first aqueducts were built as early as the 10th century B.C. by ancient communities. While primitive people lived very close to water, as people moved inland and away from direct water supplies, they created systems of water retrieval. Wells were dug to reach underground water supplies. Also, cisterns, underground collecting tanks, were used to store water. Eventually, dams were constructed to block water flow, allowing water pressure to increase, and run–off channels were constructed to guide water to specific regions. Early aqueducts redirected water by use of conduits (covered canals, or pipes, usually made of stone) that were often buried a few inches below ground for protection. Aqueducts were driven by the force of gravity pulling water downhill and extended for many miles. The use of aqueducts for drinking water, agriculture, and other uses is a part of Greek, Mexican, Roman, and Asian history. The city of ancient Rome had 11 active aqueducts traversing roughly 300 mi (485 km). Modern aqueducts use electrical power to elevate water that travels through many miles of pipes. Many modern pipes are deep beneath the ground and supply cities with water for personal and industrial use.

History

The first record of an aqueduct appeared in 691 B.C. in Assyria. This 34 mi (55 km) long aqueduct was fairly simple, consisting of a single arch over one val-

The Pont du Gard, a Roman aqueduct in Nimes, France, dates from before the fifth century A.D.

ley. At that time, Greeks were using wells to retrieve water from underground pools. Certain plants, such as fig trees, marked water sources because their roots grow in water. The first Greek aqueduct followed in 530 B.C. on the island of Samos. This aqueduct was built by an engineer named Eupalinus, who was told to supply the city with water by tunneling a pathway through a mountain. The Samos aqueduct extended for about 1 mi (1.6 km) underground, and had a diameter of 8 ft (2.4 m). These first aqueducts demonstrated an understanding of siphons and other basic hydraulic principles.

While ancient Roman aqueducts evolved into an extensive network of canals supplying the city, the first one, the Aqua Appia, was not built until 312 B.C This aqueduct was a simple subterranean covered ditch. Roman aqueducts were usually built as open troughs, covered with a top, and then covered with soil. They were made from a variety of materials including masonry, lead, terra cotta, and wood. The Appia was about 50 ft (15 m) underground to make it inaccessible to Roman enemies on the city's outskirts. The Anio Vetus, built in 272 B.C, brought more water to the city, but both the Appia and the Vetus had sewerlike designs. The Aqua Marcia, built in 140 B.C, was made of stone and had lofty arches. The Aqua Tepula of 125 B.C was made from poured concrete. Later Roman aqueducts were mainly built to meet the needs of the people or the desires of the rulers of the time. The average Roman aqueduct was 10–50 mi (16–80 km) long with a 7–15 sq ft (0.7–1.4 sq m) cross–section. Aqueducts were generally wide enough for a man to enter and clean.

Around the world, communities made advances in irrigation and water management. In the Mexican Tehuacan Valley, evidence of irrigation dates back to

Aquifer—A region of natural subterranean water collection.

Conduit—A structure such as a pipe or channel for transporting fluid.

around 700 B.C in the remains of the Purron Dam. The dam was used to direct water to domestic and crop regions for several hundred years. In the same valley, the Xiquila Aqueduct was built around 400 A.D.

Early North American aqueducts include the Potomac aqueduct in Washington, D.C. This aqueduct, which was built in 1830, extends over the Potomac River at the Key Bridge which joins Northern Virginia and the Georgetown area of the city. It was built with support from eight piers and two stone abutments to carry water from the upper Potomac to the city.

Later aqueducts of the United States include the Colorado River Aqueduct that supplies Los Angeles and the Delaware River Aqueduct that carries water into New York. In addition, aqueducts carry excess water from northern to southern California. The southwestern region of the United States is particularly dry and requires water import. Water can be collected from aquifers (underground water tables), rivers, lakes, or man–made reservoirs.

Technology

While modern water pipes are much wider (20–30 ft or 6.1–9.1 m in diameter) and significantly longer (hundreds of miles long) than the first aqueducts, the hydraulic principles governing water carriage remain essentially the same. Water flows along gradients, and its velocity depends on a number of factors. Water flows more quickly along steeper gradients, but wear and tear on such pipes is greater, resulting in the need for more frequent repair. More gradual sloping pipes result in slower–flowing water with greater sludge deposits; hence, these pipes require more cleaning with less repair.

Water velocity along conduits is also greater in larger, smoother pipes. Pipes or canals that have rough surfaces disrupt water flow, slowing it down. In addition, larger diameter passageways provide less resistance, because a smaller percentage of the flowing water is retarded by the surface friction of the conduit. Thus, smaller diameter pipes slow the flow of water compared to larger diameter pipes.

The use of water to generate other forms of power is not new at all. The ancient Greeks and Romans both used water mills for work in such places as flour factories. In such mills, aqueducts were used to supply water on a relatively continuous basis. A modern application of water power is hydroelectric power.

See also Irrigation.

Further Reading:

Hodge A. *Roman Aqueducts and Water Supply.* London: Gerald Duckworth & Co., 1992.

Hodge, A., ed. *Future Currents in Aqueduct Studies.* Great Britain: Redwood Press, 1991.

Louise Dickerson

Aquiclude see **Groundwater**

Aquifer see **Groundwater**

Arachnids

Arachnids (class Arachnida) form the second largest group of terrestrial arthropods (phylum Arthropoda) with the class Insecta being the most numerous. There are over 70,000 species of arachnids which include such familiar creatures as scorpions, spiders, harvestmen or daddy longlegs, and ticks and mites, as well as the less common whip scorpions, pseudoscorpions, and sun spiders. Arachnids are members of the subphylum Chelicerata, which also includes the phylogenetically ancient horseshoe crabs which are unusual for arachnids in that they are aquatic.

Like other arthropods arachnids have paired, jointed appendages, a hardened exoskeleton, a segmented body, and a well–developed head. They differ from other arthropods by the organization of their body into two main parts, the prosoma (equivalent to the head and thorax of insects) and the opisthosoma (or the abdomen). There are six pairs of appendages associated with the prosoma. The first pair are stabbing appendages near the mouth called chelicerae, used for grasping and cutting, and the second pair are called pedipalps or general purpose mouthparts. The last four pairs of appendages are the walking legs. Most arachnids are terrestrial and respire by means of book lungs, or by tracheae (air tubes from the outside to the tissues), or both. Most arachnids are terrestrial carnivorous predators. They feed by piercing the body of their prey, and then either directly ingesting its body fluids

A Cosmetid harvestman.

or by releasing digestive secretions onto the outside of the prey to predigest the food before ingestion.

Scorpions (order Scorpiones) are distinguished by their large, pincer–like pedipalps, and a segmented abdomen consisting of a broad anterior part and a narrow posterior part ("tail") which ends in a sharp pointed stinger. The latter contains a pair of poison glands whose ducts open at its tip. The venom is neurotoxic (attacking nerve functions) but, except in a handful of species, not potent enough to harm humans. Scorpions breathe by means of book lungs. Mating in scorpions is preceded by a complex courtship behavior. Newly–hatched scorpions are carried around by the mother on her back for one to two weeks. Scorpions are nocturnal, and feed mostly on insects. During the day they hide in crevices, under bark, and in other secluded places. They are distributed worldwide in tropical and subtropical regions.

In spiders (order Araneae) the abdomen is not segmented and it is separated from the cephalothorax by a narrow waist. The large and powerful chelicera of some spiders contains a poison gland at the base, while the tips serve as fangs to inject the poison into the prey. The pedipalps of spiders are long and leg–like. In male spiders, the pedipalps each contain a palpal organ, used to transfer sperm to the female. Some species of spider have only book lungs for respiration, while others have both book lungs and tracheae. Spiders possess silk producing glands whose secretion is drawn into fine threads by structures called spinnerets located on the lower side of the abdomen. Different types of silk are produced and used for a variety of purposes, including orb–weaving, ensnaring prey, packaging sperm to be transferred to the female, and making egg sacs. Although all spiders produce silk, not all weave orbs. The courtship patterns of spiders are quite varied.

Spiders have a worldwide distribution and are ubiquitous, living in and around human habitations, in burrows in the ground, in forests, and even under water. Spiders are predators, feeding mostly on insects. Despite their reputation as fearsome animals, spiders actually benefit humans by keeping some insect populations under control. The bite of the very few potentially harmful species of spiders is rarely fatal to humans.

Most mites and ticks (order Acari) are small, mites being microscopic, and ticks measuring only 0.2–1 in(5–25 mm) in length. The oval body of acarines consists of the fused cephalothorax and abdomen. The chelicerae and pedipalps are small, and form part of the feeding apparatus. Adult ticks and mites have four pairs of walking legs, but the larvae have only three pairs. Respiration in acarines is by tracheae. The ticks are mostly bloodsucking ectoparasites of mammals. In addition to sucking blood, and injecting poison into the host in the process, ticks transmit the agents of diseases such as Rocky Mountain spotted fever, Lyme disease, relapsing fever, typhus, and Texas cattle fever. A female tick needs to engorge by feeding on her host's blood before she can lay eggs. An engorged female is three or more times her original size. The feeding requires attachment to the host for days. The larval and nymphal stages likewise feed before they molt and progress to the next stage. Ticks have specialized sense organs which enable them to locate a host more than 25 ft (7.5 m) away.

Many mites are either ecto– or endoparasites of birds and mammals, feeding on the skin and underlying tissues. Many more mites are free living. Some, such as the chigger, are parasitic as larvae but free living in the nymph and adult stages. The ectoparasites live on the host's body surface, while the endoparasites excavate tunnels under the host's skin in which they live and reproduce. While some parasitic mites transmit disease organisms, many produce diseases such as scabies, mange, or cause an intense itch. Ticks and parasitic mites are clearly of great economic importance. Some free living mites are also of considerable importance because they cause destruction of stored grain and other products. House dust mites cause allergies in many people.

Harvestmen (order Opiliones) look superficially like spiders but differ in many respects. Harvestmen lack a waist separating the abdomen from the cephalothorax and their abdomen is segmented. They can ingest solid food as well as fluids. They do not produce silk and are non–venomous. Harvestmen feed on insects and contribute to insect control, although they are less important in this respect than spiders.

See also Arthropods; Horseshoe crabs; Mites.

Arapaima

The giant of freshwater fishes, the arapaima or pirarucu (*Arapaima gigas*) is a legend among fish. Weighing up to 40 lbs (200 kg), this species, which has only been recorded in the rivers of Brazil and the Guianas, may reach a length of some 16.5 ft (5 m), although most specimens today are less than 10 ft (3 m). The origins of the arapaima, which belongs to the bony–tongued fishes (Osteoglossidae), date back to the Cretaceous period (some 65–135 million years ago); it is one of just five remaining species of this ancient group.

In appearance the arapaima exhibits many archaic characteristic, such as an asymmetrical tail fin and a swim bladder that also functions as an air–breathing organ. Only very young arapaima have functional gills; adult fish always come to the surface to breathe in oxygen and expel carbon dioxide, usually at intervals of 10–15 minutes.

Arapaima are active predators and often seek out fish in pools that are drying out, or backwaters where the fish are slowly being starved of oxygen. Captured prey are held in the jaws and the toothed tongue is then used to press and grind the hapless prey against the roof of the mouth. When prey is abundant, arapaima gorge themselves on fish, laying down rich fat deposits that will see them through the breeding season. Reproduction is marked by vivid changes in color and the pairing of adult fish. Both male and female participate in excavating a small hole in the substrate, usually in shallow water and well concealed by vegetation. When the nest site is completed, the female proceeds to lay her eggs, which are then fertilized by the attendant male. Both parents remain in the vicinity of the nest to ward off potential predators. Upon emerging from the eggs, the young fish remain close to one or both of the adults until such time as they are able to fend for themselves. Despite such lavish parental attention, the predation rate on young arapaima is thought to be considerable.

Prior to the 19th century, this species was seldom captured as neither the techniques nor the means of preserving such a large amount of food were available. In recent decades, however, the introduction of steel–tipped harpoons and gill nets have resulted in large catches of this giant fish. Smoking and salting techniques have also developed, enabling people to store larger quantities of fish for longer periods. As a result, this species has developed as one of the most important fish caught for food throughout the Amazon basin. No estimates of the population size of this species exist, but scientists have expressed concern for its future as a result of increasingly heavy hunting pressures in some regions.

Arc

In mathematics, an arc is a segment of a curve or of the circumference of a circle.

The arc AB of a circle whose origin is O is illustrated below.

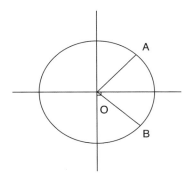

An arc whose length is shorter than the one half of the circumference of a circle is defined as the minor arc (AB traveled clockwise). An arc, whose length is longer than one half of the circumference of a circle is defined as a major arc (AB is traveled counterclockwise).

The angle which is delineated by the radius OA and OB is called the central angle. The entire central angle of a circle, a complete revolution, is equivalent to 360°, which corresponds to the entire circumference of a circle, the total arc of which has the length $2\pi r$.

A theorem of geometry states that the measure of the central angle is the measure of corresponding arc.

In addition to length and degree measures there is a third way to measure an arc, which like degrees is also used for angles. An arc, whose length equals the radius (r) of the circle, has a central angle of one radian. In degrees one radian = $360°/2\pi = 57°\ 17'\ 45''$ (given to the nearest second).

When the central angle is expressed in radians, the corresponding arc length can be calculated by the multiplication of the radian value of the angle by the radius of the circle.

See also Circle; Curve; Geometry.

Archaeoastronomy

Archaeoastronomy is the study of prescientific peoples' relation to the sky as part of their natural environment. As a formal investigation, the field of archaeoastronomy is relatively young, having begun only in the 1960s. It is often known as cultural astronomy to indicate the multidisciplinary breadth of the field and its emphasis on cultural practices and issues rather than on the "correctness" of ancient observations. Archaeoastronomers are concerned to know what observations were made by an ancient society, who made them, and how those observations were integrated into the society's political life, agricultural or hunting–gathering practices, and civic and religious customs. Thus, the tools of modern archaeoastronomers are as likely to be those of art history, sociology, or linguistics as those of the quantitative sciences, such as computer–processing algorithms, large databases, and statistical inference.

Cosmology

Most prescientific peoples developed a cosmology that explained human existence as seamlessly interwoven into the workings of the universe. This relationship of the part to the whole was usually expressed through symbols and metaphors. A simple, almost universal cosmological principle was captured in the idea of mirroring: events and powers in the sky mirrored those on Earth; the Earth was but a microcosm of the sky. In virtually all Northern Hemisphere societies, for example, earthly dwellings (the tepee, yurt, or igloo) were seen as particularized representations of the larger dwelling that arched high overhead in the heavens to create the celestial vault and which rotated around the Pole Star. An actual pole of rotation, extending from Earth to heaven, was a strong element of native North American cosmology. In Inuit cosmology, the superior plane (the mythological equivalent of the sky) was known as the Land Above. Other cosmologies have figured the universe as an endlessly folded ribbon, with Earth in the center fold; as a set of nested boxes; or as a series of interlocking spheres.

Prescientific societies held the celestial bodies in great reverence, yet were also on an intimate footing with them. Ancient peoples regarded the sky as inhabited—by Sky People, deities, departed ancestors, or simply forces. The Sky People or powers were thought to impose order on chaotic human affairs. At the same time, the sky powers could be solicited and manipulated to serve human goals. Their authority could be invoked to justify the actions of a chief priest or ruler. A moon associated with important periods in the agricultural or hunting cycle could be honored to ensure better food supplies. A desire to place the sky powers in the service of the human agenda may have been the impetus that led prescientific societies to take up regular observations of the skies—in other words, astronomy.

Early observatories

Written records are missing for many prescientific societies as they turned from noting a single celestial event to making the kinds of repeated observations that could be applied predictively to events in their own lives, such as harvesting or knowing when to expect newborns in their herds. Many ancient peoples did, however, leave physical signs of their observing activities. Among the most intriguing are the sites that, to a modern eye, seemingly could have been used as very early observatories.

Between about 3500 B.C and 1500 B.C, Bronze Age builders in Britain and the northwestern portion of France known as Brittany erected, or marked in the existing landscape, thousands of sites that invite speculation about astronomical use. The most fundamental arrangement consisted of a natural indicator on the horizon, such as a notch in a mountain (the foresight), which was aligned with another, manmade marking, such as a standing post or stone, or a hollowed–out depression in a rock (the backsight). Because distances of up to 28 mi (45 km) have been measured between foresight and backsight, these common configurations have become known as long alignments. Statistical studies show that few long alignments could have been used to establish the date of a major celestial event, such as a solstice, with certainty. Even a rough approximation, however, would have sufficed for ceremonial reasons such as sun worship.

The Neolithic builders are better known for erecting stone circles, such as Stonehenge. (A henge is an earthen mound surrounded by a low bank and a ditch; wooden or stone pillars may be arranged on the top.) Astronomical opinion is divided over the uses of Stonehenge, but the evidence for its primary use as an observatory is considered weak. Stonehenge was built in three phases over a period of about 400 years, beginning around 1700 B.C, and is one of many circles built during this period. It stands on flat Salisbury Plain, in southern England. Because the horizon lacks distinctive features, short sight lines may have been incorporated into the placement of the stones. A ritual figure such as a priest or priestess silhouetted against the rising moon, and framed between two megaliths, would also have been an impressive sight.

Astronomers believe that Stonehenge could have been used to observe the winter solstice, the time when the rising of the Sun is farthest south, and the extreme rising and setting positions of the Moon. Its primary purpose seems to have been ceremonial. That a ceremonial structure might have later evolved into an observatory in prehistoric Britain has important implications for social organization, for it suggests that an educated, elite class existed to make the observations and supervise the construction and repair of sites. Those educated observers in turn might have been the forerunners of the Druids of the Iron Age in Britain.

Culturally dissimilar groups in the American Southwest and California appear to have followed observing practices like those used in prehistoric Britain. Oral histories taken from 19th century Pueblan informants in the Four Corners region indicate that both horizon observations (that is, long alignments) and wall calendars were used. The position of the Pueblan observer was not marked by a standing stone or gouge mark or wall painting; rather, it appeared to be esoteric knowledge held by the priest–astronomer, who simply walked to the same spot every time that observations were to be made. Wall calendars were created as sunlight penetrated an opening in a house or residential cave to fall on the opposite wall. With the use of both horizon and wall calendars, the Pueblans could track the motions of the Sun, Moon, and stars and also events that occurred in the four sacred quadrants of the sky. Similar horizon and wall calendars were used by many of the estimated 300 tribes living in California before contact with Hispanic traders and explorers, which occurred in the 1760s and 1770s. Some precontact California tribes are thought to have had two calendars: a secular one, known to all, and a secret calendar to guide the timing of sacred rituals.

Simple observing stations that made use of existing sight lines and horizon marks stand at one end of the spectrum of early observatories. At the other end is elite, corporate architecture, such as is found in the northern Yucatan site of Chichn Itz. There, the highly elaborated architecture, with its steeply ascending steps and ornately carved and painted reliefs, reflects a complex union of political power and astronomical knowledge.

Chichn Itz was built over two periods that lasted, in aggregate, from about A.D. 700 to A.D. 1263. Its people were both numerate and literate, creating written works that detailed their astronomical culture. The Maya also had a warrior class, waged war regularly, took captives as slaves, and practiced ritual human sacrifice and bloodletting.

The Mayan calendar and Mayan life were dominated by the Sun and Venus, whose astrophysical activities are related to each other in a 5:8 ratio considered sacred by the Maya. The Sun was associated with warfare; Venus, a fearful power, was associated with warfare, sacrifice, fertility, rain, and maize. In the 1960s and later, glyphs from Mayan writings were interpreted as showing that raids were undertaken during important Venus stations, such as its first appearance as the Morning Star or the Evening Star. These raids have come to be called star war events. The Caracol, a building probably designed as an observatory, and several other important ceremonial buildings at Chichn Itz, such as the Great Ball Court, the Upper Temple of the Jaguars, and the Temple of the Warriors, are fairly precisely aligned to face significant Sun and Venus positions.

Mayan interest in genealogy made calendrics important. Their basic calendar consisted of two cycles, one of 260 named days and one a year of 365 days, which ran concurrently. Fifty two years of 365 days each formed the "Calendar Round." The Maya developed a system for uniquely identifying every one of the 18,980 days in the Calendar Round. A table in the Dresden Codex, one of three Mayan manuscripts to have survived the Spanish conquest, indicates ability to predict solar and lunar eclipses, as well as the behavior of certain other celestial bodies. At the time of the conquest, these predictions may have been accurate to within a day, rather than to within an hour or minute, as was then possible in Europe with the aid of advanced instrumentation. The Maya, however, did not have the concept of an hour.

See also Calendars; Seasons.

Further Reading:

Krupp, E. C., ed. *Archaeoastronomy and the Roots of Science.* AAAS Selected Symposium 71. Boulder, CO: Westview Press, 1984.

Milbrath, Susan. "Astronomical Images and Orientations in the Architecture of Chichn Itz." In *New Directions in American Astronomy. Proceedings of the 46th International Congress of Americanists.* Anthony F. Aveni, ed. Oxford, England: B.A.R., 1988.

Ruggles, Clive L. N., ed. *Archaeoastronomy in the 1990s. Papers Derived From the Third "Oxford" International Symposium on Archaeoastronomy.* Loughborough, U.K.: Group D Publications Ltd., 1993.

Ruggles, Clive L. N., ed. *Records in Stone: Papers in Memory of Alexander Thom.* Cambridge: Cambridge University Press, 1988.

Ruggles, Clive L. N., and Nicholas J. Saunders, eds. *Astronomies and Cultures.* Chicago: University Press of Chicago, 1993.

Zeilik, Michael. "Astronomy and Ritual: The Rhythm of the Sacred Calendar in the U.S. Southwest." In *New Directions in American Astronomy. Proceedings of the 46th International Congress of Americanists.* Anthony F. Aveni, ed. Oxford, England: B.A.R., 1988.

Marjorie Pannell

Archaeology

The term archaeology refers, in part, to the study of human culture and of cultural changes that occur over time. In practice, archaeologists attempt to logically reconstruct human activities of the past by systematically recovering and examining artifacts or objects of human origin. However, archaeology is a multi-faceted scientific pursuit, and includes various specialized disciplines and sub-fields of study. Depending on the specific field of interest, archaeological artifacts can mean anything from ancient Greek pottery vessels to disposable plastic bottles at modern dump sites. Thus, studies in archaeology can extend from the advent of human prehistory to the most recent of modern times. The two most common areas of study in archaeological research today, particularly in the United States, are prehistoric and historic archaeology.

Background

Although there has been a natural interest in the collection of antiquities for many hundreds of years, controlled scientific excavation and the systematic

Archaeological excavation, Eldon Pueblo, Coconino National Forest, Arizona.

tematic excavations in Virginia of prehistoric Indian "mounds" or earthworks that resemble low pyramids made from soil. His published report by the American Philosophical Society in 1799 marked the beginning of a new era in archaeological studies.

In addition to his thorough examination and recording of artifacts, Jefferson was perhaps the first researcher to observe and note a phenomenon known as *stratigraphy*, where soil and artifacts are deposited and layered one above the other like the skins of an onion. Jefferson's observation of site stratigraphy is still in use today as a basic field technique in determining the age and complexity of archaeological sites.

During the late 19th century, academic archaeology as a university subject sprang from a branch of anthropology, one of the social sciences that mainly concentrates on understanding the cultural traditions and activities of non–literate peoples.

American anthropologists of the time discovered that a better way to understand the social structure of living Native Americans was to try to reconstruct their prehistoric lifestyles. At the same time, archaeologists found that studies of contemporary Native Americans help in the interpretation of prehistoric Indian cultures, of which there are no written records. Thus, modern archaeology evolved as a result of the mutual effort between these two separate fields of academic discipline.

In addition to the many important discoveries made by researchers over the past century, perhaps the most sweeping event in the history of archaeology was the development of radiocarbon or C–14 dating in the late 1940s by Willard F. Libby.

Instead of relying solely on theories and hypotheses to date a site, scientists could derive, through laboratory analysis, highly accurate dates from small samples of organic material such as wood or bone. In many cases, radiocarbon dating proved or disproved theories regarding the postulated ages of important archaeological finds.

Today, archaeologists use a variety of techniques to unlock ancient mysteries. Some of these newly–developed techniques even include the use of space technology. The National Aeronautics and Space Administration's (NASA) ongoing project, Mission to Planet Earth, is one example. The primary objective of the project is to map global environmental changes by using specially designed SIR–C/X–SAR (Spaceborne Imaging Radar C/X–Band Synthetic Aperture Radar). However, a recent Middle East mission conducted by the space shuttle *Endeavor* resulted in several radar photographs of a series of ancient desert roadways

study of artifacts and the cultures who made them was not widely practiced until early in this century. Prior to that time, most archaeology consisted of randomly collecting artifacts that could be found lying on the surface of sites or in caves. In Europe and the Middle East, well–marked tombs and other ancient structures provided visual clues that valuable antiquities might be found hidden nearby.

Because most of these early expeditions were financed by private individuals and wealthy collectors, broken artifacts were often left behind, because only intact and highly–crafted items were thought to have any value. Consequently, early theories regarding the cultures from which artifacts originated were little more than speculation.

One of the first Americans to practice many of the techniques used in modern archaeology was Thomas Jefferson (1743–1826). Before serving his term as president of the United States, Jefferson directed sys-

leading to a central location. Field investigations, currently underway, have revealed that the roadways lead to the 5,000 year–old lost city of Ubar in southern Oman on the Arab Peninsula.

Disciplines

Over the past several decades, as new laboratory technologies have become available, so have the number of disciplines or fields of study that are linked to archaeology. Although they may seem unrelated, each is important, in that they contribute to the growing body of knowledge about humankind.

Physical anthropology, ethnobotany, DNA analysis, x ray emission microanalysis, and palynology are but a few of the dozens of specialized areas of study. However, the individual field archaeologist tends to focus his or her research on a specific culture and/or era in time.

Prehistoric archaeology

Everything that is currently known about human prehistory is derived through the excavation and study of ancient materials.

Prehistoric archaeology encompasses the study of humankind prior to the advent of written languages or written history. In effect, the job of the prehistoric archaeologist is to discover and write about the histories of ancient peoples who had no written history of their own.

However, prehistory lasted for different times in different parts of the world. In Europe, primitive written languages made their appearance around 2,500 years B.C., thus technically ending Old World prehistory. On the other hand, American prehistory came to a close only 500 years ago when explorers such as Christopher Columbus (c. 1451–1506) visited the New World for the first time. By returning to their homeland with written reports of what they had seen, those explorers ushered in the early historic era of the Western Hemisphere.

Historic archaeology

As opposed to prehistoric archaeological studies, historic archaeology is a discipline that focuses on a more detailed understanding of the recent past. Typically, any site or building over 50 years old but younger than the regional area's prehistory is considered historic. For example, Civil War battlefields are historic landmarks. Because most historic sites and buildings were used during times when records were kept, the historic archaeologist can review written doc-

umentation pertaining to that time and place as part of the overall study.

Artifactual material discovered during an historic archaeological excavation adds specific detailed information to the knowledge already gathered from existing historic documents.

A relatively new sub–discipline of historic archaeology, known as urban archaeology, attempts to quantify our current culture and cultural trends by examining material found at modern dump sites. Urban archaeology has been primarily used as a teaching aid in helping students of cultural anthropology and archaeology develop interpretive skills.

Classical archaeology

The classical archaeologist is perhaps the most popular public stereotype—the "Indiana Jones" movie character, for example, is based on the fantastic exploits of a classical archaeologist. The roots of classical archaeology can be traced to the European fascination with Biblical studies and ancient scholarship. Classical archaeologists focus on monumental art, architecture, and ancient history. Greek mythology, Chinese dynasties, and all ancient civilizations are the domain of the classical archaeologist.

This field is perhaps one of the most complex areas of the study of human culture, for it must utilize a combination of both prehistoric and historic archaeological techniques. In addition, classical studies often employ what is referred to as underwater archaeology to recover the cargo of sunken ancient sailing vessels that carried trade goods from port to port.

Cultural resource management

Beginning in the 1940s, a number of state and federal laws have been enacted in the United States to protect archaeological resources from potential destruction which could be caused by governmental developments such as highway construction. In the 1970s, additional legislation extended these laws to cover development projects in the private sector. Other countries have also passed similar laws protecting their antiquities. As a result, archaeology has moved from a purely academic study into the realm of private enterprise, spawning hundreds of consulting firms that specialize in contract archaeology or what is commonly known as cultural resource management (CRM).

CRM work has become a major economic industry in the United States, generating an estimated 250 million dollars a year in annual business through government and private contracts. Most archaeological studies conducted in the United States today are a direct result of compliance with antiquities laws.

Construction projects such as the building of dams, highways, power lines, and housing developments are a recognized and accepted pattern of human growth. It is also recognized that these activities sometimes have a detrimental affect on the evidences of human history. Both historic buildings and prehistoric sites are often encountered during the course of new construction planning. However, various steps can be taken to insure that such sites are acknowledged and investigated prior to any activities that might damage them.

The two most common measures that can be taken when a site lies in the path of development include (1) preservation by simple avoidance or (2) data recovery. Preservation by avoidance could mean re–routing a highway around an archaeological site, or moving the placement of a planned building to a different location. On the other hand, when avoidance is not possible, then data recovery by excavation becomes the next alternative.

In the case of historic structures, for example, data recovery usually includes a thorough recordation of the building. This might include photographs, scale interior and exterior drawings, and historic document searches to determine who designed and built the structure or who might have lived there. For prehistoric resources, sampling the contents of the subsurface deposit by excavation is perhaps the only method by which to determine the significance of a site.

Field methods

Archaeological survey/field reconnaissance

Prior to any archaeological excavation, whether it be prehistoric or historic, a survey or field reconnaissance must be conducted. In general terms, a survey means to systematically inspect the surface of a site to determine whether or not it is significant and may warrant further investigation. Although the determination of significance is somewhat subjective, most researchers agree that it hinges on a site's potential to yield useful information. Significance may include the ability of a site to produce new, previously unknown information, or additional data to add to what is currently known about the site's original inhabitants and their culture.

Surveys are also conducted on undeveloped properties where no sites have been previously recorded. These types of surveys are performed to verify that no sites are on the subject property, or if one is found, to record its presence and document its location, condition, size, and type. All records pertaining to archaeological surveys and sites are permanently stored at either government or university clearing houses for future reference by other archaeologists.

Test excavation

The term test excavation refers to the intermediate stage of an archaeological investigation between surveying and salvage excavation or full data recovery program. It generally incorporates the digging of units or square pits in order to sample the contents and depth of an archaeological site. Test units can be randomly located on a site or placed in specific locations. The use of test units helps the archaeologist determine what areas of a site will yield the highest quantity of artifacts or most useful information before committing time and resources to a more intensive study.

Typically, test units are measured metrically, such as in a one meter by one meter square, and excavated through the archaeological deposit to sterile soil, or soil which fails to produce any additional finds. Depending on the project and the type of site, various methods and techniques are used during an excavation. Sometimes the artifact–bearing soils (called midden) are excavated from units in 2–4 in (5–10 cm) levels, carefully peeling one layer of soil and then the next. This is known as arbitrary excavation.

In instances where natural soil layering can be observed, excavation comprises removal of each layer or strata regardless of its thickness. The purpose in both cases is to maintain a vertical control of where artifacts were recovered, as well as separating the shallow, younger materials from deeper, older materials.

Each layer or level of soil recovered from unit excavations is sifted through a wire mesh or screen. Soil falls through the screen while artifacts and other material are left on top, where they are then washed, sorted according to type, bagged, and labeled. In this way, archaeologists not only record from what unit a particular artifact was found but also at what depth.

Thus, archaeologists can reconstruct a three–dimensional view of a site layout.

Salvage excavation

Salvage excavations, or what is referred to as rescue archaeology outside the United States, generally represent the final data recovery program of an archaeological site. Although the methods used in salvage excavations are similar to those of test excavations, there are some distinctions with regard to objectives.

Whereas the term test implies an initial investigation to be followed by further study, the term salvage generally denotes that no additional research may be undertaken once the excavation is complete. This is particularly true for archaeological sites that will be destroyed as a result of construction activities.

Unfortunately, it is an accepted fact in archaeology that recovery of 100% of the contents of a site is impractical due to either time or budget constraints. In actuality, that number is estimated from less than 1% to as much as 7%, leaving the remaining bulk of the deposit unstudied. Thus, archaeologists are forced by necessity to make determinations on the most appropriate mode of data recovery and what avenues of research would best benefit from the excavation.

Traditional methods of excavation typically include the use of picks, shovels, trowels, and hand-held shaker screens.

However, archaeologists have realized that although laboratory techniques have taken full advantage of the latest technologies, field methods have not made a corresponding advancement, and in fact have not changed dramatically since the 1930s. To tackle this problem, researchers have begun to experiment with various alternative methods of data recovery. These alternatives are designed to increase sample size, lower costs to sponsors, and at the same time maintain careful scientific control over the recovery process.

One of these alternatives includes the use of earth-moving machinery. For decades, machines such as backhoes or tractor-mounted augers have been employed during test excavations to aid in determining the boundaries and depths of archaeological deposits. Recently, however, machines have been used to actually salvage excavate sites by simulating traditional digging methods, or digging level by level. As a result, new methods of hydraulic water screening have been developed to process large amounts of midden soils. Although machines have been successfully utilized in salvage excavations, the use of mechanized earth-moving machinery in archaeology is not widely practiced and cannot be applied to all sites.

Current controversy

Among many North American Indian tribes, treatment of the dead has traditionally been a matter of great concern. Some modern-day Native Americans have expressed that ancestral graves should not be disturbed or, if that cannot be prevented, then any remains and artifacts recovered should be reburied with ceremony.

KEY TERMS

Artifact—In archaeology, any human-made item that relates to the culture under study.

Classical archaeology—Archaeological research that deals with ancient history, ancient architecture, or any of the now-extinct civilizations of Greece, Egypt, Rome, Aztec, Mayan, etc.

Cultural resource management—Contract archaeology performed by privately owned and operated archaeological consulting firms.

Data recovery—An excavation intended to recover artifacts which represent the basic, raw data of any archaeological study.

Deposit—Refers to the three-dimensional, sub-surface or below-ground portion of an archaeological site.

Discipline—A specialized field or sub-field of study.

Historic archaeology—Archaeological studies focusing on the eras of recorded history.

Midden—Darkened archaeological site soil caused by organic waste material such as food refuse and charcoal from ancient campfires.

Prehistoric archaeology—Archaeological studies dealing with material which dates to before the historic era, or before the advent of written languages.

Salvage/rescue excavation—The final phase of a typical two-part series of archaeological site excavations.

Site—An archaeological resource such as an ancient Indian campsite, or an old, historic building.

Survey—A systematic surface inspection conducted to examine a known archaeological site or to verify that no site exists on the property under examination.

Test excavation—A preliminary excavation conducted to determine the size, depth, and significance of an archaeological site prior to committing to a salvage or final excavation.

However, it was not until the 1970s that this issue became a nationwide concern. By then, public attitudes in the United States had become more favorable toward both Native American interests and religious values. Passage of the Native American Religious

Freedom Act of 1978 was a reflection of this change in public attitude, as well as a result of the newly–developed political awareness and organization of Native American activist groups.

In 1990, the Native American Grave Protection and Repatriation Act (NAGPRA) was signed into federal law. In addition to applying penalties for the trafficking of illegally–obtained Native American human remains and cultural items, the law mandated that all federally–funded institutions (museums, universities, etc.) are required to repatriate or "give back" their Native American collections to tribes who claim cultural or religious ownership over those materials. These and other recently adopted state laws have sparked a heated controversy among scientists and Native American groups.

For archaeologists, physical anthropologists, and other scholars who study humankind's past, graves have provided a very important source of knowledge about past cultures. This has been particularly true in the reconstruction of prehistoric North American cultures whose peoples left no written history but who buried their dead surrounded with material goods of the time. Repatriation of this material will prevent any further studies from being conducted in the future.

Although many researchers support repatriation of historic material that can be directly linked to living tribal descendants, others have stated that it is not possible to make such determinations on very ancient materials that date to before the pyramids of Egypt. Another argument is that ongoing medical studies of diseases found in the bones of ancient remains could lead to breakthroughs in treatments to help the living.

Archaeologists have expressed that museum materials are part of the heritage of the nation, and that these new laws fail to take into consideration the many complex factors that separate ancient human remains from modern Native American cultures.

See also Dating techniques; Ethnoarchaeology.

Further Reading:

Haviland, William A. *Human Evolution and Prehistory*, 2nd ed. New York: CBS College Publishing, 1983.
Joukowsky, Marth. *A Complete Field Manual of Archaeology: Tools and Techniques of Field Work for Archaeologists*. Englewood Cliffs, NJ: Prentice–Hall, 1980.

T. A. Freeman

Archaeometallurgy

Archaeometallurgy is the study of metal artifacts, the technology that was used to smelt them, and the ways ancient societies acquired ores. In addition to understanding the history of metal technology, archaeometallurgists seek to learn more about the people who made and used metal implements and gain a broader understanding of the economic and social contexts in which the people lived. Archaeometallurgy can help to answer archaeological questions concerning the rise of craft specialization, the effects new technologies have on societies, the level of interaction between cultures, and the forces required to change societies.

Archaeometallurgy is a type of archaeometry, which is the use of scientific methods to study archaeological materials. It incorporates many different fields of study, including geology, ethnography, history, chemistry, and materials science. Archaeometallurgists reconstruct ancient smelting (ore melting) furnaces, conduct experiments, and analyze metals and slag (the glassy residue left by smelting).

It is a misconception that somehow the use of metals is limited to certain ages (e.g., the Bronze age or the Iron Age). For example, until relatively recently, there was no evidence of metallurgy in pre–Bronze Age southeast Europe. Copper artifacts had been found and there was evidence of ore mining, but because no slag had been found, some archaeologists believed the copper had been smelted elsewhere. In 1979, copper slag was discovered with material from the Vinca culture (5400–4000 B.C.). The pieces of slag were small and scattered, and had been overlooked by earlier investigators. Spectroscopic analysis of the slag showed it was similar to local ores. This is strong evidence for local smelting of the ore. In addition, a few tin bronze artifacts have been found with the Vinca and contemporary cultures of southeast Europe. This suggests that the Bronze Age, when it arrived, may have been a scaled–up version of a technology that already existed, rather than something fundamentally new. This is one example of how archaeometallurgy helps us understand ancient societies.

See also Archaeology; Metallurgy; Spectroscopy.

Architecture see **Building design/architecture**

Argan diagram see **Complex numbers**

Argon see **Rare gases**

Arithmetic

Arithmetic is a branch of mathematics concerned with the numerical manipulation of numbers using the operations of addition, subtraction, multiplication, division, and the extraction of roots. General arithmetic principles slowly developed over time from the principle of counting objects. Critical to the advancement of arithmetic was the development of a positional number system and a symbol to represent the quantity zero. All arithmetic knowledge is derived from the primary axioms of addition and multiplication. These axioms describe the rules which apply to all real numbers, including whole numbers, integers, rational, and irrational numbers.

Early development of arithmetic

Arithmetic developed slowly over the course of human history, primarily evolving from the operation of counting. Prior to 4000 B.C., few civilizations were even able to count up to ten. Over time however, people learned to associate objects with numbers. They also learned to think about numbers as abstract ideas. They recognized that four trees and four cows had a common quantity called four. The best evidence suggests that the ancient Sumerians of Mesopotamia were the first civilization to develop a respectable method of dealing with numbers. By far the most mathematically advanced of these ancient civilizations were the Egyptians, Babylonians, Indians, and Chinese. Each of these civilizations possessed whole numbers, fractions, and basic rules of arithmetic. They used arithmetic to solve specific problems in areas such as trade and commerce. As impressive as the knowledge that these civilizations developed was, they still did not develop a theoretical system of arithmetic.

The first significant advances in the subject of arithmetic were made by the ancient Greeks during the third century B.C. Most importantly, they realized that a sequence of numbers could be extended infinitely. They also learned to develop theorems which could be generally applied to all numbers. At this time, arithmetic was transformed from a tool of commerce to a general theory of numbers.

Numbering system

Our numbering system is of central importance in the subject of arithmetic. The system we use today called the Hindu–Arabic system, was developed by the Hindu civilization of India some 1500 years ago. It was brought to Europe during the middle ages by the Arabs and fully replaced the Roman numeral system during the 17th century.

The Hindu–Arabic system is called a decimal system because it is based on the number 10. This means that it uses 10 distinct symbols to represent numbers. The fact that 10 is used is not important because it could have just as easily been based on another number of symbols like 14. An important feature of our system is that it is a positional system. This means that the number 532 is different from the number 325 or 253. Critical to the invention of a positional system is perhaps the most significant feature of our system: a symbol for zero. Note that zero is a number just as any other and we can perform arithmetic operations with it.

Axioms of the operations of arithmetic

Arithmetic is the study of mathematics related to the manipulation of real numbers. The two fundamental properties of arithmetic are addition and multiplication. When two numbers are added together, the resulting number is called a sum. For example, 6 is the sum of 4 + 2. Similarly, when two numbers are multiplied, the resulting number is called the product. Both of these operations have a related inverse operation which reverses or "undoes" its action. The inverse operation of addition is subtraction. The result obtained by subtracting two numbers is known as the difference. Division is the inverse operation of multiplication and results in a quotient when two numbers are divided. The operations of arithmetic on real numbers are subject to a number of basic rules, called axioms. These include axioms of addition, multiplication, distributivity, and order. For simplicity, note that the letters a, b, c, denote real numbers in all of the following axioms.

There are three axioms related to the operation of addition. The first, called the commutative law, is denoted by the equation $a + b = b + a$. This means that the order in which you add two numbers does not change the end result. For example, 2 + 4 and 4 + 2 both mean the same thing. The next is the associative law which is written $a + (b + c) = (a + b) + c$. This axiom suggests that grouping numbers also does not effect the sum. The third axiom of addition is the closure property which states that the equation $a + b$ is a real number.

From the axioms of addition, two other properties can be derived. One is the additive identity property which says that for any real number $a + 0 = a$. The other is the additive inverse property which suggests that for every number a, there is a number $-a$ such that $-a + a = 0$.

Like addition, the operation of multiplication has three axioms related to it. There is the commutative law of multiplication stated by the equation a × b = b × a. There is also an associative law of multiplication denoted by a × (b × c) = (a × b) × c. And finally, there is the closure property of multiplication which states that a × b is a real number. Another axiom related to both addition and multiplication is the axiom of distributivity represented by the equation (a + b) × c = a × c + b × c.

The axioms of multiplication also suggest two more properties. These include the multiplicative identity property which says for any real number a, 1 × a = a, and the multiplicative inverse property that states for every real number there exits a unique number (1/a) such that (1/a) × a = 1.

The axioms related to the operations of addition and multiplication indicate that real numbers form an algebraic field. Four additional axioms assert that within the set of real numbers there is an order. One states that for any two real numbers, one and only one of the following relations is true: either a < b, a > b or a = b. Another suggests that if a < b, and b < c, then a < c. The monotonic property of addition states that if a < b, the a + c < b + c. Finally, the monotonic property of multiplication states that if a < b and c > 0, then a × c < b × c.

Numbers and their properties

These axioms apply to all real numbers. It is important to note that a real number is the general class of all numbers which include whole numbers, integers, rational numbers and irrational numbers. For each of these number types only certain axioms apply.

Whole numbers, also called natural numbers, include only numbers that are positive integers and zero. These numbers are typically the first ones to which a person is introduced, and they are used extensively for counting objects. Addition of whole numbers involves combining them to get a sum. Whole number multiplication is just a method of repeated addition. For example, 2 × 4 is the same as 2 + 2 + 2 + 2. Since whole numbers do not involve negative numbers or fractions, the two inverse properties do not apply. The smallest whole number is zero but there is no limit to the size of the largest.

Integers are whole numbers which also include negative numbers. For these numbers the inverse property of addition does apply. For these numbers, zero is not the smallest number but it is the middle number with an infinite number of positive and negative integers existing before and after it. Integers are used to measure values which can increase or decrease such as

the amount of money in a cash register. The standard rules for addition are followed when two positive or two negative numbers are added together and the sign stays the same. When a positive integer is added to a negative integer, the numbers are subtracted and the appropriate sign is applied. Using the axioms of multiplication it can be shown that when two negative integers are multiplied, the result is a positive number. Also, when a positive and negative are multiplied, a negative number is obtained.

Numbers to which both inverse properties apply are called rational numbers. Rational numbers are numbers which can be expressed as a ratio of two integers, for example, 1/2. In this example, the number 1 is called the numerator and the 2 is called the denominator. Though rational numbers represent more numbers than whole numbers or integers, they do not represent all numbers. Another type of number exists called an irrational number which cannot be represented as the ratio of two integers. Examples of these types of numbers include square roots of numbers which are not perfect squares and cube roots of numbers which are not perfect cubes. Also, numbers such as the universal constants π and e are irrational numbers.

The principles of arithmetic create the foundations for all other branches of mathematics. They also represent the most practical application of mathematics in everyday life. From determining the change received from a purchase to calculating the amount of sugar in a batch of cookies, learning arithmetic skills is extremely important.

See also Algebra; Calculus; Function; Geometry; Trigonometry.

Further Reading:
Paulos, John Allen. *Beyond Numeracy*. New York: Alfred A. Knopf, Inc., 1991.

Perry Romanowski

Armadillos

Armadillos are bony–skinned mammals native to Central and South America. Armadillos (family Dasypodidae) number 20 species in eight genera. The species include the long–nosed armadillo (six species), the naked–tailed armadillo (four species), the hairy armadillo (three species), the three–banded armadillo (two species), the fairy armadillo (two species), the six–banded or yellow armadillo (one species), the pichi (one species), and the giant armadillo (one species).

Distribution and habitat

Armadillos are found through the whole of South and Central America, from the Strait of Magellan northward to eastern Mexico.

The common long–nosed (or nine–banded) armadillo is the most widespread and is the only species found in the United States. In the 1850s several armadillos were recorded in Texas, and their descendants spread rapidly through the Gulf States toward the Atlantic in what has become the swiftest mammalian distribution ever witnessed. In 1922 a captive pair of common long–nosed armadillos escaped in Florida, and in a few decades their descendants numbered in the tens of thousands. Moving westward, the eastern population met with the Texas group only within the last decade.

Rivers and streams present no barrier to the spread of armadillos. Gulping air into their stomachs and intestines to buoy themselves, armadillos float leisurely across the water. Others have been observed walking into streams on one side and strolling out on the other side a few minutes later.

While water presents no barrier to armadillos, cold does, and winter temperatures have slowed their northern advance in the United States. Armadillos are poorly insulated and cannot withstand chilling. Cold also reduces the abundance of insects that armadillos depend on for food. Because of this, armadillos have moved northward only as far as Oklahoma and southern Kansas.

Armadillos are found in habitats ranging from pampas (grasslands) to arid deserts and from coastal prairies to rain forests and deciduous forests.

Physical appearance

Armadillos appear to be a conglomeration of other animal parts—the shell of a turtle, the ears of an aardvark, the feet of a lizard, the face of a pig, and the tail of a dinosaur. However, the patches and bands of coarse bristles and hairs on their bodies reveal them to be true mammals.

Extinct species of armadillo grew to enormous sizes and their bony shells were used as roofs and tombs by early South American Indians. Surviving species are nowhere near that large, ranging in size from the 99–132 lb (45–60 kg) giant armadillo to the 2.8–3.5 oz (80–100 g) lesser fairy armadillo. The familiar common long–nosed armadillo weighs in at 6–10 lb (2.7–4.5 kg).

The most obvious and unusual feature of armadillos is their bony skin armor, found in no other living mammal. Bands of a double–layered covering of horn and bone develop from the skin and cover most of the upper surfaces and sides of the body. These bony bands or plates are connected by flexible skin. The top of the head is capped with a bony shield and the tail is usually encased with bony rings or plates. Their underside is covered only with soft, hairy skin. Armadillos have a flattened and elongated head with a long, extendable tongue. Set in their jaws are numerous small, peglike teeth. The teeth are not covered by enamel and grow continuously. Their hind limbs have five clawed toes while the powerful forelimbs end in three, four, or five curved digging claws.

Feeding and defense

Armadillos are predominantly nocturnal in their foraging habits and their teeth dictate their diet. Those with sturdy teeth eat insects, snails, worms, small lizards, carrion, tubers, and fruits. Those with soft teeth eat primarily insects such as ants and termites. Using their long, sticky tongue to remove insects from their nests, they have been observed to eat as many as 40,000

A nine-banded armadillo (*Dasypus armadillo*) in the Aransas National Wildlife Refuge, Texas.

ants at one feeding. It is estimated that a single armadillo can eat 200 lb (90 kg) of insects in a year.

A keen sense of smell helps the armadillo locate prey as much as 6 in (10 cm) underground. Pressing its nose to the ground to keep the scent and holding its breath to avoid inhaling dust, the armadillo digs into the soil and litter with astonishing speed.

Armadillos also defend themselves by burrowing into the earth, disappearing completely in a few minutes. Once dug in, they expand their bony shell and wedge themselves into the burrow. They can also run surprisingly fast and, if cornered, will use their claws to fight. Once a predator catches an armadillo it must deal with its bony armor. The three–banded armadillo can roll up into a tight ball presenting nothing but armor to its enemies. Their armor also protects them from cactus spines and dense, thorny undergrowth.

While some species of armadillo are hunted by humans in Central and South America for their meat, the greatest danger to armadillos in the United States is the automobile. Dozens of armadillos are run down as they wander onto highways at dusk. Their habit of leaping several feet into the air when startled contributes to many of the automobile–related deaths.

Reproduction

Armadillos are solitary creatures that seek companions only during the mating season. After mating, female armadillos can suspend their pregnancy for up to two years. Another reproductive peculiarity of armadillos that has caught the attention of geneticists is the ability to produce multiple births from a single fertilized egg: depending on the species, 4, 8, or 12 genetically identical offspring may be produced.

Young armadillos are born in nest chambers within a burrow. At birth, the young are pink and have a soft, leathery skin. This soft skin hardens within a few weeks. Young armadillos stay close to their mother for about two weeks before striking out on their own.

Further Reading:

Grzimek, Bernhard. *Encyclopedia of Mammals.* Vol. 2. New York: McGraw–Hill, 1990.

Nowak, Ronald M. *Walker's Mammals of the World.* Baltimore: Johns Hopkins University Press, 1991.

Schueler, Donald G. "Armadillos Make Me Smile a Lot." *Audubon* (July 1988): 73.

Storrs, Elanor. "I'll Think about That Tomorrow." *Discover* (16 February 1990): 16.

Watson, Jim. "Rising Star." *National Wildlife* (October/November 1989): 47.

Dennis Holley

Armorheads see **Boarfish**

Arrowgrass

The arrowgrass family (Juncaginaceae) is a family of herbaceous plants whose leaves are grass–like and shaped somewhat like an arrowhead. The arrowgrass family has four genera: *Scheuchzeria* with two species; *Thrighlochin* with 12 species; *Maundia* with one species; and *Tetroncium* with one species.

All species in the arrowgrass family grow in wet or moist habitats in temperate and cold regions of the world. Many species grow in fresh water and are common in sphagnum bogs. Other species grow in brackish (semi–salty) water.

All plants in this family have thin, grass–like leaves that are flat, linear, and smooth. They have a specialized underground stem, referred to as a rhizome.

The leaves and roots arise from the rhizome. The roots of some species are fat and tuberous. Most species are perennial, in that they maintain leaves all year round.

The flowers of all species are small and inconspicuous, with clusters of individual flowers arising from an erect stalk. This inflorescence is referred to as a spike or raceme. The flowers are symmetrical, and the different parts of the flowers occur in threes or in multiples of three. Some species have bisexual flowers, in that male and female organs occur on the same flower. Other species have unisexual flowers, with male and female organs occurring in different, separate flowers. The flowers of all species are wind–pollinated.

The fertilized flowers give rise to fruits, referred to as a follicle, a dry fruit that splits along a suture on one side to release the seed(s). The follicles of plants in the arrowgrass family have one or two seeds. Each embryonic seed has one cotyledon (seed leaf).

The plants of the arrowgrass family are not of great economic significance to humans. However, the leaves or rhizomes of some species have been traditionally eaten by some aboriginal peoples of North America and Australia.

Arrowroot

Arrowroot is an edible starch obtained from the underground stems, or rhizomes, of several species of the genus *Maranta*, family Marantaceae. The most common species of arrowroot is *Maranta arundinacea*, native to the tropical areas of Florida and the West Indies, and called true, Bermuda, or West Indian arrowroot. Several relatives of true arrowroot are also known locally as arrowroot and have roots containing edible starch. For example, Brazilian arrowroot from the cassava plant (*Manihot esculenta*) is the source of tapioca. Other starches also called arrowroot are obtained from genus *Curcuma* and *Tacca*. True arrowroot and its relatives are currently cultivated in Australia, southeast Asia, Brazil, and the West Indies.

The roots of arrowroot grow underground to about 1.5 ft (46 cm) long and to two cm in diameter. Above ground, branched stems grow up to 6 ft (2 m) high, having big, ovate leaves and a few white flowers. The jointed, light yellow rhizomes are harvested after one year of growth, when they are full of starch. After harvesting, the roots are soaked in water, making their

Arrowroot cookies are a popular food product for babies because arrowroot starch digests easily.

tough, fibrous covering easier to peel off, and the remaining starchy tissue is then beaten into a pulp. The pulp is rinsed with water many times to separate the starch from the residual fiber. The liquid pulp is allowed to dry; the powder that remains is starch. One acre (0.4 ha) of arrowroot can yield 13,200 lb (6 mt) of roots. From this amount, 2,200 lb (1 mt) of starch can be obtained.

Arrowroot starch is very pure; it has no taste or odor, and has minimal nutritional value, other than as a source of energy. It is used in cooking as a thickening agent for soups, sauces, and puddings. What makes this arrowroot unique is that when boiled with a liquid such as water or broth, the gel–like mixture remains transparent, and does not become cloudy or opaque, as is the case with other starches. Arrowroot starch digests easily and is frequently used in food products for babies (for example, arrowroot cookies) or for people who need to eat bland, low protein diets because of illness. Native

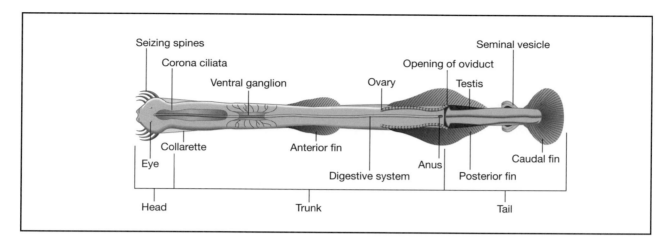

The anatomy of an arrow worm.

Americans used this root to absorb poison out of arrow wounds, giving the plant its common name.

Arsenic see **Element, chemical**

Arteries see **Circulatory system**

Arrow worms

Arrow worms are small marine planktonic animals of the phylum Chaetognatha found in tropical seas. Most of the 50 species of arrow worms belong to the genus *Sagitta*. Arrow worms have a head with eyes and hook–like spines on their jaws that identify them as predators of smaller planktonic animals and larvae. Arrow worms have an elongated body, roughly the shape of an arrow with two pairs of lateral fins and a tail fin. They are cross–fertilizing hermaphroditic animals. Sperm from one individual is received by another individual in a sperm pouch, which later fertilizes the maturing egg in the ovary.

Arrow worms are thought to be distantly related to the phylum Chordata (which includes the vertebrates) but they lack many of the other important chordate characteristics. Nevertheless, arrow worms do have a coelom (a fluid–filled body cavity) which is a characteristic of chordates and the phylum Protochordata. The coelom in arrow worms forms as an out–pocketing of the larval intestine. A similar origin of the coelom is also found in the phylum Echinodermata and the subphylum Cephalochordata (*Amphioxus*) of the phylum Chordata. However, the majority of chordates (the vertebrates in the subphylum Vertebrata) have a coelom that arises in a different way—by a splitting of the tissues to form the cavity.

Arteriosclerosis

Arteriosclerosis literally means "hardening of the arteries." In this condition, a plaque, a hardened mass of lipids, dead cells, fibrous tissue, and platelets collect in the arteries. If large enough, the plaque can block the flow of blood through the artery. If this blockage is severe, it can lead to stroke, in which an artery in the brain becomes blocked; or a heart attack, in which a coronary artery in the heart becomes blocked. Any of the plaques can lead to an embolism, in which a piece of the plaque breaks off and migrates through the artery to other sites. For instance, an embolism may form from a plaque in the leg and migrate to the lung, injuring lung tissue and leading to obstructed breathing.

Since arteriosclerosis causes strokes and heart attacks, it is considered one of the leading causes of illness and death in the United States. Arteriosclerosis has been linked to high blood cholesterol levels, lack of exercise, and smoking. Cholesterol is a substance that is similar to fat and is found in fatty foods. Although a diet low in cholesterol and fat can reduce the risk of arteriosclerosis, some people have a genetic predisposition to high cholesterol levels. This condition, called hypercholesteremia, puts people at high risk to develop arteriosclerosis. Researchers are currently working on ways to help people with hypercholesteremia lower their cholesterol levels. For now, lowering cholesterol is achieved through diet and some drug therapies. In the future, a gene that makes a cholesterol–neutralizing protein may be introduced into hypercholesteremia patients.

The cause of arteriosclerosis

Arteriosclerosis is the end stage of a condition called atherosclerosis. Atherosclerosis means "hardening of a paste–like, fatty material." The pasty, fatty material develops within arteries over a period of many years. If the condition is not treated, this material will eventually harden into arteriosclerotic plaques.

Although researchers continue to speculate about how and why this fatty material gets into arteries, a consensus has emerged in the last 20 years that points to injury of the artery walls as the underlying cause of atherosclerosis. This injury can be mechanical, such as an artery that has been nicked or cut in some way. Injury can also be in the form of exposure to various agents, such as toxins, viruses, or cholesterol. When the artery wall is injured, it tries to heal itself. The response of artery cells and the immune system to the injury leads, paradoxically, to the formation of plaques.

How plaques form

Interestingly, all middle–aged and older people have some form of atherosclerosis. In fact, some experts consider atherosclerosis part of the normal wear and tear of the arteries. Most people will not progress beyond atherosclerosis to arteriosclerosis. In some people, however, such as those with hypercholesteremia or people with high–cholesterol diets, atherosclerosis progresses to hardened plaques that block the arteries.

Researchers have formed the injury model of atherosclerosis by studying the arteries of people of all ages. In infants, for instance, a "fatty streak" consisting of lipids and immune cells is present in the innermost layer of arteries. Lipids are molecules found in cholesterol. Even at this young age, the arteries are already responding to injury, most likely the presence of cholesterol.

In teenagers and young adults at high risk for atherosclerosis, layers of macrophages (special white cells that ingest foreign material) and smooth muscle cells overlie the interior wall of arteries. In an attempt to reduce the amount of lipid within the artery, macrophages ingest the lipid. Because under a microscope the lipid within the macrophage appears to be "bubbly," or foamy, a macrophage that has ingested lipid is called a foam cell.

As time passes, more and more macrophages ingest more and more lipid, and more foam cells are present within the artery. To rid the artery of the ever increasing load of lipid, foam cells migrate through the artery wall to return the lipid to the liver, spleen, and lymph nodes. As the foam cells penetrate the artery walls, they further injure the artery. This injury attracts platelets, special components of the blood that lead to the formation of blood clots. When you cut your finger, platelets rush to the site of injury and begin forming a clot to stop the flow of blood. In an artery, platelets also rush to the site of injury and begin the process of clot formation. But instead of helping the situation, the clot further complicates the growing plaque in the artery, which at this point consists of lipid–laden macrophages, lipids, muscle cells, and platelets.

The platelets, in turn, release chemicals called growth factors. Several different growth factors are released by the platelets. One causes the cells in the artery to release proteins and other substances that eventually lead to the formation of a matrix, a collection of tough protein fibers, that further hardens the artery. Another growth factor prompts the development of blood vessels in the plaque. At this stage, the plaque is fully formed. It is large enough to block the flow of blood through the artery. At its center is a pool of lipid and dead artery cells, and it is covered by a cap of connective tissue.

Diagnosis and treatment

Most people are unaware of the atherosclerotic process going on in their arteries. The condition usually goes undiagnosed until a person develops arteriosclerosis. The progressive hardening of the arteries in the heart, for instance, can sometimes be felt as a distinct pain, called angina. Angina is a warning sign that the atherosclerosis may become life–threatening. People with angina take medication and are usually monitored by physicians to make sure the arteries do not become completely blocked. Some angina patients are able to control their arteriosclerosis with proper diet and lifestyle changes, such as quitting smoking.

The atherosclerotic plaques can be visualized by a special x ray technique. A slim tube called a catheter is inserted through an artery in the leg or other location until it reaches the plaque site. Dye that can be seen on x rays is shot through the catheter. When an x ray of the site is taken, the plaque can be clearly seen.

Currently, arteriosclerosis in the arteries of the heart is treated with drugs, surgery, or a technique called angioplasty. Like the x ray technique, angioplasty involves inserting a catheter through an artery. Instead

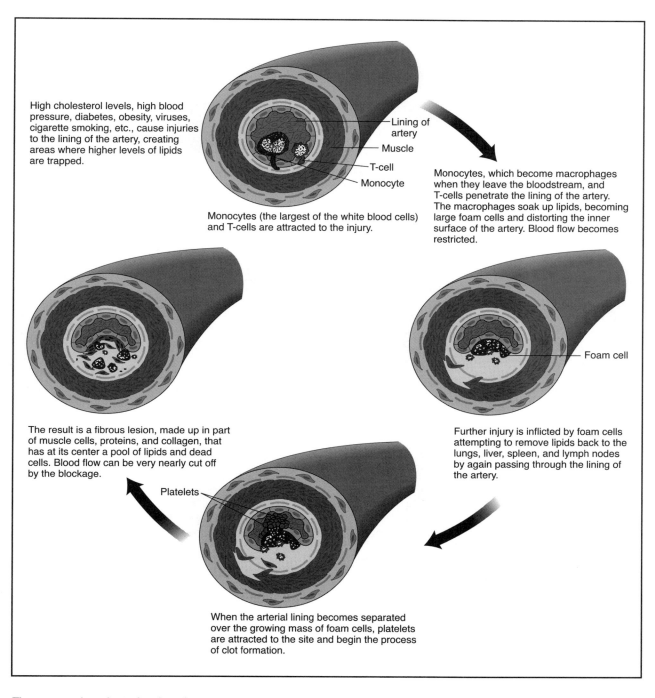

High cholesterol levels, high blood pressure, diabetes, obesity, viruses, cigarette smoking, etc., cause injuries to the lining of the artery, creating areas where higher levels of lipids are trapped.

Lining of artery
Muscle
T-cell
Monocyte

Monocytes (the largest of the white blood cells) and T-cells are attracted to the injury.

Monocytes, which become macrophages when they leave the bloodstream, and T-cells penetrate the lining of the artery. The macrophages soak up lipids, becoming large foam cells and distorting the inner surface of the artery. Blood flow becomes restricted.

Foam cell

The result is a fibrous lesion, made up in part of muscle cells, proteins, and collagen, that has at its center a pool of lipids and dead cells. Blood flow can be very nearly cut off by the blockage.

Further injury is inflicted by foam cells attempting to remove lipids back to the lungs, liver, spleen, and lymph nodes by again passing through the lining of the artery.

Platelets

When the arterial lining becomes separated over the growing mass of foam cells, platelets are attracted to the site and begin the process of clot formation.

The progression of arteriosclerosis.

of shooting dye through the catheter, the catheter is used as a "roto–rooter" to open up the narrowed arteries. Some researchers have used anti–clotting drugs delivered through the catheter to dissolve clots.

Surgery is also used to treat arteriosclerosis in the heart. Bypass surgery, in which a section of an artery in the leg is used to "bypass" a section of a hardened heart artery, is performed to correct arteriosclerosis. Because this surgery carries a risk of stroke and other serious complications, angioplasty and drug therapy, in conjunction with diet management, are tried first. If no positive results are found, surgery is performed as a last resort.

One problem with angioplasty is that the solution is often only temporary. The plaques return because angioplasty addresses only the plaques, not the process that leads to their formation. In the future, molecules that target the growth factors released by the platelets may be delivered directly to the plaques through special catheters. This treatment is some years away.

Prevention

Because arteriosclerosis may be the result of the artery's response to cholesterol, it makes sense to reduce the intake of cholesterol. Two types of cholesterol are found in foods: cholesterol that contains high density lipoprotein (the HDL's) and cholesterol that contains low density lipoprotein (the LDL's). Researchers have found that LDL cholesterol is the culprit in arteriosclerosis.

To keep the arteries healthy, eat no more than 300 mg of cholesterol a day. Cholesterol is found only in animal products; plant foods contain no cholesterol. Since many foods that are high in fat are also high in cholesterol, limiting fat intake can help reduce cholesterol levels. Knowing which foods are high in cholesterol and avoiding these foods (or limiting these foods) can also lower cholesterol. Have your blood cholesterol levels checked periodically, particularly if your family has a history of arteriosclerosis. People with hypercholesteremia or a history of heart disease may want to try a stricter diet that eliminates all fats and cholesterol. Before embarking on any major dietary change, however, consult your physician.

See also Blood; Circulatory system; Heart.

Further Reading:

Acierno, Louis J. *The History of Cardiology*. New York: Parthenon Publishing Group, 1994.

Filer, Lloyd J. Jr.; Ronald M. Lauer, and Russell L. Leupker, eds. *Prevention of Atherosclerosis and Hypertension Beginning in Youth*. Philadelphia: Lea and Febiger, 1994.

Fuster, Valentin, ed. *Progression–Regression of Atherogenesis: Molecular, Cellular, and Clinical Bases*. Dallas: American Heart Association, 1992.

Kane, John P., et. al. "Regression of Coronary Atherosclerosis During Treatment of Familial Hypercholesteremia With Combined Drug Therapies." *Journal of the American Medical Association* 264 (23): 3007, December 19, 1990.

Ross, Russell. "The Pathenogenesis of Atherosclerosis: A Perspective for the 1990s." *Nature* 362: 801 ff, April 29, 1993.

Tunis, Sean R., et. al. "The Use of Angioplasty, Bypass Surgery, and Amputation in the Treatment of Peripheral Vascular Diseases." *New England Journal of Medicine* 325 (8): 556, August 22, 1991.

Yeagle, Philip. *Understanding Your Cholesterol*. San Diego: Academic Press, 1991.

Kathleen Scogna

Arthritis

The word arthritis is a general term that literally means an inflammation of a bone joint. There are over 100 diseases that exhibit the symptom of bone joint inflammation or injury. This condition leads to such further symptoms as aches and pain, swelling, stiffness, and fatigue. Since the body sites most commonly affected are the hands, arms, shoulders, hips, and legs, any action requiring movements of these parts becomes difficult.

Diagnosis of arthritic diseases requires a knowledge of the more than 100 different types. When a patient suffers from more than one type of arthritis there may be a further complication in diagnosis.

Osteoarthritis and rheumatoid arthritis are the two most usual occurrences of the disease. Of the two forms of arthritis, osteoarthritis is more commonplace, since it is a disease of aging. It also occurs as a result of injuries or overworking certain parts of the body. Treatment of arthritis calls for pain relief with anti–inflammatory drugs, exercise, proper nutrition, and rest.

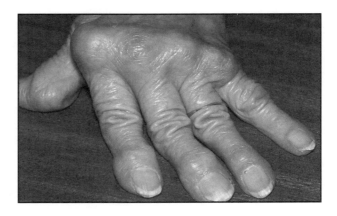

A close-up of a hand deformed by rheumatoid arthritis; the knuckles are swollen and reddened and the fingers curve away from the thumb. The ends of the middle fingers are swollen with cartilage accretion (called Heberden's nodes) that are an indication of osteoarthritis.

Osteoarthritis

Cartilage tissue surrounds the bone joints of the body. For various reasons these tissues begin to wear away or break down. That action results in the rougher surfaces of the joint bones scraping against each other, while the torn cartilage contributes further to the damage of the joint. This internal trauma (injury) releases chemicals in the body, called prostaglandins, to surround the site of injury. It is the prostaglandins along with other irritating substances from the body's immune system that cause the pain, swelling, and inflammation.

Joint sites that are most commonly subject to this disorder are the spine, knee, and hips. It also affects finger joints. Other sites are less prone but can be affected by injury or overwork. While osteoarthritis can occur at any age, it is most commonly seen in those over the age of 50, indicating the mechanism of wear and tear as one of its causes.

Osteoarthritis may be caused by a number of different factors, such as heredity, overuse of a joint, injury, disease, and diet. Though the condition is irreversible, losing weight to reduce strain on weight–bearing joints and proper exercise, along with physical therapy, can be effective in reducing pain before the use of medications is introduced.

Differences between rheumatoid arthritis and osteoarthritis

Of the more than 100 different types of arthritis, rheumatoid arthritis is one of the most crippling forms of the disease. Rheumatoid arthritis may be a disease of the immune system caused by a virus. Compared to

osteoarthritis, the pain in the joints is more intense and is also attended by swelling.

Unlike osteoarthritis, rheumatoid arthritis is seen in younger people. Three times as many women are subject to this disorder than men. Osteoarthritis develops slowly over a long period of time, while rheumatoid arthritis can occur within a short period of time—weeks or months. The joints on one side of the body are usually affected in osteoarthritis, but with rheumatoid arthritis, the same joints on both sides of the body are affected.

Inflammation (redness, warmth, swelling) of the joint is not a usual symptom of osteoarthritis, but it is of rheumatoid arthritis. Only certain joints are affected by osteoarthritis—the weight bearing ones—elbows and shoulders are seldom affected. In rheumatoid arthritis shoulders and elbows and many other joints are affected.

Rheumatoid arthritis poses a threat to the vital organs of the body, such as the heart, lungs, and visual centers. With osteoarthritis there is not an overall sense of ill–health, but rheumatoid arthritis will cause a loss of weight, fever, and a condition of general health impairment. There may also be bone nodule formation on different parts of the body with rheumatoid arthritis.

Inflammation, fever, swelling, aches and pains—the major symptoms of rheumatoid arthritis are all signs that the immune system is at work trying to ward off the attack of a foreign invader, or in terms of the body, antigens. The army of the immune system is composed of the white blood cells (leukocytes). These cells are found in the lymph nodes, spleen, and thymus. They travel to other parts of the body through the blood stream.

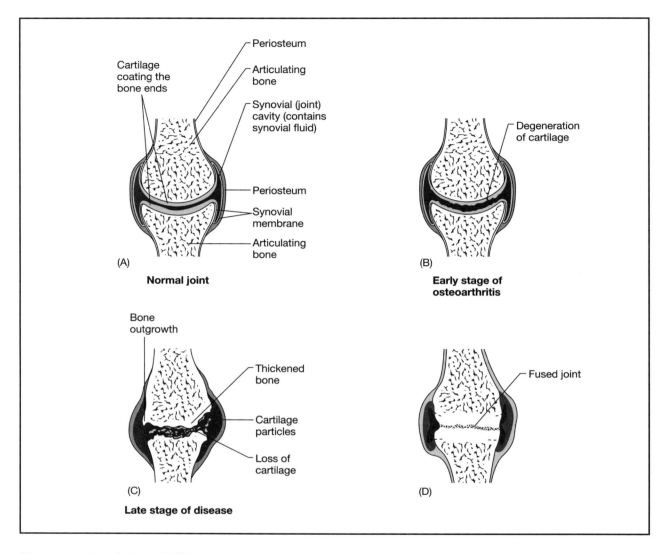

(A) **Normal joint**

Cartilage coating the bone ends

Periosteum

Articulating bone

Synovial (joint) cavity (contains synovial fluid)

Periosteum

Synovial membrane

Articulating bone

(B) **Early stage of osteoarthritis**

Degeneration of cartilage

(C) **Late stage of disease**

Bone outgrowth

Thickened bone

Cartilage particles

Loss of cartilage

(D)

Fused joint

The progression of osteoarthritis.

In its battle against antigens, the white blood cells form special cells. The B–cells produce antibodies which recognize and destroy an antigen. T–cells help the B–cells to produce antibodies, while suppressor T–cells signal the body to stop the production of antibodies. Killer T–cells destroy virus–infected cells and other T cells produce lymphokines, pain–causing chemicals that turn on the immune system.

In rheumatoid arthritis it appears that the immune system is turning against the body though there is no apparent foreign invader. This condition could be due either to a disorder of the immune system known as autoimmunity or the presence of an undetected virus or antigen that the immune system is unsuccessfully trying to fight.

People between the ages of 25 and 50 and women are more subject to rheumatoid arthritis. Inflammation occurs within the linings of the bone joints (synovial membranes). The whole joint then becomes painful. It becomes thick, red, and swollen from the inflammation. Unlike osteoarthritis, rheumatoid arthritis has a number of other bodily symptoms such as fatigue, loss of appetite and weight, and fever. It is often crippling and can deform parts of the body, especially the fingers. There are sometimes periods of remission when the disease moves in cycles.

Synovial analysis of arthritis types

Within the bone joints, tendon sheaths, and bursa, which are small closed sacs throughout the skeletal system, is a clear, thick fluid called synovia or synovial fluid. By analyzing the synovial fluid under the microscope, identifying crystal formation, and doing a white blood cell count it is possible to classify various types of arthritis. Synovial fluid that shows a departure from the normal will identify the following groups of arthritis disease:

Group 1: Noninflammatory—Osteoarthritis, traumatic arthritis; Group 2: Inflammatory–immunological—Systemic lupus erythematous, rheumatoid arthritis, Reiter's syndrome; Group 3: Inflammatory–crystalline—Gout, pseudogout; Group 4: Inflammatory–infectious—Acute bacterial arthritis, tuberculous arthritis.

Treatment of arthritis

The first line of drug treatment for osteoarthritis, as well as other types of arthritis, is nonsteroidal anti–inflammatory medicines, including aspirin and medicines that are closely related to aspirin. Some NSAIDs (pronounced en seds) are sold over–the–counter, but most containing higher dosages are sold only by prescription and have to be monitored carefully to avoid adverse side effects.

A second line of drug treatment is needed for rheumatoid arthritis and the other forms of the disease. In addition to the NSAIDs, which includes aspirin compounds and non–aspirin salicylates, corticosteroids are also used to reduce inflammation. These drugs are medicines that are like cortisone, which is produced in the adrenal cortex.

Other medicines used for rheumatoid arthritis try to slow the disease down or make it go into remission. These medicines are called immunosuppressants or cytotoxics because it is believed that they cut down the rate of cell division throughout the body. The hope then is that the immune system will turn out fewer white blood cells. These medicines usually take weeks or months to take effect. They can also suppress the growth of normal cells which could be life–threatening. Since it may take months before they work, NSAIDs and aspirin are usually taken in the interim period. They must be carefully administered and monitored to avoid any serious impairment of the body's natural defense system. As a second line of drug treatment their purpose is not only to relieve symptoms, as in the case of the NSAIDs, but to reverse or slow down the action of the disease.

In addition to being anti–inflammatories, corticosteroids are also immunosuppressants. They are used to treat a number of different forms of arthritis. The length of treatment can range from several days to years.

KEY TERMS

Anti–inflammatories—A drug used in the treatment of arthritis that counteracts inflammation.

Autoimmunity—A condition where the body's defense system attacks its own tissues and organs.

Bone joint—A place where bones are connected, such as the elbow joint, knee joint, and hip joint.

Cartilage—The tissue which surrounds the joint and degenerates in osteoarthritis.

Corticosteroids—Advanced medication to treat arthritic conditions, often injected into the area of pain.

Immune system—The body's defense system which fights off infection from outside organisms.

Leukocytes—White blood cells produced by the immune system that create antibodies to destroy foreign cells.

NSAIDs—Nonsteroidal anti–inflammatory drugs such as aspirin and ibuprofen, effective in relieving the pain of arthritis and reducing inflammation.

Stomach ulcer—Tears in the stomach lining caused by excess stomach acid.

Synovial fluid—The thick, clear, viscous fluid found in bone joints and used to identify different types of arthritic conditions.

Taken either as a pill or through injection, dosages vary according to the type of arthritis and the needs of the individual.

Corticosteroids are used for both osteoarthritis and rheumatoid arthritis. These medicines are injected into a specific site, such as a finger joint or the knee, for quick relief from pain and inflammation. In addition to blocking prostaglandin production, they also reduce the amount of white blood cells that enter into the damaged area of the joint.

Though aspirin and the other NSAIDs all work the same way to suppress prostaglandin production in the body, there are major differences in the way individuals will respond to particular NSAIDs. In long term use there may be a number of negative side effects for the stomach, kidney, and blood system. These problems have to be worked out very carefully with a patient's physician.

Stomach bleeding and irritation of the gastrointestinal tract are the two major drawbacks of aspirin and the other NSAIDs. Acetaminophen relieves pain without stomach irritation, but it is not an anti–inflammatory nor does it reduce the swelling that accompanies arthritis.

See also Inflammation; Anti–inflammatory agents; Autoimmune disease.

Further Reading:

Blechman, Wilbur J., Sanford H. Roth, and Kenneth R. Wilske. "Osteoarthritis: Are You Up–to–Date?" *Patient Care*. March 15, 1992: 99–144.

Brewerton, Derric. *All About Arthritis*. Cambridge, MA: Harvard University Press, 1992.

Fries, James F. *Arthritis*. Reading, PA: Addison–Wesley, 1990.

The Merck Manual. Rahway, NJ: Merck, 1992.

Jordan P. Richman

Arthropods

Arthropods are invertebrates such as insects, spiders and other arachnids, and crustaceans that comprise the phylum Arthropoda. The phylum Arthropoda includes three major classes—the Insecta, Arachnida, and Crustacea.

Arthropods are characterized by their external skeleton, or exoskeleton, made mostly of *chitin*, a complex, rigid carbohydrate usually covered by a waxy, waterproof cuticle. This integument is important in reducing water loss in terrestrial habitats, in providing protection, and in providing a rigid skeleton against which muscles can work in order to develop motion of the animal or in its body parts. The exoskeleton is segmented, which allows for easy movement of the body, and there are numerous paired, segmented appendages, such as legs, antennae, and external mouth parts. Periodically, the entire rigid exoskeleton is shed, the temporarily soft animal swells in size, and its new, larger exoskeleton hardens.

Most arthropods have compound eyes, each with numerous lenses capable of forming complex, composite images. Arthropods have various mechanisms for the exchange of respiratory gases which, depending on the group, include gills, chambered structures known as book lungs, tracheal tubes, and various moist areas of the body surface.

Most arthropods exhibit sexual dimorphism, in that the male animals look distinctly different from the females, at least in the appearance of their external genitalia. Arthropods have internal fertilization, and they lay eggs. Arthropods have a complex life cycle. This generally involves eggs, a juvenile larval stage, and the adult form, with complex metamorphosis occurring during the transitions between these stages. In some insects, there is an additional stage between the larva and the adult, known as a pupa.

Arthropods are extremely diverse in species richness. Approximately 874,000 living species of arthropods have been named, comprising more than 80% of all named species of animals. However, some estimates predict large numbers of species of arthropods that have not yet been described and named by biologists. Most of these unnamed species are small beetles and other inconspicuous arthropods, and most of these occur in old–growth tropical rainforests, a biome that has not yet been well explored and studied by taxonomists and ecologists.

Species of arthropods utilize an enormous variety of Earth's habitats. Most species of Crustaceans are aquatic, although a few, such as woodlice and land crabs, occur in moist habitats on land. The spiders, mites, scorpions, and other arachnids are almost entirely terrestrial animals, as are the extremely diverse insects.

Some species of arthropods are very important to humans. A few species are important as vectors in the transmission of microbial diseases, such as malaria, yellow fever, encephalitis, plague, Chagas disease, and Lyme disease. Some arthropods are venomous, and can hurt or kill people by single or more multiple stinging, for example, scorpions, some spiders, and bees and wasps. Some arthropods are a highly nutritious source of food for people, as is the case of lobsters, crayfish, shrimp, many species of crabs, and some insects.

However, the most critical importance of arthropods relates to the extremely diverse and beneficial ecological functions that they carry out. Arthropods play an important role in nutrient cycling and other aspects of ecological food webs. Earth's ecosystems would be in a great deal of trouble if there was any substantial decline in the myriad species of arthropods in the biosphere.

See also Arachnids; Crustacea; Insects.

Artichoke see **Composite family**

Artifacts see **Archaeology**

A scanning electron micrograph (SEM) of fibers of a dacron polyester material used in sleeping bags. The core of each fiber has up to seven air cavities that increase its insulating ability.

Artificial fibers

Polymeric fibers

Most synthetic fibers are polymer–based, and are produced by a process known as spinning. This process involves extrusion of a polymeric liquid through fine holes known as spinnerets. After the liquid has been spun, the resulting fibers are oriented by stretching or drawing. This increases the polymeric chain orientation and degree of crystallinity, and has the effect of increasing the modulus and tensile strength of the fibers. Fiber manufacture is classified according to the type of spinning that the polymer liquid undergoes: this may be melt spinning, dry spinning, or wet spinning.

Melt spinning is the simplest of these three methods, but it still requires that the polymer constituent be stable above its melting temperature. In melt spinning, the polymer is melted and forced through the spinnerets, which may contain from 50 to 500 holes. The diameter of the fiber immediately following extrusion exceeds the hole diameter. During the cooling process, the fiber is drawn to induce orientation. Further orientation may later be achieved by stretching the fiber to a higher draw ratio. Melt spinning is used with polymers such as nylon, polyethylene, polyvinyl chloride, cellulose triacetate, and polyethylene terephthalate, and in the multifilament extrusion of polypropylene.

In dry spinning, the polymer is first dissolved in a solvent. The polymer solution is extruded through the spinnerets. The solvent is evaporated with hot air and collected for reuse. The fiber then passes over rollers, and is stretched to orient the molecules and increase the fiber strength. Cellulose acetate, cellulose triacetate, acrylic, modacrylic, aromatic nylon, and polyvinyl chloride are made by dry spinning.

In wet spinning, the polymer solution is spun into a coagulating solution to precipitate the polymer. This process has been used with acrylic, modacrylic, aromatic nylon, and polyvinyl chloride fibers. Viscose rayon is produced from regenerated cellulose by a wet spinning technique.

Table 1, "Synthetic Polymeric Fibers," provides detailed information about each of the important classes of spun fibers.

Other synthetic fibers

Besides the polymer–based synthetic fibers described above, there are other types of synthetic fibers

TABLE 1. ARTIFICIAL POLYMERIC FIBERS

ACRYLIC

Compostion	At least 85% acrylonitrile units. Anidex is a cross-linked polyacrylate consisting of at least 50 wt% esters of a monohydric alcohol and acrylic acid.
Processing	Orlon® is made by dissolving acrylonitrile in an organic solvent. The solvent is filtered and dry-spun. Fibers are drawn at high temperature to 3 to 8 times their original length and the molecules are oriented into long parallel chains.
Properties	Resistant to dilute acids and alkalies, solvents, insects, mildew, weather. Damaged by alkalies and acids, heat above 356° F (180° C), acetone, ketones.
Uses	Sweaters, women's coats, men's winter suiting, carpets, blankets, outdoor fabrics, knits, fur-like fabrics, blankets. Orlon® and Acrilan® have been used as wool substitutes.
Trade Names	Orlon® (E.I. duPont de Nemours & Co., Inc.), Acrilan® (Monsanto Co.), Cantrece® (E.I. duPont de Nemours & Co., Inc.).

MODACRYLIC

Composition	35 to 85% acrylonitrile units.
Processing	Union Carbide makes Dynel®, a staple copolymer modacrylic fiber made from resin of 40% acrylonitrile and 60% vinyl chloride. It is converted into staple in a continuous wet-spinning process. The resin powder dissolved in acetone, filtered and spun. Fiber is dried, cut and crimped.
Uses	Dynel® resembles wool. Used for work clothing, water-softener bags, dye nets, filter cloth, blankets, draperies, sweaters, pile fabric.
Trade Names	Verel®-copolymer (Tennessee Eastman Co.), Dynel®-copolymer (E.I. duPont de Nemours & Co., Inc.)

POLYESTER

Composition	85% ester of a dihhydric alcohol and terephthalic acid.
Processing	Melt spinning.
Properties	Resistant to weak acids and alkalies, solvents, oils, mildew, moths. Damaged by phenol, heat above 338° F (170° C).
Uses	Apparel, curtains, rope, twine, sailcloth, belting, fiberfill, tire cord, belts, blankets, blends with cotton.

TABLE 1. ARTIFICIAL POLYMERIC FIBERS (cont'd)

Trade Names	Dacron® (E.I. duPont de Nemours & Co., Inc.), Kodel® (Tennessee Eastman Co.), Fortrel® (Fiber Industries, Inc.

RAYON	
Composition	The pioneer artificial fibers viscose, cuprammonium cellulose, and cellulose acetate were originally referred to as rayon. This name now is reserved for viscose. Rayon is now a generic name for a semisynthetic fiber composed of regenerated cellulose and manufactured fibers consisting of regenerated cellulose in which substituents have replaced not more than 15% of the hydroxyl group hydrogens.
Processing	Rayon was first made by denitration of cellulose nitrate fibers, but now most is made from wood pulp by the viscose process. The viscose process produces filaments of regenerated cellulose. First, a solution of cellulose undergoes chemical reaction, ageing, or solution ripening; followed by filtration and removal of air; spinning of fiber; combining of the filaments into yarn; and finishing (bleaching, washing, oiling, and drying).
Properties	Rayon can be selectively dyed in combination with cotton. Hydroxyl groups in the cellulose molecules cause the fiber to absorb water—this causes low wet strength. In the dry state, the hydroxyl groups are hydrogen bonded, and the molecules are held together. Thus the dry fibers maintain their strength even at high temperatures.
Uses	High tenacity viscose yarn is used cords for tires, hose, and belting. Strength is achieved by orienting the fiber molecules when they are made. Textile rayon is used primarily in women's apparel, draperies, upholstery, and in blends with wool in carpets and rugs. Surgical dressings.

ACETATE (CELLULOSE ACETATE)	
Composition	Cellulose acetate and its homologs are esters of cellulose and are not regenerated cellulose. Where not less than 92% of the hydroxyl groups are acetylated, the product is called a triacetate.
Processing	Cellulose is converted to cellulose acetate by treatment with a mix containing acetic anhydride. No process exists whereby the desired number of acetyl groups can be achieved directly. The process involves first producing the triacetate, then hydrolyzing a portion of the acetate groups. The desired material is usually about half way between triacetate and diacetate. Arnel® (cellulose triacetate) is produced by Celanese Corp. It is a machine-washable fiber, that shows low shrinkage when stretched, and has good crease and pleat resistance.
Uses	Blankets, carpets, modacrylic fibers, cigarette filters.
Trade Names	Arnel® (Celanese Corp.).

TABLE 1. ARTIFICIAL POLYMERIC FIBERS (cont'd)

VINYLS AND VINYLIDENES

Composition	Saran is a copolymer of vinyl chloride and vinylidene chloride (at least 80% by weight vinylidene chloride units). Vinyon is the trade name given to copolymers of 90% vinyl chloride and 10% vinyl acetate (at least 85% vinyl chloride units).
Processing	Saran is prepared by mixing the two monomers and heating. The copolymer is heated, extruded at 356° F (180° C), air-cooled, and stretched. The vinyon copolymer is dissolved in acetone to 22% solids and filtered. The fibers are extruded by dry spinning, left to stand, then wet-twisted and stretched. The fibers are resistant to acids and alkalies, sunlight, and aging. Vinyon is useful in heat-sealing fabrics, work clothing. Bayer chemists first spun polyvinyl chloride into this chemically resistant and rot-proof fiber in 1931.
Properties	These fibers are resistant to mildew, bacterial, and insect attack. Polyvinyl chloride is resistant to acids and alkalies, insects, mildew, alcohol, oils. Polyvinylidene chloride is resistant to acids, most alkalies, alcohol, bleaches, insects, mildew, and weather. Polyvinyl chloride is damaged by ethers, esters, aromatic hydrocarbons, ketones, hot acids, and heat above 158° F (70° C). Polyvinylidene chloride is damaged by heat above 194° F (90° C) and by many solvents.
Uses	Saran can be used for insect screens. Widest use is for automobile seat covers and home upholstery. Typical polyvinyl chloride uses include nonwoven materials, felts, filters, and blends with other fibers. Typical polyvinylidene chloride uses include outdoor fabrics, insect screens, curtains, upholstery, carpets, work clothes.
Trade Names	Proprietary polyvinylidene chloride names include Dynel®-copolymer (Uniroyal, Inc.). Saran is a generic name for polyvinylidene chloride.

NYLON

Composition	Nylon is a generic name for a family of polyamide polymers characterized by the presence of an amide group. Common types are nylon 66, nylon 6, nylon 4, nylon 9, nylon 11, and nylon 12.
Processing	Nylon 66 was developed by Carothers by reacting adipic acid and hexamethylenediamine in 1935. Nylon 6 is based on caprolactam. It was developed by I.G. Farbenindustrie in 1940.
Properties	Resistant to alkalies, molds, solvents, moths. Damaged by strong acids, phenol, bleaches, and heat above 338° F (170° C).
Uses	Typical uses include tire cord, carpets, upholstery, apparel, belting, hose, tents, toothbrush bristles, hairbrushes, fish nets and lines, tennis rackets, parachutes, and surgical sutures.
Trade Names	Chemstrand nylon® (Monsanto Co.).

SPANDEX

TABLE 1. ARTIFICIAL POLYMERIC FIBERS (cont'd)

Composition	At least 85% by weight segmented polyurethane.
Processing	Segmented polyurethanes are produced by reacting diisocyanates with long-chain glycols. The product is chain-extended or coupled, then converted to fibers by dry spinning.
Properties	Resistant to solvents, oils, alkalies, insects, oxidation. Damaged by heat above 284° F(140° C), strong acids.
Uses	Fibers are used in foundation garments, hose, swimwear, surgical hose, and other elastic products.
Trade Names	Proprietary names include Lycra® (E.I. duPont de Nemours & Co., Inc.), Spandelle® (Firestone Synthetic Fibers Co.).
	OLEFIN
Composition	At least 85 wt% ethylene, propylene, or other olefin units other than amorphous rubber polyolefins.
Processing	Polymer is spun from a melt at about 212° F (100° C) above the melting point because the polymer is very viscous near its melting point.
Properties	Difficult to dye. Low melting points. Polypropylene has a very low specific gravity, making it very light and suitable for blankets. It has 3 to 4 times the resistance of nylon to snags and runs, and is softer, smoother, and lighter. Polypropylene is resistant to alkalies, acids, solvents, insects, mildew. Polyethylene is resistant to alkalies, acids (except nitric), insects, mildew. Polypropylene is damaged by heat above 230° F (110° C). Polyethylene is damaged by oil and grease, heat above 212° F (100° C), oxidizers.
Uses	Olefins make excellent ropes, laundry nets, carpets, blankets, and carpet backing. Polypropylene is typically used for rope, twine, outdoor fabrics, carpets, upholstery. High density polyethylene is typically used for rope, twine, and fishnets. Low density polyethylene is typically used for outdoor fabrics, filter fabrics, decorative coverings.
Trade Names	Proprietary names for polypropylene include Herculon® (Hercules Powder Co.), Polycrest® (Uniroyal, Inc.); proprietary polyethylene names include DLP® (W. R. Grace & Co.).
	FLUOROCARBON
Composition	Long chain carbon molecules with bonds saturated by fluorine. Teflon is polytetrafluroethylene.
Processing	Fluorocarbon sheets are made by combining polytetrafluoroethylene with another microgranular material to form thin, flexible sheets. The filler is then dissolved out, leaving a pure, porous polytetrafluroethylene sheet. The pores must be small enough to be vapor permeable but large enough to extend through the fabric. The sheet has to be very thin, and is therefore fragile. GoreTex® has to protected by being sandwiched between robust fabrics such as polyester or nylon weave.

TABLE 1. ARTIFICIAL POLYMERIC FIBERS (cont'd)

Properties	As a fiber, Teflon is highly resistant to oxidation and the action of chemicals, including strong acids, alkalies, and oxidizing agents. It is nonflammable. It retains these properties at high temperatures 446°-554° F (230°-290° C). It is strong and tough. It exhibits low friction, which coupled with its chemical inertness, makes it suitable in pump packings and shift bearings. Polytetrafluoroethylene is resistant to almost all chemicals, solvents, insects, mildew. Polytetrafluoroethylene is damaged by heat above 482° F (250° C), and by fluorine at high temperatures.
Uses	Typical uses include corrosion-resistant packings, etc., tapes, filters, bearings, weatherproof outdoorwear.
Trade Name	Teflon® (E.I. duPont de Nemours & Co., Inc.) and GoreTex® (W. L. Gore & Associates) are proprietary names.
	VINAL
Composition	Vinal is the U.S. term for vinyl alcohol fibers. At least 50 wt% of the long synthetic polymer chain is composed of vinyl alcohol units. The total of the vinyl alcohol units and any one or more of the various acetal units is at least 85 wt% of the fiber.
Processing	Vinyl acetate is first polymerized, then saponified to polyvinyl alcohol. The fiber is spun, then treated with formalin and heat to make it insoluble in water. Production has remained largely confined to
Properties	The fiber has reasonable tensile strength, a moderately low melting point (432° F [222° C]), limited elastic recovery, good chemical resistance, and resistance to degradation by organisms. Has good chemical resistance, low affinity for water, good resistance to mildew and fungi. Combustible. Used for fishing nets, stockings, gloves, hats, rainwear, swimsuits. Polyvinyl alcohol is resistant to acids, alkalies, insects, mildew, oils; it is damaged by heat above 320° F (160° C), phenol, cresol, and formic acid.
Uses	Used in bristles, filter cloths, sewing thread, fishnets, and apparel. Polyvinyl alcohol is typically used for a wide range of industrial and apparel uses, rope, work clothes, fish nets.
	AZLON
Composition	Any regenerated naturally occurring protein. Azlon is the generic name for manufactured fiber in which the fiber-forming substance is composed of any regenerated naturally occurring protein. Proteins from corn, soybeans, peanuts, fish, and milk have been used. Azlon consists of polymeric amino acids.

TABLE 1. ARTIFICIAL POLYMERIC FIBERS (cont'd)

Processing	Vegetable matter is first crushed and the oil is extracted. Then the remaining protein matter is dissolved in a caustic solution and aged. The resulting viscous solution is extruded through a spinneret into an acid bath to coagulate the filaments. The fiber is cured and stretched to give it strength. Then the fiber is washed, dried, and used in a filament or staple form. Casein fibers are extracted from skim milk, then dissolved in water, and extruded under heat and pressure. The filaments are hardened and aged in an acid bath. Then they are washed, dried, and used in either filament or staple form. Seaweed fibers are made by extracting sodium alginate from brown seaweed using an alkali. The resulting solution is purified, filtered, and wet spun into a coagulating bath to form the fibers.
Properties	Azlon fibers have a soft hand, and blend well with other fibers. Combustible.
Uses	Used in blends to add a wool-like hand to other fibers, and to add loft, softness, and resiliency. Protein fibers resist moths and mildew, do not shrink, and impart a cashmere-like hand to blended fabrics.

TABLE 2. ARTIFICIAL, NONPOLYMERIC FIBERS

	GLASS
Composition	Comprised primarily of silica.
Processing	Continuous filament process—molten glass drawn into fibers, which are wound mechanically. Winding stretches the fibers. Subsequently formed into glass fiber yarns and cords. Staple fiber process—uses jets of compressed air to attenuate or draw out molten glass into fine fibers. Used for yarns of various sizes. Wool process—molten glass attenuated into long, resilient fibers. Forms glass wool, used for thermal insulation or fabricated into other
Properties	Nonflammable. Can be subjected to temperatures as high as 1200° F (650° C) before they deteriorate. Non-absorbent Impervious. They resist most chemicals, and do not break when washed in water. Mothproof, mildew-proof, do not degrade in sunlight or with age. Strong. Among the strongest man-made fibers. Derived from limestone, silica sand, boric acid, clay, coal, and fluospar. Different amounts of these ingredients result in different properties.

TABLE 2. ARTIFICIAL, NONPOLYMERIC FIBERS (cont'd)

Uses	Decorative fabrics, fireproof clothing, soundproofing, plastics reinforcement, tires, upholstery, electrical and thermal insulation, air filters, insect screens, roofing, ceiling panels.
METAL	
Composition	Whiskers are single-crystal fibers up to 2 in (5 cm) long. They are made from tungsten, cobalt, tantalum, and other metals, and are used largely in composite structures for specialized functions. Metallic yarns consist of metallized polyester film.
Processing	Filaments are alloys drawn through diamond dies to diameters as small as 0.002 cm. In ancient times, gold and silver threads were widely used in royal and ecclesiastical garments. Today, metallic yarns usually consist of a core of single-ply polyester film that is metallized on one side by vacuum-depositing aluminum. The film is then lacquered on both sides with clear or tinted colors.
Properties	Metallic whiskers may have extremely high tensile strength. Modern metallic yarns are soft, lightweight, and do not tarnish.
Uses	Whiskers are used in biconstituent structures composed of a metal and a polymeric material. Examples include aluminum filaments covered with cellulose acetate butyrate. Steels for tire cord and antistatic devices have also been developed. Metallic yarns are used for draperies, fabrics, suits, dresses, coats, ribbons, tapes, and shoelaces.
Trade Names	Producers of metallic yarns include Metlon Corp.; Metal Film Co.; and Multi-tex Products Co. Dobeckman Co. produced the first widely used metallic yarn under the tradename Lurex®.
CERAMIC	
Composition	Alumina and silica.
Processing	Insertion of aluminum ions into silica.
Properties	Retains properties to 2300° FR (1260° C), and under some conditions to 3000° F (1648° C), lightweight, inert to most acids and unaffected by hydrogen atmosphere, resilient.
Uses	Used for high temperature insulation of kilns and furnaces, packing expansion joints, heating elements, burner blocks, rolls for roller hearth furnaces and piping, fine filtration, insulating electrical wire and motors, insulating jet motors, sound deadening.
Trade Names	Fiberfrax® (Carborundum).
CARBON	
Composition	Carbonized rayon, polyacrylonitrile, pitch or coal tar.

TABLE 2. ARTIFICIAL, NONPOLYMERIC FIBERS (cont'd)	
Processing	High modulus carbon fibers are made from rayon, polyacrylonitrile, or pitch. Rayon fibers are charred at 413°-662° F (200°-350° C), then carbonized at 1832°-3632° F (1000° to 2000° C). The resulting carbon fibers are then heat treated at 5432° (3000° C) and stretched during the heat treatment. Carbon fibers are also obtained by heat treating polyacrylonitrile, coal tar or petroleum pitch.
Properties	Capable of withstanding high temperatures.
Uses	Carbon fibers come in three forms. Low modulus fibers used for electrically conducting surfaces. Medium modulus fibers used for fabrics. High modulus fibers used for stiff yarn. Used in the manufacture of heat shields for aerospace vehicles and for aircraft brakes. Carbon fibers are also used to reinforce plastics. These plastics may be used for sporting goods and engineering plastics.

that have special commercial applications. These include the fibers made of glass, metal, ceramics, and carbon described in Table 2, "Synthetic, Nonpolymeric Fibers."

See also Polymer.

Further Reading:

Austin, George T. *Shreve' Chemical Process Industries.* New York, NY: McGraw–Hill Book Company. 1984.

Lynch, Charles T. *Practical Handbook of Materials Science.* Boca Raton, Florida: CRC Press, Inc. 1989.

Sperling, L. H. *Introduction to Physical Polymer Science.* New York, NY: John Wiley & Sons, Inc. 1992.

The New Encyclopedia of Textiles, Englewood Cliffs, NJ: Prentice Hall, Inc., 1980.

Artificial heart and heart valve

The quest for a manmade device to replace a failing human heart has been a technologic goal for many decades. Although appearing simple on the surface, the construction of such a device has been unsuccessful for the most part. Estimates are that 35,000 people or more would benefit from a mechanical heart every year.

The human heart is a four–chambered, muscular organ that must function ceaselessly from before the birth of the individual until his or her death. In fact, a heart malfunction is responsible for nearly a million deaths every year in the United States alone. Day and night, during wakefulness or sleep, resting or working, the heart must pump adequate amounts of blood through the body to nourish every cell. This function

can be impaired or stopped by a heart attack, which results from a blockage in a coronary artery, or by a variety of other cardiac diseases.

Surgical procedures, now performed on a regular basis, can open or bypass a blocked coronary artery, returning an individual to his or former lifestyle, or close to it. Congestive heart failure, valvular malfunctions, and other cardiac conditions also can be treated effectively if they are diagnosed at an early stage and if the patient changes his or her lifestyle as necessary to preserve the heart muscle. The ultimate treatment for someone whose heart is beyond repair is a human heart transplant, replacing the ailing heart with one donated from a person with a healthy heart who has died because of some other ailment.

Theoretically, an artificial heart could be implanted in place of a failing natural heart and stay in place until a suitable human heart transplant became available. Such a device would need to pump blood through the lungs as well as through the rest of the body, delivering a reliable blood supply without forming clots and without damage to blood cells passing through the device. It also would require a reliable, stable power source.

The artificial heart

Prior to the development of a complete artificial heart, smaller devices had been used to help compensate for a failing heart. These devices, called left ventricular assist devices, were designed to pump in unison with the left ventricle to ease the load on that chamber of the heart. Some are designed to be implanted in the aorta, the main artery leaving the heart, and others are designed to remain outside the body with input and output tubes passing through the chest into the aorta.

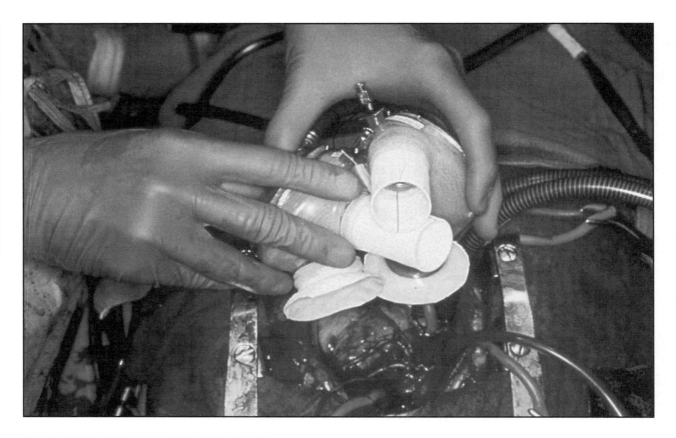

Surgical implantation of a Jarvik artificial heart.

The first use of such a device in a clinical setting was in August, 1966, when Dr. Michael DeBakey implanted a left ventricular bypass pump in a 37–year–old man. The patient had undergone surgery, but could not be disconnected from the heart–lung machine. The bypass, consisting of a single valved chamber, worked from outside the chest. Tubes passed through the chest wall to provide the pumping action. After 10 days the patient had recovered sufficient cardiac function that the device could be removed.

The first permanent implant surgeries were performed by Dr. Adrian Kantrowitz at the Maimonides Hospital in Brooklyn, New York, in 1966. The first, in February, was implanted in a 33–year–old male with left ventricular failure. The U–shaped, unvalved device fit inside the chest and had an external power source. The patient lived for 120 hours after implantation, but, having a history of alcoholism, he developed uncontrollable bleeding from his diseased liver and died. In August, Dr. Kantrowitz implanted the device for the second time in the chest of a 63–year–old woman whose congestive heart failure had left her bedridden for three years. Following the surgery she was much improved, but 10 days later she suffered a stroke and died.

Left ventricular assist devices have been improved over the years and are still used to maintain an individual's failing heart until a suitable donor heart can be located. However, they are only used for a short time and then removed.

A completely artificial heart was the object of research for a number of years, and there were many aspects of the research that were problematic. Developing a material that could withstand expansion and contraction without fail over a prolonged period of time was one. The nature of the surface over which the blood circulated was another. Opinions differed as to whether it should be rough or smooth, so both were tested to find out which would generate the fewest blood clots. Developing a device that would fit within the cavity occupied by the natural heart and yet pump sufficient volumes of blood to the body also was a consideration.

Then, in 1982, the Jarvik VII, named for its inventor, Dr. Robert Jarvik, was produced. After long research Dr. Jarvik developed a two–chambered device made of polyethylene with valves molded in. It ran on compressed air provided by an exterior air compressor connected to the artificial heart by a short, flexible tube.

Implantation of the device in a human was approved by the U.S. Food and Drug Administration under very strict guidelines. In December, 1982, Dr. William DeVries and his staff at the University of Utah implanted the first functional artificial heart in the chest of Dr. Barney Clark, a 61–year–old dentist. Dr. Clark was in the terminal stages of cardiomyopathy, a degeneration of the heart muscle. The device, successfully implanted, replaced the ventricles (two lower chambers) of Dr. Clark's heart, and operated as expected. Dr. Clark was tethered to the compressor as the device, valves audibly clicking, took over the blood circulation in his body. He lived for 112 days after surgery.

The Jarvik VII was implanted by Dr. DeVries a second time in 1984. The operation took place at Louisville, Kentucky, and the recipient, William Schroeder, aged 52, lived for only a short time after the operation. No other patients have received the artificial heart.

Today research continues, though at a reduced pace, seeking to perfect the artificial heart. A miniature, readily implantable power source is the object of much research. In an age in which human heart transplants are common, however, much work has been centered on the left ventricular assist device. In this way, the patient awaiting a suitable donor organ can be maintained for a time. The device is timed to coordinate its pumping action with that of the diseased ventricle, thus relieving the ventricle of much of the work it must accomplish.

Transplantation of a human donor heart has a number of advantages over a mechanical device. The natural heart has its own "power source" and does not require tubes or wires to an outside source. The natural heart does not damage the cellular elements of blood and does not generate blood clots under normal circumstances. On the other hand, the donated heart may initiate a rejection reaction in the recipient's body, so the patient must take medications to suppress the immune reaction. This may leave him vulnerable to other infections. Also, the number of donor organs is far short of the number of individuals who would benefit by their availability.

The artificial valve

Four one–way valves control the movement of blood into, through, and out of the human heart. All are designed to permit the flow of blood in one direction only and to prevent its backflow. Blood returning from the body to the heart enters the right atrium and from there passes through the tricuspid (or right atrioventricular) valve into the right ventricle. The right ventricle pumps the blood through the pulmonary semilunar

valve to the lungs where the blood discharges its carbon dioxide content and acquires fresh oxygen. The pulmonary circulation returns to the left atrium and is pumped into the left ventricle through the bicuspid or mitral (or left atrioventricular) valve. When the left ventricle contracts, it forces blood through the aortic semilunar valve into the aorta and on through the body.

Heart valves are made up of leaflets constructed of strong, thin, fibrous material. Each leaflet is connected by strong threads or fibers to muscular extensions within the heart called papillary muscles. The cords of the valves hold the leaflets shut against back pressure, thus allowing blood to flow only one way through them.

These valves can malfunction because of birth defects, deposits of cholesterol or calcium on the leaflets of the valves, or because of a rheumatic disease. Thickening of the valve leaflets, breaking of the cords, and tearing of the leaflets, will result in incomplete closing of the valves and backflow of blood. The physician hears this as a heart murmur through the stethoscope.

Though a small volume of backflow is not harmful, a deteriorating valve that permits greater and greater amounts of blood to pass back through it can have serious consequences on the heart itself. The ventricles may have less blood to pump if the backflow is through the atrial valves, thus depriving the body of sufficient blood flow and forcing a backup and higher blood pressure behind the valve. It is often necessary to replace the natural valve with a manmade artificial device.

A one–way valve is a rather simple device to construct, but again, to replace a heart valve requires a valve that will function ceaselessly for many years. The early mechanical valves, though adequate for controlling blood flow, tended to fracture after some years of use. The metal cage enclosing the valve broke under repeated and constant taps from the movable part of the valve. A fractured valve means a malfunctioning valve, possibly the formation of a blood clot and potential heart attack or stroke.

Artificial valves consist of a ring by means of which the valve is sewn into place in the heart and some means of controlling the flow of blood. One artificial valve known as the ball–and–cage model has a three–pronged cage within which is a ball. The ball lifts to allow blood to pass through and is pressed down into the valvular opening to seal it and prevent backflow. A disk–and–cage valve has a similar action, but the ball is replaced by a flat disk that swivels back and forth to open and close the passage. A more modern replacement valve uses the valve from a pig heart, treated to prevent rejection, mounted into a ring to be sewn into the heart. The leaflets in the pig valve behave more like those in the natural heart with less danger of breakage than occurs in the cage–type valves.

See also Heart.

Further Reading:

Gray's Anatomy. Philadelphia, Lea & Febiger, 1992.
National Heart, Lung, and Blood Institute. *The Human Heart,* Bethesda, MD (no copyright).
Yeaple, J.A. "The bionic heart." *Popular Science* 240 (April 1992): 64–69.

Larry Blaser

Artificial intelligence

Artificial intelligence (AI) is a subfield of computer science that studies ways to create software and hardware to perform some of the functions of the human brain. Some of these functions are currently accomplished better by computers. Computers can out–perform people when it comes to numerical computation and repetitive tasks. A computer is also better at storing lots of information because it can more easily and accurately retrieve data that has been stored than can our human brains. Computers were originally designed to accomplish these tasks by completing a series of clearly defined steps—called algorithms—in order to solve problems. Programmers wrote algorithmic software that carefully outlined both the problem and how to solve it. In contrast, artificial intelligence software is designed to give the computer only the problem, not the steps necessary to solve it.

The easiest problems for a computer to solve using artificial intelligence are often the hardest for people. Teachers can describe in great detail the process for multiplying two or more numbers together, and accountants can state with great accuracy the rules for completing tax forms. However, many people have a great deal of trouble with these tasks. Computers can perform them very easily, because the tasks can be broken down into a series of procedures or steps. On the other hand, tasks that seem to require no thought at all are extremely complex to describe and therefore very difficult for computers to perform. For example, most adults and older children know that a pot of boiling water on the stove is very hot and requires much care in order to handle safely. We can perhaps see steam rising and feel the heat of the burner as we approach the stove. Given this information, we plan our actions accordingly. But describing exactly how you came to this conclusion and took a certain course of action is very difficult. How to instruct a nonhuman in the appropriate handling of a situation such as this is the challenge of artificial intelligence.

Intelligent machines

A simple and conventional definition of intelligence is the acquisition and application of knowledge. We learn (acquire knowledge) and are able to act upon (apply) this learning in many ways. Computers performing artificial intelligence tasks must acquire basic knowledge from human programmers as well as the ability to use that knowledge to come to a conclusion or solution. Since computers do not acquire or act on knowledge without human intervention, can we conclude that these machines are intelligent? Are they not simply following the explicit directions given to them by human programmers? This is a hotly debated point in many areas. One issue is clear: artificial intelligence research has revolutionized computer applications.

Overview of artificial intelligence

All artificial intelligence programs are built on two foundations: a knowledge base and an inferencing capability. (Inferencing means to draw a conclusion based on facts and prior knowledge.) A knowledge base is made up of many discrete pieces of information—such as facts, concepts, theories, procedures, and relationships—on a limited area of information. Special programs are written to give the computer the ability to manipulate the information (in symbolic form) and to reason, make judgments, and reach conclusions and solutions to the particular problem at hand. Where conventional software must follow a strictly logical series of steps to reach a conclusion, artificial intelligence software uses the techniques of search and pattern matching. The process is still algorithmic in nature; that is, the computer must be told exactly where to look in its knowledge base and what constitutes a match. The computer is given some initial information and then searches the knowledge base for specific conditions or patterns that fit the criteria of the problem to be solved. This special ability of artificial intelligence programs—to reach a solution based on facts rather than on a preset series of steps—is what most closely resembles the thinking function of the human brain and causes some in the field to conclude that the computer is displaying some form of intelligence.

Microchip technology has virtually eliminated the problem of speed, allowing the program to quickly scan a huge base of possible moves and therefore provide a challenging electronic opponent. Artificial intelligence has many other applications, including problem solving, expert systems, natural language processing, vision, robotics, and education.

General problem solving

Problem solving is something AI does very well, as long as the problem is very narrow in focus and clearly defined. At first, general problem solving programs were attempted with limited success. Because all information needed to solve a problem must be reduced to symbols and programmed into the knowledge base, specific problem–solving applications are custom designed. For example, mathematicians, scientists, and engineers are often called upon to prove theorems. (A theorem is an idea that is accepted as a demonstrable truth and is part of a larger theory.) The process of proving a theorem requires that the concept be put in the simplest mathematical form. Because the formulas used are so large and complex, it can take an enormous amount of time, thought, and trial and error to prove a theorem. A specially designed AI program can reduce and simplify these formulas in a fraction of that time.

Artificial intelligence can also assist with problems in planning. An effective step–by–step sequence of actions that has the lowest cost and fewest steps is very important in business and manufacturing operations. An AI program can be designed that includes all possible steps and outcomes. The programmer must also set some criteria with which to judge the outcome, such as

whether speed is more important than cost in accomplishing the task, or if lowest cost is the desired result, regardless of how long it takes. The plan generated by this type of AI program will take less time to generate than by traditional methods.

Expert systems

The expert system is a major application of artificial intelligence today. Also known as a knowledge–based system, expert systems act as intelligent assistants to human experts, as well as serving as a resource to people who may not have access to an expert. The major difference between an expert system and a simple database containing information on a particular subject is that the database can only give the user discrete facts about the subject, whereas an expert system uses reasoning to draw conclusions from stored information. The purpose of this AI application is not to replace our human experts, but to make their knowledge and experience more widely available.

An expert system has three parts: knowledge base, inference engine, and user interface. The knowledge base contains both declarative (factual) and procedural (rules of usage) knowledge in a very narrow field. The inference engine runs the system by determining which procedural knowledge to access in order to obtain the appropriate declarative knowledge, then draws conclusions and decides when an applicable solution is found.

An interface is usually defined as the point where the machine and the human "touch." An interface is usually a keyboard. In an expert system, there are actually two different user interfaces. One is for the designer of the system—who generally has quite a bit of experience with computers; the other is for the user—generally a computer novice. Because most users are not computer–experienced, it is important that the expert system be very easy to use. All user interfaces are bi–directional; that is, able to receive information from the user and respond to the user with its recommendations. The designer's user interface must also be capable of adding new information to the knowledge base.

Natural language processing (NLP)

Natural language is the language you first learned as a child—your native tongue. This could be English or any other language. Natural language processing programs use artificial intelligence to allow a user to communicate with a computer in the user's natural language. The computer can both understand and respond to commands given in a natural language.

Most conventional computer languages consist of a combination of symbols, numbers, and some words. These languages are very complex and may take several years to master. By programming computers to respond to our natural language, they become easier to use, and many more people can use them effectively.

However, there are many problems in trying to make a computer understand people as well as people understand each other. When we communicate with each other we use a common language, and we expect to be understood by others who use the same language. For the most part, this common language is informed by a common history we share as members of a specific ethnic or racial group. To someone from another country or a non–native speaker of our language, our meaning may not be entirely clear. Four problems arise that can cause misunderstanding: ambiguity—confusion over what is meant due to multiple meanings of words and phrases; imprecision—thoughts are sometimes expressed in vague and inexact terms; incompleteness—the entire idea is not presented, and the listener is expected to "read between the lines;" and inaccuracy—spelling, punctuation, and grammar problems can obscure meaning. However, even with just a working knowledge of our language, most people could derive the correct meaning of our communication. It is much more difficult for computers having no "common history" with people to understand and respond to natural language.

To alleviate these problems, NLP programs must be able to analyze syntax—the way words are put together in a sentence or phrase; semantics—the derived meaning of the phrase or sentence; and context—the meaning of distinct words within a sentence. But this is not enough. The computer must also have access to a huge dictionary which contains definitions of every word and phrase it is likely to encounter. The computer may also use keyword analysis—a pattern–matching technique in which the program scans the text, looking for words that it has been programmed to recognize. If a keyword is found, the program responds by manipulating the text to form a reasonable response.

In its simplest form, a natural language processing program works like this: a sentence is typed in on the keyboard; if the program can derive meaning—that is, if it has a reference in its knowledge base for every word and phrase—it will respond, more or less appropriately. An example of a computer with a natural language processor is the computerized card catalog available in many public libraries. The main menu usually offers four choices for looking up information: search by author, search by title, search by subject, or search by keyword. If you want a list of books on a specific topic or subject you type in the appropriate phrase. You are asking the computer—in English—to tell you what is available on the topic. The computer usually responds in a very short time—in English—with a list of books along with call numbers so you can find what you need.

Another interesting and entertaining display of natural language processing is the Turing test. In 1950, a mathematician named Alan Turing devised a test, in the form of a game, that he thought would help decide the issue of machine intelligence. The "imitation game," as it was originally called, consisted of a questioner typing questions on a keyboard. In another room, two unseen respondents—a human and a computer—would send back answers. The questioner could pose queries to either respondent in an attempt to determine if he or she was corresponding with a human or a computer. In Turing's opinion, if the computer could fool the questioner into believing that he or she was having a dialog with a human, then the computer could be said to be intelligent.

Computer vision

Computer vision is the use of a computer to analyze and evaluate visual information. A camera is used to collect visual data. The camera translates the image into a series of electrical signals. This data is analog in nature—that is, it is directly measurable and quantifiable. A digital computer, however, operates using numbers expressed directly as digits. It cannot read analog signals, so the image must be digitized using an analog–to–digital converter (ADC). The image becomes a very long series of binary numbers which can be stored and interpreted by the computer. Just how long the series is depends on how densely packed the pixels are in the visual image. To get an idea of pixels and digitized images, take a close look at a newspaper photograph. If you move the paper very close to your eyes, you will notice that the image is a sequence of black and white dots—called pixels—arranged in a certain pattern. When you move the picture away from your eyes, the picture becomes clearly defined and your brain is able to recognize the image.

Artificial intelligence works very much the same way. Clues provided by the arrangement of pixels in the image give information as to the relative color and texture of an object, as well as the distance between objects. In this way, the computer can interpret and analyze visual images. In the field of robotics, visual analysis is very important.

Robotics

Robotics is the study of robots, which are machines that can be programmed to perform manual tasks. Most robots in use today perform various functions in an industrial setting. These robots typically are used in factory assembly lines or in hazardous waste facilities handling substances far too dangerous for humans to handle safely.

Most robots do not resemble the humanoid creations of popular science fiction. Instead they usually consist of a manipulator (arm), an end effector (hand), and some kind of control device. Industrial use robots generally are programmed to perform repetitive tasks in a highly controlled environment. However, more research is being done in the field of intelligent robots that can learn from their environment and move about it autonomously. These robots use AI programming techniques to understand their environment and make appropriate decisions based on the information obtained. In order to learn about one's environment, one must have a means of sensing the environment. Artificial intelligence programs allow the robot to gather information about its surroundings by using one of the following techniques: contact sensing, in which a robot sensor physically touches another object; noncontact sensing, such as computer vision, in which the robot sensor does not physically touch the object but uses a camera to obtain and record information; and environmental sensing, in which the robot can sense external changes in the environment, such as temperature or radiation.

The most recent robotics research centers around mobile robots that can enter environments that are hostile to humans, such as the damaged nuclear reactor at Three Mile Island or, more recently, the crater of an active volcano.

Computer–assisted instruction

Intelligent computer–assisted instruction (ICAI) has three basic components: problem–solving expertise, student model, and tutoring module. The student using this type of program is presented with some information from the problem–solving expertise component. This is the knowledge base of this type of AI program. The student responds in some way to the material that was presented, either by answering questions or otherwise demonstrating his or her understanding. The student model analyzes the student's responses and decides on a course of action. Typically this involves either presenting some review material or allowing the student to advance to the next level of knowledge presentation. The tutoring module may or may not be employed at this point, depending on the student's level of mastery of the material. The system does not allow the student to advance further than his or her own level of mastery.

Most ICAI programs in use today operate in a set sequence of presentation of new material, evaluation of student response, and employment of tutorial (if necessary). However, researchers at Yale have created software that uses a more Socratic way of teaching. These programs encourage discovery and often will not respond directly to a student's questions about a specific topic. The basic premise of this type of computer–assisted learning is to present new material only when a student needs it. This is when the brain is most ready to accept and retain the information. This is exactly the scenario most teachers hope for: students who become adroit self–educators, enthusiastically seeking the wisdom and truth that is meaningful to them. The cost of these programs, however, can be far beyond the means of most school districts. For this reason, these types of ICAI are used mostly in corporate training settings.

The question of whether computers can really think is still being debated. Even with the most sophisticated hardware and software, all the computer can do is use the information it is given in the way it is told to use it. The real question is how this technology can best serve the interests of people. The best applications of this type of software and hardware are the ones that make our lives easier. That, indeed, is the purpose all technology.

See also Automation; Computer languages; Computer software; Computer, analog; Computer, digital; Cybernetics; Robotics.

Further Reading:

Caudill, Maureen. *In Our Own Image: Building an Artificial Person*. New York: Oxford University Press, 1992.

Johnson, George. *Machinery of the Mind: Inside the New Science of Artificial Intelligence*. New York: Times Books, 1986.

Kelly, Derek. *A Layman's Introduction to Robotics*. Princeton: Petrocelli Books, 1986.

Van Horn, Mike. *Understanding Expert Systems*. New York: Bantam Books, 1986.

"The Bad Boy of Robotics," *Popular Science* (June 1995).

"Building a Baby Brain in a Robot," *Science*, (20 May 1994).

"An encounter with A. I. " *Popular Science* (June 1994).

"Electronic Intellects," *PC Novice* (December 1993).

Johanna Haaxma–Jurek

Artificial limb and joint see **Prosthetics**

Arum family (Araceae)

Arums, also called aroids, are flowering plants in the family Araceae. The 2,500 species of arums are distributed worldwide, primarily in tropical and subtropical regions, where they grow in rainforests, mostly on the ground but also commonly as epiphytes. Arums are generally absent from the arctic and deserts. Only 11 species occur in North America and other north temperate regions.

Most species are small to medium–sized perennial herbs, often climbing as vines, and a few are shrubs. The leaves of arums are generally broad, frequently dissected, and occasionally with natural holes. The leaves commonly contain abundant sharp–pointed crystals of calcium oxalate, which give the leaves an acrid smell. Calcium oxalate crystals are poisononous and irritating when chewed, thus protecting the leaves from herbivores. The tiny flowers are densely borne on a stucture called a spadix, which is accompanied by a large, often colorful leaf known as a spathe. The spathe varies in size and shape, but in the most advanced species of arums it forms a hood that encloses the spadix, as in the familiar jack–in–the–pulpit (*Arisaema triphyllum*) of North America. The fruits of arums are almost always brightly colored berries that are eaten and dispersed by animals.

Arums are famous for the variety of offensive odors they produce in association with a pollination strategy that involves deception. Arums are usually pollinated by flies or beetles that normally feed on rotting organic matter, such as decaying plants or mushrooms, dung, or animal carcasses. Arums mimic the odors of decay by emitting vapors of fatty compounds from their spadix and spathe, thereby luring insects who expect to find a tasty mass of rotting flesh or decaying plants.

Many aroids imprison the insects that they deceive. A fine example of this strategy is *Helicodiceros muscivorus,* a native of Corsica, Sardinia, and nearby Mediteranean islands. On the island of Calvioli, this plant grows in open areas between rocks, sometimes in gull colonies. Bird droppings, regurgitated seafood, the carcasses of chicks, and eggs broken by predators all contribute to breathtaking odors. *Helicodiceros* flowers when the gulls are breeding, and it produces an open spathe with the shape of a shortened, slightly compressed bullhorn. The spathe is a mottled grey–and–red color, and its appearance and odor resemble rotting meat. Excited blowflies will actually choose the stench of the arum over the gull–mess, landing on the spathe in search for food. They are eventually drawn to the dark, smelly, narrow end of the spathe, where they enter through a small

A Jack-in-the-pulpit near St. Mary's, Ontario.

opening into a chamber, which becomes their dungeon. The blowflies are unable to escape because of a dense barrier of stiff, sharp, downward–pointing hairs that guard the opening. The chamber encloses the basal portion of the spadix, on which are located the flowers. Some of the flies will have previously visited other plants and been dusted by pollen. When the flies first become trapped, only the female flowers are receptive and so they will be pollinated by the accidental stumbling of the blowflies in the dungeon. The flowers also exude a small amount of nectar, just enough to keep the flies alive. After a few days, the male flowers mature, and release their pollen onto the blowflies. Simultaneously, the sharp hairs wither, thus releasing the flies. Some of the flies will be duped a second time and cross–pollinate the arums.

Arums are unique among plants in possessing a remarkable ability to generate metabolic heat. Their spadix commonly respires fat rapidly to produce heat during pollination, apparently as a means of increasing the vaporization of their foul–smelling compounds. The philodendron (*Philodendron scandens*) can raise its spadix temperature to as high as 116°F (46°C), even when the air temperature is close to freezing. The skunk cabbage (*Symplocarpus foetidus*), which is a native of swamps and other wet places in eastern North America,

A field mouse in skunk cabbage.

flowers early in the spring, often when the ground is still covered by snow. Its spadix can generate enough heat to attain temperatures up to 77°F (25° C) above air temperatures, melt the surrounding snow, and get a head start on attracting flies.

The arum known as Jack–in–the–pulpit is a perennial plant, native to moist or wet forests throughout eastern North America, and it is sometimes cultivated as an interesting garden ornamental. The sex of individual plants depends on their size. When small, they only produce male flowers, but in later years when they are larger, they switch sex and produce only female flowers. The explanation for this phenomenon appears to be that when the plant is small, it has relatively few resources available to it, insufficient to develop the large berries that the Jack–in–the–pulpit produces. Therefore, plants are male first because pollen grains are small and take relatively little energy to produce. When the plant becomes larger, it can afford to invest in the higher costs of producing fruits. Thus, it switches its sex to female.

Several arums are important economically. The *Monstera deliciosa* produces an edible fruit and is a popular indoor plant because of its unusual leaves, which have large holes due to arrested development of parts of its growing surface. *Colocasia esculentum*, commonly

called taro or poi, is a native of Asia with many varieties that are widely cultivated in the tropics because of their large, starch–rich tubers. Many arums are cultivated as ornamentals for their interesting foliage, which is often intricately dissected, such as the *Philodendron* and *Monstera* described previously. Other species are prized as indoor plants because of their large, brightly colored spathes, which may range in color from pure white to bright red and even irridescent. Species of the genus *Cryptocoryne* are commonly used as aquarium plants.

Further Reading:

Brown, D. 1988. *Aroids: Plants of the Arum Family.* Portland, OR: Timber Press, 1988.

Dahlgren, R.M.T., H.T. Clifford, and P.F. Yeo. *The Families of the Monocotyledons: Structure, Evolution, and Taxonomy.* Berlin: Springer–Verlag, 1985.

Les C. Cwynar

Asbestos

Asbestos is the general name for a wide variety of silicate minerals, mostly silicates of calcium, magnesium, and iron. Their common characteristics are a fibrous structure and resistance to fire. The two most common families of asbestos minerals are called amphibole and serpentine. The mineral has been known and used by humans for centuries. The ancient Romans, for example, wove asbestos wicks for the lamps used by vestal virgins. The story is also told about Charlemagne's effort to impress barbarian visitors by throwing a table cloth woven of asbestos into the fire.

One of the first complete scientific descriptions of asbestos was provided by J. P. Tournefort in the early 1700s. He explained that the substance "softens in Oil and thereby acquires suppleness enough to be spun into

Threads; it makes Purses and Handkerchiefs, which not only resist the Fire, but are whiten'd and cleansed by it." Travelers to North America in the 1750s also told of widespread use of asbestos among both colonists and native Americans.

Classification and properties

The various minerals that make up the asbestos group are so diverse that they share only one major property, their fibrous character. The form known for the longest time and most widely used is chrysotile, or white asbestos, a member of the serpentine asbestos family. Its fibers are long, hollow cylinders with a diameter of about 25 nanometers (10^{-9} meter). The fibers are strong and relatively inflexible. The chemical formula assigned to chrysotile is $Mg_3Si_2O_5(OH)_4$. Like other forms of asbestos, chrysotile is noncombustible. The whole class of minerals was, in fact, named after the Greek word *asbeston*, for noncombustible. The amphibole asbestos minerals are:

riebeckite ($Na_2Fe^{2+}_3Fe^{3+}_2Si_8O_{22}(OH)_2$),
anthophyllite ($Mg_7Si_8O_{22}(OH)_2$),
actinolite ($Ca_2(Mg,Fe^{2+})_5Si_8O_{22}(OH)_2$),
and tremolite ($Ca_2Mg_5Si_8O_{22}(OH)_2$).

Riebeckite is also called crocidolite, or blue asbestos.

The asbestos amosite is sometimes included among the amphibole asbestos minerals and sometimes placed in its own group. Amosite ($Fe_7Si_8O_{22}(OH)_2$) is also called grenerite. It is typically ash–gray in color.

In general, amphibole minerals and amosite tend to have longer, more rigid fibers with a lower melting point than that of chrysotile. This fact makes them less desirable as fireproofing materials.

Occurrence and mining

The primary sources of the asbestos minerals are Quebec and the Yukon in Canada and the Ural Mountain region of Russia (chrysotile) and southern Africa (the amphiboles and amosite). Some asbestos is also found in Mexico and Italy, and in the United States, in Arizona, California, North Carolina, and Vermont.

By far the greatest fraction (95%) of asbestos produced today is chrysotile. An additional 3.5% consists of crocidolite and the final 1.5%, of amosite.

The largest supplier of asbestos minerals has traditionally been Russia or the former Soviet Union, which accounted for about half of all the asbestos mined in the world. The second largest source has been Canada (about 30% of the world's output), followed by the

European nations, Zimbabwe, China, South Africa, and the United States.

Asbestos occurs in either seams that run at or just beneath the Earth's surface or in veins that may go as deep as 300 meters. One method of quarrying the seams is known as block caving. In this process, trenches are dug underneath an asbestos seam and the whole section is then allowed to fall and break apart. In another technique, open seams of the mineral are plowed up and allowed to dry in air.

Underground veins are mined in much the same way as is coal. The distinctive fibrous character of asbestos makes it relatively easy to separate from other rocky material with which it is found.

Processing

After asbestos is removed from the earth, it is processed in order to divide it into groups according to fiber length. Longer fibers are separated out for weaving into a cloth–like material. Shorter fibers, known as shingles, are combined with each other and often with other materials to make some type of composite product. Perhaps the best known of these composites is asbestos cement, invented in the late 1800s. Asbestos cement contains about 12.5% asbestos and the remainder, portland cement, which is used for a variety of construction purposes.

The first step in making asbestos cement is to form a thick, pasty mixture of cement and asbestos in water. That mixture is then passed along a conveyor belt, where water is removed. At the end of the belt, the damp mixture of cement and asbestos is laid down on some type of base. Layers are allowed to build up until a material of the desired thickness if obtained. It is then dried.

Uses

About two–thirds of the world production of chrysotile is used to make asbestos cement. That material can be fabricated into corrugated or flat sheets for use as a building material in industrial and agricultural structures. Altering the process by which the asbestos cement is made can improve thermal, acoustical, and other properties to make it more suitable for interior structures also. Asbestos cement can also be fabricated as cylinders, making a material that is suitable for ducts and pressure pipes.

Long–fiber asbestos finds other kinds of applications. It can be woven alone or with other fibers (such as glass fibers) to make protective clothing for fire fighters, brake and clutch linings, electrical insulation, moldings for automobile components, and linings for chemical containers.

Health considerations

The deleterious health effects of asbestos have become apparent only since the end of World War II. Prior to that time, very few measurements had been made of the concentration of asbestos in the air around workplaces and other settings in which asbestos was used. In addition, the connection between the mineral and its health effects was difficult to recognize since those effects typically do not manifest themselves for 20 years or more after exposure.

Today scientists know that a rather narrow range of asbestos fiber lengths (less than two microns and five to 100 microns in length) can cause a range of respiratory problems, especially asbestosis, lung cancer, and mesothelioma. These problems begin when asbestos fibers enter the respiratory system and become lodged in the interstitial areas—the areas between the alveoli—in the lungs. As the fibers continue to accumulate in the lungs, they can cause the development of fibrous scar tissue that reduces the flow of air through the respiratory system.

Symptoms that gradually develop include coughing and shortness of breath, weight loss, and anorexia. Other respiratory conditions, such as pneumonia and bronchitis, become more common and more difficult to cure. Eventually the fibers may initiate other anatomical and physiological changes, such as the development of tumors and carcinomas.

Individuals most at risk for asbestos–related problems are those continually exposed to the mineral fibers. This includes those who work in asbestos mining and processing as well as those who use the product in some other manufacturing line, as in the production of brake linings. Over the past two decades, mammoth efforts have been made to remove asbestos–based materials from buildings where they are especially likely to pose health risks, as in school buildings and public auditoriums. Recent critics of asbestos removal maintain that if not done properly, asbestos removal spreads more asbestos fibers into the air than it actually removes. Also, there has not been a satisfactory substitute found for the asbestos materials being removed.

See also Poisons and toxins; Respiratory diseases.

Further Reading:

Brodeur, Paul. *Outrageous Misconduct: The Asbestos Industry on Trial.* New York: Pantheon Books, 1985.
Greenwood, N. N., and A. Earnshaw. *Chemistry of the Elements.* Oxford: Pergamon Press, 1984, 1990, pp. 405–406.

David E. Newton

Asexual reproduction

Sexual reproduction, involves the production of new cells by the fusion of sex cells (sperm and ova) to produce a genetically different cell. Asexual reproduction, on the other hand is the production of new cells by simple division of the parent cell into two daughter cells (called binary fission). Since there is no fusion of two different cells, the daughter cells produced by asexual reproduction are genetically identical to the parent cell.

The adaptive advantage of asexual reproduction is that organisms can reproduce rapidly, and so colonize favorable environments rapidly.

In nature

Bacteria, blue–green algae, algae, most protozoa, yeast, dandelions, and flatworms all reproduce asexually. When asexual reproduction occurs, the new individuals are called clones, because they are exact duplicates of their parent cells. Mosses reproduce by forming runners that grow horizontally, produce new stalks, and then the runner decomposes, leaving a new plant which is a clone of the original.

Starfish can regenerate and eventually produce a whole new organism from one of its severed appendages.

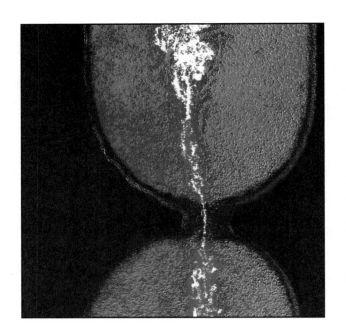

A scanning electron micrograph (SEM) of the *Salmonella typhimurium* bacterium reproducing by binary fission. The two daughter cells are still joined by a narrow neck through which DNA is passing in a thin strand. Once each cell has its full complement of DNA, they separate.

Duplication of organisms, whether sexually or asexually, involves the partitioning of the genetic material (chromosomes) in the cell nucleus.

During asexual reproduction, the chromosomes divide by mitosis, which results in the exact duplication of the genetic material into the nucleii of the two daughter cells.

Sexual reproduction involves the fusion of two gamete cells (the sperm and ova) which each have half the normal number of chromosomes, a result of reduction division known as meiosis.

Bacteria reproducing asexually double their numbers rapidly, approximately every 20 minutes. This reproduction rate is offset by a high death rate which may be the result of the accumulation of alcohol or acids that concentrate from the bacterial colonies.

Yeasts reproduce asexually by budding, as well as reproducing sexually. In the budding process, a bulge forms on the outer edge of the yeast cell as nuclear division takes place. One of these nuclei moves into the bud, which eventually breaks off completely from the parent cell. Budding also occurs in flatworms, which divide into two and then regenerate to form two new flatworms.

Bees, ants, wasps, and other insects can reproduce sexually or asexually. In Asexual reproduction eggs develop without fertilization, a process called parthenogenesis. In some species the eggs may or may not be fertilized; fertilized eggs produce females, while unfertilized eggs produce males.

There are a number of crop plants which are propagated asexually. The advantage of asexual propagation to farmers is that the crops will be more uniform than those produced from seed. Some plants are difficult to cultivate from seed and asexual reproduction in these plants makes it possible to produce crops that would otherwise not be available for commercial marketing.

The process of producing plants asexually is called vegetative propagation and is used for such crops as potatoes, bananas, raspberries, pineapples, and some flowering plants used as ornamentals. Farmers plant the so–called "eyes" of potatoes to produce duplicates of the parent. With banana plants, the suckers that grow from the root of the plant are separated and then planted as new ones. With raspberry bushes, branches are bent and covered with soil. They then grow into a separate plant with their own root system and can eventually be detached from the parent plant.

See also Algae; Bacteria; Buds and budding; Clone and cloning; Crops; Genetics; Mitosis; Parthenogenesis.

Further Reading:

Allison, Richard. "Genetic Engineering Studied." *Cancer Researcher Weekly* (21 March 1994): 13.

Leone, Francis. *Genetics: The Mystery and the Promise*. Blue Ridge Summit, Pennsylvania: Tab Books, 1992.

Nash, J. Madeleine. "Is Sex Really Necessary?" *Time* (20 January 20 1992): 47.

Robertson, John A. "The Question of Human Cloning." *The Hastings Center Report* (March/April 1994): 6.

PHASES OF MITOSIS

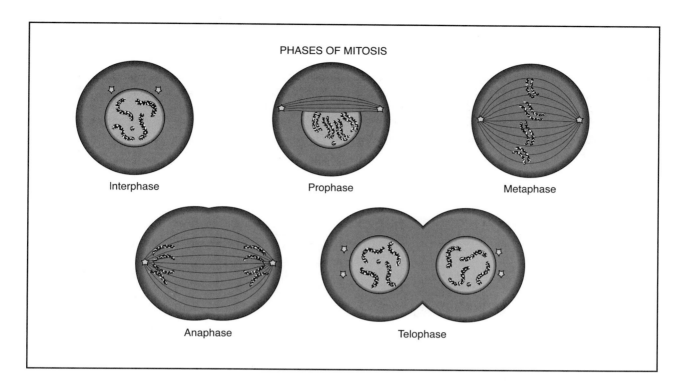

Phases of mitosis.

Taylor, Martha. *Campbell's Biology Student Study Guide.* Redwood City, California: Benjamin/Cummings, 1990.

Vita Richman

Ash see **Olive family**

Ashy-headed greenlet see **Vieros**

 Asia

Asia is the world's largest continent, encompassing an area of 44,500,000 sq. km (17,177,000 sq. mi.), 29.8% of the world's land area. The Himalayan mountains, which are the highest and youngest mountain range in the world, stretch across the continent from Afghanistan to Burma. The highest of the Himalayan peaks, called Mount Everest, reaches an altitude of 8,848 m (29,028 ft). There are many famous deserts in Asia, including the Gobi desert, the Thar desert, and Ar–Rub'al–Khali ("the empty quarter"). The continent has a wide range of climatic zones, from the tropical jungles of the south to the Arctic wastelands of the north in Siberia.

The continent of Asia encompasses such an enormous area and contains so many countries and islands that its exact borders remain unclear. In the broadest sense, it includes central and eastern Russia, the countries of the Arabian Peninsula, the far eastern countries, the Indian subcontinent, and numerous island chains. It is convenient to divide this huge region into five categories: the Middle East, South Asia, Central Asia, the Far East, and South–East Asia.

The Middle East

The Middle Eastern countries lie on the Arabian Peninsula, southwest of Russia and northeast of Africa, separated from the African continent by the Red Sea and from Europe in the northwest by the Mediterranean Sea. This area stretches from Turkey in the northwest to Yemen in the south, which is bordered by the Arabian Sea. In general, the climate is extremely dry, and much of the area is still a desert wilderness. Precipitation is low, so the fertile regions of the middle east lie around the rivers or in valleys which drain the mountains. Much of the coastal areas are very arid, and the vegetation is mostly desert scrub.

Iran

Iran is separated somewhat from the rest of the Arabian Peninsula by a great gulf which divides it from most of Saudi Arabia. This gulf is known as the Oman Gulf where it meets the Arabian Sea and is called the

Persian Gulf as it extends past the Strait of Hormuz. Most of Iran is a plateau lying about 1,200 m (4,000 ft) above sea level, and this plateau is crossed by the mountain ranges of Zagros and Elburz. These meet at an angle, forming an inverted V; between them the land is mostly salt marshes and desert. The highest elevation is Mount Damavand, which reaches 5,671 m (18,606 ft). The valleys between the mountain peaks are the main fertile regions of the country.

Iraq and Kuwait

Bordering Iran in the northeast is the country of Iraq. The west and southwest, where it borders with Syria and Saudi Arabia, is a desert region; in the northeast is a mountain range which reaches altitudes of over 3,000 m (10,000 ft). Between these two regions are fertile river plains which are watered by the Tigris and Euphrates rivers. In the southeast the two rivers join together, forming the broad Shatt al–'Arab, which flows between Iraq and Iran.

In the southeast corner of Iraq, along the tip of the Persian Gulf, is the tiny country of Kuwait. Its terrain is almost entirely made up of desert and mud flats, but along the southwestern part of the coast are a few low hills.

Saudi Arabia and Yemen

Saudi Arabia is the largest of the middle eastern countries. In the west it is bordered by the Red Sea, which lies between Saudi Arabia and the African continent. The Hijaz Mountains run parallel to this coast in the northwest, rising sharply from the sea to elevations ranging from 910–2,740 m (3,000–9,000 ft). In the south is another mountainous region called the Asir, stretching along the coast for about 370 km (230 mi) and inland about 290–320 km (180–200 mi). Between the two ranges lies a narrow coastal plain called the Tihamat ash–Sham. East of the Hijaz Mountains are two great plateaus called the Najd, which slopes gradually downward over a range of about 910 m (3,000 ft) from west to east, and the Hasa, which is only about 240 m (800 ft) above sea level. Between these two plateaus is a desert region called the Dahna.

About one third of Saudi Arabia is estimated to be desert. The largest of these is the Ar–Rub'al–Khali ("the empty quarter") which lies in the south, and covers an area of about 647,500 sq. km (250,000 sq. mi). In the north is another desert, called the An–Nafud. The climate in Saudi Arabia is generally very dry; there are no lakes and only seasonally flowing rivers. Saudi Arabia, like most of the middle eastern countries, has large oil reserves; also found here are rich gold and silver mines which are thought to date from the time of King Solomon.

Yemen, which lies along the southern border of Saudi Arabia, is divided into South Yemen, called the People's Democratic Republic of Yemen (PDRY), and North Yemen, called the Yemen Arab Republic (YAR). YAR, which lies below the Asir region of Saudi Arabia, is very mountainous. It consists mostly of plateaus and tablelands which are also the main fertile regions; but along the coast of the Red Sea is a stretch of flat coastal plains called the Tihama. This plain continues into PDRY along the gulf of Aden, and is very arid. The west of PDRY, near the YAR border, is a mountain range; and in the north PDRY borders on the great Ar–Rub'al–Khali desert. The southern plateau region is the most fertile part of the country.

Oman, UAI, and Qatar

Oman, which is bordered by the Arabian Sea and the Gulf of Oman, has three main geographical regions. These are a coastal plain, a mountain range which borders on them, and a plateau region beyond the mountains which extends inland to the Ar–Rub' al–Khali desert.

The strip of territory called United Arab Emirates (UAI) is a country divided up into different emirates or provinces. It is bordered by the Persian Gulf and a small part of the Gulf of Oman in the southwestern tip of the country, and it consists mainly of sand and gravel desert regions, but includes some fertile coastal strips and many islands. In parts of the country, the coastal sand dunes are over 90 m (300 ft) high.

North of UAI and bordered on three sides by the Persian Gulf is the country of Qatar, which is believed to have been an island before it joined with the Arabian Peninsula. It is mostly flat and sandy, with some low cliffs rising on the northeastern shore and a low chain of hills on the west coast.

Israel and Jordan

Israel contains three main regions. Along the Mediterranean Sea lies a coastal plain. Inland is a hilly area which includes the hills of Galilee in the north and Samaria and Judea in the center. In the south of Israel lies the Negev desert, which covers about half of Israel's land area. The two bodies of water in Israel are the Sea of Galilee and the Dead Sea. The latter, which takes its name from its heavy salinity, lies 393 m (1,290 ft) below sea level, and is the lowest point on the earth's landmasses. It is also a great resource for potassium chloride, magnesium bromide, and many other salts.

Jordan borders on Israel in the east near the Dead Sea, where the altitude is about 392 m (1,286 ft) below sea level. To the east of the Jordan river, which feeds the Dead Sea, is a plateau region. The low hills gradually slope downward to a large desert, which occupies most of the eastern part of the country.

Lebanon and Syria

Lebanon, which borders Israel in the north, is divided up by its steep mountain ranges. These have been carved by erosion into intricate clefts and valleys, lending the landscape an unusual rugged beauty. On the western border, which lies along the Mediterranean Sea, is the Mount Lebanon area. These mountains rise from sea level to a height of 2,000–3,000 m (6,600–9,800 ft) in less than 40 km (25 mi). On the eastern border is the Anti–Lebanon mountain range, which separates Lebanon from Syria. Between the mountains lies Bekaa Valley, Lebanon's main fertile region.

Syria has three major mountain ranges. In the southwest, the Anti–Lebanon mountain range separates the country geographically from Lebanon. In the southeast is the Jabal Ad–Duruz range, and in the northwest, running parallel to the Mediterranean coast, are the Ansariyah mountains. Between these and the sea is a thin stretch of coastal plains. The most fertile area is in the central part of the country east of the Anti–Lebanon and Ansariyah mountains; the east and northeastern part of Syria is made up of steppe and desert region.

Turkey

Turkey, at the extreme north of the Arabian Peninsula, borders on the Aegean, the Mediterranean, and the Black Seas. Much of the country is cut up by mountain ranges, and the highest peak, called Mount Ararat, reaches an altitude of 5,137 m (16,854 ft). In the northwest is the Sea of Marmara, which connects the Black Sea with the Aegean sea. Most of this area, called Turkish Thrace, is fertile and has a temperate climate. In the south, along the Mediterranean, there are two fertile plains called the Adana and the Antalya, which are separated by the Taurus mountains.

The two largest lakes in Turkey are called Lake Van, which is close to the border with Iraq, and Lake Tuz, which lies in the center of the country. Lake Tuz has such a high level of salinity that it is actually used as a source of salt. Turkey is a country of seismic activity, and earthquakes are frequent.

The Far East

Most of the far eastern countries are rugged and mountainous, but rainfall is more plentiful than in the middle east, so there are many forested regions. Volcanic activity and plate tectonics have formed many island chains in this region of the world, and nearly all the countries on the coast include some of these among their territories.

China and Taiwan

China, with a land area of 9,444,292 sq. km (3,646,448 sq. mi), is an enormous territory. The northeastern part of the country is an area of mountains and rich forest land, and its mineral resources include iron, coal, gold, oil, lead, copper, and magnesium. In the north, most of the land is made up of fertile plains. It is here that the Yellow River (Huang He) is found, which has been called "China's Sorrow" because of its great flooding. The northwest of China is a region of mountains and highlands, including the cold and arid steppes of Inner Mongolia. It is here that the Gobi Desert, the fifth largest desert in the world, is found. The Gobi was named by the Mongolians, and its name means "waterless place." It encompasses an area of 1,295,000 sq. km (500,000 sq. mi), and averages two to four inches of rainfall a year. In contrast, central China is a region of fertile land and temperate climate. Many rivers, including the great Yangtze river, flow through this region, and there are several freshwater lakes. The largest of these, and the largest in China, is called the Poyang. In the south of China the climate becomes tropical, and the land is very fertile; the Pearl River delta, which lies in this region, has some of the richest agricultural land in China. In the southwestern region, the land becomes mountainous in parts, and coal, iron, phosphorous, manganese, aluminum, tin, natural gas, copper, and gold are all found here. In the west, before the line of the Himalayas which divides China from India, lies Tibet, which is about twice as large as Texas and makes up about a quarter of China's land area. This is a high plateau region, and the climate is cold and arid. A little to the north and east of Tibet lies a region of mountains and grasslands where the Yangtze and the Yellow rivers arise.

One of the largest of the islands off the China coast is called Taiwan, which consists of Taiwan proper and about 85 additional tiny islands in the region. Because Taiwan lies on the edge of the continental shelf, the western seas are shallow (about 90 m, or 300 ft) while the eastern seas reach a depth of 4,000 m (13,000 ft) only 50 km (31 mi) from the shore. The area is prone to mild earthquakes.

Japan and Korea

Japan consists of a group of four large islands, called Honshu, Hokkaido, Kyushu, and Shikoku, and more than 3,000 smaller islands. It is a country of intense volcanic activity, with more than 60 active volcanoes, and frequent earthquakes. The terrain is rugged and mountainous, with lowlands making up only about 29% of the country. The highest of the mountain peaks is an extinct volcano found on Honshu called Mount Fuji. It attains an altitude of 3,776 m (12,388 ft).

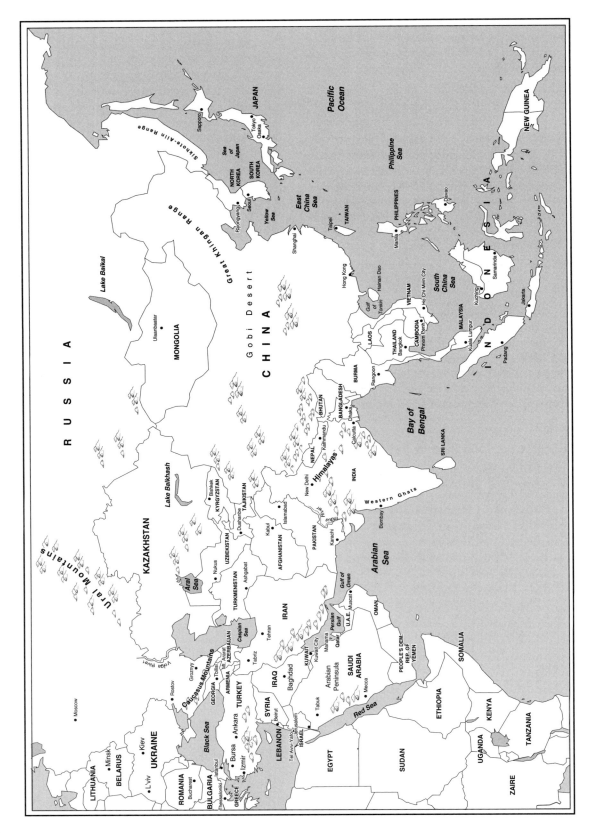

Asia.

Although the climate is generally mild, tropical cyclones usually strike in the fall, and can cause severe damage.

The two Korean republics lie between China and Japan, and are bordered by the Yellow Sea on one side and the Sea of Japan on the other. North Korea is a very mountainous region, with only 20% of its area consisting of lowlands and plains. Mt. Paektu, an extinct volcano with a lake in the crater, is the highest point in the country at 2,744 m (9,003 ft). South Korea is also quite mountainous, but with lower elevations; the highest point on the mainland is Mount Chiri, at an altitude of 1,915 m (6,283 ft). The plains region is only slightly larger than in the north, taking up about 30% of the country's land area.

Central Asia

Central Asia includes Mongolia and central and eastern Russia. This part of Asia is mostly cold and inhospitable. While only 5% of the country is mountainous, Mongolia has an average elevation of 1,580 m (5,184 ft). Most of the country consists of plateaus. The temperature variation is extreme, ranging from –40 to 104°F (–40 to 40°C). The Gobi Desert takes up about 17% of Mongolia's land mass, and an additional 28% is desert steppe. The remainder of the country is forest steppe and rolling plains.

North of China and Mongolia lies Russian Siberia. This region is almost half as large as the African continent, and is usually divided into the eastern and western regions. About the top third of Siberia lies within the Arctic circle, and the climate is very harsh. The most extreme temperatures occur in eastern Siberia, where it falls as low as –94°F (–70°C), and there are only 100 days a year when it climbs above 50°F (10°C). Most of the region along the east coast is mountainous, but in the west lies the vast West Siberian Plain.

The most important lake in this area, and one of the most important lakes in the world, is called Lake Baikal. Its surface area is about the size of Belgium, but it is a mile deep and contains about a fifth of the world's fresh water supply. The diversity of aquatic life found here is unparalleled; it is the only habitat of 600 kinds of plants and 1,200 kinds of animals, making it the home of two–thirds of the freshwater species on earth.

South–East Asia

South–East Asia includes a number of island chains as well as the countries east of India and south of China on the mainland. The area is quite tropical, and tends to be very humid. Much of the mountainous regions are extremely rugged and inaccessible; they are taken up by forest and jungle and have been left largely untouched; as a result, they are a habitat for much unusual wildlife.

Thailand

Thailand, which is a country almost twice the size of Colorado, has a hot and humid tropical climate. In the north, northeast, west, and southeast are highlands which surround a central lowland plain. This plain is drained by the river Chao Phraya, and is rich and fertile land. The highlands are mostly covered with forests, which includes tropical rain forests, deciduous forests, and coniferous pine forests. Thailand also has two coastal regions; the largest borders on the Gulf of Thailand in the east and southeast, and on the west is the shore of the Andaman Sea.

Vietnam

Vietnam, which borders on the South China Sea at the Gulf of Tonkin, consists mainly of two fertile river delta regions separated by rugged, mountainous terrain. In the south, the Mekong delta region is the largest and most fertile of the lowland areas, making up about a quarter of the total area. The northern delta region, of the Red (Hong) river, is much smaller. It is divided from the south by the Annamese Highlands, which take up the greatest part of the north. Vietnam has a moist, tropical climate, and its highlands are densely forested.

Cambodia and Laos

Between Thailand and Vietnam lies Cambodia, a country of low plains. In the center of the country is the Tonle Sap (Great Lake), and many of the rivers which water Cambodia flow into this lake. During the winter, when the Mekong river floods, it forces the flow back from the Tonle Sap into the tributaries, flooding the surrounding area with rich silt. In the north and southwest are some mountain ranges, and the Cardamom range lies along the southern coast.

North of Cambodia, lying between Thailand in the west and Vietnam in the east, is the country of Laos. The Mekong river flows along most of its western boundary with Thailand, and most of the country's rivers drain into the Mekong. On the eastern border lie the Annamese Highlands. The northern part of Laos is also very mountainous and covered with thick jungle and some coniferous forests.

Myanmar

Myanmar, formerly called Burma, lies largely between China and India, but also borders on Thailand in a strip of coast along the Andaman Sea. The country is geographically isolated by mountain ranges lying along its western and eastern borders; these run from north to south, meeting in the extreme north. Like most of the mountains in southeast Asia, these are covered with dense forest and jungle. Between the ranges is a large fertile expanse of plains watered by the Irrawaddy River; a little north of this valley below the northern mountains is a small region of dry desert.

Malaysia, Indonesia, and the Philippines

South of the mainland countries lie the island chains of Malaysia, Indonesia, and the Philippines. The latter two are both sites of much volcanic activity; Indonesia is estimated to have 100 active volcanoes. These islands, in particular Malaysia, are extremely fertile and have large regions of tropical rain forests with an enormous diversity in the native plant and wildlife.

South Asia

South Asia includes three main regions: the Himalayan mountains, the Ganges Plains, and the Indian Peninsula.

The Himalayas: Afghanistan, Pakistan, Nepal, and Bhutan

The Himalayas stretch about 3,000 km (1,860 mi) across Asia, from Afghanistan to Burma, and range from 250–350 km (150–210 mi) wide. They are the highest mountains in the world, and are still being pushed upward at a rate of about 6 cm (2.3 in) a year. This great mountain range originated when the Indian subcontinent collided with Asia, which occurred due to the subduction of the Indian plate beneath the Asian continent. The Himalayas are the youngest mountains in the world, which accounts in part for their great height. At present they are still growing as India continues to push into the Asian continent at the rate of about 6 cm (2.3 in) annually. The Indian subcontinent is believed to have penetrated at least 2,000 km (1,240 mi) into Asia thus far. The range begins in Afghanistan, which is a land of harsh climate and rugged environment.

Bordered by China, Russia, Pakistan, and Iran, Afghanistan is completely landlocked. High, barren mountains separate the northern plains of Turan from the southwestern desert region, which covers most of Afghanistan's land area. This desert is subject to violent sand storms during the winter months. The mountains of Afghanistan, which include a spur of the Himalayas called the Hindu Kush, reach an elevation of more than 6,100 m (20,000 ft), and some are snow–covered year–round and contain glaciers. The rivers of the country flow outward from the mountain range in the center of the country; the largest of these are the Kabul, the Helmand, the Hari Rud, and the Kunduz. Except for the Kabul, all of these dry up soon after flowing onto the dry plains.

To the east of Afghanistan and separated from it by the Hindu Kush, lies Pakistan. In the north of the country are the mountain ranges of the Himalayas and the Karakoram, the highest mountains in the world. Most of the peaks are over 4,580 m (15,000 ft) and almost 70 are higher than 6,700 m (22,000 ft). By comparison, the highest mountain in the United States, Mount McKinley in Alaska, is only 6,194 m (20,321 ft). Not surprisingly, many of the mountains in this range are covered with glaciers.

In the west of the country, bordering on Afghanistan, is the Baluchistan Plateau, which reaches an altitude of about 900–1,200 m (3,000–4,000 ft). Further south, the mountains disappear, replaced by a stony and sandy desert. The major rivers of Pakistan are the Kabul, the Jhelum, the Chenab, the Ravi, and the Sutlej; all of these drain into the Indus River, which flows into the Arabian Sea in the south of Pakistan.

Also found in the Himalayan Mountains are Nepal and the kingdom of Bhutan. Both of these countries border on the fertile Ganges Plains, so that in the south they are densely forested with tropical jungles; but most of both territories consists of high mountains. It is in Nepal that the highest peak in the world, called Mount Everest, is found; it is 8,848 m (29,028 ft) high.

The Ganges Plains: India and Bangladesh

South of the Himalayan mountains, India is divided up into two major regions. In the north are the Ganges Plains, which stretch from the Indus to the Ganges river delta. This part of India is almost completely flat and immensely fertile; it is thought to have alluvium reaching a depth of 3,000 m (9,842 ft). It is fed by the snow and ice from the high peaks, and streams and rivers from the mountains have carved up the northern edge of the plains into rough gullies and crevices. Bangladesh, a country to the north and east of India, lies within the Ganges Plains. The Ganges and the Brahmaputra flow into Bangladesh from India, and they are fed by many tributaries, so the country is one of the most well–watered and fertile regions of Asia. However, it is also close to sea level, and plagued by frequent flooding.

The Peninsula: India, Sri Lanka, and the Maldives

South of the plains is the Peninsula, a region of low plateaus and river valleys. It is bounded on the west, parallel to the Arabian Sea, by the Ghat mountain range; further north by the border of Pakistan is the Thar desert, which encompasses an area of 260,000 sq. km (100,387 sq. mi.). In its southern extent, the Thar borders on salt marshes and the great lava expanse

KEY TERMS

Alluvium—Deposits of water–borne substances such as silt which have been carried into a region by the flow of rivers.

Continental shelf—Part of the Earth's crust on which the continents rest, which lies above the ocean crust.

Delta—The geographical region traversed by a river and its tributaries.

Gulf—A part of the ocean which is partially enclosed by the coast.

Mud flats—A stretch of land which is alternately dampened and uncovered by the sea, so that little can grow there, but the land remains moist.

Plateau—An elevated area which is flat on top; also called "tableland."

Precipitation—Dew, rain, snow, or any other moisture which comes from the atmosphere.

Salt marshes—Marshland that is saline.

Seismic—Related to earthquakes.

Steppe—Wide expanses of relatively level plains, found in cool climates.

Strait—Part of a waterway where the channel narrows.

---

called the Deccan plateau. The island of Sri Lanka, which lies south of India, is the only other country which is part of the Peninsula, although it is separated from it by the ocean.

Off the southwestern tip of the Peninsula are the Maldives, a group of about 1,200 islands. At their highest point, they only reach an altitude of about 24 m (80 ft) above sea level; and their number and identity varies as old islands are constantly submerged and new ones created.

Further Reading:

Chapman, Graham P. and Baker, Kathleen M., ed. *The Changing Geography of Asia.* New York: Routledge, 1992.

Taylor, Robert H., ed. *Asia and the Pacific.* New York: Facts on File, 1991.

Ulack, Richard and Pauer, Gyula. *Atlas of Southeast Asia.* New York: Macmillan Publishing Company, 1989.

Sarah A. de Forest

Asparagus see **Lily family**

Aspen see **Willow family**

Aspirin see **Acetylsalicylic acid**

Assassin bugs see **True bugs**

Assembly line

An assembly line is a system of mass production in which a product is manufactured in a step–by–step process as it moves continuously past an arrangement of workers and machines. Introduced in the 19th century, it provided the basis for the modern methods of mass production of quantities of standardized, relatively low–cost goods available to great numbers of consumers. As one of the most powerful productivity concepts in history, it was largely responsible for the emergence and expansion of the industrialized, consumer–based system we have today.

History

The principle of continuous movement is perhaps the simplest and most obvious fact of an assembly line, dating back to Assyrian times, where there is evidence of a system of bucket elevators called the "chain of pots." Miners in medieval Europe also used these bucket elevators, and by the time of the Renaissance, engineers were becoming familiar with some form of the assembly line. In the 14th century, for example, the shipbuilding arsenal of Venice used moving lines of prefabricated parts to equip their war galleys. What may have been the first powered–roller conveyer system was introduced in 1804 by the British Navy's automatic production of biscuits or "hardtack." It used a steam engine to power its rollers. By the 1830s, the principle of continuous processing was starting to enter the consciousness of manufacturers, although it was by no means fully embraced until the 1870s in the United States. By then, the principles of division of labor and interchangeable parts had been successfully demonstrated by the American inventors Eli Whitney (1765–1825) and Samuel Colt (1814–1862).

The assembly line was first used on a large scale by the meat–packing industries of Chicago and Cincinnati during the 1870s. These slaughterhouses used monorail trolleys to move suspended carcasses past a line of stationary workers, each of whom did one specific task. Contrary to most factories' lines in which products are gradually put together step–by–step, this first assembly

The assembly of robots at Renault in France.

line was in fact more of a "dis–assembly" line, since each worker butchered a diminishing piece of an animal. The apparent breakthroughs in efficiency and productivity that were achieved by these meat packers were not immediately realized by any other industry until the American industrialist Henry Ford (1863–1947) designed an assembly line in 1913 to manufacture his Model T automobiles. Ford openly admitted using the meat–packing lines as a model. When the total time of assembly for a single car fell from 12.5 labor hours to 93 labor minutes, Ford was able to drastically reduce the price of his cars. His success not only brought automobile ownership within the grasp of the average person, but it served notice to all types of manufacturers that the assembly line was here to stay. The assembly line transformed in a revolutionary way the manner and organization of work, and by the end of World War I, the principle of continuous movement was sweeping mass–production industries of the world and was soon to become an integral part of modern industry.

The basic elements of traditional assembly line methods are nearly all the same. First, the sequence in which a product's component parts are put together must be planned and actually designed into the process. Then the first manufactured component passes from station to station, often by conveyor belt, and something is done or added to it. By the last station, the product is fully assembled and is identical to each one before and after it. This system ensures that a large quantity of uniform–quality goods are produced at a relatively low cost.

When manufacturers first implemented the idea of the assembly line, they enjoyed dramatic gains in productivity, and the consumer realized lower costs. However, the nature of work in a factory changed radically. Skilled workers were replaced by semi–skilled or even unskilled workers, since tasks had been minutely compartmentalized or broken down and each person was responsible only for assembling or adding one particular part. Manufacturers soon realized however, that not only were a great number of managers and supervisors required to oversee these laborers, but a high degree of preplanning on their part was absolutely essential. Overall operations had become much more complex and correct sequencing was essential. Thus, before actual assembly line production could begin, proper design of both the product and the assembly line itself had to be accomplished. Even the simplest tasks were critical to its overall success, and the apparently straightforward assembly line became a highly complex process when broken down and considered step–by–step.

Role of workers

Early 20th century assembly line systems carried the concept of division of labor to an extreme and usually restricted each worker to the repetitive performance of one simple task. These individuals had few real skills, and they were not required to know any more than their basic job demanded. This human element proved to be the weakest link in the entire system. For most people, assembly line work eventually entailed a physical and mental drudgery that became seriously counterproductive. Often the work itself was detrimental to an individual's physical and mental well–being, and from a manufacturer's standpoint, this usually resulted in diminished productivity.

Henry Ford and his fellow industrialists soon discovered this phenomenon when they tried to speed up their assembly lines. Since the pact of the assembly line was dictated by machines, supervisors often accelerated them, forcing workers to try to keep up. When this constant pressure to increase production was combined with the essentially dull and repetitive nature of the job, the result was often a drop in quality as well as output, not to mention worker unrest and dissatisfaction. By the 1920s, industry leaders realized that they could not ignore the dehumanizing aspects of the assembly line. However, it was not until after World War II that the major industries made serious attempts to make the mechanical aspects of the assembly line accommodate itself to the human physiology and nervous system.

The logical evolution of the assembly line would seem to lead to one that is fully automated. Such an automated system would ideally imply the elimination of the human element and its replacement with automatic controls that guarantee a level of accuracy and quality that is beyond human skills. In fact, this is the case today where automation has completely changed the nature of the traditional assembly line. Computer advances have resulted in assembly lines that are entirely run by computers controlling industrial robots of all kinds. Increasingly, such robots not only perform the repetitive, elementary tasks, but also are sufficiently intelligent (via feedback systems) to regulate or adjust their own performance to suit a changing situation. Especially in the automobile industry, assembly lines consist of machines that are run by machines. People are still needed of course, for quality control, repair, and routine inspection, as well as for highly specialized tasks. In fact, rather than minimizing the human skills needed to oversee these systems, today's automated

KEY TERMS

Automation—The application of self–governing machines to tasks once performed by human beings.

Division of labor—The separation of a job or task into a number of parts, with each part performed by a separate individual or machine.

Industrial robots—Programmable, multi–purpose, electromechanical machines that can perform manufacturing–related tasks that were traditionally done by human beings.

Interchangeable parts—The production of high precision parts that are identical as opposed to unique, hand–made parts; this standardization of size and shape assures its quality and quantity and permits low–cost mass–production.

Mass production—A method of organizing manufacturing processes to produce more things at a lower cost that is based on specialized human labor and the use of tools and machines.

assembly lines require more highly skilled workers to operate and maintain the sophisticated, computer–controlled equipment.

In the 1980s, Japanese and Italian automobile manufacturers so successfully automated their assembly lines that certain of their factories consisted almost entirely of robots regularly doing their jobs. On one particular Italian Fiat, only 30 of the 2,700 welds were done by human hands. In principle, they are Henry Ford's assembly lines carried to their ultimate conclusion. Starting again with the bare chassis, major components (which themselves have been automatically assembled elsewhere) are attached by robots, and the computer keeps track of exactly what is to be added to each. Each vehicle is considered unique and the central computer assures its total assembly. On the other hand, GM found that robots could not replace human workers and had to retrench from technology and focus on retraining workers. Final product assembly and delivery to the dealer offers the consumer, if not always the most affordable product, an extremely wide array of special options.

See also Industrial revolution; Mass production; Robotics.

Further Reading:
How in the World? Pleasantville, New York: Reader's Digest Association, Inc., 1990, pp. 42–43.

McNeil, Ian. *An Encyclopaedia of the History of Technology.* New York: Routledge, 1990, pp. 404–412.

Rae, John B. "The Rationalization of Production," in Melvin Kranzberg and Carroll E. Pursell, Jr. (eds). *Technology in Western Civilization: Volume II.* New York: Oxford University Press, 1967.

"Who Says the Assembly–Line Age Is History?" *U.S. News & World Report,* July 16, 1984, pp. 48–49.

Leonard C. Bruno

Asses

Asses include three of the seven genera that make up the family Equidae, which also includes horses and zebras. Wild asses are completely wary and apt to run swiftly away, so they have been difficult to study. Asses can survive in poor habitat such as scrub and near desert regions. Asses have loud voices, most notable in the raucous bray of the domestic burro and a keen sense of hearing. Male (stallion) asses tend to leave the herd and live solitary lives except during the mating season in late summer. Female asses tend to stay in the herd, especially when caring for their young. All of the species of wild asses are endangered.

The Asiatic wild ass (*Equus hemionus*) was formerly distributed in Asia from China to the Middle East.

The largest species of the kiang ass (*E. kiang*) lives in the high steppes of Tibet and China. This spieces is about 4.5 ft (1.4 m) tall at the shoulder, weighs up to 880 lbs (400 kg) with a red–brown to black back, and white sides and belly. The coat becomes thicker during the cold Tibetan winters.

The other Asiatic asses are smaller than the kiang, with narrower heads and longer ears. The onager of Iran was perhaps the first member of the horse family to be domesticated. These wild asses once lived in large herds in the deserts and grasslands of Asia, but now are limited to a few very small areas and may even be extinct in the wild, though their exact status is uncertain. The kulan is a small wild ass found in the Mongolian Desert which can run at speeds of up to 40 mph (64 kph). The khur, or Indian onager and the dziggetai of Mongolia are both endangered and probably exist today only in wildlife reserves. The small Syrian onager is the wild ass of the Bible, stands only slightly more than 3 ft (1 m) high at the shoulder, has not been seen since 1927, and is probably extinct in the wild.

The African wild ass *(E. africanus),* is the ancestor of the domesticated donkey, and is represented by a few thousand individuals in Ethiopia, Somalia, and the Sudan. The domesticated donkey is sometimes given a separate name, *E. asinus.* The African wild ass has hooves that are higher and narrower than those of other equids, allowing sure footing in its dry, hilly home. Like many desert living animals, these wild asses need little water, can withstand dehydration, even in temperatures of 125°F (50°C), and can survive two or three days without drinking.

There are two varieties of African wild ass. The Somali wild ass of Somalia and Ethiopia has a dark stripe along its back, light stripes on its legs, dark tips on its ears, and a dark, short mane. The animal's base coat color may turn yellowish or tan during the summer. The Somali wild ass is an endangered species, while the slightly smaller Nubian wild ass, which lacks stripes on its legs, is probably already extinct in the wild.

Domesticated asses are known as donkeys, jackasses, or burros. Their size varies from the tiny 2–foot (less than a meter) burro of Sicily to the Spanish donkey that stands more than 5 ft (2 m) at the shoulder. Numerous feral (wild, formerly domestic) burros live in the western United States, which are regularly rounded up and sold as pets. These sure–footed animals carry tourists on the steep narrow paths leading down into the Grand Canyon.

The hybrid offspring produced when a horse mare mates with a donkey stallion are called mules, which are as sure–footed as burros, and are even stronger than horses. However, mules, being hybrids, are almost always sterile. The offspring hybrid produced by the mating of a horse stallion with a donkey mare is called a hinny. Hinnies tend to resemble a horse more than a mule but are relatively rare because female donkeys do not easily become pregnant.

See also Donkeys.

Further Reading:
Duncan, P., ed. *Zebras, Horses and Asses: An Action Plan for the Conservation of Wild Equids.* Island Press, 1992.

Knight, Linsay. *The Sierra Club Book of Great Mammals.* San Francisco: Sierra Club Books for Children, 1992.

Patent, Dorothy Hinshaw. *Horses and Their Wild Relatives.* New York: Holiday House, 1981.

Special Publications Division. *National Geographic Book of Mammals.* Vol. 1 & 2. Washington, D.C.: National Geographic Society, 1981.

Stidworthy, John. *Mammals: The Large Plant–Eaters.* Encyclopedia of the Animal World. New York: Facts On File, 1988.

Wild Horses. Zoobooks series. San Diego: Wildlife Education, 1987.

Jean F. Blashfield

Associative property

In algebra, a binary operation is a rule for combining the elements of a set two at a time. In most important examples that combination is also another member of the same set. Addition, subtraction, multiplication, and division are familiar binary operations. A familiar example of a binary operation that is associative (obeys the associative principle) is addition (+) of real numbers. For example, the sum of 10, 2, and 35 is determined equally as well as $(10 + 2) + 35 = 12 + 35 = 47$, or $10 + (2 + 35) = 10 + 37 = 47$. The parentheses on either side of the defining equation indicate which two elements are to be combined first. Thus, the associative property states that combining a with b first, and then combining the result with c, is equivalent to combining b with c first, and then combining a with that result. A binary operation ($*$) defined on a set S obeys the associative property if $(a * b) * c = a * (b * c)$, for any three elements a, b, and c in S. Multiplication of real numbers is another associative operation, for example, $(5 \times 2) \times 3 = 10 \times 3 = 30$, and $5 \times (2 \times 3) = 5 \times 6 = 30$. However, not all binary operations are associative. Subtraction of real numbers is not associative since in general $(a - b) - c \neq a - (b - c)$, for example $(35 - 2) - 6 = 33 - 6 = 27$, while $35 - (2 - 6) = 35 - (-4) = 39$. Division of real numbers is not associative either. When the associative property holds for all the members of a set, every combination of elements must result in another element of the same set.

Astatine see **Halogens**

Aster see **Composite family**

Asteroid see **Minor planet (asteroids)**

Asthenosphere

The asthenosphere is the layer of the Earth that lies at a depth 60–150 mi (100–250 km) beneath Earth's surface. It was first named in 1914 by the British geologist J. Barrell, who divided Earth's overall structure into three major sections: the lithosphere, or outer layer of rock–like material; the asthenosphere; and the centrosphere, or central part of the planet. The asthenosphere gets its name from the Greek word for weak, asthenis, because of the relatively fragile nature of the materials of which it is made. It lies in the upper portion of Earth's structure traditionally known as the mantle.

Evidence for the existence of the asthenosphere

Geologists are somewhat limited as to the methods by which they can collect information about Earth's interior. For example, they may be able to study rocky material ejected from volcanoes and lava flows for hints about properties of the interior regions. But, generally speaking, the single most dependable source of such information is the way in which seismic waves are transmitted through Earth's interior. These waves can be produced naturally as the result of earth movements, or they can be generated synthetically by means of explosions, air guns, or other techniques.

In any case, seismic studies have shown that a type of waves known as S–waves slow down significantly as they reach a depth of about 62 mi (100 km) beneath Earth's surface. Then, at a depth of about 155 mi (250 km), their velocity increases once more. Geologists have taken these changes in wave velocity as indications of the boundaries for the region now known as the asthenosphere.

Properties of the asthenosphere

The material of which the asthenosphere is composed can be described as plastic–like, with much less rigidity than the lithosphere above it. This property is caused by the interaction of temperature and pressure on asthenospheric materials. Any rock will, of course, melt if its temperature is raised to a high enough temperature. However, the melting point of any rock (or of any material) is also a function of the pressure exerted on the rock (or the material). In general, as the pressure is increased on a material, its melting point increases.

Materials that make up the asthenosphere tend to be cooler than—but not much cooler than—their melting point. This gives them a plastic–like quality that can be compared to glass. As the temperature of the material increases or as the pressure exerted on the material increases, the material tends to deform and flow. If the pressure on the material is sharply reduced, so will be its melting point, and the material may begin to melt quickly. The fragile melting point pressure balance in the asthenosphere is reflected in the estimate made by some geologists that up to 10% of the asthenospheric material may actually be molten. The rest is so close to being molten that relatively modest changes in pressure or temperature may cause further melting.

In addition to loss of pressure on the asthenosphere, another factor that can bring about melting is an increase in temperature. The asthenosphere is heated by contact with hot materials that make up the mesosphere beneath it. Obviously, the temperature of the mesosphere is not constant. It is hotter in some places than in others. In those regions where the mesosphere is warmer than average, the extra heat may actually increase the extent to which asthenospheric materials are heated and a more extensive melting may occur. The results of such an event are described below.

The asthenosphere in plate tectonic theory

The asthenosphere is now thought to play a critical role in the movement of plates across the face of Earth's surface. According to plate tectonic theory, the lithosphere consists of a relatively small number of very large slabs of rocky material. These plates tend to be about 60 miles (100 km) thick and many thousands of miles wide. They are thought to be very rigid themselves but capable of flowing back and forth on top of the asthenosphere. The collision of plates with each other, their lateral sliding past each other, and their separation from each other are thought to be responsible for major geologic features and events such as volcanoes, lava flows, mountain building, and deep–sea rifts.

In order for plate tectonic theory to make any sense, some mechanism must be available for permitting the flow of plates. That mechanism is the semi–fluid character of the asthenosphere itself. Some observers have described the asthenosphere as the lubricating oil that permits the movement of plates in the lithosphere.

Geologists have now developed some fairly sophisticated theories to explain the changes that take place in the asthenosphere when plates begin to thin or to diverge from or converge toward each other. For example, suppose that a region of weakness has developed in the lithosphere. In that case, the pressure exerted on the asthenosphere beneath it is reduced, melting begins to occur, and asthenospheric materials begin to flow upward. If the lithosphere has not actually broken, those asthenospheric materials cool as they approach Earth's surface and eventually become part of the lithosphere itself.

On the other hand, suppose that a break in the lithosphere has actually occurred. In that case, the asthenospheric materials may escape through that break

KEY TERMS

Lithosphere—The outer layer of Earth, consisting of strong, brittle, rocky material that extends to a depth of about 60 miles (100 km).

Magma—Molten material exuded from below Earth's surface, generally consisting of rock–like materials rich in silicon and oxygen.

Seismic wave—Strictly speaking, a wave produced by an earthquake. Waves similar to seismic waves can also be produced by artificial means for the purpose of studying Earth's interior structure and composition.

and flow outward before they have cooled. Depending on the temperature and pressure in the region, that outflow of material (magma) may occur rather violently, as in a volcano, or more moderately, as in a lava flow.

Pressure on the asthenosphere may also be reduced in zones of divergence, where two plates are separating from each other. Again, this reduction in pressure may allow asthenospheric materials in the asthenosphere to begin melting and to flow upward. If the two overlying plates have actually separated, asthenospheric material may flow through the separation and form a new section of lithosphere.

In zones of convergence, where two plates are flowing toward each other, asthenospheric materials may also be exposed to reduced pressure and begin to flow upward. In this case, the lighter of the colliding plates slides upward and over the heavier of the plates, which dives down into the asthenosphere. Since the heavier lithospheric material is more rigid than the material in the asthenosphere, the latter is pushed outward and upward. During this movement of plates, pressure on the asthenosphere is reduced, melting occurs, and molten materials flow upward to Earth's surface. In any one of the examples cited here, the asthenosphere supplies new material to replace lithospheric materials that have been displaced by some other tectonic or geologic mechanism.

See also Plate tectonics; Volcano.

Further Reading:

Fuchs, Karl, and Claude Froidevaux. *Composition, Structure, and Dynamics of the Lithosphere and Asthenosphere System.* Washington, D.C.: American Geophysical Union, 1987.
White, Robert S., and Dan P. McKenzie, "Volcanism at Rifts," *Scientific American*, July 1989, pp. 62 – 71.

David E. Newton

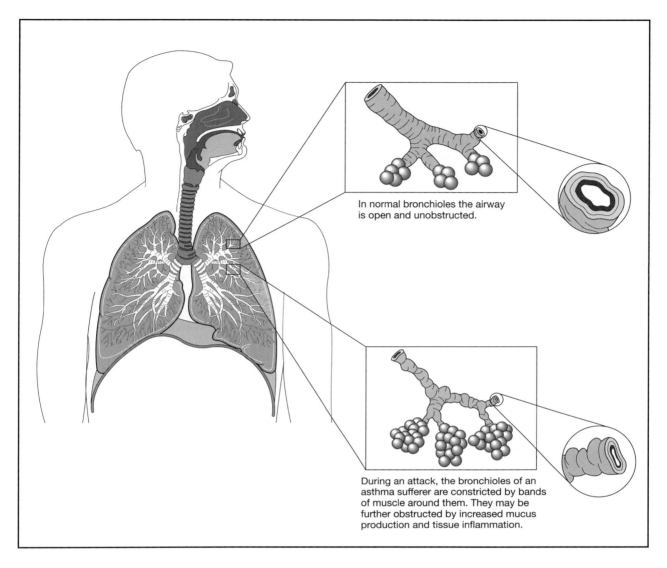

In normal bronchioles the airway is open and unobstructed.

During an attack, the bronchioles of an asthma sufferer are constricted by bands of muscle around them. They may be further obstructed by increased mucus production and tissue inflammation.

A comparison of normal bronchioles and those of an asthma sufferer.

Asthma

Asthma is a lung disease that affects approximately four million people in the United States. In people with asthma, the airways of the lungs are hypersensitive to irritants such as cigarette smoke or allergens. When these irritants are inhaled, the airways react by constricting, or narrowing. Some people with asthma have only mild, intermittent symptoms that can be controlled without drugs. In others, the symptoms are chronic, severe, and sometimes life–threatening. Although researchers have learned more about the underlying causes of asthma in recent years, a definitive treatment is still unavailable. In fact, deaths from asthma are on the rise. In the last decade, asthma deaths worldwide rose 31%.

The reasons for this increase are not clear; however, many experts believe that the lack of standard treatments and the inconsistent monitoring of asthma patients have contributed to the increased mortality rate.

What is asthma?

Asthma is sometimes referred to as a disease of "twitchy lungs," which means that the airways are extremely sensitive to irritants. The airways are the tubes that bring air from the windpipe, known as the trachea, to the lungs. These tubes are called the bronchi. Each bronchus, in turn, branches into smaller tubes called bronchioles. At the end of the bronchioles are small, balloon–like structures called alveoli. The alveoli are tiny organs that allow oxygen to diffuse into the blood and carbon dioxide to diffuse from body tissues into the lungs to be exhaled.

During an asthma attack, the bronchi and bronchioles constrict and obstruct the passage of air into the alveoli. Besides constricting, the airways may secrete copious amounts of mucus in an effort to clear the irritation from the lungs. The airway walls also swell, causing inflammation and further obstruction. Interestingly, one of the hallmarks of asthma is that the airway obstruction is reversible. This reversibility of the airway swelling is used to definitively diagnose asthma. If the swelling and inflammation can be brought under control with asthma drugs, the person has asthma and not some other upper respiratory disease.

In addition to cigarette smoke and various allergens, other triggers can cause asthma attacks. A cold or other upper respiratory infection may bring on an asthma attack. Strong emotions, such as excitement, tension, or anxiety, may trigger asthma symptoms. Exercise is linked to asthma. Even extreme weather conditions, such as very cold, very hot, or very humid weather, can cause an asthma attack.

The characteristic sign of asthma is wheezing, the noisy breathing that a person makes as he or she tries to push air in and out of narrowed airways. Other symptoms of asthma include a tight chest, shortness of breath, and a cough.

Treatment of asthma

Currently, several drugs are used to treat asthma. Not all of the asthma drugs, however, should be used by every asthma patient. Some patients with mild asthma only need to use medication occasionally to control wheezing. Patients with more serious asthma need to take medication at regular intervals to avoid life–threatening attacks. It is important for asthma patients to see their doctors if the frequency or severity of their symptoms change. It has been suggested that many of the life–threatening asthma attacks are in people who once had mild asthma—with symptoms that could be treated as they occurred—that naturally progressed to a more severe case of the disease. When this progression occurred, they did not have the medication necessary to control the severe attacks, and they tried to treat the serious asthma symptoms with the medication designed for mild asthma.

The bronchodilator controversy

Bronchodilators dilate constricted lung airways by relaxing the chest muscles. Two types of bronchodila-

tors are used to treat asthma. One type is a powder that is inhaled from a special inhaler device, and the other is taken in pill form. The bronchodilator taken in pill form is usually prescribed for severe asthma. The patient is instructed to take the drug at regular intervals, to maintain a constant level of the drug in the bloodstream. The inhaled bronchodilator is usually prescribed for milder causes of asthma. The patient inhales the drug whenever he or she feels an attack coming on. The inhaled medications are quick–acting because they are directly applied to the constricted airways.

Within in the last five years, controversy about inhaled bronchodilators has arisen in the medical field. In a study published in 1993, doctors found an increased risk of death or near–death from asthma when patients used a type of inhaled bronchodilator commonly prescribed to control asthma. This finding sent shock waves through the medical community. Although more information is still needed regarding the reasons behind the increase in deaths and near–deaths and their association with inhaled bronchodilators, some experts think that the association can be explained by several factors:

(1) More people who use inhaled bronchodilators die because their asthma suddenly becomes more severe and they do not see their doctors. These patients are treating severe asthma with a drug usually prescribed for milder forms.

(2) Bronchodilators may have long–term effects on organ systems.

(3) Bronchodilators may, over time, increase airway hyper–responsiveness.

(4) Physicians are not adequately monitoring their patients for progression from mild to severe asthma.

These factors are currently being investigated. Asthma experts stress, however, that people with asthma who use inhaled bronchodilators should continue to do so, but they should see their physicians regularly. They should also immediately contact their physicians if they notice a change in the severity and frequency of their symptoms.

A new inhaled bronchodilator, called salmeterol, combines the direct effects of inhaled bronchodilators with the long–lasting protection afforded by oral bonchodilators. Salmeterol has only recently been approved for use in the United States; it offers a new, more effective drug choice for mild and severe asthma.

Anti–inflammatory drugs

Anti–inflammatory drugs reduce the swelling and inflammation of the airways. These drugs can be inhaled or taken in pill form. Two types of anti–inflammatory drugs are prescribed for asthma patients: chromolyn sodium and corticosteroids. Chromolyn sodium is also prescribed for people with allergies, and it has few side–effects. Oral corticosteroids are a newer form of treatment, which are very effective in treating asthma but can have serious side–effects. Short–term side effects include increased appetite, weight gain, hypertension, and fluid retention. Over the long–term, corticosteroids may cause osteoporosis, cataracts, and impaired immune response. These side–effects usually preclude the use of corticosteroids for long periods of time.

Inhaled corticosteroids have few side effects. These medications are also prescribed for allergy patients. Unlike their oral counterparts, these drugs can be taken for much longer periods of time. They are especially useful in controlling moderate asthma.

Can asthma attacks be prevented?

Asthma experts are currently working to dispel many myths about asthma. For instance, it was once thought that increasing fluid intake would lessen mucus production and therefore lessen the frequency and severity of asthma attacks. But drinking lots of water does not affect asthma (although drinking a lot of water is a good idea for maintaining general health). Breathing into a paper bag is also a bad idea for someone with an asthma attack. Persons with asthma should avoid over–the–counter medications advertised to treat asthma.

Depending on the triggers associated with asthma attacks, patients can sometimes avoid attacks by taking certain preventive steps. If allergens such as dust and pollen trigger an attack, asthma can be avoided by doing the following:

(1) Avoid being outside during the early morning and late afternoon hours, when pollen levels are highest.

(2) Since dust has been associated with asthma attacks, thoroughly and frequently clean the indoor environment. Dust and vacuum every day. Wash bed linens in hot, soapy water every few days or so. Replace air filters in air conditioners and furnaces regularly.

(3) During hot weather, use air conditioning.

Eliminating the irritant is the key. If asthma is brought on by cigarette smoke, the patient must avoid this irritant. If asthma is brought on by exercise, the person should try to find a level of exertion that is comfortable. Using an inhaled bronchodilator before exercising may also control asthma symptoms.

KEY TERMS

Bronchiole—The smaller airway tubes that branch off from each bronchus.

Bronchodilator—A drug, either inhaled or taken orally, that dilates the lung airways by relaxing the chest muscles.

Bronchus—One of the two main airway tubes that branch off from the windpipe and lead to each lung.

Wheezing—The characteristic sound of asthma; results when a person tries to push air in and out of narrowed airways.

For all persons with asthma, communication with and regular visits to their physicians are essential components of treatment. Without periodic check–ups, the physician cannot monitor progress or potential worsening of symptoms. Thus, the most important aspect of prevention and treatment for asthma patients is the regular physician visit.

See also Respiratory diseases; Respiratory system.

Further Reading:

American Lung Association. *What Every Educator Should Know About Asthma.* Denver, CO: American Lung Association of Colorado, 1990.

Bartholomew, Mary Todd. "Living With Asthma." *USA Today Magazine.* vol 122 (2588): 87.

Gorman, Christine. "Asthma: Deadly but Treatable." *Time.* vol. 139 (25): 61, June 22, 1992.

National Asthma Education Program, Expert Panel. *Executive Summary: Guidelines for the Diagnosis and Management of Asthma.* Washington, D.C.: U.S. Department of Health and Human Services, Public Health Service, National Institutes of Health. June, 1991.

Spilner , Maggie. "Get Off the Asthma Tightrope." *Prevention.* vol. 46 (9): 88. September 1994.

Spitzer, Walter O. et. al. "The Use of Beta–Agonists and the Risk of Death and Near Death From Asthma." *New England Journal of Medicine.* vol. 326 (8): 501–506, February 20, 1992.

Waldron, Brian J. "Tyranny and Cruelty (Severe Asthma Attack Requires Severe Treatment)." *Discover.* vol. 14 (8): 90, August, 1993.

Kathleen Scogna

Astigmatism see **Vision disorders**

Astrapias puffin see **Auks**

An astrobleme in Arizona.

Astroblemes

Astroblemes are the scars left on the Earth's surface by the high velocity impact of large objects from outer space. Such colliding bodies are usually meteorites, but some may have been comet heads or asteroids. Few of these impacts are obvious today because our active earth tends to erode meteorite craters over short periods of geologic time. The term astrobleme was coined in 1961 by Robert S. Dietz from two Greek roots meaning "star wound."

Most geologists were not convinced until the 1930s that a mysterious handful of huge circular depressions on the earth were caused by meteorites. The most studied astrobleme during that time was Barringer Crater, a meteor crater in northern Arizona, measuring 0.7 mi (1.2 km) across and 590 ft (180 m) deep. It is now thought to have been blown out about 25,000 years ago by a nickel–iron meteorite about the size of a large house traveling at 9 mi (15 km) per second. Over the years aerial photography and satellite imagery have revealed many other astroblemes. About 100 around the world have been confirmed by various geological methods. A number have diameters 10–60 times larger than that of the Barringer Crater and are hundreds of millions of years old. The largest astrobleme is South Africa's Vredefort Ring, whose diameter spans 24 mi (40 km).

Exploding or collapsing volcanoes can make roughly circular craters, so it is not easy to interpret such features unless there are a lot of meteorite fragments present. However, because only meteorites collide with the earth at terrific speeds, geologists also have the option of searching for the effects of tremendous pressure applied in an instant of time at potential astrobleme sites. Important clues along this line are a large body of shattered rock (impact breccia) radiating downward from a central focus, similar small–scale "shatter cones," very high pressure forms of the mineral silica not found anywhere else in the earth's crust (coesite and stishovite), finely cracked, "shocked" quartz particles, and bits of impact–melted silicate rock that cool into tiny balls of glass called "tektites."

See also Comets; Meteors and Meteorites.

Astrolabe

An astrolabe is an astronomical instrument once used widely to measure stars or planets in order to determine latitude and time, primarily for navigational purposes. The original meaning of the word in Greek is "star–taker." The astrolabe was probably invented by astronomers in the second century B.C.

At least two forms of the astrolabe have existed. The older form, known as the planispheric astrolabe, consists of two circular metal disks, one representing the Earth and the other, the celestial sphere at some particular location (latitude) on the Earth's surface. The first of these disks, called the plate or tympan, is fixed in position on a supporting disk known as the mater. It shows the great circles of altitude at the given latitude. Any given plate can be removed and replaced by a plate for some other altitude with the appropriate markings for that latitude.

The second of the disks, called the rete or spider, is attached to the plate and the mater by a metal pin through its center. The metal disk that makes up the rete is primarily cut out so that it consists of a complex series of curved lines ending in points. The points indicate the location of particular stars in the celestial sphere. The rete can be rotated around the central pin to show the position of stars at various times of the day or night, as indicated by markings along the circumference of the mater.

To use the astrolabe, an observer hangs the instrument from a metal ring attached at the top of the mater. A sighting device on the back of the astrolabe, the alidade, is then lined up with some specific star in the sky. As the alidade is moved to locate the star, the rete on the front of the astrolabe is also pivoted to provide the correct setting of the celestial sphere for the given time of day. That time of day can then be read directly off the mater.

A much simpler form of the astrolabe was invented in about the 15th century by Portuguese navigators. It consisted only of the mater and the alidade, suspended from a ring attached to the mater. The alidade was used to determine the elevation of a star above the horizon and, thus, the latitude of the ship's position. This form of the astrolabe, known as the mariner's astrolabe, later evolved into the instrument known as the sextant.

More elaborate forms of the mariner's astrolabe were later developed and are still used for some specialized purposes. One of these, known as the impersonal astrolabe, was invented by the French astronomer André Danjon (1890–1967). The modern prismatic

Galileo's astrolabe.

astrolabe is based on Danjon's concept. In this form of the astrolabe, two light rays from the same star are passed through a prism, one directly and one after reflection from the surface of a pool of mercury. The star is observed as it rises (or sets) in the sky. During most of this period, the two light rays passing through the prism are out of phase with each other. At some point, the specific latitude for which the astrolabe is designed is attained and the two star images coincide with each other, giving the star's precise location at that moment.

See also Celestial coordinates.

Astrometry

Astrometry literally means measuring the stars. This type of measurement determines a specific star's location in the sky with great precision. In order to establish a star's location, it is necessary to first establish a coordinate system in which the location can be specified. Traditionally, very distant stars, which show very little motion as viewed from Earth, have been used to establish that coordinate system. However, the accuracy of the coordinate system is dependent on the accuracy of the positions of defining stars, and in recent years there has been some effort to use the extremely distant point–like objects known as quasars to establish an improved standard coordinate system. Because quasars give off radio waves, their positions can be determined with extreme accuracy, but the implementation of this system has yet to be accomplished.

Astrometry is of fundamental importance to the study of the stars. Astronomers can use the distance of the star to help determine its other properties. The annual motion of the Earth about the Sun causes nearby stars to appear to move about in the sky with respect to distant background stars. The amplitude of this apparent motion determines the distance of the star from our sun, which is known as its trigonometric parallax. The angular rate of change of the star's position is called its proper motion. If the distance to the star is also known, the proper motion can be converted into a transverse velocity relative to the Sun, which is the apparent speed of the star across the line of sight. For most stars this motion is extremely small and may require positional determinations 50 years or longer for accurate measurement. The transverse velocity may be combined with the radial velocity determined from the star's spectra to yield the true space velocity with respect to the Sun.

Occasionally the proper motion will be found to vary in a periodic manner, suggesting that the target star is orbiting another object in addition to its steady motion across the sky. Such stars are called astrometric binary stars. Stars that are orbited by planets, which are too faint to be directly observed, show this motion. However, the motion is liable to be extremely small unless the star is quite small and the planet rather large.

Often, astronomers cannot determine the distance of the star directly from the coordinate system. In this case, a method called statistical parallax is used. For example, if one independently knew the transverse velocity of a star, one could use the proper motion to obtain a distance. While it is impossible to determine the transverse velocity of a specific star without knowledge of its distance and proper motion, an estimation can be obtained by using the transverse velocity for a collection of similar stars. In addition, the radial velocity of the star can be obtained directly from its spectra without knowledge of its distance or proper motion.

These can then be combined with the observed proper motions to yield distances to the similar stars of a particular type and average values for their intrinsic properties.

A similar trick can be used on a group of stars which move together through space on more–or–less parallel tracks. Such groups of stars are called galactic, or open, clusters. Just as the parallel tracks of a railroad appear to converge to a point in the distance, so the stellar motions will appear to point to a distant convergent point in the sky. The location of this point with respect to each star specifies the angle between the radial velocity and the space velocity for that star. Knowledge of that angle allows the tangential velocity of the star to be obtained from the directly measured radial velocity. Again knowledge of the individual proper motion and tangential velocity allows for a determination of the distance to each star of the cluster. This scheme is known as the moving cluster method.

The recent introduction of adaptive optics has greatly improved the accuracy of stellar positions made from the ground. For half a century astronomers have known that it was possible in principle to undo the distortions of astronomical images generated by the atmosphere. First one had to measure those distortions, then construct a "lens" with characteristics that could be changed as fast as the atmosphere itself changed. Theoretically such a lens could then "undo" the distortions of the atmosphere, leaving the astronomer with the steady image of the star beyond the atmosphere. This seemed impossible to accomplish until very recently. Powerful lasers have now been used to produce artificial stars high in the atmosphere, enabling astronomers to measure the atmospheric distortions. Remarkable increases in computer speed have allowed the analysis of those distortions to be completed in milliseconds so that a thin mirror can be adjusted to correct for atmospheric distortions. Such systems are generally referred to as adaptive optics and in principle they allow observations of stellar positions to be made from the ground.

However, while adaptive optics systems were being developed, several satellites and satellite programs addressed the fundamental problems of astrometry. The pointing accuracy of the Hubble Space Telescope required a greatly increased "catalogue" of stars and their positions so that guide stars could be found for all potential targets of the telescope. A number of ground surveys which provided positions of several million stars were undertaken expressly to provide those guide stars. Partly in response to these surveys, machines were developed that could automatically measure star positions on the thousands of photographic glass plates that were taken for the projects. Now the determination of stellar positions can be accomplished directly by an electronic detector much like those found in a video camera, thereby replacing the photographic plate. This development also allowed the design of satellites dedicated to the determination of stellar positions. The must notable of these is Hipparcos, developed by the European Space Agency (ESA). Hipparcos was designed to measure the positions of more than 100,000 stars with an accuracy of between two and four milliarc seconds. This is easily more than 10 times the accuracy readily achievable from the ground. After nearly a decade of development, Hipparcos was launched aboard the Ariane spacecraft in 1989. Unfortunately, due to a failure of the final stage of the rocket, the satellite never achieved the geo–stationary orbit approximately 25,000 miles above the earth. Instead, its orbit is highly elliptical with its furthest point near the desired distance, but dipping down close to the earth's atmosphere at its low point. This greatly reduced the efficiency of the satellite.

Eventually satellites like Hipparcos, along with improved ground observations, will significantly enhance the number of stars for which we have good positions and other astrometrical data. Not only will this clarify our view of the local stellar neighborhood within our galaxy, it will also increase our fundamental knowledge of stars themselves.

See also Astronomical catalogs; Celestial coordinates; Parallax; Star.

Astronomical catalogs

We may define an astronomical catalog as a list of certain properties of celestial objects derived from observations. The celestial objects may be stars, planets, galaxies, x ray sources, and others, and the properties may be positions, velocities, spectra, and others. The definition emphasizes properties derived from observations. A listing of temperatures of stars determined from a computer model would not be considered a catalog nor would star positions, calculated, not observed, in a field guide for observers. Also excluded are maps of constellations, often beautiful but providing no numerical data.

Early history of astronomical catalogs

The first catalog of which we have definite knowledge is merely a listing, given in the poem *Phainomena* of Aratus (fl. third century B.C.), of the positions of 25 stars determined by Eudoxus (c. 400 B.C.–c. 350 B.C.). Hipparchus (fl. 150 B.C.) published a catalog, now lost, of positions of 850 stars. This catalog appears to be the first to not only list star positions, but also to estimate their brightness, or "magnitude" in astronomical terminology. Ptolemy's (fl. 140 A.D.) catalog of 1,023 stars, contained in the *Almagest*, may be original or, some think, largely Hipparchus's catalog corrected for precession (q.v.) and containing some additional stars. Ptolemy's catalog acquires further importance because of its scale of magnitudes, ranging from magnitude one for the brightest stars visible to the naked eye to six for the faintest. This scale, although revised, remains in use today.

The first astronomer to prepare a truly independent catalog based on new observations was Ulugh Begh (1394–1449), a grandson of Tamerlane, working in Samarkand. In Europe Tycho Brahe (1546–1601) was the first to prepare an independent catalog of 1,000 stars, although only 777 are truly independent, published in 1598; Copernicus's catalog of 1,024 stars in *De Revolutionibus* is little more than Ptolemy's catalog precessed to the contemporary era with a scattering of new observations.

Dawn of the modern era of astronomical catalogs

Brahe's catalog contained only stars visible from the Northern Hemisphere. This lacuna was filled in 1678 when Edmund Halley (1656–1752), after whom Halley's Comet is named, published a catalog of 341 southern stars he observed at St. Helena, but with a telescope.

With Halley we come to the dawn of the modern era of astronomical catalogs. The errors of positions had decreased markedly from Ptolemy, where an error of position is typically 0.5°—the angular diameter of the full Moon—to 1' or 2', roughly the angular diameter of a quarter seen at the length of a football field. But Brahe's observations represented the best that could be done pre–telescopically. Thus, while Hevelius's (1611–1687) catalog of 1,563 stars, the last observed without a telescope, incorporates a precision similar to Brahe's, Flamsteed's (1646–1720) *Historia Coelestis Britannica*, telescopic observations of 2,935 stars, gives a precision of 10", equivalent to the angular diameter of a quarter seen at the length of six football fields. Not only does the telescope permit greater precision, it also allows the observation of fainter stars; whereas magnitude six is the limit for the naked eye, a telescope with a 2–in (5–cm) lens reaches magnitude 10.

Subsequent to Flamsteed, and succeeding him as Astronomer Royal, Bradley (1693–1762) and assistants observed nearly 60,000 stars between 1750 and 1762, with a precision superior to that of Flamsteed's. These constitute the oldest observations still useful for modern research into star positions.

The nineteenth century

The nineteenth century saw a increase in the number of catalogs produced. There occurred, furthermore, a standardization of the information given. Most earlier catalogs referred star positions to the ecliptic, the apparent path of the Sun in the sky, by using celestial latitude (the angular distance measured perpendicular to the ecliptic) and celestial longitude (the angular distance measured along the ecliptic from the equinox, the intersection of the celestial equator—the projection into space of the Earth's equator—and the ecliptic).

Catalogs also became standardized into absolute catalogs, where the coordinates for each star are determined independently of previous catalogs, relative catalogs, where the coordinates are measured relative to reference stars with assumed positions, and compilation catalogs, where coordinates from individual catalogs are combined to form a single catalog. Because individual catalogs embrace observations made at different times, a compilation catalog frequently includes the "proper motions" of stars, their angular displacements perpendicular to the line of sight after the effects of the Earth's motion and atmosphere are taken into account.

The introduction of photography into astronomy represents the nineteenth century's most important contribution. Photography reaches fainter magnitudes, achieves higher precision, and registers hundreds or thousands of star images on one plate. During the nineteenth century, numerous catalogs, both visual and photographic, were produced. Toward the end of the century photography was used to determine properties other than just position and proper motion: the parallax, distance of a star; radial velocity, the motion of a star along the line of sight; and magnitude. The Henry Draper catalog, an enormous project, was undertaken to classify stars according to their spectra. Positional determinations achieved precisions of 0."3 and parallax determinations 0."02.

The twentieth century and contemporary catalogs

By the middle of the twentieth century catalogs had been published of nearly all the properties of interest for a star. Typical of these is the Wilson catalog of radial velocities and the Jenkins catalog of parallaxes. As new types of objects were discovered, such as galaxies, they were catalogued. The catalogs were usually published as large volumes of detailed information, although occasionally, especially for non–traditional objects, they were published in astronomical journals.

After WW II several developments occurred that changed both the scope and the preparation of astronomical catalogs. Emission of celestial radio waves was detected in 1932. Visible light and radio waves are the only celestial radiation that reach the surface of the Earth. But after the war, use of rockets, balloons, and, after 1957, artificial satellites, permitted the observation of gamma rays, x rays, the ultraviolet, the infrared, and microwaves. Objects observed at these wavelengths had to be catalogued, along with newly discovered objects such as quasars and pulsars.

Electronic registration has largely superseded photography. Even photographic plates can be scanned electronically and their images stored on electronic media such as computer disks. This generates, in a short time, abundant information that may, nevertheless, be analyzed quickly by computer. The old way of preparing a catalog by publishing volumes becomes inadequate: the information must first be put into machine–readable form, a tedious and error–prone process. And the sheer amount of information would generate hundreds or thousands of bulky volumes.

Modern catalogs are prepared electronically and stored on computer disks, such as CD–ROMs, where they can be accessed easily by computer. The star catalog for the Hubble space telescope affords an example. Before launch it was necessary to prepare a catalog of star positions to permit guiding the telescope during operations. The most complete catalog available at the time, the Smithsonian Astrophysical Observatory compilation catalog of 258,997 stars down to ninth magnitude, was insufficient: Hubble needed stars down to 15th magnitude. The staff of the Space Telescope Science Institute in Baltimore had 1,477 photographic plates taken of the entire sky. The plates were scanned and the information stored on optical disks. The final catalog of 18,819,291 objects, of which 15,169,873 are stars down to 15th magnitude, is published on two CD–ROMs, accessible by personal computer. If published in the traditional manner, the catalog would require over 400 volumes of 500 pages each.

Another major undertaking, the Hipparcos (high precision parallax collecting satellite) catalog, has yet to be published. This satellite, launched by the European Space Agency in August 1989 completed its mission of determining high quality parallaxes of 115,000 stars in August 1993. Positions and proper motions will also be determined, it is hoped, to great precision, perhaps 0."002. The final catalog will undoubtedly also be distributed in machine–readable form.

See also Astrometry; Parallax; Telescope.

KEY TERMS
. . . .

Celestial equator—The projection into space of the Earth's equator.

Declination—Angular distance of an object measured perpendicularly to the celestial equator.

Ecliptic—Apparent path of the Sun in the sky or, alternatively, the plane of the Earth's orbit in space.

Ecliptic latitude—Angular distance of an object measured perpendicularly to the ecliptic.

Ecliptic longitude—Angular distance measured along the ecliptic from the equinox.

Equinox—Intersection of the celestial equator and the ecliptic.

Magnitude—Brightness of an object.

Parallax—Distance of an object.

Proper motion—Change in the angular position of a star perpendicular to the line of sight after the effects of the Earth's motion and atmosphere have been removed.

Radial velocity—Motion of a star along the line of sight.

Right ascension—Angular distance measured along the equator from the equinox.

Further Reading:

Høg, E., J. Kovalevsky, and L. Lindegren. "Hipparcos Data Reduction—Construction of the Star Catalog," *ESA Bulletin*, (Nov. 69, 1992): 43.

Villard, R., "The World's Biggest Star Catalog," *Sky and Telescope*, (December 1989): 583.

Richard L. Branham, Jr.

Astronomical unit

An astronomical unit (AU) is a unit of length that astronomers use for measuring distances within the solar system. One astronomical unit is the mean distance between the Earth and the Sun, called the semimajor axis, or 92,919,000 miles (149,597,870 km).

The relative distances between the Sun and the planets, in astronomical units, were known long before the actual distances were established. Kepler, in developing his third law, showed that the ratio of the square of a planet's period (the time to make one complete revolution) to the cube of the semimajor axis of its orbit is a constant; that is, the ratio is the same for all the planets. Kepler's law can be summarized by the formula

$$a^3/p^2 = k$$

where a is the semimajor axis of the planet's orbit, p is its period, and K is the proportionality constant, a constant that holds for all bodies orbiting the Sun. By choosing the period of the Earth as one year and its orbital radius as one AU, the constant K has a numerical value of one.

Kepler's third law (in a more accurate form derived by Isaac Newton) can be used to calculate a precise value of the AU, if the exact distance between the earth and another planet can be measured. An early attempt took place in 1671, when Jean Cssini in Paris and Jean Richer about 5,000 miles (8,000 km) away in Cayenne, Guiana, simultaneously determined the parallax of Mars. Their measurements, which allowed them to calculate the distance from earth to Mars by triangulation, showed Mars to be about 50 million miles (80 million km) from Earth. Since the relative distance between Earth and Mars was known, it was a simple matter to determine the actual value of an AU in miles or kilometers. Today, the value of the AU is known very accurately. By measuring the time for a radar pulse to reach Venus and return, the distance can be calculated because radar waves travel at the speed of light.

See also Kepler's laws; Solar system.

Astrophysics

Astrophysics describes the processes which give rise to the observable features of our universe in terms of previously developed physical theories. It ties together physics and astronomy by describing astronomical phenomena in terms of the physics and chemistry we are familiar with in our everyday life.

Background

Why do the stars shine? How did our galaxy form? Will the universe expand forever? These are the types of questions asked by astrophysicists in an attempt to understand the processes which cause our universe, and everything in it, to behave the way it does. From the low–energy gravitational interactions between planets and stars, to the violent, high energy processes occurring in the centers of galaxies, astrophysical theories are used to explain what we see, and to understand how phenomena are related.

For thousands of years, astronomy was simply an observational science—humans could observe phenomena in the sky, but had no physical explanation for what they saw. Early humans could offer only supernatural explanations for what they observed, which seemed drastically different from what they experienced in everyday life. Only in the twentieth century have scientists been able to explain many astronomical phenomena in terms of detailed physical theories, relating them to the same chemistry and physics at work in our everyday lives.

Astrophysical experiments, unlike experiments in many other sciences, cannot be done under controlled conditions or repeated in a laboratory; the energies and distance scales involved are simply too great. As a result, astrophysicists are forced into the role of observer, watching events as they happen without being able to control the parameters of the experiment. For centuries, humans have made such observations and attempted to understand the forces at work. But how did scientists develop our picture of the universe if they could not reproduce what they see in the laboratory? Instead of controlling the experiments, they used what data they were able to obtain in order to develop theories based on extensions of the physical laws which govern our day–to–day experiences on earth.

Astrophysics often involves the creation of mathematical models as a means of interpreting observations. This theoretical work is important not just for explaining what has already been seen, but also for predicting other observable effects. These models are often based on well–established physics, but often must be simplified, because real astronomical phenomena can be enormously complex.

Processes in the universe

Even by looking close to the Earth, in our own solar system we see widely varying conditions. The rocky planet Mercury, very close to the Sun, has properties which differ dramatically from the gas giant Saturn, with its complex ring structure, and the cold, icy Pluto. But the scale of our solar system (and its wide variations in characteristics) is minuscule when compared to what occurs in stars, galaxies, and more exotic objects such as quasars. The properties of all of these objects, however, can be measured by observation, and an understanding of how they work can be reached by the extension and application of the same physical laws with which we are familiar.

The first astrophysical concept or law to be recognized was the law of gravity. We are all familiar with the force of gravity. Although it is a very weak force compared to the other fundamental forces of nature, it is the dominant factor determining the structure and the fate of the universe. Large structures, such as galaxies, and smaller ones, such as stars and planets, coalesced due to the force of gravity, which acts over vast distances of space. Much of the evolution of our universe is due to gravity's effects. However, scientists generally hold the view that the understanding of atomic processes marks the true beginning of astrophysics. Indeed, even such enormous objects as stars are governed by the interaction and behavior of atoms. Thus it is often said that astrophysics began in the early decades of the twentieth century, when quantum mechanics and atomic physics were born.

Importance of instrumentation

Scientists learn about distant objects by measuring the properties which we can observe directly, by detecting emissions from the objects. The most common measurements are of electromagnetic radiation, extending from radio waves, through visible wavelengths to high energy gamma rays. Each time a class of objects has been studied in a new wavelength region, new insights into the composition, structure, and properties have been gained, since different wavelength regions offer windows into different properties of the object. For this reason, the development of new instrumentation has been crucial to the development of astrophysics.

The development of space instrumentation which can detect photons before they are obscured by the Earth's atmosphere has been critical to our understanding of the universe. Large space–based observatories, such as the Hubble Space Telescope, continually lead to major advances in astrophysics due to their ability to probe parts of the electromagnetic spectrum with unprecedented sensitivity. In addition, probes such as the *Voyagers,* which visited most of the outer planets of our solar system, have provided detailed measurements of the physical environment throughout our solar system. The use of spectroscopy, which can determine the chemical composition of distant objects from their wavelength distribution is a particularly important tool of the astrophysicist.

In addition to the photons of electromagnetic radiation, emitted particles can be detected. These can be protons and electrons, the constituents of ordinary matter on Earth (though often with extremely high ener-

gies), or ghostly neutrinos, which only weakly interact with matter on Earth (and are thus extremely difficult to detect), but help us learn about the nuclear reactions which power stars. Astrophysics proceeds through hypothesis, prediction, and test (via observation), its common belief being that laws of physics are consistent throughout the universe. These laws of physics have served us well, and scientists are most skeptical of proposed explanations that violate them.

See also Cosmology; Galaxy; Gamma–ray astronomy; Infrared astronomy; Nuclear reactions; Planet; Pulsar; Quasar; Relativity, general; Relativity, special; Solar system; Spectral classification of stars; Spectral lines; Spectroscopy; Star; Sun; Telescope; Ultraviolet astronomy; X–ray astronomy.

Further Reading:

Audouze, Jean, Guy and Israël, eds. *The Cambridge Atlas of Astronomy.* Cambridge: Cambridge University Press, 1994.

Kaufmann, William J. III. *Discovering the Universe.* 2nd ed. New York: W. H. Freeman, 1990.

Pasachoff, Jay M. *Contemporary Astronomy.* 4th ed. Philadelphia: Saunders College Publishing, 1989.

David Sahnow

Asymptote

An asymptote is a straight line which is approached steadily by a curve that gets closer and closer but, although the distance between the curve and line approaches O, the two never touch. This is sometimes expressed by saying that the curve and line "meet at infinity."

Atlantic menhaden see **Herrings**

Atlantic puffin see **Auks**

Atmospheric circulation

Atmospheric circulation is the movement of air at all levels of the atmosphere over all parts of the planet. The driving force behind atmospheric circulation is solar energy, which heats the atmosphere with different intensities at the equator, the middle latitudes, and the poles. Differential heating causes air to rise in the atmosphere at some locations on the planet and then to sink back to the Earth's surface at other locations. The Earth's rotation on its axis and the unequal distribution of land and water masses on the planet also contribute to various features of atmospheric circulation.

An idealized model of atmospheric circulation

As early as the 1730s, the English lawyer and amateur scientist George Hadley described an idealized model for the movement of air in the Earth's atmosphere. It is well known, Hadley pointed out, that air at the equator is heated more strongly than at any other place on the Earth. In comparison, air above the poles is cooler than at any other location. One can hypothesize, therefore, that surface air near the equator will rise into the upper atmosphere and, above the poles, sink from the upper atmosphere to ground level. In order to balance these vertical movements of air, it was also necessary to hypothesize that air flows across the Earth's surface from each pole back to the equator and, in the upper atmosphere, from above the equator to above the poles.

The movement of air described by Hadley can be called a convection cell. The term convection refers to the transfer of heat as it is carried from place to place by a moving fluid, air in this case.

Hadley knew, of course, that surface winds do not blow from north to south in the northern hemisphere and from south to north in the southern hemisphere, as his simple model would require. He explained that winds actually tend to blow from the east or west because of the Earth's rotation. The spinning planet causes air flows that would otherwise be from the north or south to be diverted to the east or west, Hadley said.

As an analogy of how this change could occur, suppose that you are sitting on a spinning merry–go–round trying to catch a ball thrown by a friend at the center of the platform. The ball will obviously travel in a straight line from the thrower to the intended catcher on the rim. But to the catcher, the ball will appear to follow a curved path, and he or she will have to reach out to catch the ball.

A century after Hadley's initial theory was proposed, a mathematical description of this "merry–go–round effect" was published by the French physicist Gaspard Gustave de Coriolis. Coriolis was able to prove mathematically that an object in motion on any

rotating body always appears to follow a curved path in relation to any other body on the same rotating body. This discovery, now known as the Coriolis effect, provided a more exact explanation of the reason that surface winds are deflected to the east or west than did Hadley's original theory.

The three–cell model

At about the time that Coriolis published his studies on rotating bodies, scientists were beginning to realize that Hadley's single convection cell model was too simple. Atmospheric pressure and wind measurements taken at many locations around the planet did not fit the predictions made by the Hadley model.

Some important modifications in the Hadley model were suggested in the 1850s, therefore, by the American meteorologist William Ferrell. Ferrell had, of course, much more data about wind patterns than had been available to Hadley. On the basis of these data, Ferrell proposed a three–cell model for atmospheric circulation.

Ferrell's model begins where Hadley's began, with the upward flow of air over the equator and its continued flow toward the poles along the upper atmosphere. At approximately 30° latitude, however, Ferrell hypothesized that this air had become sufficiently cooled so that it began to descend to the Earth's surface. Once at surface level, some of this air would then flow back toward the equator, as in the Hadley model. Today this large convection current over the third of the globe above and below the equator is called a Hadley cell.

Ferrell's new idea, however, was that some of the air descending to the Earth near latitude 30° would flow away from the equator and toward the poles along the Earth's surface. It was this flow of air that made Ferrell's model more complex and more accurate than Hadley's. For at about 60° latitude, this surface flow of air collided with a flow of polar air to make two additional convection cells.

Ferrell had agreed with Hadley about the movement of air above the poles. That is, cool air would descend from higher altitudes and flow toward the equator along the Earth's surface. At about 60° latitude, however, this flow of polar air would collide with air flowing toward it from the 30° latitude outflow.

The accumulation of air resulting from this collision along latitude 60° would produce a region of high pressure that could be relieved, Ferrell said, by massive updrafts that would carry air high into the atmosphere. There the air would split into two streams, one flowing toward the equator and descending to the Earth's surface once more at about 30° latitude. This downward flow would complete a second convection cell covering the mid–latitudes and now known as the Ferrell cell. The second stream above 30° latitude would flow toward the poles and complete the third, or polar, cell.

One can hardly expect a model of the atmosphere developed nearly 150 years ago to be completely valid today. We know a great deal more about the atmosphere and have much more data than Ferrell knew or had. Still, his hypothesis is still valuable because it provides some general outlines about the nature of atmospheric circulation. It also explains a number of well–known circulation phenomena.

Observed patterns of circulation

One of the implications of the Ferrell hypothesis is that there should be relatively little surface wind near the equator. In this region, surface winds should be flowing toward the equator from the Hadley cells and, when they meet, rising upward into the upper atmosphere. Equatorial regions would be expected to be characterized, therefore, by relatively low pressures with weak surface winds.

But these conditions are exactly what mariners have observed for centuries. Indeed, they long ago gave the name of the doldrums to the equatorial seas. For centuries, ship captains have feared and avoided equatorial waters because winds are so weak and unreliable there that they could easily become stranded for days or weeks at a time.

A second region of calm on the Earth's surface, according to the three–cell model, would be around latitude 30°. In this region, air moving downward from both the Hadley and Ferrell cells collides as it reaches the Earth's surface, producing regions of high pressure. As in the doldrums, the regions around latitude 30° are characterized by weak, unpredictable winds.

Again, such regions have long been feared and avoided by sailors, who have given them the name of the horse latitudes. The origin of this name comes from the fact that ships bringing horses to the Americas often became becalmed in the waters around 30°N latitude. As supplies ran low, ships were forced to throw their horses overboard. Many stories are told of the waters in these latitudes being littered with the carcasses of the unfortunate animals.

The regions between the horse latitudes and the doldrums (between 0° and 30° latitude) are those in which surface winds flow toward the equator. That flow is not directly from north to south or south to north, of course, because of the Coriolis effect. Instead, winds in

these regions tend to blow from the northeast to the southwest in the northern hemisphere and from the southeast to the northwest in the southern hemisphere. Since the winds tend to be strong and dependable — the sorts of wind on which sailing ships depend — these winds have long been known as the trade winds.

The intersection of the Ferrell and polar cells around latitude 60° is another region at which surface flows of air meet. One, from the Ferrell cell, consists of relatively warm air flowing toward the poles. The other, from the polar cell, consists of much colder air flowing toward the equator. The point at which these two systems meet is called the polar front and is characterized by some of the world's most dramatic storms.

The prevailing direction of surface winds with the Ferrell and polar cells is determined by the Coriolis effect. In the former cell, winds tend to blow from the southwest to the northeast in the northern hemisphere and from the northwest to the southeast in the southern hemisphere. To residents of North America, these prevailing westerlies are well known as the mechanism by which weather systems are carried across the continent from west to east.

In the polar cell, the predominant air movements are just the opposite of the prevailing westerlies: from northeast to southwest in the northern hemisphere and from southeast to northwest in the southern hemisphere.

Patterns of surface pressure

Any student of meteorology understands that conceptual models have only limited applicability to the real world. A number of factors in the real world differ from the ideal conditions used to construct a model. These factors insure that actual weather conditions will be far more complex than the general conditions described above.

For example, both the Hadley and Ferrell models assumed that the Earth has a homogeneous composition and that the sun always shines directly over the equator. Neither condition, of course, is actually true. For example, most parts of the planet are covered with water, and land masses are distributed unequally among this watery background. The flow of air in any one cell, then, may be undisturbed for long stretches in one region (as across an ocean), but highly disrupted in another region (as across a mountainous area).

Useful tools for meteorologists interested in studying air movements are charts of air pressure at various locations on the Earth's surface. These charts are of value because, whatever models may predict, we known that in the real world air movements tend to occur from regions of higher pressure to those of lower pressure.

Such charts indicate that certain parts of the planet tend to be characterized by unusually high or low pressure centers at various times of the year. In general, about eight semipermanent high and low pressure cells have been identified. The term semipermanent is used for such cells because they seem to reappear every year on a regular basis.

For example, a semipermanent high pressure area occurs over the Bermuda Islands and persists throughout the year. A semipermanent low pressure — the Icelandic low — is usually found somewhat to the north of the Bermuda high, although it tends to shift from east to west and back again during various parts of the year. During the winter in the northern hemisphere, a semipermanent high exists over Siberia, although by summer it has disappeared and been replaced by a semipermanent low over India. The existence of these semipermanent highs and lows accounts for fairly predictable air movements over relatively large areas of the Earth's surface.

The jet streams

During World War II, an especially dramatic type of atmospheric air movement was discovered: the jet streams. On a bombing raid over Japan, a sortie of B–29 bombers found themselves being carried along with a tail wind of about 186 mph (300 kph). After the war, meteorologists found that these winds were part of permanent air movements now known as the jet streams. Jet streams are currents of air located at altitudes of 30,000 to 45,000 ft (25 to 40 km) that generally move with speeds ranging from about 30 to 75 mph (50 to 125 kph). It is not uncommon, however, for the speed of jet streams to be much greater than these average figures, as high as 300 mph (500 kph) having been measured.

The jet streams discovered in 1944 are formed along the polar front between the Ferrell and polar cells. For this reason, they are usually known as polar jet streams. Polar jet streams usually travel on a west to east direction between 30°N and 50°N latitude. Commercial aircraft often take advantage of the extra push provided by the polar jet stream when they travel from west to east, although the same winds slow down planes going in the opposite direction.

The pathway followed by jet streams is quite variable. They may break apart into two separate streams and then rejoin, or not. They also tend to meander north and south from a central west–east axis. The movement of the jet streams is an important factor in determining weather conditions in mid–latitude regions.

KEY TERMS

Convection—The transfer of heat by means of a moving fluid.

Coriolis effect—The tendency of a moving body to travel in a curved path in relation to the surface of that body.

Doldrums—A region of the equatorial ocean where winds are light and unpredictable.

Horse latitudes—A region of the oceans around 30° latitude where winds are light and unpredictable.

Jet stream—A rapidly moving band of air in the upper atmosphere.

Polar front—A relatively permanent front formed at the junction of the Ferrell and polar cells.

Trade winds—Relatively constant wind patterns that blow toward the equator at about 30° latitude.

Since the end of World War II, jet streams other than those along the polar front have been discovered. For example, a tropical easterly jet stream has been found to develop during the summer months over Africa, India, and southeast Asia. Some low–level jet streams have also been identified. One of these is located over the Central Plains in the United States, where topographic and climatic conditions favor the development of unusually severe wind systems.

Other violent wind systems

A number of air movements are not large enough to be described as forms of global circulation although they do cover extensive regions of the planet. Monsoons, for example, are heavy rain systems that sweep across the Indian subcontinent for about six months of each year. They are caused by a massive movement of air from Siberia to Africa by way of India and back again.

During the winter, cold, dry air from central Asia sweeps over India, out across the Indian Ocean, and into Africa. Relatively little moisture is transported out of Siberia during this time of the year. As summer approaches, however, the Asian land mass warms up, low pressures develop, and the winter air movement pattern is reversed. Winds blow out of Africa, across the Indian Ocean and the Indian peninsula, and back into Siberia. These winds pick up moisture from the ocean and bring nearly constant rains — the monsoons — to India for about six months.

See also Air masses and fronts; Global climate; Monsoon; Wind.

Further Reading:

Ahrens, C. Donald. *Meteorology Today*, Second Edition. St. Paul, MN: West Publishing Company, 1985.

Allen, Oliver E., and the Editors of Time–Life Books. *Planet Earth: Atmosphere*. Alexandria, VA: Time–Life Books, 1983.

Eagleman, Joe R. *Meteorology: The Atmosphere in Action*, Second Edition. Belmont, CA: Wadsworth Publishing Company, 1985.

James, I. N. *Introduction to Circulating Atmospheres*. New York: Cambridge University Press, 1994.

Lorenz, Edward N. *The Nature and Theory of the General Circulation of the Atmosphere*. Geneva: World Meteorological Organization, 1967.

Lutgens, Frederick K., and Edward J. Tarbuck. *The Atmosphere: An Introduction to Meteorology*, Fourth Edition. Englewood Cliffs, NJ: Prentice Hall, 1989.

Reiter, Elmar R. *Jet Stream Meteorology*. Ann Arbor, MI: Books on Demand, 1963.

Wagner, A. James, "Persistent Circulation Patterns," *Weatherwise*, February 1989, 18–21.

David E. Newton

Atmosphere, composition and structure

The Earth's atmosphere is composed of about 78% nitrogen, 21% oxygen, and 0.93% argon. The remainder, less than 0.1%, contains many small but important trace gases, including water vapor, carbon dioxide, and ozone. All of these trace gases have important effects on the Earth's climate. The atmosphere can be divided into vertical layers determined by the way temperature changes with height. The layer closest to the surface is the troposphere, which contains over 80% of the atmospheric mass and nearly all the water vapor. The next layer, the stratosphere, contains most of the atmosphere's ozone, which absorbs high energy radiation from the Sun and makes life on the surface possible. Above the stratosphere are the mesosphere and thermosphere. These two layers include regions of charged atoms and molecules, or ions. Called the ionosphere, this region is important to radio communications, since radio waves can bounce off the layer and travel great distances. It is thought that the present atmosphere developed from gases ejected by volcanoes. Oxygen, upon which all animal life depends, probably built up as excess emissions from plants that produce it as a waste product during photosynthesis. Human activities may be affecting the levels of some important atmospheric components, particularly carbon dioxide and ozone.

Composition of the atmosphere

Major gases

The most common atmospheric gas, nitrogen (chemical symbol N_2) accounts for about 78% of the atmosphere. Nitrogen gas is largely inert, meaning that it does not readily react with other substances to form new chemical compounds. The next most common gas, oxygen (O_2), makes up about 21% of the atmosphere. Oxygen is required for the respiration (breathing) of all animal life on earth, from humans to bacteria. In contrast to nitrogen, oxygen is extremely reactive. It participates in oxidation, a type of chemical reaction that can be observed everywhere. Some common examples of oxidation are apples turning from white to brown after being sliced, the rusting of iron, and the very rapid oxidation reaction we call fire. Just under 1% of the atmosphere is made up of argon (Ar), which is a very inert noble gas, meaning that it does not take part in any chemical reactions under normal circumstances.

Together, these three gases account for 99.96% of the atmosphere. The remaining 0.04% contains a wide variety of trace gases, several of which are crucial to life on Earth.

Important trace gases

Carbon dioxide (CO_2) affects the Earth's climate and plays a large support role in the biosphere, the collection of living things that populate the Earth's surface. Only about 0.0325% of the atmosphere is CO_2. Carbon dioxide is required by plant life for photosynthesis, the process of using sunlight to store energy as simple sugars, upon which all life on Earth depends. Carbon dioxide is also one of a class of compounds called greenhouse gases. These gases are made up of molecules that absorb and emit infrared radiation, which we feel as heat. The solar energy radiated from the Sun is mostly in the visible range, within a narrow band of wavelengths. This radiation is absorbed by the Earth's surface, then re–radiated back out to space not as visible light, but as longer wavelength infrared radiation. Greenhouse gas molecules absorb some of this radiation before it escapes to space, and re–emit some of it back toward the surface. In this way, these gases trap some of the escaping heat and increase the overall temperature of the atmosphere. If the atmosphere had no greenhouse gases, it is estimated that the Earth's surface would be 90°F (32°C) cooler.

Water vapor (H_2O) is found in the atmosphere in small and highly variable amounts. While it is nearly absent in most of the atmosphere, its concentration can range up to 4% in very warm, humid areas close to the surface. Despite its relative scarcity, atmospheric water probably has more of an impact on the Earth than any of the major gases, aside from oxygen. Water vapor participates in the hydrologic cycle, the process that moves water between the oceans, the land surface waters, the atmosphere, and the polar ice caps. This water cycling drives erosion and rock weathering, determines the Earth's weather, and sets up climate conditions that make land areas dry or wet, habitable or inhospitable. When cooled sufficiently, water vapor forms clouds by condensing to liquid water droplets, or at lower temperatures, solid ice crystals. Besides creating rain or snow, clouds affect the Earth's climate by reflecting some of the energy coming from the Sun, making the planet somewhat cooler. Water vapor is also an important greenhouse gas. It is concentrated near the surface and is much more prevalent near the tropics than in the polar regions.

Ozone (O_3) is almost all found in a layer about 9–36 mi (15–60 km) in height. Ozone gas is irritating to peoples' eyes and skin, and chemically attacks rubber and plant tissue. Nevertheless, it is vital to life on Earth because it absorbs most of the high energy radiation from the sun that is harmful to plants and animals. A portion of the energy radiated by the Sun lies in the ultraviolet (UV) region. This shorter wavelength radiation is responsible for sun tans, and is sufficiently powerful to harm cells, cause skin cancer, and burn tissue, as anyone who has had a painful sunburn knows. The ozone molecules, along with molecules of O_2, absorb nearly all the high energy UV rays, protecting the Earth's surface from the most damaging radiation. The first step in this process occurs high in the atmosphere, where O_2 molecules absorb very high energy UV radiation. Upon doing so, each absorbing molecule breaks up into two oxygen atoms. The oxygen atoms eventually collide with another O_2 molecule, forming a molecule of ozone, O_3 (a third molecule is required in the collision to carry away excess energy). Ozone in turn may absorb UV of slightly longer wavelength, which knocks off one of its oxygen atoms and leaves O_2. The free oxygen atom, being very reactive, will almost immediately recombine with another O_2, forming more ozone.

The last two steps of this cycle keep repeating but do not create any new chemical compounds; they only act to absorb ultraviolet radiation. The amount of ozone in the stratosphere is minute. If it were all transported to the surface, the ozone gas would form a layer about 0.1–0.16 in (2.5–4.0 mm) thick. This layer, as thin as it is, is sufficient to shield the Earth's occupants from harmful solar radiation.

Aerosols

In addition to gases, the atmosphere has a wide variety of tiny particles suspended in the air, known collectively as aerosols. These particles may be liquid or solid, and are so small that they may require very long times to settle out of the atmosphere by gravity. Examples of aerosols include bits of suspended soil or desert sand, tiny smoke particles from a forest fire, salt particles left over after a droplet of ocean water has evaporated, plant pollen, volcanic dust plumes, and particles formed from the pollution created by a coal burning power plant. Aerosols significantly affect the atmospheric heat balance, cloud growth, and optical properties.

Aerosols cover a very wide size range. Raindrops suspended in a cloud are about 0.04–0.24 in (1–6 mm) in diameter. Fine desert sand and cloud droplets range in diameter down to about 0.0004 in (0.01 mm). Sea salt particles and smoke particles are 1/100th of this, about 0.0001 mm, or 0.1 micrometer, in diameter (1 micrometer = one thousandth of a millimeter). Smallest of all are the particles that form when certain gases condense; that is, when several gas molecules come together to form a stable cluster. These are the Aitkin nuclei, whose diameters can be measured down to a few nanometers (1 nanometer = one millionth of a millimeter).

Some aerosols are just the right size to efficiently scatter sunlight, making the atmosphere look hazy. Under the right conditions, aerosols act as collecting points for water vapor molecules, encouraging the growth of cloud droplets and speeding the formation of clouds. They may also play a role in the Earth's climate; the aerosols are known to reflect a portion of incoming solar radiation back to space, which lowers the temperature of the Earth's surface. Current research is focused on estimating how much cooling is provided by aerosols, as well as how and when aerosols form in the atmosphere.

Atmospheric structure

The atmosphere can be divided into layers based on the atmospheric pressure and temperature profiles (the way these quantities change with height). Atmospheric temperature drops steadily from its value at the surface, about 290 K (about 63°F), until it reaches a minimum of around 220 K (−64°F) at 6 mi (10 km). This first layer is called the troposphere, and ranges in pressure from over 1,000 millibars at sea level to 100 millibars at the top of the layer, the tropopause. Above the tropopause, the temperature rises with increasing altitude up to about 27 mi (45 km). This region of increasing temperatures is the stratosphere, spanning a pressure range from 100 millibars at its base to about 10 millibars at the stratopause, the top of the layer. Above 30 mi (50 km), the temperature resumes its drop with altitude, reaching a very cold minimum of 180 K (−136°F) at around 48 mi (80 km). This layer is the mesosphere, which at its top (the mesopause) has an atmospheric pressure of only 0.01 millibars (that is, only 1/100,000th of the surface pressure). Above the mesosphere lies the thermosphere, extending hundreds of miles upward toward the vacuum of space. It is not possible to place an exact "top" of the atmosphere; air molecules simply become scarcer and more rarefied until the atmosphere blends with the material found in space.

The troposphere

The troposphere contains over 80% of the mass of the atmosphere, along with nearly all of the water vapor. This layer contains the air we breathe, the winds we observe and the clouds that bring our rain. In fact, all of what we know as "weather" occurs in the troposphere, whose name means "changing sphere." All of the cold fronts, warm fronts, high and low pressure systems, storm systems, and other features seen on a weather map occur in this lowest layer. "Severe" thunder storms may penetrate the tropopause.

Within the troposphere the temperature drops with increasing height at an average rate of about 11.7°F per every 3,280 ft (6.5°C per every 1,000 meters). This quantity is known as the lapse rate. When air begins to rise, it will expand and cool at a faster rate determined by the laws of thermodynamics. This means that if a blob of air begins to rise, it will soon find itself cooler and denser than its surroundings, and will sink back downward. This is an example of a stable atmosphere—vertical air motion is prevented. Due to the fact that air masses move around in the troposphere, a cold air mass may move into an area and have a higher lapse rate. That is, its temperature drops off more quickly with height. Under these weather conditions, air that begins rising and cooling will become warmer than its surroundings. It then is like a hot air balloon—it is less dense than the surrounding air and is buoyant, so it will

continue to rise and cool in a process called convection. If this is sustained, the atmosphere is said to be unstable and the rising blob of air will cool to the point where its water vapor condenses to form cloud droplets. The air parcel is now a convective cloud. If the buoyancy is vigorous enough, a storm cloud will develop as the cloud droplets grow to the size of raindrops and begin to fall out of the cloud as rain. Thus under certain conditions, the temperature profile of the troposphere makes possible storm clouds and precipitation.

During a strong thunderstorm, cumulonimbus clouds (the type that produce heavy rain, high winds, and hail) may grow tall enough to reach or extend into the tropopause. Here they run into strong stratospheric winds, which may shear off the top of the clouds and stop their growth. One can see this effect in the "anvil" clouds associated with strong summer thunderstorms.

The stratosphere

The beginning of the stratosphere is defined as that point where the temperature reaches a minimum and the lapse rate abruptly drops to zero. This temperature structure has one important consequence: it inhibits rising air. Any air that begins to rise will become cooler and denser than the surrounding air. The stratosphere, then, is very stable.

Although the stratosphere has very little water, clouds of ice crystals may form at times in the lower stratosphere over the polar regions. Early Arctic explorers named these clouds nacreous or mother–of–pearl clouds because of their iridescent appearance. More recently, very thin, widespread clouds have been found to form in the polar stratosphere under extremely cold conditions. These clouds, called polar stratospheric clouds, or PSCs, appear to be small crystals of ice or frozen mixtures of ice and nitric acid. PSCs play a key role in the development of the ozone hole, which is described below.

The stratosphere contains most of the ozone found in the Earth's atmosphere. In fact, the presence of ozone is the reason for the temperature profile found in the stratosphere. As described previously, ozone and oxygen gas both absorb short wave solar radiation. In the series of reactions that follow, heat is released. This heat warms the atmosphere in the layer at about 12–27 mi (20–45 km) and gives the stratosphere its characteristic temperature increase with height.

Recently the ozone layer has been the subject of some concern. In 1985, scientists from the British Antarctic Survey noticed that the amount of stratospheric ozone over the South Pole was dropping sharply during the spring months, recovering somewhat as spring turned to summer. An examination of the historical records revealed that the springtime ozone losses had begun around the late 1960s and had grown much more severe by the late 1970s. By the mid 1980s virtually all the ozone was disappearing from parts of the polar stratosphere during the late winter and early spring. These ozone losses, dubbed the ozone hole, were the subject of intense research both in the field and in the laboratory. The picture that has emerged implicates chlorine as the chemical responsible for ozone destruction in the ozone hole. Chlorine apparently gets into the stratosphere from chlorofluorocarbons, or CFCs, industrial chemicals widely used as refrigerants, aerosol propellants, and solvents. Laboratory experiments show that after destroying an ozone molecule, chlorine is tied up in a form unable to react with any more ozone. However, it can chemically react with other chlorine compounds on the surfaces of polar stratospheric cloud particles, which frees the chlorine to attack more ozone. In other words, each chlorine molecule is recycled many times so that it can destroy thousands of ozone molecules. The realization of chlorine's role in ozone depletion brought about an international agreement in 1987, the Montreal Protocol, which committed the participating industrialized countries to begin phasing out CFCs.

The mesosphere and thermosphere

The upper mesosphere and the lower thermosphere contain charged atoms and molecules (ions in a region known as the ionosphere. The atmospheric constituents at this level include nitrogen gas, atomic oxygen and nitrogen (O and N), and nitric oxide (NO). All of these are exposed to strong solar emission of ultraviolet and x ray radiation, which can result in ionization, knocking off an electron to form an atom or molecule with a positive charge. The ionosphere is a region enriched in free electrons and positive ions. This charged particle region affects the propagation of radio waves, reflecting them as a mirror reflects light. The ionosphere makes it possible to tune in radio stations very far from the transmitter; even if the radio waves coming directly from the transmitter are blocked by mountains or the curvature of the Earth, one can still receive the waves bounced off the ionosphere. After the Sun sets, the numbers of electrons and ions in the lower layers drop drastically, since the Sun's radiation is no longer available to keep them ionized. Even at night, however, the higher layers retain some ions. The result is that the ionosphere is higher at night, which allows radio waves to bounce for longer distances. This is the reason that one can frequently tune in more distant radio stations at night than during the day.

The upper thermosphere is also where the bright nighttime displays of colors and flashes known as the aurora occur. The aurora are caused by energetic particles emitted by the Sun. These particles become trapped by the Earth's magnetic field and collide with the relatively few gas atoms present above about 60 mi (100 km), mostly atomic oxygen (O) and nitrogen gas (N_2). These collisions cause the atoms and molecules to emit light, resulting in spectacular displays.

The past and future of the atmosphere

If any atmosphere was present after the Earth was formed about 4.5 billion years ago it was probably much different than that of today. Most likely it resembled those of the outer planets—Jupiter, Saturn, Uranus, and Neptune—with an abundance of hydrogen, methane, and ammonia gases. The present atmosphere did not form until after this primary atmosphere was lost. One theory holds that the primary atmosphere was blasted from the Earth by the Sun. If the Sun is like other stars of its type, it may have gone through a phase where it violently ejected material outward toward the planets. All of the inner planets, including the Earth, would have lost their gaseous envelopes. A secondary atmosphere began to form when gases were released from the crust of the early Earth by volcanic activity. These gases included water vapor, carbon dioxide, nitrogen, and sulfur or sulfur compounds. Oxygen was absent from this early secondary atmosphere.

The large amount of water vapor released by the volcanos formed clouds that continually rained on the early Earth, forming the oceans. Since carbon dioxide dissolves easily in water, the new oceans gradually absorbed most of it. (Nitrogen, being unreactive, was left behind to become the most common gas in the atmosphere.) The carbon dioxide that remained began to be used by early plant life in the process of photosynthesis. Geologic evidence indicates this may have begun about 2 to 3 billion years ago, probably in an ocean or aquatic environment. Around this time, there appeared aerobic (oxygen using) bacteria and other early animal life, which consumed the products of photosynthesis and emitted CO_2. This completed the cycle for CO_2 and O_2: as long as all plant material was consumed by an oxygen breathing organism, the two gases stayed in balance. However, some plant material was inevitably lost or buried before it could be decomposed. This effectively removed carbon dioxide from the atmosphere and left a net increase in oxygen. Over the course of billions of years, a considerable excess built

KEY TERMS

Infrared radiation—Radiation similar to visible light but of slightly longer wavelength. We sense infrared radiation as heat.

Ionosphere—Region of the atmosphere above about 48 mi (80 km) with elevated concentrations of charged atoms and molecules (ions).

Lapse rate—The rate at which the atmosphere cools with increasing altitude.

Mesosphere—The third layer of the atmosphere, lying about 30–48 mi (50–80 km) in height and characterized by small lapse rate.

Ozone hole—The sharp decease in stratospheric ozone over Antarctica that occurs every spring.

Stratosphere—The second layer of the atmosphere, lying about 6–30 mi (10–50 km) in height and characterized by a negative lapse rate, that is, temperature increase with height. This is due to heating of the layer by ozone.

Thermosphere—The top layer of the atmosphere, starting at about 48 mi (80 km) and stretching up hundreds of miles into space. Due to bombardment by very energetic solar radiation, this layer can possess very high gas temperatures.

Troposphere—The atmospheric layer closest to the surface, extending up to the tropopause at about 10 kilometers in height.

Ultraviolet radiation—Radiation similar to visible light but of shorter wavelength, and thus higher energy.

X–ray radiation—Light radiation with wavelengths shorter than the shortest ultraviolet; very energetic and harmful to living organisms.

up this way, so that oxygen now makes up over 20% of the atmosphere (and carbon dioxide makes up less than 0.033%). All animal life thus depends on the oxygen accumulated gradually by the biosphere over the past two billion years.

Future changes to the atmosphere are difficult to predict. There is currently growing concern that human activity may be altering the atmosphere to the point that it may affect the Earth's climate. This is particularly the case with carbon dioxide. When fossil fuels such as coal and oil are dug up and burned, buried carbon dioxide is released back into the air. As discussed earlier, carbon dioxide is a greenhouse gas—it acts to trap infrared (heat) energy radiated by the Earth, warming up the atmosphere. What effect will this have on future temperatures? While no one has a definite answer, this is an area of active research, using computers to model the oceans, the atmosphere, and the land areas as a very complicated climate system.

See also Aerosols; Atmospheric circulation; Atmospheric temperature; Clouds; Greenhouse effect; Hydrologic cycle; Ozone; Ozone layer depletion; Precipitation; Weather.

Further Reading:

Bohren, Craig. *Clouds in a Glass of Beer*, New York: John Wiley and Sons, 1987.

Erickson, Jon. *Greenhouse Earth*, Blue Ridge Summit, PA: Tab Books, 1990.

Firor, John. *The Changing Atmosphere*, New Haven, CT: Yale University Press, 1990.

McNeill, Robert. *Understanding the Weather*, Las Vegas, NV: Arbor Publishers, 1991.

Ramsey, Don. *Weather Forecasting*, Blue Ridge Summit, PA: Tab Books, 1990.

James Marti

Atmosphere observation

The term weather observation refers to all of the equipment and techniques used to study the properties of the atmosphere. These include such well–known instruments as the thermometer and barometer as well as less familiar devices such as the radiosonde and devices for detecting the presence of trace gases in the atmosphere.

History

The fundamental principles on which the most common atmospheric observational instruments are based were discovered during the 17th and 18th centuries. For example, the Italian physicist Evangelista Torricelli invented the first barometer in 1643, while the air hygrometer, a device for measuring atmospheric humidity, was first constructed by the Swiss physicist Horace Bénédict de Saussure in about 1780.

These instruments were useful at first in studying atmospheric properties close to the ground, but not at very high altitudes. In 1648, the French physicist asked his brother–in–law Florin Périer to carry a pair of barometers to the top of Puy–de–Dôme to make measurements of air pressure there, but that was about the limit to which humans themselves could go.

Kites

One of the first means developed for raising instruments to higher altitudes was the kite. In one of the most famous experiments in this line, Benjamin Franklin used a kite in 1752 to discover that lightning was nothing other than a form of electricity. Within a short period of time, kites were being used by other scientists to carry recording thermometers into the atmosphere, where they could read temperatures at various altitudes.

Weather balloons

An important breakthrough in atmospheric observation came in the late 18th century with the invention of the hot–air balloon. Balloon flights made it possible to carry instruments thousands of feet into the atmosphere to take measurements. Credit for the first balloon ascension for the purpose of making meteorological measurements is often given to the English physician John Jeffries, who carried a thermometer, barometer, and hygrometer to a height of 9,000 ft (2,700 m) in his balloon in 1785.

For the next 150 years, balloons were the primary means by which instruments were lifted into the atmosphere for purposes of observation. A number of devices were invented for use in weather balloons, especially the meteorograph and the radiosonde. Both devices are combinations of instruments for measuring temperature, pressure, humidity, and other atmospheric properties.

The radiosonde differs from a meteorograph in that it also includes a radio that can transmit the data collected back to the Earth. When the radiosonde is used to collect data about atmospheric winds also, it is then known as a rawinsonde. In most cases, data collected with the meteorograph is recovered only when the instrument is jettisoned from the balloon or airplane carrying it. At one time, scientists paid five dollars to anyone who found and returned one of these measuring devices.

Balloons are still an important way of transporting weather instruments into the atmosphere. Today, they are often very large pieces of equipment, made of very thin plastic materials and filled with helium gas. When the balloons are first released from the ground, they look as if they are nearly empty. However, as they rise into the atmosphere and the pressure around them decreases, they fill to their full capacity. Balloons used to study the properties of the upper atmosphere are known as sounding balloons.

Rockets and aircraft

The invention of the airplane and the rocket opened vast new avenues for the study of the atmosphere. Both devices made it possible to carry instruments far higher than they had ever gone before. At first, airplanes duplicated the work done by scientists traveling in balloons, but much more efficiently and at higher altitudes with greater safety and comfort. As technology improved, however, aircraft began to take on new and more complex tasks. For example, they might fly through a cloud and collect cloud droplets on slides for future study. Today, airplanes are also used by "hurricane hunters" who fly into the middle of a hurricane to study its properties and movement.

Some of the airplanes now used for atmospheric observation have bizarre appearances. They may carry large platforms on their tops, oversized needles on their noses, or other attachments in which an array of observational instruments can be carried. As one example, a commercial DC8 aircraft has been redesigned and outfitted to carry the equipment needed to measure levels of ozone and related chemicals over the Antarctic. Data collected from this airplane has been crucial in helping scientists to understand how ozone levels have been decreasing over the South Pole over the past decade or more.

Unmanned rockets can carry measuring devices to altitudes even greater than is possible with a manned aircraft. Again, rockets can perform the same standard measurements as a radiosonde, except at greater atmospheric heights. But they can also perform more complex measurements. For example, they can be designed to carry and release a variety of chemicals that can then be tracked by radar and other systems located on the ground. Some rockets have also released explosive devices high in the atmosphere so that scientists can study the way in which sound waves are transported there.

Weather satellites

The most sophisticated atmospheric observational systems of all are those that make use of artificial satellites. A weather satellite is a device that is lifted into Earth orbit by a rocket and that carries inside it a large number of instruments for measuring many properties of the atmosphere. The first weather satellite ever launched was put into orbit by the U.S. government on April 1, 1960. It carried the name TIROS 1 (for Television and Infrared Observation Satellite). Over the next five years, nine more satellites of the same name were launched. One of the primary functions of the TIROS satellites was to collect and transmit photographs of the Earth's cloud patterns.

In addition to the TIROS program, the U.S. government has put into operation a number of other weather satellite systems, including Nimbus, ESSA (for Environmental Sciences Service Administration), and GOES (for geosynchronous environmental satellites). The former Soviet Union also had an active program of weather observation by satellite. The first Soviet satellite was known as Kosmos 122, followed by a series of satellites known by the code name of Meteor.

Satellites can provide a variety of data about atmospheric properties that can contribute to improved weather forecasting. As an example, a satellite can track the development, growth, and movement of large storm systems, such as hurricanes and cyclones. This information can be used to warn human populations of oncoming storms and thereby save human lives and some property damage.

Satellites can also take measurements using various wavelengths of light, thereby collecting data that would not be accessible to some other kinds of instruments. As an example, a satellite can photograph a cloud cover using both visible and infrared light and, by comparing the two, predict which cloud system is more likely to produce precipitation.

Atmospheric composition

The observational systems described thus far can be used to measure more than just physical properties such as temperature, pressure, and air movements. They can also be used to determine the chemical composition of the atmosphere. Such measurements can be valuable not only in the field of meteorology, but in other fields as well.

One of the earliest examples of such research dates to 1804 when the French physicist Joseph Louis Gay–Lussac traveled in a balloon to a height of 23,000 ft (6,900 m). At this altitude, he collected an air sample which he analyzed upon his return to the ground. Gay–Lussac found that the composition of air at 23,000 ft (6,900 m) was the same as it was at sea level.

An example of this kind of research today involves the issue of climate change. Over the past decade there

---

KEY TERMS

Meteorograph—An instrument designed to be sent into the atmosphere to record certain measurements, such as temperature and pressure.

Radiosonde—An instrument for collecting data in the atmosphere and then transmitting that data back to Earth by means of radio waves.

Rawinsonde—A type of radiosonde that is also capable of measuring wind patterns.

---

has been a great deal of interest with respect to possible large scale changes in the Earth's climate. Some scientists believe that an accumulation of carbon dioxide and other gases in the atmosphere has been contributing to a gradual increase in the Earth's overall average annual temperature, called global warming. If such a change were, in fact, to occur, it might have significant effects on plant and animal (including human) life on Earth.

Many of the questions about global climate change cannot adequately be answered, however, without a fairly good understanding of the gases present in the atmosphere, changes in their concentration over time, and chemical reactions that occur among those gases. Until recently, most of those questions could not have been answered. Today, however, manned aircraft, rockets, and satellites are able to collect some of the kinds of data that will allow scientists to develop a better understanding of the chemical processes that occur in the atmosphere and the effects they may have on both weather and climate.

See also Balloon; Barometer; Global climate; Radar; Thermometer.

Further Reading:

Lutgens, Frederick K., and Edward J. Tarbuck. *The Atmosphere: An Introduction to Meteorology*, 4th ed. Englewood Cliffs, NJ: Prentice–Hall, 1989.

David E. Newton

Atmospheric inversion layers see
Atmosphere, composition and structure

Atmospheric optical phenomena

Atmospheric optical phenomena are visual events that take place in Earth's atmosphere as a consequence of the way light is reflected, refracted, and diffracted by solid particles, liquids droplets, and other materials present in the atmosphere. Such phenomena include a wide variety of events ranging from the blue color of the sky itself to mirages and rainbows to sun dogs and solar pillars.

Reflection and refraction

If Earth's atmosphere were a vacuum, the only atmospheric optical phenomenon observable would be a stream of white light from the sun. The fact that colors appear in the atmosphere is a consequence of the way that white light is broken up into its component parts—red, orange, yellow, green, blue, indigo, and violet: the spectrum—during its interaction with materials in the atmosphere. That interaction takes one of three general forms: reflection, refraction, and diffraction.

Reflection occurs when light rays strike a smooth surface and bounce off at an angle equal to that of the incoming rays. Reflection can explain the origin of color in some cases because certain portions of white light are more easily absorbed or reflected than are others. For example, an object that appears to have a green color does so because that object absorbs all wavelengths of white light except that of green, which is reflected.

One form of reflection—internal reflection—is often involved in the explanation of optical phenomena. During internal reflection, light enters one surface of a transparent material (such as a water droplet), is reflected off the inside surface of the material, and is then reflected a second time out of the material. The color of a rainbow can partially be explained in terms of internal reflection.

Refraction is the bending of light as it passes at an angle from one transparent material into a second transparent material. The process of refraction accounts for the fact that objects under water appear to have a different size and location than they have in air. Light waves passing through water and then through air are bent, causing the eye to create a visual image of the object.

Displacement phenomena

Perhaps the most common example of an atmospheric effect created by refraction is the displacement of astronomical bodies. When the Sun is directly over-

An aurora borealis display.

head, the light rays it emits pass straight through Earth's atmosphere. No refraction occurs, and no change in the Sun's apparent position takes place.

As the Sun approaches the horizon, that situation changes. Light from the Sun now enters Earth's atmosphere at an angle and is refracted. The eye sees the path of the light as it is bent and assumes that it has come from a position in the sky somewhat higher than it really is. That is, the Sun's apparent location is displaced by some angle from its true location. The same situation is true for any astronomical object. The closer a star is to the horizon, for example, the more its apparent position is displaced from its true position.

Green flash

One of the most dramatic examples of sunlight refraction is the green flash. That term refers to the fact that in the moment following sunset or sunrise, a flash of green light lasting no more than a second can sometimes be seen on the horizon on the upper part of the Sun. The green light is the very last remnant of sunlight refracted by Earth's atmosphere, still observable after all red, orange, and yellow rays have disappeared. The green light remains at this moment because the light rays of shorter wavelength—blue and violet—are scattered by the atmosphere. The green flash is rarely seen, but when it is, it makes a remarkable impression on the observer.

Scattered light

Light that bounces off very small objects is not reflected uniformly, but is scattered in all directions. The process of scattering is responsible for the fact that humans observe the sky as blue. When white light from the Sun collides with molecules of oxygen and nitrogen, it is scattered selectively. That is, light with shorter wavelengths—blue, green, indigo, and violet—is scat-

Sun dogs at sunset on the frozen sea at Cape Churchill, Hudson Bay.

tered more strongly than is light with longer wavelengths—red, orange, and yellow. No matter where a person stands on Earth's surface, she or he is more likely to see the bluish light scattered by air molecules than the light of other hues.

Twinkling

Stars twinkle; planets do not. This general, though not inviolable, rule can be explained in terms of refraction. Stars are so far away that their light reaches Earth's atmosphere as a single point of light. As that very narrow beam of light passes through Earth's atmosphere, it is refracted and scattered by molecules and larger particles of matter. Sometimes the light travels straight toward an observer, but sometimes its path is deflected. To the observer, the star's light appears to go on and off many times per second. That is, it twinkles.

Planets usually do not twinkle because they are closer to Earth. The light that reaches Earth from them consists of wider beams rather than narrow rays. The refraction or scattering of only one or two light rays out of the whole beam does not make the light seem to disappear. At any one moment, enough light rays reach Earth's surface from a planet to give a sense of one continuous beam of light.

Mirages

One of the most familiar optical phenomena produced by refraction is a mirage. One type of mirage—the inferior mirage—is caused when a layer of air close to the ground is heated more strongly than is the air immediately above it. When that happens, light rays pass through two transparent media—the hot, less dense air and the cooler, more dense air—and are refracted. As a result of the refraction, the blue sky appears to be present on Earth's surface—it may look like a body of water—and objects such as trees appear to be reflected in that water.

A second type of mirage—the superior mirage—forms when a layer of air next to the ground is much cooler than the air above it. In this situation, light rays from an object are refracted in such a way that an object appears to be suspended in air above its true position. This phenomenon is sometimes referred to as looming.

Rainbows

The most remarkable phenomenon in the atmosphere is likely to be the rainbow. To understand how a rainbow is created, imagine a single beam of white light entering a spherical droplet of water. As the light passes from air into water, it undergoes refraction (that is, it is bent). However, each color present in the white light is bent by different amounts—the blues and violets more than the reds and yellows. The light is said to be dispersed, or separated according to color. After the dispersed rays pass into the water droplet, they reflect off the rear inner surface of the droplet and exit into the air once more. As the light rays pass out of the water into the air, they are refracted a second time. As a result of this second refraction, the separation of blues and violets from reds and yellows is made more distinct.

An observer on Earth's surface can see the net result of this sequence of events repeated over and over again by billions of individual water droplets. The rainbow that is produced consists simply of the white light of the sun separated into its component parts by each separate water droplet.

Haloes, sundogs, and sun pillars

The passage of sunlight through cirrus clouds can produce any one of the optical phenomena known as haloes, sundogs, or sun pillars. One explanation for phenomena of this kind is that cirrus clouds consist of tiny ice crystals that refract light through very specific angles, namely 22° and 46°. When sunlight shines through a cirrus cloud, each tiny ice crystal acts like a glass prism, refracting light at an angle of 22° (more commonly) or 46° (less commonly).

A halo is one example of this phenomenon. Sunlight shining through a cirrus cloud is refracted in such a way that a circle of light—the halo—forms around the Sun. The halo may occur at 22° or 46°.

Sundogs are formed by a similar process, except during sunrise or sunset. When relatively large (about 30 microns) crystals of ice orient themselves horizontally in a cirrus cloud, the refraction pattern they form is

KEY TERMS

. . . .

Diffraction—The bending of light rays as they pass close to an object.

Dispersion—The separation of light into its separate colors.

Mirage—An optical illusion in which an object or scene appears to be displaced from its true position.

Reflection—The bending of light rays in a regular pattern as they bounce off the surface of a material.

Refraction—The bending of light rays as they pass at an angle from one transparent medium into a second transparent medium.

Scattering—The bending of light rays as they bounce off very small objects.

Spectrum—The band of colors that is formed when white light passes through a prism or is broken apart by some other means.

Wavelength—The distance between two troughs or two peaks in any wave.

not a circle (a halo), but a reflected image of the Sun. This reflected image is located at a distance of 22° from the actual Sun, often at or just above the horizon. Sundogs are also known as mock suns or parhelia.

Sun pillars are, as their name suggests, narrow columns of light that seem to grow out of the top or (less commonly) from the bottom of the Sun. This phenomena is a result not of refraction, but of reflection. Sunlight reflects off the bottom of flat ice crystals as they settle slowly toward Earth's surface. The exact shape and orientation of the sun pillar depends on the position of the Sun above the horizon and the exact orientation of the ice crystals to the ground.

Coronas and glories

In addition to reflection and refraction, the path of a light ray can be altered by yet a third mechanism, diffraction. Diffraction occurs when a light ray passes close to some object. For comparison, you can think of the way in which water waves are bent as they travel around a rock. Diffraction may also result in the separation of white light into its colored components.

When light rays from the Moon pass through a thin cloud, they may be diffracted. Interference of the vari-

ous components of white light that generates the colors make up the corona. The pattern formed by the diffraction rays is a ring around the Moon. The ring may be fairly sharp and crisp, or it can be diffuse and hazy. The ring is known as a corona. Coronas may also form around the Sun, although because the Sun is much brighter, they are more difficult to observe.

A glory is similar to a corona but is most commonly observed during an airplane ride. As sunlight passes over the airplane, it may fall on water droplets in a cloud below. The light that is diffracted then forms a series of colored rings—the glory—around the airplane's shadow.

See also Color; Diffraction; Light; Spectrum.

Further Reading:

Ahrens, C. Donald. *Meteorology Today*, Second Edition. St. Paul, MN: West Publishing Company, 1985.

Allen, Oliver E., and the Editors of Time–Life Books. *Planet Earth: Atmosphere*. Alexandria, VA: Time–Life Books, 1983.

Eagleman, Joe R. *Meteorology: The Atmosphere in Action*, Second Edition. Belmont, CA: Wadsworth Publishing Company, 1985.

Greenler, Robert. *Rainbows, Halos, and Glories*. New York: Cambridge University Press, 1980.

Heuer, Kenneth. *Rainbows, Halos and Other Wonders*. New York: Dodd, Mead, 1976.

Lutgens, Frederick K., and Edward J. Tarbuck. *The Atmosphere: An Introduction to Meteorology*, Fourth Edition. Englewood Cliffs, NJ: Prentice Hall, 1989.

David E. Newton

Atmospheric pressure

The Earth's atmosphere exerts a force on everything within it. This force, divided by the area over which it acts, is the atmospheric pressure. The atmospheric pressure at sea level has an average value of 1,013.25 millibars. Expressed with other units, this pressure is 14.7 pounds per square inch, 29.92 inches of mercury, or 1.01×10^5 pascals. Atmospheric pressure decreases with increasing altitude: it is half of the sea level value at an altitude of about 3.1 mi (5 km) and falls to only 20% of the surface pressure at the cruising altitude of a jetliner. Atmospheric pressure also changes slightly from day to day as weather systems move through the atmosphere.

The Earth's atmosphere consists of gases that surround the surface, and like any gas, the atmosphere exerts a pressure on everything within it. A gas is made up of molecules that are constantly in motion. If the gas is in a container, some gas molecules are always bouncing off the container walls. When they do so, they exert a tiny force on the walls. With a sufficient number of molecules, their impacts add up to make a force that can easily be measured. Dividing the total force by the area over which it is measured gives the gas pressure. Anything else the gas touches will also have this pressure exerted on it. Thus anywhere we go within the Earth's atmosphere we can detect atmospheric pressure.

Atmospheric pressure decreases as one climbs higher in the atmosphere, and increases the closer one gets to the Earth's surface. The reason for this change with altitude is that atmospheric pressure at any point is really a measure of the weight, per unit area, of the atmosphere above that point. At sea level, for example, the pressure is 14.7 pounds per square inch. This means that a slice of the atmosphere in the shape of a long, thin column, with a one square inch base and as tall as the top of the atmosphere (at least 120 mi or 200 km), would have air within the column weighing 14.7 lbs (6.7 kg). At a higher elevation, such as the top of a 10,000 ft (3,048 m) mountain, one is above some of the atmosphere. Here the atmospheric pressure is lower than at sea level, because there is less air weighing down from above. A person feels this sort of pressure effect when they dive to the bottom of a lake or deep swimming pool. As the diver descends deeper into the water, more and more water lies overhead. The extra water exerts an increasing pressure that the diver can feel on their skin (and especially on the eardrums).

Atmospheric pressure is closely related to weather. Regions of pressure that are slightly higher or slightly lower than the mean atmospheric pressure develop as air circulates around the Earth. The air rushes from regions of high pressure to low pressure, causing winds. The properties of the moving air (cool or warm, dry or humid) will determine the weather for the areas through which it passes. Knowing the location of high and low pressure areas is vital to weather forecasting, which is why they are shown on the weather maps printed in newspapers and shown on television.

Atmospheric pressure is measured by a barometer, of which there are several designs. The first barometer was made by Evangelista Torricelli in 1643, using a column closed at one end and partially filled with mercury. The column was placed vertically in a small pool of mercury with the open end downward. In this arrangement, the mercury does not run out the open end.

Rather, it stays at a height such that the pressure exerted by the suspended mercury upon the pool will equal the atmospheric pressure on the pool. The mercury barometer is still in common use today (this is the reason pressure is still given the units "inches of mercury" on weather reports). Modern barometers include the aneroid barometer, which substitutes a sealed container of air for the mercury column, and the electronic capacitance manometer, which senses pressure electronically.

See also Atmosphere, composition and structure of; Weather; Weather forecasting.

James Marti

Atmospheric temperature

The temperature of the atmosphere varies with the distance from the equator (latitude) and height above the surface (altitude). It also changes in time, varying from season to season, from day to night and irregularly due to passing weather systems. If these variations are averaged out on a global basis, a pattern of average temperatures emerges for the atmosphere. The vertical temperature profile (the way temperature changes with height) divides the atmosphere into four layers: the troposphere, the stratosphere, the mesosphere, and the thermosphere.

The vertical temperature profile

Averaging atmospheric temperatures over all latitudes and across an entire year gives us the average vertical temperature profile. This plot is sometimes called a standard atmosphere. The average vertical temperature profile suggests four distinct layers. In the first layer, called the troposphere, average atmospheric temperature drops steadily from its value at the surface, about 290 kelvin (63° F) until it reaches of minimum of around 220 K (–64° F) at a level about 6.2 mi (10 km) high. This level, known as the tropopause, is just above the cruising altitude of large commercial jet aircraft. The drop of temperature with height, called the lapse rate, is nearly steady throughout the troposphere at 6.5° Celsius per kilometer. At the tropopause, the lapse rate abruptly shrinks to very low values. Atmospheric temperature is roughly constant over the next 12 mi (20 km), then begins to rise with increasing altitude up to about 31 mi (50 km). This region of increasing temperatures is the stratosphere. At the top of the layer, called the stratopause, temperatures are nearly as warm as the

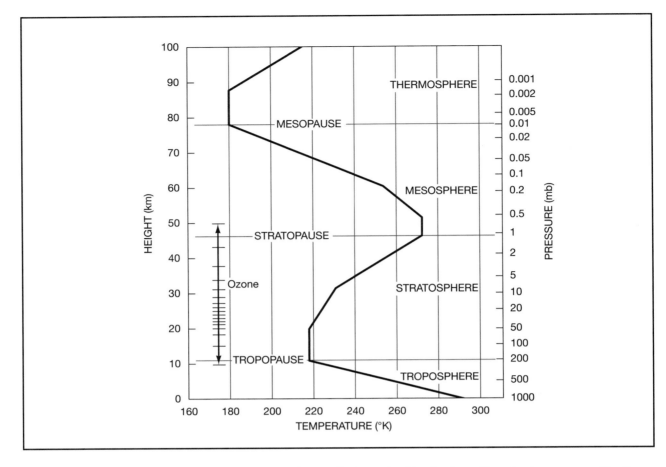

Figure 1. The temperature of the Earth's atmosphere is broadly determined by the deposition of solar energy and by the absorption of infrared (heat) radiation by "greenhouse" gases. Concern has recently been growing about increases in greenhouse warming due to human activities. This possible global warming is the subject of active research.

surface values. Between about 31–50 mi (50–80 km) lies the mesosphere, where atmospheric temperature resumes its drop with altitude and reaches a very cold minimum of 180 K (–136°F) at the top of the layer (the mesopause), around 50 mi (80 km). Above the mesopause is the thermosphere, which as its name implies is a zone of high gas temperatures. In the very high thermosphere (about 311 mi (500 km) above the Earth's surface) gas temperatures can reach from 500 K up to 2,000 K, depending on how active the Sun is. However, these figures are somewhat misleading. Temperature is a measure of the energy of the gas molecules' motion. Although they have high energies, the molecules in the thermosphere are present in very low numbers, less than one millionth of the amount present on average at the Earth's surface. If a person were in the thermosphere, it would feel to them much more like the icy cold of space because such a small number of energetic gas molecules would be unable to transfer much of their heat energy.

To add more information to the temperature graph, one can plot atmospheric temperature as a function of both latitude and altitude. Figures 2 and 3 show such plots, with latitude as the x coordinate and altitude as the y.

The Sun's role in atmospheric temperature

The reason that temperature is distributed as shown in the figures is mostly due to the Sun and the way solar energy is deposited in the atmosphere. Most of the solar radiation is emitted as visible light, with smaller portions at shorter wavelengths (ultraviolet radiation) and longer wavelengths (infrared radiation, or heat). Little of the visible light is absorbed by the atmosphere (although some is reflected back into space by clouds), so most of this energy is absorbed by the Earth's surface. The Earth is warmed in the process and radiates heat (infrared radiation) back upward. This warms the atmosphere, and just as one will be warmer when stand-

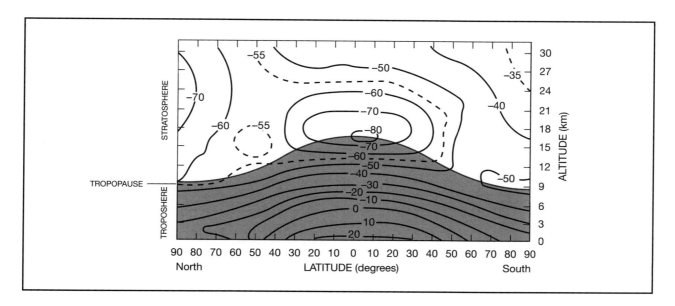

Lines are drawn on the plot connecting points of equal temperature (like contour lines on a map), given in degrees C. Figure 2 (above) is for December though February, which is winter in the northern hemisphere and summer in the southern. As one might expect, the warmest temperature is found at the surface near the equator, and drops as one travels toward either pole and/or as one increases in altitude. Surprisingly, however, the coldest spot in the lower atmosphere is at the tropopause over the equator, which is colder than even over polar regions. The temperature plot (Figure 2) for June through August (Southern hemisphere winter, Northern summer) shows that the equatorial temperature does not change much with the seasons. The middle and high latitudes have experienced much more change, as the temperature contours have shifted northward. The tropopause over the equator is still extremely cold, surpassed only by the stratosphere over the Antarctic.

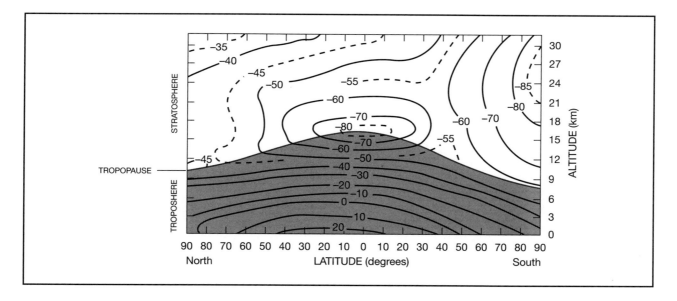

ing closer to a fire, the layers of air closest to the surface are the warmest.

According to this explanation, the temperature should continually drop as one goes higher in atmosphere. Yet Figure 1 shows that temperature rises with height in the stratosphere. The reason for this apparent contradiction is another case of solar energy deposition in the atmosphere. The stratosphere contains nearly all the atmosphere's ozone. Ozone (O_3) and molecular oxygen (O_2) absorb most of the sun's short wavelength ultraviolet radiation. In the process they are broken apart and reform again and again. The net result is that the ozone molecules transform the ultraviolet radiation to heat energy, heating up the layer and causing the increasing temperature profile observed in the stratosphere.

The mesosphere resumes the temperature drop with height. The thermosphere however is subject to very high energy, short wavelength ultraviolet and x ray solar radiation. As the atoms or molecules present at this level absorb some of this energy, they are ionized (have an electron knocked off) or dissociated (molecules are split into their component atoms). The gas layer is strongly heated by this energy bombardment, especially during periods when the Sun is active, that is, emitting elevated amounts of short wavelength radiation.

The greenhouse effect

Solar energy is not the only determinant of atmospheric temperature. As noted above, the Earth's surface, after absorbing solar radiation in the visible region, emits infrared radiation back to space. Several atmospheric gases absorb this heat radiation and re–radiate it in all directions, including back toward the surface. These so called greenhouse gases thus trap infrared radiation within the atmosphere, raising its temperature. Important greenhouse gases include water vapor (H_2O), carbon dioxide (CO_2), and methane (CH_4). It is estimated that the Earth's surface temperature would average about 32°C (90° F) cooler in the absence of greenhouse gases. Since this temperature is well below the freezing point of water, it is apparent that the planet would be much less hospitable to life in the absence of the greenhouse effect.

While greenhouse gases are essential to supporting life on the planet, more is not necessarily better. Since the beginning of the industrial revolution in the mid–nineteenth century, humans have released increasing amounts of carbon dioxide to the atmosphere through the burning of fossil fuels. The level of carbon dioxide measured in the remote atmosphere has shown a continuous increase since record keeping began in 1958. If this increase translates into a like rise in atmospheric temperature, the results would be dire indeed: melting polar ice caps and swelling seas, resulting in coastal cities being covered by the ocean; radical shifts in climate, dooming plants and animals that could not adapt quickly enough; and unpredictable changes in wind and weather patterns, posing significant challenges for agriculture. The problem in forecasting the changes that increasing greenhouse gases may bring is that the Earth's climate is a very complicated, interconnected system. The interplay of the atmosphere, the oceans, the continents and the ice caps is not completely understood. While it is known that some of the

emitted carbon dioxide is absorbed by the oceans and eventually deposited as carbonate rock (such as limestone), we do not know if this is a steady process or if it can keep pace with our constant releases. Computer models designed to mimic the Earth's climate must make many approximations. Nonetheless, calculations by these less–than–perfect models suggest that a doubling of carbon dioxide levels would mean an increase in the average Northern hemisphere surface temperatures of 39–43°F (4–6°C). While this may not sound like much, note that during the last ice age, when large ice sheets covered much of the northern hemisphere, the Earth's average temperature was only 41° F (5°C) below current levels.

KEY TERMS

Greenhouse effect—The heating of the atmosphere that occurs by the absorption and re–emission of infrared radiation by certain gases.

Infrared radiation—Radiation similar to visible light but of slightly longer wavelength. We sense infrared radiation as heat.

Lapse rate—The rate at which the atmosphere cools with increasing altitude, given in units of degrees C per kilometer.

Mesosphere—The third layer of the atmosphere, lying between about 50 and 80 kilometers in height and characterized by a small lapse rate.

Stratosphere—The second layer of the atmosphere, lying between about 10 and 50 kilometers in height and characterized by a negative lapse rate, that is, temperature increase with height. This is due to heating of the layer by ozone.

Thermosphere—The top layer of the atmosphere, starting at about 80 kilometers and stretching up hundreds of kilometers in to space. Due to bombardment by very energetic solar radiation , this layer can possess very high gas temperatures.

Troposphere—The atmospheric layer closest to the surface, extending up to the tropopause at about 6.2 mi (10 km) in height. Characterized by a lapse rate of 44° F/.621 mi (6.5°C/km).

Ultraviolet radiation—Radiation similar to visible light but of shorter wavelength, and thus higher energy.

X–ray radiation—Light radiation with wavelengths shorter than the shortest ultraviolet; very energetic and harmful to living organisms.

See also Atmosphere, composition and structure of; Greenhouse effect.

Further Reading:

Kraljic, Matthew A., ed, *The Greenhouse Effect, The Reference Shelf* Vol. 64, No. 3, New York: H.W. Wilson Co., 1992.

McNeill, Robert, *Understanding the Weather,* Las Vegas, NV: Arbor Publishers, 1991.

Newton, David E., *Global Warming,* Santa Barbara, CA: ABC–CLIO Inc, Publishers, 1993.

Ramsey, Don, *Weather Forecasting,* Blue Ridge Summit, PA: Tab Books, 1990.

Schneider, Stephen H., *Global Warming,* San Fransisco: Sierra Club Books, 1989.

James Marti

Atoll see **Coral reef**

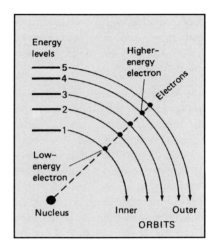

Energy levels of electrons.

Atom

Although the concept of the atom is basic to understanding the nature of matter, it took more than 2,000 years for the idea to be accepted, and most of the work on this theory was done during the last 200 years. John Dalton was the modern scientist to propose the theory of the atom. In 1808, he described atoms as small, indestructible particles of which all matter is composed. Each element, he said, has its own special kind of atom with its own specific size, shape, and weight, which are different from the atoms of every other element. Although Dalton's theory has been revised several times since its inception, the major idea of small indestructible particles has withstood the test of time and is used to successfully explain and accurately predict all of the experiments and observations of modern science.

Although it was initially thought that atoms were indivisible, it was later found that they were composed of three principle particles, the positively charged proton and the neutral neutron which contain nearly all of the mass and comprise the nucleus of an atom, and the negatively charged electrons which have very little mass and reside outside the nucleus. The current model of the atom uses wave theory to describe the probability of finding the electron at any particular place around the nucleus.

History

As early as the fifth century B.C., the Greek philosopher Leucippus wondered aloud to his student,

Democritus, whether the water of the sea could possibly be composed of small, individual particles like the sand grains of the beach. He knew that water seemed to be continuous, but so did the sand on the beach when one stood off at a distance to look at it. Perhaps, water was not really continuous as it appeared to be but was also made of small, individual particles. Democritus was perhaps the first person to use the word atom (from the Greek, *atomos,* meaning indivisible) to describe these small, ultimate particles of matter which had a definite shape and could not be subdivided.

The early Greeks believed that all things were made from only four elements: earth, fire, water, and air. The Chinese included a fifth element, metals, in this group. Greek and Roman knowledge of chemistry was based mainly on reason rather than experimentation. Their laboratories were not equipped to do complex analyses of materials and that which they did pertained only to solids and liquids, since they had no knowledge of gases. Thus, the theory of the atom gained little support and the idea of only four elements and the continuous nature of matter persisted until about the middle of the eighteenth century. Then, as experimental methods began to improve and knowledge of and about gases grew, existing theories began to lose credibility.

Robert Boyle (1627–1691) contributed much to the development of the atomical or corpuscular theory of matter, which stated that matter was made of solid, hard, impenetrable particles which were invisible and untouchable but which could join to form visible and touchable solids. Although his writings were mainly on theology and philosophy, he used chemistry to explain and understand natural phenomena. He wrote many critiques of the four–element theory of matter but since knowledge of the elements was still missing at this time, his theories were not accepted. However, it did do away with the idea that all of the possible elements were present in all matter.

With the development of the compound microscope by Robert Hooke, the argument for the existence of the atom began to gain ground. Also, the newly invented vacuum pump allowed Boyle to investigate air, and he found that the air in the atmosphere exerted great pressure on the earth. Air was also associated with breathing, rusting of iron, and tarnishing of copper. But still, air was not thought of as a chemical substance. These studies did, however, lead chemists to start thinking about elements as substances that could not be further separated by fire or any other chemical procedure. Chemists accepted the possibility that further separation could be conceivable but did not delve into this prospect.

In 1789, the element was finally defined by the French chemist, Antoine Lavoisier. Using the best scientific apparatus available at the time, he did very precise quantitative work that enabled him to develop the law of conservation of mass. He defined an element as a substance that could not be further analyzed or separated by any chemical means. As it turned out, many of his "elements" later turned out to be separable. His work with elements finally dispelled the notion of using speculation to understand nature. Instead, he showed that experimentation was really the basis for such knowledge.

In the early 1800s, Joseph Proust found evidence that substances were always formed from elements in the same ratios. Different ratios of elements always produced different substances. These ideas resulted in the law of definite proportion (also called the law of definite composition).

All of these discoveries, but especially the works of Lavoisier and Proust, led John Dalton to write his famous book, *A New System of Chemical Philosophy*, in 1808. In it, he used the atom as the basis for explaining both the law of the conservation of mass and the law of definite proportion.

Structure of the atom

Nuclear atom

With the discovery of radioactivity and electrical charges, the theory of the indivisibility of the atom was in doubt and, by the beginning of the 20th century, it was obvious that atoms were much more complex.

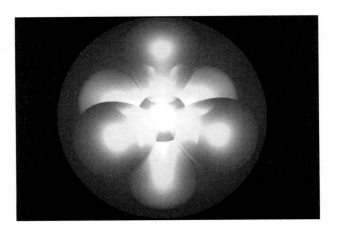

A computer generated model of a neon atom. The nucleus, at center, is too small to be seen at this scale and is represented by the flash of light. Surrounding the nucleus are the atom's electron orbitals: 1s (small sphere), 2s (large sphere), and 2p (lobed).

Michael Faraday was the first person to establish that atoms were electrical in nature. But there was no reason to relate electrical charge to a particle within the atom until experiments with cathode ray tubes gave convincing evidence for the existence of negatively charged particles. A typical cathode ray tube is a partially evacuated tube with a piece of metal attached to electrical wires at each end. When high voltage is applied to the wires, a negatively charged beam moves from the negatively charged metal plate toward the positively charged metal plate. This beam can cause metals to get red hot or fluorescent materials to glow. Scientists argued whether this beam was a form of light made up of waves or a stream of particles. The argument was finally settled in 1897 when J. J. Thomson found that the beam was deflected when very strong magnets were applied to the beam as it moved along the tube. Because it deflected, this beam is not like a light beam but must be made of particles. These particles became known as electrons.

Thomson also determined the relationship between the mass and charge of the electron. But neither of these quantities were known until 1907, when Robert A. Millikan determined the charge of the electron in his famous oil drop experiment. This allowed the mass of the electron to also be determined. It is now known that the electron has a −1 charge and is only 1/1,836 times as massive as the proton.

As early as 1886, Eugen Goldstein discovered that if the negatively charged plate in the cathode ray tube had holes in it, positive rays shot off in the opposite direction from the negative beam. It was not until 1907, though, that it was found that different gases in the tube produced particles of different masses. The lightest particle, produced by hydrogen gas, was considered to be the fundamental, positively charged particle of the atom. It was called a proton, had a charge of +1 and was assigned a mass of one atomic unit. All other atomic masses were calculated based on this unit being one.

The first detailed structure of the atom was the plum–pudding model, proposed by J. J. Thomson in 1898. In it, the atom was imagined to be a sphere of positive electricity with negatively–charged electrons evenly distributed much as plums in a pudding. Many of the properties of the atom could not be explained using this model, but it was finally disproved by the gold foil experiment performed by Ernest Rutherford and his co–workers. In this experiment, very thin sheets of gold foil were bombarded with very high–speed, positively charged particles. If the plum–pudding model was correct and the positive charge was distributed evenly throughout the atom, the speed of the bombarding particles would allow them to pass right on through, much like a BB gun fired at a sheet of tissue paper.

At first, Rutherford's experiment seemed to support this model. But upon further and more careful observation, it was found that there were a very few cases in which the bombarding particles were deflected, and some even bounced straight back in the direction from which they came. Thomson's model of the atom simply could not stand up to this experimental observation, and so Rutherford devised a new model for the atom.

What structure for the atom could have caused those few positively–charged, bombarding particles to bounce straight back? Rutherford proposed that there was a nucleus in the center of the atom that contained all of the positive charge and, since positive charges repel other positive charges, in those few cases when the incoming particles hit the nucleus, they bounced back. Rutherford also did calculations based on the number of deflections and their angles and figured that the volume of the atom was a trillion times bigger than the nucleus and that the radius of the atom was about 10,000 times bigger than the radius of the nucleus. If you imagine the atom to be about the size of a large indoor sport dome, then the nucleus of the atom would be located in the center and be about the size of a BB. All the rest of the space is occupied by very fast moving electrons that can be represented by tiny fruit flies.

The discovery of the third major particle that makes up the atom was much more difficult than the other two because it has no charge. It was discovered in 1932 by James Chadwick, an English physicist. This third particle, called a neutron, resides in the nucleus,

has about the same mass as a proton, and has no charge. With this discovery, the major building blocks for the atom were discovered and this model for the nuclear atom was complete.

The atom is composed of a very dense core called the nucleus, which contains nearly all of the mass of the atom. The nucleus consists of protons, particles with a mass of one atomic mass unit and a +1 charge, and neutrons, particles with a mass almost identical to the proton but with no charge. All atoms of the same element have the same number of protons. Electrons, which have very little mass (only 1/1,836 the mass of the proton) and a −1 charge, reside outside the nucleus and move at very high speeds, filling up nearly all the volume of the atom. The number of protons and electrons are equal, so that the atom as a whole has no net charge. But this theory of the atom had yet some major revisions to undergo.

Planetary model

Experimental observations of the simplest atom, hydrogen, did not agree with mathematical calculations concerning attractions between the positively charged protons in the nucleus and the negatively charged electrons outside the nucleus in the then current model of the atom. In fact, when using known laws that worked in the macroscopic world and applying them to the atom, the atom should collapse on itself. Obviously, this does not happen. Neils Bohr, in 1913, revised the model of the atom to include these new observations. His model, the planetary model of the atom, proposed that the arrangement of electrons around the nucleus is determined by the energy of the electrons.

In our macroscopic world, objects can have any given amount of energy, much like their weight. Weight can vary in a continuous manner. It is not restricted to discrete, fixed steps of weight. Bohr proposed that, unlike bodies in the macroscopic world which can have any amount of energy, electrons can only have particular energies, much like standing on a stepladder. You can stand on step 1, 2, or 3, etc., but all the places in between the steps are prohibited places. Bohr proposed that electrons revolve around the nucleus much like the planets orbit around the Sun, and because they have given amounts of energy, they stay in these rather stable orbits unless they receive a boost of energy from some outside force. Electrons in orbits farther from the nucleus have more energy than electrons in orbits closer to the nucleus.

Bohr's revolutionary new atomic model was widely accepted because he could use mathematical formulas to make predictions about the hydrogen atom, the one he used for all of his experimental work. However, when applying these mathematical laws to other atoms, they did not apply. The model was to be revised yet again.

Wave theory of the atom (quantum model)

In 1924 a Frenchman, Louis de Broglie, first suggested that electrons have properties like waves, and a few years later this hypothesis was confirmed by experimentation. The behavior of these subatomic particles could not be explained in the same terms as the behavior of objects in our macroscopic world. The wave theory of the atom and the behavior of the electron are understood and described mostly by very complicated mathematics. However, it is not necessary to understand the mathematics in order to understand some basic facts about this model, the quantum model for the atom. Wave theory predicts the probability of finding electrons at some given point in space with a series of four quantum numbers, but it does not tell the path by which the electron moves within the atom. Quantum numbers are much like zip codes and street addresses used by the post office to tell the region of the country, the specific post office, the street, and finally a specific house. For the electron, the first quantum number represents the energy level, or shell, and tells how far from the nucleus an electron is likely to be found. The second quantum number represents the orbital, or shape of the region of space (spherical, dumbbell shaped, double dumb–bell, etc.) where there is the greatest probability of finding an electron. The third quantum number tells the orientation of the orbital around the nucleus, and the fourth quantum number tells which way an electron is spinning.

The electron cannot be visualized in the same way objects are visualized in the macroscopic world. Wave theory tells us many things about the behavior of electrons within the atom. It allows us to know where in space an electron is most likely to be found with respect to the nucleus. It does not, however, allow us to know exactly where the electron is at any given moment or the path it takes as it moves. This model of the atom is very useful in explaining the structure of all atoms as well as predicting the structure of atoms not yet discovered. It can also be used to explain how atoms combine with other atoms to form new substances.

The theories describing the interactions between atomic particles are far from complete. The mathematical equations describing the theories generally cannot be solved exactly except in the case of very simple examples. The approximate solutions available today, however, provide results which are sufficiently accurate for most practical applications.

Many of the analytical models of atomic structure have suggested the presence of subatomic particles and interaction forces. Experiments with cosmic waves and in high–energy particle accelerators have led to the identification of two kinds of subatomic elementary matter particles, the quark and the lepton. In addition to mass and charge, these particles have unique properties called spin, flavor, and color. There are several types of quark and lepton, each with different combinations of charge, spin, flavor, and color characteristics. (To a subatomic physicist, flavor and color do not have the usual sensory meaning.) The electron and the neutrino are the lowest mass forms of leptons. Protons and neutrons are each made of three different types of quark, so that the proton has a positive charge and the neutron is neutral.

Other elementary particles have been identified which are not matter particles (leptons and quarks), but rather are particles which enable matter particles to interact. The particles, called mediator particles, include bosons, photons, and gluons and are responsible for the weak force, the electromagnetic force, and the strong force, respectively.

See also Atomic number; Atomic theory; Atomic weight; Electromagnetism; Electron; Element, chemical; Elements, formation of; Matter; Neutron; Proton; Radioactivity; Subatomic particles.

Further Reading:

Atkins, P. W. *Molecules.* New York: W. H. Freeman & Company, 1987.

Griffiths, David. *Introduction to Elementary Particles.* New York: Harper & Row, 1987.

Lederman, Leon. *The God Particle.* New York: Dell Publishing, 1993.

Leona B. Bronstein

Atomic absorbion see **Spectroscopy**

Atomic bomb see **Nulear weapons**

Repairs completed to an atomic clock. This clock is timed to the resonance frequency of cesium.

Atomic clocks

Atomic clocks are the world's most accurate time keepers. They are more accurate than astronomical time or quartz clocks. A second of time used to be defined as 1/86,400 of a mean solar day. Today it is defined as 9,192,631,770 periods or wavelengths of the radiation absorbed by the cesium 133 atom as it changes between two hyperfine energy levels. The reason for this change in definition is that atomic clocks are able to accurately measure these very short periods.

Atomic clocks have been used on jet planes and satellites to verify Einstein's theory of relativity, which states that time slows down as the velocity of one object relative to another increases. Until the advent of atomic clocks that can measure time to within one second in a million years, there was no direct way of accurately measuring the time dilation predicted by Einstein even at the velocities of space probes. Although these space vehicles reach speeds of 25,000 mi/h (40,000 km/h), such a speed is only 13% of the speed of light, and it is only at velocities close to the speed of light that time dilation becomes significant.

Atomic clocks on satellites are used in navigation. The signals sent by the atomic clocks in satellites travel at the speed of light (186,000 mi/s or 300,000 km/s). Signals from different satellites reach a ship or a plane at slightly different times because their distances from the plane or vessel are not the same. For example, by the time simultaneous signals sent from two satellites at distances of 3,100 mi (5,000 km) and 4,970 mi (8,000 km) from a ship reach the vessel, they will be separated by a time interval of 0.01 second. By knowing the position of several such satellites and the time delay between their signals, the longitude and latitude of a ship or plane can be established to within several feet.

Like all atoms, the cesium atoms used in an atomic clock are quantized; that is, they can absorb or give up only discrete quantities of energy. It is the quantum nature of the atom that is the underlying principle of atomic clocks. An atom of cesium can exist at a minimum energy level of, say, E_1, which is called its ground state. It may absorb a certain amount of energy and reach a somewhat greater energy level—E_2, E_3, E_4, and so on. Thus, an atom in its ground state can accept a quantity of energy equal to $E_2 - E_1, E_3 - E_1, E_4 - E_1$, and so on, but it cannot exist at an energy level that lies between these values. It cannot, for example, absorb a quantity of energy equal to $1/2(E_2 - E_1)$. Once an atom is at an energy level greater than its ground state, it can only release energy in the same way; that is, in quantities equal to the difference in energy levels—$E_2 - E_1, E_3 - E_1, E_4 - E_1, E_4 - E_3, E_3 - E_2,$ and so on.

When energy is emitted by an atom, it is in the form of electromagnetic radiation, such as light. Only radiation with frequencies between 4.3×10^{14} and 7.5×10^{14} Hz can be seen because those frequencies mark the ends of the range visible to the human eye. The greater the frequency of the radiation, the greater its energy. In fact, the energy, E, of the radiation is given by the equation E = hf, where f is the frequency and h is Planck's constant (6.626×10^{-34} J·s).

The energy of the radiation absorbed by the cesium atoms used in most atomic clocks is very small. It is absorbed (or released) when cesium atoms pass between two so–called hyperfine energy levels. These energy levels, which are very close together, are the result of magnetic forces that arise because of the spin of the atom's nucleus and the electrons that surround it.

The frequency of the radiation absorbed or released as atoms oscillate between two hyperfine energy states can be used as a standard for time. Such frequencies make ideal standards because they are very stable— they are not affected by temperature, air pressure, light, or other common factors that often affect ordinary chemical reactions. In atomic clocks, the atoms serve the same purpose as did pendulums or quartz crystals in earlier clocks.

Atomic clocks do not resemble ordinary clocks or watches. They do not have a set of hands that turn nor a read–out display of numbers. They simply produce electrical pulses that serve as a standard for calibrating other less accurate clocks. The newest atomic clock at the National Institute of Standards and Technology (NIST) in Boulder, Colorado, was "set" on April 22, 1993. It serves as the nation's time standard with an accuracy of about one second in a million years. The clock, which is about 7 ft (2.1 m) long, has a bright, shiny cylindrical exterior that covers several layers of magnetic shielding. The shielding prevents magnetic fields from affecting the electronic circuitry within the clock mechanism. Near one end of the long central axis of the clock is a small oven used to heat cesium metal to produce a narrow beam of atoms. As the beam moves along an evacuated tube, it passes through a laser beam before entering a 5 ft (1.5 m) long microwave cavity where microwaves at a frequency of 9,192 megahertz are reflected back and forth across the beam of cesium atoms. Upon emerging from the cavity, the atoms pass through another laser beam after which they emit radiation that is picked up by a detector.

The first laser beam through which the atoms pass is used to excite all the atoms to the proper energy level. During their passage through the microwave cavity, some of the cesium atoms absorb the energy needed to raise them to the next hyperfine level. After emerging from the cavity, energy from a second laser beam is absorbed by only those atoms at a particular energy level. That absorbed energy is quickly released and detected by a light–sensitive device that converts the radiant energy into an electric current. An electronic feedback system is used to keep the current produced by the ionized atoms at a maximum. If the frequency of the microwaves in the cavity matches the natural frequency of the energy needed to raise the cesium atoms from one hyperfine level to the next, then the current in the detector will be a maximum. If the current decreases, the feedback system will change the frequency of the microwave radiation until the current returns to its maximum level.

Time is measured by coupling the applied microwave field to a frequency divider that produces pulses separated by equal intervals of time. The microwaves acting on the atoms are similar to the vary-

---

KEY TERMS

Frequency—Number of oscillations or waves emitted per second.

Ionized atoms—Atoms that have acquired a charge by gaining or losing an electron.

Mean solar day—The average solar day; that is, the average time for the Earth to make one complete rotation relative to the Sun.

Photons—The smallest units or bundles of light energy. The energy of a photon is equal to the frequency (f) of the light times Planck's constant (h); thus, $E = hf$.

---

ing electric field that acts on the quartz crystal in a quartz watch.

International Atomic Time, based on cesium clocks, is periodically compared with mean solar time. Because the Earth's rate of rotation is slowly decreasing, the length of a solar day is increasing. Today's day is about three milliseconds longer than it was in 1900. The change is too small for us to notice; however, it is readily detected by atomic clocks. Whenever the difference between International Atomic Time and astronomical time is more than 0.9 seconds, a "leap second" is added to the mean solar time. To keep these two time systems synchronized, leap seconds have been added about every year and a half.

Further Reading:

Itano, Wayne M., and Norman F. Ramsey. "Accurate Measurement of Time." *Scientific American* 269 (July 1993): 56–65.

Morrison, Leslie. "The Day Time Stands Still." *New Scientist* (27 June 1985).

Wineland, D. J. "Trapped Ions, Laser Cooling, and Better Clocks." *Science* (26 October 1984).

Robert Gardner

Atomic fission see **Nuclear fission**
Atomic force microscope see **Microscopy**
Atomic fusion see **Nuclear fusion**
Atomic mass unit see **Atomic weight**

Atomic number

The atomic number of an element is equal to the number of protons in an atom of that element. For example, the nucleus of an oxygen atom contains eight protons and eight neutrons. Oxygen's atomic number is, therefore, eight. Since each proton carries a single positive charge, the atomic number is also equal to the total positive charge of the atomic nucleus of an element.

The atomic number of an element can be read directly from any periodic table. It is always the smaller and integral number found in association with an element's symbol in the table. In nuclear chemistry, an element's atomic number is written to the left and below the element's symbol; since an element's atomic number can always be determined simply by knowing its symbol, however, the former is often omitted from a nuclear symbol, as in ^{16}O.

The concept of atomic number evolved from the historic research of Henry Gwyn–Jeffreys Moseley in the 1910s. Moseley bombarded a number of chemical elements with x rays and observed the pattern formed by the reflected rays. He discovered that the wavelength of the reflected x rays decreases in a regular predictable pattern with increasing atomic mass. Moseley hypothesized that the regular change in wavelength from element to element was caused by an increase in the positive charge on atomic nuclei in going from one element to the next heavier element.

Moseley's discovery made possible a new understanding of the periodic law first proposed by Dmitri Mendeleev in the late 1850s. Mendeleev had said that the properties of the elements vary in a regular, predictable pattern when the elements are arranged according to their atomic masses. Although he was essentially correct, the periodic table constructed on this basis had three major flaws. Certain pairs of elements (tellurium and iodine constitute one example) appear to be misplaced when arranged according to their masses.

When atomic number, rather than atomic mass, is used to construct a periodic table, these problems disappear. The reason is that an element's chemical properties depend on the number and arrangement of electrons in its atoms. The number of electrons in an atom, in turn, is determined by the nuclear charge. It is obvious, then, that the number of protons in a nucleus (or, the nuclear charge, or the atomic number) determines the chemical properties of an element.

See also Atom; Element, chemical; Periodic table.

Atomic physics see **Physics**

Atomic spectroscopy

Atomic spectroscopy is the technique of analyzing the energy emitted by atoms in order to determine the energy levels of the atom's electrons.

Electrons can have only certain discrete energies. These energies are characteristic of each element; that is, every atom of an element has the same set of available energies. Normally, electrons in atoms are distributed in the lowest energy levels. This is called the "ground state" of the atom. If energy is added to the atom in the form of light, heat, or electricity, the electrons can move to a higher energy level. The electrons are said to be in an "excited" state. When the electrons return to their ground state distribution, they emit the excess energy in the form of light. The light carries the energy that is the difference between one energy level and another. The distribution of light energies is called a spectrum (plural spectra). The study of spectra is called spectroscopy. When light is emitted from an atom, the different colors of light can be seen after they are separated by a device like a prism or a diffraction grating. If white light passed through a prism or grating, you would see a full rainbow. But when the light emitted by an element passes through, not every color is there—only those specific colors corresponding to energy level differences. These correspond to lines in the spectrum.

A line spectrum is very useful in identifying an element because no two elements have the same line spectrum. This is how elements can be identified even on far away stars. The spectrum of light from the star is analyzed for the lines of color in its spectrum. These lines can then be matched to known line spectra of elements on earth. The element helium was discovered in this way. Its line spectrum was seen when sunlight was passed through a prism.

See also Atom; Electron; Spectroscopy.

Atomic theory

Atomic theory is the description of atoms, the smallest units of elements. The scientific evidence for the existence of atoms and its even smaller constituents is so vast that most people now consider the existence of atoms to be a fact and not just a theory.

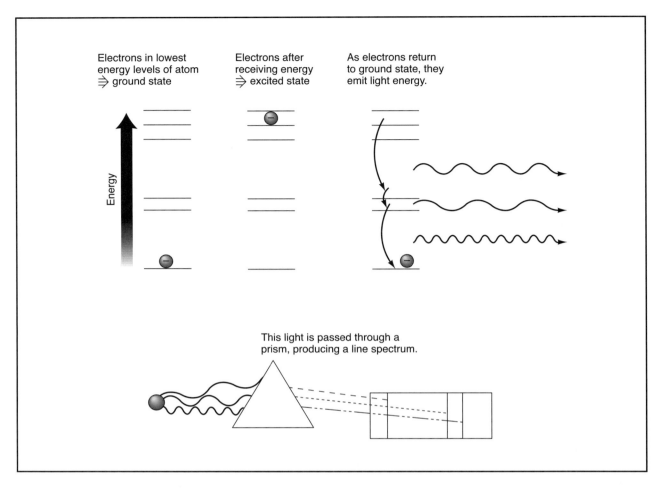

Atomic spectropscopy.

History

Beginning in about 600 B.C., many Greek philosophers struggled to understand the nature of matter. Some said everything was made of water, which comes in three forms (solid ice, liquid water, and gaseous steam). Others believed that matter was made entirely of fire in ever–changing forms. Still others believed that whatever comprised matter, it must be something that could not be destroyed but only recombined into new forms. If they could see small enough things, they would find that the same "building blocks" they started with were still there. One of these philosophers was named Democritus. He imagined starting with a large piece of matter and gradually cutting it into smaller and smaller pieces, finally reaching the smallest piece. This tiniest building block that could no longer be cut he named *a–tomos*, Greek for "no–cut." *Atomos* has been changed in modern times to "atom." The atoms Democritus envisioned differed only in shape and size. In his theory, different objects looked different because of the way the atoms were arranged. Aristotle, one of the most influential philosophers of that time, believed in some kind of "smallest part" of matter but not with Democritus's descriptions. Aristotle said there were only four elements (earth, air, fire, water) and that these had some smallest unit that made up all matter. Aristotle's teachings against the idea of Democritus's atom were so powerful that the idea of the atom fell out of philosophical fashion for the next 2,000 years.

Although atomic theory was abandoned for this long period, scientific experimentation, especially in chemistry, flourished. From the Middle Ages (1100 A.D.) onward, many chemical reactions were studied. By the seventeenth century, some of these chemists began thinking about the reactions they were seeing in terms of smallest parts. They even began using the word atom again. One of the most famous chemists of the end of the 18th century was Antoine Lavoisier. His chemical experiments involved very careful weighing of all the chemicals. He reacted various substances until they were in their simplest state. He found two important factors: (1) the simplest substances, which he called elements, could not be broken down any further, and (2) these elements always reacted with each other in the same proportions. The same more complex substances he called compounds. For example, two volumes of hydrogen reacted exactly with one volume of oxygen to produce water. Water could be broken down to always give exactly two volumes of hydrogen and one volume of oxygen. Lavoisier had no explanation for these amazingly consistent results. However, his numerous and careful measurements provided the clue to another chemist named John Dalton.

Dalton realized that if elements were made up of atoms, a different atom for each different element, atomic theory could explain Lavoisier's results. If two atoms of hydrogen always combined with one atom of oxygen, the resulting combination of atoms, called a molecule, would be water. Dalton published his explanation in 1803. This year is considered the beginning of modern atomic theory. Scientific experiments that followed Dalton were attempts to characterize how many elements there were, what the atoms of each element were like, how the atoms of each element were the same and how they differed, and, ultimately, whether there was anything smaller than an atom.

Describing characteristics of atoms

One of the first attributes of atoms to be described was relative atomic weight. Although a single atom was too small to weigh, atoms could be compared to each other. The chemist Jons Berzelius assumed that equal volumes of gases at the same temperature and pressure contained equal numbers of atoms. He used this idea to compare the weights of reacting gases. He was able to determine that, for example, oxygen atoms were 16 times heavier than hydrogen atoms. He made a list of these relative atomic weights for as many elements as he knew. He devised symbols for the elements by using the first letter or first two letters of their Latin names, a system still in use today. The symbol for hydrogen is H, for oxygen is O, for sodium (natrium, in Latin) is Na, and so on. The symbols also proved useful in describing how many atoms combine to form a molecule of a particular compound. For example, to show that water is made of two atoms of hydrogen and one atom of oxygen, the symbol for water is H_2O. One oxygen atom can even combine with one other oxygen atom to produce a molecule of oxygen with the symbol O_2.

As more and more elements continued to be discovered, it became convenient to begin listing them in symbol form in a chart. In 1869, Dmitri Mendeleev listed the elements in order of increasing atomic weight and grouped elements that seemed to have similar chemical reactions. For example, lithium (Li), sodium (Na), and potassium (K) are all metallic elements that burst into flame if they get wet. Similar elements were placed in the same column of his chart. Mendeleev began to see a pattern among the elements, where every eighth element on the atomic weight listing would belong to the same column. Because of this periodicity or repeating pattern, Mendeleev's chart is called the Periodic Table of the Elements. The Table was so regular, in fact, that when there was a "hole" in the table, Mendeleev predicted that an element would eventually be discovered to fill the place. For instance, there was a space for an element with an atomic weight of about 72 (72 times heavier than hydrogen) but no known element. In 1886, 15 years after its prediction, the element Germanium (Ge) was isolated and found to have an atomic weight of 72.3. Many more elements continued to be predicted and found in this way. However, as more elements were added to the Periodic Table, it was found that if some elements were placed in the correct column because of similar reactions, they did not follow the right order of increasing atomic weight. Some other atomic characteristic was needed to order the elements properly. Many years passed before the correct property was found.

As chemistry experiments were searching for and characterizing more elements, other branches of science were making discoveries about electricity and light that were to contribute to the development of atomic theory. Michael Faraday had done much work to characterize electricity; James Clerk Maxwell characterized light. In the 1870s, William Crookes built an apparatus, now called a Crookes tube, to examine "rays" being given off by metals. He wanted to determine whether the rays were light or electricity based on Faraday's and Maxwell's descriptions of both. Crookes's tube consisted of a glass bulb, from which most of the air had been removed, encasing two metal plates called electrodes. One electrode was called the anode and the other was called the cathode. The plates each had a wire leading outside the bulb to a source of electricity. When electricity was applied to the electrodes, rays appeared to come from the cathode. Crookes determined that these cathode rays were particles with a negative electrical charge that were being given off by the metal of the cathode plate. In 1897, J. J. Thomson discovered that these negatively charged particles were coming out of the atoms and must have been present in the metal atoms to begin with. He called these negatively charged subatomic particles "electrons." Since the electrons were negatively charged, the rest of the atom had to be

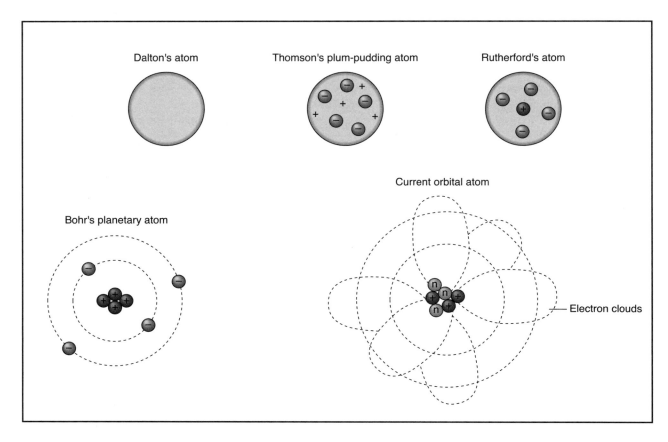

Dalton's atom

Thomson's plum-pudding atom

Rutherford's atom

Bohr's planetary atom

Current orbital atom

Electron clouds

The evolution of atomic theory.

positively charged. Thomson believed that the electrons were scattered in the atom like raisins in a positively-charged bread dough, or like plums in a pudding. Although Thomson's "plum–pudding" model was not correct, it was the first attempt to show that atoms were more complex than just homogeneous spheres.

At the same time, scientists were examining other kinds of mysterious rays that were coming from the Crookes tube that did not originate at its cathode. In 1895, Wilhelm Roentgen noticed that photographic plates held near a Crookes tube would become fogged by some invisible, unknown rays. Roentgen called these rays "x rays," using "x" for unknown as in mathematics. Roentgen also established the use of photographic plates as a way to take pictures of mysterious rays. He found that by blocking the x rays with his hand, for instance, bones would block the x rays but skin and tissue would not. Doctors still use Roentgen's x rays for imaging the human body.

Photographic plates became standard equipment for scientists of Roentgen's time. One of these scientists, Henri Becquerel, left some photographic plates in a drawer with uranium, a new element he was studying. When he removed the plates, he found that they had become fogged. Since there was nothing else in the drawer, he concluded that the uranium must have been giving off some kind of rays. Becquerel showed that this radiation was not as penetrating as x rays since it could be blocked by paper. The element itself was actively producing radiation, a property referred to as radioactivity. Largely through the work of Pierre and Marie Curie, more radioactive elements were found. The attempts to characterize the different types of radioactivity led to the next great chapter in the development of atomic theory.

In 1896, Ernest Rutherford, a student of J. J. Thomson, began studying radioactivity. By testing various elements and determining what kinds of materials could block the radiation from reaching a photographic plate, Rutherford concluded that there were two types of radioactivity coming from elements. He named them using the first two letters of the Greek alphabet, alpha and beta. Alpha radiation was made of positively charged particles about four times as heavy as a hydrogen atom. Beta radiation was made of negatively charged particles that seemed to be just like electrons. Rutherford decided to try an experiment using the alpha particles. He set up a piece of thin gold foil with photographic plates encircling it. He then allowed alpha particles to hit the gold. Most of the alpha particles went right through the gold foil. But a few of them did not. A few alpha particles were deflected from their straight course. A few even came straight backward. Rutherford wrote that it was as surprising as if one had fired a bullet at a piece of tissue paper only to have it bounce back. Rutherford concluded that since most of the alpha particles went through, the atoms of the gold must be mostly empty space, not Thomson's space–filling plum–pudding. Since a few of the alpha particles were deflected, there must be a densely packed positive region in each atom that he called the nucleus. With all the positive charge in the nucleus, the next question was the arrangement of the electrons in the atom.

In 1900, physicist Max Planck had been studying processes of light and heat, specifically trying to understand the light radiation given off by a "black–body," an ideal cavity made by perfectly reflecting walls. This cavity was imagined as containing objects called oscillators which absorbed and emitted light and heat. Given enough time, the radiation from such a black–body would produce a colored–light distribution called a spectrum that depended only on the temperature of the black–body and not on what it was made of. Many scientists attempted to find a mathematical relationship that would predict how the oscillators of a black–body could produce a particular spectral distribution. Max Planck found that correct mathematical relationship. He assumed that the energy absorbed or emitted by the oscillators was always a multiple of some fundamental "packet of energy" he called a quantum. Objects that emit or absorb energy do it in discrete amounts, called quantums.

At this same time, there was a physicist working with Thomson and Rutherford named Niels Bohr. Bohr realized that the idea of a quantum of energy could explain how the electrons in the atom are arranged. He described the electrons as being "in orbit" around the nucleus like planets around the Sun. Like oscillators in a black–body could not have just any energy, electrons in the atom could not have just any orbit. There were only certain distances that were allowed by the energy that an electron had. If an electron of a particular atom absorbed the precisely right quantum of energy, it could move farther away from the nucleus. If an electron farther from the nucleus emitted the precisely right quantum of energy, it could move closer to the nucleus. What the precisely right values were differed for every element. These values could be determined by a process

called atomic spectroscopy, an experimental technique that looked at the light spectrum produced by atoms. An atom was heated so that all of its electrons were moved far away from the nucleus. As they moved closer to the nucleus, the electrons would begin emitting their quanta of energy as light. The spectrum of light produced could be examined using a prism. The spectrum produced in this way did not show every possible color, but only those few that matched the energies corresponding to the electron orbit differences. Although later refined, Bohr's "planetary model" of the atom explained atomic spectroscopy data well enough that scientists turned their attention back to the nucleus of the atom.

Rutherford, along with Frederick Soddy, continued work with radioactive elements. Soddy, in particular, noticed that as alpha and beta particles were emitted from atoms, the atoms changed in one of two ways: 1) the element became a totally different element with completely new chemical reactions, or 2) the element maintained the same chemical reactions and the same atomic spectrum but only changed in atomic weight.

He called atoms of the second group isotopes, atoms of the same element with different atomic weights. In any natural sample of an element, there may be several types of isotopes. As a result, the atomic weight of an element that was calculated by Berzelius was actually an average of all the isotope weights for that element. This was the reason that some elements did not fall into the right order on Mendeleev's Periodic Table—the average atomic weight depended on how much of each kind of isotope was present. Soddy suggested placing the elements in the Periodic Table by similarity of chemical reactions and then numbering them in order. The number assigned to each element in this way is called the atomic number. The atomic numbers were convenient ways to refer to elements.

Meanwhile, Thomson had continued his work with the Crookes tube. He found that, not only were cathode rays of electrons produced, but so were positive particles. After much painstaking work, he was able to separate the many different kinds of positive particles by weight. Based on these measurements, he was able to determine a fundamental particle, the smallest positive particle produced, called a proton. Since these were being produced by the atoms of the cathode and since Rutherford showed that the nucleus of the atom was positive, Thomson realized that the nucleus of an atom must contain protons. A young scientist named Henry Moseley experimented with bombarding atoms of different elements with x rays. Just as in atomic spectroscopy, where heat gives electrons more energy, x rays give protons in the nucleus more energy. And just as electrons give out light of specific energies when

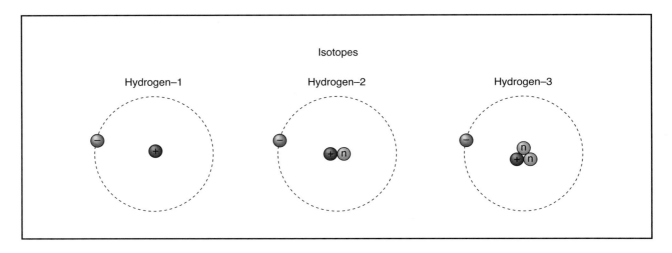

Hydrogen isotopes.

they cool, the nucleus emits x rays of a specific energy when it "de–excites." Moseley discovered that the energy of the emitted x rays for every element followed a simple mathematical relationship. The energy depended on the atomic number for that element, and the atomic number corresponded to the number of positive charges in the nucleus. So the correct ordering of the Periodic Table is by increasing number of protons in the atomic nucleus. The number of protons equals the number of electrons in a neutral atom. The electrons are responsible for the chemical reactions. Elements in the same column of the Periodic Table have similar arrangements of electrons with the highest energies, and this is why their reactions are similar.

Only one problem remained. Electrons had very little weight, 1/1,836 the weight of a proton. Yet the protons did not account for all of the atomic weight of an atom. It was not until 1932 that James Chadwick discovered the existence of a particle in the nucleus with no electrical charge but with a weight slightly greater than a proton. He named this particle the neutron. Neutrons are responsible for the existence of isotopes. Two atoms of the same element will have the same number of protons and electrons but they might have different numbers of neutrons and therefore different atomic weights. Isotopes are named by stating the name of the element and then the number of protons plus neutrons in the nucleus. The sum of the protons and neutrons is called the mass number. For example, uranium–235 has 235 protons and neutrons. We can look on a Periodic Table to find uranium's atomic number (92) which tells us the number of protons. Then by subtracting, we know that this isotope has 143 neutrons. There is another isotope of uranium, U–238, with 92 protons and 146 neutrons. Some combinations of protons and neu-

trons are less stable than others. Picture trying to hold 10 bowling balls in your arms. There will be some arrangement where you might be able to manage it. Now try holding 11 or only nine. There might not be a stable arrangement and you would drop the bowling balls. The same thing happens with protons and neutrons. Unstable arrangements spontaneously fall apart, emitting particles, until a stable structure is reached. This is how radioactivity like alpha particles is produced. Alpha particles are made of two protons and two neutrons tumbling out of an unstable nucleus.

Hydrogen has three kinds of isotopes, hydrogen–1, hydrogen–2 and hydrogen–3.

The atomic weights of the other elements were originally compared to hydrogen without specifying which isotope. It is also difficult to get single atoms of hydrogen because it usually reacts with other atoms to form molecules like H_2 or H_2O. So a different element's isotope was chosen for comparison. The atomic weights are now based on carbon–12. This isotope has six protons and six neutrons in its nucleus. Carbon–12 was defined to be 12 atomic mass units. (Atomic mass units, abbreviated amu, are units used to compare the relative weights of atoms. One amu is less than 200 sextillionths of a gram.) Every other isotope of every other element is compared to this. Then the weights of a given element's isotopes are averaged to give the atomic weights found on the Periodic Table.

Until this point in the story of the atom, all of the particles comprising the atom were thought of as hard, uniform spheres. Beginning in 1920 with the work of Louis de Broglie, this image changed. De Broglie showed that particles like electrons could sometimes have properties of waves. For instance, if water waves are produced by two sources, like dropping two pebbles into a pond, the waves can interfere with each other. This means that high spots add to make even higher spots. Low spots add to make even lower regions. When electrons were made to travel through a double slit, with some electrons going through one slit and some through the other, they effectively created two sources. The electrons showed this same kind of interference, producing a pattern on a collection plate. The ability of electrons and other particles to sometimes show properties of particles and sometimes of waves is called wave–particle duality. This complication to the nature of the electron meant that Bohr's idea of a planetary atom was not quite right. The electrons do have different discrete energies, but they do not follow circular orbits. In 1925, Werner Heisenberg stated that the precise speed and location of an electron cannot both be known at the same time. This "Heisenberg Uncertainty Principle" inspired Erwin Schrödinger to devise an equation to calculate how an electron with a certain energy moves. Schrödinger's equation describes regions in an atom where an electron with a certain energy is *likely* to be but not exactly where it is. This region of probability is called an orbital. Electrons move so fast within these orbitals that we can think of them as blurring into an electron cloud. Electrons move from one orbital into another by absorbing or emitting a quantum of energy, just as Bohr explained.

Applications of atomic theory

Early studies of radioactivity revealed that certain atomic nuclei were naturally radioactive. Some scientists wondered that if particles could come out of the nucleus, would it also be possible to force particles into the nucleus? In 1932, Cockcroft and Walton succeeded in building a particle accelerator, a device that could make streams of charged particles move faster and faster. These fast particles, protons for example, were then aimed at a thin plate of a lighter element like lithium (Li). If a lithium atom nucleus "captures" a proton, the nucleus becomes unstable and breaks apart into two alpha particles. This technique of inducing radioactivity by bombardment with accelerated particles is still the most used method of studying nuclear structure and subatomic particles. Today, accelerators race the particles in straight lines or, to save land space, in ringed paths several miles in diameter.

The spontaneous rearrangement of the atomic nucleus always results in a release of energy in the form of kinetic motion in fast–moving neutrons. When a large nucleus falls apart to form smaller atoms, the process is called fission. When lighter atoms are forced together to produce a heavier atom, the process is called

---

KEY TERMS

Accelerator—A device that causes particles to move faster and faster.

Alpha particle—A type of radioactivity, an alpha particle is made of two protons and two neutrons.

Atomic mass—The relative weight of a specific atom's isotope compared to carbon–12 = 12.000 amu.

Atomic mass units—Units used to compare the relative atomic weights of atoms, abbreviated amu.

Beta particle—A type of radioactivity, a beta particle is indistinguishable from an electron.

Electrode—A metal plate that carries electrical current.

Electron cloud—The image of an electron moving so fast that it seems to fill a region of space.

Interference—The combination of waves in which high spots combine to give even higher spots and low spots combine to give even lower spots.

Kinetic energy—The energy of a moving object.

Mass number—The sum of protons and neutrons.

Nucleus—The dense central part of an atom containing the protons and neutrons; plural is nuclei.

Orbital—The region of probability within an atom where an electron with a particular energy is likely to be.

Oscillators—Objects that can absorb or emit energy and convert it into kinetic energy.

Periodicity—Repeatability of a pattern.

Quantum—A packet or discrete amount of energy; plural is quanta.

Quarks—Believed to be the most fundamental units of protons and neutrons.

Uncertainty Principle—Heisenberg's statement that both the position and velocity of a particle cannot be known with equal precision at the same time.

Wave–particle duality—The ability of objects to show characteristics of both waves and particles.

---

fusion. In either case, fast neutrons are released. These can transfer their kinetic energy to the surroundings, heating it. This heat can be used to boil water, producing steam to run a turbine that turns an electric generator. Fusion is the process occurring in the center of the Sun and other stars. So much energy can be released quickly that the process has also been used for the hydrogen bomb. However, fusion is not yet controlled enough for running a power plant. Research continues to find a controlled method of using fusion energy.

On the other hand, fission reactions have also been used for very powerful weapons. The first atomic bomb was detonated in 1945. Since then, however, fission energy has also been controlled enough to operate the many nuclear power plants around the world.

While an atom is the smallest part of an element which still is that element, atoms are not the smallest particles that exist. Even the protons and neutrons in the atomic nucleus are believed to made of even smaller particles called quarks. Current research in atomic physics focuses on describing the internal structure of atoms. By using particle accelerators, scientists are trying to characterize quarks which may combine in a number of ways to produce other types of subatomic particles.

No one has ever seen a single atom even with the best optical microscopes. Special types of microscopes called scanning tunneling microscopes and atomic force microscopes make use of the forces produced by the electrons to obtain images of the electron clouds. These clouds indicate how atoms are arranged but we cannot "see" through the cloud to the nucleus. Because of the limitations of size, we will never see an atom with our own eyes. Everything we know about atoms must be deduced from larger–scale experiments. As a result, the description of atoms is still called a theory. However, this theory explains atomic experiments so well that we usually think of the existence of atoms as a fact.

Eileen Korenic

See also Accelerators; Atom; Atomic number; Atomic spectroscopy; Atomic weight; Electron; Element, chemical; Isotope; Mass number; Neutron; Nuclear fission; Nuclear fusion; Periodic table; Proton; Subatomic particles; X rays.

Atomic weight

Atoms are exceedingly small, so small that actual weights of atoms were not able to be determined until early in the 20th century. The weight of an atom of oxygen–16 (an oxygen atom with eight neutrons in the nucleus) was found to be 2.657×10^{-23} grams and an atom of carbon–12 (a carbon atom with six neutrons in the nucleus) was found to weigh 1.99×10^{-23} grams. Because these units are so very small, they are not practical and are seldom used in everyday laboratory work. Rather, the weight of an atom is usually calculated in units other than grams, one that is closer to the size of the particle being weighed and is therefore more practical.

The Table of Atomic Weights is based on a unit called an atomic mass unit, abbreviated u, or in older notation, amu. This unit is defined as 1/12 the mass of carbon–12 and is equal to 1.6606×10^{-24} grams. On this scale, carbon–12 weighs exactly 12 atomic mass units. But because even the smallest amount of matter contains enormous numbers of atoms, atomic weights are usually interpreted to mean grams of an element rather than atomic mass units. When interpreted in grams, the atomic weight of an element represents 6.02×10^{23} atoms, which is defined as one mole. Thus, the atomic weight in grams is the mass of an element that contains one mole or 6.02×10^{23} atoms.

Atomic weights are actually atomic masses but historically they were called atomic weights because the method used to determine them was called weighing. This terminology has persisted and is more familiar to most people even though the values obtained are actually atomic masses.

History

Although the atomic theory of matter, in its various forms, existed a good two thousand years before the time of John Dalton, he was the first to propose, in his 1808 book *A New System of Chemical Philosophy*, that atoms had weight. Atoms, as Dalton defined them, were hard, solid, indivisible particles with no inner spaces, rather than something that could not be seen, touched, or tasted. They were indestructible and preserved their identities in all chemical reactions. Furthermore, each kind of element had its own specific kind of atom different from the atoms of other elements. These assumptions led him to propose that atoms were tangible matter and therefore had weight.

Because atoms were much too small to be seen or measured by any common methods, absolute weights of atoms could not be determined. Rather, these first measurements were made by comparing weights of various atoms to hydrogen. Hydrogen was chosen as the unit of comparison because it was the lightest substance known and the weights of the other elements would be very close to whole numbers.

The weight of oxygen could then be calculated because of earlier work by Humboldt and Gay–Lussac, who found that water consisted of only two elements, hydrogen and oxygen, and that there were eight parts of oxygen for every one part of hydrogen. Lacking any knowledge about how many atoms of hydrogen and oxygen combine in a molecule of water, Dalton again had to make some assumptions. He assumed that nature is basically very simple and, therefore, one atom of hydrogen combines with only one atom of oxygen. Using this hypothesis and the fact that hydrogen was assigned a weight of one unit, it follows that oxygen, which is eight times heavier than hydrogen, would have a weight of eight units. Of course, if the ratio between hydrogen and oxygen in water were not one to one, but some other ratio, the weight of oxygen would have to be adjusted accordingly. Dalton used experimental results and similar reasoning to prepare the very first Table of Atomic Weights, but because of the lack of knowledge about the real formulas for substances, many of the weights were incorrect and had to be modified later.

Knowledge about absolute formulas of substances came mainly from the work of two chemists. In 1809, Gay–Lussac observed that gases react with each other in very simple proportions. For example, at the same temperature and pressure, two volumes of hydrogen react with one volume of oxygen and form two volumes of water. Then in 1811, Amadeo Avogadro proposed that equal volumes of gases have the same number of particles if measured at the same temperature and pressure. The difficulty of explaining how one volume of oxygen could form two volumes of water without violating the current theory that atoms were indivisible was not resolved until the 1850s when Avogadro's explanation that molecules of gases, such as hydrogen and oxygen, existed as diatomic molecules (molecules with two atoms joined together) was finally accepted. If each oxygen molecule was composed of two oxygen atoms, then it was the molecule and not the atom that split apart to form two volumes of water.

Although other scientists contributed to knowledge about atomic weights, much of the experimental work that was used to improve the Table of Atomic Weights was done by J. J. Berzelius who published his list of the weights of 54 elements in 1828. Unlike Dalton's atomic weights, the weights published by Berzelius match quite well the atomic weights used today.

So far, all the knowledge about atomic weights was relative to the weight of hydrogen as one unit. The first of the experiments to uncover knowledge about the absolute weight of parts of the atom were done early in the 20th century by J. J. Thomson and Robert Millikan.

Thomson studied rays of negative particles (later discovered to be electrons) in partially evacuated tubes. He measured how the beam deflected or bent when placed in a magnetic field and used this information to calculate mathematically the ratio of the charge on the electron to the mass of the electron.

Millikan devised a clever experiment in which he produced a very fine spray of charged oil droplets and allowed them to fall between two charged plates. By adjusting the charge on the plates as he observed the droplets under a microscope, he was able to suspend the droplets midway between the two plates and with this information calculate the charge of the electron. Now, along with the charge/mass ratio calculated by Thomson, the mass of the electron could be calculated and was found to equal 9.11×10^{-28} grams (a decimal with 27 zeros before the 9).

About five years later, the charge and mass of the proton were calculated. The proton was found to weigh 1.6726×10^{-24} grams or about 1,836 times as much as an electron. Because most atoms (hydrogen being the only exception) were heavier than would be expected from the number of protons they had, it was known that there must be another neutral particle in the atom. Because of the difficulty in observing neutral particles, the neutron was not discovered until 1932 by James Chadwick. The mass was found to be 1.6749×10^{-24} grams, about the same as the mass of the proton.

Isotopes

The atomic weight represents the sum of the masses of the particles that make up the atom, protons, neutrons, and electrons. But since the mass of the electron is so small and essentially all the weight of the atom comes from the protons and neutrons, the atomic weight is considered to represent the sum of the masses of the protons and neutrons present in the atom. These weights were given in relative units called atomic mass units (abbreviated u or, in older notation, amu) in which the protons and neutrons have nearly equal masses. Consequently, the sum of the protons and neutrons in the nucleus would be the same as the atomic weight of the atom.

Today, a very sophisticated instrument, called a mass spectrometer, is used to obtain accurate measurements of atomic masses. In this instrument, atoms are vaporized and then changed to positively charged particles by knocking off electrons. These charged particles are passed through a magnetic field which causes them to be deflected different amounts, depending on the size of the charge and mass. The particles are eventually deposited on a detector plate where the amount of deflection can be measured and compared with the charge. Very accurate relative masses are determined in this way.

When atoms of various elements were analyzed with the mass spectrometer, scientists were surprised to find that not all atoms of the same element had exactly the same mass. Oxygen, for example, was found to exist in three different forms, each differing by one atomic mass unit or about the mass of one proton or one neutron. Since the number of protons in the nucleus was known because of their association with a +1 charge, the three different masses for oxygen had to be caused by different numbers of neutrons in the nucleus. Atoms of this type were called isotopes. Both the identity of the element (since the number of protons remains the same) and the chemical properties (since the electrons remain unchanged) are identical in isotopes of the same element. However, the mass is different because of the different number of neutrons in the nucleus, and this sometimes makes the atom unstable and radioactive. Radioactive isotopes are frequently used in research because the radioactivity can be followed using a Geiger counter. They can be administered to living systems like plants or animals and the isotope is observed as it moves and reacts throughout the system. Oxygen has three isotopes with masses of 16, 17, and 18 (often written as oxygen–16, oxygen–17, and oxygen–18). Similarly, carbon exists as carbon–12, carbon–13, and carbon–14 and hydrogen as hydrogen–1, hydrogen–2, and hydrogen–3. Each of these successive isotopes have one more neutron in the nucleus than the preceding one.

Interpretation of atomic weights

Early work on atomic weights used naturally occurring oxygen, with an assigned atomic weight of exactly 16 as the basis for the scale of atomic weights. All other atomic weights were found in relation to it. Confusion arose when, in 1929, the three isotopes of oxygen were discovered. In 1961, it was finally decided to adopt carbon–12 as the basis for all other atomic weights. Under this system still in use today, the atomic weight of carbon–12 is taken to be exactly 12 and the atomic mass unit is defined as exactly one–twelfth the mass of carbon–12. All other atomic weights are measured in relation to this unit.

When examining the Table of Atomic Weights, it is found that the weight of carbon is not given as exactly 12 as would be expected, but rather 12.01. The reason is that the weights used in the table represent the average weight of the isotopes of carbon that are found in a naturally occurring sample. For example, most of the carbon found in nature, 98.89% of it to be exact, is carbon–12 and has a weight of exactly 12. The rest of it (1.11%) is carbon–13 (with an atomic weight of 13.00) and carbon–14 (which exists in quantities too minute to affect this calculation). The atomic weight of carbon is calculated by taking 98.89% of the weight of carbon–12 and 1.11% of the weight of carbon–13 to give 12.0112. All weights in the Table of Atomic Weights are calculated by using the percentage of each isotope in a naturally occurring sample.

Because atoms are so small, making it impossible for chemists to observe or weigh them, the weights of individual atoms are not very useful for experimentation. Very large numbers of atoms are involved in even the tiniest samples of matter. It is important to match the unit that is used to make a measurement to the size of the thing being measured. For example, it is useful to measure the length of a room in feet rather than miles because the unit, foot, corresponds to the length of a room. One would not measure the distance to London or Paris or to the Sun in inches or feet because the distance is so large in relation to the size of the unit. Miles would be a much more appropriate unit.

A new unit, called a mole, was created as a more useful unit for working with atoms. A mole is a counting number much like a dozen. A dozen involves 12 of anything, 12 books, 12 cookies, 12 pencils, etc. Similarly, a mole involves 6.02×10^{23} (602 with 21 zeros after it) particles of anything. The mole is such a large number that it is not a useful measurement for anything except counting very, very small particles, too small to even imagine. For example, if a mole of dollars were divided evenly among all the people of the world (5.5 billion), every single person alive would receive 1.09×10^{14} dollars! That is enough money to last nearly 300 years if a billion dollars were spent every single day of the year. Yet a mole of carbon atoms is contained in a chunk of coal about as big as a marble.

Needless to say, atoms cannot be counted in the same way that cookies or books are counted. But they can be counted by weighing, and the mole is the unit that can express this quantity. If a ping–pong ball weighs one ounce, then 12 ounces of ping–pong balls would contain 12 balls. Twenty ounces would contain 20 balls. If golf balls weigh four ounces each, then 48 ounces are needed in order to obtain 12 balls, and 80 ounces are needed in order to obtain 20 balls. Since the golf ball weighs four times as much as the ping–pong ball, it is easy to obtain equal numbers of these two balls by weighing four times as much for the golf balls as you weigh for the ping–pong balls. Actually, it is easier to count small numbers of ping–pong balls or golf balls than to weigh them. But if 10 or 20 or 30 thousand of them were needed, it would be much easier figure the weight of the balls and weigh them than it would be to count them.

Likewise, the weighing method is more useful and, in fact, is the only method by which atoms can be counted. It was discovered in the early 1800s, mostly through the work of Amadeo Avogadro, that when the atomic weight of an atom is interpreted in grams rather than atomic mass units, the number of atoms in the sample is always 6.02×10^{23} atoms or a mole of atoms. Thus, 12 grams of carbon contain one mole of carbon atoms and 16 grams of oxygen contain one mole of oxygen atoms. One mole of the lightest atom, hydrogen, weighs just one gram and one mole of the heaviest of the naturally occurring elements, uranium, weighs 238 grams.

Molecules are particles made up of more than one atom. The weight of the molecule, called the molecular weight, can be found by adding the atomic weights of each of the atoms that make up the molecule. Water is a molecule with a formula, H_2O. It is composed of two atoms of hydrogen, with an atomic weight of one, and one atom of oxygen with an atomic weight of 16. Water, therefore has a molecular weight of 18. When this molecular weight is interpreted as 18 atomic mass units, it represents the weight of one molecule in relation to one–twelfth of carbon–12. When the molecular weight is interpreted as 18 grams (less than 400 drops of water), it represents the weight of one mole or 6.02×10^{23} molecules of water. Similarly, the molecular weight of carbon dioxide (CO_2) is 44 atomic mass units or 44 grams. A chunk of solid carbon dioxide (known as dry ice) about the size of a baseball contains one mole of molecules. If this chunk were allowed to change to a gas at room conditions of temperature and pressure, this mole of carbon dioxide would take up slightly over a cubic foot.

Uses

When new substances are found in nature or are produced in the laboratory, the first thing chemists try to determine is the chemical formula for the substance. This new compound, a substance made of two or more kinds of atoms, is analyzed to find what elements it is composed of. This is usually done by chemically separating the compound into its elements and then determining how much of each element was present. Chemical formulas tell how many atoms are in a compound, not the amount of mass. So the mass of each element must be expressed as a part of a mole by comparing it to the atomic weight. When expressed in this manner, the quantity is a way of representing how many atoms are present in the compound. These numbers of moles are

---

KEY TERMS

Atomic mass—The mass of an atom relative to carbon–12 having a mass of exactly 12 atomic mass units; also the mass, in grams, of an element that contains one mole of atoms.

Atomic mass unit (u or amu)—A unit used to express the mass of atoms equal to exactly one–twelfth of the mass of carbon–12.

Molecule—The smallest particle of a compound that can exist, formed when two or more atoms join together to form a substance.

---

expressed as ratios, reduced to the lowest whole numbers and then combined with the symbols for the elements to represent the simplest chemical formula.

Companies that produce raw materials or manufacture goods use atomic and molecular weights to help determine the amounts of reactants needed to produce a given amount of product. Or they can determine how much product they can produce from a given amount of reactant. Once again, the quantities involved in chemical reactions depend on how many atoms or molecules react, not on the amount of mass of each. So the known amount of reactant or product must be expressed as a part of a mole by comparing it to the molecular weight. Although other factors are involved in these determinations, this quantity, along with the balanced equation for the chemical reaction, allows chemists to figure out how much of any other reactant or product is involved in the reaction. Calculations of this type can save manufacturers many dollars because the amounts of chemicals needed to manufacture a product can be accurately determined. If a billion tires are produced in one year and one penny can be saved on each tire by not using more of a substance than can be reacted, it would be a substantial savings to the company of $10,000,000 per year.

See also Atom; Avogadro's number; Electron; Isotope; Mass spectrometry; Molecular weight; Mole; Neutron; Periodic table; Proton.

Further Reading:

Brock, William H. *The Norton History of Chemistry*. New York: W. W. Norton & Company, 1993.
Feather, Ralph M. et. al., *Science Connections,* Columbus, OH: Merrill Publishing Company, 1990.

Leona B. Bronstein

Razor-billed auks (*Alca torda*).

ATP see **Adenosine triphosphate**

Atrium see **Heart**

Attention deficit disorder see **Hyperactivity**

Auks

Auks are penguinlike seabirds found in the Northern Hemisphere. These birds spend most of their lives in the coastal waters above 25 degrees north latitude, coming ashore only to lay their eggs and raise their young. There are 22 species of auks, including the Atlantic puffin, the common murre, the dovekie or lesser auk, and the extinct great auk.

Called alcids, the members of the auk family fill an ecological niche similar to that filled by the penguins in the southern hemisphere. However similar their role, the penguins and alcids are not closely related, the alcids being more closely related to the gulls.

Like penguins, alcids have waterproof feathers and swim and dive for their prey. Unlike penguins, auks can fly. Their wings are relatively small, and while auks are not especially graceful in flight, they are able to "fly" gracefully underwater in pursuit of prey. Auks obtain all of their food from the sea. Some of the smaller species subsist on plankton alone, but most eat fish. Like penguins, auks have deceptive coloration; when in water, their white fronts make them nearly invisible to fish below.

Auks' legs are near the rear of their bodies, giving them an upright, penguinlike posture. In some species the feet and bill are brightly colored—most notably in the Atlantic puffin, whose blue, yellow, red, and white striped bill is important to the species during the mating season. The colorful plates that make up the harlequinesque bill are shed when the bird molts. Other species, such as the rhinoceros auklet, grow special tufts of feathers during mating season. Auks mate for life and are generally monogamous, although males will attempt to copulate with a female if she is not attended by her mate.

Most auks lay their eggs on bare stone ledges, or scoop out a nest in a burrow. An exception is the marbled murrelet, which builds a simple nest in the branches of seaside pines. Depending on the species, one or two eggs are laid and incubated for 29–42 days.

A few auk species breed in solitary pairs, but most congregate in large colonies. One of the most densely populated auk colonies on record included 70 pairs of common murres in a space of 7.5 sq ft (0.65 sq m). In species that congregate in such large rookeries, each bird's egg is uniquely colored and/or patterned, allowing for easy identification. Chicks, too, are recognized individually by their voice; chicks and parents start getting to know each other's voice even before hatching. Such recognition ensures that each auk feeds only its own offspring.

Chick development varies greatly among the auks. The young of the tiny ancient murrelet take to sea with their parents just a day after they hatch. Other species brood their chicks for 20–50 days. In general, smaller auks lay proportionately larger eggs, from which hatch more precocious chicks. For example, the ancient murrelet weights just over 200 g, but lays an egg that is approximately one–fourth of the adult's body weight. The chicks reach sexual maturity in about three years.

Auks are long–lived; some birds banded as adults have been found in breeding colonies 20 years later. Their natural enemies include the great skua, the gyrfalcon, and the peregrine falcon.

Although auks are protected by law in North America, humans remain their greatest threat. In the 1500s, sailors slaughtered huge numbers of great auks for food on long sea voyages. Flightless and 2 ft (0.6 m) tall, the great auk was helpless when caught on land. Tens of millions of these birds were killed until the species became extinct in 1844, when the last great auk was killed on Eldez Island, off the coast of Iceland. More recently, hunting of other auk species has become a popular sport in Greenland.

Oil pollution—both from spills and from tanker maintenance—also kills countless birds each year. Oil destroys the waterproof quality of the auks' feathers and is swallowed by the birds when they attempt to clean themselves. Auk drownings in fishermen's gill nets have decreased in recent years. However, the decline in food–fish species such as cod and haddock have led fishermen to turn their attention to the fish species auks eat, such as sprats. Such competition does not bode well for the auks.

Further Reading:

Brooke, M., and T. Birkhead, eds. *The Cambridge Encyclopedia of Ornithology*. Cambridge: Cambridge University Press, 1991.

Encyclopedia of Birds. New York: Facts on File, 1984.

Terres, John K. *The Audubon Encyclopedia of North American Birds*. Avenel, NJ: Wings Books, 1991.

F.C. Nicholson

Australia

Of the seven continents, Australia is the flattest, smallest, and except for Antarctica, the most arid. Including the southeastern island of Tasmania, the island continent is roughly equal in area to the United States, excluding Alaska and Hawaii. Millions of years of geographic isolation from other landmasses accounts for Australia's unique animal species, notably marsupial mammals like the kangaroo, egg laying mammals like the platypus, and the flightless emu bird. Excluding folded structures (areas warped by geologic forces) along Australia's east coast, patches of the northern coastline and the relatively lush island of Tasmania, the continent is mostly dry, bleak, and inhospitable.

Topography and origin of Australia

Australia has been less affected by seismic and orogenic (mountain building) forces than other continents during the past 400 million years. Although seismic (earthquake) activity persists in the eastern and western highlands, Australia is the most stable of all continents. In the recent geological past, it has experienced none of the massive upheavals responsible for uplifting the Andes in South America, the Himalayas in south Asia or the European Alps. Instead Australia's topography is the end result of gradual changes over millions of years.

Australia's is not the oldest continent, a common misperception arising from the continent's flat, seemingly unchanged expanse. Geologically it is the same age as the Americas, Asia, Africa, Europe, and Antarctica. But Australia's crust has escaped strong earth

Ayers rock, central Australia, 1,143 ft (349 m) high.

forces in recent geological history, accounting for its relatively uniform appearance. As a result, the continent serves as a window to early geological ages.

Splitting of Australia from Antarctica

About 95 million years ago, tectonic forces (movements and pressures of the earth's crust) split Australia from Antarctica and the southern supercontinent of Gondwanaland. Geologists estimate that the continent is drifting northward at a rate of approximately 18 inches (28 cm) per year. They theorize that south Australia was joined to Antarctica at the Antarctic regions of Wilkes Land, including Commonwealth Bay. Over a period of 65 million years, beginning 160 million years ago, Australia's crust was stretched hundreds of miles by tectonics before it finally cleaved from Antarctica.

Testimony to the continental stretching and splitting includes Kangaroo Island off South Australia, made up of volcanic basalts, as well as thick layers of sediment along the coast of Victoria. Other signs are the similar geology of the Antarctic Commonwealth Bay and the Eyre Peninsula of South Australia, especially equivalent rocks, particularly gneisses (metamorphic rocks changed by heat and pressure) of identical age. The thin crust along Australia's southern flank in the Great Australian Bight also points to continental stretch.

Seismic activity and faulting

As it drifts north, the Australian plate is colliding with the Pacific and Eurasian plates, forming a subduction zone (an area where one continental plate descends beneath another). This zone, the convergence of the Australian continental plate with Papua New Guinea and the southern Indonesian islands, is studded with volcanos and prone to earthquakes. Yet Australia is unique in that it is not riven by subduction zones like other continents. There are no upwelling sections of the earth's mantle below Australia (the layer below the crust), nor are there intracontinental rift zones like the East African Rift System which threatens to eventually split Africa apart.

Overall geological structure

Furthermore, Australia and Antarctica are dissimilar to other land masses; their shapes are not rough tri-

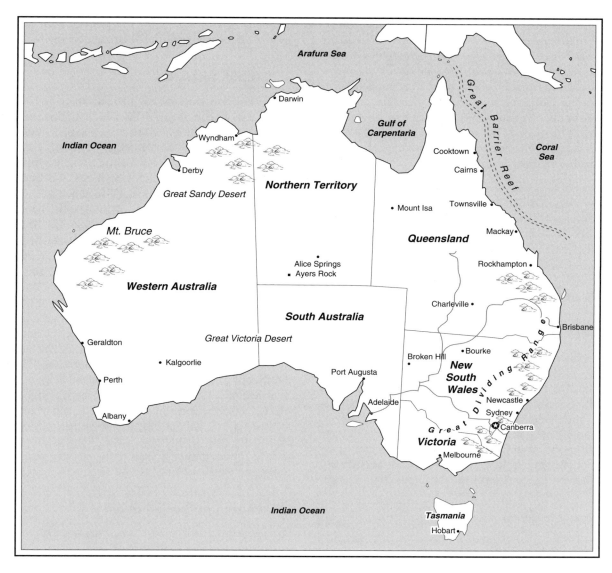

Australia.

angles with apexes pointing southward like South America, Africa, and the Indian subcontinent, Gondwanaland's other constituent parts. However, like its sister continents, Australia is composed of three structural units. These include in Western Australia a stable and ancient block of basement rock or craton as geologists call it, an ancient fold mountain belt (the Great Dividing Range along the east coast), and a flat platform–like area in–between composed of crystalline or folded rocks overlaid by flat–lying or only gently deformed sediments.

Millions of years of erosion have scoured Australia's surface features. One notable exception to Australia's flat topography is the Great Dividing Range

stretching 1,200 miles (1,931 km) along Australia's east coast. The Great Dividing Range was thrust up by geological folding like the Appalachian Mountains in the eastern U.S. The mountains are superimposed on larger geological structures including the Tasman and Newcastle geosynclines, troughs of older rocks upon which thick layers of sediment have been deposited. Those sediments in turn have been transformed by folding as well as magmatic and volcanic forces.

Great Dividing Range

Twice, during a 125 million year period beginning 400 million years ago the geosynclines were compressed, forming mountains and initiating volcanos. Volcanic activity recurred along the Great Dividing Range 20–25 million years ago during the Miocene epoch when early apes evolved as well as seals, dolphins, sunflowers, and bears. However, over millions of years the volcanic cones from this epoch have been stripped down by erosion. Still, volcanic activity persisted in South Australia until less than a million years ago. In Queensland, near Brisbane in the south and Cairns in the north of the state, the Great Dividing Range hugs the coast, creating beautiful Riviera–like vistas.

East of the Great Dividing Range, along Australia's narrow eastern coastal basin are its two largest cities, Sydney and Melbourne, as well as the capital, Canberra. The Dividing Range tends to trap moisture from easterly weather fronts originating in the Pacific Ocean. The Range is also coursed by rivers and streams. West of the Range the landscape becomes increasingly forbidding and the weather hot and dry.

The Outback

Although unrelated to geological forces, the world's largest coral formation, the Great Barrier Reef stretches for 1,245 miles (2,003 km) along Australia's northeast coast. Most of Australia is referred to as outback—monotonous desert and semi–desert flatness, broken only by scrub, salt lakes which are actually dry lakebeds most of the year, and a few spectacular sandstone proturburances like Ayers Rock (known by Australian aborigines as Uluru) and the Olgas (Kata Tjuta).

Geo–electrical current

In 1991, geologists discovered a subterranean electrical current in Australia, the longest in the world, which passes through more than 3,700 miles (6,000 km) across the Australian outback. The current is conducted by sedimentary rocks in a long horseshoe arc that skirts a huge mass of older igneous and metamorphic rock comprising most of the Northern Territory. It begins at Broome in Western Australia near the Timor Sea and then dips south across South Australia before curling northward through western Queensland where it terminates in the Gulf of Carpenteria.

A side branch runs from Birdsville in South Australia near the Flinders Ranges into Spencer Gulf near Adelaide. Geologists say the current is induced by the Earth's ever–changing magnetic field and that it runs along fracture zones in sedimentary basins which were formed as the Earth's ancient plates collided. Although the fracture zones contain alkaline fluids that are good conductors of electricity, the current is weak and cannot even light a lamp. Geologists say the current might pro-

vide clues to deposits of oil and gas and help explain the geological origins of the Australian continent.

Central Australia

Australian topography is also punctuated by starkly beautiful mountain ranges in the middle of the continent like the McDonnell and Musgrave Ranges, north and south respectively of Ayers Rock. Ayers Rock, the most sacred site in the country for Australia's aborigines, is a sandstone monolith of which two–thirds is believed to be below the surface. Ayers Rock is about 2.2 mi (3.5 km) long and 1,131 ft (339 m) high. Also in the center of the country, near Alice Springs, are the Henbury Meteorite craters, one of the largest clusters of meteorite craters in the world. The largest of these depressions, formed by the impact of an extraterrestrial rock, is about 591 ft (177 m) long and 49 ft (15 m) deep.

South Australian mountains

Other major mountain ranges rise in the eastern section of South Australia near Adelaide: the Flinders and Mount Lofty Ranges. These mountains arose from the Adelaidian Geosyncline (another large trough upon which sediments have been deposited) and were first uplifted over 500 million years ago during the Cambrian and Ordovician eras. Further thrusting occurred more recently, about 200 million years ago during the Mesozoic Era.

Western Australian shield

The continent's oldest rocks are in the Western Australian shield in southwest Australia. The basement (underlying) rocks in this area have not been folded since the Archean eon over three billion years ago, when the planet was still very young. The nucleus of this shield (called the Yilgarn craton) comprising 230,000 sq mi (59,570,000 ha), consists mostly of granite with belts of metamorphic rock like greenstones, rich in economic mineral deposits as well as intrusions of formerly molten rock.

The Yilgarn craton does not quite extend to the coast of Western Australia. It is bounded on the west by the Darling Fault near Perth. To the south and east the craton is set off by the Frazer Fault from somewhat younger rocks that were metamorphosed between 2.5 billion and two billion years ago. Both fault lines are 600 miles (960 km) long and are considered major structures on the continent.

Along the north coast of Western Australia near Port Hedland is another nucleus of ancient rocks, the

Pilbara Craton. The Pilbara craton is composed of granites over three billion years old as well as volcanic, greenstone, and sedimentary rocks. The Hammersley Range just south of the Pilbara Craton is estimated to contain billions of tons of iron ore reserves.

Basement rocks in central Australia

Other ancient rock masses in Australia are the Arunta Complex north of Alice Springs in the center of Australia which dates to 2.25 billion years ago. The MacArthur Basin, southwest of the Gulf of Carpenteria in the Northern Territory is a belt of sedimentary rocks that are between 1.8 billion and 1.5 billion years old.

The Musgrave block near the continent's center, a component of the Adelaidian geosyncline, was formed by the repeated intrusion of molten rocks between 1.4 billion to one billion years ago during the Proterozoic era when algae, jellyfish, and worms first arose. At the same time, the rocks that underlay the Adelaidian geosyncline were downwarped by geological pressures, with sediments building up through mid–Cambrian times (about 535 million years ago) when the area was inundated 400 mi (640 km) by the sea inland of the present coastline.

Adelaidian Geosyncline

The rocks of the Adelaidian geosyncline are as thick as 10 mi (16 km) with sediments that have been extensively folded and subjected to faulting during late Precambrian and Early Paleozoic times (about 600 million to 500 million years ago). Some of the rocks of the Adelaidian geosyncline, however, are unaltered. These strata show evidence of a major glacial period around 740 million years ago and contain some of the continent's richest, most diverse fossil records of soft–bodied animals.

This glaciation was one manifestation of global cooling that caused glacial episodes on other continents. Geologists say this Precambrian glacial episode was probably one of coldest, most extensive cooling periods in Earth history. They also consider the Adelaide geosyncline to be the precursor of another downwarp related to the most extensive folded belts on the continent, namely the Tasman geosyncline along Australia's east flank.

Geological time scale

Geologists determine the age of rock strata by examining the fossils they contain. Geologists and paleontologists examine rock strata and establish the age of

their surrounding sediments based on the types of fossilized specimens they find. For example, tribolites, tiny animals with shells, flourished in the Cambrian Period. So when geologists find sediments chock full of tribolite fossils they know they are dealing with Cambrian strata which they have determined to be 570 million to 500 million years old. Fossils are therefore geological signposts. Each geological period is characterized by specific types of fossilized organisms (plant and animal) the record for which has been formalized into the geologic time scale.

Such fossil testimony is spotty in eastern Australia except for a few areas including Broken Hill in western New South Wales, central Victoria and Tasmania. So while it is difficult to reconstruct an authoritative overall history of Australia in Cambrian times, some general conclusions can be withdrawn. One is that western Australia has a more stable geological history relatively speaking than the eastern section of the continent. There is much greater mobility and folding generally in the eastern half than in the west.

Geography of Victoria

Victoria is also characterized by a belt of old rocks upon which sediments have been deposited called the Lachlan geosyncline. Marine rocks were deposited in quiet water to great thicknesses in Victoria, forming black shales. Some of the sediment was built up by mud–laden currents from higher areas on the sea floor. These current–borne sediments have produced muddy sandstones called *graywackes*.

At the end of the Ordovician and early Silurian periods (about 425 million years ago) there was widespread folding of the Lachlan geosyncline called the Benambran orogeny. The folding was accompanied by granite intrusions and is thought to be responsible for the composition and texture of the rocks of the Snowy Mountains in Victoria, including Mt. Kosciusko, Australia's tallest peak at 7,310 ft (2,193 m).

The Melbourne trough in Victoria is full of Silurian graywackes and mudstones featuring graptolite fossils, cup or tube–shaped organisms with durable exoskeletons (shells) that congregated in colonies. Mid–Devonian strata (375 million years old) are abundant with armored fishes which are also found in central Australia, North America, Eurasia, and Antarctica. The sandstones of the Grampian Mountains in western Victoria were formed from the erosion of uplifted areas which were deposited in lakes and by rivers during the late Devonian, early Carboniferous periods (about 350 million years ago).

Mountain–building in eastern Australia

In eastern Australia, Paleozoic Era volcanic activity built up much of the rock strata. Mountain glaciation during the late Carboniferous period when insects, amphibians, and early reptiles first evolved, also transformed the landscape. Mountain building in eastern Australia culminated during the middle and later Permian Period (about 250 million years ago) when a huge mass of magma (underground molten rock) was emplaced in older rocks in the New England area of northeastern New South Wales. This huge mass or batholith, caused extensive folding to the west and ended the sedimentation phase of the Tasman geosyncline. It was also the last major episode of orogeny (mountain building) on the continent.

Glaciers and ocean inundations

In parts of Western Australia, particularly the Carnarvon Basin at the mouth of the Gascoyne River, glacial sediments are as thick as three miles. Western Australia, particularly along the coast, has been inundated repeatedly by the sea and has been described by geologists as a mobile shelf area. This is reflected in the alternating strata of deposited marine and non–marine layers.

Sedimentary features of Australia

In the center of Australia is a large sedimentary basin or depression spanning 450 mi (720 km) from east to west and 160 mi (256 km) north to south at its widest point. Sedimentary rocks of all varieties can be found in the basin rocks which erosion shaped into spectacular scenery including Ayres Rock and Mt. Olga. These deposits are mostly of pre–Cambrian age (over 570 million years old), while sediments along the present–day coastline including those in the Eucla Basin off the Great Australian Bight are less than 70 million years old. North of the Eucla Basin is the Nullarbor (meaning treeless) Plain which contains many unexplored limestone caves.

Dominating interior southern Queensland is the Great Artesian Basin which features non–marine sands built up during the Jurassic period (190 million to 130 million years ago), sands which contain much of the basin's Artesian water. Thousands of holes have been bored in the Great Artesian Basin to extract the water resources underneath but the salt content of water from the Basin is relatively high and the water supplies have been used for livestock only.

The Sydney Basin formed over the folded rocks of the Tasman geosyncline and is also considered to be an extension of the Great Artesian Basin. Composed of sediments from the Permian and Triassic periods (290 million to 190 million years old) it extends south and eastward along the continental shelf. The sandstone cliffs around Sydney Harbor, often exploited for building stones, date from Triassic sediments.

Geology of Tasmania

During the early to mid–Jurassic period, there was an intrusion of 2,000 cubic miles of dark, layered volcanic rocks in Tasmania, similar to the magmatic formations of the Karroo region in South Africa and the Palisades in New York. Tasmania separated from mainland Australia only 10,000 years ago, when sea levels rose after the thawing of the last ice age.

Mountain–building and glaciation in Victoria

The Glass House Mountains in southeastern Queensland and the Warbungle Mountains in northern New South Wales were formed by volcanism in recent times, during the Miocene Epoch, around 20 million years ago. Gold bearing deep leads can be found in basaltic lava flows along ancient valleys. The Flinders ranges in South Australia were uplifted in the modern geological era, the Cenozoic. About the same time the sea retreated from the Murray Basin in South Australia. During the Pleistocene (less than two million years ago), a 400 sq mi (103,600 ha) area around Mount Kosciusko was covered with glaciers.

Climate

The climatological record of Australia shows a pronounced temperature drop on the continent in the late Miocene and early Pliocene epochs between 26 and five million years ago when monkeys and early apes first evolved and saber toothed cats prowled the earth. On the Eyre Peninsula in South Australia and in Gippsland in Victoria eucalypt and acacia trees supplanted the previously dominant beech trees which had thrived in the warmer climate of the Miocene Era.

Natural resources

Of course geology is inextricably intertwined with natural resources and mineral exploitation. Minerals in Australia have had a tremendous impact on the country's human history and patterns of settlement. Alluvial gold (gold sediments deposited by rivers and streams) spurred several gold fevers and set the stage for Australia's present demographic patterns. During the post–World War II period there has been almost a continuous run of mineral discoveries, including gold, bauxite, iron, and manganese reserves as well as opals, sapphires, and other precious stones.

It is estimated that Australia has 24 billion tons (22 billion tonnes) of coal reserves, over one–quarter of which (7 billion tons/6 billion tonnes) is anthracite or black coal deposited in Permian sediments in the Sydney Basin of New South Wales and in Queensland. Brown coal suitable for electricity production in found in Victoria. Australia meets its domestic coal consumption needs with its own reserves and exports the surplus.

Natural gas fields are liberally distributed throughout the country and now supply most of Australia's domestic needs. There are commercial gas fields in every state and pipelines connecting those fields to major cities. Within three years, Australian natural gas production leapt almost 14–fold from 8.6 billion cu ft (258 million cu m) in 1969, the first year of production, to 110 billion cu ft (3.3 billion cu m) in 1972. All in all, Australia has trillions of tons of estimated natural gas reserves trapped in sedimentary strata distributed around the continent.

Australia supplies much of its oil consumption needs domestically. The first Australian oil discoveries were in southern Queensland near Moonie. Australian oil production now amounts to about 25 million barrels per year and includes pumping from oil fields off northwestern Australia near Barrow Island, Mereenie in the southern Northern Territory, and fields in the Bass Strait. The Barrow Island, Mereenie, and Bass Strait fields are also sites of natural gas production.

Australia has rich deposits of uranium ore, which is refined for use for fuel for the nuclear power industry. Western Queensland, near Mount Isa and Cloncurry contains three billion tons (2.7 billion tonnes) of uranium ore reserves. There are also uranium deposits in Arnhem Land in far northern Australia, as well as in Queensland and Victoria.

Most of Australia's substantial iron ore reserves are in Western Australia in and around the Hammersley Range. Australia has billions of tons of iron ore reserves, exporting magnetite iron from mines in Tasmania to Japan while still extracting ore from older mines on the Eyre Peninsula of South Australia and in the Koolyanobbing Range of southern Western Australia.

The Western Australian shield is rich in nickel deposits which were first discovered at Kambalda near Kalgoorlie in south Western Australia in 1964. Other nickel deposits have been found in old gold mine areas

KEY TERMS

Basalt—Dark layered, igneous rock which is often volcanic.

Batholith—Largescale geological emplacement of magma deep underground that often leads to the formation of mountains.

Craton—Structurally stable, undeformed regions of the Earth's crust usually dating to the Archean Era (2.5 billion or more years ago).

Geosyncline—Large basin or trough in the Earth's crust in which a thick succession of sedimentary and volcanic rocks have accumulated. Often the basis for orogeny or mountain building.

Gondwanaland—The ancient supercontinent comprised of present–day Africa, South America, Australia, Antarctica, and India.

Orogeny—The process of mountain formation, thrusting, folding, and faulting of the outer layers of the Earth's crust as well as metamorphic and plutonic (magma emplacements) in the middle and inner crustal layers.

Seismic—Relating to earthquakes or movements of the Earth's crust along faults.

Subduction zone—Site of the collision of continental plates where one plate is slipping underneath another.

in Western Australia. Small quantities of platinum and palladium have been extracted side–by–side with nickel reserves.

Australia is also extremely rich in lead and zinc reserves, the principal sources for which are Mt. Isa and Mt. Morgan in Queensland. The Northern Territory also has lead and zinc mines as well as vast reserves of bauxite (aluminum ore), namely at Weipa on the Gulf of Carpenteria and at Gove in Arnhem Land.

Gold production in Australia, which was substantial earlier in the century, has declined from a peak production of four million fine ounces in 1904 to several hundred thousand fine ounces nowadays. Most gold is extracted from the Kalgoorlie–Norseman area of Western Australia. The continent is also well–known for its precious stones, particularly white and black opals from South Australia and western New South Wales. There are sapphires and topaz in Queensland and in the New England District of northeastern New South Wales.

Because of its aridity, Australia suffers from leached, sandy, and salty soils. The continent's largely arid land and marginal water resources represent challenges for conservation and prudent environmental management. The challenge is to maximize the use of these resources for human beings while preserving ecosystems for animal and plant life.

Further Reading:

Drummond, Barry J., ed. *The Australian Lithosphere*. 1991.
The Geology of South Australia, South Australia: State Print, 1993.
"Underground Current Electrifies Australia," *New Scientist*, (March 30, 1991): 10.

Robert Cohen

Australian native cat see **Marsupial cats**

Autism

Autism is a profound mental disorder marked by an inability to communicate and interact with others. The condition's characteristics include language abnormalities, restricted and repetitive interests, and the appearance of these characteristics in early childhood. The disorder begins in infancy, but typically is not diagnosed until the ages two to five. Although individuals with autism are more likely to be mentally retarded than other individuals some people with the disorder have a high intelligence level. The cause of autism is unknown although it is probably biological in origin.

A singular world view

Children with autism were described as early as 1908 by Heller, a Viennese educator. Autism was not named and identified as a distinct condition until 1943. That year American psychiatrist Leo Kanner wrote about what he called "infantile autism." Kanner derived the term autism from the Latin word *aut*, meaning self. Kanner described a group of children who looked normal but showed limited communication skills and were drawn to repetitive behavior. Researchers have since discovered that the disorder is not common, occurring in two to five of every 10,000 births. The disorder is more common in males than in females.

As many as two–thirds of children with autistic symptoms are mentally deficient. But individuals with autism can be highly intelligent. Some achieve great levels of success at school and at work. The term autism is more a description of a range of behavioral traits than a term to describe a single type of person with a single level of potential.

Autistic individuals generally share a defect in "the theory of mind." This term is used to describe the way normal individuals develop a sense of what others are thinking and feeling. This sense is usually developed by about age four. Autistic individuals typically are limited in their ability to communicate nonverbally and verbally. About half of all autistic people never learn to speak. They are likely to fail in developing social relationships with peers, have limited ability to initiate conversation if they do learn how to talk, and show a need for routines and rituals.

The range of ability and intelligence among autistic individuals is great. Some individuals are profoundly withdrawn. These aloof individuals generally do not greet parents when they enter the house or seek comfort when in pain. Others can conduct a conversation but may be obsessed with strange or unusual behaviors, such as a fascination with calendars or timetables. Still others use their ability to focus on particular bodies of fact to master a job or a profession. Temple Grandin is a Ph.D. and a successful animal behavior expert who is autistic and an international expert in her field.

Certain autistic people have areas of expertise in which they are superior to normal individuals. These skills are called savant abilities and have been well documented in music, drawing, and areas where calculation is involved. The vibrant drawings of buildings by autistic British artist Stephen Wiltshire have been published to great acclaim.

Abundance of theories

The precise cause of autism is not known and many theories have emerged concerning its origin. Initially autism was believed to be caused by destructive parents. Kanner observed in 1943 that there are few "really warmhearted fathers and mothers" among parents of autistic children (Groden 1988). Other experts suggested that parents of autistic children are more likely to be cold and unsupportive of their children than parents of normal children. In the 1950s and 1960s it was still generally believed that this parental behavior caused autism. Children were therefore advised to have psychotherapy for autism. This therapy was generally unsuccessful. Some experts suggested that autistic children be removed from their parents.

In the mid–1960s experts began to challenge the assumption that parents cause autism. Evidence emerged that while autistic children look normal they have particular physical abnormalities. These include a higher–than–normal likelihood of epilepsy—it occurs in as many as 30% of children with autism. Researchers also looked at the way parents interacted with autistic children. Their findings showed that parents of autistic children are equally as skilled as parents of normal children on average.

The general belief today is that autism is a biological disorder and has nothing to do with parenting skill. Clues to what causes autism include a wealth of abnormalities documented to occur in higher percentages among autistic people than normal people. These include certain genetic conditions, epilepsy, mental disabilities, and some birth defects.

Genetics appears to play a role in autism but its role is not completely understood. Brothers or sisters of individuals with autism are slightly more likely than others to be autistic. Approximately 2%–3% of siblings of autistic people have the disorder. The twin of an autistic individual is also more likely to have autism.

The occurrence of fragile X syndrome, a genetic disorder, in about 10% of autistic people has presented researchers with a documented cause of the disorder. Fragile X victims have a gap on their X chromosome. The condition is generally linked to mental disabilities and a characteristic facial appearance (a high forehead and long ears) among other traits. Brothers or sisters of individuals with fragile X syndrome are nearly 50% more likely to be autistic than are brothers and sisters of normal children. It is not clear what causes the syndrome.

Another genetic trait more common among autistic individuals than others is neurofibromatosis, a genetic condition which affects the skin and the nerves and sometimes causes brain damage. Researchers also have noted that mothers of autistic children are more likely to receive medication during pregnancy. They have also found that autistic children are more likely to have been born with meconium (the first stool of the infant) in the amniotic fluid during labor. However these events also commonly occur among normal children. Other possible causes of autism include rubella infection in early pregnancy, herpes encephalitis (which can cause inflammation of the brain), and cytomegalovirus infection.

Whatever the cause of the damage, various abnormalities in the autistic brain have been documented. These include variations in the frontal lobes of the brain which focus on control and planning, and in the limbic system. The limbic system is a group of structures in the brain which are linked to emotion, behavior, smell, and other functions. Autistic individuals may suffer from a limited development of the limbic system. This would explain some of the difficulties faced by autistic individuals in processing information.

Studies using MRI (magnetic resonance imaging) scanners have found abnormalities in the cerebellum. Some researchers suggest that the section where abnormalities have been documented is the part of the brain concerned with attention. Other tests using electroencephalograms have found that autistic children show abnormalities in way the brain processes sound.

Teaching and learning

As theories about the cause of autism have changed so have approaches to teaching autistic individuals. Individuals with autism were once considered unteachable and were often institutionalized. Experts currently recommend early education for autistic individuals using approaches geared specifically for them. Those who cannot speak may learn sign language. Often some form of behavioral modification is suggested including offering positive reinforcement for good behavior.

Given the need for organization and repetitive behavior among autistic people, many experts suggest a structured environment with a clearly defined schedule. Some experts advocate special schools for autistic children while others recommend including them in a general school program with appropriate help.

Controversy exists concerning the best way to teach and communicate with autistic children who do not speak. In the 1980s some parents and educators claimed great success using so–called facilitated communication. This technique involves the use of a keyboard or letter board and a facilitator to help the autistic individual use the device. Some have said the device allows autistic individuals to break through the barriers of communication. Others have criticized facilitated communication as a contrived and false method of communication. The technique remains controversial.

With no cure and no prenatal test for autism, there is no prospect of eliminating this condition in the near future. Continued educational research concerning the best way to teach autistic children and continued scientific research concerning possible treatments for autism are the greatest hope for dealing with the effects of this profound developmental problem.

See also Savant.

Further Reading:
Baron–Cohen, Simon, and Patrick Bolton. *Autism: The Facts*. Oxford: Oxford University Press, 1993.

Bauman, Margaret L., and Thomas L. Kemper. *The Neurobiology of Autism.* Baltimore: Johns Hopkins University Press, 1994.

Brill, Marlene Targ. *Keys to Parenting the Child With Autism.* Hauppauge, NY: Barron's, 1994.

Cohen, Donald J., and Anne M. Donnellan. *Handbook of Autism and Pervasive Developmental Disorders.* Silver Spring, MD: V. H. Winston and Sons, 1987.

Eberlin, Michael, et al. "Facilitated Communication: A Failure to Replicate the Phenomenon." *Journal of Autism and Communication Disorders* 23 (1993): 507–528.

Groden, Gerald, and M. Grace Baron. *Autism—Strategies for Change.* New York: Gardner Press, 1988.

Harrison's Principles of Internal Medicine, edited by Kurt J. Isselbacher, et al. 13th ed. New York: McGraw–Hill, 1994.

Hart, Charles A. *A Parent's Guide to Autism.* New York: Pocket Books, 1993.

Saks, Oliver. *An Anthropologist on Mars.* New York: Knopf, 1995.

Patricia Braus

Autoimmune disease

The immune system is the body's defense system against infection from invading organisms. Autoimmune disease occurs when the immune system loses its ability to recognize the differences between self and nonself tissues, with the result that it attacks the body's own tissues and organs. The inability to make this critical distinction may lead to the partial or complete impairment of vital organs or upsets in body chemistry, culminating in a number of different diseases. Many of these diseases become chronic illnesses and may lead to death.

In a healthy individual, the immune system responds only to the presence of foreign substances, or antigens. While antigens are most commonly pathogenic bacteria and viruses, harmful organic molecules from environmental and even internal sources can also act as antigens. The presence of antigens stimulates the immune system and its array of defenses. The army of the immune system is composed of the white blood cells (leukocytes). These cells are found in the lymph nodes, spleen, and thymus. They travel to other parts of the body through the blood stream. In their battle against antigens, the white blood cells form special cells. The B cells produce antibodies which recognize and destroy an antigen. T cells help the B cells to produce antibodies, while suppressor T cells signal the body to stop the production of antibodies. Killer T cells destroy virus–infected cells and other T cells produce lymphokines, pain–causing chemicals that turn on the immune system.

Autoimmune diseases are characterized by the presence of antibodies and T cells that attack different parts of the body. When they perform in this manner, they are called autoantibodies and autoreactive T cells. The infection by viruses and bacteria in a healthy person eventually leads to the production of autoantibodies. There are, however, controls in the immune system that eliminate excess amounts of autoantibodies or other autoreactive elements created in the normal operation of the immune system throughout a person's life. When there is an environmental agent that disrupts the control mechanism for limiting autoreactive agents in the body or a genetic deficiency that impairs the autoantibody elimination mechanism, the result will be an autoimmune disease.

Although an autoimmune response is suspected as the underlying disease mechanism for a wide variety of disorders, the various causes of autoimmunity are not well understood. Among the more common causes are viral infections such as the HIV virus that causes AIDS and creates an autoimmune response that undermines the production of blood platelets (blood clotting agents) and T cells. Environmentally hazardous materials, such as toxic or carcinogenic chemicals can also trigger an autoimmune response. Some forms of cancers may have a similar effect.

The presence of autoantibodies can be predictors for the development of an autoimmune disease. For example, studies have shown that the onset of diabetes can be foreshadowed by the presence of anti–islet cells or anti–insulin antibodies.

Types

There are two types of diseases caused by autoimmunity: nonorgan–specific and organ–specific autoimmune disorder. In nonorgan–specific autoimmune disease, many organs undergo attack, thus creating simultaneous problems for different systems in the body, such as the nervous, bone and joint, and renal systems.

Of the more than 100 kinds of arthritis, many originate from nonorgan–specific autoimmunity. These include rheumatoid arthritis, systemic lupus erythematosus, scleroderma, ankylosing spondylitis, and Sjögren's syndrome. Rheumatic fever and rare muscle and skin diseases called polymyositis and dermomyositis respectively are other nonorgan–specific autoimmune diseases.

Organ–specific autoimmune diseases may occur in practically every organ. Insulin–dependent diabetes, thyroid diseases, such as Grave's disease and Hashimoto's thyroiditis, and Addison's disease are examples of organ–specific autoimmune disease. There are also some kidney and lung diseases that fall into this category.

The presence of autoantibodies and autoreactive T cells in such neurological diseases as multiple sclerosis and myasthenia gravis suggests that they too are autoimmune diseases. Uveitis (an eye disease), psoriasis (a skin disease), some forms of liver disease (such as hepatitis and cirrhosis), digestive tract disease (such as inflammatory bowel disease), and reproductive system disorders that contribute to male and female infertility all may be further examples of disease caused by the autoimmune response.

Another category of autoimmune diseases is allergic reactions: autoimmune responses to harmless substances that come into the body from the environment. The antibody responsible for allergic reactions is immunoglobulin E (IgE), which acts by attaching to cells in the skin called mast and basophil cells. Environmental substances such as certain pollens, foods, chemicals, and drugs, cause the IgE antibody to release histamines from the mast cells located in the nose, respiratory tract, skin, and other parts of the body. The histamines then cause the nasal inflammation (swollen tissues, runny nose, sneezing) and the other discomforts of hay fever or other types of allergic responses, such as hives and asthma. In rare cases, anaphylactic shock, a life–threatening condition brought on by an allergy to a drug or insect bite, can also be traced to an autoimmune response.

A theory that attempts to explain the role of IgE in allergies suggests the possibility of its usefulness to early man in preparing the immune system to fight off parasites from food. The theory maintains that, though this function may have been lost with the changes in human diet, the antibody continues to respond to harmless environmental substances as if they were harmful antigens when they are not.

Rheumatoid arthritis

Rheumatoid arthritis is one of the most crippling forms of arthritis. There are about 2.5 million Americans who have this disease. It is believed to be a disorder of the immune system caused by a virus. Compared to osteoarthritis, the pain in the joints is more intense and is also attended by swelling.

Unlike osteoarthritis, which is a degenerative disease of the cartilage in the major bone joints due to overuse and aging, rheumatoid arthritis is seen in younger people. Three times as many women are subject to this disorder than men. Osteoarthritis develops slowly over a long period of time, while rheumatoid arthritis can occur within a short period of time—weeks or months. In osteoarthritis, the joints on one side of the body only tend to be affected, but with rheumatoid arthritis the same joint on both sides of the body is affected.

Inflammation (redness, warmth, swelling) of the joint is not a usual symptom of osteoarthritis, but it is of rheumatoid arthritis. Inflammation occurs within the linings of the bone joints (synovial membranes). The whole joint then becomes painful. It becomes thick, red, and swollen from the inflammation. Only the weight–bearing joints are affected by osteoarthritis—elbows and shoulders are seldom affected. In rheumatoid arthritis, shoulders and elbows and many other joints are affected.

Rheumatoid arthritis poses a threat to the vital organs of the body, such as the heart, lungs, and visual centers. Osteoarthritis is not associated with an overall sense of ill–health, but rheumatoid arthritis will cause a loss of weight, fever, and a condition of general health impairment. There may also be bone nodule formation on different parts of the body with rheumatoid arthritis.

Inflammation, fever, swelling, aches and pains—the major symptoms of rheumatoid arthritis are all signs that the immune system is at work trying to ward off antigens. In rheumatoid arthritis it appears that the immune system is turning against the body. There is no apparent foreign invader, but the condition could be due to the presence of an undetected virus or antigen that the immune system is unsuccessfully trying to fight.

Treatment of arthritis

The first line of drug treatment for any type of arthritis is nonsteroidal anti–inflammatory medicines, including aspirin and medicines that are closely related to aspirin. Some NSAIDs (pronounced en seds) are sold over the counter, but most containing higher dosages are sold only by prescription and have to be monitored carefully to avoid adverse side effects. A second line of drug treatment is provided by corticosteroids, which are also used to reduce inflammation. These drugs are similar to cortisone, which is produced in the adrenal cortex. Corticosteroids are used for both osteoarthritis and rheumatoid arthritis. These medicines are injected into a specific site, such as a finger joint or the knee, for quick relief from pain and inflammation.

In addition to being anti–inflammatories, corticosteroids are also immunosuppressants. A variety of immunosuppressants used for rheumatoid arthritis specifically target the autoimmune response and try to slow the disease down or force it into remission. Immunosuppressants or cytotoxics cut down the rate of cell division throughout the body. The immune system may then turn out fewer white blood cells. These medicines usually take weeks or months to show an effect, and they may have life–threatening side effects in that they sometimes suppress the growth of normal cells. They must be carefully administered and monitored to avoid any serious impairment of the body's natural defense system. As a second line of drug treatment their purpose is not only to relieve symptoms, as in the case of the NSAIDs, but to reverse or slow down the action of the disease.

Other nonorgan–specific diseases

Lupus erythematosus attacks the body's connective tissues and causes inflammation. Discoid lupus is the more common form and appears in exposed areas of the skin. Systemic lupus is more serious, affecting the joints and kidneys. There is no cure for it, but many people with the disease survive for more than 10 years after the initial diagnosis is made.

Sjögren's syndrome tends to occur with rheumatoid arthritis and lupus. The exact cause of the syndrome is not known. The glands that lubricate the eyes, mouth, and vagina are impaired by the autoimmune disorder, leading to dryness, itching, and burning sensations. Ninety percent of the people who have the syndrome are postmenopausal women.

Scleroderma is a rare condition found twice as often in women, most commonly between the ages of 40–60. There are a number of different symptoms that vary in intensity. Raynaud's phenomenon, the most common symptom, is characterized by a white, red, and blue discoloration of the hands. There is no cure for this disease, but it is treated like arthritis. For more advanced cases that show high blood pressure or renal failure, antihypertensive drugs are given and dialysis may be required.

Ankylosing spondylitis is an inflammatory disease affecting the joints between the spine and pelvis. It affects less than 1% of the population and is more common in men than women. The disease runs in families and occurs between the ages of 20–40. The most prominent symptom is pain and stiffness in the back and chest. Though there is no cure for it, the condition improves with age and treatment, usually leaving only a minor deformity of the spine.

Rheumatic fever is believed to be an autoimmune disorder, even though it always occurs after a throat infection from a particular kind of bacteria. In the developed countries, rheumatic fever is now rare, though it is on the increase in some parts of the United States. It is common in poorer countries throughout the world. Children between the ages of five and 15 are the most at risk. The joint inflammation characteristic of rheumatic fever does not have crippling effects. Often there is permanent damage to the heart and sometimes to the nervous system.

Organ–specific diseases

Insulin–dependent diabetes is a common organ–specific autoimmune disease. Also referred to as type I diabetes, it appears in people below the age of 35, most often between the ages of 10–16. The insulin secreting cells of the pancreas are destroyed, and without regular injections of insulin coma and death ensue. It is believed that it is an autoimmune disorder that takes place after a viral infection.

Two thyroid diseases that may be organ–specific autoimmune disorders are Grave's disease and Hashimoto's thyroiditis. In Grave's disease, the thyroid, produces an excess of thyroxin, creating a condition known as hyperthyroidism. In Hashimoto's thyroiditis, the lymph glands begin to grow over the thyroid, thus inhibiting the production of thyroxin. That leads to a condition known as hypothyroidism. Both conditions are treatable by either curtailing the production of thyroid hormone or administering more of the hormone through daily oral doses.

Addison's disease is a disorder of the adrenal glands usually brought on by an autoimmune disorder. The adrenal cortex fails to produce sufficient amounts of two adrenal hormones, hydrocortisone and aldosterone. Symptoms include fatigue, weakness, abdominal pain, and weight loss. Treatment includes replacing the deficient hormones with corticosteroid drugs.

Neurological diseases

Multiple sclerosis is a progressive disease that is the most common nerve disease in young adults. It leads to paralysis, muscle spasms, urinary tract infections, constipation, impotence, and sharp mood swings from euphoria to depression. Multiple sclerosis is a disease of the central nervous system, in which the protective nerve fibers of the brain and spinal cord are destroyed over an extended period of time. The severity of the disease varies from case to case.The cause is unknown, though a genetic factor may be present. It occurs most frequently in temperate climates like that of the United States and Europe rather than the tropics. Researchers speculate that the individual picks it up in the first years of life from continued residency in an area that may have an infecting virus.

Myasthenia gravis is a disorder of the muscles of the eyes, face, throat, and limbs. They become weak and tire easily. It is a rare disease and affects more women than men. In mild cases, drug treatment can help deal with the condition, whereas in severe cases paralysis and arrested breathing can ensue, leading to death.

See also AIDS; Antibody and antigen; Arthritis; Diabetes mellitus; Immune system.

Further Reading:

Barrett, James T. *Textbook of Immunology.* St. Louis: Mosby, 1988.

Friedlander, Mark P. and Terry M. Phillips. *Winning the War Within.* Emmaus, Pennsylvania: Rodale Press, 1986.

Sell, Stewart. *Basic Immunology.* New York: Elsevier, 1987.

Weiner, Michael A. *Maximum Immunity.* Boston: Houghton Mifflin, 1986.

Jordan P. Richman

Automation

Delmar S. Harder, a plant manager for General Motors, is credited with first having used the term in 1935.

History

Ideas for ways of automating tasks have been in existence since the time of the ancient Greeks. The Greek inventor Hero (fl. about 50 A.D.), for example, is credited with having developed an automated system that would open a temple door when a priest lit a fire on the temple altar.

The real impetus for the development of automation came, however, during the Industrial Revolution of the early eighteenth century. Many of the steam–powered devices built by James Watt, Richard Trevithick, Richard Arkwright, Thomas Savery, Thomas Newcomen, and their contemporaries were simple examples of machines capable of taking over the work of humans.

One of the most elaborate examples of automated machinery developed during this period was the drawloom designed by the French inventor Basile Bouchon in 1725. The instructions for the operation of the Bouchon loom were recorded on sheets of paper in the form of holes. The needles that carried thread through the loom to make cloth were guided by the presence or absence of those holes. The manual process of weaving a pattern into a piece of cloth through the work of an individual was transformed by the Bouchon process into an operation that could be performed mindlessly by merely stepping on a pedal.

Types of automation

Automated machines can be subdivided into two large categories—open–loop and closed-loop machines—which can then be subdivided into even smaller categories. Open–loop machines are devices that, once started, go through a cycle and then stop. A common example is the automatic dishwashing machine. Once dishes are loaded into the machine and a button pushed, the machine goes through a predetermined cycle of operations: pre–rinse, wash, rinse, and dry, for example. A human operator may have choices as to which sequence the machine should follow—heavy wash, light wash, warm and hold, and so on—but each of these operations is alike in that the machine simply does the task and then stops.

Many of the most familiar appliances in homes today operate on this basis. A microwave oven, a coffee–maker, and a CD player are examples. Larger, more complex industrial operations also use open–cycle operations. For example, in the production of a car, a single machine may be programmed to place a side panel in place on the car and then weld it in a dozen or more locations. Each of the steps involved in this process—from placing the door properly to each of the different welds—takes place according to instructions programmed into the machine.

Closed–loop machines

Closed–loop machines are devices that are capable of responding to new instructions at some point in their operation. The instructions may come from the operation being performed itself or from a human operator. The ability of a machine to change its operation based on new information is known as feedback.

One example of a closed–loop operation is the machine used in the manufacture of paper. Paper is formed when a suspension of pulpy fibers in water is emptied onto a conveyer belt whose surface is a sieve. Water drains out of the suspension, leaving the pulp on the belt. As the pulp dries, paper is formed. The rate at which the pulpy suspension is added to the conveyer belt can be automatically controlled by a machine.

A sensing device at the end of the conveyer belt is capable of measuring the thickness of the paper and reporting back to the pouring machine on the condition of the product. If the paper becomes too thick, the sensor can tell the pouring machine to slow the rate at which pulpy suspension is added to the belt. If the paper becomes too thin, the sensor can tell the machine to increase the rate at which the raw material is added to the conveyer belt.

Many types of closed–loop machines exist, such as the paper–making machine described here. Some contain sensors, but are unable to make necessary adjustments on their own. Instead, sensor readings are sent to human operators who monitor the machine's operation and input any changes it may need to make in its functioning. Other closed–loop machines contain feedback mechanisms, like the paper–making machine described above. The results of the operation determine what changes, if any, the machine has to make. Still other closed–loop machines have feedforward mechanisms. That is, the first step they perform is to examine the raw materials that come to them and then decide what operations to perform. Letter–sorting machines are of this type. The first step such a machine takes in sorting letters is to read the zip code on the address and then send the letter to the appropriate sub–system.

The role of computers in automation

Since the 1960s, the nature of automation has undergone dramatic changes as a result of the availability of computers. For many years, automated machines were limited by the amount of feedback data they could collect and interpret. Thus, their operation was limited to a relatively small number of alternatives. When an automated machine is placed under the control of a computer, however, that disadvantage disappears. The computer can analyze a vast number of sensory inputs from a system and decide which of many responses it should make.

Artificial intelligence

The availability of computers has also made possible a revolution in the most advanced of all forms of automation, operations that are designed to replicate human thought processes. An automated machine can be said to be "thinking" if the term is used for only the simplest of mental processes: "Should I do A or B," for example. The enormous capability of a computer, however, makes it possible for a machine to analyze many more options, compare options with each other, consider possible outcomes for various options, and perform basic reasoning and problem–solving steps not contained within the machine's programmed memory. At this point, the automated machine can be said to be approaching the types of mental functions normally associated with human beings, that is, to have artificial intelligence.

The human impact of automation

The impact of automation on individuals and societies has been profound. On one level, many otherwise unpleasant and/or time–consuming tasks are now being performed by machines: dishwashing being one of the obvious examples. The transformation of the communications industry is another example of the way in which automation has made life better for the average person. Today, millions of telephone calls that would once have had to go through human operators are now handled by automatic switching machines.

However, automation has also resulted in drastic dislocations in employment patterns. When one machine can do the work of 10 workers, most or all of those people will be out of a job. In many cases, those workers will have to be retrained—often learning newer and higher skills—before they can be re–employed.

Automation has also had some positive impact on employment patterns, however. As one example, designers in many fields are now able to draw on computerized programs that will help them design and test new concepts in many fields. Automated systems also make it much easier for people to carry out the work they do in other than traditional places. They may be able to stay home, for example, and do their jobs by communicating with other individuals and machines by means of highly automated communications systems.

See also Artificial intelligence; Robotics.

Further Reading:

"Automatic Control in Industry." *The Illustrated Science and Invention Encyclopedia.* Westport, CT: H. S. Stuttman, Inc., Publishers, 1982, volume 2, pp. 192–96.

Decelle, Linda S., "Automation." *McGraw–Hill Encyclopedia of Science & Technology*, 7th edition. New York: McGraw–Hill Book Company, 1992, volume 1, pp. 300–04

Dunlop, John T. *Automation and Technological Change.* Englewood Cliffs, NJ: Prentice–Hall, 1962.

O'Brien, Robert, and the Editors of *Life* magazine. *Machines.* New York: Time Incorporated, 1964.

David E. Newton

Automobile

No invention in modern times has had as much an impact on human life as the invention of the automobile. The "auto"—or self–propelled vehicle—has become an important influence on the history, economy, and social life of much of the world. In fact, the rapid growth of the United States in the past century can be directly related to the automobile.

The modern automobile combines such features as fuel efficiency, speed, and relative safety to offer the mobility and flexibility of use demanded by an enormous variety of lifestyles and industries. Automobiles reach into every aspect of society, from the design of our cities, to police, ambulance, fire, and utility services, to such personal uses as vacation travel, dining, and shopping. Mass production techniques, first developed for the automobile, have been adapted for use in nearly every industry, providing for the fast, efficient, and inexpensive production of products. Trucks, especially the tractor–trailer, have become the major form of transporting goods across the country, allowing, for example, produce to be quickly transported to markets while still fresh. The use of automotive technology on the farm has enabled the farmer to increase the quantity, quality, and variety of our foods. Meanwhile, dozens of industries depend, directly or indirectly, on the automobile. These industries include producers of steel and other metals, plastics, rubber, glass, fabrics, petroleum products, and electronic components.

Structure of the automobile

Hundreds of individual parts make up the essential components of the modern automobile. Much like the human body, these parts are arranged into several systems, each with a different function. For example, the human circulatory system is comprised of the heart, veins, arteries, capillaries, and blood. In the automobile, the engine—the "heart" of the automobile—is comprised of pistons, cylinders, fuel, and other components. Each system is necessary for making the automobile run, keeping it safe, and reducing noise and pollution.

Henry Ford and his first automobile.

The major systems of an automobile are the engine, fuel system, transmission, electrical system, cooling and lubrication system, and the chassis, which includes the suspension system, braking system, wheels and tires, and the body. These systems will be found in every form of motor vehicle and are designed to interact with and support each other.

Design factors

When an automobile is designed, the arrangement, choice, and type of components depend on various factors. The use of the automobile is one factor. Some cars are required only for local driving. These cars may be capable of achieving good fuel economy on short trips, but they may be less comfortable to drive at high speeds. A sports car, built for speed, will have enhanced steering and handling abilities, but requires a stronger engine, more fuel, and a more sophisticated suspension system. Yet, an automobile must also be flexible enough to perform in every situation and use.

Other factors in the design of automobiles include the requirements for pollution control components that have been placed on the modern automobile. While these components are great for the environment, they are not always the best for the automobile's performance. Safety features are also a factor in the automobile's design, affecting everything from the braking and steering systems to the materials used to construct the body. The design of the body must incorporate standards of safety, size and weight, aerodynamics or ways to reduce the friction of airflow, and appearance.

The choice for front–wheel drive allows for a smaller, more fuel–efficient car. But the arrangement of the engine, and its relationship to other automobile systems will be different from a rear–wheel–driven car. Independent suspension for all four wheels improves the automobile's handling, safety, and comfort, but requires a more complex arrangement. The use of computer technology, the most recently added system to the automobile, requires changes in many of the car's other systems. Lastly, cost is an important factor in the design of a car. Many features useful for improving the various systems and characteristics of an automobile may make it too costly to produce and too expensive for many people to buy.

The design of an automobile, therefore, is a balance of many factors. Each must be taken into consideration, and compromises among features satisfy as many factors as possible. Yet, for all the variety among automobiles, the basic systems remain essentially the same.

Interaction of systems

Before examining the components of each system, it is useful to understand how the systems interact. The human body is again a good example of the interaction of systems. The heart pumps blood, which feeds the tissues of the body while at the same time helping to remove impurities. The tissues, fed by blood, are able to perform their tasks, and often are required to support the action of the heart. Muscle tissue, for example, depends on the availability of oxygen–rich blood from the heart in order to move the body.

The internal combustion engine is the heart of the automobile. The engine produces energy from fuel and converts that energy into the power to move the different components that will move the car. The engine converts the chemical energy produced by the burning of the fuel into mechanical energy. Shaking a can of soda is an example of such a conversion. The shaking motion causes a buildup of carbon dioxide—the soda's fizz—which, when the can is opened, will cause the soda to shoot out of the can.

In the engine's case, the chemical energy is used to spin a shaft. The spinning shaft, through the interaction of the transmission and other components, causes the wheels to turn and the car to move. A similar transfer of energy to motion can be seen when bicycling. The up and down motion of the feet and legs is converted to the turning motion of the pedals, which in turn pulls the chain that causes the rear wheel to spin.

Just as it is more difficult to pedal a bicycle from a standstill than it is while already rolling, the engine requires the electrical system to give it the push to move on its own. The electric starter motor of an automobile provides a powerful force to give the engine its initial movement. The battery supplies energy for the engine to use when burning the fuel needed to make it run. The alternator is driven by a belt attached to the engine, recharging the battery so there will be a constant supply of energy. The sensors of the computer control system, which governs many of the processes in an automobile, also require electricity.

The burning of fuel is a hot, noisy process that also produces as byproducts pollutants in the form of exhaust. This exhaust must be carried away from the engine and away from the automobile. The exhaust system, with its muffler, also acts to reduce the temperature and noise of the vehicle. Burning fuel produces two more results: friction and extremely high temperatures. In order to protect the parts from being worn down from the friction and from melting with the heat, they must be properly lubricated and cooled. These systems too depend on the engine and the electrical system for the power to perform their tasks.

The engine's power is used to turn the automobile's wheels. Because the tires are the only parts of the automobile that are actually in contact with the road, they must rest on a system of supports that will carry the weight of the car and respond to conditions of the road surface. At the same time, the driver must be capable of guiding the direction of the automobile. And once an automobile is moving, it will continue to move until some sort of friction, the brake, is applied to stop it.

The wheels, suspension, steering, and braking systems are all attached to the car's chassis, as is the rest of the automobile. The chassis and body, akin to the skeletal structure in the human body, provide support for all the various systems and components, while also providing safety, comfort, and protection from the elements for the automobile's passengers.

Engine

The engine operates on internal combustion; that is, the fuel used for its power is burned inside the engine. This burning occurs inside cylinders. Within the cylinder is a piston. When the fuel is burned, it creates an explosive force that causes the piston to move up and down. The piston is attached, via a connecting rod, to a crankshaft, where the up and down movement of the piston converts to a circular motion. When bicycling, the upper part of a person's leg is akin to the piston. Power from the leg is passed through the pedal in order to turn the crank.

Gasoline is the most common automobile fuel. The gasoline is pulled into the cylinder by the vacuum created as the piston moves down through the cylinder. The gasoline is then compressed up into the cylinder by the next movement of the piston. A spark is introduced through a spark plug placed at the end of the cylinder. The spark causes the gasoline to explode, and the explosion drives the piston down again into the cylinder. This movement, called the power stroke, turns the crankshaft. A final movement of the piston upward again forces the exhaust gases, the byproducts of the fuel's combustion, from the cylinder. These four movements—intake, compression, power, exhaust—are called strokes. The four–stroke engine is the most common type of automobile engine.

Most automobiles have from four to eight cylinders, although there are also two–cylinder and 12-cylinder automobiles. The cylinders work together in a sequence to turn the crankshaft, so that while one cylinder is in its intake stroke, another is in the compression stroke, and so forth. Generally, the more cylinders, the more smoothly the engine will run. The size of the automobile will affect the number of cylinders the engine uses. Smaller cars generally have the smaller four–cylinder engine. Mid–sized cars will generally require a six–cylinder engine, while larger cars need the power of an eight–cylinder engine.

The number of cylinders, however, is less important to the level of an engine's power than is its displacement. Displacement is a measure of the total volume of fuel mixture moved by all the pistons working together. The more fuel burned at one time, the more explosive the force, and thus, the power will be. Displacement is often expressed as cubic centimeters (cc) or as liters. A smaller engine will displace 1,200 cc (1.2 liters) for 60 horsepower, while a larger engine may displace as much as 4,000 cc (4 liters), generating more than 100 horsepower. Horsepower is the measurement of the engine's ability to perform work. This term reflects, perhaps, the early rivalry between the first automobiles and the traditionally horse–drawn cart. The size and weight of the car also affect its power. It takes less work to propel a lighter car than a heavier car, even if they have the same engine, just as a horse carrying a single rider can go faster with less effort than a horse drawing a cart.

Fuel system

Gasoline must be properly mixed with air before it can be introduced into the cylinder. The combination of gasoline and air creates a more volatile explosion. The fuel pump draws the gasoline from the gas tank mounted toward the rear of the car. The gasoline is drawn into a carburetor on some cars, while it is fuel–injected on others; both devices mix the gasoline with air (approximately 14 parts of air to one part of gasoline) and spray this mixture as a fine mist into the cylinders. Other parts of the fuel system include the air cleaner, which is a filter to ensure that the air mixed

into the fuel is free of impurities; and the intake manifold, which distributes the fuel mixture to the cylinders.

Exhaust system

After the fuel is burned in the pistons, the gases and heat created must be discharged from the cylinder to make room for the next infusion of fuel. The exhaust system is also responsible for reducing the noise caused by the explosion of the fuel.

Exhaust gases are discharged from the cylinder through an exhaust valve. The exhaust gathers in an exhaust manifold before eventually being channeled through the exhaust pipe and muffler and finally out the tailpipe and away from the car. The muffler is constructed with a maze of what are called baffles, specially developed walls that absorb energy, in the form of heat, force, and sound, as the exhaust passes through the muffler.

The burning of fuel creates as additional byproducts hazardous gases—hydrocarbons, carbon monoxide, and nitrogen oxide—which are extremely toxic and harmful to the engine's components and the environment. The emission control system of a car is linked to the exhaust system, and functions in two primary ways. The first is to reduce the levels of unburned fuel. This is achieved by returning the exhaust to the fuel–air mixture injected into the cylinders to burn as much of the exhaust as possible. The second method is through a catalytic converter. Fitted before the muffler, the catalytic converter contains precious metals that act as catalysts. That is, they increase the rate of conversion of the harmful gases to less harmful forms.

Cooling system

The automobile uses an additional system to reduce the level of heat created by the engine The cooling system also maintains the engine at a temperature that will allow it to run most efficiently. A liquid–cooled system is most commonly used.

The explosion of fuel in the cylinders can produce temperatures as high as $4,000°$ F ($2,204°$ C); the temperature of exhaust gases, while cooler, still reach to $1,500°$ F ($815°$ C). Liquid–cooling systems use water (mixed with an antifreeze that lowers the freezing point and raises the boiling point of water) guided through a series of jackets attached around the engine. As the water solution circulates through the jackets, it absorbs the heat from the engine. It is then pumped to the radiator at the front of the car, which is constructed of many small pipes and thin metal fins. These allow a large surface area to draw the heat from the water solution. A fan attached to the radiator uses the wind created by the movement of the car to cool the water solution further. Temperature sensors in the engine control the operation of the cooling system, so that the engine remains in its optimal temperature range.

Lubrication

Without the proper lubrication, the heat and friction created by the rapid movements of the engine's parts would quickly cause it to fail. The lubrication system of an automobile acts to reduce engine wear caused by the friction of its metal parts, as well as to carry off heat. At the bottom of the engine is the crankcase, which holds a supply of oil. A pump, powered by the engine, carries oil from the crankcase and through a series of passages and holes to all the various parts of the engine. As the oil flows through the engine, it forms a thin layer between the moving parts, so that they do not actually touch. The heated oil drains back into the crankcase, where it cools. The fumes given off by the crankcase are circulated by the PCV (positive crankcase ventilation) valve back to the cylinders, where they are burned off, further reducing the level of pollution given off by the automobile.

Electrical system

Electricity is used for many parts of the car, from the headlights to the radio, but its chief function is to provide the electrical spark needed to ignite the fuel in the cylinders. This is performed by an electrical system comprised of a battery, starter motor, alternator, distributor, ignition coil, and ignition switch. As discussed above, the starter motor is necessary for generating the power to carry the engine through its initial movements. Initial voltage is supplied by the battery, which is kept charged by the alternator. The alternator creates electrical current from the movement of the engine, much as windmills and watermills generate current from the movement of air or water.

Turning the key in the ignition switch draws current from the battery. This current, however, is not strong enough to provide spark to the spark plugs. The current is therefore drawn through the ignition coil, which is comprised of the tight primary winding and the looser secondary winding. The introduction of current between these windings creates a powerful magnetic field. Interrupting the current flow, which happens many times a second, causes the magnetic field to collapse. The collapsing of the magnetic field produces a powerful electrical surge. In this way, the 12–volt current from the battery is converted to the 20,000 volts needed as spark to ignite the gasoline.

Because there are two or more cylinders, and therefore as many spark plugs, this powerful current must be distributed—by the distributor—to each spark plug in a carefully controlled sequence. This sequence must be carefully timed, so that the cylinders and the pistons powering the crankshaft work smoothly together. For this reason, most automobiles manufactured today utilize an electronic ignition, in which a computer precisely controls the timing and distribution of current to the spark plugs.

Transmission

Once the pistons are firing and the crankshaft is spinning, this energy must be converted, or transmitted, to drive the wheels. But the crankshaft spins only within a limited range, usually between 1,000 to 6,000 revolutions per minute (rpm), and this is not enough power to cause the wheel to turn when applied directly. The transmission accomplishes the task of bringing the engine's torque, that is, the amount of twisting force the crankshaft has as it spins, to a range that will turn the wheels. One way to experience the effect of torque is by using two wrenches, one with a short handle, the other with a long handle. It may be difficult to turn a nut with the shorter wrench; but the nut turns much more easily with the longer wrench, because it allows a more powerful twisting force. The transmission has two other functions: allowing reverse, and braking the engine.

There are two types of transmission: manual and automatic. With a manual transmission, the driver controls the shifting of the gears. In an automatic transmission, as its name implies, gears are engaged automatically. Both types of transmission make use of a clutch, which allows the gears to be engaged and disengaged.

Automobiles generally have at least three gears, plus a reverse gear, although many manual transmissions have four or even five gears. Each gear provides a different ratio of the number of rpms of the crankshaft, or the input force, to the number of rpms of the output force—after the transmission—that will be directed to the wheel. In first gear, for example, which is needed to move the automobile from a standstill, the ratio of input to output is 3.5 to one or even higher. The greater the ratio, the more torque will be achieved in the output. Each successively higher gear has a lower input to output ratio. This is because once the automobile is rolling, progressively less torque is needed to maintain its movement. The fourth and fifth gears found on most cars are used when the engine has achieved higher speeds; often called overdrive gears, these gears allow the input to output ratio to sink lower than one to one. In other words, the wheels are spinning faster than the crankshaft. This allows for higher speeds and greater fuel efficiency.

Chassis

The chassis is the framework to which the various parts of the automobile are mounted. The chassis must be strong enough to bear the weight of the car, yet somewhat flexible in order to sustain the shocks and tension caused by turning and road conditions. Attached to the chassis are the wheels and steering assembly, the suspension, the brakes, and the body.

The suspension system enables the automobile to absorb the shocks and variations in the road surface, keeping the automobile stable. Most cars feature independent front suspension, that is, the two wheels in front are supported independently of each other. In this way, if one wheel hits a bump while the other wheel is in a dip, both wheels will maintain contact with the road. This is especially important because steering the automobile is performed with the front wheels. More and more cars also feature independent rear suspension, improving handling and the smoothness of the ride.

The main components of the suspension system are the springs and the shock absorbers. The springs suspend the automobile above the wheel, absorbing the shocks and bumps in the road surface. As the chassis bounces on the springs, the shock absorbers act to dampen, or quiet, the movement of the springs, using tubes and chambers filled with hydraulic fluid.

The steering system is another part of the suspension system. It allows the front wheels to guide the automobile. The steering wheel is attached to the steering column, which in turn is fitted to a gear assembly that allows the circular movement of the steering wheel to be converted to the more linear, or straight, movement of the front wheels. The gear assembly is attached to the front axle by tie rods. The axle is connected to the hubs of the wheels.

Wheels and the tires around them are the only contact the automobile has with the road. Tires are generally made of layers of rubber or synthetic rubber around steel fibers that greatly increase the rubber's strength and ability to resist puncture. Tires are inflated with air at a level that balances the greatest contact with the road surface with the ability to offer puncture resistance. Proper inflation of the tires will decrease wear on the tires and improve fuel efficiency.

Body

The body of a car is usually composed of steel or aluminum, although fiberglass and plastic are also used. The body is actually a part of the chassis, the whole

KEY TERMS

....

Catalyst—A substance that speeds up the rate of a chemical reaction.

Combustion—A chemical process producing heat; burning.

Friction—A force caused by the movement of an object through liquid, gas, or against a second object that works to oppose the first object's movement.

Gear—A wheel arrayed with teeth that meshes with the teeth of a second wheel to move it.

Ratio—A measurement in quantity, size, or speed of the relationship between two or more things.

Shaft—A rod that, when spun, can be used to move other parts of a machine.

Torque—The ability or force needed to turn or twist a shaft or other object.

Voltage—Measured in volts, the amount of electrons moved by an electric current or charge.

formed by welding stamped components into a single unit. While the body forms the passenger compartment, offers storage space, and houses the automobile's systems, it has other important functions as well. Passenger safety is achieved by providing structural support strong enough to withstand the force of an accident. Other parts of the car, such as the front and hood, are designed to crumple easily, thereby absorbing much of the impact of a crash. A firewall between the engine and the interior of the car protects the passengers in case of a fire. Lastly, the body's design contributes to reducing the level of wind resistance as the car moves, allowing the driver better handling ability, and improving the efficiency of the engine's operations.

See also Internal combustion engine.

Further Reading:

Duffy, James E. *Modern Automotive Mechanics*, Goodheart–Willcox Company, Inc., 1990.

Lewis, David L. and Laurence Goldstein, eds. *The Automobile and American Culture*, Ann Arbor, MI: University of Michigan Press, 1986.

Magliozzi, Tom and Ray. *Car Talk*, Dell Publishing, 1991.

Thiessen, Frank J. and David N. Dales. *Automotive Principles and Service*, Delmar Publishers Inc., 1993.

Waitley, Douglas. *The Roads We Travelled: An Amusing History of the Automobile*, Julian Messner, 1979.

M.L. Cohen

Autonomic nervous system see **Nervous system**

Autotroph

An autotroph is an organism able to make its own food. Autotrophic organisms take inorganic substances into their bodies and transform them into organic nourishment. Autotrophs are essential to all life because they are the primary producers at the base of all food chains. There are two categories of autotrophs, distinguished by the energy each uses to synthesize food. Photoautotrophs use light energy; chemoautotrophs use chemical energy.

Photoautotrophs

Plants are the most abundant and recognizable autotrophs on Earth. If you have noticed a houseplant on a windowsill imperceptibly turn its leaves toward the sun, you have probably guessed that plants are photoautotrophs. Plant leaves soak up the energy in sunlight and use it to make food. Plants take in water through their roots and atmospheric carbon dioxide through their leaves. Plant cells absorb light energy to fuel the synthesis of inorganic hydrogen, oxygen, and carbon into a sugar that nourishes them. This process is known as photosynthesis.

Because plants, as autotrophs, make living tissue solely out of nonliving material, they form the foundation of all food chains. Can you think of one thing you eat that does not, ultimately, come from plants? Plants are called primary producers because they create themselves out of transformed inorganic matter and, thus, are the "original food" that sustains all living things.

Chemoautotrophs

Until recently, scientists believed there existed only a few kinds of bacteria that used chemical energy to create their own food. Some of these bacteria were found living near vents and active volcanos on the lightless ocean floor. The bacteria create their food using inorganic sulfur compounds gushing out of the vents from the hot interior of the planet.

In 1993, scientists found many new species of chemoautotrophic bacteria living in fissured rock far below the ocean floor. These bacteria take carbon dioxide and water into their bodies and use the chemical energy in sulfur compounds to create nourishing carbohydrates and sugars. A unique characteristic of these chemoautotrophic bacteria is that they thrive at temperatures high enough to kill other organisms. Some scientists believe these unique bacteria should be classified in their own new taxonomic kingdom.

See also Bacteria; Photosynthesis; Plant.

Avalanche see **Mass wasting**
Avocado see **Laurel family**
Avocets see **Stilts and avocets**
Avogadro's law see **Gases, properties of**

Avogadro's number

Avogadro's number is the number of particles in one mole of any substance. Its numerical value is 6.02225×10^{23}. One mole of oxygen gas contains 6.02×10^{23} molecules of oxygen, while one mole of sodium chloride contains 6.02×10^{23} sodium ions and 6.02×10^{23} chloride ions. Avogadro's number is used extensively in calculating the volumes, masses, and numbers of particles involved in chemical changes.

The concept that a mole of any substance contains the same number of particles arose out of research conducted in the early 1800s by the Italian physicist Amadeo Avogadro (1776–1856). Avogadro based his work on the earlier discovery by Joseph Gay–Lussac that gases combine with each other in simple, whole–number ratios of volumes. For example, one liter of oxygen combines with two liters of hydrogen to make two liters of water vapor.

Avogadro argued that the only way Gay–Lussac's discovery could be explained was to assume that one liter of any gas contains the same number of particles as one liter of any other gas. To explain the water example above, he further hypothesized that the particles of at least some gases consist of two particles bound together, a structure to which he gave the name molecule.

The question then becomes, "What is this number of particles in a liter of any gas?" Avogadro himself never attempted to calculate this. Other scientists did make that effort, however. In 1865, for example, the German physicist J. Loschmidt estimated the number of molecules in a liter of gas to be 2.7×10^{22}. The accepted value today is 2.69×10^{22}.

For all elements and compounds, not just gases, a given weight must contain a certain number of atoms or molecules. A weight (in grams) equal to the atomic or molecular weight of the substance—that is, one mole of any element or compound—must contain the same number of atoms or molecules, because there is always a constant relationship between atomic weights and grams. (One atomic mass unit = 1.66×10^{-22} g.) The number of atoms or molecules in one mole of an element or compound has been named Avogadro's Number, in honor of his realization about the numbers of particles in gases. As stated above, that number has been determined to be 6.0225×10^{23}.

See also Atomic weight; Mole.

Axolotyl see **Salamanders**

Aye–Ayes

The aye–aye is a member of a group of primitive primates (Prosimians), similar to lemurs. These tree–dwelling animals are found only in Madagascar, where their range is restricted to a few localities along the northeast coast and Nosy Mangabé island. Only a handful of aye–ayes are believed to survive in the wild.

The aye–aye, *Daubentonia madagascariensis,* is the sole surviving member of the family Daubentoniidae, although the slightly larger relative *D. robusta* is thought to have become extinct only about 1,000 years ago. Habitat loss and the local belief that the aye–aye is a bad omen and should be killed on sight have caused the aye–aye's decline.

When first encountered by Europeans, the aye–aye was incorrectly classified as a rodent, because of its large ears, squirrel–like bushy tail, and large, continuously growing incisor teeth. This primate has large eyes set in a catlike face, which give it good night vision, and dark brown to black fur with long guard–hairs. Adults are approximately 3.3 ft (1 m) long and weigh about 4.4 lb (2 kg).

The aye–aye's digits end in claws, except for the big toe and thumb, which have flat nails. The middle finger of each hand is extremely long and thin with a long claw which is used to dig insect larvae out of tree bark. When aye–ayes hear insect movement under the bark, they gnaw through the wood to uncover the lar-

A young aye-aye (*Daubentonia madagascariensis*).

vae's tunnel, then insert the long finger to catch the grub. Some research indicates that by tapping a branch, aye–ayes can locate grubs with a sort of echolocation. The aye–aye also eats fruit, bamboo shoots, and other insects.

After hunting at night, the aye–aye sleeps during the day in a globe–shaped nest it makes by weaving leaves and twigs. An aye–aye may spend several days in one nest before moving on to another. Several animals may share the same home range.

Their nocturnal habits make aye–ayes difficult to observe in the wild, and so little is known about their breeding and behavior. It is thought that aye–ayes breed once every two or three years. A single infant is born after a gestation period of about 158 days (according to observations of captive aye–ayes). In April 1992, an aye–aye named "Blue Devil" was born at Duke University's primate center; named after the university mascot, it was the first aye–aye born in captivity in the Western Hemisphere.

See also Primates.

B

Babblers

Babblers are small to medium–sized passerine (perching) birds characterized by soft, fluffy plumage, strong, stout legs, and short rounded wings. Their wings make them poor fliers, and most are largely sedentary birds. Many species, particularly those that stay close to the ground, are gray, brown, or black, while the tree–living (arboreal) species are often green, yellow, or olive. Wren–babblers grow to only 3.5 in (9 cm), while the laughing–thrushes measure up to 1 ft (30 cm).

Babblers belong to Timaliidae, a large family of approximately 230 species of passerine (perching) birds that is thought to have originated in southern Asia. Babblers are most abundant in India and the Orient, but are also found in New Guinea, the Philippines, Australia, Africa, Madagascar, Saudi Arabia, and the Near East. The only species of babbler found in the New World is the wrentit, a small, reclusive brown bird found in the chaparral country west of the Rocky Mountains from Oregon south to Baja California.

Most babblers are highly social and nuzzle close to their mates and flock companions. Babblers feed primarily on insects gathered by probing and digging into the earth with their beaks; fruit and seeds round out their diet. While foraging for food, babblers keep in constant contact through the noisy chattering sounds for which they are named. The chattering pattern varies between species, some jabbering almost constantly while other remain relatively quiet. Only members of the subfamily Turdoidini are true songbirds, and their bright plumage makes them prized as cage birds.

Most babblers build dome–shaped nests on or near the ground, while the Turdoidini songbirds typically build cup–shaped nests in trees. The bareheaded rock fowl, a most unusual babbler from Africa, defies convention by plastering its mud nest to the side of a cliff.

Babirusa see **Pigs**

Baboons

Baboons are ground–living monkeys in the primate family Cercopithecidae and are found in Africa and the Arabian peninsula. Some taxonomists classify baboons in two genera, while others classify them in three or four.

All baboons have a strong torso, a snout–like face, the same dentition with long, sharp canine teeth, powerful jaws, a ground–walking habit, coarse body hair, a naked rump, and a similar social organization. Baboons live in savanna woodland, rocky plains, hill regions, and rain forests, and are mainly terrestrial. They are active during the day and eat both plant and animal materials. Male baboons are nearly twice the size of the females. Baboons form large groups that travel together foraging for food and sleep as a group.

Physical characteristics

The common savanna baboon (*Papio cynocephalus*) inhabits savanna woodlands and forest edges in Ethiopia, Angola, and South Africa. Savanna baboons eat grass, fruit, seeds, insects, and small mammals. These baboons have a gray coat with long hair covering their shoulders, and a patch of shiny black bare skin on their hips. Their tails are hook–shaped, a result of the fusion of several vertebrae. In East and Central Africa *P. cynocephalus* is yellow; in the highlands of East Africa this species is olive–colored.

The hamadryas baboon (*Papio hamadryas*) is found in the rocky and subdesert regions of Ethiopia, Somalia, Saudi Arabia, and South Yemen, with grass and thorn bush vegetation. These baboons feed on grass seeds, roots, and bulbs. Females and young hamadryas baboons have a brown coat, while adult males have a silver–gray mane over their shoulders and brilliant red bare skin on their face and around their genitals. This baboon was sacred to the ancient Egyp-

A savanna baboon (*Papio cynocephalus*) in South Luangwa National Park, Zambia.

tians; it is depicted in Egyptian art as an attendant or representative of the god Thoth, the god of letters and scribe of the gods. This species has been exterminated in Egypt and its numbers are reduced elsewhere in its range.

The Guinea baboon (*P. papio*) also feeds on grass, fruit, seeds, insects, and small animals and is found in the savanna woodlands of Senegal and Sierra Leone. These baboons have a brown coat, bare red skin around their rump, and a reddish brown face.

The drill (*Mandrillus leucophaeus*) lives in the rain forests of southeast Nigeria, western Cameroon and Gabon, and feeds on fruit, seeds, fungi, roots, insects, and small animals. Drills have a brown–black coat and a naked rump ranging from blue to purple. A fringe of white hair surrounds a black face and the long muzzle has ridges along its sides. The mandrill (*Mandrillus sphinx*) is the largest monkey. It lives in southern Cameroon, Gabon, and Congo in rain forests. Its diet includes fruit, seeds, fungi, roots, insects, and small animals. Mandrill males have a blue–purple bare rump, and a bright red stripe running down the middle of their muzzle with blue ridges on the sides, and a yellow

beard. Female and the young mandrills are similarly colored, but less brilliantly.

Gelada baboons (*Theropithecus gelada*) are found in the grasslands of Ethiopia, where they eat grass, roots, bulbs, seeds, fruit, and insects. Geladas have a long brown coat, hair that is cream colored at the tips and a long mantle of hair covering their shoulders and giving them the appearance of wearing a cape. The bare rump of both sexes is red and somewhat fat. Both sexes also have an area of bare red skin around their necks and the females have small white blisterlike lumps in this area of their bodies that swell during menstruation.

Social behavior

Baboon social behavior is matrilineal, in which a network of social relationships are sustained over three generations from the female members of the species. A troop of baboons can range in number from 30 to over 200 members, depending upon the availability of food. The baboon troop consists of related bands composed of several clans, where each clan may have a number of smaller harem families made up of mothers, their children, and a male.

Female baboons remain with the group into which they are born for the duration of their lives, while the males leave to join other troops as they become mature. Ranking within the group of females begins with the mother, with female offspring ranking below their mothers. Adult females are either nursing or pregnant for most of their lives, and they spend a great deal of their time with other female friends, avoiding the males. During a daytime rest period, the females gather around the oldest female in the troop and lie close together.

The way in which baboons huddle together while they are resting and their other movements in their troops are defense measures against outsiders and predators. The dominant males travel in the center of the troop to keep order among the females and the juveniles, while the younger males travel around the outer fringes of the group. During their rest periods baboons spend considerable time grooming one another, which helps to reinforce their social bonds. Females have male baboons that help them take care of their infants and protect them from danger. These males may not be the fathers, but they may later mate with the female.

Baboon friendships

When a young male baboon matures, he leaves the family group to join a new troop. His first gestures are toward an adult female who may make friends with him. His gestures of friendship include lip–smacking, grunting, and grooming. It will take several months of this kind of friendly behavior for a more permanent bond to become established between them.

A female may have friendships with more than one male, and when she is ready to mate she may do so with all of her male friends. Social grooming between females and males is always between friends. A female benefits from this relationship by gaining protection and help in caring for her offspring. A male benefits by having a female with which to mate. These friendships do not insure the male paternity of infants, but the social benefits seem to outweigh paternity rights in baboon societies.

There are often fights among males for the right to mate with females in estrus. Males do not have the strong ranking order that the females have among their family relatives, and males must compete for mating rights. Among some species of baboon the older males mate more than younger dominant males, because the

older males have more friendships with females, and these bonds are of a longer duration.

Food and foraging habits

Baboons have the same number of teeth and dental pattern as human beings. Baboons, like other members of the subfamily Cercopithecinae, have cheek pouches that can hold a stomach's worth of food. This enables them to literally eat on the run, and is helpful to them when they have to compete for food or avoid danger. Baboons can quickly fill up their pouches, then retreat to safety to eat at their leisure.

Baboons walk on all four limbs and their rear feet are plantigrade, which means they walk on the whole foot, not just on their toes. The walking surface of their hands is the complete surface of their four fingers. When feeding, baboons tend to stand on three of their limbs and pluck food and eat with one hand. When baboons are walking, their shoulders are higher than their hips and they are able to easily see what is going on around them as they forage for food. Baboons are well suited to walking long distances.

Young baboons learn what to eat and what not to eat, and adults intervene to prevent younger baboons from eating unusual food. Baboons are basically fruit–eaters, but they also eat seeds, flowers, buds, leaves, bark, roots, bulbs, rhizomes, insects, snails, crabs, fish, lizards, birds, and small mammals. When water is not available baboons dig up roots and tubers to find liquid and often dig holes in dry river beds to find water. It has been observed that baboons adapt their food choices to what is available in their habitats. In some regions they have developed group hunting techniques.

Communication

Baboons have a complex system of communication that includes vocalizations, facial expressions, posturing, and gesturing. These vocalizations, which baboons use to express emotions, include grunts, lip–smacking, screams, and alarm calls. The intensity of the emotion is conveyed by repetition of the sounds in association with other forms of communication.

Baboons communicate with each other primarily through body gestures and facial expressions. The most noticeable facial expression is an open–mouth threat where the baboon bares the canine teeth. Preceding this may be an eyelid signal, raising the eyebrows and showing the whites of the eyes, that is used to show displeasure. If a baboon really becomes aggressive, the hair may also stand on end, threatening sounds will be made, and the ground will be slapped. In response to aggressive facial expressions and body gestures, other baboons usually exhibit submissive gestures. A fear–face, a response to aggression, involves pulling the mouth back in what looks like a wide grin.

Presenting among baboons takes place in both sexual and nonsexual contexts. A female will approach a male and turn her rump for him to show that she is receptive. This type of presentation can lead to mating or to a special relationship between the pair. A female may also present in the same way to an infant, to let the infant know it may come close to her. She may also use this body gesture as a simple greeting to a male, indicating to him that she respects his position. A female also presents to another female when she want to fondle the other female's infant.

Males also present to other males as a greeting signal. Their tails, however, are not raised as high as those of females when they present. Presentation is also used as an invitation or request for grooming, and for protection. Baboons freely engage in embracing to show affection to infants and juveniles. The frontal embrace has also been seen as a gesture of reassurance between baboons when they are upset. Infants have their own forms of communication that involves a looping kind of walk, wrestling, and a play–face. The play–face is an open mouth gesture they use to try to bite one another.

Baboon models

Baboons were studied for a long time as models of primate behavior and used to help construct the evolution of human behavior. More recently, chimpanzees have been used as a model, because of their genetically close relationship to humans, and because they exhibit toolmaking, some language–like ability and some mathematical cognition.

Until recently, baboon troops were thought to be male–dominated. Studies have now demonstrated the cohesive nature of the matrilineal structure of baboon society. What continues to interest researchers about baboons is how adaptable they are, even when their habitats are threatened. Baboons have become skillful crop raiders in areas where their terrains have been taken up by humans for agriculture. In spite of this adaptability some species are threatened or endangered. For example, the drill is highly endangered due to habitat destruction and commercial hunting.

See also Primates.

Further Reading:

Cheney, Dorothy L., and Robert M. Seyfarth. *How Monkeys See the World.* Chicago: University of Chicago Press, 1990.

Grzimek, Bernhard. *Encyclopedia of Mammals.* Vol. 2. New York: McGraw–Hill, 1990.

Loy, James, and Calvin B. Peters. *Understanding Behavior: What Primate Studies Tell Us about Human Behavior.* New York: Oxford University Press, 1991.

Macdonald, David, ed. *The Encyclopedia of Mammals.* New York: Facts on File, 1987.

Mason, William A., and Sally P. Mendoza. *Primate Social Conflict.* Albany: State University of New York Press, 1993.

Strum, Shirley C. *Almost Human: A Journey into the World of Baboons.* New York: Random House, 1987.

Vita Richman

Backswimmers see **True bugs**

Bacteria

Bacteria are mostly unicellular organisms that lack chlorophyll and are among the smallest living things on earth—only viruses are smaller. Multiplying rapidly under favorable conditions, bacteria can aggregate into colonies of millions or even billions of organisms within a space as small as a drop of water.

The Dutch merchant and amateur scientist Anton van Leeuwenhoek was the first to observe bacteria and other microorganisms. Using single–lens microscopes of his own design, he described bacteria and other microorganisms (calling them "animacules") in a series of letters to the Royal Society of London between 1674 and 1723.

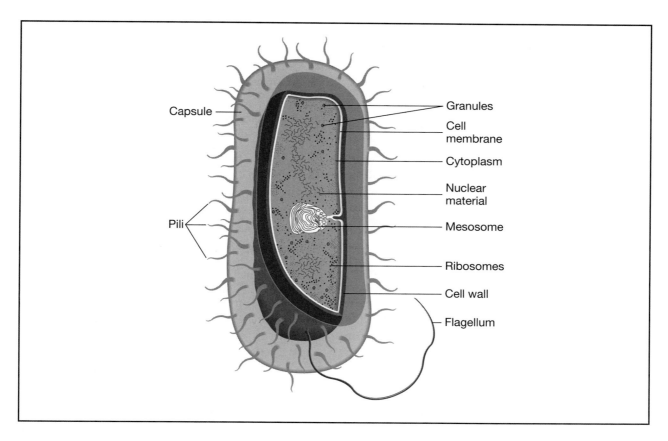

Capsule

Pili

Granules

Cell membrane

Cytoplasm

Nuclear material

Mesosome

Ribosomes

Cell wall

Flagellum

The anatomy of a typical bacteria.

Today, bacteria are classified in the kingdom Procaryotae. This taxonomic ranking reflects the fact that the genetic material of bacteria is contained in a single, circular chain of deoxyribonucleic acid (DNA) that is not enclosed within a nuclear membrane. The word prokaryote is derived from Greek meaning "prenucleus." Moreover, the DNA of prokaryotes is not associated with the special chromosome proteins called histones, which are found in higher organisms. In addition bacterial cells lack other membrane–bounded organelles, such as mitochondria.

Characteristics of bacteria

Although all bacteria share certain structural, genetic, and metabolic characteristics, important biochemical differences exist among the many species of bacteria. These differences permit bacteria to live in many different, and sometimes extreme, environments.

For example, some bacteria recycle nitrogen and carbon from decaying organic matter, then release these gases into the atmosphere to be reused by other living things. Other bacteria cause diseases in humans

and animals, help digest sewage in treatment plants, or produce the alcohol in wine, beer and liquors. Still others are used by humans to break down toxic waste chemicals in the environment, a process called bioremediation.

The cytoplasm of all bacteria is enclosed within a cell membrane that is surrounded by a rigid cell wall whose polymers, with few exceptions, include peptidoglycans—large, structural molecules made of protein carbohydrate.

Bacteria also secrete a viscous, gelatinous polymer (called the glycocalyx) on their cell surfaces. This polymer, composed either of polysaccharide, polypeptide, or both, is called a capsule when it occurs as an organized layer firmly attached to the cell wall.

Capsules increase the disease–causing ability (virulence) of bacteria by inhibiting immune system cells called phagocytes from engulfing them. One such bacterium, *Streptococcus pneumoniae*, is the cause of pneumonia.

The shape of bacterial cells includes spherical (coccus), rodlike (bacillus), spiral (spirochete), helical (spirilla) and comma–shaped (vibrio) cells. Many bacilli and vibrio bacteria have whiplike appendages (called flagella) protruding from the cell surface. Flagella are composed of tight, helical rotors made of chains of globular protein called flagellin, and act as tiny propellers, making the bacteria very mobile.

Flagella may be arranged in any of four ways, depending on the species of bacteria. There is the monotrichous condition (single flagellum at one end), the amphitrichous (single flagellum at each end of the bacterium), the lophotrichous (two or more flagella at either or both ends of the bacterium), and the peritrichous condition (flagella distributed over the entire cell).

Spirochetes are spiral–shaped bacteria which live in contaminated water, sewage, soil and decaying organic matter, as well as inside humans and animals. Spirochetes move by means of axial filaments, which consist of bundles of fibrils arising at each end of the cell beneath an outer sheath. The fibrils, which spiral around the cell, rotate, causing an opposite movement of the outer sheath that propels the spirochetes forward like a turning corkscrew. The best known spirochete is *Treponema pallidum*, the organism that causes syphilis.

On the surface of some bacteria are short, hairlike, proteinaceous projections that may arise at the ends of the cell or over the entire surface. These projections, called fimbriae, let the bacteria adhere to surfaces. For example, fimbriae on the bacterium *Neisseria gonorrhoea*, which causes gonorrhea, allow these organisms to attach to mucous membranes.

Other proteinaceous projections, called pili, occur singly or in pairs and join pairs of bacteria together, facilitating transfer of DNA between them.

During periods of harsh environmental conditions some bacteria, such as those of the genera *Clostridium* and *Bacillus*, produce within themselves a dehydrated, thick–walled endospore. These endospores can survive extremes of temperature, dryness and exposure to many toxic chemicals and to radiation. Endospores can remain dormant for long periods (hundreds of years in some cases) before being reactivated by the return of favorable conditions.

A primitive form of exchange of genetic material between bacteria involving plasmids does occur. Plasmids are small, circular, extrachromosomal DNA molecules that are capable of replication and are known to be capable of transferring genes among bacteria. For example, resistance plasmids carry genes for resistance to antibiotics from one bacterium to another, while other plasmids carry genes that confer pathogenicity. In addition, the transfer of genes via bacteriophages—

viruses that specifically parasitize bacteria—also serves as a means of genetic recombination. *Corynebacterium diphtheriae*, for example, produces the diphtheria toxin only when infected by a phage that carries the diphtherotoxin gene.

Bacteria synthesize special DNA–cutting enzymes (known as restriction enzymes) that destroy the DNA of phages that do not normally infect them. Purified restriction enzymes are used in the laboratory to slice pieces of DNA from one organism and insert them into the genetic material of another organism—a process called genetic engineering.

Bacterial growth

The term "bacterial growth" generally refers to growth of a population of bacteria rather than of an individual cell. Individual cells usually reproduce asexually by means of binary fission, in which one cell divides into two cells. Thus, bacterial growth of the population is a geometric progression of numbers of cells, with division occurring in regular intervals, called generation time, ranging from 15 minutes to 16 hours, depending upon the type of bacterium. In addition, some filamentous bacteria (actinomycetes) reproduce by producing chains of spores at their tips. Also, some filamentous species fragment into new cells.

Stages of bacterial growth

Under ideal conditions, the growth of a population of bacteria occurs in several stages termed lag, log, stationary, and death.

During the lag phase active metabolic activity occurs involving synthesis of DNA and enzymes, but no growth. Geometric population growth occurs during the log, or exponential phase, when metabolic activity is most intense and cell reproduction exceeds cell death. Following the log phase, the growth rate slows and the production of new cells equals the rate of cell death. This period, known as the stationary phase, involves the establishment of an equilibrium in population numbers and a slowing of the metabolic activities of individual cells. The stationary phase reflects a change in growing condition—for example, a lack of nutrients and/or the accumulation of waste products.

When the rate of cell deaths exceeds the number of new cells formed, the population equilibrium shifts to a net reduction in numbers and the population enters the death phase, or logarithmic decline phase. The population may diminish until only a few cells remain, or the population may die out entirely.

386

Physical and chemical requirements for bacterial growth

The physical and chemical requirements for growth can vary widely among different species of bacteria, and some are found in environments as extreme as old polar regions and hot, acid springs.

In general, the physical requirements for bacteria include proper temperature, pH and osmotic pressure. Generally, bacteria thrive only within narrow ranges of these conditions, however extreme those ranges may be.

Temperature and bacteria

Whatever temperature they prefer, bacteria grow only within a narrow temperature range. The lowest temperature at which a particular species will grow is the minimum growth temperature, while the maximum growth temperature is the highest temperature at which they will grow. The temperature at which their growth is optimal is called the optimum growth temperature. In general, the maximum and minimum growth temperatures of any particular type of bacteria are about 30° apart.

Most bacteria thrive at temperatures at or around that of the human body 98.6° F (37° C), and some, such as *Escherichia coli*, are normal parts of the human intestinal flora. These organisms are mesophiles (moderate–temperature–loving), with an optimum growth temperature between 77° F (25° C) and 104° F (40° C). Mesophiles have adapted to thrive in temperatures close to that of their host.

Psychrophiles, which prefer cold temperatures, are divided into two groups. One group has an optimal growth temperature of about 59° F (15° C), but can grow at temperatures as low as 32° F (0° C). These organisms live in ocean depths or Arctic regions. Other psychrophiles that also can grow at 32° F (0° C) have an optimal growth temperature between 68° F (20° C) and 86° F (30° C). These organisms, sometimes called psychrotrophs, are often those associated with food spoilage under refrigeration.

Thermophiles thrive in very hot environments, many having an optimum growth temperature between 122° F (50° C) and 140° F (60° C), similar to that of hot springs in Yellowstone National Park. Such organisms thrive in compost piles, where temperatures can rise as high as 140° F. Extreme thermophiles grow at temperatures above 195° F (90° C). Along the sides of hydrothermal vents on the ocean bottom 217 mi (350 km) north of the Galapagos Islands, for example, bacteria grow in temperatures that can reach 662° F (350° C).

pH and bacteria

Like temperature, pH also plays a role in determining the ability of bacteria to grow or thrive in particular environments. Most commonly, bacteria grow optimally within a narrow range of pH between 6.7 and 7.5.

Acidophiles, however, prefer acidic conditions. For example, *Thiobacillus ferrooxidans*, which occurs in drainage water from coal mines, can survive at pH 1. Other bacteria, such as *Vibrio cholera*, the cause of cholera, can thrive at a pH as high as 9.0.

Osmotic pressure and bacteria

Osmotic pressure is another limiting factor in the growth of bacteria. Bacteria are about 80% to 90% water; they require moisture to grow because they obtain most of their nutrients from their aqueous environment.

Cell walls protect prokaryotes against changes in osmotic pressure over a wide range. However, sufficiently hypertonic media at concentrations greater than those inside the cell (such as 20% sucrose) cause water loss from the cell by osmosis. Fluid leaves the bacteria causing the cell to contract, which, in turn, causes the cell membrane to separate from the overlying cell wall. This process of cell shrinkage is called plasmolysis.

Because plasmolysis inhibits bacterial cell growth, the addition of salts or other solutes to a solution inhibits food spoilage by bacteria, as occurs when meats or fish is salted.

Some types of bacteria, called extreme or obligate halophiles, are adapted to—and require—high salt concentrations, such as found in the Dead Sea, where salt concentrations can reach 30%. Facultative nalophiles do not require high salt environments to survive, but are capable of tolerating these conditions. Halophiles can grow in salt concentrations up to 2%, a level that would inhibit the growth of other bacteria. However, some facultative halophiles, such as *Halobacterium halobium* grow in salt lakes, salt flats, and other environments where the concentration of salts is up to seven times greater than that of the oceans.

When bacteria are placed in hypotonic media with concentrations weaker than the inside of the cell, water tends to enter by osmosis. The accumulation of this water causes the cell to swell and then to burst, a process called osmotic lysis.

Carbon, nitrogen and other growth factors

In addition to water and the correct salt balance, bacteria also require a wide variety of elements, especially carbon, hydrogen, and nitrogen, sulfur and phosphorus, potassium, iron, magnesium and calcium, as well as growth factors (such as vitamins and pyrimidines and purines, the building blocks of DNA).

Carbon is the fundamental building block of all of the organic compounds needed by living things, including nucleic acids, carbohydrates, proteins and fats.

Chemoheterotrophs are bacteria that use organic compounds such as proteins, carbohydrates and lipids as their carbon source, and which use electrons from organic compounds as their energy source. Most bacteria (as well as all fungi, protozoans and animals) are chemoheterotrophs. Chemoautotrophs (for example hydrogen, sulfur, iron, and nitrifying bacteria) use carbon dioxide as their carbon source and electrons from inorganic compounds as their energy source.

Saprophytes are heterotrophs that obtain their carbon from decaying dead organic matter. For example, many different soil bacteria release plant nitrogen as ammonia (ammonification). Other bacteria, the *Nitrosomonas*, convert ammonia to nitrite, while *Nitrobacter* convert nitrite to nitrate. Other bacteria, especially *Pseudomonas*, convert nitrate to nitrogen gas. These bacteria complement the activity of nitrogen–fixing bacteria (for example, *Rhizobium),* which fix nitrogen from the atmosphere and make it available to leguminous plants, and *Azotobacter*, which are also found in fresh and marine waters. Together, the activity of these bacteria underlies the nitrogen cycle, by which the gas is taken up by living organisms, used to make proteins and other organic compounds, returned to the soil during decay, then released to the atmosphere to be reused by living things.

Phototrophs use light as their primary source of energy, but may differ in their carbon sources. Photoheterotrophs (purple nonsulfur and green nonsulfur bacteria) use organic compounds as their carbon source, while photoautotrophs (for example, photosynthetic green sulfur and purple sulfur bacteria) use carbon dioxide as a source of carbon.

Aerobic and anaerobic bacteria

Oxygen may or may not be a requirement for a particular species of bacteria, depending on the type of metabolism used to extract energy from food (aerobic or anaerobic). In all cases, the initial breakdown of glucose to pyruvic acid occurs during glycolysis, which produces a net gain of two molecules of the energy–rich molecule adenosine triphosphate (ATP).

Aerobic bacteria

Aerobic bacteria use oxygen to break down pyruvic acid, releasing much more ATP than is produced during glycolysis during the process known as aerobic respiration. In addition, aerobic bacteria have enzymes such as superoxide dismutase capable of breaking down toxic forms of oxygen such as superoxide free radicals, which are also formed by aerobic respiration.

During aerobic respiration, enzymes remove electrons from the organic substrate and transfer them to the electron transport chain, which is located in the membrane of the mitochondrion. The electrons are transferred along a chain of electron carrier molecules. At the final transfer position, the electrons combine with atoms of oxygen—the final electron acceptor—which in turn combines with protons (H^+) to produce water molecules. Energy, in the form of ATP, is also made here. Along the chain of electron carriers, protons that are pumped across the mitochondrial membrane, re–enter the mitochondrion. This flow of electrons across the membrane fuels oxidative phosphorylation, the chemical reaction that adds a phosphate group to adenosine diphosphate (ADP) to produce ATP.

Obligate aerobes must have oxygen in order to live. Facultative aerobes can also exist in the absence of oxygen by using fermentation or anaerobic respiration. Anaerobic respiration and fermentation occur in the absence of oxygen, and produce substantially less ATP than aerobic respiration.

Anaerobic bacteria

Anaerobic bacteria use inorganic substances other than oxygen as a final electron acceptor. For example, *Pseudomonas* and *Bacillus* reduce nitrate ion (NO_3^-) to nitrite ion (NO_2^-), nitrous oxide (N_2O) or nitrogen gas (N_2). *Clostridium* species, which include those that cause tetanus and botulism, are obligate anaerobes. That is, they are not only unable to use molecular oxygen to produce ATP, but are harmed by toxic forms of oxygen formed during aerobic respiration. Unlike aerobic bacteria, obligate anaerobes lack the ability synthesize enzymes to neutralize these toxic forms of oxygen.

The role of bacteria in fermentation

Fermentation bacteria are anaerobic, but use organic molecules as their final electron acceptor to produce fermentation end–products. *Streptococcus*, *Lactobacillus*, and *Bacillus*, for example, produce lactic acid, while *Escherichia* and *Salmonella* produce ethanol, lactic acid, succinic acid, acetic acid, CO_2, and H_2.

Fermenting bacteria have characteristic sugar fermentation patterns, i.e., they can metabolize some sugars but not others. For example, *Neisseria meningitidis* ferments glucose and maltose, but not sucrose and lactose, while *Neisseria gonorrhoea* ferments glucose, but not maltose, sucrose or lactose. Such fermentation patterns can be used to identify and classify bacteria.

During the 1860s, the French microbiologist Louis Pasteur studied fermenting bacteria. He demonstrated that fermenting bacteria could contaminate wine and beer during manufacturing, turning the alcohol produced by yeast into acetic acid (vinegar). Pasteur also showed that heating the beer and wine to kill the bacteria preserved the flavor of these beverages. The process of heating, now called pasteurization in his honor, is still used to kill bacteria in some alcoholic beverages, as well as milk.

Pasteur described the spoilage by bacteria of alcohol during fermentation as being a "disease" of wine and beer. His work was thus vital to the later idea that human diseases could also be caused by microorganisms, and that heating can destroy them.

Identifying and classifying bacteria

The most fundamental technique for classifying bacteria is the gram stain, developed in 1884 by Danish scientist Christian Gram. It is called a differential stain because it differentiates among bacteria and can be used to distinguish among them, based on differences in their cell wall.

In this procedure, bacteria are first stained with crystal violet, then treated with a mordant—a solution that fixes the stain inside the cell (e.g., iodine–KI mixture). Then the bacteria are washed with a decolorizing agent, such as alcohol, and counterstained with safranin, a light red dye.

The walls of gram positive bacteria (for example, *Staphylococcus aureus*) have more peptidoglycans (the large molecular network of repeating disaccharides attached to chains of four or five amino acids) than do gram–negative bacteria. Thus, gram–positive bacteria retain the original violet dye and cannot be counterstained.

Gram negative bacteria (e.g., *Escherichia coli*) have thinner walls, containing an outer layer of lipopolysaccharide, which is disrupted by the alcohol wash. This permits the original dye to escape, allowing the cell to take up the second dye, or counterstain. Thus, gram–positive bacteria stain violet, and gram–negative

bacteria stain pink.

The gram stain works best on young, growing populations of bacteria, and can be inconsistent in older populations maintained in the laboratory.

Microbiologists have accumulated and organized the known characteristics of different bacteria in a reference book called *Bergey's Manual of Systematic Bacteriology* (the first edition of which was written primarily by David Hendricks Bergey of the University of Pennsylvania in 1923).

The identification schemes of *Bergey's Manual* are based on morphology (e.g., coccus, bacillus), staining (gram–positive or negative), cell wall composition (e.g., presence or absence of peptidoglycan), oxygen requirements (e.g., aerobic, facultatively anaerobic) and biochemical tests (e.g., which sugars are aerobically metabolized or fermented).

In addition to the gram stain, other stains include the acid–fast stain used to distinguish *Mycobacterium* species (for example, *Mycobacterium tuberculosis*, the cause of tuberculosis); endospore stain, used to detect the presence of endospores; negative stain, used to demonstrate the presence of capsules; and flagella stain, used to demonstrate the presence of flagella.

Another important identification technique is based on the principles of antigenicity—the ability to stimulate the formation of antibodies by the immune system. Commercially available solutions of antibodies against specific bacteria (antisera) are used to identify unknown organisms in a procedure called a slide agglutination test. A sample of unknown bacteria in a drop of saline is mixed with antisera that has been raised against a known species of bacteria. If the antisera causes the unknown bacteria to clump (agglutinate), then the test positively identifies the bacteria as being identical to that against which the antisera was raised. The test can also be used to distinguish between strains, that is slightly different bacteria belonging to the same species.

Phage typing, like serological testing, identifies bacteria according to their response to the test agent, in this case viruses. Phages are viruses that infect specific bacteria. Bacterial susceptibility to phages is determined by growing bacteria on an agar plate to which are added solutions of phages that infect only a specific species of bacteria. Areas that are devoid of visible bacterial growth following incubation of the plate represent organisms susceptible to the specific phages.

Because a specific bacterium might be susceptible to infection by two or more different phages, it may be necessary to perform several tests to definitively identify a specific bacterium.

The evolutionary relatedness of different species can also be determined by laboratory analysis. For example, analysis of the amino acids sequences of proteins from different bacteria disclose how similar the proteins are. In turn, this reflects how similar are the genes coding for these proteins.

Protein analysis compares the similarity or extent of differences between the entire set of protein products of each bacterium. Using a technique call electrophoresis, the entire set of proteins of each bacterium is separated according to size by an electrical charge applied across gel. The patterns produced when the gel is stained to show the separate bands of proteins reflects the genetic makeup, and relatedness, of the bacteria.

The powerful techniques of molecular biology have given bacteriologists other tools to determine the identity and relatedness of bacteria.

Taxonomists interested in studying the relatedness of bacteria compare the ratio of nucleic acid base pairs in the DNA of microorganisms, that is, the numbers of guanosine–cytosine pairs in the DNA. Because each guanosine on a double–stranded molecule of DNA has a complementary cytosine on the opposite strand, comparing the number of G–C pairs in one bacterium with that in another bacterium provides evidence for the extent of their relatedness.

Determining the percentage of G–C pairs making up the DNA also discloses the percentage of adenosine–thymine (A–T)—the other pair of complementary nucleic acids making up DNA (100% – [% G–C] = % A–T).

The closer the two percentages are, the more closely related the bacteria may be, although other lines of evidence are needed to make a definitive determination regarding relationships.

The principle of complementarity is also used to identify bacteria by means of nucleic acid hybridization. The technique assumes that if two bacteria are closely related, they will have long stretches of DNA that are identical.

First, one bacterium's DNA is isolated and gently heated to break the bonds between the two complementary strands. Specially prepared DNA probes representing short segments of the other organism's DNA are added to this solution of single–stranded DNA. The greater degree to which the probes combine with (hybridize) complementary stretches of the single stranded DNA, the greater the relatedness of the two organisms.

In addition to helping bacteriologists better classify bacteria, the various laboratory tests are valuable tools for identifying disease–causing organisms. This is especially important when physicians must determine which antibiotic or other medication to use to treat an infection.

Bacteria and disease

The medical community did not accept the concept that bacteria can cause disease until well into the nineteenth century. Joseph Lister, an English surgeon, applied the so–called "germ theory" to medical practice in the 1860s. Lister soaked surgical dressing in carbolic acid (phenol), which reduced the rate of post–surgical infections so dramatically that the practice spread.

In 1876, the German physician Robert Koch identified *Bacillus anthracis* as the cause of anthrax, and in so doing, developed a series of laboratory procedures for proving that a specific organism cause a specific disease. These procedures, called Koch's postulates, are still generally valid. Briefly, they state that, to prove that an organism causes a specific disease, the investigator must:

1. Find the same pathogenic microorganism in every case of the disease.

2. Isolate the pathogen from the diseased patient or experimental animal and grow it in pure culture.

3. Demonstrate that the pathogen from the pure culture causes the disease when it is injected into a healthy laboratory animal.

4. Isolate the pathogen from the inoculated animal and demonstrate that it is the original organism injected into the animal.

The ability to isolate, study, and identify bacteria has greatly enhanced the understanding of their disease–causing role in humans and animals and the subsequent development of treatments. Part of that understanding derives from the realization that since bacteria are ubiquitous and are found in large numbers in and on humans, they can cause a wide variety of diseases.

The skin and the nervous, cardiovascular, respiratory, digestive and genitourinary systems are common sites of bacterial infections, as are the eyes and ears.

The skin is the body's first line of defense against infection by bacteria and other microorganisms, although it supports enormous numbers of bacteria itself, especially *Staphylococcus* and *Streptococcus* species. Sometimes these bacteria are only dangerous if they enter a break in the skin or invade a wound, for example, the potentially fatal staphylococcal toxic shock syndrome. Among other common bacterial skin ailments are acne, caused by *Propionibacterium acnes* and superficial infection of the outer ear canal, caused by *Pseudomonas aeruginosa*.

Among the neurological diseases are meningitis, an inflammation of the brain's membranes caused by *Neisseria meningitidis* and *Hemophilus influenzae*.

Many medically important bacteria produce toxins, poisonous substances that have effects in specific areas of the body. Exotoxins are proteins produced during bacterial growth and metabolism and released into the environment. Most of these toxin–producing bacteria are gram positive.

Among the gram positive toxin–producing bacteria are *Clostridium tetani*, which causes tetanus, an often fatal paralytic disease of muscles; *Clostridium botulinum*, which causes botulism , a form of potentially lethal food poisoning; and *Staphylococcus aureus*, which also causes a form of food poisoning (gastroenteritis).

Most gram negative bacteria (for example, *Salmonella typhi*, the cause of typhoid fever) produce endotoxins, toxins that are part of the bacterial cell wall.

As the role of bacteria in causing disease became understood, entire industries developed that addressed the public health issues of these diseases.

As far back as 1810, the French confectioner Nicholas Appert proved that food stored in glass bottles and heated to high temperatures could be stored for long periods of time without spoiling. Appert developed tables that instructed how long such containers should be boiled, depending upon the type of food and size of the container. Today, the food preservation industry includes not only canning, but also freezing and freeze–drying. An important benefit to food preservation is the ability to destroy potentially lethal contamination by *Clostridium botulinum* spores.

Even as concepts of prevention of bacterial diseases were being developed, scientists were looking for specific treatments. Early in the twentieth century, the German medical researcher Paul Ehrlich theorized about the producing a "magic bullet" that would destroy pathogenic organisms without harming the host.

In 1928, the discovery by Scottish bacteriologist Alexander Fleming that the mold *Penicillium notatum* inhibited growth of *Staphylococcus aureus* ushered in the age of antibiotics. Subsequently, English scientists Howard Florey and Ernst Chain, working at Oxford

KEY TERMS

Capsule—A viscous, gelatinous polymer composed either of polysaccharide, polypeptide, or both, that surrounds the surface of some bacteria cells. Capsules increase the disease–causing ability (virulence) of bacteria by inhibiting immune system cells called phagocytes from engulfing them.

Death phase—Stage of bacterial growth when the rate of cell deaths exceeds the number of new cells formed and the population equilibrium shifts to a net reduction in numbers. The population may diminish until only a few cells remain, or the population may die out entirely.

Fimbriae—Short, hairlike, proteinaceous projections that may arise at the ends of the bacterial cell or over the entire surface. These projections let the bacteria adhere to surfaces.

Gram staining—A method for classifying bacteria developed in 1884 by Danish scientist Christian Gram which is based upon a bacterium's ability or inability to retain a purple dye.

Exotoxins—Toxic proteins produced during bacterial growth and metabolism and released into the environment.

Koch's postulates—A series of laboratory procedures, developed by German physician Robert Koch in the late nineteenth century, for proving that a specific organism cause a specific disease.

Lag phase—Stage of bacterial growth in which metabolic activity occurs but no growth.

Log phase—Stage of bacterial growth when metabolic activity is most intense and cell reproduction exceeds cell death. Also known as exponential phase.

Phage typing—A method for identifying bacteria according to their response to bacteriophages, which are viruses that infect specific bacteria.

Pili—Proteinaceous projections that occur singly or in pairs and join pairs of bacteria together, facilitating transfer of DNA between them.

Stationary phase—Stage of bacterial growth in which the growth rate slows and the production of new cells equals the rate of cell death.

Spirochetes—Spiral–shaped bacteria which live in contaminated water, sewage, soil and decaying organic matter, as well as inside humans and animals.

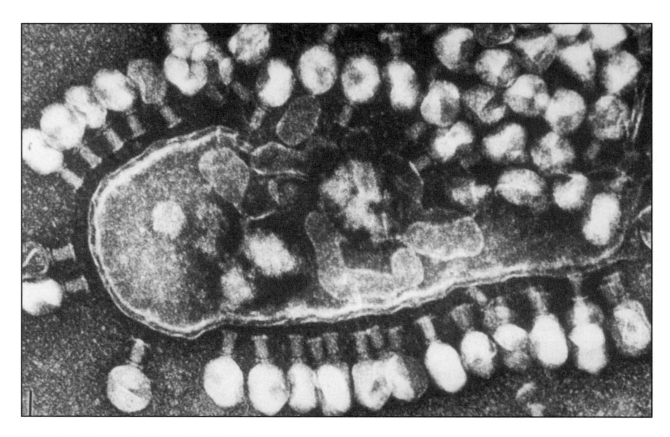

T4 bacteriophages attacking an *E. coli* bacterium.

University in England, demonstrated the usefulness of penicillin, the anti–bacterial substance isolated from *P. notatum* in halting growth of this bacterium. This inhibitory effect of penicillin on bacteria is an example of antibiosis, and from this term is derived the word antibiotic, which refers to a substance produced by microorganisms that inhibits other microorganisms.

Beginning in the 1930s, the development of synthetic anti–bacterial compounds called sulfa drugs further stimulated the field of anti–bacterial drug research. The many different anti–bacterial drugs available today work in a variety of ways, such as the inhibition of synthesis of cell–walls, of proteins, or of DNA or RNA.

Today, medical science and the multi–million dollar pharmaceutical industry are facing the problem of bacterial resistance to drugs, even as genetically engineered bacteria are being used to produce important medications for humans.

See also Aerobic; Anaerobic; Antibiotics; Antisepsis; Bioremediation; Enterobacteria; Fermentation; Flagella; Nitrogen fixation.

Marc Kusinitz

Bacteriophage

Bacteriophages (phages) are viruses that target and infect only bacterial cells. Many types of bacteriophage have been identified since their discovery in 1915, and they are named according to the type of bacteria they infect. For example, staphylophages are specific viruses of the staphylococcal bacteria, and coliphages specifically infect coliform bacteria. Bacteriophages are perhaps the most thoroughly studied and well understood viruses. They occur frequently in nature, carry out similar biological functions as other viruses, yet do not target human cells for infection. Phages have proven to be a valuable scientific research tools for a variety of applications: as models for the study of viral infectious mechanisms, as tools of biotechnology which introduce new genes to bacterial cells, and a potential treatments or human bacterial infection.

Structurally, bacteriophages (like most viruses) are composed of a protein coat surrounding a core containing DNA (deoxyribonucleic acid) or RNA (ribonucleic acid) though many variations on this basic design exist. The bacteria that these viruses infect often measure about one micron in diameter (a micron is one thousandth of a millimeter) and the phages themselves may be as small as twenty–five thousandths of a micron. Bacteriophages infect their hosts by binding to the wall of the bacterial cell. The wall is perforated by enzyme action and phage DNA is injected into the cell. This alters the genetic machinery of the cell which makes more bacteriophage DNA. Ultimately, the host cell dies when phage copies accumulate to the point of lysing (bursting) the cell membrane, releasing the phages which go forth and continue the cycle.

Much of what has been learned about the mechanisms of viral infection in general has been discerned through the study of bacteriophages. They have proved to be invaluable molecular tools for biotechnology— forming the enzymes that are used for cutting and splicing DNA in order to create new products of cellular metabolism. It is through such enzymatic cutting and pasting that human insulin was first safely and cheaply produced. Specific genes implanted in bacterial cells with the aid of phage enzymes direct bacterial cells to produce insulin and other valuable protein products in great purity and quantity. Additionally, bacteriophages are only now beginning to fulfill the dream of their discoverer, Felix d'Herelle, in combatting infection in humans and animals. The medical potential of bacteriophages is great as a treatment for blood infection and meningitis for example, along with a host of bacterial infections increasingly resistant to antibiotics.

See also Biotechnology; Virus.

Badgers

Badgers are eight species of robust, burrowing carnivores in the subfamily Meilinae of the family Mustelidae, which also includes weasels, mink, marten, otters, and skunks. There are eight species of badgers, distributed among six genera.

Badgers have a strong, sturdy body, with short, powerful, strong–clawed legs, and a short tail. The head is slender and triangular–shaped. The fur of badgers is largely composed of long, stiff, rather thin guard hairs, with relatively little underfur. Badgers are fossorial animals, meaning they are enthusiastic diggers, often constructing substantial den–complexes, usually in sandy ground. Badgers are generally crepuscular, being active at dusk, night, and dawn. Badgers are strong and tough animals and can readily defend themselves against all but the largest predators.

The American badger

The American or prairie badger (*Taxidea taxus*) is widespread in the prairies and savannas of western North America. The American badger is a stout–bodied and stubby–tailed animal. It has strong front legs armed with long, sturdy claws useful for digging and shorter–clawed hind legs. The primary color of the fur is grayish to brownish–red, with a black or dark–brown snout and feet, and bright white markings on the face and top of the head, extending over the front of the back. The hair is longest on the sides of the animal, which accentuates the rather compressed appearance of this species. Males are somewhat larger than females, and can be as long as about 3 ft ([1 m] body plus the tail) and weigh as much as 22 lbs (10 kg).

The American badger is a solitary animal during most of the year, coming together only during the breeding season. This species is highly fossorial, and it digs numerous dens. The dens may be used for breeding by successive generations of animals and can be complicated assemblages of tunnels, access holes, and chambers. The sleeping chambers are comfortably lined with grassy hay, which is renewed frequently for cleanliness. However, individual badgers may change their dens rather frequently, sometimes moving around and digging new holes over a rather extensive area. Defecation occurs in holes dug above–ground, which are then covered up. Badgers in northern and alpine parts of the range of the species will hibernate during the winter, but more southerly populations are active throughout the year. American badgers scent–mark their territory, using secretions from a pair of anal grands.

The American badger is primarily a carnivore, catching its own prey or scavenging dead animals. However, it also feeds on plant materials. Prey species include rabbits, ground squirrels, small mammals such as mice and voles, ground–nesting birds, earthworms, snails, and insects. Foraging can occur at any time of day, but most commonly around the late afternoon to dusk. Burrowing prey are excavated by vigorous, extensive digging. Baby badgers are born in the early springtime, and they disperse from the natal den in the following autumn.

The American badger has a relatively dense and lustrous fur, which in the past was of commercial value, mostly for use as a fur trim, and also for the manufacturing of shaving brushes. The American badger is considered by some farmers and ranchers to be a pest, primarily because its access holes can represent a leg–breaking hazard to large livestock. Consequently, this species has been excessively trapped and poisoned in many areas, greatly reducing the extent and abun-

A badger at its den hole.

dance of its wild populations. Attempts have been made to cultivate American badgers on fur farms, but these did not prove successful.

Other species of badgers

The natural range of the Eurasian badger (*Meles meles*) extends south of the tundra throughout most of Europe, Russia, Mongolia, Tibet, China, and Japan. The Eurasian badger is primarily a species of forests and thick scrub, although it also occurs in relatively disturbed habitats, such as parks. The Eurasian badger can reach a length of 3 ft (1 m) and a weight of 35 lbs (16 kg). It has pronounced white stripes running along the head and the forepart of its back, overlying a grayish basal color. The feet are colored dark brown or black.

The Eurasian badger digs its den or "set" in open sites with sandy soil, using its strong forelegs and stout, sharp claws. The den may be used continuously by many generations of animals, and is a complex of tunnels, with numerous exits, entrances, ventilation holes, sleeping chambers, and even an underground toilet area for use by young (adults defecate in outside pits). The sleeping areas are lined with a bedding of plant materials, which are kept clean by frequent renewals.

The Eurasian badger is monogamous and pairs for life, which can be as long as 15 years. This species is somewhat gregarious, and several pairs will live in harmony in the same complex of burrows. Once the young badgers have matured, however, they are driven from the natal den. This usually occurs after the end of their first winter, when the animals are almost one–year old.

European badgers forage at dusk and during the night, although they may also be seen basking during the day. These animals are omnivorous, with plant materials comprising about three quarters of the food consumed, and hunted and scavenged animals the

KEY TERMS

Crepuscular—Refers to animals that are most active in the dim light of dawn and dusk, and sometimes at night as well.

Fossorial—Refers to animals that spend a great deal of time digging and living underground.

Omnivore—Consumers of a wide range of foods.

remainder. If they are hand–raised as babies, European badgers will become quite tame, but wild–caught adults are not tamable.

The hog–badger (*Arctonyx collaris*) occurs in hilly, tropical and subtropical forests of northern India, Nepal, southern China, and Southeast Asia, as far south as Indonesian Sumatra. The hog–badger can weigh as much as 31 lbs (14 kg), and is an omnivorous, nocturnal animal with a pig–like snout. This species it digs enthusiastically, and climbs well.

The teludu or Malayan stink badger (*Mydaus javanensis*) is a brown animal with a broad, white stripe running along its back from the head to the tail. The teludu has well–developed anal glands, which can be used in a skunk–like fashion to deter potential predators by squirting a smelly secretion as far as 5 ft (1.5 m). This species occurs on the Malayan Peninsula, Borneo, Sumatra, and Java. The palawan or calamian stink badger (*Suillotaxus marchei*) occurs on some Philippine Islands.

The ferret badgers are various species of relatively slender, ferret–like animals, with a long, bushy tail, a face mask, and an active and inquisitive demeanor. The Chinese ferret badger (*Melogale moschata*) occurs in China and northern Southeast Asia. The Bornean or Javan ferret badger (*M. orientalis*) occurs on the Southeast Asian islands of Borneo and Sumatra. The Indian ferret badger (*M. personata*) occurs from eastern India and Nepal to Thailand and Vietnam. Ferret badgers live in open forests and savannas, and they den in holes dug in the ground or in hollow trees. Ferret badgers are predators of small mammals, birds, and invertebrates.

Further Reading:

Banfield, A. W. F. *The Mammals of Canada.* Toronto: University of Toronto Press, 1974.

Grzimek, B., ed. *Grzimek's Encyclopedia of Mammals.* London: McGraw Hill, 1990.

Hall, E. R. *The Mammals of North America,* 2nd ed. New York: Wiley & Sons, 1981.

Paradiso, J. L., ed. *Mammals of the World,* 2nd ed. Baltimore: John Hopkins Press, 1968.

Wilson, D. E. and D. Reeder. *Mammal Species of the World.* Washington, D.C.: Smithsonian Institution Press, 1993.

Bill Freedman

Baguio see **Tropical cyclone**

Baking soda see **Sodium bicarbonate**

Ballistics

Ballistics is the study of projectile motion. A projectile is an object that has been launched, shot, hurled, thrown or by other means projected and which continues in motion due to its own inertia. The path of the projectile is determined by its initial velocity (direction and speed) and the forces of gravity and air resistance. For objects projected close to Earth and with negligible air resistance, the flight path is a parabola. When air resistance is significant, however, the shape and rotation of the object are important and determining the flight path is more complicated. Ballistics influences many fields of study ranging from analyzing a curve ball to developing missile guidance systems.

Free-falling bodies

In order to understand projectile motion it is first necessary to understand the motion of free-falling bodies, that is objects which are simply dropped from a certain height above the Earth. For the simplest case, when air resistance is negligible and when objects are close to the Earth's surface, Galileo Galilei (1564–1642) was able to show that two objects fall the same distance in the same amount of time, regardless of their weights. It is also true that the speed of a falling object will increase by equal increments in equal time periods. For example, a ball dropped from the top of a building will start from rest and increase to a speed of 32 ft (9.8 m) per second after one second, to a speed of 64 ft (19.5 m) per second after two seconds, to a speed of 96 ft (29.4 m) per second after three seconds, and so on. Thus, the *change* in speed for each one second time interval is always 32 ft per second. The change in speed per time interval is known as the acceleration and is constant. This acceleration is equal to 1 g which stands for the acceleration due to the force of gravity. By comparison, a pilot in a supersonic jet pulling out of a nose dive may experience an acceleration as high as 9 g (of course, a jet is not in free fall but is being accelerated by its engines and gravity).

The acceleration of gravity, g, becomes smaller as the distance from the Earth increases. However, for most Earth bound applications, the value of g can be considered constant (it only changes by 0.5% due to a 10 mi [16 km] altitude change). Air resistance, on the other hand, can vary greatly depending on altitude, wind, and properties and velocity of the projectile itself. It is well know that sky divers may change their altitude relative to other sky divers by simply changing the shape of their body. Also, it is obvious that a rock will fall more quickly than a feather. Therefore, when treating problems in ballistics, it is necessary to separate the effects due to gravity, which are fairly simple, and the effects due to air resistance, which are more complicated.

Projectile motion without air resistance

The motion of projectiles, without air resistance, can be separated into two components. Motion in the vertical direction where the force of gravity is present, and horizontal motion where the force of gravity is zero. As Isaac Newton (1642—1727) proposed, an object in motion will remain in motion unless acted upon by an external force. Therefore, a projectile in motion will remain with the same horizontal velocity throughout its flight, since no force exists in the horizontal direction, but its velocity will change in the vertical direction due to the force of gravity. For example, a cannon ball is fired in the horizontal direction. The velocity of the cannon ball will remain constant, in the horizontal direction, but the ball will accelerate toward the Earth, in the vertical direction, with an acceleration of 1 g. The combination of these two effects produces a path which describes a parabola. Since the vertical motion is determined by the same acceleration which describes the motion of objects in free fall, a second cannon ball which is dropped, at precisely the same instant as the first cannon ball is fired, will reach the ground at precisely the same instant. Therefore, the motion in the horizontal direction does not affect the motion in the vertical direction. This fact can be confirmed by knocking one coin off the edge of the desk with a good horizontal whack, while a second coin is simultaneously knocked off the desk with a gently nudge. Both coins will reach the ground at the same time.

By increasing the amount of gun powder behind the cannon ball, one could increase the horizontal velocity of the cannon ball as it leaves the cannon and cause the cannon ball to land at a greater distance. If it were possible to increase the horizontal velocity to very high values, there would come a point at which the cannon ball would continue in its path without ever touching the ground, similar to an orbiting satellite. To attain this orbiting situation close to the Earth's sur-

---

KEY TERMS

Acceleration of gravity—The vertical downward acceleration equal to 32 ft (9.8 m) per second per second experienced by objects in flight close to the Earth.

Air resistance—The drag force on an object in flight due to the interaction with air molecules.

Free falling body—A falling object in one dimensional motion, influenced by gravity when air resistance is negligible.

Gyroscope—A device similar to a top which maintains rotation about an axis while maintaining a constant orientation of that axis in space.

Inertia—The tendency of an object in motion to remain in motion in a constant direction and at a constant speed and the tendency of an object at rest to remain at rest.

Projectile—An object which is projected close to the Earth and whose flight path is determined by gravity, air resistance, and inertia.

---

face, the cannon ball would have to be fired with a speed of 17,700 miles per hour (28,500 kph)!

In most instances, projectiles, like cannon balls, are fired at some upward angle to the Earth's surface. As before, the flight paths are described by parabolas. (The maximum range is achieved by aiming the projectile at a 45° angle above the horizontal.) Note that angles which are equally greater or less than 45° will produce flight paths with the same range (for example 30° and 60°).

Projectile motion with air resistance

If projectiles were only launched from the surface of the moon where there is no atmosphere, then the effects of gravity, as described in the previous section, would be sufficient to determine the flight path. On Earth, however, the atmosphere will influence the motion of projectiles. As opposed to the situation due to purely gravitational effects, projectile motion with air resistance will be dependent on the weight and shape of the object. As one would suspect, lighter objects are more strongly affected by air resistance. In many cases, air resistance will produce a drag force which is proportional to the velocity squared. The effects of increased air drag on an object such as a cannon ball will cause it to fall short of its normal range without air resistance. This effect may be significant. In World War I, it was realized that cannon balls would travel farther distances if aimed at higher elevations, due to the decreased air density and decreased drag.

More subtle effects of air resistance on projectile motion are related to the shape and rotation of the object. Clearly, the shape of an object can have an effect on its projectile motion, as anyone has experienced by wadding up a piece of paper before tossing it into the waste can. The rotation of an object is important also. For example, a good quarterback always puts a spin on a football when making a pass. By contrast, to produce an erratic flight, a knuckle ball pitcher in baseball puts little or no spin on the ball. The physical property which tends to keep spinning objects spinning is the conservation of angular momentum. Not only do spinning objects tend to keep spinning but the orientation of the spin axis tends to remain constant. This property is utilized in the design of rifle barrels which have spiral grooves to put a spin on the bullet. The spinning of the bullet around its long axis will keep the bullet from tumbling and will increase the accuracy of the rifle. This property is also utilized in designing guidance systems for missiles. These guidance systems consist of a small spinning device called a gyroscope which keeps a constant axis orientation and thus helps to orient the missile. Small deviations of the missile with respect to the orientation of the gyroscope can be measured and corrections in the flight path can be made.

See also Conservation laws.

Further Reading:

March, Robert. *Physics for Poets*. New York: McGraw–Hill, 1970.
Hewitt, Paul. *Conceptual Physics*. New York: HarperCollins, 1993.
Young, Hugh. *University Physics*. Reading, MA: Addison–Wesley, 1992.
Armenti, Angelo Jr. *The Physics of Sports*. New York: American Institute of Physics, 1992.
Symon, Keith. *Mechanics*. Reading, MA: Addison–Wesley, 1971.

Kurt Vandervoort

Balloon

A balloon is a nonsteerable aircraft consisting of a thin envelope inflated with any gas lighter than the surrounding air. The balloon rises from the ground similar

The balloon that carried the 3 ton, 36" Stratoscope II telescope.

to a gas bubble in a glass of soda. The physical principle underlying this ability to ascend is Archimedes' law, according to which any immersed body is pushed upward by a force equal to the weight of the displaced fluid. If this force is greater than the weight of the body itself, the body rises. The lighter the balloon is in comparison with air of the same volume, the more load (envelope, people, instruments) it can lift. The approximate lifting capacity of some lighter–than–air gases in a 1000 cu m balloon at 32° F (0° C) is shown below:

Hydrogen	Helium	Methane	Neon	Nitrogen
1203	1115	576	393	42

For example, a balloon filled with nitrogen possesses only about 1/30 of the lifting capacity of the same balloon filled with hydrogen. As a matter of fact, only hydrogen, helium, and hot air are of practical importance. Hydrogen, the lightest existing gas, would be ideal for the balloon inflation if it had not one serious demerit: inflammability. Helium is 7% less efficient than hydrogen. It is absolutely safe in usage, however, but it is not easily available and its production is not cheap. Hot air is safe and easy to obtain, making it the most often used for common manned flights. But to get from hot air a lifting power equal to at least 40% of that of helium it would be necessary to heat it to about 570° F (300°C). The ascensional force of a hot–air balloon is difficult to control, since it is very unstable sharply reacting to any variations of the inside air temperature. There is always an element of uncertainty in the balloon flight. Once airborne, it floats freely in air currents, leaving a man the possibility to regulate only the vertical motion.

For 123 years, since the first flight of a bag filled with smoke publicly launched by the Montgolfier brothers in Paris in 1783 till the first flight of the practical powered airplane of the Wright brothers in 1905, a balloon and its later modification, an airship, remained the only means of aerial navigation. This period was full of exciting achievements of courageous aeronauts. The crossing of the English Channel (1785, by Blanchard, France and Jeffries, USA), the parachute descent from the balloon (1797, by Garnerin, France), the crossing of the Irish Sea (1817, by Windham Sadler, England), and the long–distance flight from London to Nassau (1836, by Green, England) are a few of the milestones in the balloon's early history.

The suitability of balloons for making observations and for reaching the inaccessible areas was soon generally recognized. The first air force in the world was created by France in 1794, and by the end of the nineteenth century balloon corps, whose main function was reconnaissance, were the common feature of European and American armies. With the introduction of a heavier–than–air craft military interest in balloons faded. However, the most challenging pioneering and scouting missions via balloons were yet to come.

Balloons and the exploration of the unknown

In 1863, the first remarkable high–altitude ascent was made by Glaisher and Coxwell in England. The purpose of this flight was purely a scientific one: to observe and record the properties of the upper atmosphere. The explorers rose to over 33,000 ft (10,000 m). The attempt almost cost them their lives, but fortunately they survived to describe the unique experience. This outstanding attempt was followed by many others, and high–altitude scientific ascents continued until the early 1960s. A specific layer of the atmosphere between 35,000 and 130,000 ft (11,000 and 40,000 m), which is called stratosphere, for some time became a new challenge to human spirit and engineering art. The mark of 72,395 ft (22,066 m), achieved by Stevens and Anderson in 1935, was a tremendous success for that time and was surpassed only twenty years later, when the United States resumed the manned stratosphere ballooning. The last in the series was the flight of Ross and Prather, who attained the altitude of 113,740 ft (34,467 m) in 1961. The technology developed to secure man's survival in extreme conditions became a germ of future space life–support systems.

The introduction of new lightweight and very strong plastic materials made it possible to build extremely big balloons able to take aloft huge payloads. Laded with sophisticated instruments, such balloons began to carry out complex studies of the atmosphere, biomedical and geographical research, and astronomical observations.

Each day, thousands of balloonsondes measure all possible characteristics of the atmosphere around the entire globe, contributing to the worldwide meteorological database. This information is needed for understanding the laws of air–mass movement and for the accurate weather forecasting.

Balloon astronomy takes advantage of making observations in the clarity of the upper air, away from dust, water vapors, and smoke. Telescopes with a diameter of up to 3.3 ft (1 m) are placed on platforms, which are supported by mammoth balloons, as high as an eight–story building, at elevations of up to 66,000–120,000 ft (20,000–35,000 m).

The Russian mission to Venus in 1985 used two helium balloons to examine the motion of the Venusian atmosphere. For 46 hours, they floated above Venus with an attached package of scientific equipment, which analyzed the environment and transmitted the information directly to Earth. For comparison, a landing module in the mission functioned for only 21 minutes.

The success of balloons on Venus may be possibly continued on Mars. To carry a multipurpose research probe above the Martian surface, American scientists suggested an original device consisting of a big hot–air balloon and a much smaller helium–filled balloon connected together. During the day, the air–balloon, heated by the sun, would drift in the Martian atmosphere with a payload of instruments. At night, the air–balloon would cool and descend to the ground, where it would stay, supported in the upright position by the smaller gas–balloon. Thus, the same probe would perform the on–ground experiments at night and the atmospheric experiments during the day, travelling from one location to another.

See also Aerodynamics; Aircraft; Airship; Buoyancy, principle of.

Further Reading:
Jackson, D. D. *The Aeronauts*. Time–Life Books, Inc., 1980.
DeVorkin, D. H. *Race to the Stratosphere*. Springer–Verlag, 1989.
The Cambridge Encyclopedia of Space. Cambridge University Press, 1990.
Curtis, A. R. *Space Almanac*. Arcsoft Publishers, 1990.

Elena V. Ryzhov

Balsa see **Silk cotton family**
Bamboo see **Grasses**

Banana

Bananas, plantains, and their relatives are various species of plants in the family Musaceae. There are about 40 species in this family, divided among only two genera. The most diverse genus is *Musa*, containing 35 species of bananas and plantains, followed by *Ensete*, the Abyssinian bananas. The natural range of bananas and plantains is the tropics and subtropics of the Old World, but agricultural and horticultural species and varieties are now cultivated in suitable climates all over the world.

Biology of bananas

Plants in the banana family are superficially tree–like in appearance. However, they are actually tall, erect, perennial herbs, because after they flower and set fruit, they die back to the ground surface. Their perennating structure is a large, underground, branched rhizome or corm.

Bananas and their relatives have a pseudostem, so–called because it has the appearance of a tree trunk. However, the banana stem is actually herbaceous, and is comprised of the densely overlapping sheath and petiole bases of their spirally arranged leaves. The pseudostem contains no woody tissues, but its fibers are very strong and flexible, and can easily support the erect plant, which is among the tallest of any herbaceous plants.

Bananas can grow as tall as 19.7–23 ft (6–7 m), and typically have a crown of leaves at the top of their greenish stem. The leaves of bananas are large and simple, with a petiole, a stout mid–rib, and a long, expanded, roughly oval, leaf blade, which can reach several meters in length. The leaf blade has an entire (smooth) margin, although it often becomes frayed by the wind, and may develop lobe–like ingrowths along its edge.

The flowers of bananas are finger–shaped, with three petals and sepals, and are subtended by large, fleshy, bright reddish–colored scales, which fall off as the fruit matures. The flowers are imperfect (that is, unisexual), and the plants are monoecious, meaning individual plants contain both female and male flowers. The flowers are arranged in a group, in an elongate structure known as a raceme, with male flowers occurring at the tip of the structure, and female flowers below. Only one inflorescence develops per plant. The flowering stalk develops from the underground rhizome or corm, and pushes up through the pseudostem of the plant, to emerge at the apex. The flowering stalk

A banana tree. The unopened flower can be seen at the end of the stalk that comes out of the bunches of fruit.

eventually curves downwards, under the weight of the developing fruits. The central axis of the raceme continues to elongate during development, so that older, riper fruits occur lower down, while flowers and younger fruit occur closer to the elongating tip. The same is true of the male flowers, with spent flowers occurring lower down, and pollen–producing ones at the tip of the inflorescence.

The flowers of bananas are strongly scented, and produce large quantities of nectar. These attract birds and bats, which feed on the nectar, and pollinate the flowers. The mature fruits are a type of multi–seeded berry, with a leathery outer coat known as an exocarp, and a fleshy, edible interior with numerous seeds embedded.

Bananas and people

Various species in the banana family are cultivated as agricultural crops, with a world production of about 66 million tons (60 million tonnes). The best–known species is the banana (*Musa paradisiaca*; sometimes known as *M. sapientum*). The cultivated banana is a sterile triploid, and does not produce viable seeds. This

KEY TERMS

. . . .

Berry—A soft, multi–seeded fruit, developed from a single, compound ovary.

Imperfect—In the botanical sense, this refers to flowers that are unisexual, containing either male or female reproductive parts, but not both.

Monoecious—A plant breeding system in which male and female reproductive structures are present on the same plant, although not necessarily in the same flowers.

Rhizome—An underground stem.

Triploid—An organism having three sets of chromosomes. In plants, triploids develop from crosses between a diploid parent, having two sets of chromosomes, and a tetraploid parent, with four sets.

banana is believed to be derived from crosses of *Musa acuminata* and *M. balbisiana*, likely occurring in India or Southeast Asia at some prehistoric time. The banana is an ancient fruit, thought to have been cultivated for at least 3,000 years in southern Asia.

Bunches of banana fruits can be quite large, weighing as much as 110 lb (50 kg). Each bunch consists of clusters of fruits, known as hands; each hand contains 10–20 individual fruits, or fingers. After the fruits of a banana plant are harvested, the plant dies back, or is cut down, and a new stalk regenerates from the same, perennating rhizome or corm.

Bananas intended for export to temperate countries are generally harvested while the fruits are still green. As they ripen, the skin turns yellowish or reddish, depending on the variety. When dark blotches begin to appear on the skin, the fruits are especially tasty and ready for eating. Bananas are a highly nutritious food.

The cultivated banana occurs in hundreds of varieties, or cultivars, which vary greatly in the size, color, and taste of their fruits. The variety most familiar to people living in temperate regions has a rather large, long, yellow fruit. This variety is most commonly exported to temperate countries because it ripens slowly, and travels well without spoiling. However, this variety of banana has proven to be susceptible to a recently emerged, lethal fungal disease. The long, yellow banana will soon be largely replaced in the temperate marketplace by another variety, which has a smaller, reddish, apple–tasting fruit.

Most varieties of the cultivated banana occur in tropical countries, especially in southern Asia, where many may be grown in any particular locality. These varieties range greatly in their size, taste, and other characteristics, some being preferred for eating as a fresh fruit, and others for cooking by frying or baking. Plantains or platanos are a group of about 75 varieties of cultivated bananas that are only eaten after they are cooked or processed into chips or flour. Like bananas, plantains are a highly nutritious food.

Another important economic product is manila hemp or abaca, manufactured from the fibers of the large, sheathing leaf–stalks of the species *Musa textilis*, as well as from some other species of bananas and plantains. *Musa textilis* is native to the Philippines and the Moluccas of Southeast Asia, and most manila hemp comes from that general region, although it has also been introduced elsewhere, for example, to Central America. The fibers of manila hemp are tough, flexible, and elastic, and are mostly woven into rope. Because it is resistant to salt water, this cordage is especially useful on boats and ships, although its use has now been largely supplanted by synthetic materials, such as polypropylene. The fibers of manila hemp can also been woven into a cloth, used to make bags, hats, twine, and other goods.

Bananas are also sometimes cultivated as ornamental plants, in gardens and parks in warm climates, and in greenhouses in cooler climates. Some taxonomic treatments include the genus *Strelitzia* in the banana family. The best–known species in this group is the bird–of–paradise plant (*Strelitzia reginae*), a beautiful and well–known ornamental plant that is cultivated in tropical and sub–tropical climates, and in greenhouses in more temperate places.

Further Reading:

Brucher, H. *Useful Plants of Neotropical Origin and Their Wild Relatives*. New York: Springer–Verlag, 1989.

Hvass, E. *Plants That Serve and Feed Us*. New York: Hippocrene Books, 1975.

Klein, R. M. *The Green World. An Introduction to Plants and People*. New York: Harper and Row, 1987.

Woodland, D. W. *Contemporary Plant Systematics*. New Jersey: Prentice–Hall, 1991.

Bill Freedman

Bananabird see **Orioles**

Banded anteaters see **Numbat**

A Cape York bandicoot from northern Queensland, Australia, in captivity at Macquarie University, New South Wales.

Bandicoots

Australian wildlife holds many surprises, but few as intriguing as the widely distributed bandicoots. These small, rabbit–sized marsupials have a thick set body, short limbs, a pointed muzzle, short neck and short hairy tail. Their teeth are similar to those of insect– and flesh–eating mammals, but their hind feet resemble those of kangaroos and possums. The hind-feet are not only considerably longer than the front pair, which gives most bandicoots a bounding gait, but the second and third toes of the hind foot are fused together, with only the top joints and claws being free. The forefeet, in contrast, have three prominent toes, with strong claws used for digging and searching for insect prey. The fused toes of the hind limbs not only provides a strong base for a hopping animal, but also

makes a highly effective comb for grooming dirt and parasites from the fur. One species now thought to be extinct, the pig–footed bandicoot (*Chaeropus ecaudatus*), had a slightly different morphology, with only two toes on their forefeet and one on the hindfoot – adaptations for running, as this was a species of the open plains.

The taxonomic status of bandicoots is still uncertain, although two families are now recognized – the Peramelidae, with some 13 species, and the Thylacomyidae, with just one species represented, the greater bilby (*Macrotis lagotis*). All of these species are unique to the Australian region, specifically mainland Australia, Tasmania, New Guinea and several offshore islands. Within this range, however, bandicoots have adapted to a wide range of habitats, including arid and semi–arid regions, coastal and sub–coastal habitat, savannah and lowland and mid–montane rainforest. On New Guinea, some species have been recorded at an altitude of 5,000 ft (1500m). The animals themselves may also vary considerably in size and appearance. The smallest species *Microperoryctes murina* weighs less than 4 oz (100g), while one of the largest *Peroryctes broadbenti* may weigh more than 11 lbs (5kg).

Bandicoots are terrestrial and nocturnal species, constructing shallow burrows and surface nests beneath vegetation. The greater bilby is the only species that constructs a large burrow system, which may extend 7 ft (2m) underground. Bandicoots are normally solitary, with males occupying a larger home range (0.007–0.02 sq mi, or 1.7–5.2 ha) than females (0.004–0.008 sq mi, or 0.9–2.1 ha). Despite their genteel appearance males, in particular, can be very aggressive towards other males. Little is known of the social behavior of most species, but they are thought to defend a central part of their ranges, especially the area surrounding their nest, against other animals. Males do not cooperate with bringing up the litter.

In the wild, bandicoots feed mainly on insects and their larvae but they are opportunistic feeders and will also consume fruit, berries, seeds, and fungi. Prey is either dug out of the soil or gleaned from the surface; their long, pointed snout is probably an adaptation for poking into tiny crevices or foraging under leaf litter for insects. Bandicoots have a keen sense of smell which is probably the main way in which they locate food at night. Most species also have prominent ears which may also assist with locating moving prey. Some species, such as the greater bilby have long naked ears that probably help with thermoregulation, as this species is adapted to living in arid conditions.

As with all marsupials the young are born at a very early stage of development, usually after a gestation period of just 12 days – one of the shortest periods of any mammal. When they are born, young bandicoots measure less than an inch (about 1 cm) and weigh a fraction of an ounce (0.2 g). Following birth the infant, which has well developed forelimbs, crawls its way into the mother's pouch where it attaches to a nipple and where it will remain for much of its pouch life. The average litter size is four; litters of seven young have been recorded. As the young grow, the mother's pouch increases in size to accommodate her developing family. Juveniles remain in the pouch for about 50 days, after which the mother begins to wean them. By the time they are seven weeks old, they are covered with short hair and the eyes are open.

Where climate and food conditions are favorable, bandicoots may breed throughout the year – females of some species may even become pregnant before its current litter is fully weaned. Bandicoots therefore have a very specialized pattern of breeding behavior among the marsupials, with a pattern of producing many young in a short period of time and with little parental investment.

Despite these adaptations, many species are now threatened as a result of human activities. Bandicoots have proven to be highly vulnerable to habitat modification and predation from introduced predators. In Australia, large areas of former brush habitat have been converted into rough pasture for sheep and cattle grazing, whose close cropping feeding actions have had a considerable effect on the soil microhabitat. Overgrazing by rabbits has had a similar effect. Introduced predators, especially foxes, cats and dogs have also had a major impact on populations in some areas. In New Guinea, many species are trapped for their fur and meat, but current levels of exploitation are unlikely to pose a significant threat to most species.

See also Marsupials.

Baobob see **Silk cotton family**

Barbary apes see **Macaques**

Barberry

Barberries are about 600 species of plants in the genus *Berberis*, family Berberidaceae, occurring throughout the Northern Hemisphere and South America. Most species of barberry are shrubs or small trees, and many of these have persistent, evergreen leaves. The flowers are small, arranged in clusters, and insect pollinated. The fruits of barberries are multiple–seeded berries.

Barberry hybrids are often cultivated as attractive, ornamental shrubs. Some of these commonly cultivated species include the Japanese barberry (*Berberis thunbergii*), common barberry (*B. vulgaris*), Oregon grape (*Mahonia aquifolium*), and heavenly bamboo (*Nandina domestica*).

The common barberry is a native of Europe, with attractive foliage and bright–red berries. The common barberry has been widely planted in North America as a garden shrub, and it has escaped to natural habitats, where it can maintain viable populations.

The presence of wild populations of common barberry is considered a significant agricultural problem, because this species is an alternate host in the life cycle of the wheat rust (*Puccinia graminis*). This fungus is a pathogen of wheat (*Triticum aestivum*), one of the most important food–producing plants in North America, and the world. The control of populations of common barberry is critical to control of the wheat rust.

The inner bark and roots of the common barberry are bright yellow, and were once used to make a natural dye. Practitioners of folk medicine thought that this yellow color indicated that common barberry could be useful in the treatment of jaundice. However, this barberry has not proven to be useful for this purpose.

There are also native species of barberry in North America, for example, the American barberry (*Berberis canadensis*) of the eastern United States. Other native species in the barberry family include various shrubs known as Oregon grapes (for example, *Mahonia repens*). Several species of spring–flowering, herbaceous perennials occur in the understory of hardwood forests in eastern North America, including blue cohosh (*Caulophyllum thalictroides*), mayapple (*Podophyllum peltatum*), and twin–leaf (*Jeffersonia diphylla*). All of these genera of herbaceous plants of eastern North America have counterparts in the same genus is eastern Asia, but not in western North America. This represents a biogeographically interesting, disjunct pattern of distribution.

See also Rusts and smuts

Barbets

Barbets are about 76 species of medium–sized birds, divided among 13 genera. These comprise the family Capitonidae, in the order Piciformes, which also contains the woodpeckers, toucans, and their allies. Barbets are birds of tropical forests, occurring in Central and South America, Africa, and Asia as far south as Indonesia. However, none of the species of barbets occur in more than one continent. The usual habitat of barbets is tropical forests and savannahs.

Barbets are thick–set birds, with species ranging in body length from 3.5–13 in (9–33 cm). Barbets have short, rounded wings, a short tail, a large head on a short neck, and a stout, sharp–tipped bill. These birds have a distinctive "barbet" of bristles around the base of their beak. Like other birds in the order Piciformes, the barbets have short but strong legs, and feet on which two toes point backwards and two forwards. This arrangement of the toes is adaptive to clinging to bark on the sides of trees, while also using the tail feathers as a prop for additional support.

Barbets are brightly colored birds, many of them beautifully so. The basal coloration of many species is bright green, often with white, red, yellow, or blue markings, especially around the head. South American barbets have a different plumage for each sex, but the African and Asian species are not usually dimorphic in this way.

Barbets mostly eat fruits of various sorts. Although they are not migratory, barbets will move about in search of their food, especially wild figs (*Ficus* spp.), which tend to fruit seasonally. The strong bill of barbets is used to crush the hard fruits that these birds commonly feed upon. Barbets also feed on insects, and the young birds are raised almost exclusively on that high–protein diet.

Barbets nest in cavities that they excavate themselves in heart–rotted stems of trees, in termite mounds, or in earthen banks. Incubation of the two to four eggs and raising of the young is shared by both sexes of the pair. The young are dependent on their parents for a relatively long time. In some cases, older youngsters will help their parents raise a subsequent brood of babies. Barbets are noisy birds, but they are not particularly musical.

The many–colored or red–crowned barbet (*Megalaima rafflesii*) occurs over much of Southeast Asia. This species has a body length of 10 in (25 cm), and is a particularly beautiful bird, with a bright–green back, wings, and belly, bright–red cap and throat, yellow on the forehead, blue on the cheeks, and a black line through the eye. Most other species of barbets are similarly attractive in the colors and patterns of their plumage.

Barbiturates

Barbiturates are compounds derived from barbituric acid that are commonly used as sedatives. Considered addictive, these drugs operate by depressing brain activity. Phenobarbital is the most common and the longest acting of the barbiturates. Other sedatives in this group are amobarbital and the shorter–acting pentobarbital and secobarbital. Abuse of barbiturates, as well as their role in illegal drug trafficking, has led many physicians to replace them with benzodiazepines, which are considered less addictive.

Chemical name	Trade name	Street name	Chemical structure
Amobarbital	Amytal	Blue heavens	
Barbital	Veronal	Barbs	
Pentobarbital	Nembutal	Nemmies, yellow jackets	
Phenobarbital	Luminal	Goofballs	
Secobarbital	Seconal	Red devils, red birds	

Some barbiturate drugs.

In 1864, German chemist Alfred von Baeyer prepared the first barbituric acid from malonic acid. An organic compound in the pyrimidine family, barbituric acid is the parent compound of barbiturate drugs as well as the basis for the synthetic production of the B vitamin riboflavin. By adding or substituting various groups of atoms on the barbituric acid molecule, chemists were able to develop more than a dozen different synthetic barbiturates. In 1903, Emil Fischer, a student of Baeyer's, synthesized 5.5–diethylbarbituric acid, better known under its trade name, barbital. By 1912, a phenylethyl derivative was developed and commercially introduced as phenobarbital. Since then, more than 2,500 barbiturates have been developed from barbituric acid, of which only about 50 have been marketed.

When first introduced, barbiturates largely replaced bromides, compounds used at the turn of the century as sedatives, antianxiety drugs, and anticonvulsant despite their toxic effects (they were found in such popular patent medicines as Bromo Seltzer). As a treatment for depression, barbiturates were replaced in the 1950s by tranquilizers such as valium and librium. Today, the medical use of barbiturates is generally confined to anesthetic procedures and the treatment of pain in terminally ill patients (they are often the drugs used in euthanasia). One barbiturate, phenobarbital, is still used in the treatment of epilepsy.

Effect on the nervous system

The molecules of barbiturate drugs pass through the membranes of the cells in the brain. They are then able to block nerve signals that pass from cell to cell, thus inhibiting the stimulation and conduction of chemical neurotransmitters between the cells. In addition, barbiturates, especially phenobarbital, are able to reduce the effect of abnormal electrical activity in the brain which causes seizures, such as in the case of epilepsy.

Depressant drugs, like alcohol and barbiturates, just as stimulant drugs, like cocaine and amphetamines, all appear to have the ability to stimulate the brain's reward circuit. The behavioral effect of this action is to increase the need for more of the drug, usually to get the same effect (drug tolerance). If it is being taken for its effect as a sedative, more of the drug is needed each time it is taken to produce sleep. Drugs that stimulate the brain's reward centers also have the effect of excluding other types of reward sensations like those from food or sex.

The newer benzodiazapine tranquilizers reduce neuron (nerve cell) sensitivity only for cells that have specific receptor sites for the chemical gamma aminobutyric acid (GABA), but the barbiturates are able to work the sedating effect elsewhere as well. That difference in action may account for the higher degree of sedation afforded by the barbiturates over the benzodiazapines. Both types of drugs are able to affect the brain's reward center by increasing the amount of dopamine (a neurotransmitter) released into the limbic system, the part of the brain that regulates certain biological functions such as sleep and the emotions.

Adverse effects

Intoxication from barbiturates is similar to alcohol intoxication. The speech becomes slurred, grogginess and drowsiness occur, as does emotional instability, anger, suspicion, abnormal eye movements (nystagmus), and many symptoms of drug–induced mental disorder. Mental functions are seriously impaired and suicidal intentions may be traced to the drug overdose, although accidental overdose may occur by the automatic response of taking more pills to cure the related problem of insomnia. The combination of barbiturates and alcohol is especially lethal since the two drugs reinforce each other's depression of the nervous system, respiratory system, and cardiovascular system, possibly leading to deep coma.

Dependence can occur after using barbiturates even at low doses after four weeks. There are severe withdrawal symptoms when treatment is halted abruptly. Convulsions, twitching, sleeplessness, and nightmares are some of the symptoms of abrupt withdrawal. The longer an individual is on the drug, the greater his or her tolerance to it builds up, meaning more of the drug must be taken to get the desired effect.

Types of barbiturates

Barbiturates are divided into three categories: long–acting, mid–range, and a short–acting range.

Long–acting drugs last for more than six hours, mid–range for four to six hours, and short range for less than four hours. Some very short range drugs are injected intravenously and produce anesthesia within one minute. Thiopental and hexobarbital are examples of anesthetic drugs and they are not sought after by drug abusers.

Phenobarbital is an example of a long–acting barbiturate that is prescribed in an average daily adult dose of 50–300 mg. These drugs are used for insomnia, some forms of epilepsy and mental disorders, and migraine headaches. It takes about an hour for the drug to take effect and up to ten hours for the effect to wear off. One drawback is the speed with which phenobarbital builds up in the body. Fatigue and depression can result after sleep throughout the rest of the day from long–acting barbiturates or when they are being taken as an anticonvulsant.

Mid–and short–range acting barbiturates take effect within 15–40 minutes. These drugs are less likely to produce the hangover effect of the long–lasting ones. The drugs amobarbital (Amytal), which is mid–range, and pentobarbital (Nembutal), which is short–range, are used as sedatives and are the ones most likely to be found in street sale drug traffic. They also lead to high risk for dependence and tolerance and have the most severe withdrawal symptoms.

Phenobarbital and epilepsy

The cause of most brain seizures or epilepsy is not known. Electrical currents in the brain discharge creating disturbances in the normal functioning of the brain. When a epileptic event occurs, the person may collapse and convulse or the disturbance may go unrecognized unless mapped by an electroencephalogram (EEG).

In grand mal epilepsy, consciousness is lost, the individual falls, and suffers spasms and severe muscle contractions for a short period of time. *Grand mal* is a common form of epilepsy and phenobarbital is still used for its treatment along with newer drugs, like Tegretol and Dilantin. Phenobarbital is also useful for minor seizures of the body or brain without loss of consciousness.

Barbiturate abuse

The most popular barbiturates in the illegal drug trade are secobarbital, or seconal, and pentobarbital. In the street trade secobarbital is referred to as reds, red devils, or downers, while pentobarbital is called yellow jackets or nembies. A combination of the two drugs is called reds and blues. In the past, individuals addicted

KEY TERMS

Barbituric acid—Parent compound for the development of barbiturates.

Benzodiazapine tranquilizers—A newer group of antianxiety drugs considered to be safer than the barbiturates

Depressants—Drugs that depress the action of the central nervous system; the opposite of stimulants.

Dopamine—A neurotransmitter found in the brain stem that regulates many mental functions and is affected by stimulant and depressant drugs.

Euphorics—Drugs used for their psychoactive effects of making the person feel good; usually the ones sought after by the illegal market.

Gamma aminobutyric acid (GABA)—A chemical found in the brain GABA has the effect of quieting the neurons where the GABA receptors are found on the nerve cell membranes.

to barbiturates obtained their supply from physicians ignorant of the drawbacks of these drugs. Today, barbiturates are controlled under federal laws similar to those governing the use of morphine, and drug traffickers will raid warehouses or hijack legitimate shipments to supply demand for the drug on the street.

Abusers of barbiturates appear in all income and age groups. They include middle–class, middle–aged individuals who rely on doctor's prescriptions to treat anxiety or insomnia. If they have trouble getting prescription refills from one doctor they will begin to visit others. Another group of abusers are adolescents and young adults. Their use of barbiturates is the same as their use of alcohol—to obtain a high or a sense of euphoria that is a temporary state of elation or feeling good. The atmosphere in which the drug is taken, along with how the taker of the drug feels about it, will color the response of either sedation or euphoria. This group may become habituated to both alcohol and barbiturates. It is a high–risk group, since mixing barbiturates and alcohol often leads to death.

More extreme drug abusers resort to the intravenous use of barbiturates which they shoot up along with heroin and amphetamines. A preference for barbiturates over heroin may develop since these are less expensive than heroin, even at very high dosages. Abusers of barbiturates describe the effects of the high

as producing a warm and pleasant feeling along with drowsiness. As a group they resemble amphetamine abusers, so–called speed freaks, in their tendency toward asocial and violent behavior.

Injections can lead to many adverse medical complications, including allergic responses and skin sores. Heroin addicts will use the barbiturates to elevate the effects of weak heroin, or alcoholics will use barbiturates to help them with withdrawal or to elevate intoxication. Cocaine abusers seeking relief from agitated feelings of paranoia use barbiturates as sedatives.

Controversial legal use

Barbiturates figure in several ethical and social controversies. Physicians treating terminally ill patients face complex issues when choosing to administer barbiturates to their patients. On one hand, they are potent relievers of pain since they effectively induce deep sleep and loss of consciousness. On the other hand, they hasten death by slowing respiration. Barbiturates and their role in euthanasia and assisted suicide have also been a source of controversy. In addition, some states and certain countries (for example, the Netherlands) use barbiturates as a means of capital punishment. Since they are fast–acting and relatively painless they are considered to be a humane form of execution.

See also Addiction; Alcoholism; Epilepsy; Narcotic.

Further Reading:
Longenecker, Gesina L. *How Drugs Work.* Emeryville, CA: Ziff–Davis Press, 1994.
Morgan, Robert. *The Emotional Pharmacy.* Los Angeles, CA: The Body Press, 1988.
Nicholi, Armand M. Jr. *The New Harvard Guide to Psychiatry.* Cambridge, MA: Harvard University Press, 1988.
Oppenheim, Mike. *100 Drugs That Work.* Los Angeles: Lowell House, 1994.
Truog, Robert D., et al. "Barbiturates in the Care of the Terminally Ill." *The New England Journal of Medicine,* Dec 3, 1992: 1678–1683.

Jordan Richman

Barbs see **Minnows**

Bar code

Almost everyone is familiar with the striped bars found on grocery and retail store items. These are bar

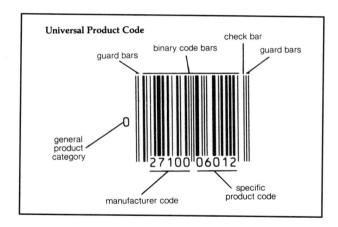

Universal Product Code

guard bars

binary code bars

check bar

guard bars

general
product
category

manufacturer code

specific
product code

The parts of the Universal Product Code (UPC).

codes, or more specifically, the Universal Product Code (UPC). UPC codes first appeared in stores in 1973 and have since revolutionized the sales industry.

The UPC code consists of ten pairs of thick and thin vertical bars that represent the manufacturer's identity, product size and name. Price information, which is not part of the bar code, is determined by the store. Bar codes are read by hand–held wand readers or fixed scanners linked to point of sale (POS) terminals.

Bar codes are also used for non retail purposes. One of the earliest uses for bar codes was as an identifier on railroad cars. Organizers of sporting events also take advantage of bar code technology. For example, as runners of the Boston Marathon complete the 26 mile course, they turn over a bar code tag that allows race officials to quickly tabulate results.

From 1965 through 1982, the United States Post Office experimented with optical character recognition (OCR) and bar code technology to speed up mail delivery. The Post Office now utilizes another type of bar code called the POSTNET bar code. Consisting of full and half height bars representing the zip–code and delivery address, the bar code allows mail to be sorted automatically at speeds of up to 700 pieces per minute.

Bareheaded rock fowl see **Babblers**

Barium see **Alkaline earth metals**

Barium sulfate

Barium sulfate ($BaSO_4$) is a white or yellow powder or crystalline salt with no taste or odor. Its density

is 4.24–4.5, and it melts at 2,876°F (1580°C), decomposing above that temperature. The compound is insoluble in water, but dissolves in hot concentrated sulfuric acid.

Barium sulfate occurs in nature as the mineral barite, or baryte, which is mined in Canada and Mexico and, in the United States in Arkansas, Missouri, Georgia, and Nevada. It is also prepared synthetically either by treating a solution of a barium salt with sodium sulfate or as a by–product in the manufacture of hydrogen peroxide.

Barium sulfate is used in diagnostic radiology of the digestive system. A suspension of barium sulfate in water is administered either orally or via an enema, which coats the lining of the upper or lower digestive tract. Because barium is a heavy metal, the compound is opaque to X–rays, and the shapes of the coated organs can be clearly seen. Although barium in solutions is highly toxic, the sulfate is so insoluble that the suspension is harmless.

Barium sulfate is also used as a filler to products such as rubber, linoleum, oil cloth, plastics, paper, and lithographic inks. The compound is also used in paints and pigments, especially in the manufacture of colored papers and wall papers. Recently, barium sulfate has become popular as a substitute for natural ivory.

Bark

Bark is a protective, outer tissue that occurs on older stems and roots of woody conifers and angiosperms. Bark is generally considered to occur on the outside of the tissue known as wood, or the water–conducting xylem tissues of woody plants. The inner cells of bark, known as phloem, grow by the division of outer cells in a generative layer called the vascular cambium, present between the bark and wood (inner cells of this cambium produce xylem cells). The outer cells of bark, known as cork, grow through the cellular division in the cork cambium, present outside of the phloem. The outer part of the bark is a layer of dead cells which can be as thick as several inches or more, and serves to protect the internal living tissues from injury, heat, and desiccation.

The macroscopic structure of bark varies greatly among species of woody plants. For example, the bark of American beech (*Fagus grandifolia*) is distinctively grey and smooth. In contrast, many species have a deeply fissured, rough bark, as in the cases of sugar maple (*Acer saccharum*) and spruces (*Picea* spp.). The color and pattern of fissuring and scaling of bark can often be used to identify species of trees and shrubs.

Some types of bark have specific uses to humans. The young, brownish, inner bark of young shoots of the cinnamon tree (*Cinnamomum zeylanicum*), native to Sri Lanka but now widely cultivated in the humid tropics, is collected, dried, and used whole or powdered as an aromatic flavoring of drinks and stews. Some barks have medicinal properties, such as that of the cinchona tree (*Cinchona calisaya*), from which quinine has long been extracted and used to reduce the fevers associated with malaria. More recently, anti–cancer chemicals have been identified in the bark of Pacific yew (*Taxus brevifolia*).

The bark of some species of trees contains large concentrations of a group of organic chemicals known as tannins, which can be reacted with animals skins to created a tough, flexible, and very useful material known as leather. Tannins will also react with certain metal salts to form dark pigments, which are used in printing and dyeing. Major sources of tannins in North America are the barks of hemlock trees, (especially *Tsuga canadensis* and *T. heterophylla*), and oaks, especially chestnut oak (*Quercus prinus*) and tanbark oak (*Lithocarpus densiflora*). Eurasian oaks and hemlocks are also used, as are several tropical species, such as red mangrove (e.g., *Rhizophora mangle*) and wattle (e.g., *Acacia decurrens*). The thick, outer bark of the cork oak (*Quercus suber*) of Europe is collected and used to manufacture bottle "corks," flotation devices, insulation, and composite materials such as parquet flooring. The bark of some conifers is used as a mulch in landscaping, for example, that of Douglas fir (*Pseudotsuga menziesii*) and redwood (*Sequoia sempervirens*).

See also Plant; Tree; Yew.

Bill Freedman

Barking squirrels see **Prairie dog**
Barley see **Grasses**

Barnacles

The rocky shores of most coastlines are liberally dotted with clusters of barnacles (phylum Arthropoda, class Crustacea). Few people take any notice of these animals, despite their common occurrence. Barnacles are exclusively marine animals: some 900 species have been identified worldwide. Many are tiny organisms measuring just a few centimeters in diameter, while others such as the South American *Balanus psittacus* may reach a height of 9 in (23 cm) and a diameter of 3 in (8 cm). Some of the smallest barnacles are parasitic, burrowing into mollusc shells and corals. The majority, however, are free–living animals that occur in distinct parts of the shoreline: while most species live within the intertidal range, some are limited to the low tide mark, while others are adapted to living in the spray zone, which only the highest tides can reach. A few species are even adapted to living in deep water.

There are two main types of barnacles – acorn and goose. Acorn barnacles are generally recognized by their squat, limpet–like appearance and extremely tough outer covering made up of five calcareous plates, which surround and protect the soft body cavity. With muscular contractions these plates can be opened or closed, depending on the state of the tide: at full tide, the plates are pushed outwards to allow the barnacle to feed, but as the tide withdraws, the barnacle closes its shell once again, leaving just a tiny opening for oxygen to enter. Thus enclosed in their shells, barnacles can resist drying at low tide.

Goose, or stalked, barnacles differ in appearance by having a long stalk (peduncle), the base of which is attached to the substratum and the main part of the body (capitulum) poised at the other end. The latter is enclosed in a toughened carapace, similar to that of acorn barnacles, while the peduncle is muscular and capable of movement.

Rocks are not the only substrate that attract barnacles. Some species attach to intertidal grasses, while others fix onto the shells of crabs or other molluscs such as clams, where they may help camouflage the host animal, and some even become attached to active–swimming species such as marine turtles or even the fins or other body parts of whales. Floating timber and flotsam, marine buoys, piers and ship's keels are also convenient anchoring points for many barnacles.

Adult barnacles remain in the same position for their lifetime. Being literally stuck in one place might prove an obstacle to many species, but barnacles have overcome this problem by having a larval dispersal phase. Most barnacles are hermaphroditic – each individual having both male and female reproductive organs and, while self–fertilization may take place in some instances, the normal pattern is for cross fertilization. Barnacles have extremely long male reproductive organs, some of which measure more than 30 times the length of the animal's body. The advantage of this is that although barnacles usually live in crowded conditions, they may also be able to reach other, more distant animals and fertilize them. Using this means to reach other barnacles, sperm are deposited in neighboring animals and the eggs brooded for about four months in a special sac within the mantle cavity. When they hatch, the tiny larvae will be released to the ocean where they drift with the currents. As many as 13,000 larvae may be released by a single individual. These larvae feed and mature through a series of six stages, following which they are ready to settle – a critical time in the life of the barnacle. As the larvae settles it attaches itself to some substrate by means of cement glands located in the base of the first antennae. It then undergoes a period of metamorphosis in which the existing larval carapace becomes covered with interlocking calcareous plates.

Locked in that position for the remainder of its life, the barnacle has evolved a simple, but effective means of feeding. When covered with water, the barnacle extends six pairs of curved, hairy legs (cirri) from the body cavity into the water column. Here they are able to trap tiny plankton and small crustaceans directly from the water. As food is captured, the cirri are withdrawn into the mouth where particles are cleaned off and the cirri unfolded once again to continue feeding. Rhythmic beating of the cirri also creates a gentle flow of water down towards the mouth, further enhancing the chances of obtaining additional food.

In spite of their small size barnacles are of considerable economic importance, particularly for shipping, as high densities of barnacles on a ship's keel can reduce its speed by as much as one–third. Similar agglomerations may form on the legs of oil rigs, piers and other semi–permanent features, causing considerable damage. A great deal of research and money has been invested in the design of anti–fouling paints which would deter barnacles from settling in the first place. Many of these products, however, have had a negative effect on the marine environment, causing poisoning among some species.

See also Arthropods; Crustacea.

Barometer

A barometer is an instrument for measuring atmospheric pressure. Two kinds of barometers are in common use, a mercury barometer and an aneroid barometer. The first makes use of a long narrow glass tube filled with mercury supported in a container of mer-

An aneroid barometer.

cury, and the second makes use of a diaphragm whose size changes as a result of air pressure.

Mercury barometers

The principle of the mercury barometer was discovered by the Italian physicist Evangelista Torricelli in about 1643. That principle can be illustrated in the following manner. A long glass tube is sealed at one end and then filled with liquid mercury metal. The filled tube is then inverted and its open end inserted into a bowl of mercury. When this happens, a small amount of mercury metal runs out of the tube, leaving a vacuum at the top of the tube.

Under normal circumstances, the column of mercury in the glass tube stands at a height of about 30 in (76 cm). The column is sustained because air pressure pushes down on the surface of the mercury in the bowl at the bottom of the barometer. At the same time, the vacuum at the top of the glass tube exerts essentially no pressure on the column of mercury. The height of the mercury column in the glass tube, then, reflects the total pressure exerted by the atmosphere at the moment of measurement.

In theory, a barometer could be made of any liquid whatsoever. Mercury is chosen, however, for a number of reasons. In the first place, it is so dense that the column sustained by air pressure is of practicable height. A similar barometer made of water, in comparison, would have to be more than 34 ft (100 m) high. Also, mercury has a low vapor pressure and does not, therefore, evaporate very easily. In a water barometer, the situation would be very different. Water has a much greater vapor pressure, and one would have to take into consideration the pressure exerted by water vapor at the top of the barometer, a factor of almost no consequence with a mercury barometer.

Two important additions needed to increase the accuracy of a barometer are a vernier scale and a thermometer. The vernier allows one to make an even more accurate measurement than is possible by reading the scale itself. The thermometer is needed because the density of mercury and other materials used in the construction of a barometer change with temperature. Most barometers come equipped with thermometers attached to them, therefore, along with conversion charts that permit one to correct barometer readings for a range of actual temperatures.

Modifications to the mercury barometer

The barometer described above is adequate for making rough measurements of atmospheric pressure. When more accurate readings are needed, however, modifications in the basic design of the barometer must be made. The most important factor to be considered in making such modifications is changes that take place in the mercury reservoir at the bottom of the barometer as a result of changes in atmospheric pressure.

When the atmospheric pressure decreases, for example, air pressure is able to sustain a slightly smaller column of mercury, and some mercury flows out of the glass tube into the reservoir. One might hope to find the new pressure by reading the new level of the mercury in the glass tube. However, the level of the mercury in the glass tube must be compared to the level of the mercury in the reservoir, and the latter has changed also as a result of a new atmospheric pressure.

This problem is dealt with in one of two ways. In one instrument, the English Kew barometer, no modification is made in the mercury reservoir itself. Instead, changes that take place in the mercury level in the reservoir as a result of changes in atmospheric pres-

sures are compensated for by making small changes in the measuring scale mounted to the glass tube. As one moves upward along the scale, the graduations between markings become slightly smaller to correct for the changing level of the mercury in the reservoir.

A second type of barometer, the Fortin barometer, contains a flexible bag that holds an extra supply of mercury metal. The flow of mercury into and out of that bag and then out of and into the glass tube is controlled by an adjustable screw whose point is moved so as just to touch the surface of the mercury in the reservoir. As atmospheric pressure and mercury levels change, modifications of the adjustable screw keep the mercury level at a constant height.

Aneroid barometer

A major disadvantage of the mercury barometer is its bulkiness and fragility. The long glass tube can break easily, and mercury levels may be difficult to read under unsteady conditions, as on board a ship at sea. To resolve these difficulties, the French physicist Lucien Vidie invented the aneroid ("without liquid") barometer in 1843.

An aneroid barometer can be compared to a coffee can whose sides have are flexible, like the bellows on an accordion. Attached to one end of the coffee can (aneroid barometer) is a pointer. As atmospheric pressure increases or decreases, the barometer contracts or expands. The movement of the barometer is reflected in the motion of the pointer, which rides up and down with changes in atmospheric pressure.

One way to observe the motion of the pointer is to attach it to the hand on a dial that moves around a circular scale, from low pressure to high pressure. The simple clock–like aneroid barometer hanging on the wall of many homes operates on this basis. Another way to observe the movement of the pointer is to have it rest on the side of a rotating cylinder wrapped with graph paper. As the cylinder rotates on its own axis, the pen makes a tracing on the paper that reflects increases and decreases in pressure. A recording barometer of this design is known as a barograph.

The altimeter

An important application of the aneroid barometer is the altimeter, an instrument used to measure one's distance above sea level. Atmospheric pressure is a function of altitude. The farther one is above sea level, the less the atmospheric pressure, and the closer one is to sea level, the greater the atmospheric pressure. A simple aneroid barometer can be used to confirm these differences. If the barometer is now mounted in an airplane, a balloon, or some other device that travels up and down in the atmosphere, one's height above the ground (or above sea level) can be found by noting changes in atmospheric pressure.

See also Atmospheric pressure.

Further Reading:

Banfield, Edwin. *Barometers: Aneroid and Barographs.* Trowbridge, Wiltshire, England: Baros Books, 1985.

Brombacher, W. G. *Mercury Barometers and Manometers.* Washington, DC: U.S. Department of Commerce, National Bureau of Standards, 1960.

Caristi, Anthony J., "Build a Portable Barometer," *Popular Electronics*, January 1994, pp. 31–6.

The Illustrated Science and Invention Encyclopedia. Westport, CT: H. S. Stuttman, Inc., Publishers, 1982, volume 2, pp. 238–40.

Middleton, W. E. Knowles. *The History of the Barometer.* Baltimore: Johns Hopkins Press, 1964.

Walker, Jearl, "Making a Barometer that Works with Water in Place of Mercury," *Scientific American*, April 1987, pp. 122–27.

David E. Newton

Barracuda

A barracuda is a long, cylindrical, silvery fish. It has two widely separated dorsal fins, in roughly the same location as the two fins on its belly, and a forked tail. The largest species, the great barracuda, seldom grows longer than 6.5 ft (2 m) and is an aggressive fearsome predator of other fish. All barracudas have an underhung jaw that houses long, incredibly sharp teeth; their teeth are conically shaped, are larger in the front, like fangs, and their horizontal mouths can open very wide. In general, the barracuda inhabits tropical and warmer temperate waters throughout the world, specifically in the Atlantic, Pacific, and Indian Oceans. Different species of barracuda thrive in a variety of specific habitats but they are common over reefs and near continental shelves. Barracudas have been known to attack humans.

Barracudas are classified in the order Perciformes, an incredibly diverse group, containing 18 suborders and nearly 7,000 species of fish. Barracudas are the only fish in the suborder Sphyraenoidei and in the family Sphyraenidae. Within their family, there is one genus, *Sphyraena*, with 20 species.

Predatory behavior

Barracudas usually swim actively in clear water searching for schools of plankton–feeding fish. Their silver coloring and elongated bodies make them difficult for prey to detect, especially when viewing them head–on. Barracudas depend heavily on their sense of sight when they hunt, noticing everything that has an unusual color, reflection, or movement. Once a barracuda sights an intended victim, its long tail and matching anal and dorsal fins enable it to move with incredibly swift bursts of speed to catch its prey before it can escape. Barracudas generally assault schools of fish, rushing at them head first and snapping their strong jaws right and left.

When barracudas are mature, they usually swim alone, however, there are circumstances when they tend to school. Two such instances are while they are young and when they are spawning. Additionally, to feed more easily, barracudas sometimes swim in groups. In this case, they can herd schools of fish into densely populated areas or chase them into shallow water; when the barracudas accomplish this, they can eat practically all the fish they want at leisure.

The great barracuda (*Sphyraenidae barracuda*)

As its name implies, the great barracuda is most notable because of its size. Like all species of barracuda, this species has a long, silvery body and very sharp teeth. It generally appears silvery with green or gray on its back and black blotches on its belly. How-

A barracuda in its reef habitat. The creature can move with great speed to slash an intended victim to ribbons with its teeth.

ever, this fish can change color to match its background environment. While individuals in most species of barracuda rarely grow longer than 5.5 ft (1.7 m), some specimens of the great barracuda have been reported to reach 10 ft (3 m) long. (Usually, members of this species average about 3 ft (0.9 m) long.)

An aggressive hunter, the great barracuda inhabits temperate and tropical waters all over the world, except in certain parts of the Pacific Ocean and Mediterranean Sea. Specifically, it is found in the west Atlantic from Brazil to New England and in the Gulf of Mexico. Also, it is one of three barracuda species found in the Caribbean. The other two species are *Sphyraenidae guachancho* and *Sphyraenidae picudilla*. These two species, much smaller and more rare, often swim in the company of jacks and are commonly named sennets.

The Pacific barracuda

A great deal is known about the Pacific barracuda (*Sphyraena argentea*). It spends its winters off Mexico and joins a school in the spring to swim up the coast and spawn. Males are sexually mature when they are two or three years old; females mature one year later. The female Pacific barracuda lays her eggs at intervals, and the eggs float freely in the water. Measuring up to 4.9 ft (1.5 m) long, Pacific barracuda eat sardines. They are caught throughout the year off the Mexican coast and in the summertime off the California coast. Their meat is reportedly very good.

Human fear of barracudas

People who dive in tropical regions are often quite afraid of barracudas, fearing them even more than sharks. Often, divers in tropical waters report feeling as if there is "someone watching them" when they are submerged. With barracudas, this is probably the case. Barracudas are curious animals and commonly follow and watch divers, noticing any strange movements or colors. Unlike sharks, barracudas only attack their prey one time, usually with one massive bite.

Barracudas are not as dangerous as many people think. Unless they are provoked, they rarely attack. Barracuda attacks usually take place under certain circumstances, including: (1) when the water is very murky; (2) when a diver is carrying a shiny reflecting object, like jewelry; (3) when the barracuda is provoked; or (4) when a diver is carrying a wounded fish. Attacks can also be caused by excessive splashing or other irregular movements in the water, especially in murky conditions. Also, some people think that the likelihood of a barracuda attack depends on location. For instance, while the great barracuda seldom attacks humans in Hawaii, it is considered more dangerous in the West Indies.

Further Reading:

Bond, Carl E. *Biology of Fishes.* Philadelphia: W. B. Saunders Company, 1979.

Grzimek, H. C. Bernard, ed. *Grzimek's Animal Life Encyclopedia.* New York: Van Nostrand Reinhold, 1993.

Hauser, Hillary. *Book of Fishes.* New York: Pisces Books, 1992.

MacMillan Illustrated Animal Encyclopedia. New York: MacMillan Publishing, 1992.

Moyle, Peter B., and Joseph J. Cech, Jr. *Fishes: An Introduction to Ichthyology.* Englewood Cliffs, NJ: Prentice–Hall, 1982.

Nelson, Joseph S. *Fishes of the World.* 3rd ed. New York: John Wiley & Sons, 1994.

The Illustrated Encyclopedia of Wildlife. London: Grey Castle Press, 1991.

The New Larousse Encyclopedia of Animal Life. New York: Bonanza Books, 1987.

Wilson, Josleen. *The National Audubon Society Collection Nature Series, North American Fish.* New York: Gramercy Books, 1991.

Kathryn Snavely

Barrier islands

A barrier island is a long, thin, sandy stretch of land, oriented parallel to the mainland coast, which protects the coast from the full force of powerful storm waves. Between the barrier island and the mainland is a calm, protected water body such as a lagoon or bay. Barrier islands are dynamic systems, constantly on the move, migrating under the influence of changing sea level, storms, waves, tides, and longshore currents. In the United States, barrier islands occur offshore where gently sloping sandy coastlines, as opposed to rocky coastlines, exist. Consequently, most barrier islands are found along the Gulf Coast and the Atlantic Coast as far north as Long Island, New York. Some of the better known barrier islands include Padre Island of Texas, the world's longest; Florida's Santa Rosa Island, composed of sugar–white sand; Cape Hatteras of North Carolina, where the first airplane was flown; and Assateague Island near Maryland, home of wild ponies.

Barrier island development

Barrier islands are young in geologic terms. They originated in the Holocene epoch, about 4000–6000 years ago. During this time, the rapid rise in sea level, associated with melting glaciers from the last ice age, slowed significantly. Although the exact mechanisms of barrier island formation aren't fully understood, this slowdown of sea level rise allowed the islands to form.

In order for barrier islands to form, several conditions must be met. First, there must be a source of sand to build the island. This sand may come from coastal deposits or offshore deposits (called shoals); in either case, the sand originated from the weathering and erosion of rock and was transported to the coast by rivers. In the United States, much of the sand composing barrier islands along Florida and the East Coast came from the Appalachian Mountains. Next, the topography of the coastline must have a broad, gentle slope. From the coastal plains of the mainland to the edge of the continental shelf, this condition is met along the Atlantic and Gulf Coasts. Finally, the forces of waves, tides and currents must be strong enough to move the sand, and of these three water movement mechanisms, waves must be the dominant force.

Several explanations of barrier island development have been proposed. According to one theory, coastal sand was transported shoreward as sea level rose, and once sea level stabilized, wave and tidal actions worked the sand into a barrier island. Another possibility is that sand was transported to its present location

A barrier island in the Cape Hatteras National Seashore Park, off the coast of North Carolina.

from shoals. Barrier islands may have formed from sandy coastal spits which separated from the mainland. Transport of sand by longshore currents flowing parallel to the beach, and breaching of low–lying areas by the sea could have aided in the creation of barrier islands from these coastal spits. Finally, barrier islands may have formed from sandy coastal ridges which became isolated from low–lying land and formed islands as sea level rose.

Once formed, barrier islands are not static land forms; they are dynamic, with winds and waves constantly reworking and moving the barrier island sand. Changes in sea level also affect these islands. Most scientists agree that sea level has been gradually rising over the last thousand years, and this rise could be accelerating today due to global warming. Rising sea level causes existing islands to migrate shoreward.

Barrier island zonation

Barrier islands do not stand alone in a geologic sense. A whole system of islands develop along favorable coastlines. The formation of these islands allows other landforms to develop, each characterized by their dominant sediment type and by the water that helps form them. For example, each barrier island has a shoreline which faces the sea and which receives the full force of waves, tides, and currents. This shoreline is often called the beach. The beach zone extends from slightly offshore (subtidal, or underwater) to the high water line. Coarser sands and gravels are deposited here, with finer sands and silts carried farther offshore.

Behind the beach are sand dunes. Wind and plants (such as sea oats) help form dunes, but occasionally dunes are inundated by high water and may be reworked by storm surges and waves. On wide barrier islands, the landscape behind the foredunes gently rolls as dunes alternate with low–lying swales (marshy wet areas). If the dunes and swales are well developed, distinct parallel lines of dune ridges and swales can be seen from overhead. These differences in topography allow some soil to develop and nutrients to accumulate despite the porous, sandy base. Consequently, some barrier islands are host to trees (which are often stunted), bushes, and herbaceous plants. Other narrower or younger barrier islands may be little more than loose sand with few plants.

KEY TERMS

Holocene epoch—An epoch of geologic time extending from 10,000 years ago through the present day.

Inlet—A narrow watery channel next to a barrier island which leads from the sea to a bay or lagoon.

Lagoon—A shallow, semi–enclosed body of water connected to the sea by an inlet.

Shoal—A sandy area submerged in shallow water.

Storm surge—A significant, sudden, and temporary rise in sea level, associated with high winds and very low pressure, accompanying hurricanes.

On the shoreward side of the main body of the island is the back–barrier. Unlike the beach, this zone does not bear the full force of ocean waves. Instead, the back–barrier region consists of a protected shoreline and lagoon which is more influenced by tides than waves. Occasionally, during storms, water may rush over the island carrying beach and dune sand and deposit the sand in the lagoon. This process, called rolling over, is vital to the existence of barrier islands. Characteristic sand overwash fans in the lagoons are evidence of rolling over. Since the back–barrier region is sheltered, salt marsh, sea grass, and mudflat communities develop. These communities teem with plant and animal life and their muddy or sandy sediments are rich with organic matter.

Finally, barrier islands are characterized by tidal inlets and tidal deltas. Tidal inlets allow water to move into and out of bays and lagoons with rising and falling tides. Tidal inlets also provide a path for high water during storms and hurricanes. As water moves through an inlet, sand is deposited at both ends of the inlet's mouth, forming tidal deltas. Longshore currents may also deposit sand at the delta. Eventually the deltas fill in with sand and the inlet closes, only to appear elsewhere on the barrier island, usually at a low–lying spot.

Can humans and barrier islands coexist?

Barrier islands bear the full force of coastal storms and hurricanes, buffering the mainland coast, often at the expense of the island. Although the processes creating and maintaining barrier islands have been occurring for thousands of years, they have only become of concern in the last few decades. Billions of dollars worth of development on barrier islands are now threatened by migrating beaches as sand continues to be reworked and transported by natural forces. Cities such as Miami Beach and Atlantic City are on barrier islands. Engineering efforts to stop erosion through beach renourishment projects, seawalls, and other means are merely temporary fixes against the powerful forces of nature. In some cases, these structures can actually accelerate the rate of erosion.

In some coastal states, laws are being written to prohibit building between the sea and the primary dune line (the dunes closest to the sea). Some laws prohibit the rebuilding of structures lost or damaged due to storms and erosion. Preservation may be the best long–term solution to insure the future of these islands, but for many people the desire for beach resorts is a more immediate, short–term concern, since many barrier islands are beautiful and desirable places to be.

See also Coast and beach; Dune; Erosion; Island.

Further Reading:

Bascom, W. *Waves and Beaches*. Garden City, New York: Anchor Press/ Doubleday , 1980.

Bennett, D. "Paying for Sand." *Audubon* (September/October 1993): 132.

Carter, R. W. G. *Coastal Environments*. San Diego: Academic Press, 1991.

Hawes, E. "Castles in the sand." *The New York Times Magazine* (July 1993): 24–32.

Kaufman, W., and O. Pilkey. *The Beaches Are Moving*. Garden City, New York: Anchor Press/ Doubleday, 1979.

Overby, P. "Beachfront Bailout." *Common Cause* (Summer 1993): 12–17.

Stuller, J. "On the Beach." *Sea Frontiers* (December 1994): 28–34.

Tibbetts, J. "On Shifting Sands." *E: The Environmental Magazine* (July/August 1993): 19–21.

Elaine L. Martin

Barrier reef see **Coral reef**

Baryon see Subatomic particles

Basal ganglia see **Brain**

Base (chemical) see **Acids and bases**

Base (exponents and logarithms) see **Exponent; Logarithms**

Base (numeration) see **Numeration systems**

Basin

A basin, or sedimentary basin, is a depressed area in the Earth's crust in which sediments tend to accumulate over a long period of time. Basins form when the crust of the Earth subsides, or becomes depressed, as a result of changes within the Earth resulting from tectonic events or other internal changes, or downward warping as sediments are loaded onto the crust. Basins can be shaped like bowls or elongate troughs, or have irregular shapes. They can be tens to hundreds of miles in diameter and can contain layers of sediment as thick as 49,000 ft (15,000 m). Much of our interest in basins results from the fact that some basins contain economically significant accumulations of petroleum. There are approximately 600 basins on Earth, of which about 150 contain petroleum.

Important petroleum–producing basins of the United States include the Anadarko Basin of Texas and Oklahoma, the Colville Basin of northern Alaska, the Gulf of Mexico Basin, the Illinois Basin, the Michigan Basin, the Permian Basin of western Texas and southeastern New Mexico, and the San Joaquin Basin of California.

Formation and types of basins

Basins are classified on the basis of where, from what type of crust, and how they form. The crust of the Earth is a thin, solid layer of rock that is generally between 3 mi (5 km) and 41 mi (60 km) thick. Continental crust, which can include mountains, is thicker and comprises less dense rock types, such as granite and relatively light sedimentary rocks. Oceanic crust tends to be thinner and more dense, with layers of rock such as basalt and gabbro overlain by sediments. When continental crust and oceanic crust collide during times of tectonic activity, the more dense oceanic crust tends to sink or subduct beneath the relatively buoyant continental crust, typically forming a trench and volcanic arc system such as we observe in Japan. If plates of continental crust collide, high mountains can form as both plates crumple and fold because the densities of the plates are similar and neither plate subducts, a phenomenon visible in the Himalayas and the remnants of the Appalachian Mountains. In areas on continental crust and in the oceans, the crust can pull apart and new crust wells up. This occurs primarily in the oceans, where the creation of new oceanic crust occurs at the mid–ocean ridges. Within the continents, the crust can sag and form depressions as it cools over long periods of time. Thus, the crust of the Earth responds in

a variety of ways to tectonic events depending on the type of crust involved and the types of tectonic events.

Basins form as a result of different processes that cause subsidence, such as tectonic activity, sediment loading, changes deeper within the Earth, changes in heating and cooling of different areas of the Earth, or a combination of these. Areas where basins form include areas where the crust is spreading (divergent regions), areas where crust is destroyed or subducted (convergent regions), areas of transform faulting, and areas within crustal plates (cratonic regions, so named because cratons are areas within continental crust that have been relatively stable for at least one billion years). Basins that form in different areas differ in the type of crust they comprise, such as continental crust, oceanic crust, or something in between.

In addition to differences in size, shape, type of crust, and presence or absence of petroleum, basins form on many different areas of the Earth such as oceans, mountains, and on flat land. As a result, the sediment that fills basins also varies widely because sediments eroded from mountain ranges and deposited in a nearby basin can come from different types of rocks than the sediment carried by rivers over long distances and deposited into the oceans. Consider the difference between sediments deposited by the Mississippi River into the Gulf of Mexico basin and the sediments transported over short distances and deposited in basins of the northern United States such as the Williston Basin, the Powder River Basin, and the Green River Basin.

Besides simple classifications of basins such as a threefold division of convergent, divergent and cratonic basins, more complicated basin classifications include seven major types of basins: Subduction basins, median basins, rift or ocean basins, pull–apart basins, deltas, interior basins, and composite basins. Convergent basins include subduction basins and median basins. Divergent basins can be rift basins, ocean basins, pull–apart basins, or deltas. Cratonic basins include interior and composite basins.

Subduction basins generally have an irregular shape. These basins form in areas where continental and oceanic crust collide and the oceanic crust subducts beneath the continental crust to create volcanic arcs and depressions where sediment can accumulate. The Aleutian Arc of Alaska is an area containing a subduction basin. Basins around Japan formed in a similar manner.

Median basins form in mountainous areas between colliding plates of continental crust. Few basins of this type exist and they do not account for much petroleum production.

KEY TERMS

Craton—Stable area of continental crust that has not experienced tectonic activity for perhaps as many as one billion years.

Crust—Relatively brittle, solid, thin, outer layer of the Earth. The crust overlies the mantle, a denser but softer layer of the Earth that is close to its melting point.

Diagenesis—Processes including compaction, cementation, and dissolution that change sediment to sedimentary rock at low temperatures.

Petroleum—Substances, such as oil, made of various molecules of hydrogen and carbon that form through the transformation of organic matter at low temperature.

Sedimentary rock—Rock made up of grains of preexisting rock or organic matter, or rocks that precipitate from water. Sandstone and limestone are common sedimentary rocks.

Seismic data—Information about the structure and composition of the Earth obtained by recording how waves reflect or refract as they travel through rock layers. The waves are generated by explosions of dynamite in shallow bore holes or by shaking the rock using large vibrator trucks.

Subsidence—Down warping of the Earth's crust produced by tectonic events, by changes in the interior of the Earth, or by ongoing accumulation of sediment that loads the crust. Subsidence can result in the formation of sedimentary basins and can occur at rates as high as 0.1 in (2.5 mm) of depression per year.

Tectonic event—Process or event that results in changes, bending, or breaking in the Earth's crust, such as collisions of crustal plates or faulting of crustal plates.

Rift or ocean basins form as plates move apart or diverge. In ocean basins, new ocean crust forms at mid–ocean ridges as plates diverge, but rifts on continental crust do not always become large enough to form new ocean basins. The Atlantic Ocean continues to widen. In the Rio Grande Rift of New Mexico, rifting has occurred, not to a degree that a new ocean could form, but enough to form a basin.

Pull–apart basins can form through rifting of preexisting zones of tectonic activity along the edges of continents. Pull–apart basins tend to be linear in shape.

Deltas form in areas where rivers drain continents and deposit sediment. The load of sediment can cause the crust to sag or warp, forming a basin. The Gulf of Mexico is an area of tremendous sediment deposition by the Mississippi River and also contains significant petroleum reserves.

Interior basins occur within cratons in areas where the crust sags or subsides. The sagging might result from cooling and shrinkage of rock over long periods of time. These basins tend to be large and circular or elliptical in shape. The Williston Basin is an interior basin that contains petroleum.

Composite basins can be linear, elliptical, or asymmetric, and result from initial extension and later compression of areas within or around cratons.

Current research

Academic institutions, governments, and petroleum companies each contribute to current research in basins. Basin analysis is a field of great interest, for it addresses questions such as how basins form, how sediments fill basins, how sediments undergo diagenesis or physical and chemical changes as sediments pile up and are subjected to higher pressures and temperatures and fluids moving through them, and how and where basins with economic accumulations of petroleum occur.

Computer models of sediment accumulation in basins, fluid movement in basins, and heat flow in basins are popular tools for basin researchers. The interplay between sedimentation, tectonic activity, climate, and changes in sea level can be assessed using computer simulations and this interplay continues to attract the attention of researchers. Examination, interpretation, and mapping of seismic data and data from exploration wells drilled in basins provide insight about the types and distribution of sediments in basins as well as information about whether or not economic accumulations of petroleum exist in a given basin. These types of questions also can be answered by examining outcrops, or exposures of rocks, at the Earth's surface.

See also Tectonics.

Further Reading:

Baird, D.J., Knapp, J.H., Steer, D.N., Brown, L.D., and Nelson, K.D., 1995, "Upper–mantle reflectivity beneath the Williston basin, phase–change Moho, and the origin of intracratonic basins." *Geology*, v. 23 n. 5: 431–34.

Middleton, Gerard V., 1995, "Clastic Sedimentology." *Geotimes*, v. 40, n. 2: 43–4.

Gretchen M. Gillis

Bass

Bass is the common name for a number of popular freshwater and salt water fish, which include the wide mouth bass, the striped bass, groupers, jewfish, and wreckfish, which are some of the finest sports and food fish in the world.

Fish known as bass actually belong to different families and are distributed worldwide in tropical and temperature waters.

The freshwater family Centrarchidae includes the black basses, crappies, and sunfish. All species have plump, oval bodies with rough scales with a comblike edge. There are two dorsal fins which are connected, the first fin with thick spines. Heavy spines are also found in the anal fin. Freshwater basses include the predatory largemouth bass *Micropterus salmoides* which is generally found in shallow waters with plenty of vegetation such as slow moving streams with muddy bottoms and lakes. The largemouth bass is widespread in the United States and southern Canada and is an important sport fish. The average size of largemouth bass varies; bass from southern regions are heavier than those from the north. In southern Georgia a specimen was caught by rod and reel weighing 22.25 lb (10 kg). The species spawns in late March in the south but in June in the north. Largemouth bass demonstrate characteristic parental care of the young. When females are about to lay their eggs males will prepare the nest. After a female has laid her eggs, the male will deposit sperm (milt) over them. He will guard the nest from potential enemies. In the course of their development the eggs are fanned to aerate them and to keep off mud and silt. After the eggs develop into fry the male guards the young for several weeks.

The largemouth bass, so called because of its large mouth compared to the other basses, is greenish with a lateral stripe on each side, the color depending on size, and water temperature and chemistry.

The smallmouth bass, *M. dolomieui,* is found in North America farther north than the largemouth bass. The smallmouth bass is found in cold, moving water, and not generally on muddy bottoms. It is a smaller species than the largemouth bass, on average weighing under a pound. It is somewhat more aggressive and provides more sport for the fisherman.

The spotted bass, *M. punctulatus* is found between Ohio and Florida and in parts of Kansas and Texas. The spotted bass may reach up to 4 lb (1.8 kg). This fish is found in cool fastflowing waters like the smallmouth bass, but may also be found in deep water (100 ft, 33 m). Three other species resemble the spotted bass. These are the Guadalupe bass, *M. treculi* reaching a weight of 1 lb (.45 kg), the Suwanee bass, *M. notius* of northern Florida weighing under a pound, and the red-eye bass, *M. coosae* of the Alabama River and nearby areas, weighing up to 2 lb (.9 kg).

The salt water basses are distinct from the fresh water basses, and most are included in the family Serranidae. Although designated as salt water fishes, some of these bass may be found in fresh or brackish water. Some of these species are prized sport fishes especially for the hook and line enthusiast. Salt water bass have the characteristic basslike or perchlike body shape with a thick spine on the first dorsal fin and a soft rayed second dorsal fin. Salt water bass vary in size from massive forms of about 1,000 lb (454 kg) to tiny individuals under 1 in (2.5 cm) long, some of which are aquarium fish.

The belted sandfish *Serranus suligarius,* matures when it reaches 2 in (5 cm) in length, and grows to a maximum of about 6 in (15 cm) long. The belted sandfish is found in the tropical Atlantic and Caribbean and may descend to deeper waters of 60 ft (20 m).

Sea basses in the genus *Morone* are occasionally found in fresh water. Some taxonomists group these fish with the grant wreckfish (*Polyprion americanus*) and the giant sea bass in the family Percichthyidae rather than the serranidae. The wreckfish reaches lengths of over 6 ft (2 m), weighs up to 100 lbs (45 kg), and descends to depths of 300 ft (1000 m).

The striped bass, *Morone saxatilis,* also called rockfish, rock bass, or striper, inhabits the waters along the mid–Atlantic coasts from the St. Lawrence River to northern Florida. Some specimens of striped bass transferred to the Pacific Ocean off California in 1879 have established themselves well and are now abundant. The striped bass may reach 100 lb (45.4 kg), although most average approximately 10 lb (4.54 kg) and are highly prized for sport and food. Striped bass spawn in fresh waters in early summer; some have become landlocked in the Santee–Cooper Reservoir in South Carolina.

Groupers (genus *Epinephelus*) frequently gather on rocky shores. Groupers are popular sport fish, caught by rod and reel as well as by hand line, and highly prized for their superb flavor. Examples are the red grouper, *E. mario,* the Nassau grouper, *E. striatus,* the red hind , *E. guttatus,* and the rock hind, *E. adscensionis.*

In Australia the Queensland grouper, *E. lanceolata,* reaches half a ton in weight and has a huge appetite. There are reports that this giant fish stalks pearl and

Striped bass.

shell divers, and there are unconfirmed tales of divers being swallowed by groupers.

A close relative of the Queensland grouper is the giant jewfish (Epinephelus itajara) which frequents the Caribbean up to Florida and also the Pacific ocean in the Gulf of California, Mexico, and Panama. Although the jewfish 's weight averages about 20 lb (9 kg), some may weigh up to 100 lb (45.4 kg) or more. A rod and reel catch of a 680 lb (309 kg) specimen has been reported. To catch the larger fish, shark hooks and ropes may be used. The large fish are cut into steaks and fillets.

The taste of the smaller fish is preferable to that of the larger specimens, which are edible but have a strong flavor.

Several species of sea bass in the Serranide are hermaphrodites, where both male and female organs are found in the same individual. Cross–fertilization is the rule since fish do not fertilize their own eggs. Examples of hermaphroditic species include *Paracentropristis cabrilla*, *P. hepatus*, and *Diplodus vulgarus* of the Mediterranean Sea. Most species of true hermaphrodite fish among the teleosts are in the Serranidae, the sea bass family.

Many species of grouper and other sea basses are fish that function as females at first which then transform into males and function as males for the rest of their lives. This explains why large specimens are all males. An example is the Atlantic or black sea bass (*Centropristis striatus*) which demonstrates this condition. It is found from Massachusetts to North Carolina with some individuals straying to Florida.

The black sea bass demonstrates a distinct form of hermaphroditism characteristic of hermaphroditic groupers, where the sexes are physically distinct. Functional males and females are easily distinguished; the female has a more pointed snout, and is a darker or duller blue color. In July, the post breeding period, some females may be brown or almost completely white. Males at spawning time in May and June may be bright blue, especially around the eyes, with an adipose (fatty) hump behind the head which is most prominent at spawning time. Early in life there is a sex change from female to male, the changeover reaching its summit at about five years of age. By the eighth year there are no females in the population, and the males continue to grow for several more years. As with the groupers this accounts for the fact that the large black sea bass are all males.

Further Reading:

Cousteau, J. "The Act of Life" in *The Ocean World of Jacques Cousteau*. Vol. 2. Canada: Prentice–Hall of Canada, 1975.

Hildebrand, S. F., and W. C. Schroeder. "Fishes of Chesapeake Bay."*Bulletin of the United States Bureau of Fisheries*. Vol XLIII, Part I, 1927.

Migdalski, E. C., and G. S. Fichter. *The Fresh and Salt Water Fishes of the World*. Arlington House, 1985.

Nathan Lavenda

Basswood

Basswoods are about thirty species of trees in the genus *Tilia*, in the linden family Tiliaceae. In North America, these trees are generally known as basswoods in forestry, and as lindens in horticulture.

Basswoods have simple, long–petioled, coarsely toothed, broadly heart–shaped leaves, arranged alternately on their twigs. The flowers occur in clusters, and emerge from a specialized leaf known as a bract. The flowers produce relatively large amounts of nectar, and are insect pollinated. The ripe fruits are grey, hard, and nut–like, and each contains one or several seeds.

Mature basswood trees issue sprouts from their roots, which develop as shoots around the tree. In addi-

tion, after a mature basswood tree is harvested, numerous sprouts arise from the surviving roots and stump, and these can develop into a new tree.

Basswoods produce a relatively light, clear, strong, and durable wood that can be used as lumber to manufacture boxes and crates, furniture, picture frames, and for carving. Basswood honey is another economic product, as is a herbal tea made from the dried flowers. North American species of basswood and the related, European linden (*Tilia cordata*) are commonly planted as shade trees in residential areas of towns and cities.

Four species of basswood are native to North America. The most widely distributed species is the American basswood (*Tilia americana*), a tree of temperate, hardwood forests of the northeastern United States and southeastern Canada. This is a relatively tall–growing species, which can reach a height of up to 82 ft (25 m). The leaves of this species are largest in relatively shaded parts of the crown, where they can achieve a length of more than 7.8 in (20 cm) and a width of 3.9 in (10 cm).

The white basswood (*T. heterophylla*) occurs in the eastern United States, while the ranges of the Carolina basswood (*T. caroliniana*) and Florida basswood (*T. floridana*) are the southeastern coastal plain of the United States.

Bill Freedman

Batfish see **Anglerfish**

Bats

Bats are one of the most diverse and widely distributed mammals on Earth, second only to rodents in number of species worldwide. Over 900 species of bats have been described; they occur almost everywhere in the world except most of the Arctic and all of Antarctica. They are the only truly flying mammals, and thus are distinct from the flying lemurs and flying squirrels, which actually glide rather than fly. Bats make up their own order, the Chiroptera, so named for the Greek words *cheir* (hand) and *pteron* (wing)—an apt name, since the wing is formed by modified bones of the hand.

The bat order is divided into two suborders. The Megachiroptera are a single family that is restricted to the tropics, and includes larger species like fruit bats or flying foxes; megachiropterans are characterized by their large eyes, simple ears, and dog–like faces. The

Looking up at fruit bats in Tasavo National Park, Kenya.

Microchiroptera are made up of 17 families, and feature small eyes, complex ears, and typically find their prey by echolocation. Certain differences in flight and in sensory capabilities between the two suborders have led some investigators to propose that they evolved independently from separate ancestral lineages, and that the megachiropteran bats are more closely related to primates. This idea remains highly controversial, however, since other morphological data and DNA evidence support the hypothesis that bats constitute one group, derived from a single common ancestor.

Basic body plan

The bodies of bats are designed for flight; but they accomplish this differently from their flying colleagues, the birds. Like birds, bats' bones are light–weight and delicate, but bats have short necks compared to birds, which is important for a toothed animal who must carry this added weight at its front end. Bats lack the deeply keeled sternum, or breastbone, where the flight muscles attach in birds. Instead, three shallow pairs of muscles on the breast power the downstroke of the wing during flight; the upstroke is provided by three pairs of muscle

on the back. Without the well–developed breastbone, bats have a flatter profile through the chest, and so they can squeeze through small openings and roost in narrow crevices.

The wing structure of birds and bats is also different; where bird wings are supported mainly by the second and third "fingers," bat wings are formed by thin, elastic skin extending from the sides of the body to the tips of all four elongated "finger" bones. Their much–reduced thumb remains free of the wing membrane and is used to manipulate food, and as a hook when the bat climbs and clings to surfaces or vegetation. The wing membranes are also supported by the hind legs, and in species with tails, the tail is entirely or partially enclosed by wing membrane stretching between the hind legs. The hind legs of bats are unique among mammals in being rotated 180°, so that the knees point backward, allowing the leg to flex in a reverse fashion; this is believed to assist in steering during flight, and in taking off from the bat's characteristic head–down roosting position.

The Megachiroptera have dog–like faces with little further elaboration; however, the faces of the

The endangered bumblebee bat (*Craseonycteris thonglongyai*).

Microchiroptera are often striking, with fleshy embell-ishments that form complicated dimples, wrinkles, and horseshoe– or leaf–like structures. Some have tubular nostrils. Biologists have suggested that these facial embellishments function in the projection of sounds produced for echolocation, like megaphones or acoustic lenses. While Megachiroptera generally have simple ears, there is huge variation in ear size, shape, and elaboration among microchiropteran bats. Microchiropteran ears may feature special folds and ridges that are thought to play a role in sound percep-tion. For instance, many of these bats possess a large tragus, the fleshy projection on the bottom front edge of the ear opening, a structure believed to aid an echolocating bat in determining the horizontal position of a target.

Most bat scientists believe that bats evolved from tree–dwelling, shrew–like ancestors who scampered along the branches and fed on insects. The proto–bat likely had long fingers supporting webs of skin attached to the body, which it used to glide or para-chute in pursuit of its insect prey. Like many birds, bats pass the food they have eaten fairly quickly through their digestive tract, so as to reduce the amount of time they must carry the extra weight of undigested food. Total output time is as little as 20 minutes in some smaller bat species (similar to birds of the same size).

Diet

The dietary diversity of bats has no match among living mammals. Most bats living in temperate areas like the United States—some 265 species—eat insects. Fruit bats or flying foxes (restricted to tropical areas) eat fruit and leaves, which they chew, swallowing the juice and spitting out the pulp. The long–tongued fruit bats (*Macroglossus*) specialize in a diet of pollen and nectar, aided by their elongated snouts and unusually long tongues (up to one–third their body length). The bulldog or fisherman bats (genus *Noctilio*) of Central and South America catch small fish, while the frog–eating bat (*Trachops cirrhosus*) uses the calls of frogs to locate this prey item, and can distinguish between the calls of poisonous and edible frogs. The large slit–faced bat (*Nycteris grandis*) of Africa may eat small birds and even other bats, caught on the wing.

The infamous vampire bats (three genera in the subfamily Desmodontinae) dine on the blood of other animals, such as domestic livestock, by making a shallow cut with the incisors and lapping the blood that drains from the wound; their saliva contains an anticoagulant that keeps the blood from clotting. These bats are quite agile on the ground, typically landing beside their sleeping victim, and crawling up onto them to feed. Vampire bats are dietary specialists, but many bats consume several food items, varying their consumption to get enough protein and other nutrients.

Sensory systems and echolocation

Contrary to popular myth, bats are not blind; the large eyes in many species suggest well–developed vision. Like most mammals, they have keen senses of taste and smell, the latter being useful in locating food items, and in identifying roost sites and other bats, including family members. They also have excellent hearing, and many species use a wide range of vocalizations to communicate with one another; some species also hunt for food simply by listening to the sounds of their prey moving about.

Perhaps their most remarkable sensory adaptation is their capacity for echolocation, which allows bats to maneuver in total darkness using the echoes of their ultrasonic calls to detect objects in their path. Human efforts to understand how bats can fly in complete darkness date back to the late eighteenth century, when Italian scientist Spallanzani, LazarroLazarro Spallanzani (1729–1799) conducted experiments that included enying bats use of their senses of smell, touch, and vision. He observed that bats lost their way only if their head was covered by a small sack, and he concluded that bats must have a sixth sense, not shared with humans.

A Swiss surgeon named Charles Jurine reported in 1794 that if a bat's ears are blocked, it cannot maneuver. Spallanzani heard this report, and taking the experiment a step further, he showed that bats with brass tubes inserted into their ears can only navigate when the tubes are open. He then concluded that bats must somehow see with their ears. How this could occur was not explained until the 1930s, when the echolocation pioneer Griffen, Donald R.Donald R. Griffen (then an undergraduate at Harvard University) detected ultrasonic signals produced by bats in the lab, using a special microphone which was capable of picking up sounds above 20 kHz—ultrasound. In a series of experiments, Griffen showed that his bats used the echoes of their calls to locate obstacles, and he coined the term 'echolocation' to describe it.

We now know that other animals echolocate—whales, dolphins, shrews, and some birds such as cave swiftlets do—and we know that some bats, including all but one of the flying foxes, do not. (The single megachiropteran genus that does use echolocation is *Rosettus*, whose sounds are produced by tongue clicks). All evidence indicates that bats see using reflected sound every bit as effectively as we see with our eyes, using reflected light. They do this by computing the time elapsed between the production of the sound (by means of the larynx) and the return of its echo, thus gauging the distance of objects around them. Of course, they do not perform these computations in a conscious way, any more than a person consciously determines the frequency of an incoming light wave to perceive an object as blue or green. Rather, the on–board computer of their brain carries out the necessary functions in a split second, providing them with a continuously updated "picture" of their surroundings.

What bats "see" in this way might best be imagined as something like what a human visitor sees in a darkened disco, where a strobe light is flickering to illuminate dancers and other objects in a pulse–like fashion. Every time the strobe light flashes, the observer gets a brief update on the position of things around them. A faster pulse rate in the strobe means that more information about these objects can be conveyed to the observer; the same is true for bats, who vary their calling rate depending on what they are doing. The rate for a bat on a routine cruise is 5–10 calls per second; as it locates and closes in on a flying insect, the call rate increases, and finally accelerates briefly to more than 200 per second in a terminal "feeding buzz" that pinpoints the location of the food item. Such a high rate of calling is only suitable for near targets, however; if an object is too distant, the outgoing signal will get mixed up with a signal returning from farther away. In addition, calling takes energy; the intensity of some bats' calls, if they were audible, would make them as loud as the beeping alarm of a home smoke detector. Expending the energy required for the feeding buzz likely does not pay off during an ordinary commute, and so the calling rate at this time is relatively low.

Meanwhile, the brain of an echolocating bat carries out some astonishing perceptual feats, and solves problems very similar to those facing early human developers of radar technology. For example, there is the problem of signal attenuation: sounds tend to degrade as they get farther away from their source. Pulses must be loud enough to survive degradation, but a loud sound overwhelms the sensitive receiver structures needed to pick up the return signal. As it turns out, bats solve this problem the same way early radar engineers did: they are equipped with a send/receive switch that momentarily disconnects the receiver function just as the loud outgoing pulse is produced; the receiver then is reconnected in time to receive the echo. This is accomplished by muscles that attach to the bones of the inner ear; when the muscles contract, these bones don't transmit sound well. When the muscles relax, the ear returns to normal sensitivity. Further signal attenuation happens within the brain itself, as neurons responsible for sound perception block the transmission of messages to higher regions of the brain at the moment that a bat vocalizes. In addition, special echo–detector cells in the brain respond more intensely to the *second* of two separate sound pulses—perfect for picking up the echo of a vocalization.

Next, there is the problem of sorting out echoes returning from near, medium, and distant objects—how can a bat tell the distance between itself and its next meal? They do it by means of frequency modulation, so the sorting can be done by differences in pitch (frequency). If a bat utters a downward–sweeping whistle call, an echo returning from a more distant object will be older, and thus higher in pitch, than echoes from near objects because the former has a longer distance to travel to return to the sender. The bat thus has a standard for comparison: lower pitch means close by, higher pitch means farther away. In addition, bats can measure the speed of a moving target by means of the Doppler effect—the phenomenon responsible for the change in pitch of an ambulance siren as it moves toward and passes a stationary observer. To do this, the bat's brain compares the pitch of an echo with the pitch of the original call; they do this reliably even in the presence of hundreds of their echolocating colleagues engaged in a midnight feeding frenzy. All this is accomplished automatically and instantaneously, with no more conscious effort than you exert in watching images on T.V. or the different lights on a traffic signal.

Of course, the system does not guarantee a 100% hunting success rate. Some flying insects, mice, and other animals can detect the bat's echolocation signals and take evasive action. However, bats also use their senses of sight and smell to find food; their other senses are also important in recognizing other bats, including their offspring, and perhaps also in identifying a roost site.

Roosting

Most bats rest during the day and disperse around dusk to feed. Bats spend over half of their lives in their roost environment, which may be a cave, mine, crevice or cavity in a rock or tree, foliage (sometimes rolled up into a tent), and human structures. Many bats roost communally, often for brooding of young or for hibernation; such colonies may range in size from just a few individuals to several million in a large cave. Females of some colonial bat species are known to share food and nursing of the young during the breeding season. For a hibernating bat in temperate areas, a communal living arrangement offers a stable microhabitat in which their body temperature may drop to within a few degrees of the ambient temperature, thus permitting conservation of critical reserves of body fat.

Reproduction and social organization

Most bats have a definite breeding season, which is spring in temperate climates. Bats may have from one to three litters in a season, depending on the species and on environmental conditions, such as the availability of food and roost sites. Females generally have just one offspring at a time; this is probably a result of the mother's need to fly when pregnant. Additionally, female bats nurse their youngster until it has achieved nearly adult size; this is because a young bat cannot forage on its own until its wings have assumed adult dimensions.

Female bats use a variety of strategies to control the timing of pregnancy and the birth of young, in an effort to make delivery coincide with maximum food ability and other ecological factors. Females of some species employ delayed fertilization, in which sperm are stored in the reproductive tract for several months after mating; in many such cases, mating occurs in the fall, but fertilization does not occur until the following spring. Other species exhibit delayed implantation, in which the egg is fertilized after mating, but remains free in the reproductive tract until external conditions become more favorable to giving birth and caring for the offspring. In yet another strategy, fertilization and implantation both occur but development of the fetus is delayed for some weeks until favorable conditions prevail, perhaps after a dry season. All of these tactics have the effect of producing the pup during times of peak local fruit or insect production.

Bats exhibit every type of breeding system that has been described for mammals. Some species are monogamous; others are polygynous, which means that one male may mate with several females. In these species, males may fight for control of preferred female roosting sites, or aggregations of females, called harems. In hammer–headed fruit bats (*Hypsignathus monstrosus*) of Africa, males assemble into leks, aggregations of displaying males at traditional sites that females visit for the purpose of selecting a mate. The males display by means of wing flapping, erecting patches of hair, and loud vocalizations. Still other bats have a promiscuous mating system, in which both males and females mate with more than one other individual.

While a mother and her young are the basic social unit, some species elaborate on this theme; for example, the social organization of the common vampire bat (*Desmodus rotundus*) is based on roosts shared by several females and their young. Roost–mates are often close relatives who groom each other, share wound sites on their prey, and regurgitate blood for consumption by the recipient.

Ecological and economic importance

In modern Western society, bats conjure up images of vampires, evil spirits, and creepy castles; people often feel that bats are dirty, dangerous, ugly creatures that can get tangled in their hair. This unfortunate image is not promoted in all societies, however; in some cultures bats are symbols of long life, good luck, and fertility. It is true that some species can carry rabies and histoplasmosis, both potentially dangerous diseases to humans and other animals; but these maligned creatures have crucial ecological and economic roles that many people overlook.

Bat guano (excrement) collected from roosts has been used for centuries as a source of saltpeter for making gunpowder and fertilizer. Gunpowder made in this way was used in this country during the War of 1812 and the Civil War. During World War II, U.S. military commanders considered using bats to carry bombs into enemy territory; however, "Project X–Ray" was abandoned when one of their own buildings was gutted by a fire caused by a stray bat–ferried bomb.

Bats have an ecological role that transcends their use in human military strategy, however. Many bat species are important pollinators and seed dispersers for plants of great economic importance, and so bats may play a keystone role in the distribution and abundance of these plants. As dispersers of "pioneer" plant species (those that colonize open or disturbed areas),

bats can play a role in the revegetation of denuded regions. In addition, bats consume vast quantities of insects, including human pests like mosquitoes, corn borers, and Jerusalem crickets.

Unfortunately, a number of bat species have already become extinct, and many others are endangered. The natural geographic ranges for many species have been drastically reduced, mainly due to loss of roosting sites, and probably also because of environmental contamination, insect control, and deforestation, all the result of human activity. The biological consequences of the continued loss of the world's bat species is unknown; but even our limited understanding of their ecological importance suggests that the outcome is not likely to be very favorable.

See also Doppler effect; Echolocation; Rodents.

Further Reading:
Fenton, M. B. *Just Bats.* Toronto: University of Toronto Press, 1983.
Nowak, Ronald M. *Walker's Mammals of the World.* 5th ed. Baltimore: Johns Hopkins University Press, 1991.
Pettigrew, J. D. "Flying Primates? Megabats Have the Advanced Pathway From Eye to Midbrain." *Science* 231 (1986): 1304–06.
Tuttle, Merlin. *America's Neighborhood Bats.* Austin: University of Texas Press, 1988.
Wilkinson, Gerald S. "The Social Organization of the Common Vampire Bat. I. Pattern and Cause of Association." *Behavioral Ecology and Sociobiology* 17 (1985): 111–21.
———. "The Social Organization of the Common Vampire Bat. II. Mating System, Genetic Structure, and Relatedness." *Behavioral Ecology and Sociobiology* 17 (1985): 123–34.

Susan Andrew

Battery

If two metals are immersed in an aqueous solution that can conduct electricity (electrolyte), they will have different tendencies to dissolve in the solution. A difference in voltage arises because one of the metals appears positive or negative relative to the other.

The combination of two metals (electrodes) in an aqueous solution for the purpose of producing electrical energy from chemical energy is referred to as a galvanic cell. A battery is a set of two or more galvanic cells connected in a series or parallel. (Though not strictly correct usage, a single galvanic cell is also fre-

A collection of batteries seen from above, with the top of the center battery cut away to show the interior. This type of battery, a dry version of the Leclanche cell, is called a carbon-zinc primary cell. A carbon rod sits upright in the center and acts as a cathode (negative electrode). The outer vessel is made of zinc, which allows it to serve as both a container and as an anode (positive electrode). The electrodes are in contact with a moist electrolytic paste (the grey material that fills the battery) consisting of ammonium and zinc chlorides, manganese dioxide and carbon particles.

quently referred to as a battery.) Each cell contains two types of electrodes, an anode (positive electrode) and a cathode (negative electrode), that together provide and absorb electrons with sufficient voltage (electromotive force) to operate useful machines or devices. The electromotive force for every cell reaction that is well understood can be calculated, and the voltage of an actual cell will not exceed this value.

Metals metaland other conductors can be arranged in an electrochemical, or electromotive, series in which each conductor's tendency to lose electrons relative to another conductor is ranked. The higher the electric potential, the more likely the metal is to appear electrically positive. In terms of electric potential, carbon has a higher potential than gold, gold a higher potential than silver; this sequence is followed in order by copper, tin, lead, iron, and zinc.

Background

Between 1790 and 1800, Luigi Galvani, lecturer in anatomy at the University of Bologna, and Alessandro Volta, professor of physics at Pavia University, began the science of electrochemistry. Galvani observed the effect of a copper probe on the muscles of a frog hung from an iron hook (the muscles twitched), and Volta interpreted this phenomena as the result of two metals being near each other, separated by an electrolyte (the blood of the frog).

Volta later built a stack of alternating zinc and silver disks separated by layers of paper or cloth soaked in a solution of sodium hydroxide or brine. He thus created a stable source of electrical current.

In 1834 Michael Faraday, inspired by Volta's results, derived the quantitative laws of electrochemistry. These established the fundamental relationships between chemical energy and electrical energy. Following Faraday's work, the following cells were developed:

- copper and zinc in sulfuric acid (1836)
- platinum cathode immersed in dilute nitric acid with a zinc anode in another compartment containing sulfuric acid
- carbon cathode immersed in dilute nitric acid with a zinc anode in another compartment containing sulfuric acid
- lead/acid battery (1859)
- Leclanche wet cell with a zinc anode and a cathode of naturally occurring manganese dioxide (1866)
- the first dry cell, consisting of a moistened cathode and a swollen starch or plaster of paris separator (1888) battery, dry cell nickel/cadmium and nickel/iron cells developed (1895-1905)
- silver oxide/zinc cell developed (1930s and 1940s)

If an incandescent lamp is connected to the two poles of a battery, an electric current flows through the lamp, illuminating it. As current flows through the electrolyte from the positive electrode to the negative one, gas bubbles are deposited on the electrodes, and an internal resistance to current flow builds up. To prevent this depolarization, the buildup of hydrogen gas at the positive electrode (anode) must be prevented to keep the cell functioning.

In the Leclanche cell, depolarization is prevented by enclosing the carbon anode with a mixture of manganese dioxide and graphite. The cell uses a zinc negative pole (cathode) and an ammonium chloride electrolyte. The potential difference between the poles is 1.3 volts. The potential difference does not depend on the size of the cell. (However, the size of the cell does affect the current intensity or amperage that can be delivered). Chemical energy, which is converted into electrical energy, results as the zinc electrode dissolves and is consumed. Thus the zinc must be renewed from time to time. Cells in which the electrodes are consumed are called primary cells.

A secondary cell can be restored to its original state by charging it, i.e., passing an electric current through it so that the electrodes are regenerated. These cells are also called storage cells or accumulators. They are usually used as groups of two or more cells. A commonly used storage cell consists of lead plates with a dilute sulfuric acid electrolyte. A layer of lead sulphate forms on the plates. When the storage cell is charged, the layer on the anode plate changes to lead dioxide, and the cathode is reduced to lead. Thus one electrode consists of lead and the other of lead dioxide. The electrodes and electrolyte together function as a galvanic cell. The stored chemical energy is converted back to electrical energy on discharging. The nickel–iron storage cell, another secondary cell, uses a potassium hydroxide electrolyte. The lead storage cell produces a potential difference of about 2 volts; the nickel–iron cell a difference of 1.36 volts.

In a dry cell, the electrolyte is in the form of a paste instead of a liquid. Higher voltages are produced by connecting the cells in series. Higher current intensities are produced by connecting cells in parallel. All cells produce direct current, i.e., electric current that flows in one direction.

Primary cells

Primary cells are designed to be discharged only once. This is so despite the fact that all electrodes must theoretically participate in a reversible reaction when current is generated. The reason that the primary cell reaction is not reversible has to do with reactions that prevent or limit the efficiency of recharging. For example, a magnesium anode decomposes to produce magnesium ions and electrons. The magnesium ions react with water to produce magnesium hydroxide, which causes the cell to swell, and hydrogen gas. Any attempt to recharge the cell would only generate more hydrogen gas at the oxide surface, because the voltage required to generate hydrogen is less than that required to redeposit the magnesium.

Moderate energy primary cells

ZINC/MANGANESE DIOXIDE SYSTEMS

The cell developed by Georges Leclanche in 1866 used inexpensive, readily available ingredients. It therefore quickly became a commercial success. The anode is a zinc alloy sheet or cup (the alloy contains small amounts of lead, cadmium, and mercury). The electrolyte is an aqueous solution of zinc chloride with solid ammonium chloride present. The cathode is manganese dioxide blended with either graphite or acetylene black to conduct electrons to the oxide. The system is relatively tolerant of many impurities. These cells are used in barricade flashers, flashlights, garage door openers, lanterns, pen lights, radios, small lighted toys and novelties, and in toys.

The zinc chloride cell without ammonium chloride was patented in 1899, but the technology from commercially producing such cells did not prove practical until about 70 years later. Currently zinc chloride cells deliver more than seven times the energy density of the original LeClanche cell. This cell is used in same applications as the LeClanche cell.

ZINC/MANGANESE DIOXIDE ALKALINE CELLS

The zinc/manganese dioxide alkaline cell's anode consists of finely divided zinc. The cathode is a highly compacted mixture of very pure manganese dioxide and graphite. The cells operate with higher efficiency than the zinc chloride or LeClanche cells at temperatures below 32° F (0° C). Manganese/manganese dioxide cells have much higher energy densities than zinc chloride systems. Cylindrical batteries are used in radios, shavers, electronic flash, movie cameras, tape recorders, television sets, cassette players, clocks, and camera motor drives. Miniature batteries are used in calculators, toys, clocks, watches, and cameras.

Medium to high energy primary cells

MERCURIC OXIDE/ZINC CELLS

Mercuric oxide/zinc cells use alkaline electrolytes and are frequently used in small button cells. The cell has about five to eight times the energy density available in the Leclanche cell and four times that in an alkaline manganese dioxide/zinc cell. The cell provides a very reliable voltage, and is used as a standard reference cell. These cells are used for walkie–talkies, hearing aids, watches, calculators, microphones, and cameras.

SILVER OXIDE/ZINC CELLS

Silver oxide/zinc cells use cellophane separators to keep the silver from dissolving and the cells from self discharging. The system is very popular with makers of hearing aids and watches because the high conductivity of the silver cathode reaction product gives the cell a very constant voltage to the end of its life. These cells are also used for reference voltage sources, cameras, instruments, watches, and calculators.

LITHIUM (NONAQUEOUS ELECTROLYTE) CELLS

Lithium/iron sulphide cells take advantage of the high electrochemical potential of lithium and low cost of iron sulfide. The high reactivity of lithium with water requires that the cells use a nonaqueous electrolyte from which water is removed to levels of 50 ppm.

Lithium/manganese dioxide cells are slowly increasing in commercial importance. The voltage provides a high energy density, and the materials are readily available and relatively inexpensive.

Lithium/copper monofluoride cells are used extensively in cameras and smaller devices. They provide high voltage, high power density, long shelf life, and good low temperature performance.

Lithium/thionyl chloride cells have very high energy densities and power densities. The cells also function better at lower temperatures than do other common cells.

Lithium/sulphur cells are used for cold weather use and in emergency power units.

AIR–DEPOLARIZED CELLS

Zinc/air cells are high energy can be obtained in a galvanic cell by using the oxygen of air as a "liquid" cathode material with an anode such as zinc. If the oxygen is reduced in the part of the cell designed for that purpose and prevented from reaching the anode, the cell can hold much more anode and electrolyte volume.

Aluminum/air cells have difficulty protecting the aluminum from the electrolyte during storage. Despite much research on this type of cell, aluminum/air cells are not in much current use.

Secondary cells

Secondary cells are designed so that the power withdrawn can be replaced by connecting the cell to an outside source of direct current power. The chemical reactions are reversed by suitably applying voltage and current in the direction opposite to the original discharge.

Moderate energy storage cells

LEAD SECONDARY CELLS

The lead/acid rechargeable battery system has been in use since the mid–1950s. It is the most widely used rechargeable portable power source. Reasons for the success of this system have included: great flexibility in delivery currents; good cycle life with high reliability over hundreds of cycles; low cost; relatively good shelf life; high cell voltages; ease of casting, welding, and recovery of lead.

The chief disadvantage of this battery is its high weight.

NICKEL ELECTRODE CELLS WITH ALKALINE ELECTROLYTES

Nickel/cadmium cells provide portable rechargeable power sources for garden, household tools, and

---

---

appliance use. The system carries exceptionally high currents at relatively constant voltage. The cells are, however, relatively expensive. These cells are used for portable hand tools and appliances, shavers, toothbrushes, photoflash equipment, tape recorders, radios, television sets, cassette players and recorders, calculators, personal pagers, and laptop computers.

ALKALINE ZINC/MANGANESE DIOXIDE CELLS

Alkaline zinc/manganese dioxide systems been developed and used as special batteries for television sets and certain portable tools or radios.

High energy storage batteries

SILVER/ZINC CELLS

Silver/zinc cells are expensive. They are chiefly used when high power density, good cycling efficiency, and low weight and volume are critical, and where poorer cycle life and cost can be tolerated. They are used in primarily four areas: under water, on the ground, in the atmosphere, and in space.

LITHIUM SECONDARY CELLS

Lithium secondary cells are attractive because of their high energy densities.

SODIUM/SULFUR SYSTEMS

Sodium/sulfur systems are high–temperature batteries that operate well even at 177 ° F (350° C).

See also Anode; Cathode; Cell, electrochemical; Electricity; Electrical conductivity; Electric conductor; Electric current; Electrolyte.

Further Reading:

Meyers, Robert A., *Encyclopedia of Physics Science and Technology*. New York, NY: Academic Press, Inc., 1992.
The Way Things Work. New York, NY: Simon and Schuster, 1967.

Randall Frost

Bayberry see **Sweet gale family**

Beach see **Coast and beach**

Beans see **Legumes**

Bear cat see **Civets**

Beardworms

Beardworms are slim, wormlike, deep–sea creatures so named for the thick cluster of long, fine, hairlike tentacles projecting from the front of the first section of a three–segmented body. There are approximately 120 species of beardworms, which belong to the phylum Pogonophora—from the Greek pogon, meaning beard, and phoron, meaning bearer.

The front section of the beardworm's body, which bears the tentacles, is quite short. The beardworm builds a protective tube around its entire body with mucus secreted from special glands in this body segment. As the worm grows (some beardworms reach a length of 5 ft/1.5 m), the tube lengthens at either end and takes on the appearance of a series of ringed sections. Visible around the worm's long narrow trunk are hundreds of tiny projections—special glands which also secrete mucus, enabling the creature to move around in its protective tube. Following behind the trunk is the third, shorter section of the body which is segmented and breaks off easily.

Beardworms have no mouth or intestines; instead, the blood–rich tentacles—as many as 200,000 on a giant beard worm of the genus Riftia—absorb all the nutrients the worm needs directly from the water. The tentacles of the female also serve a reproductive function. Although the species contains both sexes, beard-worms do not mate because they never venture from their protective tube. Instead, the male releases tiny parcels of sperm which the female captures in her tentacles. Once the packet dissolves, the sperm are released inside the tube of the female where egg fertilization takes place.

Living on the ocean floor at depths ranging from approximately 330 ft (100 m) to more than tens of thousands of feet, beardworms burrow into the sea bed, often leaving only their front section projecting above the surface.

Bears

Bears are large carnivores of the family Ursidae, related to dogs, cats, and seals. All of these mammals have special teeth called carnassials. These are a pair of modified teeth in the upper and lower jaw that, together, can rend meat into smaller chunks. Bears are not strictly meat–eaters, however, and their molars are adapted for grinding vegetation.

Bears began to evolve about 27 million years ago from a fox–sized animal called dawn bear. About 6 million years ago, bears branched into many different species, some of them huge, but most of these became extinct. Eventually only the seven species of bear known today were left on Earth. The polar bear (*Thalarctos maritimus*) is the newest bear species; it evolved from the grizzly bears. Cave bears (*Ursus spelaeus*), which were huge, were known to early humans. Their fossil remains have been found in caves where people lived 20,000 years ago.

All bears but one species live in the northern hemisphere. The spectacled bear (*Tremarctos ornatus*) lives in the northern Andes Mountains of South America. Three other small black bears are tropical animals, living within a short distance of the equator.

The giant panda (*Ailuropoda melanoleuca*) is often included with bears, although for many years it was been regarded as being a close relative of the raccoon and lesser panda. However, recent genetic studies have shown that it is, indeed, more closely related to bears.

Bears are quite variable in size. The smallest bear is the Malayan sun bear (*Helarctos malayanus*). A male sun bear is about 4 ft (1.2 m) long from head to tail tip. It stands about 28 in (70 cm) tall at the shoulder and may weigh up to 440 lb (200 kg). The largest is the polar bear, which may be up to almost 10 ft (3 m) long.

A polar bear.

A fat–padded male polar bear may weigh a ton (more than 900 kg). The layer of fat that builds up on bears may make any bear look rather lumpish and clumsy, but they can run for short distances at speeds up to 40 miles per hour (64 kph).

Most male bears, called boars, are considerably larger than the females, or sows. This is especially important when males have to compete for females to add to their harems. Sun bears and sloth bears *(Melursus ursinus)*, on the other hand, take only one mate and the males and females are more nearly the same size.

Bears from cold regions do not actually hibernate. Instead, during the coldest part of winter—when the plant food they eat is not available—they enter a long period of lethargy, or general sluggishness. Their body temperatures and pulse rates do not drop very much, as they would in true hibernation. They sleep a great deal and give up eating, living off the food that was stored as layers of fat during warmer weather. The exception

to this pattern is the polar bear, which continues to hunt for fish and seals during winter.

An additional advantage of this winter sluggishness is that the cubs born in winter are so small that they are incapable of regulating their body heat. The warm den in which the mother is wintering provides a snug place for them to grow until their body temperatures fit their northern way of life.

Most bears' bodies have an amazing ability to adjust to the seasons. Northern bears usually mate during spring or summer, but the fertilized eggs float free in the uterus, not developing. Then, in early winter, the sows find or create dens in which to sleep away the winter. The eggs implant and the actual gestation period starts. The cubs are very poorly developed when born; they are blind, nearly hairless, completely helpless, and very small. A female grizzly weighing 450 pounds (205 kg) may produce cubs weighing less than a pound (about 450 g). The female's milk, which is very rich in fat, keeps the tiny cubs warm and growing during the remainder of the winter. By the time the mother is ready to leave her den, the cubs have grown enough to follow along with her.

All bears are thickly furred, usually with a coat of a single color. With the exception of the sun bear, all species have fur on the bottoms of their feet, around the pads of the soles. This is especially important for the polar bear, which spends its life walking on ice. The sun bear, on the other hand, is aided in climbing trees by having furless feet. The print left by a bear's foot looks eerily human, five toes spread across a rounded, fleshy pad. But what may not show at first glance is the additional imprint of heavy claws digging into the soil some distance ahead of the toes. Bears walk in plantigrade fashion, which means that, like humans, they walk on the heel and sole of the foot. Most other mammals walk on their toes.

Bears have a reputation for having poor eyesight, but this probably is because they are seen to sniff at things so thoroughly. Their eyesight is good, but their sense of smell is incredible. They can identify odors of animals that passed by several days before. Unlike other carnivores, bears do not have their lips attached to their gums. This means that they can make facial expressions and use their lips to suck in food, such as insects and honey.

Grizzlies and other brown bears

Brown bears *(Ursus arctos)* live in forests across the top of the northern hemisphere. Some authorities separate them into three subspecies: the Eurasian brown bear (*U. a. arctos*); the grizzly bear (*U. a. horribilis*), which exists today only in Canada, Russia, and restricted locations in the United States; and the Kodiak bear (*U. a. middendorffi*), which lives only on Kodiak and two other islands in the Bering Sea. Although these bears may vary in color from white to cinnamon to black, their fur is mostly brown. Some brown bears have white tips on the end of the hairs, a coloring called grizzled that lends its name to the grizzly bear.

In general, a grizzly bear can be distinguished from other bears in North America by its profile. The outline of its head as seen from the side is concave, or scooped inward, and its shoulders are high from a thick layer of muscle and fat, making the back slope downward. The American black bear's facial profile does not curve inward, and its back is horizontal.

Grizzlies that live near sea–going rivers generally feed on as much salmon as they can get. Those bears that feed well tend to be huge in size. Even with their great size, they like to frolic in the water. They are adept at catching swift fish, which they carry to a bank to strip the flesh off the bones. When salmon is not available, they feed primarily on tender plant parts such as roots and berries, as well as small rodents. In the mountains, grizzlies may attack and eat such large prey as moose and even black bears. They cannot digest tough leaves very well, so they avoid fibrous plant material.

These giant bears mate in late spring. In the fall, the female makes herself a den in a cave or hollow tree, settles into it, and begins her winter lethargy. Two or three babies are born usually in February. The cubs stay close to the mother for at least two years, continuing to nurse during most of that time and often up to four and one–half years. The mother is exceedingly protective, and teaches the cubs promptly to climb trees to escape danger. Most attacks on humans have been made by sow grizzlies protecting their cubs. One of the major enemies from which she must protect them is male grizzlies, which have been known to eat cubs.

When young females are ready to leave home, they often continue to share the same feeding range as the mother. The males, however, will go off on their own, often traveling up to 100 mi (161 km) before settling down. They may have difficulty finding a place because older males will fight to keep new males out of their territory.

Formerly the range of grizzly bears extended all the way from Alaska down into Mexico. Grizzlies have long since disappeared from most of the western United States except Alaska. Only a few are left in Wyoming, Montana, Idaho, and Washington. These link up with habitat in Canada. Some residents of the San Juan Mountains in Colorado are convinced that grizzlies still live there, hidden far from human view.

Those populations of grizzlies left in the United States are in danger primarily because of lack of females of the right age to breed. In recent years, measures have been taken—despite some human objections—to import breeding bears with the hope that the populations might once more stabilize. However, a single bear may require up to 300 sq mi (about 770 sq km) to roam. Few places remain in the United States where such an area would not impinge on humans.

Eurasia brown bears, which are smaller than grizzlies, are still found throughout Europe and Asia but in rapidly decreasing numbers. Huge numbers of them were killed during World War II. Those that remain live primarily in hardwood forests on mountains. Unfortunately, such locations are being rapidly taken over by resort development. However, brown bears have a greater diversity of habitat than any other bear. They can even be found in deserts and Arctic tundra. It has been estimated that there are probably fewer than 35,000 brown bears left across the whole continent.

Eurasian brown bears vary greatly in size. The few that remain in Spain are rarely more than 250 lb (114 kg). Those in Siberia may rival the huge Kodiak bears in size. Legends abound in Russia about giant brown bears—even larger than Kodiaks—living on the Kamchatka Peninsula in far eastern Russia. They have yet to be photographed.

Polar bears

Polar bears did not appear on Earth until about 70,000 years ago, when they evolved from the grizzly and took over a very inhospitable habitat. These huge whitish bears are well adapted to life in and around the icy Arctic Ocean. They are not found near the North Pole because they must remain where their primary food—seal flesh—is found, which is near open water.

Though longer than grizzlies, polar bears are more slender. They have a longer neck and head than brown bears do. The individual hairs of a polar bear's thick fur are actually transparent, with reflected sunlight making the coat appear white. Oddly, the bear's skin is black. The sunlight that gets past the hair is absorbed by the black skin, keeping the animal warm. Many bears appear to be yellow in color instead of white from the amount of seal oil they digest. Their furry front feet are slightly webbed, helping them swim.

They swim by paddling their front feet and steering with their back feet.

Polar bears move from ice floe to ice floe, often swimming long hours in the cold sea while looking for a likely spot to find their favorite food, ringed seals (*Phoca hispida*). Their claws, much longer than those of other bears, are able to grasp and hold the biggest seals as they rise out of the water at breathing holes or along the edge of a floe. During the spring, however, the bears are more likely to break into the snowy nests where female seals have given birth to their young. The slow–moving seals have no defense against alert bears except in the water.

Bears tend to congregate in areas where ice floes move freely in the wind. In such areas, seals are more easily obtained. They will also tolerate each other's presence if one bear locates a huge stranded whale or walrus that can serve as food for more than one animal. During summer, when the ice is gone from the coastal fringes of Canada and Russia, polar bears move onto the land and feed on berries as if they were grizzlies. In recent years, some polar bears have been drawn to garbage dumps near towns. Naturalists fear that they may forget how to hunt. Also, even though polar bears look friendly when they are foraging through garbage, they are still large, dangerous bears who might attack if people get too close.

Polar bears are usually solitary, but they meet in late spring (March–June) to mate. One to three cubs are born in December or January in a snow den constructed by the mother. They are larger than grizzly cubs, averaging about 23 oz (650 g) at birth. Their weight increases to about 20 lb (9 kg) or more by the time they emerge from the den in April. This great weight gain is from the very special polar bear milk that contains more than 30% fat. The cubs will stay by the mother for at least two more years, learning to hunt and defend themselves. At that time the mother will mate again. The young females will not mate until they are at least five years old. Then they will mate with older males. Polar bears probably live to be 20 or more years old.

The five nations with polar bear territory within their boundaries—United States, Canada, Denmark (in Greenland), Norway, and Russia—have banned the hunting of these bears by airplane or large boats. Traditional methods used by Eskimos and other natives who have long depended on the polar bear are the only hunting methods allowed. Native peoples eat the bear meat and generally sell the hides.

American black bear

American black bears (*Ursus americanus*) live in forests with some open meadows across much of North America, from Alaska to Nova Scotia, south through the Rocky Mountains into Mexico, and in patches in the Appalachians and Florida. Small populations are found elsewhere, even in New Jersey. The black bear is often not black. It can be brown, even light tan, as well as black. West of the Mississippi this bear is often cinnamon in color. Several different colors may be found in the same litter of cubs. Black bears may have white markings on their chests. They have larger ears than other bears do.

Black bears are quite small, often only 4.5 ft (1.4 m) long, and weighing 125–600 lb (57–272 kg). Their weight varies considerably depending on the amount of nourishing food available. However, the male usually weighs about one–third more than the female. Because they are so much smaller than grizzly bears, black bears stay out of sight when the territories of the two species overlap. Black bears readily take over area abandoned by grizzlies.

Each black bear has a feeding territory of its own where it gathers just about anything it feels like eating. Most of its food consists of fruits and berries, but it also eats fish, carrion, insect grubs, nuts, honey, and small rodents. One male's territory will overlap those of several females. Black bears mate during the summer, with each female being visited several times.

As with most bears, the fertilized egg does not implant itself until fall. If the female bear is too thin because of a scarce food supply that year, the eggs won't implant at all. If all is well, they do implant, and after a gestation period of 8–10 weeks, one to four cubs are born in January. Young females will not become sexually mature until about four years of age if the food supply is scarce. Black bears often scratch on trees, sometimes destroying them in the process by killing their bark. This makes them especially unwelcome near tree plantations in the Northwest.

Other small black bears

The small Asiatic black bear (*Selenarctos thibetanus*) is recognized by the white crescent on its chest, which has given it the nickname of moon bear. Otherwise, it is totally black. The hair around its neck is longer than the other hair, giving it a ruff. A male may weigh up to 350 lb (159 kg), while the female usually weighs less than 200 lb (91 kg). This bear is found in usually moist mountainous forests from

Afghanistan, across China to Southeast Asia and even in Japan.

The Asiatic black bear is generally nocturnal, but it will readily go out in the daytime to pick sun–warmed fruit. However, it will also go after meat and has been known to kill fairly large game animals by breaking their necks. Northern populations of Asiatic black bears will sleep away the winter, but in the southern part of their range, they remain active all year round. Southern bears mate in fall and the cubs are born in three or four months. The cubs of these bears are able to follow their mother around much more quickly than most bear cubs do. They are weaned by four months of age.

The sun bear (*Helarctos malayanus*), also called the Malayan sun bear, is the smallest bear, often weighing no more than 100 lb (45 kg). It has black fur, a whitish snout, and often a whitish or orange–toned U–shaped mark on the chest. It has a much longer tongue than other bears, which it apparently uses to lap up honey and insects from holes in trees. The only tropical bear, the sun bear is found in rain forests of southern China and on the islands going down to Borneo and Sumatra. Sun bears climb trees and often build nests by breaking branches.

The sun bear's size does not make it any less ferocious than bigger bears. It will readily attack people when confronted in its forest habitat. Because the bear forages for honey, termites, and fruits, it is often drawn to banana and papaya plantations, where it may be shot. Sun bears are often kept as pets. These bears do not hibernate, and the cubs may be born at any time of the year after a gestation period of about 14 weeks.

The sloth bear (*Melursus ursinus*) of India and neighboring countries has the longest hair in the bear family. However, its belly is practically hairless. Otherwise, it looks very much like the Asiatic black bear, ruff, V–shaped mark, and all. The sloth bear, however, does two things that no other bear does—it carries its young on its back and the male remains with the female to help train the young. It has very strong and long claws, which it uses to break open termite nests.

The spectacled bear (*Tremarctos ornatus*) is South America's only bear. Also called the Andean bear, it can be found throughout much of the Andes Mountains, often living above 14,000 ft (4,270 m). It has a whitish eyeglasses–shaped pattern around its eyes as well as a "necklace" of white on its neck, which may extend down onto its chest. It climbs trees and may even sleep in them. A little larger than the other small black bears, male spectacled bears may reach a head–body length of almost 6 ft (1.8 m) and a weight

---

KEY TERMS

Carnassial—Of teeth, longer and sharper than nearby teeth and thus adapted for tearing meat. Carnivores have carnassial teeth.

Plantigrade—Walking on the heel and sole of the foot instead of on the toes.

---

of about 400 lb (182 kg). In profile, they can be seen to have shorter noses than other bears.

This bear is primarily nocturnal in habit, sleeping during the day in a hole or under tree roots. At night, it often climbs high into trees to pick fruit. If it finds a good supply and decides to stay awhile, it will take branches and built itself a platform to sit on. It also eats bromeliads, thick succulent plants found in rain forests, when it can't find fruit. There are probably less than 2,000 of these bears remaining in the wild. However, an international program is successfully breeding them in captivity.

Hunting bears

All bears except polar bears are regarded as sources of medicine in Asia. Fluids from the gall bladder in particular are thought to have many health–giving properties. It is also believed that an aphrodisiac, or love potion, can be made from this organ. The flesh of bear paws is also regarded as a gourmet food in the Orient.

For these reasons, the Asiatic black bear, which has long been killed for medicinal purpose, is endangered. In China, the remaining black bears often have tubes implanted into their gall bladders from which the supposedly health–giving bile fluid can be withdrawn without killing the animal. Many American black bears as well as Eurasian brown bears are also killed each year so that their gall bladders can be exported to the Orient. Even spectacled bears in South America are not safe. Native peoples regard the fat of these bears as useful against crippling arthritis.

In addition to these problems, all bears are vulnerable to habitat destruction and human invasion of their habitat. If people want to move into a area, bears are often the first animals to be eliminated.

See also Pandas.

Further Reading:

Bailey, Jill. *Polar Bear Rescue.* Austin, TX: Raintree Steck–Vaughn Publishers, 1991.

Bears. Zoobooks Series. San Diego, CA: Wildlife Education, 1982.

Brown, Gary. *The Great Bear Almanac.* New York: Lyons & Burford, 1993.

Bruemmer, Fred. *World of the Polar Bear.* Minocqua, WI: NorthWord Press, 1989.

Caras, Roger A. *North American Mammals: Fur–Bearing Animals of the United States and Canada.* New York: Meredith Press, 1967.

Domico, Terry. *Bears of the World.* New York: Facts on File, 1988.

Elman, Robert. *Bears.* Stamford, CT: Longmeadow Press, 1992.

Hunt, Joni P. *Bears.* San Luis Obispo, CA: Blake Publishing, 1993.

O'Toole, Christopher, and John Stidworthy. *Mammals: The Hunters.* New York: Facts on File, 1988.

Nowak, Ronald M. *Walker's Mammals of the World.* 5th ed. Baltimore: Johns Hopkins University Press, 1991.

Polar Bears. Zoobooks Series. San Diego, CA: Wildlife Education, 1991.

Stirling, Ian. *Bears: Majestic Creatures of the Wild.* Emmaus, PA: Rodale Press, 1993.

Van Wormer, Joe. *The World of the Black Bear.* Philadelphia: J. B. Lippincott Co., 1966.

Jean F. Blashfield

Beaufort scale see **Wind**

Beavers

The true beavers are robust, aquatic herbivores in the family Castoridae, order Rodentia. Many taxonomists believe that two, closely related species of true beavers exist—the American beaver (*Castor canadensis*) and the Eurasian beaver (*C. fiber*). Other taxonomists, however, classify these as closely related variants of the same species, under the name *Castor fiber*.

A few other rodents are also called beavers, such as the mountain beaver (*Aplodontia rufa*) of western North America, and the swamp beaver or nutria (*Myocastor coypu*) of South America. However, these two species of rodents are not in the family Castoridae, and are not true beavers.

The true beavers are large animals, weighing as much as about 88 lbs (40 kg), and they are the largest rodents to occur in Eurasia and North America. Only the capybaras of South America (family Hydrochoeri-

dae), which can weigh as much as 110 lbs (50 kg), are larger rodents. However, a now–extinct species of giant beaver in the genus *Castoroides*, which occurred in North America as recently as about 10,000 years ago at the end of the most recent ice age, is estimated to have weighed several hundred pounds. This enormous rodent was similar in size to a black bear (*Ursus americanus*).

One of the most distinctive features of beavers is their scaly, naked, paddle–like tail. The flattened beaver tail is used as a rudder while the animal swims, using its webbed hind feet to propel itself through the water. The unusual tail is also used as a support while the beaver is standing and as a brace while the animal is dragging logs to the water. If danger is perceived, the tail is energetically splashed onto the water surface to warn other beavers of the threat. However, contrary to what some people believe, the tail is not used as a trowel to daub mud onto the dams that beavers often build.

The American beaver

The American beaver (*Castor canadensis*) is widespread in North America, ranging from the limits of the boreal forest in the north, through almost all of the United States, except for the Florida peninsula and parts of the southwestern states. The American beaver has also been introduced beyond its natural range, for example, into some regions in Europe. As a result, some hybridization has occurred with the European beaver, suggesting a close evolutionary relationship between the two species.

The beaver is a large animal, with the biggest animals reaching a weight of about 88 lbs (40 kg), but more typically being 33–77 lbs (15–35 kg). The beaver has a robust body, a broad and blunt head, and a short neck and limbs. Beavers have very large, continuously growing incisor teeth and large cheek teeth used for chewing their food of plant materials. The incisor teeth meet outside of the closed lips of the mouth, enabling the animal to feed easily underwater. The nostrils and ears have skin flaps that serve as valves to keep water out when the animal is submerged. The forepaws have long fingers, useful for dextrous handling of branches and twigs while feeding and building lodges and dams. The hind feet have two serrated claws that are used in preening and oiling the fur, a task in which beavers are commonly engaged. The other three claws on the hind feet are blunt and flat. The pelage of this animal is thick and lustrous, with a dense, brown underfur and longer, coarser guard hairs.

Beavers are social animals, with the basic unit being the family, which forms a colony with a hierarchical structure among the individuals. The oldest

An American beaver (*Castor canadensis*) dragging a willow branch over his dam in Denali National Park, Alaska.

female is the central individual in the group. She establishes the colony, and, if she is killed and no daughter exists to take over the matriarchal role, the site is abandoned. The average colony size is about six animals. All of the animals in the colony work cooperatively, especially in building and maintaining the group's dams and lodge.

Beavers are famous for their industriousness and engineering skills. If an open–water wetland such as a pond is not available locally, beavers will construct one by building a dam of logs, sticks, stones, and mud-plaster across a stream, causing the water to back up. Beavers maintain their dams assiduously, and they seem to be constantly working on improving these structures. This is necessary, of course, because the beaver pond provides essential local habitat for the species, yet it is in some respects artificial, having been created by the animals themselves. Of course, many other species of wildlife benefit greatly from the habitat-creating enterprise of beavers. The dams are generally constructed to create a pool that is 6.5–10 ft (2–3 m) deep in some places, so that in the wintertime unfrozen water will occur beneath the ice, which can be as much as 3 ft

(1 m) thick. Some dams can be hundreds of feet long, and several feet high.

Beavers also build lodges of sticks and mud. Beaver lodges are commonly located in shallow, open water, and their top projects as high as several feet above the water surface. Lodges may also be located near the edge of the beaver pond, rather than in open water. The lodge has a hollow, gnawed–out core, in which the family lives. The roof of the lodge is relatively thin and porous, allowing fresh air to circulate. The interior of the lodge is reached by several underwater passageways. Beavers also burrow into mud banks, and animals living on large rivers or lakes will do this instead of building a lodge.

Beavers are crepuscular, meaning they are most active between sunset and sunrise. They have a slow lumbering gait on land, but are skilled swimmers. Beavers mostly eat the inner bark and cambium of trees and shrubs, as well as the buds, leaves, and flowers of woody plants. They also supplement this diet with aquatic plants and herbaceous terrestrial vegetation during the summer and autumn. Beavers sometimes fell quite large trees (up to 16 in [40 cm] in diameter) to get access to the relatively nutritious branches and twigs of the canopy. Trembling aspen (*Populus tremuloides*) is the food species of choice, with willows, birches, poplars, and alders also being favored.

Beavers fell trees by gnawing them at the base, often while standing erect, propped by their tail, and gripping the tree with their forepaws. The stumps of beaver–felled trees have a distinctive, conical top, with clear evidence of the large cuts made by the chisel–like incisors of the animal, which remove substantial chips of wood. The beavers do not gnaw right through the trunk—they leave a central core intact, and rely on rocking motions from a later wind to actually cause the final felling of the tree. Beavers seem unable to plan the direction of the eventual tree–fall, and they are sometimes killed when this actually happens. Beavers occasionally construct canals in wet terrain in order to make their logging areas easier to reach, and they often develop wide, well–trodden paths to facilitate the dragging of branches to their pond.

Beavers do not hibernate—they remain active in their lodges and beneath the ice of their pond. During winter these animals mostly feed on underwater piles of branches and twigs accumulated for this purpose during the previous growing summer and autumn. However, beavers will sometimes emerge above the ice and snow to feed if they run short of their stored winter food.

Many animals prey on beavers. When predators are relatively abundant, beavers are wary and do not like to forage or fell trees very far from the safety of their pond.

Beavers and the fur trade

The pelts of American beavers are valuable in the fur trade and are largely used in making coats and hats. During the first several centuries of the European colonization of North America, beaver pelts were one of the most important natural resources to be exported from the northern regions of that continent. The most important markets were in Europe, where the pelts were used to make gentlemens' hats, also known as "beavers."

In fact, most of the initial exploration and settlement of the interior of North America was undertaken by fur traders, and these intrepid men were most enthusiastically searching for beaver pelts. For many years in vast regions of North America, beaver pelts were the measure of wealth, and were even a common unity of currency. In view of the great importance of the beaver in the early colonial history of Canada, this animal has become a national symbol of that country. However, beavers were similarly important in the northeastern and central United States.

The extraordinary overharvesting of beavers for their pelts caused great reductions in the abundance of these animals, and they were widely extirpated from much of their original range in North America. Moreover, the American beaver will not breed in captivity, so fur–farming is not possible. Fortunately, the implementation of conservation measures after about the 1940s has allowed a substantial rebound in the populations of American beavers. These animals are now re–occupying much of their former range, as long as the habitat has remained suitable for their purposes. Beavers are sometimes hunted for meat, although their use in this way is usually secondary to the taking of their pelts.

Beavers can be viewed as a nuisance, their constructions flooding roads, culverts, railroads, lawns, and agricultural land. Beavers also may cut down valuable ornamental trees in some places where they are living in proximity to humans. As a result, many states and provinces will live–trap problem beavers for relocation to less built–up areas.

The Eurasian beaver

The natural range of the Eurasian beaver (*Castor fiber*) extends through most of Europe and through much of northwestern Asia. However, the modern range of the Eurasian beaver has become rather restricted and fragmented, and the species is now much less abundant than it used to be. The population declines are due to the conversion of the species' natural wetlands habitat into agricultural landscapes as well as overhunting. The European beaver has long been exploited as a natural resource, for both its thick, lustrous fur, and also a musky oil called castoreum, which is extracted from the anal or castor gland of this animal.

The mountain beaver

The mountain beaver (*Aplodontia rufa*, family Aplodontidae) occurs in the Cascade Mountains from east–central California north through Oregon and Washington to southwestern British Columbia. Other than being a large rodent, the mountain beaver is not particularly closely related to the true beavers, which are in the family Castoridae. In fact, mountain beavers are the only species in their family, and they not closely related to any other rodents. Because of their ancient evolutionary history, mountain beavers are sometimes considered to be living fossils. In body form, the mountain beaver looks like a tailless muskrat or large vole, with small ears, short legs, and a grizzled, brownish fur. Mountain beavers are terrestrial animals, digging long, complex burrows in moist, workable soil near streams, with numerous entrances and exits located in concealed places. These animals live in loose colonies, but they are not very social animals, preferring to avoid frequent, direct contact with each other. Mountain beavers eat a wide range of plant foods, including herbaceous plants and fruits, young twigs of woody plants, and conifer foliage and shoots in the wintertime. Mountain beavers store food for the winter as underground haystacks.

See also Rodents.

Further Reading:

Banfield, A. W. F. *The Mammals of Canada.* Toronto: University of Toronto Press, 1974.

Grzimek, B., ed. *Grzimek's Encyclopedia of Mammals.* London: McGraw–Hill, 1990.

Hall, E. R. *The Mammals of North America,* 2nd ed. New York: Wiley & Sons, 1981.

Paradiso, J. L., ed. *Mammals of the World,* 2nd ed. Baltimore: John Hopkins Press, 1968.

Ryden, H. *The Beaver.* London: Lyons & Burford, 1992.

Wilson, D. E. and D. Reeder. *Mammal Species of the World.* Washington, D.C.: Smithsonian Institution Press, 1993.

Bill Freedman

B cells see **Immune system; Lymphatic system**

Bed bugs see **True bugs**

Beech family (Fagaceae)

The beech family is an important group of flowering plants that includes the beeches, oaks, and sweet

A beech forest near Brussels, Belgium.

chestnuts. Most members of the family are deciduous or evergreen trees or shrubs. The leaves are arranged alternately along branches; leathery in texture, often strongly ribbed, and have margins that are entire, toothed, or deeply lobed. The flowers are unisexual. Male flowers are usually arranged in catkins (round heads in *Fagus*) whereas female flowers are in few–flowered clusters. The fruit is a one–seeded nut that is partially or completely covered by a cupule of scales or a spiny bur.

The family includes 8 genera and about 1000 species. The Fagaceae are widely distributed and most abundant in temperate and subtropical regions of the Northern Hemisphere, although there is one tropical and one south temperate (*Nothofagus*) genus. Beech (*Fagus*) and sweet chestnut are, or were in the case of American chestnut (*Castanea dentata*), prominent components of mature deciduous and mixed forests of North America and Eurasia. Much of central Europe was covered by forests of beech and oak until cleared by people for agriculture. Similar forests in the Southern Hemisphere are dominated by southern beeches in the southern Andes, eastern Australia, and New Zealand. The American chestnut was formerly a dominant species of deciduous forest in eastern North

Sweet chestnuts. The thorny husks split to release the nuts.

America. Oaks (*Quercus*) are also important in rich temperate deciduous forests as well as on droughty soils such as the sand plains of the eastern North American seaboard, where oaks grow abundantly with pines. Evergreen oaks are especially important in the arid regions of the Gulf of Mexico, southern China, and southern Japan. Evergreen species of both oaks and southern beeches are prominent in the mixed mountain forests of Southeast Asia. Given their prominence as the producers of deciduous and mixed forests, the Fagaceae are extremely important ecologically. Furthermore, their nuts are important sources of food for a variety of insects, birds, and mammals.

The beech family is among the most valuable sources of hardwood timber in the world. There are over 300 species of oaks worldwide and the characteristics of their wood varies. Nevertheless, most produce strongly grained, durable wood that polishes well. The white oaks of North America, in particular, produce fine wood that is commonly used for furniture, panelling, and flooring. The bark of oaks is often rich in tannin, which is used in tanning leather. Oak wood is used in the construction of barrels for the storage of whiskey, wine, and sherry. Oak is also valued as firewood and for making charcoal. Tropical members of the family, such as *Castanopsis* and *Lithocarpus* (called chinkapin and tanoak respectively in North America), also produce high quality wood, but they have not as yet been heavily exploited.

The bark of the Mediterranean cork oak (*Quercus suber*) is the principle source of commercial cork. Cork bark is stripped in summer by making a circular cut at the base of the trunk and another just below the first branches. A lengthwise slit is then made between the two circular cuts and the bark is carefully removed with special hatchets so as not to damage the conducting tissue of the inner bark. The stripped bark is stacked and allowed to season for a few weeks, then boiled in tanks of water, followed by the removal of the rough outer bark. The cork is then dried and ready for use. The bark is stripped from trees once every 8–10 years. Aside from its role in stoppering bottles, cork is used for gaskets, floats, non–slip walkways, corkboard, and flooring. The main cork–producing areas are Portugal and southwest Spain.

Chestnuts are especially prized for their large, sweet, edible nuts. Although there are about 10 species of sweet chestnuts, the most widely grown is *Castanea sativa*, commonly called the Italian, Spanish, or European sweet chestnut, which is a native of southern Europe. The nuts can be roasted over an open fire, used whole or sliced in stews and stuffings, or pureed into the exquisite French dessert called *marron glacé*. The American chestnut was once an important timber and nut tree, and it is said that its nuts were sweeter and tastier than those of European species. Unfortunately, this once–dominant member of the deciduous forest of eastern North America is now a rarity, struck down by chestnut blight.

Chestnut blight was introduced into eastern North America from abroad in about 1904. By 1940, the American chestnut had disappeared from most of its range, clinging in places as sprouts from the root collars of tree whose trunks had died, but although these sprouts may grow for 40 years, they do not produce fruit, and so the tree is condemned to die without leaving offspring. The disease is caused by the fungus *Endothia parasitica*, which produces spores that stick onto the beaks and feet of bark–feeding birds and on the bodies of bark beetles. The spores are carried by the birds and insects to healthy trees that become infected when spores are accidentally deposited into wounds caused by the feeding of the birds and beetles. The spores germinate and the growing fungal threads enter vital cells of the inner bark, killing them. There are no adequate control measures for chestnut blight.

Beeches (*Fagus* and *Nothofagus*) both produce valuable wood. European beeches have proved to be extremely useful in bentwood furniture, which is made by steaming laminated pieces of wood and then pressing them against forms until dry. Beech nuts were once commonly eaten by people, but now the nuts, along with acorns, are mostly fed to pigs, especially in Europe. In many parts of eastern North America, the American beech has been afflicted by a canker disease that disfigures the lovely, smooth, gray bark and obstructs the conducting tissue causing reduced rates of growth.

Further Reading:

Bateman, G., ed. *Flowering Plants of the World.* Oxford: Oxford University Press, 1978.

Mitchell, A. *The Guide to Trees of Canada and North America.* Surrey, U.K.: Dragon's World Ltd., 1987.

Les C. Cwynar

Bee–eaters

Bee–eaters are 24 species of birds that make up the family Meropidae. Bee–eaters occur in open habitats and savannas of the south–temperate and tropical zones, ranging through Africa, southern Europe, southern Asia, Southeast Asia, and many Pacific Islands. Species that breed in temperate habitats migrate to the tropics for the winter.

Bee–eaters have large, pointed wings and a long tail, usually with the two central feathers quite extended. Their bill is long, slender, down–curved, and pointed. The feet and legs are rather small and weak and are only used for perching. Bee–eaters are brightly colored, most commonly with a basal hue of green, and bold markings of yellow, blue, red, brown, black, and white. All species have a black stripe running through the eye, known as a "mask." Both sexes are similarly colored and patterned, as are the juvenile birds.

Bee–eaters tend to occur in groups, often perched in the open. They commonly feed by pursuing and catching insects in the air, a foraging strategy known as "hawking." True to their name, the principal food of most species of bee–eaters is bees and wasps. However, a wide diversity of flying insects is taken, depending on their local and seasonal availability. After a bee or wasp is captured in the bill, its abdomen is forcefully wiped against a branch, causing the venom to be discharged.

A common green bee-eater with its catch.

Bee–eaters nest in a burrow dug into an earthen bank or sand cliff. The tunnels are as long as several meters, and have a nesting chamber at the end, in which two to six eggs are laid. Nesting sites are generally colonial, with large numbers of pairs breeding in the same vicinity, commonly near water. Both sexes share in the incubation of the eggs and care of the young.

The European bee–eater (*Merops apiaster*) is a blue–bellied, cinnamon–backed, yellow–throated species of southern Europe and western Asia, wintering in sub–Saharan Africa and India.

The blue–cheeked bee–eater (*Merops persicus*) is a widespread species, occurring in Africa and Madagascar through to western Asia. This species has a lime–green body, with a bluish breast, a yellow and chestnut–brown throat, and a black eye–line.

As its name implies, the rainbow–bird (*Merops ornatus*) of Australia is an especially lovely and multi–hued bee–eater. This species migrates north to New Guinea after its breeding season in temperate Australia.

Bees

Bees belong to the insect order Hymenoptera, which includes wasps and ants. Its name is derived from Greek, meaning "winged membrane," and it is the third largest group of insects with more than a hundred thousand species in the order. Ants and bees play vital roles in agriculture, ants being useful in aerating soil and bees in pollinating plants. Wasps play an important part as predators to other insect pests and bees are the source of honey and wax, which has been highly valued by human beings since antiquity.

Hymenoptera are distinguished by having two pair of wings that are veined in cross angles creating a cell–like pattern. The rear wings are smaller than the front ones, and wing color ranges from brown with yellow markings to red, white, blue, or green marks. Male Hymenoptera have thirteen segments in their antennae, while females have only twelve. Most Hymenopterons have chewing mouthparts with a pair of mandibles, but bees have a long tongue (proboscis) to lap nectar. Bees have a complete, four–stage metamorphosis from egg, larva, pupa, to adult. Some species of bees, as well as ants and some wasps, form colonies under a *caste system*, while other species are solitary.

Bee families

The more than twenty thousand species of bees are assigned to the superfamily Apoidea, which includes eight families. The diversity of bees includes the yellow–faced, plasterer, oxaeid, andrenid, sweat, melittid, leafcutting, mason, cuckoo, digger, carpenter, bumble, and honey bees. The latter two are the most common and both belong to the family Apidae. Bees are characterized by the vein pattern on their wings and by the size of their tongues. Some have a short tongue and others a long, slender one. Bees are able to chew as well as suck with their mouthparts.

Bees mainly eat nectar and pollen, which they also store in their hives or nests for their larvae to eat. A segment of the rear legs of bees is enlarged and somewhat flattened and serves as a carrying device for the pollen they collect. Male bees have seven segments in the abdominal region, while females have only six. Hairlike setae densely cover the bodies of bees. Plants that bees pollinate include most fruits, numerous vegetables, and field crops like cotton, tobacco, and clover. While the bees that are most beneficial for commercial production of honey are social bees, many families of bees are solitary in nature. Bees are also diurnal, that is, they are active in the daytime.

Solitary bees

Among the *solitary bees*, where each queen bee builds her own nest, there is sometimes evidence of a division of labor. Some of the bee families are more sociable than others and build their nests close to one another and may even share the same entrance to the nests. In such cases, a bee might stand guard at the entrance of the group of nests to protect them from predators. This is not the same social organization as the caste system established by true social bees, where

there is only one queen bee laying eggs. Some species of solitary bees build nests, while some scavenge and use the nests of other bees or convenient crevices for laying their eggs. Nest building patterns among solitary bees vary from species to species.

Plasterer bees, members of the family Colletidae, get their name from a secretion they use to plaster the sides of their mud nests, which may be in the ground or in crevices of stones and bricks. Plasterer bees are black with light–colored body hairs. Yellow–faced bees, which belongs to the same family as the plasterer bee, builds nests in plant stalks and insect burrows. Yellow–faced bees feed their larvae on a mixture of pollen and nectar which is stored in their nests.

There are over twelve hundred species of the Andrenid bee family found in North America. These yellow, white, or black bees make their nests underground in tunnels, which may include many branches and may house large group of bees. Over five hundred species of the "sweat bee" can be found in North America. Their sting is not painful, although sweat bees have a reputation for stinging persons who are sweating. They nest in clay and sand banks of streams. Some have metallic blue or green colorations, but they are mostly black or brown.

The leafcutting bee gets its name from its habit of cutting pieces of leaves to use as a nest. It places a ball of pollen on the cut leaf and then lays its eggs on top. It locates its nests in wood, under loose bark, or in the ground. It is closely related to the mason bee, a shiny, blue–green insect, that builds its nest under stones, where it builds clusters of small cells. Mason bees also like empty snail shells and the empty nests of other bees.

Digger, cuckoo, and carpenter bees belong to the same subfamily Apidae as the honey bee and bumble bee, but they are not social. The larger carpenter bees nest in open spaces in wood, while the smaller ones use the stems of bushes in which to build their nests. They are robust in build, as is the digger and cuckoo bee. The large ones look like bumble bees. Digger bees are much more hairy than other members of the bee family and they build their nests in burrows in the ground. Cuckoo bees look like small wasps and lay their eggs in the nests of other bees.

Social bees

Honey bees and bumble bees are two of the five hundred species of bees which are *social*. Their colonies or hives range in size from several hundred to as many as eighty thousand inhabitants. They are organized within a rigid caste system, where members of a caste carry out specific tasks. The social system consists of a queen bee, male drones, and worker bees. The queen bee is responsible for laying eggs, which the drones have fertilized, and the worker bees build the nest and care for the fertilized eggs and larvae.

The female worker bees differ in structure from the queen bee. They have pollen sacs in their rear legs, which the queen bee does not have. Workers also have wax glands and other differences in their head structure. Their life span, usually a season, is shorter than that of the queen bee, who lives on the average for several years. Worker bees are not capable of mating, but if a queen bee is not present in the hive, their ovaries do develop and they become capable of laying eggs that become drones. Drones are not constructed for collecting pollen. They are hatched from unfertilized eggs that the queen lays by withholding sperm. While the queen bee has a life span of several years, the drone dies when he has impregnated the queen.

Bumble bees are social bees and are characteristically black, yellow, and hairy. After mating in the fall, a queen will hibernate over the winter, while the workers and drones from the past season's colony die before winter. In the following spring, the queen begins a new nest, lays her eggs, and spends her time protecting them and sipping from a honey pot. She is often compared to a mother hen hatching her eggs. A favorite nesting place for bumble bees is an abandoned mouse nest.

When the larvae mature in about ten days, they construct a cocoon for their pupal stage. After several weeks, female workers leave their cocoons to take up the work of building the nest. Males and potential queens are hatched later in the season. Bumble bees are important for the pollination of red clover, which is an important field crop in agriculture. Plants that bloom eight to nine weeks before clover are planted near clover fields to lure bumble bees to the area with a supply of food before the red clover comes into bloom. This ensures the bumble bees will be present when it is time to pollinate the crop.

The stingless bee flourishes in Central and South America. Before European honey bees were introduced in the Western Hemisphere, these bees supplied honey and wax to communities in these regions. The wax was also used as casting materials for the molding of gold jewelry. There are several hundred species of stingless bees in tropical regions and their colonies range from several hundred to as many as eighty thousand individual bees. They use a blend of wax, resin, and mud to build their nests, which may have walls as thick as eight inches. Eggs are laid in the nest with a

store of food and the cells are sealed. New nests are created in preparation for the departure of a new, young queen from the old nest, and workers and males follow to join her.

Honey bees

The social structure of honey bees is the caste system of queen, drones, and workers. Unlike the stingless bee, the honey bee queen is the one to leave the old colony to form a new one. The move to a new nest begins with a swarming of bees and ends when a suitable place, such as the hollow in a tree, is found to establish a new colony. A young queen will take over the old colony.

Of interest to entomologists is the so-called "dance language" of honey bees. A worker can communicate the location of a food source, how far away it is, and the type of flower that will be found. Some of this information is transmitted by the scent the flower has left on the messenger's body, but there are other features to this communication. One is a circle dance that communicates sources of the nectar. The other dance involves wagging the tail and the abdominal region, which indicates the distance. The tail wagging is accompanied by wing vibrations produced at the same rate. The closer the source of the food, the more wags. Different species of honey bees follow different dance tempos.

Direction to the food source is shown by the angle of the bee to the sun when it is wagging its tail. Besides this "dance communication," bees seem to know when flowers have a supply of nectar available. This built-in biological clock is not as well understood as their "dance language." The person responsible for unravelling the dance language of honey bees was Karl von Frisch, who received a Nobel Prize in 1973 for this work.

Honey bees are susceptible to debilitation of their honey production by bee mites, a parasite that reduces their natural pollinating and honey-making activities. In the mid 1980s, 150 million honey bees had to be destroyed in several parts of the United States to eliminate the infestation of these mites. Other diseases that honey bees are susceptible to is foulbrood, which attacks larvae or pupae, stress diseases, such as sacbrood and nosema, which can shorten the lives of adult bees, and acarine disease, another mite disease. Animal predators that are dangerous to bees are mice, birds, bears, squirrels, skunks, raccoons, and opossums. The first line of defense of a bee is of course its sting.

Beekeeping

References to bees and honey can be found in early civilizations from the Sumerians, Babylonians, Egyptians, Hindus, Greeks, Romans, and Mayans in the warmer climates to Celts, Slavs, and Northern Europe in colder climates. Honey as a sweetener was valued even in areas where sugar was available. A number of these early civilizations held the bee and its honey in high regard, using the bee as a symbol for royalty and honey for anointing their kings and for embalming the dead. Besides using honey for a sweetener in food, it was also used medicinally during the Middle Ages and Renaissance in Europe, where beeswax was also used for candle making and for molds to cast statues.

There is evidence from an Egyptian tomb dating to 2400 B.C. that this culture had learned to raise bees in man–made hives and no longer had to rely on raiding beehives for their honey. In southern climates, a round type of beehive was constructed from hollow tubes made of mud or clay and baked in the sun. The bees then built their honeycombs in these early beehives. In the northern climates of Europe, a horizontal hive was developed that was made of wicker or straw. Other materials used were cane in China, cork in Spain, and hollow tree trunks in eastern Europe. The bees were smoked out from the hive in order to collect the honey, as they frequently are today, especially with bee colonies that are aggressive in nature.

A vertical beehive was invented by François Huber in 1792 that was made of wooden frames, hinged like a book, and with glass covering the end leaves so that the bees' activities could be observed. Many other similar hives were developed, but they all shared the problem of becoming gummed together by the beeswax that was produced along with the honey. In 1851, a Pennsylvania minister solved the problem by establishing the correct measurement for *bee space* needed around the frames and other movable parts of man–made hives. This measurement is one–quarter to three–eighths of an inch or six to ten millimeters.

A subsequent innovation in beehive construction was the introduction of a fabricated wax honeycomb foundation on which the bees could accelerate the production of honey, since they did not have to spend time building the honeycomb. Further improvement in honey production was made after the introduction of a mechanical honey extractor.

Beekeeping is carried out by large–scale commercial beekeepers and by thousands of hobby beekeepers. It is estimated that the annual worldwide production of honey exceeds a million metric tons. Besides market-

ing honey as a product, beekeepers serve agricultural businesses by supplying bees for pollinating at least ninety commercially valuable crops, such as fruits, nuts, and field crops like alfalfa. Beekeepers often migrate from northern locations in the summer to southern ones in the winter. The largest honey–producing beekeepers are found in California, Florida, and Minnesota, but New York, Ohio, Michigan, and Illinois also have commercial beekeepers. While a hobbyist might have only a dozen or so hives to tend, a commercial beekeeper often has thousands of hives.

Killer bees

During the mid–1950s, a hybrid African honey bee was accidentally released in Brazil. This bee was more aggressive than the European honey bee and by the mid–1960s had gained the name of "killer bee." The African bee was introduced by Warwick Kerr in Brazil in an attempt to find a bee that was more suitable to the climate. This bee was found to be more productive than other bees and many beekeepers in South America use them for the production of honey. Bceause these bees are more aggressive, beekeepers must wear more protective clothing. By the late 1980s, the "killer bees" had migrated across the Rio Grande. While some entomologists fear that the killer bees will replace the European honey bee and upset honey production in the United States, others feel this will not happen.

KEY TERMS

. . . .

Bee space—The amount of room needed between the frames of a man–made hive for bees to move around freely.

Caste system—A system among social bees where a hierarchy of activity exists, with members of a caste assigned to specific tasks within the social structure.

Parthenogenesis—Asexual reproduction without the fertilization of eggs.

Pheromones—Alarm chemicals produced as a response to an attack by predators.

Social bees—Bees that organize themselves into colonies where they maintain a cooperative social structure with a caste system.

Solitary bees—Bees that do not colonize, but engage in individual nesting.

Further Reading:

Arnett, Ross H. *American Insects*. New York: Van Nostrand Reinhold, 1985.

Hubbell, Sue. *Broadsides from the Other Orders: A Book of Bugs*. New York: Random House, 1993.

Imes, Rick. *The Practical Entomologist*. New York: Simon & Schuster, 1992.

Morse, Roger. *The ABC and XYZ of Bee Culture*. Medina, Ohio: A.I. Root Co., 1990.

——. *Complete Guide to Beekeeping*. New York: Dutton, 1986.

Style, Sue. *Honey: From Hive to Honeypot*. San Francisco: Chronicle Books, 1992.

Winston, Mark L. *Killer Bees: The Africanized Honey Bee in the Americas*. Cambridge, Mass.: Harvard University Press, 1992.

Vita Richman

Beet

Beet belongs to the genus *Beta* in the goosefoot family, Chenopodiaceae. There are several varieties of beet and all are used as food for either animals or humans. Most species of beet are biennial and are harvested after the first growing season when the roots are most nutritious.

The wild beet, *Beta maritima*, is thought to be the species from which cultivated beets (*Beta vulgaris*), originate. Wild beet is found on the Mediterranean and the Atlantic European coasts. Although beets are native to these temperate areas, they are now cultivated in many parts of the world for food, fodder, and as a source of sugar.

The cultivated beet has several commonly used varieties. Probably the most recognizable agricultural beet (*Beta vulgaris escuelenta*) is the bulbous, reddish–purple root that shows up on the dinner table. Although these beets can be successfully stored during winter, most of the crops of red garden beets and table beets in the United States are canned, pickled or frozen. The red beetroot is often dried, made into a powder and used for food coloring and fabric dyes. Beet plants can have round globular, or long conical roots with several stems growing above ground. The leaves on the stems vary in size and from green to purple in color.

Another important variety of the cultivated beet is *B. vulgaris crassa*, the sugar beet. Sugar beets are quite large, with green leaves and white roots weighing about 2.2 lb (1 kg). The root is shredded, mixed into water, and heated. The impurities are removed and the remaining sugary liquid is concentrated and crystallized. The sugar beet has been cultivated for centuries, but its use as a primary source of sugar dates back to the beginning of the nineteenth century. France is a leading contributor to the world's sugar beet stores, which today maintains half of the world's sugar supply.

Although beets are usually grown for the root part of the plant, one type of common beet is grown for its greens. This beet is known as Swiss Chard (variety *cicla*), or spinach beet, and has large stems, fleshy red and green curly leaves, and small, branched roots. The Mangel–Wurzel beet (variety *macrorhiza*) has large roots and is grown for livestock feed. Most of the nutrients in beets are found in the tops, which are used as greens. Swiss chard, for example, is a good source of vitamins A B1, and B2, as well as calcium and iron.

Christine Miner Minderovic

Beetles

Beetles make up the large, extremely diverse order Coleoptera of the class Insecta, and comprise the largest single group of animals on Earth. There are at least 250,000 species of beetles, compared to the 5,000 known species of mammals. The weevil family of beetles alone contains about 50,000 species, and is the largest family in the animal kingdom. Thus, the order Coleoptera, representing about 40% of the known insect species, contributes greatly to making the insects the largest class of the largest phylum—Arthropoda.

Arthropods are thought to have first evolved as long as 500 million years ago in Precambrian times, while the most primitive insect fossils date to the rocks of the Middle Devonian period about 350 million years ago. Coleoptera are thought to have evolved in the early Permian period about 225–280 million years ago, and were common even before the age of reptiles.

Beetles are found in virtually all climates and latitudes throughout the world except at very high altitudes or in regions with extreme temperatures, e.g. the Antarctic. Most species of beetles occur in the tropics, but fewer individuals of a particular species are generally found in tropical regions rather than in temperate areas.

The success of the beetles is due to at least three important characteristics. First, they undergo complete metamorphosis (egg, larva, pupa, adult), with larval and adult stages usually living in different places and eating different food. This division expands greatly the number of ecological niches and food available to these insects. Second, the front pair of wings is modified into a hard cover (the elytra) that protects the soft body underneath. Third, most beetles have mouth parts capable of chewing a wide variety of solid foods. Some beetles, however, have mouth parts modified for sipping sap and nectar.

The front pair of wings, modified into horny covers (elytra), hide the rear pair of wings and abdomen, and their inner edges appose each other, creating a straight line down the back of the insect. The elytra form a rigid, closely interlocking sheath that covers the mesothorax and metathorax, and most of the abdomen. (The name Coleoptera is derived from the Greek word *koleos*, meaning sheath.) The perfect alignment of the edges of the elytra form the characteristic, straight line that seems to split the back of the beetle, and gives these insects their common name (beetle from the German word *bheid*, meaning to split).

Beetles are found on vegetation, under bark, stones, and other objects, as well as almost anywhere on or in the soil, rotting vegetation, dung, and carrion. They vary widely in size and appearance, and many have noteworthy behavior. Some beetles (e.g., Lampyridae) produce light, while others (Cerambycidae) can stridulate, that is, they can produce sound. Large beetles usually make a loud noise during flight, and some, such as the scarab beetles, have a bizarre physical form.

Varieties of beetles

The Coleoptera includes the largest and smallest insects in the world, ranging from the giant, 6.3–in (16–cm) Longhorn beetle (*Titanus giganteus*) of the Amazon region to the dot–sized, Fringed ant beetle (*Nanosella fungi*) of North America, which reaches only 0.25 mm in length—smaller than a large protozoan.

Beetles are economically important in agriculture, either feeding directly on crops and trees, or preying on other species that harm plant crops. For example, the ground beetles (Carabidae) and the rove beetles (Staphylinidae) feed on caterpillars and other larvae as well as on many soft–bodied insects and insect eggs. Many of the adult and larval forms of the ladybugs or ladybird beetles (Coccinellidae) feed on plant–sucking insects (Homoptera) such as aphids and scale insects,

while only a few of the Coccinellidae themselves (e.g., *Epilachna*) feed on plants.

Many other beetles, however, do feed on plants. Among the most important of these beetles are the leaf beetles (Chrysomelidae) and the weevils and their relatives (Curculionoidea). The larvae of leaf beetles feed on leaves, stems, or roots, while most adults chew on leaves; the larvae of weevils feed on almost every part of plants. For example, larvae and adult forms of bark beetles (Scolytidae) attack tree tissue beneath the bark.

The scarab beetles (Scarabaeidae) are important pests of crops, lawns, and pastures. One of these insects, the dung beetle, was an important religious symbol to ancient Egyptians, who considered its life cycle to be a reflection of the cyclical processes of nature, especially the "rebirth" of the sun each morning. Glazed steatite (soapstone) and other ancient Egyptian ceramic or stone representations of the beetle, called scarabs, were a symbol of the soul and used as talismans.

Many beetles act as scavengers, breaking down organic material such as wood and dead plant and animal matter. The larvae of some beetles, such as the wedge–shaped beetles, are parasitic on wasps, bees and cockroaches. The European elm bark beetle (*Scolytus multistriatus*) transmits the fungus that causes Dutch elm disease.

The vast array of forms and colors of Coleoptera ranges from the black, furry Brazilian beetle, with creamy–white and orange spots, to the squat tortoise beetle, the long–snouted Peruvian beetle, the stag beetle with its two threatening "horns," and the whirligig beetle, often found gyrating rapidly on the surface of ponds.

Click beetles (family Elateridae) are named for the sharp noise they make. When turned onto its back, a click beetle will bend its head and the upper part of its body backward, then suddenly straighten. This movement produces a click and propels the beetle into the air. This maneuver is repeated until the beetle lands right side up.

Lightning bugs or fireflies (family Lampyridae) produce light; some species produce flashes, while others produce continuous luminescence. These insect light shows, common in spring and summer, are a mating ritual through which the opposite sexes find each other.

The classification of beetles established by R. A. Crowson in 1955 (*The Natural Classification of the Families of Coleoptera*), divides the order into four suborders: Archostemata (rarely found beetles), Adephaga (the tiger beetles and various water beetles), Myxophaga (the minute bog beetles and skiff beetles), and Polyphaga (the majority of beetles, such as carrion beetles, scarab beetles, ladybugs, and long–horned beetles). The Polyphaga is the largest suborder, with 18 superfamilies. In all, there are about 135 known families of beetles, of which 120 are found in the Western Hemisphere.

Beetle anatomy and physiology

As insects, beetles share common traits with all other arthropods. The legs are jointed, and there is an external skeleton called the exoskeleton, an inert compound made mostly of a carbohydrate called chitin (polyacetylglucosamine). Those sections of the exoskeleton that do not need to be flexible to allow for movement are further strengthened by sclerotin, a hard, proteinaceous substance similar in composition to human fingernails. The exoskeleton serves in both protection and in muscle attachment. A superficial layer of wax secreted on the outside of the exoskeleton prevents water loss through evaporation.

Beetles share with all insects the body form that differentiates them from other arthropods. The body of insects is divided into three main sections: head, thorax and abdomen. In Coleoptera, however, two of the three segments of the thorax (mesothorax and metathorax) are attached to the abdomen, while the third one (prothorax) is isolated between the head and trunk and is covered by a dorsal plate called the pronotum. The insect thorax usually has three pairs of legs and two pairs of wings. This body section also contains the powerful muscles that operate both the wings and legs. The abdomen has nine or ten segments, some not externally visible, each bearing a pair of spiracles, or respiratory openings, which direct air through the exoskeleton into the body.

Beetles can fly from hostile environments, escape enemies, and seek mates over wide areas. The first pair of wings of beetles, which arise from the mesothorax, is modified as the elytra—forming the protective cover for the hind wings and abdomen. This is a particular advantage for these insects, because they spend so much time on the ground rummaging through decaying plant matter, wood, and soil. The hind wings are membranous and usually fold beneath the elytra when not in use. When the beetle flies, the elytra are held open at an angle, providing additional stability and lift as the back wings beat.

Beetle have three pairs of legs that are usually well–developed, with a strong femur and tibia, and five or fewer tarsal (end) segments tipped with a paired claw. The front pair of legs arise from cavities under the pronotum, with a spiracle positioned just to the rear of the base of each of the front legs. The mesothorax bears the second pair of legs, while the third pair of legs arise from the metathorax.

The legs of beetles may be modified for running, swimming, jumping, digging or clasping, depending on the species. For example, the hind legs of some species of water beetles are long, flattened and covered with long, matted hairs that serve as paddles for swimming. The water strider has slender legs, which, together with a lightweight body covered with tiny hairs that buoy it up, permit it to skitter over the surface of the water.

The head bears a pair of compound eyes, a pair of antennae (usually with 11 segments), and the mouthparts. The eyes consist of many tiny individual units (facets), which together resemble a honeycomb. Under each facet is a group of six or seven retinal cells surrounding a rod–like light–receptive zone (rhabdom). Each of these tiny, individual "eyes" has its own nerve, which together with the nerves of the other eyes, form the optic nerve.

The beetle eye, like that of other insects, does not move, and its lenses cannot focus. Instead, each individual eye contributes a tiny bit of the image; these combine to form a crude mosaic of the scene rather than a clear, continuous picture. In addition, insects can't close their eyes, and can see well only to a distance of a few feet (about 90 cm). The whirligig beetle, which is found on the surface of bodies of water, has eyes divided into an upper part, with which the insect observes the surface environment, and a lower part, for underwater viewing.

The antenna ("feelers") are sense organs that gather information about the touch, sound, taste, smell, temperature and humidity of the beetle's environment. The maxillae hold a pair of lobed sense organs, called palps, which may detect smells. The beetle's mouth is a simple hole that lacks jaws, but is surrounded by specialized structures for grasping and grinding. Behind the upper "lip," or labrum, a pair of jawlike appendages (called mandibles) serves as pincers. Behind the mandibles are a pair of bladelike appendages (called maxillae), followed by a second pair of maxillae that are fused in the midline to form the lower lip, or labium.

While most beetles have mouth parts designed for chewing solid food, many of the beetles of the superfamily Curculionoidea have a distinct snout that can bore into wood and suck sap. The snout has mouthparts at its end and is used for penetration and feeding, and for boring holes for egg–laying. These beetles are mostly plant feeders and are economically important pests of crops. For example, the 30,000 species of weevils in the family Curculionidae include many insect pests, such as the cotton boll weevil, the apple blossom weevil, and the rice weevil. The Curculionidae are also called true weevils, or snout weevils.

The chewed food is passed into the mouth (which secretes the digestive enzyme amylase), then into the muscular pharynx, and then to the esophagus. From there food enters the midgut, where digestive enzymes break it down further. Attached to the end of the midgut is the malpighian tubules, the insect's kidney–like organs of excretion that empty into the hindgut (located just past the midgut). The hindgut is followed by the rectum, which ends in the anus. Digested food enters the hemocoele, or body cavity, and is transported to the organs by means of the circulatory fluid, or hemolymph.

Beetles have an open circulatory system, that is, they lack an extensive system of arteries and veins and their hemolymph bathes their tissues directly. A tube–like "heart" in the abdomen pumps the hemolymph forward through a dorsal tube ("aorta") in the thorax to the head. Tiny pumps send the hemolymph to the wings, antennae and legs, after which the fluid flows back passively to the heart in the abdomen. The hemolymph transports nutrients throughout the body, and carries waste products from the organs to the malpighian tubules. Free cells called hemocytes travel in the hemolymph and serve to devour foreign microorganisms. Unlike the blood of the vertebrates, the hemolymph is not involved in oxygen transport; that function is performed by the spiracles.

Life cycle

The mouth parts, which allow beetles to utilize a wide variety of solid foods in their environment, and the elytra, which protect the hindwings, give beetles great survival advantages. Another factor that contributes to the enormous success of beetles is the fact that they undergo complete metamorphosis. Beetles pass through three distinct developmental stages—egg, larva (grub) and pupa—before becoming adults.

Beetles reproduce sexually, although a few species consist of females only and parthenogenesis sometimes occurs. The male reproductive organ is the aedeagus, a hard, tubelike structure that is inserted into the tip of the female's abdomen through the bursa copulatrix during mating. The female stores sperm in a saclike structure called the spermatheca until they are used to fertilize eggs.

The beetle larva hatches from an egg and feeds, growing until its burgeoning body splits the skin (cuticle). The larva crawls out of the old skin and forms a new one, a process called molting. This occurs several times, until the larva is mature.

Beetle larvae are always very different from adults in both form and habits. They usually have only chewing mouth parts even if as adults they develop siphoning or piercing mouth parts. Wings develop internally and are not evident until the pupal stage. Because larvae, pupas, and adults live in different places and eat different foods, they do not compete with each other.

The different larval forms of beetles reflect a wide variety of feeding habits and habitats. The predatory larvae of water beetles (dytiscids) and ground beetles (carabids) are slender or have gradually tapered bodies and long legs adapted to chasing prey, and large, slender mandibles for holding food.

The larva of the tiger beetle (Cicindelidae) lives in the ground, digging a burrow up to 2 ft (0.6 m) deep to avoid high temperatures in the subtropical and tropical environments. The head of the tiger beetle is large and is bent at right angles to the body. When the larva is poised vertically within the burrow waiting for passing prey, its lidlike head acts like a living plug flush with the surface. When a potential meal nears the burrow, the beetle springs out like a jack–in–the–box doing a partial back somersault to catch the prey in its jaws. Two barbed spines on the tiger beetle's back hook into the burrow wall and prevent a strongly struggling victim from pulling the beetle out of its burrow.

The eggs of the European stag beetle (Lucanidae) hatch in the decaying heartwood of old trees, slowly developing into plump larvae which remain in the tree when they develop into a pupa. A month later, the adult form emerges from the pupa and searches along the forest floor for prey. The large branched jaws of the adult resemble the antlers of a stag. The larvae of ambrosia beetle feed on fungus gardens cultivated by adults in the sapwood of trees.

Following the larval stage, the beetle enters the pupal stage. The pupa develops beneath the skin of the final larval stage, then emerges when the skin splits. The pupa is a soft, pale image of the adult it is to become. The pre–adult appendages are curled or loosely attached to the body and the wings are in flat bags called wing pads. After the pupa sheds its thin skin, the adult emerges, the wings stretch out to full size, and the outer skeleton hardens. The beetle has undergone complete metamorphosis—from egg to larva, to pupa, to adult.

Defense

Beetles produce a variety of noxious chemicals to protect themselves against predators. For example, members of the genus *Meloe* release an oily substance from the joints of their legs that can raise blisters on human skin. In addition, members of the genus *Eleodes* emit an offensive black fluid when disturbed. However, the bombardier beetle displays one of the most dramatic repellent devices. This beetle shoots a boiling hot mixture of liquid and vapor from a "turret" at the rear of its abdomen. Able to fire repeatedly, the beetle has been observed to shoot 29 times in rapid succession within four minutes. The spray protects the beetle from ants, frogs, spiders, and praying mantids.

Parasitic beetles

Throughout the world, beetles have evolved parasitic relationships with a wide variety of animals, feeding on epidermal secretions and the hair of vertebrate hosts. The small beetle *Leptinus testaceus* of Britain is sometimes found living on the fur of voles and mice, and has also been found in bees' nests. The American species of this beetle, *L. americanus,* is also found on small rodents. Another North American member of this genus, *L. validus,* is an ectoparasite of the common beaver; and *L. aplodontiae* is an ectoparasite of the mountain beaver. Two South American species, *Uroxys gorgon* and *Trichillium brachyporum*, in the Scarabaeidae family live in the fur of the three–toed sloth, while the Australian genus *Macropocopris* lives in the fur of kangaroos.

Beetles and humans

The vast number and variety of beetles have inevitably had an important impact on the human populations that share environments with these insects. Beetles, like some other insects, pose a threat to agriculture, feeding on crops and wood, both harvested and stored. For example, the dermestid beetles of the family Dermestidae are widely distributed and feed on cereal products, grains, stored food, rugs and carpets, upholstery, and fur coats. Although the adults of some species may be destructive, usually it is beetle larvae that do the most damage.

The grain weevil and the rice weevil are particularly destructive, having evolved a snout that can penetrate food plants and also bore holes to deposit eggs. The boll weevil *(Anthonomus grandis)* is a major cotton crop pest in North America. The boll weevil deposits up to 300 eggs at a time in cotton buds or fruit. The larvae live within the cotton boll, destroying

the seeds and the surrounding fibers. The Colorado potato beetle *(Leptinotarsa decemlineata)* attacks the leaves of potato plants; it became a major pest in the United States during the late nineteenth century.

Beetles, like other insects, also eat a variety of plants that are not of agricultural value, but may be of aesthetic value to humans. For example, two forms of ladybird beetles, the Mexican bean beetle and the squash beetle, are voracious garden pests; and some blister beetles commonly parasitize eggs or larvae of bees.

Not all beetle activity is destructive, however. Beetles, along with other insects, also help to pollinate flowers, which then produce fruits and seeds. Beetles crawling over flowers brush up against pollen–bearing organs, and carry the pollen dust to another flower of the same species.

In addition, some beetles keep gardens from being overrun by plant pests. For example, most species of ladybird beetles feed as adults and larvae on aphids, scale insects, mites, and other insect pests. These highly predatory beetles are an important factor in keeping populations of plant–feeding pests such as leaf beetle larvae and other insects from reaching plague levels. And the larvae of wedge–shaped beetles are parasitic on cockroaches.

An Australian ladybird beetle, the vedalia beetle *(Rodolia cardinalis)*, is used throughout the world to control crop pests, such as the coconut scale, sugarcane mealy bug, potato aphid, and fir aphid. In addition, certain pollen or sap beetles of the family Nitidulidae prey on the eggs, nymphs, and adult stage of a variety of whitefly and aphid species, among other insects.

See also Weevils.

Further Reading:

Johnson, Sylvia A. *Beetles*. Minneapolis: Lerner, 1982.

White, Richard E. *A Field Guide to Beetles*. Boston: Houghton Mifflin, 1983.

Marc Kusinitz

Beira see **Dwarf antelopes**

Imperfect begonia flowers (*Begonia tuberosa*).

Begonia

Begonias (genus *Begonia*) are attractive perennial herbs with soft, succulent stems, and white, pink, red, orange or yellow flowers. Begonias are members of the begonia family, Begoniaceae, order Violales, subclass Dilleniidae, class Magnoliopsida (dicotyledons), division Magnoliophyta (flowering plants). The begonia family consists of five genera and 920 true species, the majority of which belong to the genus *Begonia*. Begonia taxonomy can be ambiguous, mainly due to the enormous number of horticultural varieties and hybrids, which many gardeners treat as species. These horticultural varieties of Begonia number in the thousands.

Begonias flowers are either staminate (male) or pistillate (female), and occur on the same plant, the plants being monoecious. Wild type flowers have four or five sepals, no petals, numerous stamens in males and an inferior ovary with three fused carpels in females. The colorful begonia sepals resemble petals, and plant breeding has produced many showy flower varieties. The begonia's fruit is a dry, winged capsule which split lengthwise to release the seeds. Most begonias sprout easily from seeds and can also be propagated from leaves and stems. Leaves are simple and have wavy or serrated margins. Leaf arrangement on the stem is alternate. Two fleshy stipules occur at the base of the leaf petiole.

Horticulturists classify begonias into three categories based on rootstock: tuberous, fibrous, and rhizomatous. Unlike the tuberous and fibrous rooted begonias, which are cultivated for their flowers, rhizomatous begonias are grown for their large, attractive foliage. The cultivated Rex begonia, *Begonia x rex–cultorum*, is a rhizomatous begonia. This horticultural variety with beautiful foliage was developed in England from *Begonia rex* of India. Since most rhizomatous begonias originate from Brazil and Mexico, some people speculate that *Begonia rex* was also a cultivar. Rhizomatous begonias have striking foliage that takes many forms. Leaves can be hairy, fuzzy, or smooth, and are flecked with colorful patterns. Beefsteak begonia, *Begonia feastii*, is another example of a rhizomatous–rooted begonia.

The popular wax begonia, *Begonia semperflorens*, is a fibrous rooted begonia. Wax begonias are outdoor bedding plants that have smooth leaves and an abundance of flowers, hence the scientific name *semperflorens*, which means always flowering. Like the rex begonia, many colorful varieties of the wax begonia have been developed. The angel wing begonia, *Begonia coccinea*, with its thick, jointed stems, is another popular fibrous rooted begonia. Angel wing begonias have cane–like stems. Many cane begonias develop woody tissue in their stems.

Tuberous begonias such as *Begonia x tuberhybrida*, are best known for their showy flowers. They originate from South American begonias with large pink (*Begonia boliviensis* and *Begonia veitchii*) and yellow (*Begonia pearcei*) flowers. Cultivated tuberous begonias may resemble other popular flowers such as carnations and daffodils, and come in a range of sizes, including some varieties with large showy blossoms.

Begonias are indigenous to tropical and subtropical regions; no species is native to the United States. They occur primarily in Central and South America, Asia, and sub–Saharan Africa. The natural habitat of many begonias are moist, cool forests and tropical rainforests, but some begonias are adapted to dryer climates. Tuberous begonias are adapted to cool mountain habitats such as the Andes Mountains of Peru, where many horticultural varieties originate.

Although begonias are herbaceous perennials, they are susceptible to frost, and many varieties planted in the United States are treated as annuals. Begonias are easy to grow, both outdoors and in containers. They like bright light, not direct sun, a humid environment,

KEY TERMS
. . . .

Alternate—Leaves occur one at a time on alternating side of the stem.

Capsule—A dry, dehiscing fruit derived from two or more carpels.

Carpel—The seed bearing compartment the flower.

Hybrid—Offspring produced from the sexual union of two different species.

Inferior ovary—An ovary embedded within a flower, below the other flower parts.

Monoecious—Plants which have separate male and female flowers on the same plant.

Perennial—Plants which live for several years, often bearing fruits and flowers each year.

Rhizome—A horizontal stem at or below the soil surface.

Stipules—A modified leaf appendage occurring at the base of the leaf petiole.

and rich, aerated soil. Bright, indirect light is required to bring out the colorful patterns on rex begonia leaves. Begonias do best in mild temperatures (above 65° F (18° C) but can tolerate hot weather if they are kept in cool, shady places. Regular fertilizations keeps plants lush and healthy.

Begonias are as easy to propagate as they are to grow. Plant seeds in rich, well–drained soil, such as African violet soil and keep them protected. Many growers propagate plants from stem and leaf cuttings. Leaves are cut into wedges, each wedge with a central vein. The wedges are dusted with rooting hormone and planted in builders sand. The developing leaf wedges are given high humidity, bright indirect light, and occasional waterings. New shoot growth appears in two to three months. Cane and rhizomatous begonias may also be propagated from stem cuttings.

Begonias are susceptible to mealybugs and aphids, controllable with insecticidal soaps. Rex begonias may be infected with nematodes, soil dwelling plant parasites which are more difficult to treat. Many garden shops carry products to control nematodes. A home remedy for these pests are mothballs. Watering the plants with mothballs on the soil surface will help eliminate the nematodes.

Because of their success and popularity as ornamental bedding and container plants, begonias are eco-nomically important. Begonias are named after (1638–1710), a patron of botany. Begon also served as Governor of French Canada.

Further Reading:

Carlquist, S. "Wood anatomy of Begoniaceae, with comments on raylessness, paedomorphosis, relationships, vessel diameter, and ecology." *Bulletin of the Torrey Botanical Club*, 1985.

Heywood, V. H. *Flowering plants of the world.* New York: Mayflower Books, 1978.

Martin, T. "Rex begonias." *Horticulture*, January, 1988.

Neuman, L. "Top–notch tuberous begonias." *Horticulture*, July, 18–23, 1988.

Elaine L. Martin

Behavior

Behavior is the way that living things respond to their environment. A behavior consists of a response to a stimulus or factor in an individual's internal or external environment. Stimuli include chemicals, heat, light, pressure, and gravity. All living things exhibit behavior. When dust irritates our throats, for example, we respond with coughing behavior. Plants respond with growth behavior when light stimulates their leaves. Generally, behavior helps organisms survive. Behavior can be categorized as either innate or learned, but the distinction is frequently unclear. Learned behavior often has innate or inborn components. Behavior is considered innate when it is present and complete without the need for experience. Babies, even blind ones, at about four weeks of age smile spontaneously at a pleasing stimulus. Such innate behavior is stereotyped (always the same) and, as a result, quite predictable. Plants, protists, and animals that lack a well–developed nervous system rely on innate behavior. Higher animals use both innate and learned behavior.

Behavior in plants

The innate behavior of plants depends mainly on growth in a given direction or movement due to changes in water content. Plant behavior in which a plant organ grows toward or away from a stimulus is known as a tropism. A positive tropism is growth toward a stimulus, while a negative tropism is growth away from a stimulus. During positive phototropism, stems and leaves grow in the direction of a source of light. Roots exhibit positive gravitropism, growth toward gravity, while stems demonstrate negative grav-

Among brown bears the highest ranking animals are the large adult males. These bears are fighting to establish dominance. Overt fighting is usually brief, and serious wounds are not usually inflicted.

itropism. Since roots grow toward water, they are said to behave with positive hydrotropism. Touch stimulates positive thigmotropism, such as vines growing on supporting surfaces.

Sometimes a part of a plant moves in a specific way regardless of the direction of the stimulus. These movements are temporary, reversible, and due to changes in the water pressure inside the plant organ. The leaves of peas and beans open in the morning and close up at night. In light, ion channels open within the pulvinus, a gland present at the leaf base. Ions and water enter the leaf, causing it to open. The reverse occurs in darkness. When pollinating insects contact cornflowers, the male stamens respond by shortening rapidly, thereby releasing pollen onto the exposed female style. In the Venus flytrap, a carnivorous plant, the touch of an insect on the leaf stimulates the triggering hairs, causing the hinged lobes of the leaf to close quickly around the unsuspecting prey.

Animal behavior

The study of animal behavior is known as ethology. Ethologists investigate the mechanisms and evolu-

tion of behavior. Charles Darwin founded the scientific study of behavior, and showed by many examples that behavior, as well as morphology and physiology, is an adaptation to environmental demands, and can increase the chances of species survival.

Between 1930 and 1950, the Austrian naturalist Konrad Lorenz and the Dutch ethologist Niko Tinbergen found that certain animals show fixed–action patterns of behavior (FAP's), which are strong responses to specific stimuli. For example, male stickleback fish attack other breeding males that enter their territory. The defending male recognizes intruders by a red stripe on their underside. Tinbergen found that the male sticklebacks he was studying were so attuned to the red stripe that they would try to attack passing red British mail trucks visible through the glass of their tanks. Tinbergen termed the red stripe a behavioral releaser, that is a simple stimulus that brings about an FAP.

Once an FAP is initiated, it continues to completion even if circumstances change. If an egg rolls out of a goose's nest, the goose stretches her neck until the underside of her bill touches the egg. Then she rolls the egg back to the nest. If someone takes the egg away while she is reaching for it, the goose goes through the motions anyway without an egg. FAP's have innate components.

Complex programmed behavior involves several steps and is more complicated than FAP. When birds build nests and beavers build dams they are exhibiting complex programmed behavior.

Reflexes are also innate. A reflex is a simple, inborn, automatic response by a part of the body to a stimulus. At its simplest, a reflex involves a receptor and sensory neuron and effector organ, for example, when certain coelenterates withdraw their tentacles. More complex reflexes include processing interneurons between the sensory and motor neurons as well as specialized receptors. Complex reflexes occurs when food in the mouth stimulates the salivary glands to produce saliva, or when a hand is pulled away rapidly from a hot object. Reflexes help animals respond quickly to a stimulus, thus protecting them from harm. Learned behavior results from experience, and enables animals to adjust to new situations. Unless an animal exhibits a behavior at birth, however, it is often difficult to determine if the behavior is learned or innate. For example, pecking, an innate behavior in chicks, gets more accurate as the chicks get older. The improvement in pecking aim does not occur because the chicks learn and correct their errors, but is due to a natural maturing of muscles and eyes. Scientific studies have shown that pecking is entirely innate.

The interaction of heredity and learning can be observed in a learning program known as imprinting, seen frequently in birds. Imprinting is the learning of a behavior at a critical period early in life that becomes permanent. Such behavior was studied in the 1930s by Konrad Lorenz, an Austrian ethologist. Newly hatched geese are able to walk at birth. They survive because they follow their parents. How do young geese recognize their parents from all the objects in the environment? Lorenz found that if he removed the parents from view the first day after hatching and he walked in front of the young geese, they would follow him. This tactic did not work if he waited until the third day after hatching. Lorenz concluded that during a critical period, the goslings follow their parents' movement and learn enough about their parents to recognize them. Since Lorenz found that young geese will follow any moving object, he determined that movement is their releaser for parental imprinting.

Habituation is a type of behavior in which an animal learns to ignore a stimulus that is repeated over and over. A snail will pull its head back into its shell when touched. When touched repeatedly with no sub-

sequent harm, however, the withdrawal response ceases. Apparently, the snail's nervous system "learns" that the stimulus is not threatening and stops the reflex.

In classical conditioning, an animal's reflexes are trained to respond to a new stimulus. Ivan Pavlov, a Russian physiologist working in the early twentieth century, was the first to demonstrate this type of learning behavior. He placed powdered meat in a dog's mouth and observed that by reflex saliva flowed into the mouth. Then Pavlov rang a bell before he gave the dog its food. After doing this for a few times, the dog salivated merely at the sound of the bell. Many experiments of this type demonstrate that an innate behavior can be modified.

Further information about behavior modification came in the 1940s and 1950s with the work of B.F. Skinner, an American physiologist. He demonstrated operant conditioning, the training of certain behaviors by environmental rewards. Thistype of learning is also known as trial–and–error. During operant conditioning, a random behavior is rewarded and subsequently retained by an animal. If we want to train a dog to sit on command, all we have to do is wait until the dog sits. Then say "sit" and give the dog a biscuit. After a few times the dog will sit on command. Apparently, the reward reinforces the behavior and fosters its repetition.

Operant conditioning also occurs in nature. By watching their parents, young chimps learn to prepare a stick by stripping a twig and then using it to pick up termites from rotten logs. Their behavior is rewarded by the meal of termites, a preferred food. Operant conditioning lets animals add behaviors that are not inherited to their repertory.

Reasoning is a way to solve problems without trial–and–error.

This is accomplished by thinking. Using reasoning or insight, we apply memories of past experiences to new situations to help find answers. Memory is the storing and retrieving of learned material. The two types of memory are short–term memory, the memory of recent events, and long–term memory, the memory of events that occurred in the past. When given a phone number, we quickly forget it. This is typical of short–term memory which is temporary. Long–term memory lasts longer, days or even a lifetime. Humans use reasoning more than other animals, but primates and others have been observed to solve problems by thought processes. Researchers recently discovered that black–capped chickadees develop new brain cells to improve their memory, which helps the birds locate buried seeds in winter.

In much of their behavior, animals interact with each other.

In order to do this they communicate with each other, using their sense organs. Birds hear each other sing, a dog sees and hears the spit and hiss of a cornered cat, ants lay down scent signals (pheromones), to mark a trail that leads to food.

There are many kinds of interactive behavior. One of them is courtship behavior that usually takes place at the start of the mating season. During courtship, some animals leap and dance, others sing, still others ruffle their feathers or puff up pouches. The male peacock displays his glorious plumage to the female. Humpback whales advertise their presence under the sea by singing a song that can be heard hundreds of miles away. Courtship behavior enables an animal to find, identify, attract and arouse a mate. During courtship, animals use rituals, a series of behaviors for communication that is performed the same way by all the males or females in a species. Territorial behavior is also interactive. Here, animals use signals such as pheromones (scent signals) and visual displays to claim and defend a territory.

Some animals live together in groups and display social behavior. The group helps protect individuals from predators, and allows cooperation and division of labor.

Insects, such as bees, ants, and termites live in complex groups in which some individuals find food, some defend the colony, and some tend to the offspring. A method of reducing fighting in a group is accomplished by a dominance hierarchy or ranking system. Chickens, for example, have a peck–order from the dominant to the most submissive. Each individual knows its place in the peck–order and does not chal-lenge individuals of higher rank, thereby reducing the chances of fighting. Interactions among group members gets more complex with more intelligent species such as apes.

See also Brain; Conditioning; Courtship; Geotropism; Memory; Nervous system; Phototropism; Reflex; Territoriality.

Further Reading:

Attenborough, David. *The Trials of Life*. Boston: Little, Brown and Co., 1990.
"Leaves with Clocks." *Discover* (September 1993).
Morris, Desmond. *Animal Watching*. New York: Crown Publishers, Inc, 1990.
Simons, Paul. "Touchy Flowers Work on Elastic." *New Scientist* (10 July 1993).

Bernice Essenfeld

Belladonna see **Nightshade**

Belted sandfish see **Bass**

Bennettites

The bennettites are an extinct group of gymnosperms—seed–bearing plants whose seeds are exposed to the air, not enclosed in the ovary of a flower. Botanists hypothesize that bennettites are related to the cycads, an extant group of gymnosperms, and paleobotanists believe the bennettites originated from the seed ferns (Pteridospermales) about 220 million years ago during the Triassic period. Bennettites became extinct in the Upper Cretaceous period, about 100 million years ago.

Bennettites had palmlike leaves with stems that were thin and branched in some species, and stout and trunklike in others. Most species had stems with a large central pith. The bennettites are also distinguished by certain microscopic features of their guard cells. Guard cells are specialized cells on the surface of a leaf that regulate opening of stomata (pores) in the leaf for photosynthetic gas exchange. The bennettites had guard cells with a large amount of cutin, a naturally occurring plant wax.

The best–known genus of the bennettites is *Cycadeoidea*. Knowledge about this genus has been gleaned mostly from fossils found in the Black Hills of South Dakota. Many of these fossils were collected and studied in the early 1900s by George R. Wieland.

Wieland proposed that the strobili (reproductive structures) of *Cycadeoidea* functioned like flowers and thus that this genus was a close ancestor of the angiosperms, the flowering plants. More recent evaluation of these and other fossil strobili of the bennettites, however, indicates that they differed significantly from angiosperms. It has been shown instead that bennettite strobili were bisporangiate (containing male and female reproductive organs in the same structure) and that they probably relied on self–pollination to reproduce.

See also Cycads; Paleobotany.

Bentgrass see **Grasses**

Benzene

Benzene is an aromatic organic compound with the molecular formula C_6H_6. Credit for its discovery and identification in 1825 is usually given to the English chemist and physicist Michael Faraday.

Benzene is a clear, colorless, highly flammable liquid with a pronounced characteristic odor. It has a melting point of 41.9°F (5.5°C), a boiling point of 176.2°F (80.1°C), and a density of 0.8787 g/mL. It is only slightly soluble in water (0.18 g/100 mL at 25°C), but is completely miscible with alcohol, chloroform, ether, carbon disulfide, carbon tetrachloride, and other organic solvents. Benzene is not to be confused with benzine, which is not a pure chemical compound but a mixture of petroleum hydrocarbons used as a solvent and a fuel.

Structure

The structure of the benzene molecule proved to be a challenge for chemists for more than 40 years after the compound's discovery by Faraday. Its formula suggests the existence of multiple double and/or triple carbon–carbon bonds, because there are too few hydrogen atoms for six single–bonded carbon atoms. However, benzene exhibits none of the chemical properties associated with such a structure, the property of addition, for example. That problem was largely solved in 1865 by the German chemist Friedrich August Kekulé. Kekulé's own story is that he fell asleep in front of his fireplace and dreamed of a snake with its tail in its mouth. He awoke to the realization that the benzene molecule might be a ring consisting of six carbon atoms, with one hydrogen atom attached to each carbon atom. That general structure is still accepted today, although the concept of resonance has replaced that of simple single and double bonds between adjacent carbon atoms in the benzene ring.

Properties

The most common chemical property of benzene is that it undergoes substitution reactions. Substitution is a reaction in which an atom or group of atoms replaces a hydrogen atom in an organic molecule. The halogens, nitric acid, sulfuric acid, and alkyl halides all react with benzene to form substituted derivatives. Two, three, or more substitutions can occur on the same benzene molecule, although the ease and location on the benzene ring of these substitutions varies depending on the earlier substitutions.

Benzene derivatives

A number of the substituted benzene derivatives are well known and commercially important compounds. For example, the substitution of a single methyl, hydroxyl, or amino group in benzene results in the formation, respectively, of toluene ($C_6H_5CH_3$), phenol (C_6H_5OH), or aniline ($C_6H_5NH_2$). Probably the best known disubstituted products are the xylenes, $C_6H_4(CH_3)_2$. Three different xylene molecules are possible depending on whether the methyl groups are adjacent to each other on the benzene ring (ortho–xylene), separated by one carbon atom (meta–xylene), or opposite each other on the ring (para–xylene). The removal of one hydrogen atom from the benzene molecule results in a radical known as the phenyl group.

Benzene occurs so abundantly in and is obtained so easily from coal tar and petroleum that there is virtually no reason to make it synthetically. Although benzene had been recognized as a component of petroleum for many years, it was not produced commercially from that source until the beginning of World War II.

Uses

Benzene is used as a solvent in many commercial, industrial, and research operations. It has long been of interest as a fuel because of its high octane number. Some manufacturers, particularly in Europe, have used it as a gasoline additive to increase engine efficiency and to improve starting qualities.

By far the most important use of benzene, however, is in the production of other aromatic compounds. The word *aromatic* was originally applied to benzene because of its distinctive odor, but it later took on a broader meaning, referring to any compound whose molecular structure includes one or more benzene rings. The largest volume of compounds made from benzene goes toward the production of commercially valuable polymers, such as polystyrene, nylon, and synthetic rubber.

The benzene derivative produced in largest quantity is ethylbenzene ($C_6H_5C_2H_5$). Ethylbenzene is converted to styrene ($C_6H_5CH=CH_2$) which, in turn, is polymerized to form polystyrene. Nearly half of all benzene used in chemical synthesis is used for this process.

In another example, benzene is treated with propylene to form cumene ($C_6H_5CH[CH_3]_2$). The cumene thus formed is then oxidized to produce phenol. Phenol is the starting point for a large number of polymers known as phenolic resins.

Synthetic fibers are produced by yet a third kind of benzene substitution sequence. The addition of hydrogen to benzene converts it to cyclohexane (C_6H_{12}) which is then oxidized to adipic acid ($COOH[CH_2]_4$-$COOH$) The acid can then be treated with hexamethylene diamine to form nylon.

Health issues

The health risks associated with exposure to benzene have been known for many years. The compound has both chronic and acute effects whether ingested by mouth, taken in through the respiratory system, or absorbed through the skin. Acute effects resulting from inhalation include irritation of the mucous membranes, headache, instability, euphoria, convulsions, excitement or depression, and unconsciousness.

The ingestion of benzene has been associated with the development of bronchitis and pneumonia, while exposure through the skin can cause drying, blistering, and erythema (redness). Death can result from exposure to high concentrations of benzene. Chronic effects resulting from benzene exposure include reduced white and blood cell counts, aplasia, and more rarely, leukemia.

See also Hydrocarbon; Resonance.

Further Reading

Browning, E. *Toxicity and Metabolism of Industrial Solvents.* New York: Elsevier, 1965, pp. 3–65.

Embree, Harland D. *Brief Course: Organic Chemistry.* Glenview, IL: Scott, Foresman, 1983, pp. 97–111.

Graham, John D., Laura C. Green, and Marc J. Roberts. *In Search of Safety: Chemicals and Cancer Risk.* Cambridge, MA: Harvard University Press, 1988, Chapters 4 and 5.

Purcell, William P. "Benzene." *Kirk–Othmer Encyclopedia of Chemical Technology*, 3rd edition, volume 3. New York: John Wiley and Sons, 1978, pp. 744–71.

Solomons, T. W. Graham. *Organic Chemistry*, 2nd edition. New York: John Wiley, 1980, Chapter 11.

David E. Newton

Benzene ring see **Benzene**

Benzoic acid

Benzoic acid is a derivative of benzene with the chemical formula C_6H_5COOH. It consists of a carboxyl group atached to a phenyl group, and is thus the simplest aromatic carboxylic acid. It is also known as carboxybenzene, benzene carboxylic acid, and phenylformic acid.

In its pure form, benzoic acid exists as white needles or scales with a strong characteristic odor. It melts at 252.3°F (122.4°C), although it may also sublime at temperatures around 212° F (100°C). It dissolves only sparingly in cold water [0.4 g/100 g at 77°F (25°C)], but more completely in hot water [6.8 g/100 g at 203°F (95°C)].

Benzoic acid occurs naturally in gum benzoin, also known as benzoin resin or Benjamin gum, a brown resin found in the benzoin tree of Southeast Asia. It is also found naturally in many kinds of berries, where its concentration may reach 0.05%.

One of the most common uses of benzoic acid is as a food preservative. Both the acid and its sodium salt, sodium benzoate (usually listed on labels as benzoate of soda), are used to preserve many different kinds of foods, including fruit juices, soft drinks, pickles, and salad dressings. In fact, it is the acid rather than the sodium salt that is toxic to bacteria. Thus, the two additives can be used only in acidic solutions, where the sodium salt is converted to the acid form.

The acid and the sodium salt are both considered to be safe for human consumption in limited amounts. In the United States, foods may contain a maximum of 0.1% benzoic acid or sodium benzoate, although the limit in other nations may be as high as 1.25% in some types of prepared foods. Benzoic acid is also used in the manufacture of artificial flavors and perfumes and for the flavoring of tobacco.

See also Benzene; Carboxylic acid.

Berkelium see **Element, transuranium**

Bernoulli's principle

Bernoulli's principle states that flowing fluids like air and water press less than still fluids and that pressure decreases quadratically with speed; i.e., with speed–squared.

History

One quarter of a millennium ago, Daniel Bernoulli pioneered use of kinetic theory that molecules moved and bumped things. He also knew that flowing fluids pressed less, but he did not connect these ideas logically. In *Hydrodynamica*, Daniel's logic that flow reduced pressure was obscure, and his formula was awkward. Daniel's father Johann, amid controversy, improved his son's insight and presentation in *Hydraulica*.

This research was centered in St. Petersburg where Leonard Euler, a colleague of Daniel and a student of Johann, generalized a rate–of–change dependence of pressure and density on speed of flow. Bernoulli's Principle for liquids was then formulated in modern form for the first time.

In this same group of scientists was D'Alembert, who found paradoxically that fluids stopped ahead of obstacles, so frictionless flow did not push.

Progress then seems to have halted for about a century and a half until Ludwig Prandtl or one of his students solved Euler's equation for smooth streams of air in order to have a mathematical model of flowing air for designing wings. Here, speed lowers pressure more than it lowers density because expanding air cools, and the ratio of density times degrees–kelvin divided by pressure is constant for an ideal–gas.

More turbulent flow, as in atmospheric winds, requires an alternative solution of Euler's equation because mixing keeps air–temperature fixed.

Applying Bernoulli's principle

Bernoulli's principle is regarded by many as a paradox because currents and winds upset things, but standing a stick in a stream of water helps to clarify the enigma. You will see calm, smooth, level water ahead of the stick and a cavity of reduced pressure behind it. Calm water pushes the stick, as lower pressure downstream fails to balance the upsetting force.

Bernoulli's principle never acts alone; it also comes with molecular entrainment. Molecules in the lower pressure of faster flow aspirate and whisk away molecules from the higher pressure of slower flow. Solid obstacles such as airfoils carry a very thin stagnant layer of air with them. A swift low–pressure airstream takes some molecules from this boundary layer and reduces molecular impacts on that surface of the wing across which the airstream moves faster.

For Bernoulli's principle to dominate a dynamic situation, friction must be less dominant. Elastic molecular impacts are frictionless—no heating. Molecules of dry air, even more than those of water, collide elastically; so Bernoulli's principle with its molecular–entrainment agent is in fact, to use a vernacular cliche, the only game in town for windy air.

See also Aerodynamics.

Beryllium see **Alkaline earth metals**

Beta-blockers

Beta-blockers are medications used primarily for treating high blood pressure. These medications' usefulness rests on their ability to block the effects of a ner-

TABLE 1 FREQUENTLY USED BETA-BLOCKERS	
Generic Name	*Trade Names*
Pindolol	Visken
Propranolol	Inderal
Timolol	Blocarden
Enter Brain Poorly	
Atenolol	Tenormin
Nadolol	Corgard
Selective for Beta1 Receptors	
Metoprolol	Lopressor
Acebutolol	Sectral
Block Both Alpha and Beta Receptors	
Labetalol	Normodyne, Trandate

vous system transmitter chemical known as norepinephrine and the related "fight-or-flight" hormone epinephrine. Beta-blockers are also used to treat heart-related chest pain (*angina pectoris*, or simply angina), abnormalities of heart rhythm, and certain other conditions.

Adrenergic receptors

Like all nervous system transmitter chemicals and many hormones, norepinephrine and epinephrine exert their effects by interacting with proteins on the target cell's outer surface. Scientists refer to the ones on which epinephrine and norepinephrine act as adrenergic receptors, and group them into two major classes. These classes are formally known as α– and β–adrenergic receptors. However, many medical articles use the short forms "alpha receptors" and "beta receptors," respectively.

The most fundamental distinction between alpha and beta receptors is their response or lack of response to specific synthetic chemicals. They also respond differently to their natural stimuli: Alpha receptors are more responsive to norepinephrine than to epinephrine, while beta receptors respond equally to each.

Some cell types carry both alpha and beta receptors, while others carry only one, or neither. The two classes of receptor often have opposite effects. This allows the body to "fine–tune" its response by varying the relative amounts of circulating epinephrine and locally released norepinephrine in different tissues. In the circulatory system, however, both alpha and beta receptors raise blood pressure. Nevertheless, they do so in different ways: alpha receptors by constricting the blood vessels, beta receptors by increasing the force and rate of the heartbeat.

Mechanism of action

Beta-blockers are not general blood-pressure-lowering drugs: That is, they do not cause already normal blood pressure to go still lower. Nor do they usually affect the heartbeat of a person at rest, although they do limit the ability of exercise or emotion to make the heart beat more quickly and strongly.

Indeed, exactly how beta–blockers combat elevated blood pressure remains unclear. One important aspect is their ability to relax small arteries, thus allowing blood to flow more easily and with less pressure behind it. No one knows how beta–blockers do this, however—it would not be expected from their known actions. Furthermore, since relaxation occurs only after several days of beta–blocker use, it is very likely to be an indirect effect.

Scientists also know that beta–blockers reduce the kidney's release of renin, an enzyme essential for production of the hormone angiotensin II. Since angiotensin II raises blood pressure in several ways,

KEY TERMS

Alpha receptors (α–adrenergic receptors)—Proteins on the surface of target cells through which epinephrine and norepinephrine exert their effects.

Angina pectoris (angina)—Chest pain due to arteries carrying blood to the heart muscle being partially clogged with fatty deposits and therefore unable to supply enough blood, especially during vigorous exercise or strong emotion.

Beta receptors (β–adrenergic receptors)—Proteins on the surface of target cells through which epinephrine and norepinephrine exert their effects; beta receptors respond to the two substances to approximately the same extent.

Epinephrine (adrenaline)—The "flight–or–fight" hormone synthesized by the adrenal gland.

Norepinephrine (noradrenaline)—A substance that certain nerve cells release in order to produce their effects.

there can be little doubt that renin plays a significant role in regulating blood pressure. Unfortunately, researchers have found little relationship between blood pressure levels and the amount of renin circulating in the blood. This leaves them uncertain whether beta–blockers' ability to lower blood pressure is tied to their effect on renin release.

By contrast, reasons for beta–blockers' ability to relieve angina are obvious. This condition results from fatty deposits narrowing the arteries that carry blood to the heart muscle. As a result, the heart muscle does not get enough blood to meet its needs—especially when those needs increase because it is beating harder and faster than usual. Since beta–blockers limit the effects of exercise and emotion on the heartbeat, the gap between the amount of blood the heart receives and what it needs will be smaller. As a result, the patient will experience less pain.

Side effects

Different parts of the body contain different beta receptor subtypes, designated $beta_1$ and $beta_2$. Receptors in the circulatory system belong to the $beta_1$ subclass, while those on cells lining the small airways of the lung are of the $beta_2$ subclass. $Beta_2$ receptors help relax these small airways and therefore make breathing easier—indeed, patients with asthma and other obstructive lung diseases often inhale $beta_2$–stimulating medications to help them breath more easily. Thus, patients with such diseases should not take medications that block $beta_2$ receptors. Fortunately, several blood pressure medications that selectively block only $beta_1$ receptors are now available.

Beta–blockers are also probably not the best choice of treatment for people who have diabetes along with their high blood pressure or angina. In a hypoglycemic crisis (where blood sugar drops too low), the body pours out large amounts of epinephrine to stimulate release of stored sugar into the blood stream. This epinephrine also causes a rapid, pounding heartbeat that is often the diabetic's first indication something is wrong. Beta–blockers blunt both responses, leading to a crisis that is worse and longer–lasting than it would otherwise be.

These medications may likewise not be the best choice for people with poor circulation in their hands or feet, since beta–blockers sometimes make circulation in the extremities even worse.

About 10% of patients treated with beta–blockers may become dizzy or light–headed. More seriously, about 5% may become clinically depressed, with feelings of helplessness and hopelessness that sometimes lead to suicide. As might be expected, all such reactions are less common with beta–blockers that do not enter the brain readily.

Other moderately common side effects of beta–blockers include diarrhea, rash, slow heartbeat, and impotence or loss of sexual drive.

An additional concern with beta–blockers is their effect on blood cholesterol: They lower the amount of "good" (HDL) cholesterol while increasing the amount of "bad" (LDL) cholesterol. They also raise the amounts of fatty materials known as triglycerides in the bloodstream; some scientists believe triglycerides may increase the risk of a heart attack to almost the same extent as cholesterol. Nevertheless, there is no concrete evidence that people treated with beta–blockers are more likely to have heart attacks than those treated with other blood–pressure medications.

Summary

Beta–blockers are highly useful and relatively inexpensive medications. They remain among the most commonly used treatments for high blood pressure, although other types of medication have become more popular in recent years. Popularity of these newer medications rests almost entirely on their lower frequency of side effects: They have not been shown to treat the condition any more effectively. In fact, beta–blockers remain one of the two types of medication that have actually been shown to extend the life of people with high blood pressure.

See also Heart diseases; Hypertension.

Further Reading:

Edelson, Edward. *The ABCs of Prescription Drugs.* Garden City, NY: Doubleday & Co., 1987.
Hoffman, Brian B., and Lefkowitz, Robert J. "Adrenergic Receptor Antagonists." In Gilman, Alfred G. (ed.), *Goodman and Gilman's The Pharmacological Basis of Therapeutics,* 8th ed. New York: McGraw–Hill, 1990.
Oppenheim, Mike. *100 Drugs that Work.* Los Angeles: Lowell House, 1994.

W. A. Thomasson

Beta particle see **Radioactivity; Subatomic particles**

BHA see **Butylated hydroxyanisole**

BHT see **Butylated hyddroxytoluene**

Big bang theory

The big bang is the model that scientists use to describe the creation of the universe. It states that the universe was created in a violent event which occurred approximately 10 to 20 billion years ago. In that event, the lightest elements were formed, which provided the building blocks for all of the matter that exists in the universe today. A consequence of the big bang is that we live in an expanding universe, the ultimate fate of which cannot be predicted from the information we have at this time.

Studying the universe

Since ancient times, humans have wondered about the origin of the universe. Questions about how and when the earth and heavens formed have been pondered by philosophers, theologians, and scientists. This is now known as the science of cosmology, which is the study of the structure and origin of the universe.

There is no easy way to determine the distance to most of the objects we see in the night sky. Although different stars have different brightnesses, can we use that information to determine their distances? We know, for example, that our sun is a star like many others we see; it is much brighter only because it is so

much closer. Early astronomers assumed all stars had the same intrinsic brightness, and thus only their distance from us determined their apparent brightness. We now know that this is not true, and there are enormous variations in brightness. One of the ways this was shown was by examining binary stars—two stars in orbit about each other. When binary star systems were found in which the two stars did not have the same brightness, it was clear that the amount of light that we see is dependent on more than just distance; there must be intrinsic differences in the amount of light produced by different stars.

All measurements we make about the stars must necessarily be made from the neighborhood of the earth, since the distances involved are enormous. The nearest star other than the sun is more than four light years away (a light year is the distance that light travels in one year, about 9.5 million kilometers), and most objects we see are much farther away.

For the nearest stars, there are two direct ways to determine their distance. The first is by measuring their *parallax*, or their apparent change in position during the year. As the earth travels around the sun, we see the stars from a slightly different vantage point. The furthest objects don't appear to move, but the nearest move slightly with respect to them during the course of a year. This same effect can be seen by looking at an object many miles away. As you drive down the street, the nearby telephone poles move dramatically because they are so close to the road. But a distant mountain doesn't seem to move at all; this same effect is visible in the sky, with the nearest objects appearing to move against a fixed background. By measuring the change during a year, and knowing the radius of the earth's orbit, it is a simple matter to determine the distance to a nearby star.

Another technique is by measuring the proper motion of a star. This is simply the motion of the star with respect to other stars, due to the star's motion through the sky. Although the motions of distant stars is too small to detect, over the course of years, closer stars can be seen to change position.

These techniques are only applicable to a few of the nearest stars, however, so they tell us nothing about the large–scale structure of our universe. Instead, much more sophisticated methods have been developed, based on other astronomical observations.

Another way of learning about an object from afar is by examining its *spectrum*, or distribution of light with color. If the light from a star is divided into its component colors by use of a prism, we see a continuous rainbow of color, except for a number of dark lines. These lines, called *absorption lines*, are due to elements in the star's atmosphere. The positions and strengths of these lines can be used to learn about the temperature and other physical conditions of the object. In addition, the shift of the lines from their positions on earth can be used to calculate the velocity with which an object is moving towards or away from us. An object which is moving away from the earth will have its spectral lines shifted to longer wavelengths due to the *Doppler shift* acting on the emitted photons. Similarly, objects moving towards the earth will be shifted to shorter wavelengths. By measuring the shift of a spectrum, the velocity with which the object is moving with respect to the earth can be determined. A shift to longer wavelengths is called a *redshift*, since red light appears on the long wavelength side of the visible spectrum, while a shift to shorter wavelengths is called a *blueshift*.

Historical background

In 1905, Ejnar Hertzsprung compared the width of the stellar lines to the absolute luminosity, or brightness of the star, as found from proper motion measurements, and determined that wider lines came from larger and brighter stars. He had found a way to determine the absolute brightness of a star from its spectrum. By knowing its apparent brightness, the distance could then be determined.

In 1908, Henrietta Swan Leavitt at the Harvard College Observatory discovered that Cepheid Variables, a type of variable star in which the brightness changed in a regular manner, had a well–defined relationship between their period and their absolute luminosity. Brighter stars had longer periods, while dimmer ones had shorter periods. She later developed a simple relationship between the two. This discovery had a profound effect on stellar distance measurements. Now, any time a Cepheid could be found, its distance could be determined.

The spiral nebulae

In the early twentieth century, there was a debate among astronomers over the nature of the spiral nebulae, which were diffuse spiral–shaped structures seen in the sky. Some believed that these were relatively nearby objects, which were part of our galaxy, the Milky Way, while others thought that they were much further away, and in fact were 'island universes,' or separate galaxies, just like our own. If the distances to these objects could be measured, then the debate could be settled, and important knowledge would be gained about the structure of the universe.

In 1914, Vesto M. Slipher presented measurements of the velocities of 14 spiral nebulae, by measuring the Doppler shift of their lines, as described above. These results were surprising, because he found that most of the nebulae were moving away from the sun. If the motions were random, we would expect just as many to be moving toward us as were moving away. There was no explanation for this strange behavior. Another surprise was the large velocities at which these objects were moving. The Andromeda nebula, for example, was speeding toward us at 180 miles per second (300 km per second). Many interpreted this to mean that the nebulae must be outside our galaxy.

In 1923, Edwin Hubble, using the 60 inch and 100 inch (152 cm and 254 cm) telescopes at Mount Wilson Observatory, succeeded in identifying Cepheid Variables in the outer regions of two nebulae, M31 and M33. By measuring their periods, and using the formula developed by Leavitt several years earlier, he calculated their distances to be about 930,000 light years. From these distances and the observed sizes, it was a simple matter to calculate the actual size. These sizes were similar to that of our galaxy, so it very strongly supported the idea that the nebulae were galaxies in their own right.

In 1929, Hubble collected data on several galaxies in a graph with the distance to the galaxy along the horizontal axis, and the velocity along the vertical axis. From even this limited data, it was clear that there was a simple, linear relationship between the two quantities. On average, the velocity was proportional to the distance to the galaxy. The constant of proportionality, now called the *Hubble constant*, H, was given by the slope of the line. From those original data, it was thought to be 500 kilometers per second per megaparsec (310 miles per second per megaparsec), that is, a galaxy 1 megaparsec (one million parsecs, where one parsec = 3.26 light years) away would be moving away from our galaxy at 500 kilometers per second (310 miles per second), while one 10 times further away would be moving 10 times as fast. Modern values for H are much smaller than Hubble's estimate of 500 km/sec/mpc.

Implications of the Hubble law

What does it mean to have other galaxies moving away from us in all directions? At first, we might think that it proves that our sun is in some preferred location, in the center of the universe. But there is another explanation which is more consistent with the linear relationship that Hubble saw: all galaxies are receding from all others, that is every galaxy is getting further away from every other. There is a simple way to visualize this effect. Imagine a balloon, partially blown up, on which you draw a number of stars. As the balloon is filled with air, each star gets further away from every other. If you imagine yourself standing on any one of the stars, all the others would be moving away from you, and the ones that were further away would be moving away faster. There is no preferred direction, and no preferred position—the effect is the same for everyone.

There is a very important implication to this model. If all the galaxies are moving away from each other with a velocity proportional to their separation, then we can imagine what happened in the past. At earlier times, galaxies were closer together, and if one goes back far enough, there was a time when all were at the same position. That is, there is a beginning to the Universe. In fact, if the expansion has been constant for all time, the age of the universe is simply the inverse of the Hubble constant. Actually, scientists expect the Hubble constant to change somewhat with time, since the gravitational attraction between the galaxies will influence the rate of expansion. But this is still a good approximation.

With Hubble's original measurements, this gave an age of the universe of about two billion years. This immediately caused problems, since it was known from measurements of radioactive decay that the age of the solar system was more than twice this value. How could the solar system be formed before the universe itself? We now know that Hubble's original measurements were in error. Current measurements put the Hubble constant in the range of 50 to 100, giving an age of 10–20 billion years.

Other developments

When Einstein developed his general theory of relativity, he added a term, called the *cosmological constant*, to his equations in order to permit a static universe which was neither expanding or contracting. (He later came to regret this, calling it one of the worst mistakes he ever made). Despite his use of this extra term, however, Alexander Friedmann (in 1922 and 1924) and Georges LeMaître (in 1927) found solutions to his equations that permitted an expanding universe. After Hubble's 1929 discovery, there was a great deal of interest in these models, which could be used to explain the observations.

It should be noted that there were adherents to steady state models long after Hubble's measurements were made. One of the most promising models postulated that new galaxies were formed as the older galaxies move apart. This requires that nearby galaxies look

similar to those far away, but it was found that distant galaxies are in fact different from nearby ones, since they are older. In fact, it was one of the originators of this theory, Fred Hoyle, who coined the term "big bang," which is now used to describe the expanding universe model based on Hubble's observations. Hoyle chose the expression to ridicule the theory, but the name stuck.

The evolution of the universe

What occurred at the beginning? Our current picture of the big bang can be described briefly as follows. Because the mathematics break down close to the big bang itself, we will start one second after the event occurs. At this time, the temperature was 10,000,000,000 K. This was too hot for atoms to exist, so their elementary particle constituents (electron, protons, and neutrons) existed separately, along with *photons* (particles of light), and other exotic particles. Over the next 100 seconds, the temperature dropped by a factor of ten, which was enough to allow nuclei of light elements, such as deuterium (an isotope of hydrogen) and helium to form. As further cooling took place, the electrons and nuclei combined into atoms.

It should be stressed that the expansion of the universe means that space itself is expanding—this is different than an explosion, for instance, in which matter expands into empty space. This difference has many important implications. For example, as space expands, the temperature drops with it. One consequence of this is known as the *cosmic background radiation*. Early in the history of the universe, when the density was extremely high, particles and radiation were in equilibrium, meaning that there was a very uniform temperature distribution. Such a distribution gives rise to a particular spectrum, called a *blackbody spectrum*, with a well–defined shape, and a peak wavelength dependent on the temperature. Due to expansion of the universe, this blackbody spectrum is now shifted to below 3 K (−270°C), or three degrees above absolute zero, despite its initial high temperature. This cosmic background radiation was first detected in the microwave region of the spectrum by Arno Penzias and Robert Wilson in 1965. Measurements from the COBE spacecraft have shown that the spectrum is a nearly perfect blackbody at 2.73 K (−270.27°C).

As described above, only the lightest elements with which we are familiar were created in the big bang. As the universe expanded, eventually inhomogeneities developed, and regions of more dense and less dense gas formed. Gravity eventually caused the high density areas to coalesce into galaxies and eventually stars, which became luminous due to nuclear reactions in their cores. These reactions take the hydrogen and create some of the heavier elements. Once the nuclear fuel is exhausted, a star can explode in a supernova, creating still heavier elements in the process. It is these heavy elements from which the solar system, the earth, and humans are made. Every atom in your body was processed through a star billions of years ago.

What will be the ultimate fate of the universe? Will it continue to expand forever, or will it eventually contract in a 'big crunch'? We can use the analogy to a rocket being launched from the surface of the earth to understand this question. If a rocket is launched with enough energy, we know it will escape the earth's gravity, and travel on forever. If it has less energy than is required, however, gravity will pull it back to ground. This same effect is at work in the universe today. If there is enough mass in the universe, the force of gravity acting between the constituents will eventually cause the expansion to slow, and then stop; finally, the expansion will reverse, and the universe will become smaller and smaller until it ultimately collapses. When astronomers make estimates of the mass in the universe based on the luminous objects they see, they calculate a total mass much less than that required to close the universe. But from other measurements, they know that there is a unseen mass, called *dark matter*. The amount of this dark matter is not known, however, and the ultimate fate of the universe is unknown.

Future work

Although the big bang model has done a good job of explaining what we see in the universe, there are still many unanswered questions. As described above, there is still disagreement about the exact value of the Hubble constant by approximately a factor of two. The Hubble Space Telescope is making observations similar to those made by Edwin Hubble in order to try to measure this quantity more accurately, and preliminary results have been announced, but it will be some time before a value can be accurately determined. These measurements are very difficult to make, since they are at the limits of the telescope's ability to observe.

Another open question is how galaxies actually form from what was very close to a uniform, homogeneous medium in the early universe. From the uniformity of the microwave background radiation, we know that this uniformity was better than one part in a thousand. But just by looking at the sky we can see that today there is a great deal of structure in the universe, and this structure is seen up to very large size scales of clusters of galaxies and beyond. There must have been some type of clumping which occurred to start the process (with gravity helping the process along), but what started it?

See also Blackbody radiation; Cosmic background radiation; Cosmology; Dark matter; Doppler effect; Elements, formation of; Redshift.

Further Reading:

Hawking, Stephen W. *A Brief History of Time*. Toronto: Bantam Books, 1988.

Peebles, P. James E.; Schramm, David N.; Turner, Edwin L.; and Kron, Richard G. "The Evolution of the Universe," *Scientific American*. (October 1994): 53.

Silk, Joseph. *A Short History of the Universe*. New York: Scientific American Library, 1994.

Weinberg, Steven. *The First Three Minutes: A Modern View of the Origin of the Universe*. New York: Basic Books, 1977.

David Sahnow

Big-eyed shad see **Mooneyes**

Bigmouth buffalo (fish) see **Suckers**

Binary arithmetic see **Numeration systems**

Binary star

Binary stars, often called double stars, refer to pairs of stars sufficiently close to each other in space to be gravitationally bound together. Following the laws of gravitation, each of the components revolves around the common center of mass of the system. At least 50% of the stars are found to exist as binary systems, according to conservative statistics. There seems to be no obvious preference for particular combinations of brightness, size, or mass differences and a wide range in periods of

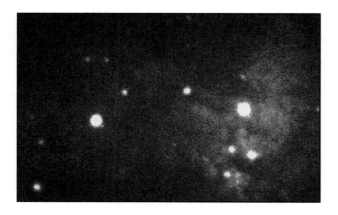

An x-ray image of the x-ray binary star system LMC X-1 in the Large Magellanic Cloud (LMC). LMC X-1 is seen as the two bright objects at center left and center right. The Tarantula Nebula is at the top of the cloud at left. The picture was taken by the ROSAT x-ray astronomy satellite. ROSAT discovered 15 new x-ray sources in the LMC, which is 163,000 light years from our galactic center and 33,000 light years in diameter. ROSAT was launched on June 1, 1990, and is a collaboration between Germany, UK, and USA.

revolution from less than a day to thousands of years. Likewise, there is a large range in separations from those stars in contact to those separated by thousands of times the Earth to Sun distance. Historically visual binaries, those which appear as double stars when seen through a telescope, were discovered to be gravitationally bound by William Herschel around 1800.

Techniques of observation

There are a number of telescopic techniques used to discover and study binary stars. No one telescopic method can be used because of the wide range in the separations exhibited in the systems. The desired information about the orbital motion and the physical quantities of the stars themselves must come from different ways of observing. Hence, there are descriptive classifications of binary stars as determined by the various modes of study discussed below.

Importance

The importance of binaries lies in a number of areas: 1) The analysis of a visual binary (where the two components can be seen visually through a telescope) leads to the only direct method for the evaluation of stellar mass, one of the most important parameters of the physical universe. In some cases the mass of the system is found, in other situations the mass ratio of the components, and in some the individual masses can

be determined. 2) Stellar duplicity plays an important role in the study of the physical aspects of stars, such as relative diameters, surface brightness, the genesis and evolution of stars; and the study of stellar–mass loss.

Visual binaries

Visual binaries are those stellar systems which appear as two stars in the eyepiece of a telescope. They are traditionally observed by manually measuring, at the eyepiece of a telescope, the angular separation of the two components. The angle the fainter stars make with respect to the brighter component is also taken into account, and refers to the north direction on the plane of the sky. If the measurements of each component are made photographically compared to background stars, the masses of each star can be found. Many observations are needed over a period of time commensurate to the period of revolution of the pair.

Study of orbital motion

The first goal generally is to determine the period of revolution, then when feasible the geometric elements (relating the apparent orbit on the plane of the sky to that on the true plane of the orbit) and the dynamical orbital elements of the system as far as possible, which will lead to the physical characteristics of the stellar components. The simple laws which govern the dynamics of orbital motion of double stars stem from the three Kepler laws which were originally formulated by Johann Kepler to describe the motions in our solar system. They had far–reaching implications of gravitational forces explained later by Newton. The laws of Kepler, as used in binary star analysis are: 1) The orbit described by the fainter component (often called B) around the brighter (A component) is an ellipse with the A component at one of the foci; 2) The component sweeps over equal areas, throughout its orbital path, in equal lengths of time; 3) The sum of the masses of the two components (in units of the solar mass) is equal to the scale or semi–major axis cubed (in units of the earth–sun distance) divided by the period squared (in unit of years). The mass of the binary system from Kepler's third law is the only direct way stellar mass can be determined.

Astrometric binaries

Astrometric binaries are double star systems visible on astrometric photographs as single stars. They have a telltale wavy motion across the sky indicating that the visible star is revolving around the center of mass of the visible star and its invisible companion, and thus its motion over an interval of time is analyzed for gravitational orbital motion. This process is a slightly modified form of the method for visual binaries. Generally, the companion star is either too faint to be seen or too close to the primary star to be resolved as two stars. The largest ground telescopes and also the Hubble Space Telescope are used to try and "see" the fainter component which might turn out to be a brown dwarf or a planet. The star Sirius is a fine example of a visual binary, discovered first as an astrometric binary in 1844 by the German astronomer F. Bessel.

Spectroscopic binaries

Spectroscopic binaries are pairs which are too close to each other as seen from the earth to be resolved into two stars. However, when the light from the star is analyzed with a spectrograph, which spreads the light into a continuous spectrum of colors with dark absorption lines superimposed, these spectral lines are alternately shortened or lengthened indicating Doppler motion, a to–and–fro motion as seen from Earth. This shift in the wavelengths results from the periodic motion, in the line of sight, of the visible star revolving around the center of mass of the system. When only the brighter component has sufficient light to show on the spectrogram the system is known as a single–lined spectroscopic binary. When the spectra of the fainter component is also recorded the name double–line spectroscopic binary is used.

Eclipsing binaries

Eclipsing binaries are those systems, seen as a single star, which show periodic changes in brightness. This occurs when one component eclipses the other during their orbital motions around the center of mass of the system. The plane of the orbital motion must necessarily be close to perpendicular to our line of sight; eclipses are further facilitated when their separation is small. By analyzing the brightness with the passage of time, the resulting light curve can indicate some geometric and dynamical components of orbital motion. Astrophysical properties can be determined such as the relative brightness of the two components, their relative diameters, and some aspects of their atmospheres.

Mass exchange binaries

Mass exchange binaries are short period pairs whose components are virtually in contact with each other so that they interact with each other; their large gaseous atmospheres may touch forming a figure eight

---

KEY TERMS

mass—The quantity of matter in the star as exhibited by its gravitation pull on another object. Stellar mass is usually measured in units of the sun's mass.

geometrical orbital elements—Used in equations to describe the orbital path of a binary star component as seen on the plane of the sky.

dynamical orbital elements—Used in equations to describe the true orbital path of a binary star component in the plane of the orbit.

astrometric photographs—Photos taken with "telephoto type" telescopes yielding large scale portrayal suitable for accurate measurements of positions of stellar images.

Doppler shift—The wavelengths of the radiation of a source receding from the viewer appear lengthened to the viewer and when the source is approaching the wavelengths appear shortened.

Dark absorption lines—Part of the stellar spectrum coming from different atomic elements in the atmosphere of the star.

---

in three dimensions. Sometimes the atmospheres overlap to such an extent that they make an envelope around the entire system. Mass from one component flows into the other resulting in mass loss and exchange. This in turn affects a change in the period of revolution of the pair. Generally, the components are of different stages in their evolutionary track. X–ray binaries described below also are binaries which exchange mass. Much remains to be done to understand the details of the physics of the interaction.

X–ray binaries

X–ray binaries are discovered through space telescopes which focus on very short–wave energy radiation sources. The International Explorer and the Einstein X–Ray Observatory and other satellites have been used. Some semi–detached pairs emit X–rays provided by mass transfer in a common atmospheric envelope. Close pairs with one component, a neutron star or a black hole, are likely indicated from enormous energy output in the form of ultraviolet and X–rays which are generated around the massive star as gas from the companion, unevolved star, is sucked toward the massive central degenerate component. This type of binary may have a period of revolution around two days or less.

See also Black Hole; Brown dwarf; Doppler Effect; Gravity and gravitation; Neutron Star; X–ray astronomy.

Further Reading:
Batten, Alan H. *Binary and Multiple Star Systems.* Pergamon Press, 1973.

Couteau, Paul. *Observing Double Stars.* Cambridge, MA: The MIT Press, 1981.

McAlister, H.A. and Hartkopf, Wm. I., eds. *Complementary Approaches to Double and Multiple Star Research, IAV Colloquium 135.* ASP Conference Series, Vol. 32, 1992. Published by the Astronomical Society of the Pacific.

Pringle, J.E and Wade, R., eds. *Interacting Binary Stars.* Cambridge University Press, 1985.

van de Kamp, Peter. *Stellar Paths.* Astrophysics and Space Science Library 85, Dordrecht, Holland: D. Reidel Publishing Company, 1981.

Zeilik, M. and Gaustad, J. *Astronomy, the Cosmic Perspective.* New York: John Wiley, 1990.

Sarah Lee Lippincott

Binomial theorem

The binomial theorem provides a simple method for determining the coefficients of each term in the expansion of a binomial with the general equation $(A + B)^n$. Developed by Isaac Newton, this theorem has been used extensively in the area of probability and statistics. The main argument in this theorem is the use of the combination formula to calculate the desired coefficients.

The question of expanding an equation with two unknown variables called a binomial was posed early in the history of mathematics. One solution, known as Pascal's Triangle, was determined in China as early as the thirteenth century by the mathematician Yang Hui. His solution was independently discovered in Europe 300 years later by Blaise Pascal whose name has been permanently associated with it since. The binomial theorem, a simpler and more efficient solution to the problem, was first suggested by Isaac Newton. He developed the theorem as an undergraduate at Cambridge and first published it in a letter written for Gottfried Leibniz, a German mathematician.

Expanding an equation like $(A + B)^n$ just means multiplying it out. By using standard algebra the equation $(A + B)^2$ can be expanded into the form $A^2 + 2AB + B^2$. Similarly, $(A + B)^4$ can be written $A^4 + 4A^3B + 6A^2B^2 + 4AB^3 + B^4$. Notice that the terms for A and B follow the general pattern A^nB^0, $A^{n-1}B^1$, $A^{n-2}B^2$, $A^{n-3}B^3$,

..., A^1B^{n-1}, A^0B^n. Also observe that as the value of n increases, the number of terms increases. This makes finding the coefficients for individual terms in an equation with a large n value tedious. For instance, it would be cumbersome to find the coefficient for the term A^4B^3 in the expansion of $(A + B)^7$ if we used this algebraic approach. The inconvenience of this method led to the development of other solution for the problem of expanding a binomial.

One solution, known as Pascal's Triangle, uses an array of numbers (shown below) to determine the coefficients of each term.

$(A+B)^0$						1					
$(A+B)^1$					1		1				
$(A+B)^2$				1		2		1			
$(A+B)^3$			1		3		3		1		
$(A+B)^4$		1		4		6		4		1	
$(A+B)^5$	1		5		10		10		5		1

Pascal's Triangle

This triangle of numbers is created by following a simple rule of addition. Numbers in one row are equal to the sum of two numbers in the row directly above it. In the fifth row the second term, 4 is equal to the sum of the two numbers above it, namely $3 + 1$. Each row represents the terms for the expansion of the binomial on the left. For example, the terms for $(A+B)^3$ are $A^3 + 3A^2B + 3AB^2 + B^3$. Obviously, the coefficient for the terms A^3 and B^3 is 1. Pascal's Triangle works more efficiently than the algebraic approach, however, it also becomes tedious to create this triangle for binomials with a large n value.

The binomial theorem provides an easier and more efficient method for expanding binomials which have large n values. Using this theorem the coefficients for each term are found with the combination formula. The combination formula is

$$_nC_r = \frac{n!}{r!(n-r)!}$$

The notation n! is read "n factorial" and means multiplying n by every positive whole integer which is smaller than it. So, 4! would be equal to $4 \cdot 3 \cdot 2 \cdot 1 = 24$. Applying the combination formula to a binomial expansion $(A + B)^n$, n represents the power to which the formula is expanded, and r represents the power of B in each term. For example, for the term A^4B^3 in the expansion of $(A + B)^7$, n is equal to 7 and r is equal to 3. By substituting these values into the combination formula we get $7!/(3! \cdot 4!) = 35$ which is the coefficient

KEY TERMS

. . . .

Binomial—An equation consisting of two unknowns such as (A + B).

Coefficient—A number which is multiplied by terms in an algebraic equation.

Expansion—Multiplying out terms in an equation.

Factorial—An operation represented by the symbol !. The term n! would be equal to multiplying n by all of the positive whole number integers which are less than it.

Pascal's Triangle—An array of integers which represents the expansion of a binomial equation.

for this term. The complete binomial theorem can be stated as the following

$$(A + B)^n = \Sigma_n C_r A^{n-r} B^r$$

The binomial theorem has been applied to many areas of science and mathematics. It is particularly useful for determining values for the square root of numbers. It is also extensively used in probability and statistics to describe the distribution of values about a mean.

See also Coefficient; Factorial; Statistics.

Further Reading:

Carrie, Dennis. *Precalculus*. Boston: Houghton Mifflin Company, 1990.

Newman, James R., ed. *The World of Mathematics*. New York: Simon and Schuster, 1956.

Dunham, William. *Journey Through Genius*. New York: John Wiley & Sons, 1990.

Perry Romanowski

Binturong see **Civits**

Bioaccumulation

Bioaccumulation is the accumulation of chemicals from the air, water, or soil in animal or plant tissues. The result is that the concentration of the chemical in living tissues is substantially greater than in the environmental medium from which it came.

Bioaccumulation can include two processes: bioconcentration and biomagnification. Bioconcentration is the direct uptake of a chemical, by inhalation, ingestion, or absorption, by organisms such as algae, bacteria, plants, crustaceans, fish, birds, or humans. The bioconcentration factor (BCF) is defined as the concentration of a chemical in tissue divided by its concentration in the air, water, or soil. The degree of bioconcentration depends upon the species in question—its size, unique metabolism, and fat content—and upon the properties of the chemical contaminant. Some chemicals, classified as hydrophilic, or "water–hating," are attracted to and concentrated in the lipid or fatty phase of plant or animal tissues. BCFs measured by scientists after spraying DDT (an insecticide commonly used from the 1940s through the 1970s) on a pond were 5,900 for algae, 110,000 for snails, and 26,000 for fish.

Organisms can also bioconcentrate metals and inorganic compounds, but the degree of accumulation depends upon the chemical speciation—the form the chemical takes in the water, air, or soil. For example, bacteria in water take up mercury 20 times more effectively than sediment, and they convert it to methylmercury, which is easily taken up by other organisms. Fish can accumulate methyl mercury through their food, as well as through the water. BCFs for mercury in aquatic plants and animals range from 1,000 to 100,000.

The progressively increasing concentrations of a chemical as it is transferred to tissues of organisms at higher levels of the food web is called biomagnification. As larger organisms eat smaller ones, the bioaccumulated chemical is concentrated further in the tissues of the predator, thus amplifying the effect of bioconcentration. Clear Lake in California was sprayed with DDD (an organochlorine pesticide with chemical properties similar to those of DDT) in the 1940s and 1950s to control aquatic insects. Microscopic algae absorbed the insecticide from the water and were then eaten by minute crustaceans, which were in turn consumed by frogs and sunfish. The resulting concentration of DDD in sunfish was 12,000 times the concentration in the water.

See also Biomagnification.

Bioassay

The biological assay or bioassay is a test system which uses living organisms to determine the presence and biological activity of chemical substances. Bioassays make quantitative estimations of biologically active substances by determining their biological effects on a parameter in an organism (such as growth or reproduction) under standardized conditions. Frequently bioassays are used to determine the risks associated with the use of a drug or biological substance by studying the effects produced on organisms of standard size. Pharmaceutical companies frequently use rats or mice to determine the possible consequences of drug application. Biological assays are employed to test the effects of environmental pollutants, plant growth regulators, chemical substances, and to detect the presence mutagens and carcinogens. A mutagen can be any substance that damages the DNA of the genome, whereas a carcinogen acts to produce a malignant growth identified as a cancer. Using bacteria as the test organism, approximately 90% of organic carcinogens identified have been recognized as mutagens.

Animal bioassays

Identifying the agents that act as mutagens and carcinogens in humans is difficult because of the long time required from the time of exposure to a carcinogen and the subsequent appearance of the cancer. The animal bioassay is the classical method for detecting carcinogens and relies on mice and rats as the test organisms. Organic chemicals identified as human carcinogens also have been demonstrated to cause cancer in the experimental animals; however, there are limitations to animal cancer tests. To meet statistical requisites of comparing tumors caused by chemicals versus tumors caused by chance, thousands of animals are required at astounding costs. Instead, to overcome the statistical number of difficulties, and to demonstrate relative safety of the questioned substance, a small sample size of test animals are exposed to very high doses of suspected cancer causing substances.

The use of animals to test environmental chemicals is a Herculean enterprise demanding large numbers of experimental animals, along with the technicians and pathologists to supervise the undertaking. Because it is time consuming, awkward, controversial and extremely costly to use small mammals as the test organisms in bioassays for mutagens and carcinogens, bioassays on microorganisms were developed to prescreen a wide variety of chemicals.

Microbial bioassays

In 1970 Bruce Ames developed the Ames test, which is a widely used, cost effective bioassay technique to test for carcinogens. Based on the recognition that cancer causing agents also act as mutagens, this test holds the advantage over the animal tests by employing bacterial selection techniques which require short generation times. The Ames test uses special tester strains of the *Salmonella* bacteria which have mutational differences in their cell walls allowing greater permeability to the test substances. These auxotrophic *Salmonella* test organisms lack the ability to synthesize the amino acid histidine.

Cultures of these organisms are plated out on two culture media. The control medium contains nutrient agar enriched with histidine, the testing medium contains the nutrient medium plus the test mutagen and a small concentration of histidine. After incubation, the organisms will grow in the presence of the test substance until the histidine is consumed, at this point only mutants which have regained the ability to synthesize histidine will form colonies. A comparison between the counts of the visible colonies of the test substance to those of the control gives a measure of the relative mutagenicity of the substance—the greater the number of colonies, the greater the mutagenicity.

Plant growth regulator bioassays

Bioassays are considered to be indispensable tools for research in the field of plant growth regulators. Using this technique, plant growth response is related to the nature of the chemical inducing the response. Gibberellins are plant growth promoters that cause cell division and elongation. When externally applied to dwarf plants at the appropriate concentrations, gibberellin induces plants to grow taller and faster. Using a series of dwarf pea plants treated with a graded range of identified gibberellin concentrations, a series of plants with heights corresponding to the dosage of the applied chemicals result after a specific growth time. The height of the plant treated with the unknown gibberellin concentration is compared to the height of the dwarfs treated with the known concentration. This growth response determines the concentration of the plant hormone. Using bioassay techniques the concentration of the applied chemical can be determined by grading the response of plants to different concentrations of the test substance.

Water quality bioassay

Recently the bacteria *Heliobacter pylori* has been identified as the agent causing stomach and intestinal ulcers and may also be associated with an increased rate of stomach cancer. Because the incidence of *H. pyloric* infection is common in Lima, Peru where the stomach cancer rate is four times higher than in North America, investigators sought to isolate the source of infection. Studying 400 children, 48 percent were found to be infected. High–income families showed a 32 percent infection rate compared to 56 percent in low income families.

The infection rate appeared to be related to the source of drinking water in the home rather than to the family's socio–economic level. The infection rate was three times higher in those children receiving water from external sources compared with those receiving water supplies inside their homes. Those high–income families supplied with municipal reservoir water showed a 12 times higher rate of infection than children from similar high–income families supplied with water from community wells. This water quality bioassay relating incidence of infection to source of water supply concluded that the municipal water supply was the major source of *H. Pylari* infection in Lima.

See also Ames test; Carcinogen; Mutagen.

Further Reading:

Ames, Bruce. "Environmental Chemicals Causing Cancer and Genetic Birth Defects: Developing a Strategy to Minimize Human Exposure." California Policy Seminar Monograph Number 2, UC Berkeley, 1978.

Campbell, Neil. *Biology.* New York: Benjamin/Cumings, 1993.

Glass, Gary, ed. *Bioassay Techniques and Environmental Chemistry.* Ann Arbor: Ann Arbor Science Publishers, 1973.

Klein, Peter, David Graham, Alvaro Gaillour, Antone Opekun, and E. Smith. "Water Source as Risk Factor for *Heliobacter pylori* Infection in Peruvian Children." *The Lancet* 337 (1991): 1503–507.

Prescott, Lansing; Harley, John; Klein, Donald. *Microbiology.* Dubuque: Wm. C. Brown, 1993.

Yopp, John, Louis Aung, and George Steffens, eds. *Bioassays and Other Special Techniques for Plant Hormones and Plant Growth Regulators.* Plant Growth Regulator Society of America, 1986.

Rita Hoots

Biochemical oxygen demand

Oxygen helps liberate biochemical energy from food by acting as the electron acceptor for the reaction that metabolizes adenosine triphosphate, ATP, one of the body's major chemical energy sources. Metabolic processes which require oxygen are called aerobic. Naturally occurring oxygen is in the form of molecular oxygen, O_2. Atmospheric oxygen is obtained by the body in the lungs in tiny air sacs called alveoli. Within the alveoli, red blood cells (rbc's) in narrow blood vessels absorb oxygen and carry it to cells throughout the body. Respiration, inhaling and exhaling of air, is subconsciously controlled by the brain in response to fluctuations in carbon dioxide levels. The average human body of 139 pounds consumes 250 ml of O_2 each minute. The major single organ oxygen consumers are the liver, brain, and heart (consuming 20.4%, 18.4%, and 11.6%, respectively). While the sum total of all the body's skeletal muscles consume about 20% In addition, the kidneys use up about 7.2%, and the skin uses 4.8% The rest of the body consumes the remaining 17.6% of the oxygen. Oxygen use can also be measured per 100 gm of an organ to indicate concentrations of use; as such, heart usage is highest, followed by the kidneys, then the brain, and then the liver. During exercise, the biochemical oxygen demand increases for active tissues including the heart and skeletal muscles.

Oxygen is the molecule used by animals as a final electron acceptor for metabolism. Two electrons (one at a time) from metabolic products can chemically bind each oxygen molecule. While numerous molecules combine with oxygen in the human body, one of the major chemical reactions involving oxygen is the synthesis of the high–energy phosphate bonds in ATP. ATP is the cell's currency for generating muscle contractions and driving certain ions through membrane–bound ion channels. Oxygen facilitates aerobic ATP production in mitochondria of cells throughout the body. Aerobic production of 36 molecules of ATP from one glucose molecules occurs in the citric acid metabolic cycle. About 1 liter of oxygen can release the chemical energy stored in 1 gram of food.

Oxygen is carried through the body in a number of chemical forms including simple O , water (H_2O), carbon dioxide (CO_2), and oxyhemoglobin. Unbound oxygen radicals can be highly toxic to cells. Allowing random oxidation reactions to occur throughout the cell, these radicals can be very destructive, and cellular defenses have evolved to combat them. In fact, the oxygen radical H_2O_2 is highly toxic to cells and can be used as a bactericidal agent. H_2O and CO_2 are end products for several aerobic reactions. And oxyhemoglobin is the oxygen shuttle complex that carries oxygen to needy cells. One rbc contains around 350 million hemoglobin molecules. Hence, one rbc can carry about 1.5 billion oxygen molecules.

Hemoglobin is a large globular protein made up of four polypeptide chains (two alpha and two beta hemoglobins, in adults) that each contain one heme complex. Heme complexes are sophisticated ring structures that contain a central ferrous iron atom. The iron atoms can each bind one O_2 molecule. Hence, one hemoglobin molecule can bind four O_2 molecules. This is conventionally represented as Hb_4O_8 . The four Hb components can alter their orientation to favor uptake or release of the oxygen. When the Hb bonds are relaxed, they favor uptake, and when they are tense they favor release. Affinity is the chemical term used to indicate how eager multiple units are to interact with one another. The chemical affinity for the first oxygen to bind is lower than the affinity for the later oxygens to bind: in other words, once one oxygen has bound to the hemoglobin, the binding of the other three oxygen molecules is more favorable. In addition, the amount of oxygen bound or released depends on the concentration of oxygen in two locations (where it is coming from and where it is being absorbed).

Oxygen flow is greatly determined by local partial pressure gradient. Just like it is more difficult to push water up a waterfall, so is it difficult to absorb oxygen into an area that already has more oxygen than the place it is coming from. In both cases, a certain amount of pressure is causing something to flow one way. As rbc's travel through arteries and veins around the human body, they collect oxygen in the alveoli where the partial pressure of oxygen is higher than it is in the rbc's. Usual average atmospheric pressure is measured as 1 atmosphere (1 atm) or 14.7 pounds per square inch (14.7 psi). Since oxygen makes up about 21% of atmospheric air, the partial pressure of oxygen is 0.21 atm or 3.09 psi. Because venous oxygen partial pressure is less than 3.09 psi, oxygen is driven into the blood in the lungs. Although a small amount of O_2 gas dissolves into the plasma (the fluid surrounding the blood cells) most is bound by hemoglobin. The reverse process occurs as capillaries supply tissues with oxygen. The partial pressure of oxygen in the tissue is lower than in the blood, so oxygen flows into the tissue. CO_2 travels a reverse course where high tissue partial pressures push CO_2 out into the veins that carry it to the lungs for release into the atmosphere. The CO_2 partial pressure of the atmosphere is significantly lower than that of body tissues. The relationship of gaseous absorption to atmospheric pressure makes it crucial for mountain climbers and

scuba divers to calculate their expected partial pressure gaseous exposure before climbing or diving. Miscalculations could lead to death.

Body tissues vary in their oxygen dependency. Hypoxia is the condition of existing with a lowered oxygen supply. The brain and heart are the two most hypoxia sensitive organs. A severe drop in available oxygen can cause brain death in five minutes. Less severe hypoxia can lead to other mental problems such as dizziness, headache, disorientation, drowsiness, or impaired judgment. Although basic brain functions may recover fully from a short hypoxic period, higher neural functions can be severely impaired.

During rigorous exercise, oxygen demand may increase to up to 15 times normal demand. As muscles deplete their oxygen supplies, the lowered muscular oxygen partial pressure steepens the pressure gradient so that even more oxygen leaves the blood and enters the muscles. If aerobic metabolism is unable to supply enough ATP to muscle cells, then anaerobic metabolism can provide some ATP. However, anaerobic metabolism temporarily adds lactic acid to the muscle creating an oxygen debt whereby the muscle fatigues and requires a recovery period to rid of the lactic acid. An initial oxygen debt is also always present for about the first 30 seconds of exercise until circulation can accelerate to provide additional oxygen.

Various life forms are classified on the basis of their tolerance or requirement of oxygen. Different types of bacteria are aerobic, facultatively aerobic, or anaerobic. Aerobes use oxygen to generate energy. Facultative aerobes can use oxygen but survive without it. Oxygen is highly toxic to anaerobes which die rapidly when exposed to it.

See also Aerobic; Blood; Cellular respiration; Circulatory system; Metabolism; Respiratory system.

Further Reading:

Ganong W, ed. *Review of Medical Physiology*, 15th ed. Norwalk, CT: Appleton & Lange, 1991.

Rhoads R and Pflanzer R, eds. *Physiology*, 2nd ed. New York: Saunders College Publishing, 1992.

Louise Dickerson

Biochemistry

Biochemistry is the branch of chemistry that deals with the chemical substances and chemical processes of living things. It is the scientific study of the chemistry of plant, animal, and microbial life at the molecular level. This science investigates the composition, structure, properties, and the changes in properties, of living organisms. The study of biochemistry includes the knowledge of the structure and function of molecules found in the biological world and an understanding of the precise biochemical pathways by which organic molecules are either put together or broken down.

The biochemistry of digestion, for example, includes the study of the stepwise pataways involving changes in molecular structure, and all enzyme interactions, that take place when large food molecues (proteins, lipids, or carbohydrates) are broken down into smaller molecules capable of uptake and use by the cells of a living body.

Biochemistry also involves the study of the relationship between how a living substance behaves and how its atoms are connected. An example of molecular structure influencing the function of an organism can be seen in the various physical traits that an offspring inherits from its parents.

These traits are determined by the way the nitrogenous bases are lined up one after the other in the lengths of DNA (deoxyribonucleic acid) molecules that make up the genes in the chromosomes that each offspring gets from its parents. The structure of the DNA molecule is remarkably well suited to its ability to make more copies of itself. The hydrogen bonds between the base pairs of the DNA double helix enable the two–stranded double helix molecule to unzip easily so that each piece can act as a pattern to build new DNA molecules. The study of biochemistry investigates the relationship between molecular structure and function or in living things on a molecular level.

See also Amino acid; Carbohydrate; Deoxyribonucleic acid; Enzyme; Hormones; Lipid; Metabolism; Molecular biology; Photosynthesis; Proteins; Ribonucleic acid.

Biodegradable

The term *biodegradable* is used to describe substances which are capable of decomposing through the agency of bacteria, fungi, and other living organisms.

Temperature and sunlight may also play a role in the decomposition of biodegradable substances. When substances are not biodegradable, they remain in the environment for a long time, and, if toxic, may pollute the soil and water. Some biodegradable pollutants may be capable of causing harm to organisms in the environment.

Common, everyday substances that are biodegradable include food refuse, tree leaves, and grass clippings. Many communities now encourage people to compost these materials and use them as humus (an organic–rich material in soil) for gardening. Because plant and animal materials are biodegradable, this is one way to reduce solid waste problems for towns and cities.

The development of detergents and the problem their surfactants (surface–acting substances) created in sewage systems raised the issue of biodegradability of these chemicals. A complex phosphate, sodium tripolyphosphate, was responsible for a build up of foam in sewage plants and streams. Environmental concerns led to the development of new detergents that are more easily biodegradable. Detergent manufacturers have responded to the issue of biodegradable detergents by replacing phosphates with enzymes like protease and amylase.

In efforts to control the use of non–biodegradable materials, governments and industries have taken various measures. For example, the plastic rings that bind six–packs of soda and beer must now by biodegradable by law in Oregon and Alaska. Italy has banned all non-biodegradable plastics. Manufacturers have responded to the issue by experimenting with biodegradable packaging of food.

See also Aerobic; Composting; Hazardous wastes; Landfill; Recycling; Waste management.

Biodiversity

Biodiversity is the total richness of biological variation. Usually the scope of biodiversity is considered to range from the genetic variation of individual organisms within and among populations of a species to different species occurring together in ecological communities. Some definitions of biodiversity also include the spatial patterns and temporal dynamics of populations and communities on the landscape. The geographical scales at which biodiversity can be considered range from local to regional, state or provincial, national, continental, and ultimately to global.

Biodiversity at all scales is severely threatened by human activities, making it one of the most important aspects of the global environmental crisis. Humans have already caused permanent losses of biodiversity through the extinction of many species and the loss of distinctive, natural communities. Ecologists predict that unless there are substantial changes in the ways that humans affect ecosystems, there will be much larger losses of biodiversity in the near future.

Species richness of the biosphere

About 1.7 million of Earth's species have been identified and designated with a scientific name. About 6% of the identified species live in boreal or polar latitudes, 59% in the temperate zones, and the remaining 35% in the tropics. However, knowledge of Earth's species is highly incomplete, especially for tropical countries. According to some estimates there could be as many as 30–50 million species on Earth, 90% of them occurring in tropical ecosystems. Tropical ecosystems are richer in species than are those at higher latitudes.

Most of the described species on Earth are invertebrates, especially insects, and most of the insects are beetles (Coleoptera). The famous scientist J.B.S. Haldane was once asked by a theologian to briefly explain what his knowledge of biology told of God's purpose. Haldane reputedly said that God has "an inordinate fondness of beetles," reflecting the fact these insects are so much more speciose than any other creatures on Earth. Some biologists believe that beetles account for most of the undescribed tropical insects.

The suggestion of enormous numbers of undescribed insects in tropical forests has mostly emerged from the work of Terry Erwin. This entomologist performed experiments in which tropical–forest canopies were treated with an insecticide, and the subsequent "rain" of dead arthropods was collected using ground–level sampling devices. This innovative sampling procedure indicated that: (1) a large fraction of the insect species of tropical rainforests is unknown to science; (2) most insect species are confined to a single type of tropical forest, or even to particular tree species that are themselves of local distribution; and (3) most species of tropical–forest insects have little ability to disperse very far. Erwin's studies of tropical rainforest in Amazonia found that beetles accounted for most of the insect species and that most of the beetles are narrowly endemic, that is, of a local distribution and found nowhere else. The tree *Luehea seemanii,* for example, had more than 1,100 species of beetle in its canopy of which 15% were specific to that plant. The

emerging conclusion from this and other descriptive research is that there is an enormous abundance of undescribed species of insects and other invertebrates living in tropical forests.

Compared with invertebrates, the numbers of species, that is, the species richness, of other groups of tropical–forest organisms is better known. Although it is very difficult to do so, the numbers of species of vascular plants have been described for a few tropical forests. For example: a plot of only 0.0004 sq mi (0.1 ha) in a moist forest in Ecuador had 365 species of vascular plants; there were 98 species of large trees in 0.006 sq mi (1.5 ha) of forest in Sarawak, Malaysia; there were 90 tree species in 0.0032 sq mi (0.8 ha) of forest in Papua New Guinea; 742 woody species occurred in 0.012 sq mi (3 ha) of forest in Sarawak with 50% of the species recorded as single individuals; and more than 300 species of woody plants were discovered on a 50–ha area of forest in Panama. These tropical forests are much richer than temperate forests which typically support fewer than 12–15 species of trees. The Great Smokies of the eastern United States have some of the richest temperate forests in the world, and they typically contain 30–35 species, far fewer than in tropical rainforests.

It is extraordinarily difficult to determine the numbers of birds in tropical forests because the dense foliage and darkness of the understory make it inconvenient to see small animals, even if they are brightly colored. As a result, very few studies have been made of the birds of tropical rainforests. However, one study in Peru discovered 245 resident and 74 transient species in 0.4 sq mi (97 ha) of Amazonian forest. Another study of rainforest in French Guiana recorded 239 species of birds, and another found 151 species in a forest in Sumatra. In comparison, temperate forests in North America typically support only 15–30 species of birds.

Almost no systematic surveys have been made of all of the species of tropical ecosystems. In one case, a 42 sq mi (108 sq km) reserve of dry forest in Costa Rica was estimated to support about 700 plant species, 400 vertebrate species, and 13,000 species of insects, including 3,140 species of moths and butterflies.

Why is biodiversity important?

Biodiversity is valuable for the following classes of reasons:

(1) Intrinsic Value. Biodiversity has its own intrinsic values, regardless of its worth in terms of human needs. Because of this intrinsic merit, there are ethical considerations to any degradation of biodiversity. For

example, do humans have the "right" to diminish or exterminate elements of biodiversity, all of which are unique and irretrievable? Is the human existence itself diminished by losses of biodiversity? Ethical issues cannot be resolved through science, but enlightened persons would mourn any loss of species, or of natural, ecological communities.

(2) Direct Utilitarian Value. Humans have an absolute requirement for the products of other species. Because of this need, wild and domesticated species and their communities are exploited in many ways to provide food, materials, energy, and other goods and services. This fact can be illustrated in many ways. In the United States, for example, about one–quarter of prescription drugs have active ingredients obtained from higher plants, and these uses contributed about $14 billion per year to the U.S. economy, and $40 billion per year worldwide. Potentially, harvests of biodiversity can be conducted in ways that foster renewal. Unfortunately, potentially renewable biodiversity resources are often harvested too intensively or inadequate attention is paid to regeneration, so the resource is consequently degraded or becomes extinct.

(3) Provision of Ecological Services. Biodiversity provides many ecological services that are directly and indirectly important to human welfare. Examples of these services include biological productivity, nutrient cycling, cleaning of water and air, control of erosion, provision of atmospheric oxygen, removal of carbon dioxide, and other functions related to the integrity of ecosystems. According to the biologist Peter Raven: "Biodiversity keeps the planet habitable and ecosystems functional."

There are many cases of the discovery of bio–products useful to humans as food, medicine, or for other purposes through research on previously unexploited plants and animals. Consider the case of the rosy periwinkle (*Catharantus roseus*), a small plant native to the tropical island of Madagascar. During an extensive screening of wild plants for anti–cancer chemicals, an extract of rosy periwinkle was observed to inhibit the growth of cancerous cells. The active biochemicals are several alkaloids in foliage of the plant, probably used to deter herbivores. These natural substances are now used to prepare the drugs vincristine and vinblastine, which can be successfully used to treat childhood leukemia and a lymphatic cancer known as Hodgkin's disease. In this case, a species of wild plant known only to a few botanists has proven to be of great benefit to humans by treating previously incurable diseases in the process sustaining a large pharmaceutical economy. There is a tremendous undiscovered wealth of other biological products useful to humans in unexplored biodiversity.

BIODIVERSITY AND EXTINCTION

Extinction refers to the loss of some species or other taxonomic unit (e.g., subspecies, genus, family, etc.; each is known as a taxon) occurring over all of its range on Earth. (Extirpation refers to a more–local disappearance, with the taxon still surviving elsewhere.) The extinction of any species is an irrevocable loss of part of the biological richness of Earth, the only place in the universe known to support living creatures. Extinction can be a natural occurrence caused by unpredictable catastrophes, chronic environmental stresses, or ecological interactions such as competition, disease, or predation. However, there have been dramatic increases in extinction rates since humans have become Earth's dominant large animal and the perpetrators of global environmental changes.

Extinction has always occurred naturally. Almost all species that have ever lived on Earth have become extinct. Perhaps they could not cope with changes occurring in their environment such as climate changes or in the intensity of predation or disease. Alternatively, many extinctions may have occurred simultaneously as a result of unpredictable catastrophes. From the geological record it is known that species, families, and even phyla have appeared and disappeared over time. For example, numerous phyla of invertebrates proliferated during an evolutionary radiation at the beginning of the Cambrian era about 570 million years ago, but most of these are now extinct. The 15–20 extinct phyla from that period are known from the Burgess Shale of British Columbia, and they represent unique experiments in invertebrate form and function. Similarly, entire divisions of plants have appeared, radiated, and disappeared, such as the seed ferns Pteridospermales, the cycad–like Cycadeoidea, and woody plants known as Cordaites. Of the twelve orders within the class Reptilia, only three survive today: crocodilians, turtles, and snakes/lizards. Clearly, the fossil record displays a great deal of evidence of natural extinctions.

Overall, the geological record suggests that there have been long periods of time characterized by uniform rates of extinction but punctuated by about nine catastrophic episodes of mass extinction. The most intense extinction event occurred at the end of the Permian period some 245 million years ago when 54% of marine families, 84% of genera, and 96% of species are estimated to have become extinct.

Another famous, apparently synchronous extinction of vertebrate animals occurred about 65 million years ago at the end of the Cretaceous period. The most renowned extinctions were of the last of the reptilian dinosaurs and pterosaurs, but many plants and invertebrates also became extinct at the same time. In total, perhaps 76% of species and 47% of genera became extinct in the end–of–Cretaceous crisis. One hypothesis to explain the cause of this mass extinction involves a meteorite impacting the Earth, causing great quantities of fine dust to be spewed into the atmosphere, and resulting in a climatic deterioration that most large animals could not tolerate. However, some scientists believe that the extinctions of the last dinosaurs were more gradual.

More recently, humans have been responsible for most of Earth's extinctions. These extinctions are occurring so quickly that they represent a modern mass extinction of similar intensity to those documented in the geological record. Recent extinctions caused by humans include well–known cases such as the dodo, passenger pigeon, and great auk. Many other high–profile species have been taken to the brink of extinction, including the plains bison, whooping crane, ivory-billed woodpecker, right whale, and other marine mammals. These losses have been caused by insatiable overhunting and intense disturbance or conversion of natural habitats.

Beyond these well–known and tragic cases involving large animals, Earth's biodiversity is experiencing an even larger loss. This ruin is mostly being caused by extensive conversions of tropical ecosystems, particularly rainforests, to agricultural habitats that sustain few of the original species. As was described previously, tropical ecosystems have very large numbers of species, most of which have restricted distributions. The conversion of tropical forests to habitats unsuitable for specialized, native species inevitably causes the loss of most of the locally endemic biota. This is a great tragedy, and the lost species will never again occur.

The most important human influences causing the extinction or endangerment of species are: (1) excessive exploitation, (2) effects of introduced predators, competitors, and diseases, and (3) habitat disturbance and conversion. These stressors can result in small and fragmented populations which experience the deleterious effects of inbreeding and population instability and then decline further, ultimately to extirpation or extinction. The increased rate of extinction and endangerment of biodiversity during the past several centuries is best documented for vertebrates because, as noted previously, most invertebrate species, particularly insects, have not yet been described by scientists. During the last four centuries there have been more than 700 known extinctions globally, including about 100 species of mammals and 160 species of birds, all because of human influences.

A much larger number of species is facing imminent extinction; they are endangered. For example, more than one thousand species of birds are considered to be threatened with extinction. Of this total, 46% live on isolated oceanic islands, a situation in which species are especially vulnerable to extinction caused by stresses associated with human activities. Birds of tropical forests account for 43% of the threatened bird species, wetland species for 21%, grassland and savannah species 19%, and other habitats 17%. Only 1.5% of the threatened species are North American, 4.2% are European and Russian, 33% Central and South American, 18% African, 30% Asian, and 14% from Australasia and the Pacific.

Protection of threatened biodiversity

Biodiversity can be protected in ecological reserves. These are protected areas established for the preservation of natural values, usually the known habitat of endangered species, threatened ecological communities, or representative examples of widespread communities. In the early 1990s there were about 7,000 protected areas globally with an area of 651 million hectares. Of this total, about 2,400 sites comprising 379 million ha were fully protected and could be considered to be true ecological reserves.

Ideally, the design of a national system of ecological reserves would provide for the longer–term protection of all native species and their natural communities including terrestrial, freshwater, and marine systems. So far, however, no country has implemented a comprehensive system of ecological reserves to fully protect its natural biodiversity. Moreover, in many cases existing reserves are relatively small and are threatened by environmental change and other stressors such as illegal poaching of animals and plants and sometimes tourism.

The World Conservation Union, World Resources Institute, and United Nations Environment Program are three important agencies whose mandates center on the conservation and protection of the world's biodiversity. These have developed the *Global Biodiversity Strategy,* an international program to help protect biodiversity. The broad objectives are to: (1) preserve biodiversity; (2) maintain Earth's ecological processes and life–support systems; and (3) ensure that natural resources will be sustainable used by humans. The *Global Biodiversity Strategy* is a mechanism by which countries and peoples can initiate meaningful actions to protect biodiversity to benefit present and future

KEY TERMS

. . . .

Binomial—The scientific name of organisms consists of two words, and is therefore a binomial. Humans, for example, are designated as *Homo sapiens,* which designates our genus as *Homo,* and our species within that genus as *sapiens.* Binomials are always latinized words, and are written in italics, or are underlined.

Endangerment—Refers to a situation in which a species is vulnerable to extinction or extirpation.

Endemic—Refers to species with a relatively local distribution, sometimes occurring as small populations confined to a single place, such as an oceanic island. Endemic species are more vulnerable to extinction than are more widespread species.

Extinction—Refers to a situation in which there are no longer any living individuals of a species anywhere on Earth. Extirpation means that a species no longer occurs in a place or country, although it survives elsewhere.

Species diversity—An indicator of biodiversity at the community level, which accommodates both the number of species present (i.e., richness) and their relative abundance. Ecologists consider species diversity to be a good indicator of biodiversity within communities, because it accommodates differences amongst species in rarity and commonness.

Species richness—The number of species in some place or area. Often ecologists estimate this as the number of species encountered during a systematic search of a distinctive community or a larger area, such as a park or ecological reserve.

generations and for intrinsic reasons as well. Because it only began in the late 1970s, it is too early to evaluate the success of this program. However, the existence of this comprehensive international effort is encouraging as is the participation of most of Earth's countries, representing all stages of socioeconomic development.

Important progress is being made, and the progressive worldwide development of activities intended to identify, conserve, and preserve biodiversity will hopefully come to be regarded as an ecological "success story."

See also Biological community; Ecosystem; Endangered species; Extinction.

Further Reading:

Freedman, B. *Environmental Ecology, 2nd edition.* San Diego: Academic Press, 1994.

Wilson, E.O., ed. *BioDiversity.* Washington, D.C.: National Academy Press, 1988.

Wilson, E.O. *The Diversity of Life.* Cambridge: Harvard University Press, 1992.

Bill Freedman

Bioenergy

Bioenergy is energy derived from using organic material, especially plant matter, as fuel. The material burned or processed to produce bioenergy (the "feedstock") is called biomass. Biomass has been an energy source ever since humans used wood fires to warm themselves and cook food. Wood is still the most common biomass fuel. In developing countries, a dried mixture of straw and animal dung is also a common biomass fuel.

Unlike most other sources of energy, biomass is a potentially renewable resource. By definition, bioenergy sources should include coal, petroleum, and naturally occurring gases because these fossil fuels were derived from plants laid down in early geologic ages. However, these are nonrenewable sources of energy and thus are omitted when discussing bioenergy. In fact, the big advantage of bioenergy is that its use reduces the use of such nonrenewable energy sources.

Primary ways of using bioenergy

There are currently three major ways in which the energy in plants can be utilized: direct burning, conversion to gas, and conversion to alcohol.

Direct burning

Biomass materials can be burned directly as fuel, as when logs are put on a fire. A major environmental problem in many developing countries is that forests have disappeared as people have used up the trees as fuel for cooking. Without forests to hold soil, the land erodes and becomes desertlike, making it almost impossible to raise crops. Some environmentalists think this contributed to widespread famine in Africa. Direct burning of biomass also releases many of the same pollutants into the air as does the burning of fossil fuels.

More useful than cutting forests is using biomass that is grown specifically for the purpose. These bioenergy crops may be a great source of energy in the future. The incineration of municipal and industrial wastes can be an inexpensive method for obtaining energy as well as for disposing of these "wastes."

Conversion to gas

Biomass can also be converted into methane gas, called biogas, which is, in turn, burned for energy. When bacteria digest organic materials without the presence of oxygen (*anaerobic digestion*), gas is produced that is about two–thirds methane, CH_4, which is the main component in natural gas. Methane is also produced in landfills as waste is digested anaerobically. The gas must be collected and piped out of landfills to prevent explosions, so it can easily be used as fuel. Biogas can also be obtained from the anaerobic digestion of sewage sludge.

In China, many farmers use small closed pits as anaerobic digesters. Agricultural waste and sewage is placed in the pits, and the biogas given off is used as a fuel for cooking. On a larger scale, some dairy farmers in the United States have begun to produce biogas from cow manure. The gas is used to run electrical generators, and the heat given off by the generators is fed back into the manure digesters to speed up the process as well as into the barns for general space heating.

Conversion to alcohol

About one–fourth of all energy use in the United States is for transportation. Biomass can be converted by fermentation into liquid alcohol, which can be used in vehicle engines. In the same natural process that has been used to make alcoholic beverages since civilization began, yeast feeds on the sugars and starches in the plants, producing ethyl alcohol, or ethanol, (C_2H_6O; also written CH_3CH_2OH). Ethanol is added to gasoline, usually in a ratio of 1 part ethanol to 9 parts gasoline, to produce gasohol, which can be used in standard automobile engines. Ethanol can be used alone only in engines that have been slightly modified. Brazil, which makes ethanol from sugarcane, has many cars that run on gasohol. Ethanol has a higher octane rating and produces less carbon monoxide than gasoline.

Most ethanol in the United States has been produced from corn and sorghum. However, most of it has been made by the fermentation of the grain only. This is useful in the U.S. where farmers can acquire an additional source of farm income with extra land, but in nations without enough cropland, the land is needed for food. Researchers are working on solving the problems of converting cornstalks, instead of grains, into ethanol. Another hazard is the pollutants that are

expelled into the atmosphere if fossil fuels are used in the distillation process. However, the burning of ethanol in vehicles in major cities can reduce the amount of carbon monoxide polluting the atmosphere.

Fermentation of organic materials gives off carbon monoxide and hydrogen gas, which can be heated in the presence of a catalyst to synthesize a poisonous but energy–efficient alcohol called *methanol* or wood alcohol (CH_4O or CH_3OH). Methanol can be substituted for gasoline in motor vehicles and other machinery, but the process is not yet efficient. Factories to convert biomass into methanol without using fossil fuels are not yet commercially realistic. Also, emissions given off by burning methanol includes the highly toxic formaldehyde. However, this can probably be eliminated by emissions control equipment on the vehicles.

Sources of biomass

There are four major sources of biomass: agricultural and forest residues, municipal solid waste, industrial waste, and bioenergy crops.

Agricultural and forest residues

The conversion of crop–quality biomass to energy does not have significant benefits. It is less efficient to produce biofuel than food on the Earth's limited arable land, and the burning of biomass releases pollutants into the atmosphere just as the burning of fossil fuels does. However, many people in developing countries use crop residues and the branches of leaves left behind after logging operations as a fuel source. Although it may seem a viable resource, crop and forest residues are often the parts of the plants containing many nutrients. If the residues are taken as fuel, the nutrients are lost to the field or forest, and synthetic chemical fertilizers must be used. However, the burning of secondary wastes from processing, such as rice hulls or wood pulp, makes an efficient use of materials which would have been wasted.

Municipal solid waste

Municipal solid waste (MSW), most of which is organic in origin, is currently being incinerated in some cities both as a means of keeping the waste out of landfills and as a way to acquire relatively inexpensive fuel for electrical power. On average, the burning of one ton of normal MSW produces as much heat as one barrel of oil. There are more than 70 waste–to–energy plants in use in the United States and about that many others are being planned.

Unexpected problems have arisen in those cities that do such a good job of recycling that not enough high–energy waste is available for the incinerator. Plastics, for example, are a particularly high–energy waste that can be efficiently recycled. Another problem is that the content of MSW is usually not known. It can contain materials that send toxins into the air or that make the final residue toxic, which must then be treated as hazardous waste.

Industrial waste

Some industrial wastes can also be a good source of bioenergy, especially if its use is planned as a part of a cogeneration project. Cogeneration is the use of heat or materials left over from manufacturing to produce electricity. The electricity can then be used to run the factory, with any power left over put into the municipal grid. The U.S. paper and pulp industry currently derives about 8% of its energy from cogeneration of wood waste.

In South Florida's Palm Beach County, the country's largest biomass cogeneration project is being built. When it is functioning in 1996, it is expected to produce enough electricity to power 46,000 homes. It will burn *bagasse*, a byproduct of milling sugar, plus wood waste from building and demolition firms.

Bioenergy crops

Wood and other high–energy crops can be grown specifically for use as bioenergy sources. The growing of annual crops such as corn is probably not efficient enough in the long run; too much labor and energy are required. Perennial grasses such as switchgrass, on the other hand, can readily be harvested for bioenergy. Grasses may be compressed into pellets, rather like coal chunks, and burned. Woody crops, such as poplar trees, can be grown in plantations with tree harvested on a 3–to–10–year cycle and then regrown from stump sprouts. New trees would have to be replanted about every 15–20 years.

Good biomass crops grow fast, use nutrients and water efficiently, are dense and hardy, and, preferably, are perennial and regenerate easily after harvesting. Ideally, they would also have nitrogen–fixing capability, which would limit the need for fertilizer application. It is hoped that in the future bioengineering will increase the nitrogen–fixing capabilities of various plants and speed the rate at which bioenergy sources grow. Bioengineering has already improved the bioenergy qualities of such trees as black cottonwood. Among other trees that have good potential as bioenergy sources are eucalyptus, sweetgum, and black locust.

KEY TERMS

Biogas—Methane derived from the anaerobic digestion of biological material.

Biomass—Any material, living in origin, used to produce energy.

Cogeneration—Generation of electricity from the heat derived from an industrial process. The electricity generated is used to carry out the industrial processes.

Digester—A sealed, enclosed space in which anaerobic digestion of biological material is carried out.

Emissions—Any byproduct of combustion, especially from industrial processes and internal combustion engines.

Fermentation—The conversion of sugar to ethyl alcohol and carbon dioxide by special enzymes found in the tiny plants called yeast.

Gasohol—A mixture of ethanol or methanol and gasoline, used to increase the octane rating of the gasoline and reduce carbon dioxide emissions.

Methane—A gas resulting from the anaerobic digestion of organic matter by bacteria; CH_4; also called biogas.

Methanol—Methyl alcohol, CH_4O (also written CH_3OH).

Municipal solid waste—The entire waste of a municipality, its homes, and offices, but not including industry or sewage; also called MSW.

Octane—A number that indicates the ability of a petroleum compound to burn smoothly in an engine instead of with power–losing explosions. The higher the octane number, the smoother the engine burns.

Organic—Made of or requiring the materials of living things. In pure chemistry, organic refers to compounds that include carbon, whether or not they are biological in origin.

Advantages and disadvantages of bioenergy

Although the burning or conversion of biomass does not relieve pollution of the atmosphere, it does have several major benefits. Biomass is more reliable than either sunshine or wind energy. That is because the energy in plants is already captured and stored, while in solar and wind energy this must be done by humans. Another advantage of bioenergy is that it can be produced using organic waste materials that would otherwise have to be thrown away, saving the environmental and economic expense of their disposal. Used in mass quantities, bioenergy could help the economy of any nation that must now import fossil fuels. If crops grown for their biomass increase the amount of growing plants on the planet, they can reduce the amount of carbon dioxide in the atmosphere. The most significant advantage of bioenergy is that it is a potentially renewable and natural resource that could supply the world's energy needs indefinitely.

However, there are some disadvantages to using bioenergy. Biomass has much less energy content for its bulk than fossil fuels. Therefore, labor, transportation, and storage costs would be higher. Also, water, which is in short supply in many areas, must be used in producing the biomass crops. Fortunately, such aquatic "crops" as kelp and water hyacinths have potential as bioenergy sources.

Perhaps the major difficulty with bioenergy, however, is the same problem that has arisen with recycling. People won't demand bioenergy until there is a considerable savings in doing so, and there won't be a savings in using bioenergy until there is a demand for it. In the meantime, research must continue into the most efficient ways of harvesting, transporting, and utilizing the world's oldest source of energy.

See also Alcohol; Alternative energy sources; Hazardous wastes; Hydrocarbon; Landfill; Pollution.

Further Reading:

Blashfield, Jean F., and Wallace B. Black. *Recycling.* Saving Planet Earth series. Chicago: Childrens Press, 1991.

Miller, Alan. *Growing Power: Bioenergy for Development and Industry.* Washington, DC: World Resources Institute, 1986.

Pack, Janet. *Fueling the Future.* Saving Planet Earth series. Chicago: Childrens Press, 1992.

Rickard, Graham. *Bioenergy.* Alternative Energy series. Milwaukee, WI: Gareth Stevens, 1991.

Jean F. Blashfield

Bioethics see **Environmental ethics**

Biofeedback

Biofeedback is a means by which a person can mentally influence a natural physiologic process that may or may not be consciously regulated under normal conditions. This could include lowering blood pressure, regulating the heart rate, or influencing the skin temperature.

Deliberate control of bodily functions is not a new accomplishment. Many historical accounts exist of Indian yogis who controlled their body temperature with such precision that they could make the palm of one hand warmer or cooler on one side than the other. Biofeedback also played a role in the performances of the famous escape artist Harry Houdini who consciously suppressed his gag reflex to suspend a key in his throat so as to regurgitate it later to unlock his elaborate bindings.

Development of modern biofeedback methods

As a form of therapy, biofeedback is a relatively recent development that has begun to gain acceptance among some members of the medical community. Research in the topic began in the 1960s, and by the end of the decade a number of research projects had demonstrated its effectiveness. While some early studies indicated that physiologic processes not usually under conscious control could not be influenced by biofeedback, subsequent research soon disproved this assumption.

During the 1970s biofeedback developed a devout following and as a result an entire industry was created for the manufacture and marketing of the instruments used to measure biofeedback alterations and alpha rhythms in the brain. Alpha rhythms are electrical waves formed by the brain at the rate of 8–13 cycles per second. Because they are associated with the state of meditation attained by practitioners of yoga or transcendental meditation, they were accepted as the optimal state of biofeedback. Instruments to detect and measure alpha rhythms soon became readily available.

Biofeedback training

Biofeedback training must begin with an auditory or visual signal to measure the activity of the organ being influenced and to indicate any changes that take place in it. Heart rate, for example, can be signaled by a beeping sound that occurs with each heartbeat. A subject can detect any increase or decrease in the number of heartbeats per minute by the increasing or decreasing rapidity of the beeping. A visual signal also could be devised—for example, spikes in a horizontal line that appear closer together or farther apart as the heartbeat changes. The ultimate objective is to develop a such a high level of consciousness that such changes can be determined without the signal device.

Biofeedback can be separated into three processes or steps. The first involves detecting the biological process being measured and amplifying it so as to be seen or heard. The second step is to convert the electrical signal into an easily understood form from which its alterations can be read. The third step is to make this signal available to the subject as soon as possible after the event being measured has occurred.

Uses of biofeedback

Clinical applications for biofeedback include the control of blood pressure for patients with hypertension, relief or control of migraine headaches, easing of muscle cramps, and relief of insomnia.

Biofeedback training begins with the basic control of heart rate or other readily accessible and controllable functions. The subject is provided an auditory or visual signal at first and is gradually weaned from it as he becomes more skillful at the practice. Once the basic skill has been learned he or she can then shift concentration to a specific problem. Ideally, the patient will continue to practice biofeedback techniques and so increase their effectiveness over time.

Biofeedback has gained acceptance in the United States as its clinical use has increased. Most major cities have a biofeedback association, and practitioners can be certified by a national certification institute. Certification standards are rigorous to assure that the practitioner has a thorough understanding of physiology and psychology to better apply the methodology.

See also Alternative medicine.

Further Reading:

Burton Goldberg Group. *Alternative Medicine: The Definitive Guide.* Puyallup, WA: Future Medicine Publishing, 1993.

Fugh–Berman, A. "The Case for 'Natural' Medicine." *The Nation* 257 (6–13 September 1993): 240–244.

Morrow, J. and Wolff, R. "Wired for Wonders." *Readers Digest* 140 (May 1992): 105–108.

Larry Blaser

Biological community

A biological (or ecological) community consists of the populations of different species that occur together in the same place and time. Communities vary over space and time, depending on environmental conditions, history of disturbance, and the species locally available to colonize available habitat. These factors all influence the species composition of communities, as well as the relative abundance and productivity of particular species. Community ecology is the study of spatial and temporal patterns and dynamics of assemblages of species, and the biological and physical factors that influence these.

Properties of communities

Ecologists refer to community structure in terms of species composition and the relative abundance of species, while community functions refer to the diverse interactions that can occur amongst individuals and species.

Ecological communities have collective properties related to the characteristics of their individual organisms and species. Examples of such composite properties are community biomass, density, productivity, and species diversity and richness. However, communities also have emergent properties that are associated with complex interactions of individuals and species. Emergent properties cannot be predicted through separate consideration of the parts.

The structural and functional attributes of communities have analogues in the attributes of individual organisms, which to some degree can be understood through separate studies of cells, tissues, organs, and the whole individual. Within limits, an understanding of a particular, hierarchical level within an organism can be gained from consideration of the others. However, each level also has properties that demand an isolated, focused investigation, and that cannot be otherwise understood.

The designation of ecological communities

It must be emphasized that ecological communities are a notion, that is, a theoretical idea that is broadly understood, but impossible to define precisely. This attribute of communities is partly due to the fact that in nature, communities cannot usually be objectively delineated, because to some degree they intergrade with each other along continuously varying environmental gradients. In this sense, communities are always a perceptual or mathematical construct of humans. Because of the inevitable, human–centered bias that is involved, the delineation of communities is an abstraction of the actual, natural reality of continuous ecological variation over space and time.

This idea can be appreciated by considering a conceptual analysis of forest communities. A forest ecologist may be interested in studying the communities of trees in some large area or landscape. Strictly speaking, a forest community is an assemblage of all of the individual organisms occurring together in some place and time. However, forest ecologists may be especially interested in some particular component of the community, often trees. As such, the forest ecologist may focus on those large plants, which clearly dominate the biomass and productivity of the forest community. Different ecologists, however, might be interested in other components of the larger community, such as the smaller ground vegetation, lichens and mosses living upon the trees, or arthropods, amphibians, birds, or small mammals. Even smaller subcommunities can be designated, for example, the community of microorganisms in the gut of a deer, or in a rotting log on the forest floor. The point being made here is that communities are often functionally defined by ecologists, on the basis of their particular interests and research needs.

Community designations may also be influenced by sampling artifacts and particular mathematical procedures that might be used in an ecological analysis. For example, a forest ecologist might randomly select and sample a large number of individual stands. Each stand is, of course, unique and different from all of the others. Because stands are usually subsampled during data collection (it is too expensive and time consuming to conduct a complete survey of large stands), the data are always an inexact approximation of the true nature of the stands. Usually, the stand data are analyzed mathematically in order to aggregate the stands into groups, on the basis of their similarity of composition and relative abundance of species. However, the nature of these groupings will be influenced by the specific choice of the various, alternative mathematical procedures that are available to ecologists in their research. As a result of both of these factors (that is, subsampling and choice of mathematical analysis), the resulting "communities" that are identified and reported are only an interpretation of the ecological reality.

Large–scale similarities of community structure and function are aggregated by ecologists into broad categories. The largest of these are global in scale, and are known as biomes. For example, the biome known as northern coniferous forest (also called boreal forest, or taiga) occurs in many parts of the world wherever climate, soil, and other environmental factors are appro-

priate to its development. Although the actual species occurring in boreal forest vary among different parts of the world, they are often of the same genus, and are generally of a similar physical form and have a similar ecophysiology. The common genera of conifers of the boreal forest include pines, spruces, firs, and larches. In much of northern North America, for example, white or black spruce (*Picea glauca* and *P. mariana*) are dominant, while in northwestern Europe it might be the closely related Norway spruce (*Picea abies*).

Ecological interactions

The structure and function of ecological communities are greatly influenced by interactions amongst their component individuals and species, through competition, herbivory, predation, parasitism, disease, and social interactions.

Competition is a process of interaction among organisms, occurring whenever the capability of the environment to supply essential resources (such as space, light, nutrients, mating partners, etc.) is less than the potential, biological demand. Because of these constraints, organisms interfere with each other in a quest for resources. Intraspecific competition occurs among individuals of the same species and, because these have virtually identical requirements of environmental resources (because they occupy the same, species–specific niche), this type of competition can be very intense. Interspecific competition occurs among individuals of different species. Interspecific competition may be quite weak and inconsequential, or it may be intense if the species have similar needs for resources. Competition–related interactions are said to be symmetric if they involve organisms of similar size and ability to exploit resources. Competition is asymmetric if there are substantial differences in these abilities, as in the case of stresses exerted by trees of a forest canopy on small plants of the understory.

Herbivory, predation, parasitism, and disease are all trophic interactions, in which individuals of one species exploit individuals of another species. Usually, these exploitative interactions result in a selective harvest of particular species or size classes of organisms from a community. The primary, direct effect of exploitation stress is the injury or removal of individuals, populations, or even entire communities (especially in some cases of harvesting by humans). There may also, however, be secondary consequences of exploitation. For example, the removal of nutrients contained in the biomass of plants may be large enough to cause a reduction in fertility of the site, as often occurs in agriculture. Especially large, indirect effects occur if selectively harvested organisms are disproportionately important in the structure and function of their community.

Disturbance and other environmental stresses

The structure and function of communities are also greatly influenced by natural, disruptive events of disturbance, such as a windstorm or wildfire. Disturbance often results in a great deal of mortality of the component species of a community, along with other ecological damages. After disturbance, there is usually a tendency for the regenerating community to progressively recover towards its original condition. This tendency is referred to as community stability, and the process of post–disturbance recovery is called succession. Primary succession occurs after disturbance that has been so devastating that no organisms survived to regenerate, so that ecological recovery requires re–invasion of the site from elsewhere. Primary succession occurs after the melting of glaciers exposes new land for ecological development, or after a very severe wildfire. Secondary succession follows less severe disturbances, which may disrupt the original community but not kill all individuals of its component species, so that they can contribute to the recovery. Not surprisingly, community development during secondary succession is much more rapid and vigorous than occurs during primary succession.

If a sufficiently long time passes without another event of catastrophic disturbance, then the rate of successional change slows. Eventually, a relatively stable community occurs that is in an approximate equilibrium with environmental conditions. This terminal, end–point of succession is known as the climax community. For example, in regions of the world with a climate suitable to the development of forest, the climax state is an old–growth forest of some sort. Although at the stand or landscape level old–growth communities are rather stable, they should not be considered to be static. The dynamics of old–growth communities are largely associated with local influences, for example the micro–successional changes that occur in conjunction with the death of a single, dominant tree in the forest overstory.

The structure and function of communities are also greatly influenced by environmental stresses associated with human activities. These can include disturbances associated with, for example, commercial harvesting by humans of some component of the community, such as trees, deer, or fish. Other stresses associated with human activities include toxic pollution by pesticides, heavy metals, or gases such as sulfur dioxide and ozone. The dumping of waste heat

Community—In ecology, a community is an assemblage of populations of different species that occur together in the same place and at the same time.

Competition—An interaction between organisms of the same or different species, associated with the need for a mutually required resource that occurs in a supply that is smaller than the potential demand.

Niche—The role that an individual or species plays in its community, including its activities, resource demands, and interactions with other organisms.

Population—In ecology, a population is a group of organisms of the same species, utilizing the same habitat and interbreeding without spatial isolation.

Succession—A process that occurs after disturbance, and that involves the progressive replacement of earlier species and communities with others. In the absence of further disturbance succession culminates in a stable climax community that is determined by climate, soil, and the nature of the participating species.

from power plants is another stressor of ecological communities, as is the disposal of large quantities of nutrients into water or onto land. All of these environmental stressors distort the pre–existing structure and function of the affected community, causing a general degradation of its ecological integrity.

Ecologists have identified some commonly observed responses of communities to an intensification of environmental stress. These effects include the following: (1) increased rates in mortality of some or all species, leading to changes in species composition and relative abundance; (2) reductions of the number of species; (3) increased loss of nutrients and biomass from the community, for example, through leaching deep into the soil or into streamwater, or by erosion; (4) a change in the balance of community respiration and production, so that net production becomes negative and the quantity of biomass declines; and (5) replacements of sensitive individuals or species with tolerant ones, again leading to community change.

Communities that are continuously subject to severe stress also develop some commonly observed characteristics. Such communities are typically: (1) relatively stable over time; (2) simple in terms of species richness and structural complexity; (3) composed of longer–lived species with a small biomass; (4) have few so–called ruderal species with opportunistic life styles; and (5) have relatively small rates of productivity, decomposition, and nutrient cycling.

See also Biome; Ecological integrity; Ecology; Habitat; Stress, ecological.

Further Reading:

Begon, M., Harper, J.L., and Townsend, C.R. *Ecology. Individuals, Populations and Communities. 2nd ed.* London: Blackwell Sci. Pub., 1990.

Freedman, B. *Environmental Ecology. 2nd ed.* San Diego, CA: Academic Press, 1994.

Ricklefs, R.E. *Ecology.* New York: W.H. Freeman and Co., 1990.

Bill Freedman

Biological warfare

Biological warfare is the use of pathogenic (disease–causing) agents as military weapons. One of the earliest recorded uses of biological weapons occurred in the spring of 1346. A Mongol army had laid siege to the Crimean city of Kaffia for three years without success. Trying a new approach, the Monguls gathered a number of their own people who had died of the plague, laid them on their catapults, and hurled them into the walled town. Eventually the plague spread through Kaffia and residents began to flee the city in order to escape from the disease. Historians point out that the successful conquest of the town by the Mongols incidentally may have resulted in the eventual spread of the plague to Constantinople and to the rest of Europe.

Biological weapons are among the most terrible and least commonly used parts of a military arsenal. For centuries most military leaders have been reluctant to let loose the microorganisms that might cause a widespread epidemic that could include friendly and enemy citizens.

Yet stories similar to the Mongol siege can be found throughout military history. During a rebellion among American Indians in the 1760s, Lord Jeffrey Amherst is said to have given blankets that had been taken from a small pox hospital to members of an Ohio tribe. When the disease broke out among the Indians the rebellion came to an end.

More recent examples of biological warfare also exist. During the 1979 invasion of Afghanistan by the Soviet Union, attacking armies were accused of dropping toxins from the air on the Afghans.

Pathogenic agents

The microorganisms generally considered suitable for biological warfare include viruses, bacteria, protozoa, rickettsiae, and fungi. Toxins and poisonous chemicals produced by microorganisms also are considered biological weapons. Toxins have one important advantage over pathogens themselves: they are not alive, more stable, and easier to produce and distribute.

Some of the most likely candidates for biological weapons are summarized below. This list is only suggestive, since a very large number of potential biological agents have been investigated by scientists in many countries.

Anthrax

Anthrax is caused by the bacterium *Bacillus anthracis*. It occurs widely in soil in the form of a virtually indestructible spore. The bacterium enters the body of an animal in one of two ways. It can pass through an opening in a skin, such as a cut, and enters into the bloodstream. Such an infection produces fever, chills, nausea, vomiting, and a general feeling of poor health. The infection is not fatal and an animal soon recovers its health.

The inhalation of anthrax spores is another matter. The spores accumulate in the lungs, release toxins, and causes suffocation. The death rate from this type of anthrax infection approaches 100%. This form of anthrax is thought to be the most useful as a weapon. During the 1930s and 1940s, Japan and Great Britain are known to have constructed and tested biological weapons carrying anthrax spores.

Botulism

Botulism is a disease produced by the bacterium known as *Clostridium botulinum*. It is best known as a form of food poisoning that kills about 100 people worldwide each year. The bacterium develops when food is improperly cooked or canned. The toxin released by the bacterium is regarded as the most powerful nerve poison known to science.

The United States Army has tested the use of bullets covered with *botulinum* and an aerosol containing the toxin. The organism's sensitivity to sunlight hinders its use as a biological weapon.

Brucellosis

Like most potential biological weapons brucellosis occurs naturally among domestic and wild animals. It is spread by one of three varieties of the *Brucella* bacterium. It is not fatal but causes a long–term, debilitating illness characterized by fever, loss of weight, general lassitude, and depression. Brucellosis is a biological weapon that does not kill people but renders them so ill that they are unable to resist an attack effectively. The disease can be treated with tetracycline but until treatment is administered a person is not strong enough to fight any attacker.

Q Fever

Q (for query because its cause was not known at first) fever is an example of a biological agent that is not particularly harmful but highly infectious. It is caused by the rickettsial organism *Coxiella burnetii,* and produces headache, fever, chills, sweats, and lack of appetite. Scientists believe that the condition is often mistaken for the flu.

Like brucellosis, the value of Q fever is not in its toxicity but its ability to be easily spread. No more than a dozen microbes are needed to initiate an infection.

Saxitoxin

From time to time coastal waters in various parts of the world develop a reddish tinge because of one–celled organisms called dinoflagellates. These so–called "red tides" are a warning that seafood from these waters is not safe to eat. The dinoflagellates release a variety of toxins including saxitoxin. These toxins act very quickly in the human body, causing a type of paralysis that may bring death in less than an hour. American military scientists prepared and tested shellfish toxins including saxitoxin for possible use as a biological weapon in the post–World War II years.

Staphylococcus

Many forms of the *Staphylococcus* microorganism exist, some harmless and some quite dangerous. In the latter category are the organisms responsible for some forms of food poisoning and toxic shock syndrome. The form of *Staphylococcus* most often tested as a possible biological weapon is one that causes illness within a matter of hours. A person infected with the disease experiences severe nausea, vomiting, diarrhea, and is essentially incapacitated for two or three days. *Staphylococcus* has a practical advantage: it can be dried and stored for up to a year without losing its toxicity.

Tularemia

Tularemia is a plague–like disease caused by the bacterium *Pasteurella tularensis*. After an incubation period of about a week a person infected with the bacterium begins to develop a fever accompanied by chills and headaches. If the bacterium has been inhaled symptoms also include chest pain and difficulty in breathing. The death rate is relatively low when exposure occurs through the skin but much higher when inhaled. The United States Army considered tularemia as one of the most promising of all biological weapons at one time.

Genetically engineered weapons

In the last 40 years the development of genetic engineering has greatly expanded the possibilities of biological warfare. Genetic engineering is the process by which an organism's fundamental make–up is changed for a purpose that is regarded as desirable. One way in which genetic engineering could be used by military scientists is in the transforming of microorganisms that currently have no effects on human health into new forms that are pathogenic or lethal. The transformed organisms could be responsible for the development of new disorders for which no treatment is available and against which an enemy could not protect itself.

Genetic engineering could also be used to make existing pathogens more useful as weapons. Some potentially useful microorganisms cannot be used now for non-biological reasons, such as their inability to be stored for long periods of time or their sensitivity to heat, light, or other environmental factors.

The use and control of biological weapons

The largely unspoken ban against the use of biological weapons and chemical weapons has been broken on only rare occasions in modern history. According to some reports, German spies attempted to spread the bacteria that cause plague in Russia during 1915–16. But largely, biological warfare was not accorded much attention until the 1920s.

At that point, the newly formed League of Nations decided to take a formal stand on the threat of chemical and biological warfare. In 1925 the League adopted the Geneva Protocol, a treaty prohibiting the development and use of any form of biological weapon. The treaty was ratified by every member of the League with the exception of Japan and the United States. In fact, the United States government did not ratify the Geneva Protocol until 50 years later in April 1975.

Experimentation on biological weapons

It made relatively little difference whether nations ratified the Geneva Protocol or not. Some who signed the treaty began their own research on biological weapons, as did Japan and the United States. When confronted with the discovery of such research nations usually defended their work by claiming that studies of biological weapons were necessary to develop defenses against such weapons.

For many decades, this rationale has been offered by the United States for its very aggressive research program on biological weapons. While promising never to build such weapons for offensive use, the government has explained that research on defensive measures had to be continued. The corollary to such an argument is that biological weapons first must be developed and manufactured before scientists can research defenses against them.

The most serious transgressor of the Geneva Protocol was the Japanese government during the 1930s and 1940s. Evidence now shows that the Japanese tested and used biological weapons in its conquest of China in the 1930s, and that American soldiers captured in World War II were subjected to biological weapons' tests.

The United States has maintained a large and aggressive program of biological weapons research in the decades following World War II. According to authority Jeanne McDermott: "From coast to coast the army sprayed the country with the microorganisms *Serratia*, *Bacillus globigii*, and *Aspergillus fumigatus* ... [and] targeted every ecological niche and demographic profile. ... They put military bases to the biological test as well, dropping simulated germ weapons on forts, schools, air force bases, camps and test stations in [eight states]."

During the years between the end of World War II and 1969, the U.S. army conducted experiments and tests at dozens of American bases. Its most important center of research was Fort Detrick outside of Frederick, Maryland. Some reports claim that several deaths occurred at Fort Detrick as a result of exposure to potential biological weapons. Hundreds of more cases of serious illness may also have occurred.

In 1969, President Richard Nixon announced that the United States was ceasing from further research on biological and chemical weapons and that certain installations engaged in this type of research were being closed down. The Commandant at the Army's Chemical Center and School in Fort McClellan, Alabama, pointed out that Nixon's comments did not mean that the United States was no longer interested in research on biological weapons. "Nothing could be further from the truth," he said as he pointed out that research on defensive responses to biological weapons would continue.

By the early 1970s concerns about the use of biological weapons reached a peak. In 1972, 87 nations—including the United States—signed the Biological Weapons Convention Treaty which banned the development, testing, and storage of such weapons. For a time it appeared that the nations of the world agreed to ban these instruments of war.

By the 1980s the political mood had changed. The election of Ronald Reagan as President of the United States signalled a return to an aggressive view of foreign policy. In 1982, Reagan declared that the world situation justified research on biological and chemical weapons and that the United States would return to a more ambitious program in this area.

See also Bacteria; Botulism; Brucellosis; Chemical warfare; Poisons and toxins; Virus.

KEY TERMS

Epidemic—The spread of a disease that occurs so rapidly that many people have the disease at the same time.

Microorganism—An organism so small that it can be seen only with the aid of a microscope.

Pathogen—Any organism capable of causing a disease.

Plague—A highly contagious disease that spreads rapidly through a population; also, a well–known specific example of that kind of epidemic, a disease caused by the bacterium *Yersinia pestis*.

Toxin—A poisonous substance secreted by an organism, often a microorganism.

Further Reading:

Douglass, Joseph D., Jr., and Neil C. Livingstone. *America the Vulnerable: The Threat of Chemical/Biological Warfare*. Lexington: Lexington Books, 1987.

Harris, Robert, and Jeremy Paxman. *A Higher Form of Killing*. New York: Hill and Wang, 1982.

Hersh, Seymour M. *Chemical and Biological Warfare: America's Hidden Arsenal*. New York: Bobbs–Merrill, 1968.

McCuen, Gary E. *Poison in the Wind: The Spread of Chemical and Biological Weapons*. Hudson: GEM Publications, Inc., 1992.

McDermott, Jeanne. *The Killing Winds: The Menace of Biological Warfare*. New York: Arbor House, 1987.

Pillar, Charles. *Gene Wars: Military Control over the New Genetic Technologies.* New York: Beech Tree Books, 1988.

Taylor, L. B., Jr., and C. L. Taylor. *Chemical and Biological Warfare.* New York: Franklin Watts, 1985.

Biology

Biology is the scientific study of all forms of life, including plants, animals, or microorganisms.

Among the numerous fields in biology are microbiology, the study of microscopic organisms like bacteria; cytology, the study of cells; embryology, the study of development; genetics, the study of heredity; biochemistry, the study of the chemical structures in living things; morphology, the study of the anatomy of plants and animals; taxonomy, the identification, naming, and classification of organisms; and physiology, the study of how organic systems function and respond to stimulation. Biology often interfaces with subjects like psychology. For example, animal behaviorists would need to understand the biological nature of the animal they are studying in order to evaluate the animal's behavior.

Important discoveries in biological science

The history of biology begins with the careful observation of the external aspects of organisms and continues with investigations into the functions and interrelationships of living things.

The ancient Greek philosopher Aristotle is credited with establishing the importance of observation and analysis as the basic approach for scientific investigation. By 200 A.D., studies in biology were centered in the Arab world. Most of the investigations during this period were made in medicine and agriculture. Arab scientists continued this activity throughout the Middle Ages.

When ancient Greek and Roman writings were revived in Europe during the Renaissance, scientific investigations began to accelerate. Leonardo da Vinci and Michelangelo, Italian Renaissance artists, produced detailed anatomical drawings of human beings. At the same time others were dissecting cadavers (dead bodies) and describing internal anatomy. By the seventeenth century, formal experimentation was introduced into the study of biology. William Harvey, an English physician, demonstrated the circulation of the blood and so initiated the biological discipline of physiology.

So much work was being done in biological science during this period that academies of science and

---

KEY TERMS

Genetic engineering—The science of altering the genetic code of an organism.

Germ theory of disease—The belief that disease is caused by germs.

Metabolism—The chemical changes within cells that produces energy for vital organism activity and the assimilation of nutrients.

Microorganisms—Living units that cannot be seen without magnification under a microscope.

Molecular biology—The study of the cellular structure of living units.

Prokaryote—A cell that does not have a distinct nucleus, such as bacteria or alga.

Spontaneous generation—The theory that disease was caused spontaneously, not from germs.

---

scientific journals were formed, the first of which being the Academy of the Lynx in Rome in 1603. In Massachusetts, the Boston Philosophical Society was founded nearly a hundred years before the American Revolution. The first scientific journals were established in 1665 with the *Journal des Savants* (France) and in Great Britain with the *Philosophical Transactions of the Royal Society.*

The invention of the light microscope opened the way for biologists to investigate living organisms at the cellular level, and ultimately at the molecular level. The first drawings of magnified life were made by Francesco Stelluti, an Italian who published drawings of a honeybee at a ten–times magnification in 1625.

During the eighteenth century, Carl Linnaeus proposed a system for naming and classifying plants and animals which is still used today. In his book, *Species plantarum*, which was written in 1753, Linnaeus described six thousand plants, each one assigned a binomial name–genus and species. For example, the binomial name for the wolf is *Canis lupus*, and for humans, *Homo sapiens*.

In the nineteenth century, many explorers contributed to biological science by collecting plant and animal specimens from around the world. In 1859, Charles Darwin published *On the Origin of Species*, in which he outlined the theory of evolution by means of natural selection. This was an important discovery; it disproved the idea that organisms generated spontaneously. Later, French chemist Louis Pasteur confirmed

Darwin's findings by the discovery of certain bacteria-causing diseases. Pasteur also developed the first vaccines. By the end of the nineteenth century the germ theory of disease was established by Robert Koch, and by the early twentieth century, chemotherapy was developed. The use of antibiotics began with penicillin in 1928 and steroids were discovered in 1935.

From the nineteenth century until the present, the amount of research and discovery in biology has been voluminous. Two fields of rapid growth in the biological science today are molecular biology and genetic engineering.

See also Biochemistry; Botany; Ecology; Embryology; Evolution; Genetics; Molecular biology; Physiology; Taxonomy.

Further Reading:

Ambrose, E. J. *The Nature and Origin of the Biological World*. New York: John Wiley & Sons, 1982.

Carson, Rachel. *Under the Sea Wind*. New York: Dutton, 1991.

Davis, P. William. *The World of Biology*. Philadelphia: Saunders, 1990.

Edwards, Gabrielle I. *Biology the Easy Way*, 2nd ed. New York: Barron's, 1990.

Jackson, Francis. *Life in the Universe*. New York: Norton, 1989.

Smith, John M. *The Problems of Biology*. New York: Oxford University Press, 1986.

Taylor, Martha R. *Campbell's Biology*, 2nd ed. Redwood City, California: The Benjamin/Cummings Publishing Company, 1990.

Vita Richman

Bioluminescence

Bioluminescence is the production of light by living organisms. Some single celled organisms (bacteria and protista) as well as many multicellular animals and fungi demonstrate bioluminescence.

Bioluminescence in nature

Marine environments support a number of bioluminescence organisms including species of bacteria, dinoflagenates, jellyfish, coral, shrimp, and fish. On any given night one can see the luminescent sparkle produced by the single-celled dinoflagellates when water is disturbed by a ship's bow or a swimmer's motions. Many multicellular marine organisms have specialized light emitting organs that project light in a

Fireflies have a bioluminescent organ in their abdomen that they use to attract mates. Enzymes within the organ react with oxygen to produce light. The insect controls the flashes by regulating the flow of oxygen.

particular direction or convey a unique shape to the light. The anglerfish has a light–emitting organ that projects from its head which serves as a bait to attract smaller prey fish. The light emitted from this organ in the anglerfish is actually produced by bacteria, living in a symbiotic relationship in which both the fish and bacteria profit from their shared existence.

Bioluminescent organisms in the terrestrial environment include species of fungi and insects. The most familiar of these is the firefly, which can often been seen glowing during the warm summer months. In some instances organisms use bioluminescence to communicate, such as in fireflies, which use light to attract members of the opposite sex. Certain reef fish use light produced from organs under their eyes to illuminate the interior of crevices and caves. This not only helps the fish to navigate but also allows it to locate prey. Organisms that are unpalatable or dangerous, such as jellyfish, use bioluminescence as a signal to warn off attacks by predators.

Biochemical mechanism

Light is produced by most bioluminescent organisms when a chemical called luciferin reacts with oxygen to produce light and oxyluciferin. The reaction between luciferin and oxygen is catalyzed by the enzyme luciferase. Luciferases, like luciferins, usually have different chemical structures in different organisms.

In addition to luciferin, oxygen, and luciferase other molecules (called cofactors) must be present for the bioluminescent reaction to proceed. Cofactors are molecules required by an enzyme (in this case luciferase) to perform its catalytic function. Common cofactors required for bioluminescent reactions are calcium and ATP, a molecule used to store and release energy that is found in all organisms.

The terms luciferin and luciferase were first introduced in 1885. The French scientist Raphael Dubois obtained two different extracts from bioluminescent clams and beetles. When Dubois mixed these extracts they produced light. He also found that if one of these extracts was first heated no light would be produced upon mixing. Heating the other extract had no effect on the reaction, so Dubois concluded that there are at least two components to the reaction. Dubois hypothesized that the heat resistant chemical undergoes a chemical change during the reaction, and called this compound luciferin. The heat sensitive chemical, Dubois concluded, was an enzyme which he called luciferase.

Bioluminescence as a research tool

The two basic components needed to produce a bioluminescent reaction, luciferin and luciferase, can be isolated from the organisms that produce them. When they are mixed in the presence of oxygen and the appropriate cofactors these components will produce light with an intensity dependent on the quantity of luciferin and luciferase added as well as the oxygen and cofactor concentrations.

Scientists have used isolated luciferin and luciferase to determine the concentrations of important biological molecules such as ATP and Calcium. After adding a known amount of luciferin and luciferase to a blood or tissue sample, the cofactor concentrations may be determined from the intensity of the light emitted. Scientists have also found numerous other uses for the bioluminescent reaction such as using it to quantify specific molecules which do not directly participate in the bioluminescence reaction. To do this, scientists have attached luciferase to antibodies, which are molecules produced by the immune system that bind to specific molecules called antigens. The antibody–luciferase complex is added to a sample where it binds to the molecule which is to be quantified. Following washing to remove unbound antibodies, the molecule of interest can be quantified indirectly by adding luciferin and measuring the light emitted. Methods used to quantify particular compounds in biological samples such as the ones described here are called assays.

Further Reading:

Herring, Peter, ed. *Bioluminescence in Action.* New York: Academic Press, 1978.
Herring, Peter, Anthony Campbell, Michael Whitfield, and Linda Maddock, eds. *Light and Life in the Sea.* Cambridge, England: Cambridge University Press, 1990.

KEY TERMS

Antibodies—Molecules produced by the immune system that bind specific molecules called antigens.

Antigen—Any molecule that is bound by an antibody.

Assay—Method used to quantify a biological compound.

ATP—Adenosine triphosphate, a molecule used to store or release energy that is found in all living organisms.

Cofactor—Molecule required by an enzyme to perform its catalytic function.

Dinoflagellate—Chloroplast containing protists that primarily inhabit marine environments.

Enzyme—A protein that speeds up or catalyzes a specific reaction.

Extract—Solution from a biological material that contains an active compound.

Luciferase—An enzyme that catalyzes the reaction between oxygen and luciferin.

Luciferin—Complex carbon molecules that produce light when oxidized.

Oxidation—The process where a molecule loses one or more electrons.

Oxyluciferin—An oxidized luciferin molecule which is the product of a bioluminescent reaction.

Protista—Kingdom composed of single-celled organisms whose DNA is enclosed by a nucleus.

Purves, William, Gordon Orians, and H. Heller. *Life: The Science of Biology.* 3rd ed. Sunderland, Massachusetts: Sinaur Associates, Inc., 1992.
Smith, D. C., and A. E. Douglas. *The Biology of Symbiosis.* Baltimore: Edward Arnold, 1987.

Steven MacKenzie

Biomagnification

Biomagnification (or bioaccumulation) refers to the ability of living organisms to accumulate certain chemicals to a concentration larger than that occurring in their inorganic, non–living environment, or in the case of animals, in the food that they eat. Of course,

DDT in fish
eating birds 25 ppm

Aquatic
contamination

DDT in water
0.000003 ppm
or 0.003 ppb

DDT in
zooplankton 0.04 ppm

DDT in
large fish 2 ppm

DDT in small fish
(minnows) 0.5 ppm

Biomagnification accounts for higher toxin levels in animals the higher they are on the food chain.

organisms accumulate any chemical needed for their nutrition. In environmental science, however, the major focus of biomagnification is the accumulation of certain non–essential chemicals, especially certain chlorinated hydrocarbons that are persistent in the environment, insoluble in water, but highly soluble in fats. Because almost all fats within ecosystems occur in the living bodies of organisms, chlorinated hydrocarbons such as DDT and PCBs tend to selectively accumulate in organisms. This can lead to ecotoxico-

logical problems, especially for top predators at the summit of ecological food webs.

Biomagnification and food–web accumulation

Organisms are exposed to a myriad of chemicals in their environment. Some of these chemicals occur in trace concentrations in the environment, and yet they may be selectively accumulated by organisms to much larger concentrations that can cause toxicity. This tendency is referred to as biomagnification, or bioaccumulation.

Some of the biomagnified chemicals are elements such as selenium, mercury, or nickel, or organic compounds of these such as methylmercury. Diverse others are in the class of chemicals known as chlorinated hydrocarbons (or organochlorines). These are extremely insoluble in water, but are freely soluble in organic solvents, including animal fats and plant oils (these are collectively known as lipids). Many of the chlorinated hydrocarbons are also very persistent in the environment, because they are not easily broken down to simpler chemicals through the metabolism of microorganisms, or by ultraviolet radiation or other inorganic processes. Common examples of bioaccumulating chlorinated hydrocarbons are the insecticides DDT and dieldrin, and a class of industrial chemicals known as PCBs.

Food–web accumulation is a special case of biomagnification, in which certain chemicals occur in their largest ecological concentration in predators at the top of the food web. An ecological food web is a complex of species that are linked through their trophic interactions, that is, their feeding relationships. In terms of energy flow, food webs are supported by inputs of solar energy, which is fixed by green plants through photosynthesis. Some of this fixed energy is used by the plants in their own respiration, and the rest, as plant biomass, is available to be passed along to animals, which are incapable of metabolizing any other type of energy. Within the food web, animals that eat plants are known as herbivores. These are eaten by first–level carnivores, which in turn may be eaten by higher–level carnivores. Top predators occur at the summit of the food web. In general, food webs have a pyramidal structure, with plant productivity being much greater than that of herbivores, and these being more productive than their predators. Top predators are usually quite uncommon. Within food webs, biomagnifying chemicals such as DDT, dieldrin, and PCBs have their largest concentrations, and cause their greatest damages in top predators.

Biomagnification of some inorganic chemicals

All of the naturally occurring elements occur in the environment in at least trace concentrations. This ubiquitous contamination is always be detectable, as long as the analytical chemistry methodology has detection limits that are small enough. About 25 of the elements are required by plants and/or animals, including the micronutrients copper, iron, molybdenum, zinc, and rarely, aluminum, nickel, and selenium. However, under certain ecological conditions these micronutrients can biomagnify to very large concentrations, and even cause toxicity to organisms.

One such case refers to serpentine soil and the vegetation that grows in it. Serpentine minerals contain relatively large concentrations of nickel, cobalt, chromium, and iron, and soils derived from this mineral can be toxic to plants. However, some plants that grown on serpentine soils are physiologically tolerant of these metals, and can bioaccumulate them to very large concentrations. For example, the normal concentration of nickel in plants is about 1–5 ppm (parts per million, a concentration equivalent to mg/kg). However, on sites with serpentine soils much larger concentrations of nickel occur in plant foliage and other tissues. Nickel concentrations as large as 16% occur in tissues of a plant in the mustard family, *Streptanthus polygaloides,* in California, and 11–25% nickel occurs in the blue–colored latex of *Sebertia acuminata* on the island of New Caledonia in the Pacific Ocean. It is common for plants growing on serpentine soils to have nickel concentrations of thousands of parts per million, which is usually considerably larger than the concentration in soil.

Another case of biomagnification occurs on some sites in semiarid regions in which the soil is contaminated by selenium, which may then be hyperaccumulated (i.e., extremely accumulated) by specialized species of plants. These plants are poisonous to grazing livestock and other large animals, causing a toxic reaction called "blind staggers." The most important selenium–accumulating plants in North America are milk vetches in the genus *Astragalus,* in the legume family. There are 500 species of *Astragalus* in North America, of which 25 are accumulators of selenium. The foliage of these plants can contain thousands of ppm of selenium, to a maximum of about 15–thousand ppm, much larger than the concentration in soil. Sometimes, accumulator and non–accumulator *Astragalus* species grow together, as in the case of a place in Nebraska with 5 ppm selenium in soil, and 5560 ppm in *Astragalus bisulcatus,* but only 25 ppm in *A. missouriensis.*

Mercury can also be biomagnified from trace concentrations in the environment. In this case, trace concentrations of mercury in water can result in large contaminations of fish and other predators. For example, fish species known to bioaccumulate mercury in off-shore waters of North America include Atlantic swordfish, Pacific blue marlin, tunas, and halibut, among others. These fish can accumulate mercury from trace concentrations in seawater (less than 0.1 ppb, equivalent to 0.0001 ppm or 0.1 μg/L) to concentrations in flesh that commonly exceed 0.5 ppm fresh weight (f.w.), the maximum acceptable concentration in fish for human consumption. The contamination of oceanic fish by mercury is probably natural, and is not only a modern phenomenon. Studies have found no difference in mercury contaminations of modern tuna and museum specimens collected between before 1909, or concentrations in feathers of pre–1930 and post–1980 seabirds collected from islands in the northeast Atlantic Ocean. In this phenomenon of mercury biomagnification, there is a tendency for larger, older fish to have relatively large concentrations. In a study Atlantic swordfish, for example, the average mercury concentration of animals smaller than 23 kg was 0.55 ppm, compared with 0.86 ppm for those 23 to 45 kg in weight, and 1.1 ppm for those heavier than 45 kg. Large concentrations of mercury also occur in fish–eating marine mammals and birds that are predators at or near the top of the marine food web.

Mercury biomagnification has also been observed in many freshwater ecosystems, even in some relatively remote lakes where this may be a natural occurrence. Mercury concentrations exceeding 0.5 ppm are often measured in fish from lakes and rivers in many parts of the United States and Canada. For example, about three–quarters of 1500 lakes monitored in Ontario had at least some fish that exceeded 0.5 ppm f.w. in flesh. In one remote lake in northern Manitoba, the mercury concentration averaged 2 ppm f.w. in northern pike, and one individual had 5 ppm. As in the marine case, fresh–water fish that are top predators have the largest concentrations of mercury, and older and larger individuals are the most contaminated. Because of the common occurrence of large mercury concentrations in fish in certain regions, some governments have developed fish–consumption advisories and/or restrictions. In Sweden about 250 lakes have been "blacklisted" in terms of fish consumption, and 9400 other lakes are candidates for that status. In Ontario about 1200 lakes have restrictions on fish consumption. Some fish–eating wildlife, such as loons and mink, may also be affected by mercury in their food.

Biomagnificaiton of some chlorinated hydrocarbons

Chlorinated hydrocarbons such as the insecticides DDT, DDD, dieldrin, and methoxychlor, the dielectric fluids known as PCBs, and the chlorinated dioxin, TCDD have a very sparse solubility in water. As a result, these chemicals cannot be "diluted" into this ubiquitous solvent, which is so abundant on the surface of the Earth and in organisms. Therefore, even situations considered to be highly contaminated by chlorinated hydrocarbons have very small concentrations of these chemicals in water, typically less than 1 ppb, and in the case of the dioxin TCDD smaller than 1 ppt (i.e., 0.001 ppb). However, chlorinated hydrocarbons are highly soluble in lipids. Because most lipids within ecosystems occur in biological tissues, the chlorinated hydrocarbons have a strong affinity for living organisms, and they tend to biomagnify by many orders of magnitude from vanishingly small aqueous concentrations. Furthermore, because chlorinated hydrocarbons are persistent in the environment, they accumulate progressively as organisms grow older, and they food–web accumulate into especially large concentrations in top predators, as described previously. In some cases, older individuals of top–predator animals such as raptorial birds and fish–eating marine mammals have been found to have thousands of ppm of DDT and PCBs in their fatty tissues. The toxicity caused to these animals by their accumulated exposures to DDT, PCBs, and other chlorinated hydrocarbons is a well–recognized environmental problem.

The biomagnification and food–web accumulation characteristics of DDT are especially well known. Typically, DDT has extremely small concentrations in air and water, and to lesser degree in soil. However, concentrations are much larger in organisms, especially in animals at or near the top of their food web, such as humans and predatory birds. The food–web biomagnification of DDT can be illustrated by the case of Lake Kariba, Zimbabwe. Although banned in most industrialized countries since the early 1970s, DDT is still used in many tropical countries for agriculture purposes and to control insect vectors of human diseases. The use of DDT in agriculture was banned in Zimbabwe in 1982, but DDT continues to be used to control mosquitoes and tsetse fly, insects that spread malaria and diseases of livestock. The concentration of DDT in the water of Lake Kariba was less than 0.002 ppb, but concentrations in sediment were 0.4 ppm (because sediment contains a relatively large concentration of organic matter, it contains much more DDT than the overlying water). Planktonic algae contained 2.5 ppm. A filter–feeding mussel had 10 ppm (values for animal tissues are for DDT in fat), while two species of plant–eating fish contained 2 ppm, and a bottom–feeding fish contained 6 ppm. A predatory fish and a fish–eating bird, the great cormorant, contained 5–10 ppm. The Nile crocodile is the top predator in Lake Kariba (other than humans), and it had 34 ppm. Therefore, the data for Lake Kariba illustrates a substantial biomagnification of DDT from

KEY TERMS

Biomagnification—Tendency of organisms to accumulate certain chemicals to a concentration larger than that occurring in their inorganic, non–living environment, such as soil or water, or in the sake of animals, larger than in their food.

Ecotoxicology—Direct and indirect effects of toxic chemicals on ecosystem structure and function. Indirect ecotoxicological effects of toxic substances occur, for example, through changes in the physical structure or species composition of habitats, or in the abundance of food. These can affect species, even if they are not directly affected by the toxic chemical.

Food–Web Accumulation—Tendency of certain chemicals to occur in their largest concentration in predators at the top of the ecological food web. As such, chemicals such as DDT, PCBs, and mercury in the aquatic environment have their largest concentrations in predators, in comparison with the non–living environment, or with plants and herbivores.

Hyperaccumulation—A syndrome in which a chemical is bioaccumulated to an extraordinary degree.

water, and to a lesser degree from sediment, as well as a marked food–web accumulation from herbivores to top carnivores.

The widespread occurrence of food–web biomagnification of DDT and other chlorinated hydrocarbons caused chronic, ecotoxicological damages to birds and mammals of many species, even in habitats remote from sprayed sites. In some species, effects on predatory birds were severe enough to cause large declines in abundance beginning in the early 1950s, and resulting in local or regional losses of populations. Prominent examples of North American birds that suffered population decreases because of exposure to chlorinated hydrocarbons include bald eagle, golden eagle, peregrine falcon, osprey, brown pelican, and double–crested cormorant, among others. However, since the banning of the use of DDT in North America in the early 1970s, these birds have increased in abundance. In the case of the peregrine falcon, this increase was enhanced by a captive–breeding and release program over much of its former range in eastern North America.

See also Bioaccumulation; Food chain/web.

Further Reading:

Freedman, B. 1994. *Environmental Ecology, 2nd ed.* Academic Press, San Diego.

Moriarty, F. 1988. *Ecotoxicology, 2nd ed.* Academic Press, London.

Smith, R.P. 1992. *A Primer of Environmental Toxicology.* Lea & Febiger, Philadelphia, PA.

Bill Freedman

Biome

A biome is a major, geographically extensive ecosystem, structurally characterized by its dominant life forms. Terrestrial biomes are usually distinguished on the basis of the major components of their mature or climax vegetation, while aquatic biomes, especially marine ones, are often characterized by their dominant animals.

Biomes can occur in widely divergent places as long as the environmental conditions are appropriate for their development. Often, different species having similar, convergent growth forms will dominate at different places within the same biome. For example, the boreal coniferous forest occurs in suitable environments of northern North America and Eurasia. In northeastern North America this biome is dominated by stands of black spruce, while in the northwest white spruce is dominant. Norway spruce is most important in this biome in northwestern Europe, while in parts of Siberia species of pine and larch are dominant. Because biomes are described according to structural characteristics of their dominant organisms (in this example, coniferous trees growing under a particular climatic regime) all of these different forest types are convergent ecosystems within the same biome, the boreal coniferous forest.

Major biomes and their characteristics

Most biomes are delineated on the basis of their naturally occurring communities of plants, animals, and microorganisms. Exceptions are the so–called anthropogenic biomes, which are strongly influenced by humans and their activities, as is the case of cities and agroecosystems. However, it should be remembered that to some degree, all of Earth's biomes have been influenced by human activities. All organisms, for example, contain trace contaminations of certain organochlorine chemicals of human manufacture, such

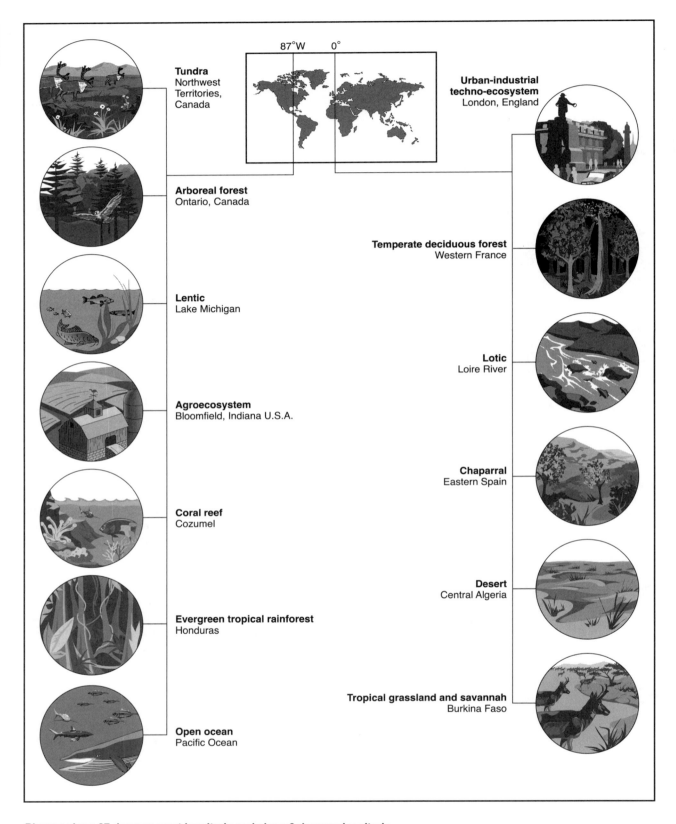

Tundra
Northwest Territories, Canada

Arboreal forest
Ontario, Canada

Lentic
Lake Michigan

Agroecosystem
Bloomfield, Indiana U.S.A.

Coral reef
Cozumel

Evergreen tropical rainforest
Honduras

Open ocean
Pacific Ocean

87°W   0°

Urban-industrial techno-ecosystem
London, England

Temperate deciduous forest
Western France

Lotic
Loire River

Chaparral
Eastern Spain

Desert
Central Algeria

Tropical grassland and savannah
Burkina Faso

Biomes along 87 degrees west longitude and along 0 degrees longitude.

organochlorine chemicals of human manufacture, such as DDT and PCBs.

Ecologists have used a number of systems to divide the biosphere into major biomes. A classification of global biomes, modified from one proposed by E.P. Odum, is described below:

Terrestrial biomes

Tundra

Tundra is a treeless biome occurring in a cold climate with short growing seasons. Alpine tundra occurs at high altitude on mountains, while arctic tundra occurs at high latitude. Most tundras have very small inputs of water as precipitation, but their soil may nevertheless be moist or wet because there is little evaporation, and deep drainage may be prevented by frozen soil. The coldest, most northern, high–arctic tundras are very unproductive and dominated by long–lived but short–statured plants, typically less than 1.97–3.94 in (5–10 cm) tall. Low–arctic tundras are dominated by shrubs as tall as 3.28 ft (1 m), while wet sites develop relatively productive meadows of sedge, cottongrass, and grass. In North America, arctic tundras can support small densities of mammalian herbivores such as caribou and muskox (although during migration these animals can occur in locally large densities), and even smaller numbers of their predators, such as wolves.

Boreal coniferous forest

The boreal coniferous forest, or taiga, is an extensive northern biome occurring in moist climates with cold winters. The boreal forest is dominated by coniferous trees, especially species of fir, larch, pine, and spruce. Some broad–leaved, angiosperm trees are also important in the boreal forest, especially species of aspen, birch, poplar, and willow. Usually, particular stands of boreal forest are dominated by only one or several species of trees. Most regions of boreal forest are subject to periodic events of catastrophic disturbance, most commonly caused by wildfire, and sometimes by insects, such as spruce budworm, that kill trees through intensive defoliation. Montane forests, also dominated by conifers and similar in structure to the boreal forest, can occur at sub–alpine altitudes on mountains in southerly latitudes.

Temperate deciduous forest

Forests dominated by species–rich mixtures of broad–leaved trees occur in relatively moist, temperate climates. Because these forests occur in places where the winters can be cold, the foliage of most species is seasonally deciduous, meaning that all leaves are shed each autumn and re–grown in the springtime. Common trees of this forest biome in North America are species of ash, basswood, birch, cherry, chestnut, dogwood, elm, hickory, magnolia, maple, oak, tulip–tree, and walnut, among others. These various tree species segregate into intergrading communities on the basis of site variations of soil moisture, fertility, and air temperature.

Temperate rainforest

Temperate rainforests develop under climatic regimes characterized by mild winters and an abundance of precipitation. Because these systems are too moist to support regular, catastrophic wildfires, they often develop into old–growth forests, dominated by coniferous trees of mixed age and species composition. Individual trees can be extremely large, and in extreme cases can be more than one thousand years old. Common trees of this biome are species of Douglas–fir, hemlock, cedar, redwood, spruce, and yellow cypress. In North America, temperate rainforests are best developed on the humid west coast.

Temperate grassland

These grasslands occur under temperate climatic regimes that are intermediate to those that support forest and desert. In the temperate zones grasslands typically occur where rainfall is 9.9–24 in (25–60 cm) per year. Grasslands in North America are called prairie (they are often called steppe in Eurasia), and this biome occupies vast regions in the interior. The prairie is often divided into three types according to height of the dominant vegetation – tallgrass, mixedgrass, and shortgrass. The once extensive tallgrass prairie is dominated by various species of grasses and herbaceous broadleaved plants such as sunflowers and blazing stars, some as tall as 9.8–13.1 ft (3–4 m). Fire was an important natural factor that prevented much of the tallgrass prairie from developing into an open forest. The tallgrass prairie is now an endangered natural ecosystem, because it has been almost entirely converted to agriculture. The mixedgrass prairie occurs where rainfall is less, and it supports shorter species of grasses and other herbaceous plants. The shortgrass prairie has even less precipitation, and is subject to unpredictable years of severe drought.

Tropical grassland and savannah

Tropical grasslands can occur in regions with as much as 47.2 in (120 cm) of rainfall per year, but under highly seasonal conditions with a pronounced dry season. Savannahs are dominated by grasses and other herbaceous plants, but they also have scattered shrub and tree–sized woody plants, which form a very open canopy. Tropical grasslands and savannahs can support a great seasonal abundance of large, migratory mammals, as well as substantial populations of resident animals. This is especially true of Africa, where this biome supports a diverse assemblage of large mammals, including gazelles and other antelopes, rhinos, elephant, hippopotamus, and buffalo, and various predators of these, such as lion, cheetah, wild dog, and hyena.

Chaparral

Chaparral is a temperate biome that develops in environments with seasonally extreme moisture gradients, characterized by a so–called Mediterranean climate with winter rains and summer drought. Chaparral is typically characterized by dwarf forest and shrubs and interspersed herbaceous vegetation, and is highly prone to events of catastrophic wildfire. In North America, chaparral is best developed in parts of the southwest, especially coastal southern California.

Desert

Desert is a temperate or tropical biome, commonly occurring in the centers of continents, and in the rain shadows of mountains. The distribution of this biome is determined by the availability of water, generally occurring where there is less than 9.9 in (25 cm) of precipitation per year. Not surprisingly, the productivity of desert ecosystems is strongly influenced by the availability of water. The driest deserts support almost no plant productivity, while less–dry situations may support communities of herbaceous, succulent, and annual plants, and somewhat moister places will allow a shrub–dominated ecosystem to develop.

Semi–evergreen tropical forest

This type of tropical forest develops when there is a seasonality of water availability, due to the occurrence of pronounced wet and drier seasons during the year. Because of this seasonality, most of the trees and shrubs of this biome are seasonally deciduous, meaning that they shed their foliage in anticipation of the drier season. This biome supports a great richness of species of plants and animals, though somewhat less than in tropical rainforests.

Evergreen tropical rainforest

This biome occurs under tropical climates with abundant precipitation and no seasonal drought. Because wildfire and other types of catastrophic disturbance are uncommon in this sort of climate regime, tropical rainforests usually develop into old–growth

forests. As such, they contain a diverse size range of trees, a great richness of species of trees and other plants, as well as an extraordinary diversity of animals and microorganisms. Many ecologists consider this biome to represent the epitome of ecosystem development on land, because of the enormous variety of species that are supported under relatively benign climatic conditions in old–growth tropical rainforests.

Freshwater biomes

Lentic ecosystems such as lakes and ponds occur in basins containing standing water. Depending on the rates of input and output of water, the flushing time of these ecosystems can range from days, in the case of small pools, to centuries, in the case of the largest lakes. The biological character of lentic ecosystems is strongly influenced by water chemistry, especially nutrient concentration and water transparency. Waters with a large nutrient supply are highly productive, or eutrophic, while infertile waters are unproductive, or oligotrophic. Commonly, shallow waterbodies are much more productive than deeper waterbodies of the same surface area. However, plant productivity is also influenced by the penetrance of light into the water column. This factor is restricted in waters with large concentrations of turbidity associated with silt, or with a brown color caused by dissolved organic matter. In such cases primary productivity is smaller than might be expected on the basis of nutrient supply. The ecosystems of lentic waters are usually highly zonal in two dimensions. Horizontal zonation is associated with variations of water depth, usually related to slope and length of the shoreline. Vertical zonation of deeper waters is determined by light availability, water temperature, and nutrient and oxygen concentrations. There are also distinct, benthic ecosystems in the sediment of lentic ecosystems.

Lotic

The character of this running–water biome is determined by physical factors, especially the quantity, velocity, and seasonal variations of water flow. These hydrologic characteristics influence other important characteristics of lotic ecosystems. For example, the bottom type tends to be muddy in places with calm water flows where silt is deposited, and rocky in more vigorous places where fine particles are selectively eroded from the bottom. Similarly, turbidity is great during high water flows, and this interferes with the penetration of light, and restricts plant productivity. Although they sustain some primary productivity of aquatic plants, the common lotic ecosystems such as rivers, streams, and brooks are not usually self–supporting in terms of fixed energy. These ecosystems typically rely on inputs of organic matter from their surrounding, terrestrial watershed or from upstream lakes to support much of their productivity of aquatic invertebrates and fish.

Wetlands

Freshwater wetlands (or mires) occur in shallow waters, usually having pronounced seasonal variations of water depth, sometimes including dry periods during which water does not occur at the surface. The four major wetland types are: marsh, swamp forest, bog, and fen. Marshes are the most productive wetlands, and are typically dominated by relatively tall, emergent species of angiosperm plants such as reed, cat–tail, and bulrush, and by floating–leaved plants such as water lily and lotus. Swamps are forested wetlands, seasonally or permanently flooded, and in North America dominated by tree–sized plants such as bald cypress or silver maple. Bogs are acidic, unproductive wetlands that develop in relatively cool but wet climates. Bogs depend on atmospheric inputs for their supply of nutrients, and are typically dominated by species of sphagnum moss. Fens also develop in cool and wet climates, but they have a better nutrient supply than bogs, and are consequently less acidic and more productive.

Marine biomes

Open ocean

The character of the open–water, or pelagic oceanic biome is determined by physical and chemical environmental factors, particularly waves, tides, currents, salinity, temperature, light intensity, and nutrient concentration. Primary productivity of this biome is small, and comparable to some of the least productive terrestrial biomes, such as deserts. Primary production in the open ocean is carried out by phytoplankton of diverse species, ranging in size from extremely small photosynthetic bacteria, to larger but microscopic unicellular and colonial algae. The phytoplankton are grazed by small crustaceans known as zooplankton, and these are eaten in turn by small fish. At the top of the pelagic food web are very large predators such as bluefin tuna, sharks, squid, and whales. The deep benthic ecosystems of this biome are supported by a sparse rain of dead biomass from its surface waters. The benthic ecosystems are not well known, but they appear to be extremely stable, rich in species, and low in productivity.

Continental shelf waters

Nearshore waters of the oceans are relatively shallow, because they overlie continental shelves. Compared with the open ocean, waters over continental shelves are relatively warm, and are well supplied with nutrients. The nutrients originate with inputs from rivers, and from occasional movements of deeper, more fertile waters to the surface, stirred from the bottom by turbulence caused by storms. Mostly as a result of the nutrient inputs, the phytoplankton of these waters are relatively productive, and they support a larger biomass of animals than occurs in the open ocean. Some of the world's most important pelagic and benthic fisheries are supported by the continental shelf biome, for example, those in the North Sea and Barents Sea of western Europe, the Grand Banks and other shallow waters of northeastern North America, the Gulf of Mexico, and inshore waters of much of western North America.

Upwelling regions

In certain places or regions, oceanographic conditions favor upwellings to the surface of relatively deep, nutrient rich waters. Because of the enhanced nutrient supply, upwelling areas are relatively fertile, and they sustain this highly productive, open–ocean biome. Because of their large foundation of primary production, upwelling regions support sizeable populations of animals, including large species of fish and shark, marine mammals, and seabirds. Some of Earth's most productive fisheries occur in upwelling areas, such as that off the west coast of Peru and elsewhere off South America, and large regions of the Antarctic Ocean.

Estuaries

Estuaries are a complex group of coastal ecosystems that are semi–enclosed, but open to the sea. Estuaries display characteristics of both marine and freshwater biomes, because they typically have substantial inflows of fresh water from the nearby land, along with large fluctuations of salt water resulting from tidal cycles. Examples of estuaries include coastal bays, sounds, river mouths, salt marshes, and tropical mangrove forests. Because their large water–borne inputs of terrestrial nutrients are partially retained by their semi–enclosed water circulation, estuaries are highly productive ecosystems. Estuaries provide important habitat for juvenile stages of many commercially important species of fish, shellfish, and crustaceans, and they are often characterized as "nursery" habitat for these species.

Seashores

The seashore biome is a complex of ecosystems occurring at the interface of terrestrial and oceanic biomes. The local character of the seashore biome is determined by environmental factors, such as the intensity of wave action, the frequency of major events of disturbance, and bottom type. In temperate waters, hard–rock and cobble bottoms often develop ecosystems dominated by large species of macroalgae, broadly known as seaweeds, or kelp. In some cases, so–called kelp "forests" can develop. These are highly productive ecosystems, which maintain large quantities of biomass, mostly of macroalgae. In situations characterized by softer bottoms of sand or mud, ecosystems are typically dominated by benthic invertebrates, especially mollusks, echinoderms, crustaceans, and marine worms.

Coral reefs

Coral reefs are a distinctive marine biome of tropical seas, occurring locally in shallow but relatively infertile areas close to land. The physical structure of coral reefs is provided by the calcium carbonate exoskeletons of dead coral polyps. This structure supports a species–rich population of living coral, crustose algae, invertebrates, and fish. This biome is dominated by corals, a diverse group of coelenterate animals, living in symbiosis with unicellular algae. Because this symbiosis is highly efficient in the acquisition and recycling of nutrients, coral reefs typically sustain a high productivity, even though they occur in nutrient–poor waters.

Human–dominated biomes

Urban–industrial techno–ecosystems

This anthropogenic biome consists of large metropolitan districts, dominated by humans, human dwellings, businesses, factories, and other types of infrastructure. This biome supports many species in addition to humans, but, with few exceptions, these are non–native plants and animals that have been introduced from other places, and that cannot live independently outside of this biome, unless they are returned to their native biome.

Rural techno–ecosystems

This is another anthropogenic biome, occurring outside of intensively built–up areas, and consisting of certain components of the extensive technological infrastructure of civilization. This biome is comprised of transportation corridors (such as highways, railways, transmission corridors, and aqueducts), small towns, and industries involved in the extraction, processing, and manufacturing of products from natural resources. Typically, this biome supports mixtures of introduced species and those native species that are tol-

erant of the disturbances and other stresses associated with human activities.

Agroecosystems

This biome consists of ecosystems that are managed and harvested for human use. The components of this biome are uneven in their anthropogenic influence. The most intensively managed agroecosystems typically involve monocultures of non–native crop species of plants or animals in agriculture, aquaculture, or forestry, and are no favorable to native wildlife. The management objective is to cultivate the economically valuable species under conditions that ensure optimal growth. Less–intensively managed agroecosystems involve mixtures of species, or polycultures, and these may provide habitat for some native wildlife species.

See also Continental shelf; Coral reef; Desert; Ecosystem; Forests; Grasslands; Lake; Ocean; Rain forest; Savanna; Tundra; Wetlands.

Further Reading:

Barbour, M.G. and Billings, W.D. *North American Terrestrial Vegetation.* New York: Cambridge University Press, 1988.

Begon, M., Harper, J.L., and Townsend, C.R. *Ecology. Individuals, Populations and Communities. 2nd ed.* London: Blackwell Sci. Pub., 1990.

Walter, H. *Vegetation of the Earth.* New York: Springer–Verlag, 1977.

Odum, E.P. *Ecology and Our Endangered Life–Support Systems.* Sunderland, MA: Sinauer Assoc. Ltd.1993.

Bill Freedman

Biophysics

Biophysics is the integration and application of the principles of physics to explain and explore the form and function of living things. The most familiar examples of the role of physics in biology are the use of lenses to correct visual defects and the use of x rays to reveal the structure of bones. Principles of physics have been used to explain some of the most basic processes in biology such as osmosis, diffusion of gases, and the function of the lens of the eye in focusing light on the retina.

The understanding that living organisms obey the laws of physics as non–living systems do has had profound effects on the study of biology. The discovery of the relationship between electricity and muscle contraction by Luigi Galvani, an eighteenth–century physician, initiated a field of research that had continued to give information about the nature of muscle contraction and nerve impulses. It has led to the development of such instruments and devises as the electrocardiograph, electroencephalograph, and cardiac pacemaker. Medical technology in particular has benefited from the association of physics and biology. Medical imaging with 3–D diagnostic techniques such as computer tomographic (CAT) scanning, magnetic resonance imaging and positron emission tomography have permitted researchers to look inside living things without disrupting life processes. Today, lasers and x rays are routinely used in medical treatments.

The use of a wide array of instruments and techniques futhered by discoveries in physics, especially electronics, has helped biology to change from a descriptive science to an analytical one. An example of this is one of the most important events of this century, deciphering the structure of the DNA molecule using x–ray diffraction, a technique which has also been used to determine the structure of hemoglobin, viruses, and a variety of other biological molecules and microorganisms. The ability to apply information discovered in physics to study of living things led to the development and use of the electron microscope and ultracentrifuge, instruments which have revealed much about information about cell structure and function. Other applications have been sensors for heat and pressure detection that give information about body functions under a variety of conditions which have been of great importance in the space program.

See also Computerized axial tomography; Laser; Microscopy; Physics; Ultracentrifuge; X rays.

Bioremediation

Bioremediation is a type of biotechnology in which living organisms or ecological processes are utilized to deal with some environmental problem. The most common use of bioremediation is to metabolically break down or otherwise remove toxic chemicals before or after they have been discharged into the environment. In such uses, bioremediation takes advantage of the fact that certain microorganisms can utilize such toxic chemicals as metabolic substrates, in the process rendering them into simpler, less toxic compounds. Bioremediation is a relatively new and actively developing technology.

In general, bioremediation methodologies focus on: (1) enhancing the abundance of certain species or groups of microorganisms that can metabolize toxic chemicals (this is also known as *bioaugmentation*) and/or (2) optimizing environmental conditions for the actions of these organisms (also known as *biostimulation*). Bioaugmentation may involve the deliberate addition of strains or species of microorganisms that are specifically effective at treating particular toxic chemicals, but are not indigenous to or abundant in the treatment area. Biostimulation usually involves fertilization, aeration, or irrigation in order to decrease the importance of environmental factors in limiting the activity of microorganisms. Biostimulation focuses on rapidly increasing the abundance of naturally occurring, ubiquitous microorganisms that are capable of dealing with certain types of environmental problems.

Bioremediation of spilled hydrocarbons

Accidental spills of petroleum or other hydrocarbons on land and water are regrettable but frequent occurrences. Such spills can range in size from a few gallons that may be spilled during refueling to enormous spillages of millions of tons as occurred to both the sea and land during the Gulf War of 1991. Once spilled, petroleum and its various refined products can be persistent environmental contaminants. However, these organic chemicals can also be metabolized by microorganisms which in the process transform them into simpler compounds, ultimately to carbon dioxide, water, and other inorganic chemicals.

Numerous attempts have been made to increase the rates by which microorganisms break down spilled hydrocarbons. In some cases, specially prepared concentrates of bacteria that are highly efficient at metabolizing hydrocarbons have been "seeded" into spill areas in an attempt to increase the rate of degradation of the spill residues. Although this technique has sometimes been effective, it commonly is not. This occurs because the indigenous microbial communities of soils and aquatic sediments contain many species of bacteria and fungi that are capable of utilizing hydrocarbons as a metabolic substrate. After a spill the occurrence of large concentrations of hydrocarbons in soil or sediment stimulates rapid growth of those microorganisms. Consequently, seeding of microorganisms that are metabolically specific to hydrocarbons does not always make much of a difference to the overall rate of degradation.

More important, however, is the fact that the environmental conditions under which spill residues occur are almost always highly sub–optimal for their degradation by microorganisms. Most commonly, the rate of microbial breakdown of spilled hydrocarbons is limited by the availability of oxygen or of certain nutrients such as nitrate and phosphate. Therefore, the microbial breakdown of spilled hydrocarbons on land can be greatly enhanced by occasionally tilling the soil to keep conditions aerated and by fertilizing with nitrogen and phosphorus while keeping conditions moist but not wet. Therefore, bioremediation systems for dealing with soils contaminated by spilled gasoline or petroleum can be based on simple tillage and fertilization.

Similarly, petroleum refineries may utilize a bioremediation process called landfarming in which oily wastes are spread onto land which is then tilled and fertilized until microbes reduce the residue concentrations to an acceptable level.

After some petroleum spills, more innovative approaches may prove to be useful. For example, it is difficult to fertilize aquatic habitats, because the nutrients simply wash away and are therefore not effective for very long. In the case of the *Exxon Valdez* spill in Alaska in 1989, research demonstrated that nutrients could be applied to soiled beaches as an oleophilic (that is, oil–seeking), nitrogen and phosphorus–containing fertilizer. Because of its oleophilic nature, the

fertilizer adhered to the petroleum residues and was able to significantly enhance the rate of oil degradation by the naturally occurring community of microorganisms. This treatment was applied to about 73 m (118 km) of oiled beach and proved to be successful in speeding up the process of degradation of the residues by increasing the rate of oxidation by about 50%. No attempts were made in this case to "seed" the microbial community with species that are specifically adapted to metabolizing hydrocarbons. It was believed that hydrocarbon–specific microbes were naturally present in the beach sediment and that their activity and that of species with broader substrate tolerances only had to be enhanced by making the ecological conditions more favorable, that is, by fertilizing.

Bioremediation of metal pollution

Metals are common pollutants of water and land when they are emitted by many industrial, agricultural, and domestic sources. In some situations, organisms or ecological processes can be successfully utilized to concentrate metals that are dispersed in the environment, especially in water. The metals can then be removed from the system by harvesting the organisms. For example, metal polluted waste waters can be treated by encouraging the vigorous growth of certain types of algae, fungi, or vascular plants, usually by fertilizing the water within some sort of constructed lagoon. This bioremediation system works because the growing plants and microorganisms absorb metals from the water (acting as so–called biosorbents), and thereby reduce their concentrations to a more tolerable range. The plants can then be harvested to remove the metals from the bioremediation system. In some cases, the plant biomass may even be processed to yield metal products of economic value.

Bioremediation of acidification

In some situations, artificial wetlands can be engineered to treat acidic waters associated with coal mining or other sources of acidity. Coal mining disturbs soil and fractures rocks and exposes large quantities of pyritic sulfur to atmospheric oxygen. Under such conditions, certain species of bacteria oxidize the sulfide of the mineral pyrites to sulfate generating large quantities of acidity in the process which is known as *acid mine drainage*. The resulting acidity is often treated by adding large quantities of acid–neutralizing chemicals such as lime or limestone. However, it has also been recently demonstrated that natural, acid–consuming, ecological processes operate in wetlands. These processes can be taken advantage of in constructed wetlands to decrease much of the initial acidity of acid mine drainages and thereby reduce the costs of conventional treatments with acid–neutralizing chemicals. The microbial processes that consume acidity are various, but they include: (1) the chemical reduction of sulfate to sulfide at the oxygen–poor interface between the sediment and the water column and around plant roots, (2) the reduction of ferric iron to ferrous in the same anoxic microhabitats, as well as (3) the primary productivity of phytoplankton, which also consumes some acidity.

A less intensive type of bioremediation can be used to mitigate some of the deleterious ecological effects associated with the acidification of surface waters, such as lakes and ponds. In almost any fresh waters, fertilization with phosphate will greatly increase the primary productivity of algae and vascular plants. In acidic waters, this process can be taken advantage of to reduce the acidity somewhat, but the most important ecological benefit occurs through enhancement of the habitat of certain aquatic animals. Ducks and muskrat, for example, can breed very successfully in fertilized acidic lakes, because their habitat is improved through the vigorous growth of vegetation and of aquatic insects and crustaceans. However, the productive but still acidic habitat remains toxic to fish. In this case, manipulation of the ecosystem by fertilization mitigates some but not all of the negative effects of acidification.

Bioremediation of sewage

Sewage represents a very complex mixture of wastes, usually dominated by fecal materials but also containing toxic chemicals that have been dumped into the disposal system by industries and home owners. Many advanced sewage–treatment technologies utilize microbial processes to both oxidize the organic matter associated with fecal wastes and to decrease the concentrations of soluble compounds or ions of metals, pesticides, and other toxic chemicals. The latter effect,

decreasing the aqueous concentrations of toxic chemicals, is accomplished by a combination of chemical adsorption as well as microbial biodegradation of complex chemicals into their simpler, inorganic constituents. Microbial processes are relied upon in many sewage treatment systems including activated sludges, aerated lagoons, anaerobic digestion, trickling filters, waste stabilization ponds, composting, and disposal on land.

See also Bacteria; Biotechnology; Hazardous wastes; Microorganisms; Oil spills; Sewage treatment.

Further Reading:

Frederick, R.J., and M. Egan. "Environmentally Compatible Applications of Biotechnology." *BioScience,* 44 (1994): 529–535.

Freedman, B. *Environmental Ecology,* 2nd ed. San Diego: Academic Press, 1994.

Bill Freedman

Biological rhythms

Biological rhythms are often referred to as biological clocks, since they operate on time schedules on a daily, monthly, seasonal, or annual basis. Some biological rhythms even occur on the basis of fractions of seconds. These internal clocks operate independent of the environment, but they are controlled by environmental conditions in changing situations. During times of change, such as seasonal decreases of light, or those caused by travel in an east–west or west–east direction, human beings are able to reset their biological clocks to become synchronized with the environment.

The study of biological rhythms is called chronobiology, a relatively new scientific specialty that began in the 1950s when researchers used new heart and lung monitors to answer some of the basic questions that chronobiologists ask. Some of these questions deal with sleep/wake cycles, time of day energy and productivity levels, and mood changes. Other important areas of study in chronobiology deal with growth patterns, hormone secretions, and menstruation.

Types of internal clocks

Some biological rhythms occur more than once a day and are called ultradian rhythms. The release of hormones from the male pituitary gland of mammals occurs about every one to two hours during the day. Sleep cycles, that is, the cycle from drowsiness to

REM (rapid eye movement, dream sleep) to dozing, then light and deep sleep, and finally slow–wave sleep, is a 90–minute sleep cycle that repeats itself during a night's sleep. Constant breathing and the beating of our hearts are also ultradian rhythms, but these activities are also affected by the daily sleep/wake cycle, which is a circadian rhythm. Heart rate and breathing both slow during sleep.

Circadian rhythms are those that occur once a day and relate to the sun. The one that dominates our activities is the sleep/wake cycle that people experience every 24 hours. Body temperature, response to medications, alcohol blood level, alertness, and fatigue all have a daily up and down cycle. Circadian rhythms also control such daily activities as eating. Chronobiologists explain the synchronizing of circadian rhythms to sunlight. This external factor helps the body regulate its daily activities. When people travel in an east or west direction through many time zones, they may suffer from jet lag and will need several days to adjust their sleep/wake cycle to the new daylight and darkness in their new environment.

Infradian cycles are monthly cycles, the most common of which is the monthly menstruation of females. Illness and death has been correlated to certain times within infradian cycles, with more deaths occurring in the second half of the menstrual cycle. Research with men has shown that weight fluctuations, hormone levels, growth of beards, body temperature, pain threshold, lung capacity, and physical strength all demonstrate monthly cyclical patterns. More men experience symptoms of prostate enlargement during the new moon period, while more deaths and accidents occur around the time of a full moon.

The longest cycle is of course the life cycle, which has the distinct stages of growth, maturation, decline, and death in all forms of life. Lunar cycles are somewhat longer than circadian ones. They last about twenty–four hours and fifty minutes. Some marine invertebrates, such as the fiddler crab, synchronizes its daily activity to the tides which are affect by the moon. The change in water levels during the tides influence the activity of many marine invertebrates (animals without a spinal column).

The circannual cycle is a yearly occurring one. Some people and animals periodically gain or lose weight at certain times of the year. Transplant patients respond better to certain drug treatments at certain times of the year than at others.

A disorder called SAD (seasonal affective disorder) afflicts many people during the winter months of the year when the days are shorter. It is the hormone called melatonin that is secreted from the pineal gland, which is located just behind the hypothalamus in the brain. Melatonin affects our moods. Its greatest production is during the night and when there is more darkness during a twenty–four hour period, as it is in winter in the norther hemisphere, there is a tendency for some people to become depressed. An effective treatment is to expose the person to intense bright light.

Adaptations to time

The basic time adaptation in biological rhythms is entrained, which means that it is influenced by external cues. Other aspects of out biological rhythms are so influential that most of us adapt our activities to the time of day during which we function best. Some people are morning people, while others are night people. Morning people (sometimes called larks) wake up with lots of energy and perform their best work in the morning. Night people are sluggish in the morning and do their best work late in the day or in the evening. They are often called owls. Work environments in our society are not adjusted to these differences, though, and many people have to work at times when they are least likely to be productive.

An experiment that took place in New Mexico in 1989, when a woman spent 130 days in isolation in a cave that had not natural light, demonstrated how external cues affect our biological clocks. After six weeks, she was functioning within a 44 hour cycle of sleeping and wakefulness. Her perception of time was also compressed to a considerable degree. In other experiments, volunteers drifted into a 25 hour day, while others have experienced 50 hour days or irregular cyclical patterns.

Medical uses

The work of chronobiologists in the area of biological rhythms has been useful to medical science in helping them diagnose illness more accurately. Twenty–four hour monitoring of heart rate and blood pressure gives the treating physician a better picture of health problems. Newborn infants to families with histories of heart disease can be monitored and abnormalities can be seen. Early detection of breast cancer can be made through the recording of skin temperature fluctuations over breasts. Noncancerous temperatures of the skin of breasts has a greater fluctuation cycle than temperatures recorded of the skin of cancerous breasts.

Another important way that chronobiology has helped medical science has been in determining the

KEY TERMS

Chronobiology—The study of biological clocks.

Circadian rhythm—The daily biological cycle.

Infradian cycle—The monthly biological cycle.

Entrainment—Regulation of the biological cycle to the environment.

Free–running clock—Response to internal clocks without any influence from the external world.

Lunar rhythm—The regulation of the biological cycle to the movement of the moon.

Synchrony—The adjustment of biological rhythms to the environment.

Ultradian rhythm—Biological cycles of less than a day.

best times of day for certain drug treatments. For example, cortisone injections are given in the morning for the treatment of adrenal gland malfunctions. Hormones in various glands throughout the human body are released when they are needed by major organs and, the chemical changes that occur manage our biological rhythms. As new ways of monitoring them are discovered, early warning signs of disease will become more apparent to diagnosing physicians.

See also Depression; Hormones; Menstrual cycle; Sleep; Tides.

Further Reading:
Campbell, Jeremy. *Winston Churchill's Afternoon Nap.* New York: Simon and Schuster, 1986.
Dotto, Lydia. *Losing Sleep.* New York: William Morrow, 1990.
Hughes, Martin. *Body Clock.* New York: Facts on File, 1989.
Orlock, Carol. *Inner Time.* New York: Birch Lane Press, 1993.
Perry, Susan L. *The Secrets Our Body Clocks Reveal.* New York: Rawson Associates, 1988.
Shafii, Mohammad and Shafii, Sharon Lee. *Biological Rhythms, Mood Disorders, Light Therapy, and the Pineal Gland.* Washington, D.C.: American Psychiatric Press, 1990.

Vita Richman

Biosphere

The biosphere is the space on or near the Earth's surface which contains and supports living organisms. It is typically subdivided into the lithosphere, atmosphere, and hydrosphere. The lithosphere is the Earth's surrounding layer composed of solid substance such as soil and rock, the atmosphere is the surrounding gaseous envelope, and the hydrosphere refers to liquid environments such as lakes and oceans which lie between the lithosphere and atmosphere. The biosphere's creation and continuous existence results from chemical, biological, and physical processes. To study these processes a multi disciplinary effort has been employed by scientists from fields such as chemistry, biology, geology, and ecology.

History

The term biosphere was first used by Austrian geologist Eduard Suess (1831–1914) in 1875 to describe the space on Earth which contains life. The concept introduced by Suess had little impact on the scientific community until it was resurrected by Russian scientist Vladimir Vernadsky (1863–1945) in 1926 with the publication of *La biosphere*. In this work, Vernadsky extensively developed the modern concepts which recognize the interplay between geology, chemistry, and biology in biospheric processes.

Requirements for life

For organisms to live appropriate environmental conditions (e.g., temperature, moisture, etc.) must exist, and the organisms must be supplied with energy and nutrients. In a biosphere such as the Earth's where no external nutrient supply exists, nutrients contained in dead organisms or waste products from living cells must be transformed back into compounds which living matter can reutilize for the biosphere to continue to support life. Mineral sources of nutrients are also important.

Energy is needed for the functions which organisms perform, such as growth, movement, waste removal and reproduction. It is the only requirements for life which is supplied from a source outside the biosphere. This energy, in the form of light or solar radiation received from the Sun, is captured and stored by plants in a process called photosynthesis. Photosynthesis refers to the light induced chemical reaction between carbon dioxide and water which produces oxygen and large carbon compounds called organic molecules. Energy is stored in the chemical bonds of organic molecules and can be released in the process of respiration; the enzymatic chemical reaction between organic molecules and oxygen to form carbon dioxide, water and energy. Organic molecules may also be used for growth since they are the major component of most tissues. Plants and some microorganisms are the only organisms which can form organic molecules by photosynthesis. Heterotopic organisms like humans rely on plants for their energy needs.

The major elements or chemical building blocks which comprise all living organisms are carbon, oxygen, nitrogen, phosphorus and sulfur. Organisms are able to acquire these elements only if they occur in useable chemical forms termed nutrients. In a process called the nutrient cycle the elements are transformed from one chemical form to another and back to the original form. The different chemical forms in which carbon occurs illustrate this process. Carbon occurs in the gaseous molecule carbon dioxide or in the organic molecules which compose living and dead organisms. Gaseous carbon dioxide is transformed to solid organic compounds (simple sugars) by the process of photosynthesis as mentioned previously. When organisms grow they deplete the atmosphere of carbon dioxide. If this process were to continue without carbon dioxide being resupplied at the same rate that it is consumed eventually the atmosphere would no longer contain carbon dioxide and organisms could no longer use the energy supplied by the Sun to sustain life. Fortunately, carbon dioxide is returned to the atmosphere at the same rate that it is consumed when organisms respire their own stores of organic molecules, when microorganisms respire tissue from organisms which have died in a process known as decomposition, or when wildfires occur.

Biosphere evolution

During the Earth's long history, life forms have drastically altered the chemical composition of the biosphere and at the same time the biosphere's chemical composition has influenced which life forms inhabit the Earth. In the past, the rate that nutrients were transformed from one chemical form to another was not always the same as the transformation back to the original chemical form. This has resulted in a change in the relative concentrations of chemicals in the biosphere. For example, when life first evolved approximately 3.8 billion years ago, the atmospheric carbon dioxide concentration was much greater than what we find today and there was virtually no free oxygen. The decrease in carbon dioxide and increase in atmospheric oxygen which occurred over time was due

---

KEY TERMS

Decomposition—The breakdown of the complex molecules which compose dead organisms into simple nutrients which can be reutilized by living organisms.

Energy—The ability to do work. Energy appears in forms, the most important in biospheric processes are solar, kinetic, heat, and chemical bond energies.

Global warming—Atmospheric warming which results from an increase in the concentration of gases which store heat such as carbon dioxide.

Nutrients—The molecules organisms obtain from their environment which are used for growth, energy, and various other cellular processes.

Nutrient cycle—The cycling of biologically important elements from one molecular form to another and back to the original form.

Photosynthesis—Sunlight induced chemical reaction between carbon dioxide and water which produces oxygen and organic molecules.

Respiration—Chemical reaction between organic molecules and oxygen which produces carbon dioxide, water, and energy.

---

to photosynthesis occurring at a faster rate than respiration. The carbon which was present in the atmosphere as carbon dioxide now lies in fossil fuel deposits and limestone rock.

Scientists believe that the increase in atmospheric oxygen concentration influenced the evolution of life. It was not until oxygen reached high concentrations such as we find on the Earth today that multicellular organisms like ourselves could have evolved. We require high oxygen concentrations to accommodate our high respiration rates and would not be able to survive had the biosphere not been altered by the organisms which came before us.

Current developments

Most research concerning the biosphere is being done to determine the effects which human activities have on our environment. Pollution, fertilizer application, land use, and fuel consumption affect nutrient cycles and may damage components of the biosphere such as the ozone layer which protects us from ultraviolet radiation. Fertilizer application increases the amount of nitrogen, phosphorus and other nutrients which organisms can use for growth. These excess nutrients damage lakes as demonstrated by large algal blooms and fish kills. Fuel consumption and land clearing increases carbon dioxide levels in the atmosphere and may cause global warming as a result of carbon dioxide's excellent ability to trap heat.

Recent interest in long term manned space operations has spawned research into the development of artificial biospheres. Extended missions will require that nutrients be cycled in a space no larger than a building. The Biosphere 2 project which received a great deal of press in the early 1990s should provide insights into the feasibility of such biospheres as well as the function and evolution of our own.

See also Atmosphere, composition and structure of; Lithosphere; Nutrients; Photosynthesis; Respiration.

Further Reading:

Allen, John. *Biosphere 2: The Human Experiment*. New York: Viking, 1991.
Bradbury, I. K. *The Biosphere*. London/New York: Bellhaven Press, 1991.
Clark, W. C., and R. E. Munn, eds. *Sustainable Development of the Biosphere*. Cambridge: Cambridge University Press, 1986.
Odum, Eugene. *Ecology and Our Endangered Life–Support Systems*. 2nd ed. Sunderland, MA: Sinauer Associates, 1993.
Piel, G. "The Biosphere." In *Only One World: Our Own to Make and to Keep*. New York: W. H. Freeman, 1992.
Salthe, S. N. "The Evolution of the Biosphere: Towards a New Mythology." *World Futures* 30 (1990): 53–67.
Tudge, Colin. *Global Ecology*. New York: Oxford University Press, 1991.

Steven MacKenzie

Biotechnology

Few developments in science have had the potential for such profound impact on research, technology, and society in general as has biotechnology. Yet authorities do not agree on a single definition of this term. Sometimes, writers have limited the term to techniques used to modify living organisms and, in some instances, the creation of entirely new kinds of organisms.

In most cases, however, a broader, more general definition is used. The Industrial Biotechnology Asso-

ciation, for example, uses the term to refer to any "development of products by a biological process." These products may indeed be organisms or they may be cells, components of cells, or individual and specific chemicals. A somewhat more detailed definition is that of the European Federation of Biotechnology, which defines biotechnology as the "integrated use of biochemistry, microbiology, and engineering sciences in order to achieve technological (industrial) application of the capabilities of microorganisms, cultured tissue cells, and parts thereof."

History of biotechnology

By almost any definition, biotechnology has been used by humans for thousands of years. Some of the oldest manufacturing processes known to humankind make use of biotechnology. Beer, wine, and breadmaking, for example, all occur because of the process of fermentation. During fermentation, microorganisms such as yeasts, molds, and bacteria are mixed with natural products which they use as food. In the case of wine–making, for example, yeasts live on the sugars found in some type of fruit juice, most commonly, grape juice. They digest those sugars and produce two new products, alcohol and carbon dioxide.

The alcoholic beverages produced by this process have been, for better or worse, a mainstay of human civilization for untold centuries. In breadmaking, the products of fermentation are responsible for the wonderful odor (the alcohol) and texture (the carbon dioxide) of freshly–baked bread. Cheese and yogurt are two other products formed when microorganisms act on a natural product, in this case milk—changing its color, odor, texture, and taste.

Biotechnology has long been used in a variety of industrial processes also. As early as the 17th century, bacteria were used to remove copper from its ores. Around 1910, scientists found that bacteria could be used to decompose organic matter in sewage, thus providing a mechanism for dealing efficiently with such materials in solid waste. A few years later, a way was found to use microorganisms to produce glycerol synthetically. That technique soon became very important commercially, since glycerol is used in the manufacture of explosives and World War I was about to begin.

Not all forms of biotechnology depend on microorganisms. Hybridization is an example. Farmers long ago learned that they could control the types of animals bred by carefully selecting the parents. In some cases, they actually created entirely new animal forms that do not occur in nature. The mule, a hybrid of horse and donkey, is such an animal.

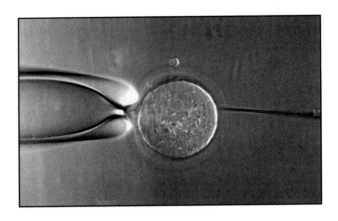

An animal cell being microinjected with foreign genetic material.

Hybridization

Hybridization has also been used in plant growing for centuries. Farmers found that they could produce food plants with any number of special qualities by carefully selecting the seeds they plant and by controlling growing conditions. As a result of this kind of process, the 2–3 in (5–7.5 cm) vegetable known as maize has evolved over the years into the 12 in (30 cm), robust product we call corn. Indeed, there is hardly a fruit or vegetable in our diet today that has not been altered by long decades of hybridization.

Until the late 19th century, hybridization was largely a trial–and–error process. Then the work of Gregor Mendel became known. Mendel's research on the transmission of hereditary characteristics soon gave agriculturists a solid factual basis on which to conduct future experiments in cross–breeding.

Modern principles of hybridization have made possible a greatly expanded use of biotechnology in agriculture and many other areas. One of the greatest successes of the science has been in the development of new food crops that can be grown in a variety of less–than–optimal conditions. The dramatic increase in harvests made possible by these developments has become known as the agricultural revolution or green revolution.

Three decades after the green revolution first changed agriculture in many parts of the world, a number of problems with its techniques have become apparent. The agricultural revolution forced a worldwide shift from subsistence farming to cash farming, and many small farmers in developing countries lack the resources to negotiate this shift. A farmer must make significant financial investments in seed, agricultural chemicals (fertilizers and pesticides), and machinery to make use of new farming techniques. In developing countries, peasants do not have and cannot borrow the necessary capital. The seed, chemicals, machinery, and oil to operate the equipment must commonly be imported, adding to already crippling foreign debts. In addition, the new techniques often have harmful effects on the environment. In spite of problems such as these, however, the green revolution has clearly made an important contribution to the lessening of world hunger.

Modern methods of hybridization have application in many fields besides agriculture. For example, scientists are now using controlled breeding techniques and other methods from biotechnology to insure the survival of species that are threatened or endangered.

The discovery of DNA

The nature of biotechnology has undergone a dramatic change in the last half century. That change has come about with the discovery of the role of DNA in living organisms. DNA is a complex molecule that occurs in many different forms. The many forms that DNA can take allow it to store a large amount of information. That information provides cells with the direction they need to carry out all the functions they have to perform in a living organism. It also provides a mechanism by which that information is transmitted efficiently from one generation to the next.

As scientists learned more about the structure of the DNA molecule, they discovered precisely and in chemical terms how genetic information is stored and transmitted. With that knowledge, they have also developed the ability to modify DNA, creating new instructions that direct cells to perform new and unusual functions. The process of DNA modification has come to be known as genetic engineering. Since genetic engineering normally involves combining two different DNA molecules, it is also referred to as recombinant DNA research.

Genetic engineering—the new biotechnology

There is little doubt that genetic engineering is the best known form of biotechnology today. Indeed, it is easy to confuse the two terms and to speak of one when it is the other that is meant. However, the two terms are different in the respect that genetic engineering is only one type of biotechnology.

502

In theory, the steps involved in genetic engineering are relatively simple. First, scientists decide what kind of changes they want to make in a specific DNA molecule. They might, in some cases, want to alter a human DNA molecule to correct some error that results in a disease such as diabetes. In other cases, a researcher might want to add instructions to a DNA molecule that it does not normally carry. He or she might, for example, want to include instructions for the manufacture of a chemical such as insulin in the DNA of bacteria that normally lack the ability to make insulin.

Second, scientists find a way to modify existing DNA to correct errors or add new information. Such methods are now well developed. In one approach, enzymes that "recognize" certain specific parts of a DNA molecule are used to cut open the molecule and then insert the new portion.

Third, scientists look for a way to insert the "correct" DNA molecule into the organisms in which it is to function. Once inside the organism, the new DNA molecule may give correct instructions to cells in humans (to avoid genetic disorders), in bacteria (resulting in the production of new chemicals), or in other types of cells for other purposes.

Accomplishing these steps in practice is not always easy. One major problem is to get an altered DNA molecule to express itself in the new host cells. That the molecule is able to enter a cell does not mean that it will begin to operate and function (express itself) as scientists hope and plan. This means that many of the expectations held for genetic engineering may not be realized for many years.

In spite of problems, genetic engineering has already resulted in a number of impressive accomplishments. Dozens of products that were once available only from natural sources and in limited amounts are now manufactured in abundance by genetically engineered microorganisms at relatively low cost. Insulin, human growth hormone, tissue plasminogen activator, and alpha interferon are examples. In addition, the first trials with the alteration of human DNA to cure a genetic disorder were begun in 1991.

The prospects offered by genetic engineering have not been greeted with unanimous enthusiasm by everyone. Many people believe that the hope of curing or avoiding genetic disorders is a positive advance. But they question the wisdom of making genetic changes that are not related to life–threatening disorders. Should such procedures be used for helping short children become taller or for making new kinds of tomatoes? Indeed, there are some critics who oppose all forms of genetic engineering, arguing that humans

never have the moral right to "play God" with any organism for any reason. As the technology available for genetic engineering continues to improve, debates over the use of these techniques in practical settings are almost certainly going to continue—and to escalate—in the future.

As progress in genetic engineering goes forward, so do other forms of biotechnology. The discovery of monoclonal antibodies is an example. Monoclonal antibodies are cells formed by the combination of tumor cells with animal cells that make one and only one kind of antibody. When these two kinds of cells are fused, they result in a cell that reproduces almost infinitely and that recognizes one and only one kind of antigen. Such cells are extremely valuable in a vast array of medical, biological, and industrial applications, including the diagnosis and treatment of disease, the separation and purification of proteins, and the monitoring of pregnancy.

See also Endangered species; Fermentation; Genetic engineering; Hybrid; Sewage treatment.

KEY TERMS

Hybridization—Development of new breeds of plants or animals achieved by combining the desired traits of two or more species in controlled breeding.

Monoclonal antibodies—Antibody formed by the combination of tumor cells and animal cells. Each recognizes only one specific antibody.

Recombinant DNA research—A process of DNA modification by which two different DNA molecules are combined.

Further Reading:

Fox, M. W. *Superpigs and Wondercorn: The Brave New World of Biotechnology and Where It May All Lead.* New York: Lyons and Buford, 1992.

Kessler, D. A., et al. "The Safety of Foods Developed by Biotechnology." *Science* (26 June 1992): 1747–749+.

Kieffer, G. H. *Biotechnology, Genetic Engineering, and Society.* Reston, VA: National Association of Biology Teachers, 1987.

Marx, J., ed. *A Revolution in Biotechnology.* New York: Cambridge University Press, 1989.

Weintraub, P. "The Coming of the High–Tech Harvest." *Audubon* (July–August 1992): 92–103.

David E. Newton

Birch family (Betulaceae)

The birch family is a group of flowering plants of tree or shrub form that includes the birches (*Betula*), alders (*Alnus*), hornbeams (*Carpinus*) and hazels (*Corylus*). Members of the birch family have simple and alternate leaves that bear appendages (stipules) where they join the branch. The leaves are also deciduous, generally thin and often doubly toothed along the margin. The flowers are densely borne on elongate, spike–like structures called catkins. Each catkin bears flowers of only one sex but male and female catkins occur on the same plant. Female catkins are stiffer and fewer–flowered than male catkins. The flowers lack petals or sepals, although some species have small scale–like appendages that represent reduced perianth parts. Pollination occurs in the spring by the wind. The fruit is a one–seeded nut or nutlet which is often winged and enclosed or surrounded at the base by leaflike appendages called bracts.

The family includes six genera and about 170 species worldwide. The Betulaceae occur throughout the temperate and boreal regions of the Northern Hemisphere, where they are prominent members of forest communities. Some alders and dwarf birches extend into the southern Arctic where they are common shrubs. Members of the family occur only in a few regions of the Southern Hemisphere, notably in the tropical mountains of the northern Andes of Columbia and in Argentina.

Ecologically, this an important family. Many members of the Betulaceae play pivotal roles in early successional stages following disturbance. In North America, for example, the paper or white birch (*Betula papyrifera*) is a transcontinental species which rapidly recolonizes areas disturbed by fire or logging, thus stabilizing the soil and providing suitable conditions for recolonization by other species. Paper birch is able to invade disturbed areas by dispersal of its winged seeds. In addition, birches typically resprout from the base when the main trunk is killed. Birches grow fast and die young; paper birch, for example, reaches maturity in 60–75 years and seldom lives longer than 140 years.

Alders are also important early successional species. In northern regions, cold soils limit the activity of nitrogen–producing soil bacteria, thus, northern soils frequently lack adequate quantities of nitrogen for vigorous plant growth. Alders are among the few plants that form symbiotic relationships with nitrogen–fixing bacteria. In alders, filamentous bacteria known as actinomycetes form nodules on the roots. The nitrogen compounds produced by the actinomycetes are in a

A birch tree (*Betula peudola*).

form directly usable by the host alder plant. In addition, some of the nitrogen compounds are leached from the nodules or released when nodule–bearing roots die. These compounds accumulate in the soil where they remain available for use by other plants of later successional stages that cannot produce their own nitrogenous compounds.

In the United States there are five genera and about 25 species of Betulaceae. Yellow birch (*Betula alleghaniensis*) and paper birch are common in the northern hardwood forests of northern New England. The American hornbeam, also called blue beech, is the only North American member of the genus *Carpinus* (*C. caroliniana*). It grows in moist woods as a tall shrub or small tree reaching heights of 39 ft (10 m) and with a smooth, gray, ridged trunk that is often described as fluted. American hornbeam has a curious range that covers much of eastern north America, parts of Texas, and then skips to southern Mexico, Guatemala, and Honduras. Eastern hop hornbeam

(*Ostrya virginiana*) has a similar distribution to American hornbeam. However, eastern hop hornbeam is taller, reaching heights of 65 ft (20 m), and has scaly bark that breaks off in short strips. The wood of eastern hop hornbeam is extremely dense, making it difficult to drive a nail into it, hence its other common name of ironwood. A variety of alder species occur as shrubs in moist ground throughout North America. In the Pacific Northwest, however, red alder (*A. rubra*) is an abundant, fast–growing tree of disturbed areas that attains heights of 131 ft (40 m). Hazel (*Corylus*) is a widespread shrub (3–10 ft [1–3m] tall) in eastern North America and parts of the Midwest, with the beaked hazel (*C. cornuta*) reaching Oregon.

The birch family is economically valuable. In North America, yellow and sweet birch are important sources of wood for cabinet–making, furniture of various kinds, floors, and doors. Paper birch is excellent as firewood and is used in the making of plywood and boxes. The bark of paper birch was once used by indigenous North Americans for making canoes. In northern Europe and especially in Russia, birch switches are traditionally used to beat one's skin during sauna baths. The sap of birches is sweet and can be collected and condensed into syrup. Hazels produce edible nuts that are sometimes called filberts or cobnuts. Store–bought hazelnuts generally come from cultivated European species, most commonly *Corylus avellana*, *C. colurna*, and *C. maxima*. Turkey is the largest producer of hazelnuts at 300,000 metric tons annually, followed by Spain and Italy. In the United States, hazelnuts are produced mostly in Oregon with annual harvests of about 10,000 metric tons.

Most species of alder are shrubs of no commercial value, but red alder of the Pacific Northwest and a number of European species reach tree–size and are valuable sources of wood. Alder wood produces a superior charcoal that imparts a delicious flavour to meat. Charcoal made from red alder is preferred for smoking salmon on the west coast of North America.

Further Reading:

Bateman, G., ed. *Flowering Plants of the World*. Oxford: Oxford University Press, 1978.
Mitchell, A. *The Guide to Trees of Canada and North America*. Surrey, U.K.: Dragon's World Ltd., 1987.

Les C. Cwynar

Birds

Birds are vertebrate animals in the class Aves. There are approximately 8,800 species of birds, divided among 28 living orders. One order, the Passeriformes or perching birds, accounts for more than one–half of the living species of birds.

The skin of birds is covered with specialized structures known as feathers. Feathers are a highly modified, epidermal structure, and are analogous to the scales of reptiles. The presence of feathers is diagnostic of birds—no other animals have these structures. Feathers are important as insulation to help keep the body warm and in providing a light, strong, surface area for the wings, which are the major aerodynamic surface of these flying animals. The feathers of most species are colored, often brightly so, and commonly in beautiful patterns. In this sense, feathers are also important in social displays and camouflage.

Birds have four limbs, and are therefore tetrapods. However, the fore limbs are highly modified into structures known as wings, which are mostly used for flying or gliding. The hind limbs are mostly used for walking or hopping, so these animals are bipedal when moving on the ground. Some species of birds are flightless, but most can fly or soar well.

The bones of all of the flying birds are modified for flight, and are relatively light and have many hollow regions. The flying birds have a strongly keeled breastbone or sternum, to which the flight muscles are attached. Their pelvic bones are fused into a structure known as a synsacrum. Birds have a relatively long neck and their mandibles are modified into a keratinous beak. Birds do not have any teeth. Birds have a four–chambered heart and a double circulation of the blood, with complete separation of oxygenated and de–oxygenated blood.

Birds have internal fertilization, and they are oviparous, laying relatively large, hard–shelled eggs, with a discrete yolk. The eggs are incubated by one or both parents. The young of almost all species of birds are cared for by their parents.

Birds are believed to have evolved from saurischian dinosaurs, about 150 million years ago. The first truly bird–like animal was *Archaeopteryx lithographica*, which lived during the Jurassic period, about 130 million years ago. This 3 ft (1 m) long animal is considered to be an evolutionary link between the birds and the dinosaurs. *Archaeopteryx* had teeth and other dinosaurian characters, but it also had a feathered body and could fly.

See also Birds of prey; Chordates; Shore birds; Song birds.

Birds of paradise

The birds of paradise are some of the most fascinating birds in the world, both because of the striking coloration of the males of many species, and because of the wide range of behaviors demonstrated in the group. Researchers of animal behavior are particularly interested in the elaborate mating displays performed by the males in most species of birds of paradise.

Birds of paradise is the common name given to this group of species in the Paradisaeidae family. The birds of paradise probably evolved on the island of New Guinea; the family is comprised of 43 species, 38 of which are found mainly or entirely on New Guinea. Two species are found only in the Moluccan Islands to the west of New Guinea, and four species are found mainly or entirely in northeastern Australia. Included within the family are such birds as sicklebills, parotias, manucodes, paradisaeas, riflebirds, and astrapias.

Description

The birds of paradise in general have a crowlike or starling–like form with strong feet and bills. In some species this basic pattern has been modified in different ways. For example, the sicklebills have evolved a long, curved bill mainly used to probe for insects in moss and tree bark. In many species the plumage of the males is modified with fantastic, almost unreal–looking plumes, streamers, and wiry head or tail extensions. Although the bodies of most of the birds of paradise are 10–17 in (25–45 cm) long, the head plumes of some males may reach 16 in (40 cm) in length, and tail feathers may be up to 27 in (70 cm) long.

An Emperor of Germany's bird of paradise in Baiyer River Sanctuary, New Guinea.

The females of many species are drab buff to black, with patterning that helps them remain hidden in the forest while sitting on a nest. (This type of patterning is called cryptic.) Nests of most species are cup–shaped, and are built in the forks of trees using leaves, twigs, and other plant materials. Females usually lay 1 or 2 eggs, which average 1.4 in (36.5 mm) long and 1 in (26 mm) wide. Incubation periods in the wild are unknown, but captive bird incubation periods are 17–21 days, and young birds remain in the nest 17–30 days.

Habitat and diet

New Guinea is a relatively young island (5–6 million years old), and it is extremely mountainous. Its location just south of the equator creates a generally warm climate, but ice caps remain on top of the highest peaks. Ocean winds carry moisture–laden air over the island, and some sites receive over 27 ft (8.5 m) of rain per year. Sites on lee sides of mountains, however, may be extremely dry. This variation in climate creates many different types of habitat, and the species of birds of paradise found on New Guinea are fairly specific to the types of habitats they prefer. For example, the crested bird of paradise is found in upper montane forest or subalpine shrubs, the trumpet manucode is found only in lowlands and lower mountains, and the blue bird of paradise prefers the mid–montane forest.

In addition to inhabiting different zones throughout the island, the various birds of paradise may also use different food resources. The two basic types of foods eaten by birds of paradise are fruits and insects. The two main groups of fruits are simple fruits rich in carbohydrates, such as figs, and complex fruits with high levels of fats and proteins, such as mahogany and nutmeg fruits. Species of birds of paradise tend to eat either mainly simple fruits (e.g., trumpet manucode), mainly complex fruits (e.g., raggiana bird of paradise), or complex fruits plus significant quantities of insects (e.g., magnificent bird of paradise).

When animals eat tree fruits, they may also digest the seeds contained in the fruit, or they may leave the seeds unharmed. If they leave the seeds, a new tree seedling may sprout from the seeds, helping the forest regenerate. In most forest habitats worldwide, the main fruit–dispersing animals are mammals. However, New Guinea lacks fruit–eating mammals, and instead this role is filled by birds of paradise. Birds of paradise eat the fruits and distribute the unharmed seeds; in their flight they spread the seeds ensuring that the different species of forest trees sprout throughout the birds' habitats.

Mating behavior

Polygynous birds of paradise

As mentioned above, many species of birds of paradise are sexually dimorphic, which means the male and females have different appearances. Males have elaborate plumage patterns, which are used in mating displays. Females of these species are relatively drab and cryptic. Sexually dimorphic species are usually also polygynous (the males may mate with more than one female). To attract females, the adult males may perform mating dances on the ground in clearings, may perch on shrubs, or may hang upside down on tree trunks or tree branches, all while conspicuously displaying their plumage and calling to the females. Males may perform these displays alone, or in groups in areas called leks. The females watch the displays and decide whether or not to mate with a particular male. Females seem to choose males based on the vigor of the male's display, or the condition or color of his feathers. By choosing a healthy, vigorous father for her offspring, the female presumably ensures that her offspring will be healthy and vigorous as well. The strongest, most brightly–feathered males will be chosen as mates by many females, while the less attractive males are sometimes passed over completely. The elaborate plumages of the males are thought to have evolved through this process of sexual selection (females choosing mates from among males who compete for their attention with displays). After mating, a female in these species returns to her nest and raises her offspring alone.

Researchers have noticed a relationship between mating system and diet in the birds of paradise. Polygynous bird of paradise species that display in leks (such as raggiana birds of paradise) tend also to be those that eat mainly complex fruits, because females searching for these fruits fly long distances in the forest and thus are likely to see large groups of males displaying together. Polygynous species in which solitary males display (such as magnificent birds of paradise) tend to be those which eat insects plus complex fruits. To get insects, females need not fly long distances, so a male is more likely to be seen and chosen as a mate by a female if he displays alone near her small home territory.

Interestingly, the polygynous birds of paradise also show sexual bimaturism. This means that males and females become sexually mature at different ages. Females in these species are thought to begin to breed when 2–3 years old, while males do not acquire mature plumage (and, therefore, do not breed) until age 4–7 years. However, males of these species have been observed to grow adult plumage at a younger age when kept alone in captivity. This suggests that the delay in male maturation in the wild is due to some form for hormonal suppression from the already–mature adult males.

Monogamous birds of paradise

Nine species of birds of paradise, including the manucodes, are sexually monomorphic. The males and females have the same or nearly the same coloring (they tend to be brown or black), and both lack the elaborate plumage that characterizes many other birds of paradise. These species are monogamous (the males and females mate with only one partner at a time), and some species may pair for life. As in most monogamous species, the males in these species help the females raise the young.

These species also are typically those that feed mainly on simple fruits such as figs. This type of fruit is relatively low in nutrients, compared to complex fruits and insects. Scientists think that the monogamous mating system may have developed in these species because two parents are necessary to provide enough nutrients to successfully raise the young. Thus, in the birds of paradise, it appears that the diet of a species may have influenced the evolution of its social system.

Habitat loss

Although much of New Guinea is still covered with rain forest, due in part to the seed dispersal abilities of birds of paradise, some areas are beginning to be logged and habitat destruction will doubtless increase in the future. Some species of birds of paradise are only found in such limited ranges that any disturbance to their habitat could result in extinction. Others are

KEY TERMS

. . . .

Cryptic—Drab, usually brownish coloration which makes an organism difficult to see in its natural habitat and allows it to hide from predators.

Lek—A central area in which many males of a species perform mating displays simultaneously.

Montane—Habitat on relatively cool, moist mountain slopes below the treeline.

Sexual bimaturism—Condition in which the males and females of a species become sexually mature at different ages.

Sexual dimorphism—Condition in which the males and females of a species differ significantly in appearance.

Subalpine—Habitat on high mountain slopes, above the treeline.

Further Reading:

Beehler, Bruce M. *A Naturalist in New Guinea.* Austin, TX: University of Texas Press, 1991.

Beehler, Bruce M. "The Birds of Paradise." *Scientific American* 261 (December 1989): 116–123.

Beehler, Bruce M., Thane K. Pratt, and Dale A. Zimmerman. *Birds of New Guinea.* Princeton, NJ: Princeton University Press, 1986.

Perrins, C. M., and A. L. A. Middleton, eds. *The Encyclopedia of Birds.* New York: Facts on File, 1985.

Amy Kenyon–Campbell

found throughout the island, but only at certain altitudes. For example, the blue bird of paradise is only found between altitudes of 4,200 and 5,900 ft (1,300–1,800 m). The species is under pressure from human colonization at these altitudes.

In addition to habitat loss, many species have been threatened by overhunting in the past. After Europeans discovered the birds, the demand for their plumage to use as decoration increased so that by 1900 population sizes of many species were greatly reduced. At present importation of bird of paradise feathers into the United States and most of Europe is illegal. However, bird of paradise feathers and plumes continue to be of great cultural importance for the native highlanders of New Guinea, who use the feathers in headdresses and other decorations.

Six of twenty–four species on a 1985 list of New Guinea birds that may require conservation action in the future were birds of paradise. Because of this, and because birds of paradise are so visible and are found throughout the various New Guinea habitats, Bruce Beehler, a noted expert on birds of paradise, suggested creating a series of rain forest reserves centered around the known habitats of all New Guinea birds of paradise. These reserves would also provide habitat for the many other rare species of New Guinea birds which are not as well–known or charismatic as the birds of paradise. For any such reserves to be successfully established, they must be planned in such a way as to provide sustainable livelihood to the indigenous peoples of the area. The challenge in the future will be to balance human development with environmental conservation.

Birds of prey

Birds of prey are predators that catch and eat other animals. These birds are called raptors (from the Latin *rapere*, meaning to snatch), a reference to their specialized, powerful feet for seizing prey. Raptorial birds eat birds, small mammals, reptiles, amphibians, fish, and even large insects.

Birds of prey are members of five avian families within the order Falconiformes. The Accipitridae includes the hawks, eagles, kites, harriers, and Eurasian vultures. Some widespread North American species in this family are the bald eagle (*Haliaeetus leucocephalus*), the red–tailed hawk (*Buteo jamaicensis*), the sharp–shinned hawk (*Accipiter striatus*), and the northern harrier (*Circus cyaneus*). The Falconidae includes the falcons and caracaras, such as the peregrine falcon (*Falco peregrinus*) and the merlin (*F. columbarius*). The Pandionidae includes only one species, the osprey (*Pandion haliaetus*), which has an almost worldwide distribution. The Sagittariidae of Africa includes only the secretary bird (*Sagittarius serpentarius*). Finally, the Cathartidae (American vultures) live only in North and South America and include the turkey vulture (*Cathartes aura*), the black vulture (*Coragyps atratus*), and the endangered California condor (*Gymnogyps californianus*).

Owls are also birds of prey. The order Strigiformes includes two families, the Tytonidae (barn owls), represented in North America by the barn owl (*Tyto alba*), and the Strigidae, including the eastern screech–owl (*Otus asio*), the great horned owl (*Bubo virginianus*), the snowy owl (*Nyctea scandiaca*), and the tiny elf owl (*Micrathene whitneyi*), which is only 5 in (13 cm) long.

As a group, birds of prey eat large numbers of small mammals that would otherwise be pests of agriculture or homes. Many people find raptors fascinating because of the grace, speed, ferocity, and power that many species display as predators. However, some people dislike birds of prey because certain species hunt game birds and songbirds, and in the past, raptors have been killed in large numbers. Large numbers of raptors have also been indirectly poisoned by the use of insecticides. For example, the widespread agricultural use of persistent bioaccumulating chlorinated–hydro-carbon insecticides such as DDT and dieldrin has caused the collapse of populations of peregrine falcons, bald eagles, and other species of birds. The use of pesticides is now restricted, and their effect on raptors is becoming less significant. However, populations of many birds of prey remain perilously small, indicating declines in the populations below the top predators.

See also Condors; Eagles; Falcons; Hawks; Owls; Vultures.

Birth

Birth, or parturition, in mammals is the process in which a fully developed fetus is expelled from the mother's uterus by the force of strong, rhythmic muscle contractions. The birth of live offspring is a reproductive feature shared by mammals, some fishes, and selected invertebrates (such as scorpions), as well as some reptiles and amphibians. Animals who give birth to live offspring are called viviparous (meaning "live birth").

In contrast to viviparous animals, other animals give birth to eggs; these animals are called oviparous (meaning "egg birth"). Some oviparous species, such as birds, retain their eggs inside their bodies for long periods of time; in these animals, the eggs are laid at an advanced stage of development. Other animals, such as frogs, give birth to less developed eggs, which undergo development outside the mother's body.

Viviparous animals

In both viviparous animals and oviparous animals, fertilization of the mother's egg with the father's sperm takes place inside the mother's body. One of the advantages to giving birth to live young is that the mother protects the fetus inside her body as it develops. The developing fetus derives nutrients from the mother's body, and so is assured of receiving all the nourishment it needs to complete development.

The length of time between fertilization and birth in viviparous animals is called the gestation period.

The length of the gestation period varies according to species. The gestation period of mice is 21 days, of rabbits is 30–36 days, and of dogs and cats is 60 days. The largest mammal, the baleen whale, has a gestation period of 12 months—only three months longer than the gestation period of humans. Elephants have one of the longest gestation periods of all animals, 22 months.

Some viviparous animals such as humans, horses, and cows give birth to only one offspring at a time, although occasionally these animals produce twins or triplets. Other animals give birth to many offspring at a time. Usually, the multiple offspring in a litter are each derived from a separate egg, but the armadillo gives birth to four identical offspring that are derived from the same fertilized egg.

How does birth begin?

At the end of the gestation period, the mother's uterus begins to contract rhythmically, a process called labor. The initiation of labor leading up to birth is the result of a number of hormones, notably oxytocin.

Maternal progesterone

Shortly after fertilization the hormone progesterone increases and is maintained at high levels in the mother's bloodstream. The high levels of progesterone prevent the uterus from contracting. The progesterone prepare the lining of the uterus (the endonestrium) for its supporting role in nurturing the developing fetus, and helps form the placenta. Maternal progesterone levels begin to drop during the last weeks of gestation, while the levels of estrogen begin to rise. When progesterone levels drop to very low levels and estrogen levels are high, the uterus begins to contract.

Oxytocin

Oxytocin is a hormone released from the pituitary gland in the brain, which stimulates uterine contractions and also controls the production of milk in the mammary glands of the breast (a process called lactation). Synthetic oxytocin is sometimes given to women in labor to induce labor.

The mechanism that prompts the secretion of oxytocin from the pituitary during labor is thought to be initiated by the pressure of the fetus's head against the cervix, the opening of the uterus. As the fetus's head presses against the cervix, the uterus stretches, and relays a message along nerves to the pituitary, which responds by releasing oxytocin. The more the uterus stretches, the more oxytocin is released.

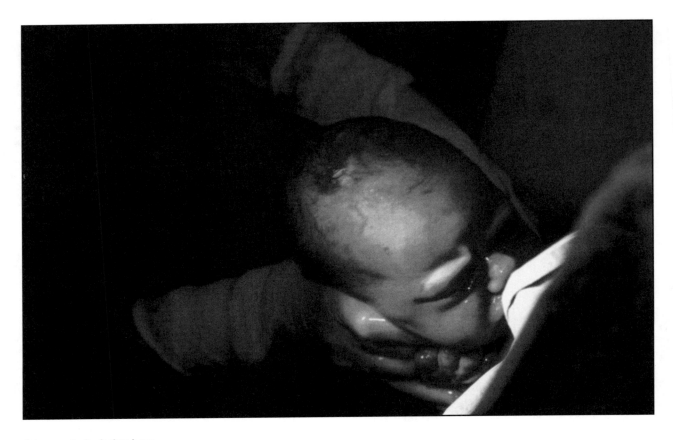

A human baby being born.

Fetal endocrine control

Fetal hormones are also thought to play a role in initiating labor. At the end of gestation, the fetal adrenal glands secrete steroid hormones called cortico steroids, which cause the hormone–like substances known as prostaglandins. Prostaglandins contribute to the contraction of the uterus during labor.

Birth in humans

Labor culminating in birth in humans begins with the rhythmic contractions of the uterus which dilate the cervix. This causes the fetus to move down the birth canal, and to be expelled together with the placenta—which had supplied the developing fetus with nutrients from the mother. These events can take anywhere from 48 hours to less than one hour but more usually the entire birth process takes about 16 hours.

The first stage: dilation of the cervix

In order for the fetus to leave the uterus and to enter the birth canal, it must pass through the cervix, the opening of the uterus. The cervix is normally tightly closed, and is sealed with a plug of mucus during gesta-

tion to protect the fetus from invading microorganisms. During the first stages of labor, the contractions of the uterus dilate the cervix which widens to about 4 in (10 cm), which can accommodate the passage of the fetal head.

In the last weeks of pregnancy, before labor begins, the uterus undergoes irregular contractions, which serve to exercise the muscles of the uterus and may even dilate the cervix; it's not unusual for a woman to go into active labor with a cervix that's already one or two centimeters dilated. During the last weeks of pregnancy, the cervix also thins out (or effaces) which makes dilation easier.

In preparation for birth, the fetus moves further down into the mother's pelvis. When labor begins, the fetus is usually positioned with its head engaged with the top of the cervix. This engagement is called "lightening" or "dropping." When labor begins, the contractions loosen the mucus plug in the cervix, which causes small capillaries in the cervix to break, and the mucus and blood are discharged from the vagina. This discharge is sometimes called "bloody show" and signals the onset of labor.

The Holstein calf being born here, unlike a newborn human child, will walk almost immediately.

Another sign that may signal the beginning of labor is the rupturing of the amniotic sac. In the uterus the fetus is encased in a membrane (the amniotic sac) and literally floats in amniotic fluid. When uterine contractions begin, this sac ruptures and the amniotic fluid can leak from the uterus. Not all women experience an abrupt rupturing of the amniotic sac; in some the amniotic fluid gradually leaks out as labor progresses. Once the amniotic sac has ruptured, or the amniotic fluid begins to leak, labor usually progresses more rapidly.

During the first stage of labor, the cervix dilates about 0.5–0.6 in (1.2–1.5 cm) an hour. The uterine contractions are about 5–30 minutes apart, and last for 15–40 seconds. The end of the first stage of labor is associated with the strongest uterine contractions. Contractions are two to five minutes apart, and last for 45–60 seconds. The cervix opens rapidly at this point. This period of labor, sometimes called transition, is usually the most difficult for the mother. The contractions are very strong and close together, and nausea and vomiting are common. After the cervix has dilated to its full width of 4 in (10 cm), the contractions slow down somewhat to about three to five minutes apart.

The fetus is then ready to be born, and the second stage of labor begins.

The second stage: birth

During the second stage, lasting about one to two hours, the mother uses her abdominal muscles to push the fetus through and out of the birth canal.

The pushing is actually a reflex action, but if a woman can help the reflex by actively using her muscles, birth goes much faster. As the fetus moves down the birth canal to the vaginal opening, the head begins to appear. The appearance of the head at the opening of the vagina is called crowning. After the head is delivered, first one shoulder is delivered, then the other. The rest of the body follows.

After the baby is born, the umbilical cord that has attached the fetus to the placenta is clamped. The clamping cuts off the circulation of the cord, which eventually stops pulsing due to the interruption of its blood supply. The baby now must breathe air through its own lungs.

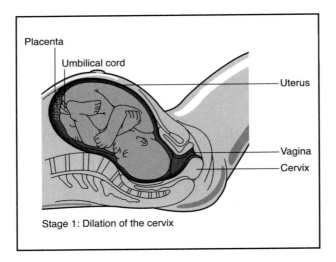

Stage 1: Dilation of the cervix

Stage 1: Dilation of the cervix.

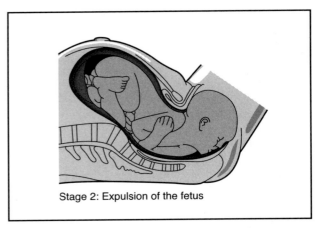

Stage 2: Expulsion of the fetus

Stage 2: Expulsion of the fetus.

The third stage: delivery of the placenta

Before delivery, the placenta separates from the wall of the uterus.

Since the placenta contains many blood vessels, its separation from the wall of the uterus causes bleeding. This bleeding, if not excessive, is normal. After the placenta separates from the uterine wall, it moves into the birth canal and is expelled from the vagina. The uterus continues to contract even after the placenta is delivered, and it is thought that these contractions serve to control bleeding.

Birth interventions: how humans manage labor and delivery

History of childbirth

Until the 20th century, childbirth was the province of women. A woman giving birth was attended by her female relatives and perhaps a woman in the community known for her midwifing skills. As the scientific revolution of the 17th century took place, concerned physicians noticed that childbirth was sometimes a dangerous, often fatal, process. Infections, injury to the baby and mother, and death occurred when unskilled midwives attempted to manage complications. Gradually, childbirth changed from a wholly female–centered activity to a medical process overseen by predominately male physicians. By the early 20th century, childbirth moved from the home to the hospital. By the mid–20th century, childbirth had become a completely medical process, attended by physicians and managed by medical equipment and procedures, such as fetal monitors, anesthesia, and surgical interventions.

Later in the 20th century, some women became dissatisfied with this medical approach to birth. Many felt that the medical establishment had taken control of a natural biological process. Women wanted more control over labor and birth and new ways of giving birth that sought to reduce or eliminate the medical interventions became popular. With the increasing concern about the effect of anesthesia on the fetus, many women refused artificial means of controlling pain, and instead relied on breathing and relaxation techniques. Fathers, once banished from labor and delivery rooms, were now welcomed as partners in the birth process.

Today, women have many options for labor and birth. Some women deliver in a hospital with doctors and nurses close by to supervise the birth process. Others choose a nurse–midwife, a person who has been trained to deliver babies but who is not a doctor. Still others choose home birth, attended either by a doctor or midwife, or sometimes both. Whatever option a woman chooses, it is important to get good medical care throughout pregnancy. Periodic prenatal checkups are one of the best ways to avoid birth complications.

Types of childbirth preparation

Many childbirth experts believe that the more a mother knows about the birth process, the less fear and apprehension she will feel giving birth. Many childbirth preparation methods prepare both mother and father for the birth experience and teach relaxation and breathing techniques. The Read method, for instance (named after its founder, British physician Grantley Dick–Read), is based on the notion that fear leads to pain. The Read method includes childbirth education, exercises to improve muscle tone, and relaxation techniques. The Lamaze method (named for Dr. Ferdinand

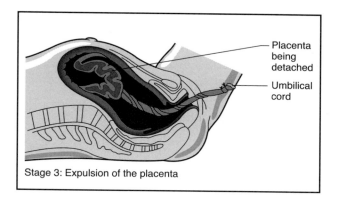

Stage 3: Expulsion of the placenta

Stage 3: Expulsion of the placenta.

Lamaze) takes a psychological approach to managing labor. The Lamaze method teaches women to relax and breathe in response to pain, the theory being that this substitution of favorable activity for negative sensations reduces pain. The Bradley method focuses on deep relaxation and slow, deep breathing, and ascribes an important role to the father.

Types of anesthesia

Two types of anesthesia are commonly used during labor and birth. In general anesthesia, the mother is given drugs that put her to sleep, but this type of anesthesia is rarely used today, since the drugs can depress the fetal heart beat. In regional anesthesia, drugs are injected to deaden sensation around the spinal nerves that carry sensations from the pelvic region. Controversy about whether these drugs affect the fetus is ongoing, although some kinds of regional anesthesia affect the fetus less than others.

See also Embryo and embryonic development; Fertilization; Hormones; Oviparous; Reproductive system; Sexual reproduction; Viviparity.

Further Reading:
"Deciding to Be Born." *Discover* 13 (10 May 1992).

Bean, Constance A. *Methods of Childbirth*, second edition. Garden City, New York: Doubleday, 1990.

Bradley, Robert A. *Husband–Coached Childbirth*. New York: Harper and Row, 1981.

Dick Read, Grantley. *Childbirth Without Fear*. New York: Harper and Row, 1984.

Fischman, Joshua. "Putting a New Spin on the Birth of Human Birth." *Science* 264 (20 May 1994): 1082.

Karmel, Marjorie. *Thank You, Dr. Lamaze*. New York: Harper and Row, 1993.

Knobil, Ernst and Neill, Jimmy D., eds. *The Physiology of Reproduction*, second edition. New York: Raven Press, 1994.

Mitford, Jessica. *The American Way of Birth*. New York: Dutton, 1992.

Kathleen Scogna

Birth control see **Contraception**

Birth defects

Birth defects or congenital defects are present at birth. They result from heredity, environmental influences, or maternal illness. Such defects range from very minor, such as a dark spot or birthmark that may appear anywhere on the body, to more serious conditions that may result in marked disfigurement or limit the lifespan of the child.

A number of factors individually or in combination may cause birth defects. Heredity plays a major role in passing birth defects from one generation to the next. Conditions such as sickle cell anemia, color blindness, deafness, and extra digits on the hands or feet are hereditary. The condition may not appear in every generation, but the defective gene usually is passed on.

Causes of defects

Low birth weight is the most common birth defect, with one in every 15 babies being born at less than their ideal weight. A baby who weighs 5 lb, 8 oz (2,500 g) at birth has a low birth weight. One who is born weighing 3 lb, 5 oz (1,500 g) has a very low birth weight. Low birth weight may occur if the baby is born before the normal gestation period of 38 weeks has elapsed, in which case the baby is preterm or premature. A low birth weight baby born after a normal gestation period is called a small–for–date or small–for–gestational–age baby. Premature birth, other than being a birth defect in itself, also may have accompanying defects. A baby born before the 28th week of gestation, for example, may have great difficulty breathing because the lungs have not developed fully.

Exposure of the mother to chemicals such as mercury or to radiation during the first three months of pregnancy may result in an abnormal alteration in the growth or development of the fetus. The mother's diet may also be a factor in her baby's birth defect. A balanced and healthy diet is essential to the proper formation of the fetus because the developing baby receives all of its nutrition from the mother.

Prenatal development of the fetus may also be affected by disease that the mother contracts, especially those that occur during the first trimester (three months) of pregnancy. For example, if a pregnant woman catches rubella, the virus crosses the placenta and infects the fetus. In the fetus, the virus interferes with normal metabolism and cell movement and can cause blindness (from cataracts), deafness, heart malformations, and mental retardation. The risk of the fetal damage resulting from maternal rubella infection is greatest during the first month of pregnancy (50%) and declines with each succeeding month.

It is especially important that the mother not smoke, consume alcohol or take drugs while she is pregnant. Drinking alcohol heavily can result in fetal alcohol syndrome (FAS), a condition that is physically apparent. FAS newborns have small eyes and a short, upturned nose that is broad across the bridge, making the eyes appear farther apart than normal. These babies also are underweight at birth and do not catch up as time passes. They often have some degree of mental retardation and may exhibit behavior problems. A mother who continues to take illicit drugs such as heroin, crack, or cocaine will have a baby who is already addicted to its mother's drug. The addiction may not be fatal, but the newborn will be uncomfortable and disagreeable until the addiction is controlled.

Some therapeutic drugs taken by pregnant women have also been shown to produce birth defects. The most notorious example is thalidomide, a mild sedative. During the 1950s women in more than 20 countries who had taken this drug gave birth to more than 7,000 severely deformed babies. The principal defect these children suffered from is a condition called phocomelia, characterized by extremely short limbs often with no fingers or toes.

Physical birth defects

Clubfoot

Approximately one newborn out of every 400 has a form of clubfoot. In the most serious form, known as equinovarus, the foot is twisted inward and downward and the foot itself is cupped or flexed. If both feet are clubbed in this manner the toes point to each other rather than straight ahead. Often the heel cord or Achilles tendon is taut so that the foot cannot be straightened without surgery.

A milder and more common type of clubfoot is called calcaneal valgus, in which the foot is bent upward and outward in the same way that you would flex your foot at the ankle. Still other forms include the talipes cavus in which the instep is abnormally elevated; talipes valgus in which the heel is turned outward, and talipes varus in which the heel is turned inward.

The seriously deformed clubfoot requires surgery to realign the bones and ligaments. The milder forms often can be cured by fitting the baby with corrective shoes to gradually move the bones back into alignment.

Cleft lip and cleft palate

Approximately 7,000 newborns (one of every 700 births) are born with cleft lip and/or cleft palate each year in the United States. Cleft lip and palate describe a condition in which a split remains in the lip and roof of the mouth. During growth *in utero* (in the womb) the lip or palate, which develop from the edges toward the middle, fail to grow together. The defect occurs most often among Asians and certain Native American groups, less frequently among whites, and least often among African Americans.

Approximately 25% of infants born with cleft palate have inherited the trait from one or both parents. The cause for the other 75% remains unknown, but probably is a combination of heredity, poor nutrition, use of drugs, or a disease the mother contracted while pregnant. The cleft may involve only the upper lip, may extend into the palate, or may be located on the back of the palate.

Surgery is especially important to correct the defect in the palate. Feeding a baby with cleft palate is difficult because the food can pass through the palate into the nasal cavity and may be inhaled and cause choking. In the newborn, whose bones have not completely hardened, surgery is relatively simple. As the child ages, however, surgical correction is more difficult and the child will require a speech therapist.

Spina bifida

Spina bifida or open spine occurs once in 2,000 births in the United States. It occurs because, as in cleft palate, the edges of the spine growing around the spinal cord do not meet. An open area remains which in the worst case of this disease leaves the spinal cord unprotected. The mildest form of spina bifida may be so slight that the defect does not have any effect on the child and is discovered by accident, usually when an x–ray is taken for another reason. The term spinal bifida means the spine is cleft, having an opening or space, in two parts.

Spina bifida may present itself as a cyst, ranging in size from a walnut to a grapefruit, in which some parts of the meninges (layers of connective tissue covering the spinal cord), spinal cord, or both are contained. The lump can be removed surgically. In the most serious form, the lump or cyst has little skin or covering so spinal fluid may leak from it. Roots of the spinal nerves are contained within the cyst and the cyst may be covered with sores. Infection is a serious risk until surgery has been performed and the area has healed. Unfortunately, this leaves the child's legs paralyzed and without feeling. Problems may develop later in control of the bowels and bladder.

Newborns with spina bifida often have a condition called hydrocephalus, which literally means water in the head. In this condition, cerebrospinal fluid collects in and around the brain and will not drain. Mental retardation can result if the fluid is not drained regularly. This can be accomplished by implanting a special tube (called a shunt) leading from the brain down into a vein in the child's neck or into the child's chest to allow the fluid to drain harmlessly. Hydrocephaly also can occur in infants who do not have spina bifida. The cause of spina bifida is not known, nor is any means of prevention. It can be diagnosed before birth by amniocentesis or ultrasound.

Heart defects

Congenital heart defects occur in one of every 175 births in the United States. The defect may be so mild that it is not detected for some years or it may be fatal. A baby with a heart defect may be born showing a bluish tinge around the lips and on the fingers. This condition, called cyanosis, is a signal that the body is not receiving enough oxygen. The blue color may disappear shortly after birth, indicating that all is normal or it may persist, indicating that further testing is needed to determine the nature of the heart defect.

A normal heart has four chambers; two upper, called the atria (singular: atrium) and two lower called the ventricles. Veins returning blood from the body lead into the upper right chamber, and from the lower right chamber to the lungs. From the lungs vessels flow into the left upper chamber, and the main blood vessel of the body, the aorta, leads out of the left lower chamber.

In the womb there are changes in this cycle because the fetus' blood does not need to flow through its lungs. It receives its oxygen from the mother through the placenta via the umbilical cord. A special shunt in place during development of the fetus closes at birth so the blood is cycled in the right direction. Failure of this shunt to close allows blood to back up into the lungs with serious consequences. Surgery is required to close the shunt and restore normal circulation.

If it is undetected at birth, a heart defect may impair the growth of a child. He will be unable to exert the energy that other children do at play because he cannot supply sufficient blood to his body. He may become breathless at small amounts of exertion and may squat frequently because it is easier to breathe in that position.

Some minor defects may disappear over time as the child grows. A small hole in the wall between the left and right sides of the heart, for example, may grow closed. A larger defect will require surgical patching.

Some newborns may have only one upper chamber or only a single lower chamber of the heart. The aorta, where it begins at the heart, may be pinched and impair the flow of blood from the heart. Some of the heart valves may not function correctly and occasionally the vessels of the heart may be transposed so that the aorta leads from the right side of the heart.

These are only a few of the heart anomalies that can be present in the newborn. The heart is a complicated organ and its formation can be influenced by hereditary factors as well as by alcohol consumption or smoking. Fortunately, most heart defects correct themselves over time or can be corrected with surgery.

Other physical deformities

Physical defects in newborns are common. They can affect any of the bones or muscles in the body and may or may not be correctable. Among the more common are the presence of extra fingers or toes (poly-dactyly), which presents no health threat and can be corrected surgically. Similarly, webbed fingers and toes, a genetic disorder, seen in approximately one of every 1,700 to 2,000 births, can be treated surgically to resemble a normal appendage.

A more serious, though relatively rare, condition is called achondroplasia; this term means without carti-lage formation and refers to the supposed lack of carti-lage growth plates near the ends of a child's bones. In fact in the plates are present, but grow poorly. Achon-droplasia is a type of dwarfism. This genetic disorder of bone growth is seen in one in 25,000–40,000 births and is one of the oldest known birth defects. Ancient Egyptian art shows individuals with this condition.

The cause of achondroplasia is not known, nor is there a cure. The child who has this condition will be slow at walking and sitting because of his short arms and legs, and this may be interpreted as mental retarda-tion. However, these individuals have normal intelli-gence.

Hereditary diseases and syndromes

In addition to physical deformities, certain dis-eases and syndromes also are passed to the infant through the parents' genes. Some of these conditions can be controlled or treated while others are untreat-able and fatal.

Sickle cell anemia

Sickle cell anemia is an inherited disease of the blood cells that occurs in one of every 400–600 African Americans. An individual can be a carrier of sickle cell anemia, in which case he or she has the gene but does not show any active signs of the disease. If two carriers become parents, however, some of their children may have sickle cell anemia.

The disease gets its name because certain red blood cells assume a sickle shape and lodge in small blood vessels. This altered shape is a function of the hemoglo-bin molecule present in red blood cells. Two forms of hemoglobin make up these cell: hemoglobin A (Hb A) and hemoglobin B (Hb B). In individuals with sickle cell anemia, Hb B transforms into Hb S, a form of hemoglobin with a rigid, sickle shape that deforms the red blood cell. When the cell becomes wedged in a small blood vessel it prevents the flow of blood through the vessel and can initiate what is called a sickle cell crisis. The lack of blood flow to the tissues being blocked causes pain and degeneration of the tissue.

Abnormal red blood cells are removed from the circulatory system by the spleen, but removal of large numbers of such cells can lead to anemia, a lack of adequate numbers red blood cells. Unfortunately, the breakdown of abnormal red blood cells can in itself cause a serious condition in which excess iron, scav-enged from the hemoglobin molecule, is deposited in tissues such as the heart and liver. So, although replacement of the destroyed red blood cells could be achieved with blood transfusion, the replacement cells will only add to the iron content of blood. There is no cure for sickle cell anemia, though scientists are learn-ing how to better control it to prevent sickling of the blood cells.

Tay–Sachs disease

Tay–Sachs disease affects Jews of eastern Euro-pean origin, the Ashkenazi Jews, and is a condition that is fatal at an early age. A carrier of the disease will have a gene for Tay–Sachs disease and another gene that is normal. If two carriers have children, one in four will be normal, two in four can carry the trait and pass it on without showing any effects from it, and one in four may have the disease.

The newborn Tay–Sachs child lacks a blood enzyme called hexosaminidase A, which breaks down certain fats in the brain and nerve cells. When first born the baby may appear normal, but over a short period of time, as the brain cells become clogged with fatty deposits, the child will no longer smile, crawl or turn over and will become blind and unaware of his surroundings. Usually the child is dead by the age of three or four years.

Obviously there is no cure for Tay–Sachs disease, but carriers can be detected by a simple blood test that measures the amount of hexosaminidase A. A carrier will have half the amount of the enzyme as a normal person, and two carriers can be counseled to explain the probability of producing an offspring with Tay–Sachs disease. Researchers are trying to find a way to provide sufficient levels of the missing enzyme in the newborn, or to find a suitable substitute that could be supplied as the child ages, much like insulin is used to treat dia-betes. A more technologically advanced line of research is examining the possibility of transplanting a normal gene to replace the defective one in carriers.

Down's syndrome

One of every 800–1,000 babies is born with Down's syndrome. Down's syndrome babies may have eyes that slant upward, small ears that may turn over at the top, a small mouth and nose that also is flattened between the eyes (at the bridge). Mental retardation is present in varying degrees, but most Down's syndrome children have only mild to moderate retardation. Generally these children walk, talk, dress themselves, and are toilet trained later than children with normal intelligence.

Down's syndrome results when either the egg or the sperm that fertilizes it has an extra chromosome. Normally a human has 23 pairs of chromosomes, for a total of 46. An extra chromosome, specifically an extra number 21 chromosome, present when the egg is fertilized, leads to a baby with Down's syndrome. Of course, if either parent has Down's syndrome, the probability of passing the condition on to the offspring is increased. Also, parents who have had one Down's syndrome child and mothers older than 35 years of age are at increased risk of having a Down's syndrome baby. There is no cure, though many of these children can go on to attend school and hold jobs as do unaffected individuals.

It should be apparent from this small sample, that some birth defects are hereditary, passed from parents to offspring; little can now be done to prevent or cure these conditions, but genetic therapy offers hope that this situation may change in the future. Other birth defects result from maternal diseases or from maternal consumption of alcohol or drugs, use of tobacco, or exposure to radiation or chemicals during pregnancy. In some cases, these birth defects can be prevented through education or improved prenatal care.

See also Chorionic villus sampling; Congenital; Down's syndrome; Embryo and embryonic development; Fetal alcohol syndrome; Genetics; Sickle cell anemia; Spina bifida; Thalidomide.

Further Reading:

Drinking During Pregnancy: Fetal Alcohol Syndrome and Fetal Alcohol Effects. March of Dimes/Birth Defects Foundation, 1991.

Gorman, C. "Thalidomide's Return." *Time* 143 (13 June 1994): 67.

Grogen, D. "The Baby Killer." (Outbreak of Anencephaly in Texas). *People Weekly* 40 (27 September 1993): 86–89.

Down's Syndrome. March of Dimes/Birth Defects Foundation, 1993.

Low Birth Weight. March of Dimes/Birth Defects Foundation, 1991.

Purdy, C. "Birth Defects: Life Goes On." *Current Health* 2 (October 1993): 12–13.

Larry Blaser

Bismuth see **Element, chemical**

Bison

The American bison *(Bison bison)* is a large, herbivorous land mammal native to the grasslands of North America. Bisons are members of the family Bovidae, which also includes cattle, sheep, and goats. When French explorers first saw these large, shaggy cow–like animals, they called them *boeufs,* the French word for "cattle." This was anglicized into the English word "buffalo" which is still applied to the bison, despite the fact that there are other animals in Africa and Asia known by this name.

There are two subspecies of American bison, the plains bison, *B. b. bison,* and the wood bison, *B. b. athabascae.* The wood bison historically lived west and north of the plains bison, is larger and darker in color. Because of its woodland habitat, it did not live in such huge herds as the plains bison. Some taxonomists do not recognize wood bison and plains bison as separate subspecies.

Bison probably came to North America across a land bridge in the region of the present–day Bering Straits from Eurasia during the Ice Ages when sea levels were lower, perhaps 25,000 years ago. The only remnant of the Eurasian population is the European bison, or wisent, *(B. bonasus),* which still lives in the forests of eastern Europe. A population of bisons in the Caucasus Mountains became extinct in 1925. A large captive–bred population of wisents live in the protected Bialowiecza Forest on the border between Poland and Russia. The wisent is somewhat smaller than the American bison and does not have as large a hump.

Bison (*Bison bison*) in Golden Gate Park, California.

America's largest mammal

The male bison can reach 6.5 ft (2 m) in height and measure up to 12 ft (3.7 m) long, and is twice as large as the female. Male bisons weigh up to 2,000 lbs (900 kg) and animals almost twice as large have been reported. American bison have a huge hump across the shoulders that rises sometimes a foot (30 cm) or more higher than the top of the head. The dark brown hair growing on the hump is long and shaggy, and the bison's thick winter fur allows it to withstand temperatures as low as –49°F (–45°C). In spring and fall, the bisons molt and great quantities of this hair falls off. The back half of the body has only short, lighter–colored hair. The head is covered with a helmet of thick black hair that terminates under the chin in a "goatee." Very rare white bison are revered by Native Americans of the Plains, and when one was born in 1994, people traveled long distances to Wisconsin to see it. As the calf grew, its fur turned darker.

Growing sideways from their large heavy heads bison have large curved hollow horns, which are never shed. The horns may reach 24–26 in (60–65 cm) long but are usually much shorter. The female's horns curve back toward the head more than the male's. Bison have no front teeth, and eat grass by wrapping it around their tongues and pulling or breaking it off. Bison are ruminants, which have a four–chambered stomach and which chew a cud.

Their short tails are used both as flyswatters and as indicators of excitement, for the normally drooping tail rises into the air when the animal is angry or excited. Bison are subject to attack by numerous prairie insects, so they have a habit of rolling in dust or mud to relieve the annoyance. They can't roll over completely, probably because of their humps, so they rock and kick first on one side and then on the other. This procedure is called wallowing. Wallowing also helps the animals get rid of their molting hair.

Life in the herds

Estimates of the numbers of bison on the American plains before the arrival of Europeans vary from 30–80 million. They were a "pantry on the hoof" for the Plains tribes of Native Americans, who used the animals for food, clothing, fuel, and shelter, killing only the animals they needed to survive.

Bison herds move around constantly in search of food and water, and may travel about 2 mi (3 km) a day. Unlike many migrating animals, bison did not follow set paths each year, and anything could change their direction—a fearful scent on the wind, a strange animal crossing their path, the fact that a water hole had dried up. The only set pattern to their migration is that they meander north to find a good place to raise their young in the summer, and then south to ride out the winter. The herd follows the lead bison, and bison in herds continually make noises to each other, with roars, grunts, sneezing, snorts, and bawling communicating different meanings.

The least hint of danger might set an entire herd stampeding across the plains. Their stampede speed might reach 35 mph (56 kph), though they usually can not keep up that speed for more than about half an hour at a time. If running does not shake their pursuers, bison will turn abruptly and charge. The animal's skull bone in the forehead is double–thick, which protects the brain from damage during impact.

The continuing generations

In the early summer, bulls and cows gather for the rut. During the rut, the bulls challenge each other for

518

KEY TERMS

Bovid—An animal of the Bovidae, or cow, family, characterized by grazing and having hollow horns.

Molt—To lose one type of hair in preparation for a new type to grow in. Bison molt twice a year as the seasons change.

Ruminant—An animal that has teeth especially adapted for grazing and has a four–chambered stomach.

Rut—The period during which males challenge each other to acquire mates.

Wallowing—Rolling and kicking in the dust to eliminate insect pests.

the right to mate with the cows. Cows mate when they are about two years old, but bulls mate when they are older and strong enough to challenge dominant males. A few loud roars and a demonstration of kicking and wallowing is usually enough to convince a lower ranked male to look elsewhere for a mate. Only rarely does an actual fight occur, when bison lock horns and charge each other.

When a dominant male selects a mate, he bonds with her by grazing side by side for some hours, away from the rest of the herd. After a brief nocturnal mating, the companionship may continue for a brief time, but then the male departs, looking for another female. The females usually mate only once.

The gestation period lasts nine–and–a–half months, so new calves are born in spring, starting about mid–April, though births continue on into early autumn. Newborn cinnamon–colored calves weighing about 50 lbs (23 kg) can walk and nurse within two or three hours of birth. The calves start to eat grass within about 15 days and at about two months old their humps and horns begin to show and their coats darken to the adult color. Bison will live to be an average of about 20 years old in the wild though they can reach 40 years in captivity.

The disappearing bison

The large bison herds of North America shrank rapidly in the face of westward migration. The presence of bison conflicted with the aims of the people looking for land to settle, and with those of the government that wanted to eliminate the native tribes. As the railroads were built through the Central Plains, travelers were encouraged to shoot bison from the windows of the train, killing as many animals as they could. The

carcasses were often just left to rot. By 1905, there were only about 500 bison left on the range in the United States. A herd of endangered wood bison, discovered in northern Canada in 1957, lives protected in Wood Buffalo National Park, and other locales.

Although bison are still a threatened species, today there are wild herds of sufficient size to allow some ranchers to raise domestic herds and to sell buffalo meat, which has less cholesterol than beef. It has been suggested that large herds of bison once again be allowed to roam free in the North American Plains, so creating a major tourist industry to bring money to an economically depressed region.

Further Reading:
Berman, Ruth. *American Bison.* Minneapolis: Carolrhoda Books, 1992.
Caras, Roger A. *North American Mammals: Fur–Bearing Animals of the United States and Canada.* New York: Meredith Press, 1967.
Green, Carl R., and William R. Sanford. *The Bison.* New York: Crestwood House, 1985.
McHugh, Tom. *The Time of the Buffalo.* Lincoln: University of Nebraska Press, 1972.
Time–Life Books, eds. *Lords of the Plains.* Alexandria, VA: Time–Life Books, 1993.
Stidworthy, John. *Mammals: The Large Plant–Eaters.* New York: Facts On File, 1988.

Jean F. Blashfield

Biting lice see **Lice**

Bitterns

Bitterns are about 12 species of wading birds in the subfamily Botaurinae of the family Ardeidae, which also includes herons and egrets. There are two genera: four species of the relatively large and stocky true bitterns (*Botaurus* spp.), and eight species of the much smaller and more slender, least bitterns (*Ixobrychus*).

Bitterns have brown–and–black, vertically streaked plumage, which renders them well camouflaged in their marshy or reed–fringed habitats. Male and female bitterns have identical plumage. When a potential predator is in the vicinity, bitterns will try to blend in with their surroundings by extending their neck and bill upright, compressing their brownish–streaked breast plumage, and facing the intruder. Bitterns may also sinuously wave their body to emulate the movements of the surrounding, wind–blown reeds and bulrushes.

Bitterns are unobtrusive animals, and many people are unaware of the presence of these animals, even in marshes where they are breeding. Bitterns fly with a slow wingbeat, low over the tops of the marsh vegetation, and then suddenly drop down out of sight to land.

Bitterns mostly eat fish, but they also take aquatic invertebrates, snakes, frogs, baby birds, and small mammals when these are available. Bitterns slowly and deliberately stalk their prey, and then capture their victim by quickly spearing it with a rapid thrust of the beak.

Bitterns usually nest on rough platforms that they construct out of sticks or marsh vegetation. The nest may be placed in a concealed place on the ground, or in a shrub or low tree. Bitterns lay three to six eggs, which are incubated by the female, who is also mostly or totally responsible for rearing the brood.

Species of bitterns

The American bittern (*Botaurus lentiginosus*) breeds in freshwater and brackish marshes over most of the temperate zone of North America, and as far south as central Mexico. Most North American populations migrate to the southern United States and Central America to spend their non–breeding season. American bitterns mostly eat fish, but they will also predate on other appropriately sized, aquatic prey. Male American bitterns have a distinctive "song" in the springtime, when they are establishing a breeding territory and attempting to attract a mate. This booming call can be heard over a distance of several miles, and more or less sounds like a pumping, "ong–ka–chonk." Some local names of the American bittern reflect its call: "thunder pump" and "stake driver."

Other species of *Botaurus* occur in non–overlapping ranges on other continents. These species are all rather similar, and although considered to be taxonomically distinct, they form a closely–related, "superspecies." The other species of bitterns include the Eurasian bittern (*Botaurus stellaris*) of Europe and Asia, the Australian bittern (*B. poiciloptilus*), and the South American bittern (*B. pinnatus*).

The least bittern (*Ixobrychus exilis*) is the smallest species of heron in North America. This secretive species breeds widely in freshwater and coastal marshes in the eastern United States and southeastern Canada. Least bitterns also breed in a disjunct, western range in California and Oregon, and south to Brazil, Paraguay, and northern Argentina. Northern populations of the least bittern migrate to northern Mexico and Baha California for the winter. The least bittern mostly feeds on small fish, which it stalks patiently and then spears with its bill.

An American bittern in Florida.

The various species of *Ixobrychus* also have non–overlapping ranges, and also form a closely–related "superspecies." The species include the little bittern (*I. minutus*) of Europe, Asia, Africa, and Australia, and the Chinese little bittern (*I. sinensis*) of eastern Asia.

Conservation of bitterns

Habitat losses associated with the drainage of wetlands for agricultural and residential developments are the most important threats to bitterns in North America and elsewhere. Pollution may also be significant in degrading habitat in some regions.

As a result of these and other stressors, the populations of both American bitterns and least bitterns are widely acknowledged as having declined substantially in North America. There is significant concern about the population status of both species in most parts of their ranges in the United States and Canada.

KEY TERMS

Marsh—A type of productive wetland that is dominated by tall, emergent plants, such as reeds, bulrushes, and cattails.

Superspecies—This refers to a complex of taxonomically distinct, but closely related, and anatomically and behaviorally similar species, usually occupying non–overlapping ranges. Both of the genera of bitterns are considered to be superspecies.

Wader—This is a general term for various long–legged, long–necked, long–beaked, short–tailed birds of marshes and swamps that stand in shallow water while stalking their prey. Waders include species in the heron family, as well as birds in other families, such as storks, ibises, flamingos, spoonbills, and cranes.

Like so many other species that require wetlands as habitat, the survival of bitterns can only be ensured by caring for the ecosystems of which they are an integral part. In this case, the key is the conservation and protection of wetlands.

Further Reading:

Ehrlich, P. R., D. S. Dobkin, D. Wheye. *Birds in Jeopardy.* Stanford, CA: Stanford University Press, 1992.
Hancock, J. and J. Kushlan. 1984. *The Herons Handbook.* London: Croom Helm, 1984.
Harrison, C. J. O., ed. *Bird Families of the World.* New York: H.N. Abrams Pubs., 1978.
Marquis, M. *Herons.* London: Colin Baxter, 1993.

Bill Freedman

Bivalves

Bivalve molluscs belong to the class Bivalvia or Lamellibranchia of the phylum Mollusca. Known by such common names as clams, mussels, cockles, oysters, and scallops, bivalves are among the most familiar aquatic invertebrates, occurring in large numbers in marine, estuarine, and freshwater habitats all over the world. Over 30,000 living species of bivalves have been described. The main divisions of the Bivalvia are the Protobranchia (the primitive nutshells), the Filibranchia (the mussels, scallops, and oysters) and the Enamellibranchia (the cockles, clams, venus shells, razor shells, and shipworms).

The name bivalve refers to the limy shell, which consists of two pieces or valves, right and left, held closed by a pair of adductor muscles, and joined together by an elastic hinge ligament. The compressed body is completely enclosed by the shell valves, except for a hatchet–shaped, muscular foot, which extends between their lower edges so that the animals can burrow in soft sand or mud. The two halves of the shells are secreted by the two lobes of the body wall (the mantle), and consist of layers of calcium carbonate crystals embedded in a protein matrix. The innermost shell layer, which is often shiny and iridescent, is called mother of pearl. If a grain of sand or other foreign matter gets lodged between the mantle and the shell, a layer of this pearly material is secreted around it, forming, in some species, a pearl. The space between the body wall and the mantle is known as the mantle cavity. This cavity contains a pair of large, perforated, platelike gills which have a ciliated surface and which function in both respiration and feeding. The posterior edges of the mantle lobes join to form two tubes, or siphons. The beating of the gill cilia causes water to be drawn into the mantle cavity through the lower incurrent siphon; after passing across the gills where oxygen is extracted, the water is expelled by the excurrent siphon. They lack a well–developed head, and so their sense organs (such as eyes) are located on the fringe of the mantle.

Bivalves are filter feeders, using their perforated gills as a sieve, which collects minute algae or other food particles suspended in the incoming respiratory water. These particles are trapped in strings of mucus secreted by the gills and conveyed to the mouth by cilia. Marine bivalves reproduce by external fertilization, releasing prodigious numbers of eggs and sperm into the water which float in the surface plankton. Within 48 hours after fertilization, embryos develop into minute planktonic trochophore larvae. This stage is followed by another larval form, the veliger, which settles to the seabed and transforms into an adult. In freshwater bivalves, the eggs are retained in the gill chambers of the female, where they undergo fertilization and develop into a peculiar larval form, the glochidium. Upon its release, the larva attaches to passing fish, and lives as an ectoparasite for several weeks before settling.

Mussels and oysters do not burrow, but remain permanently fixed to hard substrata. Mussels are attached to rocks by clumps of byssus threads. In oysters, only the left valve is cemented to the rock. Scallops are able to swim by clapping their valves and ejecting water through an opening near the hinge area to produce a jet action. Scallops also have rows of eyes

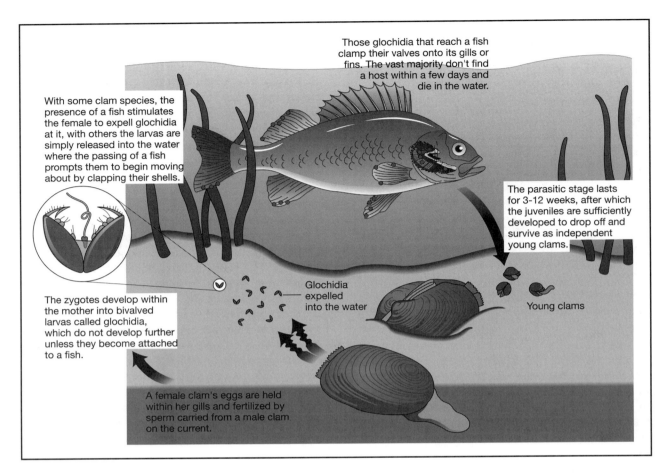

Those glochidia that reach a fish clamp their valves onto its gills or fins. The vast majority don't find a host within a few days and die in the water.

With some clam species, the presence of a fish stimulates the female to expel glochidia at it, with others the larvas are simply released into the water where the passing of a fish prompts them to begin moving about by clapping their shells.

The parasitic stage lasts for 3-12 weeks, after which the juveniles are sufficiently developed to drop off and survive as independent young clams.

The zygotes develop within the mother into bivalved larvas called glochidia, which do not develop further unless they become attached to a fish.

Glochidia expelled into the water

Young clams

A female clam's eggs are held within her gills and fertilized by sperm carried from a male clam on the current.

The life cycle of a typical freshwater clam. For species that don't have the parasitic larval stage, the fertilized eggs develop into young clams within the gills of the mother.

on the lower edges of the mantle. Other bivalves are able to bore into limestone, clay, or wood. Bivalves range in size from the fingernail–sized "nut shells" of the Atlantic coast of North America to the giant clam of the Indo–Pacific which measures up to 4.9 ft (1.5 m) in length and weighs more than 495 lb (225 kg).

Bivalves are of great economic importance as a food source, as a source of valuable products such as pearls, and, in the case of shipworms, because of their for destroying the wooden hulls of ships and wharf pilings.

See also Mollusks.

Blackberry see **Rose family**

Blackbirds

The blackbird family (Icteridae) consists of 94 medium–sized species of birds that occur only in the Americas. Blackbirds are found in widespread habitats, ranging from wetlands, to prairies, to forests. The most common members of the family are various species of blackbirds, grackles, cowbirds, orioles, meadowlarks, bobolink, and others.

Biology of blackbirds

Blackbirds tend to have conical shaped, pointed beaks. Most species are sexually dimorphic, particularly the relatively northern, migratory species. Males often have brilliant hues in their plumage and are commonly iridescent, while female blackbirds are usually relatively drab and cryptically marked. Some male blackbirds incorporate splendid yellow, orange, and red colors in their plumage.

Some species of the blackbirds are accomplished vocalists, displaying a complex repertoire of loud and clear whistles and calls. Orioles are among the most

bird (*Xanthocephalus xanthocephalus*) are typical of marshes and some other wet habitats.

The most widespread species is the red–winged blackbird, which ranges from the subarctic to Central America. This common and familiar bird breeds in tall marshes and other wet places. The male red–winged blackbird is colored as its name implies, with a jet–black body and richly red epaulets on the shoulders. Female red blackbirds have a streaky, brown plumage, and look much like large sparrows. After the breeding season, red–winged blackbirds aggregate into large flocks which forage widely for small grains, and can cause agricultural damage. Red–winged blackbirds generally spend the winter in these flocks, mostly in southern parts of their range, where they forage during the day and roost communally at night in woodlands and marshes.

The most northerly blackbird is the rusty blackbird (*Euphagus carolinus*), which in some places breeds as far as the limits of the mainland in the western Arctic. The most southerly species is the red–breasted blackbird (*Leistes militaris*) of the Falkland Islands.

Blackbirds that breed in the north are migratory. The longest migrations are undertaken by the bobolink. This species breeds in prairies and hayfields as far north as southern Canada, and winters in pampas and other grasslands as far south as Argentina. Tropical members of the blackbird family are not migratory, but they may undertake local, seasonal movements.

Cowbirds, such as the brown–headed cowbird (*Molothrus ater*) of North America, are species of open habitats. As their name implies, these birds often associate with grazing livestock, feeding on insects that these animals flush as they move through vegetation. Cowbirds have an unusual breeding strategy. Instead of building their own nest and raising their young, cowbirds are nest parasites. They surreptitiously lay single eggs in the nests of other species, and sometimes remove eggs of the host bird. If the host birds do not recognize the cowbird egg as being alien, they will brood it and care for the hatchling until it fledges. Many of the approximately 200 species of birds known to be parasitized by the brown–headed cowbird are relatively small, such as vireos, warblers, and thrushes. The nestlings of these birds suffer as a result of the disproportionate demands placed by the voracious cowbird chick on its foster parents, and in many cases this causes the reproductive effort of the host birds to fail. The cowbird chick develops rapidly, and can fly in only nine or ten days after hatching.

A male brown-headed cowbird in Kirtland's warbler breeding territory near Mio, Michigan. Because the cowbird lays its eggs in the nests of other birds, where its aggressive hatchlings often out-compete their nest mates for food, the cowbird has been identified as a factor in the decline of the Kirtland's warbler, an endangered species known only to nest in north-central Michigan.

musical of the blackbirds, producing rather pleasing, flute–like melodies.

Species of blackbirds

Blackbirds exploit a wide range of habitats. Most species occur in tropical forests of various sorts, but virtually all types of terrestrial and wetland habitats are utilized by some species. In North America, the northern oriole (*Icterus galbula*) is a species of open forests, where it builds its characteristic, pendulous nests, often in elm trees. The bobolink (*Dolichonyx oryzivorus*) and meadowlarks (*Sturnella* spp.) are more typical of open grasslands and prairies, while the red–winged blackbird (*Agelaius phoeniceus*) and yellow–headed black-

Outside of the Americas, the blackbird (*Turdus merula*) of Europe, is actually a member of the thrush family, Turdidae.

Blackbirds and humans

Cowbirds are considered to be an important pest in those parts of North America to which the species has expanded its range as a result of the fragmentation of the initially forested landscape by humans. Birds in those regions tend not to be well adapted to cowbird parasitism, and the reproductive success of their populations can be markedly reduced by this relationship. In some cases, cowbirds are sought out and killed by conservation biologists, in order to reduce the negative impact of parasitism on rare and endangered species of birds, such as the Kirtland's warbler (*Dendroica kirtlandii*) of Michigan.

Some species of blackbirds are highly gregarious, especially during autumn and winter when they aggregate into flocks that can contain millions of birds. Winter flocks of the red–winged blackbird are sometimes regarded as an agricultural nuisance because of damages caused to fields of winter wheat and some other crops. Sometimes, pest–control actions are mounted against these flocks, and millions of these native birds may be killed when they are sprayed with chemicals are their communal roost sites.

See also Thrushes.

Further Reading:

Brooke, M., and T. Birkhead. *The Cambridge Encyclopedia of Ornithology.* Cambridge: Cambridge University Press, 1991. U.K.

Harrison, C. J. O., ed. *Bird Families of the World.* New York: H. N. Abrams, 1978.

Orians, G. H. *Blackbirds of the Americas.* Seattle: Washington University Press, 1986.

Bill Freedman

Blackbody radiation

The term blackbody radiation refers to electromagnetic radiation emitted by a completely opaque object. Such an object is referred to as a blackbody since it absorbs all of the radiation that falls on it and thus appears to be colorless, or black. According to Kirchoff's law, any object that qualifies as a blackbody must also be a perfect emitter of radiation.

In fact, no real object fits the definition of a blackbody since even the most opaque of materials reflects some small fraction of the light incident upon it. Soot, carbon black, platinum black, and carborundum are among the materials that come closest to a blackbody in the real world. the concept of an idealized blackbody is still of major importance in physics. It serves as a standard for heat and temperature measurements just as the wavelength of light emitted by krypton–86 atoms is a standard for measurements of length.

For research purposes, physicists replicate the principle of a blackbody with a device known as a cavity radiator. A cavity radiator is a hollow sphere with a small hole through which radiation can enter and leave. Radiation that enters the hole is reflected continuously within the sphere until it is completely absorbed (as would be the case with a blackbody). It follows, then, that any radiation emitted by the cavity radiator corresponds to the definition of blackbody radiation.

The study of blackbody radiation was of considerable interest to physicists in the late 1800s. Experiments showed that for any given temperature, the intensity (brightness) of blackbody radiation is a maximum for a relatively narrow range of wavelengths, dropping off sharply at shorter and longer wavelengths. A number of attempts were made to use classical electromagnetic theory to derive a mathematical formula that would describe the intensity/wavelength relationship, but all failed for one or another part of the curve. Finally, in 1900, the German physicist Max Planck solved the problem. By assuming that radiation travels not in continuous waves, but in discrete "packages" (called quanta), Planck was able to derive a formula for the blackbody radiation curve. That formula is:

$$I = (\hbar c^2/\lambda^5)[\exp(\hbar c/\lambda kT - 1]^{-1}$$

where $\hbar$ is Planck's constant, k is Boltzmann's constant, λ is the wavelength of the radiation, and T is the absolute temperature.

Black hole

Anyone who has ever watched the launch of a rocket is familiar with the concept that escape from a gravitational field requires the expenditure of energy. The stronger the gravitational field, more energy is required to escape from its clutches. If the rocket has insufficient fuel, it will return to Earth and escape is impossible. Thus, it is not hard to imagine a gravitational field strong enough to prevent the escape of any object with a finite amount of energy.

The gravitational force of an object is governed by a combination of the amount of matter it contains and its volume. The more the matter is confined in progressively smaller volume, the larger the gravitational field at the surface of the object. Since even a light beam has a finite amount of energy, one can imagine a massive object in a sufficiently small volume that would posses a gravitational field strong enough to prevent the escape of that light. The French mathematician Simon Laplace reasoned in 1795 that, if Newton's corpuscular theory of light were correct, there could exist massive object from which light could not escape.

Indeed, any theory of gravity should contain the notion of such an object. In the case of Einstein's theory of General Relativity, we call such an object a black hole.

However, in the case of general relativity, the path taken by a light beam defines the geometry of space–time for it represents the "shortest distance between two points." Such a path is called a geodesic. Thus, for a black hole in general relativity, a light beam originating on the surface that cannot escape really travels nowhere. In some sense, all "surface" points can be viewed as the same point and the object can be said to have been sealed off from the ordinary space and time of outside observers. The point from which light can no longer escape is known as the event horizon since knowledge of events beyond that point can never be transmitted to the outside world by a light beam or any other mechanism. The event horizon imposes a form of censorship on the makeup of a black hole. Indeed, the only aspects of a black hole that may be ascertained from outside are its mass, net charge, and rate of spin. No internal processes that depend on time in any way can be detected in the external environment, for that would constitute sending signals from inside the black hole to the outside when not even light can escape. This "censorship" is what is responsible for the small number of measurable properties of the black hole itself—mass, spin, and charge.

While there are complications in defining the size of a black hole, one can uniquely specify its circumference and thus define a radius as just the circumference divided by 2π. This radius is known as the Schwarzschild radius after Karl Schwarzschild, who first defined it as $R_s = 2GM/c^2$. Here M is the mass of the black hole, G is the Newtonian constant of gravity, and c is the speed of light. However, R_s should not be viewed as the distance from the event horizon of the black hole to its center. The geometry of space–time in the interior of the black hole is so warped that Euclidean notions of distance no longer apply. Nevertheless,

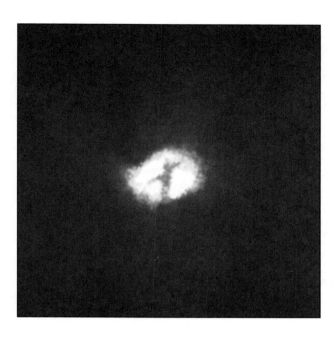

An image of the core of the Whirlpool galaxy M51 (NGC 5194) taken by the Wide Field Planetary Camera onboard the Hubble Space Telescope. It shows an immense ring of dust and gas (the x-shaped dark lanes at center) which is thought to surround and hide a giant black hole, 1 million times the mass of the Sun, in the center of the galaxy. The ring forms an accretion disc of gas, about 100 light years across, falling toward the black hole. The two brighter areas perpendicular to the widest dark lane are two jets of particles accelerated by the black hole.

R_s does provide a measure of the space around a particular mass M that will be seriously warped. R_s for an object having the mass of the Sun is about 3 km. Thus, to turn the Sun into a black hole, one would have to cram all of its mass into a sphere having about a 3 km radius. Squeezing any such mass into a volume dictated by its Schwarzschild radius posses a serious assembly problem. In fact, about the only processes which might lead to the formation of a black hole involve the death of moderately massive normal stars or the formation of supermassive stars.

As evolving stars exhaust the nuclear fuel which enables them to support their own weight and shine at the same time, they begin a rapid collapse. It is believed that the crushing self–gravity of the collapsing star may be sufficient to form a black hole with the mass of several times that of the Sun. Such black holes would have Schwarzschild radii of several to perhaps a few tens of kilometers. Considering their mass, they are really tiny things. If one were to replace the Sun with a black hole of the same mass as the Sun, there would be a region of space a few kilometers in size located where the center of the Sun currently resides where space would be extremely warped. However, the gravitational field of this object, measured at the distance of the Earth, would be exactly that of the present–day Sun. The Earth and planets would continue in their orbits and except for it being rather dark, the solar system would continue much as it does today. If one were to launch a rocket from the Earth to hit the black hole, the task would be immensely more difficult than hitting the Sun. The Sun presents a target nearly one and a half million kilometers across while the black hole would be more than one hundred thousand times smaller. This emphasizes just how difficult it is to feed matter into a black hole.

Normally, one must get within a few Schwarzschild radii in order to feel the major effects of the black hole. Indeed, one of the observational tests for the presence of a black hole in binary systems involves observing heated matter as it is unmercifully squeezed during its final plunge into the black hole. Such matter will emit fluctuating amounts of x rays as a result of being squeezed. The rate of fluctuation is tied to the size of the emitting region and we find in such systems that the x rays come from a volume of space only a few kilometers in size. These are the dimensions of the environment surrounding a black hole of stellar proportions. In several instances, further analysis of the orbital motion in the binary system indicates that the dark unseen member of the binary system is much more massive than the Sun. A dark stellar component more massive than the Sun confined to a volume smaller than a few kilometers is a prime candidate for a black hole.

There is at least one other situation where astronomers suspect the existence of a black hole. Again, since it does not radiate light, we must detect it through the effect its gravitational field has on neighboring objects. In the centers of some galaxies the stars, gas and dust of the galaxy are moving at very high speeds, suggesting they are being pulled about by the gravity of some very massive object. If the object was a collection of massive stars, it would shine so brightly as to dominate the light from the galactic center. The absence of light from the massive object suggests it is a black hole. In one active galaxy, the Hubble Space Telescope has even observed disks of matter that appear be accreting onto a central massive dark object which is likely to be a black hole. Recently a large team of astronomers reported the results of a world-wide study involving the Hubble Space Telescope, the International Ultraviolet Explorer satellite (IUE) and many ground based telescopes which were able to detect light which was emitted by the accreting matter

as it spirals into the black hole which was subsequently absorbed and re–emitted by the orbiting clouds just a few light–days away from the central source. Mass estimates of the central source determined from the motion of these clouds suggests that the object has a mass of at least several million times the mass of the Sun. So much material contained in a volume of space no larger than a few light days provides the best evidence yet for the existence of a black hole at the center of this galaxy.

The concept of massive black holes at the centers of some galaxies is supported by theoretical investigations of the formation of very massive stars. Stars of more than about one hundred time the mass of the Sun cannot form because they will explode from nuclear energy released during their contraction before the star can shrink far enough for its self–gravity to hold it together. However, if cloud of interstellar material collapsing to form a star contains about a million time the mass of the Sun, the collapse will occur so fast that the nuclear processes initiated by the collapse will not stop the collapse and disrupt the star. The collapse will continuum unrestrained until the object formed is a black hole with a mass a million times the mass of the Sun or more.

Such objects appear to be required to understand the behavior of the material in the center of some galaxies. Indeed, it seems likely that black holes may reside at the centers of normal galaxies such as our own Milky Way. Again, the best evidence comes from the motion of gas clouds near the galactic center. However, the presence of a black hole at the center of our own galaxy is further supported by the observation of certain energetic gamma rays emanating from the galactic center. The origin of these rays requires an extremely energetic environment such as is found in the immediate neighborhood of a black hole.

All that has been said so far involves black holes as described by the general theory of relativity. However, in the realm of the very small, quantum mechanics has proved to be the proper theory to describe the physical world. To date, no one has successfully combined general relativity with quantum mechanics to produce a fully self consistent theory of quantum gravity. However, in 1974 Stephen Hawking suggested that an application of quantum principles to a black hole showed that it would radiate energy like a perfect radiator having a temperature inversely proportional to its mass. While the amount of radiation for any astrophysical black hole is pathetically small (e.g. a radiation temperature for a black hole with the mass of the sun would be $10–7K$), the possibility of it happening at all was revolutionary. It suggested the first link between quantum theory and general relativity and has spawned a host of new ideas which expand the relationship between the two theories. It represents a classical example of a concept which may have little if any direct practical application, but revolutionizes the way in which we view the physical world.

See also Relativity, general; Stellar evolution; Supernova.

George W. Collins II

Black smoker see **Hydrothermal vents**

Bleach

Bleaches are substances that whiten textiles and paper by chemical reaction. These reactions usually involve processes that degrade color. They may destroy or modify chemical bonds or groups that give fabrics their characteristic colors. This process degrades color bodies into smaller, more soluble units that are easily removed in laundering. Conventional bleaching agents, include two types: chlorine–based bleaches, such as sodium hypochlorite, and peroxygen bleaching agents such as hydrogen peroxide and sodium perborate.

Textile bleaching

The bleaching of textiles appears to have been known as early as 300 B.C. when soda ash was prepared from burned seaweed and used to clean cloth. Then the cloth was treated with soured milk to reduce its alkalinity. The bleaching process was completed when the cloth was exposed to the Sun. This type of sun bleaching typically took several weeks.

A Swedish chemist discovered chlorine gas in 1784 and succeeded in demonstrating its use for decolorizing vegetable dyes. Fifteen years later a patent was awarded for a bleaching powder formed by the absorption of chlorine gas into dry hydrate of lime. Following World War I the technology for shipping liquid chlorine was developed. This allowed for on–site production of sodium hypochlorite in textile mills and led to the development of other chlorine–based bleaches. In 1928, the first dry calcium hypochlorite bleach containing 70% available chlorine was produced in the United States. This material largely replaced bleaching powder in commercial bleaching.

Hydrogen peroxide was prepared as early as 1818 but did not find use in the bleaching of textiles until much later. By 1930, the prices of peroxides had dropped sufficiently to allow the use of hydrogen peroxide in the bleaching of cotton, wool, and silk. By 1940, 65% of all cotton bleaching was done with hydrogen peroxide.

Pulp bleaching

There are many parallels in the histories of pulp and textile bleaching because early paper commonly was made from rags. In the 1700s sunlight was used to bleach paper. After 1800 bleaching powder was used to whiten the rags used to make paper. In the early 1800s wood came into use as a source of paper and calcium hypochlorite was used as the bleaching agent.

After World War I chlorine bleaching came into use in paper production because compressed chlorine gas became available. By the 1950s, chlorine dioxide had become the principal pulp bleaching agent. More recently, peroxygens such as hydrogen peroxide have been used.

Household and commercial laundering

Before the twentieth century, home laundry bleaching in the United States was done by the same method used by the Romans and Gauls in ancient times: clothes were first laundered in a mildly alkaline bath then subjected to sunlight. In 1910–20 sodium hypochlorite solutions were developed and distributed regionally in the United States. By the mid–1930s these solutions had become available nationwide. In the 1950s, dry sources of hypochlorite were introduced but these products had disappeared by the late 1960s because consumers preferred liquid hypochlorites.

In Europe sodium perborate was first used as a bleaching agent in the early 1900s. The perborate dissolves during bleaching to release hydrogen peroxide. Sodium perborate continues to be used in European laundering because their laundering temperatures tend to be higher than those used in America.

See also Chlorine; Hydrogen peroxide; Paper; Sodium chloride; Sodium hypochlorite.

Further Reading:

Kirk–Othmer Encyclopedia of Chemical Technology, vol. 4, 4th ed. New York: John Wiley & Sons, Inc., 1992.

Blennies

Blennies are small, primarily tropical and subtropical marine fish. They are elongated and often eel–like in shape, with a dorsal fin running from the back of the head almost to the tail fin, and small abdominal fins; the pelvic fin is often completely absent. Many species also lack scales. The blenny's anatomy is well suited for hiding in cracks and crevices along shallow, rocky shorelines, their preferred habitat. Some species, however, dwell in deeper waters. Living and foraging close to the ocean floor, blennies are either carnivorous (meat eaters) or omnivorous (eating both meat and vegetation). A wide variety of body shapes, colors, patterns, and behaviors are displayed by the more than 732 species in the six families belonging to the suborder Blennioidei.

Many species of scaleless blennies (family Blenniidae) are distributed throughout the world. Scaleless blennies are often found in tide pools and complete their entire life cycle in one general location. These species are divided into two groups—the subfamily Blenniinae, which have immovable teeth firmly rooted in the jaw, and the subfamily Salariinae which have moveable teeth rooted in the gums.

Scaled blennies belong to the very large family Clinidae, or clinids. They inhabit temperate oceans primarily south of the Equator. Dazzling and varied colors and markings differentiate the species. The largest clinid, one of the many pointy–headed blennies, is the 24–inch (61–cm) kelpfish (*Heterostichus rostratus*) which inhabits the Pacific shoreline from British Columbia to Southern California, while the 8–inch (20–cm), blunt–headed, hairy blenny (*Labrisomus nuchipinnis*) lives in the tropical waters off both Atlantic coastlines. The pike blenny (*Chaenopsis ocellata*) is a tube–dwelling species found in Florida. Male pike blennies jealously defend their territories from other intruding males by aggressively displaying a stiffly raised dorsal fin and a widely gaping mouth. Two males may literally face off, gaping mouths touching, until one snaps its mouth shut on the other. Some of the smallest blennies are also found in the Clinidae family—the female of the species *Tripterygion nanus* found in the Marshall Islands, is fully grown at less than 0.75 in (1.9 cm) in length.

The largest blennies, often reaching 9 ft (2.7 m) in length, are found among the nine species of wolf fish and wolf eels belonging to the family Anarhichadidae. These cold water fish are found in the northern hemisphere. They have prominent canine teeth in the front of their jaws and massive grinding teeth in the back of their mouths. Two species, the Atlantic wolf fish (*Anarhichas lupus*) and the spotted wolf fish (*A. minor*), are fished commercially along the European coasts.

Blimp see **Airship**

Blindness see **Vision disorders**

Blindsnakes

These tiny, primitive burrowers live underground and forage for ants, termites, soft–bodied insects, and insect larvae. The eyes of most blindsnakes are degenerate; they are covered by scales and do not function. However, the eyes do have light–sensitive cells (rods), so these snakes may not be completely blind. The head is large and the mouth, like a shark's, is below and behind the snout, which is blunt or hooked. There is a tiny spine under the snake's stubby tail which anchors the animal while burrowing. The body is covered with smooth, shiny, tough scales, which even cover the belly, making it difficult for the snake to slither on solid surfaces. The body is cylindrical, either thin or thick. Blindsnakes are commonly black or brown, although some species completely lack any pigment.

The blindsnakes are classified in three families—the Typhlopidae (wormsnakes), the Leptotyphlopidae (threadsnakes), and the Anolmalepidae. The Typhlopidae and Leptotyphlopidae are so similar that most herpetologists include both in the Scolecophidia. Both families have a remnant pelvic girdle, one lung, and one oviduct. Threadsnakes have large teeth in the lower jaw and none in the upper jaw, while wormsnakes have teeth only on the upper jaw. The 15 species of threadlike Anomalepidae of tropical South America are also included in the Scolecophidia, but this family has teeth on both jaws and no vestigial pelvic girdle.

The 80 species of threadsnakes are found in tropical South America, Africa, and the southern United States, and range in length from 6–16 in (15–41 cm). Some species release foul–smelling excretions which ward off ravaging predators such as army ants. The Texas threadsnake incubates her eggs by muscular shivering to raise its body temperature, a strategy found in only one or two species of python.

The 200 species of worm snakes occur in tropical and temperate South America, Africa, Madagascar, southern Europe, Asia, and Australia. Wormsnakes range in length from 4.5 in (11.5 cm) to about 3 ft (91.5 cm). The Brahminy wormsnake is parthenogenic, the only species of snake to reproduce without mating, and every specimen found so far is female. This tiny species lives among plant roots and is transported by unsuspecting humans carrying potted plants from place to place. A single Brahminy wormsnake can populate an entirely new region.

Blindsnakes are harmless to humans, except for a species from India which is reputed to crawl into the ears of people sleeping on the ground.

See also Reptiles; Snakes.

Further Reading:

Bellairs, Angus. *The Life of Reptiles*. Vols. I and II. New York: Universe Books, 1970.

Mattison, Christopher. *Snakes of the World*. New York/Oxford: Facts on File Publications, 1986.

Parker, H. W. *Snakes: A Natural History*. Ithaca/London: Cornell University Press, 1977.

Porter, Kenneth R. *Herpetology*. Philadelphia/London/Toronto: W. B. Saunders Co., 1972.

Zug, George R. *Herpetology: An Introductory Biology of Amphibians and Reptiles*. San Diego: Academic Press, 1993.

Marie L. Thompson

BL Lacertae object

BL Lacertae objects, abbreviated BL Lac, are one subclass of active galactic nuclei (AGN), the extremely energetic nuclei of active galaxies. Roughly 40 BL Lac objects are known. Perhaps the most obvious property of BL Lac objects is that they look like stars. Astronomers originally thought the prototype, BL Lac, was a star. In fact, BL Lacertae is normally a variable star designation, two letters followed by a constellation name, because astronomers originally thought that BL Lac was a star whose brightness varies, a variable star. BL Lac objects do however have properties that are clearly not stellar. Unlike most stars, BL Lac objects are very strong sources of radio and infrared emission. This emission, which is called synchrotron emission, arises from electrons traveling near the speed of light in spiral paths in strong magnetic fields. Synchrotron emission generally is polarized, so BL Lac objects have polarized emission. When light or other electromagnetic radiation is polarized, the directions of the oscillations are the same. The amount of polarization and the brightness of BL Lac objects is highly variable. This variability is very rapid and erratic. They can change very significantly in times as short as 24 hours or less. The rapid variability tells us that the energy source is very small. Nothing can travel faster than the speed of light, including whatever signal or mechanism causes the BL Lac object to change its brightness. Therefore, if a BL Lac object changes its brightness significantly in a day its energy source must be less than one light day in radius. The spectrum of a BL Lac object contains very few if any absorption or emission lines, which are caused by interstellar gas. Their essentially featureless spectra tell us that there is very little interstellar gas around BL Lac objects. There is evidence for a faint fuzziness in some pictures of BL Lac objects. This fuzziness is most likely the host galaxy, of which the BL Lac object is the active nucleus. The currently most popular explanation of BL Lac objects is that they are the central very energetic nuclei of galaxies. The small central energy source in the nucleus is probably a supermassive black hole. However, astronomers are still very uncertain of their nature. We need to continue studying BL Lacertae objects to better understand them.

See also: Active Galactic Nuclei; Electromagnetic waves; Polarized light.

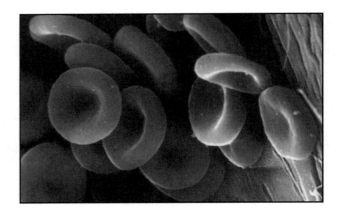

Red blood cells alongside the wall of the blood vessel.

Blood

Blood is a liquid connective tissue that performs many functions in the body, including transport of oxygen, carbon dioxide, nutrients, waste products, and hormones; clotting; and defense against microorganisms. Blood consists of formed elements, or blood cells suspended in plasma, a watery liquid that contains proteins, salts, and other substances. When a blood sample is placed in a test tube and spun rapidly (a process called centrifugation), the heavier blood cells sink to the bottom of the test tube, while the straw–colored plasma floats on top.

Kinds of blood found in the animal kingdom

All vertebrates circulate blood within blood vessels. Because blood is enclosed within blood vessels, the circulatory systems of vertebrates are called closed circulatory systems. Some animals without vertebrae, called invertebrates, have circulatory systems that do not contain blood vessels. In these open circulatory systems, the fluid analogous to blood is called hemolymph (Greek, *hemo*, blood + *lympha*, water). Examples of animals that circulate hemolymph include insects and aquatic arthropods such as lobsters and crawfish. Like blood, hemolymph transports oxygen and carbon dioxide and has a limited clotting ability. Unlike blood, hemolymph is colorless. Other invertebrates have no true circulatory system. In these animals, it is not possible to distinguish blood or hemolymph from the watery fluid that bathes the tissues. This fluid contains a few defensive cells, proteins, and salts. However, oxygen and carbon dioxide are not transported in this fluid.

The composition of human blood

The human body contains about 4 to 6.3 qt (4 to 6 l) of blood. Men have more blood than women, due to the presence of higher levels of testosterone, a hormone that regulates sex characteristics and function and also stimulates blood formation. Plasma makes up 55% of the blood, while the blood cells constitute the other 45%.

Plasma

Plasma contains mostly water, which accounts for 91.5% of the plasma content. The water acts as a solvent for carrying other substances.

Proteins account for 7% of plasma. The most prevalent of these proteins in plasma is albumin, a protein also found in egg white. Albumin concentration is four times higher in the blood than in the interstitial fluid (the watery fluid that bathes tissues, but is located outside and between cells). This high concentration of albumin in plasma serves an important osmotic function. The higher concentration of protein in blood prevents water from moving from the blood into the interstitial fluid. Without this osmotic protection, water would move from the interstitial fluid into the blood, diluting the plasma and swelling the blood volume. A high blood volume could have disastrous consequences, because the circulatory system can only pump so much blood before it becomes overloaded.

Other proteins that are present in plasma are immunoglobins and fibrinogen. Immunoglobins, also called antibodies, are proteins that function in the immune response. Antibodies attach to invading bacteria and other microorganisms, marking them for destruction by other immune cells. Fibrinogen is a protein that functions in a complex series of reactions that leads to the formation of blood clots.

The other components of plasma are salts, nutrients, enzymes, hormones, and nitrogenous waste products. Together, these substances account for 1.5% of plasma. The salts present in plasma include sodium, potassium, calcium, magnesium, chloride, and bicarbonate. These salts function in many important body processes. For instance, calcium functions in muscle contraction; sodium, chloride, and potassium function in nerve impulse transmission in nerve cells; and bicarbonate regulates pH. These salts are also called electrolytes. An imbalance of electrolytes, which can be caused by dehydration, can be a serious medical condition. Many gastrointestinal illness, such as cholera, cause a loss of electrolytes through severe diarrhea. When electrolytes are lost, they must be replaced with intravenous solutions of water and salts or by having the patient drink solutions of salts and water.

The remaining substances present in plasma are elements that the plasma is transporting from one place to another. For instance, plasma contains nutrients that nourish tissues. The nutrients found in plasma include amino acids, the building blocks of proteins; glucose, or sugars; and fatty acids and glycerol, the components of lipids (fats). In addition to nutrients, plasma also contains enzymes, or small proteins that function in chemical reactions, and hormones, which are transported from glands to body tissues. Waste products from the breakdown of proteins are also found in plasma. These waste products include creatinine, uric acid, and ammonium salts. Blood transports these waste products from the body tissues to the kidneys, where they are filtered from the blood and excreted in the urine.

Formed elements, or blood cells

Blood cells make up 45% of the total composition of blood. The various types of blood cells are erythrocytes, or red blood cells; leukocytes (also spelled leucocytes), or white blood cells; and platelets.

Red blood cells

The human body contains an estimated 25 trillion red blood cells; approximately 4.8 to 5.4 million are found in every liter of blood. The structure of a red blood cell is eminently suited to its primary function, the transport of oxygen from the lungs to body tissues. Red blood cells are very small (about 6 nanometers wide), disk–shaped, and contain a small depression on either side. Their small size allows them to squeeze through the tiniest blood vessels, called capillaries. In

KEY TERMS

ABO blood groups—Blood types established by the A and B antigens present on the plasma membrane of red blood cells; ABO blood groups include A, B, AB, and O.

Agranular leukocyte—A white blood cell without granules in its cytoplasm; these white blood cells include the monocytes and lymphocytes.

Aerobic metabolism—Metabolic processes that require oxygen.

Albumin—A protein found in plasma.

Antibody—An immune protein that marks foreign microorganisms in the body for destruction by other immune cells.

Antigen—A protein that is attached to a cell's plasma membrane.

B lymphocyte—A type of white blood cell that gives rise to antibodies.

Basophil—A type of white blood cell; functions in the inflammatory response by releasing histamines and other chemicals that have specific effects on tissues.

Capillary—The smallest blood vessels.

Centrifugation—A laboratory procedure in which a test–tube of blood or other liquid is spun at a high speed.

Circulatory system—The body system that circulates blood pumped by the heart through the blood vessels to the body tissues.

Clotting factor—A set of substances released by platelets that function in the clotting mechanism.

Cytotoxic T lymphocyte—A type of white blood cell that attacks and kills cells infected by a foreign microorganism.

Electrolytes—The salts and other substances present in the plasma that function in crucial body processes.

Eosinophil—A type of white blood cell that counteracts the effects of histamine and other inflammatory chemicals; also phagocytizes bacteria tagged by antibodies.

Erythrocyte—A red blood cell.

Fibrin—A protein that functions in the clotting mechanism; forms mesh–like threads that trap red blood cells.

addition, the small size of red blood cells allows a greater diffusion of oxygen across the blood cells' plasma membranes than if the cells were larger. Because blood contains so many of these small cells, the combined surface area of these many blood cells translates into an extremely large amount of surface area for the diffusion of oxygen. The disk shape and the depressions on either side also contribute to a greater surface area.

Red blood cells are unusual in that they do not contain nuclei or mitochondria, the cellular organelle in which aerobic metabolism (the breakdown of nutrients that requires oxygen) is carried out. Red blood cells acquire energy through metabolic process that do not require oxygen. The lack of nuclei and mitochondria therefore allow the red blood cell to function without depleting its cargo of oxygen, leaving more oxygen for the body tissues.

The molecule that binds oxygen in red blood cells is called hemoglobin. Hemoglobin is a large, globular protein consisting of four protein chains surrounding an iron core. Hemoglobin is densely packed inside the red blood cell; in fact, hemoglobin accounts for a third of the weight of the entire red blood cell. Each red blood cell contains about 250 molecules of hemoglobin. In the lungs, oxygen diffuses across the red blood cell membrane and binds to hemoglobin. As blood circulates to the tissues, oxygen diffuses out of the red blood cells and enters tissues. The waste product of aerobic metabolism, carbon dioxide then diffuses across red blood cells and binds to hemoglobin. Once circulated back to the lungs, the red blood cells discharge their load of carbon dioxide, which is then breathed out of the lungs. However, only 7% of carbon dioxide generated from metabolism is transported back to the lungs for exhalation by red blood cells; the majority is transported in the form of bicarbonate, a component of plasma.

Sickle cell anemia is an inherited disorder caused by a defect in one of hemoglobin's four protein chains. The sickle hemoglobin distorts the shape of the red blood cells and injuries the red blood cell membrane. Water and potassium leak from the cells, causing the red blood cells to become "sickle–shaped." The cells also become inflexible and rigid. As a result of these changes, oxygen transport is severely interrupted and circulation of the blood through the blood vessels can become blocked. These irregular blood cells do not carry as much oxygen as their normally–shaped counterparts. They also tend to become stuck in capillaries, leading to blood vessel blockage. Sickle cell anemia is invariably fatal; most people with the disease die in early adulthood.

KEY TERMS (cont'd)

Fibrinogen—The inactive form of fibrin present in plasma; activated by clotting factors released by platelets.

Formed elements—The cells present in blood.

Granular leukocyte—A white blood cell that contains granules in its cytoplasm; includes basophils, eosinophils, and neutrophils.

Helper T lymphocyte—A type of white blood cell that activates the immune system when it encounters an invading microorganism.

Hemoglobin—The protein found in red blood cells that binds oxygen; consists of four protein chains surrounding an iron core.

Hemolymph—The blood–like liquid present in the open circulatory systems of certain invertebrates.

Hemophilia—A genetic disorder in which one or more clotting factors are not released by the platelets; causes severe bleeding from even minor cuts and bruises.

Hemopoiesis—The process of red blood cell formation in the bone marrow.

Histamine—A chemical released by basophils during the inflammatory response; causes blood vessels to dilate.

Human leukocyte–associated (HLA) antigens—Antigens present on the plasma membrane of white blood cells.

Immunoglobin—An antibody.

Inflammatory response—A type of non–specific immune response; involves the release of chemicals from basophils that increase blood circulation and white blood cell migration to the affected area.

Interstitial fluid—The fluid that bathes cells.

Leukocyte—A white blood cell.

Red blood cells are formed in red bone marrow from precursor cells called pluripotent stem cells. The process of red blood cell formation is called hemopoiesis or hematopoiesis. In adults, hemopoiesis takes place in the marrow of ribs, vertebrae, breast bone, and pelvis. On average, a red blood cell lives only 3–4 months. Constant wear and tear on the red blood cell membrane, caused by squeezing through tiny capillaries, contribute to the red blood cell's short life span.

KEY TERMS (cont'd)

Lymph node—A small structure located at several points in the body; consists of lymphatic tissue that filters blood and remove microorganisms.

Lymphocyte—A type of white blood cell; includes B and T lymphocytes.

Lysozyme—An enzyme released by neutrophils that kills cells.

Macrophage—A type of phagocytic cell derived from monocytes.

Monocyte—A type of white blood cell that phagocytizes foreign microorganisms.

Neutrophil—A type of white blood cell that phagocytizes foreign microorganisms; also releases lysozyme.

Lymphoid stem cell—The cell from which B and T lymphocytes are derived.

Phagocytize—To engulf and digest a cell.

Plasma—The straw colored liquid portion of the blood that contains water, proteins, salts, nutrients, hormones, and metabolic wastes.

Plasma cell—The cell derived from the B lymphocyte which secretes antibodies.

Platelet—A piece of a cell that contains clotting factors.

Pluripotent stem cell—The type of stem cell from which red blood cells and more white blood cells are derived in the bone marrow.

Sickle cell anemia—A genetic disorder caused by a defect in one of hemoglobin's four protein chains; causes red blood cells to be sickle-shaped.

T lymphocyte—A type of lymphocyte that plays a key role in the immune response.

Thymus—The organ in which T cells undergo further development and maturation.

Worn out red blood cells are destroyed by phagocytic cells (cells that engulf and digest other cells) in the liver. Parts of red blood cells are recycled for use in other red blood cells, such as the iron component of hemoglobin.

An interesting aspect of red blood cells is that they carry certain proteins, called antigens, on their plasma membranes. These antigens are responsible for the vari-

ous blood groups known as A, B, AB, and O. A person with A antigens is type A; a person with B antigens is type B; a person with both antigens is type AB; and a person with none of the antigens is type O. A individuals have antibodies to B antigens; B individuals have antibodies to A antigens; AB individuals don't have antibodies to the antigens, and O individuals have antibodies to both A and B antigens. These combinations are necessary to know for blood transfusions. For instance, if a type A individual donates blood to a type B individual, the A antibodies in the recipient's B blood will react with the A antigens of the donor's A blood. This reaction, called the agglutination reaction, causes the blood cells to clump together. Agglutination can be fatal. Until blood typing was worked out early in this century, many deaths from blood transfusions occurred due to incompatibility of antigens and antibodies.

White blood cells

White blood cells are less numerous than red blood cells in the human body; each liter of blood contains 500–1000 white blood cells. The number of white blood cells increases, however, when the body is fighting off infection. White blood cells, therefore, are maintained at a stable number until the immune system detects the presence of a foreign invader. When the immune system is activated, chemicals called lymphokines stimulate the production of more white blood cells.

White blood cells function in the body's defense against invasion and are key components of the immune system. They usually do not circulate in the blood vessels, and are instead found in the interstitial fluid and in lymph nodes. Lymph nodes are composed of lymphatic tissue and are located at strategic places in the body. Blood filters through the lymph nodes, and the white cells present in the nodes attack and destroy any foreign invaders.

The human body contains five types of white blood cells: monocytes, neutrophils, basophils, eosinophils, and lymphocytes. Each type of white blood cells plays a specific role in the body's immune defense system.

Under a microscope, three kinds of white blood cells appear to contain granules within their cytoplasm. These three types are the neutrophils, basophils, and eosinophils. Together, these three types of white blood cells are called the granular leukocytes. The granules are specific chemicals released by these white blood cells during the immune response. The other two types of white blood cells, the monocytes and lymphocytes, do not contain granules. These types are known as the agranular leukocytes.

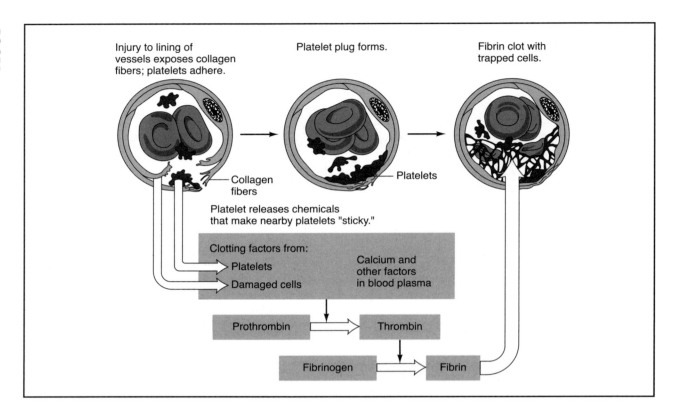

Figure 1. The clotting process.

Monocytes, which comprise 3–8% of the white blood cells, and neutrophils, which comprise 60–70% of white blood cells, are phagocytic cells. They ingest and digest cells, including foreign microorganisms such as bacteria. Monocytes differentiate into cells called macrophages. Macrophages can be fixed in one place, such as the brain and lymph nodes, or can "wander" to areas where they are needed, such as the site of an infection. Neutrophils have an additional defensive property: they release granules of lysozyme, an enzyme that destroys cells.

Basophils comprise 0.5–1% of the total composition of white blood cells and function in the body's inflammatory response. Allergies are caused by an inflammatory response to relatively harmless substances, such as pollen or dust, in sensitive individuals. When activated in the inflammatory response, basophils release various chemicals that cause the characteristic symptoms of allergies. Histamines, for instance, cause the runny nose and watery eyes associated with allergic reactions; heparin is an anticoagulant that slows blood clotting and encourages the flow of blood to the site of inflammation, inducing swelling.

Eosinophils, which comprise 2–4% of the total composition of white blood cells, are believed to coun-

teract the effects of histamine and other inflammatory chemicals. They also phagocytize bacteria tagged by antibodies.

Lymphocytes, which comprise 20–25% of the total composition of white blood cells, are divided into two types: B lymphocytes and T lymphocytes. The names of these lymphocytes are derived from their origin. T lymphocytes are named for the thymus, an organ located in the upper chest region where these cells mature; and B lymphocytes are named for the bursa of Fabricus, an organ in birds where these cells were discovered. T lymphocytes play key roles in the immune response. One type of T lymphocyte, the helper T lymphocyte, activates the immune response when it encounters a macrophage that has ingested a foreign microorganism. Another kind of T lymphocyte, called a cytotoxic T lymphocyte, kills cells infected by foreign microorganisms. B lymphocytes, when activated by helper T lymphocytes, become plasma cells, which in turn secrete large amounts of antibodies.

All white blood cells arise in the red bone marrow. However, the cells destined to become lymphocytes are first differentiated into lymphoid stem cells in the red bone marrow; from the red bone marrow, these stem cells undergo further development and maturation in the spleen, tonsils, thymus, adenoids, and lymph nodes.

HIV, the virus that causes Acquired Immune Deficiency syndrome (AIDS), attacks and kills T lymphocytes. This disease cripples the immune system and leaves the body helpless to stave off infections. As AIDS progresses, the number of helper T lymphocytes drops from a normal 1000 to 0.

Like red blood cells, the plasma membranes of white blood cells also contain antigens. These surface antigens are called the human leukocyte associated (HLA) antigens. Like the red blood cell types, these HLA antigens represent different white blood cell "groups." When a person receives an organ transplanted from a donor, the recipient and the donor must have the same HLA antigen group for the transplant to be successful. If the donor and recipient are two different HLA antigen groups, the recipient's body will "reject" the organ; in other words, the recipient's immune system will be activated by the foreign cells of the organ and initiate an immune response against the organ.

Platelets

Platelets are not cells; they are fragments of cells that function in blood clotting. Platelets number about 250,000 to 400,000 per liter of blood. Blood clotting is a complex process that involves a cascade of reactions that leads to the formation of a blood clot. Platelets contain chemicals called clotting factors. These clotting factors first combine with a protein called prothrombin. This reaction converts prothrombin to thrombin. Thrombin, in turn, converts fibrinogen (present in plasma) to fibrin (Figure 1).

Fibrin is a thread–like protein that traps red blood cells as they leak out of a cut in the skin. As the clot hardens, it forms a seal over the cut. This process works for relatively small cuts in the skin. When a cut is large, or if an artery is severed, blood loss is so severe that the physical pressure of the blood leaving the body prevents clots from forming. In addition, in the inherited disorder called hemophilia, one or more clotting factors are lacking in the platelets. This disorder causes severe bleeding from even the most minor cuts and bruises.

Platelets have a short life span; they survive for only 5–9 days before being replaced. Platelets are produced in red bone marrow and are broken off from other red blood cells.

See also Anemia; Anticoagulants; Blood gas analysis; Blood supply; Circulatory system; Connective tissue; Heart; Hematology; Hemophilia; Plasma; Respiratory system; Sickle–cell anemia.

Further Reading:

Agre, Peter C. and Cartron, Jean–Pierre, eds. *Protein Blood Group Antigens of the Human Red Cell: Structure, Function, and Clinical Significance.* Baltimore: Johns Hopkins University Press, 1992.

Belcher, Anne E. *Blood Disorders.* St. Louis: Mosby Year–Book, 1993.

Kapff, Carola R. *Blood: Atlas and Sourcebook of Hematology,* 2nd edition. Boston: Little, Brown. 1991.

Long, Michael W. and Wicha, Max S., eds. *The Hematopoietic Microenvironment: The Functional and Structural Basis of Blood Cell Development.* Baltimore: Johns Hopkins University Press, 1993.

Roush, Wade. An "Off–Switch" for Red Blood Cells. *Science* 268: 27, April 7, 1995.

Ware, Anthony J. and Heistad, Donald D. "Platelet–Endothelium Interactions." *New England Journal of Medicine* 328: 628, March 4, 1993.

Weller, Peter F. "The Immunobiology of Eosinophils." *New England Journal of Medicine* 324: 110, April 18, 1991.

Kathleen Scogna

Blood circulation see **Circulatory system**

Blood gas analysis

Blood gas analysis is a means of determining the amount of oxygen or carbon dioxide being carried in the blood, and in some cases, of discovering the identity of a toxic gas, such as carbon monoxide, that may be present. Also, the determination can be made as to whether the blood is too acidic or too alkaline, which may help the physician in his diagnosis.

Among other functions, blood carries oxygen to the body's tissues and removes carbon dioxide. The blood laden with carbon dioxide passes through the right side of the heart into the lungs and exchanges the carbon dioxide for fresh oxygen. The oxygenated blood then is pumped by the left side of the heart out into the body to repeat the cycle.

The red blood cells, or erythrocytes, carry the blood gases. Hemoglobin, the substance that gives blood its red color, is the molecular substance in the erythrocyte that attaches to oxygen and exchanges it for carbon dioxide.

Carbon monoxide, a colorless, very toxic gas, can displace oxygen in the bloodstream. Hemoglobin has approximately 12 times the affinity for carbon monoxide as it does for oxygen, so it will pick up carbon monoxide if both gases are present. This means that the body does not get the oxygen it needs, and eventually death will occur.

Testing blood gases is a means to determine whether an acid–base (biochemical) disturbance is of respiratory or metabolic origin. Respiratory conditions such as pneumonia, bronchitis, emphysema, or severe asthma can cause the blood to become more acid. Respiratory conditions such as aspirin toxicity, strenuous exercise, fever, or overactive thyroid can cause the blood to be more alkaline. Kidney failure, burns, heart attack, or starvation are the metabolic reasons for the blood to become acid, and liver failure, vomiting, ulcer, or cystic fibrosis cause metabolic alkaline blood.

To determine blood gases, the blood specimen must be taken from an artery (usual blood specimens are taken from a vein) and the blood specimen is placed in ice to prevent any changes in blood gases, and rushed to the laboratory for analysis.

See also Blood; Bronchitis; Circulatory system; Emphysema; Pneumonia.

Blood supply

Blood supply refers to the blood resources in blood banks and hospitals that are critical to the health care community. The blood supply consists of donated blood units (in pints) that are used to replace blood lost during surgery or from trauma.

Blood transfusions were attempted as early as 1667 when Jean–Baptiste Denis, a French physician, transfused 12 fl oz (355 ml) of lamb's blood into a 15–year–old male patient. While Denis's subject improved immediately, later attempts to transfuse blood met with mixed results. Prior to the end of the nineteenth century, some patients who received blood from another person improved while others died quickly. In 1900, Austrian physician Karl Landsteiner discovered the four types of human blood, A, B, O, and AB, and the rules that govern their compatibility. Type O can be given to any recipient and is called the universal donor. Type A can be given to type A and AB recipients, and type B to type B and AB recipients. Transfusing blood of a type not compatible with the patient's blood can be fatal.

Donating blood

Blood units are collected in the United States by the American Red Cross and by blood banks at local hospitals. Donations are always needed due to the con-

stant demands of hospitals and their trauma units as well as to the brief shelf–life of stored blood. Some 12 million units are used every year in the U.S.

Blood is collected by simply inserting a needle into a vein and allowing the blood to flow into a plastic bag that has been specially treated to prevent the blood from clotting. The average adult human has approximately 6 qt (5.7 l) of blood in their body, so the loss of one pint will have little effect on them. The liquid portion of the blood is quickly replaced from fluid the donor drinks afterwards and the blood cells are regenerated from the bone marrow. Healthy donors can make blood donations about every six to eight weeks without suffering any ill effects.

Once the blood has been collected in the bag, other small specimens are collected for testing. Blood is tested for hepatitis viruses, syphilis, AIDS, or other diseases and classified as to type. Technicians also run a series of antigen tests to provide information on the presence of any factor that may provoke a reaction in the recipient.

After the blood is tested and found satisfactory it is refrigerated for use. Blood in blood banks is distributed to medical facilities in the region of the blood bank. Patients undergoing surgery have blood tests to determine their blood type and antigen structure so that compatible blood can be selected to replace that which is lost during surgery. Patients who arrive in the emergency room following a trauma such as an automobile accident also are tested for possible blood replacement. Loss of between 1–2 qt (1–2 l) of blood will result in shock and require the immediate transfusion of blood. Loss of up to 3 qt (2.8 l), half the blood supply in the human body, can be fatal.

Blood components

Not all of the collected blood is used as whole–blood transfusions. Some of the supply is broken down into its components. Blood plasma, the liquid part of blood that remains once the blood has coagulated (clotted), can be dried into a powder and used as a replacement for blood volume lost from wounds. Blood plasma need not be refrigerated so it is useful in situations such as battlefields and areas that lack proper refrigeration. The plasma powder is reconstituted by mixing it with sterile water. It is then infused into the wounded or injured patient.

Thousands of units of blood can be combined and the clotting factor (Factor VIII) refined from the mixture. Factor VIII is used by hemophiliacs to provide the ingredient they lack to make their blood clot. Without the clotting factor a hemophiliac can bleed uncontrollably.

Blood cells also can be separated and used. Concentrated red blood cells can improve the blood count of an anemic patient. White blood cells and platelets also are isolated and transfused into needy patients.

AIDs and the blood supply

When Acquired Immune Deficiency (AIDS) entered the U.S. population in the late 1970s and early 1980s, much was unknown about the disease and no test existed to detect the virus in blood. While initially confined to populations demonstrating high risk behavior, such as homosexuals and intravenous drug users, AIDS began to infect hemophiliacs and surgical patients who did not fit into such high risk categories. Members of the medical community soon determined that these patients had contracted the disease from donated blood and that the process used to break blood into its components did not kill the AIDS virus. Because of its minute size the virus passed through the filters used in the extraction process.

In 1985 a test was developed to detect the HIV virus in blood, and immediately every unit of donated blood was tested and those tainted with the virus removed from the blood supply. Donors are now carefully screened to eliminate any who might be at high risk of contracting AIDS. To eliminate the possibility of contracting this or any other blood–borne disease, patients who are scheduled to undergo surgery are urged to donate blood ahead of time so that their own blood can be transfused into them if needed.

It is important to know that a blood donor cannot contract AIDS or any other disease by donating blood. The equipment used to collect donated blood is used only the once and then discarded.

See also AIDS; Blood.

Larry Blaser

Blue-backed fairy bluebird see **Orioles**
Blueberry see **Heath family**

Bluebirds

Bluebirds are small blue–colored perching birds in the thrush family (Turdidae). There are three species of bluebirds in North America. All of these bluebirds nest

A male mountain bluebird flying to its nest.

in natural cavities or nest boxes. They tend to feed from perches, flying down to catch insects as they see them, and sometimes hawking insects in the air.

The eastern bluebird (*Sialia sialis*) occurs in shrubby habitats, old orchards, recent clear–cuts and burns, and other open habitats with woody plants in eastern and central North America and south to Nicaragua in Central America. The male of this species has a bright, blue back and a brick–red breast, while the female has a somewhat similar, but more subdued coloration. Northern populations of the eastern bluebird are migratory, wintering in the southeastern United States or further south.

The male western bluebird (*S. mexicana*) is rather similar in coloration to the eastern bluebird, but it has a blue throat, and a red shoulder. This species and the mountain bluebird (*S. currucoides*) are western in their distributions. The male mountain bluebird is a striking, sky–blue color, and this species tends to occur at relatively higher elevations than the western bluebird during the breeding season.

Populations of bluebirds have declined greatly in large parts of their ranges. In part, this has been caused by modifications of their habitat by humans, especially agricultural and forestry activities that have reduced the availability of the nesting cavities that bluebirds require. The use of pesticides has also affected bluebirds in some ares.

Bluebirds have also suffered badly from competition for their essential nesting cavities with common starlings (*Sturnus vulgaris*), and to a lesser degree the house sparrow (*Passer domesticus*). Both of these species were introduced to eastern North America from Europe in the later nineteenth century. The common starling is now the most abundant bird in North America, and populations of bluebirds have declined drastically throughout the range of this invasive pest. Fortunately, bluebird populations have been increasing in many areas during the past several decades, although they are still generally depressed. The population recovery of bluebirds has been substantially assisted by volunteer programs that provide these lovely and interesting birds with artificial nest boxes.

See also Thrushes.

Blue-green algae see **Algae**
Blue-hooded euphonia see **Tanagers**

Blue revolution (aquaculture)

The blue revolution refers to the remarkable emergence of aquaculture as an important and highly productive agricultural activity. In the sense used here, aquaculture refers to all forms of active culturing of aquatic animals and plants, occurring in marine, brackish, or freshwaters.

Aquaculture has long been practiced in China and other places in eastern Asia, where freshwater fish have been grown as food in managed ponds for thousands of years. In recent decades, however, the practice of aquaculture has spread around the world, and many new species of freshwater and marine organisms are being cultivated as highly productive and nutritious crops. The tremendous growth of aquaculture as an economic activity, contributing large amounts of food for consumption by humans, is sometimes referred to as the "blue revolution."

In part, the growth of aquaculture has been stimulated by knowledge that there are intrinsic limitations to the productivity of the wild, unmanaged aquatic ecosystems that humans have traditionally exploited as sources of fish, aquatic invertebrates, and seaweeds. Moreover, in a depressingly large number of cases, the useful productivity of natural aquatic ecosystems has been overexploited or otherwise degraded by humans, so that harvested yields have declined substantially.

In many cases, however, the productivity of valuable aquatic species can be greatly increased under managed conditions, and by the genetic selection for varieties having desirable traits, such as high productivity. The principle goal of aquaculture science is to develop systems by which aquatic organisms can be grown and harvested at large but sustainable rates, while not causing unacceptable environmental damages.

Fish farming.

Aquaculture production

By far, the greatest productivity of aquaculture occurs in Asia, which had 11.2 million tons of aquaculture production in 1989, compared with 1.23 million tons in Europe, 0.94 million tons in North America, and 0.37 million tons in the rest of the world. Of the global production of 13.7 million tons, about 42.4% was freshwater fish, 8.6% was anadromous and marine fish, 21.5% was molluscs, 4.5% was crustaceans, and 23.0% were other organisms, mostly kelps and other algae.

In comparison, the global landings of marine fishes in 1989 were about 84.2 million tons, while 13.3 million tons were produced by the world's freshwater fisheries. Clearly, aquaculture is a very large and rapidly growing enterprise.

Fish farming

Fish farming is a relatively intensive enterprise, commonly involving the management of all steps in the life cycle of the cultivated fish, from the production of eggs and larvae, through to growth and eventual harvest of a high–quality, market–sized fish. In this sense, fish farming is different from fish ranching, which is a less–intensive enterprise that usually involves the confinement and feeding of wild captured fish in order to increase their market value. This is done, for example, with bluefin tuna (*Thunnus thynnus*) in some places.

Fish have many potential benefits as cultivated species. Because they are cold–blooded (or *poikilothermic*), fish divert little energy to the maintenance of body temperature, and they can therefore convert a relatively large proportion of their food into their growing biomass. In other words, populations of fish can be very productive, especially under conditions where the animals are well–fed, and the rates of mortality from diseases and predation are kept small. Moreover, fish are a tasty and very nutritious food for humans. Consequently, the economic value of fish is great, as are the potential profits of cultivating them in large quantities.

Various species of fish are grown in aquaculture using a variety of cultivation systems. These systems most commonly involve confinement in artificial ponds, or in cages or pens set into larger bodies of water, including the ocean. The fish are fed with a nutritious diet, sometimes to excess so that growth rates are maximized. When the fish are economically mature, they are carefully harvested and processed so that the highest–value economic products can be delivered to consumers.

The oldest fish–farming systems were developed in Asia, and involved several species of freshwater fishes. The first writings about methods of fish culture are dated from about 2,500 years ago and were written by Fan Lei, a wealthy Chinese fish farmer. The first species to be grown in aquaculture was probably the common carp (*Cyprinus carpio*), a species native to China but now spread throughout the world, and still a very important species in aquaculture. Other so–called Chinese carps are also important in Asian fish–farming, including the grass carp (*Ctenopharyngodon idella*), bighead carp (*Aristichtys nobilis*), and silver carp (*Hypophthalmichtys molitrix*), along with tilapia (*Tilapia mossambica* and other *Tilapia* spp.) and Asian catfish (*Clarias* spp.).

Freshwater fish are also cultivated in North America and Europe. Most commonly grown are species of trout, especially brook trout (*Salvelinus fontinalis*) and rainbow trout (*Salmo gairdneri*). Also important are channel catfish (*Ictalurus punctatus*), and the common carp.

Fewer species and quantities of fish are grown under brackish–water conditions in Asia, but they include the milkfish (*Chanos chanos*). Brackish and saltwater fish farming are larger enterprises in northern Europe and North America, where species of trout and salmon are commonly cultivated, sometimes in large, open–water complexes of cages supported by rafts. Especially important species are Atlantic salmon (*Salmo salar*), brown trout (*S. trutta*), and Pacific salmon (*Oncorhynchus* spp.).

Invertebrate culture

Many species of molluscs, crustaceans, and other invertebrates are commonly grown in aquaculture, particularly in Asia, but increasingly in other regions as well.

The most important crops are molluscs, especially species of oysters (*Crassostrea* spp.) and mussels (*Mytilis* spp.). Most crustacean production occurs in Asia, where many species of oriental shrimps are cultivated (*Penaeus* spp., *Metapenaeus* spp.), along with giant freshwater prawn (*Macrobrachium rosenbergii*). In Europe and North America, attention has focussed on American and European lobsters (*Homarus americanus*, *H. gammarus*), and on various species of crayfishes.

Seaweed culture

Seaweeds are also grown in large quantities as food, as feedstocks for the production of alginates and other industrial products. Most aquaculture production occurs in Asia, although there is also a significantly growing industry in North America.

Environmental impacts of aquaculture

Aquaculture provides many benefits to people, mostly through access to a rather large production of nutritious, high–quality foods. However, as with conventional, terrestrial agriculture, there are many adverse environmental impacts of aquaculture.

The most important effects are ecological, and are associated with the conversion of natural ecosystems into intensively managed aquacultural ecosystems. For example, the conversion of tropical mangrove forests into aquacultural facilities for the raising of shrimp or prawns represents a net loss of natural habitats. This conversion has important consequences for native species, and it often causes damages to offshore ecosystems through increased rates of siltation and pollution. These sorts of environmental damages are severe, and they are associated with all natural ecosystems that have been dominated and converted by humans and their activities.

In addition, aquaculture operations often degrade local water quality in various ways. Oxygen concentrations may be lowered to unacceptably small concentrations because of the consumption of this gas during the decomposition of waste feed and animal feces. Other impacts are associated with toxic chemicals that are applied to aquaculture cages in order to prevent them from being colonized or eaten by marine organisms. Local waters and species may also become contaminated with antibiotics and other medicines that may be used to keep animal crops healthy. In addition, non–native species may escape from aquaculture and establish themselves in new habitats, possibly competing with or degrading the habitat of native species.

These and other environmental effects of aquaculture are important considerations, and they must be dealt with in an effective manner if this enterprise is to be judged sustainable in the proper, ecological sense.

See also Carp; Trout-perch.

Further Reading:

Brown, E.E. *World Fish Farming: Cultivation and Economics.* Westport, Conn.: AWI Pub. Co., 1983.

Pillay, T.V.R. *Aquaculture. Principles and Practices.* Cambridge: Fishing News Books, The University Press, 1990.

Pillay, T.V.R. *Aquaculture and the Environment.* New York: J. Wiley & Sons, 1992.

Swift, D.R. *Aquaculture Training Manual.* Farnham, England: Fishing News Books Ltd., 1988.

Bill Freedman

Blue sky see **Rayleigh scattering**

B lymphocytes see **Blood; Immune system; Lymphatic system**

Boarfish

Boarfish is a common name, so it is not surprising that fish from two different marine families, from two different orders, with superficially similar snout–shaped faces share this name.

One group of species which bear the common name boarfish comprise the few species of the genus *Antigonia*, which according to some experts is the only

genus in the family Caprioidae. Others add the genus *Capros* to this family. The family falls in the order Zeiformes, which extends back into the fossil record at least to the Eocene, the time when mammals assumed their present position as the dominant land animals. This order also includes the families Zeniontidae, Oreosomatidae, and Zeidae (dories), all of which are known as zeomorph fishes. Similar in shape to other members of the Zeiformes, boarfishes possess diamond– or rhombus–shaped bodies of medium size, up to 8–9 in (22 cm) long. Their bodies are relatively thin or compressed, and are covered with ctenoid scales—scales with saw–toothed edges. The boarfishes take their name from the snout–like shape of the end of their heads which makes them look like boars, or male pigs.

Boarfishes from the Caprioidae live in salt water, again like other species in the order Zeiformes, and they are commonly found swimming near the bottom of their marine environment. Boarfishes inhabit such areas from India to the western Pacific and also in the Atlantic Ocean.

Besides the boarfishes of the Caprioidae, this common name is also applied to members of the marine family Pentacerotidae, or Histiopteridae, order Perciformes. Another common name for these fishes is armorheads. This family includes the silver–colored fishes of the genera *Pseudopentaceros* and *Zanclistus* which are sought by commercial fishermen. Some of these fishes undergo a marked change in shape as they mature, which includes the development of an elongate snout resembling the snout of a pig. Some species from the Pentacerotidae can reach almost a meter in length.

The giant boarfish (*Paristiopterus labiosus*) is a relatively rare member of the Pentacerotidae which is known in Australia and New Zealand for excellent eating quality and sweet taste. Similarly popular for eating is the long–snouted boarfish (*Pentaceropsis recurvirostris*) from the waters off southern Australia.

Boars see **Pigs**

Boas

Boas are a group of nonvenomous, constricting snakes (family Boidae), most of which are found in tropical America and in Madagascar. Boas bear live young, and in this way they differ from the Old World pythons, which lay eggs. Boas are of ancient derivation, retaining some of the features of their lizard–like ancestors, such as paired lungs (modern snakes have only one), tiny remnants of hind limbs (often called

An anaconda in Venezuela, swimming.

spurs), and a characteristic bone in their lower jaw, the coronoid, which is not found in advanced snakes. Boas have no poison fangs, and they kill their prey by squeezing, though their prey is often bitten first.

Boas, pythons, and wood snakes are classified in the family Boidae, whose members have small nostrils and small eyes with elliptical, vertical pupils. Boas are among the most ancient groups of living snakes, having been present in the Cretaceous period, 200 million years ago, when dinosaurs still stalked the earth. Although boas made up a major part of the snake fauna in the past, today only about 40 species of boas are known. Two quite distinct subfamilies are recognized, the true boas, which are mainly tropical rainforest animals from South America and Madagascar, and the Sandboas from the deserts and other arid regions of the northern hemisphere. The reticulated python (*Reticulatus*) of Asia grows up to 33 ft (11 m) and is one the world's largest snakes.

True boas

All primitive snakes (other than the burrowing blindsnakes) have eyes with vertically elliptic pupils (cat–eyes) that can open widely in the dark. Boas have a stout body, short tail, and a green, brown, or yellow body with either blotches or diamond patterns. They tend to be most active at night, whether they inhabit deserts or rainforests. Beyond this general similarity, however, the South American boas are highly varied in their habits as well as in their overall appearance.

The boa constrictor, (*Constrictor constrictor*) and the West Indian boas (*Epicrates*) are primarily ground–dwellers, although they may also climb trees, but they show no specializations for a particular life–style. As in other boas, the young feed on small animals such as lizards, whereas the large adults tend to feed on larger mammals and birds.

The West Indian boas are found on many Caribbean islands. In general, each island has a single, unique species. The exception is the island of Hispaniola (Haiti and the Dominican Republic) which has three species; *Epicrates fordi* and *E. gracilis*, each only about 3 ft (1 m) long, and *E. striatus*, a much larger snake that reaches a length of 8 ft (2.5 m) or more. The latter species is also found on a number of islands in the Bahamas. On several Caribbean islands boas gather at cave entrances at night, snatching bats out of the air as they exit or enter the cave.

Probably the best known representative of the true boas is the boa constrictor of tropical America, from Mexico to Argentina. Although often depicted as a giant, man–eating snake in lurid stories or movies, this boa seldom grows to a length of more than 10 ft (3 m); the record is 16 ft (5 m). Boa constrictors are gentle and easy to care for, and have become one of the favorite pet snakes in recent years.

The green anaconda (*Eunectes murinus*) of South America may be the largest snake in the world. It has fairly reliably been reported to grow to 35 ft (11 m) long, although 18–20 ft (5.5–6 m) is the maximum seen in recent times. These dark green snakes with black marking are river–dwellers, and are highly adapted for an aquatic existence. The anaconda's eyes and nostrils are positioned on top of its head to allow it to see and breathe while the rest of its body is completely submerged. Anacondas lie submerged in the water at night waiting for peccaries (pigs) to come down to drink. Besides feeding on mammals, anacondas are also known to eat birds, crocodilians (caimans), and turtles. Like other boas, anacondas give birth to 40 or more live young.

The tree boas (*Corallus* and relatives) are highly modified for a life in the trees. Tree boas have slender bodies and their prehensile tails make them excellent climbers. They also have large eyes for nocturnal foraging, and long teeth for catching sleeping birds and other tree–dwellers, such as lizards, rodents, and opossums. Tree boas, like all boas, have heat–sensitive grooves between the labial scales under their nostrils that locate warm–blooded prey, even in total darkness. The emerald tree boa (*Corallus caninus*)) and the green tree boa (*Boa canina*) are especially well–adapted for an arboreal life, with green, white–marked coloration making them almost invisible in the trees.

The West Indian boas (*Epicrates*) are common on those islands lacking the snake–eating Indian mongoose, which was introduced on several islands in the 1800s to control the rats in the sugarcane fields. However, boas are almost extinct on most islands where the mongoose occurs. As is the case with so many attempts to introduce exotic animals for a particular purpose, the mongoose did not do the job that was expected. Instead of eating rats, the mongoose preferred chickens. and also ate ground–nesting birds and terrestrial lizards and snakes, some of which have been driven to extinction.

The distribution of the true boas is rather odd. Although most of them inhabit tropical America, there is one group of three species, the Pacific boas (*Can-*

doia), that are found on the other side of the Pacific Ocean, in the Fiji islands and on other islands north and east of New Guinea. Although they appear to be closely related to the American species, these Pacific boas live in an area more than 4,000 mi (6,440 km) away. It is not easy to explain this disjunct distribution, but a parallel case is found in the Fiji iguanas (*Brachylophus*), whose closest relatives are also in tropical America.

Sandboas (family Erycidae)

Most sandboas are relatively small snakes, less than 3 ft (1 m) in length, currently found in southern Asia and northern Africa, and in western North America. In most ways the sandboas are very much like the true boas of South America, but because most of them live in relatively treeless areas, they are more adapted to burrowing in the sand than to climbing. Like the South American boas, they feed on small animals, such as lizards and rodents, which they kill by constriction. Because of their subterranean habits, however, the sandboas tends to have small, compact heads that can be pushed through the soil, and short, stubby tails that can act as "pushers." Their tail vertebrae are specialized and can be recognized in the fossil members of this family. Such sandboa fossils are known from many localities in western Europe and eastern North America that are very distant from the areas which sandboas currently inhabit. The two American sandboas are the rubber boa of the dry pine forests of the western states of Washington and Oregon, and the rosy boa of the southwestern desert regions. The latter is a handsome snake that is a favorite of pet owners.

As in the true boas, there is a strange situation in sandboa distribution and relationship. On the island of Madagascar, off the southeast coast of Africa, there are two boas that resemble those of South America. One of these is specialized as a tree boa, the other is so similar in appearance to the South American boa constrictor that some experts have placed it in the same genus. Recent research, however, suggests that despite their superficial similarities the Madagascan boas are related to the sandboas, and probably represent an ancient division of that group.

See also Reptiles; Snakes.

KEY TERMS

Constricting snake—One that kills its prey by wrapping its body around it to stop its breathing movements.

TABLE I. TYPICAL BOND ENERGIES

Type of bond or attraction	Range of bond energies, kJ/mol
Ionic bonds	700-4000
Covalent triple bonds	800-1000
Covalent double bonds	500-700
Covalent single bonds	200-500
Dipole attractions between molecules	40-400
Hydrogen bonds	10-40

Further Reading:

Halliday, Tim, and Kraig Adler, eds. *The Encyclopedia of Reptiles and Amphibians.* New York: Facts on File, 1986.

Minton, S. A., and M. R. Minton. *Giant Reptiles.* New York: Charles Scribner's Sons, 1973.

Ross, R. A., and G. Marzec. *The Reproductive Husbandry of Pythons and Boas.* Stanford, CA: Institute for Herpetological Research, 1990.

Tolson, P. J., and R. W. Henderson. *The Natural History of West Indian Boas.* Excelsior, MN: R & A Publ., 1994.

Trutnau, Ludwig. *Nonvenomous Snakes.* New York: Barron's Educational Series, 1986.

Herndon G. Dowling

Bobcat see **Cats**

Boiling point see **States of matter**

Bond energy

Bond energy is the strength of a chemical bond between atoms, expressed as the amount of energy required to break it apart. It's just as if the bonded atoms were glued together: the stronger the glue is, the more energy you'd have to use to break them apart. A higher bond energy, therefore, means a stronger bond.

Bond energies are usually expressed in kilojoules per mole (kJ/mol): the number of kilojoules of energy that it would take to break apart exactly one mole of those bonds is 6.02×10^{23}.

KEY TERMS

Kilojoule—An amount of energy equal to a thousand joules. One kilojoule is equivalent to 0.239 kilocalorie. Or in electrical terms, a kilojoule is the amount of energy used by one kilowatt of power operating for one second.

There are several kinds of "glues," or attractions, by which atoms and molecules can stick together. Table I shows the approximate ranges of their strengths, from the strongest to the weakest.

Notice that ionic bonds are stronger than covalent bonds. Among covalent bonds, triple bonds are stronger than double bonds and double are stronger than single bonds. Hydrogen bonds are weaker than all, but they play a big role in determining the properties of important compounds such as proteins and water.

Bonds of the same type can vary quite a bit in their strengths. The bond energies of several specific bonds are shown in Table II.

Bond energies between certain pairs of atoms vary somewhat, depending on the particular molecule they are part of, because adjacent atoms can affect their bonding slightly. The values in Table II are average bond energies for the listed bonds.

See also Chemical bond; Dipole.

Robert L. Wolke

TABLE 2. AVERAGE BOND ENERGIES OF COMMON BONDS	
Bond	*Bond energy, kJ/mol*
C–C	347
C=C	615
C≡C	812
C–O	360
C=O	728
F–F	158
Cl–Cl	244
C–H	414
H–H	436
H–O	464
O=O	498

Bonitos see **Tuna**

Bonobo see **Chimpanzees**

Bony fish

Bony fish (Osteichthyes) are distinguished from other fish species that have a cartilaginous skeleton (Chondrichthyes—sharks, rays and chimaeras, for example) by the presence of true bone—a mixture of calcium phosphates and carbonates—in their skeletons. Other differences between the two groups are modifications in the structure and arrangement of the scales and fins and the presence of more specialised teeth in bony fish. When feeding, bony fish display a far wider range of adaptations than cartilaginous species: the former may be either carnivorous (like most cartilaginous species), plant–eating, or both. Combined, these features have helped them to exploit a much wider range of feeding and living habitats.

Fish breathe and feed in order to obtain sufficient energy to meet their daily physical requirements. Much of this energy is required for swimming, which can range from simple short distances to much greater seasonal migrations. However, considerable amounts of energy are also required for finding food and mates, as well as for avoiding predators. To conserve energy, bony fish have evolved a special swim bladder which is a gas–filled chamber that provides buoyancy and helps keeps them weightless in the water column. Through this system they may remain at the same level of water for several hours without expending too much valuable energy.

With few exceptions all, bony fish require a constant source of oxygen for respiration. Dissolved oxygen is freely available in salt and freshwater and to extract this, fish pass the water through specialised gill chambers that are richly supplied with blood vessels. As the water passed over the highly convoluted surface of the gills, the oxygen passes across the thin membranes and enters the red hemoglobin cells of the blood stream.

The classification of bony fish is complex and outside the scope of this present account. Basically there are two main groups of bony fish: the Crossopterygii and Actinopterygii. The latter contains some additional small groups of distinct fish such as the Polypteridae (bichirs), Acipenseridae (sturgeons), Polyodontidae (paddle fish) and Lepisosteidae (gar or pikes). It also includes the teleost fish, which are by far the most numerous of all fishes, with more than 20,000 species identified from a wide range of habitats—aquatic, marine and terrestrial. Although these species vary considerably in size, appearance and structure, they are all much lighter than primitive species, largely through the loss of heavy body armor and thickened scales. The smallest known teleost fish is the Philippine goby (*Pandaka pygmaea*) which reaches a length of just 0.5 in (12 mm); the largest is the arapamia or pirarucu (*Arapamia gigas*) of the Amazonian waterways, which has been known to measure 16 ft (5 m).

In addition to the wide range of modern bony fish, a few primitive representatives still survive and, for taxonomic purposes, have been grouped together in the Crossopterygii. One of these is the coelacanth (*Latimera chalumnae*), a large blue–gray fish that may reach a length of 6.5 ft (2 m). Known only from the deep ocean trenches off the tiny Comoros Archipelago around northwest Madagascar, this sluggish species lives in complete darkness and preys on other fish. Many of its features are similar to fossil species, the most notable of which are its arrangement of fins. The rays of the second dorsal fin, the anal fin, and the paired fins rest on a muscular, scale–covered lobe, while the powerful tail fin is symmetrical in appearance. Almost nothing is known about the ecology of this species. A recent discovery showed that coelacanths actually give birth to live young.

Other unusual species of this same group are the lung fish of Africa, Australia and South America, the only living representatives of a widespread group of fish that lived on Earth some 350 million years ago. In some of these, the dorsal, anal, and caudal fins are fused and modified to form a continuous median fin. Some species come to the surface to gulp in air, while others have developed a gill system that enables them to breathe when submerged. During periods of dry weather, the African and South American species dig deeply into the mud at the base of lakes and swamps and envelop themselves in a thick coat of mucus. As this dries out it provides a protective covering for the fish, enabling it to survive periods of drought in a state of aestivation. When the rains return, the mucus coating is softened and the fish reemerges.

While features such as these enabled some species to withstand periods of adverse weather, or avoid excessive predation through the development of toughened skins that were often reinforced with bulky scales, as the world's climate changed and new species continued to evolve, most of these primitive features

were lost and an explosion of new life forms spread throughout the seas and freshwater ecosystems. Witness to this is the present staggering diversity and numbers of bony fish that occur in almost every aquatic habitat on Earth, from the warm tropical waters to the frozen seas of the poles and from the margins of the tides to the deepest oceanic trenches.

See also Cartilaginous fish; Fish.

Boobies and gannets

Boobies and gannets are nine species of marine birds that make up the family Sulidae, in the order Pelecaniformes, which also includes the pelicans, cormorants, anhingas, tropic birds, and frigate birds.

Boobies and gannets have a narrow, cigar–shaped body, a longish, pointed tail, and long, narrow wings. Their feet are fully webbed, and are used in swimming. The beak is strong, pointed, has a serrated edge for gripping slippery prey, and is brightly colored in some species. Unlike some of the other groups in the order Pelecaniformes, boobies and gannets have fully waterproof plumage.

Gannets and boobies feed on fish, which they find by flying over the surface of the ocean at an altitude of up to 98 ft (30 m). These birds then catch their prey by spectacular, head–long, angled–winged plunges into the surface of the sea, seizing their quarry in their beak, and swallowing it underwater. During the breeding season, gannets and boobies are found in near–coastal waters. In their non–breeding season, however, these birds may occur far out to sea. Almost all species of gannets and boobies are colonial nesters.

Gannets (*Morus* spp.) are birds of temperate and subarctic oceans, and they breed in colonies on rocky cliffs and ledges. Both birds of a mated pair incubate their single egg, which they cover with their webbed feet before snuggling down to brood. After the chick develops its flight feathers and is ready to fledge, it is abandoned by its parents. It soon leaps into the sea from its cliff–top nest and begins to fish for itself.

The six species of boobies (*Sula* spp.) are all tropical and subtropical birds. Boobies breed in nests built on near–shore shrubs, or on coastal cliffs.

Species of gannets

The northern gannet (*Morus bassana*) breeds in north–temperate and subarctic waters on both sides of the Atlantic Ocean. In North America, the largest

Blue-footed boobies in the Galapagos Islands.

colonies of these birds occur at Cape Saint Mary's on Newfoundland and on Bonaventure Island in the Gulf of the Saint Lawrence River. There are another four smaller colonies of northern gannets in the western Atlantic Ocean and another 28 in the eastern Atlantic.

Adult northern gannets have a white body, with black wing–tips. The head is a bright lemon–yellow. During the first year after birth gannets are a dark–brown color, while older sub–adults have a dirty–white plumage and lack the yellow head of the sexually mature adults. The tail of gannets is pointed, as is the profile of their head, giving the bird a dou-ble–ended shape in flight.

The populations of northern gannets in some of their breeding colonies can be quite large. These birds are aggressively territorial, and their nests are therefore spaced at about twice the distance that a sharp beak can be thrust towards a neighbor. Other displays involve birds engaging in ritualized posturings to impress their neighbors, or to infatuate a potential mate.

In healthy colonies, all of the suitable space may be covered with nests. At Cape Saint Mary's, popula-tion growth in recent decades has resulted in all of the

prime nesting habitat on cliffs to be fully utilized. This has forced many birds to nest on adjacent coastal meadows, an accessible habitat in which they are vul-nerable to land–borne predators.

After their breeding season, northern gannets occur widely in waters of the continental shelves. Dur-ing the winter, gannets range as far south as the north-ern Gulf of Mexico and the southeastern United States.

Other species of gannets include the Cape gannet (*Morus capensis*) of South Africa, and the Australian gannet (*M. serrator*) of Australia. These species are rather similar to the northern gannet, and some taxono-mists consider all of these taxa to be subspecies of *Morus bassana*.

Species of boobies

Three species of boobies are relatively widespread in tropical waters. The brown booby (*Sula leucogaster*) is the most common species, breeding in all of the trop-ical oceans. This species has dark–brown upper parts and breast, and a white belly. Male birds have a dark–blue face, while that of females is yellow. Imma-ture birds are more uniformly brown.

The blue–faced or masked booby (*Sula dactylatra*) is the largest species. This species breeds in the tropics of the Pacific and Indian Oceans. The blue–faced booby has a mostly white body, but the flight feathers are all black, resulting in a black stripe running the length of the back of the wings. The "mask" is an area of black feathers just behind the beak.

The red–footed booby (*Sula sula*) is a species of the tropical Pacific, Indian, and Atlantic Oceans. This species is named after its bright–red feet and legs. The red–footed booby nests in shrubs and trees.

Other, less–widespread species are the Peruvian booby (*Sula variegata*) of offshore islands and coastal headlands of Peru, the blue–footed booby (*S. nebouxii*) of western Mexican and Central and South American waters, and Abbott's booby (*S. abbotti*), which only occurs in the vicinities of Assumption and Christmas Islands in the Indian Ocean. Peruvian boobies can nest in huge colonies, which can contain as many as one million pairs of birds.

Boobies do not breed in North America, but several species are regular visitors to coastal waters during their non–breeding season. The blue–faced booby occurs most frequently in the vicinity of the Dry Tortugas off extreme southern Florida, and also in the Caribbean Sea, the Gulf of Mexico, and Baha California, as well as farther south of all of those places. The brown booby and blue–footed booby are also occasional visitors to the extreme southern United States.

Boobies, gannets, and people

Guano is a commercially important product obtained by digging the surface of the huge colonies of Peruvian boobies and other seabirds off northern South America, and at colonies of Cape Gannets off South Africa. Guano is a natural, phosphorus–rich compound derived from the excrement of seabirds, and is used as a fertilizer.

For many years, gannets, and to a much lesser degree boobies, were considered to be serious competitors with humans for commercially important marine fish. For this reason, gannets were often killed, and only a few decades ago their numbers were perilously small. This sort of indiscriminate killing is not much of a problem anymore, except in a few remote places.

In some regions, gannets and boobies may be killed for their meat and feathers, and where they are accessible, their eggs may be collected for eating.

Boobies and gannets are also vulnerable to collapses in the populations of the fish that they feed upon. For example, Peruvian boobies and other seabirds have suffered precipitous population declines

---

KEY TERMS

Overfishing—Harvesting of fish at a rate that is greater than their productivity, leading to a collapse in the size of the stocks.

Plunge–diver—A bird that dives head–long into the water to catch prey swimming fairly close to the surface.

---

when their most important prey of anchovies collapsed as a result of oceanographic changes associated with El Niño. El Niño is a warm–water phenomenon that impedes nutrient cycling, greatly reducing the productivity of phytoplankton, and ultimately, causing a collapse of fish stocks.

Since the beginning of the 1990s, there has also been a collapse of many fish stocks in coastal waters off eastern Canada. The reasons for this ecological change are not known for certain, but the leading hypotheses include the effects of overfishing and climate change. The collapse of the fisheries of the northwest Atlantic has led to severe economic hardship for many people who are dependent on that natural resource for their livelihood. However, there have also been severe effects on northern gannets and other seabirds, which depend on those fish stocks as a source of food, particularly when they are raising their young. Consequently, these birds have experienced unsuccessful reproduction, and this may pose a threat to the longer–term health of their populations in that region.

Further Reading:

Ehrlich, P. R., D. S. Dobkin, D. Wheye. *Birds in Jeopardy.* Stanford, CA: Stanford University Press, 1992.

Harrison, C. J. O., ed. *Bird Families of the World.* New York: H. N. Abrams Pubs., 1978.

Harrison, P. *Seabirds: An Identification Guide.* U.K.: Croom Helm, Beckenham, 1983.

Nelson, B. *The Sulidae: Gannets to Boobies.* London: Harrell Bokks, 1978.

Bill Freedman

Booklice see **Lice**

Boolean algebra

Boolean algebra is often referred to as the algebra of logic, because the English mathematician George Boole, who is largely responsible for its beginnings,

---

was the first to apply algebraic techniques to logical methodology. Boole showed that logical propositions and their connectives could be expressed in the language of set theory. Thus, Boolean algebra is also the algebra of sets. Algebra, in general, is the language of mathematics, together with the rules for manipulating that language. Beginning with the members of a specific set (called the universal set), together with one or more binary operations defined on that set, procedures are derived for manipulating the members of the set using the defined operations, and combinations of those operations. Both the language and the rules of manipulation vary, depending on the properties of elements in the universal set. For instance, the algebra of real numbers differs from the algebra of complex numbers, because real numbers and complex numbers are defined differently, leading to differing definitions for the binary operations of addition and multiplication, and resulting in different rules for manipulating the two types of numbers. Boolean algebra consists of the rules for manipulating the subsets of any universal set, independent of the particular properties associated with individual members of that set. It depends, instead, on the properties of sets. The universal set may be any set, including the set of real numbers or the set of complex numbers, because the elements of interest, in Boolean algebra, are not the individual members of the universal set, but all possible subsets of the universal set.

Properties of sets

A set is a collection of objects, called members or elements. The members of a set can be physical objects, such as people, stars, or red roses, or they can be abstract objects, such as ideas, numbers, or even other sets. A set is referred to as the universal set (usually called I) if it contains all the elements under consideration. A set, S, not equal to I, is called a proper

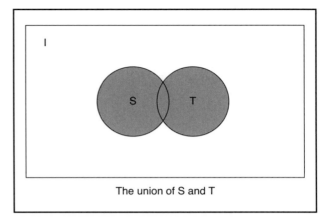

The union of S and T

Figure 2.

subset of I, if every element of S is contained in I. This is written and read "S is contained in I" (see figure 1).

If S equals I, then S is called an improper subset of I, that is, I is an improper subset of itself (note that two sets are equal if and only if they both contain exactly the same elements). The special symbol is given to the set with no elements, called the empty set or null set. The null set is a subset of every set.

When dealing with sets there are three important operations. Two of these operations are binary (that is, they involve combining sets two at a time), and the third involves only one set at a time. The two binary operations are union and intersection. The third operation is complementation. The union of two sets S and T is the collection of those members that belong to either S or T or both (see figure 2).

The intersection of the sets S and T is the collection of those members that belong to both S and T, and is written (see figure 3).

The complement of a subset, S, is that part of I not contained in S, and is written S' (see figure 4).

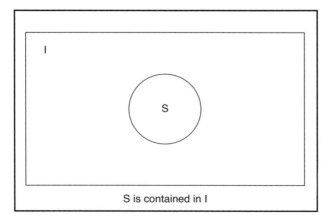

S is contained in I

Figure 1.

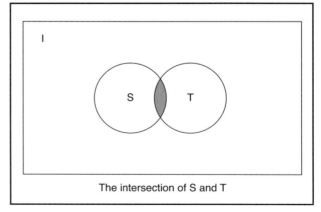

The intersection of S and T

Figure 3.

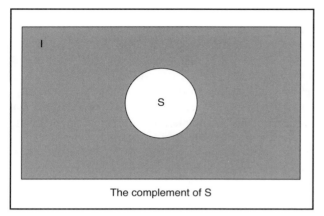

The complement of S

Figure 4.

Properties of Boolean algebra

The properties of Boolean algebra can be summarized in four basic rules.

(1) Both binary operations have the property of commutativity, that is, order doesn't matter.

$S \cap T = T \cap S$, and $S \cup T = T \cup S$.

(2) Each binary operation has an identity element associated with it. The universal set is the identity element for the operation of intersection, and the null set is the identity element for the operation of union.

$S \cap I = S$, and $S \cup \emptyset = S$.

(3) each operation is distributive over the other.

$S \cup (T \cap V) = (S \cup T) \cap (S \cup V)$, and $S \cap (T \cup V) = (S \cap T) \cup (S \cap V)$.

This differs from the algebra of real numbers, for which multiplication is distributive over addition, $a(b+c) = ab + ac$, but addition is not distributive over multiplication, $a+(bc) \neq (a+b)(a+c)$.

(4) each element has associated with it a second element, such that the union or intersection of the two results in the identity element of the other operation.

$A \cup A' = I$, and $A \cap A' = \emptyset$.

This also differs from the algebra of real numbers. Each real number has two others associated with it, such that its sum with one of them is the identity element for addition, and its product with the other is the identity element for multiplication. That is, $a + (-a) = 0$, and $a(1/a) = 1$.

Applications

The usefulness of Boolean algebra comes from the fact that its rules can be shown to apply to logical statements. A logical statement, or proposition, can either be

true or false, just as an equation with real numbers can be true or false depending on the value of the variable. In Boolean algebra, however, variables do not represent the values that make a statement true, instead they represent the truth or falsity of the statement. That is, a Boolean variable can only have one of two values. In the context of symbolic logic these values are true and false. Boolean algebra is also extremely useful in the field of electrical engineering. In particular, by taking the variables to represent values of on and off (or 0 and 1), Boolean algebra is used to design and analyze digital switching circuitry, such as that found in personal computers, pocket calculators, compact disc players, cellular telephones, and a host of other electronic products.

See also Algebra; Computer, digital; Set theory.

Further Reading:

Christian, Robert R. *Introduction to Logic and Sets*. Waltham MA: Blaisdell Publishing Co., 1965.

Garfunkel, Soloman A., ed. *For All Practical Purposes: Introduction to Contemporary Mathematics*. New York: W. H. Freeman, 1988.

Hoernes, Gerhard E. and Melvin F Heilweil. *Boolean Algebra and Logic Design*. New York: McGraw Hill, 1964.

Ryan, Ray and Lisa A. Doyle. *Basic Digital Electronics, 2nd ed*. Blue Ridge Summit, PA: Tab Books, 1990.

J.R. Maddocks

Bootlace worms see **Ribbon worms**

Boric acid

Boric acid, also known as boracic acid and arthoboric acid, is a very weak acid with the formula H_3BO_3, often used as a mild antiseptic. Chemically, it acts as a tribasic acid—an acid that can dissociate successively to produce three hydrogen ions in solution. However, because it dissociates to such a small extent, it is a very weak acid that is actually used in water solution as an eye wash. Pure boric acid is a colorless, odorless, white powder or transparent crystals that melt at about 340° F (171° C). Boric acid loses water as it is heated, changing first into metaboric acid (HBO_2) and then into pyroboric acid ($H_2B_4O_7$). The three acids can be thought of as hydrates of boric oxide (B_2O_3). Orthoboric acid is fairly soluble in water (especially hot water), alcohol, and glycerine.

Boric acid has a wide variety of industrial applications. It is used in the manufacture of heat–resistant borosilicate glass and other ceramics, such as crockery, porcelains, enamels, and artificial gemstones. It also used in waterproofing wood and fireproofing textiles. It also finds application as an insecticide for cockroaches and black carpet beetles and as an fungicide on citrus fruits.

Its use in the last of these applications is carefully monitored, however, because of the compound's toxicity. When swallowed, boric acid can cause nausea, vomiting, diarrhea, and other intestinal problems. In large doses, it can cause coma and death. The toxic level of boric acid in infants can be less than 0.2 oz (5 g) and in adults, from 0.2 oz (5 g) to 0.7 oz (20 g).

Boring machine see **Machine tools**

Boron see **Element, chemical**

Boson see **Subatomic particles**

Bosun bird see **Tropic birds**

Botany

Botany is the study of plants. It is one of the major fields of biology, together with zoology (the study of animals) and microbiology (the study of bacteria and viruses). Specializations within the field of botany includes the study of mosses, algae, lichens, ferns, and fungi. Other specialties in botany include plant physiology, the study of the vital processes of plants, such as photosynthesis, respiration, and plant nutrition. Biochemists study the effects of soil, temperature, and light on plants, while plant morphologists study of the evolution and development of leaves, roots, and stems with a focus on the tissues at the tips of stems where the cells have the ability to divide.

Plant *pathology* studies the causes and control of plant diseases. Pathologists may work with a specific group of plants, such as forest trees, vegetable crops, grain, or ornamental plants, and they may concentrate on the interactions between host plants and pathogens, the carriers of disease. Economic botanists study the economic impact of plants as they relate to human needs for food, clothing, and shelter, while plant geneticists investigate the structure and behavior of genes in plants and plant heredity in order to develop crops that are resistant to diseases and pests. Paleobotany deals with the biology and evolution of plants by studying the fossil record in order to reconstruct the 600 million year history of plant life on this planet.

The relationship between plants and animals is one of interdependence. Without the evolution of plants, animals would not have been able to subsist. Animals, in turn, contribute to plant distribution, plant pollination, and every other aspect of plant growth and development. It is through this interdependence that plants continue to adapt and change. Human intervention in the cultivation of plants has contributed equally to plant development. Today, the study of botany is only one aspect of ecology, the study of the environment. Plant ecologists are concerned with the effects of the environment on plants.

History of botany

Aristotle and Theophrastus, living in ancient Greece about the fourth century B.C., were both involved in identifying plants and describing them. Theophrastus is called the "father of botany," because of two of his surviving works on plant studies. While Aristotle also wrote about plants, he received more recognition for his studies of animals.

The early study of plants was not limited to Western cultures. The Chinese developed the study of botany along lines similar to the ancient Greeks at about the same time. In 60 A.D., another Greek, Dioscorides, wrote *De Materia Medica*, a work that described a thousand medicines, 60% of which came from plants. It remained the guidebook on medicines in the Western world for 1,500 years until the compound microscope was invented in the late sixteenth century, opening the way to the careful study of plant anatomy.

During the seventeenth century progress was made in experimenting with plants. Johannes van Helmont measured the uptake of water in a tree during the 1640s, and in 1727 Stephen Hales, an Englishman who is credited with establishing plant physiology as a science, published his experiments dealing with the nutrition and respiration of plants in a work entitled *Vegetable Staticks*. He developed techniques to measure area, volume, mass, pressure, gravity, and temperature in plants. In the latter part of the eighteenth century, Joseph Priestley laid the foundation for the chemical analysis of plant metabolism.

During the nineteenth century advances were made in the study of plant diseases because of the potato blight that killed potato crops in Ireland in the 1840s, an event that led to a mass migration of Irish to America. The study of plant diseases developed rapidly after this event. When the work in genetics by Gregor Mendel, an Austrian monk, was applied after 1900 to plant breeding, the development of modern plant genetics began. During the early part of the nineteenth century, progress in the study of plant fossils was made, and ecology began to develop as a science in the late nineteenth and early twentieth centuries.

Technology has helped specialists in botany to see and understand the three–dimensional nature of cells, and genetic engineering of plants has improved agricultural output. The study of plants continues as botanists try to both understand the structure, behavior, and cellular activities of plants in order to develop better crops, find new medicines, and explore ways of maintaining an ecological balance on the Earth to continue to sustain both plant and animal life.

See also Paleobotany; Plant; Plant diseases; Taxonomy.

Further Reading:

Evans, Howard Ensign. *Pioneer Naturalists*. New York: Holt, 1993.

Heiser, Charles B. *Of Plants and People*. Norman: University of Oklahoma Press, 1985.

Morton, A. G. *History of Botanical Science*. London: Academic Press, 1981.

Roth, Charles E. *The Plant Observer's Guidebook*. Englewood Cliffs, NJ: Prentice–Hall, 1984.

Taylor, Martha R. *Campbell's Biology*, 2nd ed. Redwood City, California: The Benjamin/Cummings Publishing Company, 1990.

Vita Richman

Botulism

Botulism is a extremely serious disease caused by the bacterium *Clostridium botulinum*. *C. botulinum* release the most potent toxin known—one gram of botulinum toxin theoretically can kill one million people. The toxin is swift–acting. It kills by binding to nerve cells, thereby causing paralysis of the muscles that are used in breathing.

First coined in the 1870s, the term botulism comes from the Latin word for sausage, *botulus*, since botulism used to be associated with eating sausage. Although botulism is still commonly associated with food contamination in the United States, it is more likely to occur from eating plants, not meat.

The canning connection

Plant foods associated with botulism are canned vegetables. In a typical scenario vegetables contaminated with *C. botulinum* from the soil are not washed adequately and subjected to temperatures inadequate for killing the bacteria. As the vegetable sits on the shelf botulinum toxin is released into the can. Because the toxin is odorless and colorless, the unsuspecting person eats the contaminated vegetable.

Fortunately, this scenario is rare as modern commercial canning techniques virtually have eliminated the risk of botulism. However, many home canners do not know the proper prevention techniques. About 10 outbreaks of botulism still occur each year in the United States. Most of these outbreaks are traced to food poisoning. More infrequently botulism in humans stems from wound infections, or even more rarely a gastrointestinal infection of newborns. In animals, botulism can be traced to the eating of contaminated animal carcasses or hay or grass that has been contaminated by a dead, toxic animal. Animals that characteristically feed on dead animals, such as vultures, are apparently resistant to the effects of botulinum toxin.

Clostridium botulinum

Clostridium botulinum has been classified into eight different strains. Each strain releases the deadly toxin but in slightly different forms. Humans are susceptible to four of these eight toxins; the other four are deadly in cattle, sheep, and horses. *C. botulinum* is a strict anaerobe, meaning it survives only in conditions completely lacking oxygen. In fact the presence of oxygen kills *C. botulinum*. However the bacteria can survive for long periods of time by producing endospores. Endospores are small, protective capsules that surround the bacteria. They can withstand incredible extremes of temperature. The *C. botulinum* endospore can survive several hours at 212°F (100°C, the boiling point of water) and 10 minutes at 248°F (120°C). *C. botulinum* endospores also can survive at –374°F (–190°C). The endospores can even resist radiation. The botulism endospore is one of the most hardy organisms on earth.

The botulinum toxin that the bacteria produces is a neurotoxin—it binds to nerve cells. Once bound the toxin prevents the release of a neurotransmitter called acetylcholine from the nerve cell. Since nerve cells use the release of acetylcholine to transmit nerve impulses, preventing the release of acetylcholine stops the transmission of nerve impulses. Muscle paralysis eventually results.

The toxin targets nerve cells of the peripheral nervous system which govern the muscles associated with breathing. The muscles that control the tongue, pharynx, and ribs succumb swiftly to the toxin, becoming paralyzed within hours of ingestion of contaminated food. If rapid diagnosis is not made and treatment with an antitoxin (a substance that blocks the binding of the toxin to nerve cells) is not started, death can result quickly.

Symptoms

Symptoms can occur anywhere from 12–36 hours to eight days after eating toxin–contaminated food. The early symptoms of botulism are mild. Dizziness, fatigue, and weakness are common complaints. None of the early symptoms indicate the seriousness of the disease. Later, neurological symptoms develop, including difficulty in speaking and swallowing, and double vision. Fever rarely is present. Abdominal distension can further complicate the diagnosis leading to the incorrect conclusion of appendicitis. As more toxin binds to more nerve cells paralysis sets in. Weakness of the muscle groups in the neck, extremities, and respiratory muscles is followed by complete paralysis.

Treatment

Because botulism is caused by a toxin and not the effects of the bacteria, antibiotics are not usually prescribed. The treatment for botulism is the antitoxin that neutralizes the toxin in the body. The antitoxin must be given early in the course of the disease to be effective. The antitoxin is useless if given too late, for too many nerve cells already are affected by the toxin. A botulism patient also must receive intensive, supportive care such as a respirator to assist breathing. Sometimes

---

KEY TERMS

Antitoxin—A substance that neutralizes a toxin.

Endospore—A small, protective capsule surrounding a bacterium.

Toxin—A poison released by some organisms such as bacteria.

---

dialysis, a process that artificially cleanses the blood, is used to assist the kidneys in removing the toxin from the bloodstream.

Prevention

The risk of botulism virtually has been eliminated from the commercial canning industry which uses sterilization techniques to kill the *C. botulinum* spores. For the home canner it is essential to follow recommended guidelines to prevent the growth of *C. botulinum*. These guidelines are:

(1) All non–acidic foods such as green beans and corn must be canned using a pressure cooker. Acidic foods such as tomatoes and citrus fruits contain natural acids that kill the botulism bacteria.

(2) To can non–acidic foods cook them at 10 pounds of pressure at a temperature of 248°F (120°C) for 80 minutes.

Obviously canning non–acidic foods requires special equipment. If you are not sure about the origin or safety of any home–canned food do not eat it. Dispose of the can safely and be sure to wash hands and touched surfaces thoroughly with bleach or ammonia.

The toxin can also be inactivated if the canned vegetable is cooked at 176°F (80°C) for five minutes or boiled for one minute before eating.

It is also wise to be wary of uncooked fish and meats. Sushi, a popular Japanese dish of raw fish, and venison have been known to spread botulism. All meats should be cooked thoroughly to kill the botulism endospores.

See also Food poisoning; Poisons and toxins.

Further Reading:

Houschild, Andreas H. W., and Karen L. Dodds, eds. *Clostridium botulinum: Ecology and Control in Foods.* New York: M. Dekker, 1993.

Jankovic, Joseph, and Mitchell F. Brin. "The Therapeutic Uses of Botulinum Toxin." *New England Journal of Medicine* 324 (25 April 1991): 1186.

Lance, Simpson L., ed. *Botulinum Neurotoxin and Tetanus Toxin.* San Diego: Academic Press, 1989.

Morse, Dale L., et. al. "Garlic–in–Oil Associated Botulism: Episode Leads to Product Modification." *American Journal of Public Health* 80 (November 1990): 1372.

Nebel, Diane. "Case Study: Botulism in Home–Canned Food." *Journal of Environmental Health* 54 (July–August 1991): 9.

Kathleen Scogna

Bowerbirds

The 18 species of bowerbirds are unique in that the males build and decorate a bower, a structure of sticks or grass on the ground, for the purpose of attracting and courting females. Members of the bowerbird family (Ptilonorhynchidae) are found in Australia and New Guinea, and are related to lyrebirds and birds of paradise. Most bowerbirds are about the size of a blue jay or grackle, and as a group they show a wide variety of plumage characteristics, vocal behavior, and bower–building styles. The bowers of some species are quite large (3.3–6.6 ft/1–2 m) in length, and are decorated with a variety of objects, making them some of the most remarkable examples of animal architecture.

Naturalists have been fascinated by bowerbirds for decades. Early observers believed that the bower was a nest; however, in 1865, the ornithologist John Gould suggested that the bower was used for sexual display and mating. Not all bowerbirds build a bower; some, such as the toothbilled bowerbird of eastern Australia, simply clear a display court on the ground, and decorate it with leaves.

Bowers occur in several forms, each built by species that appear to share closer genealogical relationships with each other than with those species that build a different type of bower. Avenue bowers (constructed by the satin bowerbird) have two vertical walls running parallel to each other, with one end opening onto a display area where most of the decorations are arranged. Maypole bowers consist of sticks woven around a central pole, formed by a sapling or fern, surrounded by a circular, raised court. Two species, the striped gardener bowerbird and Vogelkop's bowerbird, build massive hutlike structures (up to 6.6 ft/2 m across) around the central maypole, opening onto a cleared exhibition area. The golden bowerbird places sticks against adjacent saplings which are joined by a crossbranch; this he uses as a display perch. A variety of objects are used to decorate the bowers of different species of bowerbird, including fruits, flowers, feathers, moss, snail shells, colored stones and bark; the recent presence of humans has added coins, bottle tops, pieces of glass, teaspoons, nails and screws to the bowers.

Female bowerbirds visit the bowers of numerous males in the process of selecting a mate. When a female arrives, she will take up a position within the bower, while the owner launches into a stereotyped display that is unique for each species. The male emits varied chirps, whistles, buzzes and mechanical sounds, while performing a series of dance–like movements which have been described as "rooster walks" and "penguin walks." Males of some species pick up and hold decorations in their beak during their display, bobbing their heads or tossing the items with considerable vigor. One especially vigorous species, the spotted bowerbird, actually rushes at the visitor watching from within the bower, crashing bodily into the wall that separates the two birds. When the visiting female is ready to mate, she crouches low in the bower, lifting her tail, and the male approaches from the rear of the bower to mount her and copulate for just one or two seconds.

It is clear that a bower can be extremely valuable to its owner, for bowerbirds spend hours constructing, decorating, and maintaining their bowers, and no male has ever been reported to successfully court a female without one. However, success is not guaranteed. Males in some species are highly competitive, and are observed to steal decorations from the bowers of other males, and to destroy rival bowers. Many bowerbird males simply fail to mate with even one visiting female during a breeding season, even though the males have been tending bowers.

Researchers have sought to understand why some individuals enjoy high mating success, while most others do not, and the functional role of the bower in female mate choice. Elaborate display traits, such as bowers, suggest the influence of sexual selection—the process of evolutionary change due to competition between members of one sex (usually males), and selective mate choice by the other sex (usually females). In species where males give little or no parental care to their offspring (as is the case for most bowerbirds), researchers have attempted to address the question: What is the female choosing when she selects a mate? Bowerbird observers have attempted to ascertain whether certain features of bowers or of male display are reliable predictors of a male's success in obtaining mates.

Gerald Borgia and his collaborators have used an ingenious method to investigate this question in the

A female satin bowerbird (*Ptilonorhynchus violaceus*) visiting a bower.

field. A video camera, positioned a short distance in front of the bower, was outfitted with a motion–sensitive infrared detector, which turned on the camera whenever there was movement at the bower. Such continuous monitoring compiled a comprehensive record of activity at the bower, and allowed Borgia to measure and compare the courtship of many individuals. The results showed that female bowerbirds differentiated among males, at least in part on the basis of the quality of the bowers and the display. In satin bowerbirds, for instance, the number of decorations, especially snail shells and blue feathers, as well as the degree of bower symmetry and the density of the sticks used to construct it, were excellent predictors of male mating success. The more decorations, and the more symmetrical and densely constructed the bower, the more matings were achieved by the bower owner. The importance of decorations was underscored when the researchers experimentally removed decorations from some bowers. The owners of the manipulated bowers had far less success in attracting females. Clearly, female choice could exert a potent effect on the evolution of male display in bowerbirds, helping shape the elaborate courtship structures and behaviors observed in these animals.

Further Reading:

Borgia, Gerald. "Sexual Selection in Bowerbirds." *Scientific American* 254 (1986): 92–101.

Bowfin

The bowfin is a bony fish (*Amia calva*, family Amiidae) found in eastern North America. It is a relic species—the sole living representative of the order Amiiformes, which first appeared in the Triassic period more than 200 million years ago.

Members of this family were common in Europe and Asia, as well as North America, during the Cretaceous and the early part of the Cenozoic. Fossil species of the genus *Amia* occurred in Europe as recently as the Miocene (about 20 million years ago) but this single species in North America is the only one of its group still living.

The bowfin is a relatively common fish in swamps and slow–moving streams in the southeastern United

A male Pacific boxfish (*Ostracion meleagris*) near Cocos island, Costa Rica.

States, and is often caught by fishermen. Often called a grennel or mudfish, it is very bony and seldom used as food if there is an alternative. In appearance it is a rather stout cylindrical fish, with a distinctive bony head and a wide mouth with many sharp–pointed teeth. It differs from most freshwater fishes in having a very long dorsal fin and widely separated pectoral and pelvic fins.

The bowfin preys on other fishes, and because its swim bladder is connected with its esophagus, it can gulp air in situations when the oxygen in the water is depleted. Thus, it can survive in warm isolated pools during a drought and feed on the other fishes that cannot withstand these conditions. The male bowfin builds a circular nest in shallow water and guards the eggs until they hatch. He continues to guard the young for some time. They can be seen following him in shallow water like so many baby chicks following their mother hen.

Box elder see **Maples**

Box elder bug see **True bugs**

Boxfish

Boxfish, also called trunkfish or cowfish, are a small group of shallow–water, marine fish in the family Ostraciontidae (order Tetraodontiformes). The family includes the genera *Lactoria, Ostracion,* and *Tetrosomus* and is closely related to the poisonous puffer fish of the family Tetraodontidae. To avoid confusion with these poisonous relatives, some people avoid eating boxfish despite their being good for food. Boxfish are generally oval in shape when seen from the side; while being viewed from one end, different species of boxfish resemble triangles, squares or pentagons.

Boxfish take their shared common name from the hard shell or carapace, composed of strongly joined plates corresponding to the scales of other fish, which surrounds their bodies. Only the eyes, the low–set mouth, the fins, and the tail are not covered by this rigid shell. Boxfish reach lengths of up to 2 ft (61 cm). They inhabit warm waters from the Pacific Ocean to the Caribbean. Boxfish usually prefer shallow waters, and are often found around coral reefs. In some areas the boxfish are dried and used as decorations.

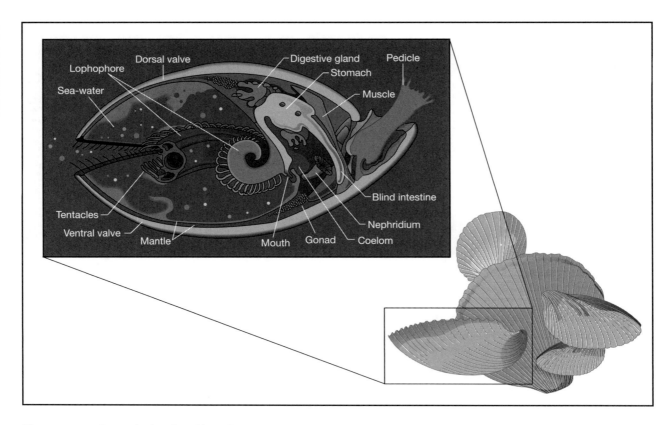

The anatomy of an articulate brachiopod.

Boxfish possess an intriguing method of defense against predators, such as sharks. Like other species of fish, when disturbed boxfish can secrete molecules known as icthyocrinotoxins or ichthyotoxins—literally, fish poisons—from their skin. The toxins of two Pacific boxfish species, *Ostracion immaculatus* from Japan and *O. lentiginosus* from Hawaii, have been characterized by biochemists. These toxins turn out to be esters of choline chloride. Choline is a vitamin in the b complex that makes up part of many of the fatty acids found in the membranes of human cells.

Similar to the ichthyotoxic compounds of fish from other families, boxfish toxins are surfactants. In general they act as biological detergents, promoting the dissolution of fatty acids in water. This occurs because surfactants, like all detergents, include parts which can interact with water and parts which can interact with fats. Thus, fats and water can mix, something which normally does not occur. By this mechanism, these ichthyotoxins cause hemolysis in the laboratory by dissolving cell membranes. When these membranes dissolve, cells break down and die. This irritates and deters predators, saving the boxfish from being eaten.

Brachiopods

Brachiopods, or lampshells, are a phylum of small marine animals with a two–valved shell that, at first glance, resemble bivalved mollusks such as clams. The resemblance, however, is quite superficial. The orientation of the shells of brachiopods is very different from that of bivalved molluscs, and brachiopods have two additional structures virtually unique to them, the lophophore (a ciliated feeding apparatus) and pedicle (a muscular stalk). The valves of the brachiopod shell are asymmetrical–being dorsal and ventral and covering the upper and lower parts of the body, with the hinge at the posterior end. In contrast, shells of a clam are on the right and left sides of the body, with the hinge dorsal.

The lophophore is a complex feeding apparatus with minute tentacles and cilia that separate food particles from the sea water, and convey them to the mouth. The other phyla of marine invertebrates—moss animals or bryozoans (Ectoprocta) and phoronid worms (Pheronida)—also feed by means of ciliated tentacles on a lophophore, and the three groups are sometimes collectively known as the lophophorates.

The pedicle is a kind of stalk for attachment to firm surfaces, such as the wall of an underwater canyon or to the shell of another brachiopod. The distal end of the pedicle secretes a sticky substance which some brachiopods use to form a sand anchor, enabling them to withdraw deeper into the sediment by contracting the pedicle when threatened by a potential predator. The pedicle ranges from about 0.1 in (a few millimeters) in some species to more than 7.9 in (20 cm) in others. Some bivalved molluscs, such as oysters, also attach themselves to the substratum, but they lack a pedicle.

Brachiopods had a spectacular heyday in the Paleozoic era, 500 million years ago, as shown by their common occurrence as fossils in many parts of the world. This accounts for their great interest to geologists. Most of the 260 living species of lampshells are found in deep water, so their shells are not commonly found on the beach. In the Pacific, *Lingula unguis* is commonly found living in vertical burrows in sand and mud. In Maine, *Terebratulina septentrionalis* is sometimes exposed to the air at low tide. In Florida, an unrelated species, *Glottidia pyramidata,* lives in shallow water, especially in the sand beneath eel–grass plots. Five species of brachiopods are readily collected from rocks off the shores of the South Island of New Zealand.

The food of brachiopods is mainly algal cells of the phytoplankton, which are strained out of water currents passing over the lophophore, in a process called filter–feeding. Clearance rates of several species are in the same range or a little lower than rates shown by bivalve mollusks. Research on the physiology of brachiopods is heavily slanted toward comparisons with mussels and clams because of the obvious similarity in protective shell and mode of feeding. The fossil record indicates the rise of one group followed by the decline of the other, as if they might have been competitors. Unlike mollusks, brachiopods are not significantly preyed upon or harvested. Some observations suggest that fish find lampshells distasteful.

Since brachiopods are fixed in position after the larval phase, there is little observable behavior beyond the opening and closing of valves. The valves may remain closed for periods of 5–22 hours, during which there is no feeding and little or no oxygen uptake. Lampshells obtain oxygen from the water that passes over the lophophore which functions as a respiratory surface although brachiopods tolerate lack of oxygen (anoxia) well.

Oxygen consumption rates of brachiopods are generally lower than those of bivalves of similar size. The same is true of feeding rates. In addition to the sudden

KEY TERMS

Lophophore—A complex feeding apparatus with minute tentacles and cilia that separates food particles from sea water; this apparatus is found in brachiopods, bryozoans, and phoronid worms.

Pedicle—A kind of stalk that anchors a brachiopod to a firm surface.

shortening of the pedicel, a very slow contraction of the pedicle has also been observed.

See also Lamp shells.

Further Reading:

Hammen, C. S. "Brachiopod Metabolism and Enzymes." *American Zoologist* 17 (1977): 141–147.

Morris, S. C. "The Fossil Record and the Early Evolution of the Metazoa." *Nature* 361 (1993): 219–225.

Pearse, V., et al. *Living Invertebrates.* Palo Alto, CA: Blackwell, 1987.

Rhodes, M. C., and R. J. Thompson. "Comparative Physiology of Suspension–Feeding in Living Brachiopods and Bivalves: Evolutionary Implications. *Paleobiology* 19 (1993): 322–334.

Rudwick, M. J. S. *Living and Fossil Brachiopods.* London: Hutchinson University Library, 1970.

Wilson, E. O. 1994. "Biodiversity: Challenge, Science, Opportunity." *American Zoologist* 34 (1994): 5–11.

C. S. Hammen

Boyle's law see **Gases, properties of**

Brackish

Brackish refers to water with a salinity intermediate to that of fresh water and sea water (the latter has a salt concentration of about 3.5%, or 35 parts per thousand). Brackish waters originate by the mixing of sea water and fresh water, and are most common near the coasts of the oceans.

Brackish waters can occur as enclosed systems such as lakes and ponds that receive occasional inputs of oceanic water during severe storms. Brackish waters also occur as coastal estuaries or salt marshes that are more frequently flooded with saline water as a result of tidal cycles. Sometimes, brackish waters can occur far inland, for example, in parts of the prairies of North America where saline ponds and wetlands have variable salt concentrations depending on the diluting effects of recent rains or snowmelt.

The salt concentration of water is highly influential on the transport of ions across cellular membranes, the availability of nutrients in soil, and for other reasons. Most species can tolerate either salty water or fresh water, but not both. However, organisms that live in brackish habitats must be tolerant of a wide range of salt concentrations (such species are known as *euryhaline*). For example, the small fish known as killifish (*Fundulus* spp.) are common residents of brackish coastal habitats known as estuaries, where within any day the salt concentration in tidal pools and creeks can vary from that typical of fresh water to that of the open ocean. Other fish such as salmon (e.g., *Salmo* spp.) and eels (*Anguilla* spp.) move to or from marine waters during their spawning migrations, in the process moving from environments characterized by the salt concentration of full seawater, through brackish, to fresh water. Animals that live in or move through estuaries must be tolerant of the physiological stresses associated with such large and rapid changes in salinity, as must the plants of those habitats, such as the aquatic eelgrass (*Zostera* spp.) and the cord grass of salt marshes (*Spartina* spp.).

The environmental conditions of brackish waters are highly stressful for organisms that cannot tolerate such wide swings of salinity. However, for those relatively few species that are tolerant of such difficult environmental conditions, brackish habitats represent a relatively uncompetitive, ecological opportunity to be exploited as a livelihood.

See also Freshwater; Saltwater.

Brain

The brain is a mass of nerve tissue located in an animal's head that controls the body's functions. In simple animals, the brain functions like a switchboard picking up signals from sense organs and passing the information to muscles. In more advanced forms, particularly vertebrates, a more analytical brain coordinates complex behaviors. The brain is part of an animal's central nervous system, which receives and transmits impulses. It works with the peripheral nervous system, which carries impulses to and from the brain and spinal cord via nerves which run throughout the body.

Invertebrate brain

Nematodes (roundworms) have a simple brain and nervous system consisting of approximately 300 nerve cells, or neurons. Sensory neurons located in the head end of the animal detect stimuli from the environment and pass messages to the brain. The brain then sends out impulses through a ventral nerve cord to muscles which respond to the stimulus. The way that the interneurons of the brain process the data determines the response.

The earthworm and other annelids, as well as insects and other arthropods, have more complex nervous systems. In these animals, there are paired ventral nerve cords that run from head to tail on the animal's underside. Cell bodies of neurons in the cords form pairs of ganglia in each body segment. Four of the most anterior ganglia fuse in the head to form a brain. As a result, the brain ganglia are larger than the segmental ganglia, and also contain a larger proportion of sensory motor neurons. The brain ganglia have some dominance over the segment ganglia. The ventral nerve cords, brain, and segmental ganglia comprise the central nervous system. Neuronal fibers in the cords, bundled into nerves that carry communications between ganglia, make up the peripheral nervous system.

The earthworm's brain consists of paired ganglia in the head end. An impulse, such as touch, light, or moisture, is detected by receptor cells in the skin. A pair of nerves in each of the earthworm's segments carries the signal to the brain and smaller ganglia in each segment, where the signals are analyzed. The central nervous system then transmits impulses on nerves that coordinate muscle action, causing the earthworm to move.

In insects, specialized sense organs detect information from the environment and transmit it to the central nervous system. Such sense organs include simple and compound eyes, sound receptors on the thorax or in the legs, and taste receptors. The brain of an insect consists of a ganglion in the head. Some of the segmental ganglia are fused, allowing better communication between the segments. The information that insects use for behaviors such as walking, flying, mating, and stinging is stored in the segmental ganglia. In experiments in which heads are cut off of cockroaches and flies, these insects continue to learn.

Vertebrate brain

The central nervous system of vertebrates consists of a single spinal cord, which runs in a dorsal position

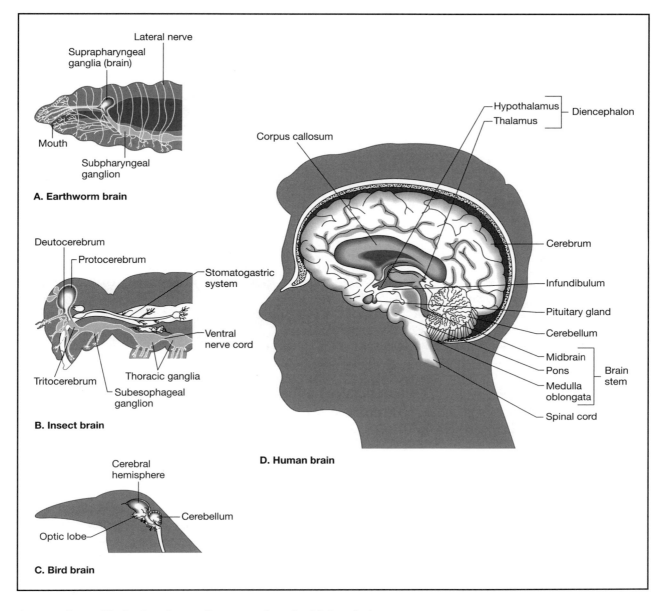

A comparison of the brains of an earthworm, an insect, a bird, and a human.

along the back, and a highly developed brain. The brain is the dominant structure of the nervous system. It is the master controller of all body functions, and the analyzer and interpreter of complex information and behavior patterns. We can think of the brain as a powerful neural computer. The peripheral nervous system, composed of nerves which run to all parts of the body, transmits information to and from the central nervous system.

The vertebrate brain is divided into three main divisions: the forebrain, the midbrain, and the hindbrain. The hindbrain connects the brain to the spinal cord, and a portion of it, called the medulla oblongata, controls important body functions such as the breathing rate and the heart rate. Also in the hindbrain, the cerebellum controls balance. The forebrain consists of the cerebrum, thalamus, and hypothalamus. The forebrain controls, among other things, the sense of smell in vertebrates.

During the first few weeks of development, the brain of a vertebrate looks like a series of bulges in the neural tube. It is hard to see a difference when we examine the early embryonic brains of fish, amphibians, reptiles, birds, and mammals. As the brain develops, the bulges enlarge, and each type of vertebrate acquires its own specific adult brain that helps it survive in its environment. In the forebrain of fish, the olfactory (smell) sense is well developed, whereas the cerebrum serves merely as a relay station for impulses. In mammals, on the other hand, the olfactory division is included in the limbic system, which also controls emotions, and the cerebrum is highly developed, operating as a complex processing center for information. Optic lobes are well–developed in the midbrain of nonmammalian vertebrates, whereas in mammals the vision centers are mainly in the forebrain. In addition, a bird's cerebellum is large compared to the rest of its brain, since it controls coordination and balance in flying.

Human brain

The living human brain is a soft, shiny, grayish white, mushroom–shaped structure. Encased within the skull, it is a 3 lb (1.4 kg) mass of nerve tissue that keeps us alive and functioning. On average, the brain weighs 13.7 oz (390 g) at birth, and by age 15 grows to approximately 46 oz (1,315 g). The human brain is composed of up to one trillion nerve cells—100 billion of them are neurons, and the remainder are supporting (glial) cells. Neurons receive, process, and transmit impulses, while glial cells (neuroglia) protect, support, and assist neurons. The brain is protected by the skull and by three membranes called the meninges—the outermost the dura mater, the middle the arachnoid, and the innermost the pia mater. Also protecting the brain is cerebrospinal fluid, a liquid that circulates between the arachnoid and pia mater in the subarachnoid space. Many bright red arteries and bluish veins on the surface of the brain penetrate inward. Glucose, oxygen, and certain ions pass easily from the blood into the brain, whereas other substances, such as antibiotics, do not. The capillary walls are believed to create a blood–brain barrier that protects the brain from a number of biochemicals circulating in the blood.

The parts of the brain can be studied in terms of structure and function. Four principal sections of the human brain are the brain stem (the hindbrain and midbrain), the diencephalon, the cerebrum, and the cerebellum.

The brain stem

The brain stem is the stalk of the brain, and is continuous with the spinal cord. It consists of the medulla oblongata, pons, and midbrain. A part of the brain stem, the medulla oblongata is a continuation of the spinal cord. All the messages that are transmitted between the brain and spinal cord pass through the medulla via fibers in the white matter. The fibers on the right side of the medulla cross to the left and those on the left cross to the right. The result is that each side of the brain controls the opposite side of the body. There are three vital centers in the medulla which control the heartbeat, the rate of breathing, and the diameter of the blood vessels. Centers that help coordinate swallowing, vomiting, hiccoughing, coughing, and sneezing are also located in the medulla. The reticular formation occurs partially in the medulla and in other parts of the central nervous system. The reticular formation operates in maintaining our conscious state. The pons (meaning bridge) conducts messages between the spinal cord and the rest of the brain, and between the different parts of the brain. The midbrain conveys impulses from the cerebral cortex to the pons and spinal cord. It also contains visual and audio reflex centers involving the movement of eyeballs and head.

Twelve pairs of cranial nerves originate in the underside of the brain, mostly from the brain stem. They leave the skull through openings and extend as peripheral nerves to their destinations. Cranial nerves include the olfactory nerve that brings messages about smell from the nose and the optic nerve that conducts visual information from the eyes.

The diencephalon

The diencephalon lies above the brain stem, and embodies the thalamus and hypothalamus. In the diencephalon, the thalamus is an important relay station for sensory information for the cerebral cortex from other parts of the brain. The thalamus also interprets sensations of pain, pressure, temperature, and touch, and is concerned with some of our emotions and memory. It receives information from the environment in the form of sound, smell, and taste. The hypothalamus performs numerous important functions. These include the control of the autonomic nervous system (a branch of the nervous system involved with control of a number of body functions, such as heartbeat rate and digestion). The hypothalamus helps regulate the endocrine system and controls normal body temperature. It tells us when we are hungry, full, and thirsty. It helps regulate sleep and wakefulness, and is involved when we feel angry and aggressive.

The cerebrum

The cerebrum, constituting about 87.5% of the brain weight, spreads over the diencephalon. The cerebral cortex is the outer layer of the brain and is composed of gray matter made up of nerve cell bodies. It is about 0.08 in (2 mm) thick and its surface area is about 5 sq ft (1.5 sq m)—around half the size of an office desk. White matter, composed of nerve fibers covered with myelin sheaths, lies beneath the gray matter. With the rapid growth of the brain during embryonic development, the gray matter grows faster than the white matter and folds on itself. The folds are called convolutions or gyri, and the grooves between them are known as sulci. A deep longitudinal fissure separates the cerebrum into a left and right hemisphere. Each cerebral hemisphere is divided into frontal, temporal, parietal, and occipital lobes. The corpus callosum, a large bundle of fibers, connects the two cerebral hemispheres. The thalamus and subcortical nuclei, or basal ganglia, are areas of gray matter that exist below the white matter.

Sensory areas of the cerebrum interpret sensory impulses. Spoken and written language are transmitted to a part of the cerebrum called Wernicke's area where meaning is extracted, and sent to Broca's area, one of the motor areas of the cerebrum. Motor areas of the cerebrum control muscle movements. Within Broca's area, thoughts are translated into speech, and muscles are coordinated for speaking. Impulses from other motor areas direct our hand muscles when we write, and our eye muscles when we scan the page for information.

Association areas of the cerebrum are concerned with emotions and intellectual processes, by connecting sensory and motor functions. In our association areas, innumerable impulses are processed that result in memory, emotions, judgment, personality, and intelligence.

Certain structures in the cerebrum and diencephalon make up the limbic system. These regions function in memory and emotions, and are associated with pain and pleasure.

By studying patients whose corpus callosum had been destroyed, scientists realized that differences existed between the left and right sides of the cerebral cortex. The left side of the brain functions mainly in speech, logic, writing, and arithmetic. The right side of the brain, on the other hand, is more concerned with imagination, art, symbols, and spatial relations.

The cerebellum

The cerebellum is located below the cerebrum and behind the brain stem, and is shaped like a butterfly. The "wings" are the cerebellar hemispheres, and each consists of lobes that have distinct grooves or fissures. The cerebellum controls the movements of our muscular system needed for balance, posture, and maintaining posture.

Studying the brain

At the end of the nineteenth century, Santiago Ramon y Cajal, a Spanish scientist, studied neurons using stain developed by Camillo Golgi. Cajal realized that the brain was made up of individual units and not a continuous net as was believed at the time. His studies uncovered a large variety of neurons that differed in size and shape. He explained that neurons received signals on dendrites and transmitted impulses on axons. Since his work, researchers have learned that neurons carry information in the form of brief electrical impulses called action potentials that result when positively charged sodium ions travel across the axon membrane from the fluid outside to the cytoplasm inside. When a nerve impulse reaches the end of an axon, neurotransmitters are released at junctions called synapses. The neurotransmitters are chemicals that bind to receptors on the receiving neurons, triggering the continuation of the impulse. Fifty different neurotransmitters have been discovered since the first one was identified in 1920. By studying the chemical effects of neurotransmitters in the brain, scientists have made advances in finding medicines for the treatment of mental disorders, and determining the actions of drugs on the brain.

Researchers today are able to trace various molecules that are transported along axons during action potentials. Microelectrodes are used to detect the currents that cross synapses. Using this information, wiring diagrams are created which model the patterns of information flow within the brain.

Considerable knowledge about the human brain has been obtained during brain surgery by stimulating specific areas with a mild electric current, and from the observation of patients with brain damage. In the 1920s, a Canadian neurosurgeon named Wilder Penfield electrically stimulated different parts of the brains of some of his patients. He found this caused them to remember specific events from the past. For example, one patient heard someone from the past singing a particular song. From this and other studies, scientists realized that specific functions are localized in specific parts of the brain. Recently, scientists observed the behavior of a woman whose amygdala (an almond–shaped group of cells in the cerebrum) was destroyed. The amygdala plays a role in emotions and social relationships. The researcher realized that without an amygdala, the patient could not read facial expressions. As a result, she couldn't judge the intentions of others, and often made poor social decisions.

Until recently, scientists believed that brain cells do not regenerate, thereby making brain injuries and brain diseases untreatable. Researchers are now trying to help such patients with neuron transplants, introducing nerve tissue into the brain. They are also studying substances, such as nerve growth factor (NGF), that someday may be used to help regrow nerve tissue.

Since the 1950s, scientists have begun to understand the process of sleep. They find that sleep occurs in different stages. One stage is called rapid eye movement (REM) sleep. We dream during REM sleep, a period when there is a lot of brain activity and eye movements and the body is inactive. The pons, an area of the brainstem, sets off REM sleep and dreaming. During REM sleep, the brain emits characteristic brain waves. Non–REM sleep usually comes first, takes up about 75% of our sleep, and is much quieter. Its stages get deeper and deeper. Non–REM sleep also has its own particular brain waves. The two types of sleep alternate during the night. Scientists are beginning to understand the factors that control sleep and wakefulness. These include a biological clock, a group of about 10,000 neurons in the hypothalamus that trigger off waking up; homeostasis, the body's tendency to maintain equilibrium in physiological systems; and changes in the level of norepinephrine and serotonin, neurotransmitters in the brain.

Where and how does memory occur? This is another question that has puzzled scientists for decades. Recent information suggests that memory is not stored in a single brain center, but instead is part of numerous processing systems in the cerebral cortex. Scientists believe that memory involves chemical and structural changes in neurons, as well as changes in the strength of synapses.

Technology provides useful tools for researching the brain and helping patients with brain disorders. An electroencephalogram (EEG) is a record of brain waves, electrical activity generated in the brain. An EEG is obtained by positioning electrodes on the head and amplifying the waves with an electroencephalograph, and is valuable in diagnosing brain diseases such as epilepsy and tumors.

Scientists use three different techniques that involve scans to study and understand the brain and diagnose disorders:

(1) Magnetic resonance imaging (MRI) depends on the use of a magnetic field to display the living brain at various depths as if in slices. Not blocked by bone, MRI allows the viewer to zoom in on any region and obtain reliable pictures of brain tissue.

(2) Positron emission tomography (PET) results in color images of the brain displayed on the screen of a monitor. During this test, a technician injects a small

KEY TERMS
Broca's area—Area in the cerebrum that organizes thought and coordinates muscles for speech.
Ganglion—A structure comprised of neuron cell bodies, usually sited outside of the central nervous system.
Glial cells—Nerve cells (other than neurons) located in the brain that protect, support, and assist neurons.
REM sleep—Rapid eye movement sleep that is characterized by dreaming, active brain activity, and numerous eye movements.
Wernicke's area—Area in the cerebrum that processes information from written and spoken language.

amount of a substance, such as glucose, that is marked with a radioactive tag. The marked substance shows where glucose is consumed in the brain. PET is used to study the chemistry and activity of the normal brain and to diagnose abnormalities such as tumors.

(3) Magnetoencephalography (MEG) measures the electromagnetic fields created between neurons as electrochemical information is passed along. When under the machine, if the subject is told, "wiggle your toes," the readout is an instant picture of the brain at work. Concentric colored rings appear on the computer screen that pinpoint the brain signals even before the toes are actually wiggled.

Using an MRI along with MEG, physicians and scientists can look into the brain without using surgery. They hope to use these techniques for the early diagnosis of disorders such as Alzheimer's and Parkinson's disease. They foresee that these techniques could help paralysis victims move by supplying information on how to stimulate their muscles, or indicating the signals needed to control an artificial limb.

In spite of recent advances, many questions about brain function remain. How is inherited information wired into the brain during embryonic development? What happens in the brain when we learn? How is memory stored? What causes degeneration and disorders of brain cells? Further research may hold the answers.

See also Electrocardiogram (ECG); Electroencephalogram (EEG); Nervous system; Neuron; Neurotransmitter; Nuclear medicine; Sleep.

Further Reading:

Carey, Joseph, ed. *Brain Facts*. Washington, D.C.: Society for Neuroscience, 1993.

Jackson, Carolyn, ed. *How Things Work: The Brain*. Alexandria, Va.: Time–Life Books, 1990.

"Mind and Brain." *Scientific American* (September, 1992).

The Nature of the Nerve Impulse. Films for the Humanities and Sciences, 1994–95. Videocassette.

Bernice Essenfeld

Brambling see **Finches**

Brant see **Geese**

Bream see **Carp**

Brewing

Brewing is a multi–stage process during which the brewer encourages a grain such as barley to germinate briefly, steeps the grain in water to release its sugars, and adds yeast to the mixture, which ferments the sugar, turning it into alcohol and carbon dioxide. Around the world, people have brewed grains and starchy vegetables for thousands of years from ingredients as varied as rice, corn, cassava, pumpkins, sorghum, and millet, and brewed beverages are staples in the diets of many cultures.

History

Archaeologists have turned up evidence that the Summarian people in the Middle East were brewing barley as long as 8,000 years ago. These early brewers may have discovered the fundamental processes of brewing as they observed — or tasted — what happened when they left fruit juices or cereal extracts exposed to the wild yeasts that naturally float in the air. Native Americans made a beer from corn, which they softened by chewing and mixing into a pulpy mass with saliva. They then set this masticated corn out in a vessel to ferment, and enjoyed the resulting drink.

Throughout Europe, breweries sprang up where there was good water for brewing. During the Middle Ages, monasteries became the centers for brewing, and the monks originated brewing techniques and created

A brewmeister and fellow worker inspect the current brew of a local beer in a brewery in the Dominican Republic.

many of the beers still popular today. Early European settlers in North America brought with them from Europe a taste for beer, but followed the Native Americans' example and initially made beer from corn and pumpkins, which they flavored with such local additives as the tops of spruce trees.

With the spread of the British empire and rise of industrialization over the past 150 years, traditional European beer began to move from its local markets to towns, pubs, and countries far away from its place of origin. This emigration was aided with the introduction of bottled beer in 1875 by the Joseph Schlitz Brewing Company in Milwaukee, Wisconsin, and the later advent of canned beer in the 1930s.

Brewing process

The brewer's first step in making a beer is to wet the kernels of grain, promoting their germination, or sprouting. During this process, the germ or embryo of the grain breaks down slightly, releasing the enzymes that turn starches, complex sugars, into simple sugars. The brewer allows the grain to germinate for a short period and dries it quickly in a kiln. Dried, malted grain is very durable and easily stored.

The brewer next mixes the dried malt with water to create a porridgy substance called mash. During this phase, the mash is brought to a temperature of around 150° F (66° C) and is kept there a number of hours. The starchy components of the grain break down during mashing, and are converted into simple sugars, which yeast will be able to digest during the fermentation phase.

The brewer now adds more water to the mash and rinses out a watery sugar solution called wort, which is heated to a boil. At this point, the brewer adds hops, the flower of the *Humulus lupulus* vine, which give beer its characteristic bitter flavor and aroma.

When the wort has cooled to the temperature most friendly to yeast (50–60° F [10–16° C]), these organisms are added and go to work consuming the sugars in the wort, growing to be as much as five to ten times their original weight. They fuel their growth with the sugar and in the process, change it from carbohydrate to ethanol, a form of alcohol, and carbon dioxide, the gas that is responsible for beer's foam and bubbles.

Types of beer

Most familiar beers are barley–based beverages. In Europe and the United States, beer is usually one of two types, ale or lager. Ale is a traditional British beer that until the latter part of the nineteenth century was not flavored with hops. Ale is made with a variety of yeast that rises to the top of the fermentation tank, and that produces a higher alcohol content than lagers. Ales range from pale ales such as Kolsch (from a district around Cologne, Germany) which is strongly hopped and not sweet, to strong, dark, ales such as porter and stout. Lager (which means cellar in German) originated in the Bavarian region of Germany. Lager is made with bottom–fermenting yeast, and is lower in alcohol content than ales. Lagers include: pilsner, a pale beer with a distinctive hop flavor; bock, a strong dark beer; weiss, a pale beer made with wheat that is usually served with slices of lemon or flavored with fruit juices.

Future developments

Current research in brewing technology is focusing on events at the cellular level. For example, brewery researchers are working on methods that will rapidly and accurately detect the presence and identity of unwanted yeasts or other microorganisms that find their way into the beer during brewing, and that change the flavor of the beer. (Potentially problematic organisms include *Lactobacillus, Pediococcus,* and *Obesumbacterium.*) Some of the methods already available or soon to be available include those using DNA probes, and protein and chromosome fingerprinting. Some of these techniques are already used in tests designed for at–home pregnancy testing, drug screening, AIDS testing, and tests for the presence of environmental contaminants such as pesticides.

Breweries are also using biotechnological techniques and genetic engineering to select and propagate choice characteristics in barley, rice, corn, yeast, and hops. Some of the characteristics that brewery researchers are working toward include disease resis-

---

KEY TERMS

Ale—A top–fermented beer that until the latter part of the nineteenth century was not flavored with hops; traditionally British has a higher alcohol content than lagers.

Lager—Lager (which means cellar in German) is a traditional Bavarian beer made with bottom– fermenting yeast. These beers are lighter in color and lower in alcohol content than ales. Over the past few decades, lager surpassed ale in popularity.

Hops—Comes from the cone of the flower of the vine *Humulus lupulus,* which is cultivated throughout temperate regions for use in brewing. The addition of hops gives beer its characteristic bitter flavor and aroma.

Malt—Grain that has germinated, or sprouted, for a short period and is then dried. During germination, the enzymes in the germ of the grain are released, which will make the sugars in the grain available to the yeast.

Wort—The sugar water solution made when malted barley is steeped in water and its complex sugars break down into simple sugars.

Fermentation—The process during which yeast consume the sugars in the wort and release alcohol and carbon dioxide as byproducts.

Yeast—A microorganism of the fungus family that promotes alcoholic fermentation, and is also used as a leavening in baking.

---

tance in the crops, and in yeast, the ability to resist contamination and to ferment carbohydrates that yeasts have been incapable of fermenting. Micropropagation is a new and experimental technique that involves making any number of genetically identical copies of a plant, by removing minute quantities of its growth points and placing them in a medium that encourages the rapid growth of shoots. This process is then repeated again and again. Mutation breeding is a process for creating mutations, some of which may be desirable, by exposing the plant to X–rays or chemical mutagens; and transformation technologies, which allow the breeder to make a change in a single gene by adding or deleting it.

See also Fermentation; Yeast.

Further Reading:

Briggs D.E. and J.S. Hough. *Malting and Brewing Science,* Volumes 1 & 2. London: Chapman and Hall, 1981.

Adobe bricks on a flatbed truck in Taos, New Mexico.

Gourish and Wilson. *The British Brewing Industry, 1830–1980.* Cambridge: Cambridge University Press, 1994.

Gump, Barry, ed. *Beer and Wine Production: Analyses, Characterization, and Technological Advances.* American Chemical Society Symposium Series 536, American Chemical Society, Washington D.C., 1993.

Hough, J.S. *Biotechnology of Brewing.* Cambridge: Cambridge University Press, 1985.

Beth Hanson

Brick

Bricks are one of the oldest types of building blocks. They are an ideal building material because they are relatively cheap to make, very durable, and require little maintenance. Bricks are usually made of kiln–baked mixtures of clay. In ancient times, bricks were made of mud and dried in the sun; modern bricks are made from concrete, sand and lime, and glass. The physical and chemical characteristics of the raw materials used to make bricks, along with the temperature at which they are baked, determine the color and hardness of the finished product. Bricks are made in standard sizes, are usually twice as long as they are wide and, since most bricklaying is done manually, are made small enough to fit in the hand. Bricklayers use a trowel to cover each brick with mortar—a mixture of cement, sand, and water. The mortar hardens when dry and keeps the bricks in place. Bricks are arranged in various patterns, called bonds, for strength.

History

Archaeologists have found bricks in the Middle East dating to 10,000 years ago. Scientists suggest that these bricks were made from mud left after the rivers in that area flooded. The bricks were molded by hand and left in the sun to dry. Structures were built by layering the bricks using mud and tar as mortar. The ancient city of Ur (modern Iraq) was built with mud bricks around 4,000 B.C. The Bible (Exodus 1:14; 5:4–19) provides the earliest written documentation of brick production—the Israelites made bricks for their Egyptian rulers. These bricks were made of clay dug from the

Earth, mixed with straw, and baked in crude ovens or burned in a fire. Many ancient structures made of bricks, such as the Great Wall of China and remnants of Roman buildings, are still standing today. The Romans further developed kiln–baked bricks and spread the art of brickmaking throughout Europe.

The oldest type of brick in the Western Hemisphere is the adobe brick. Adobe bricks are made from adobe soil, comprised of clay, quartz, and other minerals, and baked in the sun. Adobe soil can be found in dry regions throughout the world, but most notably in Central America, Mexico, and the southwestern United States. The Pyramid of the Sun was built of adobe bricks by the Aztecs in the fifteenth century and is still standing. In North America, bricks were used as early as the seventeenth century. Bricks were used extensively for building new factories and homes during the Industrial Revolution. Until the 19th century, raw materials for bricks were mined and mixed, and bricks were formed, by manual labor. The first brickmaking machines were steam powered, and the bricks were fired with wood or coal as fuel. Modern brickmaking equipment is powered by gas and electricity. Some manufacturers still produce bricks by hand, but the majority are machine made.

Brick manufacturing

The manufacture of bricks entails several steps and starts with obtaining the raw materials. Clays are mined from open pits or underground mines. Storage areas are located at the mining site so that portions from various "digs" can be blended. The clay mixture goes through a process called primary crushing, where the clay is put through giant rollers that break the clay into small chunks. This mixture is transported to the manufacturing site, where the clay mixture is pulverized and screened to remove impurities. Further blending of materials may take place at this time.

There are three methods of forming bricks. The most common is the stiff–mud process where the clay blend is put into a machine called a pug mill that mixes the clay with water (12–15% by weight), kneads the mixture, removes trapped air, and transfers the mixture to an auger machine. The auger forces or extrudes the wet clay through a die that forms a continuous rectangle–shaped column. The column is cut with steel wires into desired lengths. The newly formed bricks are place on drying racks for a few days and then fired in a kiln. The soft–mud process is used when the mined clay is naturally too wet (20–30% by weight) to undergo the stiff–mud process. The clay is mixed, extruded, and placed in lubricated molds. Each mold makes six to eight bricks. The drying process takes more time than with stiff mud, but the firing procedure is the same. The third method is the dry–press process, which is most commonly used when making refractory bricks. The clay has minimal water content (up to 10% by weight) and is exposed to high pressure (in a hydraulic or mechanical press) while in the molds. The bricks are dried and fired. While still damp and moldable, textures, designs, or functional grooves can be pressed into the brick. Special glazes can be applied for decorative and for functional purposes.

Firing or burning the bricks takes two to five days. The most common type of kiln used to fire bricks is the tunnel kiln, where the bricks, stacked on cars, move slowly though a long chamber or tunnel. Many changes in the physical properties occur during the firing process. During firing, any residual water evaporates, some minerals melt, blend, and fuse, and organic matter oxidizes. The hardness of the brick increases and the color develops. The whole process of making bricks takes 10–12 days.

With handmade bricks, the clay is kneaded and put into molds. Excess clay is skimmed off the top of the mold, and the brick is then dumped out, dried, and fired. Handmade bricks are usually more expensive than machine–made bricks. They are often used in special projects, such as historical restoration.

Types of brick

Some bricks are made for specific purposes and are made of certain raw materials, formed in a particular shape, or with added special textures or glazes. Common brick is the everyday building brick. They are not made of special materials, and do not have special marks, color, or texture. Common brick is typically red and sometimes used as a "backup" brick, depending on the quality. Face brick is often applied on top of common backup brick. Face brick can be obtained in a variety of colors, has a uniform surface appearance and color, is more durable, and is graded according to its ability to withstand freezing temperatures and moisture. Refractory bricks are made from fireclays—clays with a high alumina or silica content or nonclay minerals such as bauxite, zircon, silicon carbide, or dolomite. Fireclays are heat resistant and are used in various types of furnaces, kilns, and fireplaces. Calcium silicate bricks are often made in areas where clay is not readily available. Glazed bricks are made primarily for walls in buildings such as dairies, hospitals, and laboratories, where easy cleaning is necessary.

See also Building design/Architecture; Concrete; Stone and masonry.

Further Reading:

Adams, J. T. *The Complete Concrete, Masonry, and Brick Handbook.* New York: Arco Publishing, 1979.

Cowan, Henry J. *The Master Builders.* New York: Wiley, 1977.

Olin, Harold B. *Construction; Principles, Materials and Methods.* Danville, Ill.: Interstate Printers and Publishers, 1980.

Christine Miner Minderovic

A bowstring arch bridge in Arizona. The deck is supported from the arch by hangers. The load is transmitted to the abutments by the outward thrust of the arch.

Bridges

Bridges are structures that join two otherwise inaccessible points of land, such as the two shores of a river or lake, or the two sides of a canyon or deep gully. Bridges are designed to carry railroad cars, motor vehicle traffic, or foot travel by pedestrians and/or animals, or to support pipes, troughs, or other conduits used for the movement of goods and materials, such as an oil pipeline or a water aqueduct.

Humans have been constructing bridges since ancient times. The earliest bridges were probably nothing more than felled trees used to cross rivers or ditches. As civilization advanced, artisans discovered ways to use stone, rock, mortar, and other naturally occurring materials in the construction of longer and stronger bridges. Finally, as physicists and engineers began to develop the principles underlying bridge construction, they incorporated other materials such as iron, steel, and aluminum into the bridges they built.

Bridges can be classified in a number of different ways, according to their intended use (railroad bridge or pedestrian walkway, for example), according to the material of which they are made (steel, wood, or concrete, for example), or according to whether they are fixed or moveable. Moveable bridges are used when the height of ships traveling on a waterway will be greater than the floor of the bridge. In such cases, the bridge is built so that the roadway can be raised or pivoted to allow marine traffic to pass under or through it. Probably the most useful way to classify bridges for technical purposes, however, is according to their structural form. There are three major types of bridges: arch, cantilever, and suspension.

Forces acting on a bridge

Three kinds of forces operate on any bridge: the dead load, the live load, and the dynamic load. The first of these terms refers to the weight of the bridge itself. Like any other structure, a bridge has a tendency to collapse simply because of the gravitational forces acting on the materials of which the bridge is made—wood, concrete, steel, or aluminum, for example. The second term refers to traffic that moves across the bridge as well as normal environmental factors such as changes in temperature, precipitation, and winds. The third factor refers to environmental factors that go beyond normal weather conditions, factors such as sudden gusts of wind and earthquakes. All three factors must be taken into consideration in the design of a bridge.

For example, suppose that it is necessary to build a bridge across a span that is 325 ft (100 m) wide. It would not be possible to build a beam bridge, one that consists of a single slab of steel 325 ft (100 m) long, of that length. The weight of the material used to construct the bridge plus the weight of the traffic on the bridge would be too great for the bridge to remain standing. An engineer would have to design some other kind of bridge—an arch or suspension bridge, for example—that would be able to hold up that amount of weight.

Dynamic loads

Dynamic loads can present special problems for the bridge designer. A bridge has to be able to withstand not only the forces of normal, everyday traffic, but also unusual forces of unexpected magnitude. In California, as an example, bridges require special kinds of reinforcement to withstand possible earthquakes. The fact that engineers have not completely solved the problems presented by dynamic loads is reconfirmed from time to time. For example, during the 1989 earthquake in the San Francisco Bay area, a section of the

Dame Point bridge in Jacksonville, Florida, is a cable-stayed bridge. The deck is supported by cables which transmit the load to the towers.

San Francisco–Oakland Bay Bridge collapsed, leaving a gaping hole. A freeway overpass in Oakland also failed during the earthquake, taking the lives of about two dozen motorists.

Wind gusts have been responsible for a number of bridge failures in the past. Even if wind speeds are relatively low, dynamic loads may become too great for a bridge to withstand. One reason for this phenomenon is that the bridge may begin to vibrate so violently that it actually shakes itself apart. Such was the case, for example, with the Tacoma Narrows Bridge in 1941. On November 7 of that year, with wind speeds registering only about 40 mph (25 kph), the bridge vibrated so badly that it collapsed. The actual force experienced by the bridge was considerably less than the dead and live forces for which it had been designed. But the oscillations produced by wind gusts on the day in question were sufficient to shake the bridge apart.

As a result of failures such as those in the Bay Bridge and the Tacoma Narrows Bridge, engineers have developed methods for making bridges more aerodynamically sound. For example, lighter materials arranged in geometric structures that are aerodynamically more stable are now used in bridges where earthquakes, wind gusts, or other unusually severe environmental problems can be expected.

Model testing

At one time, the only test of a bridge design was actual use. Engineers could incorporate all the scientific knowledge and technological craftsmanship they had to produce a sound design. But how well the bridge would stand up under actual use and dynamic loads could only be discovered in the real world.

Today, engineers have two powerful tools with which to test their ideas: wind tunnels and computer–aided design (CAD). Wind tunnels have long been used by aeronautical engineers for the testing of aircraft designs. Now they are routinely used also for the testing of bridge designs. A wind tunnel is an enclosed space in which rapidly moving air from giant fans is made to pass over the model of a bridge. Possible structural and design problems can be detected by photographing and studying patterns of air movement over the model.

As in so many other fields, bridge design has benefitted greatly from the growth and development of computer programs. Such programs can incorporate huge amounts of information about various ways in which bridges and the materials of which they are made will react to various kinds of stresses. CAD can be used to actually draw and test bridge designs on screen without even making the models needed for wind tunnel testing.

Types of bridges

The simplest type of bridge corresponds to the felled tree mentioned above. It consists of a single piece of material that stretches from one side of the gap to be bridged to the other side. That piece of material—the beam, or girder—rests directly on the ground on each side or is supported on heavy foundations known as piers. The length of a beam bridge of this kind is limited by the weight of the beam itself plus the weight of the traffic it has to bear. Longer beam bridges can be constructed by joining a number of beams to each other in parallel sections.

The concept of a beam bridge can be extended to make a stronger product, the continuous bridge. A continuous bridge differs from a beam bridge in that the latter has at least one additional point of support beyond the two found in a beam bridge. The longest existing continuous bridges now in use are the Astoria Bridge that crosses the Columbia River near Astoria, Oregon, and the Oshima Bridge that connects Oshima Island to the mainland in Japan.

Cantilever bridges

A cantilever bridge is a variation of the simple beam bridge. A cantilever is a long arm that is anchored at one end and is free to move at the opposite end. A diving board is an example of a cantilever. When anchored firmly, a cantilever is a very strong structure. Imagine a 200 lb (91 kg) man standing on the end of a diving board. The board bends only slightly, showing that it can hold a relatively large weight (the 200 pound man).

A cantilever bridge consists of three parts: the outer beams, the cantilevers, and the central beam. Each of the outer beams of the bridge is somewhat similar to a short beam bridge. The on–shore edge of the bridge is attached to the ground itself or to a pier that is sunk into the ground. The opposite edge of the outer beam is attached to a second pier, sunk into the ground at some distance from the shore.

Bridge piers are vertical columns, usually made of reinforced concrete or some other strong material. In many cases, they are sunk into massive supporting structures known as abutments. Abutments are constructed in large holes in the ground, in contact with bedrock if possible, to withstand the forces created by the dead and live loads created by bridges and the traffic they carry.

Also attached to the off–shore pier is one end of a cantilever. The free end of the cantilever extends outward into the middle of the gap between the shores. An incomplete cantilever bridge consists, therefore, of two halves, one anchored to each side of the gap to be bridged and consisting of a cantilever facing toward the middle of the gap. The space between the two cantilevers, finally, is bridged by another beam, similar to that of a short beam bridge joining the two cantilevers to each other.

The distribution of forces in a cantilever bridge is fairly straightforward. The dead load and live load of the bridge is born by the two sets of piers that hold up the bridge, the outermost piers that hold up the outer edges of the bridge, and the inner piers that anchor the fixed end of the cantilever.

The two longest cantilever bridges in the world are the Forth Railway Bridge in Scotland, completed in 1890, and the Quebec Bridge in Canada, built in 1917. The former is 1,700 ft (520 m) in length and the latter, 1,800 ft (550 m) long.

Trusses

The strength of a cantilever bridge can be increased by the use of trusses. A truss is structure that consists of a number of triangles joined to each other. The triangle is an important component of many kinds of structures because it is the only geometric figure that can not be pulled or pushed out of shape without actually changing the length of one of its sides. By combining a number of triangles into a single unit, then, the unit is given a great deal of strength.

The cantilever beam, end beams, and joining beams in a cantilever bridge are often strengthened by adding trusses to them. The trusses act somewhat like an extra panel of iron or steel, adding strength to the bridge with relatively little additional weight. The open structure of a truss also allows the wind to blow through them, preventing additional stress on the bridge from this factor.

Trusses are used not only in cantilever bridges, but in all other kinds of bridges also. In fact, you have probably noticed the complex pattern of intersecting triangles on bridges over which you have passed. These truss patterns are one of the most efficient ways of adding strength to any type of bridge an engineer designs.

Arch bridges

As its name suggests, the main supporting structure in an arch bridge is one or more curved elements. The dead and live forces that act on the arch bridge are transmitted along the curved line of the arch into abutments at either end. These abutments are sunk deep into the earth, into bedrock if at all possible. They are, therefore, essentially immovable and able to withstand very large forces exerted on the bridge itself. This structure is so stable that piers are generally unnecessary in an arch bridge.

The deck of an arch bridge can be placed anywhere with relationship to the arch: on top of it, beneath it, or somewhere within the arch. The deck is attached to the arch by vertical posts (ribs and columns) if the deck is above the arch, by ropes or cables (suspendors) if the deck is below the arch, and by some combination of the two if the deck is somewhere within the arch.

Most arch bridges today are made either of steel or of reinforced concrete. The longest existing steel arch bridge is the New River Gorge Bridge in Fayetteville, West Virginia, built in 1977. It is 1,700 ft (518 m) long. The longest reinforced concrete bridge is the Jesse H. Jones Memorial Bridge at the Houston Ship Channel, Texas, with a length of 1,500 ft (455 m).

Suspension bridges

The longest bridges in the world are all suspension bridges. Some examples are the Humber Bridge in Hull, England, with a length of 4,626 ft (1,410 m), the Verrazano–Narrows Bridge in lower New York Bay (4,620 ft [1,298 m]); the Golden Gate Bridge over the entrance to San Francisco Bay (4,200 ft [1,280 m]); and the Mackinac Straits Bridge connecting the Upper and Lower Peninsulas of Michigan (3,800 ft [1,158 m]).

In a suspension bridge, the dead and live loads are carried by thick wire cables that run across the top of at least two towers and are anchored to the shorelines within heavy abutments. In some cases, the bridge deck is supported directly by suspendors from the cables, while in other cases, the suspendors are attached to a truss, on top of which the deck is laid. In either case, the dead and light load of the bridge are transmitted to the cables which, in turn, exert stress on the abutments. That stress is counteracted by attaching the abutments to bedrock.

The towers in a suspension bridge typically rest on massive foundations sunk deep into the river bed or sea bed beneath the bridge itself. The wire cables that carry the weight of the bridge and its traffic are made of parallel strands of steel wire woven together to make a single cable. Such cables typically range in diameter from about 15 in (38 cm) to as much as 36 in (91 cm). Smaller cables can be ordered from a factory, while thicker cables may have to be assembled on the construction site itself.

An interesting hybrid of the cantilever and suspension bridge is known as the cable–stayed bridge. The 1,200 ft (366 m) Sunshine Skyway across the entrance to Tampa Bay in Florida is one of the most beautiful examples of the cable–stayed bridge. In a cable–stayed bridge, the deck is cantilevered outward in both directions from a central tower. The deck is then attached to the tower by a series of cables, similar to those in a suspension bridge. Often, a cable–stayed bridge will make use of two towers. In that case, the cantilevered sections extending towards each other in the middle of the bridge can be joined together, producing an unusually long central span. The advantage of the cable–stayed bridge is that support for dead and live loads come from three distinct places: the towers, the cables, and the abutments to which the bridge is attached at each end.

Pontoon bridges

Pontoon bridges are bridges that float on water. They find use primarily in two situations. First, they find application during wars when engineers need to construct a simple bridge quickly and easily. In such instances, they can be assembled from inflatable rubber or plastic and put into place in a matter of hours. Second, they can be used in rivers and lakes where the river bottom makes it very difficult or impossible to install piers. Lake Washington, in the state if Washington, for example, once had three floating bridges. All were made of large hollow concrete blocks tied to each other.

KEY TERMS

Abutment—Heavy supporting structures usually attached to bedrock and supporting bridge piers.

Cable–stayed bridge—A type of bridge that is a mix of cantilever and suspension bridge, in which the deck is supported both by one or more central towers and cables suspended from the tower(s).

Dead load—The force exerted by a bridge as a result of its own weight.

Dynamic load—The force exerted on a bridge as a result of unusual environmental factors, such as earthquakes or strong gusts of wind.

Live load—The force exerted on a bridge as a result of the traffic moving across the bridge.

Piers—vertical columns, usually made of reinforced concrete or some other strong material, on which bridges rest.

Suspendors—Ropes or steel wires from which the deck of a bridge is suspended.

Truss—A structure that consists of a number of triangles joined to each other.

Movable bridges

Traditionally, three kinds of movable bridges have been constructed. In one, the swing bridge, the deck is rotated around a central span, a large, heavy pier sunk into the river bottom. The swing bridge has one serious disadvantage. The central pier, on which the bridge rotates, is usually located in the deepest part of the waterway. Ships with significant drafts may, therefore, have difficulty passing through such bridges. The swing bridge also has one important advantage. Since it never moves upward in a vertical direction, it will not interfere with air traffic that might be present in the area.

In the second type of movable bridge, the bascule bridge, the deck is raised, either at one end or at two ends. The bascule bridge acts, therefore, something like a cantilever in which the free end is raised to permit passage of seagoing vessels.

In the third type of movable bridge, the vertical–lift bridge, the whole central portion of the bridge is raised straight up by means of steel ropes. One disadvantage of the vertical–lift bridge, of course, is that it can not open entirely above the waterway, but can only be raised to a given maximum height.

Further Reading:

Brash, Sarah, Matthew Cope, Charles Foran, Dónal Kevin Gordon, and Peter Pocock. *How Things Work: Structures.* Alexandria, VA: Time–Life Books, 1991.

"Bridge," *McGraw–Hill Encyclopedia of Science & Technology*, 7th edition. New York: McGraw–Hill Book Company, 1992, volume 2, pp. 49–58.

Corbett, Scott. *Bridges.* New York: Four Winds Press, 1978.

DeLony, Eric. *Landmark American Bridges.* Boston: Little, Brown and Company, 1993.

MacGregor, Anne and Scott. *Bridges: A Project Book.* New York: Lothrop, Lee & Shephard Books, 1980.

David E. Newton

Bristletails

Bristletails are about 300–400 species of small, elongate, terrestrial insects in the order Thysanura. Bristletails have an ancient evolutionary lineage, and they are believed to be relatively primitive, that is, similar in form and function to the most early evolved insects.

Bristletails have a simple metamorphosis, with three life–history stages: egg, nymph, and adult. Both the nymphal and adult stages are wingless, and they are rather similar in their physical appearance, the main difference being in size and sexual maturity. The adults are large and mature.

Bristletails are easily distinguished by the three thread–like appendages that emerge from the end of their abdomen, by their long, backward–pointing antennae, and by their body covering of glistening scales. Bristletails have chewing mouth parts, and they feed on a wide range of types of soft, usually decaying organic matter. Bristletails hide during the day, and if they are disturbed they run quickly away to seek a new hiding place. Otherwise, bristletails are active at night. Bristletails are unusual in that they continue to grow and molt even after they have become sexually mature adults. Almost all other insects stop growing after they become breeding adults.

The most familiar bristletails are those in the family Lepismatidae, including the light–colored, common silverfish (*Lepisma saccharina*) and the darker–colored firebrat (*Thermobia domestica*), which often occurs in warm, moist places, for example, near hearths, stoves, and furnaces. Both of these species can be common in moist places in buildings, where they feed on a wide variety of starchy foods, and can some-

times cause significant damages to books, wallpaper, fabrics, and stored foods.

The jumping bristletails (family Machilidae) are widespread in North America, living under organic debris in various types of natural, terrestrial habitats. The primitive bristletails (Lepidotrichidae) and nicoletiid bristletails (Nicoletiidae) are all rather rare in North America.

Brittle star

Brittle stars are starfishlike echinoderms (phylum Echinodermata) in the family Ophiodermatidae, whose star–shaped bodies are radially symmetrical and are supported by a hard endoskeleton made of calcium salts. Brittle stars are closely related to basket stars, and more distantly related to starfish, sand dollars, and sea urchins. Brittle stars are named for the ease by which their arms fall off when touched; these animals, known collectively as ophioroids, are also called serpent stars (*ophis* means snake in Greek) because their long arms resemble serpents. The brittle stars comprise the largest number of species (about 1,000) of echinoderms and are found on the seabed in all of the world's oceans. Brittle stars also inhabit the dark high–pressure environments on the floor of the abyssal zone, the deepest part of the ocean where few other living things can survive. Some species of brittle star can swim, but most species simply crawl along the ocean floor. Brittle stars in shallow seas tend to avoid light and prefer to hide in dark crevices, becoming more active at night, or they inhabit the ocean depths where it is always dark. Brittle stars usually have five long, thin, jointed arms covered with spines; sometimes they have six or seven arms. Brittle stars can be as large as 2 ft (0.6 m) in diameter or as small as a few millimeters. Ophioroids are usually a drab green, grey, or brown, but some have variegated color patterns. Some species of brittle stars glow in the dark—a bright green luminescence appears if they are disturbed. Others can change their color.

The arms of brittle stars are attached to a central disklike body that houses on the underside the mouth and jaws, stomach, and saclike body cavities called bursae, which are peculiar to ophioroids. The mouth is surrounded by five moveable jaw segments, making the mouth opening look like a star. Some brittle stars are carnivorous, while others feed on small particles of plankton. The food enters the mouth and goes directly into the stomach, and there is no intestine and no anus; absorption and excretion are carried out instead by the five pairs of bursae located at the base of each of the arms. Water circulates in the bursae and there is an exchange of respiratory gases and excretion of wastes. The coelomic walls of the bursae contain the gonads that discharge sex cells in the water for fertilization. The larva, which develops from a fertilized egg, is called an ophiopluteus and is free swimming in the plankton until it transforms into the juvenile stage when it settles on the bottom of the ocean. Brittle stars are either male or female, although a few individuals are hermaphrodites. Brittle stars spawn at the end of summer, and most species release their eggs into the plankton and invest no parental care thereafter. They can also reproduce asexually; if an arm breaks off and it still has a small piece of the central disk attached, the arm can regenerate into a whole new brittle star.

Brittle stars are among the most active of the echinoderms and, unlike starfish and sea urchins, can move easily and quickly. The arms of a brittle star reach out in pairs to pull the animal along. Each arm is supported by a central internal skeletal support (ossicle). Like starfish, brittle stars have tube feet, but those of brittle stars lack suckers. The tube feet help more with feeding than with locomotion. Like other echinoderms, brittle stars can regenerate lost parts. If an arm is broken off, a new one grows in its place within months. If an arm is injured, the star can cast off the injured arm (autotomy) and then eventually grow a new one.

Broadbill see **Swordfish**

Broca's area see **Brain**

Bromeliad family (Bromeliadaceae)

The pineapple family (Bromeliadaceae) consists of about 1,500 species of flowering plants. Most species are medium–sized herbs with tightly packed, thick, stiff, spiralling leaves that usually have spiny margins. Some species are semi–woody, and a few rare ones, such as *Puya raimondii,* are trees that can reach 33 ft (10 m) in height. Most species of bromeliads are epiphytes in rain forests, while others are terrestrial, inhabiting dry habitats in mountainous and coastal regions. Bromeliads are native to tropical and subtropical regions of North and South America. The only exception may be *Pitcairnia feliciana* of coastal west Africa; this species appears to represent a remarkable example of long–distance, natural dispersal, although it may have been introduced into Africa by humans. The range of the bromeliads extends from Tierra del Fuego in southernmost South America, northward into Mexico, then through the southeastern United States to their northernmost limit in southern Maryland.

The most commercially valuable member of this family is the common pineapple, *Ananus comosus.* A native of South America, the pineapple has been widely planted as a cash crop throughout tropical and subtropical regions, especially in the Hawaiian Islands, the Philippines, South Africa, and southern Asia. The pineapple is a biennial plant, that is, it usually lives for only two years. In the first year this species produces a dense growth of sharp–pointed, overlapping leaves. During the second year a short stalk with many flowers is produced. Each flower gives rise to fruits that are technically berries, but then the stalk bearing the fruit begins to swell. This results in the development of a thick, sweet, fleshy mass, within are embedded the fruits. This whole thing is the "pineapple," which is therefore an aggregation of fruits within an accessory structure (the thickened stem). When you buy a pineapple at the market you notice at the top of the "fruit" a tuft of prickly, reduced leaves or bracts, and a cleanly cut–off base. This may lead you to believe that the pineapple was cut off from the plant at ground level, but this was not the case. Pineapples grow at the end of shoots, two to four per plant, so they are cut off from an underlying, large–leafed shoot.

Bromeliads are xerophytes and possess many of the usual, water–conserving adaptations of such plants: a thick epidermis covered with wax, water–storage cells that cause the leaves to appear succulent (that is thick and fleshy), and sheathing leaf bases. One of the notable characteristics of bromeliads is the distinctive, water–absorbing scales on their leaves and stems. These thin scales occur in grooves in the epidermis, and they resemble opened umbrellas. Their thinness and large surface area make the scales ideal for rapidly absorbing water.

Equally important in terms of water economy are the shape and arrangement of the leaves of bromeliads. In many species the leaves are wide and deeply U–shaped where they join the stem, forming a series of vessel–like compartments. When it rains, water flows down the leaves and pools in the compartments, where it can be absorbed by the umbrella scales. Especially remarkable are the "tank plants," such as *Nidularium* and *Billbergia*. In these species the stem is greatly reduced and the densely packed leaves have broad, overlapping bases, resulting in a pitcher or vase–like center—the tank. Rainwater fills the tank, where some of the moisture is absorbed by the umbrella scales. Because the tank is shaded by the dense crown of leaves around it, the water does not evaporate quickly

Spanish moss in Louisiana.

and can persist, enabling the plant to survive periods of drought. Interestingly, some species of mosquitoes breed nowhere else but in these tanks.

Another important adaptation of some bromeliads to drought–prone environments is seen in their stomata. Stomata allow gaseous carbon dioxide, a necessary ingredient for photosynthesis, into the leaf. In most plants the stomata are open during daylight hours, because that is when light is available to drive photosynthesis. When open during the day, however, stomata also lose water, which is a disadvantage for plants growing in environments where water is scarce. Many plants, including the bromeliads pineapple and Spanish moss, have evolved stomata that are closed during the heat of the day but open at night when temperatures are cooler. These plants trap the carbon dioxide that enters through their stomata and store the gas until daylight,

when light energy is available for further processing through photosynthesis.

Why are some plants of wet tropical and subtropical regions, such as bromeliads, specially adapted to dry conditions? The key is that most bromeliads are epiphytic, occurring high in the crowns of forest trees. When it is not raining and the sun is out, these plants can dry out rapidly because their roots are not in soil. In addition most bromeliads that are terrestrial generally occur in rocky habitats, where rainwater rapidly percolates through the soil, leaving it dry.

Spanish moss (*Tillandsia usneoides*) is not a true moss but rather is one of the interesting bromeliads known as "air plants." Most of these species grow as epiphytes high in the crowns of trees, where of course there is no soil. In order to obtain the nutrients necessary for growth, air–plants absorb some directly from the atmosphere, such as gases of sulfur and nitrogen. Other nutrients must be absorbed from rainwater or atmospheric dusts. Air–plants are commonly available in flower shops. These attractive plants need to be misted occasionally with a sprayer, because their foliar scales must be moistened to absorb the nutrients. Because they derive most of their nutrients directly or indirectly from the atmosphere, these bromeliads are called air plants. Spanish moss commonly grows in the southeastern United States, where it often forms large and beautiful drapes in tree canopies. The roots of Spanish moss serve to hold the plant to the tree on which it is growing, and do not function in obtaining water and nutrients.

Bromeliads have become increasingly popular as indoor plants. Air plants are appealing novelty items, but many of the other, leafier bromeliads are also now prized. These have attractive, usually bright–red flowers, designed to attract birds as pollinators, and often surrounded by brightly colored modified leaves. Furthermore, as xerophytic plants, bromeliads can withstand the benign neglect of forgetful watering.

Further Reading:

Dahlgren, R. M. T., H. T. Clifford, and P. F. Yeo. *The Families of the Monocotyledons: Structure, Evolution, and Taxonomy.* Berlin: Springer–Verlag, 1985.

Les C. Cwynar

Bromine see **Halogens**

Bronchi see **Respiratory system**

A bromeliad growing on the bole of a cypress tree in Everglades National Park, Florida.

Bronchitis

Bronchitis is the inflammation of the bronchi and is a commonly seen winter condition. The bronchi (the air passages leading into the lungs) are formed by the division of the trachea (the main windpipe leading from the larynx (adam's apple) down through the neck into the chest). The trachea branches left and right into the bronchi which branch to supply lung lobe with the means for air to pass in and out.

Like the trachea, the bronchi are formed of cartilage rings overlain with muscle. One layer of muscle runs lengthwise along the tube; the other layer is circular. These muscles regulate the diameter of the air passages.

A common cold or extended exposure to cold temperatures or air pollution over time may lead to bronchitis (the suffix "–itis" means inflammation). A cough and sore throat are the primary symptoms but difficulty in breathing and development of a fever are also characteristics. This sudden and short–lived bronchitis is called acute bronchitis. This is easily cured with aspirin in more serious cases an antibiotic. Acute bronchitis usually causes no long–term problems.

Chronic bronchitis is a more serious condition. Chronic means that it is a condition persists over a long period of time. Chronic bronchitis is a disease of cigarette smokers and is often accompanied by emphysema. Emphysema is a condition in which lung tissue is destroyed and the capacity to breathe is seriously impaired.

The form of bronchitis associated with emphysema is called chronic obstructive pulmonary disease (COPD) and is difficult to cure. It is often difficult to tell whether the respiratory problems associated with COPD are the result of emphysema or chronic bronchitis. Some physicians consider the two conditions to be synonymous: if one has chronic bronchitis one also has emphysema.

See also Emphysema; Respiratory diseases; Respiratory system.

Brotulid fish see **Cave fish**

Brown dwarf

What is more than a planet but less than a star? A brown dwarf is. Jupiter has about 0.001 times the mass of the Sun and is nearly the most massive a giant gas planet can be. A planet like Jupiter but with slightly less mass, such as Saturn, will be smaller in size. If it has slightly more mass it will be larger in size up to about twice Jupiter's mass. Beyond this point, a more massive object will actually be smaller in size. These objects having more than twice Jupiter's mass are brown dwarfs rather than planets. They are smaller because the additional mass provides enough inward gravitational force that the pressure pushing out from the core of brown dwarfs is not enough to support their extra mass. Brown dwarfs therefore collapse to a smaller size than giant Jupiter-like planets when they form.

The smallest stars are a little less than one tenth the mass of the Sun. To be a star, a ball of hydrogen must have enough mass to compress and heat the core to the point where nuclear fusion reactions ignite. A star wannabe that does not have enough mass to ignite the fusion reactions will become a brown dwarf. It will collapse and warm up but will not be as hot as a star. It also will have no hydrogen fusion reactions in the core. Brown dwarfs occupy the mass range between the most massive planets and the least massive stars, about 0.002 to 0.08 times the mass of the Sun.

Do brown dwarfs really exist? Astronomers think that they should be fairly common. Why? Astronomers have observed that the less massive stars are far more common than the more massive stars. If this trend continues, then brown dwarfs should be more common than even the least massive stars. Brown dwarfs are so cool, small, and faint however, that they are quite difficult to find. Hot stars are blue; cool stars are red. Brown dwarfs, cooler than the coolest stars, should be brightest in the infrared. Therefore one way to find brown dwarfs is to search for faint infrared objects. It is however difficult to tell if a faint infrared object is just above or just below the dividing mass between brown dwarfs and the least massive stars because we have no good way to find the object's mass. Another strategy for finding brown dwarfs is looking for evidence of a low mass companion orbiting a star. This is the same strategy as that used for looking for planets outside the solar system. An astronomer finding such an object could estimate its mass from the orbital properties to decide if it were a planet, brown dwarf, or a very low mass star.

In June 1995 three astronomers, Gibor Basri, Geoffrey Marcy, and James Graham, reported observations made with the newly completed Keck 400 in (10 m) telescope. They feel that their data confirms a previously suspected brown dwarf candidate is indeed a brown dwarf. They used a technique that was made possible by the new Keck telescope, which is currently the largest in the world by a significant margin. They observed the spectrum of a suspected brown dwarf called PPL 15 that is located in the cluster of stars known as the seven sisters of the Pleiades. Their technique gets around the problem of finding the mass by looking at the amount of lithium in the brown dwarf candidate's spectrum to see if hydrogen fusion reactions are occurring in the core. When a star initially forms it contains some lithium near its surface. For low mass stars, convection currents mix the surface lithium with the core where it is destroyed by the hydrogen fusion reactions. For brown dwarfs the lithium still mixes with the core, but the core has no hydrogen fusion reactions to destroy the lithium. Hence a brown dwarf will show lithium in its spectrum, but only the very youngest low mass stars will. The stars in the Pleiades cluster are old enough that the low mass stars will have no lithium in their spectra. Basri's team found lithium in the spectrum of the brown dwarf candidate PPL 15. Hence their assertion that it is a brown dwarf rather than a low mass star.

What difference does it make whether brown dwarfs exist? A major problem in modern astronomy is the dark matter. Roughly 90% of the matter in the universe is unaccounted for. We can't see it, so it is called dark matter. We know that it is there because its mass affects the orbits of objects near the visible edge of galaxies and of galaxies within clusters of galaxies. If

Brown Dwarf—An object with a mass in a range that is intermediate between planets and stars.

Cluster of galaxies—A group of galaxies that is gravitationally bound.

Cluster of stars—A group of stars that is gravitationally bound and in which all members formed at essentially the same time

Dark Matter—Unseen matter that we know is there in part because we see its gravitational effect on the motions of galaxies within clusters of galaxies.

Infrared—Wavelengths slightly longer than visible light, often used in astronomy to study cool objects.

Nuclear Fusion—Nuclear reactions that fuse two or more smaller atoms into a larger one. Hydrogen fusion reactions provide the energy for the Sun and other stars.

brown dwarfs really are as common as astronomers think, then their total mass might be enough to account for the dark matter. If improved detection techniques allow us to find a large number of brown dwarfs, then we will go a long way towards solving a major mystery of modern astronomy.

See also Infrared astronomy; Stellar evolution.

Further Reading:

"Making Sense of The Smallest Stars." *Sky & Telescope* 89, May, 1995, p. 12–13.

Morrison, David, Wolff, Sidney, and Fraknoi, Andrew. *Abell's Exploration of the Universe,* 7th ed. Philadelphia: Saunders College Publishing, 1995.

Wilford, John N. "Big Telescope is First to Find Brown Dwarf, Team Reports." *The New York Times,* June 14, 1995, p. B7.

Zeilik, Michael. *Astronomy: The Evolving Universe.* 7th ed. New York: Wiley, 1994.

Paul A. Heckert

Brownian motion

Brownian motion is the constant but irregular zigzag motion of small colloidal particles such as smoke, soot, dust, or pollen that can be seen quite clearly through a microscope.

In 1827, Robert Brown, a Scottish botanist, prepared a slide by adding a drop of water to pollen grains. As he watched the tiny particles of pollen under his microscope, Brown noticed that they were constantly jiggling about. He thought that the motion might be related to life processes within the pollen, but later he observed the same kind of zigzag motion with pollen from plants that had been dead for many years. Others found the same strange motion when they observed tiny inanimate particles of dye, dust, smoke, or soot.

Brown could offer no explanation for his observation, which became known as Brownian motion, nor could anyone else until James Clerk Maxwell and others developed the kinetic molecular theory a generation later. According to this theory, Brownian motion was the result of collisions between the small microscopic particles and the invisible but constantly moving water or air molecules surrounding them. Since particles such as pollen are thousands of times larger than water molecules, we would expect that on the average the particle would be hit as many times by water molecules on one side as it would be by molecules striking it from the opposite direction. However, since molecular motion is random, there will be moments when the particle is struck by more molecules moving in one direction than in any other. When that happens, the particle will respond to the unbalanced force and move accordingly.

Imagine yourself caught in the middle of a large crowd of people who are undecided as to which way they should go. You would find people bumping into you from all sides. Sometimes pushes from all directions would be equal and you would not move. At other times, more people would be bumping you from the right than from the left and so you would move to the left. A short time later, there might be more people pushing from behind than from in front, and you would move forward. Your motion would be similar to that of a tiny pollen particle suspended in, and constantly being struck by randomly moving molecules of water.

The fact that the jiggling movement of a particle exhibiting Brownian motion increases with temperature provided evidence that its motion could be explained by the kinetic molecular theory. Early in the twentieth century, Albert Einstein published a series of papers in which he statistically analyzed the expected velocity of particles of various sizes and masses undergoing Brownian motion at various temperatures in liquids with different viscosities. In an effort to verify Einstein's theoretical work, Jean Perrin carried out a number of experiments using small uniform particles of known size and mass. His results confirmed Einstein's analysis and put to rest forever any doubts about the molecular nature of matter.

See also Molecule; Motion.

Further Reading:

The Encyclopedia of Physics. Edited by Robert M. Besançon. New York: Reinhold, 1966, p. 86.

Haber–Schaim et. al. *Introductory Physical Science.* 5th ed. Englewood Cliffs, N.J.: Prentice–Hall, 1987, pp. 268–275.

Parsegian, Meltzer, Luchins, and Kinerson. *Introduction to Natural Science Part One: The Physical Sciences.* New York: Academic Press, 1968, pp. 336–337.

Rogers, Eric M. *Physics for the Inquiring Mind.* Princeton, N.J.: Princeton University Press, 1960, pp. 362, 364, 447.

Science and Technology Illustrated. Chicago: Encyclopaedia Britannica, Inc., 1984.

Wheeler, Gerald F. and Kirkpatrick, Larry D. *Physics: Building a World View.* Englewood Cliffs, N.J.: Prentice–Hall, 1983, pp. 142–142.

Brucellosis

Brucellosis is a disease caused by bacteria in the genus *Brucella.* The disease infects animals such as swine, cattle, and sheep; humans can become infected indirectly through contact with infected animals or by drinking *Brucella*–contaminated milk. In the United States, most domestic animals are vaccinated against the bacteria, but brucellosis remains a risk with imported animal products.

Characteristics of *Brucella*

Brucella are rod–shaped bacteria that lack a capsule around their cell membranes. Unlike most bacteria, *Brucella* cause infection by actually entering host cells. As the bacteria cross the host cell membrane, they are engulfed by host cell vacuoles called phagosomes. The presence of *Brucella* within host cell phagosomes initiates a characteristic immune response, in which infected cells begin to stick together and form aggregations called granulomas.

Brucella species

Three species of *Brucella* cause brucellosis in humans: *Brucella melitensis*, which infects goats; *B. abortis*, which infects cattle and, if the animal is pregnant, causes the spontaneous abortion of the fetus; and *B. suis*, which infects pigs. In animals, brucellosis is a self–limiting disease, and usually no treatment is necessary for the resolution of the disease. However, for a period of time from a few days to several weeks, infected animals may continue to excrete brucella into their urine and milk. Under warm, moist conditions, the bacteria may survive for months in soil, milk, and even seawater.

Because the bacteria are so hardy, humans may become infected with *Brucella* by direct contact with the bacteria. Handling or cleaning up after infected animals may put a person with contact with the bacteria. *Brucella* are extremely efficient in crossing the human skin barrier through cuts or breaks in the skin.

Symptoms and treatment of brucellosis

The incubation period of *Brucella*—the time from exposure to the bacteria to the start of symptoms—is typically about three weeks. The primary complaints are weakness and fatigue. An infected person may also experience muscle aches, fever, and chills.

The course of the disease reflects the location of the *Brucella* bacteria within the human host. Soon after the *Brucella* are introduced into the bloodstream, the bacteria seek out the nearest lymph nodes and invade the lymph node cells. From the initial lymph node, the *Brucella* spread out to other organ targets, including the spleen, bone marrow, and liver. Inside these organs, the infected cells form granulomas.

Diagnosing brucellosis involves culturing the blood, liver, or bone marrow for *Brucella* organisms. A positive culture alone does not signify brucellosis, since persons who have been treated for the disease may continue to harbor *Brucella* bacteria for several months. Confirmation of brucellosis, therefore, includes a culture positive for *Brucella* bacteria as well as evidence of the characteristic symptoms and a history of possible contact with infected milk or other animal products.

In humans, brucellosis caused by *B. abortus* is a mild disease that resolves itself without treatment. Brucellosis caused by *B. melitensis* and *B. suis*, however, is chronic and severe. Brucellosis is treated with administration of an antibiotic that penetrates host cells to destroy the invasive bacteria.

Prevention

Since the invention of an animal vaccine for brucellosis in the 1970s, the disease has become somewhat rare in the United States. Yet the vaccine cannot prevent all incidence of brucellosis. In 1989, the Centers for Disease Control reported only 95 total cases in the

United States. Most of these were reported in persons who worked in the meat processing industry. Brucellosis remains a risk for those who work in close contact with animals, including veterinarians, farmers, and dairy workers.

Brucellosis also remains a risk when animal products from foreign countries are imported into the United States. Outbreaks of brucellosis have been linked to unpasteurized feta and goat cheeses from the Mediterranean region and Europe. In the 1960s, brucellosis was linked to bongo drums imported from Africa: drums made with infected animal skins can harbor *Brucella* bacteria, which can be transmitted to humans through cuts and scrapes in the human skin surface.

In the United States, preventive measures include a rigorous vaccination program that involves all animals in the meat processing industry. On an individual level, people can avoid the disease by not eating animal products imported from other countries. If this is not possible or desirable, make sure that imported cheeses have been made with pasteurized milk. If the package does not indicate pasteurization, do not eat the cheese.

Further Reading:

Joklik, Wolfgang K., et al. *Zinsser Microbiology.* 20th ed. Norwalk, Conn.: Appleton and Lange, 1992.

Kiel, Frank W. and M. Yousouf Khan. "Brucellosis in Saudi Arabia." *Social Science and Medicine* 29 (1989): 999–1001.

Olle–Goig, Jaime E., and Jaume Canela–Soler. "An Outbreak of *Brucella melitensis* Infection by Airborne Transmission Among Laboratory Workers." *American Journal of Public Health* 77 (8 March 1987): 335–38.

Thimm, Bernhard M. *Brucellosos: Distribution in Man, Domestic, and Wild Animals.* Berlin: Springer–Verlag, 1982.

Wright, Paul. "Brucellosis." *American Family Physician* 35 (May 1987): 155–59.

Kathleen Scogna

Brush-tailed tuans see **Marsupial rats and mice**

Brushtail possum see **Phalangers**

Bryophyte

Bryophytes include the mosses, liverworts, and hornworts. Bryophytes are the simplest of plants (excluding the algae, which are not considered plants by most botanists). Bryophytes are small, seldom exceeding 6–8 in (15–20 cm) in height, and usually much smaller. They are attached to the substrate (ground, rock, or bark) by *rhizoids,* which are one or a few–celled, root–like threads that serve only for anchoring and are not capable of absorbing water and nutrients from the substrate. Brypohytes lack *vascular tissue* (the specialized cells grouped together to pipe water and nutrients to various parts of the body), or in the rare cases when this tissue is present, it is not well differentiated. The leaves of bryophyte are technically not true leaves, because in most species they lack vascular tissue. However, they are functionally equivalent to leaves, containing chlorophylls a and b for photosynthesis. Leaves are usually one–cell thick, except for the midrib, which may be up to 15 cells thick. Bryophytes satisfy their nutritional requirements by absorbing minerals from dust, rainfall, and water running over their surface.

The life cycle of bryophytes is characterized by an alternation of generations, one of which is a multicellular, diploid individual called a *sporophyte,* having two of each type of chromosome per cell. This stage alternates with multicellular, haploid individual called the *gametophyte,* with only one of each type of chromosome per cell, as is also the case with animal sperm. Bryophytes are unique among plants in that the dominant, conspicuous generation is the haploid gametophyte. In all other plants, the dominant stage is the diploid sporophyte.

Most reproduction of bryophytes is asexual, occurring by fragmentation of body parts, and by the production of specialized vegetative units called *gemmae.* Gemmae may be produced as microscopic plates (in the genus *Tetraphis*), as bulbils in the axils of leaves (in

Pohlia), or as microscopic filaments (in *Ulota*). When sexual reproduction occurs, it always involves a flagellated sperm (produced in a specialized organ called an *antheridium*) that must swim through water to reach an egg located in a specialized, flask–shaped organ (the *archegonium*). The antheridia and archegonia are surrounded by a layer of sterile cells, which protects the sex organs from mechanical damage and desiccation.

The union of the sperm and egg results in a diploid zygote, i.e., a new sporophyte. This is nourished by the gametophyte and grows on it in a parasitic fashion, although the sporophytes of some bryophytes photosynthesize and make some contribution to their own growth. Initially, as the young sporophyte grows, the archegonium also enlarges. However, it ultimately fails to keep pace with the growth of the sporophyte and becomes detached from its base, forming a cap–like structure called a *calyptra*.

Classification, characteristics, and habitats of bryophytes

The classification of bryophytes has been controversial among botanists. Traditionally, the division Bryophyta has included the true mosses, liverworts, and hornworts. However, some scientists consider each of these groups sufficiently distinct to deserve their own division: Bryophyta for the mosses, Hepatophyta for the liverworts, and Anthoceratophyta for the hornworts. The latter view is followed here, although the bryophyte is used as a collective term for all of these.

About 15,000 species of bryophytes have been described. They are distributed throughout the world, and are especially abundant in arctic and boreal regions, where they often dominate the ground vegetation. Bryophytes also occur in humid tropical regions where they commonly grow on other plants, especially in higher–elevation forests. Bryophytes are considered the amphibians of the plant world, because they require abundant moisture to grow. This requirement for water results from a number of their characteristic features. Their stems and leaves are thin, and either lack a cuticle (that is, a waxy surface layer) or have a very thin one, making them prone to drying out. Because bryophytes lack roots and a vascular system, they cannot obtain water from the soil and transport it to above–ground tissues; for this same reason, bryophytes are necessarily small. In addition, their sperm require free water in order to swim from their parent plant to the egg on another plant.

Division Hepatophyta (liverworts)

Hepatophyta means "liver plant" and refers to the body of some common species of liverworts, whose lobing is reminiscent of a liver. During Medieval and earlier times, many people followed the doctrine of signatures—a belief that the superficial resemblance of a plant to some part of the human anatomy indicated that the plant possessed medicinal properties related to the organ it resembled. Liverworts are the simplest of the living plants, and range in size from minuscule, leafy filaments less than 0.02 in (0.5 mm) in diameter, to plants exceeding 8 in (20 cm) in size. Liverworts lack specialized conducting tissues, cuticles, and stomates, and their rhizoids are always unicellular. The gametophytes arise directly from spores in most species. Most liverworts (75%) have 9 chromosomes in their haploid cells. There are two kinds of liverworts based on body form: thallose and leafy.

Thallose liverworts have gametophytes with an undifferentiated body called a thallus which has a ribbon–like appearance. *Marchantia* is one of the most widely distributed thallose liverworts, especially in habitats that provide ideal conditions of light and high humidity. The body is typically 30 cells thick at the midrib, and only 10 cells thick elsewhere. A thin, upper, green layer contains chlorophyll–rich cells, arranged in polygonal or diamond–shaped patterns each centered on a permanently open pore. Below each polygon is an airspace connected to the outside by the pore, and within the chamber are erect threads of photosynthetic cells. Below the relatively thin, upper photosynthetic layer is a lower layer that is colorless and stores the products of photosynthesis. Most reproduction is asexual by fragmentation, usually caused by wind or by animals breaking the plants apart while eating them or when stepping on them or when trampling them. Thallose liverworts also commonly reproduce asexually by producing small balls of cells called gemmae, within bowl–like structures called *gemma cups*. The balls become detached and are splashed out by raindrops, dispersing away to colonize favorable habitats.

Leafy liverworts grow in wet or humid habitats, and are especially common in the tropics and subtropics, although they also occur in temperate areas. They are the simplest of the plants with leaflike structures. Their leaves lack vascular tissue, each is deeply cleft so as to appear two–lobed, and they are arranged in two rows along a much branched stem. Unlike the true mosses, which typically appear somewhat erect, leafy liverworts form small, flat mats. Asexual reproduction by fragmentation is common.

Hornworts (division Anthocerophyta)

The hornworts are the smallest of the three groups of bryophytes with only about 100 species in six genera. Hornworts are especially diverse in the tropics, although *Anthoceros* occurs in temperate regions.

The gametophyte of hornworts is saucer–shaped, with upturned edges, and only 0.4–0.8 in (1–2 cm) in diameter. These interesting little plants are more similar to algae than are any other plants, especially because they have only one, large chloroplast in association with a pyrenoid in each photosynthetic cell. Yet, the hornworts are more advanced in some ways than liverworts, for example, they possess *stomates*, which exchange gases between the plant and the air. They are also unique among plants in having stomates on their gametophytes. Unlike the liverworts in which internal spaces between cells are filled with air, in hornworts the cavities are filled with *mucilage*, a water–absorbing material within which the cyanobacterium *Nostoc* can be found. This symbiotic relationship greatly benefits the hornwort, because cyanobacteria are among the few organisms that can fix molecular nitrogen (as N_2) into nitrogen compounds that are in a form useable to plants as nutrients; no plants can produce these essential compounds on their own.

Hornworts derive their name from their sporophyte, which has the appearance of a tapered horn. The sporophyte has a mass of undifferentiated tissue called a *meristem* at its base. The meristem can actively grow, so that the sporophyte can continue to increase in height, especially if damaged at the top, and can reach a height of 0.4–1.6 in (1–4 cm). The sporophyte of hornworts possesses stomate–like openings and remains photosynthetic for several months. It is, therefore, only semi–dependent on the gametophyte to which it remains attached. The sporophyte of hornworts represents a transitional stage to more highly evolved plants such as ferns, in which the sporophyte is for the most part independent of the gametophyte.

Mosses (division Bryophyta)

Only members of the division Bryophyta are considered "true" mosses. Many other plants and some algae are commonly called mosses, because they superficially resemble the true mosses, but they are not in fact even closely related to them. For example, Spanish moss (*Tillandia uneoides*) is a flowering plant in the pineapple family, Irish moss (*hardrus crnpa*) is a red alga that is collected for the extraction of *carageenan*, a starch–like substance used in food preparation, reindeer moss (*Cladina* spp.) is a lichen, and club mosses (*Lycopodium* spp.) are advanced plants with well developed vascular systems.

A number of characteristics distinguish two mosses from other bryophytes. Their gametophytes are leafy, whereas those of hornworts and thallose liverworts are not. The leaves of mosses occur in three ranks on the stem, but because the stem twists, they appear to have *radial symmetry,* the ability to be bisected into identical halves in more than one way. In contrast, leafy liverworts, whose leaves are two–ranked, only have one set of mirror images (*bilateral symmetry*). Furthermore, leaves of mosses are not lobed as in leafy liverworts. The rhizoids of mosses are multicellular, compared with single–celled in liverworts.

Mosses are distributed throughout the world, and are among the ecosystem dominants in boreal, arctic, and alpine environments. Mosses occur in a wide variety of habitats. They commonly grow on mineral and organic soils, and they can occur on volcanically heated soil that may reach temperatures of 131°F (55° C), on rocks in Antarctica where the temperature during the growing season does not exceed 14°F (–10°C), as epiphytes that grow on other plants, especially in tropical and subtropical regions, and in freshwater habitats. No mosses are truly marine, although some live within the spray zone of coastal habitats. The luminous moss *Schistoste* occurs within caves near the entrance where it concentrates the limited available light wing the curved, lens–like surface of its leaves. The dung–loving species of the genus *Splachnum* are among the rarest and most beautiful of mosses. Their capsules occur on long, flimsy stalks, and the base of each capsule bears a thin, papery, brightly colored, umbrella–like structure— yellow in *S. luteum* and red in *S. rubrum*.

The smallest mosses reach only 0.04–0.8 in (1–2 mm) in height, whereas the largest can grow to 20 in (50 cm). In temperate regions, mosses grow during cooler, wetter parts of the year, primarily during the autumn, mild spells in winter, and in early spring. The mosses naturally fall into three distinctive groups, taxonomically referred to as classes: Bryidae, the true mosses; Sphagnidae, the peat mosses; and Andreaeidae, the granite mosses.

True Mosses. One of the most distinctive features of true mosses involves the development of their gametophytes. Spores germinate to produce a characteristic mass of algal–like threads, called *protonema*, which looks like a loose ball of wool. Bud–like structures develop later, and give rise to the familiar leafy gametophyte. Although mosses are considered to be non–vascular plants, many true mosses in fact have a primitive vascular system consisting of a central strand of water–conducting cells called *hydroids*. Some also have specialized cells around the column of hydroids called *leptoids,* which function in the transport of carbohydrates, the products of photosynthesis. The stems of true mosses are more–or–less uniformly leafy and erect. Their leaves usually have a midrib, and their sporophytes possess capsules that are borne on stalks that are made of sporophytic tissue. Also, the capsules contain one or two rows of toothlike appendages (*peristome*) over the opening of the capsule, which are exposed when the lid is shed. This is by far the largest group of mosses.

Peat Mosses. This is a small, but extremely important group of mosses, numbering about 350 species. Their stems are branched at nodes, with the nodes closely spaced at the tips, giving the plants a tufted appearance. Their gametophytes develop from the margins of plate–like protonema, in contrast to the filamentous protonema of true mosses. The leaves of peat mosses lack a midrib, and the bulk of the leaf mass is composed of large, translucent cells that are dead. These hyaline cells contain pores, allowing them to readily take up water. Some peat mosses can absorb an amount of water equal to 26 times their dry weight. Narrower, living cells that photosynthesize occur in networks between the hyaline cells. The sporophytes of peat mosses are distinct in that the stalk on which the capsule sits is part of the gametophyte and not the sporophyte itself as in the true mosses. The capsule also characteristically disperses its spores by a minute explosion. At maturity, the globular capsules begin to dry so that the middle portion contracts inward. The contraction produces great internal pressure on the air trapped inside, which eventually increases enough to blow off the lid with an audible pop, shooting the spores into the air. The capsules lack a peristome.

Granite mosses. This is the smallest group of mosses containing only about 100 species. Granite mosses are small, dark, tufted plants that grow on exposed rocks in alpine and arctic regions. Their leafy gametophytes arise from a lobed structure, rather than from a filamentous protonema. Their sporophytes generally are stalks that are derived from the gametophyte, as in the peat mosses. Their tiny capsules typically have four vertical sutures that split at maturity to release the spores. This method of spore dispersal is unique among the mosses.

Importance of mosses

Mosses are extremely important during the early stages of ecological succession. Succession begins with the generation of a new environment. This can occur,

for example, by the formation of sand dunes, the exposure of land by deglaciation, or by the radical disturbance of a previously vegetated landscape as when an area is logged or burned by wildfire. In such cases, the ground becomes vegetated by the process of succession, during which various different plant communities dominate the site in turn. Because of their ability to reproduce asexually by fragmentation and gemmae combined with sexual reproduction, which produces enormous numbers of tiny, easily–dispersed spores, mosses play a vital role in being among the first colonizers of disturbed sites. They stabilize the soil surface, thereby reducing erosion, while at the same time reducing the evaporation of water, making more available for succeeding plants. Mosses are not an important source of food for vertebrate herbivores. Peat mosses are the dominant plants of extensive northern wetland areas, and are largely responsible for the development of bogs.

Most species of mosses are not of any direct economic importance, and none is a food source for humans. Peat mosses are economically the most important mosses. Peat mosses are an important source of fuel in some countries. Peat is abundant in northern regions and represents a vast reservoir of potential energy. In northern Europe, peat has historically been dried, and in some cases compressed into briquettes for use in fireplaces and stoves. In Ireland, peat is still extensively used for cooking. One great advantage of peat as a fuel is that it burns very cleanly. About 95% of peat harvested in Ireland burned to generate electricity. Peat is also highly valued as a conditioner of inorganic soils. Because it absorbs large amounts of water readily, pest improves the water–holding capacity of soil. Peat mosses are characteristically acidic which prevents the growth of most bacteria. They have therefore been used by indigenous peoples for diapers, and during the World Wars, when bandages were in short supply, peat mosses were a commonly used antiseptic dressing for wounds.

In recent years, mosses have become important in monitoring the health of ecosystems, especially in relation to atmospheric contamination. Because bryophytes lack roots, many of their nutritional requirements are met by nutrients deposited from the atmosphere. Thus, they are sensitive indicators of atmospheric pollutants. Changes in the distributions of mosses (and lichens) are therefore an early–warning signal of serious effects of atmospheric pollution.

See also Asexual reproduction; Liverwort; Moss; Succession; Symbiosis; Wetlands.

Further Reading:

Longton, R.E. *The Biology of Polar Bryophytes and Lichens.* U.K.: Cambridge University Press, 1988.
Richardson, D.H.S. *The Biology of Mosses.* New York: John Wiley and Sons, Inc., 1981.
Schofield, W.B. *Introduction to Bryology.* New York: Macmillan Publishing Co., 1985.

Les C. Cwynar

Bubble chamber see **Particle detectors**

Bubonic plague

Bubonic plague is a contagious, deadly disease caused by the bacterium *Yersinia pestis*. Sometimes referred to simply as "the plague," this disease has played a major role in world history. Because plague is highly contagious, it is easily transmitted from one person to another. Worldwide epidemics of the disease (called pandemics) have decimated populations since 542 A.D., when the first evidence of plague was recorded. Plague is rarely seen in the United States today, but is still epidemic in Southeast Asia.

Transmission of bubonic plague bacteria

Yersinia pestis is an intracellular parasite. In contrast to other kinds of bacteria, it enters cells. The bacterium that causes tuberculosis is also an intracellular parasite, as is the bacterium that causes chlamydia, a sexually transmitted disease.

Humans are not the "first choice" of host for *Yersinia pestis*. The *Yersinia pestis* bacterium infects the bloodstream of rats and other wild rodents such as squirrels and prairie dogs. Humans become infected only through the bite of a flea that has ingested blood from an infected rodent. Another route of transmission is through person–to–person contact. If a person's lungs are infected with the bacteria, the disease can be transmitted easily to another person through a cough or a sneeze. This form of transmission is extremely quick: cases have been recorded of persons dying from the disease within 24 hours of exposure to an infected person.

Symptoms of bubonic plague

In humans, plague can take two forms. One form, called the bubonic form, usually results from a flea bite and is characterized by a sore called a bubo. The bubo is actually the infected lymph node that drains the area through which the bacteria was introduced by the infected flea. The lymph node enlarges and turns black. Other symptoms of this form of plague include fever and congestion of the blood vessels of the eye. As the disease progresses, the bacteria spread to other parts of the body, resulting in septicemia, or widespread infection. The fatality rate of the bubonic plague is 15%.

In another form of plague, called the pneumonic form, the bacteria infect the lungs. This form of plague can follow the bubonic form, as the bacteria spreads to the lungs. Or, a person may simply contract the pneumonic form only, and show no evidence of a bubo. The pneumonic form is highly contagious and especially virulent: the average length of time from the first appearance to symptoms to death is less than two days.

For both types of plague, antibiotics can cure the disease. A vaccine is also available to protect those who are at risk of contracting plague. People who work with *Yersinia pestis* in laboratories and in environments where wild rodents are infected with the bacteria usually are vaccinated against plague. United States soldiers who fought in the Vietnam war in the 1960s and 1970s were vaccinated against plague. However, the vaccine only protects against the bubonic form, not the pneumonic form. People who are exposed to the pneumonic disease should take antibiotics as a precautionary measure.

Plague pandemics

Plague has played a major role in world history. Some evidence exists that a plague pandemic took place about 2000 years ago, but the first recorded pandemic of plague occurred in 542 A.D. in Egypt and Ethiopia. This pandemic killed 100 million people.

Burning of houses where plague had ocurred during the last world-wide pandemic of plague, which started in China in the 1890s. This outbreak of plague spread from the East to the West through the trade routes.

The next great plague pandemic occurred in the 14th century in Europe, Central Asia, the North East, India, and China. In this pandemic, trading ships from China carried infected rats to Europe. About 25 million people in Europe alone died from plague; some experts estimate that this number constitutes a third of the European population. Because so many people died, the plague had a major impact on the economy and political structure of Europe. The scarcity of workers led to a scarcity of food; workers, previously given little compensation for their labors, began to demand higher wages. Some historians feel that the unrest of workers and the middle class in Europe that culminated in the beheading of King Charles I in England in the 17th century and the beheading of Louis XVI in France in the 18th century had its roots in the economic aftermath of the 14th plague pandemic.

The third plague pandemic began in Burma in 1894; from there, the plague spread to China and through Hong Kong to North America. One hundred million people in India died from plague over a period of 20 years. During this pandemic, the United States saw its first case of plague in 1900 in San Francisco. In 1907, 167 cases of plague in San Francisco were recorded. As a result of the pandemic, rats and other wild rodents in the areas around San Francisco became reservoirs of *Yersinia pestis*.

Today, isolated cases of plague are still found in Kansas, Oklahoma, and Texas. The majority of cases worldwide—90%—occur in Southeast Asia: Burma, South Vietnam, Nepal, and Indonesia. Brazil also has a high number of plague cases. A recent outbreak in Surat, India, in 1994, killed 56 people and caused widespread panic.

Prevention

Plague pandemics can be prevented by the disinfection of ships, aircraft, and persons who are known to have the plague. The classic route of transmission that leads to pandemics is the transportation of infected rodents aboard transcontinental vehicles. Since many countries have instituted rigorous disinfection practices for ships and planes, plague cases have dropped dramatically.

KEY TERMS

. . . .

Bubo—The characteristic sign of bubonic plague; the infected lymph node that drains the site through which plague bacteria are introduced by an infected flea.

Epidemic—An outbreak of a disease contained within a country or region.

Intracellular parasite—A bacterium that enters cells.

Pandemic—A worldwide outbreak of a disease.

Quarantine—Isolation of an individual with a contagious disease to avoid transmission of the disease to others.

Septicemia—Widespread infection of the body.

If a person is diagnosed with plague, most countries, including the United States, require that the governmental health agency be notified. The person is usually kept under strict quarantine until the disease is brought under control with antibiotics.

Another way to prevent plague is to control rodent and flea populations in cities. Fleas are easier to control than rodents, since most homes can be easily decontaminated. Many cities, especially in the United States, have instituted rodent–control programs aimed at decreasing the numbers of rodents that roam the streets. Since rodents also carry rabies and other deadly diseases, controlling their numbers makes sense for a variety of reasons.

Further Reading:

Epstein, Richard. "A Persistent Pestilence." *Geographical Magazine* 63 (April 1994): 18.

Jayaramen, K. S. "Indian Plague Poses Enigma to Researchers." *Nature* (13 October 1994): 547.

Mee, Charles L. "How a Mysterious Disease Laid Low Europe's Masses." *Smithsonian* (February 1990): 66.

Richardson, Sarah. "The Return of the Plague." *Discover* 16 (January 1995): 69.

Kathleen Scogna

Buckeye see **Horse chestnut**

Buckminsterfullerene

As recently as 1984, carbon was thought to exist in only two solid forms. There was graphite, in which the carbon atoms arranged themselves as layered sheets of hexagonally bonded atoms, and there was diamond, in which the carbon atoms formed octahedral structures in which each carbon atom had four nearest neighbors.

Then, in 1985, chemists R. E. Smalley, R. F. Curl, J. R. Heath, and S. O'Brien at Rice University, and H. W. Kroto of the University of Sussex in England observed that a hollow truncated icosahedron, similar in shape to a soccer ball, and consisting of 60 carbon atoms, tends to form spontaneously when carbon vapor condenses. In 1990, physicists D. R. Huffman and L. Lamb of the University of Arizona, working with W. Kratschmer and K. Fostiropoulos of the Max Planck Institute in Germany, discovered a way to make bulk quantities of this ^{60}C molecule, which investigations using high resolution electron microscopes have shown to have sizes of about one billionth of a meter.

As ^{60}C has the same structure as the geodesic dome developed by American engineer and philosopher R. Buckminster Fuller, these molecules were christened buckminsterfullerenes by the group at Rice University. The Swiss mathematician Leonhard Euler had proved that a geodesic structure must contain 12 pentagons to close into a spheroid, although the number of hexagons may vary. Later research by Smalley and his colleagues showed that there should exist an entire family of these geodesic–dome–shaped carbon clusters. Thus, ^{60}C has 20 hexagons; whereas its rugby–ball shaped cousin ^{70}C has 25. Research has since shown that laser vaporization of graphite produces clusters of carbon atoms whose sizes range from two to thousands of atoms. These molecules are now known as fullerenes. All the even numbered species between ^{3}C and ^{600}C are hollow fullerenes, but below ^{32}C, the fullerene cage is too brittle to remain stable. Helical microtubules of graphitic carbon have also been found.

Why ^{60}C?

Although many examples are known of five–membered carbon rings attached to six–membered rings in stable organic compounds (for example, the nucleic acids adenine and guanine), only a few occur whose two five–membered rings share an edge. The smallest fullerene in which the pentagons need not share an edge is ^{60}C; the next is ^{70}C. ^{72}C and all larger fullerenes adopt structures in which the five–membered carbon rings are well separated, but the pentagons in these larger fullerenes occupy strained positions. This makes the carbon atoms at such sites particularly vulnerable to chemical attack. Thus, it turns out that the truncated icosahedral structure of ^{60}C distributes the strain of closure equally, producing a molecule of great strength

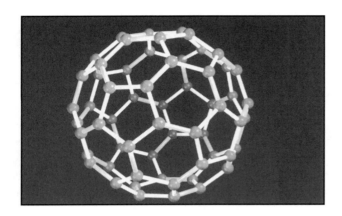

A supercomputer simulation of the atomic structure of a molecule of Buckminsterfullerene. Carbon molecules appear as small spheres; double bonds between them are darker than single bonds.

and stability. This molecule will, however, react with certain free radicals.

When compressed to 70% of its initial volume, the buckminsterfullerene is expected to become harder than diamond. After the pressure has been released, the molecule would be expected to take up its original volume. Experiments in which these molecules were thrown against steel surfaces at about 17,000 m/h (25,744 km/h) showed them to just bounce back.

Fullerenes are, in fact, the only pure, finite form of carbon. Diamond and graphite both form infinite networks of carbon atoms. Under normal circumstances, when a diamond is cut, the surfaces are instantly covered with hydrogen, which tie up the unattached surface bonds. The same is true of graphite. Because of their symmetry, fullerenes need no other atoms to satisfy their surface chemical bonding requirements.

The buckminsterfullerene seems to have an incredible range of electrical properties. It is currently thought that it may alternately exist in insulating, conducting, semiconducting, or superconducting forms.

Fullerenes with metal atoms trapped inside the carbon cage have also been studied. These are referred to as endohedral metallofullerenes. Reports of uranium, lanthanum, and yttrium metallofullerenes have appeared in the literature. It has been exceptionally difficult to isolate pure samples of these shrink–wrapped metal atoms, however.

Production of fullerenes

For reasons that are not yet fully understood, ^{60}C seems to be the inevitable result of condensing carbon slowly at high temperatures. At high temperatures when carbon is vaporized, most of the atoms initially coalesce into clusters of 2–15 atoms. Small clusters from chains, but clusters containing at least 10 atoms commonly form monocyclic rings. Although these rings are favored at low temperatures, at very high temperatures they break open to form linear chains of up to 25 carbon atoms. These carbon chains may then link together at high temperatures to form graphite sheets, which somehow manage to form the geodesic fullerenes. One theory has it that the carbon sheets, when heated sufficiently, close in on themselves to form fullerenes.

Kratschmer and his coworkers in Germany managed to prepare the first concentrated solution of fullerenes in 1990 by mixing a few drops of benzene with specially prepared carbon soot.

Scientists later demonstrated that fullerenes can be conveniently generated by setting up an electric arc between two graphite electrodes. In their method, the tips of the electrodes are screwed toward each other as fast as the graphite is evaporated to maintain a constant gap. The process has been found to work best in a helium atmosphere in which other gases such as hydrogen and water vapor have been eliminated.

Fullerenes have been reported to occur naturally in certain coals, as well as in structures produced by lightening known as fulgurites, and in the soot of many flames.

Uses

Fullerenes have so far failed to realize their commercial potential. This is partly for reasons of cost and partly because it has proven difficult to isolate large quantities of sought–after types. At the beginning of 1994, fullerenes were actively being studied for the following applications: optical devices, hardening agents for carbides, chemical sensors, gas separation devices, thermal insulation, diamonds, batteries, catalysts, hydrogen storage media, polymers and polymer additives, and medical applications.

It has been predicted the first large–scale applications for fullerenes will not be found until manufacturing cost are close to those of aluminum (a few dollars per pound). At the end of 1993, fullerenes sold for $100 to $200 per gram.

See also Carbon; Platonic solids; Polyhedron; Polymer.

Further Reading:

Baggott, J. *Perfect Symmetry*. New York: Oxford University Press, 1994.

Curl, Robert F., and Richard E. Smalley. "Fullerenes." *Scientific American* (October 1991).

Fuller, Buckminster. *Ideas and Integrities.* Toronto: Collier Books, 1963.

Stewart, Ian, and Martin Golubitsky. *Fearful Symmetry: Is God a Geometer?* Oxford: Blackwell, 1992.

Randall Frost

Buckthorn

Buckthorns are various species of shrubs and small trees in the family Rhamnaceae, a mostly tropical and subtropical family of about 600 species. Most of the buckthorns are in the genus *Rhamnus*.

Buckthorns have a few economic applications, although none of these are very important. A dye known as sap green is made from the fruits of the European buckthorn (*Rhamnus cathartica*). Another pigment known as Chinese green is made from the bark of several Chinese species of buckthorn (*Rhamnus globosus* and *R. utilis*). A laxative and tonic known as cascara is made from the bark of the western buckthorn (*R. purshiana*) of the United States, and from a European species, the alder buckthorn (*R. frangula*). The wood of some buckthorns may also be carved, for example, as pipe stems.

There are a number of native species of buckthorns in North America. The Carolina buckthorn (*Rhamnus caroliniana*) occurs widely in the eastern United States. Cascara buckthorn (*R. purshiana*) occurs relatively broadly in forested areas of the west coast. Western species of more restricted distributions in the southwestern United States include birchleaf buckthorn (*R. betulaefolia*) and California buckthorn (*R. californica*).

The European buckthorn (*Rhamnus cathartica*) and glossy buckthorn (*R. frangula*) are European species that were introduced to North America through horticulture, and have now become invasive weeds in some areas. These shrubs can form dense stands that exclude native species of shrubs and other plants, and that represent severely degraded ecosystems. The European buckthorn is also an alternate host of oat rust, a fungus that causes an economically important disease of oats (*Avena sativa*).

Bill Freedman

Buckwheat

Buckwheat, *Fagopyrum esculentum*, is not really a wheat at all—it belongs to the family Polygonaceae, and hence is a dicotyledonous plant, not a monocotyledonous species. However, the starchy seeds of buckwheat are utilized in much the same way as the cereal grains of cultivated grasses, such as wheat (*Triticum aestivum*).

The seeds of buckwheat can be used directly as poultry or animal feed. Processed, the seeds can be cooked as porridge for humans, or they can be milled to yield a nutritious flour that can be made into a variety of foods, such as pancakes and biscuits. Technically, the seeds of buckwheat are achenes (simple, dry, one–celled, one–seeded fruits), as they are surrounded by dry, brown fruit coats, and are slightly winged.

Fagopyrum esculentum was probably derived from the wild species *F. cymosum*, a perennial species with rhizomes (underground storage organs) that occurs naturally in China and northern India. Buckwheat has been cultivated in China for about 1,500 years, and was introduced to Europe (via Germany) in the fifteenth century, and arrived in England about 1600 A.D. From Europe it was taken to the American colonies and to Africa. The production of buckwheat has been declining in countries where it has been popular in the recent past, such as the former Soviet Union,

Buckwheat (*Fagopyrum esculentum*) flowering.

France and the United States, but against this trend, production has increased in Canada since the 1960s.

Cultivated buckwheat is an annual plant that grows well in poor soils, reaching a height of about 24 in (60 cm). Another attractive feature to farmers is the excellent resistance of buckwheat to many insect pests and diseases. Possession of such resistance is fortunate, since breeding for improvements by conventional methods has proved to be difficult.

See also Crops.

Buckyball see **Buckminsterfullerene**

Buds and budding

Bud is a term used to refer to three different types of undeveloped forms described in this article.

Plant buds

Plant buds, such as the buds of flowers, trees, and scrubs, are small, rounded, incompletely developed, dormant parts of a plant consisting of cells capable of rapid cell division when conditions are right for growth. They first appear in the spring when sap starts to flow, causing the buds to swell, which makes them more noticeable. These buds are first formed by the plant in late summer and early fall but remain small over the winter. When spring arrives, the structures for new shoot and floral growth are already formed and are tightly packaged and ready for quick growth when days lengthen and temperatures rise. The delicate, immature structures of these plant buds are covered with tough protective scales formed from modified leaves, that enable the tender structures to get through winter in a dormant, resting state.

Plant buds can be classified in two ways, either according to their location on the plant, or according to the type of tiny immature structures that are contained within the bud. Buds on the tip of stems are called terminal buds, those at the sides of stems are called lateral buds, while those formed in the angle the leaf makes with the plant stem are known as axillary buds. When buds are classified according to their internal structures, those that contain only the beginning of a flower are called flower buds. Those that contain only immature leaves are called leaf buds, while those buds containing both flowers and leaves in the earliest stages of development are termed mixed buds. Flower buds on herbaceous plants and on woody plants are made up of undeveloped and tightly packed groups of cells that are the precursors of the various floral parts—petals, stamens, and pistils—with a whorl of sepals or outer leaf bracts covering and protecting the inner parts of the flower bud. Some small buds can produce a surprising amount of growth when attached to, and growing out from, a piece of the parent plant that is put into suitable soil. People familiar with growing potatoes by planting small sections of potato that contain "eyes" (sunken buds) know that the sprouts that grow from these buds will develop into whole new potato plants. Because of this remarkable ability for vegetative reproduction, these fertile pieces of potato are referred to as seed potatoes. The little sunken bud (the potato "eye") draws its nourishment to sprout from the stored starchy food contained in the piece of parent potato tuber.

The buds that woody plants such as shrubs, woody vines, and trees produce contain miniature shoots with a short stem and small, undeveloped, tightly packed leaves or immature floral structures covered with tough protective, overlapping scales. A terminal bud on a

A hydra, budding.

woody twig overwinters and grows out during the next spring and summer into a whole new shoot that extends the length of the twig and may also produce flowers. Apple and cherry blossoms are well known examples of this type of bud growth. Growth from a lateral bud will produce either a branch, or just a leaf on the side of the twig depending upon the nature of the precursor cells that were packaged in the bud during the previous fall.

Animal buds

Buds and budding are also found in the asexual reproduction (involving only one parent) of some animals, such as the freshwater hydra and species of marine colonial jellyfish, where a single parent gives rise to one or more new individuals. When a single hydra reaches maturity and is well fed, outpocketings of the animal's body wall begin to form a rounded growth projecting from the tube–like section or stalk of the adult's body. This growth, called a bud, develops in time into a miniature hydra whose body layers and inner body cavity, the digestive cavity, are continuous with that of the parent individual. Food captured and gathered in by the adult parent also supports the growth of the bud. Early in this budding process tiny tentacles appear on the free end of the hydra bud. It is not

unusual to find two or more buds on an adult hydra in different stages of growth and development. An adult hydra may have its body and tentacles fully extended while its bud may have its whole form contracted into a rounded mass. Conversely the bud may be stretched out, while the adult is contracted. The bud will, however, sometimes contract soon after the adult contracts as the nerve net in the mesoglea (middle jelly layer) of the two individuals is continuous. When a newly budded hydra offspring is fully formed and sufficiently developed to take up an independent existence, the base of the new hydra seals off and thus allows the new individual to break off from the parent hydra.

Buds and budding also refers to the extensions of microscopic yeast cells and some types of bacterial cells produced during asexual reproduction, forming the beginning of daughter cells. The taste buds of the mammalian tongue, are so called because of their small size and bud–like shapes, but bear no relationship to the buds of plants and animals discussed above.

See also Asexual reproduction; Hydra; Plant; Yeast.

Further Reading:

BSCS. *Biological Science: An Ecologic Approach.* Dubuque, Iowa: Kendall /Hunt, 1992.

Mader , Sylvia S. *Introduction to Biology.* Dubuque , Iowa: Wm . C. Brown Communications, Inc., 1994.

Raven, Peter H., Ray F. Evert , and Susan E. Eichorn . *Biology of Plants.* 5th ed. New York: Worth Publishers, 1992.

Julia M. Van Denack

Buffalo see **Bison; Cattle family**

Buffalo gnats see **True flies**

Buffer

In chemistry, a buffer is a system, usually an aqueous (water) solution, that resists having its pH changed when an acid or a base is added to it.

Normally, the addition of acid to a solution will lower its pH and the addition of a base will raise its pH. If the solution is a buffer, however, its pH will be changed to a much lesser extent than would be expected from the amounts of acid or base that are added. So–called "buffered aspirin" is not really a buffer, because it doesn't resist acids and bases. It is simply aspirin combined with a basic compound, such as magnesium carbonate or aluminum hydroxide, which neutralizes some stomach acid.

Almost all chemical reactions that take place in aqueous solution—and that means almost all chemical reactions—are sensitive to the concentrations of hydrogen ions and hydroxide ions, that is, to the pH of the solution. That's because hydrogen and hydroxide ions are the ions of water itself. In particular, many biochemical processes that are essential to life are quite sensitive to the acidities of various body fluids. A variety of natural buffer systems keep the body's pH values within the limits that are necessary for health. For example, a system of several buffers holds the pH of human blood between 7.33 and 7.43 in a healthy person. A blood pH below 7.0 or above 7.8 can be fatal.

How buffers work

There are two common kinds of buffer solutions: solutions that contain a weak acid plus one of its salts (e.g., acetic acid plus sodium acetate) and solutions that contain a weak base plus one of its salts (e.g., ammonia plus ammonium chloride). Their workings can be understood in terms of LeChâtelier's principle.

Weak acid buffers

When a weak acid is dissolved in water, only a few of its molecules dissociate to form only a few hydrogen ions; the rest of the acid molecules remain as undissociated, neutral molecules that don't affect the pH. For example, whenever acetic acid is added to water, the following three species will be in the solution:

$$HC_2H_3O_2 \longleftrightarrow H^+ + C_2H_3O_2^-$$

| many acetic acid molecules | a few hydrogen ions | a few acetate ions |

To make a buffer solution out of this system, we can add many more acetate ions to the solution in the

form of sodium acetate, which is a strong electrolyte and dissociates completely. Ignoring the sodium ions that come along with the sodium acetate because they don't affect the acidity at all, we then have:

Buffer solution

$$HC_2H_3O_2 \longleftrightarrow H^+ + C_2H_3O_2^-$$

| many acetic acid molecules | a few hydrogen ions | many acetate ions |

This solution will resist having its hydrogen ion concentration changed. To see how that works, first consider what would happen if we were to add some acid—some extra hydrogen ions—to this solution. According to LeChâtelier's principle, the equilibrium will be shifted to the left. That is, the added hydrogen ions will react with some of the acetate ions to form more acetic acid molecules. The result is that almost all of the added hydrogen ions are used up to form "harmless" neutral molecules; they therefore aren't available to increase the acidity of the solution. The solution has resisted having its pH lowered more than a little bit.

What if we were to add some base—hydroxide ions—to the buffer solution? Hydroxide ions just love to react with hydrogen ions, because the resulting molecule, H_2O, is so stable.

$$OH^- + H^+ \rightarrow H_2O$$

| hydroxide ion | hydrogen ion | water |

Therefore, the added hydroxide ions will quickly remove hydrogen ions from the buffer solution, which according to LeChâtelier's principle will then shift its equilibrium to the right, making more acetate ions out of acetic acid molecules. Thus, the added hydroxide ions will have been used up, and only "harmless" acetate ions will have been formed. (Acetate ions are slightly basic, however, so the pH of the buffer solution does increase slightly.)

Weak base buffers

When ammonia gas is added to water, it forms a solution of a weak base whose equilibrium can be represented as follows:

$$NH_3 + H_2O \longleftrightarrow NH_4^+ + OH^-$$

| many ammonia molecules | water | a few ammonium ions | a few hydroxide ions |

To make a buffer solution out of this system, we can add many more ammonium ions to the solution in the form of ammonium chloride, which is a strong electrolyte and dissociates completely. Ignoring the chloride ions that come along with the ammonium chloride because they don't affect the acidity at all, we'll then have

Buffer solution

$$NH_3 + H_2O \longleftrightarrow NH_4^+ + OH^-$$

| many ammonia molecules | water | many ammonium ions | a few hydroxide ions |

If we add hydrogen ions to this buffer solution, they will be neutralized by reacting with the hydroxide ions to form water. According to LeChâtelier's principle, this removal of hydroxide ions will shift the equilibrium to the right, producing more ammonium ions, which don't affect the pH. (But ammonium ions are slightly acid.)

If we add hydroxide ions to the ammonia buffer solution, they will shift the equilibrium to the left, which uses up the added hydroxide ions and forms more whole NH_3 molecules, which don't affect the pH.

Some important buffers

Common weak acid buffer systems are based upon carbonic acid (H_2CO_3), citric acid ($H_3C_6H_5O$), and phosphoric acid (H_3PO_4). Common weak base buffer systems are based upon amines (organic bases) or amino acids, which can act as both acids and bases.

A buffer solution based upon a dibasic or tribasic acid (an acid that can produce two or three hydrogen ions per molecule) may be made from two different ions of the same acid, rather than from the acid itself and one salt ion. For example, the phosphoric acid ions $H_2PO_4^-$ and HPO_4^{2-} can form what is known as the phosphate buffer system, which is one of the buffers that control the pH of human blood. In this system the $H_2PO_4^-$ ion plays the role of the weak acid and the HPO_4^{2-} ion plays the role of its salt. The relevant equilibrium is

$$H_2PO_4^- \longleftrightarrow H^+ + HPO_4^{2-}$$

| dihydrogen phosphate | hydrogen ion | monohydrogen phosphate ion |

The main buffer that is involved in controlling blood pH, however, is the carbonate system, which is based on the following equilibrium:

$$H_2CO_3 \longleftrightarrow H^+ + HCO_3^-$$

| carbonic acid | hydrogen ion | bicarbonate ion |

The carbonic acid in the blood comes from dissolved carbon dioxide:

$$CO_2 + H_2O \longleftrightarrow H_2CO_3$$

| carbon dioxide | water | carbonic acid |

Our breathing (oxygen in, carbon dioxide out) controls the amount of carbon dioxide that is available to dissolve in the bloodstream. Therefore, our lungs also play an important part in controlling our blood's pH through the carbonate buffer system.

See also Acids and bases; Equilibrium, chemical; Hydrolysis.

Further Reading:
Brown, William H., and Elizabeth Rogers. *General, Organic and Biochemistry.* Boston: Willard Grant, 1980.

Creedy, John. *A Laboratory Manual for Schools and Colleges.* London: Heinemann, 1977.

Hill, John W., and Dorothy M. Feigl. *Chemistry and Life.* 2nd edition. Minneapolis: Burgess, 1978.

Widom, Joanne M., and Stuart J. Edelstein. *Chemistry: An Introduction to General, Organic, and Biological Chemistry.* San Francisco: W. H. Freeman, 1981.

Robert L. Wolke

Bugs see **True bugs**

Building design/architecture

Architects design buildings, but architecture is more than just building design and more than just art on a massive scale. Architecture is about light and space. It is about stimulating emotions in the people who see and inhabit the structure. Architecture creates an environment, whether it is the uplifted spirituality of the Chartres Cathedral, the drama and anticipation of the Schauspielhaus auditorium, or tranquil serenity of Fallingwater. It is experiential. When you approach or enter a building you move through the space, the scale changes, the proportions shift around you. This is what makes architecture glorious; the way it manipulates light.

Structure is fundamental to architecture. For a design to move from the mind of the architect to reality, there must be a method of building it. The development of structural forms has thus been a driving force in architecture, every bit as much as changes in social order and historical events. Through history there have been relatively quiet periods of stylistic development, interspersed with almost muscular leaps of structural innovation such as the Roman period, the Gothic period or the Industrial Revolution.

Prehistory

The architecture of prehistory is largely one of tombs and temples, though mudbrick Neolithic settlements have been discovered. Houses in these settlements were one story, rectangular structures with a hole in the roof that served as both chimney and entry. The doorway, with its horizontal lintel and vertical posts, was developed somewhat later and constitutes the first significant leap forward in architecture, making all future styles possible. The architectural term for post–and–lintel construction is trabeation. Trabeated passages, some involving enormous stones, were built into huge mounds of earth to form burial tombs called barrows.

The thought of the ancient Egyptians immediately brings the image of the pyramids to mind, but architecturally speaking the advances they made with materials and design were far more important. The Egyptians built structures as we know them, with walls, trabeated doorways and small window openings. They eventually developed the freestanding column, which allowed them to build enormous halls with trabeated roofs, structures that essentially consisted of parallel rows of post–and–lintel constructions.

The emphasis of ancient Egyptian architecture was on mass rather than space, typified by the Hypostyle hall where some of the columns are 11 or 12 ft (3.5–4 m) in diameter. The structural strength of the lintel in a trabeated roof limits the expanse of open space that can be spanned by this method. When the lintel is too long, the load carried by the stone is greater than its strength, and it fails. Thus, the open space in Egyptian halls was very limited, though the ceilings soared to heights of almost 70 ft (21 m) and the actual halls were hundreds of feet wide.

The Egyptians were the first structural designers with an identifiable visual style. Their temples and tombs had such a strong identity and coherence that architects still echo their designs in modern structures. They drew some of their inspiration from nature, carving columns to look like palms, or plants crowned with papyrus or lotus blossoms. Structures were also designed to elicit emotions in the viewers, such as the temples interiors that progressed from the bright, relatively open spaces allowed to the public, to the dim, confined spaces of the inner sanctum, accessible only to the priests and rulers. Both the use of nature in architectural decoration and the use of design to control emotion were themes that would be repeated over and over in coming centuries.

The architecture of the Near–Eastern civilizations that coexisted with the Egyptians evolved distinct identities. The Sumerians, for example, had little access to stone. Their available building material was mudbrick, a structurally weak material that could not produce the lintels required for trabeated roofing. To solve the problem of roofing, the Sumerians are believed to have developed the curved arch and tunnel vault to enclose narrow interior spaces. The ancient Persians had access to a variety of building materials, and they were influenced by the architecture of the Egyptians, the Greeks, and the other civilizations that inhabited their enormous empire. With such rich source material, they were able to develop a unique, fanciful architectural style, and structurally refine the approach of the ancient Egyptians. In the royal audience hall in Persopolis, the ancient capital, the pillars were half the diameter of the Egyptian columns, with a significantly wider spacing than the Egyptian version. The ceiling was still trabeated, but the effect is of a much lighter, much more open space.

Classical architecture

The Greeks

Ancient Greek architecture was a miracle of style, balance, and harmony, with a powerful simplicity whose influence persists in architecture to this day. It is distinctive and immediately recognizable, a graceful massing that creates a sense of dignity, wisdom, and timelessness. The Greeks believed in human intellect and rational thought, in community, and the achievements of the living, rather than the cult of death featured in earlier civilizations. Accordingly, their architectural focus was on public buildings: temples, theaters, civic structures. They were the pioneers of city planning.

Greek society was built upon democracy, stressing the involvement of the individual in government and culture. This was reflected in their architecture. Structures were rarely aligned with one another but were instead set at angles to enhance the individuality of the structures and draw the viewer into participating in the process. The viewer's viewpoint was not strictly regimented, as we will see in later eras, but instead allowed to form naturally.

The elements of classical Greek structures are simple and few, yet carefully organized to create an overall effect. The primary structural form was trabeation — stone columns supporting lintels. There were three styles, or orders, of Greek architecture: the Doric, the Ionic, distinct styles that originated in different parts of the country, and the Corinthian, which is essentially a spin–off of the Ionic order. The structural elements, proportions, and composition of a building were defined by its order. Doric structures, in particular, followed a rigidly prescribed design, evolving toward the ideal Doric form expressed in the Parthenon. Symmetry of proportion runs through the structures, with set ratios of building length to width, and column height, diameter, and spacing. The Ionic style was less rigidly defined than the Doric, though proportion was still important, and the Corinthian order differed from the Ionic only in column design. In fact, the names of the orders are most often associated with the capitals or decorative tops of the columns used in the buildings. Doric columns are simple angled tops, Ionic columns are delicate scrolls, and Corinthian columns are crowned with a delicate, leafy capital.

The Romans

It has been said that the Romans excelled in drains, not brains. Perhaps the ancient Romans did not reach the heights of art, drama, and philosophy that the Greeks did, but they were great engineers and builders who fundamentally changed the way people thought about architecture. The Romans took previously invented structural elements, such as the arch and vault, to the limits of their potential. The Greeks, for example, dabbled with concrete and in later periods

occasionally used arches, but only as freestanding decorative elements. In the hands of the Romans, these same two concepts were used to build the Colosseum.

The development of the rounded arch was critical to Roman architecture. In our earlier discussion of trabeation, we pointed out the lintel as the weak element of the structure. The tensile strength of the lintel limits the size of the opening and the load that can be carried, because the load on the lintel is only supported at the ends. In the non–supported portion of the lintel, the lines of force are aimed through the lintel to the ground. In an arch, on the other hand, the lines of force from the load are directed through the curve of the arch to the supporting piers, and from there to the ground. The supporting pier strength is limited by the compressive strength of the stone, which is far greater than its tensile strength. Moreover, the form of the arch and arch elements is such that the structure actually becomes stronger with a uniform load placed on top of it.

Rounded arches can be placed in a row to make a barrel vault, which means that a significant amount of space can be roofed over. The Romans developed a number of variations on the barrel vault, changing the way that space could be enclosed. The disadvantage of the barrel vault is that it requires continuous support along the sides, limiting the number of window openings permitted in the sidewalls. One answer to this was the groin vault, a structure consisting of two intersecting barrel vaults. Whereas the weight and force of the barrel vault is carried all along the line of the supporting wall, the groin vault concentrates weight and force in the corners of the structure, permitting a more open space and windows. The hemispherical dome, which can be thought of as an arch in three dimensions, was another variation on roofing. This form appears time and time again in Roman architecture, most notably in the Pantheon.

Another important Roman development was that of improved concrete. For several centuries, a concrete made of lime, sand, and water had been used sporadically by various builders. The Romans added a volcanic ash called pozzolana to their concrete, obtaining a stronger mortar that had the added advantage of setting up in water, allowing underwater construction. The Romans mixed this concrete with gravel or chips of stone and molded it into blocks or even arches and vaults, simplifying construction methods.

The Romans thought about architecture differently than the Greeks. The Greeks thought about structure and form, the Romans thought about space. Whereas Greek architecture was exterior, focused on the outside, on creating an experience for the viewer, Roman architecture was interior, based on the idea of creating an environment for the inhabitants. The Romans were more pragmatic than spiritual. Rather than focusing on temples, they built sumptuous bath houses, theaters, and other public spaces. Great administrators, they created the basilica to house government offices. The interiors of their buildings focused on space, on creating spaces to serve man, spaces that were emotionally and functionally pleasing. The Romans were also sophisticated urban planners, designing freeform civic centers, or forums, and rigidly styled *castrum*, a combination military outpost/colonial settlement in newly conquered territory.

Byzantine

After the fall of the western Roman Empire, the creative focus of architecture moved to Constantinople, located at the site of the Hellenic city of Byzantium. Most of the surviving structures from this period are churches. Rather than the long, axial floorplan characteristic of Roman barrel vaulted structures, Byzantine designs tended toward a centralized, vertically focused structure crowned with a dome that flooded the interior with light. Light, form, and structure in these churches were orchestrated to express the spiritual ideas of the new Christian religion, to exhalt the worshippers.

Byzantine churches achieved the floating effect of the central dome by the use of pendentives and pendentive domes. A hemispherical dome requires a circular base to support it fully, like that on the Pantheon. Interior spaces, however, tend to be square. Ancient architects wishing to top a non–circular space by a spherical dome added diagonal elements across the corners, called squinches, which helped support the structure. The Romans developed a more sophisticated method of support called the pendentive. A pendentive is a spherical, inverted triangle that rises from its point and curves downward. It is essentially a section of a domed surface and as such can be constructed to fully support a hemispherical dome. More important than the full support, though, is the nature of that support. The structural support of a dome on a cylinder or on squinches is visually dense, giving a sense of massing and of enclosure. A dome on pendentives appears to rise from only four points, giving the impression of floating overhead, adding to the otherworldly effect of the church interior.

The spiritual effect of the floating domes was enhanced by the use of light and ornamentation. Hagia Sophia, the most spectacular of the Byzantine churches, is flooded with light from a multitude of wall openings. A row of windows around the base of the dome adds to the impression of a magically hovering surface, as do the additional half domes and colonnades in the lower levels. To look up from the floor of the building is to look into a gleaming, billowing surface that appears to follow no known rules of structure, generating an exaltation of religion in its intensity.

Medieval architecture—Romanesque and Gothic

In the medieval period, European architects were profoundly influenced by the Roman structures dotting the countryside. A style known as Romanesque emerged, featuring the Roman hallmarks of rounded arches and barrel vaults. Because barrel vaults must be supported continuously along the sides, these structures had few windows. The focus was on an almost claustrophobic massing: thick walls, small windows, heavy, ponderous piers.

The lines of force in an arch are designed to run down into the supporting column or piers. When the load is too extreme, as in the case of the large vaults of the Romanesque cathedrals, the lines of force are shifted laterally, with the result that the base of the arch tends to push outward from its supporting column. To prevent this, the Romanesque designers added buttresses, massive piers of masonry built against the walls at critical points to resist the lateral stress. Structurally it was effective, but it only added to the oppressive feel of the buildings.

Romanesque was primarily an adaptation of existing ideas, but the Gothic period was one of profound innovation. Elements were developed that allowed interior space to be approached in a way it had not been before. In contrast to the heavy inertness of the Romanesque structures, the Gothic cathedrals were open and buoyant, with a dynamic use of space. If Byzantine churches like Hagia Sophia gave an impression of the otherworldly, to the medieval peasant unused to any but the smallest interior spaces, the soaring lines of the Gothic cathedrals with their brilliantly colored walls of glass and traceries of stone must have felt like heaven.

The rounded arch is a powerful structural element but it has its limitations. Force applied to the rounded arch is carried along the full arc and driven into the supports of the arch. When the applied load is too high, however, the lines of force move outside of the structure of the arch; in such a case, the arch fails. The arch developed by the Gothic cathedral builders was pointed, rather than round. Its lines described a catenary arc rather than a hemisphere, keeping the lines of force within the structure of the arch so that the load applied to the arch was deflected straight down through the arch supports to the ground. The Gothic arch is more stable and can be thinner than the same size rounded arch. This allowed the cathedral designers to build larger, lighter looking structures.

A second important development of the Gothic period was the rib vault. Romanesque naves were roofed with barrel vaults, essentially a line of rounded arches. Load applied to the vault was carried all along the wall holding up the arch. This limited the number of openings possible in the wall, leading to the claustrophobically small and infrequent windows of the Romanesque churches. Groin vaults made from the intersection of two barrel vaults permitted a somewhat wider open space, but again the load on the vault was carried by the arches. Groin vaults carried the load in the corners, allowing more openings in the walls, but they were difficult to build and could only span a square area. The rib vault represented a new concept in structure.

The rib vault consists of six arches: the arches on each side and a pair of transverse arches. The roofing of the vault is just a thin, relatively lightweight layer of stone webbed over this supporting structure. Load is minimized and carried at the corners of the vault. Construction is dramatically simplified. Design of the rib vault is facilitated by the pointed arch, which allows the vault to be any variety of rectangle, as opposed to the square vault dictated by use of rounded arches. The development of the rib vault allowed the cathedral architects to roof over enormous spaces. Because the vaults carried the load to the corners of the vault, the need for massive load–bearing walls was gone. The Gothic builders were able to open enormous holes in the walls without compromising the structure, and the cathedrals became traceries of stone filled with stained glass.

The third major development of Gothic architecture was the flying buttress. Romanesque churches used massive piers to support their sidewalls, the inertial bulk resisting the side forces created by the load of the ceiling. The flying buttress is a half arch that connects to a massive pier. It allowed the Gothic architects to apply resistive force to the ceiling loads at the point needed, rather than simply building huge piers and hoping they wouldn't fail. The flying buttresses allowed the cathedrals to soar to heights well over a hundred feet. Moreover, they lightened the feel of the cathedral exteriors, making them appear like lacework, fragile and airy.

The Renaissance and the Baroque

Renaissance architecture was a response to the ornamentation of the Gothic period and a homage to the new values of symmetry, balance, logic, and order. Man was once again exerting control over his environment, and the structures of this time reflected the dedication to mathematical forms and the ordering of space. The innovations of Renaissance architecture are less structural than paradigmatical. Leon Battista Alberti (1404–1472) codified what was known of architecture, emphasizing the theoretical aspects, turning it from a trade into a profession. More importantly, he developed perspective drawing techniques that allowed architects to draw accurate architectural renderings, techniques that are still used today.

Like the Renaissance, the Baroque period in architecture was marked by design rather than structural innovation. In response to the bareness of Renaissance architecture, Baroque buildings were lavishly decorated. Rather than the approach of form following function, designers of this period approached architecture as theater, emphasizing effects, interpretations, and movement. The Spanish Steps in Rome, for instance, were designed to mimic the movements of a popular dance of the time, with sidewalls that moved in, moved out, met, separated, and met again. The design elements became more emotional and dynamic, and the focus was on energy versus balance. At the same time, underlying the ornateness of the Baroque was the logic of Renaissance design.

One notable aspect of Baroque architecture was its use of controlled viewing to emphasize a building. The approach to St. Peter's in Rome is a classic example. It was carefully orchestrated, beginning some blocks away with the Ponte S. Angelo, progressing through a tangle of narrow streets that heighten anticipation by providing only glimpses of St. Peter's. Finally, the pilgrim emerged into an enormous oval piazza that permitted a clear view of St. Peter's for the first time, framed by the curved colonnade. The sequence was designed to enhance the religious experience of St. Peter's by intensifying the emotions – creating a sense of anticipation and delayed gratification – felt during the approach.

The Industrial Revolution—new materials

After the Baroque faded slowly away, eighteenth–century architecture consisted primarily of revivals of previous periods. This time was to be the calm before the storm, for the approaching Industrial Revolution was to change everything about the world as it was then, including architecture. Previously, building materials had been restricted to a few man-made materials along with those available in nature: timber, stone, timber, lime mortar, and concrete. Metals were not available in sufficient quantity or consistent quality to be used as anything more than ornamentation. Structure was limited by the capabilities of natural materials. The Industrial Revolution changed this situation dramatically.

In 1800, the worldwide tonnage of iron produced was 825,000 tons. By 1900, with the Industrial Revolution in full swing, worldwide production stood at 40,000,000 tons, almost 50 times as much. Iron was available in three forms. The least processed form, cast iron, was brittle due to a high percentage of impurities. It still displayed impressive compressive strength, however. Wrought iron was a more refined form of iron, malleable, though with low tensile strength. Steel was the strongest, most versatile form of iron. Through a conversion process, all of the impurities were burned out of the iron ore, then precise amounts of carbon were added for hardness. Steel had tensile and compressive strength greater than any material previously available, and its capabilities would revolutionize architecture.

This change did not happen over night. Prior to the introduction of bulk iron, architecture relied on compressive strength to hold buildings up. Even great structures like the Chartres Cathedral or the Parthenon were essentially orderly piles of stone. Architects were accustomed to thinking of certain ways of creating structure, and though they glimpsed some of the possibilities of the new materials, the first applications were made using the old ideas.

The explosion in the development of iron and steel structures was driven initially by the advance of the railroads. Bridges were required to span gorges and rivers. In 1779, the first iron bridge was built across the Severn River in Coalbrookdale, England. It was not an iron bridge as we might conceive of it today, but rather a traditional arch made of iron instead of stone. The compressive strength of limestone is 20 tons per square foot. The compressive strength of cast iron is 10 tons per square inch, 72 times as high, permitting significantly larger spans. Later, the truss, long used in timber roofs, became the primary element of bridge building. A triangle is the strongest structural element known, and applied force only makes it more stable. When a diagonal is added to a square, the form can be viewed as two triangles sharing a side, the fundamental element of a truss. Trusses were used to build bridges of unprecedented strength throughout the 19th century, including cantilever bridges consisting of truss com-

plexes balanced on supporting piers. A third, more attractive type of steel bridge was the suspension bridge, in which the roadway is hung from steel cables strung from supporting towers in giant catenary arcs.

As with bridges, some of the first structural advances using steel were prompted by the railroads. Trains required bridges and rails to get them where they were going, but once there, they required a depot and storage sheds. These sheds had to be of an unprecedented scale, large enough to enclose several tracks and high enough to allow smoke and fumes to dissipate. Trusses spanned the open area of the tracks, creating a steel skeleton hung with steel–framed glass panes. The structures were extraordinarily light and open. Some of the sheds were huge, such as St. Pancras Station, London, England. To the people of the nineteenth century these sheds were breathtaking, the largest contiguous enclosed space the world had ever seen.

At this point the capabilities of iron and steel had been proven and it was natural to extend the idea to another utilitarian application—factories. The first iron frame factory was built in 1796-97 in Shrewsbury, England, followed rapidly by a seven story cotton mill with cast iron columns and ceiling beams. Wrought iron beams were developed in 1850, a significant advance over brittle cast iron versions.

The new materials were not just used as skeletal elements. In the 1850s, 60s, and 70s, cast iron was used as a facade treatment, especially in the Soho district of New York City. Buildings such as the Milan Galleria, an indoor shopping area, and the Bibliotheque Nationale in Paris used iron as an internal structural and decorative element. In 1851, the Crystal Palace was built for the London Exposition, truly the Chartres Cathedral of its time. In 1889, Gustav Eiffel built the Eiffel Tower for the Exposition Universelle in Paris, initially the target of harsh criticism and now the symbol of Paris.

The Industrial Revolution provided more than just ferrous building materials. A stronger, more durable and fire resistant type of cement called Portland Cement was developed in 1824. The new material was still limited by low tensile strength, however, and could not be used in many structural applications. By a stroke of good fortune, the thermal expansion properties of the new cement were almost identical to those of iron and steel. In a creative leap, nineteenth century builders came up with the idea of reinforced concrete. Though expensive, iron and steel had high tensile strength and could be easily formed into long, thin bars. Enclosed in cheap, easily formed concrete, the bars were protected from fire and weather. The result was a strong, economical, easily produced structural member that could take almost any form imaginable, including columns, beams, arches, vaults, and decorative elements. It is still one of the most common building materials used today.

The modern era

In the mid–nineteenth century, Viollet–le–Duc published a series of tracts on architecture. He decried the fact that with the notable exception of engineers like Eiffel, new structures were being built with old methods. In the face of the new material, architects had either substituted the new material for the old (the Coalbrookdale Bridge), or adapted old methods to the new material (the truss). What architecture needed, according to Viollet, was to uncover new methods that tapped the potential of the new materials.

Some of the most significant advances in architecture at this point were made by a group of architects collectively known as the Chicago School, developers of the modern skyscraper. The skyscraper was developed in response to the rising price of city land. To maximize use of ground space, it was necessary to construct buildings sixteen or more stories tall. Initial attempts included iron frame construction with heavy masonry walls requiring massive, space consuming piers. This was an extension of the traditional methods in which the exterior walls of a building added structural support, unnecessary in the face of iron/steel framing. The approach was merely an adaptation, at a time when a completely new approach was needed.

The solution, developed in Chicago, was to separate the load–bearing frame of the building from a non–structural facade. The facade became a curtain wall that was supported by the steel frame story by story. Because the facade material on a given story supported only itself, it could be very light and thin. The further evolution of this approach by architects of the Chicago School led to the modern skyscraper, with its fireproof steel frame, curtain wall facade, and internal wind bracing.

Much of the architecture of the twentieth century has been a process of refinement, of learning to work with the multitude of new materials and techniques presented by the Industrial Revolution. The various movements, such as art nouveau, art deco, modernism, and postmodernism have all been about design and ornamentation rather than major structural innovation. Certainly architects during this period have explored the possibilities of the new materials and construction techniques. Most recently, however, architecture has been working through a revival period in which old

styles are being reinterpreted, similar to the 18th century. Perhaps, like the eighteenth century, we are poised at the start of a new period of innovation.

This entry is only a brief discussion of the role of technical advances in the history of architecture. It is by no means a thorough discussion of architecture itself. Technology permits architecture, but architecture is not about technology. What is architecture? It can perhaps best be expressed in the words of Le Corbusier, one of the most influential architects of the twentieth century: "You employ stone, wood, concrete, and with these materials you build houses and palaces. This is construction. Ingenuity is at work. But suddenly you touch

---

KEY TERMS

Barrel vault—A vault made of a series of rounded arches.

Buttress—A masonry pier designed to give extra lateral support to walls supporting arches.

Curtain wall—A non–loadbearing facade that is supported by the steel frame of the building.

Flying buttress—A buttress incorporating arches that applies force at the arch/column interface.

Groin vault—A vault made of the intersection of two barrel vaults.

Nave—The long central portion of a church or cathedral.

Pendentive—An inverted concave masonry triangle used to support a hemispherical dome.

Pier—A vertical support element, usually extremely massive.

Piazza—Italian for plaza or square.

Post and lintel—A structural form consisting of a horizontal element (lintel) resting on two support posts. Also called trabeation.

Squinch—Diagonal elements crossing the corners of a rectangular room to supply additional support for a dome.

Trabeation—A structural form consisting of a horizontal element (lintel) resting on two support posts. Also called post and lintel construction.

Truss—A very light, yet extremely strong structural form consisting of triangular elements, usually made of iron, steel, or wood.

Vault—A roof made using various types of arches.

---

my heart, you do me good, I am happy and I say 'This is beautiful.' That is Architecture. Art enters in."

See also Brick; Bridges; Concrete; Cranes; Industrial Revolution; Stone and masonry.

Further Reading:

Allen, Edward. *The Architect's Studio Companion*; New York, NY: John Wiley & Sons, 1989.

Allen, Edward. *Fundamentals of Building Construction*; New York, NY: John Wiley & Sons, 1985.

Ching, Francis D. *Architecture: Space, Form, and Order*; New York, NY: Van Nostrand Reinhold, 1979.

McCoy, Esther. *Case Study Houses, 1945–1962*; Santa Monica, CA: Hennessey & Dyalls Inc., 1977.

Trachtenberg, Marvin, and Isabelle Hyman, *Architecture from Prehistory to Postmodern*; Englewood Cliffs, NJ: Prentice Hall Inc., 1986.

Kristin Lewotsky and Stephen K. Lewotsky

Bulbuls

Bulbuls are about 120 species of medium–sized, perching birds, distributed among fifteen genera, and making up the family Pyncnontidae. The most diverse genus is *Pycnonotus*, with about 50 species. Bulbuls are mostly tropical and subtropical birds, occurring in Africa, Asia, and Southeast Asia. Some relatively northern species are migratory, but most species of bulbuls are local birds.

Bulbuls have rather short, rounded wings, a long tail, small, relatively delicate legs and feet, a small, slender bill, and prominent bristles about the base of the top mandible (these are known as rictal bristles). The body size of bulbuls ranges from 6–11 in (15–28 cm).

The coloration of bulbul species is commonly black or grey, often with reddish markings, and sometimes with a distinctive crest on the top of the head. Male and female birds look very similar, as do juvenile birds, although their coloration is more subdued than that of adults.

Bulbuls build a cup–shaped nest in a bush or tree, and lay two to four eggs. Both parents share in the incubation and care of the young.

Species of bulbuls occur in diverse tropical habitats, but not in deserts. They may occur in dense vegetation in tropical forests or in more open habitats, such as gardens in towns or even city parks. Some species of

bulbuls are accomplished singers, and they are among the more pleasing avian vocalists in tropical towns and parks where habitat is available for these birds.

Most species of bulbuls eat small fruits, but they may also feed on insects, particularly when they are raising babies, which require high–protein foods. Both parents feed and care for the young, which typically fledge about two weeks after hatching. During the non–breeding season, bulbuls often occur in mixed–species flocks with other bulbuls, and sometimes with birds of other families.

The black bulbul (*Hypsipetes madagascariensis*) is a wide–ranging species, occurring in young forests and other disturbed habitats from Madagascar to Southeast Asia. This species has an all–black plumage, but red legs, feet, bill, and eyes.

The red–whiskered bulbul (*Pycnonotus jocosus*) is a common and familiar species of open habitats from India, through south China, to mainland Southeast Asia. This distinctively head–crested species has also been introduced to Australia, Mauritius, Fiji, and southern Florida.

The yellow–crowned bulbul (*Pycnonotus zeylanicus*) of Malaya, Borneo, Sumatra, and Java is an especially accomplished singer, and is sometimes kept in that region as a caged songbird.

Bulimia see **Eating disorders**
Bullheads see **Catfish**
Bullrushes see **Sedges**

Bunsen burner

Named after the German chemist Robert Wilhelm Bunsen, who contributed to its development, the Bunsen burner was already known to Michael Faraday, who may have created the first design. The idea behind the Bunsen burner is to reduce the considerable loss in heat energy typical in ordinary gas burners. This reduction of energy waste is accomplished by using a mixture of gas and air, the optimal proportion being three volumes of air to one of gas, instead of pure gas. As a result, combustion is intensified, producing a nonluminous but remarkably hot flame.

The Bunsen burner consists essentially of a long metal tube set on a flat base. Gas enters the burner through a hole in the bottom of the tube. Some burners have a gas adjustment screw that allows one to control the amount of gas entering the tube. With burners lacking a gas adjustment screw, gas flow can be controlled only at the supply valve. A second opening at the bottom of the metal tube allows air to enter and mix with the gas. The air inlet may be the bottom opening of the tube itself, or it may be a pair of holes cut into the tube, near the base. The amount of air entering the tube in the former design with controlled by a flat piece of metal that can be slid across the hole to allow more or less air to enter. Some burners have threaded bases that allow the air supply to be controlled by turning the tube. In the second design described above, air supply is controlled by a collar that covers the hole in the tube. The collar can be rotated to allow more or less air to enter the tube.

The gas–air mixture is ignited at the top of the barrel. The flame produced at this point commonly consists of two cones. The outer cone is blue, while the inner remains quite pale, almost invisible. The hottest part of the burner flame is at the tip of the inner cone, where a rich supply of air ensures the nearly total combustion of the gas. The temperature at this point may be in excess of 3272° F (1800° C) in an inexpensive laboratory burner.

Beyond the laboratory, the the principle of Bunsen combustion is widely used in industry, in gas furnaces, and in everyday life, as exemplified by the kitchen gas range.

See also Combustion.

Buntings see **Sparrows and buntings**

Buoyancy, principle of

The principle of buoyancy is called Archimedes' Principle, since it was discovered by this Greek mathematician in the third century B.C. The principle states that the buoyant force acting on an object placed in a fluid is equal to the weight of the fluid displaced by the object. An object completely immersed in a fluid (liquid or gas) displaces a volume of fluid exactly equal to the volume of the object. The weight of that volume of displaced fluid is the buoyant force acting on the object.

The high salt content of the Dead Sea contributes to increased buoyancy.

What causes buoyancy?

Fluids such as water or air exert pressure in all directions and the amount of pressure depends on the depth of the fluid. The pressure on the bottom of an object immersed in a fluid will be greater than the pressure on the top of the object. The imbalance of pressure acting on the object creates an upward force called the buoyant force. If the buoyant force is greater than the weight of the object, the object will float. If the buoyant force is less than the weight of the object, the object will sink in the fluid.

The density of a fluid is its weight per unit of volume. Liquids and gases exhibit widely different densities. The buoyant force, or the weight of the volume of displaced fluid, will depend on the density of the fluid as well as the displaced volume. Fresh water has a density of 62.4 pounds per cubic foot (pcf), salt water density is, on average, 64 pcf. Air at sea level has a density of 0.08 pcf and at 10,000 ft (3,050 m), 0.06 pcf. Salt water is denser than fresh water because of its salt content, and, as a result, a swimmer is more buoyant in the ocean than in a fresh water lake. The density of salt water depends on its salinity and varies around the world. The molecular structure of water expands when it freezes, therefore, ice is less dense than liquid water. As a result, ice cubes float and lakes freeze from the top down rather than the bottom up.

Boats and bladders and blimps

Steel has a density of 487 pcf, about eight times that of water. Steel boats float, however, because they are hollow and shaped to displace a volume of water that weighs more than the boat's weight. Ships are often rated by their displacement. Displacement is measured in units called tons which are the weight of

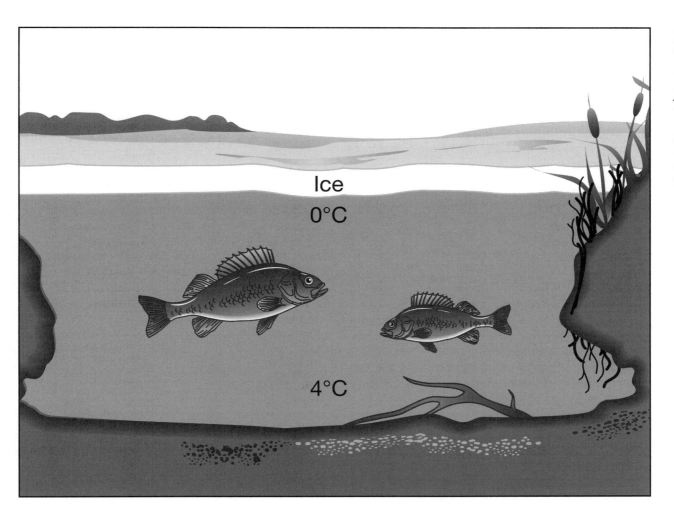

The molecular structure of water begins to expand once it cools beyond 4°C (39.4°F) and continues to expand until it becomes ice. For this reason, ice is less dense than water, floats on the surface, and retards further cooling of deeper water, which accounts for the survival of freshwater plant and animal life through the winter.

the water displaced by the ship. As a ship is loaded with cargo, it settles deeper into the water. This displaces an additional volume of water and produces the greater buoyant force required to support the added load. Plimsoll marks are painted onto the hull of cargo ships to indicate the depth to which the ship could be loaded. The different marks refer to fresh and salt water and to the various seasons where temperature also effect water density.

Fish can alter their buoyancy by changing the volume of their internal swim bladder. Scuba divers can inflate their external buoyancy compensator vest to change its volume. Both of these changes alter the amount of displaced water and, thus, the buoyant force acting on the body. With this control, divers and fish can ascend or descend at will as they observe each other at play.

The principle of buoyancy applies to all fluids, including gases. A blimp is filled with very light helium gas with a density of 0.01 pcf. As a result, the weight of the blimp is less than the weight of the air that it displaces and the blimp will float in air. By dropping ballast or venting helium, the blimp can control its buoyancy and, thus, its altitude. A hot air balloon gets it buoyancy because hot air is less dense than cold air. The density of air at 200°F (93°C) at sea level is 0.06 pcf and serves the same function as the light helium gas in the blimp. Although highly flammable, hydrogen gas is much less dense than helium and was used for lift in dirigibles up until 1937, when the German airship *Hindenberg* burned and crashed.

See also Balloon; Density; Pressure

Richard A. Jeryan

Buret

A buret (also spelled burette) is a long glass tube open at both ends, that is used to measure out precise volumes of liquids or gases. Most burets are about 1 mm in diameter and 75 cm long. The bottom of a buret is tapered so that its diameter is only about 0.1 mm in diameter. Burets are most commonly designed to hold volumes of 1 mL or less.

Fluid is dispensed form a buret through a glass stopcock at the lower end of the glass tube. The stopcock consists of an inner piece of ground glass that fits tightly into the glass tube and that can be rotated in a tightly fitting casing. The stopcock allows a fluid to be released in very small, precise amounts. Commercially available burets can usually be read with an accuracy of ±0.01 mL.

Probably the most familiar application of a buret is in the process known as titration. In this process, accurately measured amounts of two solutions are allowed to react with each other in order to determine the concentration of one. Burets have far more uses, however. A single buret can be used, for example, to release a known volume of a solution of known concentration in order to determine the mass of an unknown solid. Oxidation–reduction reactions can also be studied quantitatively using burets.

Gas–dispensing burets consist of arrangements in which some gas is contained by and forced out of a graduated cylindrical tube by means of some liquid, such as mercury. In their appearance, gas burets look something like an upside–down version of their liquid counterparts.

Burets became necessary in chemical research only with the development of relatively precise analytical techniques in the eighteenth century. Credit for their invention is usually given to the French chemist Joseph Louis Gay–Lussac, who first developed them for the purpose of assaying silver.

Burn

A burn is damage to an area of the body, internal or external, resulting from application of excess heat, overexposure to sunlight or other radiation, or contact with a caustic chemical. A burn can be a minor, hardly noticeable irritation or it can be of such severity as to be life threatening. Burns are classified as first–, second–, or third–degree (now called full–thickness) depending upon the depth of the burn and damage to the tissue. A full–thickness burn is a severe burn.

The skin

To understand burns and their severity, one must first explore the functions of the skin. The skin is the largest organ of the body. It covers the outer surface and serves multiple purposes.

Its primary function is that of protection. The skin prevents bacteria, dirt, and other foreign materials from getting into the body and initiating an infection. Probably trillions of bacterial cells rest on the human skin at any one time. Cutting or puncturing the skin offers bacteria and viruses an entry into the area of the body that is most hospitable to them. An intact skin is the outermost defense against this occurrence.

The skin is far more than simply a dry envelope, however. It aids in regulating the body temperature by sweating. The inner layer of the skin contains sweat and oil glands that discharge their products through pores in the outer skin. The oil keeps skin supple and the sweat aids in ridding the body of waste products and also, on hot days, helps to cool the internal temperature. Evaporation of the sweat cools the skin surface.

Beneath the skin the body fluids circulate between and in and out of the cells. Blood, serum, lymph, water, and other materials can move from place to place because the outer skin prevents their loss. Destruction of wide areas of the outer skin, as occurs in full–thickness burns, however, allows the body fluids to drain and evaporate at a great rate. If the burn is extensive enough the loss of fluids can become critical.

First–degree burns

A first–degree burn is the mildest burn and seldom poses any problem other than an irritation. A mild sunburn or a small burn received by touching a hot pan are examples of first–degree burns. The affected area of skin turns a darker color. No blisters are evident and the skin is not broken.

An extensive sunburn, affecting the entire back, back of the legs and arms, and back of the neck, while widespread, still is a first–degree burn. It will be tender to touch, irritated and by clothing, but it poses no hazard and usually will not require medical attention. Application of a soothing antisunburn agent available at most drugstores will dampen the heat and ease the area back to normalcy.

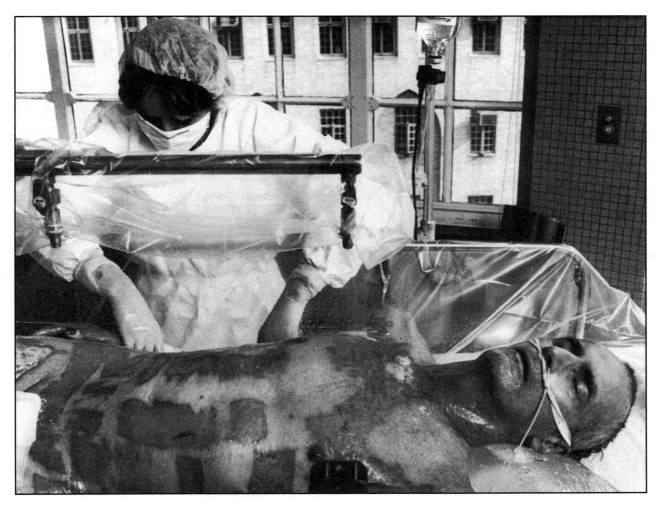

A burn sufferer undergoes debridement (the removal of dead skin). The patterns on his chest are from skin grafts.

A sunburn is the reaction of the skin to ultraviolet light rays of a wavelength of about 3,000 angstroms. Skin reaction will be apparent in one to 24 hours, and even the most severe reactions will peak in about 72 hours. However, after such a sunburn the skin will be more susceptible to another such burn because the original sunburn resulted in skin cells being shed and some protection lost. A subsequent sunburn may be much more severe than the first one because of the newly exposed underlayer of skin. Fair–skinned individuals will not tan, but will shed the outer layer of skin. These individuals are especially susceptible to sunburn and should stay out of the Sun or well wrapped.

Second–degree burns

A slightly more severe condition than first–degree burns, the appearance of blisters on the skin indicates that the burn is second degree. The burn damage extends through the outer layer of the skin to the underlying dermis. Vesicles or blisters form, indicating the loss of fluid from the cells.

Second–degree burns are more painful and slower to heal, but not significantly, than lighter burns. The damage does not interfere with replacement of lost skin cells and the pain can be relieved by over–the–counter burn relief medications. Extensive second–degree burns may result in lost work time because tight clothing can break the blisters and irritate the underlying raw tissue. Loose, nonbinding clothing is necessary if one has a second–degree burn on the trunk or legs.

Again, the skin is more susceptible to another burn if the original burn was the result of overexposure to sunlight. Some of the protective outer layer of skin cells have been sloughed off and the inner layer, not yet hardened, burns easily.

Touching the hand or other part of the body to a hot object or having hot embers contact the skin also can result in second–degree burns. The result is the same as if sunburn had caused the lesion: the skin changes color and fluid leaks from between the cells under the skin and forms liquid–filled blisters on the surface of the skin. It is best that the blisters be punctured and drained from a pinhole than to wear chafing clothing over them that will rub off the entire skin surface. If need be a light bandage can be placed over the burned area to protect it.

Full–thickness burns

Third–degree, or full–thickness burns are the most severe. Sunburns are never so advanced. The burn damage includes destruction of the epidermis and dermis and possibly underlying tissue. At first, these burns may be difficult to distinguish from second–degree burns because blisters may form early, but they soon will slough off and the area of tissue destruction will become evident.

A more serious category of full–thickness burns, called fourth–degree burns, are those that penetrate the skin and burn into the underlying muscles and perhaps even into bones. Such burns will require extensive therapy, grafts, and rebuilding of the affected tissues as well as follow–up physical therapy to restore full function to the affected limb. Burns of this severity can result in loss of function of an extremity because muscle and nerve are destroyed.

Such burns result most often from the direct exposure of skin to open flame or very hot substances such as molten metal. Tissue destruction can be deep and, if widespread, dangerous. A full–thickness burn, even a very localized one, will require medical attention because of the distinct possibility that an infection will develop in the burned area. In addition, a widespread full–thickness burn allows the escape of fluid from the burn area and may result in dehydration of the patient. Special measures may need to be applied to hydrate the burned person.

These burns often require skin transplants to cover the burn area. The depth of the burn allows blood and fluid to escape and also provides a very easy route for invasion of infectious agents. If left unattended, the burn area may start to heal from the edges and formation of scar tissue will result. This will draw the wound area together in a taut and painful scar that may interfere with normal function of a hand, for example. Skin grafting prevents such a result and allows the area to heal in a way that will preserve function.

Third– and fourth–degree burns, if they involve a large enough area of the body, are life threatening. Someone who has suffered a third–degree burn over, say, 50% of his body is facing a long and painful course of recovery that must be carefully monitored to prevent secondary infections. The loss of fluid through such a widespread area of damage may be more rapid than the fluid can be replaced. Surprisingly, there is usually little pain with such burns because the nerve endings have been burned away with the tissue. The pain involved results from the therapy that must be applied. Debriding the area, which is the removal of destroyed tissue, charred skin, and any foreign material in the burn, is a painful and time–consuming process.

Widespread full–thickness burns offer the double hazard of entry for infectious agents and an open area for body fluids to escape. Covering the burned area with grafts will help to seal it, will protect the interior of the body from infection, and will prevent the formation of scars. Scar tissue is a nonfunctional tissue that has little elasticity, which means that it can interfere with proper functioning of an extremity. For moderate burns the needed skin graft can be obtained from other areas of the patient's body. A thin patch of skin is removed and is put through a machine that punctures the graft so that it can be expanded, somewhat like the lattice topping of a pie. The area covered by the perforated skin is much greater than is the area that could be covered by the intact skin patch.

Man–made materials also can be used as skin grafts. Individuals who have a full–thickness burn that covers most of their body cannot spare the skin for a graft. Man–made materials can be applied to the burned area to seal it off and allow natural skin to grow back. Whatever the method, treatment of a full–thickness burn is a long and involved procedure that must be closely followed to achieve the desired cure.

Scalds

Scalding, that is burning by steam or hot liquid, differs from contact burns or sunburns. Small children are especially prone to scalds because in their curiosity they may pull a pan from the stove and spill hot water or grease on themselves.

The scalded skin will be painful and in severe cases the skin will be of a lighter color than normal. Skin reaction eventually will parallel that of sunburn or contact burn. A minor scald will result in skin color change and little else. A more severe one will result in the formation of blisters and even tissue destruction. Inhaling steam can burn the lining of the nose, larynx, and trachea, and if hot enough, the bronchi and lungs. Formation of scar tissue following a burn inside the respiratory tract is a serious and possibly lethal situation.

Preventing burns

Obviously, burn prevention is the best measure. Avoiding first– and second–degree burns can be accomplished by spending shorter time spans in the Sun, using an effective sunscreen, and taking care in the kitchen or other areas in which one is at risk for burn.

Light–skinned individuals are more prone to painful sunburn than are people with darker skins. The lack of melanin in the lighter skin offers less protection from the burning ultraviolet rays. Some individuals do not burn readily, but tan quickly when exposed to the Sun. This is the reaction of the melanin–producing cells in the lower level of the skin, which release the dark melanin granules to spread into the epidermis and shield the skin from damaging sun rays. Redhaired people do not have a sufficient number of melanin–producing cells to provide a protective layer. Light–skinned people will burn instead of tan and the burn will be painful and may blister.

Skin that is repeatedly exposed to sunlight is at higher risk for the development of skin cancer. Though it is usually not fatal, skin cancer requires medical attention to prevent its spreading. Those who have close relatives who have had skin cancer are at increased risk for developing it. These individuals should avoid "sunbathing" or they should wear an effective sunscreen when out of doors.

Chemical burns

Chemical burns differ from radiant burns in that the skin has no protective mechanism to prevent them. With radiation, the melanin cells spread melanin in the skin to block ultraviolet light from penetrating. With chemical burns no such protective measure exists.

Chemical burns can occur with the application of acids, strong alkali (such as lye), or other agents. Some 25,000 industrial chemicals (of about 300,000 in use) can produce chemical burns, either internal or external. Also, the eyes are vulnerable to chemical burns. Ideally the worker who is using dangerous materials wears goggles and other protective gear, but the home craftsman may not. Alkalis burn into the eyes rapidly and deeply. Acids burn rapidly, but usually are neutralized by the tears before they burn deeply.

KEY TERMS

Angstrom—A unit of length equal to 100–millionth of a centimeter, usually applied to electromagnetic wavelengths.

Dermis—The internal layer of skin. It contains the sweat and oil glands, hair follicles, and provides replacement cells for those that are shed from the outer layer.

Epidermis—The outer layer of the skin consisting of dead cells. It is the primary protective barrier against sunlight, chemicals, and other possible harmful agents. The epidermal cells are constantly being shed and replenished.

Graft—The attachment of skin to an injured area. The new skin, natural or artificial, will prevent the loss of fluids and provide the means for a new, intact layer of skin to form.

Hydration—Restoring fluids to the body. Deep and extensive burns allow the escape of fluids needed for proper body functions. Restoring those fluids is called hydration.

Initially chemical burns may appear to be mild, but during the following day or so the injured tissue may slough off and the extent of the injury will be revealed. Chemical burns may occur from unexpected sources. Dry cement, for example, because of its lime content, is capable of causing burns if one's skin is exposed to it for hours. Gasoline can penetrate skin and cause a burn if one is exposed to it for some hours. Never use fuel to clean the hands or use it in any other way that would result in long–term exposure. Surprisingly, air bags in automobiles have burned some accident victims. The bags inflate explosively upon impact to cushion the car's occupants. However, the gas that inflates the bag is hot when it is released from the cylinder. Several burns from contact with inflating air bags have been reported.

Household chemicals can be as dangerous as industrial ones. Drain openers, for example, are based on lye with other additives and can be responsible for serious burns. Lawn fertilizer should never be handled with bare hands, and any that gets on the skin should be rinsed off immediately.

Obviously, chemicals present a ready source for burns, internal and external. It is important that these materials be stored out of reach of young people and that they be used with great care. Protective clothing, gloves, and goggles should be worn whenever one is working with such chemicals. Spills and splashes should be cleaned up immediately and any chemical that contacts the skin should be rinsed off quickly. Excess chemicals or empty containers should be disposed of with care and in accordance with existing regulations. Empty containers should not be saved for reuse.

Further Reading:

Englebardt S.L. "A Rage against Dying." *Reader's Digest* 144 (May 1994): 161–162+.

Larry Blaser

Burro see **Asses**

Bushbabies see **Lorises**

Bushbuck see **Antelopes and gazelles**

Bushmaster see **Snakes**

Bustards

Bustards are 22 species of tall birds that make up the family Otidae. Bustards occur in relatively open habitats in Africa, central and southern Europe and Asia, Southeast Asia, and Australia. Most species, however, are African.

Bustards are large birds, with species ranging in body length from 14.5–52 in (37–132 cm), and in weight from 1–48 lbs (0.6–22 kg). Bustards have a stocky body, a long neck, and stout legs and feet, with three toes pointing forward, and no hind toe. The wings are broad, and the tail is short. The bill is stout, flattened, and blunt.

Bustards are colored in various subdued hues and patterns of brown, buff, grey, black, and white. Bustards are sexually dimorphic, with males being larger and more brightly colored than females.

Some species of bustards occur during the non-breeding season in flocks of various size. Bustards walk while feeding, and although they can fly, they tend to run to escape from predators. Bustards have keen vision, and are wary and difficult to approach closely on foot. Bustards are omnivores, eating a wide range of plant and animal foods. Bustards predate on large insects such as grasshoppers and beetles, as well as on small reptiles and nestling birds.

Bustards nest on the ground, and lay one to five eggs. The female incubates the eggs and cares for the young birds, which are precocious and can leave their nest soon after hatching.

Species of bustards

The great bustard (*Otis tarda*) occurs in scattered populations in Eurasia. Its present distribution is greatly reduced compared with several centuries ago because of overhunting and conversions of its natural habitat to agriculture. However, this species is still abundant in some places where its seasonal flocks can contain as many as 500 birds. The male great bustard has a spectacular courtship display in which internal air sacs are expanded to greatly puff out the chest while white plumes are erected on the wings, tail, breast, and head. This strutting display is generally performed on slightly raised ground, in front of a hopefully appreciative audience of as many as six female birds.

The little bustard (*Otis tetrax*) is another Eurasian species with a similarly wide distribution as the great bustard. This and the preceding species undertake seasonal migrations, flying south from the northern parts of their range. The Houbara or MacQueen's bustard (*Chlamydotis undulata*) occurs from the Canary Islands off western Africa, through North Africa, as far as southwestern Asia.

The Australian bustard (*Ardeotis australis*) is the only species to occur on that continent. This species

A Kori bustard (*Ardeotis kori*) near Masai Mara, Kenya.

utilizes rather dense, shrubby habitat, in contrast to the open spaces preferred by other species of bustards.

The smallest bustards are the lesser florican (*Sypheotides indica*) and the Bengal florican (*Houbaropsis bengalensis*) of India. The world's heaviest flying bird is the great bustard, which can achieve a weight of 48 lbs (22 kg). Other large species include those in the genus *Ardeotis*, such as the Kori bustard (*A. kori*) of Southern Africa.

Bustards and humans

Bustards are large, palatable birds, and they are hunted for sport or as food in most parts of their range. Some species of bustards have become endangered through the combined effects of overhunting and conversions of their habitat to agricultural land uses. Other species, while not endangered, have had their breeding ranges significantly reduced. The great bustard, for example, was extirpated in England in 1832.

Further Reading:

Brooke, M. and T. Birkhead. *The Cambridge Encyclopedia of Ornithology.* Cambridge, U.K.: Cambridge University Press, 1991.
Harrison, C. J. O., ed. *Bird Families of the World.* New York: H.N. Abrams Pubs., 1978.
Johnsgard, P. A. *Bustards, Hemipodes, and Sandgrouse.* Oxford, U.K.: Oxford University Press, 1991.

Bill Freedman

Butane see **Hydrocarbon**

Butcher-birds see **Shrikes**

Buttercup

Buttercups and crowfoots are about 275 species of plants in the genus *Ranunculus*, family Ranunculaceae. Buttercups mostly occur in cool and temperate regions of both hemispheres of the world, including mountains in tropical latitudes.

Buttercups are annual or perennial, and they are herbaceous plants, dying back to the ground surface before the winter. The leaves of terrestrial species are simple or compound. However, the underwater leaves of aquatic buttercups can be very finely divided. Some of the aquatic buttercups have dimorphic foliage, with delicately divided leaves in the water, and distinctly broader leaves in the atmosphere.

The flowers of buttercups have numerous stamens and pistils, arranged in a spiral fashion on a central axis. The flowers of most species of buttercups are radially symmetric and showy, owing to their large, yellow petals. However, some species have red or white petals. The petals secrete nectar, important in attracting the insects that are the pollinators of most buttercups. There are usually five sepals, but these generally fall off the flower relatively soon. The fruits are loose heads of one–seeded fruits called achenes.

Many species of buttercups are native to North America. The wood buttercup (*Ranunculus abortivus*) is a widespread species of rich, temperate forests. The yellow water–crowfoot (*R. gmelini*) is a widespread species of freshwater marshes and shores, while the seashore–buttercup (*R. cymbalaria*) occurs in salt marshes and estuaries. Many native species of buttercups occur in alpine and arctic tundras, for example, the Lapland buttercup (*R. lapponicus*) and snow buttercup (*R. nivalis*).

Several species of Eurasian buttercups have been introduced to North America, where they have become widespread weeds of lawns, fields, and other disturbed places. Some of the more familiar introduced species are the tall or meadow buttercup (*R. acris*), the creeping buttercup (*R. repens*), and the corn crowfoot or hunger–weed (*R. arvensis*).

A few species of buttercups are used in horticulture. The most commonly used species for this purpose is the garden buttercup (*R. asiaticus*), available in varieties with white, red, or yellow–colored flowers. Aquatic buttercups, such as the water crowfoot (*R. aquatilis*), are sometimes cultivated in garden pools. Various alpine species of buttercups can be planted in rock gardens.

Meadow buttercups (*Ranunculus acris*).

Butterfly fish

Butterfly fish (family Chaetodontidae) are some of the most colorful and varied fish of the oceans, the majority of which live on or close to coral reefs. Most species measure from 5–9.5 in (13–24 cm) in length and have deep, flattened bodies that are frequently adorned by extended fins. In some species these may form a large arc over the body. In addition to refinements in the body shape, the colors and patterns of most butterfly fish are quite enthralling. The head and body is usually a dark background color which is broken up by a series of stripes and other patterns. Coloration varies considerably but often includes patches of yellow, orange, blue, and white. A "false eye" is commonly seen on some butterfly fish; this is usually located towards the back of the fish or even on a fin, the objective being to distract a striking predator from the butterfly fish's own head.

Like the parrotfish and wrasses, butterfly fish swim by synchronous rowing strokes of the pectoral fins, while the tail fin is used as a rudder for direction and balance. They are capable of very rapid movement and rely largely on their agility to avoid capture from other larger species. Butterfly fish are strictly diurnal, exploiting the diversity of feeding and living spaces in and around coral reefs and atolls. As dusk approaches, however, most begin to seek out a safe hiding place where they will rest for the night.

Butterfly fish are specialist feeders: many species have the mouth placed at the end of a short, tubular snout that facilitates the animals poking into tiny crevices in coralline reefs and extracting prey from seemingly inaccessible places. Their diet may either be restricted to living polyps plucked from just a few coral species, while other members of the family spare the polyps themselves, preferring to graze on algae growing on the corals. Some even actively pursue small shrimps and copepods that lurk within the many crevices of the reef face.

The social behavior of butterfly fish varies according to the particular species. Many species are solitary, but some do form stable monogamous relationships with a member of the opposite sex. In the latter case, the two fish commonly patrol and defend a particular patch of coral against other members of the same species. A series of threat and aggressive gestures including color changes have evolved in these species which help prevent aggressive encounters from developing. Spawning frequently occurs at dusk—a strategy that may have evolved to increase the survival rates of young butterfly fish, as many of the tiny plankton feeders are less active in the evening.

Butterflies

Butterflies are insects in the order Lepidoptera, which also includes the moths. Butterflies at rest fold their wings vertically over their heads, whereas moths at rest hold their wings horizontally, and most butterflies are active during daylight hours, while moths are mostly nocturnal. Butterflies undergo complete metamorphosis, that is, eggs give rise to the larva (caterpillar), which pupates in a chrysalis, from which emerges the adult (imago) butterfly.

Evolution

Butterflies probably evolved about 150 million years ago, appearing about the same time as flowering plants. Butterflies are found throughout the world, except in Antarctica, and are especially numerous in the tropics. Of the 220,000 species of Lepidoptera, only 45,000 species are butterflies, which probably evolved from moths. They fall into eight families—Papilionidae (swallowtails), Pieridae (whites), Danaidae (milkweeds), Satyridae (browns), Morphidae (morphos), Nymphalidae (nymphalids), Lycaenidae (blues), and Hesperidae (skippers).

Development and life cycle

The butterfly's brief adult life—one week for some species and up to 10 months for a few others—is spent in mating and, for the female, egg laying. The female lays eggs on the food plant upon which the caterpillar must feed, selecting plants in the most favorable stage of development. Eggs are laid on leaves, flowers, or stems; some species of butterfly lay eggs on tree bark or even stones, leaving the newly hatched caterpillars to find their own specific food plant. A few species of butterfly even lay their eggs while in flight, the eggs attaching to grasses as they fall.

The egg

By the time most female butterflies emerge from the chrysalis, their eggs are fully mature, permitting immediate fertilization. Following mating, minute pores in the egg allow entry of the male sperm for fertilization. Eggs are laid singly, in rows, in clusters, or in rings around a plant stem, and are highly vulnerable to predators and parasites. Each female lays up to 600 eggs at a time. A sticky substance produced by the female during egg laying glues the eggs to the plant. Most eggs hatch within a few days, although those of some species remain dormant over winter, and hatch in spring.

The caterpillar

The larval stage of butterflies is the caterpillar, which emerges from the egg fully formed. Caterpillars see by means of groups of tiny eyes on each side of the head. The body of the caterpillar is protected by bristly hairs and has 16 legs. Three pairs of legs, called the true legs because they become the legs of the adult butterfly, are on the thorax behind the head; four pairs of legs are found on the abdomen, and are known as false, or prolegs; and there is a single pair of legs, called claspers, at the tip of the abdomen which grip tightly to the food plant. Prolegs and claspers also carry tiny hooks, which catch a silk thread spun by the larva as it moves about its food plant and which help keep it from falling. The silk thread is produced as a thick liquid,

A monarch butterfly (*Danaus plexippus*) in Livonia, Michigan. The larvae of this butterfly feed on the leaves of the milkweed, ingesting substances that make them toxic to birds and other predators.

excreted through glands near the mouth, which is then spun into a thread by the spinneret located behind the jaws.

The caterpillar spends most of its time eating. Its large jaws (the mandibles) move sideways, to consume its plant diet. The caterpillar munches its way through life—first eating its own egg shell (from which it gets important nutrients), then continuously consuming its favorite food plants. A small number of butterfly species have caterpillars that eat insects and other caterpillars. Caterpillars will eat more than twice their own weight each day, stopping only to shed their old skin, in order that they may grow. Skin shedding (molting or ecdysis) occurs about four times before the caterpillar is fully grown, with growth rates depending on temperature—faster in warm weather, and slower in cool temperatures. The caterpillar then seeks a protected place in which to pupate, forming a protective

shell and becoming dormant. Some caterpillars travel long distances (330 ft or 100 m) across roads, fields, and footpaths seeking a safe sheltered place to pupate.

The chrysalis

This protective case surrounding the pupating caterpillar takes many shapes, is usually brownish green in color, and is sometimes speckled to aid in camouflage. With a few exceptions, butterfly larvae pupate above ground, usually attached to a leaf or stem by a sticky silk thread. Inside the chrysalis the pupated caterpillar gradually transforms into a butterfly. The process takes two weeks for some species, several years for others. The developed butterfly inside the chrysalis swallows air, inflating its body and splitting the pupal skin. The perfectly formed adult butterfly struggles out shortly after dawn, its wet wings hanging limply from its thorax. Crawling to a place where it can hang by its legs, the newly emerged butterfly pumps up its wings (by once again swallowing air), increasing its blood pressure and forcing blood through the tiny veins in the wings. Within a couple of hours the expanded wings dry and harden, and the butterfly excretes the waste products produced during pupation. The butterfly is now free to begin the life cycle all over again.

The adult (imago)

Butterflies, like all insects, have an external skeleton, known as an exoskeleton, to which muscles are attached. The exoskeleton provides the butterfly's body with support and reduces water loss through evaporation. The respiratory system does not have a pumping mechanism. The sides of the thorax and abdomen have tiny pores (spiracles) through which air enters and leaves the body via tubes (tracheae). The insect's blood (hemolymph) is pumped as it passes through the long, thin heart, leaving the heart through tiny holes along its sides before bathing the organs inside the body cavity.

Two large compound eyes, made up of hundreds of tiny units (ommatidia) completely cover the butterfly's head and allow vision in all directions, including partially backward. However, the butterfly's eyes cannot distinguish detail nor determine distance, but readily identify color and movement, both of which are vital for the butterfly's survival. Colors aid in the identification of flowers, larval food plants, and the opposite sex, while detecting movement may save butterflies from attacks by predators.

The long, coiled proboscis (tongue) of the butterfly is projected into the center of flowers in search of nectar (liquid food). Above the eyes and on either side of the head are two antennae covered with microscopic

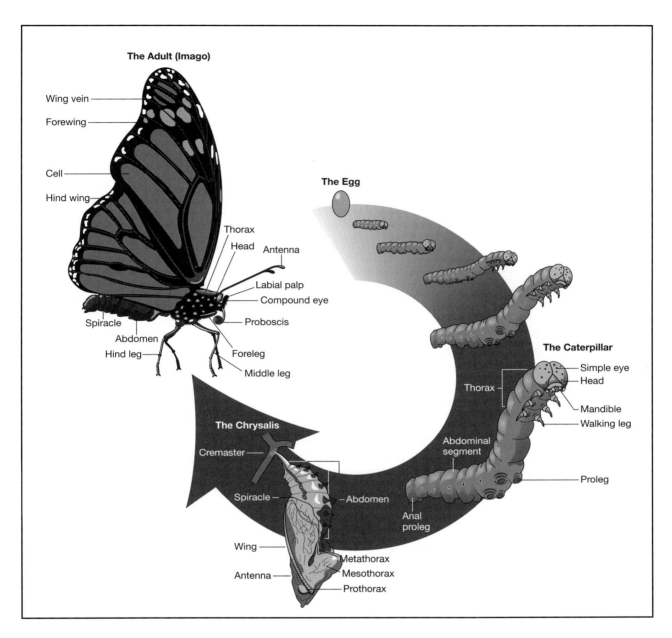

The Adult (Imago)

Wing vein

Forewing

Cell

Hind wing

Thorax

Head

Antenna

Labial palp

Compound eye

Spiracle

Proboscis

Abdomen

Hind leg

Foreleg

Middle leg

The Egg

The Caterpillar

Simple eye

Head

Thorax

Mandible

Walking leg

Abdominal
segment

Proleg

Anal
proleg

The Chrysalis

Cremaster

Spiracle

Abdomen

Wing

Metathorax

Antenna

Mesothorax

Prothorax

The life cycle of a butterfly.

sense organs. Antennae are often incorrectly called feelers; smellers would be more accurate, for it is through the antennae that the butterfly sniffs out its favorite food and potential mate. The antennae can detect pheromones—chemical signals released by the opposite sex—from great distances.

The butterfly's thorax is divided into three segments, each having one pair of legs. Each leg ends in a claw, enabling the butterfly to hold on while feeding and egg laying. Sensory receptors on the leg just above the claw detect the chemical makeup of plants and help to identify food plants.

The wings are the most spectacular part of the butterfly, and are extremely large compared to its body. The wings attach at the two rear segments of the thorax. Tough veins provide the framework which supports the wing membrane, which is covered by millions of microscopic scales arranged in rows like shingles on a roof. It is the wing scales—about 99,000 per sq in (2.5 sq cm)—which form the color and pattern of the wing and body. Brown, orange, and black tones are the basic pigments, while the brilliant, iridescent blues and greens are actually light waves bouncing off tiny facets on the surface of each scale, creating colors like light shining through a prism. The wing colors provide camouflage against predators and aid in identifying mates. Scales also cover the segmented abdomen in which the digestive organs and reproductive organs are located.

Reproduction

Reproduction in butterflies begins with courtship, with the male vigorously flapping its wings, releasing above the female's antennae a dust of microscopic scales carrying pheromones. These male pheromones act as a sexual stimulant to the female. Some males release additional pheromones from "hair pencils" under the abdomen. Female butterflies that are ready to mate dispense with courtship. Some species, however, perform complicated courtship maneuvers, one reason being, perhaps, to find a mate strong enough to endure the rigorous rituals, thereby increasing the chance of strong offspring. Males usually must wait one or two days after emerging from the chrysalis before mating, but then they may mate many times. Females can mate immediately after emerging, some species mating several times; the last male to mate fertilizes the eggs. Females of other species mate once only.

Migration

Most butterfly species live and die within a narrow geographic range, since their brief life span allows little time for wandering. A few species, however, such as the Monarch, migrate thousands of miles from Washington state to Mexico, the round trip taking two or three generations to complete because of the short individual life span. Each butterfly must find its own way, having no living guide, yet one species will follow the same migratory route year after year, century after century. It is not known what drives butterflies to migrate in massive numbers, forming colossal clouds of color sometimes a mile wide and a mile long; millions perish in the process.

Vulnerability and defense

Eggs, larvae, pupae, and adults are all vulnerable to disease, predators, environmental changes, and human intervention. Stable populations mean that only two eggs laid by each female will reach adulthood. Brilliantly colored butterflies are often toxic when ingested, so predators learn to leave them alone. Occasionally, a nonpoisonous species evolves that mimics the appearance of a poisonous species, thus being less susceptible to prey. Dark colors, displayed by butter-

flies in cooler climates (as far north as the Arctic Circle), readily absorb sunlight, so the cold-blooded insect warms up quickly.

Some butterflies are well camouflaged and almost undetectable among the flowers of their particular food plant. A variety of spots resembling eyes on the outer edges of the wings serve to startle or perhaps distract predators, drawing the point of attack by the beak of a swooping bird away from the butterfly's soft body. Some butterflies do a 180-degree turn before landing, so the eye-spots on the wings are positioned where a predator may think the head should be. Butterflies surviving bird attacks can fly well even with a small piece of wing missing.

The underpart of the wing is usually duller than the surface, so that when the butterfly assumes its resting position with wings folded high above its head, it is cryptically colored, blending into the background on which it alights. Some butterflies use the clubs on the end of the antennae to knock other small predators off their body.

The hairy spines on the caterpillar deter predators, and their colors often blend in with the leaves of their food plant. Some pupae develop hornlike appendages on the head and rear of the chrysalis which appear to point menacingly at predators, and a chrysalis hanging from a twig may look exactly like a dead leaf.

Conservation

Sunshine and habitat are the most important conditions in the butterfly's existence. Habitat loss to agriculture, deforestation, construction of cities and reservoirs, draining of wetlands and the like is the foremost threat to butterfly populations. Although pollution, pesticides, and specimen collection pose serious threats to some species, none is as dangerous a threat as habitat loss. The butterfly's short life span usually makes it impossible for a displaced population to find another appropriate habitat before it dies. Although no species of butterfly is known to have been brought to extinction, some species have been completely exterminated in some areas; some subspecies of butterflies are actually extinct, and small, isolated populations of rare species are particularly endangered. Protection of habitat is the most effective way to prevent major reductions in populations or, in some cases, extinction.

Further Reading:

Barbour, Spider. "Overnight Sensation." *Natural History* (May 1989): 24–28.
Boppre, Michael. "Sex, Drugs, and Butterflies." *Natural History* (January 1994): 28–33.

Feltwell, John. *The Natural History of Butterflies.* New York: Facts on File, 1986.

Pollard, Ernest. *Monitoring Butterflies for Ecology and Conservation.* London: Chapman & Hall, 1993.

Riley, Norman, ed. *Butterflies and Moths.* Rev. ed. New York: Viking Press, 1970.

Scott, James A. *The Butterflies of North America.* Stanford: Stanford University Press, 1986.

Marie L. Thompson

Butylated hydroxyanisole

Butylated hydroxyanisole is a food additive much more widely known by its abbreviation, BHA. BHA is an aromatic organic compound with the chemical names of 2– and 3–tert–butyl–4–methoxyphenol. It can exist in either of the two isomeric forms or as a mixture of the two isomers. In its pure form, BHA is a waxy white or pale yellow solid with a melting point of 121.5°–134°F (48°–55°C) and a boiling point of 510°–521°F (264°–270°C). It is normally insoluble in water, but can be treated in order to make it so.

The chemical property of BHA that is of greatest commercial interest is its tendency to reduce the rate at which other substances undergo oxidation. It has long been used as a preservative in foods containing fats, which turn rancid by oxidation. First used as an antioxidant in 1947, it is now added to a wide variety of foods, including beverages, ice cream, candy, baked goods, instant mashed potatoes, edible fats and oils, breakfast cereals, dry yeast, and sausages. The compound is sometimes used in conjunction with a related antioxidant, butylated hydroxytoluene (BHT).

Some studies have found that BHA can produce allergic reactions and, in larger doses, affect liver and kidney functions. The Select Committee on GRAS (Generally Regarded as Safe) Substances of the U.S. Food and Drug Administration (FDA) reported in 1980 that no evidence exists to indicate that BHA is a health hazard. However, it recommended caution in its use and suggested additional studies on possible risks to human health. Currently FDA regulations limit the concentration of BHA in commercial foods to 0.02% in products containing fats and oils and to somewhat higher concentrations in other food products. In spite of current FDA regulations, some nutrition experts have recommended that BHA be banned from use in foods on the grounds that safer antioxidant alternatives are available.

See also Butylated hydroxytoluene.

Butylated hydroxytoluene

Butylated hydroxytoluene (BHT) is a derivative of cresol, an aromatic organic compound in which two additional hydrogen atoms in the benzene ring are replaced by tertiary butyl groups. Its technical name is 2,6–di–tert–butyl–p–cresol. In its pure form BHT is a white crystalline solid with a melting point of 158° F (70° C) and a boiling point of 509° F (265° C). It is normally insoluble in water, but for commercial applications, it can be converted to a soluble form.

BHT was first used as an antioxidant food additive in 1954. An antioxidant is a substance that prevents the oxidation of materials with which it occurs. BHT, therefore, prevents the spoilage of food to which it is added.

BHT has grown to be very popular among food processors and is now used in a great range of products that include breakfast cereals, chewing gum, dried potato flakes, enriched rice, potato chips, candy, sausages, freeze–dried meats, and other foods containing fats and oils. BHT is sometimes used in conjunction with a related compound, butylated hydroxyanisole (BHA) as a food additive.

Some evidence exists that BHT may be harmful to human health. Studies suggest that the compound may damage the liver and kidneys. However, the U.S. Food and Drug Administration has deemed that BHT is safe enough when used in limited concentrations. It currently permits its use in concentrations of about 0.01% to 0.02% in most foods. As an emulsion stabilizer in shortening, it may be used in a somewhat higher concentration, 200 parts per million. Some authorities suggest that BHT poses too large a health risk and that it should be banned in foods. That policy has been adopted in some other nations, such as England and Australia, where its use is permitted as a food additive only in special cases.

BHT does have other commercial uses, as in animal feeds and in the manufacture of synthetic rubber and plastics, where it also acts as an antioxidant.

See also Butylated hydroxyanisole (BHA); Food preservation.

Butyl group

Butyl group consists of the group of atoms C_4H_4. It is derived by removing one hydrogen atom from either of the isomers of butane, C_4H_{10}, and exists in four isomeric forms. Two isomers of butane exist, n–butane, also called 1–butane ($CH_3CH_2CH_2CH_3$), and iso–butane, also called 2–methylpropane ($CH_3CH(CH_3)CH_3$).

Removing a hydrogen atom from the first isomer can result in the formation of two different butyl groups, one designated as n–butyl, and the other as sec–butyl (secondary butyl). The structure of the n–butyl group is $CH_3CH_2CH_2CH_2$; the structure of the sec–butyl group is $CH_3CHCH_2CH_3$. The difference is that the n–butyl group bonds to other atoms via an end carbon atom, while the sec–butyl group bonds via an "inner" carbon atom.

Removal of a hydrogen atom from the iso–butane isomer can result in the formation of two different butyl groups. One of these groups has the structural formula at the left below and is commonly known as tert–butyl or 1, 1–dimethylethyl. The tert– prefix stands for tertiary, indicating that the open bond is from a carbon atom that is attached to three other carbon atoms. The other butyl group that can be formed from iso–butane is the isobutyl or 2–methylpropyl group.

Butyl compounds

A large number of compounds containing the butyl group exist. Many of them are relatively simple and can be represented by the formula C_4H_9X, where X

stands for a halogen, a hydroxyl group, an amine, or some other group. The following sections review some of the most important of these compounds.

Butyl alcohols

Four butyl alcohols exist, each formed by the addition of a hydroxyl group (OH) to one of the four butyl isomers discussed above. Their names and structures are as follows:

TABLE 1. BUTYL COMPOUNDS AND USES

Compound	Use
n–butyl acetate	manufacture of photographic film, safety glass, artificial leather, perfumes, and flavoring agents
N–butyl pthalateinsect	repellant
n–butyltrichlorosilane	production of silicones
4–tert–butyl catechol	used to slow down or stop polymerization reactions in the production of certain plastics and synthetic rubbers
butylate (bis [2–methyl–propyl] carbamothoic acid S–ethyl ester) herbicide t–butyl acetate	gasoline additive
4–tert–butylphenyl salicylate	light absorber in plastic food wrappings
n–butylamine	raw material in the synthesis of many products, including dyes, pharmaceuticals, insecticides, and rubber chemicals
sec–butylamine	prevents the growth of fungi
n–butyl citrate	anti–foaming agent; plasticizer; manufacture of inks and polishes
1–butyl–3–metanilyurea	treatment of hypoglycemia (an abnormally low blood sugar level)
butylmethoxydibenzoyl–methane	screens out ultraviolet light
t–butyl nitrate	jet propellant
n–butyl strearate	used to soften cosmetics, plastics, textiles, and other types of polymers

n–butyl alcohol (or 1–butanol) $CH_3CH_2CH_2CH_2OH$; iso–butyl alcohol (or 2–methyl–1–propanol) $CH_3CH(CH_3)CH_2OH$; sec–butyl alcohol (or 2–butanol) $CH_3CHOHCH_2CH_3$; tert–butyl alcohol (or 2–methyl–2–propanol) $CH_3C(CH_3)(OH)CH_3$.

The boiling points of the butyl alcohols decrease regularly in moving down the above list, from 244°F (118°C) for n–butyl alcohol to 226°F (108°C) for iso–butyl alcohol to 212°F (100°C) for sec–butyl alcohol to 180°F (82°C) for tert–butyl alcohol. A similar pattern exists for solubility of the alcohols, increasing from 8 g per 100 g of water for n–butyl alcohol to 10 g per 100 g of water and 12.5 g per 100 g of water for the next two forms to complete miscibility for tert–butyl alcohol.

The four butyl alcohols undergo very different reactions in many instances. As an example, n–butyl and iso–butyl alcohol can be oxidized rather easily to yield aldehydes. Oxidation of sec–butyl alcohol, however, results in the formation of a ketone. Oxidation of tert–butyl alcohol occurs only under the most extreme conditions, resulting in the complete oxidation of the compound to carbon dioxide and water.

Of the four butyl alcohols, n–butyl alcohol is in the greatest demand commercially. It is used as a solvent for fats, waxes, gums, shellac, varnish, and other materials in many industrial processes. It is also used as the starting point in the preparation of other butyl compounds. All of the butyl alcohols are of some interest in the synthetic flavoring industry since they can react with organic acids to make pleasant smelling esters. For example, n–butyl butanoate has the odor of pineapple; 2–methylpropyl propanoate smells like rum; 2–methylpropyl methanoate, like apple; n–butyl methanoate, like banana; and n–butyl ehtanoate, like strawberry.

The accompanying table summarizes some butyl compounds and their most important uses.

See also Isomer; Oxidation–reduction reaction.

Further Reading:

Budavari, Susan, ed.. *The Merck Index*, 11th edition. Rahway, NJ: Merck and Company, 1989, pp. 236–242.

Embree, Harland D.. *Brief Course: Organic Chemistry*. Glenview, IL: Scott, Foresman, 1983, Chapter 6 and passim.

Hawley, Gessner G., ed. *The Condensed Chemical Dictionary*, 9th edition. New York: Van Nostrand Reinhold, 1977, pp. 133–142.

Solomons, T.W. Graham. *Organic Chemistry*, 2nd edition. New York: John Wiley, 1980, Chapter 15 and passim.

Buzzards

The true buzzards are diurnal birds of prey in the genus *Buteo*, sub–family Buteonidae, family Accipitridae. In North America, buzzards are also commonly known as hawks, although other genera in the family Accipitridae are also given this common name, for example, the *Accipiter* hawks. There are 25 species of buzzards.

Buzzards are in the order Falconiformes, which also includes other types of hawks, eagles, osprey, falcons, and vultures. All of these birds have strong, grasping (or raptorial) talons, a hooked beak, extremely good vision, and a fierce demeanor. However, buzzards can be distinguished by their relatively large size, wide, rounded tail, broad wings, and their soaring flight. The usual color of the feathers is a barred pattern of browns and black, with some buff or red. The sexes are colored similarly, but females are substantially larger than males.

Buzzards occur on all of the continents, except for Antarctica. However, most species of buzzards occur in the Americas. Buzzards are most common seen in relatively open habitats, such as prairies, savannahs, and forest edges.

Buzzards are mostly predators of small mammals, rabbits and hares, and to a lesser degree, snakes, lizards, birds, and larger insects, such as grasshoppers. Buzzards commonly soar in huge circles at great heights, looking for prey in the open, using their extremely acute vision. If prey is seen, an attempt may be made to catch it by undertaking a steep dive, known as a stoop. Some species also hunt regularly from perches in trees or on posts. The prey is generally killed by the powerful, sharp–clawed, grasping talons of these birds.

Migrating buzzards also soar during their long–distance movements, utilizing the lift obtained from high thermals during sunny days to achieve a relatively effortless flight. Some species migrate in large groups, and occasionally thousands of individuals can be seen at one time. These birds seem to fill the sky as they soar to great heights on one thermal and then glide slowly to pick up the next thermal along their path of travel, using the presence of other birds to identify the otherwise invisible habitat of rising, warm air.

Buzzards defend a territory during their breeding season. The territory is proclaimed by aerial displays and by loud, harsh screams. Buzzards nest in trees. Often the nest was built by another species, such as crows or ravens, and is then appropriated by the buzzard. However, buzzards will also build their own nests. The same pair may continue to utilize a nest for several seasons.

Species of buzzards

The largest, most widespread and familiar species of buzzard in North America is the red–tailed hawk (*Buteo jamaicensis*). This species breeds in almost all regions below the arctic tundra, and as far south as Panama and the West Indies. The red–tailed hawk nests in trees at or near the edge of a woodland, but feeds in open country. The plumage of the red–tailed hawk is quite variable, but adults have a reddish top of their tail. Northern populations migrate to the south in winter, although they will stay quite far north if an abundance of their prey of small mammals is available.

The red–shouldered hawk (*B. lineatus*) is a common species of the eastern United States and southeastern Canada, with a separate, disjunct population in coastal California and Oregon. This species commonly hunts from perches. Northern populations winter in the southeastern states.

The broad–winged hawk (*B. platypterus*) is a relatively small and common woodland species of the eastern United States and southeastern Canada. This species usually hunts for small mammals, reptiles, and insects from a perch in a tree. During the autumn the broad–winged hawk migrates in spectacular flocks, which occur as large groups riding thermals in a southerly direction. This species winters from southern Mexico to northern South America.

The rough–legged hawk (*B. lagopus*) breeds in the northern tundra of Canada and Alaska and winters in open habitats of the United States. This species also breeds throughout the tundra of northern Eurasia, from Scandinavia to eastern Siberia. The rough–legged hawk commonly hunts while hovering in the air.

The ferruginous hawk (*B. regalis*) is a buzzard of prairies and other open habitats of western North America, wintering in the southwestern States and Mexico. Swainson's hawk (*B. swainsoni*) is another western species of open habitats, breeding from central

A common buzzard (*Buteo buteo*) perched in a spruce.

Alaska to northern Mexico. This species migrates in flocks, and winters in Argentina.

Other species of buzzards in North America are relatively uncommon and localized in their distributions. These include the Harlan's hawk (*B. harlani*), Harris' hawk (*B. unicinctus*), and the zone–tailed hawk (*B. albonotatus*).

The common buzzard (*Buteo buteo*) breeds widely in Europe and northern Asia. Northern populations of this species are migratory, but southern populations are sedentary, as long as there is sufficient prey of small mammals available to support their needs. The long–legged buzzard (*B. rufinus*) has a more southern Eurasian distribution.

Buzzards and humans

Some people consider all hawks to be pests, believing that they eat game birds such as grouse and ducks, or that they kill song birds. For these essentially misguided reasons, buzzards and other hawks have been killed in large numbers in some regions. Fortunately, however, this is rarely the case today, and few people now go out of their way to kill these magnificent predators.

To some degree, buzzards have also been detrimentally affected by the toxic effects of insecticide use in agriculture and forestry. However, these birds have been somewhat less damaged by pesticides than some other types of raptors, such as falcons and eagles.

In fact, because they eat large numbers of small mammals, which can cause serious agricultural damages, buzzards provide a useful service to humans.

Because of buzzards' large size and fierce demeanor, many bird–watchers avidly seek out quality sightings of individuals, which can represent a highlight of a day's field expedition.

See also Birds of prey.

Further Reading:

Clark, W. S. and B. K. Wheeler. *A Field Guide to the Hawks of North America.* Boston: Houghton–Mifflin, 1987.

Freedman, B. *Environmental Ecology,* 2nd ed. San Diego: Academic Press, 1994.

Johnsgard, P. A. *Hawks, Eagles, and Falcons of North America. Biology and Natural History.* Washington, D.C.: Smithsonian Press, 1990.

Scholz, F. *Birds of Prey.* Harrisburg, PA: Stackpole Books, 1993.

Bill Freedman

By-the-wind-sailor see **Hydrozoa**

C

Cabbage see **Mustard family**

Cacomistle see **Raccoons**

Cactus

The cactus family or Cactaceae is made up of about 2,000 species of perennial plants with succulent stems, most of which are well–armed with sharp spines. The natural distribution of most cacti is American, ranging from southern British Columbia and southern Ontario in Canada, through much of the United States, to the tip of southern South America. One genus, *Rhipsalis*, occurs in Africa, Madagascar, and India, and is probably native there. Cacti usually inhabit deserts and other dry, open places. The major use of cacti by humans is as attractive, ornamental plants in gardens, or as indoor house plants. A few species produce edible fruits, and one yields peyote, a hallucinogenic drug.

Biology of cacti

Cacti are perennial plants. Their stems are fleshy or succulent, and are cylindrical or flattened in shape. The stems are green–colored, and are photosynthetic, usually performing this function instead of leaves, which are greatly reduced in abundance or even absent in most mature cacti. Most species of cactus are well–protected by sharp bristles and spines, which serve to deter most herbivores.

The stems of cactus plants have numerous cushion– or pit–like structures known as areoles on their surface, from which usually emerge clusters of spines. In terms of developmental biology, areoles are usually interpreted as being incompletely developed, axillary stem branches. The spines are actually modified leaves. The areoles may also be protected by hook–like barbs

known as glochidia. The roots of cacti are shallow and may be widely spread in the soil.

The flowers of cacti are usually perfect (bisexual), containing both male reproductive organs (stamens) and female parts (a pistil). The flowers occur singly, rather than in groups, although many discrete flowers may be present on a cactus at the same time. The flowers of most species of cacti are large and showy, and they can be colored white, red, pink, orange, or yellow, but not blue. The sepals of the calyx are petal–like in shape and color, and they combine with the numerous petals to form an attractive, often richly scented, nectar–producing flower, designed to lure such pollinators as hawk–moths, bees, bats, and birds, especially hummingbirds and small doves. The fruit is a many–seeded berry.

Cacti are xerophytic plants, meaning they are physiologically and morphologically adapted to coping with the extreme water deficiencies of dry habitats, such as deserts. The xerophytic adaptations of cacti include: (1) their succulent, water–retaining stems, (2) a thick, waxy cuticle and few or no leaves to greatly reduce the losses of water through transpiration, (3) stems that are photosynthetic, so leaves are not required to execute this function, (4) stems that are cylindrical or spherical in shape, which reduces the surface to volume ratio, and helps to preserve moisture, (5) tolerance of high tissue temperatures, (6) protection of the biomass and moisture reserves from herbivores by an armament of stout spines, (7) a physiological tolerance of long periods of drought, and (8) a periodic pattern of growth, productivity, and flowering, which takes advantage of the availability of moisture during the brief, rainy season, while the plant remains dormant at drier times of the year.

Cacti have a so–called crassulacean–acid metabolism, in which atmospheric carbon dioxide is only taken up during the night, when the stomates are open. The carbon dioxide is fixed into four–carbon, organic acids,

A prickly pear cactus (*Opuntia humifusa*) in Big Bend National Park, Texas. The prickly pear is the only widespread eastern cactus in the United States. It can be found as far north as southern Ontario.

and can later be released within the plant, to be fixed into sugars by photosynthesis when the sun is shining during the daylight hours. Because this system allows stomates to be kept tightly closed during the day, crassulacean–acid metabolism is an efficient way of conserving water in dry environments.

Some plant species of dry habitats that are not related to cacti are nevertheless remarkably similar in appearance (at least, apart from their flowers and fruits, which are always distinctive among plant families). This is the result of convergent evolution, the similar evolutionary development of unrelated species or families that are subjected to comparable types of environmental selective pressures. Some species of spurges (family *Euphorbiaceae*) that grow in dry habitats are commonly thought by non–botanists to be cacti, even though they are quite unrelated.

Species of cacti in North America

Species of cacti are prominent in many arid and semi–arid habitats in the Americas. Cacti provide important elements of the habitat for many species of animals, especially larger species such as saguaro and candelabra cacti.

One of the most familiar groups of cacti are the prickly–pears, beaver–tails, or chollas (*Opuntia* spp.), of which there are about 300 species. These species have flattened, succulent, segmented stems (sometimes known as stem–joints), and are usually well–armed with spines of various sizes. *Opuntia lindheimeri* is a red– or yellow–flowered species that grows in Louisiana, Texas, and northeastern Mexico. This plant can reach a height of almost 13 ft (4 m) and can sometimes form dense thickets. *Opuntia macrorhiza* is a yellow–flowered species that grows in dry prairies from Kansas and Missouri to Texas. *Opuntia imbricata* has cylindrical instead of flattened stems, grows as tall as 6.6 ft (2 m), has red– or purple–colored flowers, and is commonly known as the tree or candelabra cactus. *Opuntia compressa* or the beaver–tail is a low–growing, yellow–flowered, eastern species that ranges from Massachusetts to Georgia. *Opuntia fulgida* or cholla occurs in the Sonora and other deserts of the southwestern United States and Mexico.

The pin–cushion cacti (*Mammillaria* spp.) are about 300 species of relatively small cacti that have spherical stems, with numerous, small, spiny, nipple–like protuberances on their surface. *Mammillaria microcarpa* and *M. thornberi* are species native to the southwestern states and Mexico.

The hedge or candelabra cacti (*Cereus* spp.) are made up of about 40 species. The barbed–wire cactus (*Cereus pentagonus*) is an arching, sometimes climbing species that grows in southern Florida, while the organ–pipe cactus (*C. thurberi*) is an erect, multi–stemmed species of deserts of Arizona and Mexico, which can achieve a height greater than 39 ft (12 m). The desert night–blooming cereus (*C. greggii*) occurs in deserts of the southwestern United States and Mexico. The odorous, nectar–rich, white flowers of this species open synchronously on only a few nights each year, and are pollinated by bats and hawk moths.

The saguaro, giant, or tall cactus (*Carnegiea giganteus*, sometimes known as *Cereus giganteus*) is a spectacular, multi–columnar species that dominates the landscape of deserts of Arizona and down into Mexico. This candelabra–like species can grow as tall as 49 ft (15 m) and has showy flowers that are pollinated by bats, birds, moths, and bees. The saguaro is an important component of the habitat of many species of animals. The gila woodpecker (*Centurus uropygalis*) and gilded flicker (*Colaptes chrysoides*) excavate nesting cavities in the saguaro cactus, and when these are abandoned they may be used secondarily by elf owls (*Micrathene whitneyi*) and other species of birds. The cactus wren (*Campylorhynchus brunneicapillus*) is another prominent species in saguaro–dominated deserts. In addition, many species of animals feed on the nectar of the saguaro, and on the bright–red, juicy pulp of its ripened fruits.

The barrel cacti (*Echinocactus* spp.) are seven species with stout, rotund, barrel–like stems. The barrel cactus (*Echinocactus polycephalus*) is a relatively large species of the southwestern states and Mexico, while the horse crippler (*E. texensis*) and star cactus (*E. asterias*) are smaller species. The hedgehog cacti (*Echinocereus* spp.) are 70 species with relatively small, densely aggregated, spiny stems. The red–flowered hedgehog cactus (*E. triglochidiatus*) occurs widely in arid habitats of the southwestern United States and Mexico. The organ–pipe cacti (*Lemaireocereus* spp.) are 25 species of tall, multi–stemmed, columnar cacti, including the candebobe (*L. weberi*) of Mexico. The barrel cacti (*Ferocactus* spp.) are 35 species of stout, short–columnar species, including *F. acanthodes, F. wislizenii,* and *F. covillei* of the southwestern states and Mexico.

Economic importance of cacti

Many species of cacti are highly prized by horticulturalists as botanical oddities and ornamental plants. These may be cultivated for their beautiful flowers, the aesthetics of their stems and spines, or merely because the plants have a strange–looking appearance. In addition, many people like to grow cacti because they are relatively easy to maintain—it doesn't matter much if you forget to water your cacti for a few days, or even a few weeks or more. In fact, over–watering is usually the greatest risk to most cacti that are kept as house plants, because too much moisture will pre–dispose these drought–adapted plants to developing fungal and bacterial diseases, such as soft–rot.

Virtually any of the native species of cacti of North America may be used in horticulture, as are many of the species of Central and South America. The genera *Mammillaria* and *Opuntia* are most commonly grown, but virtually any species may be found in cultivation around or in homes and greenhouses. One of the most common and familiar species is the Christmas cactus (*Zygocactus elegans*), a flat–stemmed, red–, pink–, or white–flowered species that is grown as a garden and house plant. This species blooms during the winter, and florists often induce this plant to bloom around Christ-

---

KEY TERMS

Berry—A multi–seeded fruit, developed from a single, compound ovary.

Cuticle—A waxy, superficial layer that covers the foliage of vascular plants, and the stems of cacti.

Monoecious—This is a plant breeding system in which male and female reproductive structures are present on the same plant, and in the case of cacti, in the same flowers.

Perfect—In the botanical sense, this refers to flowers that are bisexual, containing both male and female reproductive parts.

Stomate—These are microscopic pores in the leaf or stem cuticle, bordered by guard cells which control opening or closing of the pore.

Succulent—This refers to specialized plant tissues that are fleshy, and adaptive for the storage and conservation of water.

Xerophyte—A plant that is adapted to tolerating dry environmental conditions.

---

mas–time, when it is commonly sold as a living ornament to brighten homes during that festive season. The candelabra cactus (*Cereus peruvianus*) is a tree–sized species native to South America that is commonly cultivated outdoors in hot climates, or in greenhouses in colder climates.

Many species of cacti can be rather easily transplanted from natural habitats into the vicinities of homes and businesses, where they may be used as central components of low–maintenance gardens in places where rainfall is sparse, and the development of grassy lawns would require an excessive use of scarce and expensive water. Wild cacti are also collected to grow in or around the home, and to develop private collections of these interesting plants.

Unfortunately, most species of cacti re–colonize disturbed sites very slowly and infrequently. Extensive losses of cactus habitat to industrial and residential developments, coupled with excessive collections of wild plants, have resulted in the populations of some species of cacti becoming endangered. In some areas, populations of wild cacti must be guarded against illegal, often nocturnal collecting of valuable plants for horticultural purposes. Unfortunately, it is difficult to protect many endangered cacti from poaching. This is because of the extensive areas that must be patrolled, in

A CAD system used for Boeing airplanes.

the face of multi–million–dollar profits that can potentially be made in the illicit cactus trade. Some species of cactus are now critically endangered in the wild because of excessive, illegal collecting, and this represents an important ecological problem in many areas.

The most commonly edible cactus fruit is that of *Opuntia* species, especially *O. ficus–indica*. The fruits of prickly–pears, sometimes known as apples or tunas, can be eaten directly or used to make a jelly. Prickly–pear fruits are considered to be a delicacy around Christmas time in some regions.

Peyote or mescal buttons (*Lophophora williamsii*) is a cactus containing several alkaloids in its tissues that are used as a hallucinogen and folk medicine. Peyote is important in the culture of some tribes of native Amerindians in the southwestern United States and Mexico, especially in the vicinity of the Rio Grande River. These aboriginal peoples use peyote to induce religious experiences and revelations. Peyote is also commonly used as a recreational drug by many people, and by several religious cults.

Some species of spiny cacti, such as *Opuntia*s, are used as living fences, for example, to keep livestock out of gardens. The long, sharp spines of other cacti were used as needles in some of the earliest types of phonographs. The "wood" of the saguaro cactus has long been used by Amerindian peoples, and is still utilized to make crafts and novelty furniture.

A few species of cacti have become pests, or weeds, when they escaped from cultivation in places where they were not native, and were not controlled by diseases or herbivores. The best known example is that of a prickly pear cactus (*Opuntia* spp.) that was imported to Australia from North America for use as an ornamental plant and living fence, but became invasive and a serious weed of rangelands. This pest has now been almost completely controlled through the introduction of one of its natural herbivores, the moth *Cactoblastis cactorum*, whose larvae feed on the cactus.

See also Desert; Hallucinogens; Spurge family.

Further Reading:

Benson, L. *The Cacti of the United States and Canada.* Stanford, CA: Stanford University Press, 1982.

Klein, R. M. *The Green World. An Introduction to Plants and People.* New York: Harper and Row, 1987.

Weniger, D. *Cacti of the Southwest.* Austin: University of Texas Press, 1975.

Woodland, D. W. *Contemporary Plant Systematics.* New Jersey: Prentice–Hall, 1991.

Bill Freedman

CAD/CAM/CIM

CAD/CAM is an acronym for computer–aided design and computer–aided manufacturing. The use of computers in design and manufacturing applications makes it possible to remove much of the tedium and manual labor involved. For example, the many design specifications, blueprints, material lists, and other documents needed to build complex machines can require thousands of highly technical and accurate drawings and charts. If the engineers decide structural components need to be changed, all of these plans and drawings must be changed. Prior to CAD/CAM, human designers and draftspersons had to change them manually, a time consuming and error–prone process. When a CAD system is used, the computer can automatically evaluate and change all corresponding documents instantly. In addition, by using interactive graphics workstations, designers, engineers, and architects can create models or drawings, increase or decrease sizes, rotate or change them at will, and see results instantly on screen.

CAD is particularly valuable in space programs, where many unknown design variables are involved. Previously, engineers depended upon trial–and–error testing and modification, a time consuming and possibly life–threatening process. However, when aided by computer simulation and testing, a great deal of time, money, and possibly lives can be saved. Besides its use in the military, CAD is also used in civil aeronautics, automotive, and data processing industries.

CAM, commonly utilized in conjunction with CAD, uses computers to communicate instructions to automated machinery. CAM techniques are especially suited for manufacturing plants, where tasks are repetitive, tedious, or dangerous for human workers.

Computer integrated manufacturing (CIM), a term popularized by Joseph Harrington in 1975, is also known as autofacturing. CIM is a programmable manufacturing method designed to link CAD, CAM, industrial robotics, and machine manufacturing using unattended processing workstations. CIM offers uninterrupted operation from raw materials to finished product, with the added benefits of quality assurance and automated assembly.

CAE (computer aided engineering), which appeared in the late 1970s, combines software, hardware, graphics, automated analysis, simulated operation, and physical testing to improve accuracy, effectiveness, and productivity.

See also Automation; Robotics.

Caddisflies

North America's streams, rivers, and lakes are home to more than 1,200 different species of caddisflies, which are aquatic insects in the order *Trichoptera.* Adaptations to different water conditions and food types allow this group of insects to populate a variety of habitats in America's waters.

Caddisflies are best known and most easily identified in their larval stages. Most caddisfly larvae either spin shelters of silk or build tubular cases. The type of shelter can be used to assign caddisflies to their different families. Some species make shelters from the hollow stems of grasses. Others inhabit shelters constructed from rock fragments, pieces of bark, or other available materials. Some species of caddisfly carry their shelters with them as they graze on the algae on rocks; others remain anchored to a rock. Caddisflies that spin silk shelters also spin nets that filter out food particles from the flowing water.

Immature caddisflies are aquatic and must obtain oxygen from the water. Mobile caddisfly larvae move water through their gills. Sedentary caddisfly larvae make undulating movements to move water across their gills. The larval cases of sedentary caddiflies restrict or direct flow in some essential way, for if the cases are removed, the larvae usually die.

Like many other insects, caddisflies undergo complete metamorphosis, from egg to larva to pupa to adult. The aquatic larvae eventually spin a cocoon or pupal case and become dormant. At the end of the pupation period, adult caddisflies break free of their cocoons and swim to the surface. There, the new adults dry their wings and begin their short adult lives as active, sexually mature air–breathing insects.

Most adult caddisflies live less than a month. During that time, they are inactive during the day, and active at night. Adult caddisflies feed on plant nectar, or other plant liquids. After the females have mated they lay their eggs. Where they lay their eggs depends on their species: One species of caddisfly remains underwater for more than 15 minutes as she lays her eggs.

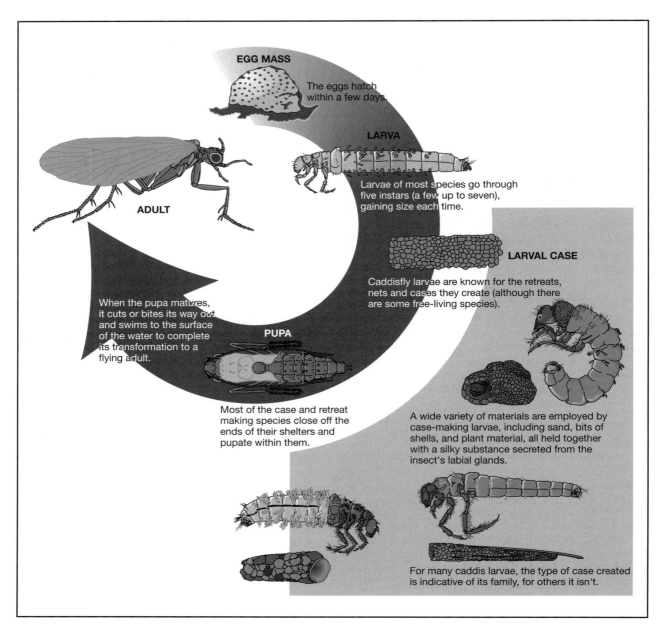

The life cycle of a caddisfly.

Another species deposits her eggs on plants above water, while another species lays her eggs on the water surface–the mass of eggs then absorbs water, sinks, and adheres to an underwater rock or other surface.

As an order, caddisflies are associated with a variety of aquatic habitats: rushing mountain streams, ephemeral spring seeps, slow moving rivers and tranquil lakes. A single habitat such as a stream, can support several different species of caddisflies as part of a complex aquatic food web. The larvae of a species grazes on algae on rocks, another feeds on leaves and other plant parts that fall into the water, shredding the material into fine particles. Another species filters food from the fast moving rapids, while another species catches of food items that flow by in slower–moving waters.

Caddisflies specialize in how they acquire food rather than in the type of food they ingest. These specializations make caddisflies one of the most varied and abundant species of aquatic insects in North America.

Cadmium see **Element, chemical**

Caecilians

Caecilians are long, worm–like legless amphibians in the order Gymnophiona (sometimes known as Apoda, meaning without legs). There are 163 species of caecilians, in 35 genera. Little is known about these animals, and few species have common names. Most of the caecilians are tropical or sub–tropical, and occur in Central and South America, Africa, and south and southeast Asia.

Caecilians grow up to 5 ft (1.5 m) in length in the case of *Caecilia thompsoni* of Colombia. Caecilians are virtually all body, with almost no tail. Caecilians do not even have rudimentary leg or girdle bones, and have probably been a distinct amphibian lineage for a very long time. However, caecilians have almost no fossil record, so little is known about their evolutionary history.

Caecilians are generally a uniformly or mottled gray in color, and somewhat lighter beneath. They have a small mouth, nostrils, and small eyes incapable of movement, covered by skin, and are probably only able to sense changes in light intensity. Caecilians have numerous ring–like, segmental grooves along their body, which enhance their superficial resemblance to earthworms.

Most caecilians live secretively in burrows made in moist soil or in forest litter, often near streams and wetlands. Some species occur in aquatic habitats, where they also burrow in soft substrates. Caecilians feed on invertebrates, some species specializing in earthworms or termites. The skull of caecilians is heavily boned, and the skin adheres to the skull—both of these are adaptations to the chisel–like burrowing methods of these animals.

Caecilians have internal fertilization, a relatively uncommon trait among amphibians. About one–half of caecilian species lay eggs that are guarded by the female, which coils around them until hatching occurs. The other species of caecilians are viviparous, meaning the eggs are retained within the reproductive tract of the female, where they develop and hatch into miniature adults. The larvae feed on their egg yolk, on a rich maternal secretion known as "uterine milk," and by scraping nutritious material from the lining of the reproductive tract of their mother. After a relatively long gestation period of 9–11 months, the baby caecilians emerge as fully metamorphosed but miniature replicas of the adults.

See also Amphibians.

Caffeine

Caffeine is an alkaloid found in coffee, tea, chocolate, and other natural foods. It is also a component of cola soft drinks. Caffeine has been a part of the human diet for many centuries and is one of the most widely used central nervous system stimulants in the world. In recent years, research has raised questions about possible deleterious health effects of caffeine, but no definitive conclusions have been reached about the harmfulness of moderate amounts.

Chemistry of caffeine

Caffeine's chemical name is 3,7–dihydro–1,3,7–trimethyl–1H–purine–2,6–dione. It is also known as theine, methyl theobromine, and 1,3,7–trimethylxanthine. Its molecular formula is $C_8H_{10}N_4O_2 \cdot H_2O$, and it consists of bicyclic molecules derived from the purine ring system.

In its pure form, caffeine is a fleecy white solid or long silky crystals. It is odorless, but has a distinctive bitter taste. When heated, caffeine loses water at 179°F (80°C), sublimes at 355.5°F (178°C), and/or melts at 461°F (236.8°C). It is only slightly soluble in water and alcohol, but dissolves readily in chloroform. Water solutions of caffeine are essentially neutral (pH = 6.9).

Caffeine is a member of the alkaloid family, a group of compounds obtained from plants whose molecules consist of nitrogen–containing rings. In general, alkaloids tend to have identifiable physiological effects on the human body, although these effects vary greatly from compound to compound.

History

The pleasures of coffee, tea, and chocolate drinking have been known to humans for centuries, but the isolation of caffeine from these beverages was accomplished only in the early 1800s. During the 1820s, researchers identified the active agents in tea and chocolate and gave them a variety of names such as guaranin and thenin. In 1840, T. Martins and D. Berthemot independently showed that these compounds are all identical with caffeine. Caffeine itself was originally called cofeine or caffein and only in the late 1820s was given the name by which we know it today.

Much of the work leading to the full characterization of caffeine's molecular structure was completed by the German chemist Emil Fischer (1852–1919). Fischer first synthesized the compound from raw materials in 1895, and two years later derived its precise structural formula.

Sources

Of all the commercial sources of caffeine, guarana paste has the highest concentration of the pure compound, about 4%. Guarana paste is made from the seed of the Paullinia tree, found primarily in Brazil. More common sources of caffeine contain lower concentrations of the compound: 1.1–2.2% in coffee beans; 3.5% in tea leaves; and 1.5% in kola nuts. Other less common sources of caffeine include maté leaves, obtained from the Ilex plant (less than 0.7% caffeine), and yoco bark, obtained from the Paullinia yoco tree (2.7% caffeine).

Because of the way in which these foods are prepared, the above data do not give an accurate picture of the amount of caffeine that people consume. The average cup of coffee, for example, contains approximately 100–150 mg of caffeine; the average cup of tea, 50 mg of caffeine; and the average cup of cocoa, about 5 mg of caffeine. Cola drinks tend to contain 35–55 mg of caffeine, and the average chocolate bar contains about 20 mg of the compound.

Pharmacological effects

The most important physiological effect of caffeine is that it stimulates nerve cells, particularly those in the brain. It appears that caffeine molecules bind to neurotransmitter receptor sites in nerve cells, causing the continual stimulation of those cells. This property explains the most common clinical symptoms of caffeine ingestion: wakefulness, excitability, increased mental awareness, and restlessness.

Caffeine affects nerve tissue in the brain much more quickly than it does nerve tissue anywhere else in the body. As a result, it will bring about muscular changes such as convulsions only with very high doses of the drug—10 g or more, the equivalent of drinking 70–100 cups of coffee in a short time. Death from caffeine overdose is, therefore, extremely unlikely.

Teratogenic and mutagenic effects

Concerns about the possible health effects of consuming caffeine have been expressed for well over a hundred years. Recent concern about its physiological effects tend to focus on mutagenic and teratogenic effects. Mutagenic effects are those that change the reproductive genes, producing mutations in subsequent generations. Scientific reports have also appeared connecting the consumption of large doses of caffeine with particular types of cancer. However, the significance of such findings to the average coffee or tea drinker is unclear.

The situation with teratogenic effects—those that affect the fetus while it is still in the womb—is somewhat clearer. Caffeine passes readily across the placental lining, exposing the fetus to concentrations of the stimulant that are comparable to those in the mother's blood. Since the developing nervous system of the fetus is more likely to be affected by the drug than is the mother's, a reduction in caffeine intake is often recommended for pregnant women.

See also Alkaloid.

Further Reading:
Brecher, Edward M., and the editors of *Consumer Reports. Licit and Illicit Drugs*. Mt. Vernon, N.Y.: Consumers Union, 1972.
Dews, Peter B., ed. *Caffeine: Perspectives from Research*. Berlin: Springer–Verlag, 1984.
Gilbert, Richard J. *Caffeine: The Most Popular Stimulant*. New York: Chelsea House, 1986.
Goulart, Francis Sheridan. *The Caffeine Book: A User's and Abuser's Guide*. New York: Dodd Mead, 1984.
Selinger, Ben. *Chemistry in the Marketplace*. 4th ed. Sydney: Harcourt Brace Jovanovich, 1989.

David E. Newton

Caimans see **Crocodiles**

Caisson

A caisson is a hollow structure made of concrete, steel, or other materials that can be sunk into the earth. It used as the substructure for a bridge, a building, or other large structures. Caissons come in many sizes and shapes depending on their future use. The one shared feature is that their bottom edges are sharp so they easily can be sunk into the ground. These sharp edges are known as the cutting edges of the caisson.

General principle

The purpose of using a caisson in construction is to provide a temporary structure from which earth, water, and other materials can be removed and into which concrete or some other fill material can be placed. For example in the construction of a bridge it may be necessary to burrow into the soil at the bottom of a river until bedrock is reached. One way of doing this is to sink a caisson filled with compressed air into the river until it reaches the river bottom. Workers then can go into the caisson and dig soil out of the river bed until they come to bedrock. As they remove soil it can be transported upward out through the caisson. During this process the caisson continues to sink more deeply into the river bed until it reaches bedrock. At that point concrete may be poured into the caisson to form the lowest section of the new bridge pier.

Caissons may consist of a single unit looking like a tin can with both ends cut out. Or they may be subdivided into a number of compartments similar to a honeycomb. One factor in determining the shape of the caisson is the area it must cover. The larger the size of the caisson the more necessary it may be to subdivide it into smaller compartments.

Types of caissons

All caissons feature the shape of a tube, often with a cylindrical contour but it may also be rectangular, elliptical, or some other form. Some caissons are open at both ends, some are open only at the top, and some are open only at the bottom. It depends on the way each type of caisson is to be used.

A caisson open at both ends might be used to lay down a pier for a new skyscraper. The caisson would be driven into the ground to a certain depth and the earthy material inside the caisson would be scooped out. Depending on the depth of the pier required one long open cylindrical caisson could be used or a sequence of shorter caissons could be laid down one on top of the other. When the caisson(s) have been inserted to the desired depth and all the soil within them removed they might be filled with concrete. The decision as to whether to remove the caissons themselves before adding concrete would depend on the surrounding soil's nature. If the soils were too unstable to hold their shape the caisson would be left in place. With stable soils the caisson could be removed.

A caisson closed at the bottom and open at the top is a floating caisson. This type of caisson often is used in the construction of bridge piers. The caisson is constructed on land of concrete, steel, wood, or some other material and floated to its intended position in a river, lake, or other body of water. The caisson then is filled with gravel, concrete, or some other material and allowed to sink to the river bed. The filled caisson then becomes the lowest portion of the new bridge pier. A floating caisson can be used only if engineers can be assured that the soil beneath and around the filled caisson will not wash away.

One interesting application of the floating caisson is in the reclamation of land from the North Sea around the Netherlands. In the first stage of this process a series of floating caissons are moved into the ocean where they are arranged to form a new dike system. Ocean water trapped within the line of caissons is pumped out to form new farmland.

A caisson closed at the top and open at the bottom is a pneumatic caisson. This type of caisson generally is used in underwater construction projects. It can be used only if air is pumped in to produce a pressure greater than water pressure outside. Workers entering a pneumatic caisson must first pass through an intermediate chamber that allows their bodies to adjust from normal atmospheric pressure to the higher pressure within the caisson or vice versa. Pneumatic caissons can not be used at a depth of more than 120 ft (36.6 m). Beyond that point the air pressure needed inside the caisson to keep out water is too great for the human body to withstand.

See also Bridges.

Further Reading:

How Things Work: Structures. Alexandria: Time–Life Books, 1991.

McGraw–Hill Encyclopedia of Science & Technology, vol. 3, 6th ed. New York: McGraw–Hill Book Co., 1987.

Owen, Wilfred, Ezra Bowen, and the editors of LIFE. *Wheels.* New York: Time Inc., 1967.

David E. Newton

Calcium

The metallic chemical element of atomic number 20. Symbol Ca, atomic weight 40.08, specific gravity 1.55 at 71°F (20°C), melting point 1545±3°F (839±2°C), boiling point 2706°F (1484°C).

Calcium (from the Latin *calx*, meaning lime) is a fairly soft, silvery white metal in group 2 of the periodic table, the group known as the alkaline earth metals. It consists of six stable isotopes with mass numbers between 40 and 48. By far the most abundant, however, is ^{40}Ca, which constitutes 96.941% of all the calcium atoms that we find in nature.

Calcium is the fifth most abundant element (after oxygen, silicon, aluminum and iron), in the Earth's crust, making up 3.63% of the crust by weight. It occurs in the form of minerals such as limestone (calcium carbonate, $CaCO_3$), gypsum (calcium sulfate, $CaSO_4 \cdot 2H_2O$) and fluorite (calcium fluoride, CaF_2).

In living things, calcium is a component of leaves, bones, teeth, shells, and coral. It constitutes 1.4% by weight of the human body, with 99% located in the bones and teeth. A necessary element in the human diet, calcium also plays a role in the clotting of blood, the contraction of muscles, and the regulation of heartbeat. It can be obtained by eating foods such as green vegetables and dairy products, after which it is utilized by the body with the help of vitamin D. Calcium supplements are often recommended to prevent osteoporosis, a loss of bone density in older people, mostly women, which can lead to brittle and easily broken bones.

Calcium oxide (CaO) or lime, was known to the Romans, who made it by heating limestone. The element itself wasn't isolated and identified until 1808, however, when Sir Humphry Davy (1778–1829) prepared it by electrolyzing (passing electricity through) a mixture of calcium oxide and mercuric oxide, and then heating the resulting amalgam to drive off the mercury.

(An amalgam is a mixture of mercury with another metal or metals. Dentists use an amalgam of silver for filling teeth.) Today, calcium metal is obtained by electrolyzing molten calcium chloride ($CaCl_2$) or by reducing calcium oxide with aluminum metal.

Calcium is a very active metal and is never found uncombined in nature. It tarnishes quickly when exposed to air and burns with a bright yellowish red flame, forming mostly calcium nitride (Ca_3N_2). It reacts directly with water to form calcium hydroxide [$Ca(OH)_2$] and hydrogen gas. Because of its strong reducing power it is used to produce other metals such as thorium and uranium by reducing their compounds, and to purify various alloys by removing oxides and sulfides. Calcium forms useful alloys with aluminum, copper and lead.

Many calcium compounds have important uses. Calcium oxide or lime is widely used to make cement (lime+clay), mortar (cement+sand+water) and concrete (cement+sand+gravel+water). It is also used in the manufacture of glass. When water is added to calcium carbide (CaC_2) the highly flammable gas acetylene (C_2H_2) is produced; it is used in lamps and welding torches, and as a starting material in the synthesis of many organic compounds. Calcium chloride ($CaCl_2$) is used as a drying agent, because it is a *deliquescent* solid: it can absorb so much water from the air that it turns into a liquid. It is also used as a more effective and less corrosive substitute for common salt (NaCl) for melting ice on roads in the winter. Calcium hypochlorite [$Ca(OCl)_2$] is used as a bleach. Calcium phosphate [$Ca_3(PO_4)_2$] and calcium cyanamide [$Ca(CN)_2$] are used in the production of fertilizers.

See also Alkaline earth metals; Alloy; Calcium carbonate; Calcium oxide; Calcium propionate; Calcium sulfate; Element, chemical; Hard water; Osteoporosis.

Calcium carbonate

Calcium carbonate, $CaCO_3$, is one of the most common compounds on earth, making up about 7% of Earth's crust. It occurs in a wide variety of mineral forms, including limestone, marble, travertine, and chalk. Calcium carbonate also occurs combined with magnesium as the mineral dolomite, $CaMg(CO_3)_2$. Stalactites and stalagmites in caves are made of calcium carbonate. A variety of animal products are also made primarily of calcium carbonate, notably coral, sea shells, egg shells, and pearls.

Calcium carbonate has two major crystalline forms—two different geometric arrangements of the calcium ions and carbonate ions that make up the compound. These two forms are called aragonite and calcite. All calcium carbonate minerals are conglomerations of various–sized crystals of these two forms, packed together in different ways and containing various impurities. The large, transparent crystals known as Iceland spar, however, are pure calcite.

In its pure form, calcium carbonate is a white powder with a specific gravity of 2.71 in the calcite form or 2.93 in the aragonite form. When heated, it decomposes into calcium oxide (CaO) and carbon dioxide gas (CO_2). It also reacts vigorously with acids to release a froth of carbon dioxide bubbles. It is said that Cleopatra, to show her extravagance, dissolved pearls in vinegar (acetic acid).

Every year in the United States alone, tens of millions of tons of limestone are dug, cut, or blasted out of huge deposits in Indiana and elsewhere. It is used mostly for buildings and highways and in the manufacture of steel, where it is used to remove silica (silicon dioxide) and other impurities in the iron ore; the calcium carbonate decomposes to calcium oxide in the heat of the furnace, and the calcium oxide reacts with the silica to form calcium silicates (slag), which float on the molten iron and can be skimmed off.

Deposits of calcium carbonate can be formed in the oceans when calcium ions dissolved from other minerals react with dissolved carbon dioxide (carbonic acid, H_2CO_3). The resulting calcium carbonate is quite insoluble in water and sinks to the bottom.

However, most of the calcium carbonate deposits that we find today were formed by sea creatures millions of years ago when oceans covered much of what is now land. From the calcium ions and carbon dioxide in the oceans, they manufactured shells and skeletons of calcium carbonate, just as clams, oysters, and corals still do today. When these animals die, their shells settle on the sea floor where, long after the seas have gone, we now find them compressed into thick deposits of limestone. The White Cliffs of Dover in England are chalk, a soft, white porous form of limestone made from the shells of microscopic sea creatures called Foraminifera that lived about 136 million years ago. Blackboard "chalk" isn't made of chalk; it is mostly gypsum, $CaSO_4$.

In pearls—which mollusks make out of their shell–building material when they are irritated by a foreign body in their flesh—and in sea shells, the individual $CaCO_3$ crystals are invisibly small, even under a microscope. But they are laid down in such a perfect order that the result is smooth, hard, shiny, and sometimes even iridescent, as in the rainbow colors of abalone shells. In many cases, the mollusk makes its shell by laying down alternating layers: calcite, aragonite, calcite, aragonite, and so on. This gives the shell great strength, as in a sheet of plywood where the grain of the alternating wood layers runs in crossed directions.

See also Calcium; Corals; Mollusks.

Calcium oxide

Calcium oxide (CaO), more commonly known as lime or quick lime, has been studied by scholars as far back as the pre–Christian era. In his book *Historia Naturalis,* for example, Pliny the Elder discussed the preparation, properties, and uses of lime. Probably the first scientific paper on the substance was Dr. Joseph Black's "Experiments Upon Magnesia, Alba, Quick–lime, and Some Other Alkaline Substances," written in 1755.

Lime does not occur naturally since it reacts so readily with water (to form hydrated lime) and carbon dioxide (to form limestone). It is produced in very large quantities synthetically, however, by the heating of limestone. For many years, calcium oxide has ranked among the top ten chemicals in the United States in terms of production. Other common names by which the compound is known include burnt lime, unslaked lime, fluxing lime, and calx.

In its pure form, calcium oxide occurs as white crystals, white or gray lumps, or a white granular powder. It has a very high melting point of 4662° F (2572° C) and a boiling point of 5162° F (2850° C). It dissolves in and reacts with water to form calcium hydroxide and is soluble in acids and some organic solvents.

Like other calcium compounds, calcium oxide is used for many construction purposes, as in the manufacture of bricks, mortar, plaster, and stucco. Its high melting point makes it attractive as a refractory material, as in the lining of furnaces. The compound is also used in the manufacture of various types of glass. Common soda–lime glass, for example, contains about 12% calcium oxide, while high–melting aluminosilicate glass contains about 20% calcium oxide. One of the new forms of glass used to coat surgical implants contains an even higher ratio of calcium oxide, about 24% of the compound.

Among the many other applications of calcium oxide are its uses in the production of pulp and paper, in the removal of hair from animal hides, in clarifying cane and beet sugar, in poultry feeds, and as a drilling fluid.

See also Calcium.

Calcium propionate

Calcium propionate is an organic salt formed by the reaction of calcium hydroxide with propionic acid (also known as propanoic acid). Its chemical formula is $Ca(OOCCH_2CH_3)_2$. The compound occurs in either crystalline or powder form. It is soluble in water and only very slightly soluble in alcohol.

Calcium propionate is used as a food preservative in breads and other baked goods because of its ability to inhibit the growth of molds and other microorganisms. It is not toxic to these organisms, but does prevent them from reproducing and posing a health risk to humans.

Propionic acid occurs naturally in some foods and acts as a preservative in those foods. Some types of cheese, for example, contain as much as 1% natural propionic acid.

Studies indicate that calcium propionate is one of the safest food additives used by the food industry. Rats fed a diet containing nearly 4% calcium propionate for a year showed no ill effects. As a result, the U.S. Food and Drug Administration has placed no limitations on its use in foods. In addition to baked goods, it is commonly used as a preservative in chocolate products, processed cheeses, and fruit preserves. The tobacco industry has also used calcium propionate as a preservative in some of its products.

Beyond its role as a food additive, calcium propionate finds some application in the manufacture of butyl rubber. Adding it to the raw product makes it easier to process the rubber and protects the rubber from scorching during manufacture.

See also Food preservation; Salt.

Calcium sulfate

Calcium sulfate ($CaSO_4$) occurs in nature in both the anhydrous and the hydrated form. The former is found primarily as the mineral known as anhydrite, while the latter is probably best known as alabaster or gypsum. Calcium sulfate also occurs in forms known as selenite, terra alba, satinite, satin spar, and light spar.

Gypsum was well known to ancient cultures. Theophrastus of Eresus (about 300 B.C.), for example, described its natural occurrence, its properties, and its uses. The Persian pharmacist Abu Mansur Muwaffaq is believed to have first described one of the major products of gypsum, plaster of Paris, around 975 A.D.

Calcium sulfate occurs as a white odorless powder or as crystals that may be tinged with color by impurities. It has a melting point of 2642° F (1450° C) and is only slightly soluble in water. When heated, the hydrated forms of calcium sulfate lose 1.5 molecules of water and form the hemihydrate, $CaSO_4 \cdot 1/2H_2O$, commonly known as plaster of Paris. When added to water, plaster of Paris forms a hard mass used in making plaster casts, quick–setting cements, molds, wall plasters and wall board, and inexpensive art objects. Neither the anhydrous nor the hydrated calcium sulfate will react with water as does the hemihydrate.

Among the many other uses of calcium sulfate are as a pigment in white paints, as a soil conditioner, in Portland cement, as a sizer, filler, and coating agent in papers, in the manufacture of sulfuric acid and sulfur, in the metallurgy of zinc ores, and as a drying agent in many laboratory and commercial processes.

See also Calcium.

Calculator

The calculator is a computing machine. Its purpose is to do mathematics; basic calculators do the basic mathematical functions (addition, subtraction, division, and multiplication) while the more advanced ones, which are relatively new in the history of computing machines, do advanced calculations such as solving polynomials. The odometer, or mileage counter, in your car is a counting machine as is the calculator in your backpack and the computer on your desk. They may have different ability levels, but they all tally numbers.

Early calculators

Perhaps the earliest calculating machine was the Babylonian rod numerals. Not only was it a notational device, but administrators carried rods of bamboo, ivory, or iron in bags to help with their calculations. Rod numerals used nine digits (Figure 1).

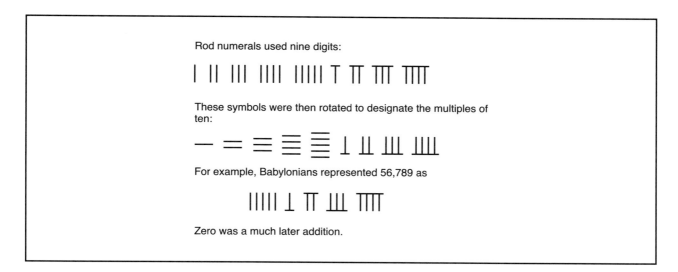

Rod numerals used nine digits:

These symbols were then rotated to designate the multiples of ten:

For example, Babylonians represented 56,789 as

Zero was a much later addition.

Figure 1.

The next invention in counting machines was the abacus. A counting board dating from approximately 500 BCE now resides in the National Museum in Athens. It is not an abacus, but the precursor of the abacus. Oriental cultures have documents discussing the abacus (the Chinese call it a *suan phan* and the Japanese the *soroban*) as early as the 1500s CE; however, they were using the abacus at least a thousand years earlier. While experts disagree on the origin of the name (from either the Semitic *abq*, or dust, or the Greek *abax*, or sand tray), they do agree the word is based upon the idea of a sand tray which was used for counting.

A simple abacus has rows (or wires) and each row has ten beads. Each row represents a unit ten greater than the previous. Thus, the first stands for units of one; the second, units of ten; the third, units of hundred; and so on. The appropriate number of beads are moved from left to right on the wire representing the unit. When all ten beads on a row have been moved, they are returned to their original place and one bead on the next row is moved. The soroban divides the wires into two unequal parts. The beads along the lower, or larger, part represent units, tens, hundreds, and so on. The bead at the top represent five, fifty, five hundred, and so on. These beads are stored away from the central divider, and as needed are moved toward it.

Finger reckoning must not be ignored as a basic calculator. Nicolaus Rhabda of Smyrna and the Venerable Bede (both of the 8th century CE) wrote, in detail, how this system using both hands could represent numbers up to one million. The numbers from 1 to 99 are created by the left and the numbers from 100 to 9900 by the right hand. By bending the fingers at their various joints and using the index finger and thumb to represent the multiples of ten, combinations of numbers can be represented. Similar systems were devised much earlier than the 8th century, probably by merchants and traders who could not speak each other's languages but needed a system to communicate: their fingers. Multiplication using the fingers came much later; well into the 15th century CE such complex issues, as multiplication, were left to university students, who were forced to learn a different finger reckoning system to accommodate multiplication.

Early calculators

Schickard, a German professor and Protestant minister, seems to have been the first to create an adding machine in the 1620s. It performed addition, subtraction, and carrying through the use of gears and preset multiplication tables. The machine only computed numbers up to six digits. Once the operator surpassed this limit, he was required to put a brass ring around his finger to remind him how many carries he had done. Schickard made sure to include a bell, so that the user would not forget to add his rings. His drawings of the machine were lost until the mid–1960s when a scrap of paper was located inside a friend's book which had a drawing of his machine. With this drawing and Schickard's letters, a reconstruction was made in 1971 to honor the adding machine's 350th anniversary.

Finished in 1642, Blaise Pascal's calculating machine also automatically carried tens and was limited to six digit numbers. The digits from 0 to 9 were represented on dials; when a one was added to a nine the gear turned to show a zero and the next gear, representing the next higher tens unit, automatically turned. Over fifty of these machines were made. A few remain in existence.

Gottfried Wilhelm Leibniz, a German, created a machine in 1671 which did addition and multiplication. For over two hundred years this machine was lost; then it was discovered by some workmen in the attic of one of the Göttingen University's buildings.

Charles Xavier Thomas de Colmar, in 1820, devised a machine which added subtraction and division to a Leibniz type calculator. It was the first mass produced calculator and became a common sight in business offices.

Difference engine

The great English mathematician Charles Babbage tried to build a machine which would calculate mathematical tables to 26 significant figures; he called it the Difference Engine. However, in the early 1820's his plans were stalled when the British government pulled its funding. His second attempt, in the 1830's, failed because some of the tools he needed had yet to be invented. Despite this, Babbage did complete part of this second machine, called the Analytical Engine, in the early 1840s. It is considered to be the first modern calculating machine. The difference between the Difference and Analytical Engines is that the first only performed a certain number of functions, which were built into the machine, while the second could be programmed to solve almost any algebraic equation.

By 1840 the first difference engine was finally built by the Swedish father and son team of George and Edvard Scheutz. They based their machine on Babbage's 1834 publication about his experiments. The Scheutz's three machines produced the first automatically created calculation tables. In one 80 hour experiment, the Scheutz's machine produced the logarithms of 1 to 10,000; this included time to reset the machine for the 20 polynomials needed to do the calculations.

Patents

The first patent for a calculating machine was granted to the American Frank Stephen Baldwin in 1875. Baldwin's machine did all four basic mathematical functions and did not need to be reset after each computation. The second patent was given in 1878 to Willgodt Theophile Odhner from Sweden for a machine of similar design to Baldwin's. The modern electronic calculators are based on Baldwin's design.

In 1910, Babbage's son, Henry P. Babbage, built the first hand held printing calculator based on his father's Analytical Engine. With this machine, he was able to calculate and then print multiples of π to 29 decimal places.

In 1936, a German student, Konrad Zuse, built the first automatic calculating machine. Without any knowledge of previous calculating machines, Zuse built the Z1 in his parents' living room. He theorized that the machine had to be able to do the mathematical fundamentals. To do this, he turned to binary mathematics, something no other scientist or mathematician had contemplated. (The mathematics we use in every day life, decimal, is based on 10 digits. Binary mathematics uses two digits: 0 and 1.) By using binary mathematics, the calculating machine became a series of switches rather than gears, because a switch has two options: on (closed or 1) or off (open or 0). He then connected these switches into logic gates, a combination of which can be selected to do addition or subtraction. Zuse's third model (finished in 1941) was not only programmable, but hand held; it added, subtracted, multiplied, divided, discovered square roots, and converted from decimal to binary and back again. However, to add it took a third of a second, and to subtract an additional three to five seconds. By changing his relays into vacuum tubes he believed he could speed his machine up 1000 times, but he could not get the funding from the Third Reich government to rebuild his machine.

Electronic predecessor to computer

In 1938, the International Business Machine Corporation (IBM) team of George Stibitz and S. B. Williams began building the Complex Number Calculator. It could add, subtract, multiply, and divide complex numbers. They completed the project in 1940 and until 1949 these calculators were used by Bell Laboratories. It was the first machine to use remote stations (terminals, or input units, not next to the computer) and to allow more than one terminal to be used. The operator typed the request onto a teletype machine and the response was sent back to that teletype. The relays inside the machine were basic telephone relays.

The IBM Automatic Sequence Controlled Calculator (ASCC) was based upon Babbage's ideas. This machine, completed in 1944, was built for the United States Navy by Harvard University and IBM. It weighed about 5 tons (10,000 kg) and was 51 ft (15.5 m) long and 8 ft (2.4 m) high. A second, more useful version, was completed in 1948.

The Electronic Numerical Integrator and Computer (ENIAC), also based on Babbage's concepts, was completed in 1945 at the University of Pennsylvania for the United States Army. It weighted over 30 tons (27,240) kg and filled a 30 by 55 ft (9 by 17 m) room. In one second it could do 5000 additions, 357 multiplications, or 38 divisions. However, to reprogram ENIAC meant rewiring it, which caused up to two days in delays.

The first electronic calculator was suggested by the Hungarian turned American John von Neumann. Von Neumann introduced the idea of a stored memory for a computer which allowed the program and the data to be inputted to the machine. This resolved problems with rewiring computers and permitted the computer to move directly from one calculation to another. This type of machine architecture is called "von Neumann." The first completed computer to use von Neumann architecture was the English Electronic Delay Storage Automatic Calculator (EDSAC) finished in 1949. An added feature of the EDSAC was that it could be programmed in a type of shorthand, which it then converted into binary code, rather than its precursors which demanded the programmer actually write the program in binary code, a laborious process.

Inside calculators

The early counting machines, items like the car's odometer, work with a set of gears and wheel. A certain number of wheels are divided in ten equal parts on each of which one of the ten digits appears. (Windows are placed on top of these wheels so that only one digit appears at a time.) These wheels are then attached to gears which as they turn rotate the wheel so that the digit being displayed changes. When the right most wheel changes from 9 to 0, a mechanism is set in motion which turns the wheel to the left one unit, so that the digit it displays changes. This is the carry sequence. When this second wheel changes from 9 to 0, it too has a mechanism to carry to the next left wheel.

Electronic calculators have the four major units van Neumann created: input, processing, memory, and output. The input unit accepts the numbers keyed in, or sent through the reader in the case of the punch card, by the operator. The processing unit performs the calculations. When the processing unit encounters a complex calculation, it uses the memory unit to store intermediary results or to locate arithmetic instructions. At the completion of the calculation, the final answer is sent to the output unit which informs the operator of the result; this may be through a display, paper, or a combination. Since the calculator thinks in binary, the output unit must convert the result into decimal units.

Modern advances

At the end of 1947, the transistor was invented, eventually making the vacuum tube obsolete. This tiny

KEY TERMS

Binary—The base 2 system of counting using two digits: 0 and 1. Each unit is a 2 to the n+1 power. For example, the first unit is 2^0 or 1; the second 2^1 or 2; the third 2^2 or 4; the forth 2^3 or 8; and so forth. Thus 221 in binary is 11011101 or 1 hundreds twenty–eight (2^7), 1 sixty–four (2^6), no thirty–twos (2^5), 1 sixteen (2^4), 1 eight (2^3), 1 four (2^2), no twos (2^1), and 1 one (2^0). This unit of counting was invented by Gottfried Leibniz in the 1600s.

Decimal—The base 10 system of counting using ten digits: 0, 1, 2, 3, 4, 5, 6, 7, 8, 9. Each unit is 10 to the n+1 power. For example, the first unit is 10^0 or 1; the second 10^1 or 10; the third 10^2 or 100; and so forth. Thus, 221 is 2 hundreds (10^2), 2 tens (10^1), and 1 one (10^0).

Punch cards—Made of a heavy cardboard, these rectangular cards have holes punched in them. Each hole is placed in a designated area which the computer then translates into a binary code. A series of such punched cards contain a sequence of events, or a program. The first punch cards were invented by Jacquard, a weaver, who wanted to automate the creation of patterns in his fabric. Thus, his loom was the first machine to use these cards.

creation, composed of semiconductors, were much faster and less energy consumptive than the tubes. Problems arose with the connections between the components with size, speed, and reliability as more complex machines needed more complex circuitry which in turn required more components soldered to more boards (the actual board to which the pieces were attached). The next breakthrough came with the invention of the integrated circuit (IC) in 1959 by Texas Instruments (TI) and Fairchild (a semiconductor manufacturing company). The integrated circuit is akin to a solid mass of transistors, resistors, and capacitors. Again, the speed of computation increased (since the resistance in the circuit was reduced) and the energy required by the machine was decreased. Finally, a computer could fit on a spaceship (they were part of the Apollo computer) or missile. In 1959, an IC cost over $1,000 but by 1965 they were under $10.

Ted Hoff, an electrical engineer for Intel conceived of a radical new concept—the microprocessor. This incorporated the circuitry of the integrated circuit and the programs used in a computer onto a single chip, or piece of silicon. This model of this microprocessor was finished in 1970. The idea of a disposable piece of a calculator was revolutionary. Its compactness and speed changed the face of the computing industry.

The creation of ICs allowed calculators to become much faster and smaller. By the 1960s, they were hand held and affordable. By the late 1980s, calculators were found on watches. However, once again engineers are being blocked by the size factor. The limits are now the size of the chip which in turn limits the speed and programmability of the calculator, or computer.

See also Computer, analog; Computer, digital.

Further Reading:

Adler, Irving. *Thinking Machines: A Layman's Introduction to Logic, Boolean Algebra, and Computers.* New York: John Day, 1961.

Macaulay, David. *The Way Things Work.* Boston: Houghton Mifflin, 1988.

Palfreman, Jon, and Doron Swade. *The Dream Machine: Exploring the Computer Age.* London: BBC Books, 1991.

Williams, Michael R. *A History of Computing Technology.* Englewood Cliffs, New Jersey: Prentice–Hall, 1985.

Mara W. Cohen Ioannides

Calculus

Calculus is the branch of mathematics that deals with rates of change and motion. It grew out of a desire to understand various physical phenomena, such as the orbits of planets, and the effects of gravity. The immediate success of calculus in formulating physical laws and predicting their consequences led to development of a new division in mathematics called analysis, of which calculus remains a large part. Today, calculus is the essential language of science and engineering, providing the means by which physical laws are expressed in mathematical terms. As a scientific tool it is invaluable in the further analysis of physical laws, in predicting the behavior of electrical and mechanical systems governed by those laws, and in discovering new laws.

Calculus divides naturally into two parts, differential calculus and integral calculus. Differential calculus is concerned with finding the instantaneous rate at which one quantity changes with respect to another, called the derivative of the first quantity with respect to the second. For example, determining the speed of a falling body at a particular instant of time, say that of a skydiver or bungi jumper, is equivalent to calculating the instantaneous rate of change in his or her position with respect to time. In general, evaluating the derivative of a function, $f(x)$, involves finding another function, $f'(x)$, such that $f'(x)$ is equal to the slope of the tangent to the graph of $f(x)$ at each x. This is accomplished, for each 2, by determining the slope of an approximating line segment in the limit that its length approaches zero.

Integral calculus deals with the inverse of the derivative, namely, finding a function when its rate of change is known. For example, if a skydiver's velocity is a known function of time, then we may ask what is his or her position at any given time after jumping. Finding the original function, given its derivative, is called integration, and the function is called the indefinite integral. Evaluating the indefinite integral of any function between specific limits leads to definition of the definite integral, which is equal to the area under the graph of the function between the specified limits. The latter is developed as a natural consequence of approximating an area by summing the areas of a number of inscribed rectangles. The approximation becomes exact in the limit that the number of rectangles approaches infinity. Thus, both differential and integral calculus are based on the theory of limits.

The usefulness of calculus is indicated by its widespread application. For example, it is used in the design of navigation systems, particle accelerators, and synchrotron light sources. It is used to predict rocket trajectories, and the orbits of communications satellites. Calculus is the mathematical tool used to test theories about the origins of the universe, the development of tornadoes and hurricanes, and salt fingering in the oceans. It has even found extensive application in business, where it is used, among other things, to optimize production.

History

Calculus was invented, more or less simultaneously, by Isaac Newton, and Gottfried Leibniz. Some of the essential ingredients, however, had their beginnings in ancient Greece. In the 4th century B.C., Eudoxus invented the so called method of exhaustion, in order to furnish proofs of certain geometric theorems without having to resort to arguments involving the infinite. Approximately a century later, Archimedes used the same method to find a formula for the area of a circle. Archimedes' method consisted of inscribing a polygon with n sides inside a circle, and circumscribing a similar polygon, again with n sides, outside the circle. Then, allowing n, in other words the number of sides, to get very large, he was able to show that the area of the circle was always greater than the area of the inscribed polygon and less than the area of the circumscribed polygon. As n grew very large, the areas of the two polygons tended to become equal, thus leading him to the area of a circle. The method of Archimedes persisted from the 3rd century B.C. until the beginning of the 17th century A.D. when the work of Johannes Kepler, a German Astronomer, led to the discovery of general principles for the calculation of areas and volumes. Kepler's contribution was the notion of infinitesimals. He envisioned the inscribed polygons of Archimedes as being a collection of infinitely many, vanishingly small triangles. Thus, the area of a circle could be calculated by summing the areas of these triangles. While, Eudoxus and Archimedes had worked hard to avoid the infinite, Kepler embraced it. Simultaneous work on infinite sequences and sums of infinite sequences led the French mathematician Fermat, and others, to discover general methods for evaluating areas and volumes as the sums of infinite sequences rather than the sums of areas of common geometric figures. Finally, around the middle of the seventeenth century, Isaac Newton, in attempting to develop a universal theory of gravitation, discovered the derivative, a general method for determining the instantaneous rate of change of a function, based on the notion of infinitesimals. Though he did not explicitly define the integral at the time, Newton did recognize the need to solve differential equations. As a result, he invented methods of evaluating indefinite integrals very soon after introducing the derivative. It was Leibniz, however, whose work postdated that of Newton by some 10 years, who recognized and formulated the definite integral as an infinite sum of "lines," that is, as an area calculated by summing an infinite number of infinitely narrow rectangles.

Differential calculus

Differential calculus involves the analysis of functions, specifically, determining their instantaneous rates of change. An important feature of any function is its rate of change. Geometrically, rate of change is associated with the graph of a function. The rate of change of a straight line (the simplest kind of real valued function) is the slope of the line. The slope is defined as the ratio of the vertical change, or "rise," to the horizontal change, or "run," that occurs between any two points on the line. Because the slope is the same between any two points, the rate of change of such a function is said to be constant. In general, however, any function whose graph is not a straight line has a varying rate of change. The rate of change in the vicinity of a particular point

on the graph of curve can be approximated by drawing a straight line through two points in the neighborhood of that point, and determining the slope of the line. Suppose we are interested in the rate of change at the point $(x, f(x))$. First, choose a second nearby point, say $(x+h, f(x+h))$. Then the slope of the line segment connecting these two points is $[f(x+h) - f(x)] \div [(x+h) - x]$. The shorter the approximating line segment becomes, the more accurate the approximation of the rate of change at the point $(x, f(x))$ becomes. In the limit that h approaches zero the slope of the approximating line segment becomes exactly the rate of change of the function at the point $(x, f(x))$. Thus, the instantaneous rate of change of a function, called the derivative of the function, is defined by:

$$f'(x) \;=\; \frac{df(x)}{dx} \;=\; \lim_{h \to 0} \frac{f(x+h) - f(x)}{h}$$

where the notation $df(x)$ is intended to indicate that the derivative is the ratio of an infinitesimal change in $f(x)$ (the rise) to the corresponding infinitesimal change in x (the run). The derivative of a function is itself a function, and so may also have a derivative. Often times the derivative of the derivative is an important quantity. Called the second derivative of the original function f, it is denoted by $f''(x)$.

An important application of differential calculus involves using information about the first and second derivatives, and the appropriate geometric interpreta-

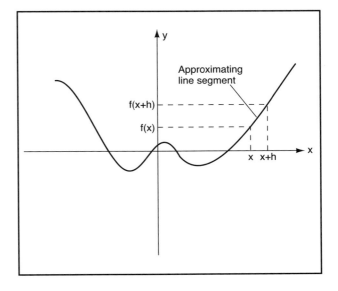

Figure 1. The rate of change in the vicinity of a particular point on the graph of a curve can be approximated by drawing a straight line through two points in the neighborhood of that point, and determining the slope of the line.

tions, to graph functions. For example, the first derivative of a function is its rate of change. The value of the first derivative at a given point is equal to the slope of the tangent to the graph of the function at that point. When the derivative is positive, the function is said to be increasing (the value of the function increases with increasing x). When the derivative is negative, the function is said to be decreasing (the value of the function decreases with increasing x). When the value of the derivative is zero at a point, the tangent is horizontal, and the function changes from increasing to decreasing, or vice versa, depending on the sign of the second derivative. The second derivative is the rate of change of the rate of change, and thus contains information about the curvature of the function. When the second derivative is positive, the function is concave upward (as though it would hold water). When the second derivative is negative, the function is concave downward. With this knowledge, and a few points in the function, a reasonable graph can be drawn without having to plot hundreds of points.

Other applications of differential calculus include the solution of rate problems and optimization problems. In general, a rate is the ratio of change in one quantity to the simultaneous change in a second quantity. Thus, the derivative, being an instantaneous rate, is applicable to any problem in which the rate of change of one quantity with respect to another is of interest. Innumerable applications in engineering and science affect our daily lives. For instance, the instantaneous velocity of an orbiting communications satellite is calculated from knowledge of its position as a function of time. The acceleration of a falling body is calculated from knowledge of its velocity as a function of time, which in turn is calculated from knowledge of its position as a function of time. The force required to deliver natural gas through a pipeline, over large distances, is calculated using the derived of the gas pressure with respect to distance.

Optimization problems are problems that require knowledge of maximum or minimum values of functional relationships. For example, it can be shown that a sphere has the least surface area for a given volume of any geometric solid. Thus, the optimum shape for a raindrop is spherical because this shape contains the most water, but has the least amount of surface area, hence the least surface energy (a measure of the work required to form the drop).

Integral calculus

Integral calculus is the study of integration and methods for evaluating integrals. Integrals come in two kinds, definite and indefinite. The definite integral of a function, interpreted geometrically, corresponds to the area under the curve of the function between any two limits. Thus, it has a definite value depending on the limits chosen, The indefinite integral of a function is the inverse of the derivative of that function. That is, integrating (finding the integral) undoes differentiating (finding the derivative f'(x)). Integrating the derivative of a function returns the original function.

Indefinite Integral

The indefinite integral is the inverse of the derivative, that is, the integral of the derivative of a function is the original function. From the definition of derivative, $f'(x) = df(x)/dx$, we find $f'(x)dx = df(x)$. To obtain the original function from this second equation, we "integrate" both sides, and write, $\int f'(x)dx = \int df(x) = f(x) + C$. The integral sign, $\int$, is intended to symbolize the summing, integrating, or putting together of the infinitesimal pieces $df(x)$ to obtain the original function $f(x)$. The constant, C, arises because functions that differ only by a constant are "parallel" to one another, and so have the same derivative (or slope) at each value of x. Defined in this manner, integrating amounts to guessing original functions based on prior knowledge of their derivatives. For example, if $f(x) = x^2$ then $f'(x) = 2x$. Thus, if asked to integrate the function $g(x) = 2x$, it is apparent that $\int 2x dx = x^2 + C$. In order to determine the value of C it is necessary to have an additional piece of information. Such information is referred to as an initial condition or a boundary condition, and is sufficient to determine which of the parallel curves is the desired one.

The primary application of indefinite integrals is in the solution of differential equations. A differential equation is any equation that contains at least one derived. The equation $f'(x) = ax^2+bx+c$ is an example of a differential equation. Many natural relationships are described by differential equations. For instance, heat conduction is related to the derivative of the temperature with respect to distance; the velocity of a fluid flowing through a pipe is related to the derivative of the pressure with respect to length of pipe; and the force on any massive body is related to the derivative of its momentum with respect to time.

Definite Integral

The definite integral corresponds to the area under the graph of a function, above the x–axis and between two vertical lines called the limits of integration. Consider approximating the area under the graph of a function f(x) by drawing a series of rectangles, and summing their areas to arrive at the total area, A(x) (see Figure 2). The height of each rectangle is the value of the function at x, namely f(x). The width of each rectangle is $\Delta x = (b–a)/n$, where n is the number of rectangles chosen. If we wish to know the area between x=a and x=b, then the area is given by the sum

$$A(x) = \sum_{k=1}^{n} f(x_k)\, \Delta x$$

(the Greek letter Σ (sigma) is used to indicate that the n products $f(x_k)\, \Delta x$ corresponding to the n rectangles are to be summed). In the limit that n approaches infinity, Δx approaches 0, and the sum is exactly equal to the are. Since Δx approaches 0, it represents an infinitesimal change in the variable x, so the same notation used in defining the derivative is used to replace Δx with d. The product $f(x)\, \Delta x$ becomes $f(x)dx$, and corresponds to an infinitesimal area, $dA(x)$. The total area, then, is the sum of an infinite number of an infinite number of infinitesimal areas. Thus, the area $A(x)$ between a and b is equal to the integral of $f(x)dx$, written,

$$A(x) = \int_{a}^{b} dA(x) = \int_{a}^{b} f(x)dx$$

The limits included above and below the integral sign indicate that the indefinite integral of $f(x)d$ is to be evaluated at a and b and the values subtracted, that is,

$$\int_{a}^{b} f(x)dx = A(b) - A(a)$$

This is interpreted as the area under the curve to the left of b minus the area under the curve to the left of a. Comparing this with the form of the indefinite integral

we see that a function $f(x)$ is the derivative of its "Area function", the constant C being evaluated by use of boundary conditions, namely the values a and b. There are many applications of definite integrals, among the most common are the determination of areas and volumes of revolution.

Further Reading:

Abbot, P. and M.E. Wardle. *Teach Yourself Calculus*. Lincolnwood, IL: NTC Publishing, 1992.
Moore, A.W. "A Brief History of Infinity." *Scientific American* 272 (1995): 112–116.
Silverman, Richard A. *Essential Calculus With Applications*. New York: Dover, 1989.
Swokowski, Earl W. *Pre Calculus, Functions, and Graphs*, 6th. edition. Boston, MA: PWS–KENT Publishing Co., 1990.
Thomas, George B., Jr. and Ross L. Finney. *Elements of Calculus and Analytic Geometry*, 6th edition. Reading, MA: Addison Wesley, 1989.

J. R. Maddocks

Calendars

There are three units of time which have a direct basis in astronomy. The Day, which is the time interval in which the Earth makes one rotation around its axis of rotation. The Month, which is the time interval for the Moon to revolve around the Earth. The Year, which is the time interval in which the Earth makes one revolution around the Sun.

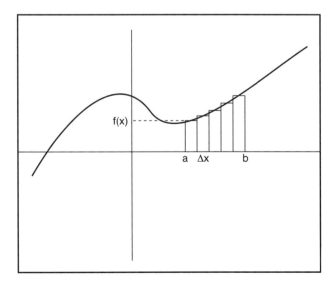

Figure 2. Consider approximating the area under the graph of a function f(x) by drawing a series of rectangles, and summing their areas to arrive at the total area.

The week has an indirect basis in astronomy; the seven days of the week probably were named for the seven objects which the ancients saw moving on the zodiac, which were the Sun, Moon, and the five naked eye planets.

A calendar is a system for measuring long units of time, usually in terms of days, weeks, months, and years. The year is the most important time unit in most calenders, since the cycle of seasons, which are associated with change of climate in the Earth's temperate and frigid zones, repeat in a yearly cycle with the change in the Sun's apparent position on the ecliptic as the Earth revolves around the Sun.

Types of calendars

There are three main types of calendars. One type of calendar is the Lunar Calendar, which is based on the month (Moon). A lunar calendar year is 12 synodic months long, where a synodic month is the time interval in which the phases of the Moon repeat (from one Full Moon to the next), and which averages 29.53 days. Thus, a lunar calendar year averages 354.37 days long. Since the Earth takes slightly longer than 365 days to revolve completely around the Sun, a lunar calendar soon gets out of phase with the seasons. Thus, most lunar calendars have died out over the centuries. The main exception is the Muslim Calendar, which is used in Islamic countries, most of which are in or near the Earth's torrid zone, where seasonal variation of climate is slight or non–existent, and the climate is usually consistently hot.

The second type of calendar is the Luni–Solar Calendar, in which most years are 12 synodic months long, but a thirteenth month is inserted every few years to keep the calendar in phase with the seasons. There are two important surviving luni–solar calendars: the Hebrew (Jewish) Calendar, which is used by the Jewish religion, and the Chinese Calendar, which is used extensively in eastern Asia.

The third type of calendar is the Solar Calendar, which is based on the length of the year. Our present calendar is of this type; however, it evolved from the ancient Roman calendar, which passed through the stage of being a luni–solar calendar. Let us summarize its early history.

In the first centuries after Rome was founded (753 B.C.), the Roman calendar consisted of ten synodic months; the year began near the start of spring with March and ended with December (the tenth month). The remaining 70 winter days were not counted in the calendar. Some centuries later two more months, January, named for Janus, the two–faced Roman god of gates and doorways, and February, named for the Roman festival of purification, were added between December and March. An occasional thirteenth month was later inserted into the calendar; at this stage the Roman calendar was luni–solar calendar. It was quite complicated and somewhat inaccurate even by the year 45 B.C.

That year, Julius Caesar (100–44 B.C.) Commissioned the Greek astronomer Sosigenes (c. 50 B.C.) from Alexandria to plan a sweeping reform of the Roman Calendar. The calendar which Sosigenes devised and Caesar installed for the Roman Empire had the following main features.

The months January, March, May, July, August, October, and December each have 31 days. The months April, June, September, and November each have 30 days. February has 28 days in ordinary years, which have 365 days.

Every fourth year is a Leap year with 366 days. The 366th day appears in the calendar as February 29th.

The calendar year begins on January 1 instead of March 1. January 1 is set by the time of year when the Sun seems to set about half an hour later than its earliest setting seen in Rome, which occurs in early December.

This calendar was named the Julian calendar for Julius Caesar. He also had the month Quintilis (the fifth month) renamed July for himself. Augustus Caesar (63 B.C. – 14 A.D.) clarified the Julian calendar rule for leap year by decreeing that only years evenly divisible by four would be leap years. He also renamed the month Sextilis (the sixth month) August for himself.

The average length of the Julian calendar year over a century or more is 365.25 days. This time interval is between the lengths of two important astronomical years. The shorter one is the tropical year, or the year of the seasons; it is defined as the time interval between successive crossings of the Vernal Equinox by the Sun (which mark the beginning of spring in the Earth's northern hemisphere) and averages 365.2422 days long. The sidereal year, which is defined as the time interval needed for the Earth to make a complete 360° orbital revolution around the Sun, is slightly longer, being 365.25636 days long. The small difference between the lengths of the sidereal and tropical years arises because the Earth's rotation axis is not fixed in space but describes a cone around the line passing through the Earth's center that is perpendicular to the Earth's orbit plane (the ecliptic); the rotation axis describes a complete cone in 25,800 years. This phenomenon is called precession, and it causes the equinoxes (the intersections of the celestial equator and ecliptic) to shift westward on the ecliptic by 50.”2 (O°0139) each year and also the celestial poles to describe small circles around the ecliptic poles. Since the Sun appears to move eastward on the ecliptic at an average rate of 0°.9856/day, the Sun moves only 359°.9861 eastward along the ecliptic in an average tropical year, whereas it moves 360° eastward in a sidereal year, making the tropical year about 20 minutes shorter than the sidereal year. Precession is caused by stronger gravitational pulls of the Sun and Moon on the closer parts of the Earth's equatorial bulge than on its more distant parts. This effect tries to turn the Earth's rotation axis towards the line perpendicular to the ecliptic, but since the Earth is rotating, the Earth precesses like a rapidly spinning top, producing the effects described above.

An astronomer wants to make the average length of the calendar year equal to the length of the tropical year in order to keep the calendar in phase with the seasons. Sosigenes knew that precession of the equinoxes existed; it had been discovered by his predecessor Hipparchus (c. 166–125 B.C.). From his observations and records of earlier observations, Sosigenes allowed for precession of the equinoxes by making the average length of the Julian calendar year slightly shorter (0.00636 day, or about nine minutes) than the length of the sidereal year. But he did not know the physical cause of precession (a gravitational tidal effect), so he could not calculate what the annual rate of the precession of the equinoxes should be. The crude astronomical observations existing at that time may have led Sosigenes to believe that the rate of precession of the equinoxes was about half its true value, and therefore, that the 365.25 day average length of the Julian calendar year was an adequate match to the length of the tropical year. Unfortunately, this is not true for a calendar intended for use over time intervals of many centuries.

The development of our present (Gregorian) calendar

The Sun appeared to reach the Vernal Equinox about March 25 in the years immediately after the Roman Empire adopted the Julian calendar. It continued to be the official Roman calendar for the rest of the empire's existence. The Roman Catholic Church adopted the Julian calendar as its official calendar at the Council of Nicaea in 325 A.D., soon after the conversion of the emperor Constantine I, who then made Christianity the Roman Empire's official religion. By that time, the Sun was reaching the Vernal equinox about March 21; the fact that the tropical year is 0.0078 day shorter than the average length of the Julian calendar year had

accumulated a difference of three to four days from the time when the Julian calendar was first adopted. The Council of Nicaea also renumbered the calendar years; the numbers of the Roman years were replaced by a new numbering system in an effort to have had Christ's birth occur in the year 1 A.D. (Anno Domini). This effort was somewhat unsuccessful; the best historical evidence indicates that Christ probably was born sometime between 7 B.C. (before Christ) and 4 B.C. Another feature of this modified Julian calendar is that it has no year zero; the 1 B.C. is followed by the year 1 A.D.

This Julian calendar remained the official calendar of the Roman Catholic Church for the next 1,250 years. By the year 1575, the Sun was reaching the Vernal Equinox about March 11. This caused concern among both church and secular officials because, if this trend continued, by the year 11,690, Christmas would have become an early spring holiday instead of an early winter one, and would be occurring near Easter.

This prompted Pope Gregory XIII to commission the astronomer Clavius to reform the calendar. Clavius studied the problem, then he made several recommendations. The rate of the precession of the equinoxes was known much more precisely in the time of Clavius than it had been in the time of Sosigenes. The calendar which resulted from the study by Clavius is known as the Gregorian calendar; it was adopted in 1583 in predominantly Roman Catholic countries. It distinguished between century years, that is, years such as 1600, 1700, 1800, 1900, 2000, etc., and all other years, which are non–century years. The Gregorian calendar has the following main features.

All non–century years evenly divisible by four, such as 1988, 1992, and 1996 are leap years with February 29th as the 366th day. All other non–century years are ordinary years with 365 days.

Only century years evenly divisible by 400 are leap years; all other century years are ordinary years. Thus, 1600 was and 2000 will be leap years with 366 days, while 1700, 1800, and 1900 had only 365 days.

The Gregorian calendar was reset so that the Sun reaches the Vernal Equinox about March 21. To accomplish this, ten days were dropped from the Julian calendar; in the year 1582 in the Gregorian calendar, October 4 was followed by October 15.

The Gregorian calendar is the official calendar of the modern world. From the rules for the Gregorian calendar shown above, one finds that, in any 400–year interval, there are 97 leap years and 303 ordinary years, and the average length of the Gregorian calendar year is 365.2425 days. This is only 0.0003 day longer than the tropical year. This will lead to a discrepancy of a day in about the year 5000. Therefore, the Sun has usually reached the Vernal Equinox and northern hemisphere Spring has begun about March 21 according to the Gregorian calendar.

The Gregorian calendar was not immediately adopted beyond the Catholic countries. For example, the British Empire (including the American colonies) did not adopt the Gregorian calendar until 1752, when 11 days had to be dropped from the Julian calendar, and the conversion to the Gregorian calendar did not occur in Russia until 1917, when 13 days had to be dropped.

One feature of the Gregorian calendar is that February is the shortest month (with 28 or 29 days), while the summer months July and August have 31 days each. This disparity becomes understandable when one learns that the Earth's orbit is slightly elliptical with eccentricity 0.0167, and the Earth is closest to the Sun (at perihelion) in early January, while it is most distant from the Sun (at aphelion) in early July. It follows from Kepler's Second Law that the Earth, moving fastest in its orbit at perihelion and slowest at aphelion, causing the Sun to seem to move fastest on the ecliptic in January and slowest in July. The fact that the Gregorian calendar months January, February, and March have 89 or 90 days, while July, August, and September have 92 days makes some allowance for this.

Possible future calendar reform and additions

Although the Gregorian calendar partially allows for the eccentricity of the Earth's orbit and for the dates of perihelion and aphelion, the shortness of February introduces slight inconveniences into daily life. An example is that a person usually pays the same rent for the 28 days of February as is paid for the 31 days of March. Also the same date falls on different days of the week in different years. These and other examples have led to several suggestions for calendar reform.

Perhaps the best suggestion for a new calendar is the World Calendar, recommended by the Association for World Calendar Reform. This calendar is divided into four equal quarters that are 91 days (13 weeks) long. Each quarter begins on a Sunday on January 1, April 1, July 1, and October 1. These four months are each 31 days long; the remaining eight months all have 30 days. The last day of the year, a World Holiday (W–Day), comes after Saturday December 30 and before January 1 (Sunday) of the next year; it is the 365th day of ordinary years and the 366th day of leap years. The extra day in leap years appears as a second

World Holiday (Leap year or L–Day) between Saturday June 30 and Sunday July 1. The Gregorian calendar rules for ordinary, leap, century, and non–century years would remain unchanged for the foreseeable future.

One should mention a future Mars calendar for the human colonization of Mars in future centuries. There are about 668.6 sols (mean Martian solar days which average 24 hours 39 minutes 35.2 seconds of Mean Solar Time long) in a Martian sidereal year. At least one Martian calendar has been suggested, but much more must be done before an official Martian calendar is adopted.

The Julian day calendar

This calendar should be mentioned because of the extensive use of the Julian date (J.D.) in astronomy, oceanography, and perhaps some other sciences. It must not be confused with the Julian civil calendar.

This calendar was devised in 1582 by Josephus Justus Scaliger; the Julian date for a given calendar date is the number of days which have elapsed for that date since noon (by Universal Time [U.T.]) on January 1, 4713 B.C. It is based on a time interval 7980 years long, which Scaliger called the Julian period. For example, noon (12:00 U.T.) on January 1, 1996 is Julian Day J.D. 2,450,084.0 = 1.5 January 1996 U.T.

Further Reading:

Oriti, Ronald A. and Starbird, William B., *Introduction to Astronomy,* Encino, California: Glencoe Press, 1977, pp. 45–51.

Alter, Dinsmore, Cleminshaw, Clarence H., and Phillips, John G., *Pictorial Astronomy.*

Branley, Franklyn M., Chartrand III, Mark R., and Wimmer, Helmut K. *Astronomy,* New York, NY: Thomas Y. Crowell Co., 1975, pp. 407–415.

Proposed Reform Calendar taken from *Survey of the Universe,* Menzel, Donald H. Whipple, Fred L., and de Vaucouleurs, Gerard, Englewood Cliffs, New Jersey, 1970, p. 60.

Frederick R. West